Employment Discrimination

ASPEN CASEBOOK SERIES

Employment Discrimination

Procedure, Principles, and Practice

Second Edition

Joseph A. Seiner

Professor of Law and
Oliver Ellsworth Professor of Federal Practice
University of South Carolina School of Law

Wolters Kluwer

Published by Wolters Kluwer in New York.

Wolters Kluwer Legal & Regulatory U.S. serves customers worldwide with CCH, Aspen Publishers, and Kluwer Law International products. (www.WKLegaledu.com)

To contact Customer Service, e-mail customer.service@wolterskluwer.com, call 1-800-234-1660, fax 1-800-901-9075, or mail correspondence to:

Wolters Kluwer
Attn: Order Department
PO Box 990
Frederick, MD 21705

Printed in the United States of America.

1 2 3 4 5 6 7 8 9 0

ISBN 978-1-5438-0092-0

Library of Congress Cataloging-in-Publication Data

Names: Seiner, Joseph A., author.
Title: Employment discrimination : procedure, principles, and practice /
   Joseph A. Seiner, Professor of Law, University of South Carolina School of Law.
Description: Second edition. | New York : Wolters Kluwer, [2019] |
Series: Aspen casebook series | Includes bibliographical references and index.
Identifiers: LCCN 2018055938 | ISBN 9781543800920 (casebound)
Subjects: LCSH: Discrimination in employment—Law and legislation—
   United States. | LCGFT: Casebooks (Law)
Classification: LCC KF3464.S45 2019 | DDC 344.7301/133—dc23
LC record available at https://lccn.loc.gov/2018055938

About Wolters Kluwer Legal & Regulatory U.S.

Wolters Kluwer Legal & Regulatory U.S. delivers expert content and solutions in the areas of law, corporate compliance, health compliance, reimbursement, and legal education. Its practical solutions help customers successfully navigate the demands of a changing environment to drive their daily activities, enhance decision quality and inspire confident outcomes.

Serving customers worldwide, its legal and regulatory portfolio includes products under the Aspen Publishers, CCH Incorporated, Kluwer Law International, ftwilliam.com and MediRegs names. They are regarded as exceptional and trusted resources for general legal and practice-specific knowledge, compliance and risk management, dynamic workflow solutions, and expert commentary.

I dedicate this book to my children, my wife, and my parents. Joseph and Mary Elizabeth – you have brought so much happiness to my life. Megan – thank you for your endless support and for being my best friend. Mom and Dad – thank you for all of your love and guidance over the years.

—J.A.S.

■ SUMMARY OF CONTENTS

■ CONTENTS

PART TWO   ANALYTICAL FRAMEWORKS

Chapter 3: Disparate Treatment   79

Chapter 4: Disparate Impact   169

Chapter 5: Harassment   207

PART THREE   ENFORCEMENT BY PROTECTED CLASS

Chapter 6: Race and Color Discrimination   279

Chapter 7: Sex Discrimination   319

PART FOUR ■ REMEDIES

PART FIVE ■ BEST PRACTICES

■ PREFACE

This book seeks to provide a new approach to teaching employment discrimination law. My goal with this text is to fill a void in the academic book market: offering a procedural-based approach to employment discrimination doctrine. Employment discrimination cuts across traditional subject matter boundaries and cannot be considered a completely distinct area of the law. Indeed, business law, contract law, and tort law all play important roles in this field. Most notably, however, civil procedure is inextricably intertwined with employment questions. This is particularly true as the major focus of employment discrimination law has shifted from whether (and how) the field should exist to how cases are actually litigated in the courts. Unfortunately, the textbooks currently available often fail to address this important shift in the area. Students thus frequently struggle with the basic principles of employment discrimination law as they are unable to see how the theory explained in the text is actually applied by advocates and the courts. Procedure is therefore too often omitted from a law student's introduction to employment discrimination, a result that leaves them without a complete understanding of the area and without the necessary tools to practice in this growing field.

This book does, in many ways, take a traditional approach to employment discrimination law, addressing the core statutory and regulatory provisions in the field. The book explores the federal protections found in Title VII, the Age Discrimination in Employment Act, the Americans with Disabilities Act, and the Equal Pay Act, which combine to prohibit discrimination on the basis of race, color, sex, national origin, religion, age, and disability. Beyond this traditional approach, however, this book integrates procedural issues throughout. By examining actual cases that have been litigated in the courts, this text highlights those core procedural issues and questions facing the courts and litigants. This book also offers a detailed review of the administrative process.

Similarly, the book explores those Supreme Court cases that have arisen outside of the employment arena, but have nonetheless redefined workplace litigation. While these cases are of substantial importance to the discrimination field, they are too often omitted from instructional materials simply because they did not originate in the employment context. For example, the Supreme Court's controversial pleading decisions in *Bell Atlantic Corp. v. Twombly* and *Ashcroft v. Iqbal* have had a profound effect on the way plaintiffs allege discrimination claims. And, the Court's decisions *in Exxon Shipping Co. v. Baker* and *Philip Morris USA v. Williams* have altered the way that damages are calculated for civil rights claims, despite the fact that these cases arose outside of the employment context. Again, these cases all address procedural issues that change the way workplace cases are litigated, and this text highlights how these cases fit into the overall scheme of employment litigation.

Also, unlike any other major text in this area, this book includes a chapter on "best practices" in the industry. This chapter examines some of the best ways to address discrimination in the workplace—both from a practical and legal perspective. Among other issues, this section examines the proper training and complaint procedures that employers should have in place. It explores policies and procedures for responding to employee reference requests. It looks at emerging trends in the workplace for policies related to email, social media and other technology. And it looks at problems employers face that are not necessarily addressed by statute—including employee bullying. It also examines how to discipline employees that have gone astray of company policies, and how to document these types of corrective measures. This section thus goes beyond the law on the books, and discusses the best ways for management and employees to address everyday workplace problems.

Additionally, this book provides a number of practical elements that will help students to comprehend this complex material. In particular, this text integrates the following features into the material:

Interactive Problems. Each chapter begins with a hypothetical interactive problem that introduces the students to the area of the law that is being addressed. The problem can be used by the instructor to explore many of the issues that arise in the particular area that is discussed. The problem can also be used as a group activity to allow students to work together when formulating their opinions on the topic. Throughout the chapter, the interactive problem is revisited multiple times with differing facts that will help the students to focus in on different areas of the particular statute that is being addressed. These problems thus bring to life the material for the students, and give them an opportunity to work through the many different issues of employment discrimination law in a much more practical way.

Practice and Procedural Tips. This book contains dozens of specific practice and procedural tips for the students. The tips cover all areas of employment discrimination law—from practical suggestions on filing a charge and complaint of discrimination to ways of avoiding potential retaliation claims. These helpful hints in the area take a much more practical view of the topic of employment discrimination. These tips allow students to get a sense of the potential issues that can arise in this field, and provide guidance on how to address these concerns.

Class Exercises. This text includes numerous class exercises that the instructor can use to help emphasize the materials in the course. These exercises vary in their content and include such topics as drafting a hypothetical complaint of discrimination, writing a motion for summary judgment in a discrimination case, and formulating an anti-harassment policy. These exercises are often meant to be performed in a group setting and will help students to become more comfortable with the employment discrimination field.

Historical Notes. This text further raises many historical notes that address the evolution of employment discrimination law. This field has a rich and interesting history that is explored in these notes, which help bring some context to the issues being addressed. While the goal of the text is to focus on many of the modern developments and procedural twists currently dominating the area, it is impossible to discuss the field of employment discrimination law without providing an overview of its origins.

Summary Graphs and Charts. This text provides a number of graphs and charts that help summarize the particular topics being addressed. For example, this text provides a breakdown of how to impute claims of harassment to an employer in a graphical format. Another chart displays the differential in damages between Title VII and ADEA claims. Yet another graph summarizes the potential claims that can be brought by individuals with disabilities. Students often find this type of visual summary to be extremely helpful when learning the material.

Best Practices Chapter. This employment discrimination book is completely unique in including an entire chapter on the "best practices" in the industry. This chapter examines some of the best ways to address discrimination in the workplace—both from a theoretical and legal perspective. Among other issues, this section examines the proper training and complaint procedures that employers should have in place. It also looks at emerging trends in the workplace for policies related to email, social media and other technology. It examines the problems employers face that are not necessarily addressed by statute—including employee bullying. And it looks at how to discipline employees that have gone astray of company policies and how to document these types of corrective measures. This section goes beyond the laws on the books and discusses the best ways for management to address everyday workplace problems. And, this chapter explores the "best practices" from the worker's perspective, examining the potential pitfalls plaintiffs often face when pursuing workplace claims.

Chapter-in-Review. Each chapter begins with an introduction to the material, and ends with a review of the materials that were addressed. This review allows the instructor to make certain that she has covered all of the relevant materials in each chapter. More importantly, however, it allows students the opportunity to review and verify that they have understood the materials addressed in that section.

These various elements of the book all work together to allow students to better understand the topic of employment discrimination law. Through the use of interactive problems, practice and procedural tips, and visual reviews, this text takes a unique approach to this material. The book is designed to have both a theoretical and practical perspective. Both are necessary to gain a full understanding of this critical topic.

The second edition of this book continues all of the important elements found in the original text and includes a number of updates to evolving and emerging areas of the law. The new edition includes a robust discussion of the #MeToo movement, an examination of the recent federal appellate cases on sexual orientation discrimination, a look at recent appearance discrimination case law, and a note on workplace discrimination in the technology sector.

I have greatly enjoyed putting together these materials in a new and unique way. I have dedicated the course of my career exclusively to employment discrimination law and have a true love for this field. Employment claims have a human element that is absent from many other areas of the law. We often define who we are by what we do for a living. And, for better or worse, we often judge others by their jobs. For that reason, employment issues cut to the core of who we are as individuals. I hope that you will enjoy using and learning the materials presented here as much as I have enjoyed preparing them.

Joseph Alan Seiner
Columbia, South Carolina
2019

■ ACKNOWLEDGMENTS

This book would not have been possible without the tremendous assistance of others. There are numerous individuals who were instrumental in the preparation of this book. In particular, I would like to thank the research and support staff at the University of South Carolina School of Law. The tireless efforts, dedication, long hours, and weekend work of Carol Young specifically made the first edition of this book possible. The enormously generous assistance, hard work, helpful advice and tremendous efforts of Vanessa McQuinn greatly enhanced both editions of this text. Shannon Palmore was also extraordinarily helpful in reviewing the new edition of the text and providing substantial input and suggestions.

I would also like to thank my research assistants who were very helpful in the preparation of this text. Specifically, over two editions, this book—and the accompanying materials—have benefited greatly from the extraordinary research and drafting contributions of Brigid Benincasa, Elliot Condon, Axton Crolley, Michael Parente, Adair Patterson, Sarah Specter, Chris Trusk, Matthew Turk, Erin Waldron, and Mary Skahan Willis.

Many of my colleagues provided important advice during this process. Professors Josh Eagle, Derek Black, and Ned Snow were tremendously generous of their time in helping to guide me through the production process. Benjamin Gutman and Daniel Vail graciously (and thankfully) responded to numerous requests from me for information related to specific topics in this text. Professor Suja Thomas provided uniquely insightful advice on how to structure a book that approached employment discrimination from a procedural perspective.

I would also like to acknowledge the wonderful assistance provided by Wolters Kluwer in helping to get this project off the ground. The entire production team provided valuable contributions during this process. Kathy Langone, Carianne King, and Kaesmene Banks were instrumental in helping to fine tune this work, and in providing critical editorial guidance along the way.

Finally, I would like to give special thanks to University of South Carolina School of Law Dean Robert Wilcox for supporting and encouraging this book project and for providing the research assistance and other administrative help necessary for this effort.

Thanks to all of you, I really appreciate all of your help!

Joseph Alan Seiner

Sherman, Rowland / U.S. Information Agency / National Archives at College Park, MD. "Civil Rights March on Washington, D.C.," August 28, 1963. Photograph. http://research.archives.gov/description/542014.

National Archives at College Park, MD. "President George H. W. Bush Signs the Americans with Disabilities Act," July 26, 1990. Photograph. http://research.archives.gov/description/6037489#.

Gibbons, Tony / flickr. "City and County Building – Salt Lake City," June 23, 2009. Photograph. https://www.flickr.com/photos/ftzgene/3869484352/in/photostream/. Reprinted with permission.

National Archives at College Park, MD. "Eleanor Roosevelt, Franklin D. Roosevelt Jr; and Franklin D. Roosevelt III," 1962. Photograph. http://research.archives.gov/description/196361.http://research.archives.gov/description/6037489#.

Highsmith, Carol / Photographs in the Carol M. Highsmith Archive, Library of Congress, Prints and Photographs Division. "Crew of Amtrak's new Acela Express trainset model their new uniforms. Washington, D.C." Photograph. http://www.loc.gov/pictures/item/2011633271/.

drummerboy / morgueFile. "Stethoscope_fullview." Photograph. http://www.morguefile.com/archive/display/42955.

Highsmith, Carol / Photographs in the Carol M. Highsmith's America, Library of Congress, Prints and Photographs Division. "Chrysler Building detail, New York, New York," Sept. 16, 2007. http://www.loc.gov/pictures/item/2010630430/.

Highsmith, Carol / Photographs in the Carol M. Highsmith's America, Library of Congress, Prints and Photographs Division. "Aerial view of World Trade Center, New York, New York, taken a couple of months before 9/11 tragedy," 2001. http://www.loc.gov/pictures/item/2011634887/.

Thorman, Mary / morgueFile. "Bitterlivesbittermen." http://www.morguefile.com/archive/display/84029.

Sloan, Lester / AARP. "Percy Green, II. St. Louis, Missouri," 2004.

National Park Service. "Gateway Arch in the Spring." http://www.nps.gov/media/photo/gallery.htm?id=68B91F4A-155D-4519-3EF693EC657D9F13.

Bergeron, Ronnie / morgueFile. Warehouse. Photograph. http://www.morguefile.com/archive/display/85631.

Caputo, Joey / Brave New Films. "A Protest in Utah against Wal-Mart," July 14, 2005. http://commons.wikimedia.org/wiki/File%3AWal-Mart_protest_in_Utah.jpg.

West, Liz / flickr. "Fire Fighter Gear," December 20, 2005. Photograph. https://www.flickr.com/photos/calliope/75703700/.

Petteway, Steve / Collection of the Supreme Court of the United States. "Sonia Sotomayor, U.S. Supreme Court," Aug. 21, 2009. Photograph. http://en.wikipedia.org/wiki/File:Sonia_Sotomayor_in_SCOTUS_robe.jpg.

VWAmFot / Wikimedia Commons. "Vrouwe Justitia-beeld op de Civiele Griffie," Oct. 29, 2008. [CC-BY-SA-3.0 (http://creativecommons.org/licenses/by-sa/3.0)]. Photograph. http://commons.wikimedia.org/wiki/File%3AVrouwe_Justitia-beeld_op_de_Civiele_Griffie%2C_Burg_11_2%2C_Brugge.JPG.

Alexandrowicz, John L., / Environmental Protection Agency / National Archives at College Park, MD. "West Penn Power Plant North of Pittsburgh." September 1975. Photograph. http://research.archives.gov/description/557295.

Bubley, Esther / Library of Congress, Prints & Photographs Division, FSA/OWI Collection, LC-DIG-fsa-8d33365. "Sign at bus station. Rome, Georgia," Sept. 1943. Photograph. http://www.loc.gov/pictures/item/owi2001035842/PP/.

Highsmith, Carol / The Jon B. Lovelace Collection of California Photographs in Carol M. Highsmith's America Project, Library of Congress, Prints and Photographs Division. "Folsom State Prison is a California State Prison in Folsom, California." Photograph. http://www.loc.gov/pictures/item/2011631970/.

The National Oceanic and Atmospheric Administration. "Salmon Cannery and Herring Reduction Plant." Photograph. http://www.photolib.noaa.gov/htmls/fish5700.htm.

Collection of the Supreme Court of the United States. Photograph. http://commons.wikimedia.org/wiki/File:Anthony_Kennedy_official_SCOTUS_portrait.jpg.

Library of Congress, Prints & Photographs Division, HABS CAL, 41-REDWO , 1–9. "Interior Tellers' Windows - Bank of San Mateo County 2000-2002." Photograph. http://www.loc.gov/pictures/item/ca0847.photos.017653p/.

Jefferies, Rupert / morgueFile. "Knebworth05." Photograph. http://www.morgue-file.com/archive/display/79410. Reprinted by permission.

Department of Defense / American Forces Information Service / Defense Visual Information Center / National Archives at College Park, MD. "AFIS BILLBOARD POSTERS. SEXUAL HARASSMENT! DEFENSE BILLBOARD #27," January 1, 2000. Illustration. http://research.archives.gov/description/6507449.

Richie, Robert Yarnall / Robert Yarnall Richie Photograph Collection / Southern Methodist University / Central University Libraries / DeGolyer Library. "Gulf Oil Corp., Gulf Service Boat & Fixed Platform Rig," July 15, 1956. Photograph. https://www.flickr.com/photos/smu_cul_digitalcollections/8222024652/.

Clarita / morgueFile. Mannequin couple. Photograph. http://www.morguefile.com/archive/display/219875.

Sawyer, Jane M. / morgueFile. ATM sign. Photograph. http://www.morguefile.com/archive/display/27851. Reprinted with permission.

Petteway, Steve / Collection of the Supreme Court of the United States. Justice Clarence Thomas. Photograph. http://web.archive.org/web/20080523184218/ http:/www.supremecourthistory.org/02_history/subs_current/images_b/008.html.

McNeely, Bob, The White House. Bill Clinton. Photograph. http://en.wikipedia.org/wiki/File:Bill_Clinton.jpg.

skmeljin / morgueFile. Lifeguard chair. Photograph. http://www.morguefile.com/archive/display/606900.

Jade0620 / morgueFile. Lifeguards in chairs. Photograph. http://www.morguefile.com/archive/display/606900.

Riggan, Phil. Virginia Civil Rights Memorial. Photograph. Reprinted with permission.

Rowe, Abbie / White House Photographs / John F. Kennedy Presidential Library and Museum, Boston. "Meeting with Robert F. Kennedy (RFK), Martin Luther King, Jr. (MLK), and Burke Marshall, 10:30AM," June 22, 1963. Photograph. http://www.jfklibrary.org/Asset-Viewer/Archives/JFKWHP-1963-06-22-A.aspx.

Rice, Don / Library of Congress Prints and Photographs Division, LC-USZ62-111165. "Martin Luther King, Jr., half-length portrait, facing left, speaking at microphones, during anti-war demonstration, New York City," 1967. Photograph. http://www.loc.gov/pictures/item/94505369/.

Liberman, Howard / Library of Congress, Prints & Photographs Division, FSA/OWI Collection, LC-USW3-054153-D. "A Transit-Mixed Concrete Company truck displaying a United States Truck Conservation Corps pledge on the door," Oct. 1942. Photograph. http://www.loc.gov/pictures/item/owi2001040568/PP/.

Shahn, Ben / Library of Congress, Prints & Photographs Division, FSA/OWI Collection, LC-USF33- 006392-M4. "Sign on restaurant, Lancaster, Ohio," Aug. 1938. Photograph. http://www.loc.gov/pictures/item/fsa1997017528/PP/.

Clarita / morgueFile. Lady with basket statue. Photograph. http://www.morgue-file.com/archive/display/143870.

Illinois: Federal Art Project, 1936 or 1937, Library of Congress Prints and Photographs Division. Photograph. "Girls - are you interested in a job?" http://www.loc.gov/pictures/item/98517815/.

Work Projects Administration Poster, Library of Congress Prints and Photographs Division. "Expecting? Get the right advice from the right sources, your doctor or health bureau," September 1938. Photograph. http://www.loc.gov/pictures/item/98513524/.

Vosper, Gretta / morgueFile. "Expectancy." Photograph. http://www.morguefile.com/archive/display/757315. Reprinted with permission.

Saatchi & Saatchi / Library of Congress, Prints & Photographs Division, LC-USZC4-2857. "Would you be more careful if it was you who got pregnant?" Photograph. http://www.loc.gov/pictures/item/yan1996000207/PP/.

Black, Kevin / morgueFile. "Random aisle photos." Photograph. http://www.morguefile.com/archive/display/910480. Reprinted with permission.

Highsmith, Carol / The Jon B. Lovelace Collection of California Photographs in Carol M. Highsmith's America Project, Library of Congress, Prints and Photographs Division. "2012 Gay Pride Parade, San Francisco, California," 2012. Photograph. http://www.loc.gov/pictures/item/2013633371/.

Library of Congress, Prints & Photographs Division, HABS MASS, 13-BOST, 144A–12. Photograph. http://www.loc.gov/pictures/item/ma1445.photos.336409p/.

Farr, Larry / morgueFile. Razor wire. Photograph. http://www.morguefile.com/archive/display/872477. Reprinted with permission.

Highsmith, Carol / Photographs in the Carol M. Highsmith Archive, Library of Congress, Prints and Photographs Division. "Harrah's Hotel and Casino, Las Vegas, Nevada." Photograph. http://www.loc.gov/pictures/item/2011634602/.

Highsmith, Carol / Photographs in the Carol M. Highsmith Archive, Library of Congress, Prints and Photographs Division. "Hilton Hotel casino sign, Las Vegas." Photograph. http://www.loc.gov/pictures/item/2011631856/.

Highsmith, Carol / Photographs in the Carol M. Highsmith Archive, Library of Congress, Prints and Photographs Division. "Tropicana Casino, Las Vegas, Nevada." Photograph. http://www.loc.gov/pictures/item/2011636069/.

Library of Congress. "The sky is now her limit," Oct. 1920. Illustration. http://www.morguefile.com/archive/display/872477http://www.loc.gov/pictures/item/2002716769/.

Library of Congress, Rare Book and Special Collections Division, America Singing: Nineteenth-Century Song Sheets. "No Irish need apply," 1862. Sheet Music. http://www.loc.gov/item/amss002378/.

U.S. War Manpower Commission, Library of Congress Prints and Photographs Division. "Americans All," 1942. Illustration. http://www.loc.gov/pictures/item/96502727/.

Courtesy of The Bancroft Library, University of California, Berkeley; Call no. AP2 H3 Vol. 13:512. "Pacific Chivalry." Illustration. http://content.cdlib.org/ark:/13030/hb9n39p05s/.

Adams, Ansel / Library of Congress, Prints & Photographs Division, LC-DIG-ppprs-00309. "Butcher shop, Manzanar Relocation Center," 1943. Photograph. http://www.loc.gov/pictures/item/2002695118/.

Edouarado / morgueFile. Angel Statue. Photograph. http://www.morguefile.com/archive/display/601589.

Bain News Service / Library of Congress, Prints & Photographs Division, LC-DIG-ggbain-04403. "Prayer at meeting of House of Representatives, interior of chamber, Washington," Dec. 6, 2009. Photograph. http://www.loc.gov/pictures/item/ggb2004004403/.

Matson Photo Service / Library of Congress, Prints & Photographs Division, LC-DIG-matpc-22819. "Mount of Olives, Bethphage and Bethany. Mt. of Olives, tablets in the Church of the Lord's Prayer." http://www.loc.gov/pictures/item/mpc2010000198/PP/.

Lee, Russell / Library of Congress, Prints & Photographs Division, FSA/OWI Collection, LC-USF34-035276-D. "Agricultural workers union at Tabor, Oklahoma, opens with a prayer," Feb. 1940. Photograph. http://www.loc.gov/pictures/item/fsa2000016540/PP/.

Lee, Russell / Library of Congress, Prints & Photographs Division, FSA/OWI Collection, LC-USF34-036686-D. "The school day opens with prayer at private school at the Farm Bureau building," June 1940. Photograph. http://www.loc.gov/pictures/item/fsa2000018000/PP/.

Highsmith, Carol / Carol M. Highsmith's America, Library of Congress, Prints and Photographs Division. Lee, Russell / Library of Congress, Prints & Photographs Division, FSA/OWI Collection, LC-USF34-036686-D. "General Motors Building, Detroit, Michigan," June 4, 2006. Photograph. http://www.loc.gov/pictures/item/2010630931/.

Herr, John / Library of Congress, Prints & Photographs Division, HAER PA, 51-PHILA, 713--7. "Detail of Fly Twa Sign Mounted on Northwest Edge of Roof," 1999. Photograph. http://www.loc.gov/pictures/item/pa3780.photos.362321p/.

sideshowmom / morgueFile. TWA plane. Photograph. http://www.morguefile.com/archive/display/70338.

Connors, Kevin / morgueFile. School lockers. Photograph. http://www.morguefile.com/archive/display/611007. Reprinted with permission.

Miltenberg, Joni /morgueFile. "Apple dictionary." Photograph. http://morguefile.com/archive/display/872873. Reprinted with permission.

Connors, Kevin / morgueFile. Classroom. Photograph. http://www.morguefile.com/archive/display/610885. Reprinted with permission.

Highsmith, Carol / Photographs in the Carol M. Highsmith Archive, Library of Congress, Prints and Photographs Division. "The University of Notre Dame is a Catholic research university located in Notre Dame, an unincorporated community north of the city of South Bend, in St. Joseph County, Indiana," October 2012. Photograph. http://www.loc.gov/pictures/item/2013650737/.

Library of Congress, Prints & Photographs Division, HABS, HABS CAL,38-SANFRA,203A--1. "Contextual view from east-southeast, showing cathedral house and cathedral in rear - Grace Cathedral, George William Gibbs Memorial Hall, 1051 Taylor Street, San Francisco, San Francisco County, CA." Photograph. http://www.loc.gov/pictures/item/ca1806.photos.323019p/.

Connors, Kevin / morgueFile. Metropolitan Cathedral doors. Photograph. http://www.morguefile.com/archive/display/866664. Reprinted with permission.

Connors, Kevin / morgueFile. Steps. Photograph. http://www.morguefile.com/archive/display/221600. Reprinted with permission.

Library of Congress, Prints & Photographs Division. "Helen Keller, three-quarter length, seated, facing right; holding hand of her teacher, Mrs. John A. Macy (Anne Mansfield Sullivan)." Photograph. http://www.loc.gov/pictures/item/2002706661/.

miguelwhee / morgueFile. United Airlines plane. Photograph. http://www.morguefile.com/archive/display/147442.

Library of Congress, Prints & Photographs Division, HABS CAL, 1-OAK,1600–7. "Interior, Kitchen/Galley, From Near Southeast Corner of Room, Looking West, With Passages to Refrigeration And Food Preparation Rooms At Center." http://www.loc.gov/pictures/item/ca2222.photos.182775p/.

Library of Congress, Prints & Photographs Division, Detroit Publishing Company Collection, LC-DIG-det-4a09249. "Methodist church, Streator, Ill." Photograph. http://www.loc.gov/pictures/item/det1994014869/PP/.

Tarleton, Gary / Library of Congress, Prints & Photographs Division, HAER ORE, 2-MONR, 1--60 (CT). "GENERAL VIEW OF SITE FROM EAST OVER LUMBER YARD," 1997. Photograph. http://www.loc.gov/pictures/item/or0449.color.570338c/.

Lee, Russell / Library of Congress, Prints & Photographs Division, FSA/OWI Collection, LC-USF34-070620-D. "Long Bell Lumber Company, Cowlitz County, Washington. Yarding logs," Oct. 1941. Photograph. http://www.loc.gov/pictures/item/fsa2000047330/PP/.

Indrelunas, Brian / flickr. U.S. Airways headquarters. Jan. 15, 2009. Photograph. https://www.flickr.com/photos/btindrelunas/3205391788/.

Anderson, Paul / morgueFile. "Caution sign." Photograph. http://www.morguefile.com/archive/display/700322.

Navarro, Paula / Freeimages. "The Grandfather Sculpture," Sept. 17, 2006. Photograph. http://www.freeimages.com/photo/618387.

Sprout, Susan / Sunbriar Beagles / morgueFile. "Faye and Dick." Photograph. http://www.morguefile.com/archive/display/798346. Reprinted with permission.

Lee, Russell / Library of Congress, Prints & Photographs Division, FSA/OWI Collection, LC-USF33-012762-M2. "Elderly man who has lived in Mogollon, New Mexico from its earliest days," June 1940. Photograph. http://www.loc.gov/pictures/item/fsa1998001188/PP/.

Brewster, Robert / Library of Congress, Prints & Photographs Division, HAER MASS, 11 - QUI, 10C--6,2-MONR,1--60 (CT). "View from west side of Hammerhead crane," 1989. Photograph. http://www.loc.gov/pictures/item/ma1533.photos.336964p/.

Department of Defense / National Archives at College Park, MD. "A team of US Air Force (USAF) fire fighters, in proximity suits, from the 185th Civil Engineer Squadron (CES) spray water on a mock aircraft at the North Dakota Air National Guard (NDANG) Regional Training Site (RTS) in Fargo, North Dakota (ND)," June 15, 2004. Photograph. http://research.archives.gov/description/6664795.

Mconnors / morgueFile. Gavel. Photograph. http://www.morguefile.com/archive/display/734782.

Pittman, Blair / Environmental Protection Agency / National Archives at College Park, MD. "Fishing in the Houston Ship Channel," September 1973. http://research.archives.gov/description/550902.

Wright, Martin, Mass Communication SPECIALIST 1ST Class U.S. Navy / Department of Defense. "U.S. Navy Reserve Construction Mechanic 2nd Class Brian Seaverns, assigned to Naval Mobile Construction Battalion 18 (NMCB-18), power washes a vehicle engine clean before starting to do any further maintenance in the Construction Mechanic Shop, at Camp Fallujah, Al Anbar Province, Iraq," Jan. 31, 2007. Photograph. http://research.archives.gov/description/6704001.

Highsmith, Carol / Photographs in the Carol M. Highsmith Archive, Library of Congress, Prints and Photographs Division. "Dental office." Photograph. http://www.loc.gov/pictures/item/2011634399/.

Vachon, John / Library of Congress, Prints & Photographs Division, FSA/OWI Collection, LC-USW3-018258-D. "New York, New York. Camel cigarette advertisement at Times Square," Feb. 1943. Photograph. http://www.loc.gov/pictures/item/owi2001020004/PP/.

Melki, Serge / flickr. "Justice Statue with light painting," Nov. 22, 2008. Photograph. https://www.flickr.com/photos/sergemelki/3056656393. Reprinted with permission.

Federal Bureau of Investigation. Photograph. http://www.fbi.gov/news/stories/2007/october/snipers_102207.

Lock, Jeremy T. / Tech. Sgt. / U.S. Air Force. Federal Bureau of Investigation. "Firefighters in Iraq," June 8, 2006. Photograph. http://commons.wikimedia.org/wiki/File:Firefighters_in_Iraq.JPG.

Library of Congress, Prints & Photographs Division, Detroit Publishing Company Collection, LC-DIG-det-4a25852. "Couple at champagne supper." Photograph. http://www.loc.gov/pictures/item/det1994022159/PP/.

Library of Congress, Prints & Photographs Division, Detroit Publishing Company Collection, LC-DIG-det-4a27658. "Young couple on rock holding hands, full-length portrait." Photograph. http://www.loc.gov/pictures/item/det1994024103/PP/.

Photographs in the Carol M. Highsmith Archive, Library of Congress, Prints and Photographs Division. "Willis Tower, long known as Sears Tower, Chicago, Illinois." Photograph. http://www.loc.gov/pictures/item/2011634501/.

Kandell, Alice S. / Library of Congress, Prints & Photographs Division. Dr. Alice S. Kandell Collection of Sikkim Photographs, LC-DIG-ppmsca-30783. "Nepalese woman wearing purple headscarf and nose ring, holding baby, Sikkim." Photograph. http://www.loc.gov/pictures/item/2011646465/.

Highsmith, Carol / The Jon B. Lovelace Collection of California Photographs in Carol M. Highsmith's America Project, Library of Congress, Prints and Photographs Division. "Colorful liquor-store sign in North Hollywood, California," 2013. Photograph. http://www.loc.gov/pictures/item/2013631377/.

Henderson, Win / Federal Emergency Management Agency/ National Archives at College Park, MD, October 6, 2005. "New Orleans, October 6, 2005 - A medical simulation set up in one of the 12 operating rooms available on the hospital ship USS Comfort," Oct. 6, 2005. Photograph. http://research.archives.gov/description/5691777.

—J.A.S.

■ PRACTICE AND PROCEDURAL TIPS

■ A NOTE ABOUT THE CASES INCLUDED AND CASE EDITING

It is worth briefly addressing the manner in which the cases are presented in this book. The cases have often been heavily edited due to space constraints and in an effort to help the material flow more smoothly for the students. In this regard, most (if not all) of the subheadings used by the courts have been deleted. Many individual paragraphs, sentences, citations, and quotations by the courts have also been omitted, and some paragraphs have been merged in certain instances. This book further avoids many of the traditional signals of deleted materials (such as the use of ellipses) in its presentation of the cases to allow the material to be set forth in a more straightforward and unobtrusive way. Many of the concurrences and dissenting opinions have also been removed. In some instances, there have been small additions made (such as including a full case citation). I would refer the reader back to the original case, then, before citing directly to the material or quoting any of the language in the text. These changes are in no way intended to alter the meaning of the different courts' decisions, but rather to present these decisions in a more concise and effective way for educational purposes.

I would also like to note that I worked for many years as an attorney for the U.S. Equal Employment Opportunity Commission in Washington, D.C. While at the EEOC, I gained an enormous respect for the work of the Commission and its efforts to help prevent and eradicate employment discrimination. In some instances, I served as lead counsel in some of the cases that are presented in this material. In certain other instances, colleagues of mine were heavily involved in some of the cases presented here. The views that are expressed in this text are solely my own and in no way represent the views of the EEOC, the federal government, or any other individual or entity.

PART ONE

Introduction & The Administrative Process

Employment Discrimination

A. Introduction

Employment discrimination has a lengthy and troubled history under the laws of the United States. Discrimination has long been a problem in this country, and it continues to thrive to this day. Employment discrimination can take many forms, and depending upon societal issues or concerns, has ebbed and flowed in particular geographical areas, affecting different segments of the population at different times in our nation's history. For example, in the midst of World War II, this country saw a swift and immediate backlash against Japanese Americans. *See* Korematsu v. United States, 323 U.S. 214 (1944) (upholding the constitutionality of the Japanese internment, which included a racially based military system of curfew and exclusion, following the attack on Pearl Harbor). The Iran hostage crisis in 1979 led to Iranian Americans becoming the primary target of xenophobic Americans, resulting in a spate of hate crimes and widespread discrimination. Similarly, in the days and months following September 11, 2001, Muslim Americans experienced heightened levels of discrimination. *See* Shoba Sivaprasad Wadhia, *Business as Usual: Immigration and the National Security Exception*, 114 PENN. ST. L. REV. 1485, 1505 (2010) (noting that both "airport discrimination" and "employment discrimination" against Arab, Muslim, and South Asian populations heightened following September 11, 2001). And, race discrimination against African Americans (and others) has long been a major problem in this country. This open, overt form of discrimination led to the widespread civil rights protests and riots in the 1960s. Ultimately, backlash against this form of discrimination resulted in substantial legislative reform.

The creation of Title VII of the Civil Rights Act of 1964 — which prohibits many forms of discrimination — was largely a result of the civil rights movement, which was energized in 1954 after the Supreme Court's landmark decision in *Brown v. Board of Education*, 347 U.S. 483 (1954), as well as Dr. Martin Luther King's legacy of fighting against racial discrimination and bias in society. During the 1950s and 1960s, members of the public organized peaceful protests, boycotts, and sit-ins to end racial segregation in buses, public places, and even some schools. The resistance, however, often responded violently and countless protestors and innocent civilians lost their lives during the movement. In the spring of 1963, Dr. King was arrested in Birmingham, Alabama, and imprisoned, during which time he wrote his famous "Letter from Birmingham Jail," urging for equal rights between blacks and whites. In June 1963, President Kennedy addressed the nation and vowed to pave the way for equality in American society by proposing a civil rights bill that would

Civil Rights March at the Lincoln Memorial

guarantee all Americans a right to be served in public establishments and would authorize the federal government to be more involved in school segregation cases. After the President's remarks, even more violence erupted — a prominent civil rights advocate was murdered outside of his home and, after King's famous "I Have a Dream Speech" in August 1963, members of the Ku Klux Klan bombed a Birmingham church, leaving four young girls dead and twenty-one others injured. In the meantime, Congress continued to debate the President's bill, and a subcommittee eventually strengthened the bill by adding a guarantee to equal employment. On November 20, 1963, the House Judiciary Committee issued a favorable report regarding the bill, but only two days later President Kennedy was killed. President Lyndon Johnson picked up where President Kennedy left off, promising to make civil rights a focus of his presidency. The President urged Congress to pass the bill, including the employment section of the statute. Debate continued, with critics arguing that Title VII was unconstitutional and would essentially result in a dictatorship that controlled what employers could and could not do. While Title VII was primarily designed to end employment discrimination on the basis of race and color, it covers other protected classes as well — religion, national origin, and sex. The scope of protection afforded by the Act was also hotly debated, with proponents supporting its extension to several characteristics and opponents criticizing it.

Dramatic filibustering followed the long and heated debates, but finally ended with a 71–29 vote in the Senate. Social unrest did not immediately cease, but President Johnson signed the bill into law on July 2, 1964, in a groundbreaking moment in support of the civil rights movement and Dr. King's cause. Title VII, along with the EEOC's implementation of it and other similar employment discrimination statutes, such as the Americans with Disabilities Act and Age Discrimination in Employment Act, has led to definite progress with respect to equal employment opportunities and workplace environments free of discrimination and harassment. Although this book does not purport to provide a complete historical overview, there are a number of wonderful sources that do provide in-depth accounts of the emergence of Title VII. *See, e.g.,* Eric S. Dreiband, *Celebration of Title VII at Forty*, 36 U. MEM. L. REV. 5 (2005); Francis J. Vaas, *Title VII: Legislative History*, 7 B.C. INDUS. & COM. L. REV. 431 (1966).

As a nation, we have struggled not only with discrimination, but also with how to combat it. Various laws have emerged during different political and economic climates. Civil rights statutes now cover a wide range of different activities, including public accommodations, voting laws, and housing legislation. More important to this text, however, Congress passed a number of federal laws targeted at discrimination in the workplace. These laws would supplement both the constitutional protections that have always been in place, as well as state and local prohibitions against workplace discrimination. *See* Jeffrey M. Hirsch, *Revolution in Pragmatist Clothing: Nationalizing Workplace Law*, 61 ALA. L. REV. 1025 (2010) (arguing in support of nationalizing workplace law to create an ideal level of regulation).

B. Current Debate — Theory Versus Procedure

For years, there has been a substantial debate as to whether employment discrimination laws were appropriate in the workplace. Many argued that enacting such laws was not the place of the federal government, and that state and local jurisdictions should address these concerns on a more regional level. Others believed that discrimination was best addressed not by the legislature, but by the economy. *See, e.g.,* Richard A. Posner, *The Efficiency and the Efficacy of Title VII*, 136 U. PA. L. REV. 513 (1987). These commentators argued that those companies that discriminated against their workers were inherently inefficient, and would eventually be supplanted by more effective businesses that did not discriminate against their personnel. Still others maintained that discrimination was a vestige of the past, and any remaining practices were merely de minimis and not warranting the resources necessary to intervene.

These arguments — whether valid or not — have largely gone by the wayside over time. At present, there remains little credible debate over whether antidiscrimination laws should exist in the workplace. The debate over whether the "theory" of employment discrimination should even exist has largely been resolved, and it is clear that workplace laws are here to stay. While some might still attempt to argue against the value of these laws, there is little chance that such laws will cease to exist any time soon.

This is not to say that the field of employment discrimination is without controversy. Much to the contrary, workplace laws have always been — and continue to be — a source of great debate in the legislature and judiciary. The debate has moved, however. There is now very little focus on the issue of whether employment discrimination should exist as a theory. Instead, the argument now focuses more on how these laws should be applied to both employers and employees. The question has now moved to the appropriate scope and breadth of the laws, and how these laws should be interpreted. While some may still use basic principles of economics to argue against antidiscrimination statutes, these arguments have failed to gain any traction. Discrimination law is now solidly entrenched in our society as a recognized exception to the employment-at-will principle.

In many ways, the real debate has moved to one that is largely about policy and procedure. The debate that is currently taking place seems to center on what type of policy we should have when it comes to employment discrimination. Should the laws serve as a shield to proactively protect workers from all forms of workplace discrimination, or should they be used more infrequently and only in instances where the discrimination is both egregious and widespread? Should antidiscrimination laws be used aggressively to ferret out unlawful conduct, or should we be hesitant to intrude on business operations with excessive workplace litigation?

Civil Rights Protest

In more recent years, these policy questions — which have focused on how vibrant the antidiscrimination laws should be — have been largely debated in the context of civil procedure. The controversial questions in this area now center on how cases should be litigated, and the manner in which procedural mechanisms should be used in workplace disputes. We have thus seen a monumental shift from arguments over whether the laws should exist, to how the laws should be implemented and enforced.

These procedural questions have come in many different forms, but the basic policy question of the breadth and scope of the laws remains the same. For example, questions have been raised over whether the judicial forum is even the right place for workplace disputes, or whether these claims are better suited for an arbitrator with expertise in the area. When claims have been permitted in the courts, we have seen debate over the specificity with which the case must be alleged, and how plausible the particular claim must be to survive dismissal. We have also seen a dramatic rise over time in the extent to which summary judgment is used as a tool to prevent a jury from deciding a particular case. And, we have seen controversial decisions on class-action workplace disputes that make it much more difficult for workers to band together when bringing claims of discrimination.

The list goes on, and the procedural disputes have now taken center stage in the ongoing debate over the purpose and scope of antidiscrimination laws. From an educational standpoint, we must now study these laws from a different perspective as well. We should fully consider and understand these procedural concerns and issues, and how procedure can play a unique role in the context of antidiscrimination laws.

C. Employment Statutes

Unlike many other industrialized nations, the United States operates under the principle of at-will employment. At-will employment means that an employee can be fired at any time for any reason, and that the employee can leave employment at any time for any reason. This rule has become a core principle in the operation of the workplace. Over time, several exceptions have been carved out. One major exception that now exists is for employment discrimination. As a society, this country has determined that this form of discrimination should not be permitted under the eyes of the law. There are several bases that now exist for this exception. *See generally* Joseph E. Slater, *The "American Rule" that Swallows the Exceptions*, 11 Emp. Rts. & Emp. Pol'y J. 53 (2007) (arguing that employment at-will undermines anti-discrimination law); Ellen Dannin, *Why at-Will Employment Is Bad for Employers and Just Cause Is Good for Them*, 58 Lab. L.J. 5 (2007) (arguing that the at-will regime ill serves employees, our economy, and our national interests); Scott A. Moss, *When There's At-Will, There Are Many Ways: Redressing the Increasing Incoherence of Employment At Will*, 67 U. Pitt. L. Rev. 295 (2005) (suggesting how courts can retain employment at-will while also lessening the doctrinal incoherence).

In particular, there are several federal laws prohibiting workplace discrimination that will form the basis of this text. Though constitutional law, state law, and local statutes are also an integral part of an employment discrimination practice, federal law is typically at the heart of this field. This text will thus focus primarily on federal law and the statutes that prohibit discrimination in the workplace.

Title VII of the Civil Rights Act of 1964. This statute forms the basis for much of what is considered antidiscrimination law, and was highly controversial at the time of passage. The rise of the civil rights era largely started at the end of World War II. The labor shortage at the time resulted in stronger employment opportunities for minority workers. The nation also saw a shift in attitude toward black and women workers at this time, and the Supreme Court's decision in *Brown v. Board of Education* signaled a cultural shift toward equality in this country. Various forms of civil rights legislation were debated in the 1950s and 1960s, and President Kennedy originally proposed an early version of Title VII, though this first proposal was largely seen as ineffective.

Following President Kennedy's death, President Lyndon B. Johnson aggressively backed more sweeping employment reforms. At the time, the heart of Title VII was seen as its prohibitions against race discrimination, though the bill would outlaw various other forms of discrimination as well. A fierce legislative battle was waged over the legislation, and vigorous negotiations avoided filibusters and other proposed blocks to the statute. President Johnson, who became a surprise advocate of enhanced civil rights protections, quickly supported the legislation. Five days after President Kennedy's assassination, President Johnson addressed Congress, stating:

> We have talked long enough in this country about civil rights. It is time to write the next chapter and to write it in the books of law . . . . No eulogy could more eloquently honor President Kennedy's memory than the earliest possible passage of the civil rights bill for which he fought so long.

EEOC, *Pre 1965: Events Leading to the Creation of EEOC*, www.eeoc.gov/eeoc/history/35th/pre1965/index.html.

Title VII of the Civil Rights Act was passed into law as part of sweeping civil rights legislation. In passing this statute, Congress looked to some of the laws that had already been passed by other states, and also considered other federal legislation on worker rights. The statute is quite unique, however, in its coverage of workers and in its remedial scheme. The statute prohibits discrimination against employees on the basis of race, color, sex, national origin, and religion. The law further prohibits retaliation against those who participate in a discrimination claim or oppose discrimination in the workplace. To qualify for coverage under Title VII, an employer must employ at least fifteen workers. In addition to its substantive prohibitions, the statute also created the Equal Employment Opportunity Commission (EEOC). The EEOC was charged with helping to interpret the law. Subsequent legislation also gave the EEOC litigation authority, and the agency has been largely responsible for enforcing the employment provisions of the Civil Rights Act.

Dr. Martin Luther King, Jr. at the Civil Rights March on Washington, D.C.

As the original statute did not provide the EEOC with independent litigation authority, Title VII provides a robust private right of action. Individuals may thus bring their own claims against their employers once they have successfully navigated the administrative process and received a right-to-sue letter from the EEOC. The statute was subsequently amended, and employers may now also be subject to suit by the federal government. In 1991, Title VII was further amended to include the opportunity for plaintiffs to secure compensatory and punitive damages in intentional discrimination cases, and also to provide the right to a jury trial. The 1991 amendments also codified disparate impact claims, which provide a cause of action where a facially neutral policy or practice has an adverse effect on a protected group for which there is no legitimate business justification.

The number of charges filed under Title VII have varied over time. As demonstrated by the chart below, however, the recent trend has been for discrimination claims to be on the rise in recent years:

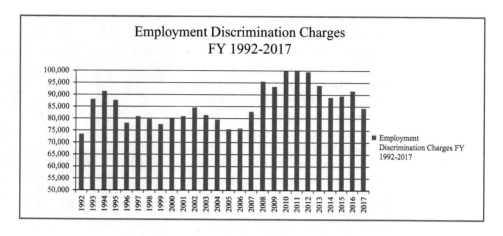

Source: EEOC, Charge Statistics FY 1992 Through FY 1996 & Charge Statistics FY 1997 Through FY 2017, http://eeoc.gov/eeoc/statistics/enforcement/charges.cfm & http://eeoc.gov/eeoc/statistics/enforcement/charges-a.cfm.

The Age Discrimination in Employment Act of 1967 (ADEA). In addition to Title VII's protections for workers on the basis of race, color, sex, national origin, and religion, Congress debated legislation at the time that would outlaw age-based discrimination as well. Early attempts to include age discrimination as part of Title VII were unsuccessful. Instead of including age as part of this earlier statute, the Secretary of Labor was charged with conducting a study on the issue to determine the extent of the problem.

The Secretary's report revealed widespread discrimination on the basis of age that was based largely on stereotypes and not on actual worker performance. While passage of Title VII was highly controversial, the ADEA was not nearly as contentious. Indeed, the statute was passed with little opposition, and prohibits discrimination in the workplace on the basis of age. The statute covers workers who are forty years of age or older. In addition, the statute covers employers that employ twenty or more workers. The damages provisions of the ADEA differ dramatically from Title VII, as will be discussed later in this text.

The Americans with Disabilities Act (ADA). The ADA is the most recent of the civil rights legislation that will be thoroughly discussed in this book. In the ADA, Congress stated that 43 million Americans have at least one disability, and that this number is on the rise. The statute was backed with almost uniform political support, and signed by the first President Bush on July 26, 1990. A narrow reading of the statute by several Supreme Court decisions led to amendments of the statute as part of the ADA Amendments Act of 2008 (ADAAA). The ADAAA expanded the scope of the statute and rebuffed these Supreme Court cases.

The ADA prohibits discrimination against individuals with disabilities in the workplace. The statute contains numerous technical terms that have been defined by the courts and regulations, and will be discussed later in this text. The statute provides coverage for employers with fifteen or more employees. In many ways, the statute is patterned after Title VII, and mirrors many of the damages provisions of this statute.

Other Federal Legislation. Other federal statutes provide additional protections from discrimination for many workers. Such provisions include, for example, the Rehabilitation Act of 1973, which was the precursor to the ADA. The Uniformed Services Employment and Reemployment Rights Act of 1994 (USERRA) prohibits discrimination against military personnel. And, the Immigration Reform and Control Act of 1986 provides for cer-

President George H. W. Bush signs the ADA, July 26, 1990

tain discrimination claims on the basis of national origin. Additionally, Congress more recently acted to prohibit genetic discrimination in the workplace with the Genetic Information Nondiscrimination Act of 2008 (GINA). This text will also touch on the Equal Pay Act, which prohibits pay discrimination on the basis of gender. Finally, it should be noted that federal legislation is routinely proposed in Congress, with varying degrees of success. For example, several attempts to pass legislation prohibiting discrimination on the basis of sexual orientation have been made, though these attempts have all been unsuccessful.

It is also worth noting that 42 U.S.C. § 1981 is a statutory provision that prohibits racial discrimination arising from an employment contract. Per the statute, "[a]ll persons within the jurisdiction of the United States shall have the same right in every State and Territory to make and enforce contracts." This statute allows private and public workers to pursue discrimination claims against their employers specifically on the basis of race. Unlike many of the other federal statutes discussed above, there is no minimum employee threshold for claims brought under 42 U.S.C. § 1981, and the statute of limitations gives individuals four years to file a claim.

All of these "other" statutes thus provide important aspects of employment discrimination laws, but nonetheless are not a major focus of this book. Title VII, the ADEA, and the ADA are the major statutory provisions that are emphasized in this text.

D. Constitutional Claims

In addition to the various federal statutory prohibitions against discrimination, the U.S. Constitution also provides a basis for bringing employment discrimination claims. In particular, 42 U.S.C. § 1983 provides workers with a basis for suing a governmental employer under the Fourteenth Amendment. Thus, for the most part, such suits are brought not against private employers (as authorized under Title VII), but against individual states and state officials.

Section 1983 provides that where a state entity subjects "any citizen of the United States or other person within the jurisdiction thereof to the deprivation of any rights, privilege, or immunities secured by the Constitution and laws, [it] shall be liable to the party injured in an action at law, suit in equity, or other proper proceeding for redress." Lawsuits brought under § 1983 can include any of the bases protected by federal law, including race, color, sex, national origin, and religion. Many of the earlier cases invoking this provision focused on discrimination on the basis of race and sex. It is important to note that § 1983 claims are broader than those simply arising in the employment context. This provision can be used wherever a governmental actor violates an individual's statutory or constitutional rights. For example, unlawful search and seizure cases often arise under § 1983.

Though this text will focus primarily on claims brought under the federal statutes rather than the U.S. Constitution, it is important to highlight some of the differences of pursuing a § 1983 claim. Most notably, such claims do not involve the exhaustion of complex administrative requirements, as required under Title VII (and as discussed in the following chapter). It can thus be much more straightforward to bring these claims, since plaintiffs need not navigate the difficult procedural hoops involved with Title VII litigation. Where an individual has failed to properly follow the administrative requirements of Title VII, a § 1983 suit may be an attractive alternative if the other eligibility requirements have been satisfied.

Similarly, the timelines for filing a § 1983 claim are far more generous than with Title VII litigation, as the administrative requirements (which involve short deadlines for bringing a discrimination charge) are not implicated. The damages provisions of a Title VII claim and a § 1983 claim are also quite different. In particular, no statutory caps exist for claims brought pursuant to the Constitution, whereas Title VII limits the relief available for compensatory and punitive damages.

It should be noted that in many ways § 1983 claims are far more limited than claims brought under Title VII. This is true because § 1983 allows suit only against the state or state officials. Thus, only public workers may bring suit under this section. By contrast, Title VII allows for suit against private corporations. Interestingly, a § 1983 claim also permits injunctive relief against specific individuals acting in their official capacity for the state. No individual liability is permitted under Title VII. Notably, both Title VII and § 1983 provide the right to a jury trial and the possibility of attorneys' fees.

Thus, § 1983 provides an attractive basis of litigation for state workers. There are certain limitations on these suits, however, though these constitutional claims do not require navigating the same complex administrative process set up under Title VII. If an employee works for a state entity and has experienced discrimination, litigation under this provision should be considered.

E. State and Local Claims

In addition to constitutional and federal causes of action, workplace plaintiffs may often avail themselves of certain state and local laws. Depending upon the jurisdiction, some states or municipalities may have more favorable laws that plaintiffs may consider pursuing. In some circumstances, a state or local law may have better remedies than federal law. Or, the state or local law may be wider in scope than its federal counterpart.

For example, the state of California is known for its expansive civil rights protections. These protections extend to the workplace as well. The state prohibits employment discrimination on the basis of marital status, gender identity, and gender expression, among others. *See* Cal. Fair Emp't & Hous. Act. Thus, the scope of the state statute expands well beyond that of federal law. Similarly, the city of Washington, D.C., makes it unlawful for employers to discriminate on the basis of appearance, family responsibilities, matriculation, or political affiliation. *See* D.C. CODE § 2-1402.11 (2012). Again, these workplace protections are well beyond those found under federal law. And, many state statutes apply to a wider swath of employers that are often exempted from Title VII.

It is important to closely consider state and local law when determining whether to pursue a cause of action, or when advising a particular client. Local law is often forgotten as a source of worker rights, but it can be a vibrant (and important) consideration for any employment claim.

F. This Book and Employment Discrimination Law

This book is divided into three broad sections. First, it will focus on the broad theory of employment discrimination, explaining the administrative process and the way that intentional and unintentional discrimination claims are structured. It will further discuss the analytical framework for harassment claims established by the federal government and federal court system. Second, it will examine the different categories of discrimination, evaluating claims brought on the basis of race, color, sex, national origin, religion, age, and disability. Finally, the text will look at the remedies available to employment plaintiffs, as well as the "best practices" that should prevail in the workplace.

The text also focuses on a procedural and problem-based approach to employment discrimination. Thus, each chapter will look at different litigation strategies involved in these cases, and examine various practice tips and procedural points that can arise. Each chapter will begin with an interactive problem that introduces the topic. The interactive problem will be revisited throughout the chapter, highlighting various aspects of a case that can be of importance to a court or litigant.

Finally, the book will also introduce several class exercises that are designed to emphasize the importance of specific research on particular issues. These class exercises will help you to develop your ability to analyze specific issues that can arise in the employment discrimination field.

As opposed to a traditional case book, this text seeks to be much more interactive in nature. It attempts to engage the learning processes through many different vehicles, and to engage the reader in the debate over the current role of employment discrimination in the courts.

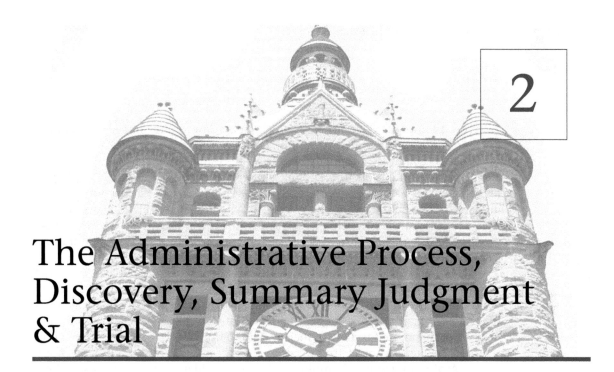

2

The Administrative Process, Discovery, Summary Judgment & Trial

 Interactive Problem

Caroline Cook has worked as a chef for over twenty years. For the past decade, she has been employed by Le Fancy Restaurant, which serves upscale French cuisine in an intimate atmosphere. Caroline has received excellent evaluations on her work ethic and food preparation. Indeed, she was recognized as one of the best chefs in the country by a major food critic. One of the managers of the restaurant recently resigned to pursue other opportunities in another city. Because she had always wanted to open her own restaurant one day, Caroline believed that pursuing a career in restaurant management might be beneficial for her long-term ambitions. Consequently, Caroline applied for the management opening with the restaurant's proprietor, Ollie Owner. Ollie immediately laughed at Caroline's request, saying that this business is "cut-throat" and is no place for inexperienced "girls." Ollie noted that there had only ever been one female manager in the restaurant's history, and that she had been the "worst" employee that the company had ever employed. Ollie concluded by telling Caroline that she should stick with what she does best, and to get back in the kitchen where she belongs.

Has the restaurant violated federal law? If so, how? What should Caroline do if she believes that she has been discriminated against? Where should she go to pursue her claims? How long does she have to do so?

A. Introduction

One often-overlooked aspect of civil rights law is the procedural requirements of filing a discrimination claim. Too often these requirements are treated carelessly by plaintiffs, often with devastating results. The deadlines for filing a charge of discrimination in a lawsuit are very stringent. Failure to comply will result in dismissal of the suit. Recently, the Supreme Court has become increasingly restrictive on the requirements necessary to file a viable claim of discrimination. This case law is still being developed in the lower courts, and there are now several additional strategic decisions that attorneys must consider when drafting a complaint.

When an individual believes that she has been discriminated against in the workplace, she should initially consider addressing the issue internally. Depending upon the nature of the discrimination, a discussion with the individual's supervisor or the human resources department may quickly resolve the issue without a need to pursue more formal channels. Additionally, the company may have procedures or policies in place that would permit an internal resolution of the complaint. Again, an aggrieved employee should consider whether to pursue these policies.

Regardless of whether an internal resolution of a discrimination claim is possible, once an individual has been discriminated against, the timeline for filing a charge of discrimination with the federal government begins to run immediately. As a result, it is critical—irrespective of whether the employee proceeds with internal dispute resolution—that the worker simultaneously consider whether to complain outside of the company as well.

When complaining of discrimination, a worker must first file a claim with the Equal Employment Opportunity Commission (EEOC), or with an equivalent state agency.

B. The Equal Employment Opportunity Commission and the Department of Justice

The EEOC is a federal governmental agency that was created to enforce the provisions of Title VII of the Civil Rights Act of 1964. The Commission currently enforces not only Title VII, but also the ADA, the ADEA, the Equal Pay Act, and the Genetic Information Nondiscrimination Act (GINA). The EEOC also issues regulatory guidelines on each of the statutes that it enforces, as well as policy guidance on discrimination principles. *See* Anne Noel Occhialino & Daniel Vail, *Why the EEOC (Still) Matters*, 22 Hofstra Lab. & Emp. L.J. 671 (2005) (outlining the history and modern impact of the EEOC).

The EEOC is comprised of five individual Commissioners appointed by the President, one of whom serves as chair of the agency. The first chair of the agency was Franklin D. Roosevelt, Jr., who served from May 26, 1965 to May 11, 1966. Roosevelt was the son of the former United States President, and was instrumental in helping to get the fledgling agency off the ground.

The EEOC has long held independent litigation authority. Title VII did not originally provide for this authority. As such, Title VII was written to provide a robust *private* right of action, and many important early cases did not involve the agency. The statute was amended in 1972, however, allowing the EEOC to bring suit against those that ran afoul of the statute. The EEOC also has broad subpoena powers that allow it to review employer records and documents. The Commission, thus, has

Franklin and Eleanor Roosevelt with son Franklin

the power to litigate on its own behalf and to sue in federal court those employers that it believes have not complied with of one of the statutes that it enforces. The EEOC primarily handles cases brought against private entities. Though the statistics vary from year to year, the Commission typically files between one and five hundred cases a year against various private employers. Also, the EEOC is relatively successful in its cases. For example, in 2017, the agency recovered over $355 million in monetary benefits for victims of discrimination. The vast majority of states also have some type of agency that is roughly equivalent to the EEOC. These states have workshare agreements with the EEOC to help coordinate the intake and investigation of charges of discrimination.

Beyond processing charges and litigating cases of employment discrimination, the EEOC also issues rules, regulations and guidance on all of the statutes that it enforces. While varying degrees of deference are given to these materials, they provide a helpful interpretation to this often confusing area of the law. Therefore, the courts frequently look to—and often rely on—the various promulgations of the EEOC.

Where an individual believes that she has been discriminated against by a public organization—such as a school district, fire department, or police agency—relief should be sought through the Department of Justice (DOJ). The Civil Rights Division of the DOJ handles employment discrimination claims that are filed against public or governmental agencies. The DOJ enforces civil rights laws that prohibit discriminatory treatment "in voting, public accommodations, public facilities, public schools, state and local government employment, housing, and credit." BRIAN K. LANDSBERG, ENFORCING CIVIL RIGHTS: RACE DISCRIMINATION AND THE DEPARTMENT OF JUSTICE (1997).

C. The Administrative Process

Where discrimination has occurred, a plaintiff cannot simply file a lawsuit in federal court. A complex administrative process has been established which a plaintiff must successfully navigate prior to bringing a federal claim. A plaintiff must exhaust her administrative remedies prior to proceeding to court. Failing to do so can result in dismissal of the claim.

When an individual believes that she has been discriminated against, she should strongly consider filing a "charge" of discrimination against her employer with the EEOC. As discussed at the end of this text, there are numerous legal and practical considerations of whether an individual should file a charge of discrimination against her employer. Assuming that the employee decides to pursue governmental intervention, that employee must act relatively quickly in filing a charge.

Title VII requires that an individual file a charge within 180 days of the discriminatory event. If a state or local equivalent of the EEOC exists in a particular jurisdiction, as it does in the vast majority of states, the individual will have 300 days to file a discrimination charge. The number of charges that the agency receives in a typical year varies tremendously. However, in recent years, the number has hovered around the 80,000 mark. For example, in fiscal year 2017, the Commission received 84,254 charges of discrimination. A blank EEOC charge form is set forth below, which illustrates the simple nature of this document:

EEOC Form 5 (5/01)

CHARGE OF DISCRIMINATION This form is affected by the Privacy Act of 1974. See enclosed Privacy Act Statement and other information before completing this form.	Charge Presented to: Agency(ies) Charge No(s): ___ FEPA _X_ EEOC

_____ and EEOC
State or local Agency, if any

Name (*indicate Mr. Ms. Mrs.*)	Home Phone (Incl. Area Code)	Date of Birth

Street Address	City, State and ZIP Code	

Named is the Employer, Labor Organization, Employment Agency, Apprenticeship Committee, or State or Local Government Agency That I believe Discriminated Against Me or Others. (*If more than two, list under PARTICULARS below.*)

Name	No. Employees, Members	Phone No. (Include Area Code)

Street Address	City, State and ZIP Code	

Name	No. Employees, Members	Phone No. (Include Area Code)

Street Address	City, State and ZIP Code	

DISCRIMINATION BASED ON (*Check appropriate box(es).*)

__ RACE __ COLOR __ SEX __ RELIGION __ NATIONAL ORIGIN

__ RETALIATION __ AGE __ DISABILITY __ OTHER (Specify below.)

DATE(S) DISCRIMINATION TOOK PLACE
Earliest   Latest

__ CONTINUING ACTION

THE PARTICULARS ARE (*If additional paper is needed, attached extra sheet(s)*):

I want this charge filed with both the EEOC and the State or local Agency, if any. I will advise the agencies if I change my address or phone number and I will cooperate fully with them in the processing of my charge in accordance with their procedures.

NOTARY – *When necessary for State and Local Agency Requirements*

I declare under penalty of perjury that the above is true and correct.

I swear or affirm that I have read the above charge and that it is true to the best of my knowledge, information and belief.
SIGNATURE OF COMPLANANT

_____ _____
Date   *Charging Party Signature*

SUBSCRIBED AND SWORN TO BEFORE ME THIS DATE (*month, day, year*)

Figure 2.1 **EEOC Form 5 (www.eeoc.gov)**

Given the overwhelming number of discrimination charges filed each year, and the limited government resources to handle this intake, not all discrimination charges will be fully investigated. When the Commission receives a charge of discrimination, it will typically be triaged. The Commission treats "A" claims as those that are extremely strong and will be thoroughly investigated. Claims designated as "B" charges will require additional information to determine their validity. "C" charges typically have little merit or fail on the face of the claim itself.

Once an investigation of the charge is complete, the Commission will issue a letter of determination. This determination will include one of two possible findings: that there is cause to believe that discrimination has occurred, or, based on the record before the EEOC, that there is no reasonable cause to find discrimination. The number of cases where cause is found varies from year to year. Typically, however, the Commission finds cause in approximately two to ten percent of the charges that it receives. It is important to remember that this determination by the EEOC is not binding. It simply reflects whether the agency has found cause to believe that discrimination has occurred based on its limited investigation into the events in question. The investigation will not typically be as extensive when seeking discovery as it would in a federal proceeding. Thus, it is not unusual for a plaintiff to later establish discrimination even after a no-cause finding has been entered by the Commission. Indeed, given the massive workload of the agency, it is often difficult for the EEOC to fully explore many of the charges it receives.

By statute, the EEOC has the authority to settle a charge of discrimination. What is typically known as conciliation is an effort by the government to settle a discrimination charge before it reaches federal court. Conciliation is usually attempted in those cases where the Commission has found cause to believe discrimination has occurred. These settlements can result in the recovery of hundreds of millions of dollars collectively for the charging parties. In 2017, for example, the agency recovered over $355 million for victims as a result of settlements. *See* EEOC, ALL STATUTES, FY 1997–FY 2017, http://www.eeoc.gov/eeoc/statistics/enforcement/all.cfm. *See also* Minna J. Kotkin, *Outing Outcomes: An Empirical Study of Confidential Employment Discrimination Settlements*, 64 WASH. & LEE L. REV. 111 (2007) (analyzing employment discrimination claims in federal courts). In *Mach Mining, LLC v. EEOC*, 135 S. Ct. 1645 (2015), the Supreme Court addressed whether the federal courts have the authority to review the EEOC's conciliation efforts. The Court held that it is appropriate for the lower courts to examine "whether the EEOC satisfied its statutory obligation to attempt conciliation before filing suit." The extent of the lower court's review is quite limited, however. The Supreme Court concluded that this narrow scope helps "recognize[] the EEOC's extensive discretion to determine the kind and amount of communication with an employer appropriate in any given case."

When conciliation fails, the EEOC must determine whether to litigate a particular claim. The Commission has the right of first refusal in determining whether to litigate a case. When the EEOC sues an employer, it is acting on behalf of the government. Thus, while its interests may be closely aligned with the charging party, they are not always identical. For example, the government may be more interested in injunctive and prospective relief in assuring that the employer no longer discriminates, whereas the individual may have a more substantial interest in monetary benefits. *See* EEOC v. Waffle House, Inc., 534 U.S. 279 (2002). Charging parties may intervene in the case to make sure that their interests are being adequately represented. The Commission does not charge attorneys' fees when it takes a case on, and it turns over any award that it receives to the victims of discrimination.

When determining whether to file a lawsuit, the agency usually considers three primary factors. First, it tends to pursue claims that are on the cutting edge of employment discrimination. Thus, it considers closely those cases where the law is not well developed and where it may advance novel legal theories. Second, the Commission also looks closely at those cases where the facts are particularly egregious or where the discrimination has occurred companywide. Where the employer's actions seem harsh, or where the actions impact multiple individuals, the Commission may be more likely to bring suit. Finally, the agency also closely considers those cases that may implicate its enforcement authority. Thus, for example, the Commission might want to litigate where there is an issue as to the validity of one of its regulations.

The numbers vary, but the EEOC usually brings about 300 cases a year. *See* EEOC, LITIGATION STATISTICS, FY 1997–FY 2017, http://www.eeoc.gov/eeoc/statistics/enforcement/litigation.cfm (EEOC brought cases averaging 310 a year from FY 1997–FY 2017). Though this number seems large on its face, it is important to keep in mind that this is a relatively small percentage of those charges that actually walk through the door. For example, in a year where in which 100,000 charges of discrimination are filed, the Commission will bring suit in approximately 0.30 percent of those cases. Thus, for any individual filing a charge with the agency, the likelihood is extremely low that the Commission will actually take the case to federal court. When the agency does sue, it is extremely successful. It is not unusual for the Commission to have a success rate in excess of 90 percent of the cases where it brings suit. This is not surprising, however, given that the agency is selecting from among the very best charges that it receives.

Where the agency does not file suit or where the EEOC does not find cause to believe that discrimination has occurred, it will issue what is known as a right-to-sue letter to the charging party. Once an individual receives a right-to-sue letter, she will have 90 days to file a complaint of discrimination in federal or state court. If the individual misses this deadline, the case will be dismissed. At any time in the administrative process, an individual may also request that the EEOC suspend its investigation and issue an early right-to-sue letter. This may occur, for example, where a charging party is represented by counsel and there is a strong desire to move forward with the litigation.

Practice and Procedural Tip

1: Time Deadlines and the Administrative Process

The administrative process for filing discrimination claims is rife with the potential for missteps by a charging party. From a procedural standpoint, plaintiffs and defendants must be careful in assuring that all relevant deadlines have been satisfied. For plaintiffs, these deadlines must be closely followed to make sure that the case is allowed to proceed. For defendants, these deadlines represent an opportunity to have the case dismissed—regardless of the merits—where the charging party has not closely adhered to the requirements of the administrative process.

Though each step of the process should be closely monitored by both parties, there are two specific time periods that should be closely examined. First, as noted above, a plaintiff has 180 or 300 days to file a charge of discrimination depending upon the jurisdiction. This is a relatively short period of time compared to other types of civil actions. For example, it is not unusual for a plaintiff to have three years to file a tort cause of action. Congress wanted to make sure that the time period for filing these claims was limited as memories fade quickly, employees change jobs, and documents are misplaced or destroyed. Given this short deadline, individuals must act quickly if they believe that discrimination has occurred. A company should make certain that a plaintiff has satisfied this initial deadline in the case. The consequence for failing to timely file is dismissal regardless of the merits of the claim. Thus, this deadline presents an excellent opportunity for employers to prevail in the case where a plaintiff has missed this important time period.

Second, plaintiffs have 90 days to file a lawsuit after they have received a right-to-sue letter from the EEOC. Thus, once a plaintiff has received this letter, she must file her complaint in state or federal court within this time deadline. Again, the consequence for failing to meet this requirement is dismissal of the case. Plaintiffs should thus be extremely cautious to make sure that their cause of action has been filed in a timely manner. And, defendants should observe the potential opportunity to have the case dismissed where this deadline has not been satisfied.

The administrative process thus presents potential pitfalls for plaintiffs and significant opportunities for defendants as the case proceeds. The parties should closely monitor the case to determine whether or not the relevant deadlines have been satisfied. Although the deadlines arise early in the case, the administrative process is a critical procedural component of the cause of action.

Though the administrative requirements seem fairly straightforward, there can be substantial debate over whether a particular deadline has been satisfied. It is generally a best practice for plaintiffs to file a claim as soon as practical, and to not wait until the last minute to pursue their action. This may avoid any subsequent question over whether a deadline has been met. The courts are replete with cases interpreting the administrative process and how to determine whether the requirements have been satisfied. Nonetheless, plaintiffs must make certain to fully investigate their claims and develop their theories of the case. Doing so in an expedient manner will help avoid any subsequent questions on timing.

The administrative process is thus fairly straightforward in employment discrimination cases, but it can be confusing to navigate at times. The chart below helps summarize how the process works and the deadlines that must be met:

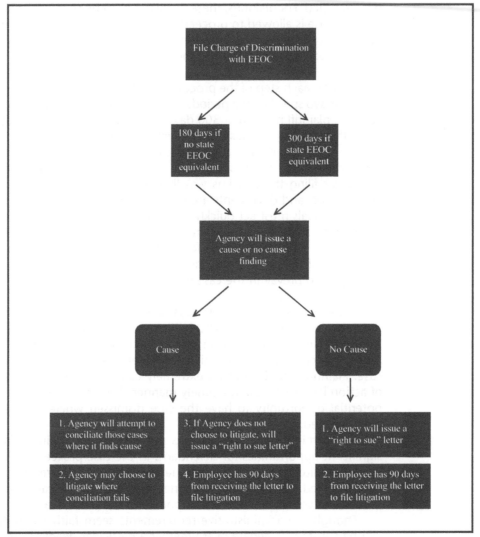

Figure 2.2: **EEOC Administrative Process.**

As discussed above, the timeline for filing a charge of discrimination is relatively short—180 or 300 days depending on the jurisdiction. There has been substantial disagreement over the years as to what type of discriminatory event is necessary to start this clock running in employment discrimination cases. As seen below, the Supreme Court would distinguish between "discrete" acts and "continuing violations" when defining the charge-filing window. This distinction, highlighted by the Court in the following case, continues to play a critical role in many discrimination cases.

National Railroad Passenger Corp. v. Morgan
536 U.S. 101 (2002)

Justice THOMAS delivered the opinion of the Court.

Respondent Abner Morgan, Jr., sued petitioner National Railroad Passenger Corporation (Amtrak) under Title VII alleging that he had been subjected to

discrete discriminatory and retaliatory acts and had experienced a
racially hostile work environment
throughout his employment.
Section 2000e–5(e)(1) requires
that a Title VII plaintiff file a charge
with the Equal Employment
Opportunity Commission (EEOC)
either 180 or 300 days "after the
alleged unlawful employment
practice occurred." We consider
whether, and under what circumstances, a Title VII plaintiff may file
suit on events that fall outside this
statutory time period.

On February 27, 1995, Abner J. Morgan, Jr., a black male, filed a charge of
discrimination and retaliation against Amtrak with the EEOC and cross-filed with
the California Department of Fair Employment and Housing. Morgan alleged that
during the time period that he worked for Amtrak he was "consistently harassed
and disciplined more harshly than other employees on account of his race." The
EEOC issued a "Notice of Right to Sue" on July 3, 1996, and Morgan filed this
lawsuit on October 2, 1996. While some of the allegedly discriminatory acts about
which Morgan complained occurred within 300 days of the time that he filed his
charge with the EEOC, many took place prior to that time period. Amtrak filed a
motion, arguing, among other things, that it was entitled to summary judgment
on all incidents that occurred more than 300 days before the filing of Morgan's
EEOC charge. The District Court granted summary judgment in part to Amtrak,
holding that the company could not be liable for conduct occurring before May
3, 1994, because that conduct fell outside of the 300-day filing period. The court
employed a test established by the United States Court of Appeals for the Seventh
Circuit in *Galloway v. General Motors Service Parts Operations*, 78 F.3d 1164 (C.A.
7 1996): A "plaintiff may not base [the] suit on conduct that occurred outside
the statute of limitations unless it would have been unreasonable to expect the
plaintiff to sue before the statute ran on that conduct, as in a case in which the
conduct could constitute, or be recognized, as actionable harassment only in the
light of events that occurred later, within the period of the statute of limitations."
The District Court held that "[b]ecause Morgan believed that he was being discriminated against at the time that all of these acts occurred, it would not be
unreasonable to expect that Morgan should have filed an EEOC charge on these
acts before the limitations period on these claims ran."

Morgan appealed. The United States Court of Appeals for the Ninth Circuit
reversed, relying on its previous articulation of the continuing violation doctrine,
which "allows courts to consider conduct that would ordinarily be time barred 'as
long as the untimely incidents represent an ongoing unlawful employment practice.'" Contrary to both the Seventh Circuit's test, used by the District Court, and a
similar test employed by the Fifth Circuit, the Ninth Circuit held that its precedent

"precludes such a notice limitation on the continuing violation doctrine." Morgan v. Nat'l R. R., 232 F.3d 1008, 1015 (2000).

An individual must file a charge within the statutory time period and serve notice upon the person against whom the charge is made. In a State that has an entity with the authority to grant or seek relief with respect to the alleged unlawful practice, an employee who initially files a grievance with that agency must file the charge with the EEOC within 300 days of the employment practice; in all other States, the charge must be filed within 180 days. A claim is time barred if it is not filed within these time limits.

For our purposes, the critical sentence of the charge filing provision is: "A charge under this section *shall be filed* within one hundred and eighty days *after the alleged unlawful employment practice occurred.*" § 2000e–5(e)(1). The operative terms are "shall," "after . . . occurred," and "unlawful employment practice." "[S]hall" makes the act of filing a charge within the specified time period mandatory. "[O]ccurred" means that the practice took place or happened in the past. The requirement, therefore, that the charge be filed "after" the practice "occurred" tells us that a litigant has up to 180 or 300 days *after* the unlawful practice happened to file a charge with the EEOC.

The critical questions, then, are: What constitutes an "unlawful employment practice" and when has that practice "occurred"?

We take the easier question first. A discrete retaliatory or discriminatory act "occurred" on the day that it "happened." A party, therefore, must file a charge within either 180 or 300 days of the date of the act or lose the ability to recover for it. Morgan argues that the statute does not require the filing of a charge within 180 or 300 days of each discrete act, but that the language requires the filing of a charge within the specified number of days after an "unlawful employment *practice.*" "Practice," Morgan contends, connotes an ongoing violation that can endure or recur over a period of time. In Morgan's view, the term "practice" therefore provides a statutory basis for the Ninth Circuit's continuing violation doctrine. This argument is unavailing, however, given that 42 U.S.C. § 2000e–2 explains in great detail the sorts of actions that qualify as "[u]nlawful employment practices" and includes among such practices numerous discrete acts. *See, e.g.,* § 2000e–2(a) ("It shall be an unlawful employment practice for an employer—(1) to fail or refuse to hire or to discharge any individual, or otherwise to discriminate against any individual with respect to his compensation, terms, conditions, or privileges of employment, because of such individual's race, color, religion, sex, or national origin . . . "). There is simply no indication that the term "practice" converts related discrete acts into a single unlawful practice for the purposes of timely filing.

> Prior to this decision, there was substantial conflict in the lower courts over how to define an "unlawful employment practice." Similarly, there was also significant confusion in determining when such a practice began.

We have repeatedly interpreted the term "practice" to apply to a discrete act or single "occurrence," even when it has a connection to other acts. We derive several principles from [our prior] cases. First, discrete discriminatory acts are not actionable if time barred, even when they are related to acts alleged in timely filed charges. Each discrete discriminatory act starts a new clock for filing charges alleging that act. The charge, therefore, must be filed within the 180- or 300-day time period after the discrete discriminatory act occurred. The existence of past acts and the employee's prior knowledge of their occurrence, however, does not bar employees from filing charges about related discrete acts so long as the acts are independently discriminatory and charges addressing those acts are themselves timely filed. Nor does the statute bar an employee from using the prior acts as background evidence in support of a timely claim.

As we have held, however, this time period for filing a charge is subject to equitable doctrines such as tolling or estoppel. Courts may evaluate whether it would be proper to apply such doctrines, although they are to be applied sparingly.

The Court of Appeals applied the continuing violations doctrine to what it termed "serial violations," holding that so long as one act falls within the charge filing period, discriminatory and retaliatory acts that are plausibly or sufficiently related to that act may also be considered for the purposes of liability. With respect to this holding, therefore, we reverse.

Discrete acts such as termination, failure to promote, denial of transfer, or refusal to hire are easy to identify. Each incident of discrimination and each retaliatory adverse employment decision constitutes a separate actionable "unlawful employment practice." Morgan can only file a charge to cover discrete acts that "occurred" within the appropriate time period. While Morgan alleged that he suffered from numerous discriminatory and retaliatory acts from the date that he was hired through March 3, 1995, the date that he was fired, only incidents that took place within the timely filing period are actionable. Because Morgan first filed his charge with an appropriate state agency, only those acts that occurred 300 days before February 27, 1995, the day that Morgan filed his charge, are actionable. During that time period, Morgan contends that he was wrongfully suspended and charged with a violation of Amtrak's "Rule L" for insubordination while failing to complete work assigned to him, denied training, and falsely accused of threatening a manager. All prior discrete discriminatory acts are untimely filed and no longer actionable.

> The Court distinguishes between discrete acts and continuing violations when it comes to the charge filing deadlines.

Hostile environment claims are different in kind from discrete acts. Their very nature involves repeated conduct. The "unlawful employment practice" therefore cannot be said to occur on any particular day. It occurs over a series of days or perhaps years and, in direct contrast to discrete acts, a single act of harassment may not be actionable on its own. Such claims are based on the cumulative effect of individual acts.

In determining whether an actionable hostile work environment claim exists, we look to "all the circumstances," including "the frequency of the discriminatory conduct; its severity; whether it is physically threatening or humiliating, or a mere offensive utterance; and whether it unreasonably interferes with an employee's work performance." To assess whether a court may, for the purposes of determining liability, review all such conduct, including those acts that occur outside the filing period, we again look to the statute. It provides that a charge must be filed within 180 or 300 days "after the alleged unlawful employment practice occurred." A hostile work environment claim is composed of a series of separate acts that collectively constitute one "unlawful employment practice." 42 U.S.C. § 2000e–5(e)(1). The timely filing provision only requires that a Title VII plaintiff file a charge within a certain number of days after the unlawful practice happened. It does not matter, for purposes of the statute, that some of the component acts of the hostile work environment fall outside the statutory time period. Provided that an act contributing to the claim occurs within the filing period, the entire time period of the hostile environment may be considered by a court for the purposes of determining liability.

That act need not, however, be the last act. As long as the employer has engaged in enough activity to make out an actionable hostile environment claim, an unlawful employment practice has "occurred," even if it is still occurring. Subsequent events, however, may still be part of the one hostile work environment claim and a charge may be filed at a later date and still encompass the whole.

It is precisely because the entire hostile work environment encompasses a single unlawful employment practice that we do not hold, as have some of the Circuits, that the plaintiff may not base a suit on individual acts that occurred outside the statute of limitations unless it would have been unreasonable to expect the plaintiff to sue before the statute ran on such conduct. The statute does not separate individual acts that are part of the hostile environment claim from the whole for the purposes of timely filing and liability. And the statute does not contain a requirement that the employee file a charge prior to 180 or 300 days "after" the single unlawful practice "occurred." Given, therefore, that the incidents constituting a hostile work environment are part of one unlawful employment practice, the employer may be liable for all acts that are part of this single claim. In order for the charge to be timely, the employee need only file a charge within 180 or 300 days of any act that is part of the hostile work environment.

The following scenarios illustrate our point: (1) Acts on days 1–400 create a hostile work environment. The employee files the charge on day 401. Can the employee recover for that part of the hostile work environment that occurred in the first 100 days? (2) Acts contribute to a hostile environment on days 1–100 and on day 401, but there are no acts between days 101–400. Can the act occurring on day 401 pull the other acts in for the purposes of liability? In truth, all other things being equal, there is little difference between the two scenarios as a hostile environment constitutes one "unlawful employment practice" and it does not matter whether nothing occurred within the intervening 301 days so long as each act is part of the whole. Nor, if sufficient activity occurred by day 100 to make out a claim, does it matter that the employee knows on that day that an actionable claim happened; on day 401 all incidents are still part of the same claim. On the other hand, if an act on day 401 had no relation to the acts between days 1–100, or for some other reason, such as certain intervening action by the employer, was no longer part of the same hostile environment claim, then the employee cannot recover for the previous acts, at least not by reference to the day 401 act.

Simply put, § 2000e–5(e)(1) is a provision specifying when a charge is timely filed and only has the consequence of limiting liability because filing a timely charge is a prerequisite to having an actionable claim. A court's task is to determine whether the acts about which an employee complains are part of the same actionable hostile work environment practice, and if so, whether any act falls within the statutory time period.

With respect to Morgan's hostile environment claim, the Court of Appeals concluded that "the pre- and post-limitations period incidents involve[d] the same type of employment actions, occurred relatively frequently, and were perpetrated by the same managers." 232 F.3d at 1017. To support his claims of a hostile environment, Morgan presented evidence from a number of other employees that managers made racial jokes, performed racially derogatory acts, made negative comments regarding the capacity of blacks to be supervisors, and used various racial epithets. Although many of the acts upon which his claim depends occurred outside the 300 day filing period, we cannot say that they are not part of the same actionable hostile environment claim. On this point, we affirm.

Our holding does not leave employers defenseless against employees who bring hostile work environment claims that extend over long periods of time. Employers have recourse when a plaintiff unreasonably delays filing a charge. As noted in *Zipes v. Trans World Airlines, Inc.*, 455 U.S. 385 (1982), the filing period is not a jurisdictional prerequisite to filing a Title VII suit. Rather, it is a requirement subject to waiver, estoppel, and equitable tolling "when equity so requires." These equitable doctrines allow us to honor Title VII's remedial purpose "without negating the particular purpose of the filing requirement, to give prompt notice to the employer."

■ NOTES AND QUESTIONS

1. The Court notes that "[d]iscrete acts such as termination, failure to promote, denial of transfer, or refusal to hire" each start their own separate charge filing deadline. Depending upon the jurisdiction, then, a plaintiff has 180 or 300 days to file a charge of discrimination where a discrete act has occurred.

2. The Court also notes that where a discrete act falls outside of the charge filing time limits, it may still be used as background evidence by the plaintiff. What does this mean? How can an untimely act be used as evidence of timely discrimination?

3. Would the introduction of untimely discriminatory background evidence encourage a jury to give a higher award? Could this create jury nullification?

4. The Court notes that "[h]ostile environment claims are different in kind from discrete acts. Their very nature involves repeated conduct." In what way is this true? Do other discrete acts involve any type of repeated conduct as well? Does a hostile work environment always require repeated actions?

5. The Court holds that as long as a single discriminatory event occurs within the 180/300-day charge filing window, the entire hostile work environment is timely. Assume, then, that a supervisor harasses an employee on a daily basis for several years, and then takes a year off work to go on sabbatical. Upon his return, he immediately resumes harassing the same subordinate. Is all of the supervisor's conduct actionable?

6. Do you agree with the distinction the Court makes between those cases involving a continuing violation and those involving a discrete act? Can you think of any other continuing violation cases other than hostile work environment claims?

7. In discriminatory pay cases, should the charge filing deadline begin to run on the day that the employer decides to pay an employee less because of her protected characteristic? Or should each separate, lower paycheck create its own discriminatory act and thus a separate charge filing deadline? *See* Ledbetter v. Goodyear Tire & Rubber Co., 550 U.S. 618 (2007); Lilly Ledbetter Fair Pay Act, Pub. L. No. 111-2 (Jan. 29, 2009) (amending Title VII at 42 U.S.C. § 2000e-5).

8. As seen in the adjacent table, the EEOC typically receives between 75,000 and 100,000 charges of discrimination each year.

Year	Charges
2000	79,896
2001	80,840
2002	84,442
2003	81,293
2004	79,432
2005	75,428
2006	75,768
2007	82,792
2008	95,402
2009	93,277
2010	99,992
2011	99,947
2012	99,412
2013	93,727
2014	88,778
2015	89,385
2016	91,504
2017	84,254

Figure 2.3 **General Rise of EEOC Charges in Recent Years**
Source: EEOC, Charge Statistics FY 1997 Through FY 2017

 Interactive Problem

Looking back at the facts of the interactive problem, does the restaurant's conduct toward Caroline represent a discrete act of discrimination or a continuing violation? Assume that while Caroline was working in the kitchen, another chef repeatedly groped her and made inappropriate sexual comments to her. Would this conduct be actionable? If so, when would the statutory period for filing a claim based on this conduct begin to run?

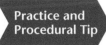

Practice and Procedural Tip

2: A Brief Note on Charge Filing and Retaliation

Later in this text, in Chapter 13, an extensive discussion is included on the best practices for employers to address employee complaints. It is worth noting here, however, the importance of properly handling the receipt of a charge of discrimination. As already discussed, about 80,000 charges of discrimination are received by the EEOC each year. Employers across the country will thus routinely receive notice of a charge of discrimination by one of their workers. When this occurs, the employer must be reminded of the importance of not retaliating against the complaining employee. This can be difficult for employers, particularly where they believe that no discrimination has occurred. In essence, an employer may perceive that a worker has gone outside the company to a federal agency to file an erroneous claim. The employer's natural reaction may be to lash out against the worker and either change his job duties or terminate his employment altogether.

Employers should be strongly counseled against this kind of retaliatory conduct. While an employer need not treat a worker any better because the worker has filed a complaint, an employer must be extremely cautious not to take an adverse action against the worker *because* of a complaint. The applicable legal standard prohibits employers from taking any adverse action that would dissuade a reasonable worker from filing a charge of discrimination. *See* Burlington N. & Santa Fe Ry. Co. v. White, 548 U.S. 53, 57 (2006). Given this standard, employers must walk a delicate line in making certain that the charge filing does not alter the working relationship.

The case law is replete with instances where an employer is vindicated on a charge of discrimination, but is held liable based on the company's subsequent retaliatory acts. Thus, even though no initial discrimination is ultimately found, the employer is still subject to damages and attorneys' fees. Congress and the courts are serious about enforcing the anti-retaliation provisions. When employers receive a charge of discrimination, they must be reminded by their attorneys of the importance of not retaliating.

D. Standing and Coverage Requirements

When filing a case of discrimination, a plaintiff will only be permitted to proceed if that worker has standing to bring a claim and the employer is covered by the statute. It is not always easy to determine whether standing and coverage exist in a particular case. These elements must be examined closely by both the employer and employee early in any proceeding.

To be covered by Title VII, an employer must have fifteen or more employees. The ADA similarly requires fifteen or more employees for coverage. The ADEA has a slightly different number, and requires twenty or more employees to be included under the terms of the statute. As defined by Title VII:

"The term 'employee' means an individual employed by an employer."

42 U.S.C. § 2000e(f) (2012).

This definition of "employee" under Title VII is the same as it is under the ADEA. 29 U.S.C. § 630(f) (2012). Unfortunately, the guidance provided by the statute—"an individual employed by an employer"—is not particularly helpful in discerning who is or is not an employee. The case law has helped fill this gap and has provided substantial guidance on the question of whether there is coverage under the statute.

Clackamas Gastroenterology Associates v. Wells
538 U.S. 440 (2003)

Justice STEVENS delivered the opinion of the Court.

The Americans with Disabilities Act of 1990 (ADA or Act), like other federal antidiscrimination legislation, is inapplicable to very small businesses. Under the ADA an "employer" is not covered unless its work force includes "15 or more employees for each working day in each of 20 or more calendar weeks in the current or preceding calendar year." § 12111(5). The question in this case is whether four physicians actively engaged in medical practice as shareholders and directors of a professional corporation should be counted as "employees."

Petitioner, Clackamas Gastroenterology Associates, P. C., is a medical clinic in Oregon. It employed respondent, Deborah Anne Wells, as a bookkeeper from 1986 until 1997. After her termination, she brought this action against the clinic alleging unlawful discrimination on the basis of disability under Title I of the ADA. Petitioner denied that it was covered by the Act and moved for summary judgment, asserting that it did not have 15 or more employees for the 20 weeks required by the statute. It is undisputed that the accuracy of that assertion depends on whether the four physician-shareholders who own the professional corporation and constitute its board of directors are counted as employees.

The District Court, adopting the Magistrate Judge's findings and recommendation, granted the motion. Relying on an "economic realities" test adopted by the Seventh Circuit in *EEOC v. Dowd & Dowd, Ltd.*, 736 F.2d 1177 (1984), the District Court concluded that the four doctors were "more analogous to partners in a partnership than to shareholders in a general corporation" and therefore were "not employees for purposes of the federal antidiscrimination laws."

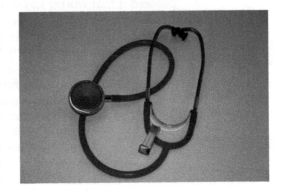

A divided panel of the Court of Appeals for the Ninth Circuit reversed. Noting that the Second Circuit had rejected the economic realities approach, the majority held that the use of any corporation, including a professional corporation, "'precludes any examination designed to determine whether the entity is in fact a partnership.'" It saw "no reason to permit a professional corporation to secure the 'best of both possible worlds' by allowing it both to assert its corporate status in order to reap the tax and civil liability advantages and to argue that it is like a partnership in order to avoid liability for unlawful employment discrimination."

"We have often been asked to construe the meaning of 'employee' where the statute containing the term does not helpfully define it." *Nationwide Mut. Ins. Co. v. Darden*, 503 U.S. 318 (1992). The definition of the term in the ADA simply states that an "employee" is "an individual employed by an employer." 42 U.S.C. § 12111(4). That surely qualifies as a mere "nominal definition" that is "completely circular and explains nothing." *Darden*, 503 U.S. at 323. As we explained in *Darden*, our cases construing similar language give us guidance on how best to fill the gap in the statutory text.

> The statutory definition of employee is circular and provides only that an employee is someone "employed by an employer."

In *Darden* we were faced with the question whether an insurance salesman was an independent contractor or an "employee" covered by the Employee Retirement Income Security Act of 1974 (ERISA). Because ERISA's definition of "employee" was "completely circular," 503 U.S. at 323, we followed the same general approach that we had previously used in deciding whether a sculptor was an "employee" within the meaning of the Copyright Act of 1976, see *Community for Creative Non-Violence v. Reid*, 490 U.S. 730 (1989), and we adopted a common-law test for determining who qualifies as an "employee" under ERISA. Quoting *Reid*, 490 U.S. at 739–740, we explained that " 'when Congress has used the term "employee" without defining it, we have concluded that Congress intended to describe the conventional master-servant relationship as understood by common-law agency doctrine.' " *Darden*, 503 U.S. at 322–323.

Rather than looking to the common law, petitioner argues that courts should determine whether a shareholder-director of a professional corporation is an "employee" by asking whether the shareholder-director is, in reality, a "partner." The question whether a shareholder-director is an employee, however, cannot be answered by asking whether the shareholder-director appears to be the functional equivalent of a partner. Today there are partnerships that include hundreds of members, some of whom may well qualify as "employees" because control is concentrated in a small number of managing partners. Thus, asking whether shareholder-directors are partners—rather than asking whether they are employees—simply begs the question.

Nor does the approach adopted by the Court of Appeals in this case fare any better. The majority's approach, which paid particular attention to "the broad purpose of the ADA," 271 F.3d at 905, is consistent with the statutory purpose of ridding the Nation of the evil of discrimination. *See* 42 U.S.C. § 12101(b). Nevertheless, two countervailing considerations must be weighed in the balance. First, as the dissenting judge noted below, the congressional decision to limit the coverage of the legislation to firms with 15 or more employees has its own justification that must be respected—namely, easing entry into the market and preserving the competitive position of smaller firms. Second, as *Darden* reminds us, congressional silence often reflects an expectation that courts will look to the common law to fill gaps in statutory text, particularly when an undefined term has a settled meaning at common law. Congress has overridden judicial decisions that went beyond the common law in an effort to correct "'the mischief'" at which a statute was aimed.

Perhaps the Court of Appeals' and the parties' failure to look to the common law for guidance in this case stems from the fact that we are dealing with a new type of business entity that has no exact precedent in the common law. State statutes now permit incorporation for the purpose of practicing a profession, but in the past "the so-called learned professions were not permitted to organize as corporate entities." 1A W. Fletcher, Cyclopedia of the Law of Private Corporations § 112.10 (rev. ed. 1997–2002). Thus, professional corporations are relatively young participants in the market, and their features vary from State to State. Nonetheless, the common law's definition of the master-servant relationship does provide helpful guidance. At common law the relevant factors defining the master-servant relationship focus on the master's control over the servant. The general definition of the term "servant" in the Restatement (Second) of Agency § 2(2) (1957), for example, refers to a person whose work is "controlled or is subject to the right to control by the master." *See also id.* § 220(1) ("A servant is a person employed to perform services in the affairs of another and who with respect to the physical conduct in the performance of the services is subject to the other's control or right to control"). In addition, the Restatement's more specific definition of the term "servant" lists factors to be considered when distinguishing between servants and independent contractors, the first of which is "the extent of control" that one may exercise over the details of the work of the other. *Id.* § 220(2)(a). We think that the common-law element of control is the principal guidepost that should be followed in this case.

This is the position that is advocated by the Equal Employment Opportunity Commission (EEOC), the agency that has special enforcement responsibilities under the ADA and other federal statutes containing similar threshold issues for determining coverage. Specific EEOC guidelines discuss both the broad question of who is an "employee" and the narrower question of when partners, officers, members of boards of directors, and major shareholders qualify as employees. With respect to the broad question, the guidelines list 16 factors—taken from *Darden*, 503 U.S. at 323–324,—that may be relevant to "whether the employer controls the means and manner of the worker's work performance." The guidelines list six factors to be considered in answering the narrower question, which they frame as "whether the individual acts independently and participates in managing the organization, or whether the individual is subject to the organization's control."

We are persuaded by the EEOC's focus on the common-law touchstone of control, see *Skidmore v. Swift & Co.*, 323 U.S. 134, 140 (1944), and specifically by its submission that each of the following six factors is relevant to the inquiry whether a shareholder-director is an employee:

> The Court observes that control is the most important factor in the employment relationship, and provides several ways to determine whether sufficient control exists.

"Whether the organization can hire or fire the individual or set the rules and regulations of the individual's work[;] Whether and, if so, to what extent the organization supervises the individual's work[;] Whether the individual reports to someone higher in the organization[;] Whether and, if so, to what extent the individual is able to influence the organization[;] Whether the parties intended that the individual be an employee, as expressed in written agreements or contracts[;] Whether the individual shares in the profits, losses, and liabilities of the organization." EEOC Compliance Manual § 605:0009.

As the EEOC's standard reflects, an employer is the person, or group of persons, who owns and manages the enterprise. The employer can hire and fire employees, can assign tasks to employees and supervise their performance, and can decide how the profits and losses of the business are to be distributed. The mere fact that a person has a particular title—such as partner, director, or vice president—should not necessarily be used to determine whether he or she is an employee or a proprietor. Nor should the mere existence of a document styled "employment agreement" lead inexorably to the conclusion that either party is an employee. Rather, as was true in applying common-law rules to the independent-contractor-versus-employee issue confronted in *Darden*, the answer to whether a shareholder-director is an employee depends on "'all of the incidents of the relationship . . . with no one factor being decisive.'" 503 U.S. at 324 (quotation omitted).

Some of the District Court's findings—when considered in light of the EEOC's standard—appear to weigh in favor of a conclusion that the four director-shareholder physicians in this case are not employees of the clinic. For example, they apparently control the operation of their clinic, they share the profits, and they are personally liable for malpractice claims. There may, however, be evidence in the record that would contradict those findings or support a contrary conclusion under the EEOC's standard that we endorse today. Accordingly, as we did in *Darden*, we reverse the judgment of the Court of Appeals and remand the case to that court for further proceedings consistent with this opinion.

■ NOTES AND QUESTIONS

1. Why does Congress set any limit at all on the number of employees an employer must have to be covered? Shouldn't an employer be subject to the provisions of the statute even where it only has ten employees? Five employees? One employee?

2. It is important to remember that while Title VII, the ADA, and the ADEA all have statutory thresholds that set a minimum number of employees for coverage, many state laws have different coverage provisions. For example, Virginia requires a minimum of six employees to file a claim under state law; and New York, Pennsylvania, Delaware, and Rhode Island require that an employer have a minimum of four employees to file a claim. The state of Michigan requires only a single employee for coverage. Colorado, Montana, New Jersey, North Dakota, South Dakota, and Oregon have no employee requirement for coverage. Thus, an employer might not be covered under Title VII, but may still be covered by a state antidiscrimination statute.

See Discrimination Claims—State Laws, WORKPLACEFAIRNESS, http://www.workplacefairness.org/minimum#CA (last visited May 23, 2018).

3. It is interesting that Title VII and the ADA both require fifteen employees for coverage while the ADEA requires twenty employees. Why is there a different requirement for the two statutes?

4. The Court lists multiple different factors that the EEOC uses to determine whether someone is an employee. It notes that the most important determination is that of control. How would you determine whether or not sufficient control exists to warrant an employer-employee relationship? Which of the factors that the Court lists would you consider the most important in this determination? *See generally* Matthew T. Bodie, *Participation as a Theory of Employment,* 89 NOTRE DAME L. REV. 661 (2014) (arguing for a definition for "employee" based on the concept of participation rather than control).

5. Is a doctor an employee in the traditional sense of the word? What about a lawyer? Does it depend on the particular environment where the professional works? *See generally* Steven L. Willborn, *College Athletes as Employees: An Overflowing Quiver,* 69 U. MIAMI L. REV. 65 (2014) (discussing the Northwestern University case that questions whether college athletes are employees under the NLRA).

6. The EEOC establishes special rules for whether "Partners, Officers, Members of Boards of Directors, and Major Shareholders" are employees. The agency suggests an examination of the following factors for these workers:

> Whether the organization can hire or fire the individual or set the rules and regulations of the individual's work
>
> Whether and, if so, to what extent the organization supervises the individual's work
>
> Whether the individual reports to someone higher in the organization
>
> Whether and, if so, to what extent the individual is able to influence the organization
>
> Whether the parties intended that the individual be an employee, as expressed in written agreements or contracts
>
> Whether the individual shares in the profits, losses, and liabilities of the organization

EEOC Compl. Man. (CCH) § 2-III(A)(1)(d) (2009).

7. Is a volunteer an employee under the statute? Why or why not? Should whether an employee is paid have any impact on whether or not he would have a cause of action for discrimination? If an employer does not pay a worker, does she have any control over that individual? *See* Howard S. Lavin & Elizabeth E. DiMichele, *Split Circuits: Are Volunteers "Employees" for Purposes of Title VII?,* 39 EMP. RELATIONS L.J. 101 (2013) (summarizing the current split among circuit courts); David C. Yamada, *The Employment Law Rights of Student Interns,* 35 CONN. L. REV. 215 (2002) (examining the implications of the FLSA and other employment laws on the "intern economy"); Cynthia Grant Bowman & MaryBeth Lipp, *Legal Limbo of the Student Intern: The Responsibility of Colleges*

and Universities to Protect Student Interns Against Sexual Harassment, 23 Harv. Women's L.J. 95 (2000) (discussing the inapplicability of antidiscrimination provisions to sexual harassment for unpaid interns).

From the EEOC:

> Volunteers usually are not protected "employees." However, an individual may be considered an employee of a particular entity if, as a result of volunteer service, s/he receives benefits such as a pension, group life insurance, workers' compensation, and access to professional certification, even if the benefits are provided by a third party.

EEOC Compl. Man. (CCH) § 2-III(A)(1)(c) (2009).

8. Why was Congress not more explicit in the statute in defining who is an employee? Why did it leave this definition fairly ambiguous?

9. The courts commonly use the "payroll method" to determine who is an employee under the statute. Thus, it is critical to determine whether an individual is actually paid by the corporation and shows up on the employer's payroll. *See* Walters v. Metro. Educ. Enters., Inc., 519 U.S. 202 (1997); Mitchell H. Rubinstein, *Employees, Employers, and Quasi-Employers: An Analysis of Employees and Employers Who Operate in the Borderland Between an Employer-and-Employee Relationship,* 14 U. Pa. J. Bus. L. 605 (2012) (reviewing theories of quasi-employer responsibility); Ann C. McGinley, *Functionality or Formalism? Partners and Shareholders as "Employees" Under the Anti-Discrimination Laws,* 57 SMU L. Rev. 3, 6 (2004) ("[T]he theoretical foundation upon which *Clackamas* stands must fall and Congress should overrule *Clackamas* and establish a test for determining employee status that considers both the power of the individual within the partnership and the connection to the partnership.").

10. The Supreme Court's decision highlights the importance of the EEOC's factors on determining whether or not someone is an employee. In its guidance, the agency provides substantial information on the types of factors that should be used to trigger the employment relationship. The EEOC provides:

Factors indicating that a worker is in an employment relationship with an employer include the following:

- The employer has the right to control when, where, and how the worker performs the job.
- The work does not require a high level of skill or expertise.
- The employer furnishes the tools, materials, and equipment.
- The work is performed on the employer's premises.
- There is a continuing relationship between the worker and the employer.
- The employer has the right to assign additional projects to the worker.
- The employer sets the hours of work and the duration of the job.
- The worker is paid by the hour, week, or month rather than the agreed cost of performing a particular job.
- The worker does not hire and pay assistants.
- The work performed by the worker is part of the regular business of the employer.

- The employer is in business.
- The worker is not engaged in his/her own distinct occupation or business.
- The employer provides the worker with benefits such as insurance, leave, or workers' compensation.
- The worker is considered an employee of the employer for tax purposes (i.e., the employer withholds federal, state, and Social Security taxes).
- The employer can discharge the worker.
- The worker and the employer believe that they are creating an employer-employee relationship.

This list is not exhaustive. Other aspects of the relationship between the parties may affect the determination of whether an employer-employee relationship exists. Furthermore, not all or even a majority of the listed criteria need be met. Rather, the determination must be based on all of the circumstances in the relationship between the parties, regardless of whether the parties refer to it as an employee or as an independent contractor relationship.

EEOC Compl. Man. (CCH) § 2-III(A)(1) (2009).

 ## Interactive Problem

Looking back at the facts of the interactive problem, assume that Ollie calls Caroline into his office and says, "I've been thinking a lot about your desire to be a manager. It really upsets me as I want someone that is dedicated purely to cooking. There's no way that I'm going to have a silly girl as a manager here, and I'm certainly not going to have an undedicated woman working in my kitchen either. Consider yourself dismissed." Assume further that the restaurant only employs fourteen individuals. Would Caroline have any recourse against Ollie? Could she look anywhere other than federal law for potential relief?

The lower courts have continued to apply and refine the *Clackamas* decision. In the case below, the Third Circuit Court of Appeals addresses the question of who an "employee" is in a case brought under Title VII. The court thus addresses the applicability of *Clackamas* to Title VII cases.

Mariotti v. Mariotti Building Products, Inc.
714 F.3d 761 (3d Cir. 2013)

SMITH, Circuit Judge.

In *Clackamas Gastroenterology Associates, P.C. v. Wells*, 538 U.S. 440 (2003), the Supreme Court set out a test for determining whether a shareholder-director of a professional corporation is an "employee" for purposes of the Americans with Disabilities Act (ADA). This appeal allows us to consider whether that test applies to business entities that are not professional corporations in a Title VII employment action. We hold that it does.

Mariotti Building Products, Inc., is a "closely held family business." Louis S. "Babe" Mariotti started the family business in 1947, operating "a small lumber yard." In the 1960s, Babe's sons, Plaintiff Robert A. Mariotti, Sr. (Plaintiff), and his two brothers, Eugene L. Mariotti, Sr. and Louis C. Mariotti "joined the business." Babe and his sons continued to develop the business, eventually incorporating it as Mariotti Building Products, Inc. (MBP). The business "experienced substantial growth" over the years with "annual sales skyrocketing from less than $250,000 to over $60 Million." MBP, according to the amended complaint, is "recognized as the area's best source for building materials[.]" Plaintiff averred that he was "responsible for developing and growing a number of areas" of MBP's business, "principally manag[ing] the manufactured housing sales division of the company together with customer credit, bill paying, and purchasing and inbound transportation of product lines[.]" Plaintiff further averred that the divisions he managed "earned profit" of more than $15 million in the six years preceding termination of his employment, and that that amount exceeded the profit of the divisions managed by his brother Eugene.

As "one of the founders of MBP," Plaintiff was an officer of the corporation, serving as both vice-president and secretary. He also served as a member of the board of directors, and was a shareholder pursuant to a written agreement executed by the parties on July 23, 2007. Plaintiff averred that he and his brothers "were not at-will employees" of MBP because they were employed pursuant to an agreement that provided for termination "only for cause."

Plaintiff alleged that he had a "spiritual awakening" in 1995. His newfound spirituality, he claimed, resulted in "a systematic pattern of antagonism" toward him. It took the form of "negative, hostile and/or humiliating statements" about him and his religious affiliation. MBP's officers, directors, and some employees were the source of this harassment. In 2005, the harassment increased.

Babe Mariotti, the family patriarch, died either at the end of 2008 or in the first days of January 2009. On January 4, 2009, while the family was making arrangements for the funeral, Eugene Mariotti, derided Plaintiff and his faith. At the funeral on January 6, Plaintiff delivered a eulogy, which included comments about his own faith, and his "father's good example." The eulogy upset members of the family. On January 8, the shareholders of the closely held family business convened a meeting in Plaintiff's absence and decided to terminate his employment.

Two days later on January 10, 2009, Plaintiff received written notice of the termination of his employment. The notice recited that the shareholders had met to discuss his future status as an employee and that the vote to terminate his employment had been unanimous and was effective immediately. The letter explained that various benefits would cease, including the use of a company car, health insurance coverage, a cellular telephone, access to company credit cards, and the availability of an office. Finally, the letter explained that "[y]our share of any draws from the corporation or other entities will continue to be distributed to you."

Despite his termination in January of 2009, Plaintiff continued to serve as a member of MBP's board of directors "until August 6, 2009, when the shareholders did not re-elect him as a director" of the closely held family corporation. On October 22, 2009, Plaintiff filed a timely charge of religious discrimination in violation of Title VII of the Civil Rights Act of 1964, as amended. 42 U.S.C. § 2000e–2(a)(1). Thereafter, Plaintiff filed suit against MBP, asserting

Title VII claims of religious discrimination and a hostile work environment. He also asserted several state law claims. MBP moved to dismiss the complaint under Federal Rule of Civil Procedure 12(b)(6), arguing that Plaintiff was not an "employee" for purposes of Title VII and could not invoke its protections. An amended complaint followed, and was met with a second motion to dismiss asserting the same argument.

In *Clackamas*, the Supreme Court considered whether the shareholder-directors of a professional corporation should be counted as employees in determining whether the business entity met the threshold number of employees, and thereby qualified as an employer under the ADA. 538 U.S. at 442. Consistent with precedent, the Supreme Court looked to the "'conventional master-servant relationship as understood by common-law agency doctrine'" in deciding what Congress intended the term "employee" to mean.

The Court observed that "the common law's definition of the master-servant relationship," focusing as it does on the "master's control over the servant," provided "helpful guidance." *Id.* at 448. It concluded that "the common-law element of control is the principal guidepost that should be followed" in deciding whether an individual is an employee. After considering the guidelines of the Equal Employment Opportunity Commission (EEOC) applicable to determining whether "partners, officers, members of boards of directors, and major shareholders qualify as employees[,]" *id.*, the Court declared that six factors in the EEOC guidelines were "relevant to the inquiry whether a shareholder-director is an employee," *id.* at 449.

Plaintiff contends that *Clackamas* should not be applied in this case. He is correct that there are several differences between *Clackamas* and this case. None of those differences, however, provides a sound basis for disregarding the Supreme Court's guidance in *Clackamas*.

First, Plaintiff argues *Clackamas* concerned the ADA, not Title VII. This distinction is without significance. The Supreme Court granted certiorari in *Clackamas* to address the conflict among the courts in determining whether an individual qualifies as an employee under the ADA, as well as under other antidiscrimination statutes, including Title VII and the Age Discrimination in Employment Act (ADEA). 538 U.S. at 444 n. 3. Because Title VII's definition of employee is the same as the ADA's definition, *see* 42 U.S.C. §§ 2000e(f), 12111(4), and because the EEOC's guidelines, on which the *Clackamas* Court relied, apply to coverage under Title VII, the ADEA, the ADA, and the Equal Pay Act, *see Clackamas*, 538 U.S. at 449 n. 7, we conclude that the analysis set out in *Clackamas* applies to Title VII as well.

Second, we recognize that *Clackamas* concerned whether an individual was an employee for purposes of determining if the employee threshold had been met, thereby subjecting the business entity to the ADA's prohibitions against discrimination. As Plaintiff correctly notes, there is no dispute in this case that MBP, which has more than 15 employees, qualifies as an employer covered by Title VII. Nonetheless, *Clackamas* remains applicable here because neither the ADA nor Title VII define the term "employee" solely for purposes of deciding which business entities may be subject to the proscriptions against employment discrimination. Rather, the definitions in the ADA and Title VII also apply to the statutory provisions establishing enforcement mechanisms that may be exercised by the EEOC or the aggrieved employee. 42 U.S.C. §§ 2000e–5, 12117. Thus, the definitions of "employer" and "employee" set forth in both the ADA and Title VII are relevant in resolving (1) whether an entity qualifies as an "employer" under Title VII, and (2) whether an individual is an "employee" who "may invoke [Title VII's] . . . protections against discrimination[.]" *Clackamas*, 538 U.S. at 446 n. 6. As a consequence, even though *Clackamas* considered the question of whether certain individuals were employees of a covered entity, its test informs our determination as to whether Plaintiff is entitled to invoke Title VII's protections.

Third, we consider Plaintiff's contention that the *Clackamas* test applies only to professional corporations. Because MBP is not a professional corporation, Plaintiff asserts that the District Court erred by applying the *Clackamas* test.

We are not persuaded. We agree with our sister Courts of Appeals that *Clackamas*'s application is not limited to professional corporations. The EEOC Manual on which the Court relied in *Clackamas* considered multiple business enterprises. Furthermore, the Supreme Court's analysis pointed out that the form of the business entity was not the key element, emphasizing that the determination of one's status cannot be decided simply on the basis of titles, such as an individual's status as a partner, director, or officer, or the existence of documentary evidence. "Rather, . . . the answer to whether [an individual] is an employee depends on all of the incidents of the relationship with no one factor being decisive." 538 U.S. at 451 (internal quotation marks, ellipsis and citations omitted). We therefore conclude that the nature of the business entity is simply an attribute of the employment relationship that must be considered in applying the *Clackamas* test to determine whether an individual is an employee or an employer. For that reason, MBP's status as a closely held family business informs our analysis. Consistent with *Clackamas*, our analysis focuses on the element of control and the six factors discussed in that precedent.

> Generally speaking, the *Clackamas* test has been applied broadly by the lower courts to all employment discrimination situations, and has not been limited to professional settings.

Our review of the allegations of Plaintiff's amended complaint confirms that Plaintiff's status as a shareholder, a director, and a corporate officer gave him both substantial authority at MBP and the right to control the enterprise. He was entitled to participate in the management, development, and governance of MBP. By sitting on the board of directors and serving as a corporate officer, Plaintiff had the ability to participate in the fundamental decisions of the business. We cannot ignore Plaintiff's allegation, which we must accept as true, that after his termination in January of 2009, he continued to serve as a director of the closely held family corporation until August 6, 2009. Furthermore, the termination letter he received did not mention the cessation of any salary. Instead, it stated that "[y]our shares of any draws from the corporation or other entities will continue to be distributed to you." We conclude that Plaintiff's amended complaint fails to allege that he is "the kind of person that the common law would consider" an employee. *Clackamas*, 538 U.S. at 445 n. 5. He has not alleged a claim that entitles him to relief.

We recognize that Plaintiff's amended complaint alleges that he did not have exclusive control of MBP. Exclusive control, however, is merely one attribute of the employment relationship. Its absence does not compel a conclusion that an individual who lacks it is an employee entitled to invoke Title VII's protections. Such a conclusion would ignore that the EEOC guidelines, which the Court embraced in *Clackamas*, pertained to business entities that do not vest exclusive control in any one individual. *Id.* at 448 (noting the guidelines applied to "partners, officers, members of boards of directors, and major shareholders").

The allegations in the amended complaint make plain that Plaintiff was entitled to participate in the development and governance of the business. His averment that he continued to serve after his termination on January 9, 2009 as a member of the board of directors confirms that he remained entitled by virtue of his position "to a say in the fundamental decisions" of the closely held family corporation for months after his termination. For that reason, we conclude that the District Court did not err in its determination that the allegations in Plaintiff's complaint did not establish that he was an employee under Title VII.

■ NOTES AND QUESTIONS

1. This case makes clear that the Supreme Court's test on who is an employee applies to all of the federal antidiscrimination statutes—including the ADA, Title VII, the Equal Pay Act, and the ADEA.

2. As the Supreme Court noted, and as the Third Circuit reiterates here, a job title is not dispositive of whether or not someone is an employee at a company. Rather, the courts will look at the element of control to determine whether or not the employment relationship exists.

3. The court here also acknowledges that the determination of whether or not a worker is an employee is fact intensive. If you were an employment attorney attempting to demonstrate the existence of an employer–employee relationship, what facts would be relevant to persuading the court?

4. This decision further emphasizes the breadth of the Supreme Court's decision. *Clackamas* is not restricted simply to professional corporations and will apply to all businesses.

5. **Technology and employment.** Recent years have seen a rise in companies based in the technology sector. Many of these corporations are platform-based and involve customers using an app to make a purchase for a product or service. Companies such as Uber, Lyft, GrubHub and DoorDash have transformed the landscape of the traditional brick-and-mortar employment setting. As this more modern economy emerges, questions arise as to whether workers in this industry should be protected by traditional employment laws. The question is highly fact specific and turns on the particular company involved. The courts are currently struggling with how to define employment in the sector, and litigation in this area will help define more clear parameters in the coming years. *See generally* Benjamin Means & Joseph Seiner, *Navigating the Uber Economy*, 49 U.C. Davis L. Rev. 1511 (2016).

Class Exercise: Establishing the Employment Relationship

Breaking up into small groups, discuss what factors a court might look to when determining whether a worker is in fact an "employee." Do any of the factors that you propose go to anything other than the "control" of the employer? Did everyone in your group agree on the relevancy of the same factors? Why or why not?

Practice and Procedural Tip

3: Employee versus Independent Contractor

One critical issue for an employer to consider when establishing its workforce is whether to employ full-time workers or independent contractors. There are numerous benefits in having actual "employees" work for a corporation. Most notably, full-time workers will typically be more loyal to the company, which can result in a greater quality and quantity of work itself. Employees may also have longer tenures at a particular company, and employers can thus benefit from greater institutional knowledge.

Using independent contractors also has a number of advantages. These workers are more fungible and allow employers to better handle variations in workload and economic conditions. Thus, more independent contractors can be used during a company's busy season and fewer when times are more lean. An employer may also avoid giving the same benefit package to independent contractors. Similarly, as noted above, these workers are not covered by the antidiscrimination laws, thus limiting an employer's potential exposure to liability. In some ways, employing independent contractors can actually hurt *full-time* employees. Indeed, employers can avoid coverage under various antidiscrimination statutes by hiring many independent contractors and fewer actual employees. At the end of the day, this will only disadvantage full-time employees who are unable to avail themselves of these protections, because the employer is considered too "small" to be an employer under the particular statute.

Whether to employ independent contractors or full-time workers is a strategic decision that each corporation must assess. There are both practical and legal consequences tied to this decision. An employer is best advised to carefully weigh these costs and benefits before making an employment decision. It is also important to keep the line clear between employees and independent contractors. An employer does not want to fall into the trap of hiring an independent contractor only to find out later in the litigation that it has blurred the line as to that worker's employment status and subjected itself to potential liability.

The issue of employees versus independent contractors is one that is hotly debated in both the literature and the courts. In some instances, depending upon the jurisdiction at issue and the nature of the work involved, employers may ultimately not be able to "choose" whether to employ a worker as an employee or as an independent contractor. Thus, an employer should examine the law of its jurisdiction and the nature of the workplace to determine how much "control" it has over this issue. *See* Steven J. Arsenault et al., *An Employee by Any Other Name Does Not Smell as Sweet: A Continuing Drama*, 16 LAB. LAW. 285 (2000); Myra H. Barron, *Who's an Independent Contractor? Who's an Employee?*, 14 LAB. LAW. 457 (1999).

E. Filing the Complaint

Once the administrative process is complete, and the individual has received a right-to-sue letter, she may proceed to federal court. Once there, she must file a complaint of discrimination under one of the federal antidiscrimination statutes. At this stage of the proceedings, the complainant is like any other litigant in civil court. In the complaint, the plaintiff must sufficiently allege that she has been discriminated against under federal law and is entitled to relief. If the employer believes that the claim fails to satisfy this standard, it may move for dismissal under Federal Rule of Civil Procedure 12(b)(6).

Filing a complaint has become a much more onerous and confusing process than it once was. Supreme Court case law has made clear that plaintiffs must state a plausible claim to relief if they want to be permitted to proceed with their claims. What is plausible will obviously vary on the facts of the case, and can be particularly difficult for employment litigants to determine. In 2002, the Supreme Court addressed what a plaintiff must allege in an employment discrimination complaint.

Swierkiewicz v. Sorema N.A.

534 U.S. 506 (2002)

Justice THOMAS delivered the opinion of the Court.

This case presents the question whether a complaint in an employment discrimination lawsuit must contain specific facts establishing a prima facie case of discrimination under the framework set forth by this Court in McDonnell *Douglas Corp. v. Green*, 411 U.S. 792 (1973). We hold that an employment discrimination complaint need not include such facts and instead must contain only "a short and plain statement of the claim showing that the pleader is entitled to relief." Fed. Rule Civ. Proc. 8(a)(2).

Petitioner Akos Swierkiewicz is a native of Hungary, who at the time of his complaint was 53 years old. In April 1989, petitioner began working for respondent Sorema N.A., a reinsurance company headquartered in New York and principally owned and controlled by a French parent corporation. Petitioner was initially employed in the position of senior vice president and chief underwriting officer (CUO). Nearly six years later, François M. Chavel, respondent's Chief Executive Officer, demoted petitioner to a marketing and services position and transferred the bulk of his underwriting responsibilities to Nicholas Papadopoulo, a 32-year-old who, like Mr. Chavel, is a French national. About a year later, Mr. Chavel stated that he wanted to "energize" the underwriting department and appointed Mr. Papadopoulo as CUO. Petitioner claims that Mr. Papadopoulo had only one year of underwriting experience at the time he was promoted, and therefore was less experienced and less qualified to be CUO than he, since at that point he had 26 years of experience in the insurance industry.

Following his demotion, petitioner contends that he "was isolated by Mr. Chavel . . . excluded from business decisions and meetings and denied the opportunity to reach his true potential at SOREMA." Petitioner unsuccessfully attempted to meet with Mr. Chavel to discuss his discontent. Finally, in April 1997, petitioner sent a memo to Mr. Chavel outlining his grievances and requesting a severance package. Two weeks later, respondent's general counsel presented petitioner with two options: He could either resign without a severance package or be dismissed. Mr. Chavel fired petitioner after he refused to resign. Petitioner filed a lawsuit alleging that he had been terminated on account of his national origin in violation of Title VII, and on account of his age.

Applying Circuit precedent, the Court of Appeals required petitioner to plead a prima facie case of discrimination in order to survive respondent's motion to dismiss. In the Court of Appeals' view, petitioner was thus required to allege in his complaint: (1) membership in a protected group; (2) qualification for the job in question; (3) an adverse employment action; and (4) circumstances that support an inference of discrimination.

> The four-part *McDonnell Douglas* burden shifting test is discussed in greater detail in Chapter 3.

The prima facie case under *McDonnell Douglas*, however, is an evidentiary standard, not a pleading requirement. In *McDonnell Douglas*, this Court made clear that "[t]he critical issue before us concern[ed] the order and allocation of *proof* in a private, non-class action challenging employment discrimination." 411 U.S. at 800 (emphasis added). In subsequent cases, this Court has reiterated that the prima facie case relates to the employee's burden of presenting evidence that raises an inference of discrimination.

This Court has never indicated that the requirements for establishing a prima facie case under *McDonnell Douglas* also apply to the pleading standard that plaintiffs must satisfy in order to survive a motion to dismiss. For instance, we have rejected the argument that a Title VII complaint requires greater "particularity," because this would "too narrowly constric[t] the role of the pleadings." *McDonald v. Santa Fe Trail Transp. Co.*, 427 U.S. 273, 283, n. 11 (1976). Consequently, the ordinary rules for assessing the sufficiency of a complaint apply.

In addition, under a notice pleading system, it is not appropriate to require a plaintiff to plead facts establishing a prima facie case because the *McDonnell Douglas* framework does not apply in every employment discrimination case. For instance, if a plaintiff is able to produce direct evidence of discrimination, he may prevail without proving all the elements of a prima facie case. Under the Second Circuit's heightened pleading standard, a plaintiff without direct evidence of discrimination at the time of his complaint must plead a prima facie case of discrimination, even though discovery might uncover such direct evidence. It thus seems incongruous to require a plaintiff, in order to survive a motion to dismiss, to plead more facts than he may ultimately need to prove to succeed on the merits if direct evidence of discrimination is discovered.

Moreover, the precise requirements of a prima facie case can vary depending on the context and were "never intended to be rigid, mechanized, or ritualistic." *Furnco Constr. Corp. v. Waters*, 438 U.S. 567 (1978). Before discovery has unearthed relevant facts and evidence, it may be difficult to define the precise formulation of the required prima facie case in a particular case. Given that the prima facie case operates as a flexible evidentiary standard, it should not be transposed into a rigid pleading standard for discrimination cases.

Furthermore, imposing the Court of Appeals' heightened pleading standard in employment discrimination cases conflicts with Federal Rule of Civil Procedure 8(a)(2), which provides that a complaint must include only "a short and plain statement of the claim showing that the pleader is entitled to relief." Such a statement must simply "give the defendant fair notice of what the plaintiff's claim is and the grounds upon which it rests." *Conley v. Gibson*, 355 U.S. 41, 47 (1957). This simplified notice pleading standard relies on liberal discovery rules and summary judgment motions to define disputed facts and issues and to dispose of unmeritorious claims. *See id.* at 47–48; *Leatherman v. Tarrant County Narcotics Intelligence and Coordination Unit*, 507 U.S. 163, 168–169 (1993). "The provisions for discovery are so flexible and the provisions for pretrial procedure and summary judgment so effective, that attempted surprise in federal practice is aborted very easily, synthetic issues detected, and the gravamen of the dispute brought frankly into the open for the inspection of the court." 5 C. Wright & A. Miller, Federal Practice and Procedure § 1202, p. 76 (2d ed. 1990).

Rule 8(a)'s simplified pleading standard applies to all civil actions, with limited exceptions. Rule 9(b), for example, provides for greater particularity in all averments of fraud or mistake. This Court, however, has declined to extend such exceptions to other contexts. In *Leatherman* we stated: "[T]he Federal Rules do address in Rule 9(b) the question of the need for greater particularity in pleading certain actions, but do not include among the enumerated actions any reference to complaints alleging municipal liability under § 1983. Expressio unius est exclusio alterius." 507 U.S. at 168. Just as Rule 9(b) makes no mention of municipal liability under Rev. Stat. § 1979, 42 U.S.C. § 1983 (1994 ed., Supp. V), neither does it refer to employment discrimination. Thus, complaints in these cases, as in most others, must satisfy only the simple requirements of Rule 8(a).

Other provisions of the Federal Rules of Civil Procedure are inextricably linked to Rule 8(a)'s simplified notice pleading standard. Rule 8(e)(1) states that "[n]o technical forms of pleading or motions are required," and Rule 8(f) provides that "[a]ll pleadings shall be so construed as to do substantial justice." Given the Federal Rules' simplified standard for pleading, "[a] court may dismiss a complaint only if it is clear that no relief could be granted under any set of facts that could be proved consistent with the allegations." *Hishon v. King & Spalding*, 467 U.S. 69 (1984). If a pleading fails to specify the allegations in a manner that provides sufficient notice, a defendant can move for a more definite statement under Rule 12(e) before responding. Moreover, claims lacking merit may be dealt with through summary judgment under Rule 56. The liberal notice pleading of Rule 8(a) is the starting point of a simplified pleading system, which was adopted to focus litigation on the merits of a claim.

Applying the relevant standard, petitioner's complaint easily satisfies the requirements of Rule 8(a) because it gives respondent fair notice of the basis for petitioner's claims. Petitioner alleged that he had been terminated on account of his national origin in violation of Title VII and on account of his age in violation of the ADEA. His complaint detailed the events leading to his termination, provided relevant dates, and included the ages and nationalities of at least some of the relevant persons involved with his termination. These allegations give respondent fair notice of what petitioner's claims are and the grounds upon which they rest.

> In *Swierkiewicz*, the Court repeatedly relies on the *Conley* decision. The *Conley* decision was called into question by the Court a number of years later.

Respondent argues that allowing lawsuits based on conclusory allegations of discrimination to go forward will burden the courts and encourage disgruntled employees to bring unsubstantiated suits. Whatever the practical merits of this argument, the Federal Rules do not contain a heightened pleading standard for employment discrimination suits. A requirement of greater specificity for particular claims is a result that "must be obtained by the process of amending the Federal Rules, and not by judicial interpretation." Furthermore, Rule 8(a) establishes a pleading standard without regard to whether a claim will succeed on the merits. "Indeed it may appear on the face of the pleadings that a recovery is very remote and unlikely but that is not the test."

For the foregoing reasons, we hold that an employment discrimination plaintiff need not plead a prima facie case of discrimination and that petitioner's complaint is sufficient to survive respondent's motion to dismiss. Accordingly, the judgment of the Court of Appeals is reversed, and the case is remanded for further proceedings consistent with this opinion.

■ NOTES AND QUESTIONS

1. In *Swierkiewicz*, the Court makes clear that a plaintiff need not plead a prima facie case under *McDonnell Douglas* to proceed under Title VII. This text will look more closely at the *McDonnell Douglas* elements in Chapter 3. For now, it is worth noting that to establish a prima facie case under *McDonnell Douglas*, a plaintiff must show that she is (a) a member of a protected class; (b) qualified for the position; (c) suffered an adverse action; and (d) there is other evidence that would give rise to an inference of discrimination. Where the plaintiff satisfies this test, the burden of production shifts to the employer to show a legitimate nondiscriminatory reason for taking the adverse action. The plaintiff carries the ultimate burden of persuasion of showing that this reason is pretextual.

2. *Swierkiewicz* does not clarify exactly what a plaintiff must establish to survive a dismissal motion. The Court is clear, though, that the requirements do not include all four parts of the traditional prima facie case.

3. The Court also explains that *McDonnell Douglas* "is an evidentiary standard, not a pleading requirement." Thus, the Court makes clear that a traditional prima facie case for discrimination is only one way of establishing unlawful conduct. There may be other ways for the plaintiff to prove her case as well.

4. The Court here also emphasizes the notice pleading requirements of the federal rules. In the Court's view, it should not be an onerous burden on the plaintiff to simply notify its employer of the claims against it.

5. In some ways, *Swierkiewicz* creates a safe harbor for employment discrimination litigants. If, as the case holds, a plaintiff need not plead all of the elements of the *McDonnell Douglas* prima facie case, a plaintiff that does sufficiently plead all of these elements should survive dismissal. Following this decision, then, plaintiffs should be advised to *at least* plead all of the elements of a prima facie case where possible.

6. Plaintiffs have also been wary of putting *too much* information into the complaint. Doing so could potentially hurt a plaintiff's case and subject it to early dismissal. Plaintiffs were thus cautious to avoid over-pleading their facts before discovery had occurred.

 ## Interactive Problem

Looking back at the facts of the interactive problem, which facts should Caroline include in her complaint to sufficiently allege a Title VII violation? Should her complaint satisfy all of the elements of the prima facie case? Are there enough facts available for her to do so at this time?

In two controversial decisions, the Supreme Court addressed the pleading standard for federal civil cases. The Court adopted the now well-known plausibility standard, which is discussed below. This standard disturbed well-settled procedural law that had been in place for decades, now requiring that a plaintiff plead enough facts to state a *plausible* claim to relief.

Ashcroft v. Iqbal
556 U.S. 662 (2009)

Justice KENNEDY delivered the opinion of the Court.

Respondent Javaid Iqbal is a citizen of Pakistan and a Muslim. In the wake of the September 11, 2001, terrorist attacks he was arrested in the United States on criminal charges and detained by federal officials. Respondent claims he was deprived of various constitutional protections while in federal custody. To redress the alleged deprivations, respondent filed a complaint against numerous federal officials, including John Ashcroft, the former Attorney General of the United States, and Robert Mueller, the Director of the Federal Bureau of Investigation (FBI). Ashcroft and Mueller are the petitioners in the case now before us. As to these two petitioners, the complaint alleges that they adopted an unconstitutional policy that subjected respondent to harsh conditions of confinement on account of his race, religion, or national origin.

In the District Court petitioners raised the defense of qualified immunity and moved to dismiss the suit, contending the complaint was not sufficient to state a claim against them. The District Court denied the motion to dismiss, concluding the complaint was sufficient to state a claim despite petitioners' official status at the times in question. Petitioners brought an interlocutory appeal in the Court of Appeals for the Second Circuit. The court, without discussion, assumed it had jurisdiction over the order denying the motion to dismiss; and it affirmed the District Court's decision.

Respondent's account of his prison ordeal could, if proved, demonstrate unconstitutional misconduct by some governmental actors. But the allegations and pleadings with respect to these actors are not before us here. This case instead turns on a narrower question: Did respondent, as the plaintiff in the District Court, plead factual matter that, if taken as true, states a claim that petitioners deprived him of his clearly established constitutional rights. We hold respondent's pleadings are insufficient.

Following the 2001 attacks, the FBI and other entities within the Department of Justice began an investigation of vast reach to identify the assailants and prevent them from attacking anew. The FBI dedicated more than 4,000 special agents and 3,000 support personnel to the endeavor.

In the ensuing months the FBI questioned more than 1,000 people with suspected links to the attacks in

John Ashcroft, former U.S. Attorney General

particular or to terrorism in general. Of those individuals, some 762 were held on immigration charges; and a 184-member subset of that group was deemed to be "of 'high interest'" to the investigation. The high-interest detainees were held under restrictive conditions designed to prevent them from communicating with the general prison population or the outside world.

Respondent was one of the detainees. According to his complaint, in November 2001 agents of the FBI and Immigration and Naturalization Service arrested him on charges of fraud in relation to identification documents and conspiracy to defraud the United States. *Iqbal v. Hasty*, 490 F.3d 143, 147–148 (C.A.2 2007). Pending trial for those crimes, respondent was housed at the Metropolitan

Detention Center (MDC) in Brooklyn, New York. Respondent was designated a person "of high interest" to the September 11 investigation and in January 2002 was placed in a section of the MDC known as the Administrative Maximum Special Housing Unit (ADMAX SHU). As the facility's name indicates, the ADMAX SHU incorporates the maximum security conditions allowable under Federal Bureau of Prison regulations. ADMAX SHU detainees were kept in lockdown 23 hours a day, spending the remaining hour outside their cells in handcuffs and leg irons accompanied by a four-officer escort.

Respondent pleaded guilty to the criminal charges, served a term of imprisonment, and was removed to his native Pakistan. He then filed a *Bivens* action in the United States District Court for the Eastern District of New York against 34 current and former federal officials and 19 "John Doe" federal corrections officers. See *Bivens v. Six Unknown Fed. Narcotics Agents*, 403 U.S. 388 (1971). The defendants range from the correctional officers who had day-to-day contact with respondent during the

World Trade Center prior to 9/11/2001

term of his confinement, to the wardens of the MDC facility, all the way to petitioners—officials who were at the highest level of the federal law enforcement hierarchy.

The 21-cause-of-action complaint does not challenge respondent's arrest or his confinement in the MDC's general prison population. Rather, it concentrates on his treatment while confined to the ADMAX SHU. The complaint sets forth various claims against defendants who are not before us. For instance, the complaint alleges that respondent's jailors "kicked him in the stomach, punched him in the face, and dragged him across" his cell without justification; subjected him to serial strip and body-cavity searches when he posed no safety risk to himself or others; and refused to let him and other Muslims pray because there would be "[n]o prayers for terrorists."

The allegations against petitioners are the only ones relevant here. The complaint contends that petitioners designated respondent a person of high interest on account of his race, religion, or national origin, in contravention of the First and Fifth Amendments to the Constitution. The complaint alleges that "the [FBI], under the direction of Defendant Mueller, arrested and detained thousands of Arab Muslim men . . . as part of its investigation of the events of September 11." It further alleges that "[t]he policy of holding post-September-11th detainees in highly restrictive conditions of confinement until they were 'cleared' by the FBI was approved by Defendants Ashcroft and Mueller in discussions in the weeks after September 11, 2001." Lastly, the complaint posits that petitioners "each knew of, condoned, and willfully and maliciously agreed to subject" respondent to harsh conditions of confinement "as a matter of policy, solely on account of [his] religion, race, and/or national origin and for no legitimate penological interest." The pleading names Ashcroft as the "principal architect" of the policy, and identifies Mueller as "instrumental in [its] adoption, promulgation, and implementation."

Petitioners moved to dismiss the complaint for failure to state sufficient allegations to show their own involvement in clearly established unconstitutional conduct. The District Court denied their motion.

The Court of Appeals considered *Twombly*'s applicability to this case. Acknowledging that *Twombly* retired the *Conley* no-set-of-facts test relied upon by the District Court, the Court of Appeals' opinion discussed at length how to apply this Court's "standard for assessing the adequacy of pleadings." It concluded that *Twombly* called for a "flexible 'plausibility standard,' which obliges a pleader to amplify a claim with some factual allegations in those contexts where such amplification is needed to render the claim *plausible*." The court found that petitioners' appeal did not present one of "those contexts" requiring amplification. As a consequence, it held respondent's pleading adequate to allege petitioners' personal involvement in discriminatory decisions which, if true, violated clearly established constitutional law.

> The *Twombly* decision required that a federal complaint contain a "plausible" basis for relief.

We turn to respondent's complaint. Under Federal Rule of Civil Procedure 8(a)(2), a pleading must contain a "short and plain statement of the claim showing that the pleader is entitled to relief." As the Court held in *Twombly*, 550 U.S. 544, the pleading standard Rule 8 announces does not require "detailed factual allegations," but it demands more than an unadorned, the-defendant-unlawfully-harmed-me accusation. *Id.* at 555. A pleading that offers "labels and conclusions" or "a formulaic recitation of the elements of a cause of action will not do." 550 U.S. at 555. Nor does a complaint suffice if it tenders "naked assertion[s]" devoid of "further factual enhancement." *Id.* at 557.

To survive a motion to dismiss, a complaint must contain sufficient factual matter, accepted as true, to "state a claim to relief that is plausible on its face." *Id.* at 570. A claim has facial plausibility when the plaintiff pleads factual content that allows the court to draw the reasonable inference that the defendant is liable for the misconduct alleged. *Id.* at 556. The plausibility standard is not akin to a "probability requirement," but it asks for more than a sheer possibility that a defendant has acted unlawfully. *Ibid.* Where a complaint pleads facts that are "merely consistent with" a defendant's liability, it "stops short of the line between possibility and plausibility of 'entitlement to relief.'" *Id.* at 557 (brackets omitted).

Two working principles underlie our decision in *Twombly*. First, the tenet that a court must accept as true all of the allegations contained in a complaint is inapplicable to legal conclusions. Threadbare recitals of the elements of a cause of action, supported by mere conclusory statements, do not suffice. Rule 8 marks a notable and generous departure from the hyper-technical, code-pleading regime of a prior era, but it does not unlock the doors of discovery for a plaintiff armed with nothing more than conclusions. Second, only a complaint that states a plausible claim for relief survives a motion to dismiss. Determining whether a complaint states a plausible claim for relief will, as the Court of Appeals observed, be a context-specific task that requires the reviewing court to draw on its judicial experience and common sense. But where the well-pleaded facts do not permit the court to infer more than the mere possibility of misconduct, the complaint has alleged—but it has not "show[n]"—"that the pleader is entitled to relief." Fed. Rule Civ. Proc. 8(a)(2).

In keeping with these principles a court considering a motion to dismiss can choose to begin by identifying pleadings that, because they are no more than conclusions, are not entitled to the assumption of truth. While legal conclusions can provide the framework of a complaint, they must be supported by factual allegations. When there are well-pleaded factual allegations, a court should assume their veracity and then determine whether they plausibly give rise to an entitlement to relief.

Our decision in *Twombly* illustrates the two-pronged approach. There, we considered the sufficiency of a complaint alleging that incumbent telecommunications providers had entered an agreement not to compete and to forestall competitive entry, in violation of the Sherman Act, 15 U.S.C. § 1. Recognizing that § 1 enjoins only anticompetitive conduct "effected by a contract, combination, or conspiracy," the plaintiffs in *Twombly* flatly pleaded that the defendants "ha[d] entered into a contract, combination or conspiracy to prevent competitive entry . . . and ha[d] agreed not to compete with one another." 550 U.S. at 551 (internal quotation marks omitted). The complaint also alleged that the defendants' "parallel course of conduct . . . to prevent competition" and inflate prices was indicative of the unlawful agreement alleged.

The Court held the plaintiffs' complaint deficient under Rule 8. In doing so it first noted that the plaintiffs' assertion of an unlawful agreement was a "'legal conclusion'" and, as such, was not entitled to the assumption of truth. *Id.* at 555. Had the Court simply credited the allegation of a conspiracy, the plaintiffs would have stated a claim for relief and been entitled to proceed perforce. The Court next addressed the "nub" of the plaintiffs' complaint—the well-pleaded, nonconclusory factual allegation of parallel behavior—to determine whether it gave rise to a "plausible suggestion of conspiracy." *Id.* at 565–566. Acknowledging that parallel conduct was consistent with an unlawful agreement, the Court nevertheless concluded that it did not plausibly suggest an illicit accord because it was not only compatible with, but indeed was more likely explained by, lawful, unchoreographed free-market behavior. *Id.* at 567. Because the well-pleaded fact of parallel conduct, accepted as true, did not plausibly suggest an unlawful agreement, the Court held the plaintiffs' complaint must be dismissed.

Under *Twombly*'s construction of Rule 8, we conclude that respondent's complaint has not "nudged [his] claims" of invidious discrimination "across the line from conceivable to plausible."

We begin our analysis by identifying the allegations in the complaint that are not entitled to the assumption of truth. Respondent pleads that petitioners "knew of, condoned, and willfully and maliciously agreed to subject [him]" to harsh conditions of confinement "as a matter of policy, solely on account of [his] religion, race, and/or national origin and for no legitimate penological interest." The complaint alleges that Ashcroft was the "principal architect" of this invidious policy, and that Mueller was "instrumental" in adopting and executing it. These bare assertions, much like the pleading of conspiracy in *Twombly*, amount to nothing more than a "formulaic recitation of the elements" of a constitutional discrimination claim, 550 U.S. at 555, namely, that petitioners adopted a policy "'because of,' not merely 'in spite of,' its adverse effects upon an identifiable group." As such, the allegations are conclusory and not entitled to be assumed true. To be clear, we do not reject these bald allegations on the ground that they are unrealistic or nonsensical. We do not so characterize them any more than the Court in *Twombly* rejected the plaintiffs' express allegation of a "'contract, combination or conspiracy to prevent competitive entry,'" *Id.* at 551, because it thought that claim too chimerical to be maintained. It is the conclusory nature of respondent's allegations, rather than their extravagantly fanciful nature, that disentitles them to the presumption of truth.

We next consider the factual allegations in respondent's complaint to determine if they plausibly suggest an entitlement to relief. The complaint alleges that "the [FBI], under the direction of Defendant Mueller, arrested and detained thousands of Arab Muslim men . . . as part of its investigation of the events of September 11." It further claims that "[t]he policy of holding post-September-11th detainees in highly restrictive conditions of confinement until they were 'cleared' by the FBI was approved by Defendants Ashcroft and Mueller in discussions in the weeks after September 11, 2001." Taken as true, these allegations are consistent with petitioners' purposefully designating detainees "of high interest" because of their race, religion, or national origin. But given more likely explanations, they do not plausibly establish this purpose.

The September 11 attacks were perpetrated by 19 Arab Muslim hijackers who counted themselves members in good standing of al Qaeda, an Islamic fundamentalist group. Al Qaeda was headed by another Arab Muslim—Osama bin Laden—and composed in large part of his Arab Muslim disciples. It should come as no surprise that a legitimate policy directing law enforcement to arrest and detain individuals because of their suspected link to the attacks would produce a disparate, incidental impact on Arab Muslims, even though the purpose of the policy was to target neither Arabs nor Muslims. On the facts respondent alleges the arrests Mueller oversaw were likely lawful and justified by his nondiscriminatory intent to detain aliens who were illegally present in the United States and who had potential connections to those who committed terrorist acts. As between that "obvious alternative explanation" for the arrests, *Twombly*, *supra* at 567, and the purposeful, invidious discrimination respondent asks us to infer, discrimination is not a plausible conclusion.

But even if the complaint's well-pleaded facts give rise to a plausible inference that respondent's arrest was the result of unconstitutional discrimination, that inference alone would not entitle respondent to relief. It is important to recall that respondent's complaint challenges neither the constitutionality of his arrest nor his initial detention in the MDC. Respondent's constitutional claims against petitioners rest solely on their ostensible "policy of holding post-September-11th detainees" in the ADMAX SHU once they were categorized as "of high interest." To prevail on that theory, the complaint must contain facts plausibly showing that petitioners purposefully adopted a policy of classifying post-September-11 detainees as "of high interest" because of their race, religion, or national origin.

This the complaint fails to do. Though respondent alleges that various other defendants, who are not before us, may have labeled him a person of "of high interest" for impermissible reasons, his only factual allegation against petitioners accuses them of adopting a policy approving "restrictive conditions of confinement" for post-September-11 detainees until they were " 'cleared' by the FBI." *Ibid.* Accepting the truth of that allegation, the complaint does not show, or even intimate, that petitioners purposefully housed detainees in the ADMAX SHU due to their race, religion, or national origin. All it plausibly suggests is that the Nation's top law enforcement officers, in the aftermath of a devastating terrorist attack, sought to keep suspected terrorists in the most secure conditions available until the suspects could be cleared of terrorist activity. Respondent does not argue, nor can he, that such a motive would violate petitioners' constitutional obligations.

To be sure, respondent can attempt to draw certain contrasts between the pleadings the Court considered in *Twombly* and the pleadings at issue here. In *Twombly*, the complaint alleged general wrongdoing that extended over a period of years, *id.* at 551, whereas here the complaint alleges discrete wrongs—for instance, beatings—by lower level Government actors. The allegations here, if true, and if condoned by petitioners, could be the basis for some inference of wrongful intent on petitioners' part. Despite these distinctions, respondent's pleadings do not suffice to state a claim. Unlike in *Twombly*, where the doctrine of *respondeat superior* could bind the corporate defendant, here, as we have noted, petitioners cannot be held liable unless they themselves acted on account of a constitutionally protected characteristic. Yet respondent's complaint does not contain any factual allegation sufficient to plausibly suggest petitioners' discriminatory state of mind. His pleadings thus do not meet the standard necessary to comply with Rule 8.

Respondent says that our decision in *Twombly* should be limited to pleadings made in the context of an antitrust dispute. This argument is not supported by *Twombly* and is incompatible with the Federal Rules of Civil Procedure. Our decision in *Twombly* expounded the pleading standard for "all civil actions," *ibid.* and it applies to antitrust and discrimination suits alike.

> The Court is clear here that the plausibility standard announced in *Twombly* applies to cases involving discrimination.

Respondent [also] maintains that the Federal Rules expressly allow him to allege petitioners' discriminatory intent "generally," which he equates with a conclusory allegation. It follows, respondent says, that his complaint is sufficiently well pleaded because it claims that petitioners discriminated against him "on account of [his] religion, race, and/or national origin and for no legitimate penological interest." Were we required to accept this allegation as true, respondent's complaint would survive petitioners' motion to dismiss. But the Federal Rules do not require courts to credit a complaint's conclusory statements without reference to its factual context.

We hold that respondent's complaint fails to plead sufficient facts to state a claim for purposeful and unlawful discrimination against petitioners.

■ NOTES AND QUESTIONS

1. In *Twombly*, the Supreme Court abrogated its long-standing language from *Conley* that a plaintiff should be permitted to proceed in a civil case where it can allege "any set of facts" that will support the claim. In place of the "any set of facts" language, the *Twombly* Court adopted a plausibility standard. Under this new standard, a plaintiff must allege sufficient facts to establish a plausible claim to relief. *See* Melanie A. Goff & Richard A. Bales, *A "Plausible" Defense: Applying* Twombly *and* Iqbal *to Affirmative Defenses*, 34 Am. J. Trial Advoc. 603 (2011) (addressing whether the new pleading standards apply to pleadings filed by either party or whether they apply only to a plaintiff's filings); Scott Dodson, *Pleading Standards After* Bell Atlantic Corp. v. Twombly, 93 Va. L. Rev. in Brief 135 (2007) (considering the future implications of the new pleading standard).

2. It was unclear whether *Twombly*—which was an antitrust case—applied outside of the context of the Sherman Act. Scholars differed on the applicability of *Twombly* outside of antitrust cases. *Iqbal* clarifies that the plausibility standard applies to "all civil actions," including "antitrust and discrimination suits alike." Following *Iqbal*, there can be little doubt that the plausibility pleading standard applies to all federal discrimination cases, including Title VII, the ADA and the ADEA. *But see* Suja A. Thomas, *Oddball* Iqbal *and* Twombly *and Employment Discrimination*, 2011 U. Ill. L. Rev. 215 (arguing that the new pleading standard should not apply to employment discrimination cases).

3. The *Swierkiewicz* decision relies heavily on the Supreme Court's decision in *Conley*—which was overruled by *Twombly* and *Iqbal*. There is a serious question, then, whether *Swierkiewicz* is still good law following the more recent Supreme Court decisions. Scholars and courts are already divided on this issue. *See generally* David Noll, *The Indeterminacy of* Iqbal, 99 Geo. L.J. 117, 143–147 n.162 (2010) (noting that several courts and commentators have questioned whether *Swierkiewicz* remains good law, but ultimately concluding that the essential holding of *Swierkiewicz* remains intact); Adam N. Steinman, *The Pleading Problem*, 62 Stan. L. Rev. 1293, 1310 (2010) (doubting the "continued vitality of pre-*Twombly* authorities" like *Swierkiewicz*).

4. Given the current debate on the viability of *Swierkiewicz*, it is again unclear whether a plaintiff must plead a prima facie case of discrimination to survive dismissal. It is even unclear whether a plaintiff in certain instances must go above and beyond pleading a prima facie case by including additional facts to state a plausible claim.

5. The plaintiff in *Iqbal* appears to have detailed fairly comprehensive facts of the conspiracy that was being alleged. These facts were still deemed insufficient to permit the plaintiff to proceed. As a motion to dismiss is often brought before discovery, how will a plaintiff in a Title VII action be able to gather enough facts to survive dismissal? In many employment discrimination cases, isn't it true that most of the important facts are in the possession of the employer?

6. It is also clear, following *Iqbal*, that a plaintiff cannot simply parrot the language of the statute that the defendant purportedly violated and expect to survive dismissal. The plaintiff must state more than conclusory allegations and should support the claim with any relevant facts. As the *Iqbal* Court held, "[t]hreadbare recitals of the elements of a cause of action, supported by mere conclusory statements, do not suffice."

7. Does *Iqbal* make it more difficult for plaintiffs to prevail in Title VII cases? There are many empirical attempts to answer this question, but the results of those studies have been unclear. Anecdotally, however, there have been numerous cases where the courts have appeared to raise the pleadings bar following *Twombly* and *Iqbal*. *See generally* Joseph A. Seiner, *The Trouble with* Twombly: *A Proposed Pleading Standard for Employment Discrimination Cases*, 2009 U. Ill. L. Rev. 1011; David Freeman Engstrom, *The* Twiqbal *Puzzle and Empirical Study of Civil Procedure*, 65 Stan. L. Rev. 1203 (2013) (summarizing studies).

8. What does it mean to plead a plausible claim of employment discrimination? What facts would you typically expect to see to satisfy this type of standard?

9. If an employee's complaint simply alleged that "the employee was terminated on a [specified date] because of her age," would such a complaint be sufficient to survive dismissal? Why or why not?

 # Interactive Problem

Looking back at the facts of the interactive problem, does the *Iqbal* decision change your view of the type of facts Caroline should plead in her complaint in order to survive dismissal? If so, what additional facts would you suggest that she allege?

Practice and Procedural Tip

4: Constructing the Federal Complaint

As seen above, there is substantial confusion over what must be alleged in a Title VII complaint. Prior to *Twombly* and *Iqbal*, *Swierkiewicz* had created a safe harbor for plaintiffs. If an employment discrimination litigant was able to establish the four elements of *McDonnell Douglas* in the complaint, that plaintiff should have been able to survive dismissal. *Swierkiewicz* stated that a Title VII plaintiff need *not* plead a prima facie case to avoid dismissal—those that do plead such a case should inherently survive such a motion.

This standard created an excellent template for plaintiffs—allege the prima facie case but no more. Doing so would insulate the complaint from dismissal, but also ensure that the plaintiff was not pleading too many facts and thus pleading herself out of court. More troubling, the key element in many employment discrimination cases is that of intent. It can be very difficult to establish this intent element without access to discovery. In employment cases in particular, many of the witnesses and critical documents are in the possession of the employer. Without discovery it can be an uphill battle for plaintiffs to gather sufficient facts to plead a plausible case early in the proceedings.

In Chapter 13, we will discuss the "best practices" for what to include in a complaint of discrimination. There is no simple or correct answer as to what should be included in the complaint. Jurisdictions vary as the law is in a state of flux on this issue. The short answer, however, is that at the current time plaintiffs should be cautious to plead as many facts as are available in the case to support their claims. As it is unclear how much factual support a court will require early on, it is best for plaintiffs to err on the side of inclusiveness.

From a practical standpoint, this may mean that plaintiffs will have to do substantial work prior to filing a claim. Individuals will want to make sure that they have gathered enough evidence to survive a dismissal motion. At a minimum, this will require pleading enough facts to establish the *McDonnell Douglas* prima facie case. But in certain instances—in some jurisdictions—it may mean even more. Simply put, it is better to over-plead than under-plead until the case law becomes more settled. Additionally, plaintiffs should do their best to educate themselves about the judge in the particular case and research the types of facts that the particular jurisdiction requires to survive dismissal. *See generally* John Hendrickson, *What Lies Ahead? Notice Pleading and* Iqbal *in EEOC Employment Discrimination Litigation,* ABA (2010), http://www.americanbar.org/content/dam/aba/administrative/labor_law/meetings/2010/annualconference/053.authcheckdam.pdf.

Class Exercise: Pleading a Discrimination Claim

Breaking up into small groups, discuss the types of facts a plaintiff in a typical race discrimination discharge lawsuit would need to plead to survive dismissal. What types of facts should appear in the complaint? How should the plaintiff go about gathering these facts?

 # F. Discovery, E-Discovery, and Summary Judgment

After a case has been filed in federal court and has survived any initial dismissal motions, it will typically proceed to discovery. In discovery, the parties will exchange interrogatories and documents. Witnesses will also be deposed on their knowledge of the facts involved in the particular case. Discovery in employment discrimination cases is identical to any other civil action. The parties involved will exchange information in advance of trial. This information takes the form of written responses, document requests, and witness testimony.

One unique aspect of discovery in employment discrimination cases is the importance of the deposition of the plaintiff. As the alleged victim of discrimination will have substantial information about the nature of the case and the perceived wrongdoing, this deposition will be critical to almost every case of workplace discrimination. Additionally, as the issue of intent is important to these claims, discovery in employment discrimination cases is often targeted at uncovering evidence of the defendant's potential animus. Documents, emails, and testimony will typically be sought by the plaintiff in discovery to help shed light on the employer's true motivations for its behavior.

E-discovery is a particularly important aspect of litigation in employment cases in the digital age. Uncovering important information in emails, texts, and other digital forms has become an increasingly critical skill. While employers may believe that such information has been "deleted," it can often be recovered by experts in the area. This type of information can often reveal the bias of certain workers, and can quickly become a central piece of evidence in a case.

At the close of discovery, it is common for defendants in an employment discrimination case to move for summary judgment. While either party can move for summary judgment under Federal Rule of Civil Procedure 56, it is much more common for defendants to use this procedural tool. When the defendant "moves for summary judgment," that employer will argue that even if the facts as revealed during discovery are taken in the light most favorable to the plaintiff, the case should still be dismissed. Essentially, when a defendant moves for summary judgment in the case, it is asking the court to dismiss the plaintiff's claim because the facts (even when viewed in the plaintiff's favor) simply fail to support it. *See* Robinson v. BGM Am., Inc., 964 F. Supp. 2d 552, 564 (D.S.C. Aug. 8, 2013) (citing Dennis v. Columbia Colleton Med. Ctr., Inc., 290 F.3d 639, 645 (4th Cir. 2002)) ("In discrimination cases, a party is entitled to summary judgment if no reasonable jury could rule in the non-moving party's favor.").

While it is common for employers to seek summary judgment and dismissal of an entire case, individual issues can also be decided under Rule 56. In this regard, it is not uncommon for workers to move for summary judgment on more specific issues in the case. From a practical perspective, the case is often won or lost at the summary judgment stage of the proceedings. Where a plaintiff survives summary judgment, she empirically has a better-than-average chance of prevailing before a jury. Thus, employers often attempt to settle a case when they are unsuccessful in having the matter dismissed before trial. To prevail on a summary judgment motion, the defendant must show that there is no material issue of fact in dispute, and that the case should be resolved in the employer's favor.

When deciding whether to grant summary judgment in a case, courts are often faced with a difficult question. The one unique issue in employment discrimination cases is that the question of intent is often at stake. *See* Hernandez v. City of Corpus Christi, 820 F. Supp. 2d 781, 800 (S.D. Tex. 2011) ("Summary judgment in employment discrimination cases is rarely appropriate."). It may be particularly difficult for the courts to resolve the question of intent without the assistance of a jury. *See* EEOC v. RJB Props., Inc., 857 F. Supp. 2d 727, 739 (N.D. Ill. 2012) (quoting EEOC v. Int'l Profit Ass'ns, Inc., 654 F. Supp. 2d 767, 783 (N.D. Ill. 2009)) ("Because intent and credibility are typically crucial issues in employment discrimination cases, summary judgment must be approached with caution, and heightened scrutiny of the record is appropriate.").

Nonetheless, the courts do routinely grant summary judgment in federal employment discrimination cases, although many of these dismissals are on administrative or procedural grounds. While the data is constantly changing and not always easily accessible, it is clear that very few cases actually make it to trial. One federal appellate court concluded that less than 10 percent of employment discrimination cases survive summary judgment. *See* Wallace v. SMC Pneumatics, Inc., 103 F.3d 1394, 1396 (7th Cir. 1997). There are numerous other studies that show the difficulty that plaintiffs encounter surviving summary judgment and ultimately proceeding to trial. *See generally* Kevin M. Clermont & Stewart J. Schwab, *How Employment Discrimination Plaintiffs Fare in Federal Court*, 1 J. Empirical Legal Stud. 429 (2004); Wendy Parker, *Lessons in Losing: Race Discrimination in Employment*, 81 Notre Dame L. Rev. 889 (2006) (analyzing different categories of employment discrimination cases' outcomes); Laura Beth Nielsen et al., *Individual Justice or Collective Legal Mobilization? Employment Discrimination Litigation in the Post-Civil Rights United States*, 7 J. Empirical Legal Stud. 175 (2010); Michael Selmi, *Why Are Employment Discrimination Cases So Hard to Win?*, 61 La. L. Rev. 555 (2001).

The following case looks at the use of summary judgment in a claim involving pregnancy discrimination. We will look more closely at the contours of pregnancy discrimination in our subsequent chapter exploring sex discrimination under Title VII. This case, however, provides an excellent example of how a federal appellate court will go about analyzing a summary judgment motion in an employment discrimination case.

EEOC v. Houston Funding II, Ltd.

717 F.3d 425 (5th Cir. 2013)

E. GRADY JOLLY, Circuit Judge:

The question we must answer in this appeal is whether discharging a female employee because she is lactating or expressing breast milk constitutes sex discrimination in violation of Title VII. We hold that it does.

The Equal Employment Opportunity Commission ("EEOC"), on behalf of Donnicia Venters ("Venters"), sued Houston Funding II, Ltd. and Houston Funding Corp. ("Houston Funding"), alleging Houston Funding unlawfully discharged Venters because she was lactating and wanted to express milk at work. The district court granted summary judgment in favor of Houston Funding, finding that, as a matter of law, discharging a female employee because she is lactating or expressing milk does not constitute sex discrimination. We VACATE and REMAND.

Venters worked as an account representative/collector for Houston Funding from March 2006 until she was fired in February 2009. In December 2008, she took a leave of absence to have her baby. Houston Funding has no maternity leave policy, and Venters and her supervisors did not specify a date for her return. Shortly after giving birth, Venters told Harry Cagle ("Cagle"), Houston Funding's Limited Partner, that she would return to work as soon as her doctor released her. Venters suffered complications from her C-section, however, and ended up staying home through mid February.

During her absence, Venters regularly contacted her supervisor, Robert Fleming ("Fleming"), as well as other Houston Funding managers. Venters' mobile phone records reflect that she spent 115 minutes on the phone with the Houston Funding office between January 7, 2009, and February 6, 2009. Fleming testified that Venters called him at least once a week from the beginning of her

NURSE THE BABY
YOUR PROTECTION AGAINST TROUBLE
INFORM YOURSELF THROUGH THE HEALTH
BUREAU PUBLICATIONS
AND CONSULT YOUR DOCTOR

leave in December 2008 through his departure from the company in January 2009. During one conversation, Venters told Fleming that she was breastfeeding her child and asked him to ask Cagle whether it might be possible for her to use a breast pump at work. Fleming stated that when he posed this question to Cagle, Cagle "responded with a strong 'NO. Maybe she needs to stay home longer.'"

On February 17, 2009, Venters called Cagle and told him her doctor had released her to return to work. Again, she mentioned she was lactating and asked whether she could use a back room to pump milk. After asking this question, Venters testified that there was a long pause, and when Cagle finally responded, he told her that they had filled her spot. The record reflects no denial of this conversation. On February 20, Houston Funding mailed a termination letter dated February 16 to Venters. This letter stated Venters was discharged due to job abandonment, effective February 13.

Venters subsequently filed a charge of sex discrimination with the EEOC. Houston Funding responded to this charge by asserting Venters had not contacted her supervisor during her maternity leave and had not attempted to return to work. After investigating Venters' charge, the EEOC brought a Title VII action against Houston Funding in district court, asserting that Houston Funding unlawfully discriminated against Venters based upon her sex, including her pregnancy, childbirth, or related medical conditions, by ending her employment.

Houston Funding argued Title VII does not cover "breast pump discrimination" and moved for summary judgment. The district court granted the motion, finding that, even if Venters' allegations were true, "[f]iring someone because of lactation or breast-pumping is not sex discrimination," and that lactation is not a related medical condition of pregnancy. The EEOC timely appealed.

We review a grant of summary judgment *de novo*, applying the same standard as the district court. *Rachid v. Jack In The Box, Inc.*, 376 F.3d 305 (5th Cir. 2004). Summary judgment is properly granted if, viewing the facts in the light most favorable to the nonmoving party, the movant shows that there is no genuine issue of material fact and that the movant is entitled to judgment as a matter of law. *Id.*; Fed. R. Civ. P. 56(c).

Title VII of the Civil Rights Act "prohibits various forms of employment discrimination, including discrimination on the basis of sex." Almost immediately after the Supreme Court, in *General Electric Co. v. Gilbert*, 429 U.S. 125 (1976), held that discrimination on the basis of pregnancy is not sex discrimination, Congress amended Title VII to include the Pregnancy Discrimination Act ("PDA"). 42 U.S.C. § 2000e–(k). The PDA provides that "[t]he terms 'because of sex' or 'on the basis of sex' include, but are not limited to, because of or on the basis of pregnancy, childbirth, or related medical conditions[.]" 42 U.S.C. § 2000e–(k). And the Supreme Court has recognized that this amendment "unambiguously expressed [Congress'] disapproval of both the holding and the reasoning of the Court in the *Gilbert* decision." *Newport News Shipbuilding & Dry Dock Co. v. EEOC*, 462 U.S. 669, 678 (1983).

> The Pregnancy Discrimination Act amended Title VII to make clear that pregnancy, childbirth, and related medical conditions are included in sex discrimination.

As such, courts have since interpreted Title VII to cover a far wider range of employment decisions entailing female physiology. This Court, for example, found in *Harper v. Thiokol Chemical Corp.*, 619 F.2d 489 (5th Cir. 1980), that "Thiokol's policy of requiring women who have been on pregnancy leave to have sustained a normal menstrual cycle before they can return to work clearly deprives female employees of employment opportunities and imposes on them a burden which male employees need not suffer." 619 F.2d at 491–92. The court accordingly held Thiokol violated Title VII as amended by the PDA.

In this case, the parties focus upon whether Houston Funding's conduct violated Title VII generally, as well as upon whether lactation is a related medical condition of pregnancy for purposes of the PDA. Given our precedent, we hold the EEOC's argument that Houston Funding discharged Venters because she was lactating or expressing milk states a cognizable Title VII sex discrimination claim. An adverse employment action motivated by these factors clearly imposes upon women a burden that male employees need not—indeed, could not—suffer.

Moreover, we hold that lactation is a related medical condition of pregnancy for purposes of the PDA. Lactation is the physiological process of secreting milk from mammary glands and is directly caused by hormonal changes associated with pregnancy and childbirth. It is undisputed in this appeal that lactation is a physiological result of being pregnant and bearing a child.

The PDA does not define the statutory term "medical condition" ("pregnancy, childbirth, or related medical conditions"), but "[i]t is well-settled that 'we should give words of statutes their plain meaning.'" *United States v. Ferguson*, 369 F.3d 847 (5th Cir. 2004) (quotation omitted). In discerning words' plain meaning, we may consult the dictionary. The McGraw-Hill Concise Dictionary of Modern Medicine defines "medical condition" as a "disease, illness, or injury" such as:

> physiological, mental, or psychologic conditions or disorders—e.g., orthopedic, visual, speech, or hearing impairments, cerebral palsy, epilepsy, muscular dystrophy, multiple sclerosis, CA, CAD, DM, mental retardation, emotional or mental illness, specific learning disabilities, HIV disease, TB, drug addiction, alcoholism.

JOSEPH SEGEN, MCGRAW-HILL CONCISE DICTIONARY OF MODERN MEDICINE 405 (2006). This definition is consistent with those of other medical dictionaries, which also broadly construe these terms. Given that this definition includes any physiological condition, it is difficult to see how it could not encompass lactation.

Furthermore, our precedent follows this interpretation. For example, although this Court in *Harper* did not explicitly find menstruation was a related medical condition of pregnancy under the PDA, it did find

> noteworthy that Thiokol's maternity leave policy is in contravention of the regulations of the Equal Employment Opportunity Commission. The 1972 guidelines, as amended, specify that '(w)ritten or unwritten employment policies and practices involving matters such as . . . reinstatement . . . shall be applied to disability due to *pregnancy, childbirth or related medical conditions* on the same terms and conditions as they are applied to other disabilities.' 29 C.F.R. § 1604.10(b) (1979).

619 F.2d at 493 n. 2 (alterations in original) (emphasis added). Accordingly, the Court did, at least implicitly, hold that menstruation was "pregnancy, childbirth or [a] related medical condition," given the facts of that case.

Menstruation is a normal aspect of female physiology, which is interrupted during pregnancy, but resumes shortly after the pregnancy concludes. Similarly, lactation is a normal aspect of female physiology that is initiated by pregnancy and concludes sometime thereafter. If an employer commits unlawful sex-based discrimination by instituting a policy revolving around a woman's post-pregnancy menstrual cycle, as in *Harper*, it is difficult to see how an employer who makes an employment decision based upon whether a woman is lactating can avoid such unlawful sex discrimination. And as both menstruation and lactation are aspects of female physiology that are affected by pregnancy, each seems readily to fit into a reasonable definition of "pregnancy, childbirth, or related medical conditions."

Because discriminating against a woman who is lactating or expressing breast milk violates Title VII and the PDA, we find that the EEOC has stated a *prima facie* case of sex discrimination with a showing that Houston Funding fired Venters because she was lactating and wanted to express milk at work. The EEOC has further proffered evidence showing that Houston Funding's stated reason for discharging Venters—i.e., job abandonment—was pretextual. There is, therefore, triable evidence from which a factfinder may conclude that Houston Funding violated Title VII by discharging Ms. Venters. The EEOC has thus satisfied the requirements of the *McDonnell Douglas* inferential test for Title VII discrimination such that she may proceed to trial. *McDonnell Douglas Corp. v. Green*, 411 U.S. 792 (1973).

For these reasons, we VACATE the judgment of the district court and REMAND for further proceedings not inconsistent with this opinion.

■ NOTES AND QUESTIONS

1. Was the appellate court correct in overturning the district court's grant of summary judgment?

2. As the Fifth Circuit notes, the lower court had concluded that " '[f]iring someone because of lactation or breast-pumping is not sex discrimination,' and that lactation is not a related medical condition of pregnancy." In the lower court's view, there was no material dispute of fact that would allow this case to go to trial. Disagreeing with this approach, the appellate court overturned the lower court's decision, permitting the case to proceed.

3. Who has the stronger case at trial—the EEOC or the defendant?

4. What evidence could the defendant offer at trial to defend this case?

5. What type of documents would have been exchanged during discovery in this case? What types of interrogatories would have been asked? Which witnesses would have been deposed?

6. It is interesting that this case is brought under Title VII. In many ways, it appears that an even stronger claim could have been brought under the Family and Medical Leave Act. In a footnote omitted from the case, the court noted that the employer was too small to be covered by that statute. While Title VII requires only fifteen employees for coverage, the FMLA requires fifty workers. The FMLA, however, only provides a right to twelve weeks of unpaid leave (and job preservation).

7. The court holds that "discriminating against a woman who is lactating or expressing breast milk violates Title VII." Given this conclusion, the court found that the Commission had satisfied its prima facie case and had provided further evidence to demonstrate that "Houston Funding's stated reason for discharging Venters—i.e., job abandonment—was pretextual." What evidence did the EEOC introduce to satisfy the prima facie case? What evidence shows that the employer's stated reason for termination was pretextual?

8. Should an employer routinely move for summary judgment in employment discrimination cases? What strategies can employers use during discovery to bolster their chances of prevailing on a summary judgment motion?

9. Citing Federal Rule of Civil Procedure 56, the court notes that "[s]ummary judgment is properly granted if, viewing the facts in the light most favorable to the nonmoving party, the movant shows that there is no genuine issue of material fact and that the movant is entitled to judgment as a matter of law." This standard has been widely accepted and applied in the courts. As this case clearly demonstrates, however, there are varying opinions as to when summary judgment is appropriate.

10. As many employment discrimination cases are fact intensive and involve questions of intent, they may be difficult to resolve prior to trial. Nonetheless, plaintiffs often have limited success in getting past the summary judgment stage of the proceedings. *See generally* Hon. Mark W. Bennett, *Essay: From the "No Spittin', No Cussin' and No Summary Judgment" Days of Employment Discrimination Litigation to the "Defendant's Summary Judgment Affirmed Without Comment" Days: One Judge's Four-Decade Perspective*, 57 N.Y.L. Sch. L. Rev. 685 (2012–2013); Vivian Berger, Michael O. Finkelstein & Kenneth Cheung, *Summary Judgment Benchmarks for Settling Employment Discrimination Lawsuits*, 23 Hofstra Lab. & Emp. L.J. 45 (2005); Hon. Bernice B. Donald & J. Eric Pardue, *Bringing Back Reasonable Inferences: A Short, Simple Suggestion for Addressing Some Problems at the Intersection of Employment Discrimination and Summary Judgment*, 57 N.Y.L. Sch. L. Rev. 749 (2012–2013).

11. Is summary judgment even constitutional? Does it deny civil rights plaintiffs the right to a jury trial? *See* Suja A. Thomas, *Why Summary Judgment Is Unconstitutional*, 93 Va. L. Rev. 139 (2007).

Interactive Problem

Looking back at the facts of the interactive problem, assume that the restaurant has been losing a substantial amount of business due to a downturn in the economy. Rather than fill the management position for which Caroline applied, the company decides to simply go out of business. In response to Caroline's complaint of discrimination, could the company move to dismiss? Could it file a summary judgment motion in the case? Why or why not?

Class Exercise: The Motion for Summary Judgment

Breaking up into small groups, draft a short motion for summary judgment by an employer in a case where a plaintiff has alleged racial discrimination. During discovery, the plaintiff established that she was black, that her employer fired her, and that her supervisor had been heard saying to a co-worker, "I've never been comfortable working with too many black people." During his deposition, this supervisor stated that the reason for the plaintiff's discharge was tardiness, that he had the time cards to establish that she had been late to work ten times in the past year, and that all other workers with this type of attendance record had similarly been fired. What would your summary judgment motion look like? What other facts not given here would you like to have to prevail?

G. Jury Trial

The Civil Rights Act of 1964 did not provide the right to a jury trial for Title VII litigants. Thus, these cases were often decided before the trial court itself. This would all change with the Civil Rights Act of 1991, which altered Title VII in numerous important respects. One of the most notable changes to the statute was the inclusion of the right to a jury trial. The statute, at 42 U.S.C. § 1981a(c), now provides: "If a complaining party seeks compensatory or punitive damages under this section—any party may demand a trial by jury."

When an employment discrimination case does proceed to trial, it is litigated like any other civil action. The Federal Rules of Civil Procedure apply to these cases just as they would in any other type of federal cause of action.

Empirically, plaintiffs are very successful in employment discrimination cases that are brought to trial. Typically, depending upon the exact claim, approximately 60 percent of the cases that do go to trial result in a favorable judgment for the plaintiff. *See* Joseph A. Seiner, *The Failure of Punitive Damages in Employment Discrimination Cases: A Call for Change*, 50 WM. & MARY L. REV. 735, 764 (2008). And, plaintiffs are very successful in the amount of recovery when they do win at trial. It is common for jury verdicts in employment discrimination cases to reach into six figures.

Despite these success rates, only an extremely small percentage of employment discrimination cases actually make it to trial. For example, one well-known study found that 3.7 percent of employment cases go to trial. *See* Kevin M. Clermont & Stewart J. Schwab, *How Employment Discrimination Plaintiffs Fare in Federal Court*, 1 J. EMPIRICAL LEGAL STUD. 429, 438 (2004). The vast majority of cases are either dismissed based on the complaint, thrown out at summary judgment, or settled between the parties. Thus, while the right to a jury trial is of critical importance to civil rights litigants, it is a vehicle that is seldom used in the courts for employment discrimination cases.

One critical issue on the right to jury trials is whether an employer can attempt to require workers to waive this right in advance. The scholarship in this area has done an excellent job of outlining this question. *See, e.g.*, Robert Frankhouser, *The Enforceability of Pre-Dispute Jury Waiver Agreements in Employment Discrimination Cases*, 8 DUQ. BUS. L.J. 55 (2006) (describing jury waiver agreements and concluding that they are valid under federal and Pennsylvania law); Michael H. LeRoy, *Jury Revival or Jury Reviled? When Employees Are Compelled to Waive Jury Trials*, 7 U. PA. J. LAB. & EMP. L. 767 (2005) (discussing the history and validity of waivers to employees' rights to a jury trial).

The following matter looks at one case that alleged particularly egregious facts of discrimination. The case was subsequently decided by a jury that sided with the plaintiff. Both the defendant and the plaintiff appealed to the U.S. Court of Appeals for the Seventh Circuit following post trial motions made in the district court.

May v. Chrysler Group, LLC
716 F.3d 963 (7th Cir. 2013)

PER CURIAM.

To understand the particular nature of [Otto] May's harassment, it is helpful to know a little about May's family story. We therefore begin, briefly, with May's grandfather, who moved to Cuba from Germany around 1911. Although he was Jewish, he married a Protestant woman from Cuba, and May's father was raised as a Protestant. Two years after Fidel Castro took power, when May was eleven, May and his family moved to Florida. When May was seventeen, he converted to Judaism so he could marry his girlfriend (she was Jewish). He has since divorced and remarried several times, but his connection to Judaism has endured, and he identifies as a Messianic Jew. Since 1988, May has worked at Chrysler's Belvidere Assembly Plant, in Belvidere, Illinois, as a pipefitter, repairing and maintaining equipment used to paint and assemble cars.

The events that produced this case started early in 2002 with vandalism to May's car and then to the loaner cars he used as replacements. The first car broke down on his drive home from work—sugar in the gas tank, according to the mechanic. He drove a second car for a few weeks before sugar was discovered in its tank too. That second car also had a tire disintegrate, as did the tire of a third car he drove while the first two were in the shop. All this was reported to the local police and to Chrysler in February 2002. Three months later, May drove over a homemade spike hidden by rags and placed under his tire. He reported the incident to security and police the next day. May didn't notice a response from Chrysler, so he complained to a person in human resources at Chrysler's headquarters in Michigan. Approximately ten days later, Kim Kuborn, a human resources supervisor who eventually became the principal HR person on May's case, called May and told him he could park in the salaried lot, which is monitored by cameras. This solution didn't much please May, however, because a Chrysler security officer told him that some of the cameras did not record, that some did not work, and that the ones that did were not monitored.

The threatening messages started in the first half of 2002, with words "fuck" and "sucks" written on the tag of May's coveralls. In June 2002, a heart with "Chuck + Otto" was found on the wall of a materials elevator. (Chuck was one of May's closest friends at the plant.) May complained to management, but the writing was not removed until August 29. Two days later, May saw "Cuban fag Jew" on the wall of the same elevator. May reported the graffiti and it was cleaned four days later, on September 3. That same day, May found a printout of a chain email titled, "Yes, I'm a Bad American" tucked into one of the drawers of his toolbox. The document had some handwritten additions. For example, next to a printed line that said, "I think being a minority does not make you noble or victimized, and does not entitle you to anything" was handwritten "Cuban sucks cock fag." Next to the printed line "I've never owned a slave, or was a slave, I didn't wander forty years in the desert after getting chased out of Egypt. I haven't burned any witches or been persecuted by the

Chrysler Building, New York City

Turks and neither have you! So, shut-the-Hell-up already" was written "Cuban Jew [swastika] kill Jew Heil Hitler." May told his supervisor, labor relations, security and provided Chrysler a copy of the note. May found another note in his toolbox on September 12. It said: "no one can help you fucken Cuban Jew We will get you Death to the Jews Cuban fag Die." Chrysler and the police were informed. Additional threatening graffiti targeting May was found on September 19 and 22.

On September 26, the head of human resources, Richard McPherson, and the head of labor relations, Bob Kertz, held two meetings (one with the first and third shifts, one with the second shift) with about sixty people from the skilled trades. McPherson addressed the groups about Chrysler's harassment policy. Some didn't appreciate the reminder; they were upset that skilled trades was being singled out and complained that McPherson was telling them they could not have "fun" at work anymore. The meeting was just a meeting; McPherson did not meet with the attendees or interview them individually, even those who were upset by his lecture. May, for his part, was upset that McPherson gathered so few people. More than a thousand plant employees had access to the areas where the notes and graffiti were found. May told McPherson and others that he thought Chrysler needed to do more. In particular, he thought installing surveillance cameras and swipe-key door locks (to monitor who was coming and going from particular areas) would be a good idea.

Just a few days after the meeting, on September 30, there was more graffiti: "Otto Cuban Jew die." At least five similar incidents with the same threatening theme—"a good Jew is a dead Jew"—occurred between September 30 and November 11. On December 7, May found another menacing note in his toolbox. This one told May that his "time is short" and proclaimed "death to the Jews" and "we hate the Jews" signing off with a "Heil Hitler" and swastika.

Soon after receiving the December 7 note, feeling that nothing was being done to stop the harassment, May contacted the Anti-Defamation League, a civil rights organization focused on combating anti-Semitism. In January 2003, the letter from the Anti-Defamation League reached Scott Huller, a staff advisor in Chrysler's corporate diversity office. Huller's responsibilities included investigating civil rights issues at Chrysler's manufacturing facilities. The letter prompted Huller to travel to the plant to interview May, and they met for a few hours on January 16 and 17. May told him he genuinely feared for his life and was distressed and depressed. Once again, May recommended security cameras. According to May, Huller was focused on getting a list of suspects. He wanted names. So Huller got what he wanted from May—a list of names. Huller, however, did not interview anyone on the list or instruct the local HR employees to do so (and none did).

Four days after Huller's meeting with May, more graffiti appeared. And later that same month (January 2003), May reported that someone was calling his work extension and making derogatory remarks in a disguised voice (essentially the same message as the notes and graffiti). May reported the calls but nobody from Chrysler discussed the details with him.

In March, there were two graffiti incidents and May found another death-threat note in one of his toolbox drawers. The note seemed to comment on the absence of harassment in February: "Otto Cuban Jew muther fucker not forget about you your time is coming we will get YOU death to the Jews [swastika]." Chrysler's incident report documented that a police officer who came to the plant to collect the note said that a security camera should be installed to record future harassment.

Sometime in 2003, Chrysler implemented a protocol for handling incidents involving May. According to McPherson (the head of HR at the plant), the person who found the graffiti or note was to notify HR and security, and a picture would be taken. After the incident was documented, someone from HR or security would talk to whoever found the graffiti or the note to establish when it was found. If the incident involved graffiti, the area would be cleaned. Pictures of the incident and details about when and where it happened (including when the area was last seen without graffiti) were collected by Kim Kuborn, who kept a detailed but not quite complete record of May's harassment in a large binder.

In May 2003, Chrysler's lawyers retained Jack Calvert, a forensic document examiner. Chrysler initially gave Calvert pictures (or copies of pictures) of graffiti. Soon Chrysler provided Calvert with an original note from June 2003, which Kim Kuborn collected quickly after its discovery, before the police arrived on the scene to take it themselves, and he went to the police to view more originals. Chrysler also gave him logbooks containing daily entries from many employees on different shifts. After reviewing this material, Calvert told Chrysler's counsel that he thought only one person was responsible for the graffiti and notes, but that he couldn't identify who. Based on what he had seen from the logbooks, he wanted additional "exemplars" (samples of handwriting) from approximately sixty employees. Chrysler responded with a variety of documents, including old job applications. (To jump ahead a bit, Calvert continued to collect exemplars throughout 2004 and into 2005. He ultimately issued his report in July 2007. It was inconclusive. More on this soon.) The incidents continued through 2004 and ended in 2005[.]

Chrysler's outward response to May's harassment involved McPherson's September 2002 group meetings, Huller's January 2003 interviews with May, ongoing documentation of the incidents, and (usually) prompt cleaning of graffiti. Behind the scenes, Kim Kuborn reviewed gate records to see who may have been around the plant when incidents occurred and Calvert was given more handwriting samples to analyze. Chrysler also wanted the jury to know that the employees at the Belvidere plant valued May as a colleague and cared about him as a person. For example, Kim Kuborn testified that "this behavior was completely unacceptable in our eyes, and we wanted to stop it and find out who was responsible for it. We certainly didn't want this kind of activity going on in the plant and making one of our team members as uncomfortable as it clearly was."

Beyond cataloguing the actions it took in response to May's harassment, and somewhat at odds with the empathy expressed by some employees for May's predicament, Chrysler's defense had another (rather unsettling) theme: *May did it all to himself.* Chrysler kept this defense in the background and at times seemed to deny it was part of its defense at all. For example, when confronted about whether Chrysler really believed May was the culprit, Kim Kuborn said, "I have no evidence that he did this himself." Chrysler left it primarily to Jack Calvert, the forensic document examiner, and Rosalind Griffin, a psychiatrist hired by Chrysler to analyze May, to make the case *against* May, to argue that May was not being victimized by death threats and suffering because of Chrysler's inaction, but that, more likely, *Chrysler* was actually the victim of May's lies.

We have already summarized the mechanics of Jack Calvert's operation. He was given samples of graffiti and notes and known exemplars (handwriting samples from plant employees), and carefully compared the two. After his initial look at the materials, there were approximately sixty employees he could not rule out, and he requested more samples of their writing. He was given more samples and, during 2004 and 2005, whittled his list down to three. He was never able to reach a conclusion about who did it, but he could only say that there was more evidence "that [this person] did author the material than that he did not" about one employee—Otto May, Jr. Calvert's testimony was challenged, of course. The jury heard that Calvert's list of possible authors was reduced not just by his own professional opinion but also by Chrysler informing him that twenty-six employees could be removed from consideration because they were not at the plant at the time of one of the incidents. The jury heard that those removed included Eldon Kline, John Myers, and Dave Kuborn. The jury also heard testimony that May was not eliminated as a possible perpetrator even though he, too, was not present when some of the incidents occurred. Chrysler never gave that information about May to Calvert. Chrysler did, however, give Calvert a large number of samples of May's writing, including May's notes documenting the harassment where, according to May's testimony, he tried to copy graffiti exactly as printed.

> As discussed later in this text, punitive and compensatory damages in Title VII cases are capped at $300,000 for the largest employers.

After a seven-day trial, the jury also rejected Chrysler's implication. And beyond that, the jury decided that Chrysler's efforts to stop the harassment were inadequate, and substantially so, and accordingly returned a large verdict for May. As explained in our opening summary, the jury awarded May $709,000 in compensatory damages and $3.5 million in punitive damages. The compensatory damage award was remitted to $300,000 and the district court granted Chrysler's Rule 50(b) motion for judgment as a matter of law on punitive damages. Both parties appeal.

We review de novo a district court's grant or denial of a Rule 50(b) motion for judgment as a matter of law. Thus, like the district court, we decide whether the jury had "a legally sufficient evidentiary basis" for its verdict. In this case, the jury was presented ample evidence to conclude that Chrysler did not "promptly and adequately" respond to the harassment. Consider only the death-threat notes and graffiti. By June 2002, there had been two relatively minor incidents. The graffiti was not pleasant, but it had not yet turned threatening. Its tenor started to change at the end of August when "Cuban fag Jew" appeared. A few days later, May found the "Yes, I am a Bad American" note in his toolbox. That note, recall, included, among other things, the phrase "kill Jew." Approximately one week later, on September 12, May received a more alarming threat: "no one can help you fucken Cuban Jew We will get you Death to the Jews Cuban fag Die." A full two weeks later, Chrysler held two short meetings with about sixty employees total. Within days of those meetings, the graffiti and death threats resumed. There were more than half-a-dozen incidents between the McPherson meetings and the next notable action by Chrysler in January 2003, when Scott Huller, prompted by a letter from the Anti-Defamation League, traveled from Chrysler's corporate offices in Michigan to interview May. Huller came away from those meetings with May's list of suspects. Huller took that information and created a template for HR at the plant to use in its investigation. But nobody on May's list was interviewed. Within days of Huller's meetings with May, there was more graffiti. And soon after that graffiti, there were threatening calls to May on his work extension. There were seven more incidents—including another death-threat note in May's tool-box—before Chrysler took the next step in its investigation, retaining Jack Calvert, the handwriting analyst. That was in May 2003. Every month for the rest of 2003 brought more graffiti, death-threat notes, or both.

For the purposes of Chrysler's liability, we can stop here. During the first year of written threats and harassment, what had Chrysler done? They held a meeting. They interviewed May. And, one year in, they hired Calvert. Did that amount to a "prompt and adequate" response to multiple racist and anti-Semitic death threats? Especially in light of the gravity of the harassment, the jury was presented with more than enough evidence to conclude that Chrysler had not done enough.

[T]he jury [also] heard about what Chrysler did not do. Two things stand out. First, the jury heard that Chrysler did not interview *anyone* on May's list. Not one person. Second, Chrysler did not install a single surveillance camera.

What about the idea that May himself was the culprit? [T]o be sure, Chrysler presented some evidence of May's guilt, but that evidence certainly did not (and does not) force any particular conclusion. At most, it raised a question. It was for the jury to answer, and it did, and we will not (and on these facts cannot) second-guess that judgment here.

■ NOTES AND QUESTIONS

1. Do you agree with the court that there was enough evidence in this case to support the jury's verdict? Why or why not?

2. How persuasive was Chrysler's argument that the plaintiff conjured the incidents himself? What type of evidence would have been necessary to overcome the jury's verdict and accept Chrysler's version of events?

3. How common is this type of discrimination in this day and age? The events alleged here were both disturbing and widespread. Is it alarming that the alleged behavior still occurs decades after Title VII was enacted?

4. The court notes that the standard for these types of claims is whether there is "'a legally sufficient evidentiary basis' for its verdict." What does this standard mean? How would it be applied in cases of employment discrimination?

5. Did Chrysler do a good job of presenting its defense? What type of evidence could have been sought and presented to help defend its case?

6. Should the company have sought to settle this claim? Why do you believe that the case proceeded to trial?

7. When faced with this type of harassment claim, what should the company have done in response? What actions could it have taken to help insulate itself from liability?

8. We will address the standard for harassment in Chapter 5. For purposes of this case, however, it is sufficient to understand that a company must take reasonable steps to prevent harassing conduct of which it is aware (or should have been aware).

9. Was the jury's assessment of damages proper here? Would a greater or lesser judgment have been more appropriate?

 Interactive Problem

Looking back at the facts of the interactive problem, assume that Caroline's Title VII claim is permitted to proceed to trial. What witnesses would the plaintiff put on to establish her case before the jury? What exhibits would be entered into evidence? How would the defendant try to persuade the jury that no violation has occurred? If you were the defendant in the case, would you try to settle in advance of trial?

H. Arbitration

One area of recent interest is the desire of some employers to defend employment discrimination claims in an arbitration setting rather than in federal court. When parties agree to arbitrate their employment claims, they typically waive the right to go to federal court. Instead, a neutral decision maker is selected and empowered to make a final and binding decision in the matter.

Arbitration tends to be much more informal than federal court proceedings. The rules on discovery, the introduction of evidence, and other procedural requirements tend to be much more relaxed. The arbitrator maintains significant power in the case. An arbitrator's decision is binding and only reviewable on very narrow grounds. For this reason, arbitration tends to be much quicker and far less expensive than federal court litigation for employment discrimination cases.

If an employer decides that arbitration is preferable, that employer will usually prepare an arbitration agreement for its workers and new hires to sign. A typical arbitration agreement will require an employee to waive her rights to go to trial and instead agree to resolve all disputes before an arbitrator. Employers seeking to invoke these agreements will be best served to have them signed at the beginning of employment when there is less doubt as to whether the element of consideration is satisfied. An arbitration agreement is nothing more than a contract and there must be a meeting of the minds and adequate consideration for that agreement to be enforceable.

In addition, as a contract, arbitration agreements will be subject to many of the additional requirements of contract law. Similarly, the agreements must comply with the Federal Arbitration Act, which imposes additional obligations on employers. The case below examines one arbitration contract that was heavily weighted in favor of the employer, and rejected by the court on fairness concerns.

Hooters of America, Inc. v. Phillips
173 F.3d 933 (4th Cir. 1999)

WILKINSON, Chief Judge:

Annette R. Phillips alleges that she was sexually harassed while working at a Hooters restaurant. After quitting her job, Phillips threatened to sue Hooters in court. Alleging that Phillips agreed to arbitrate employment-related disputes, Hooters preemptively filed suit to compel arbitration under the Federal Arbitration Act, 9 U.S.C. § 4. Because Hooters set up a dispute resolution process utterly lacking in the rudiments of even-handedness, we hold that Hooters breached its agreement to arbitrate. Thus, we affirm the district court's refusal to compel arbitration.

Appellee Annette R. Phillips worked as a bartender at a Hooters restaurant in Myrtle Beach, South Carolina. She was employed since 1989 by appellant Hooters of Myrtle Beach (HOMB), a franchisee of appellant Hooters of America (collectively Hooters).

Phillips alleges that in June 1996, Gerald Brooks, a Hooters official and the brother of HOMB's principal owner, sexually harassed her by grabbing and slapping her buttocks. After appealing to her manager for help and being told to "let it go," she quit her job. Phillips then contacted Hooters through an attorney claiming that the attack and the restaurant's failure to address it violated her Title VII rights. Hooters responded that she was required to submit her claims to arbitration according to a binding agreement to arbitrate between the parties.

This agreement arose in 1994 during the implementation of Hooters' alternative dispute resolution program. As part of that program, the company conditioned eligibility for raises, transfers, and promotions upon an employee signing an "Agreement to arbitrate employment-related disputes." The agreement provides that Hooters and the employee each agree to arbitrate all disputes arising out of employment, including "any claim of discrimination, sexual harassment, retaliation, or wrongful discharge, whether arising under federal or state law." The agreement further states that the employee and the company agree to resolve any claims pursuant to the company's rules and procedures for alternative resolution of employment-related disputes, as promulgated by the company from time to time ("the rules"). Company will make available or provide a copy of the rules upon written request of the employee.

The employees of HOMB were initially given a copy of this agreement at an all-staff meeting held on November 20, 1994. HOMB's general manager, Gene Fulcher, told the employees to review the agreement for five days and that they would then be asked to accept or reject the agreement. No employee, however, was given a copy of Hooters'

arbitration rules and procedures. Phillips signed the agreement on November 25, 1994. When her personnel file was updated in April 1995, Phillips again signed the agreement. After Phillips quit her job in June 1996, Hooters sent to her attorney a copy of the Hooters rules then in effect. Phillips refused to arbitrate the dispute.

Hooters filed suit in November 1996 to compel arbitration under 9 U.S.C. § 4. Phillips defended on the grounds that the agreement to arbitrate was unenforceable. Phillips also asserted individual and class counterclaims against Hooters for violations of Title VII and for a declaration that the arbitration agreements were unenforceable against the class. In response, Hooters requested that the district court stay the proceedings on the counterclaims until after arbitration, 9 U.S.C. § 3.

In March 1998, the district court denied Hooters' motions to compel arbitration and stay proceedings on the counterclaims. The court found that there was no meeting of the minds on all of the material terms of the agreement and even if there were, Hooters' promise to arbitrate was illusory. In addition, the court found that the arbitration agreement was unconscionable and void for reasons of public policy. Hooters filed this interlocutory appeal, 9 U.S.C. § 16.

The benefits of arbitration are widely recognized. In support of arbitration, Congress passed the Federal Arbitration Act (FAA). When a valid agreement to arbitrate exists between the parties and covers the matter in dispute, the FAA commands the federal courts to stay any ongoing judicial proceedings, and to compel arbitration.

Predispute agreements to arbitrate Title VII claims are [] valid and enforceable. The question remains whether a binding arbitration agreement between Phillips and Hooters exists and compels Phillips to submit her Title VII claims to arbitration. The FAA provides that agreements "to settle by arbitration a controversy thereafter arising out of such contract or transaction . . . shall be valid, irrevocable, and enforceable, save upon such grounds as exist at law or in equity for the revocation of any contract." 9 U.S.C. § 2. "It [i]s for the court, not the arbitrator, to decide in the first instance whether the dispute [i]s to be resolved through arbitration." *AT & T Techs., Inc. v. Communications Workers of Am.*, 475 U.S. 643 (1986). In so deciding, we " 'engage in a limited review to ensure that the dispute is arbitrable—i.e., that a valid agreement to arbitrate exists between the parties and that the specific dispute falls within the substantive scope of that agreement.' "

Hooters argues that Phillips gave her assent to a bilateral agreement to arbitrate. That contract provided for the resolution by arbitration of all employment-related disputes, including claims arising under Title VII. Hooters claims the agreement to arbitrate is valid because Phillips twice signed it voluntarily. Thus, it argues the courts are bound to enforce it and compel arbitration.

We disagree. The judicial inquiry, while highly circumscribed, is not focused solely on an examination for contractual formation defects such as lack of mutual assent and want of consideration. Courts also can investigate the existence of "such grounds as exist at law or in equity for the revocation of any contract." 9 U.S.C. § 2. However, the grounds for revocation must relate specifically to the arbitration clause and not just to the contract as a whole. In this case, the challenge goes to the validity of the arbitration agreement itself. Hooters materially breached the arbitration agreement by promulgating rules so egregiously unfair as to constitute a complete default of its contractual obligation to draft arbitration rules and to do so in good faith.

Hooters and Phillips agreed to settle any disputes between them not in a judicial forum, but in another neutral forum-arbitration. Their agreement provided that Hooters was responsible for setting up such a forum by promulgating arbitration rules and procedures. To this end, Hooters instituted a set of rules in July 1996.

The Hooters rules when taken as a whole, however, are so one-sided that their only possible purpose is to undermine the neutrality of the proceeding. The rules require the employee to provide the company notice of her claim at the outset, including "the nature of the Claim" and "the specific act(s) or omissions(s) which are the basis of the Claim." Rule 6-2(1), (2). Hooters, on the other hand, is not required to file any responsive pleadings or to notice its defenses. Additionally, at the time of filing this notice, the employee must provide the company with a list of all fact witnesses with a brief summary of the facts known to each. The company, however, is not required to reciprocate.

The Hooters rules also provide a mechanism for selecting a panel of three arbitrators that is crafted to ensure a biased decisionmaker. Rule 8. The employee and Hooters each select an arbitrator, and the two arbitrators in turn select a third. Good enough, except that the employee's arbitrator and the third arbitrator must be selected from a list of arbitrators created exclusively by Hooters. This

> What rules did Hooters establish that "undermine the neutrality" of the proceeding?

gives Hooters control over the entire panel and places no limits whatsoever on whom Hooters can put on the list. Under the rules, Hooters is free to devise lists of partial arbitrators who have existing relationships, financial or familial, with Hooters and its management. In fact, the rules do not even prohibit Hooters from placing its managers themselves on the list. Further, nothing in the rules restricts Hooters from punishing arbitrators who rule against the company by removing them from the list. Given the unrestricted control that one party (Hooters) has over the panel, the selection of an impartial [decisionmaker] would be a surprising result.

Nor is fairness to be found once the proceedings are begun. Although Hooters may expand the scope of arbitration to any matter, "whether related or not to the Employee's Claim," the employee cannot raise "any matter not included in the Notice of Claim." Rules 4-2, 8-9. Similarly, Hooters is permitted to move for summary dismissal of employee claims before a hearing is held whereas the employee is not permitted to seek summary judgment. Rule 14-4. Hooters, but not the employee, may record the arbitration hearing "by audio or videotaping or by verbatim transcription." Rule 18-1. The rules also grant Hooters the right to bring suit in court to vacate or modify an arbitral award when it can show, by a preponderance of the evidence, that the panel exceeded its authority. No such right is granted to the employee.

In addition, the rules provide that upon 30 days notice Hooters, but not the employee, may cancel the agreement to arbitrate. Rule 23-1. Moreover, Hooters reserves the right to modify the rules, "in whole or in part," whenever it wishes and "without notice" to the employee. Rule 24-1. Nothing in the rules even prohibits Hooters from changing the rules in the middle of an arbitration proceeding.

We hold that the promulgation of so many biased rules—especially the scheme whereby one party to the proceeding so controls the arbitral panel—breaches the contract entered into by the parties. The parties agreed to submit their claims to arbitration—a system whereby disputes are fairly resolved by an impartial third party. Hooters by contract took on the obligation of establishing such a system. By creating a sham system unworthy even of the name of arbitration, Hooters completely failed in performing its contractual duty.

Moreover, Hooters had a duty to perform its obligations in good faith. By agreeing to settle disputes in arbitration, Phillips agreed to the prompt and economical resolution of her claims. She could legitimately expect that arbitration would not entail procedures so wholly one-sided as to present a stacked deck. Thus we conclude that the Hooters rules also violate the contractual obligation of good faith.

Given Hooters' breaches of the arbitration agreement and Phillips' desire not to be bound by it, we hold that rescission is the proper remedy. As we have explained, Hooters' breach is by no means insubstantial; its performance under the contract was so egregious that the result was hardly recognizable as arbitration at all. We therefore permit Phillips to cancel the agreement and thus Hooters' suit to compel arbitration must fail.

Our decision should not be misread: We are not holding that the agreement before us is unenforceable because the arbitral proceedings are too abbreviated. An arbitral forum need not replicate the judicial forum.

Nor should our decision be misunderstood as permitting a full-scale assault on the fairness of proceedings before the matter is submitted to arbitration. Generally, objections to the nature of arbitral proceedings are for the arbitrator to decide in the first instance. Only after arbitration may a party then raise such challenges if they meet the narrow grounds set out in 9 U.S.C. § 10 for vacating an arbitral award. In the case before us, we only reach the content of the arbitration rules because their promulgation was the duty of one party under the contract. The material breach of this duty warranting rescission is an issue of substantive arbitrability and thus is reviewable before arbitration. This case, however, is the exception that proves the rule: fairness objections should generally be made to the arbitrator, subject only to limited post-arbitration judicial review as set forth in section 10 of the FAA.

By promulgating this system of warped rules, Hooters so skewed the process in its favor that Phillips has been denied arbitration in any meaningful sense of the word. To uphold the promulgation of this aberrational scheme under the heading of arbitration would undermine, not advance, the federal policy favoring alternative dispute resolution. This we refuse to do.

■ NOTES AND QUESTIONS

1. The court here acknowledges many of the benefits associated with arbitration. The court states that arbitration offers more "streamlined proceedings and expeditious results." Do you agree?

2. The court here questions the arbitration agreement, noting that "[t]he Hooters rules when taken as a whole . . . are so one-sided that their only possible purpose is to undermine the neutrality of the proceeding." The court further maintains that the agreement is so "one-sided as to present a stacked deck." Are the rules as articulated in this agreement truly that offensive to one's sensibilities of fairness? In what way are the rules so strongly biased against the plaintiff?

3. The plaintiff here entered into an agreement with the defendant to abide by the arbitration rules. Why shouldn't this contract be enforced? Couldn't the plaintiff have simply chosen to pursue employment elsewhere if she did not like the agreement?

4. The court further concludes in this case that, "[g]iven Hooters' breaches of the arbitration agreement and Phillips' desire not to be bound by it, we hold that rescission is the proper remedy." Why is this the case? Should the court have rescinded the entire agreement? Why didn't the court simply rewrite the rules or require the parties to arbitrate under a neutral agreement? Doesn't sending this case to litigation undercut policies in favor of arbitration?

5. The court maintains that there is a "federal policy favoring alternative dispute resolution." What would the basis be for this policy? Shouldn't individuals be encouraged to "have their day in court" if that is what they desire? *See generally* Ann C. Hodges, *Trilogy Redux: Using Arbitration to Rebuild the Labor Movement*, 98 Minn. L. Rev. 1682 (2014) (analyzing the possibility of creating a program to provide representation to employees bound to arbitrate their legal disputes with their employees, while simultaneously building a movement to challenge the practice of compulsory arbitration and its impact on employees' rights).

6. There are many forms of alternative dispute resolution (ADR). This text does not attempt to provide an exhaustive review of the various ADR techniques that can be used in the employment context. It is important to consider, however, the difference between arbitration and mediation. Arbitration puts an employment dispute in the hands of a neutral decision maker or decision makers. The decision of the neutral decision maker is final and binding. Mediation, however, involves an attempt to settle the dispute informally between the parties. A mediator does not have the authority to issue a binding decision in the case. Rather, the mediator's role is to attempt to resolve the matter informally between the parties. For a leading textbook on alternative dispute resolution in employment, see Laura Cooper, Dennis R. Nolan, Richard Bales, & Stephen Befort, ADR in the Workplace (3d ed. 2014).

7. Mediation and arbitration are very common in employment discrimination cases. This is likely because workplace claims are often complex and fact intensive. It can be far less expensive and time-consuming to resolve these matters more informally. *See, e.g.,* Susan A. FitzGibbon, *Arbitration, Mediation, and Sexual Harassment,* 5 PSYCHOL. PUB. POL'Y & L. 693 (1999) (suggesting that mediation and arbitration are appropriate procedures to resolve sexual harassment claims).

8. If an employee agrees to arbitrate a claim, can the EEOC still sue on that individual's behalf in federal court? In *EEOC v. Waffle House,* 534 U.S. 279 (2002), the Supreme Court held that the Commission is the "master of its own case" and may thus pursue employment discrimination claims even where there is a private arbitration agreement in place. *Id.* at 280. Thus, an employer could potentially be subjected to arbitration by a private individual—and federal court litigation by the EEOC—over the same set of facts.

9. The Supreme Court has made it more difficult for individuals to act collectively in arbitration. *See* Epic Sys. Corp. v. Lewis, 138 S. Ct. 1612 (May 21, 2018); AT&T Mobility LLC v. Concepcion, 563 U.S. 333 (2011). Though this case arose outside of the employment context, its principles will likely still be applied to discrimination cases.

10. While this text only touches on the importance of arbitration in employment cases, the academic literature is replete with excellent articles outlining the importance of this area, and the controversies that still exist. *See, e.g.,* Michael Z. Green, *Measures to Encourage and Reward Post-Dispute Agreements to Arbitrate Employment Discrimination Claims,* 8 NEV. L.J. 58 (2007) (advocating legislative incentives for post-dispute arbitration agreements as well as a ban on pre-dispute arbitration agreements); Dennis R. Nolan, *Employment Arbitration After* Circuit City, 41 BRANDEIS L.J. 853 (2003); David Sherwyn, *Because It Takes Two: Why Post-Dispute Voluntary Arbitration Programs Will Fail to Fix the Problems Associated with Employment Discrimination Law Adjudication,* 24 BERKELEY J. EMP. & LAB. L. 1 (2003); Stephen J. Ware, *Consumer and Employment Arbitration Law in Comparative Perspective: The Importance of the Civil Jury,* 56 U. MIAMI L. REV. 865 (2002).

 Interactive Problem

Looking back at the facts of the interactive problem, assume that Caroline decides to pursue a sex discrimination claim against her employer. Looking through her employee manual, Caroline realizes that upon acceptance of employment, she agreed to arbitrate any disputes with her employer. The arbitration agreement simply requires that the rules of the American Arbitration Association be adopted in full. The agreement also provides for the selection of an arbitrator, who will be "either one of the owners of the restaurant." Will this arbitration agreement be upheld if contested? If there is a problem with the agreement, should the entire agreement be rescinded, or should the agreement simply be revised?

5: Mandatory Employment Arbitration Agreements

From a practical standpoint, employers must decide whether to adopt a policy requiring workers to sign a binding arbitration agreement. In this way, employers should decide—weighing all of the pros and cons—whether they would prefer to have employment disputes resolved in federal court or before a more informal neutral decision maker. There is no straightforward answer as to the best approach to use, and employers should consider multiple factors when deciding on the best course of action. In the end, it is really a multifaceted business decision.

There are a number of benefits to employers in resolving cases in an arbitral forum. As noted earlier, these cases tend to be more quickly resolved, they are frequently less expensive to litigate, and they can be decided by individuals with specific expertise in the area of the law. At the same time, there are numerous drawbacks. In particular, plaintiffs may be more likely to prevail in this type of setting (at least on some level), and the cases may not be as frequently dismissed on procedural or other grounds. Thus, while federal court litigation is expensive, it may also result in a higher success rate for employers. It is hard to speak empirically on the best approach to take on this issue, as the data on this question is difficult to gather and the results are often mixed.

Finally, employers should be cognizant of the possibility of being subjected to both private arbitration and federal court litigation over the same set of facts. As the EEOC is not bound by private agreements, an employer can face federal litigation by the government as well as private arbitration with the individual over the same dispute. This is likely a worst-case scenario for many employers and one that they would very much like to avoid.

Employers must thus make a strategic decision of whether to attempt to have any discrimination claims considered in arbitration rather than federal court. And this question must simply be decided on a company-specific basis. This decision will ultimately depend on several factors. Employers should look at industry practice, overall costs, and the implications of litigating in the particular jurisdiction where the employer resides. By considering these variables that are specific to each corporation—as well as the overall benefits and drawbacks of arbitration—employers can make an informed decision on the best approach to take on this issue.

 # I. Chapter-in-Review

One of the most critical aspects of filing an employment discrimination claim is properly navigating the administrative and procedural hurdles. In particular, victims of discrimination must make certain to file a charge within 180/300 days of the discriminatory event, and a lawsuit within 90 days of receiving the right-to-sue letter. Failure to do so will result in dismissal of the case. To satisfy the standing and coverage requirements of Title VII, the plaintiff must be an "employee" under the statute, and the defendant must be an "employer." An employee is separate and distinct from an independent contractor and the courts primarily look to the element of control to make this determination. To be covered by Title VII and the ADA, a company must employ fifteen or more employees. The ADEA requires twenty workers for coverage.

After the Supreme Court's decisions in *Twombly* and *Iqbal*, filing a complaint of employment discrimination can be a difficult endeavor. Plaintiffs must make certain to provide enough facts in the complaint to state a "plausible" claim. At a minimum, plaintiffs should do their best to provide facts sufficient to support the prima facie case.

Discovery is a critical aspect of employment discrimination claims. Particular importance is placed on the deposition of the plaintiff in these cases. Additionally, discovery is often targeted at uncovering any discriminatory intent of the employer, which can be a challenging aspect of the case. Summary judgment is frequently a decisive procedural moment in a Title VII case. If a plaintiff can show that there is a question of fact, the case can be given to a jury. Most cases are either dismissed or settled prior to going before a jury.

Arbitration appears to be an increasingly popular way of settling employment discrimination claims. Employers often include mandatory arbitration provisions in employment agreements. Such provisions must be fair in application.

PART TWO

Analytical Frameworks

3

Disparate Treatment

 ## Interactive Problem

Bob was born in Ireland and remains a citizen of that country. Bob began working in Utah as a regional sales director for a software company, Computers, Inc., in August 2016. Bob was the only sales director for his particular region. The company, which employs about two hundred workers, is headquartered in Utah and is a wholly owned subsidiary of the Technology World Corporation, which is located in Bombay, India. Computers, Inc. sells software for its parent company. Approximately 95 percent of the employees of Computers, Inc. are Indian nationals. In the fall 2018, an officer of Technology World Corporation, who shortly thereafter became president of Computers, Inc., stated that "this is an Indian company, it was Indian from the start, the majority of the employees are Indian, and I could see this, in the future, being a wholly Indian company." In addition, shortly after being terminated by the company but before he was replaced by an Indian worker, Bob's immediate supervisor, a white male, told him that while there is no document that states that Americans are being forced out of the company, "it is the practice." Moreover, a supervisor of another department told Bob that Americans have never worked out at the company because "they don't commit the way that Indians do." And, another white salesperson was told that she needed too much "hand-holding," and that if an Indian salesperson had her position "she would just do her job." Bob also felt that the company was interfering with his territory and his ability to do his job, and concedes that his overall sales were low. In November 2018, Computers, Inc. terminated Bob's employment for poor sales performance.

Bob subsequently brought an action under Title VII for national origin discrimination. How would the analysis proceed? How would Bob establish his claim? *See* Keelan v. Majesco Software, Inc., 2004 WL 370225 (N.D. Tex. Feb. 26, 2004).

A. Introduction

Generally speaking, there are two different types of employment discrimination claims—disparate treatment (or intentional discrimination) and disparate impact (or unintentional discrimination). This part of the text will address these two models of discrimination. It is important to gain a thorough understanding of how cases proceed under each of these two models before turning to the specific categories of discrimination. These models were developed through statutory enactment and years of contentious litigation. These analytical frameworks help formulate the "language" of employment discrimination, and must be considered before examining the intricacies of the law inherent to each protected class.

We begin with disparate treatment, where an individual attempts to prove that an employer discriminated on the basis of a protected characteristic. Disparate treatment cases are critical to understand as most employment discrimination claims are brought under this theory. One major basis for intentional discrimination claims can be found in § 703(a)(1) of Title VII, which provides that

> [it] shall be an unlawful employment practice for an employer . . . to fail or refuse to hire or to discharge any individual, or otherwise to discriminate against any individual with respect to his compensation, terms, conditions, or privileges of employment, because of such individual's race, color, religion, sex, or national origin.

42 U.S.C. § 2000e-2(a).

One key to this operative language of Title VII is that the employer must take an adverse action *because of* the individual's protected characteristic. The courts have interpreted this "because of" showing to mean establishing that the employer intended to discriminate. But how does a plaintiff establish intent? For many years following the enactment of Title VII, the courts were undecided when evaluating this element of the plaintiff's cause of action. The Supreme Court would eventually take up the issue in a case examining circumstantial evidence of discrimination.

B. Circumstantial Evidence of Discrimination

Though the law has evolved on this issue, there have traditionally been two primary ways to establish claims of intentional discrimination: direct and circumstantial evidence. Direct evidence occurs where there is no room for inference or presumption on the issue of discriminatory intent. For example, direct evidence would be present where an employer issues an employee a memorandum that states he is being fired "because he is black." In the vast majority of cases, plaintiffs attempt to establish their claims circumstantially, because there is typically no "smoking gun."

There are many important Supreme Court cases in employment discrimination law. One case stands out as being of seminal importance to all discrimination claims, *McDonnell Douglas Corp. v. Green*, 411 U.S. 792 (1973), where the Court was called upon to develop a method for determining whether a plaintiff should be allowed to proceed with a discrimination claim. This decision would forever shape the way employment discrimination claims were litigated.

McDonnell Douglas Corp. v. Green
411 U.S. 792 (1973)

Mr. Justice POWELL delivered the opinion for a unanimous Court.

Petitioner, McDonnell Douglas Corp., is an aerospace and aircraft manufacturer headquartered in St. Louis, Missouri, where it employs over 30,000 people. Respondent, a black citizen of St. Louis, worked for petitioner as a mechanic and laboratory technician from 1956 until August 28, 1964 when he was laid off in the course of a general reduction in petitioner's work force. Respondent, a long-time activist in the civil rights movement, protested vigorously that his discharge and the general hiring practices of petitioner were racially motivated. As part of this protest, respondent and other members of the Congress on Racial Equality illegally stalled their cars on the main roads leading to petitioner's plant for the purpose of blocking access to it at the time of the morning shift change.

Percy Green II, Civil Rights Advocate and Plaintiff in Case

On July 2, 1965, a "lock-in" took place wherein a chain and padlock were placed on the front door of a building to prevent the occupants, certain of petitioner's employees, from leaving. Though respondent apparently knew beforehand of the "lock-in," the full extent of his involvement remains uncertain.

Some three weeks following the "lock-in," on July 25, 1965, petitioner publicly advertised for qualified mechanics, respondent's trade, and respondent promptly applied for re-employment. Petitioner turned down respondent, basing its rejection on respondent's participation in the "stall-in" and "lock-in." Shortly thereafter, respondent filed a formal complaint with the E.E.O.C., claiming that petitioner had refused to rehire him

> **Are the use of lock-ins and stall-ins during civil rights protests lawful activities?**

because of his race and persistent involvement in the civil rights movement, in violation of §§ 703(a)(1) and 704(a) of the Civil Rights Act of 1964.

On April 15, 1968, respondent brought the present action, claiming initially a violation of § 704(a) and, in an amended complaint, a violation of § 703(a)(1) as well. The District Court dismissed the latter claim of racial discrimination in petitioner's hiring procedures on the ground that the Commission had failed to make a determination of reasonable cause to believe that a violation of that section had been committed. The District Court also found that petitioner's refusal to rehire respondent was based solely on his participation in the illegal demonstrations and not on his legitimate civil rights activities. The court concluded that nothing in Title VII or § 704 protected "such activity as employed by the plaintiff in the 'stall in' and 'lock in' demonstrations."

On appeal, the Eighth Circuit affirmed that unlawful protests were not protected activities under § 704(a), but reversed the dismissal of respondent's § 703(a)(1) claim relating to racially discriminatory hiring practices, holding that a prior Commission determination of reasonable cause was not a jurisdictional prerequisite to raising a claim under that section in federal court. The court ordered the case remanded for trial of respondent's claim under § 703(a)(1).

The critical issue before us concerns the order and allocation of proof in a private, non-class action challenging employment discrimination. The language of Title VII makes plain the purpose of Congress to assure equality of employment opportunities and to eliminate those discriminatory practices and devices which have fostered racially stratified job environments to the disadvantage of minority citizens.

In this case respondent, the complainant below, charges that he was denied employment "because of his involvement in civil rights activities" and "because of his race and color." Petitioner denied discrimination of any kind, asserting that its failure to re-employ respondent was based upon and justified by his participation in the unlawful conduct against it. Thus, the issue at the trial on remand is framed by those opposing factual contentions. The two opinions of the Court of Appeals and the several opinions of the three judges of that court attempted, with a notable lack of harmony, to state the applicable rules as to burden of proof and how this shifts upon the making of a prima facie case. We now address this problem.

The complainant in a Title VII trial must carry the initial burden under the statute of establishing a prima facie case of racial discrimination. This may be done by showing (i) that he belongs to a racial minority; (ii) that he applied and was qualified for a job for which the employer was seeking applicants; (iii) that, despite his qualifications, he was rejected; and (iv) that, after his rejection, the position remained open and the employer continued to seek applicants from persons of complainant's qualifications. In the instant case, we agree with the Court of Appeals that respondent proved a prima facie case. Petitioner sought mechanics, respondent's trade, and continued to do so after respondent's rejection. Petitioner, moreover, does not dispute respondent's

> The four-part prima facie case created by the Supreme Court in this case is critical to employment discrimination law.

[handwritten margin note: FEOC claim → DC court inadmissible overruled]

qualifications and acknowledges that his past work performance in petitioner's employ was "satisfactory."

The burden then must shift to the employer to articulate some legitimate, nondiscriminatory reason for the employee's rejection. We need not attempt in the instant case to detail every matter which fairly could be recognized as a reasonable basis for a refusal to hire. Here petitioner has assigned respondent's participation in unlawful conduct against it as the cause for his rejection. We think that this suffices to discharge petitioner's burden of proof at this stage and to meet respondent's prima facie case of discrimination.

> As addressed in the next case, the employer has only a burden of production, not persuasion, to articulate its legitimate nondiscriminatory reason for taking the adverse action.

[We] think the court below seriously underestimated the rebuttal weight to which petitioner's reasons were entitled. Respondent admittedly had taken part in a carefully planned "stall-in," designed to tie up access to and egress from petitioner's plant at a peak traffic hour. Nothing in Title VII compels an employer to absolve and rehire one who has engaged in such deliberate, unlawful activity against it.

Petitioner's reason for rejection thus suffices to meet the prima facie case, but the inquiry must not end here. While Title VII does not, without more, compel rehiring of respondent, neither does it permit petitioner to use respondent's conduct as a pretext for the sort of discrimination prohibited by § 703(a)(1). On remand, respondent must, as the Court of Appeals recognized, be afforded a fair opportunity to show that petitioner's stated reason for respondent's rejection was in fact pretext. Especially relevant to such a showing would be evidence that white employees involved in acts against petitioner of comparable seriousness to the "stall-in" were nevertheless retained or rehired. Petitioner may justifiably refuse to rehire one who was engaged in unlawful, disruptive acts against it, but only if this criterion is applied alike to members of all races.

Other evidence that may be relevant to any showing of pretext includes facts as to the petitioner's treatment of respondent during his prior term of employment; petitioner's reaction, if any, to respondent's legitimate civil rights activities; and petitioner's general policy and practice with respect to minority employment. On the latter point, statistics as to petitioner's employment policy and practice may be helpful to a determination of whether petitioner's refusal to rehire respondent in this case conformed to a general pattern of discrimination against blacks. In short, on the retrial respondent must be given a full and fair opportunity to demonstrate by competent evidence that the presumptively valid reasons for his rejection were in fact a cover-up for a racially discriminatory decision.

In sum, respondent should have been allowed to pursue his claim under § 703(a)(1). If the evidence on retrial is substantially in accord with that before us in this case, we think that respondent carried his burden of establishing a prima facie case of racial discrimination and that petitioner successfully rebutted that case.

But this does not end the matter. On retrial, respondent must be afforded a fair opportunity to demonstrate that petitioner's assigned reason for refusing to re-employ was a pretext or discriminatory in its application. If the District Judge so finds, he must order a prompt and appropriate remedy. In the absence of such a finding, petitioner's refusal to rehire must stand.

As the Court notes, the burden of persuasion stays with the plaintiff throughout the case.

■ NOTES AND QUESTIONS

1. **Historical note.** On April 26, 2005, Percy Green II (the respondent in *McDonnell Douglas*) was recognized before the U.S. House of Representatives for his lifetime achievements in the civil rights movement—particularly his role in the fight to end racial discrimination in the workplace as demonstrated by the facts that led to *McDonnell Douglas*. Green's protest against the McDonnell Douglas Corp. was only one of several acts of civil disobedience that he and others participated in—including marches, sit-ins, and public demonstrations—aimed at equalizing social and economic opportunities for minorities in America. In one well-known protest, Green climbed the Gateway Arch in St. Louis to protest the lack of minority contractors in its construction. Even today, Green remains devoted to promoting equality, and his actions

Gateway Arch, St. Louis, MO

leading to the *McDonnell Douglas* decision not only made a lasting contribution to employment discrimination law, but also to the nation. 151 Cong. Rec. E757 (Apr. 26, 2005), Tribute to Percy Green II, Civil & Human Rights Activist, http://www.gpo.gov/fdsys/pkg/CREC-2005-04-26/pdf/CREC-2005-04-26-pt1-PgE757-2.pdf.

2. The *McDonnell Douglas* framework created what is likely the most important test in all of employment discrimination law—establishing how an employer intended to discriminate against an employee through circumstantial evidence

of discrimination. This case arose in a failure to hire context, but the lower courts have extended the doctrine to *all* adverse actions including promotion denials, terminations, and unequal wages, among other things. What would the test look like in a case involving a termination? A failure to promote case?

3. The *McDonnell Douglas* test establishes the prima facie case of discrimination in circumstantial evidence cases. The Court's decision has been refined over the years, and it is now commonly accepted that to establish a prima facie case of discrimination, the plaintiff must show that (a) she was a member of a protected class; (b) she was qualified for the job; (c) she suffered an adverse action; and (d) there is some other evidence of discrimination in the case.

4. Once the plaintiff carries the burden of persuasion of establishing the four elements of the prima facie case, an inference of discrimination arises, and the defendant must assert (through a burden of production) that there was a legitimate nondiscriminatory reason for the adverse action. If the defendant successfully articulates this reason, the inference of discrimination drops from the case. The burden of persuasion—which remains with the plaintiff throughout—is then to establish that the legitimate nondiscriminatory reason is pretextual for true discrimination.

5. Why do we even need a test to determine whether discrimination has occurred circumstantially?

6. What does it mean to be in a protected class? Will this be a fairly straightforward inquiry in most cases? *See* Nancy Levit, *Changing Workforce Demographics and the Future of the Protected Class Approach*, 16 Lewis & Clark L. Rev. 463 (2012) (suggesting that individuals will face increasing difficulty proving membership in a protected group as demographic changes blur group lines).

7. Qualified. What does it mean to be qualified for a job? How would the plaintiff go about establishing this element? What if an employer established a set of criteria for a job for which no one could qualify?

8. What is an adverse action? Some adverse actions are easy to identify. All courts would recognize that if you are not hired, or if you are fired, demoted, or transferred with significantly different job responsibilities because of your protected characteristic, an adverse action has occurred. But would it be an adverse action if an employer gave a worker a desk that was a quarter inch smaller than other employees because of her gender? What if an employer paid a worker fifty cents a year less because she was Hispanic? The Supreme Court has never resolved these issues, though as we will see later in this text, the Court has weighed in on what constitutes an adverse action in the retaliation context. All courts require something more than an action that is simply de minimis. Some courts require something that is materially adverse. Others require an ultimate employment action. *See, e.g.*, McCoy v. City of Shreveport, 492 F.3d 551, 560 (5th Cir. 2007) ("recognizing only 'ultimate employment decisions' as actionable adverse employment actions remains controlling for Title VII *discrimination* claims"). Most courts tie the adverse action to economic disadvantage or deprivation or stigmatization. *See generally* Peter Siegelman, *The Compromised Worker and the Limits of Employment Discrimination Law*, U. Chi. Symposium on Law & Econ. of Race (May 15, 2010) (discussing how a substantial amount of

all employment discrimination plaintiffs are "compromised workers," in that they have done something on the job that might plausibly justify the adverse treatment about which they are complaining).

9. **Fourth prong.** How would you establish the fourth element of the prima facie case? In a failure to hire case, such as *McDonnell Douglas*, it would be sufficient to show that the position you were seeking remained open and that the employer continued looking at other applicants. For a discussion on the interpretation of the fourth element in age-discrimination cases, see Stephen E. Gruendel, *Rejecting the Requirement That ADEA Plaintiffs Demonstrate Replacement from Outside Protected Class:* O'Connor v. Consolidated Coin Caterers Corp., 38 B.C. L. Rev. 381 (1997). In other contexts, when looking at the fourth prong, the courts will often examine evidence as to whether a similarly situated employee from a different protected class was treated in a dissimilar manner. For example, assume that two workers with the same job on an assembly line—one male and one female—got into a fight, and the female was terminated while the male was only disciplined. If the female worker could establish that she was similarly situated to the male (same history of previous offenses, same culpability for the fight, etc.), it would be sufficient to establish the fourth prong of the prima facie case. Courts vary as to how similarly situated the individuals have to be, but the courts seem to agree that they need not be *identical. See* Coleman v. Donahoe, 667 F.3d 835, 846 (7th Cir. 2012) ("Similarly situated employees must be 'directly comparable' to the plaintiff 'in all material respects,' but they need not be identical in every conceivable way."); Wright v. Murray Guard, Inc., 455 F.3d 702, 709 (6th Cir. 2006) ("[T]o establish that an employee is an appropriate comparator, 'the plaintiff [must] demonstrate that he or she is similarly situated to the [claimed comparator] in all relevant respects.'"). Other ways of showing the fourth element of the prima facie case include through discriminatory comments made in the workplace or by statistical evidence that might bolster a case. And, plaintiffs can also establish this element in termination or failure to promote cases by showing that they were replaced with someone outside of their protected class.

10. Once the plaintiff establishes the prima facie case, the Supreme Court has said that an inference of discrimination arises. To combat this, the defendant must (through a burden of production) assert the existence of a legitimate nondiscriminatory reason for taking the adverse action. What would be some common legitimate nondiscriminatory reasons articulated by employers? Several exist. Among others, employers often assert that the employee was a poor performer, that others performed better, that the employee was excessively tardy or absent, that the employee was insubordinate, or that a reduction in force was necessary for economic reasons.

11. *McDonnell Douglas* facts. Is it a nondiscriminatory reason for the employer to argue that Green was fired because of his participation in civil rights activities? Is this rationale too closely tied to discrimination based on race? How important is it that the activities engaged in by the plaintiff were arguably illegal?

12. **Pretext.** Once the employer asserts the legitimate nondiscriminatory reason, the inference of discrimination drops from the case, and the plaintiff must carry her burden of persuasion of establishing that the reason was pretextual. What type of evidence would you need to establish pretext? Is it enough to show that the employer's legitimate nondiscriminatory reason is untrue?

13. Does the *McDonnell Douglas* test favor plaintiffs or defendants? Which side would prefer to use the test?

 ## *Interactive Problem*

Looking back at the facts of the interactive problem outlined at the beginning of this chapter, how would you argue that the *McDonnell Douglas* factors had been satisfied if you represented the plaintiff? If you were representing the defendant, how would you respond?

Practice and Procedural Tip ## 6: "Bulletproofing" Employment Decisions

From a procedural standpoint, a thorough understanding of the *McDonnell Douglas* test can be very helpful. For a plaintiff, the test can help formulate the best way to articulate the particular case. For a defendant, the framework allows several opportunities to attack the plaintiff's case. One procedural benefit of the *McDonnell Douglas* test is the ability to use the framework before an adverse decision is ever made.

If a defendant is considering taking an adverse action against an employee, it can evaluate the risks involved before actually making that decision. As an attorney, it is important to encourage your clients to come to you before effectuating a tangible employment action, so that you can best advise them on how to proceed. If a decision to go forward is made, the reasons for the decision should be well documented. For example, what is the legitimate nondiscriminatory reason that the decision is based on? This reason should be clearly articulated to the employee and backed up in writing by the employer.

Similarly, where the employer is considering a reduction in force, that company should closely evaluate the workforce when considering whom to lay off. The potential liability for the company should be carefully considered. Each potential target of the layoff should be evaluated, and comparators should be considered. Is the employer fairly treating everyone from all protected groups when considering the reduction in force? Will one group be more adversely impacted than another? Beyond intentional discrimination claims, it will also be important to assess whether this type of layoff will have a disparate impact on a protected group—an issue that will be explored in more detail in the following chapters.

Another interesting procedural consideration is the potential to use the *McDonnell Douglas* test to "bulletproof" employment decisions. For example, many courts rely heavily on the use of comparators in deciding whether to allow a discrimination claim to proceed. If there is no similarly situated individual who has been treated differently, it will be an uphill battle for the plaintiff to prevail in many courts. With this knowledge, employers can take steps—before an adverse action is ever made or a lawsuit even contemplated—to make it difficult for a plaintiff to point to a comparator. In this regard, employers can make all positions slightly different from one another, allowing them to make the argument that there is no comparator to point to. If no two positions are the same, it will be a challenge for plaintiffs to satisfy the similarly situated requirement in the case. While the courts have generally held that a comparator need not be identical, this procedural strategy still makes it a difficult task for employees, as the burden of persuasion remains with them throughout the case.

All workplaces are different, and no single strategy will work for everyone. The key is for the attorney to understand the potential upside of the *McDonnell Douglas* test long before litigation is contemplated. Is there a way—from either the defense or plaintiff side—that the test can be used in advance to help guide how that party will proceed? By considering these issues in advance, attorneys can use this test to maximize the potential benefit to their clients.

The *McDonnell Douglas* case represents the Supreme Court's first attempt to articulate the prima facie case in employment discrimination cases, and to set forth the burdens of proof for both plaintiffs and defendants in these matters. Over the years, the Supreme Court has continued to refine the *McDonnell Douglas* test. In the case below, it examines the contours of the defendant's legitimate nondiscriminatory reason.

Texas Department of Community Affairs v. Burdine
450 U.S. 248 (1981)

Justice POWELL delivered the opinion of the Court.

This case requires us to address again the nature of the evidentiary burden placed upon the defendant in an employment discrimination suit brought under Title VII. The narrow question presented is whether, after the plaintiff has proved a prima facie case of discriminatory treatment, the burden shifts to the defendant to persuade the court by a preponderance of the evidence that legitimate, nondiscriminatory reasons for the challenged employment action existed.

Petitioner, the Texas Department of Community Affairs (TDCA), hired respondent, a female, in January 1972, for the position of accounting clerk in the Public Service Careers Division (PSC). PSC provided training and employment opportunities in the public sector for unskilled workers. When hired, respondent possessed several years' experience in employment training. She was promoted to Field Services Coordinator in July 1972. Her supervisor resigned in November of that year, and respondent was assigned additional duties. Although she applied for the supervisor's position of Project Director, the position remained vacant for six months.

PSC was funded completely by the United States Department of Labor. The Department was seriously concerned about inefficiencies at PSC. In February 1973, the Department notified the Executive Director of TDCA, B. R. Fuller, that it would terminate PSC the following month. TDCA officials, assisted by respondent, persuaded the Department to continue funding the program, conditioned upon PSC's reforming its operations. Among the agreed conditions were the appointment of a permanent Project Director and a complete reorganization of the PSC staff.

After consulting with personnel within TDCA, Fuller hired a male from another division of the agency as Project Director. In reducing the PSC staff, he fired respondent along with two other employees, and retained another male, Walz, as the only professional employee in the division. It is undisputed that respondent had maintained her application for the position of Project Director and had requested to remain with TDCA. Respondent soon was rehired by TDCA and assigned to another division of the agency. She received the exact salary paid to the Project Director at PSC, and the subsequent promotions she has received have kept her salary and responsibility commensurate with what she would have received had she been appointed Project Director.

Respondent filed this suit in the United States District Court for the Western District of Texas. She alleged that the failure to promote and the subsequent decision to terminate her had been predicated on gender discrimination in violation of Title VII. After a bench trial, the District Court held that neither decision was based on gender discrimination.

The Court of Appeals for the Fifth Circuit reversed in part. The court held that the District Court's "implicit evidentiary finding" that the male hired as Project Director was better qualified for that position than respondent was not clearly erroneous. Accordingly, the court affirmed the District Court's finding that respondent was not discriminated against when she was not promoted. The Court of Appeals, however, reversed the District Court's finding that [the Executive Director's] testimony sufficiently had rebutted respondent's prima facie case of gender discrimination in the decision to terminate her employment at PSC. The court reaffirmed its previously announced views that the defendant in a Title VII case bears the burden of proving by a preponderance of the evidence the existence of legitimate nondiscriminatory reasons for the employment action and that the defendant also must prove by objective evidence that those hired or promoted were better qualified than the plaintiff. The court found that [the Executive Director's] testimony did not carry either of these evidentiary burdens. It, therefore, reversed the judgment of the District Court and remanded the case for computation of backpay.

In *McDonnell Douglas Corp. v. Green,* we set forth the basic allocation of burdens and order of presentation of proof in a Title VII case alleging discriminatory treatment. First, the plaintiff has the burden of proving by the preponderance of the evidence a prima facie case of discrimination. Second, if the plaintiff succeeds in proving the prima facie case, the burden shifts to the defendant "to articulate some legitimate, nondiscriminatory reason for the employee's rejection." Third, should the defendant carry this burden, the plaintiff must then have an opportunity to prove by a preponderance of the evidence that the legitimate reasons offered by the defendant were not its true reasons, but were a pretext for discrimination.

The nature of the burden that shifts to the defendant should be understood in light of the plaintiff's ultimate and intermediate burdens. The ultimate burden of persuading the trier of fact that the defendant intentionally discriminated against the plaintiff remains at all times with the plaintiff. The *McDonnell Douglas* division of intermediate evidentiary burdens serves to bring the litigants and the court expeditiously and fairly to this ultimate question.

The Court has repeatedly emphasized that the prima facie case is not a stringent test.

The burden of establishing a prima facie case of disparate treatment is not onerous. The plaintiff must prove by a preponderance of the evidence that she applied for an available position for which she was qualified, but was rejected under circumstances which give rise to an inference of unlawful discrimination. The prima facie case serves an important function in the litigation: it eliminates the most common nondiscriminatory reasons for the plaintiff's rejection. Establishment of the prima facie case in effect creates a presumption that the employer unlawfully discriminated against the employee. If the trier of fact believes the plaintiff's evidence, and if the employer is silent in the face of the presumption, the court must enter judgment for the plaintiff because no issue of fact remains in the case.

The burden that shifts to the defendant, therefore, is to rebut the presumption of discrimination by producing evidence that the plaintiff was rejected, or someone else was preferred, for a legitimate, nondiscriminatory reason. The defendant need not persuade the court that it was actually motivated by the proffered reasons. It is sufficient if the defendant's evidence raises a genuine issue of fact as to whether it discriminated against the plaintiff. To accomplish this, the defendant must clearly set forth, through the introduction of admissible evidence, the reasons for the plaintiff's rejection. The explanation provided must be legally sufficient to justify a judgment for the defendant. If the defendant carries this burden of production, the presumption raised by the prima facie case is rebutted, and the factual inquiry proceeds to a new level of specificity. Placing this burden of production on the defendant thus serves simultaneously to meet the plaintiff's prima facie case by presenting a legitimate reason for the action and to frame the factual issue with sufficient clarity so that the plaintiff will have a full and fair opportunity to demonstrate pretext. The sufficiency of the defendant's evidence should be evaluated by the extent to which it fulfills these functions.

The Court of Appeals has misconstrued the nature of the burden that *McDonnell Douglas* and its progeny place on the defendant. We stated in [prior case law] that "the employer's burden is satisfied if he simply 'explains what he has done' or 'produc[es] evidence of legitimate nondiscriminatory reasons.'" It is plain that the Court of Appeals required much more: it placed on the defendant the burden of persuading the court that it had convincing, objective reasons for preferring the chosen applicant above the plaintiff.

We have stated consistently that the employee's prima facie case of discrimination will be rebutted if the employer articulates lawful reasons for the action; that is, to satisfy this intermediate burden, the employer need only produce admissible evidence which would allow the trier of fact rationally to conclude that the employment decision had not been motivated by discriminatory animus. The Court of Appeals would require the defendant to introduce evidence which, in the absence of any evidence of pretext, would *persuade* the trier of fact that the employment action was lawful. This exceeds what properly can be demanded to satisfy a burden of production.

The court placed the burden of persuasion on the defendant apparently because it feared that "[i]f an employer need only *articulate*—not prove—a legitimate, nondiscriminatory reason for his action, he may compose fictitious, but legitimate, reasons for his actions." [Citation omitted.] We do not believe, however, that limiting the defendant's evidentiary obligation to a burden of production will unduly hinder the plaintiff. First, as noted above, the defendant's explanation of its legitimate reasons must be clear and reasonably specific. Second, although the defendant does not bear a formal burden of persuasion, the defendant nevertheless retains an incentive to persuade the trier of fact that the employment decision was lawful. Thus, the defendant normally will attempt to prove the factual basis for its explanation. Third, the liberal discovery rules applicable to any civil suit in federal court are supplemented in a Title VII suit by the plaintiff's access to the Equal Employment Opportunity Commission's investigatory files concerning her complaint.

> As the Court makes clear in this case, the employee's rebuttal burden is one of production, not persuasion.

In summary, the Court of Appeals erred by requiring the defendant to prove by a preponderance of the evidence the existence of nondiscriminatory reasons for terminating the respondent and that the person retained in her stead had superior objective qualifications for the position. When the plaintiff has proved a prima facie case of discrimination, the defendant bears only the burden of explaining clearly the nondiscriminatory reasons for its actions.

> The Court notes that from a practical perspective, the defendant will still present its best case regardless of its legal burden.

■ NOTES AND QUESTIONS

1. In *Burdine*, the Court makes clear that the employer's legitimate, nondiscriminatory reason is only a burden of production, not persuasion. Thus, the employer must introduce enough evidence of a legitimate, nondiscriminatory reason to have the issue decided by the fact-finder, but the employer does not have to go so far as to convince the fact-finder to view the facts in a way that favors the employer.

2. Would the evidence presented by the employer in this case satisfy the burden of production? What about the burden of persuasion?

3. The Court notes in this dispute that the prima facie case is a low threshold for plaintiffs. The Court has reemphasized this point over the years. Nonetheless, many of the lower courts continue to apply a more rigorous standard, and seemingly make the prima facie test a more onerous burden than what the Supreme Court intended.

⟳ *Interactive Problem*

Looking back to the facts of the interactive problem, what will the company's legitimate nondiscriminatory reason be for terminating Bob? Would this reason satisfy the company's burden of production? Why or why not?

The Supreme Court again visited the parameters of the prima facie case in the decision below. While the Court had already provided substantial guidance on how to apply the test, it would continue to refine the test over time. In the case below, the Court explores the plaintiff's ultimate burden of persuasion in employment discrimination matters.

St. Mary's Honor Center v. Hicks
509 U.S. 502 (1993)

Justice SCALIA delivered the opinion of the Court.

We granted certiorari to determine whether, in a suit against an employer alleging intentional racial discrimination in violation of § 703(a)(1) of Title VII of the Civil Rights Act of 1964, the trier of fact's rejection of the employer's asserted reasons for its actions mandates a finding for the plaintiff.

Petitioner St. Mary's Honor Center (St. Mary's) is a halfway house operated by the Missouri Department of Corrections and Human Resources (MDCHR). Respondent Melvin Hicks, a black man, was hired as a correctional officer at St. Mary's in August 1978 and was promoted to shift commander, one of six supervisory positions, in February 1980.

In 1983 MDCHR conducted an investigation of the administration of St. Mary's, which resulted in extensive supervisory changes in January 1984. Respondent retained his position, but John Powell became the new chief of custody (respondent's immediate supervisor) and petitioner Steve Long the new superintendent. Prior to these personnel changes respondent had enjoyed a satisfactory employment record, but soon thereafter became the subject of repeated, and increasingly severe, disciplinary actions. He was suspended for five days for violations of institutional rules by his subordinates on March 3, 1984. He received a letter of reprimand for alleged failure to conduct an adequate investigation of a brawl between inmates that occurred during his shift on March 21. He was later demoted from shift commander to correctional officer for his failure to ensure that his subordinates entered their use of a St. Mary's vehicle into the official log book on March 19, 1984. Finally, on June 7, 1984, he was discharged for threatening Powell during an exchange of heated words on April 19.

Respondent brought this suit in the United States District Court for the Eastern District of Missouri, alleging that petitioner St. Mary's violated § 703(a)(1) of Title VII of the Civil Rights Act of 1964, 42 U.S.C. § 2000e–2(a)(1), and that petitioner Long violated Mo. Rev. Stat. § 1979, 42 U.S.C. § 1983, by demoting and then discharging him because of his race. After a full bench trial, the District Court found for petitioners. The United States Court of Appeals for the Eighth Circuit reversed and remanded, and we granted certiorari.

Respondent does not challenge the District Court's finding that petitioners sustained their burden of production by introducing evidence of two legitimate, nondiscriminatory reasons for their actions: the severity and the accumulation of rules violations committed by respondent. Our cases make clear that at that point the shifted burden of production became irrelevant: "If the defendant carries this burden of production, the presumption raised by the prima facie case is rebutted," *Burdine*, and "drops from the case." The plaintiff then has "the full and fair opportunity to demonstrate," through presentation of his own case and through cross-examination of the defendant's witnesses, "that the proffered reason was not the true reason for the employment decision," and that race was. He retains that "ultimate burden of persuading the [trier of fact] that [he] has been the victim of intentional discrimination."

The District Court, acting as trier of fact in this bench trial, found that the reasons petitioners gave were not the real reasons for respondent's demotion and discharge. It found that respondent was the only supervisor disciplined for violations committed by his subordinates; that similar and even more serious violations committed by respondent's co-workers were either disregarded or treated more leniently; and that Powell manufactured the final verbal confrontation in order to provoke respondent into threatening him. It nonetheless held that respondent had failed to carry his ultimate burden of proving that *his race* was the determining factor in petitioners' decision first to demote and then to dismiss him. In short, the District Court concluded that "although [respondent] has proven the existence of a crusade to terminate him, he has not proven that the crusade was racially rather than personally motivated."

In the nature of things, the determination that a defendant has met its burden of production (and has thus rebutted any legal presumption of intentional discrimination) can involve no credibility assessment. For the burden-of-production determination necessarily *precedes* the credibility-assessment stage. At the close of the defendant's case, the court is asked to decide whether an issue of fact remains for the trier of fact to determine. None does if, on the evidence presented, (1) any rational person would have to find the existence of facts constituting a prima facie case, and (2) the defendant has failed to meet its burden of production — *i.e.*, has failed to introduce evidence which, *taken as true*, would *permit* the conclusion that there was a nondiscriminatory reason for the adverse action. In that event, the court must award judgment to the plaintiff as a matter of law under Federal Rule of Civil Procedure 50(a)(1) (in the case of jury trials) or Federal Rule of Civil Procedure 52(c) (in the case of bench trials). If the defendant has failed to sustain its burden but reasonable minds could *differ* as to whether a preponderance of the evidence establishes the facts of a prima facie case, then a question of fact *does* remain, which the trier of fact will be called upon to answer.

If, on the other hand, the defendant has succeeded in carrying its burden of production, the *McDonnell Douglas* framework — with its

> Does the Court's language suggest that disproving the legitimate nondiscriminatory reason is enough for the plaintiff to prevail in the case?

presumptions and burdens—is no longer relevant. To resurrect it later, after the trier of fact has determined that what was "produced" to meet the burden of production is not credible, flies in the face of our holding in *Burdine* that to rebut the presumption "[t]he defendant need not persuade the court that it was actually motivated by the proffered reasons." The presumption, having fulfilled its role of forcing the defendant to come forward with some response, simply drop out of the picture. The defendant's "production" (whatever its persuasive effect) having been made, the trier of fact proceeds to decide the ultimate question: whether plaintiff has proven "that the defendant intentionally discriminated against [him]" because of his race. The factfinder's disbelief of the reasons put forward by the defendant (particularly if disbelief is accompanied by a suspicion of mendacity) may, together with the elements of the prima facie case, suffice to show intentional discrimination. Thus, rejection of the defendant's proffered reasons will *permit* the trier of fact to infer the ultimate fact of intentional discrimination, and the Court of Appeals was correct when it noted that, upon such rejection, "[n]o additional proof of discrimination is *required*" (emphasis added). But the Court of Appeals' holding that rejection of the defendant's proffered reasons *compels* judgment for the plaintiff disregards the fundamental principle of Rule 301 that a presumption does not shift the burden of proof, and ignores our repeated admonition that the Title VII plaintiff at all times bears the "ultimate burden of persuasion."

The principal case on which the dissent relies is *Burdine*. While there are some statements in that opinion that could be read to support the dissent's position, all but one of them bear a meaning consistent with our interpretation, and the one exception is simply incompatible with other language in the case. *Burdine* describes the situation that obtains after the employer has met its burden of adducing a nondiscriminatory reason as follows: "Third, should the defendant carry this burden, the plaintiff must then have an opportunity to prove by a preponderance of the evidence that the legitimate reasons offered by the defendant were not its true reasons, but were a pretext for discrimination."

450 U.S. at 253. The dissent takes this to mean that if the plaintiff proves the asserted reason to be *false*, the plaintiff wins. But a reason cannot be proved to be "a pretext *for discrimination*" unless it is shown *both* that the reason was false, *and* that discrimination was the real reason *Burdine*'s later allusions to proving or demonstrating simply "pretext" are reasonably understood to refer to the previously described pretext, *i.e.*, "pretext for discrimination."

> **Does the Court's language also suggest that disproving the defendant's legitimate nondiscriminatory reason is not enough for the plaintiff to prevail?**

We turn, finally, to the dire practical consequences that the respondents and the dissent claim our decision today will produce. What appears to trouble the dissent more than anything is that, in its view, our rule is adopted "for the benefit of employers who have been found to have given false evidence in a court of law," whom we "favo[r]" by "exempting them from responsibility for lies." *Post* at 2762. As we shall explain, our rule in no way gives special favor to those employers whose evidence is disbelieved. But initially we must point out that there is no justification for assuming (as the dissent repeatedly does) that those employers whose evidence is disbelieved

[margin note: pretext - may approach]

are perjurers and liars. *See ibid.* ("the employer who lies"; "the employer's lie"; "found to have given false evidence"; "lies"); *post*, at 2764 ("benefit from lying"; "must lie"; "offering false evidence"), 2764 n. 13 ("employer who lies"; "employer caught in a lie"; "rewarded for its falsehoods"), 2764 ("requires a party to lie"). Even if these were typically cases in which an individual defendant's sworn assertion regarding a physical occurrence was pitted against an individual plaintiff's sworn assertion regarding the same physical occurrence, surely it would be imprudent to call the party whose assertion is (by a mere preponderance of the evidence) disbelieved, a perjurer and a liar. And in these Title VII cases, the defendant is ordinarily *not* an individual but a company, which must rely upon the statement of an employee—often a relatively low-level employee—as to the central fact; and that central fact is *not* a physical occurrence, but rather that employee's state of mind. To say that the company which in good faith introduces such testimony, or even the testifying employee himself, becomes a liar and a perjurer when the testimony is not believed, is nothing short of absurd.

■ NOTES AND QUESTIONS

1. The *Hicks* decision helped clarify that judgment need not be entered for the plaintiff where the employer's legitimate nondiscriminatory reason is disbelieved. It is the plaintiff that ultimately carries the burden of persuasion in the case, and more may be needed than simply establishing that the company's articulated reason is false.

2. **Pretext-may versus pretext-plus.** The *Hicks* case did provide some clarification for employment discrimination litigants, but it also created significant confusion. Following *Hicks*, a substantial divide remained in the lower courts as to whether a pretext-may or a pretext-plus approach should be followed. Under the pretext-may approach, some courts took the approach that if the employer's legitimate nondiscriminatory reason was disbelieved, this (combined with the prima facie case) was sufficient for the trier of fact to rule in the plaintiff's favor. Under pretext-may, the trier of fact *may* find for the plaintiff in this circumstance, but it does not have to. Those courts following the pretext-plus approach, however, believed that in addition to disproving the employer's legitimate nondiscriminatory reason, some other evidence of pretext must be produced in the case to show the employer's discriminatory intent. Under this approach, more is needed than a simple disbelief of the employer's articulated reason for the adverse action.

3. Does *Hicks* support the pretext-may or pretext-plus view? Is there language in the Court's decision that would help resolve this debate? Does the statute support a particular view? What about equity? Compare the Court's language that "[t]he factfinder's disbelief of the reasons put forward by the defendant . . . together with the elements of the prima facie case, suffice to show intentional discrimination" with its statement that "a reason cannot be proved to be 'a pretext *for discrimination*' unless it is shown *both* that the reason was false, *and* that discrimination was the real reason."

7: Shifting Reasons for an Adverse Action

From a procedural standpoint, an employer puts itself in an awkward position when it flip-flops between different rationales for taking an adverse action against a plaintiff. As *Burdine* and *Hicks* make clear, the defendant has only a burden of production—not persuasion—to articulate a legitimate, nondiscriminatory rationale for an adverse action. Nonetheless, from a practical standpoint, the employer will want to be as convincing as possible with its stated reason.

The more convincing the employer's reason for the adverse action, the more likely it is that the employer will persuade a judge or jury of the rationale for its decision. Establishing the legitimate, nondiscriminatory reason should begin long before litigation is filed in a case. Before any adverse action is ever officially taken, the employer should make certain to have its explanation clearly determined. The reason for the adverse action must be plainly articulated to the employee and it should be explained in writing. As with all employment decisions, the key is to document, document, document. Whatever reason is given to the employee, it must be backed up in writing. This is critical as it helps prevent the worker from maintaining that she was not informed of the reason for the action, or was given a different reason from the one that was truly conveyed.

Beyond this, it is critical to be honest and forthcoming with the worker. This may seem obvious on its face, but in practice it can be difficult to implement. This is particularly true as employers strive to maintain a harmonious working environment. Suppose, for example, that an employer decides not to promote a Hispanic female because she is only an average employee, and it instead promotes a white male who has been an outstanding worker. Not wanting to discourage the Hispanic worker, the employer might tell the worker that the true reason for the failure to promote her is that she does not have the requisite experience for the new position—this might be a way of letting her down lightly. Once the employee sues, however, the company will no longer be concerned with making the employee happy, and further will want to use the true reason for the failure to promote—average work performance. These types of "shifting reasons," however, can get the employer into trouble, as they create a question of fact for the jury to decide (which is always a risky proposition). The employer will be asked, "You stated initially that the decision was based on the employee's lack of qualifications; now you are telling the court the true reason is her performance. Which is the true rationale, or is the true rationale really discrimination?" Courts from numerous circuits have held that inconsistent reasons offered for an adverse employment action can support a claim of actionable pretext in disparate treatment cases. *See, e.g.*, Hitchcock v. Angel Corps., Inc., 718 F.3d 733 (7th Cir. 2013); Velez v. Thermo King de Puerto Rico, Inc., 585 F.3d 441 (1st Cir. 2009); Raad v. Fairbanks N. Star Borough Sch. Dist., 323 F.3d 1185 (9th Cir. 2003).

The key practice tip to take away from this discussion is the importance of (1) deciding on a reason for the adverse action early; (2) documenting that reason; and (3) remaining consistent about the reason—from the time it is conveyed to the worker through the end of the litigation. Similarly, from a plaintiff's perspective, if the defendant has failed to remain consistent, there is an opportunity to challenge the company on its true motivations for a particular employment decision.

As discussed, the Court's articulation of the prima facie case still left substantial ambiguity for the lower courts to attempt to resolve. The Court finally addressed the pretext-may versus pretext-plus question head on in the decision below, providing substantial guidance in this area. This case not only answers the question, but it provides helpful guidance on analyzing employment discrimination cases generally.

Reeves v. Sanderson Plumbing Products, Inc.
530 U.S. 133 (2000)

Justice O'CONNOR delivered the opinion of the Court.

In October 1995, petitioner Roger Reeves was 57 years old and had spent 40 years in the employ of respondent, Sanderson Plumbing Products, Inc., a manufacturer of toilet seats and covers. Petitioner worked in a department known as the "Hinge Room," where he supervised the "regular line." Joe Oswalt, in his mid-thirties, supervised the Hinge Room's "special line," and Russell Caldwell, the manager of the Hinge Room and age 45, supervised both petitioner and Oswalt. Petitioner's responsibilities included recording the attendance and hours of those under his supervision, and reviewing a weekly report that listed the hours worked by each employee.

In the summer of 1995, Caldwell informed Powe Chesnut, the director of manufacturing and the husband of company president Sandra Sanderson, that "production was down" in the Hinge Room because employees were often absent and were "coming in late and leaving early." Because the monthly attendance reports did not indicate a problem, Chesnut ordered an audit of the Hinge Room's timesheets for July, August, and September of that year. According to Chesnut's testimony, that investigation revealed "numerous timekeeping errors and misrepresentations on the part of Caldwell, Reeves, and Oswalt." Following the audit, Chesnut, along with Dana Jester, vice president of human resources, and Tom Whitaker, vice president of operations, recommended to company president Sanderson that petitioner and Caldwell be fired. In October 1995, Sanderson followed the recommendation and discharged both petitioner and Caldwell.

In June 1996, petitioner filed suit in the United States District Court for the Northern District of Mississippi, contending that he had been fired because of his age in violation of the Age Discrimination in Employment Act of 1967. At trial, respondent contended that it had fired petitioner due to his failure to maintain accurate attendance records, while petitioner attempted to demonstrate that respondent's explanation was pretext for age discrimination. Petitioner introduced evidence that he had accurately recorded the attendance and hours of the employees under his supervision, and that Chesnut, whom Oswalt described as wielding "absolute power" within the company had demonstrated age-based animus in his dealings with petitioner.

During the trial, the District Court twice denied oral motions by respondent for judgment as a matter of law under Rule 50 of the Federal Rules of Civil Procedure, and the case went to the jury. The court instructed the jury that "[i]f the plaintiff fails to prove age was a determinative or motivating factor in the decision to terminate him, then your verdict shall be for the defendant." So charged, the jury returned a verdict in favor of petitioner, awarding him $35,000 in compensatory damages, and found that respondent's age discrimination had been "willfu[l]." The District Court accordingly entered judgment for petitioner in the amount of $70,000, which included $35,000 in liquidated damages based on the jury's finding of willfulness. Respondent then renewed its motion for judgment as a matter of law and alternatively moved for a new trial, while petitioner moved for front pay. The District Court denied respondent's motions and granted petitioner's, awarding him $28,490.80 in front pay for two years' lost income.

The Court of Appeals for the Fifth Circuit reversed, holding that petitioner had not introduced sufficient evidence to sustain the jury's finding of unlawful discrimination. 197 F.3d at 694. After noting respondent's proffered justification for petitioner's discharge, the court acknowledged that petitioner "very well may" have offered sufficient evidence for "a reasonable jury [to] have found that [respondent's] explanation for its employment decision was pretextual." *Id.* at 693. The court explained, however, that this was "not dispositive" of the ultimate issue—namely, "whether Reeves presented sufficient evidence that his age motivated [respondent's] employment decision." *Ibid.* Addressing this question, the court weighed petitioner's additional evidence of discrimination against other circumstances surrounding his discharge. Specifically, the court noted that Chesnut's age-based comments "were not made in the direct context of Reeves's termination"; there was no allegation that the two other individuals who had recommended that petitioner be fired (Jester and Whitaker) were motivated by age; two of the decisionmakers involved in petitioner's discharge (Jester and Sanderson) were over the age of 50; all three of the Hinge Room supervisors were accused of inaccurate recordkeeping; and several of respondents management positions were filled by persons over age 50 when petitioner was fired. On this basis, the court concluded that petitioner had not introduced sufficient evidence for a rational jury to conclude that he had been discharged because of his age.

We granted certiorari to resolve a conflict among the Courts of Appeals as to whether a plaintiff's prima facie case of discrimination (as defined in *McDonnell Douglas Corp. v. Green*, 411 U.S. 792), combined with sufficient evidence for a reasonable factfinder to reject the employer's nondiscriminatory explanation for its decision, is adequate to sustain a finding of liability for intentional discrimination.

> The primary issue addressed in this case is whether the lower courts should follow a pretext-may or pretext-plus approach.

Although intermediate evidentiary burdens shift back and forth under this framework, "[t]he ultimate burden of persuading the trier of fact that the defendant intentionally discriminated against the plaintiff remains at all times with the plaintiff." *Burdine*, 450 U.S. at 253. And in attempting to satisfy this burden, the plaintiff—once the employer produces sufficient evidence to support a nondiscriminatory explanation for its decision—must be afforded the "opportunity to prove by a preponderance of the evidence that the legitimate reasons offered by the defendant were not its true reasons, but were a pretext for discrimination." *Ibid.; see also St. Mary's Honor Center v. Hicks,* 509 U.S. 502, 507–508 (1993). That is, the plaintiff may attempt to establish that he was the victim of intentional discrimination "by showing that the employer's proffered explanation is unworthy of credence." *Burdine, supra* at 256. Moreover, although the presumption of discrimination "drops out of the picture" once the defendant meets its burden of production, *St. Mary's Honor Center, supra* at 511, the trier of fact may still consider the evidence establishing the plaintiff's prima facie case "and inferences properly drawn there from . . . on the issue of whether the defendant's explanation is pretextual," *Burdine, supra* at 255, n. 10.

In this case, the evidence supporting respondent's explanation for petitioner's discharge consisted primarily of testimony by Chesnut and Sanderson and documentation of petitioner's alleged "shoddy record keeping." Chesnut testified that a 1993 audit of Hinge Room operations revealed "a very lax assembly line" where employees were not adhering to general work rules. As a result of that audit, petitioner was placed on 90 days' probation for unsatisfactory performance. In 1995, Chesnut ordered another investigation of the Hinge Room, which, according to his testimony, revealed that petitioner was not correctly recording the absences and hours of employees. Respondent introduced summaries of that investigation documenting several attendance violations by 12 employees under petitioner's supervision, and noting that each should have been disciplined in some manner. Chesnut testified that this failure to discipline absent and late employees is "extremely important when you are dealing with a union" because uneven enforcement across departments would keep the company "in grievance and arbitration cases, which are costly, all the time." He and Sanderson also stated that petitioner's errors, by failing to adjust for hours not worked, cost the company overpaid wages. Sanderson testified that she accepted the recommendation to discharge petitioner because he had "intentionally falsif[ied] company pay records."

Petitioner, however, made a substantial showing that respondent's explanation was false. First, petitioner offered evidence that he had properly maintained the attendance records. Most of the timekeeping errors cited by respondent involved employees who were not marked late but who were recorded as having arrived at the plant at 7 A.M. for the 7 A.M. shift. Respondent contended that employees arriving at 7 A.M. could not have been at their workstations by 7 A.M., and therefore must have been late. But both petitioner and Oswalt testified that the company's automated timeclock often failed to scan employees' timecards, so that the timesheets would not record any time of arrival. On these occasions, petitioner and Oswalt would visually check the workstations and record whether the employees were present at the start of the shift. They stated that if an employee arrived promptly but the timesheet contained no time of arrival, they would reconcile the two by marking "7 A.M." as the employee's arrival time, even if the employee actually arrived at the plant earlier. On cross-examination, Chesnut acknowledged that the timeclock sometimes malfunctioned, and that if "people were there at their work station[s]" at the start of the shift, the supervisor "would write in seven o'clock." Petitioner also testified that when employees arrived before or stayed after their shifts, he would assign them additional work so they would not be overpaid.

Petitioner similarly cast doubt on whether he was responsible for any failure to discipline late and absent employees. Petitioner testified that his job only included reviewing the daily and weekly attendance reports, and that disciplinary writeups were based on the monthly reports, which were reviewed by Caldwell. Sanderson admitted that Caldwell, and not petitioner, was responsible for citing employees for violations of the company's attendance policy. Further, Chesnut conceded that there had never been a union grievance or employee complaint arising from petitioner's recordkeeping, and that the company had never calculated the amount of overpayments allegedly attributable to petitioner's errors. Petitioner also testified that, on the day he was fired, Chesnut said that his discharge was due to his failure to report as absent one employee, Gina Mae Coley, on two days in September 1995. But petitioner explained that he had spent those days in the hospital, and that Caldwell was therefore responsible for any overpayment of Coley. Finally, petitioner stated that on previous occasions that employees were paid for hours they had not worked, the company had simply adjusted those employees' next paychecks to correct the errors.

Based on this evidence, the Court of Appeals concluded that petitioner "very well may be correct" that "a reasonable jury could have found that [respondent's] explanation for its employment decision was pretextual." Nonetheless, the court held that this showing, standing alone, was insufficient to sustain the jury's finding of liability: "We must, as an essential final step, determine whether Reeves presented sufficient evidence that his age motivated [respondent's] employment decision." And in making this determination, the Court of Appeals ignored the evidence supporting petitioner's prima facie case and challenging respondent's explanation for its decision. The court confined its review of evidence favoring petitioner to that evidence showing that Chesnut had directed derogatory, age-based comments at petitioner, and that Chesnut had singled out petitioner for harsher treatment than younger employees. It is therefore apparent that the court believed that only this additional evidence of discrimination was relevant to whether the jury's verdict should stand. That is, the Court of Appeals proceeded from the assumption that a prima facie case of discrimination, combined with sufficient evidence for the trier of fact to disbelieve the defendant's legitimate, nondiscriminatory reason for its decision, is insufficient as a matter of law to sustain a jury's finding of intentional discrimination.

In so reasoning, the Court of Appeals misconceived the evidentiary burden borne by plaintiffs who attempt to prove intentional discrimination through indirect evidence. This much is evident from our decision in *St. Mary's Honor Center.* There we held that the factfinder's rejection of the employer's legitimate, nondiscriminatory reason for its action does not *compel* judgment for the plaintiff. The ultimate question is whether the employer intentionally discriminated, and proof that "the employer's proffered reason is unpersuasive, or even obviously contrived, does not necessarily establish that the plaintiff's proffered reason . . . is correct." *Id.* at 524. In other words, "[i]t is not enough . . . to disbelieve the employer; the factfinder must *believe* the plaintiff's explanation of intentional discrimination." *Id.* at 519.

In reaching this conclusion, however, we reasoned that it is *permissible* for the trier of fact to infer the ultimate fact of discrimination from the falsity of the employer's explanation. Specifically, we stated:

> The factfinder's disbelief of the reasons put forward by the defendant (particularly if disbelief is accompanied by a suspicion of mendacity) may, together with the elements of the prima facie case, suffice to show intentional discrimination. Thus, rejection of the defendant's proffered reasons will *permit* the trier of fact to infer the ultimate fact of intentional discrimination. *Id.* at 511.

Proof that the defendant's explanation is unworthy of credence is simply one form of circumstantial evidence that is probative of intentional discrimination, and it may be quite persuasive. In appropriate circumstances, the trier of fact can reasonably infer from the falsity of the explanation that the employer is dissembling to cover up a discriminatory purpose. Such an inference is consistent with the general principle of evidence law that the factfinder is entitled to consider a party's dishonesty about a material fact as "affirmative evidence of guilt." *Wright v. West,* 505 U.S. 277 (1992). Moreover, once the employer's justification has been eliminated, discrimination may well be the most likely alternative explanation, especially since the employer is in the best position to put forth the actual reason for its decision.

> The Court determined that disproving the employer's legitimate nondiscriminatory reason is a form of circumstantial evidence.

This is not to say that such a showing by the plaintiff will *always* be adequate to sustain a jury's finding of liability. Certainly there will be instances where, although the plaintiff has established a prima facie case and set forth sufficient evidence to reject the defendant's explanation, no rational factfinder could conclude that the action was discriminatory. For instance, an employer would be entitled to judgment as a matter of law if the record conclusively revealed some other, nondiscriminatory reason for the employer's decision, or if the plaintiff created only a weak issue of fact as to whether the employer's reason was untrue and there was abundant and uncontroverted independent evidence that no discrimination had occurred.

Whether judgment as a matter of law is appropriate in any particular case will depend on a number of factors. Those include the strength of the plaintiff's prima facie case, the probative value of the proof that the employer's explanation is false, and any other evidence that supports the employer's case and that properly may be considered on a motion for judgment as a matter of law. For purposes of this case, we need not—and could not—resolve all of the circumstances in which such factors would entitle an employer to judgment as a matter of law. It suffices to say that, because a prima facie case and sufficient evidence to reject the employer's explanation may permit a finding of liability, the Court of Appeals erred in proceeding from the premise that a plaintiff must always introduce additional, independent evidence of discrimination.

[I]t is apparent that respondent was not entitled to judgment as a matter of law. In this case, in addition to establishing a prima facie case of discrimination and creating a jury issue as to the falsity of the employer's explanation, petitioner introduced additional evidence that Chesnut was motivated by age-based animus and was principally responsible for petitioner's firing. Petitioner testified that Chesnut had told him that he "was so old [he] must have come over on the Mayflower" and, on one occasion when petitioner was having difficulty starting a machine, that he "was too damn old to do [his] job." According to petitioner, Chesnut would regularly "cuss at me and shake his finger in my face." Oswalt, roughly 24 years younger than petitioner, corroborated that there was an "obvious difference" in how Chesnut treated them. He stated that, although he and Chesnut "had [their] differences," "it was nothing compared to the way [Chesnut] treated Roger." Oswalt explained that Chesnut "tolerated quite a bit" from him even though he "defied" Chesnut "quite often," but that Chesnut treated petitioner "[i]n a manner, as you would . . . treat . . . a child when . . . you're angry with [him]." Petitioner also demonstrated that, according to company records, he and Oswalt had nearly identical rates of productivity in 1993. Yet respondent conducted an efficiency study of only the regular line, supervised by petitioner, and placed only petitioner on probation. Chesnut conducted that efficiency study and, after having testified to the contrary on direct examination, acknowledged on cross-examination that he had recommended that petitioner be placed on probation following the study.

Further, petitioner introduced evidence that Chesnut was the actual decisionmaker behind his firing. Chesnut was married to Sanderson, who made the formal decision to discharge petitioner. Although Sanderson testified that she fired petitioner because he had "intentionally falsif[ied] company pay records," respondent only introduced evidence concerning the inaccuracy of the records, not their falsification. A 1994 letter authored by Chesnut indicated that he berated other company directors, who were supposedly his coequals, about how to do their jobs. Moreover, Oswalt testified that all of respondent's employees feared Chesnut, and that Chesnut had exercised "absolute power" within the company for "[a]s long as [he] can remember."

In holding that the record contained insufficient evidence to sustain the jury's verdict, the Court of Appeals misapplied the standard of review dictated by Rule 50. Again, the court disregarded critical evidence favorable to petitioner—namely, the evidence supporting petitioner's prima facie case and undermining respondent's nondiscriminatory explanation. The court also failed to draw all reasonable inferences in favor of

> The Court emphasized that the prima facie case, combined with disproving the legitimate nondiscriminatory reason, may be enough to get to a jury.

petitioner. For instance, while acknowledging "the potentially damning nature" of Chesnut's age-related comments, the court discounted them on the ground that they "were not made in the direct context of Reeves's termination." And the court discredited petitioner's evidence that Chesnut was the actual decisionmaker by giving weight to the fact that there was "no evidence to suggest that any of the other decision makers were motivated by age." Moreover, the other evidence on which the court relied—that Caldwell and Oswalt were also cited for poor recordkeeping, and that respondent employed many managers over age 50—although relevant, is certainly not dispositive. In concluding that these circumstances so overwhelmed the evidence favoring petitioner that no rational trier of fact could have found that petitioner was fired because of his age, the Court of Appeals impermissibly substituted its judgment concerning the weight of the evidence for the jury's.

The ultimate question in every employment discrimination case involving a claim of disparate treatment is whether the plaintiff was the victim of intentional discrimination. Given the evidence in the record supporting petitioner, we see no reason to subject the parties to an additional round of litigation before the Court of Appeals rather than to resolve the matter here. The District Court was therefore correct to submit the case to the jury, and the Court of Appeals erred in overturning its verdict.

Justice GINSBURG, concurring.

The Court today holds that an employment discrimination plaintiff *may* survive judgment as a matter of law by submitting two categories of evidence: first, evidence establishing a "prima facie case," as that term is used in *McDonnell Douglas Corp. v. Green*, 411 U.S. 792 (1973); and second, evidence from which a rational factfinder could conclude that the employer's proffered explanation for its actions was false. Because the Court of Appeals in this case plainly, and erroneously, required the plaintiff to offer some evidence beyond those two categories, no broader holding is necessary to support reversal.

I write separately to note that it may be incumbent on the Court, in an appropriate case, to define more precisely the circumstances in which plaintiffs will be required to submit evidence beyond these two categories in order to survive a motion for judgment as a matter of law. I anticipate that such circumstances will be uncommon. As the Court notes, it is a principle of evidence law that the jury is entitled to treat a party's dishonesty about a material fact as evidence of culpability. Under this commonsense principle, evidence suggesting that a defendant accused of illegal discrimination has chosen to give a false explanation for its actions gives rise to a rational inference that the defendant could be masking its actual, illegal motivation. *Ibid.* Whether the defendant was in fact motivated by discrimination is of course for the finder of fact to decide; that is the lesson of *St. Mary's Honor Center*. But the inference remains—unless it is conclusively demonstrated, by evidence the district court is required to credit on a motion for judgment as a matter of law, that discrimination

> Justice Ginsburg appears to try to limit the number of circumstances that would follow the pretext-plus approach.

could not have been the defendant's true motivation. If such conclusive demonstrations are (as I suspect) atypical, it follows that the ultimate question of liability ordinarily should not be taken from the jury once the plaintiff has introduced the two categories of evidence described above. Because the Court's opinion leaves room for such further elaboration in an appropriate case, I join it in full.

■ NOTES AND QUESTIONS

1. *Reeves* helps put to rest the debate over pretext-may versus pretext-plus. Though the Court does not specifically answer the question, it certainly sides heavily in favor of a pretext-may analysis. The Court holds that "in appropriate circumstances, the trier of fact can reasonably infer from the falsity of the explanation that the employer is dissembling to cover up a discriminatory purpose. . . . [O]nce the employer's justification has been eliminated, discrimination may well be the most likely alternative." *Reeves*, 530 U.S. at 147.

2. Nonetheless, *Reeves* still leaves some room for a pretext-plus approach. The Court notes that there can still "be instances where, although the plaintiff has established a prima facie case and set forth sufficient evidence to reject the defendant's explanation, no rational factfinder could conclude that the action was discriminatory." *Reeves*, 530 U.S. at 148. What would some of these instances be?

3. In her concurrence, Justice Ginsburg states that "evidence suggesting that a defendant accused of illegal discrimination has chosen to give a false explanation for its actions gives rise to a rational inference that the defendant could be masking its actual, illegal motivation. Whether the defendant was in fact motivated by discrimination is of course for the finder of fact to decide." *Reeves*, 530 U.S. at 154. Justice Ginsburg appears to be highlighting the fact that there are very few situations where a pretext-plus approach would be appropriate, and that the pretext-may analysis should likely be followed in most instances.

Class Exercise: *McDonnell Douglas* Test

One issue that has remained controversial is what it takes to establish an adverse employment action in an employment discrimination case analyzed under *McDonnell Douglas*. As discussed in this chapter, all courts now require something more than a de minimis action by the employer. The Supreme Court, however, has never weighed in on what it takes to rise to the level of an adverse action. This has resulted in substantial disagreement in the lower courts.

Breaking up into small groups, discuss whether the following actions rise to the level of being sufficiently adverse: (1) A supervisor will not have lunch with an employee because she is African American; (2) an employee is transferred to another part of the company because she is female, but she retains the same job responsibilities, title, and pay status; and (3) an employee is fired because he is Muslim.

 Interactive Problem

Looking back at the facts of the interactive problem, what if the true reason that Bob was fired was that he had information that could result in the company CEO being charged with tax evasion? If this reason was never given to Bob (to cover up the illegal dealings), but was suspected by the court, would a pretext-plus approach be more appropriate?

C. Direct Evidence of Discrimination

Traditionally, intentional discrimination cases were examined through the dual lens of circumstantial and direct evidence of discrimination. The vast majority of discrimination cases arise in the context of circumstantial evidence. And, as employers have become more knowledgeable over time, the likelihood of a plaintiff uncovering direct evidence of discrimination has greatly diminished. Nonetheless, direct evidence remains an extremely important tool for analyzing discrimination claims, and there are a number of situations where this type of evidence is critical.

Under the black letter law, direct evidence of discrimination can be defined as "evidence which reflects a discriminatory or retaliatory attitude correlating to the discrimination or retaliation complained of by the employee . . . that, if believed, proves the existence of a fact without inference or presumption." Hamilton v. Southland Christian Sch., Inc., 680 F.3d 1316, 1320 (11th Cir. 2012) (quotations, citations, and alterations omitted). The key for direct—as opposed to circumstantial—evidence is that such evidence leaves no leeway for doubt as to whether intentional discrimination occurred. Under direct evidence, there can thus be no room for inference or presumption on the issue of discriminatory intent. The ultimate piece of direct evidence of discrimination would be a notarized document sent from the employer to the employee, informing her that "she is being terminated because she is a woman." Such evidence, however, rarely surfaces in this day and age.

A key question that often arises during the litigation of an employment discrimination case, then, is how we distinguish between direct and circumstantial evidence. Often these cases arise in the context of discriminatory comments that are made by a supervisor. When discriminatory remarks are specifically at issue, the jurisdictions have each adopted a test for what constitutes direct evidence. While these tests vary between the courts, they do tend to have substantial overlap. An excellent summary of these tests was recently articulated by the U.S. Court of Appeals for the Fifth Circuit in *Reed v. Neopost USA, Inc.*, 701 F.3d 434, 441 (5th Cir. 2012):

> Where a plaintiff offers remarks as direct evidence, we apply a four-part test to determine whether they are sufficient to overcome summary judgment [by looking at whether the comments are] 1) []related [to the protected class]; 2) proximate in time to the terminations; 3) made by an individual with authority over the employment decision at issue; and 4) related to the employment decision at issue.

Thus, for comments to constitute direct evidence of discrimination, they must pertain to the protected class, be made close to the time of the adverse action, be made by an individual with authority, and be related to the decision. It is important to note that where a comment does not satisfy this test, it is considered a "stray remark." Despite this terminology, such stray remarks can still be powerful circumstantial evidence of discrimination that must be analyzed under the *McDonnell Douglas* framework.

Where there is direct evidence of discrimination, there is no need to follow the *McDonnell Douglas* test. Keep in mind the purpose of the *McDonnell Douglas* framework—to determine whether intentional discrimination has occurred. Where direct evidence is present, this determination has already been made, and there is no need to consider the circumstantial evidence.

Price Waterhouse v. Hopkins
490 U.S. 228 (1989)

Justice BRENNAN announced the judgment of the Court and delivered an opinion, in which Justice MARSHALL, Justice BLACKMUN, and Justice STEVENS join.

Ann Hopkins had worked at Price Waterhouse's Office of Government Services in Washington, D.C., for five years when the partners in that office proposed her as a candidate for partnership. Of the 662 partners at the firm at that time, 7 were women. Of the 88 persons proposed for partnership that year, only 1—Hopkins—was a woman. Forty-seven of these candidates were admitted to the partnership, 21 were rejected, and 20—including Hopkins—were "held" for reconsideration the following year. Thirteen of the 32 partners who had submitted comments on Hopkins supported her bid for partnership. Three partners recommended that her candidacy be placed on hold, eight stated that they did not have an informed opinion about her, and eight recommended that she be denied partnership.

In a jointly prepared statement supporting her candidacy, the partners in Hopkins' office showcased her successful 2-year effort to secure a $25 million contract with the Department of State, labeling it "an outstanding performance" and one that Hopkins carried out "virtually at the partner level." Despite Price Waterhouse's attempt at trial to minimize her contribution to this project, Judge Gesell specifically found that Hopkins had "played a key role in Price Waterhouse's successful effort to win a multi-million dollar contract with the Department of State." Indeed, he went on, "[n]one of the other partnership candidates at Price Waterhouse that year had a comparable record in terms of successfully securing major contracts for the partnership."

The partners in Hopkins' office praised her character as well as her accomplishments, describing her in their joint statement as "an outstanding professional" who had a "deft touch," a "strong character, independence and integrity." Clients appear to have agreed with these assessments. At trial, one official from the State Department described her as "extremely competent, intelligent," "strong and forthright, very productive, energetic and creative." Another high-ranking official praised Hopkins' decisiveness, broadmindedness, and "intellectual clarity"; she was, in his words, "a stimulating conversationalist." Evaluations such as these led Judge Gesell to conclude that Hopkins "had no difficulty dealing with clients and her clients appear to have been very pleased with her work" and that she "was generally viewed as a highly competent project leader who worked long hours, pushed vigorously to meet deadlines and demanded much from the multidisciplinary staffs with which she worked."

On too many occasions, however, Hopkins' aggressiveness apparently spilled over into abrasiveness. Staff members seem to have borne the brunt of Hopkins' brusqueness. Long before her bid for partnership, partners evaluating her work had counseled her to improve her relations with staff members. Although later evaluations indicate an improvement, Hopkins' perceived shortcomings in this important area eventually doomed her bid for partnership. Virtually all of the partners' negative remarks about Hopkins—even those of partners supporting her—had to do with her "interpersonal skills." Both "[s]upporters and opponents of her candidacy," stressed Judge Gesell, "indicated that she was sometimes overly aggressive, unduly harsh, difficult to work with and impatient with staff."

> Is the plaintiff's so-called aggressiveness more of a traditionally male characteristic?

There were clear signs, though, that some of the partners reacted negatively to Hopkins' personality because she was a woman. One partner described her as "macho"; another suggested that she "overcompensated for being a woman"; a third advised her to take "a course at charm school." Several partners criticized her use of profanity; in response, one partner suggested that those partners objected to her swearing only "because it's a lady using foul language." Another supporter explained that Hopkins "ha[d] matured from a tough-talking somewhat masculine hard-nosed mgr to an authoritative, formidable, but much more appealing lady ptr candidate." But it was the man who, as Judge Gesell found, bore responsibility for explaining to Hopkins the reasons for the Policy Board's decision to place her candidacy on hold who delivered the *coup de grace*: in order to improve her chances for partnership, Thomas Beyer advised, Hopkins should "walk more femininely, talk more femininely, dress more femininely, wear make-up, have her hair styled, and wear jewelry."

In previous years, other female candidates for partnership also had been evaluated in sex-based terms. As a general matter, Judge Gesell concluded, "[c]andidates were viewed favorably if partners believed they maintained their femin[in]ity while becoming effective professional managers"; in this environment, "[t]o be identified as a 'women's lib[b]er' was regarded as [a] negative comment." In fact, the judge found that in previous years "[o]ne partner repeatedly commented that he could not consider any woman seriously as a partnership candidate and believed that women were not even capable of functioning as senior managers—yet the firm took no action to discourage his comments and recorded his vote in the overall summary of the evaluations."

Judge Gesell found that Price Waterhouse legitimately emphasized interpersonal skills in its partnership decisions, and also found that the firm had not fabricated its complaints about Hopkins' interpersonal skills as a pretext for discrimination. Moreover, he concluded, the firm did not give decisive emphasis to such traits only because Hopkins was a woman; although there were male candidates who lacked these skills but who were admitted to partnership, the judge found that these candidates possessed other, positive traits that Hopkins lacked.

The judge went on to decide, however, that some of the partners' remarks about Hopkins stemmed from an impermissibly cabined view of the proper behavior of women, and that Price Waterhouse had done nothing to disavow reliance on such comments. He held that Price Waterhouse had unlawfully discriminated against Hopkins on the basis of sex by consciously giving credence and effect to partners' comments that resulted from sex stereotyping. Noting that Price Waterhouse could avoid equitable relief by proving by clear and convincing evidence that it would have placed Hopkins' candidacy on hold even absent this discrimination, the judge decided that the firm had not carried this heavy burden.

The Court of Appeals affirmed the District Court's ultimate conclusion, but departed from its analysis in one particular: it held that even if a plaintiff proves that discrimination played a role in an employment decision, the defendant will not be found liable if it proves, by clear and convincing evidence, that it would have made the same decision in the absence of discrimination. Under this approach, an employer is not deemed to have violated Title VII if it proves that it would have made the same decision in the absence of an impermissible motive, whereas under the District Court's approach, the employer's proof in that respect only avoids equitable relief. We decide today that the Court of Appeals had the better approach, but that both courts erred in requiring the employer to make its proof by clear and convincing evidence.

The specification of the standard of causation under Title VII is a decision about the kind of conduct that violates that statute. According to Price Waterhouse, an employer violates Title VII only if it gives decisive consideration to an employee's gender, race, national origin, or religion in making a decision that affects that employee. On Price Waterhouse's theory, even if a plaintiff shows that her gender played a part in an employment decision, it is still her burden to show that the decision would have been different if the employer had not discriminated. In Hopkins' view, on the other hand, an employer violates the statute whenever it allows one of these attributes to play any part in an employment decision. Once a plaintiff shows that this occurred, according to Hopkins, the employer's proof that it would have made the same decision in the absence of discrimination can serve to limit equitable relief but not to avoid a finding of liability. We conclude that, as often happens, the truth lies somewhere in between.

To say that an employer may not take gender into account is not, however, the end of the matter, for that describes only one aspect of Title VII. The other important aspect of the statute is its preservation of an employer's remaining freedom of choice. We conclude that the preservation of this freedom means that an employer shall not be liable if it can prove that, even if it had not taken gender into account, it would have come to the same decision regarding a particular person. The statute's maintenance of employer prerogatives is evident from the statute itself and from its history, both in Congress and in this Court.

As to the employer's proof, in most cases, the employer should be able to present some objective evidence as to its probable decision in the absence of an impermissible motive. An employer may not prevail in a mixed-motives case by offering a legitimate and sufficient reason for its decision if that reason did not motivate it at the time of the decision. Finally, an employer may not meet its burden in such a case by merely showing that at the time of the decision it was motivated only in part by a legitimate reason. The very premise of a mixed-motives case is that a legitimate reason was present, and indeed, in this case, Price Waterhouse already has made this showing by convincing Judge Gesell that Hopkins' interpersonal problems were a legitimate concern. The employer instead must show that its legitimate reason, standing alone, would have induced it to make the same decision.

The courts below held that an employer who has allowed a discriminatory impulse to play a motivating part in an employment decision must prove by clear and convincing evidence that it would have made the same decision in the absence of discrimination. We are persuaded that the better rule is that the employer must make this showing by a preponderance of the evidence.

In finding that some of the partners' comments reflected sex stereotyping, the District Court relied in part on Dr. Fiske's expert testimony. Without directly impugning Dr. Fiske's credentials or qualifications, Price Waterhouse insinuates that a social psychologist is unable to identify sex stereotyping in evaluations without investigating whether those evaluations have a basis in reality. This argument comes too late. At trial, counsel for Price Waterhouse twice assured the court that he did not question Dr. Fiske's expertise and failed to challenge the legitimacy of her discipline. Without contradiction from Price Waterhouse, Fiske testified that she discerned sex stereotyping in the partners' evaluations of Hopkins and she further explained that it was part of her business to identify stereotyping in written documents. We are not inclined to accept petitioner's belated and unsubstantiated characterization of Dr. Fiske's testimony as "gossamer evidence" based only on "intuitive hunches" and of her detection of sex stereotyping as "intuitively divined." Nor are we disposed to adopt the dissent's dismissive attitude toward Dr. Fiske's field of study and toward her own professional integrity.

Indeed, we are tempted to say that Dr. Fiske's expert testimony was merely icing on Hopkins' cake. It takes no special training to discern sex stereotyping in a description of an aggressive female employee as requiring "a course at charm school." Nor, turning to Thomas Beyer's memorable advice to Hopkins, does it require expertise in psychology to know that, if an employee's flawed "interpersonal skills" can be corrected by a soft-hued suit or a new shade of lipstick, perhaps it is the employee's sex and not her interpersonal skills that has drawn the criticism.

Price Waterhouse also charges that Hopkins produced no evidence that sex stereotyping played a role in the decision to place her candidacy on hold. As we have stressed, however, Hopkins showed that the partnership solicited evaluations from all of the firm's partners; that it generally relied very heavily on such evaluations in making its decision; that some of the partners' comments were the product of stereotyping; and that the firm in no way disclaimed reliance on those particular comments, either in Hopkins' case or in the past. Certainly a plausible—and, one might say, inevitable—conclusion to draw from this set of circumstances is that the Policy Board in making its decision did in fact take into account all of the partners' comments, including the comments that were motivated by stereotypical notions about women's proper deportment.

Price Waterhouse appears to think that we cannot affirm the factual findings of the trial court without deciding that, instead of being overbearing and aggressive and curt, Hopkins is, in fact, kind and considerate and patient. If this is indeed its impression, petitioner misunderstands the theory on which Hopkins prevailed. The District Judge acknowledged that Hopkins' conduct justified complaints about her behavior as a senior manager. But he also concluded that the reactions of at least some of the partners were reactions to her as a *woman* manager. Where an evaluation is based on a subjective assessment of a person's strengths and weaknesses, it is simply not true that each evaluator will focus on, or even mention, the same weaknesses. Thus, even if we knew that Hopkins had "personality problems," this would not tell us that the partners who cast their evaluations of Hopkins in sex-based terms would have criticized her as sharply (or criticized her at all) if she had been a man. It is not our job to review the evidence and decide that the negative reactions to Hopkins were based on reality; our perception of Hopkins' character is irrelevant. We sit not to determine whether Ms. Hopkins is nice, but to decide whether the partners reacted negatively to her personality because she is a woman.

We hold that when a plaintiff in a Title VII case proves that her gender played a motivating part in an employment decision, the defendant may avoid a finding of liability only by proving by a preponderance of the evidence that it would have made the same decision even if it had not taken the plaintiff's gender into account. Because the courts below erred by deciding that the defendant must make this proof by clear and convincing evidence, we reverse the Court of Appeals' judgment against Price Waterhouse on liability and remand the case to that court for further proceedings.

Justice O'CONNOR, concurring in the judgment.

I agree with the plurality that, on the facts presented in this case, the burden of persuasion should shift to the employer to demonstrate by a preponderance of the evidence that it would have reached the same decision concerning Ann Hopkins' candidacy absent consideration of her gender. I further agree that this burden

> As *Price Waterhouse* was announced by a plurality of the Court, Justice O'Connor's concurrence was widely relied upon.

shift is properly part of the liability phase of the litigation. I thus concur in the judgment of the Court. My disagreement stems from the plurality's conclusions concerning the substantive requirement of causation under the statute and its broad statements regarding the applicability of the allocation of the burden of proof applied in this case.

In my view, in order to justify shifting the burden on the issue of causation to the defendant, a disparate treatment plaintiff must show by direct evidence that an illegitimate criterion was a substantial factor in the decision. Requiring that the plaintiff demonstrate that an illegitimate factor played a substantial role in the employment decision identifies those employment situations where the deterrent purpose of Title VII is most clearly implicated. As an evidentiary matter, where a plaintiff has made this type of strong showing of illicit motivation, the factfinder is entitled to presume that the employer's discriminatory animus made a difference to the outcome, absent proof to the contrary from the employer. Where a disparate treatment plaintiff has made such a showing, the burden then rests with the employer to convince the trier of fact that it is more likely than not that the decision would have been the same absent consideration of the illegitimate factor. The employer need not isolate the sole cause for the decision; rather it must demonstrate that with the illegitimate factor removed from the calculus, sufficient business reasons would have induced it to take the same employment action. This evidentiary scheme essentially requires the employer to place the employee in the same position he or she would have occupied absent discrimination. If the employer fails to carry this burden, the factfinder is justified in concluding that the decision was made "because of" consideration of the illegitimate factor and the substantive standard for liability under the statute is satisfied.

Thus, stray remarks in the workplace, while perhaps probative of sexual harassment cannot justify requiring the employer to prove that its hiring or promotion decisions were based on legitimate criteria. Nor can statements by non-decisionmakers, or statements by decisionmakers unrelated to the decisional process itself, suffice to satisfy the plaintiff's burden in this regard. In addition, in my view testimony such as Dr. Fiske's in this case, standing alone, would not justify shifting the burden of persuasion to the employer. Race and gender always "play a role" in an employment decision in the benign sense that these are human characteristics of which decisionmakers are aware and about which they may comment in a perfectly neutral and nondiscriminatory fashion. For example, in the context of this case, a mere reference to "a lady candidate" might show that gender "played a role" in the decision, but by no means could support a rational factfinder's inference that the decision was made "because of" sex. What is required is what Ann Hopkins showed here: direct evidence that decisionmakers placed substantial negative reliance on an illegitimate criterion in reaching their decision.

> Justice O'Connor's requirement that the plaintiff produce direct evidence to proceed in a mixed-motives case became a source of substantial controversy.

■ NOTES AND QUESTIONS

1. *Price Waterhouse* provides excellent guidance on what type of evidence constitutes "direct evidence" of discrimination. Do you agree with the Court here that Hopkins was able to establish direct evidence?

2. The *Price Waterhouse* decision quickly came under fire by civil rights groups, and part of the decision was ultimately reversed by the Civil Rights Act of 1991, as discussed in greater detail below. For a personal account by the plaintiff in *Price Waterhouse*, as well as a brief discussion of the parts of *Price Waterhouse* that were reversed by the Civil Rights Act of 1991, see Ann Hopkins, Price Waterhouse v. Hopkins: *A Personal Account of a Sexual Discrimination Plaintiff,* 22 Hofstra Lab. & Emp. L.J. 357 (2005).

3. Would a comment that an employee was an "old, gray-haired fart" made by a high-ranking company official a year prior to that employee's termination constitute direct evidence? Given the passage of time between the comment and the adverse act, at least one court said no. Jackson v. Cal-Western Packaging Corp., 602 F.3d 374 (5th Cir. 2010). Do you agree?

4. Employers have generally become more familiar with discrimination laws over the years, and it is less common to have direct evidence of discrimination. Where might such claims still arise? Sometimes, employers see the need to discriminate on the basis of some type of authenticity argument (e.g., hiring Italian waiters for an upscale Italian restaurant); other employers see safety as a rationale to discriminate in certain circumstances (e.g., no one over seventy allowed to work as an airline pilot). Can you think of other instances where employers might feel that they have a legitimate basis to discriminate?

5. Do you agree with Justice O'Connor that *direct* evidence is needed to proceed under a motivating factor analysis?

6. For an interesting outlook on female law students' and lawyers' encounters with gender norms during law school and in practice, see Ann Bartow, *Still Not Behaving like Gentlemen*, 49 U. Kan. L. Rev. 809 (2001); Ann Bartow, *Some Dumb Girl Syndrome: Challenging and Subverting Destructive Stereotypes of Female Attorneys*, 11 Wm. & Mary J. Women & L. 221 (2005); and Lani Guinier et al., *Becoming Gentlemen: Women's Experiences at One Ivy League Law School*, 143 U. Pa. L. Rev. 1 (1994).

7. Much controversy surrounded world-famous chef and television personality, Paula Deen, with regard to alleged discrimination claims brought by a former employee. Deen was sued by a former manager of one of her restaurants for racial harassment. In her deposition in the case, Deen admitted to having used the "N" word in a conversation with her husband but maintained that she has not used that particular slur in a while. Would use of this language constitute direct evidence of discrimination? Why or why not? Would we need to know more? *See* Alan Duke, *Celeb Chef Paula Deen Admits Using "N word,"* CNN (July 3, 2013), http://www.cnn.com/2013/06/19/showbiz/paula-deen- racial-slur/index.html; Dorothy Brown, Op-Ed., *Paula Deen's Alternative Universe*, CNN (Mar. 17, 2014), http://www.cnn.com/2014/03/04/opinion/brown-deen-12-years-a-slave/ (noting how Paula Deen's own words demonstrate a bizarre misreading of slavery's damage and lasting racial implications).

Interactive Problem

Looking back at the interactive problem, suppose that Bob overheard his direct supervisor tell another supervisor at the company that he "never really liked Bob because he is white, and whites just don't fit in here at the company." Suppose further that Bob is terminated the next day. Would the direct supervisor's comment constitute direct evidence of discrimination? Why or why not?

Practice and Procedural Tip

8: Defenses to Direct Evidence of Discrimination

It may seem that when a plaintiff is able to uncover direct evidence of discrimination, the case is lost for the defendant. After all, once discriminatory intent has been established, shouldn't the plaintiff automatically prevail? In many instances, the presence of direct evidence of discrimination does put the defendant in an unwinnable position. Nonetheless, there are at least two popular procedural ways that a defendant may either avoid liability or minimize its impact where the plaintiff has established direct evidence of discrimination. *See, e.g.,* E. Ericka Kelsaw, *Help Wanted: 23.5 Million Unemployed Americans Need Not Apply*, 34 Berkeley J. Emp. & Lab. L. 1, 56–60 (2013) (discussing the bona fide occupational qualification defense).

First, the defendant can acknowledge that it discriminated, but argue that the discrimination was a bona fide occupational qualification (BFOQ). The BFOQ defense will be discussed in detail in Chapter 7, but it is worth noting here as well. Section 703e(1) of Title VII provides that "[n]otwithstanding any other provision of this title . . . it shall not be an unlawful employment practice for an employer to hire and employ employees . . . on the basis of religion, sex, or national origin in those certain instances where religion, sex, or national origin is a bona fide occupational qualification reasonably necessary to the normal operation of that particular business or enterprise."

As we will see later in this text, the Supreme Court has interpreted the BFOQ to apply to Title VII claims where the discrimination is (1) job related and (2) goes to the essence or central mission of what the employer does. A classic example of the BFOQ would apply where a theatrical playhouse would want to hire a woman to play the role of Joan of Arc to bring authenticity to a production. Keep in mind, however, that the BFOQ's statutory language does not apply to race or color. The defendant has the difficult burden of establishing a BFOQ. Where the defendant is successful in doing so, it is a complete bar to recovery for the plaintiff. Thus, even where direct evidence of discrimination is present in a case, the employer may still be able to prevail by conceding discrimination and arguing for a BFOQ.

Second, the defendant can also limit damages in a case involving direct evidence of discrimination by successfully arguing that it would have taken the same adverse action against the plaintiff even in the absence of any discriminatory motive. These types of "mixed-motives" cases occur where a defendant has both a legitimate and illegitimate rationale for taking a particular employment action. *See* 42 U.S.C. § 2000e–2(m). It is important to keep in mind that this type of argument will not be a complete bar to recovery for the plaintiff, but will minimize the defendant's liability exposure as outlined below.

D. Mixed-Motives Analysis/Civil Rights Act of 1991

Along with several other Supreme Court cases issued around the same time, the *Price Waterhouse* decision resulted in substantial controversy and debate. Congress ultimately decided to intervene as part of the Civil Rights Act of 1991, which amends Title VII. This statute now provides that

> an unlawful employment practice is established when the complaining party demonstrates that race, color, religion, sex, or national origin was a motivating factor for any employment practice, even though other factors also motivated the practice.

42 U.S.C. § 2000e–2(m).

Thus, a plaintiff will prevail where she can show that a protected characteristic was a "motivating factor" in an employment decision. If a plaintiff proceeds under this provision, however, the employer will have a limited affirmative defense available that can restrict the relief the plaintiff receives. If an employer is able to "demonstrat[e] that [it] would have taken the same action in the absence of the impermissible motivating factor," 42 U.S.C. § 2000e–5(g)(2)(B), the plaintiff's relief will be limited to declaratory relief, injunctive relief, attorneys' fees and costs. *Id.* Notably, compensatory and punitive damages are not available where the defendant has successfully established this defense.

After the Civil Rights Act of 1991, Title VII now provides for this type of intermediate approach. In a traditional disparate treatment case, a plaintiff can prevail by showing—either through direct or circumstantial evidence—that she was discriminated against because of a protected characteristic. Alternatively, the plaintiff can argue that a protected characteristic was a motivating factor in the case. If the plaintiff successfully prevails on the motivating factor argument, the defendant can limit the damages available to the plaintiff by establishing (through an affirmative defense) that it would have taken the same action absent the discriminatory motive.

The classic mixed-motives situation arises where there is both a legitimate and illegitimate rationale for the employment decision, for example, where an employer dislikes Hispanic employees, and a particular Hispanic worker is also frequently tardy to work. Thus, the employer has a discriminatory motivation, but likely would have taken an adverse action against the employee even in the absence of this motivation. The law is clear that the employer is not completely absolved of liability in these situations, but the employee cannot recover compensatory and punitive damages.

Desert Palace, Inc. v. Costa
539 U.S. 90 (2003)

Justice Thomas delivered the opinion of the Court.

The question before us in this case is whether a plaintiff must present direct evidence of discrimination in order to obtain a mixed-motive instruction under Title VII of the Civil Rights Act of 1964. We hold that direct evidence is not required.

In *Price Waterhouse v. Hopkins*, 490 U.S. 228 (1989), the Court considered whether an employment decision is made "because of" sex in a "mixed-motive" case, *i.e.*, where both legitimate and illegitimate reasons motivated the decision. The Court concluded that, under § 2000e–2(a)(1), an employer could "avoid a finding of liability . . . by proving that it would have made the same decision even if it had not allowed gender to play such a role." *Id.* at 244. The Court was divided, however, over the predicate question of when the burden of proof may be shifted to an employer to prove the affirmative defense. [U]nder Justice O'Connor's view, "the burden on the issue of causation" would shift to the employer only where "a disparate treatment plaintiff [could] show by *direct evidence* that an illegitimate criterion was a substantial factor in the decision." *Ibid.* (emphasis added).

Two years after *Price Waterhouse*, Congress passed the 1991 Act "in large part [as] a response to a series of decisions of this Court interpreting the Civil Rights Acts of 1866 and 1964." *Landgraf v. USI Film Products*, 511 U.S. 244, 250 (1994). In particular, § 107 of the 1991 Act, which is at issue in this case, "respond[ed]" to *Price Waterhouse* by "setting forth standards applicable in 'mixed motive' cases" in two new statutory provisions.

[In this case, p]etitioner Desert Palace, Inc., dba Caesar's Palace Hotel & Casino of Las Vegas, Nevada, employed respondent Catharina Costa as a warehouse worker and heavy equipment operator. Respondent was the only woman in this job and in her local Teamsters bargaining unit.

Respondent experienced a number of problems with management and her co-workers that led to an escalating series of disciplinary sanctions, including informal rebukes, a denial of privileges, and suspension. Petitioner finally terminated respondent after she was involved in a physical altercation in a warehouse elevator with fellow Teamsters member Herbert Gerber. Petitioner disciplined both employees because the facts surrounding the incident were in dispute, but Gerber, who had a clean disciplinary record, received only a 5-day suspension.

Respondent subsequently filed this lawsuit against petitioner in the United States District Court for the District of Nevada, asserting claims of sex discrimination and sexual harassment under Title VII. The District Court dismissed the sexual harassment claim, but allowed the claim for sex discrimination to go to the jury. At trial, respondent presented evidence that (1) she was singled out for "intense 'stalking'" by one of her supervisors, (2) she received harsher discipline than men for the same conduct, (3) she was treated less favorably than men in the assignment of overtime, and (4) supervisors repeatedly "stack[ed]" her disciplinary record and "frequently used or tolerated" sex-based slurs against her.

This case provides us with the first opportunity to consider the effects of the 1991 Act on jury instructions in mixed-motive cases. Specifically, we must decide whether a plaintiff must present direct evidence of discrimination

Warehouse Facility

in order to obtain a mixed-motive instruction under 42 U.S.C. § 2000e–2(m). Our precedents make clear that the starting point for our analysis is the statutory text. Section 2000e–2(m) unambiguously states that a plaintiff need only "demonstrat[e]" that an employer used a forbidden consideration with respect to "any employment practice." On its face, the statute does not mention, much less require, that a plaintiff make a heightened showing through direct evidence. Indeed, petitioner concedes as much.

> As the Court states, the primary question in this case is whether the "plaintiff must present direct evidence of discrimination in order to obtain a mixed-motive instruction."

Moreover, Congress explicitly defined the term "demonstrates" in the 1991 Act, leaving little doubt that no special evidentiary showing is required. Title VII defines the term "'demonstrates'" as to "mee[t] the burdens of production and persuasion." § 2000e(m). If Congress intended the term "'demonstrates'" to require that the "burdens of production and persuasion" be met by direct evidence or some other heightened showing, it could have made that intent clear by including language to that effect in § 2000e(m). Its failure to do so is significant, for Congress has been unequivocal when imposing heightened proof requirements in other circumstances, including in other provisions of Title 42.

In addition, Title VII's silence with respect to the type of evidence required in mixed-motive cases also suggests that we should not depart from the "[c]onventional rul[e] of civil litigation [that] generally appl[ies] in Title VII cases." That rule requires a plaintiff to prove his case "by a preponderance of the evidence," using "direct or circumstantial evidence," *Postal Service Bd. of Governors v. Aikens*, 460 U.S. 711 (1983). We have often acknowledged the utility of circumstantial evidence in discrimination cases. For instance, in *Reeves v. Sanderson Plumbing Products, Inc.*, 530 U.S. 133 (2000), we recognized that evidence that a defendant's explanation for an employment practice is "unworthy of credence" is "one form of *circumstantial evidence* that is probative of intentional discrimination." *Id.* at 147 (emphasis added). The reason for treating circumstantial and direct evidence alike is both clear and deep rooted: "Circumstantial evidence is not only sufficient, but may also be more certain, satisfying and persuasive than direct evidence." *Rogers v. Missouri Pacific R. R. Co.*, 352 U.S. 500 (1957).

In order to obtain an instruction under § 2000e–2(m), a plaintiff need only present sufficient evidence for a reasonable jury to conclude, by a preponderance of the evidence, that "race, color, religion, sex, or national origin was a motivating factor for any employment practice." Because direct evidence of discrimination is not required in mixed-motive cases, the Court of Appeals correctly concluded that the District Court did not abuse its discretion in giving a mixed-motive instruction to the jury. Accordingly, the judgment of the Court of Appeals is affirmed.

It is so ordered.

Justice O'Connor, concurring.

I join the Court's opinion. In my view, prior to the Civil Rights Act of 1991, the evidentiary rule we developed to shift the burden of persuasion in mixed-motive cases was appropriately applied only where a disparate treatment plaintiff "demonstrated by direct evidence that an illegitimate factor played a substantial role" in an adverse employment decision. *Price Waterhouse v. Hopkins*, 490 U.S. 228, 275 (1989) (O'CONNOR, J., concurring in judgment). This showing triggered "the deterrent purpose of the statute" and permitted a reasonable fact-finder to conclude that "absent further explanation, the employer's discriminatory motivation 'caused' the employment decision."

> Justice O'Connor acknowledges that her opinion in *Price Waterhouse* is no longer good law after the 1991 amendments.

As the Court's opinion explains, in the Civil Rights Act of 1991, Congress codified a new evidentiary rule for mixed-motive cases arising under Title VII. I therefore agree with the Court that the District Court did not abuse its discretion in giving a mixed-motive instruction to the jury.

■ NOTES AND QUESTIONS

1. As *Costa* clearly shows, the Civil Rights Act of 1991 resolves any dispute as to whether a plaintiff can use the motivating factor analysis, and provides a limited affirmative defense for employers. *See* Harold S. Lewis, Jr., *Walking the Walk of Plain Text: The Supreme Court's Markedly More Solicitous Treatment of Title VII Following the Civil Rights Act of 1991*, 49 St. Louis U. L.J. 1081 (2005) (discussing the 1991 amendment's impact on Title VII).

2. *Costa* also clarifies that direct evidence of discrimination is no longer needed to receive a mixed-motives jury instruction in a Title VII case.

3. Many commentators thought that *Costa* went even further, however, and argued that the Civil Rights Act and the *Costa* decision would open up the floodgates to litigation. If direct evidence is no longer needed to proceed in a mixed-motives Title VII case, would this invite additional litigation?

4. Of particular note in *Costa* is the Court's emphasis on the importance of circumstantial evidence. As the Court notes, "[c]ircumstantial evidence is not only sufficient, but may also be more certain, satisfying and persuasive than direct evidence." Can you envision situations where circumstantial evidence would be more persuasive than direct evidence?

5. It has also been argued that, after *Costa*, the *McDonnell Douglas* framework is no longer relevant. *See* William R. Corbett, McDonnell Douglas, *1973-2003: May You Rest In Peace?*, 6 U. Pa. J. Lab. & Emp. L. 199 (2003). *But see* Martin J. Katz, *Reclaiming* McDonnell Douglas, 83 Notre Dame L. Rev. 109 (2007) (defending the *McDonnell Douglas* framework). Do you agree? Rather than applying the framework, should a court simply weigh the evidence to determine whether the plaintiff has satisfied her burden by a preponderance of the evidence?

6. Justice O'Connor acknowledges in her concurrence that the evidentiary burden portion of her opinion in *Price Waterhouse* is no longer good law after the 1991 amendments to Title VII.

Interactive Problem

Looking back at the facts of the interactive problem, would Bob be able to establish that race was a "motivating factor" in the decision to terminate him? Could he also establish "but-for" causation? If you were the plaintiff's attorney handling the case, would you ask for a mixed-motives jury instruction, or would you seek to instruct the jury on but-for causation? Would you ask for both of these instructions?

Practice and Procedural Tip

9: Handling Mixed-Motives Cases

A key procedural issue that arises in mixed-motives cases is *when* a plaintiff would want to seek this type of jury instruction. On its face, the answer might be "always." After all, it is easier to show that a protected characteristic was a "motivating factor" in a decision rather than the "sole" factor. But a deeper look at the question reveals that the answer is not always this straightforward. *See* Kaitlin Picco, *The Mixed-Motive Mess: Defining and Applying a Mixed-Motive Framework*, 26 ABA J. Lab. & Emp. L. 461 (2011).

In those instances where a plaintiff has a particularly strong case, that plaintiff may be somewhat leery of including a mixed-motives jury instruction request. It is important to keep in mind that when the plaintiff proceeds in a mixed-motives case, the defendant has the ability to limit damages if it can show that it would have taken the same action even in light of the unlawful motivation. From a practical standpoint, allowing the jury to consider this "intermediate" approach might be problematic, as—in an effort to reach conciliation—jurors might rush to this middle ground. The elimination of punitive and compensatory damages (where the defendant successfully establishes its defense) can thus be a powerful disincentive to employees to proceed under this theory.

It is also important to keep in mind that from a procedural standpoint it is entirely possible to present to the jury both options—that discrimination was the sole cause or that discrimination was only a motivating factor for the employment decision. The two different theories can thus be given to the jury, and they can decide which (if either) is appropriate. Again, however, while including the motivating factor instruction may be tempting from the plaintiff's side, this instruction also comes with the possibility that the jury will reach this middle ground in an attempt to quickly settle on a verdict and thus potentially limit the damages to the plaintiff.

Another interesting aspect that has not largely been addressed in the literature is the question of whether an employer might ever want to request that a mixed-motives instruction be given to the jury. This may seem counterintuitive—why would the defendant want to create a lower burden for the plaintiff? The answer again comes in the form of damages. In those cases where the facts are particularly bad for the employer, it may want to consider giving the jury a middle ground in the form of the motivating factor analysis. In this way, the employer can attempt to limit its potential exposure to liability.

In the case below, one appellate court merges the *McDonnell Douglas* and *Desert Palace* frameworks into a single test. The decision provides an interesting analysis of how to apply these two critical Supreme Court decisions. While the decision is instructive, the appellate courts have taken varying approaches to their application of *Desert Palace* to employment discrimination cases.

Keelan v. Majesco Software, Inc.
407 F.3d 332 (5th Cir. 2005)

DeMoss, Circuit Judge:

This Circuit has adopted use of a "modified *McDonnell Douglas* approach" in cases where the mixed-motive analysis may apply. *See Rachid v. Jack In The Box, Inc.*, 376 F.3d 305, 312 (5th Cir. 2004). After the plaintiff has met his four-element prima facie case and the defendant has responded with a legitimate nondiscriminatory reason for the adverse employment action:

> [T]he plaintiff must then offer sufficient evidence to create a genuine issue of material fact either (1) that the defendant's reason is not true, but is instead a pretext for discrimination (pretext alternative); or (2) that the defendant's reason, while true, is only one of the reasons for its conduct, and another motivating factor is the plaintiff's protected characteristic (mixed-motive[s] alternative).

Id. (internal quotation marks and citations omitted). The question of pretext versus mixed-motive treatment is only reached after a plaintiff has met his *prima facie* showing under the modified *McDonnell Douglas* standard and the defendant has responded with a legitimate nondiscriminatory reason. *Id.* If the plaintiff demonstrates the protected characteristic was a motivating factor in the employment decision (meets the mixed-motive showing), which pursuant to *Desert Palace* may be achieved through circumstantial evidence, *Rachid*, 376 F.3d at 311–12, "it then falls to the defendant to prove that the same adverse employment decision would have been made regardless of discriminatory animus. If the employer fails to carry this burden, plaintiff prevails." *Id.* at 312 (internal quotation marks and citation omitted). In *Rachid*, this Court determined that enough fact issues still remained at the summary judgment stage, after plaintiff had met his *prima facie* case and the employer had replied with a nondiscriminatory reason, such that Rachid's case could not be adequately determined to be either pretext or mixed-motive. *Id.* at 316.

Appellants desire that their case be analyzed under *Desert Palace*, which is a mixed-motive case, but they also erroneously argue that *Desert Palace* changed *McDonnell Douglas*, which governs disparate treatment cases premised on pretext. The district court acknowledged Appellants' request. However, the court denied such mixed-motive treatment primarily because it found "no evidence that Majesco had legitimate *and* illegitimate reasons for discharging Keelan."

Both Keelan and Sullivan failed to raise sufficient evidence to support their *prima facie* cases of discrimination. Therefore, this case is distinguishable from *Rachid* because here the district court did not need to reach the question of whether Appellants created fact issues on either or both of pretext or mixed-motive. We thus find no error.

■ NOTES AND QUESTIONS

1. In *Majesco*, the Fifth Circuit merges the frameworks of *McDonnell Douglas* and *Costa* into a single test that occurs at the pretext stage of the analysis. Do you agree with this approach?

2. Should the courts always analyze employment discrimination cases under this type of merged analysis, or, as the Fifth Circuit suggests, only use this type of framework where there is some type of evidence of mixed motives? *See* David A. Drachsler, *Proof of Disparate Treatment Under Federal Civil Rights Law*, 56 Lab. L.J. 229 (2005).

3. As noted above, the courts have taken varying approaches to the application of *Costa* to employment discrimination cases. *Majesco* provides an interesting look at one appellate court's approach.

E. After-Acquired Evidence

The mixed-motive analysis and *Costa* decision represent a specific type of case—where the employer has both legitimate and illegitimate reasons for taking an adverse action *at the time that decision is made*. But what happens when the defendant takes an adverse action based solely on discriminatory motives, and information later comes to light that would have justified the employer's decision? Specifically, what if the employer does not learn until much later (sometimes even at trial) that the employee was acting inappropriately while employed?

These types of situations represent after-acquired evidence cases. In both the mixed-motives case and the after-acquired evidence case, the employee has acted in a way that justifies the adverse action. It is the *timing* of the employer learning about the employee's behavior that distinguishes these two types of situations.

McKennon v. Nashville Banner Publishing Co.
513 U.S. 352 (1995)

Justice KENNEDY delivered the opinion of the Court.

The question before us is whether an employee discharged in violation of the Age Discrimination in Employment Act of 1967 is barred from all relief when, after her discharge, the employer discovers evidence of wrongdoing that, in any event, would have led to the employee's termination on lawful and legitimate grounds.

For some 30 years, petitioner Christine McKennon worked for respondent Nashville Banner Publishing Company. She was discharged, the Banner claimed, as part of a work force reduction plan necessitated by cost considerations. McKennon, who was 62 years old when she lost her job, thought another reason explained her dismissal: her age. She filed suit in the United States District Court for the Middle District of Tennessee, alleging that her discharge violated the Age Discrimination in Employment Act of 1967.

In preparation of the case, the Banner took McKennon's deposition. She testified that, during her final year of employment, she had copied several confidential documents bearing upon the company's financial condition. She had access to these records as secretary to the Banner's comptroller. McKennon took the copies home and showed them to her husband. Her motivation, she averred, was an apprehension she was about to be fired because of her age. When she became concerned about her job, she removed and copied the documents for "insurance" and "protection." A few days after these deposition disclosures, the Banner sent McKennon a letter declaring that removal and copying of the records was in violation of her job responsibilities and advising her (again) that she was terminated. The Banner's letter also recited that had it known of McKennon's misconduct it would have discharged her at once for that reason.

For purposes of summary judgment, the Banner conceded its discrimination against McKennon. The District Court granted summary judgment for the Banner, holding that McKennon's misconduct was grounds for her termination and that neither backpay nor any other remedy was available to her under the ADEA. The United States Court of Appeals for the Sixth Circuit affirmed on the same rationale. We now reverse.

We shall assume, as summary judgment procedures require us to assume, that the sole reason for McKennon's initial discharge was her age, a discharge violative of the ADEA. Our further premise is that the misconduct revealed by the deposition was so grave that McKennon's immediate discharge would have followed its disclosure in any event.

As we have said, the case comes to us on the express assumption that an unlawful motive was the sole basis for the firing. McKennon's misconduct was not discovered until after she had been fired. The employer could not have been motivated by knowledge it did not have and it cannot now claim that the employee was fired for the nondiscriminatory reason. Mixed motive cases are inapposite here, except to the important extent they underscore the necessity of determining the employer's motives in ordering the discharge, an essential element in determining whether the employer violated the federal antidiscrimination law.

> The Court notes here the distinction between mixed-motive and after-acquired evidence cases.

Our inquiry is not at an end, however, for even though the employer has violated the Act, we must consider how the after-acquired evidence of the employee's wrongdoing bears on the specific remedy to be ordered. The proper boundaries of remedial relief in the general class of cases where, after termination, it is discovered that the employee has engaged in wrongdoing must be addressed by the judicial system in the ordinary course of further decisions, for the factual permutations and the equitable considerations they raise will vary from case to case. We do conclude that here, and as a general rule in cases of this type, neither reinstatement nor front pay is an appropriate remedy. It would be both inequitable and pointless to order the reinstatement of someone the employer would have terminated, and will terminate, in any event and upon lawful grounds.

The proper measure of backpay presents a more difficult problem. Resolution of this question must give proper recognition to the fact that an ADEA violation has occurred which must be deterred and compensated without undue infringement upon the employer's rights and prerogatives. The object of compensation is to restore the employee to the position he or she would have been in absent the discrimination, but that principle is difficult to apply with precision where there is after-acquired evidence of wrongdoing that would have led to termination on legitimate grounds had the employer known about it. Once an employer learns about employee wrongdoing that would lead to a legitimate discharge, we cannot require the employer to ignore the information, even if it is acquired during the course of discovery in a suit against the employer and even if the information might have gone undiscovered absent the suit. The beginning point in the trial court's formulation of a remedy should be calculation of backpay from the date of the unlawful discharge to the date the new information was discovered. In determining the appropriate order for relief, the court can consider taking into further account extraordinary equitable circumstances that affect the legitimate interests of either party. An absolute rule barring any recovery of backpay, however, would undermine the ADEA's objective of forcing employers to consider and examine their motivations, and of penalizing them for employment decisions that spring from age discrimination.

> In after-acquired evidence cases, backpay is cut off when the employer learns of the improper behavior.

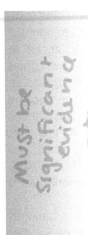

(handwritten margin note: Must be significant evidence)

■ NOTES AND QUESTIONS

1. *McKennon* emphasizes the important distinction between mixed-motives cases and after-acquired evidence cases. In a mixed-motives case, the employer relies on an employee's misconduct in making the employment decision. In after-acquired evidence cases, the employer does not learn of the inappropriate employee conduct until after the decision is made. The type of evidence typically uncovered in an after-acquired evidence case can vary, but includes such things as lying on a job application or making material misrepresentations in a résumé. *See generally* Sachin S. Pandya, *Unpacking the Employee-Misconduct Defense,* 14 U. Pa. J. Bus. L. 867 (2012) (examining the arguments for and against the defense and arguing that there is "no sound reason" for "continuing to apply it").

2. Note the distinction in damages between mixed-motives and after-acquired evidence cases. In particular, the Court here holds that the plaintiff in an after-acquired evidence case may be entitled to some backpay. In a mixed-motives case, the plaintiff will not receive any backpay if the defendant is successful in proving its affirmative defense. Does it make sense to have these two different recovery regimes for these two different types of cases?

3. Note that after firing McKennon, the defendant learned of the plaintiff's inappropriate conduct. It then terminated her again. Was this the right procedural decision? Did it need to take this action? Does it make any sense to fire the plaintiff twice?

 *Interactive Problem*

Looking back at the interactive problem, assume that during discovery, the company learns that Bob misrepresented on his employment application that he was a college graduate. Under *McKennon*, could this affect the outcome or damages in the case? In what way?

Class Exercise: Defending a Lawsuit

Assume that you represent a Fortune 500 company, and that you are sued by a female employee for sex discrimination after she has been terminated. Your internal investigation reveals that there is a strong possibility that discriminatory motivations were in play as part of the adverse decision. In light of *McKennon*, what type of evidence could you seek in discovery to try to limit your potential liability? What documents would you ask for, and what other investigation could you undertake? Are there any risks in probing too much into the employee's background?

F. Intentional Discrimination Framework: Summary Review

As seen throughout this chapter, analyzing intentional discrimination claims can be a complex endeavor. *See generally* Brian S. Clarke, *A Better Route Through the Swamp: Causal Coherence in Disparate Treatment Doctrine*, 65 Rutgers L. Rev. 723 (2013) (arguing that the many routes involved in disparate treatment cases are imperfect and proposing a new, more unified route). It can be helpful to briefly summarize the way that the courts and litigants typically review these claims.

First, as discussed above, the most common form of discrimination involves allegations based on circumstantial evidence of discrimination. Where this occurs, the plaintiff has the burden of persuasion of establishing the four factors set forth in the *McDonnell Douglas* test. This includes establishing that (a) the plaintiff was a member of a protected class; (b) she was qualified for the job; (c) she suffered an adverse action; and (d) there is some other evidence of discrimination in the case. Once the plaintiff carries the burden of persuasion of establishing the four elements of the prima facie case, an inference of discrimination arises, and the defendant must show (through a burden of production) that there was a legitimate nondiscriminatory reason for the adverse action. If the defendant successfully articulates this reason, the inference of discrimination drops from the case. The burden of persuasion—which remains with the plaintiff throughout—is then to establish that the legitimate nondiscriminatory reason is pretextual for true discrimination.

The *McDonnell Douglas* test can be avoided where the plaintiff can show direct evidence of discrimination in the case. Where direct evidence is present, there is no room for inference or presumption on the issue of discriminatory intent (and thus no need to consider the *McDonnell Douglas* factors). Direct evidence often comes in the form of discriminatory comments. To be considered direct evidence, such comments must be related to the protected class, proximate in time, made by an individual with authority to take the employment decision, and related to the employment decision at issue. One major defense to direct evidence of discrimination is the bona fide occupational qualification (BFOQ) defense—an affirmative defense that will be discussed in greater detail in Chapter 7.

One other possible approach includes a mixed-motives analysis, where the plaintiff establishes that discrimination was a motivating factor in the employer's decision, rather than the sole cause of the adverse action. In these cases, the employer can limit the plaintiff's relief by affirmatively demonstrating that it would have taken the same adverse action in the absence of the impermissible motive.

Finally, it is also important to consider after-acquired evidence cases. These claims typically arise where the defendant discovers—after taking the alleged discriminatory adverse action—that the worker had engaged in some type of misconduct. In these cases, damages are cut off on the date of the employer's discovery of the misconduct.

It should be noted that these different types of claims are not mutually exclusive. Thus, a plaintiff can pursue an employment discrimination case by alleging both direct and circumstantial evidence of discrimination. Similarly, the plaintiff could maintain that discrimination was both the sole factor in the employer's decision as well as a motivating rationale. Numerous strategic considerations factor into how the plaintiff will ultimately frame her cause of action.

It can be helpful to review this framework in a flow chart, which is set forth below:

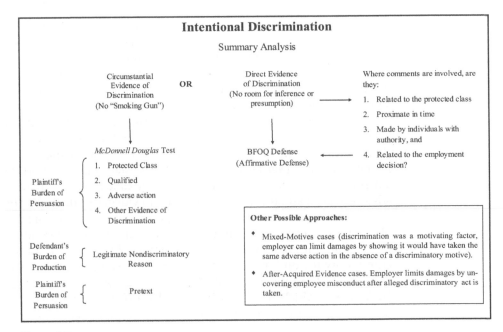

Figure 3.1

G. Systemic Litigation

When we talk about systemic litigation in the employment context, we are referring to claims that are brought on behalf of multiple individuals. Much litigation involves only a single plaintiff filing suit. Other claims, however, can involve numerous litigants filing against the same employer. As Professor Melissa Hart has correctly observed, "[c]lass litigation has the added benefit that it can go beyond an individual instance of discrimination to challenge the intrusion of both conscious and unconscious discrimination into the culture and structure of the workplace." Melissa Hart, *Subjective Decisionmaking and Unconscious Discrimination*, 56 ALA. L. REV. 741, 778 (2005). Though the same basic principles for analyzing employment discrimination claims apply in the systemic context, these types of claims are important to consider because they do involve unique procedural considerations.

From a more practical standpoint, systemic litigation also deserves special attention. If the number of plaintiffs in a particular suit is large enough, the potential liability to the employer can be devastating. Indeed, successful systemic litigation can threaten the business itself. Employers should thus be very cautious of these types of claims, cognizant of how to prevent them, and aware of the procedural avenues that must be pursued.

It is also important to understand the two different types of systemic claims that exist. First, the government (typically the DOJ or EEOC) can bring suit on behalf of multiple individuals alleging discrimination against a single employer. When the government brings this type of systemic suit, it is clear that it is not subject to the requirements of Federal Rule of Civil Procedure 23 with which private litigants must comply. This means that the common class-action requirements like numerosity and commonality do not apply to the government. Thus, for example, the government can bring a claim on behalf of four or five individuals without any concern over an objection to numerosity.

The second type of class-action claim that can arise occurs in the private litigation context. These types of claims occur where many individuals file suit—as part of a common claim—against an employer. In these types of suits, many courts require the plaintiffs to satisfy the elements of Federal Rule of Civil Procedure 23(a) to certify the class. This rule provides that, as a prerequisite to class certification, the following elements must be satisfied:

(1) the class is so numerous that joinder of all members is impracticable;
(2) there are questions of law or fact common to the class;
(3) the claims or defenses of the representative parties are typical of the claims or defenses of the class; and
(4) the representative parties will fairly and adequately protect the interests of the class.

All of these factors are critical to pursuing a class-action claim in the employment discrimination context. Rules 23(a)(1) and 23(a)(2) can give discrimination plaintiffs particular trouble, however. The courts vary as to how many plaintiffs are necessary to satisfy the numerosity requirement, so an individual analysis of the particular jurisdiction is critical to understanding how many individuals are necessary in a particular case. It has been noted that, generally speaking, classes with over forty-one plaintiffs will be sufficient to meet this test. *See, e.g.*, Hillary Jo Baker, *No Good Deed Goes Unpunished: Protecting Gender Discrimination Named Plaintiffs from Employer Attacks*, 20 HASTINGS WOMEN'S L.J. 83, 91 (2009). Again, however, satisfying numerosity will depend on the specific facts of the case, and on the particular jurisdiction in which the case is filed.

Commonality is another potential stumbling block for plaintiffs in discrimination cases. How common must the claims be of the litigants involved in the case? Must the plaintiffs have worked at the same office location, or can plaintiffs pursue claims against various branches of a corporation across the country? These issues were addressed in a massive sex discrimination class-action case brought against Wal-Mart.

Wal-Mart Stores, Inc. v. Dukes
564 U.S. 338 (2011)

Justice SCALIA delivered the opinion of the Court.

We are presented with one of the most expansive class actions ever. The District Court and the Court of Appeals approved the certification of a class comprising about one and a half million plaintiffs, current and former female employees of petitioner Wal-Mart who allege that the discretion exercised by their local supervisors over pay and promotion matters violates Title VII by discriminating against women. In addition to injunctive and declaratory relief, the plaintiffs seek an award of backpay. We consider whether the certification of the plaintiff class was consistent with Federal Rules of Civil Procedure 23(a) and (b)(2).

Petitioner Wal-Mart is the Nation's largest private employer. It operates four types of retail stores throughout the country: Discount Stores, Supercenters, Neighborhood Markets, and Sam's Clubs. Those stores are divided into seven nationwide divisions, which in turn comprise 41 regions of 80 to 85 stores apiece. Each store has between 40 and 53 separate departments and 80 to 500 staff positions. In all, Wal-Mart operates approximately 3,400 stores and employs more than one million people.

Pay and promotion decisions at Wal-Mart are generally committed to local managers' broad discretion, which is exercised "in a largely subjective manner." *Dukes v. Wal-Mart Stores*, 222 F.R.D. 137, 145 (N.D. Cal. 2004). Local store managers may increase the wages of hourly employees (within limits) with only limited corporate oversight. As for salaried employees, such as store managers and their deputies, higher corporate authorities have discretion to set their pay within pre-established ranges.

> Is the size of the class a major factor in the Court's decision?

Promotions work in a similar fashion. Wal-Mart permits store managers to apply their own subjective criteria when selecting candidates as "support managers," which is the first step on the path to management. Admission to Wal-Mart's management training program, however, does require that a candidate meet certain objective criteria, including an above-average performance rating, at least one year's tenure in the applicant's current position, and a willingness to relocate. But except for those requirements, regional and district managers have discretion to use their own judgment when selecting candidates for management training. Promotion to higher office—e.g., assistant manager, co-manager, or store manager—is similarly at the discretion of the employee's superiors after prescribed objective factors are satisfied.

The named plaintiffs in this lawsuit, representing the 1.5 million members of the certified class, are three current or former Wal-Mart employees who allege that the company discriminated against them on the basis of their sex by denying them equal pay or promotions, in violation of Title VII.

These plaintiffs, respondents here, do not allege that Wal-Mart has any express corporate policy against the advancement of women. Rather, they claim that their local managers' discretion over pay and promotions is exercised disproportionately in favor of men, leading to an unlawful disparate impact on female employees, see 42 U.S.C. § 2000e–2(k). And, respondents say, because Wal-Mart is aware of this effect, its refusal to cabin its managers' authority amounts to disparate treatment, see § 2000e–2(a). Their complaint seeks injunctive and declaratory relief, punitive damages, and backpay. It does not ask for compensatory damages.

Importantly for our purposes, respondents claim that the discrimination to which they have been subjected is common to *all* Wal-Mart's female employees. The basic theory of their case is that a strong and uniform "corporate culture" permits bias against women to infect, perhaps subconsciously, the discretionary decisionmaking of each one of Wal-Mart's thousands of managers—thereby making every woman at the company the victim of one common discriminatory practice. Respondents therefore wish to litigate the Title VII claims of all female employees at Wal-Mart's stores in a nationwide class action.

Rule 23(a) ensures that the named plaintiffs are appropriate representatives of the class whose claims they wish to litigate. The Rule's four requirements—numerosity, commonality, typicality, and adequate representation—"effectively 'limit the class claims to those fairly encompassed by the named plaintiff's claims.'" *General Telephone Co. of Southwest v. Falcon,* 457 U.S. 147 (1982). The crux of this case is commonality—the rule requiring a plaintiff to show that "there are questions of law or fact common to the class." Rule 23(a)(2). That language is easy to misread, since "[a]ny competently crafted class complaint literally raises common 'questions.'" [Richard A.] Nagareda,

> Do you agree with the majority or the dissent on the question of whether the facts present sufficient "glue" to hold the class action together?

Class Certification in the Age of Aggregate Proof, 84 N.Y.U. L. REV. 97, 131–132 (2009). Their claims must depend upon a common contention—for example, the assertion of discriminatory bias on the part of the same supervisor. That common contention, moreover, must be of such a nature that it is capable of classwide resolution—which means that determination of its truth or falsity will resolve an issue that is central to the validity of each one of the claims in one stroke.

In this case, proof of commonality necessarily overlaps with respondents' merits contention that Wal-Mart engages in a *pattern or practice* of discrimination. That is so because, in resolving an individual's Title VII claim, the crux of the inquiry is "the reason for a particular employment decision," *Cooper v. Federal Reserve Bank of Richmond*, 467 U.S. 867, 876 (1984). Here respondents wish to sue about literally millions of employment decisions at once. Without some glue holding the alleged *reasons* for all those decisions together, it will be impossible to say that examination of all the class members' claims for relief will produce a common answer to the crucial question *why was I disfavored*.

This Court's opinion in *Falcon* describes how the commonality issue must be approached. There an employee who claimed that he was deliberately denied a promotion on account of race obtained certification of a class comprising all employees wrongfully denied promotions and all applicants wrongfully denied jobs. 457 U.S. at 152. We rejected that composite class for lack of commonality and typicality, explaining:

> Conceptually, there is a wide gap between (a) an individual's claim that he has been denied a promotion [or higher pay] on discriminatory grounds, and his otherwise unsupported allegation that the company has a policy of discrimination, and (b) the existence of a class of persons who have suffered the same injury as that individual, such that the individual's claim and the class claim will share common questions of law or fact and that the individual's claim will be typical of the class claims. *Id.* at 157–158.

Falcon suggested two ways in which that conceptual gap might be bridged. First, if the employer "used a biased testing procedure to evaluate both applicants for employment and incumbent employees, a class action on behalf of every applicant or employee who might have been prejudiced by the test clearly would satisfy the commonality and typicality requirements of Rule 23(a)." Second, "[s]ignificant proof that an employer operated under a general policy of discrimination conceivably could justify a class of both applicants and employees if the discrimination manifested itself in hiring and promotion practices in the same general fashion, such as through entirely subjective decisionmaking processes." We think that statement precisely describes respondents' burden in this case. The first manner of bridging the gap obviously has no application here; Wal-Mart has no testing procedure or other companywide evaluation method that can be charged with bias. The whole point of permitting discretionary decisionmaking is to avoid evaluating employees under a common standard.

The second manner of bridging the gap requires "significant proof" that Wal-Mart "operated under a general policy of discrimination." That is entirely absent here. Wal-Mart's announced policy forbids sex discrimination, and as the District Court recognized the company imposes penalties for denials of equal employment opportunity. The only evidence of a "general policy of discrimination" respondents produced was the testimony of Dr. William Bielby, their sociological expert. Relying on "social framework" analysis, Bielby testified that Wal-Mart has a "strong corporate culture," that makes it "vulnerable" to "gender bias." He could not, however, "determine with any specificity how regularly stereotypes play a meaningful role in employment decisions at Wal-Mart. At his deposition . . . Dr. Bielby conceded that he could not calculate whether 0.5 percent or 95 percent of the employment decisions at Wal-Mart might be determined by stereotyped thinking."

The only corporate policy that the plaintiffs' evidence convincingly establishes is Wal-Mart's "policy" of *allowing discretion* by local supervisors over employment matters. On its face, of course, that is just the opposite of a uniform employment practice that would provide the commonality needed for a class action; it is a policy *against having* uniform employment practices. It is also a very common and presumptively reasonable way of doing business—one that we have said "should itself raise no inference of discriminatory conduct," *Watson v. Fort Worth Bank & Trust*, 487 U.S. 977, 990 (1988).

Respondents have not identified a common mode of exercising discretion that pervades the entire company—aside from their reliance on Dr. Bielby's social frameworks analysis that we have rejected. In a company of Wal-Mart's size and geographical scope, it is quite unbelievable that all managers would exercise their discretion in a common way without some common direction. Respondents attempt to make that showing by means of statistical and anecdotal evidence, but their evidence falls well short. The statistical evidence consists primarily of regression analyses performed by Dr. Richard Drogin, a statistician, and Dr. Marc Bendick, a labor economist.

> As is the case here, statistical evidence can be critical in class action claims.

Even if they are taken at face value, these studies are insufficient to establish that respondents' theory can be proved on a classwide basis. In *Falcon*, we held that one named plaintiff's experience of discrimination was insufficient to infer that "discriminatory treatment is typical of [the employer's employment] practices." A similar failure of inference arises here. As Judge Ikuta observed in her dissent, "[i]nformation about disparities at the regional and national level does not establish the existence of disparities at individual stores, let alone raise the inference that a company-wide policy of discrimination is implemented by discretionary decisions at the store and district level." 603 F.3d at 637. A regional pay disparity, for example, may be attributable to only a small set of Wal-Mart stores, and cannot by itself establish the uniform, store-by-store disparity upon which the plaintiffs' theory of commonality depends.

Respondents' anecdotal evidence suffers from the same defects, and in addition is too weak to raise any inference that all the individual, discretionary personnel decisions are discriminatory. In *Teamsters v. United States*, 431 U.S. 324 (1977), in addition to substantial statistical evidence of company-wide discrimination, the Government (as plaintiff) produced about 40 specific accounts of racial discrimination from particular individuals. That number was significant because the company involved had only 6,472 employees, of whom 571 were minorities, and the class itself consisted of around 334 persons, *United States v. T.I.M.E.-D.C., Inc.,* 517 F.2d 299, 308 (C.A.5 1975), overruled on other grounds, *Teamsters, supra.* The 40 anecdotes thus represented roughly one account for every eight members of the class. Moreover, the Court of

Appeals noted that the anecdotes came from individuals "spread throughout" the company who "for the most part" worked at the company's operational centers that employed the largest numbers of the class members. 517 F.2d at 315, and n. 30. Here, by contrast, respondents filed some 120 affidavits reporting experiences of discrimination—about 1 for every 12,500 class members—relating to only some 235 out of Wal-Mart's 3,400 stores. 603 F.3d at 634 (Ikuta, J., dissenting). More than half of these reports are concentrated in only six States (Alabama, California, Florida, Missouri, Texas, and Wisconsin); half of all States have only one or two anecdotes; and 14 States have no anecdotes about Wal-Mart's operations at all. Even if every single one of these accounts is true, that would not demonstrate that the entire company "operate[s] under a general policy of discrimination," *Falcon, supra,* at 159, n. 15, which is what respondents must show to certify a companywide class.

Justice GINSBURG, with whom Justice BREYER, Justice SOTOMAYOR, and Justice KAGAN join, concurring in part and dissenting in part.

The District Court, recognizing that "one significant issue common to the class may be sufficient to warrant certification," found that the plaintiffs easily met that test. Absent an error of law or an abuse of discretion, an appellate tribunal has no warrant to upset the District Court's finding of commonality.

The District Court certified a class of "[a]ll women employed at any Wal-Mart domestic retail store at any time since December 26, 1998." 222 F.R.D. at 141–143 (internal quotation marks omitted). The named plaintiffs, led by Betty Dukes, propose to litigate, on behalf of the class, allegations that Wal-Mart discriminates on the basis of gender in pay and promotions. They allege that the company "[r]eli[es] on gender stereotypes in making employment decisions such as . . . promotion[s] [and] pay." Wal-Mart permits those prejudices to infect personnel decisions, the plaintiffs contend, by leaving pay and promotions in the hands of "a nearly all male managerial workforce" using "arbitrary and subjective criteria." Further alleged barriers

to the advancement of female employees include the company's requirement, "as a condition of promotion to management jobs, that employees be willing to relocate." Absent instruction otherwise, there is a risk that managers will act on the familiar assumption that women, because of their services to husband and children, are less mobile than men.

Women fill 70 percent of the hourly jobs in the retailer's stores but make up only "33 percent of management employees." 222 F.R.D. at 146. "[T]he higher one looks in the organization the lower the percentage of women." The plaintiffs' "largely uncontested descriptive statistics" also show that women working in the company's stores "are paid less than men in every region" and "that the salary gap widens over time even for men and women hired into the same jobs at the same time."

The District Court identified "systems for . . . promoting in-store employees" that were "sufficiently similar across regions and stores" to conclude that "the manner in which these systems affect the class raises issues that are common to all class members." The selection of employees for promotion to in-store management "is fairly characterized as a 'tap on the shoulder' process," in which managers have discretion about whose shoulders to tap. Vacancies are not regularly posted; from among those employees satisfying minimum qualifications, managers choose whom to promote on the basis of their own subjective impressions.

Wal-Mart's compensation policies also operate uniformly across stores, the District Court found. The retailer leaves open a $2 band for every position's hourly pay rate. Wal-Mart provides no standards or criteria for setting wages within that band, and thus does nothing to counter unconscious bias on the part of supervisors.

Wal-Mart's supervisors do not make their discretionary decisions in a vacuum. The District Court reviewed means Wal-Mart used to maintain a "carefully constructed . . . corporate culture," such as frequent meetings to reinforce the common way of thinking, regular transfers of managers between stores to ensure uniformity throughout the company, monitoring of stores "on a close and constant basis," and "Wal-Mart TV," "broadcas[t] . . . into all stores."

The plaintiffs' evidence, including class members' tales of their own experiences, suggests that gender bias suffused Wal-Mart's company culture. Among illustrations, senior management often refer to female associates as "little Janie Qs." One manager told an employee that "[m]en are here to make a career and women aren't." 222 F.R.D. at 166 (internal quotation marks omitted). A committee of female Wal-Mart executives concluded that "[s]tereotypes limit the opportunities offered to women."

Finally, the plaintiffs presented an expert's appraisal to show that the pay and promotions disparities at Wal-Mart "can be explained only by gender discrimination and not by . . . neutral variables." Using regression analyses, their expert, Richard Drogin, controlled for factors including, *inter alia*, job performance, length of time with the company, and the store where an employee worked. The results, the District Court found, were sufficient to raise an "inference of discrimination."

The District Court's identification of a common question, whether Wal-Mart's pay and promotions policies gave rise to unlawful discrimination, was hardly infirm. The practice of delegating to supervisors large discretion to make personnel decisions, uncontrolled by formal standards, has long been known to have the potential to produce disparate effects. Managers, like all humankind, may be prey to biases of which they are unaware. The risk of discrimination is heightened when those managers are predominantly of one sex, and are steeped in a corporate culture that perpetuates gender stereotypes.

Wal-Mart's delegation of discretion over pay and promotions is a policy uniform throughout all stores. The very nature of discretion is that people will exercise it in various ways. A system of delegated discretion, *Watson* held, is a practice actionable under Title VII when it produces discriminatory outcomes. A finding that Wal-Mart's pay and promotions practices in fact violate the law would be the first step in the usual order of proof for plaintiffs seeking individual remedies for company-wide discrimination. That each individual employee's unique circumstances will ultimately determine whether she is entitled to backpay or damages should not factor into the Rule 23(a)(2) determination.

> How much deference should be given to the district court to make the class determination?

■ NOTES AND QUESTIONS

1. Historical note. Sixty-two-year old Betty Dukes worked forty hours a week as a greeter at Wal-Mart. After eighteen years with the company, her yearly salary approached approximately $35,000. When she first began in 1994, she made about $5.00 an hour, which increased to approximately $16.00 at the time she brought the class action against Wal-Mart. After subtracting her living expenses and caring for her elderly mother, Dukes claimed that she barely had enough money to survive. *See* Dave Jamieson, *Betty Dukes, Renowned* Dukes v. Walmart *Plaintiff, Takes Her Fight Back to Capitol Hill*, HUFFINGTON POST (June 6, 2012, 4:46 P.M.), http://www.huffingtonpost.com/2012/06/20/betty-dukes-walmart-supreme- court_n_1613305.html.

2. The Court here seems to have imposed a high standard for commonality in class-action discrimination claims. Will it ever be possible for plaintiffs to meet this standard against massive corporations? *See* Suzette M. Malveaux, *How Goliath Won: The Future Implications of* Dukes v. Wal-Mart, 106 Nw. U. L. REV. ONLINE 34, 40 (2011), http://www.law.northwestern.edu/lawreview/colloquy/2011/18/ (finding it "hard to imagine what type and quantity of evidence would satisfy the new 'significant proof' standard for an employment discrimination case of large scope and magnitude"); George Rutherglen, Wal-Mart, AT&T Mobility, *and the Decline of the Deterrent Class Action*, 98 VA. L. REV. IN BRIEF 24 (2012) (suggesting that the frequency of class actions after *Wal-Mart* will diminish); Michael Selmi, *Theorizing Systemic Disparate Treatment Law: After* Wal-Mart v. Dukes, 32 BERKELEY J. EMP. & LAB. L. 477, 479 (2011) (noting that the *Wal-Mart* decision likely made nationwide class actions far more difficult to certify); A. Benjamin Spencer, *Class Actions, Heightened Commonality, and Declining Access to Justice*, 93 B.U. L. REV. 441, 447 (2013) (arguing that the heightened commonality standard makes it more difficult for plaintiffs to bring claims and have them heard).

3. The Court also seems to reject the plaintiff's statistical evidence. What type of statistical proof would have been more persuasive?

4. Assume that the plaintiffs were successful in certifying the class. How would the case be litigated? Would a massive class action on behalf of over a million plaintiffs effectively force Wal-Mart to settle the case?

5. If all one and a half million plaintiffs filed suit individually against Wal-Mart, would the company be in a better or worse position than if it had subjected itself to the class action?

6. Is the commonality standard adopted by the Court applicable only to those cases where over a million individuals are bringing suit? Or is the standard more broadly applicable to all discrimination cases?

7. While numerosity and commonality are important (and often contested) aspects of Title VII class-action litigation, it is also important for plaintiffs to address the remaining aspects of certification under Rule 23(a)—typicality and adequacy of representation. There is obviously substantial overlap between the questions of commonality and typicality, but a plaintiff must adequately argue both. And, plaintiff attorneys must be able to demonstrate that they will be able to successfully and adequately handle the claims of the entire class on behalf of whom the lawsuit is brought.

8. The discussion of damages by the Court is omitted here. It is important to note that when addressing damages on behalf of a class, the rules apply differently from individual litigation. More importantly, the issue of damages is highly jurisdiction specific, and litigants must carefully analyze the specific rules of the particular jurisdiction where the case arises when seeking relief. *See generally* Suzette M. Malveaux, *Class Actions at the Crossroads: An Answer to* Wal-Mart v. Dukes, 5 HARV. L. & POL'Y REV. 375 (2011) (discussing relief in Title VII class-action cases).

9. *Wal-Mart* **as a constitutional floor.** Some employer groups have argued that the commonality standard created by *Wal-Mart* creates a constitutional floor for class-action claims. Thus, these groups argue that the *Wal-Mart* case applies beyond Rule 23 to all federal and state law systemic claims. Do you agree?

 Interactive Problem

Looking back at the facts of the interactive problem, assume that Bob becomes aware of ten or fifteen other Caucasian employees at the company that were similarly treated with regard to their race. Would Bob be able to become part of a class-action lawsuit against the company? Why or why not?

As discussed above, Federal Rule of Civil Procedure 23 places various requirements on plaintiffs trying to proceed in a class-action employment discrimination case. These rules apply specifically to *private* litigants. In the following case, the Seventh Circuit Court of Appeals looks at the applicability of Rule 23 to systemic cases brought by the EEOC, a government entity. The federal government has typically not been required to comply with this rule. The appellate court revisits the sensibility of this application of the procedural rules, and discusses the role of the government's complex actions.

In re Bemis Co.
279 F.3d 419 (7th Cir. 2002)

Posner, Circuit Judge.

Rule 23(f) of the Federal Rules of Civil Procedure authorizes us to accept appeals from orders granting or denying motions for class certification in Rule 23 class actions. The EEOC has brought a Title VII suit against Bemis Company on behalf of five named, and a "class" of other, black employees of the company. The complaint seeks compensatory and punitive damages and other relief for what it claims is racial harassment of the employees constituting the class. Bemis answered, contending that the EEOC had failed to comply with Rule 23 and could not do so because the case does not meet the requirements of the rule. The EEOC moved to strike this part of the answer on the ground that the Supreme Court had held in *General Telephone of the Northwest, Inc. v. EEOC*, 446 U.S. 318 (1980), that suits brought by the EEOC on behalf of a class are not subject to Rule 23. The district court granted the motion and Bemis has petitioned us to accept an appeal from that order under Rule 23(f).

[W]e cannot grant the relief sought by Bemis because the EEOC is indeed exempt from Rule 23. That is the holding of *General Telephone* and of course we have no authority to overrule decisions of the Supreme Court. The distinctions that Bemis urges are threadbare: *General Telephone* did not involve harassment, the EEOC here is not alleging an intentional company-wide pattern or practice of discrimination, and it is seeking compensatory and punitive damages rather than merely injunctive relief and back pay as in *General Telephone* (which was decided before common-law-type damages could be awarded in Title VII suits). We do not begin to see what these differences have to do with the reasoning of *General Telephone*. The main reason the Supreme Court thought Rule 23 inapplicable to EEOC class actions was that the EEOC is not an exact or even close counterpart to the class representative (and class lawyer) in a Rule 23 class action.

The EEOC's primary role is that of a law enforcement agency and it is merely a detail that it pays over any monetary relief obtained to the victims of the defendant's violation rather than pocketing the money itself and putting them to the bother of suing separately. Having to persuade the district court that the class was numerous and homogeneous and that the EEOC's interest was aligned with that of the class members, the sort of things that compliance with Rule 23 would entail, would interfere with the Commission's exercise of its prosecutorial discretion. It would be like a court's undertaking to decide whether the Justice Department, in bringing a suit attacking price fixing, was being adequately solicitous of the private interests of the victims of the defendant's conduct. "[T]he EEOC is authorized to proceed in a unified action and to obtain the most satisfactory overall relief even though competing interests are involved and particular groups may appear to be disadvantaged. The individual victim is given his right to intervene for this very reason. The EEOC exists to advance the public interest in preventing and remedying employment discrimination, and it does so in part by making the hard choices where conflicts of interest exist." *General Telephone, supra,* 446 U.S. at 331.

That at any rate was the line taken by the Court in *General Telephone* and we cannot find anything in the present case that would have led the Court to carve an exception for this case. It is of course possible that this case is less *appropriate* for class treatment—maybe as Bemis argues there is a huge variance in the nature and extent of the injuries suffered by the members of the class. But the Court did not hold in *General Telephone* that the case before it met the standards of Rule 23. The whole point was that the EEOC doesn't *have* to meet those standards, a holding that embraces this case as well. What Bemis's argument comes down to is that if the Court had known about a case like this, maybe it would have decided *General Telephone* differently. Maybe so, though we greatly doubt it; but we cannot disregard Supreme Court holdings on the basis of such conjectures.

Any doubt about the validity or scope of *General Telephone* has been laid to rest by the Supreme Court's decision, rendered just days after our order denying Bemis's petition, in *EEOC v. Waffle House, Inc.,* 534 U.S. 279 (2002). In the course of holding, with many approving references to *General Telephone,* that even after the addition of compensatory and punitive damages to the EEOC's arsenal of remedies the EEOC does not sue as the representative of the discriminated-against employees who may benefit from the relief it obtains and hence is not barred from suing by the fact that the employees had agreed to submit their claims to binding arbitration, the Court stated that Title VII "makes the EEOC the master of its own case and confers on the agency the authority to evaluate the strength of the public interest at stake." "The EEOC does not stand in the employee's shoes."

■ NOTES AND QUESTIONS

1. In this case, Judge Posner reaffirms the general rule that the EEOC is not subject to the requirements of Rule 23.

2. Under the law of *General Telephone* (and this case), the government is given a lot of leeway in deciding how to proceed in a systemic discrimination case. How common the issues are in a case, or how many individuals the government decides to sue on behalf of, are widely within the discretion of the government.

3. Should the EEOC be more aggressive in pursuing class-action type claims after *Wal-Mart*? If it is now more difficult for individuals to pursue these actions, should the agency attempt to fill this gap, as it is not subject to the Rule 23 requirements? As Professor Melissa Hart notes:

   For the immediate future, the question is how litigants and courts can move forward to address claims of systemic discrimination in the light of this decision and without new legislation. One possibility is a greater reliance on the enforcement efforts of the E.E.O.C. Given that pattern or practice claims pursued by the E.E.O.C. are not subject to the requirements of Rule 23, these actions may be a more effective tool for addressing structural discrimination than private litigation subject to the post-*Wal-Mart* interpretation of Rule 23. Of course, the challenge in E.E.O.C. litigation will be whether defendants can successfully argue that they are entitled to present individualized defenses as to every specific employee in these cases as well.

Melissa Hart, *Civil Rights and Systemic Wrongs*, 32 Berkeley J. Emp. & Lab. L. 455, 475 (2011).

4. Would the reasoning of *Wal-Mart* (and the Court's commonality standard) apply to governmental agencies?

 Interactive Problem

Looking back at the facts of the interactive problem, assume again that Bob becomes aware of ten or fifteen other employees at the company who were similarly treated because of their race. Could the government bring a systemic claim on behalf of these employees? Why or why not?

Practice and Procedural Tip

10: EEOC Litigation—An Overview

As Judge Posner points out above, the Supreme Court considers the EEOC to be the "master of its own case." From a procedural standpoint, it is critical to remember that the EEOC is separate and apart from the individuals on whose behalf it brings suit. Thus, when the government sues a large company on behalf of Sue Jones, it is the government, not Ms. Jones, that is the plaintiff in the case. More importantly, the government represents itself in these cases, and it has its own interests in mind. While the interests of the alleged victim and the government often overlap, they are not always identical. For example, the government may be far more interested in obtaining injunctive and prospective relief—such as training of a company's employees to prevent future discrimination—than the individual, who may want to primarily pursue monetary damages.

For this reason, individuals on whose behalf the EEOC sues should strongly consider retaining their own counsel in the case. Individuals can intervene in the EEOC litigation, and private counsel can assure that their rights are being adequately represented. The individual may have reservations about doing so, however, as she will then have to compensate her attorney to represent her. There is thus no easy answer as to whether an alleged victim should seek separate counsel in this type of case, and it may largely depend on the particular facts and the EEOC's interests in the matter. It should be noted that where the EEOC does recover monetary damages on a victim's behalf, it typically turns those funds over to the individual. The EEOC also does not "charge" the individual any type of attorneys' fees in a case. Again, however, it is important to emphasize that the EEOC is not actually representing the alleged victim.

Similarly, defense counsel should be cognizant of who it is that is bringing suit in this type of litigation. Where the EEOC is involved, it must be remembered that the government will typically have different interests from the individual in the case. This can lead to different settlement expectations than those found in a typical employment discrimination suit. And, where the alleged victim does intervene in the matter, it can complicate matters further from the defense perspective.

H. Further Defining Discrimination

In *Ricci v. DeStefano*, the Supreme Court further refined what it means to discriminate against an employee because of a protected characteristic. The decision proved to be highly controversial. Indeed, the case was at center stage in Justice Sotomayor's confirmation hearings, as she was a member of the appellate court panel whose decision was subsequently vacated by the Court. The decision raises many questions, and helps shed new light on how discrimination claims are evaluated.

Ricci v. DeStefano
557 U.S. 557 (2009)

Justice KENNEDY delivered the opinion of the Court.

In the fire department of New Haven, Connecticut—as in emergency-service agencies throughout the Nation—firefighters prize their promotion to and within the officer ranks. An agency's officers command respect within the department and in the whole community; and, of course, added responsibilities command increased salary and benefits. Aware of the intense competition for promotions, New Haven, like many cities, relies on objective examinations to identify the best qualified candidates.

In 2003, 118 New Haven firefighters took examinations to qualify for promotion to the rank of lieutenant or captain. Promotion examinations in New Haven (or City) were infrequent, so the stakes were high. The results would determine which firefighters would be considered for promotions during the next two years, and the order in which they would be considered. Many firefighters studied for months, at considerable personal and financial cost.

When the examination results showed that white candidates had outperformed minority candidates, the mayor and other local politicians opened a public debate that turned rancorous. Some firefighters argued the tests should be discarded because the results showed the tests to be discriminatory. They threatened a discrimination lawsuit if the City made promotions based on the tests. Other firefighters said the exams were neutral and fair. And they, in turn, threatened a discrimination lawsuit if the City, relying on the statistical racial disparity, ignored the test results and denied promotions to the candidates who had performed well.

In the end the City took the side of those who protested the test results. It threw out the examinations.

Certain white and Hispanic firefighters who likely would have been promoted based on their good test performance sued the City and some of its officials. Theirs is the suit now before us. The suit alleges that, by discarding the test results, the City and the named officials discriminated against the plaintiffs based on their race, in violation of both Title VII of the Civil Rights Act of 1964, and the Equal Protection Clause of the Fourteenth Amendment. The City and the officials defended their actions, arguing that if they had certified the results, they could have faced liability under Title VII for adopting a practice that had a disparate impact on the minority firefighters. The District Court granted summary judgment for the defendants, and the Court of Appeals affirmed.

> The City threw out its promotion exam out of fear of a disparate impact suit.

We conclude that race-based action like the City's in this case is impermissible under Title VII unless the employer can demonstrate a strong basis in evidence that, had it not taken the action, it would have been liable under the disparate-impact statute. The respondents, we further determine, cannot meet that threshold standard. As a result, the City's action in discarding the tests was a violation of Title VII. In light of our ruling under the statutes, we need not reach the question whether respondents' actions may have violated the Equal Protection Clause.

> The key issue in this case is whether an overt attempt to avoid a disparate impact claim can result in disparate treatment.

[A detailed factual analysis of the case is omitted.]

The decision not to certify the examination results led to this lawsuit. The plaintiffs—who are the petitioners here—are 17 white firefighters and 1 Hispanic firefighter who passed the examinations but were denied a chance at promotions.

Petitioners raise a statutory claim, under the disparate-treatment prohibition of Title VII, and a constitutional claim, under the Equal Protection Clause of the Fourteenth Amendment. A decision for petitioners on their statutory claim would provide the relief sought, so we consider it first. Title VII of the Civil Rights Act of 1964, as amended, prohibits employment discrimination on the basis of race, color, religion, sex, or national origin. Title VII prohibits both intentional discrimination (known as "disparate treatment") as well as, in some cases, practices that are not intended to discriminate but in fact have a disproportionately adverse effect on minorities (known as "disparate impact").

[An amendment to Title VII] included a provision codifying the prohibition on disparate-impact discrimination. That provision is now in force along with the disparate-treatment section already noted. Under the disparate-impact statute, a plaintiff establishes a prima facie violation by showing that an employer uses "a particular employment practice that causes a disparate impact on the basis of race, color, religion, sex, or national origin." 42 U.S.C. § 2000e–2(k)(1)(A)(i). An employer may defend against liability by demonstrating that the practice is "job related for the position in question and consistent with business necessity." *Ibid.* Even if the employer meets that burden, however, a plaintiff may still succeed by showing that the employer refuses to adopt an available alternative employment practice that has less disparate impact and serves the employer's legitimate needs.

Petitioners allege that when CSB refused to certify the captain and lieutenant exam results based on the race of the successful candidates, it discriminated against them in violation of Title VII's disparate-treatment provision. The City counters that its decision was permissible because the tests "appear[ed] to violate Title VII's disparate-impact provisions." Our analysis begins with this premise: The City's actions would violate the disparate-treatment prohibition of Title VII absent some valid defense. All the evidence demonstrates that the City chose not to certify the examination results because of the statistical disparity based on race—i.e., how minority candidates had performed when compared to white candidates. As the District Court put it, the City rejected the test results because "too many whites and not enough minorities would be promoted were the lists to be certified." Without some other justification, this express, race-based decisionmaking violates Title VII's command that employers cannot take adverse employment actions because of an individual's race.

Whatever the City's ultimate aim—however well-intentioned or benevolent it might have seemed—the City made its employment decision because of race. The City rejected the test results solely because the higher scoring candidates were white. The question is not whether that conduct was discriminatory but whether the City had a lawful justification for its race-based action. We consider, therefore, whether the purpose to avoid disparate-impact liability excuses what otherwise would be prohibited disparate-treatment discrimination. Courts often confront cases in which statutes and principles point in different directions. Our task is to provide guidance to employers and courts for situations when these two prohibitions could be in conflict absent a rule to reconcile them. In providing this guidance our decision must be consistent with the important purpose of Title VII—that the workplace be an environment free of discrimination, where race is not a barrier to opportunity.

With these principles in mind, we turn to the parties' proposed means of reconciling the statutory provisions. Petitioners take a strict approach, arguing that under Title VII, it cannot be permissible for an employer to take race-based adverse employment actions in order to avoid disparate-impact liability—even if

the employer knows its practice violates the disparate-impact provision. Petitioners would have us hold that, under Title VII, avoiding unintentional discrimination cannot justify intentional discrimination. That assertion, however, ignores the fact that, by codifying the disparate-impact provision in 1991, Congress has expressly prohibited both types of discrimination. We must interpret the statute to give effect to both provisions where possible. We cannot accept petitioners' broad and inflexible formulation.

Petitioners next suggest that an employer in fact must be in violation of the disparate-impact provision before it can use compliance as a defense in a disparate-treatment suit. Again, this is overly simplistic and too restrictive of Title VII's purpose. The rule petitioners offer would run counter to what we have recognized as Congress's intent that "voluntary compliance" be "the preferred means of achieving the objectives of Title VII." *Firefighters v. Cleveland*, 478 U.S. 501 (1986). Forbidding employers to act unless they know, with certainty, that a practice violates the disparate-impact provision would bring compliance efforts to a near standstill. Even in the limited situations when this restricted standard could be met, employers likely would hesitate before taking voluntary action for fear of later being proven wrong in the course of litigation and then held to account for disparate treatment.

At the opposite end of the spectrum, respondents and the Government assert that an employer's good-faith belief that its actions are necessary to comply with Title VII's disparate-impact provision should be enough to justify race-conscious conduct. But the original, foundational prohibition of Title VII bars employers from taking adverse action "because of . . . race." § 2000e–2(a)(1). And when Congress codified the disparate-impact provision in 1991, it made no exception to disparate-treatment liability for actions taken in a good-faith effort to comply with the new, disparate-impact provision in subsection (k). Allowing employers to violate the disparate-treatment prohibition based on a mere good-faith fear of disparate-impact liability would encourage race-based action at the slightest hint of disparate impact. A minimal standard could cause employers to discard the results of lawful and beneficial promotional examinations even where there is little if any evidence of disparate-impact discrimination. That would amount to a de facto quota system, in which a "focus on statistics . . . could put undue pressure on employers to adopt inappropriate prophylactic measures." *Watson v. Fort Worth Bank & Trust*, 487 U.S. 977 (1988) (plurality opinion). Even worse, an employer could discard test results (or other employment practices) with the intent of obtaining the employer's preferred racial balance. That operational principle could not be justified, for Title VII is express in disclaiming any interpretation of its requirements as calling for outright racial balancing. § 2000e–2(j). The purpose of Title VII "is to promote hiring on the basis of job qualifications, rather than on the basis of race or color." *Griggs v. Duke Power Co.*, 401 U.S. 424 (1971).

In searching for a standard that strikes a more appropriate balance, we note that this Court has considered cases similar to this one, albeit in the context of the Equal Protection Clause of the Fourteenth Amendment. The

> The Court does not wholesale adopt either the plaintiff's or defendant's approach in this case.

Court has held that certain government actions to remedy past racial discrimination—actions that are themselves based on race—are constitutional only where there is a "'strong basis in evidence'" that the remedial actions were necessary. *Richmond v. J.A. Croson Co.*, 488 U.S. 500 (1989). This suit does not call on us to consider whether the statutory constraints under Title VII must be parallel in all respects to those under the Constitution. That does not mean the constitutional authorities are irrelevant, however. Our cases discussing constitutional principles can provide helpful guidance in this statutory context. Writing for a plurality in *Wygant v. Jackson Bd. of Educ.*, 476 U.S. 267, 290 (1986), and announcing the strong-basis-in-evidence standard, Justice Powell recognized the tension between eliminating segregation and discrimination on the one hand and doing away with all governmentally imposed discrimination based on race on the other.

Applying the strong-basis-in-evidence standard to Title VII gives effect to both the disparate-treatment and disparate-impact provisions, allowing violations of one in the name of compliance with the other only in certain, narrow circumstances. The standard leaves ample room for employers' voluntary compliance efforts, which are essential to the statutory scheme and to Congress's efforts to eradicate workplace discrimination. And the standard appropriately constrains employers' discretion in making race-based decisions: It limits that discretion to cases in which there is a strong basis in evidence of disparate-impact liability, but it is not so restrictive that it allows employers to act only when there is a provable, actual violation.

Resolving the statutory conflict in this way allows the disparate-impact prohibition to work in a manner that is consistent with other provisions of Title VII, including the prohibition on adjusting employment-related test scores on the basis of race. Examinations like those administered by the City create legitimate expectations on the part of those who took the tests. As is the case with any promotion exam, some of the firefighters here invested substantial time, money, and personal commitment in preparing for the tests. Employment tests can be an important part of a neutral selection system that safeguards against the very racial animosities Title VII was intended to prevent. Here, however, the firefighters saw their efforts invalidated by the City in sole reliance upon race-based statistics. For the foregoing reasons, we adopt the strong-basis-in-evidence standard as a matter of statutory construction to resolve any conflict between the disparate-treatment and disparate-impact provisions of Title VII.

> The middle ground reached by the Court is the strong-basis-in-evidence standard. Do you agree with this approach?

Our statutory holding does not address the constitutionality of the measures taken here in purported compliance with Title VII. We also do not hold that meeting the strong-basis-in-evidence standard would satisfy the Equal Protection Clause in a future case. As we explain below, because respondents have not met their burden under Title VII, we need not decide whether a legitimate fear of disparate impact is ever sufficient to justify discriminatory treatment under the Constitution.

Nor do we question an employer's affirmative efforts to ensure that all groups have a fair opportunity to apply for promotions and to participate in the process by which promotions will be made. But once that process has been established and employers have made clear their selection criteria, they may not then invalidate the test results, thus upsetting an employee's legitimate expectation not to be judged on the basis of race. Doing so, absent a strong basis in evidence of an impermissible disparate impact, amounts to the sort of racial preference that Congress has disclaimed, § 2000e–2(j), and is antithetical to the notion of a workplace where individuals are guaranteed equal opportunity regardless of race.

Title VII does not prohibit an employer from considering, before administering a test or practice, how to design that test or practice in order to provide a fair opportunity for all individuals, regardless of their race. And when, during the test-design stage, an employer invites comments to ensure the test is fair, that process can provide a common ground for open discussions toward that end. We hold only that, under Title VII, before an employer can engage in intentional discrimination for the asserted purpose of avoiding or remedying an unintentional disparate impact, the employer must have a strong basis in evidence to believe it will be subject to disparate-impact liability if it fails to take the race-conscious, discriminatory action.

The City argues that, even under the strong-basis-in-evidence standard, its decision to discard the examination results was permissible under Title VII. That is incorrect. Even if respondents were motivated as a subjective matter by a desire to avoid committing disparate-impact discrimination, the record makes clear there is no support for the conclusion that respondents had an objective, strong basis in evidence to find the tests inadequate, with some consequent disparate-impact liability in violation of Title VII.

On this basis, we conclude that petitioners have met their obligation to demonstrate that there is "no genuine issue as to any material fact" and that they are "entitled to judgment as a matter of law." Fed. Rule Civ. Proc. 56(c). In this Court, the City's only defense is that it acted to comply with Title VII's disparate-impact provision. To succeed on their motion, then, petitioners must demonstrate that there can be no genuine dispute that there was no strong basis in evidence for the City to conclude it would face disparate-impact liability if it certified the examination results.

The racial adverse impact here was significant, and petitioners do not dispute that the City was faced with a prima facie case of disparate-impact liability. On the captain exam, the pass rate for white candidates was 64 percent but was 37.5 percent for both black and Hispanic candidates. On the lieutenant exam, the pass rate for white candidates was 58.1 percent; for black candidates, 31.6 percent; and for Hispanic candidates, 20 percent. The pass rates of minorities, which were approximately one-half the pass rates for white candidates, fall well below the 80-percent standard set by the EEOC to implement the disparate-impact provision of Title VII. Based on how the passing candidates ranked and an application of the "rule of three," certifying the examinations would have meant that the City could not have considered black candidates for any of the then-vacant lieutenant or captain positions.

Based on the degree of adverse impact reflected in the results, respondents were compelled to take a hard look at the examinations to determine whether certifying the results would have had an impermissible disparate impact. The problem for respondents is that a prima facie case of disparate-impact liability—essentially, a threshold showing of a significant statistical disparity, *Connecticut v. Teal*, 457 U.S. 440 (1982), and nothing more—is far from a strong basis in evidence that the City would have been liable under Title VII had it certified the results. That is because the City could be liable for disparate-impact discrimination only if the examinations were not job related and consistent with business necessity, or if there existed an equally valid, less-discriminatory alternative that served the City's needs but that the City refused to adopt. We conclude there is no strong basis in evidence to establish that the test was deficient in either of these respects. There is no genuine dispute that the examinations were job related and consistent with business necessity. The City's assertions to the contrary are "blatantly contradicted by the record." *Scott v. Harris*, 550 U.S. 372 (2007). The City, moreover, turned a blind eye to evidence that supported the exams' validity. Respondents also lacked a strong basis in evidence of an equally valid, less discriminatory testing alternative that the City, by certifying the examination results, would necessarily have refused to adopt.

On the record before us, there is no genuine dispute that the City lacked a strong basis in evidence to believe it would face disparate-impact liability if it certified the examination results. In other words, there is no evidence—let alone the required strong basis in evidence—that the tests were flawed because they were not job related or because other, equally valid and less discriminatory tests

> The Court emphasizes that more is needed here than simply fear of litigation.

were available to the City. Fear of litigation alone cannot justify an employer's reliance on race to the detriment of individuals who passed the examinations and qualified for promotions. The City's discarding the test results was impermissible under Title VII, and summary judgment is appropriate for petitioners on their disparate-treatment claim.

The record in this litigation documents a process that, at the outset, had the potential to produce a testing procedure that was true to the promise of Title VII: No individual should face workplace discrimination based on race. Respondents thought about promotion qualifications and relevant experience in neutral ways. They were careful to ensure broad racial participation in the design of the test itself and its administration. As we have discussed at length, the process was open and fair.

The problem, of course, is that after the tests were completed, the raw racial results became the predominant rationale for the City's refusal to certify the results. The injury arises in part from the high, and justified, expectations of the candidates who had participated in the testing process on the terms the City had established for the promotional process. Many of the candidates had studied for months, at considerable personal and financial expense, and thus the injury caused by the City's reliance on raw racial statistics at the end of the process was all the more severe. Confronted with arguments both for and against certifying the test results—and threats of a lawsuit either way—the City was required to make a difficult inquiry. But its hearings produced no strong evidence of a disparate-impact violation, and the City was not entitled to disregard the tests based solely on the racial disparity in the results.

Our holding today clarifies how Title VII applies to resolve competing expectations under the disparate-treatment and disparate-impact provisions. If, after it certifies the test results, the City faces a disparate-impact suit, then in light of our holding today it should be clear that the City would avoid disparate-impact liability based on the strong basis in evidence that, had it not certified the results, it would have been subject to disparate-treatment liability. Petitioners are entitled to summary judgment on their Title VII claim, and we therefore need not decide the underlying constitutional question. The judgment of the Court of Appeals is reversed, and the cases are remanded for further proceedings consistent with this opinion.

It is so ordered.

■ NOTES AND QUESTIONS

1. **Historical note.** Justice Sotomayor was a member of the Second Circuit panel that issued the decision in *Ricci v. DeStefano* that was later vacated by the Supreme Court. When Sotomayor was considered for a position on the Supreme Court in 2009, she received considerable criticism regarding the decision. During her confirmation she was grilled by Senate Republicans, who categorized her as a judicial activist. On the other hand, supporters of Sotomayor's nomination believed that her action in *Ricci* demonstrated a sense of restraint, in that the three-judge panel interpreted the law narrowly and complied with well-established Second Circuit precedent. *See Sotomayor Completes Testimony with Grace*, ALLIANCE FOR JUSTICE (July 16, 2009), http://afjjusticewatch.blogspot.com/2009/07/sotomayor-completes-testimony-with.html; Joan Biskupic, *Firefighter Case May Keep Sotomayor in Hot Seat*, USA TODAY (June 1, 2009), http://usatoday30.usatoday.com/news/washington/judicial/2009-05-31-firefighters_N.htm.

Justice Sonia Sotomayor

2. The primary question raised by *Ricci* is "whether the purpose to avoid disparate-impact liability excuses what otherwise would be prohibited disparate-treatment discrimination." From a policy standpoint, should we

excuse an employer's discrimination if it is done to avoid other discrimination? How can the employer avoid this type of Catch-22 scenario?

3. The Court's primary holding in *Ricci* is that a "race-based action like the City's in this case is impermissible under Title VII unless the employer can demonstratea strong basis in evidence that, had it not taken the action, it would have been liable under the disparate-impact statute." Where is the Court getting the "strong basis in evidence standard"? Can it be found in the statute or regulations? *See* Herman N. (Rusty) Johnson, Jr., *The Evolving Strong-Basis-in-Evidence Standard*, 32 Berkeley J. Emp. & Lab. L. 347 (2011).

4. What would it take to establish a "strong basis in evidence"? What type of factors could the City point to in establishing that it had satisfied this standard? How could the plaintiffs argue against the standard?

5. When it comes to standardized tests that are administered to a company's personnel, how important is it to have the test validated by an outside group? What is the validation study trying to show? *See* Daniel A. Biddle & Patrick M. Nooren, *Validity Generalization vs. Title VII: Can Employers Successfully Defend Tests Without Conducting Local Validation Studies?*, 57 Lab. L.J. 216 (2006); Richard E. Biddle & Daniel A. Biddle, Ricci v. DeStefano: *New Opportunities for Employers to Correct Disparate Impact Using Croson Studies*, 61 Lab. L.J. 67 (2010) (part one of a two-part series); Creola Johnson, *Credentialism and the Proliferation of Fake Degrees: The Employer Pretends to Need a Degree; the Employee Pretends to Have One*, 23 Hofstra Lab. & Emp. L.J. 269, 327–330 (2006).

6. Justice Scalia's concurrence is omitted from the opinion above. In his separate opinion, Justice Scalia questions whether disparate-impact doctrine can hold up under the Equal Protection Clause. Is disparate impact constitutional?

7. For an in-depth analysis of *Ricci*, including a discussion on the majority opinion, concurrences, and dissent, as well as the impact on race discrimination in employment, see Marcia L. McCormick, *Back to Color Blindness: Recent Developments in Race Discrimination Law in the United States*, 20 Revue des Affaires Européennes (2010). *See also* Michael J. Zimmer, Ricci's *"Color-Blind" Standard in a Race Conscious Society: A Case of Unintended Consequences?*, 2010 B.Y.U. L. Rev. 1257 (discussing the Supreme Court's "color-blind" standard of disparate-treatment liability for Title VII and the equal protection consequences for Title VII's disparate-impact provisions).

I. Retaliation

Retaliation is one of the most critical aspects of employment discrimination law. Congress recognized the importance of prohibiting not just discrimination itself, but retaliation against those who were subjected to retaliatory acts for their complaints. If individuals were afraid to avail themselves of Title VII for fear of retribution, the statute would have very little meaning. Retaliation is thus strictly prohibited by Title VII, which provides:

> It shall be an unlawful employment practice for an employer to discriminate against any of his employees . . . because he has opposed any practice made an unlawful employment practice by this subchapter, or because he has made a charge, testified, assisted, or participated in any manner in an investigation, proceeding, or hearing. . . . 42 U.S.C. § 2000e–3(a).

2 clauses

Retaliation claims are now the most common type of discrimination claim brought to the EEOC, even surpassing race and sex discrimination claims, which have historically been the highest. In 2017, 48.8 percent of all EEOC charges included a claim of retaliation under one of the discrimination statutes (Title VII, ADA, ADEA, Equal Pay Act, and Genetic Information Nondiscrimination Act), whereas race discrimination claims amounted to 33.9 percent of total charges and sex discrimination claims accounted for 30.4 percent. *See* EEOC, *Charge Statistics,* FY 1997–FY 2017, http://www.eeoc.gov/eeoc/statistics/enforcement/charges.cfm. Moreover, retaliation charges have a slightly higher rate of success than other discrimination charges with regards to settlements. In 2017, the EEOC settled 6.3 percent of retaliation claims and conducted successful conciliations in 0.9 percent of retaliation cases. *See* EEOC, *Retaliation-Based Charges, FY 1997–FY 2017,* http://www.eeoc.gov/eeoc/statistics/enforcement/retaliation. cfm. On the other hand, the EEOC settled 5.7 percent of race claims and successfully conciliated 0.9 percent of race cases. *See* EEOC, *Race-Based Charges, FY 1997–FY 2017,* http://www.eeoc.gov/eeoc/statistics/enforcement/race.cfm. Although the data regarding whether employees who allege retaliation are more successful at trial than employees alleging discrimination based on other protected classes is not readily available, *see* David Sherwyn et al., *Experimental Evidence That Retaliation Claims Are Unlike Other Employment Discrimination Claims,* 44 SETON HALL L. REV. 455, 486 (2014), several sources suggest that retaliation claims are more successful with juries, *see, e.g.,* Jamie Darin Prenkert et al., *Retaliatory Disclosure: When Identifying the Complainant Is an Adverse Action,* 91 N.C. L. REV. 889, 898 n.35 (2013) (stating that "[r]etaliation claims have been successful with juries").

The courts have articulated the prima facie case for a retaliation claim in varying ways. One common interpretation states that the plaintiff must establish, by a preponderance of the evidence, that "(1) he engaged in protected activity; (2) he was subjected to an adverse employment action; and (3) there was a causal link between the protected activity and the adverse action." *See* Hamilton v. Geithner, 666 F.3d 1344, 1357 (D.C. Cir. 2012). Once the plaintiff establishes these factors, the case proceeds as it would under the *McDonnell Douglas* framework—the defendant must articulate a legitimate nondiscriminatory reason for the adverse action, and the plaintiff will then respond by showing that this reason is pretextual. Retaliation claims—like all other areas of discrimination law—have generally been on the rise in recent years. The chart below shows the number of retaliation charges that the EEOC has received between 1992 and 2017, thus demonstrating the importance of this issue:

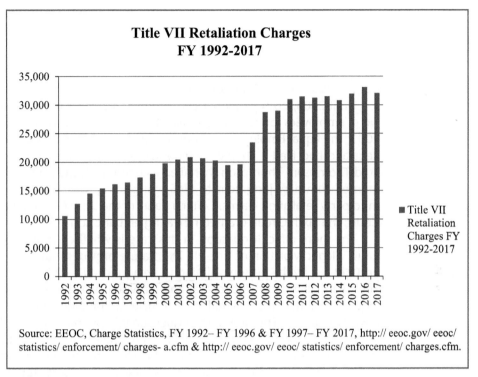

Title VII Retaliation Charges
FY 1992-2017

■ Title VII
Retaliation
Charges FY
1992-2017

Source: EEOC, Charge Statistics, FY 1992– FY 1996 & FY 1997– FY 2017, http:// eeoc.gov/ eeoc/ statistics/ enforcement/ charges- a.cfm & http:// eeoc.gov/ eeoc/ statistics/ enforcement/ charges.cfm.

Figure 3.2

1. Coverage

A critical first inquiry in a retaliation case is whether the plaintiff is actually covered by the statute. This can be particularly tricky in the retaliation context, as there is not always a direct link between the person who complains and the retaliation itself. The Supreme Court has held that former employees are covered by the statute. Thus, if a worker were to leave a company after complaining of discrimination, he would still maintain anti-retaliation protection under the statute. *See* Robinson v. Shell Oil Co., 519 U.S. 337 (1997). Protection can also extend not only to those who are retaliated against because of their complaints, but to those who refuse to engage in discriminatory conduct. The EEOC maintains that "refusal to obey an order constitutes protected opposition if the individual reasonably believes that the order requires him or her to carry out unlawful employment discrimination." EEOC Compl. Man. (CCH) ¶ 8005, § 8-II(B)(2) (1998).

Thus, coverage is not always a straightforward issue. One question that frequently arises in a retaliation case is whether coverage extends to individuals who are retaliated against because a loved one has complained of discrimination. This question often comes up when two individuals who are related work for the same employer, or where married couples share the same workplace. This issue was resolved by the Supreme Court.

Thompson v. North American Stainless, LP
562 U.S. 170 (2011)

Justice Scalia delivered the opinion of the Court.

Until 2003, both petitioner Eric Thompson and his fiancée, Miriam Regalado, were employees of respondent North American Stainless (NAS). In February 2003, the Equal Employment Opportunity Commission (EEOC) notified NAS that Regalado had filed a charge alleging sex discrimination. Three weeks later, NAS fired Thompson. Thompson then filed a charge with the EEOC. The District Court granted summary judgment to NAS, concluding that Title VII "does not permit third party retaliation claims." After a panel of the Sixth Circuit reversed the District Court, the Sixth Circuit granted rehearing en banc and affirmed by a 10-to-6 vote.

The more difficult question in this case is whether Thompson may sue NAS for its alleged violation of Title VII. The statute provides that "a civil action may be brought . . . by the person claiming to be aggrieved." 42 U.S.C. § 2000e– 5(f)(1). The Sixth Circuit concluded that this provision was merely a reiteration of the requirement that the plaintiff have Article III standing. We do not understand how that can be. The provision unquestionably permits a person "claiming to be aggrieved" to bring "a civil action." It is arguable that the aggrievement referred to is nothing more than the minimal Article III standing, which consists of injury in fact caused by the defendant and remediable by the court. But Thompson's claim undoubtedly meets those requirements, so if that is indeed all that aggrievement consists of, he may sue.

We have suggested in dictum that the Title VII aggrievement requirement conferred a right to sue on all who satisfied Article III standing. *Trafficante v. Metropolitan Life Ins. Co.*, 409 U.S. 205 (1972), involved the "person aggrieved" provision of Title VIII (the Fair Housing Act) rather than Title VII. In deciding the case, however, we relied upon, and cited with approval, a Third Circuit opinion involving Title VII, which, we said, "concluded that the words used showed 'a congressional intention to define standing as broadly as is permitted by Article III of the Constitution.'" *Id.* at 209 (quoting *Hackett v. McGuire Bros., Inc.*, 445 F.2d 442, 446 (1971)). We think that dictum regarding Title VII was too expansive. Indeed, the *Trafficante* opinion did not adhere to it in expressing its Title VIII holding that residents of an apartment complex could sue the owner for his racial discrimination against prospective tenants. The opinion said that the "person aggrieved" of Title VIII was coextensive with Article III "insofar as tenants of the same housing unit that is charged with discrimination are concerned." Later opinions, we must acknowledge, reiterate that the term "aggrieved" in Title VIII reaches as far as Article III permits, though the holdings of those cases are compatible with the "zone of interests" limitation that we discuss below. In any event, it is Title VII rather than Title VIII that is before us here, and as to that we are surely not bound by the *Trafficante* dictum.

We now find that this dictum was ill-considered, and we decline to follow it. If any person injured in the Article III sense by a Title VII violation could sue, absurd consequences would follow. For example, a shareholder would be able to sue a company for firing a valuable employee for racially discriminatory reasons, so long as he could show that the value of his stock decreased as a consequence. At oral argument Thompson acknowledged that such a suit would not lie. We agree, and therefore conclude that the term "aggrieved" must be construed more narrowly than the outer boundaries of Article III.

> Do you agree that these earlier comments of the Court were "ill-considered dictum?"

At the other extreme from the position that "person aggrieved" means anyone with Article III standing, NAS argues that it is a term of art that refers only to the employee who engaged in the protected activity. We know of no other context in which the words carry this artificially narrow meaning, and if that is what Congress intended it would more naturally have said "person claiming to have been discriminated against" rather than "person claiming to be aggrieved." We see no basis in text or prior practice for limiting the latter phrase to the person who was the subject of unlawful retaliation. Moreover, such a reading contradicts the very holding of *Trafficante*, which was that residents of an apartment complex were "person[s] aggrieved" by discrimination against prospective tenants. We see no reason why the same phrase in Title VII should be given a narrower meaning.

In our view there is a common usage of the term "person aggrieved" that avoids the extremity of equating it with Article III and yet is fully consistent with our application of the term in *Trafficante*. The Administrative Procedure Act, 5 U.S.C. § 551 *et seq.*, authorizes suit to challenge a federal agency by any "person . . . adversely affected or aggrieved . . . within the meaning of a relevant statute." § 702. We have held that this language establishes a regime under which a plaintiff may not sue unless he "falls within the 'zone of interests' sought to be protected by the statutory provision whose violation forms the legal basis for his complaint."

> Does the "zone of interest" test accurately capture what Congress intended in prohibiting retaliation?

Lujan v. National Wildlife Federation, 497 U.S. 871, 883 (1990). We have described the "zone of interests" test as denying a right of review "if the plaintiff's interests are so marginally related to or inconsistent with the purposes implicit in the statute that it cannot reasonably be assumed that Congress intended to permit the suit." *Clarke v. Securities Industry Assn.*, 479 U.S. 388, 399–400 (1987). We hold that the term "aggrieved" in Title VII incorporates this test, enabling suit by any plaintiff with an interest "arguably [sought] to be protected by the statutes," *National Credit Union Admin. v. First Nat. Bank & Trust Co.*, 522 U.S. 479, 495 (1998) (internal quotation marks omitted), while excluding plaintiffs who might technically be injured in an Article III sense but whose interests are unrelated to the statutory prohibitions in Title VII.

Applying that test here, we conclude that Thompson falls within the zone of interests protected by Title VII. Thompson was an employee of NAS, and the purpose of Title VII is to protect employees from their employers' unlawful actions. Moreover, accepting the facts as alleged, Thompson is not an accidental victim of the retaliation—collateral damage, so to speak, of the employer's unlawful act. To the contrary, injuring him was the employer's intended means of harming Regalado. Hurting him was the unlawful act by which the employer punished her. In those circumstances, we think Thompson well within the zone of interests sought to be protected by Title VII. He is a person aggrieved with standing to sue.

■ NOTES AND QUESTIONS

1. Does the zone of interest test make sense in the Title VII context? Is it too broad? *See* Jessica K. Fink, *Protected by Association? The Supreme Court's Incomplete Approach to Defining the Scope of the Third-Party Retaliation Doctrine*, 63 Hastings L.J. 521 (2012).

2. Suppose that an employer fires a worker's second cousin after that worker complains of race discrimination. Is the cousin within the zone of interest?

3. Would best friends or BFFs fall within the zone of interest?

 Interactive Problem

Looking back at the facts of the interactive problem, assume that Bob's fiancée (Sylvia Smith) also works for the company. The day after Bob files his Title VII claim against the corporation, Sylvia's direct supervisor informs her that she will not be getting the promotion for which she recently applied. Sylvia is told that the company doesn't reward "troublemakers," or "friends of troublemakers," so she doesn't have "much of a future here anymore." Would Sylvia have a cause of action under Title VII?

2. Protected Activity

Beyond showing coverage under the statute, there are two primary ways for a plaintiff to establish that she was engaged in protected activity under Title VII. First, she can claim that she was retaliated against because she "opposed" an unlawful practice; second, she can allege that she was retaliated against because she "participated" in the more formal enforcement processes of the statute. Both provisions are critical to the workings of anti-retaliation law and will be discussed below.

a. Participation Clause

As already noted, Title VII makes it unlawful to retaliate against an individual who "has made a charge, testified, assisted, or participated in any manner in an investigation, proceeding, or hearing." The participation clause prohibits employers from punishing workers who take part in the more formal enforcement processes contemplated by the statute. Thus, for example, it is unlawful to retaliate against someone because they have filed a charge of discrimination with the EEOC, testified in a Title VII case, or given an interview to an EEOC investigator. The participation clause is both broader and narrower than the opposition clause. It is broader in the sense that it provides absolute protection—if you are retaliated against because of your involvement in the enforcement process or legal proceedings, you will be protected. It is narrower in the sense of the activities that it protects—coverage extends to only those formal processes involving the EEOC or federal courts.

The EEOC has nicely summarized the protection provided by the participation clause as follows:

> The anti-discrimination statutes do not limit or condition in any way the protection against retaliation for participating in the charge process. While the opposition clause applies only to those who protest practices that they reasonably and in good faith believe are unlawful, the participation clause applies to *all* individuals who participate in the statutory complaint process. Thus, courts have consistently held that a[n employer] is liable for retaliating against an individual for filing an EEOC charge regardless of the validity or reasonableness of the charge. To permit an employer to retaliate against a charging party based on its unilateral determination that the charge was unreasonable or otherwise unjustified would chill the rights of all individuals protected by the anti-discrimination statutes.

EEOC Compl. Man. (CCH) ¶ 8005, § 8-II(C)(2) (1998).

The participation clause covers not only those that file a discrimination charge, but all individuals involved in the legal process, such as witnesses. And the protection also applies where there is no reasonable basis for filing the charge in the first place. This is a critical distinction from charges filed under the opposition clause—from a practical perspective, employers might be even more likely to want to retaliate against someone that has filed a charge in what they perceive to be bad faith.

 Interactive Problem

Looking back at the facts of the interactive problem, assume that Bob files a charge of discrimination against the company. He then applies for a job with ComputerZone—another wholly owned subsidiary of his former employer, Technology World Corporation. His application is rejected, and he is told that he will not be considered for employment while there is "a federal case" pending against the company. Would Bob have a retaliation claim?

b. Opposition Clause

Title VII also makes it unlawful to retaliate against a worker who "has opposed any practice made unlawful under the employment discrimination statutes." The retaliation is much broader in terms of the types of acts it covers. To avail yourself of protection under the opposition clause, you must make your employer aware of your belief that a violation of Title VII has occurred. As the EEOC provides, this provision "applies if an individual explicitly or implicitly communicates to his or her employer or other covered entity a belief that its activity constitutes a form of employment discrimination that is covered by any of the statutes enforced by the EEOC." EEOC Compl. Man. § 8-II(B)(1) (1998).

There are numerous ways for an individual to gain protection under the opposition clause. The classic way to invoke this provision is to complain to your supervisor or the human resources department that you believe your Title VII rights have been violated. But coverage is much broader than this—you can also complain to management outside your chain of command, or even engage in peaceful picketing of the business for its unlawful activities. The key is that you are making your employer aware of your belief that it is engaging in activities that run afoul of Title VII.

The key distinction between the opposition clause and the participation clause is that to fall within the ambit of the opposition clause, the individual must have a *reasonable good faith belief* that Title VII has been violated. The participation clause requires no such good faith belief. Thus, a completely frivolous claim under the opposition clause will not gain a worker any protection. As "reasonable good faith belief" is a subjective inquiry, the courts vary as to what a plaintiff must establish to prevail under this terminology. Some courts have been particularly restrictive in their reading of what constitutes a good faith belief, while other courts have been more liberal in their approach.

In *Clark County School District v. Breeden*, 532 U.S. 268 (2001), the U.S. Supreme Court addressed a retaliation claim with the following facts:

> [The female plaintiff's] male supervisor met with respondent and another male employee to review the psychological evaluation reports of four job applicants. The report for one of the applicants disclosed that the applicant had once commented to a co-worker, "I hear making love to you is like making love to the Grand Canyon." At the meeting respondent's supervisor read the comment aloud, looked at respondent and stated, "I don't know what that means." The other employee then said, "Well, I'll tell you later," and both men chuckled. Respondent later complained about the comment to the offending employee, to Assistant Superintendent George Ann Rice, the employee's supervisor, and to another assistant superintendent of petitioner. Her first claim of retaliation asserts that she was punished for these complaints.

Breeden, 532 U.S. at 269–270.

Would these facts support a claim for retaliation? Do they provide a good faith reasonable belief that Title VII has been violated? The Supreme Court held:

> No reasonable person could have believed that the single incident recounted above violated Title VII's standard. The ordinary terms and conditions of respondent's job required her to review the sexually explicit statement in the course of screening job applicants. Her co-workers who participated in the hiring process were subject to the same requirement, and indeed, in the District Court respondent "conceded that it did not bother or upset her" to read the statement in the file. Her supervisor's comment, made at a meeting to review the application, that he did not know what the statement meant; her co-worker's responding comment; and the chuckling of both are at worst an "isolated

inciden[t]" that cannot remotely be considered "extremely serious," as our cases require.

Breeden, 532 U.S. at 271. Should the employee in *Breeden* have waited to complain until there was another hostile comment? Should the employee have gone directly to the EEOC to gain protection?

Class Exercise: The Opposition Clause

Breaking up into small groups, try to identify at least five different ways that an individual can complain of discrimination internally at a company, without going to the EEOC or courts. What ways are workers able to complain easily of discrimination? Would complaint through the channels that you identified satisfy the opposition clause of the statute?

---

3. Adverse Action

Once a plaintiff has established that she has engaged in protected conduct, she must further demonstrate that she suffered an adverse action. Establishing an adverse action pursuant to a retaliation claim is different than it is for a traditional disparate treatment claim analyzed under *McDonnell Douglas*. Because Congress is particularly concerned with preventing retaliation against those that avail themselves of Title VII, the standard for what constitutes an adverse action is arguably somewhat lower in the retaliation context. The Supreme Court specifically addressed this distinction in the case below.

Burlington Northern & Santa Fe Railway Co. v. White

548 U.S. 53 (2006)

Justice Breyer delivered the opinion of the Court.

The Courts of Appeals have come to different conclusions about the scope of the Act's antiretaliation provision, particularly the reach of its phrase "discriminate against." Does that provision confine actionable retaliation to activity that affects the terms and conditions of employment? And how harmful must the adverse actions be to fall within its scope?

We conclude that the antiretaliation provision does not confine the actions and harms it forbids to those that are related to employment or occur at the workplace. We also conclude that the provision covers those (and only those) employer actions that would have been materially adverse to a reasonable employee or job

applicant. In the present context that means that the employer's actions must be harmful to the point that they could well dissuade a reasonable worker from making or supporting a charge of discrimination.

This case arises out of actions that supervisors at petitioner Burlington Northern & Santa Fe Railway Company took against respondent Sheila White, the only woman working in the Maintenance of Way department at Burlington's Tennessee Yard. In June 1997, Burlington's roadmaster, Marvin Brown, interviewed White and expressed interest in her previous experience operating forklifts. Burlington hired White as a "track laborer," a job that involves removing and replacing track components, transporting track material, cutting brush, and clearing litter and cargo spillage from the right-of-way. Soon after White arrived on the job, a co-worker who had previously operated the forklift chose to assume other responsibilities. Brown immediately assigned White to operate the forklift. While she also performed some of the other track laborer tasks, operating the forklift was White's primary responsibility.

In September 1997, White complained to Burlington officials that her immediate supervisor, Bill Joiner, had repeatedly told her that women should not be working in the Maintenance of Way department. Joiner, White said, had also made insulting and inappropriate remarks to her in front of her male colleagues. After an internal investigation, Burlington suspended Joiner for 10 days and ordered him to attend a sexual-harassment training session.

On September 26, Brown told White about Joiner's discipline. At the same time, he told White that he was removing her from forklift duty and assigning her to perform only standard track laborer tasks. Brown explained that the reassignment reflected co-workers' complaints that, in fairness, a "'more senior

> Would the reassignment of duties constitute an adverse action in a traditional (non-retaliation) adverse action case?

man'" should have the "less arduous and cleaner job" of forklift operator. *White v. Burlington N. & Santa Fe Ry. Co.*, 364 F.3d 789, 792 (C.A. 6 2004) (case below).

On October 10, White filed a complaint with the Equal Employment Opportunity Commission (EEOC or Commission). She claimed that the reassignment of her duties amounted to unlawful gender-based discrimination and retaliation for her having earlier complained about Joiner. In early December, White filed a second retaliation charge with the Commission, claiming that Brown had placed her under surveillance and was monitoring her daily activities. That charge was mailed to Brown on December 8.

A few days later, White and her immediate supervisor, Percy Sharkey, disagreed about which truck should transport White from one location to another. The specific facts of the disagreement are in dispute, but the upshot is that Sharkey told Brown later that afternoon that White had been insubordinate. Brown immediately suspended White without pay. White invoked internal grievance procedures. Those procedures led Burlington to conclude that White had not been insubordinate. Burlington reinstated White to her position and awarded her backpay for the 37 days she was suspended. White filed an additional retaliation charge with the EEOC based on the suspension.

After exhausting administrative remedies, White filed this Title VII action against Burlington in federal court. As relevant here, she claimed that Burlington's actions—(1) changing her job responsibilities, and (2) suspending her for 37 days without pay—amounted to unlawful retaliation in violation of Title VII. § 2000e–3(a). A jury found in White's favor on both of these claims. It awarded her $43,500 in compensatory damages, including $3,250 in medical expenses. The District Court denied Burlington's post-trial motion for judgment as a matter of law. See Fed. Rule Civ. Proc. 50(b). Initially, a divided Sixth Circuit panel reversed the judgment and found in Burlington's favor on the retaliation claims. 310 F.3d 443 (2002). The full Court of Appeals vacated the panel's decision, however, and heard the matter en banc. The court then affirmed the District Court's judgment in White's favor on both retaliation claims.

[W]e conclude that Title VII's substantive provision and its antiretaliation provision are not coterminous. The scope of the antiretaliation provision extends beyond workplace-related or employment-related retaliatory acts and harm. We therefore reject the standards applied in the Courts of Appeals that have treated the antiretaliation provision as forbidding the same conduct prohibited by the antidiscrimination provision and that have limited actionable retaliation to so-called "ultimate employment decisions."

The antiretaliation provision protects an individual not from all retaliation, but from retaliation that produces an injury or harm. As we have explained, the Courts of Appeals have used differing language to describe the level of

> What would constitute an "ultimate" employment decision?

seriousness to which this harm must rise before it becomes actionable retaliation. We agree with the formulation set forth by the Seventh and the District of Columbia Circuits. In our view, a plaintiff must show that a reasonable employee would have found the challenged action materially adverse, "which in this context means it well might have 'dissuaded a reasonable worker from making or supporting a charge of discrimination.'"

We speak of material adversity because we believe it is important to separate significant from trivial harms. Title VII, we have said, does not set forth "a general civility code for the American workplace." *Oncale v. Sundowner Offshore Services, Inc.*, 523 U.S. 75, 80 (1998); *see Faragher v. Boca Raton*, 524 U.S. 775, 788 (1998) (judicial standards for sexual harassment must "filter out complaints attacking 'the ordinary tribulations of the workplace, such as the sporadic use of abusive language, gender-related jokes, and occasional teasing'"). An employee's decision to report discriminatory behavior cannot immunize that employee from those petty slights or minor annoyances that often take place at work and that all employees experience. *See* 1 B. Lindemann & P. Grossman, Employment Discrimination Law 669 (3d ed. 1996) (noting that "courts have held that personality conflicts at work that generate antipathy" and "'snubbing' by supervisors and co-workers" are not actionable under § 704(a)). The antiretaliation provision seeks to prevent employer interference with "unfettered access" to Title VII's remedial mechanisms. *Robinson v. Shell Oil Co.*, 519 U.S. 337, 346 (1997). It does so by prohibiting employer actions that are likely "to deter victims of discrimination from complaining to the EEOC," the courts, and their employers. *Ibid.* And normally petty slights, minor annoyances, and simple lack of good manners will not create such deterrence. *See* 2 EEOC 1998 Manual § 8, p. 8–13.

We refer to reactions of a *reasonable* employee because we believe that the provision's standard for judging harm must be objective. An objective standard is judicially administrable. It avoids the uncertainties and unfair

> What makes an employer's conduct "materially adverse"?

discrepancies that can plague a judicial effort to determine a plaintiff's unusual subjective feelings. Applying this standard to the facts of this case, we believe that there was a sufficient evidentiary basis to support the jury's verdict on White's retaliation claim. The jury found that two of Burlington's actions amounted to retaliation: the reassignment of White from forklift duty to standard track laborer tasks and the 37-day suspension without pay.

First, Burlington argues that a reassignment of duties cannot constitute retaliatory discrimination where, as here, both the former and present duties fall within the same job description. We do not see why that is so. Almost every job category involves some responsibilities and duties that are less desirable than others. Common sense suggests that one good way to discourage an employee such as White from bringing discrimination charges would be to insist that she spend more time performing the more arduous duties and less time performing those that are easier or more agreeable. That is presumably why the EEOC has consistently found "[r]etaliatory work assignments" to be a classic and "widely recognized" example of "forbidden retaliation." 2 EEOC 1991 Manual § 614.7. Based on this record, a jury could reasonably conclude that the reassignment of responsibilities would have been materially adverse to a reasonable employee.

Second, Burlington argues that the 37-day suspension without pay lacked statutory significance because Burlington ultimately reinstated White with backpay. White did receive backpay. But White and her family had to live for 37 days without income. They did not know during that time whether or when White could

> Is it important to the outcome of this case that the plaintiff was ultimately paid?

return to work. Many reasonable employees would find a month without a paycheck to be a serious hardship. And White described to the jury the physical and emotional hardship that 37 days of having "no income, no money" in fact caused. Indeed, she obtained medical treatment for her emotional distress. A reasonable employee facing the choice between retaining her job (and paycheck) and filing a discrimination complaint might well choose the former. That is to say, an indefinite suspension without pay could well act as a deterrent, even if the suspended employee eventually received backpay. Thus, the jury's conclusion that the 37-day suspension without pay was materially adverse was a reasonable one.

■ NOTES AND QUESTIONS

1. One key take away from the *Burlington Northern* decision is the Court's articulation of the formulation for an adverse action brought pursuant to a retaliation claim under Title VII. The plaintiff must show that "a reasonable employee would have found the challenged action materially adverse, which in this context means it well might have dissuaded a reasonable worker from making or supporting a charge of discrimination." *Burlington N.*, 548 U.S. at 68 (internal quotations omitted). Does the standard adopted by the Court make sense? Is it a high enough standard?

2. The plaintiff in this case failed to receive pay for 37 days, but then was provided with the full amount of backpay due. Does this rise to the level of an adverse action?

3. What should the standard be for an adverse action for a claim brought outside of the retaliation context? Should the Court's retaliation standard be imported to the more traditional disparate treatment cases?

 Interactive Problem

Look back at the facts of the interactive problem for this chapter. Assume that another worker at Computers, Inc. complained of national origin discrimination, and as a result, her direct supervisor refused to have lunch with her any more. Her employment in all other respects remained the same. Would this constitute an adverse action under *Burlington Northern*?

4. Causation

Once employees establish that they have engaged in protected conduct and suffered an adverse action, they can complete the prima facie case by showing the causal link between the two. The plaintiff must thus show that the adverse act by the employer was caused by the complaint. Establishing causation can be relatively straightforward in certain cases. Often employers are angry that an employee is complaining of discrimination, and will directly retaliate against him for doing so, providing the employee with direct evidence of discrimination. Or, the employer may make offhanded comments that might be suggestive of retaliation and prove to be valuable circumstantial evidence of discrimination.

Other times, the *timing* of the adverse act itself can be suspicious. For example, if an employee were fired within two hours of complaining of pay discrimination, those circumstances may raise serious questions about the employer's motivations. *See, e.g.*, Love v. RE/MAX of Am., Inc., 738 F.2d 383 (10th Cir. 1984). How much time is too much between the protected conduct and the adverse action is a question for which there is no ready answer, and the courts vary on their approach to the timing issue. *See* Lisa Cooney, *Understanding and Preventing Workplace Retaliation*, 88 Mass. L. Rev. 3, 14 (2003). Generally speaking, when the adverse act occurs within months of the employee's complaint, the courts may be suspicious of the timing. When it occurs more than a year after the complaint, however, the timing begins to appear too tenuous. And of course, this is all a very fact- and jurisdiction-specific inquiry. Where there is a lack of an immediate adverse action by the employer, the courts tend to look for something in addition to timing to support the prima facie case. *See id.* ("The plaintiff cannot meet the burden of causation merely by relying on chronology.") (internal citation omitted). Even where there is a lengthy period between the complaint and the adverse act, other evidence, such as discriminatory comments, may be sufficient to support a prima facie case. And, in all jurisdictions, regardless of timing, the employer's knowledge of the complaint will be critical to proving a retaliation claim. An employer cannot retaliate against that which it has no knowledge of.

Another issue that reached the Supreme Court is whether but-for causation is necessary to establish a retaliation claim. A close textual reading of the statute is necessary to resolve this question.

University of Texas Southwestern Medical Center v. Nassar
570 U.S. 338 (2013)

Justice KENNEDY delivered the opinion of the Court.

Petitioner, the University of Texas Southwestern Medical Center (University), is an academic institution within the University of Texas system. The University specializes in medical education for aspiring physicians, health professionals, and scientists. Over the years, the University has affiliated itself with a number of healthcare facilities including, as relevant in this case, Parkland Memorial Hospital (Hospital). As provided in its affiliation agreement with the University, the Hospital permits the University's students to gain clinical experience working in its facilities. The agreement also requires the Hospital to offer empty staff physician posts to the University's faculty members, and, accordingly, most of the staff physician positions at the Hospital are filled by those faculty members.

Respondent is a medical doctor of Middle Eastern descent who specializes in internal medicine and infectious diseases. In 1995, he was hired to work both as a member of the University's faculty and a staff physician at the Hospital. He left both positions in 1998 for additional medical education and then returned in 2001 as an assistant professor at the University and, once again, as a physician at the Hospital.

In 2004, Dr. Beth Levine was hired as the University's Chief of Infectious Disease Medicine. In that position Levine became respondent's ultimate (though not direct) superior. Respondent alleged that Levine was biased against him on account of his religion and ethnic heritage, a bias manifested by undeserved scrutiny of his billing practices and productivity, as well as comments that "'Middle Easterners are lazy.'" *Nassar v. Univ. Texas Sw. Med. Ctr.*, 674 F.3d 448, 450 (C.A. 5 2012). On different occasions during his employment, respondent met with Dr. Gregory Fitz, the University's Chair of Internal Medicine and Levine's supervisor, to complain about Levine's alleged harassment. Despite obtaining a promotion with Levine's assistance in 2006, respondent continued to believe that she was biased against him. So he tried to arrange to continue working at the Hospital without also being on the University's faculty. After preliminary negotiations with the Hospital suggested this might be possible, respondent resigned his teaching post in July 2006 and sent a letter to Dr. Fitz (among others), in which he stated that the reason for his departure was harassment by Levine. That harassment, he asserted, "'stems from . . . religious, racial and cultural bias against Arabs and Muslims.'" *Id.* at 451. After reading that letter, Dr. Fitz expressed consternation at respondent's accusations, saying that Levine had been "publicly humiliated by th[e] letter" and that it was "very important that she be publicly exonerated."

Meanwhile, the Hospital had offered respondent a job as a staff physician, as it had indicated it would. On learning of that offer, Dr. Fitz protested to the Hospital, asserting that the offer was inconsistent with the affiliation agreement's requirement that all staff physicians also be members of the University faculty. The Hospital then withdrew its offer.

After exhausting his administrative remedies, respondent filed this Title VII suit in the United States District Court for the Northern District of Texas. He alleged two discrete violations of Title VII. The first was a status-based discrimination claim under § 2000e–2(a). Respondent alleged that Dr. Levine's racially and religiously motivated harassment had resulted in his constructive discharge from the University. Respondent's second claim was that Dr. Fitz's efforts to prevent the Hospital from hiring him were in retaliation for complaining about Dr. Levine's harassment, in violation of § 2000e–3(a). The jury found for respondent on both claims. It awarded him over $400,000 in backpay and more than $3 million in compensatory damages. The District Court later reduced the compensatory damages award to $300,000.

On appeal, the Court of Appeals for the Fifth Circuit affirmed in part and vacated in part. The court first concluded that respondent had submitted insufficient evidence in support of his constructive-discharge claim, so it vacated that portion of the jury's verdict. The court affirmed as to the retaliation finding, however, on the theory that retaliation claims brought under § 2000e–3(a)—like claims of status-based discrimination under § 2000e–2(a)—require only a showing that retaliation was a motivating factor for the adverse employment action, rather than its but-for cause. It further held that the evidence supported a finding that Dr. Fitz was motivated, at least in part, to retaliate against respondent for his complaints against Levine. The Court of Appeals then remanded for a redetermination of damages in light of its decision to vacate the constructive-discharge verdict. Four judges dissented from the court's decision not to rehear the case en banc, arguing that the Circuit's application of the motivating-factor standard to retaliation cases was "an erroneous interpretation of [Title VII] and controlling caselaw" and should be overruled en banc. 688 F.3d 211, 213–214 (C.A.5 2012) (Smith, J., dissenting from denial of rehearing en banc). Certiorari was granted.

> The district court reduced the award in this case to comply with the statutory caps for compensatory and punitive damages, which will be discussed in Chapter 12.

This case requires the Court to define the proper standard of causation for Title VII retaliation claims. Causation in fact—i.e., proof that the defendant's conduct did in fact cause the plaintiff's injury—is a standard requirement of any tort claim. In the usual course, this standard requires the plaintiff to show "that the harm would not have occurred" in the absence of—that is, but for—the defendant's conduct. It is thus textbook tort law that an action "is not regarded as a cause of an event if the particular event would have occurred without it." W. KEETON, D. DOBBS, R. KEETON, & D. OWEN, PROSSER AND KEETON ON LAW OF TORTS 265 (5th ed. 1984). This, then, is the background against which Congress legislated in enacting Title VII, and these are the default rules it is presumed to have incorporated, absent an indication to the contrary in the statute itself.

Since the statute's passage in 1964, it has prohibited employers from discriminating against their employees on any of seven specified criteria. Five of them—race, color, religion, sex, and national origin—are personal characteristics and are set forth in § 2000e–2. (As noted at the outset, discrimination based on these five characteristics is called status-based discrimination in this opinion.) And then there is a point of great import for this case: The two remaining categories of wrongful employer conduct—the employee's opposition to employment discrimination, and the employee's submission of or support for a complaint that alleges employment discrimination—are not wrongs based on personal traits but rather types of protected employee conduct. These latter two categories are covered by a separate, subsequent section of Title VII, § 2000e–3(a).

[The Court here summarizes the *Price Waterhouse* debate over but-for causation.] [I]n short, the 1991 Act substituted a new burden-shifting framework for the one endorsed by *Price Waterhouse* [in § 2000e–2(m)]. Under that new regime, a plaintiff could obtain declaratory relief, attorney's fees and costs, and some forms of injunctive relief based solely on proof that race, color, religion, sex, or nationality was a motivating factor in the employment action; but the employer's proof that it would still have taken the same employment action would save it from monetary damages and a reinstatement order.

> As discussed earlier in this Chapter, the *Price Waterhouse* decision was a motivating force behind the Civil Rights Act of 1991, which amended Title VII in several important ways.

After *Price Waterhouse* and the 1991 Act, considerable time elapsed before the Court returned again to the meaning of "because" and the problem of causation. This time it arose in the context of a different, yet similar statute, the ADEA, 29 U.S.C. § 623(a), *Gross v. FBL Fin. Servs., Inc.*, 557 U.S. 167 (2009).

Concentrating first and foremost on the meaning of the phrase "'*because of . . .* age,'" the Court in *Gross* explained that the ordinary meaning of "'because of'" is "'by reason of'" or "'on account of.'" Thus, the "requirement that an employer took adverse action 'because of' age [meant] that age was the 'reason' that the employer decided to act," or, in other words, that "age was the 'but-for' cause of the employer's adverse decision."

In the course of approving this construction, *Gross* declined to adopt the interpretation endorsed by the plurality and concurring opinions in *Price Waterhouse*. Noting that "the ADEA must be 'read . . . the way Congress wrote it,' [citation omitted], the

Court concluded that "the textual differences between Title VII and the ADEA" "prevent[ed] us from applying *Price Waterhouse* . . . to federal age discrimination claims," *Gross*, 557 U.S. at 175, n. 2. As noted, Title VII's antiretaliation provision, which is set forth in § 2000e–3(a), appears in a different section from Title VII's ban on status-based discrimination. The antiretaliation provision states, in relevant part:

> It shall be an unlawful employment practice for an employer to discriminate against any of his employees . . . because he has opposed any practice made an unlawful employment practice by this subchapter, or because he has made a charge, testified, assisted, or participated in any manner in an investigation, proceeding, or hearing under this subchapter.

This enactment, like the statute at issue in *Gross*, makes it unlawful for an employer to take adverse employment action against an employee "because" of certain criteria. *Cf.* 29 U.S.C. § 623(a)(1). Given the lack of any meaningful textual difference between the text in this statute and the one in *Gross*, the proper conclusion here, as in *Gross*, is that Title VII retaliation claims require proof that the desire to retaliate was the but-for cause of the challenged employment action.

The principal counterargument offered by respondent and the United States relies on their different understanding of the motivating-factor section, which — on its face — applies only to status discrimination, discrimination on the basis of race, color, religion, sex, and national origin. In substance, they contend that: (1) retaliation is defined by the statute to be an unlawful employment practice; (2) § 2000e–2(m) allows unlawful employment practices to be proved based on a showing that race, color, religion, sex, or national origin was a motivating factor for — and not necessarily the but-for factor in — the challenged employment action; and (3) the Court has, as a matter of course, held that "retaliation for complaining about race discrimination is 'discrimination based on race.'"

There are three main flaws in this reading of § 2000e–2(m). The first is that it is inconsistent with the provision's plain language. It must be acknowledged that because Title VII defines "unlawful employment practice" to include retaliation, the question presented by this case would be different if § 2000e–2(m) extended its coverage to all unlawful employment practices. As actually written, however, the text of the motivating-factor provision, while it begins by referring to "unlawful employment practices," then proceeds to address only five of the seven prohibited discriminatory actions — actions based on the employee's status, i.e., race, color, religion, sex, and national origin. This indicates Congress' intent to confine that provision's coverage to only those types of employment practices.

The second problem with this reading is its inconsistency with the design and structure of the statute as a whole. Just as Congress' choice of words is presumed to be deliberate, so too are its structural choices. When Congress wrote the motivating-factor provision in 1991, it chose to insert it as a subsection within § 2000e–2, which contains Title VII's ban on status-based discrimination and says nothing about retaliation. The title of the section of the 1991 Act that created § 2000e–2(m) — "Clarifying prohibition against impermissible consideration of race, color, religion, sex, or national origin in employment practices" — also indicates that Congress determined to address only claims of status-based discrimination, not retaliation.

The third problem with respondent's and the Government's reading of the motivating-factor standard is in its submission that this Court's decisions interpreting federal antidiscrimination law have, as a general matter, treated bans on status-based discrimination as also prohibiting retaliation. In support of this proposition, both respondent and the United States rely upon decisions in which this Court has "read [a] broadly worded civil rights statute . . . as including an antiretaliation remedy." These decisions are not controlling here.

The proper interpretation and implementation of § 2000e–3(a) and its causation standard have central importance to the fair and responsible allocation of resources in the judicial and litigation systems. This is of particular significance because claims of retaliation are being made with ever-increasing frequency. The number of these claims filed with the Equal Employment Opportunity Commission (EEOC) has nearly doubled in the past 15 years—from just over 16,000 in 1997 to over 31,000 in 2012. EEOC, Charge Statistics FY 1997 Through FY 2012, http://www.eeoc.gov/eeoc/statistics/enforcement/charges.cfm (as visited June 20, 2013, and available in Clerk of Court's case file). Indeed, the number of retaliation claims filed with the EEOC has now outstripped those for every type of status-based discrimination except race.

The facts of this case also demonstrate the legal and factual distinctions between status-based and retaliation claims, as well as the importance of the correct standard of proof. Respondent raised both claims in the District Court. The alleged wrongdoer differed in each: In respondent's status-based discrimination claim, it was his indirect supervisor, Dr. Levine. In his retaliation claim, it was the

> The Court notes a dramatic rise in the number of retaliation claims filed over the past fifteen years. What accounts for this increase?

Chair of Internal Medicine, Dr. Fitz. The proof required for each claim differed, too. For the status-based claim, respondent was required to show instances of racial slurs, disparate treatment, and other indications of nationality-driven animus by Dr. Levine. Respondent's retaliation claim, by contrast, relied on the theory that Dr. Fitz was committed to exonerating Dr. Levine and wished to punish respondent for besmirching her reputation. Separately instructed on each type of claim, the jury returned a separate verdict for each, albeit with a single damages award. And the Court of Appeals treated each claim separately, too, finding insufficient evidence on the claim of status-based discrimination.

If it were proper to apply the motivating-factor standard to respondent's retaliation claim, the University might well be subject to liability on account of Dr. Fitz's alleged desire to exonerate Dr. Levine, even if it could also be shown that the terms of the affiliation agreement precluded the Hospital's hiring of respondent and that the University would have sought to prevent respondent's hiring in order to honor that agreement in any event. That result would be inconsistent with the both the text and purpose of Title VII.

The text, structure, and history of Title VII demonstrate that a plaintiff making a retaliation claim under § 2000e–3(a) must establish that his or her protected activity was a but-for cause of the alleged adverse action by the employer. The University claims that a fair application of this standard, which is more demanding than the motivating-factor standard adopted by the Court of Appeals, entitles it to judgment as a matter of law. It asks the Court to so hold. That question, however, is better suited to resolution by courts closer to the facts of this case. The judgment of the Court of Appeals for the Fifth Circuit is vacated, and the case is remanded for further proceedings consistent with this opinion.

Justice GINSBURG, with whom Justice BREYER, Justice SOTOMAYOR, and Justice KAGAN join, dissenting.

Title VII makes it an "unlawful employment practice" to "discriminate against any individual . . . *because of* such individual's race, color, religion, sex, or national origin." § 2000e–2(a) (emphasis added). Backing up that core provision, Title VII also makes it an "unlawful employment practice" to discriminate against any individual *"because"* the individual has complained of, opposed, or participated in a proceeding about, prohibited discrimination. § 2000e–3(a) (emphasis added). This form of discrimination is commonly called "retaliation," although Title VII itself does not use that term. The Court has recognized that effective protection against retaliation, the office of § 2000e–3(a), is essential to securing "a workplace where individuals are not discriminated against because of their racial, ethnic, religious, or gender-based status." *Burlington N. & S.F. Ry. Co. v. White*, 548 U.S. 53 (2006) (*Burlington Northern*). That is so because "fear of retaliation is the leading reason why people stay silent" about the discrimination they have encountered or observed.

Similarly worded, the ban on discrimination and the ban on retaliation against a discrimination complainant have traveled together: Title VII plaintiffs often raise the two provisions in tandem. Today's decision, however, drives a wedge between the twin safeguards in so-called "mixed-motive" cases. To establish discrimination, all agree, the complaining party need show only that race, color, religion, sex, or national origin was "a motivating factor" in an employer's adverse action; an employer's proof that "other factors also motivated the [action]" will not defeat the discrimination claim. § 2000e–2(m). But a retaliation claim, the Court insists, must meet a stricter standard: The claim will fail unless the complainant shows "but-for" causation, i.e., that the employer would not have taken the adverse employment action but for a design to retaliate.

> The dissent emphasizes the strong relationship between status discrimination and retaliation over the years.

In so reining in retaliation claims, the Court misapprehends what our decisions teach: Retaliation for complaining about discrimination is tightly bonded to the core prohibition and cannot be disassociated from it. Indeed, this Court has explained again and again that "retaliation in response to a complaint about [proscribed] discrimination *is* discrimination" on the basis of the characteristic Congress sought to immunize against adverse employment action.

The Court shows little regard for the trial judges who will be obliged to charge discrete causation standards when a claim of discrimination "because of," e.g., race is coupled with a claim of discrimination "because" the individual has complained of race discrimination. And jurors will puzzle over the rhyme or reason for the dual standards. Of graver concern, the Court has seized on a provision, § 2000e–2(m), adopted by Congress as part of an endeavor to strengthen Title VII, and turned it into a measure reducing the force of the ban on retaliation.

The Court holds, at odds with a solid line of decisions recognizing that retaliation is inextricably bound up with status-based discrimination, that § 2000e–2(m) excludes retaliation claims. It then reaches outside of Title VII to arrive at an interpretation of "because" that lacks sensitivity to the realities of life at work. In this endeavor, the Court is guided neither by precedent, nor by the aims of legislators who formulated and amended Title VII. Indeed, the Court appears driven by a zeal to reduce the number of retaliation claims filed against employers. Congress had no such goal in mind when it added § 2000e–2(m) to Title VII. Today's misguided judgment, along with the judgment in *Vance v. Ball State University*, should prompt yet another Civil Rights Restoration Act.

■ NOTES AND QUESTIONS

1. Do you agree with the majority that a textual analysis of the statute supports a but-for causation standard for retaliation claims? Why or why not?

2. The Court emphasized the substantial rise in retaliation claims over the prior fifteen-year period. All charge data is available on the government's website. *See* EEOC, *Charge Statistics FY 1997–FY 2017*, http://eeoc.gov/eeoc/statistics/enforcement/charges.cfm.

3. Did the Court properly apply the standard that it announced here to the facts of the case? Why or why not?

4. How convincing do you find the dissent's argument that status-based discrimination and retaliation claims are more or less intertwined and should carry the same standard of proof?

5. The dissent also asserts that the majority's new standard will create confusion for the courts and juries. Do you agree?

6. The dissent further advocates for "yet another Civil Rights Restoration Act," given this case and another recent decision. Should Congress act to overturn this case?

Interactive Problem

Looking back at the facts of the interactive problem, assume that Bob tries to secure new employment with Super Computers Corporation, where he would perform the same type of work he had done in the past. When Super Computers contacts Computers, Inc., for a reference, they are told that "Bob is a troublemaker and will sue you for discrimination the first chance he gets—avoid hiring him at all costs." If Bob were able to enter this conversation into evidence, would but-for causation be established? Would the other elements of a retaliation claim similarly be present?

Class Exercise: Researching Causation/Timing

The federal courts vary in their views about the importance of the timing of the adverse action in relation to the protected conduct. Is there an inference of discrimination if an adverse act is taken within a week of the employee's complaint? A month? Six months? A year? Breaking up into small groups, discuss what period of time would make the most sense to set as an outer limit to support retaliatory motivations. How did you arrive at this time period?

---

5. Completing the *McDonnell Douglas* Framework for Retaliation Claims

Once the plaintiff establishes all of the elements of the prima facie case, an inference of discrimination is raised. The case then proceeds like a typical *McDonnell Douglas* case, as the defendant has the burden of production to establish a legitimate nondiscriminatory reason for the adverse act. As the EEOC has provided: "Common non-retaliatory reasons offered by respondents for challenged actions include: poor job performance; inadequate qualifications for the position sought; violation of work rules or insubordination; and, with regard to negative job references, truthfulness of the information in the reference." EEOC Compl. Man. (CCH) § 8-II(E)(2) (1998).

Once the employer establishes the legitimate nondiscriminatory reason, the employee has the opportunity to show — through a burden of persuasion — that the employer's stated reason is pretext for discrimination. Like any case of discrimination, there are a variety of ways that an employee can attempt to show pretext. *See id.* ("Typically, pretext is proved through evidence that the respondent treated the complainant differently from similarly situated employees or that the respondent's explanation for the adverse action is not believable. Pretext can also be shown if the respondent subjected the charging party's work performance to heightened scrutiny after she engaged in protected activity.").

Practice and Procedural Tip

11: Handling Retaliation Claims

Being a good lawyer starts well before litigation ever occurs. This is particularly true in the employment discrimination context, where litigation can be avoided in many instances by properly handling a given employment situation. Retaliation claims are particularly important to address in an appropriate manner.

When an employer receives an internal complaint of discrimination, it must be carefully addressed. This means performing a full investigation of the complaint by an independent party. It is imperative to remember — and to advise those individuals taking part in the investigation — that retaliation against the individual filing the complaint can be damaging to the company. When discrimination is uncovered, it should be quickly addressed to prevent further occurrences. Where no discrimination is found, the results of the investigation should be conveyed to the complaining party.

The situation can be particularly difficult to handle where the employee goes outside the company and files a charge with the EEOC. As a defense attorney, you must quickly advise your client on how to handle these situations. In particular, employers tend to be angry when receiving these complaints. This anger is only heightened if they did not actually discriminate ("How can he accuse me of breaking federal law? I'll get him!"). It is thus critical to advise clients that they must not react by trying to punish the employee for complaining. While this may seem obvious to an attorney who is cognizant of the law, it may not be as obvious to managers that are not as knowledgeable of the statute (and who are frustrated by the situation). The company must be made aware of the consequences of improper retaliation, and advised that an independent investigation into the allegations should commence.

6. Retaliation Review

As retaliation is a critical concept in employment discrimination, it can be helpful to briefly summarize the elements of a typical case of retaliation under Title VII. The chart below helps provide a visual summary of this area of the law:

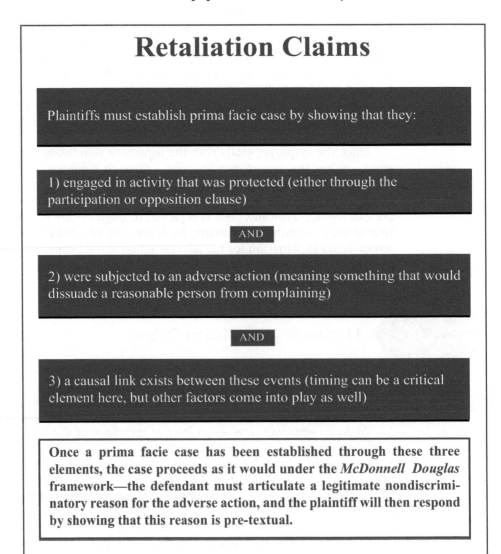

Retaliation Claims

Plaintiffs must establish prima facie case by showing that they:

1) engaged in activity that was protected (either through the participation or opposition clause)

AND

2) were subjected to an adverse action (meaning something that would dissuade a reasonable person from complaining)

AND

3) a causal link exists between these events (timing can be a critical element here, but other factors come into play as well)

Once a prima facie case has been established through these three elements, the case proceeds as it would under the *McDonnell Douglas* framework—the defendant must articulate a legitimate nondiscriminatory reason for the adverse action, and the plaintiff will then respond by showing that this reason is pre-textual.

Figure 3.3

J. Chapter-in-Review

The vast majority of employment discrimination claims are analyzed through the *McDonnell Douglas* framework, which examines cases of circumstantial evidence. To establish a prima facie case under this standard, plaintiffs must show that they are (a) in a protected class; (b) qualified; (c) suffered an adverse action; and (d) that there is some other evidence of discrimination. Once the plaintiff satisfies this test, the burden of production shifts to the employer to articulate a legitimate nondiscriminatory reason for the action. The plaintiff, who carries the burden of persuasion throughout the case, must then show that this reason is pretextual.

Plaintiffs may also show discrimination through direct evidence. This evidence leaves no room for inference or doubt on the question of discriminatory intent.

Mixed-motives cases are a unique form of Title VII action. In these cases, plaintiffs need not show but-for causation, but can instead establish that discrimination was a motivating factor in the decision. Defendants can limit damages in these cases through an affirmative defense—showing that they would have made the same decision even in the absence of the discriminatory motive. In after-acquired evidence cases, the employer does not discover that the employee has engaged in some type of wrongdoing until after the discriminatory employment decision is made. Damages are typically cut off in these cases on the date that the wrongdoing is discovered.

Systemic litigation is a controversial area in employment discrimination cases. To bring a class-action claim, a plaintiff must satisfy all of the elements of Rule 23 of the Federal Rules of Civil Procedure. Governmental entities are not bound by this procedural rule.

Retaliation claims are critical to employment discrimination cases. To bring a claim of retaliation, plaintiffs must show (a) that they engaged in protected conduct under either the participation or opposition clause; (b) that they suffered an adverse action; and (c) that there is causation. Just like any other case under *McDonnell Douglas*, the defendant must articulate a legitimate nondiscriminatory reason, and the plaintiff must show that this reason is pretextual.

Disparate Impact

Interactive Problem

Susan Hernandez, a Hispanic female, applies to work as a "moving specialist" at a major moving company—Big Trucking, Inc. As part of the application process, Susan must take a 200-question standardized test demonstrating that she is capable of driving a truck, that she understands the rules of the road, and that she is familiar with the policies of the company. After completing the exam, Susan is told that she has not passed the test, and thus cannot be employed at the company. She is further informed that she should never have been allowed to take the test in the first place, as she also fails to satisfy the physical requirements of the job. To ensure that its workers are strong enough to move heavy furniture, Big Trucking requires that its movers be at least six feet tall and weigh 140 pounds. Susan is only five foot five inches tall and weighs 130 pounds. Susan believes that both the standardized test and the height and weight policies are discriminatory, and files a charge alleging that these policies have a disparate impact on a protected group. What evidence would Susan need to establish her claim? How would the claim be analyzed?

A. Introduction

It is unusual to think of negligence and employment discrimination in the same context, but there is a close connection. Though the vast majority of discrimination claims involve allegations of discriminatory intent, establishing intent is not always necessary in these types of cases. Thus, an employer can be found liable under Title VII even where it does not necessarily mean to discriminate. The Supreme Court has defined disparate impact as those "'employment practices that are facially neutral in their treatment of different groups but that in fact fall more harshly on one group than another and cannot be justified by business necessity.'" Raytheon Co. v. Hernandez, 540 U.S. 44, 52 (2003) (quoting Teamsters v. United States, 431 U.S. 324, 335–336 n.15 (1977)). Thus, the key for disparate impact claims is that there is a "'facially neutral employment policy [that] has a discriminatory impact on protected classes. . . .'" *Id.* at 53 (quoting Texas Dep't of Cmty. Affairs v. Burdine, 450 U.S. 248, 252 n.5 (1981)).

Though most allegations of discrimination involve intent, disparate impact is a critical theory of discrimination. As an employer's policies and practices can impact a protected group, these types of lawsuits invite systemic litigation, which can be expensive for an employer. Businesses should thus be extremely cautious when implementing a policy or practice to make sure that it does not run afoul of the statute.

Early on, disparate impact lacked any solid statutory underpinning. Title VII was silent on whether unintentional discrimination could prove to be a viable cause of action. Many civil rights groups orchestrated a well-organized campaign in the 1960s and early 1970s to have disparate impact claims acknowledged by the courts. It was recognized early in the statute's history that without disparate impact claims, sophisticated employers could conceal intentional discrimination under the guise of facially neutral policies or practices. Not surprisingly, the lower courts differed in their approach to disparate impact claims. Ultimately, the Supreme Court visited the issue in one of the most important employment discrimination cases the Court would ever consider.

Griggs v. Duke Power Co.

401 U.S. 424 (1971)

Mr. Chief Justice BURGER delivered the opinion of the Court.

We granted the writ in this case to resolve the question whether an employer is prohibited by the Civil Rights Act of 1964, Title VII, from requiring a high school education or passing of a standardized general intelligence test as a condition of employment in or transfer to jobs when (a) neither standard is shown to be significantly related to successful job performance, (b) both requirements operate to disqualify Negroes at a substantially higher rate than white applicants, and (c) the jobs in question formerly had been filled only by white employees as part of a longstanding practice of giving preference to whites.

Congress provided, in Title VII of the Civil Rights Act of 1964, for class actions for enforcement of provisions of the Act and this proceeding was brought by a group of incumbent Negro employees against Duke Power Company. All the petitioners are employed at the Company's Dan River Steam Station, a power generating facility located at Draper, North Carolina. At the time this action was instituted, the Company had 95 employees at the Dan River Station, 14 of whom were Negroes; 13 of these are petitioners here.

The District Court found that prior to July 2, 1965, the effective date of the Civil Rights Act of 1964, the Company openly discriminated on the basis of race in the hiring and assigning of employees at its Dan River plant. The plant was organized into five operating departments: (1) Labor, (2) Coal Handling, (3) Operations, (4) Maintenance, and (5) Laboratory and Test. Negroes were employed only in the Labor Department where the highest paying jobs paid less than the lowest paying jobs in the other four "operating" departments in which only whites were employed. Promotions were normally made within each department on the basis of job seniority. Transferees into a department usually began in the lowest position.

> Prior to the enactment of Title VII, the company here *openly* discriminated on the basis of race.

In 1955 the Company instituted a policy of requiring a high school education for initial assignment to any department except Labor, and for transfer from the Coal Handling to any "inside" department (Operations, Maintenance, or Laboratory). When the Company abandoned its policy of restricting Negroes to the Labor Department in 1965, completion of high school also was made a prerequisite to transfer from Labor to any other department. From the time the high school requirement was instituted to the time of trial, however, white employees hired before the time of the high school education requirement continued to perform satisfactorily and achieve promotions in the "operating" departments. Findings on this score are not challenged.

The Company added a further requirement for new employees on July 2, 1965, the date on which Title VII became effective. To qualify for placement in any but the Labor Department it bec[a]me necessary to register satisfactory scores on two professionally prepared aptitude tests, as well as to have a high school education. Completion of high school alone continued to render employees eligible for transfer to the four desirable departments from which Negroes had been excluded if the incumbent had been employed prior to the time of the new requirement. In September 1965 the Company began to permit incumbent employees who lacked a high school education to qualify for transfer from Labor or Coal Handling to an "inside" job by passing two tests—the Wonderlic Personnel Test, which purports to measure general intelligence, and the Bennett Mechanical Comprehension Test. Neither was directed or intended to measure the ability to learn to perform a particular job or category of jobs. The requisite scores used for both initial hiring and transfer approximated the national median for high school graduates.

The District Court had found that while the Company previously followed a policy of overt racial discrimination in a period prior to the Act, such conduct had ceased. The District Court also concluded that Title VII was intended to be prospective only and, consequently, the impact of prior inequities was beyond the reach of corrective action authorized by the Act.

> The District Court found no *intentional* discrimination based on the facts in this case. Do you agree?

The Court of Appeals was confronted with a question of first impression, as are we, concerning the meaning of Title VII. After careful analysis a majority of that court con- cluded that a subjective test of the employer's intent should govern, par- ticularly in a close case, and that in this case there was no showing of a dis- criminatory purpose in the adoption of the diploma and test requirements. On this basis, the Court of Appeals concluded there was no violation of the Act.

Power Plant Facility

The Court of Appeals reversed the District Court in part, rejecting the holding that residual discrimination arising from prior employment practices was insulated from remedial action. The Court of Appeals noted, however, that the District Court was correct in its con- clusion that there was no showing of a racial purpose or invidious intent in the adoption of the high school diploma requirement or general intelligence test and that these standards had been applied fairly to whites and Negroes alike. It held that, in the absence of a discriminatory purpose, use of such requirements was permitted by the Act. In so doing, the Court of Appeals rejected the claim that because these two requirements operated to render ineligible a markedly dispro- portionate number of Negroes, they were unlawful under Title VII unless shown to be job related.

The objective of Congress in the enactment of Title VII is plain from the lan- guage of the statute. It was to achieve equality of employment opportunities and remove barriers that have operated in the past to favor an identifiable group of white employees over other employees. Under the Act, practices, procedures, or tests neutral on their face, and even neutral in terms of intent, cannot be main- tained if they operate to "freeze" the status quo of prior discriminatory employ- ment practices.

The Court of Appeals' opinion, and the partial dissent, agreed that, on the record in the present case, "whites register far better on the Company's alternative requirements" than Negroes. This consequence would appear to be directly traceable to race. Basic intelligence must have the means of articulation to manifest itself fairly in a testing process. Because they are Negroes, petition- ers have long received inferior education in segregated schools and this Court expressly recognized these differences in Gaston County v. United States, 395 U.S. 285, (1969). There, because of the inferior education received by Negroes in North Carolina, this Court barred the institution of a literacy test for voter registration on the ground that the test would abridge the right to vote indi- rectly on account of race. Congress did not intend by Title VII, however, to guarantee a job to every person regardless of qualifications. In short, the Act does not command that any person be hired simply because he was formerly the subject of discrimination, or because he is a member of a minority group. Discriminatory preference for any group, minority or majority, is precisely and only what Congress has proscribed. What is required by Congress is the removal of artificial, arbitrary, and unnecessary barriers to employment when the barriers operate invidiously to discriminate on the basis of racial or other impermissible classification.

Congress has now provided that tests or criteria for employment or promotion may not provide equality of opportunity merely in the sense of the fabled offer of milk to the stork and the fox. On the contrary, Congress has now required that the posture and condition of the job-seeker be taken into account. It has—to resort again to the fable—provided that the vessel in which the milk is proffered be one all seekers can use. The Act proscribes not only overt discrimination but also practices that are fair in form, but discriminatory in operation. The touchstone is business necessity. If an employment practice which operates to exclude Negroes cannot be shown to be related to job performance, the practice is prohibited.

On the record before us, neither the high school completion requirement nor the general intelligence test is shown to bear a demonstrable relationship to successful performance of the jobs for which it was used. Both were adopted, as the Court of Appeals noted, without meaningful study of their relationship to job-performance ability. Rather, a vice president of the Company testified, the requirements were instituted on the Company's judgment that they generally would improve the overall quality of the work force.

The evidence, however, shows that employees who have not completed high school or taken the tests have continued to perform satisfactorily and make progress in departments for which the high school and test criteria are now used. The promotion record of present employees who would not be able to meet the new criteria thus suggests the possibility that the requirements may not be needed even for the limited purpose of preserving the avowed policy of advancement within the Company. In the context of this case, it is unnecessary to reach the question whether testing requirements that take into account capability for the next succeeding position or related future promotion might be utilized upon a showing that such long range requirements fulfill a genuine business need. In the present case the Company has made no such showing.

> The Court notes that employees hired before the new policies were put in place were performing well. Why is this important?

The Court of Appeals held that the Company had adopted the diploma and test requirements without any "intention to discriminate against Negro employees." We do not suggest that either the District Court or the Court of Appeals erred in examining the employer's intent; but good intent or absence of discriminatory intent does not redeem employment procedures or testing mechanisms that operate as "built-in headwinds" for minority groups and are unrelated to measuring job capability.

The Company's lack of discriminatory intent is suggested by special efforts to help the undereducated employees through Company financing of two-thirds the cost of tuition for high school training. But Congress directed the thrust of the Act to the consequences of employment practices, not simply the motivation. More than that, Congress has placed on the employer the burden of showing that any given requirement must have a manifest relationship to the employment in question.

The facts of this case demonstrate the inadequacy of broad and general testing devices as well as the infirmity of using diplomas or degrees as fixed measures of capability. History is filled with examples of men and women who rendered highly effective performance without the conventional badges of accomplishment in terms of certificates, diplomas, or degrees. Diplomas and tests are useful servants, but Congress has mandated the commonsense proposition that they are not to become masters of reality.

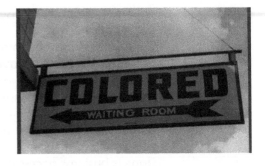

Nothing in the Act precludes the use of testing or measuring procedures; obviously they are useful. What Congress has forbidden is giving these devices and mechanisms controlling force unless they are demonstrably a reasonable measure of job performance. Congress has not commanded that the less qualified be preferred over the better qualified simply because of minority origins. Far from disparaging job qualifications as such, Congress has made such qualifications the controlling factor, so that race, religion, nationality, and sex become irrelevant. What Congress has commanded is that any tests used must measure the person for the job and not the person in the abstract. The judgment of the Court of Appeals is, as to that portion of the judgment appealed from, reversed.

■ NOTES AND QUESTIONS

1. The disparate impact theory is recognized as one of the most significant, as well as controversial, developments in antidiscrimination law. While the theory is generally associated with the *Griggs* decision, its origins run deeper. The academic scholarship, judicial case law, and the strategic decision by the EEOC to introduce the theory as an alternative to intentional discrimination claims, all led to the creation of the disparate impact theory. *See* Michael Selmi, *Was the Disparate Impact Theory a Mistake?*, 53 UCLA L. Rev. 701 (2006).

2. This case discusses unintentional discrimination, but do you believe that Duke Power actually *intended* to discriminate when it adopted the standardized test and high school diploma requirement? Why or why not?

3. Do you agree with the Court that disparate impact should be permitted under the statute? Shouldn't an employer be required to *purposely* discriminate to have liability imposed?

4. This case pre-dates *McDonnell Douglas*. How would you analyze this case under the *McDonnell Douglas* framework presented in the previous chapter?

5. Disparate impact claims have been criticized as creating quota-like systems in the workplace. Do you agree with this critique? *See generally* Kingsley R. Browne, *The Civil Rights Act of 1991: A "Quota Bill," a Codification of* Griggs, *a Partial Return to* Wards Cove, *or All of the Above?*, 43 Case W. Res. L. Rev. 287 (1993); Charles J. Cooper, Wards Cove Packing Co. v. Atonio: *A Step Toward Eliminating Quotas in the American Workplace*, 14 Harv. J.L. & Pub. Pol'y 84 (1991); Michael H. Gottesman, *Twelve Topics to Consider Before Opting for Racial Quotas*, 79 Geo. L.J. 1737 (1991); Lino A. Graglia, *Title VII of the Civil Rights Act of 1964: From Prohibiting to Requiring Racial Discrimination in Employment*, 14 Harv. J.L. & Pub. Pol'y 68 (1991); Mark H. Grunewald, *Quotas, Politics, and Judicial Statesmanship: The Civil Rights Act of 1991 and Powell's* Bakke, 49 Wash. & Lee L. Rev. 53, 54–56 (1992) (discussing generally *Griggs* and *Wards Cove,* particularly with respect to quotas).

6. The Court here establishes a two-part test for disparate impact claims: (1) The plaintiff must show that the defendant has adopted a facially neutral policy or practice that has a discriminatory impact on a protected group; and (2) the defendant can still prevail by establishing that the requirement is job related and consistent with business necessity.

7. The Court does not discuss in this case the commonly accepted third prong of the disparate impact test; that even in the face of a business necessity the employee can still show that there are policies available that have less discriminatory impact but still serve the employer's business needs. How important is this last prong? How would it have been applied in *Griggs*?

8. An argument can be made that Duke Power was intentionally discriminating in this case, but that it was impossible to prove. As the Court notes, prior to the enactment of Title VII, the company had openly discriminated. Does the Court create a policy, then, that is really targeting those situations that seem suspicious but are difficult to prove? Or, is disparate impact meant to apply more broadly? *See* Ian Haney-López, *Intentional Blindness*, 87 N.Y.U. L. Rev. 1779 (2012); Stacy E. Seicshnaydre, *Is the Road to Disparate Impact Paved with Good Intentions?: Stuck on State of Mind in Antidiscrimination Law*, 42 Wake Forest L. Rev. 1141 (2007).

9. Among the determinative factors in the Court's decision in *Griggs* was the sense that a ruling that prohibited the EEOC from closely examining practices that worked a greater disadvantage on under-represented groups would allow employers to use those practices to continue discriminatorily designed programs. Samuel Estreicher, *The Story of* Griggs v. Duke Power Co., *in* Employment Discrimination Stories 153, 164–166 (Joel M. Friedman ed., 2006).

10. **Historical Note.** Chief Justice Burger initially designated the *Griggs* case as "dead listed": those cases not discussed among the Justices for review. However, Justice Brennan, who was recused as former counsel for Duke Power, convinced Justice Stewart to advocate for a discussion of *Griggs*. After arguments, the Chief Justice assigned the opinion to himself, apparently in the hope of combating his popular portrayal as a "conservative," cast opposite the role of his predecessor, Earl Warren. Bob Woodward & Scott Armstrong, The Brethren: Inside the Supreme Court 122–123 (1979).

Interactive Problem

Looking back at the interactive problem at the beginning of the chapter, assume that the company also has a policy that no applicant that has ever been convicted of an alcohol- or drug-related driving violation can become a "moving specialist." How would this policy be analyzed under the Court's test?

Some employers have adopted policies that—while having a discriminatory impact—are perceived to be in the best interests of public safety. These policies frequently seem to come with an important rationale to the business and larger community safety concerns. The Supreme Court considers one such case below. The case was brought by the plaintiff as one of both disparate impact and intentional sex discrimination. The disparate impact portion of the decision is set forth below, and the Court's discussion of intentional sex discrimination is addressed in Chapter 6.

Dothard v. Rawlinson
433 U.S. 321 (1977)

Mr. Justice STEWART delivered the opinion of the Court.

Dianne Rawlinson sought employment with the Alabama Board of Corrections as a prison guard. Called in Alabama a "correctional counselor."

At the time she applied for a position as correctional counselor trainee, Rawlinson was a 22-year-old college graduate whose major course of study had been correctional psychology. She was refused employment because she failed to meet the minimum 120-pound weight requirement established by an Alabama statute. The statute also establishes a height minimum of 5 feet 2 inches.

After her application was rejected because of her weight, Rawlinson filed a charge with the Equal Employment Opportunity Commission, and ultimately received a right-to-sue letter. She then filed a complaint in the District Court on behalf of herself and other similarly situated women, challenging the statutory height and weight minima as violative of Title VII and the

> Would a 120 lb. 5' 2" guard necessarily be able to control an unruly prisoner?

Equal Protection Clause of the Fourteenth Amendment. A three-judge court was convened. While the suit was pending, the Alabama Board of Corrections adopted Administrative Regulation 204, establishing gender criteria for assigning correctional counselors to maximum-security institutions for "contact positions," that is, positions requiring continual close physical proximity to inmates of the institution. Rawlinson amended her class-action complaint by adding a challenge to regulation 204 as also violative of Title VII and the Fourteenth Amendment.

Like most correctional facilities in the United States, Alabama's prisons are segregated on the basis of sex. Currently the Alabama Board of Corrections operates four major all-male penitentiaries: Holman Prison, Kilby Corrections Facility, G. K. Fountain Correction Center, and Draper Correctional Center. The Board also operates the Julia Tutwiler Prison for Women, the Frank Lee Youth Center, the Number Four Honor Camp, the State Cattle Ranch, and nine Work Release Centers, one of which is for women. The Julia Tutwiler Prison for Women and the four male penitentiaries are maximum-security institutions. Their inmate living quarters are for the most part large dormitories, with communal showers and toilets that are open to the dormitories and hallways. The Draper and Fountain penitentiaries carry on extensive farming operations, making necessary a large number of strip searches for contraband when prisoners re-enter the prison buildings.

State Prison

A correctional counselor's primary duty within these institutions is to maintain security and control of the inmates by continually supervising and observing their activities. To be eligible for consideration as a correctional counselor, an applicant must possess a valid Alabama driver's license, have a high school education or its equivalent, be free from physical defects, be between the ages of 20 1/2 years and 45 years at the time of appointment, and fall between the minimum height and weight requirements of 5 feet 2 inches, and 120 pounds, and the maximum of 6 feet 10 inches, and 300 pounds. Appointment is by merit, with a grade assigned each applicant based on experience and education. No written examination is given.

At the time this litigation was in the District Court, the Board of Corrections employed a total of 435 people in various correctional counselor positions, 56 of whom were women. Of those 56 women, 21 were employed at the Julia Tutwiler Prison for Women, 13 were employed in noncontact positions at the four male maximum-security institutions, and the remaining 22 were employed at the other institutions operated by the Alabama Board of Corrections. Because most of Alabama's prisoners are held at the four maximum-security male penitentiaries, 336 of the 435 correctional counselor jobs were in those institutions, a majority of them concededly in the "contact" classification. Thus, even though meeting the statutory height and weight requirements, women applicants could under Regulation 204 compete equally with men for only about 25% of the correctional counselor jobs available in the Alabama prison system.

The gist of the claim that the statutory height and weight requirements discriminate against women does not involve an assertion of purposeful discriminatory motive. It is asserted, rather, that these facially neutral qualification standards work in fact disproportionately to exclude women from eligibility for employment by the Alabama Board of Corrections.

[T]o establish a prima facie case of discrimination, a plaintiff need only show that the facially neutral standards in question select applicants for hire in a significantly discriminatory pattern. Once it is thus shown that the employment standards are discriminatory in effect, the employer must meet "the burden of showing that any given requirement (has) . . . a manifest relationship to the employment in question." Griggs v. Duke Power Co., 401 U.S. 424, 432 (1971). If the employer proves that the challenged requirements are job related, the plaintiff may then show that other selection devices without a similar discriminatory effect would also "serve the employer's legitimate interest in 'efficient and trustworthy workmanship.'" Albemarle Paper Co. v. Moody, 422 U.S. 405, 425 (1975), quoting McDonnell Douglas Corp. v. Green, 411 U.S. 792, 801 (1973).

Although women 14 years of age or older compose 52.75% of the Alabama population and 36.89% of its total labor force, they hold only 12.9% of its correctional counselor positions. In considering the effect of the minimum height and weight standards on this disparity in rate of hiring between the sexes, the District Court found that the 5'2" requirement would operate to exclude 33.29% of the women in the United States between the ages of 18-79, while excluding only 1.28% of men between the same ages. The 120-pound weight restriction would exclude 22.29% of the women and 2.35% of the men in this age group. When the height and weight restrictions are combined, Alabama's statutory standards would exclude 41.13% of the female population while excluding less than 1% of the male population. Accordingly, the District Court found that Rawlinson had made out a prima facie case of unlawful sex discrimination.

The appellants argue that a showing of disproportionate impact on women based on generalized national statistics should not suffice to establish a prima facie case. They point in particular to Rawlinson's failure to adduce comparative statistics concerning actual applicants for correctional counselor positions in Alabama. There is no requirement, however, that a statistical showing of disproportionate impact must always be based on analysis of the characteristics of actual applicants. See Griggs v. Duke Power Co., *supra*, 401 U.S. at 430. The application process might itself not adequately reflect the actual potential applicant pool, since otherwise qualified people might be discouraged from applying because of a self-recognized inability to meet the very standards challenged as being discriminatory. See International Brotherhood of Teamsters v. United States, 431 U.S. 324, 365–367 (1977). A potential applicant could easily determine her height and weight and conclude that to make an application would be futile. Moreover, reliance on general population demographic data was not misplaced where there was no reason to suppose that physical height and weight characteristics of Alabama men and women differ markedly from those of the national population.

For these reasons, we cannot say that the District Court was wrong in holding that the statutory height and weight standards had a discriminatory impact on women applicants. The plaintiffs in a case such as this are not required to exhaust every possible source of evidence, if the evidence actually presented on its face conspicuously demonstrates a job requirement's grossly discriminatory impact. If the employer discerns fallacies or deficiencies in the data offered by the plaintiff, he is free to adduce countervailing evidence of his own. In this case no such effort was made.

We turn, therefore, to the appellants' argument that they have rebutted the prima facie case of discrimination by showing that the height and weight requirements are job related. These requirements, they say, have a relationship to strength, a sufficient but unspecified amount of which is essential to effective job performance as a correctional counselor. In the District Court, however, the appellants pro-

> Is strength generally correlated with height and weight? Should the Court be substituting its judgment where safety is an issue?

duced no evidence correlating the height and weight requirements with the requisite amount of strength thought essential to good job performance. Indeed, they failed to offer evidence of any kind in specific justification of the statutory standards.

If the job-related quality that the appellants identify is bona fide, their purpose could be achieved by adopting and validating a test for applicants that measures strength directly. Such a test, fairly administered, would fully satisfy the standards of Title VII because it would be one that "measure(s) the person for the job and not the person in the abstract." *Griggs*, 401 U.S. at 436. But nothing in the present record even approaches such a measurement.

Mr. Justice REHNQUIST, with whom THE CHIEF JUSTICE and Mr. Justice BLACKMUN join, concurring in the result and concurring in part.

Appellants argued only the job-relatedness of actual physical strength; they did not urge that an equally job-related qualification for prison guards is the appearance of strength. As the Court notes, the primary job of correctional counselor in Alabama prisons "is to maintain security and control of the inmates . . . ," a function that I at least would imagine is aided by the psychological impact on prisoners of the presence of tall and heavy guards. If the appearance of strength had been urged upon the District Court here as a reason for the height and weight minima, I think that the District Court would surely have been entitled to reach a different result than it did. For, even if not perfectly correlated, I would think that Title VII would not preclude a State from saying that anyone under 5 foot 2 inches or 120 pounds, no matter how strong in fact, does not have a sufficient appearance of strength to be a prison guard.

But once the burden has been placed on the defendant, it is then up to the defendant to articulate the asserted job-related reasons. Because of this burden, a reviewing court is not ordinarily justified in relying on arguments in favor of a job qualification that were not first presented to the trial court. As appellants did not even present the "appearance of strength" contention to the District Court as an asserted

> Even though the plaintiffs did not make the "appearance" argument raised here, couldn't the Court have taken judicial notice of it?

job-related reason for the qualification requirements, I agree that their burden was not met. The District Court's holding thus did not deal with the question of whether such an assertion could or did rebut appellee Rawlinson's prima facie case.

■ NOTES AND QUESTIONS

1. Why is the height and weight requirement adopted by the facility for prison guards in contact positions not job related and consistent with business necessity? Isn't there a strong relationship between size and strength, as the defendants argue?

2. The concurrence seems to suggest that if the defendants had argued that size gives the "appearance of strength," this would have been a viable defense to the disparate impact claim. Is this argument really that different from the one articulated by the defendants?

3. If the Court believes that the appearance of strength is important, shouldn't it be able to consider this factor regardless of whether it was argued by the defendant? Isn't the defendant simply losing on a mere technicality here?

4. Should the law be intervening in these types of cases? After all, there is no suggestion that the prison system and state were not trying to act in the best interests of public safety in a difficult prison environment. Shouldn't a state be given wide discretion in how to best operate its prison system?

5. Was disparate impact law—when created by *Griggs*—intended to be used in this type of public safety context?

6. The question of whether sex is a bona fide occupational qualification in this prison context was addressed by the Supreme Court, and is discussed in Chapter 7.

7. Is this case more appropriately considered as one of intentional or unintentional discrimination? Why?

Practice and Procedural Tip

12: Using Arrest and Conviction Records in Employment Decisions, and the "Ban the Box" Movement

The use of arrest records in making a hiring decision has always been controversial. The potential issue in using these records is that they could result in an unlawful disparate impact against certain minority groups. While the courts have largely upheld the use of criminal convictions in hiring, arrest records are a more difficult question. *See* Roberto Concepcíon, Jr., *Need Not Apply: The Racial Disparate Impact of Pre-Employment Criminal Background Checks*, 19 Geo. J. on Poverty L. & Pol'y 231 (2012); Alexandra Harwin, *Title VII Challenges to Employment Discrimination Against Minority Men with Criminal Records*, 14 Berkeley J. Afr.-Am. L. & Pol'y 2 (2012).

The EEOC has found that "[n]ational data supports a finding that criminal record exclusions have a disparate impact based on race and national origin." The Commission further advises that "an exclusion based on an arrest, in itself, is not job related and consistent with business necessity." And the Commission notes that "an employer may make an employment decision based on the conduct underlying the arrest if the conduct makes the individual unfit for the position in question. The conduct, not the arrest, is relevant for employment purposes." *See EEOC Enforcement Guidance, Consideration of Arrest and Conviction Records in Employment Decisions Under Title VII of the Civil Rights Act of 1964* § V(B)(2) (Apr. 25, 2012).

Thus, employers should be very cautious when using arrest records in making employment decisions. In particular, they should closely review any policies that completely exclude applicants with criminal arrests on their records. A more careful inquiry into the arrest and the conduct underlying it are necessary to comply with the statute. The EEOC has already taken on high-profile cases against major companies based on the use of criminal records, and an employer should seek to avoid this type of litigation.

The National Employment Law Project also recently provided data showing that approximately 150 local jurisdictions across the nation have followed the well-known "ban the box" movement, adopting legislation that prohibits employers from soliciting information about an individual's conviction history on a job application. *See* Nat'l Emp't Law Project, Ban the Box (Apr. 20, 2018), http://www.nelp. org/publication/ban-the-box-fair-chance-hiring-state-and-local-guide/. There is substantial concern that such information can also lead to disparate impact discrimination, and many feel that this information should not be considered until the later stages of the hiring process. For example, the state of North Carolina enacted legislation that prohibits employers or educational institutions from asking, "in any application, interview, or otherwise . . . an applicant for employment or admission to disclose information concerning any arrest, criminal charge, or criminal conviction of the applicant that has been expunged." N.C. Gen. Stat. Ann. § 15A-153.

Similarly, a 2013 EEOC lawsuit against BMW alleged that workers at a South Carolina plant were fired (or not hired) based on a newly implemented background check policy that disparately impacted black employees. In sum, the EEOC alleged that BMW's criminal background check policy, which prohibited workers from having misdemeanor or felony convictions on their records, disproportionately excluded black individuals from working at the company. Many workers who had already worked for the company for years—in some cases over a decade—were fired, even if the criminal offense was not serious in nature. The EEOC argued that the gross disparity in the rates at which black employees were denied access to jobs compared to white employees was significant—about 80 percent of those adversely impacted by the policy were black. *See* David Dykes, *Lawsuit Alleges Workers at South Carolina Plant Were Fired or Deprived of Jobs*, USA Today (June 12, 2013, 1:22 p.m.), http://www.usatoday.com/story/news/nation/2013/06/12/federal-agency-sues-bmw-over-background-checks/2415333/; Michelle Singletary, *For Ex-cons Seeking Work, Let's "Ban the Box,"* Wash. Post, June 14, 2013, http://www.washingtonpost.com/business/for-ex-cons-seeking-work-lets-ban-the-box/2013/06/13/cc46146e-d2f4-11e2-a73e-826d299ff459_story.html. *See generally* Press Release, U.S. E.E.O.C., BMW to Pay $1.6 Million and Offer Jobs to Settle Federal Race Discrimination Lawsuit, EEOC.gov (Sept. 8, 2015), https://www.eeoc.gov/eeoc/newsroom/release/9-8-15.cfm ("The U.S. District Court for the District of South Carolina today entered a consent decree ordering [BMW] to pay $1.6 million and provide job opportunities to alleged victims of race discrimination as part of the resolution of a lawsuit filed by the [EEOC]. The lawsuit . . .

alleged that BMW excluded African-American logistics workers from employment at a disproportionate rate when the company's new logistics contractor applied BMW's criminal conviction records guidelines to incumbent logistics employees."). Thus, even when using conviction records in an employment decision, employers must be cautious to follow state and local law, as well as making sure that there has been no disparate impact violation of Title VII.

Griggs saw the height of disparate impact theory. Because disparate impact lacks intentional discrimination (and arguably promotes a quota-like system), it has been a source of continued controversy. *See* Richard A. Primus, *Equal Protection and Disparate Impact: Round Three*, 117 HARV. L. REV. 493 (2003); Richard Primus, *The Future of Disparate Impact*, 108 MICH. L. REV. 1341 (2010); Charles A. Sullivan, *Disparate Impact: Looking Past the* Desert Palace *Mirage*, 47 WM. & MARY L. REV. 911 (2005). For this reason, as the political climate changed in the early and mid-1980s (along with the make-up of the federal courts), many lower courts began to pull back on *Griggs*. This was easy to do as the decision was not based on any solid statutory basis — rather, it was judicially created. Courts were free, then, to distinguish *Griggs* on its facts and limit the reach of its holding. This political wrangling eventually reached the Supreme Court in *Wards Cove*. By the time the *Wards Cove* decision was issued, the make-up of the Court had become more politically conservative than when *Griggs* was decided.

As the Court grew increasingly more conservative after the *Griggs* decision, it revisited the contours of the disparate impact theory. The case below proved to be one of the most divisive civil rights decisions of the decade, resulting in a backlash against the Court. *Wards Cove*, while later largely overturned by Congress, marks a key historical point in the development of employment discrimination law.

Wards Cove Packing Co. v. Atonio
490 U.S. 642 (1989)

Justice WHITE delivered the opinion of the Court.

The claims before us are disparate-impact claims, involving the employment practices of petitioners, two companies that operate salmon canneries in remote and widely separated areas of Alaska. The canneries operate only during the salmon runs in the summer months. They are inoperative and vacant for the rest of the year. In May or June of each year, a few weeks before the salmon runs begin, workers arrive and prepare the equipment and facilities for the canning operation. Most of these workers possess a variety of skills. When salmon runs are about to begin, the workers who will operate the cannery lines arrive, remain as long as there are fish to can, and then depart. The canneries are then closed down, winterized, and left vacant until the next spring. During the off-season, the companies employ only a small number of individuals at their headquarters in Seattle and Astoria, Oregon, plus some employees at the winter shipyard in Seattle.

The length and size of salmon runs vary from year to year, and hence the number of employees needed at each cannery also varies. Estimates are made as early in the winter as possible; the necessary employees are hired, and when the time comes, they are transported to the canneries. Salmon must be processed soon after they are caught, and the work during the canning season is therefore intense. For this reason, and because the canneries are located in remote regions, all workers are housed at the canneries and have their meals in company-owned mess halls.

Salmon Cannery Facility in Alaska

Jobs at the canneries are of two general types: "cannery jobs" on the cannery line, which are unskilled positions; and "noncannery jobs," which fall into a variety of classifications. Most noncannery jobs are classified as skilled positions. Cannery jobs are filled predominantly by nonwhites: Filipinos and Alaska Natives. The Filipinos are hired through, and dispatched by, Local 37 of the International Longshoremen's and Warehousemen's Union pursuant to a hiring hall agreement with the local. The Alaska Natives primarily reside in villages near the remote cannery locations. Noncannery jobs are filled with predominantly white workers, who are hired during the winter months from the companies' offices in Washington and Oregon. Virtually all of the noncannery jobs pay more than cannery positions. The predominantly white noncannery workers and the predominantly nonwhite cannery employees live in separate dormitories and eat in separate mess halls.

In 1974, respondents, a class of nonwhite cannery workers who were (or had been) employed at the canneries, brought this Title VII action against petitioners. Respondents alleged that a variety of petitioners' hiring/promotion practices—*e.g.,* nepotism, a rehire preference, a lack of objective hiring criteria, separate hiring channels, a practice of not promoting from within—were responsible for the racial stratification of the work force and had denied them and other nonwhites employment as noncannery workers on the basis of race. Respondents also complained of petitioners' racially segregated housing and dining facilities. All of respondents' claims were advanced under both the disparate-treatment and disparate-impact theories of Title VII liability.

The District Court held a bench trial, after which it entered 172 findings of fact. It then rejected all of respondents' disparate-treatment claims. It also rejected the disparate-impact challenges involving the subjective employment criteria used by petitioners to fill these noncannery positions, on the ground that those criteria were not subject to attack under a disparate-impact theory. Petitioners' "objective" employment practices (*e.g.,* an English language requirement, alleged nepotism in hiring, failure to post noncannery openings, the rehire preference, etc.) were found to be subject to challenge under the disparate-impact theory, but these claims were rejected for failure of proof. Judgment was entered for petitioners.

On appeal, a panel of the Ninth Circuit affirmed, but that decision was vacated when the Court of Appeals agreed to hear the case en banc. The en banc hearing was ordered to settle an intra-circuit conflict over the question whether subjective hiring practices could be analyzed under a disparate-impact model; the Court of

Appeals held—as this Court subsequently ruled in *Watson v. Fort Worth Bank & Trust*, 487 U.S. 977 (1988)—that disparate-impact analysis could be applied to subjective hiring practices. The Ninth Circuit also concluded that in such a case, "[o]nce the plaintiff class has shown disparate impact caused by specific, identifiable employment practices or criteria, the burden shifts to the employer," to "prov[e the] business necessity" of the challenged practice. Because the en banc holding on subjective employment practices reversed the District Court's contrary ruling, the en banc Court of Appeals remanded the case to a panel for further proceedings.

On remand, the panel applied the en banc ruling to the facts of this case. It held that respondents had made out a prima facie case of disparate impact in hiring for both skilled and unskilled noncannery positions. The panel remanded the case for further proceedings, instructing the District Court that it was the employer's burden to prove that any disparate impact caused by its hiring and employment practices was justified by business necessity. Neither the en banc court nor the panel disturbed the District Court's rejection of the disparate-treatment claims.

It is clear to us that the Court of Appeals' acceptance of the comparison between the racial composition of the cannery work force and that of the non-cannery work force, as probative of a prima facie case of disparate impact in the selection of the latter group of workers, was flawed for several reasons. Most obviously, with respect to the skilled noncannery jobs at issue here, the cannery work force in no way reflected "the pool of *qualified* job applicants" or the "*qualified* population in the labor force." Measuring alleged discrimination in the selection of accountants, managers, boat captains, electricians, doctors, and engineers—and the long list of other "skilled" noncannery positions found to exist by the District Court, by comparing the number of nonwhites occupying these jobs to the number of nonwhites filling cannery worker positions is nonsensical. If the absence of minorities holding such skilled positions is due to a dearth of qualified nonwhite applicants (for reasons that are not petitioners' fault), petitioners' selection methods or employment practices cannot be said to have had a "disparate impact" on nonwhites.

The Court of Appeals also erred with respect to the unskilled noncannery positions. Racial imbalance in one segment of an employer's work force does not, without more, establish a prima facie case of disparate impact with respect to the selection of workers for the employer's other positions, even where workers for the different positions may have somewhat fungible skills (as is arguably the case for cannery and unskilled noncannery workers). As long as there are no barriers or practices deterring qualified nonwhites from applying for noncannery positions, if the percentage of selected applicants who are nonwhite is not significantly less than the percentage of qualified applicants who are nonwhite, the employer's selection mechanism probably does not operate with a disparate impact on minorities. Where this is the case, the percentage of nonwhite workers found in other positions in the employer's labor force is irrelevant to the question of a prima facie statistical case of disparate impact. As noted above, a contrary ruling on this point would almost inexorably lead to the use of numerical quotas in the workplace, a result that Congress and this Court have rejected repeatedly in the past.

Moreover, isolating the cannery workers as the potential "labor force" for unskilled noncannery positions is at once both too broad and too narrow in its focus. It is too broad because the vast majority of these cannery workers did not seek jobs in unskilled noncannery positions; there is no showing that many of them would have done so even if none of the arguably "deterring" practices existed. Thus, the pool of cannery workers cannot be used as a surrogate for the class of qualified job applicants because it contains many persons who have not (and would not) be noncannery job applicants. Conversely, if respondents propose to use the cannery workers for comparison purposes because they represent the "qualified labor population" generally, the group is too narrow because there are obviously many qualified persons in the labor market for noncannery jobs who are not cannery workers.

The peculiar facts of this case further illustrate why a comparison between the percentage of nonwhite cannery workers and nonwhite noncannery workers is an improper basis for making out a claim of disparate impact. Here, the District Court found that nonwhites were "overrepresent[ed]" among cannery workers because petitioners had contracted with a predominantly nonwhite union (local 37) to fill these positions. As a result, if petitioners (for some permissible reason) ceased using local 37 as its hiring channel for cannery positions, it appears (according to the District Court's findings) that the racial stratification between the cannery and noncannery workers might diminish to statistical insignificance. Under the Court of Appeals' approach, therefore, it is possible that *with no change whatsoever* in their hiring practices for noncannery workers—the jobs at issue in this lawsuit—petitioners could make respondents' prima facie case of disparate impact "disappear." But *if* there would be no prima facie case of disparate impact in the selection of noncannery workers absent petitioners' use of local 37 to hire cannery workers, surely petitioners' reliance on the union to fill the cannery jobs not at issue here (and its resulting "overrepresentation" of nonwhites in those positions) does not—standing alone—make out a prima facie case of disparate impact. Yet it is precisely such an ironic result that the Court of Appeals reached below.

Consequently, we reverse the Court of Appeals' ruling that a comparison between the percentage of cannery workers who are nonwhite and the percentage of noncannery workers who are nonwhite makes out a prima facie case of disparate impact. Of course, this leaves unresolved whether the record made in the District Court will support a conclusion that a prima facie case of disparate impact has been established on some basis other than the racial disparity between cannery and noncannery workers. This is an issue that the Court of Appeals or the District Court should address in the first instance.

Since the statistical disparity relied on by the Court of Appeals did not suffice to make out a prima facie case, any inquiry by us into whether the specific challenged employment practices of petitioners caused that disparity is pretermitted, as is any inquiry into whether the disparate impact that any employment practice may have had was justified by business considerations. Because we remand for further proceedings, however, on whether a prima facie case of disparate impact has been made in defensible fashion in this case, we address two

> The Court's instructions on remand are a critical part of this case.

other challenges petitioners have made to the decision of the Court of Appeals. First is the question of causation in a disparate-impact case. The law in this respect was correctly stated by Justice O'CONNOR's opinion in *Watson*, 487 U.S. at 994.

> [T]he plaintiff's burden in establishing a prima facie case goes beyond the need to show that there are statistical disparities in the employer's work force. The plaintiff must begin by identifying the specific employment practice that is challenged. . . . Especially in cases where an employer combines subjective criteria with the use of more rigid standardized rules or tests, the plaintiff is in our view responsible for isolating and identifying the specific employment practices that are allegedly responsible for any observed statistical disparities.

Indeed, even the Court of Appeals—whose decision petitioners assault on this score—noted that "it is . . . essential that the practices identified by the cannery workers be linked causally with the demonstrated adverse impact." Notwithstanding the Court of Appeals' apparent adherence to the proper inquiry, petitioners contend that that court erred by permitting respondents to make out their case by offering "only [one] set of cumulative comparative statistics as evidence of the disparate impact of each and all of [petitioners' hiring] practices."

Our disparate-impact cases have always focused on the impact of *particular* hiring practices on employment opportunities for minorities. Just as an employer cannot escape liability under Title VII by demonstrating that, "at the bottom line," his work force is racially balanced (where particular hiring practices may operate to deprive minorities of employment opportunities), see *Connecticut v. Teal*, 457 U.S. 440, 450 (1982), a Title VII plaintiff does not make out a case of disparate impact simply by showing that, "at the bottom line," there is racial *imbalance* in the work force. As a general matter, a plaintiff must demonstrate that it is the application of a specific or particular employment practice that has created the disparate impact under attack. Such a showing is an integral part of the plaintiff's prima facie case in a disparate-impact suit under Title VII.

Here, respondents have alleged that several "objective" employment practices (*e.g.*, nepotism, separate hiring channels, rehire preferences), as well as the use of "subjective decision making" to select noncannery workers, have had a disparate impact on nonwhites. Respondents base this claim on statistics that allegedly show a disproportionately low percentage of nonwhites in the at-issue positions. However, even if on remand respondents can show that nonwhites are underrepresented in the at-issue jobs in a manner that is acceptable under the standards set forth, this alone will *not* suffice to make out a prima facie case of disparate impact. Respondents will also have to demonstrate that the disparity they complain of is the result of one or more of the employment practices that they are attacking here, specifically showing that each challenged practice has a significantly disparate impact on employment opportunities for whites and nonwhites. To hold otherwise would result in employers being potentially liable for "the myriad of innocent causes that may lead to statistical imbalances in the composition of their work forces." *Watson v. Fort Worth Bank & Trust, supra*, 487 U.S. at 992.

If, on remand, respondents meet the proof burdens outlined above, and establish a prima facie case of disparate impact with respect to any of petitioners' employment practices, the case will shift to any business justification petitioners offer for their use of these practices. This phase of the disparate-impact case contains two components: first, a consideration of the justifications an employer offers for his use of these practices; and second, the availability of alternative practices to achieve the same business ends, with less racial impact.

Though we have phrased the query differently in different cases, it is generally well established that at the justification stage of such a disparate-impact case, the dispositive issue is whether a challenged practice serves, in a significant way, the legitimate employment goals of the employer. The touchstone of this inquiry is a reasoned review of the employer's justification for his use of the challenged practice. A mere insubstantial justification in this regard will not suffice, because such a low standard of review would permit discrimination to be practiced through the use of spurious, seemingly neutral employment practices. At the same time, though, there is no requirement that the challenged practice be "essential" or "indispensable" to the employer's business for it to pass muster: this degree of scrutiny would be almost impossible for most employers to meet, and would result in a host of evils we have identified above.

> Note the limited "reasoned review" standard applied here by the Court.

In this phase, the employer carries the burden of producing evidence of a business justification for his employment practice. The burden of persuasion, however, remains with the disparate-impact plaintiff. To the extent that the Ninth Circuit held otherwise in its en banc decision in this case, suggesting that the persuasion burden should shift to petitioners once respondents established a prima facie case of disparate impact—its decisions were erroneous. "[T]he ultimate burden of proving that discrimination against a protected group has been caused by a specific employment practice remains with the plaintiff *at all times.*" *Watson, supra,* 487 U.S. at 997 (O'Connor, J.) (emphasis added). This rule conforms with the usual method for allocating persuasion and production burdens in the federal courts, *see* Fed. Rule Evid. 301, and more specifically, it conforms to the rule in disparate-treatment cases that the plaintiff bears the burden of disproving an employer's assertion that the adverse employment action or practice was based solely on a legitimate neutral consideration. We acknowledge that some of our earlier decisions can be read as suggesting otherwise. But to the extent that those cases speak of an employers' "burden of proof" with respect to a legitimate business justification defense, *see, e.g., Dothard v. Rawlinson,* 433 U.S. 321, 329 (1977), they should have been understood to mean an employer's production—but not persuasion—burden. The persuasion burden here must remain with the plaintiff, for it is he who must prove that it was "because of such individual's race, color," etc., that he was denied a desired employment opportunity. *See* 42 U.S.C. § 2000e–2(a).

> Wasn't *Griggs* clear that the burden on the defendant was one of persuasion? How is that undercut here?

Finally, if on remand the case reaches this point, and respondents cannot persuade the trier of fact on the question of petitioners' business necessity defense, respondents may still be able to prevail. To do so, respondents will have to persuade the factfinder that "other tests or selection devices, without a similarly undesirable racial effect, would also serve the employer's legitimate [hiring] interest[s]"; by so demonstrating, respondents would prove that "[petitioners were] using [their] tests merely as a 'pretext' for discrimination." *Albemarle Paper Co. v. Moody*, 422 U.S. 405, 425 (1975). If respondents, having established a prima facie case, come forward with alternatives to petitioners' hiring practices that reduce the racially disparate impact of practices currently being used, and petitioners refuse to adopt these alternatives, such a refusal would belie a claim by petitioners that their incumbent practices are being employed for nondiscriminatory reasons. Of course, any alternative practices which respondents offer up in this respect must be equally effective as petitioners' chosen hiring procedures in achieving petitioners' legitimate employment goals.

For the reasons given above, the judgment of the Court of Appeals is reversed, and the case is remanded for further proceedings consistent with this opinion.

It is so ordered.

Justice Stevens, with whom Justice Brennan, Justice Marshall, and Justice Blackmun join, dissenting.

Fully 18 years ago, this Court unanimously held that Title VII of the Civil Rights Act of 1964 prohibits employment practices that have discriminatory effects as well as those that are intended to discriminate. *Griggs v. Duke Power Co.*, 401 U.S. 424. Federal courts and agencies consistently have enforced that interpretation, thus promoting our national goal of eliminating barriers that define economic opportunity not by aptitude and ability but by race, color, national origin, and other traits that are easily identified but utterly irrelevant to one's qualification for a particular job. Regrettably, the Court retreats from these efforts in its review of an interlocutory judgment respecting the "peculiar facts" of this lawsuit. Turning a blind eye to the meaning and purpose of Title VII, the majority's opinion perfunctorily rejects a longstanding rule of law and underestimates the probative value of evidence of a racially stratified work force. I cannot join this latest sojourn into judicial activism.

> Note that the tensions seem particularly high at this point on the Court between the conservative and more liberal Justices.

■ NOTES AND QUESTIONS

1. Though *Wards Cove* changed the understood meaning of disparate impact law in many ways, two particular points stand out. First, the case holds that a plaintiff must "identify[] the specific employment practice that is challenged."

This can be burdensome for plaintiffs, who may see that a clear disparate impact exists, but are unable to specifically identify the policy or practice that is causing the impact. Second, the Court concludes that the "touchstone" of the business necessity defense "is a reasoned review of the employer's justification for his use of the challenged practice." *Wards Cove*, 490 U.S. at 659. And, the Court reasons that this is a burden of production, not persuasion. This change in the case law was dramatic, as it substantially lowered the defendant's burden in disparate impact cases from how the law was articulated in *Griggs*. As the Court itself conceded, "some of our earlier decisions can be read as suggesting otherwise." *Id.* at 660.

2. What does a "reasoned review" of an employer's business practice mean? What type of evidence would it take to satisfy the reasoned review? How critical is it that this test is one of production for the employer, not of persuasion?

3. How often will it be difficult for a plaintiff to "identify[ ] the specific employment practice that is challenged"? Shouldn't an employee be required to have this information before she files suit?

4. The dissent accuses the majority of "[t]urning a blind eye to the meaning and purpose of Title VII" and engaging in a "sojourn into judicial activism." These are harsh words from these dissenting Supreme Court Justices, but is it a fair assessment of the majority's decision?

5. The majority in *Wards Cove* substantially alters the state of disparate impact law. Yet it purports to not undo the Court's earlier decision in *Griggs*. Does *Wards Cove* overturn *Griggs*?

6. Does the lack of a solid statutory underpinning make it easier for the Court to reach its decision here? Does the decision discuss—at any length—a disagreement over statutory terms? Why or why not?

7. As noted in the following section, *Wards Cove* was largely overturned by the Civil Rights Act of 1991. The case still likely remains good law as to the Age Discrimination in Employment Act, however, as the subsequent amendments apply *only* to Title VII.

8. **Historical Note.** "The replacement of Lewis Powell, a moderate conservative essentially sympathetic to race-conscious remedies, by Anthony Kennedy, a conservative apparently more opposed to preferential treatment, may help partially to explain the Court's action [in *Wards Cove*]." Herman Belz, Equality Transformed: A Quarter-Century of Affirmative Action 226 (1991).

Justice Anthony Kennedy

The chart below shows the make-up of the Court in these key cases. The dissent is depicted in red. Does the chart suggest that the case was decided politically, or does Justice White's opinion reflect a more subtle shift in jurisprudence?

Griggs		Wards Cove	
Justice	Nominated by	Justice	Nominated by
Burger	Nixon (R)	Rehnquist	Reagan (R)
Black	F. Roosevelt (D)	White	Kennedy (D)
Douglas	F. Roosevelt (D)	O'Connor	Reagan (R)
Harlan	Eisenhower (R)	Scalia	Reagan (R)
Stewart	Eisenhower (R)	Kennedy	Reagan (R)
White	Kennedy (D)	Brennan	Eisenhower (R)
Marshall	L. Johnson (D)	Marshall	L. Johnson (D)
Blackmun	Nixon (R)	Blackmun	Nixon (R)
Brennan (abstained)	Eisenhower (R)	Stevens	Ford (R)

 ## *Interactive Problem*

Looking back at the interactive problem at the beginning of this chapter, Big Trucking asserts that its height and weight policy are necessary to assure that its movers are strong enough to lift heavy objects. Would this rationale satisfy the "reasoned review" standard established in *Wards Cove*? If so, would it also satisfy the more rigorous job-related and consistent with business necessity test?

 # B. Statutory Framework

Wards Cove was just one of several controversial Supreme Court decisions that impacted civil rights and employment cases in the late 1980s. These controversial decisions would ultimately culminate in congressional intervention. Congress went on to pass the Civil Rights Act of 1991, which amended Title VII. Though the Civil Rights Act made many important changes to Title VII, one particularly noteworthy change was the addition of disparate impact to Title VII. Following this amendment, disparate impact would specifically be codified as part of Title VII for the first time.

The Civil Rights Act would undo much of what *Wards Cove* had done. Specifically, the revised statute would restore the burden-shifting framework originally created by *Griggs*—namely that once the plaintiff establishes the prima facie case, the defendant must show (through a burden of persuasion) that the policy or practice in question is job related and consistent with business necessity. This business necessity standard also replaces the more watered down "reasoned review" approach advocated by *Wards Cove*. The statute further provides that even where an employer can satisfy its burden, the employee has the opportunity to articulate alternative practices that are less discriminatory but still serve the same business goals. In sum, Title VII now adopts a three-part test for analyzing all disparate impact claims:

> First, the plaintiff must establish that an identified employment practice results in a disparate impact on a protected group. Second, the employer must prove that the employment practice is "job related for the position in question and consistent with business necessity." Finally, even if the employer satisfies its burden on the job-relatedness question, the plaintiff can still prevail by establishing that there is an alternative employment practice available with less discriminatory impact that still satisfies the employer's business needs.

Joseph A. Seiner & Benjamin N. Gutman, *Does* Ricci *Herald a New Disparate Impact?*, 90 B.U. L. Rev. 2181, 2194 (2010).

Though it is tempting to think that the Civil Rights Act completely overruled *Wards Cove*, this is simply not the case. It is important to remember that this amendment only impacts Title VII. Thus, the standard articulated by *Wards Cove* likely applies to the Age Discrimination in Employment Act. (The ADA, however, follows the Title VII model in most respects.) The new framework created by the revised statute, however, does go a long way toward clarifying this area of the law. While there is still much subjectivity in the statute, disparate impact now has a clear statutory basis. A summary of how disparate impact claims are analyzed is set forth below:

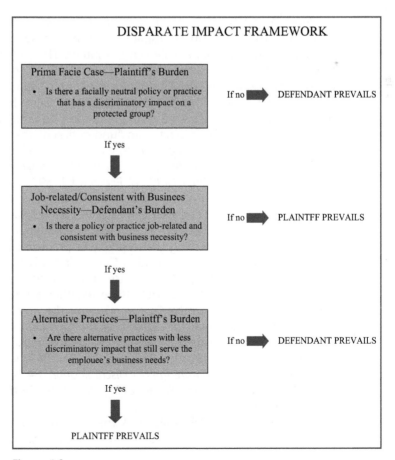

Figure 4.1

Class Exercise: Establishing Company Policy

Disparate impact claims come in many different shapes and sizes. Sometimes these claims arise where an employee is simply unable to find a "smoking gun" in an intentional discrimination case. In other instances, employers fail to recognize how a particular policy or practice might have an adverse effect on their workforce.

Working in small groups, try to formulate an employment policy that an employer might innocently establish that could have a disparate impact on a protected group. Once you have agreed on a policy, work through the three-part test created by the Civil Rights Act of 1991. Has the employee established its prima facie case? If so, would the employer be able to carry its burden of persuasion of showing that the policy or practice is job related and consistent with business necessity? Finally, can the employee still show that there are alternative practices available that have less discriminatory impact but still serve the employer's business needs?

Practice and Procedural Tip

13: Examining the Lack of Disparate Impact Cases

From a plaintiff's perspective, disparate impact appears to be an attractive way to pursue a case. Unlike disparate treatment cases, unintentional discrimination claims do not require a showing of intent. Thus, employees need not prove this element when pursuing these claims. Intent is often one of the most difficult things for a plaintiff to establish in an employment discrimination case.

Why then do we see so few disparate impact claims brought when the burden of proof seems so much lower than in a traditional disparate treatment case? Why do scholars decry disparate impact as an "underutilized" theory? *See generally* Michael Selmi, *Was the Disparate Impact Theory a Mistake?*, 53 UCLA L. Rev. 701 (2006); Elaine W. Shoben, *Disparate Impact Theory in Employment Discrimination: What's Griggs Still Good for? What Not?*, 42 Brandeis L.J. 597, 598 (2004). There may be several responses to this question, but the answer likely lies in at least two important cost-related areas: (1) expense of litigation and (2) lack of damages.

Disparate impact cases are often difficult and expensive to litigate. The most common way of establishing that a policy or practice has an adverse effect on a protected group is through statistics. Generating this type of data can be expensive and time-consuming. The data itself must be gathered, and an expert often needs to analyze the data to determine whether a disparate impact exists. *See* Reginald C. Govan, *Honorable Compromises and the Moral High Ground: The Conflict Between the Rhetoric and the Content of the Civil Rights Act of 1991*, 46 Rutgers L. Rev. 1 (1993); Julia Lamber, *Discretionary Decisionmaking: The Application of Title VII's Disparate Impact Theory*, 1985 U. Ill. L. Rev. 869; Jennifer L. Peresie, *Toward a Coherent Test for Disparate Impact Discrimination*, 84 Ind. L.J. 773 (2009); Elaine W. Shoben, *Differential Pass-Fail Rates in Employment Testing: Statistical Proof Under Title VII*, 91 Harv. L. Rev. 793 (1978).

Disparate impact claims also lack the potential damages of a traditional disparate treatment claim. In particular, compensatory and punitive damages are unavailable in unintentional discrimination claims. After all, it would be inconsistent with the nature of an unintentional act to punish an employer with punitive damages. Given that disparate impact cases are more expensive to litigate and often yield lower damages, there is a disincentive for employment lawyers to pursue this type of litigation. It is thus not surprising that we see far more disparate treatment claims litigated in the employment discrimination context.

Nonetheless, this should not be an invitation for employers to let their guard down. These claims are still brought by private litigants. And, the government—which is often interested primarily in broad injunctive relief—may not be dissuaded by the potential lack of monetary damages in a case. Moreover, disparate impact claims can also be extremely expensive for employers to defend against. Thus, despite the overall lack of litigation in this area, employers should still be very cautious when implementing a proposed policy or practice to assure that it does not create an unlawful disparate impact.

C. Subjective Criteria

One critical question that arises in the disparate impact context is defining exactly what constitutes a policy or practice. Early on, there was some debate over the issue of whether a "subjective" policy could satisfy the disparate impact standard. Thus, for example, if an employer simply had a policy of hiring the "best worker available," could this subjective practice still run afoul of the disparate impact provisions of Title VII? The lower courts were divided on this particular issue, which was ultimately resolved by the Supreme Court.

Watson v. Fort Worth Bank & Trust
487 U.S. 977 (1988)

Justice O'CONNOR announced the [portions of the Court's judgment excerpted below]:

This case requires us to decide what evidentiary standards should be applied under Title VII in determining whether an employer's practice of committing promotion decisions to the subjective discretion of supervisory employees has led to illegal discrimination.

Petitioner Clara Watson, who is black, was hired by respondent Fort Worth Bank and Trust (the Bank) as a

Bank Teller Windows

proof operator in August 1973. In January 1976, Watson was promoted to a position as teller in the Bank's drive-in facility. In February 1980, she sought to become supervisor of the tellers in the main lobby; a white male, however, was selected for this job. Watson then sought a position as supervisor of the drive-in bank, but this position was given to a white female. In February 1981, after Watson had served for about a year as a commercial teller in the Bank's main lobby, and informally as assistant to the supervisor of tellers, the man holding that position was promoted. Watson applied for the vacancy, but the white female who was the supervisor of the drive-in bank was selected instead. Watson then applied for the vacancy created at the drive-in; a white male was selected for that job. The Bank, which has about 80 employees, had not developed precise and formal criteria for evaluating candidates for the positions for which Watson unsuccessfully applied. It relied instead on the subjective judgment of supervisors who were acquainted with the candidates and with the nature of the jobs to be filled. All the supervisors involved in denying Watson the four promotions at issue were white.

Watson filed a discrimination charge with the Equal Employment Opportunity Commission (EEOC). After exhausting her administrative remedies, she filed this lawsuit in the United States District Court for the Northern District of Texas. She alleged that the Bank had unlawfully discriminated against blacks in hiring, compensation, initial placement, promotions, terminations, and other terms and conditions of employment.

The District Court addressed Watson's individual claims under the evidentiary standards that apply in a discriminatory treatment case. See *McDonnell Douglas Corp. v. Green*, 411 U.S. 792 (1973), and *Texas Dept. of Community Affairs v. Burdine*, 450 U.S. 248 (1981). It concluded, on the evidence presented at trial, that Watson had established a prima facie case of employment discrimination, but that the Bank had met its rebuttal burden by presenting legitimate and nondiscriminatory reasons for each of the challenged promotion decisions. The court also concluded that Watson had failed to show that these reasons were pretexts for racial discrimination. Accordingly, the action was dismissed.

A divided panel of the United States Court of Appeals for the Fifth Circuit affirmed in part. The majority concluded that there was no abuse of discretion in the District Court's class decertification decisions. In order to avoid unfair prejudice to members of the class of black job applicants, however, the Court of Appeals vacated the portion of the judgment affecting them and remanded with instructions to dismiss those claims without prejudice. The majority affirmed the District Court's conclusion that Watson had failed to prove her claim of racial discrimination under the standards set out in *McDonnell Douglas, supra*, and *Burdine, supra*.

Watson argued that the District Court had erred in failing to apply "disparate impact" analysis to her claims of discrimination in promotion. Relying on Fifth Circuit precedent, the majority of the Court of Appeals panel held that "a Title VII challenge to an allegedly discretionary promotion system is properly analyzed under the disparate treatment model rather than the disparate impact model." Other Courts of Appeals have held that disparate impact analysis may be applied to hiring or promotion systems that involve the use of "discretionary" or "subjective" criteria.

In *Griggs v. Duke Power Co.*, 401 U.S. 424 (1971), this Court held that a plaintiff need not necessarily prove intentional discrimination in order to establish that an employer has violated § 703. In certain cases, facially neutral employment practices that have significant adverse effects on protected *groups* have been held to violate the Act without proof that the employer adopted those practices with a discriminatory intent. The factual issues and the character of the evidence are inevitably somewhat different when the plaintiff is exempted from the need to prove intentional discrimination. The evidence in these "disparate impact" cases usually

> The critical question addressed by the *Watson* court was whether the disparate impact model applies to subjective criteria.

focuses on statistical disparities, rather than specific incidents, and on competing explanations for those disparities.

The distinguishing features of the factual issues that typically dominate in disparate impact cases do not imply that the ultimate legal issue is different than in cases where disparate treatment analysis is used. *See, e.g., Washington v. Davis*, 426 U.S. 229 (1976) (STEVENS, J., concurring). Nor do we think it is appropriate to hold a defendant liable for unintentional discrimination on the basis of less evidence than is required to prove intentional discrimination. Rather, the necessary premise of the disparate impact approach is that some employment practices, adopted without a deliberately discriminatory motive, may in operation be functionally equivalent to intentional discrimination.

Perhaps the most obvious examples of such functional equivalence have been found where facially neutral job requirements necessarily operated to perpetuate the effects of intentional discrimination that occurred before Title VII was enacted. In *Griggs* itself, for example, the employer had a history of overt racial discrimination that predated the enactment of the Civil Rights Act of 1964. Such conduct had apparently ceased thereafter, but the employer continued to follow employment policies that had "a markedly disproportionate" adverse effect on blacks. The *Griggs* Court found that these policies, which involved the use of general aptitude tests and a high school diploma requirement, were not demonstrably related to the jobs for which they were used. Believing that diplomas and tests could become "masters of reality," which would perpetuate the effects of pre-Act discrimination, the Court concluded that such practices could not be defended simply on the basis of their facial neutrality or on the basis of the employer's lack of discriminatory intent.

This Court has repeatedly reaffirmed the principle that some facially neutral employment practices may violate Title VII even in the absence of a demonstrated discriminatory intent. We have not limited this principle to cases in which the challenged practice served to perpetuate the effects of pre-Act intentional discrimination. Each of our subsequent decisions, however, like *Griggs* itself, involved standardized employment tests or criteria. In contrast, we have consistently used conventional disparate treatment theory, in which proof of intent to discriminate is required, to review hiring and promotion decisions that were based on the exercise of personal judgment or the application of inherently subjective criteria.

Our decisions have not addressed the question whether disparate impact analysis may be applied to cases in which subjective criteria are used to make employment decisions. As noted above, the Courts of Appeals are in conflict on the issue. In order to resolve this conflict, we must determine whether the reasons that support the use of disparate impact analysis apply to subjective employment practices, and whether such analysis can be applied in this new context under workable evidentiary standards.

The parties present us with stark and uninviting alternatives. Petitioner contends that subjective selection methods are at least as likely to have discriminatory effects as are the kind of objective tests at issue in *Griggs* and our other disparate impact cases. Furthermore, she argues, if disparate impact analysis is confined to objective tests, employers will be able to substitute subjective criteria having substantially identical effects, and *Griggs* will become a dead letter. Respondent and the United States (appearing as *amicus curiae*) argue that conventional disparate treatment analysis is adequate to accomplish Congress' purpose in enacting Title VII. They also argue that subjective selection practices would be so impossibly difficult to defend under disparate impact analysis that employers would be forced to adopt numerical quotas in order to avoid liability.

We are persuaded that our decisions in *Griggs* and succeeding cases could largely be nullified if disparate impact analysis were applied only to standardized selection practices. However one might distinguish "subjective" from "objective" criteria, it is apparent that selection systems that combine both types would generally have to be considered subjective in nature. Thus, for example, if the employer in *Griggs* had consistently preferred applicants who had a high school diploma and who passed the company's general aptitude test, its selection system could nonetheless have been considered "subjective" if it also included brief interviews with the candidates. So long as an employer refrained from making standardized criteria absolutely determinative, it would remain free to give such tests almost as much weight as it chose without risking a disparate impact challenge. If we announced a rule that allowed employers so easily to insulate themselves from liability under *Griggs*, disparate impact analysis might effectively be abolished.

We are also persuaded that disparate impact analysis is in principle no less applicable to subjective employment criteria than to objective or standardized tests. In either case, a facially neutral practice, adopted without discriminatory intent, may have effects that are indistinguishable from intentionally discriminatory practices. It is true, to be sure, that an employer's policy of leaving promotion decisions to the unchecked discretion of lower level supervisors should itself raise no inference of discriminatory conduct. Especially in relatively small businesses like respondent's, it may be customary and quite reasonable simply to delegate employment decisions to those employees who are most familiar with the jobs to be filled and with the candidates for those jobs. It does not follow, however, that the particular supervisors to whom this discretion is delegated always act without discriminatory intent. Furthermore, even if one assumed that any such discrimination can be adequately policed through disparate treatment analysis, the problem of subconscious stereotypes and

> Doesn't the comment in the case that there was "a lot of money . . . for blacks to have to count" suggest intentional discrimination, rather than disparate impact?

prejudices would remain. In this case, for example, petitioner was apparently told at one point that the teller position was a big responsibility with "a lot of money . . . for blacks to have to count." Such remarks may not prove discriminatory intent, but they do suggest a lingering form of the problem that Title VII was enacted to combat. If an employer's undisciplined system of subjective decisionmaking has precisely the same effects as a system pervaded by impermissible intentional discrimination, it is difficult to see why Title VII's proscription against discriminatory actions should not apply. In both circumstances, the employer's practices may be said to "adversely affect [an individual's] status as an employee, because of such individual's race, color, religion, sex, or national origin." 42 U.S.C. § 2000e–2(a)(2). We conclude, accordingly, that subjective or discretionary employment practices may be analyzed under the disparate impact approach in appropriate cases.

■ NOTES AND QUESTIONS

1. Should subjective practices be covered by disparate impact law? Isn't it hard to quantify what is or is not a subjective policy?

2. If only objective policies or practices were considered under the statute, would it (as the plaintiff here argues) largely negate disparate impact law? Couldn't the employer always add a subjective component to the policy in question to avoid liability?

3. How would this case be analyzed under *McDonnell Douglas*? Does the alleged comment that "the teller position was a big responsibility with 'a lot of money . . . for blacks to have to count'" suggest that this was more of an intentional than unintentional case of discrimination?

4. In the wake of the 2014 fatal shooting of a young, African-American male by a Caucasian police officer in Ferguson, Missouri, where the police force had an extremely low percentage of black officers, national attention has focused on the difficulty police and fire departments across the nation face in hiring and retaining minority police officers. While some argue this signals systemic racism, substantial evidence indicates that it is the result of discriminatory hiring practices, such as written and physical tests, background checks, and a lack of resources to review hiring practices. Some aggressive efforts by local police departments to alleviate the disparate impact of their hiring practices have been shown to be successful in attempting to achieve racial diversification. Despite these relatively successful efforts by a small number of jurisdictions, an overwhelming majority of departments across the nation still have lacked the initiative to change their hiring practices and continue to show evidence of disparate impact discrimination against minority applicants. *See* Shaila Dewan, *Mostly White Forces in Mostly Black Towns: Police Struggle for Racial Diversity*, N.Y. Times, Sept. 9, 2014, at A1.

Interactive Problem

Looking back at the interactive problem at the beginning of this chapter, assume that in addition to the written test and the height and weight requirements, the employer also integrated an oral interview as part of the hiring process. Could the company's policies and practices still be challenged under disparate impact law?

Practice and Procedural Tip

14: Deciding Between Disparate Impact and Disparate Treatment Litigation

As already discussed, there is a significant difference between disparate treatment and disparate impact claims. The models of proof are substantially different, as are the damages available. Often it can be difficult to determine which theory to allege. As the facts from *Watson* show, a case can often be characterized as either intentional or unintentional discrimination.

The decision of whether to pursue a case as disparate treatment, disparate impact, or both is often a strategic one for the plaintiff. Factors that should be considered are whether there is sufficient evidence to show intent in the case, whether statistical evidence can be gathered to show disparate impact, and the expense of litigating the case itself. Certainly, plaintiffs also weigh the availability of punitive and compensatory damages (in intentional discrimination cases) in deciding how to plead the case. It may also be unclear, at the beginning stages of a case, whether the evidence turned up in discovery will ultimately reveal intentional or unintentional discrimination.

It should also be considered that a plaintiff may plead both disparate impact and disparate treatment. The theories are not mutually exclusive. However, plaintiffs should be wary of waiting too long to allege a particular theory in the case. The Supreme Court has made clear that disparate impact should be alleged at the earlier stages of the litigation, or it is waived. *See* Raytheon Co. v. Hernandez, 540 U.S. 44 (2003); Hazen Paper Co. v. Biggins, 507 U.S. 604 (1993). Ultimately, plaintiffs should not just blindly allege one theory without giving the strategic implications serious thought. And, defendants should similarly understand the best approach to litigating a particular type of claim brought by a plaintiff.

 # D. Defenses

Perhaps the most common defense to a disparate impact claim is to show that the policy or practice in question is job related and consistent with business necessity. Where the defendant is able to satisfy this showing, all that remains for a plaintiff is to establish alternative practices that are available. Over time, however, other defenses have been asserted by defendants.

1. The Bottom-Line Defense

One well-known defense attempted by defendants was the so-called-bottom-line defense. This defense asserts that even if a particular practice has a disparate impact on the workforce, the employer should still prevail because it has made adjustments in an effort to alleviate the negative effects of the practice in question. The Supreme Court ultimately took up the question of the bottom-line defense in *Connecticut v. Teal*.

Connecticut v. Teal
457 U.S. 440 (1982)

Justice BRENNAN delivered the opinion of the Court.

We consider here whether an employer sued for violation of Title VII of the Civil Rights Act of 1964 may assert a "bottom-line" theory of defense. Under that theory, as asserted in this case, an employer's acts of racial discrimination in promotions—effected by an examination having disparate impact—would not render the employer liable for the racial discrimination suffered by employees barred from promotion if the "bottom-line" result of the promotional process was an appropriate racial balance. We hold that the "bottom line" does not preclude respondent employees from establishing a prima facie case, nor does it provide petitioner employer with a defense to such a case.

Four of the respondents, Winnie Teal, Rose Walker, Edith Latney, and Grace Clark, are black employees of the Department of Income Maintenance of the State of Connecticut. Each was promoted provisionally to the position of Welfare Eligibility Supervisor and served in that capacity for almost two years. To attain permanent status as supervisors, however, respondents had to participate in a selection process that required, as the first step, a passing score on a written examination. This written test was administered on December 2, 1978, to 329 candidates. Of these candidates, 48 identified themselves as black and 259 identified themselves as white. The results of the examination were announced in March 1979. With the passing score set at 65, 54.17 percent of the identified black candidates passed. This was approximately 68 percent of the passing rate for the identified white candidates. The four respondents were among the blacks who failed the examination, and they were thus excluded from further consideration for permanent supervisory positions. In April 1979, respondents instituted this action in the United States District Court for the District of Connecticut against petitioners, the State of Connecticut, two state agencies, and two state officials. Respondents alleged, *inter alia*, that petitioners violated Title VII by imposing, as an absolute condition for consideration for promotion, that applicants pass a written test that excluded blacks in disproportionate numbers and that was not job related.

More than a year after this action was instituted, and approximately one month before trial, petitioners made promotions from the eligibility list generated by the written examination. In choosing persons from that list, petitioners considered past work performance, recommendations of the candidates' supervisors and, to a lesser extent, seniority. Petitioners then applied what the Court of Appeals characterized as an affirmative-action program in order to ensure a significant number of minority supervisors. Forty-six persons were promoted to permanent supervisory positions, 11 of whom were black and 35 of whom were white. The overall result of the selection process was that, of the 48 identified black candidates who participated in the selection process, 22.9 percent were promoted and of the 259 identified white candidates, 13.5 percent were promoted. It is this "bottom-line" result, more favorable to blacks than to whites, that petitioners urge should be adjudged to be a complete defense to respondents' suit.

After trial, the District Court entered judgment for petitioners. [T]he court found that, although the comparative passing rates for the examination indicated a prima facie case of adverse impact upon minorities, the result of the entire hiring process reflected no such adverse impact. Holding that these "bottom-line" percentages precluded the finding of a Title VII violation, the court held that the employer was not required to demonstrate that the promotional examination was job related. The United States Court of Appeals for the Second Circuit reversed, holding that the District Court erred in ruling that the results of the written examination alone were insufficient to support a prima facie case of disparate impact in violation of Title VII. The Court of Appeals stated that where "an identifiable pass-fail barrier denies an employment opportunity to a disproportionately large number of minorities and prevents them from proceeding to the next step in the selection process," that barrier must be shown to be job related. We granted certiorari, and now affirm.

Petitioners' examination, which barred promotion and had a discriminatory impact on black employees, clearly falls within the literal language of § 703(a)(2), as interpreted by *Griggs*. The statute speaks, not in terms of jobs and promotions, but in terms of *limitations* and *classifications* that would deprive any individual of employment *opportunities*. A disparate-impact claim reflects the language of § 703(a)(2) and Congress' basic objectives in enacting that statute: "to achieve equality of employment *opportunities* and remove barriers that have operated in the past to favor an identifiable group of white employees over other employees." *Griggs v. Duke Power Co.*, 401 U.S. 424, 429–430 (1971) (emphasis added). When an employer uses a nonjob-related barrier in order to deny a minority or woman applicant employment or promotion, and that barrier has a significant adverse effect on minorities or women, then the applicant has been deprived of an employment *opportunity* "because of . . . race, color, religion, sex, or national origin." In other words, § 703(a)(2) prohibits discriminatory "artificial, arbitrary, and unnecessary barriers to employment," *Griggs*, 401 U.S. at 431, that "limit . . . or classify . . . applicants for employment . . . in any way which would deprive or tend to deprive any individual of employment *opportunities*." (Emphasis added.)

> In *Teal*, the Supreme Court rejected the application of the so-called bottom-line defense to disparate impact claims.

Our conclusion that § 703(a)(2) encompasses respondents' claim is reinforced by the terms of Congress' 1972 extension of the protections of Title VII to state and municipal employees. Although Congress did not explicitly consider the viability of the defense offered by the state employer in this case, the 1972 amendments to Title VII do reflect Congress' intent to provide state and municipal employees with the protection that Title VII, as interpreted by *Griggs*, had provided to employees in the private sector: equality of *opportunity* and the elimination of discriminatory *barriers* to professional development. The Committee Reports and the floor debates stressed the need for equality of opportunity for minority applicants seeking to obtain governmental positions. Congress voiced its concern about the widespread use by state and local governmental agencies of "invalid selection techniques" that had a discriminatory impact.

The decisions of this Court following *Griggs* also support respondents' claim. In considering claims of disparate impact under § 703(a)(2) this Court has consistently focused on employment and promotion requirements that create a discriminatory bar to *opportunities.* This Court has never read § 703(a)(2) as requiring the focus to be placed instead on the overall number of minority or female applicants actually hired or promoted.

In short, the District Court's dismissal of respondents' claim cannot be supported on the basis that respondents failed to establish a prima facie case of employment discrimination under the terms of § 703(a)(2). The suggestion that disparate impact should be measured only at the bottom line ignores the fact that Title VII guarantees these individual respondents the *opportunity* to compete equally with white workers on the basis of job-related criteria. Title VII strives to achieve equality of opportunity by rooting out "artificial, arbitrary, and unnecessary" employer-created barriers to professional development that have a discriminatory impact upon individuals. Therefore, respondents' rights under § 703(a)(2) have been violated, unless petitioners can demonstrate that the examination given was not an artificial, arbitrary, or unnecessary barrier, because it measured skills related to effective performance in the role of Welfare Eligibility Supervisor.

The United States, in its brief as *amicus curiae*, apparently recognizes that respondents' claim in this case falls within the affirmative commands of Title VII. But it seeks to support the District Court's judgment in this case by relying on the defenses provided to the employer in § 703(h). Section 703(h) provides in pertinent part:

> Notwithstanding any other provision of this subchapter, it shall not be an unlawful employment practice for an employer . . . to give and to act upon the results of any professionally developed ability test provided that such test, its administration or action upon the results is not designed, intended or used to discriminate because of race, color, religion, sex or national origin.

The Government argues that the test administered by the petitioners was not "used to discriminate" because it did not actually deprive disproportionate numbers of blacks of promotions. But the Government's reliance on § 703(h) as offering the employer some special haven for discriminatory tests is misplaced. We considered the relevance of this provision in *Griggs*. After examining the legislative history of § 703(h), we concluded that Congress, in adding § 703(h), intended only to make clear that tests that were *job related* would be permissible despite their disparate impact. *Griggs*, 401 U.S. at 433–436. As the Court recently confirmed, § 703(h), which was introduced as an amendment to Title VII on the Senate floor, "did not alter the meaning of Title VII, but 'merely clarifie[d] its present intent and effect.'" *American Tobacco Co. v. Patterson*, 456 U.S. 63 (1982), quoting 110 Cong. Rec. 12723 (1964) (remarks of Sen. Humphrey). A nonjob-related test that has a disparate racial impact, and is used to "limit" or "classify" employees, is "used to discriminate" within the meaning of Title VII, whether or not it was "designed or intended" to have this effect and despite an employer's efforts to compensate for its discriminatory effect. See *Griggs*, 401 U.S. at 433.

In sum, respondents' claim of disparate impact from the examination, a pass-fail barrier to employment opportunity, states a prima facie case of employment discrimination under § 703(a)(2), despite their employer's nondiscriminatory "bottom line," and that "bottom line" is no defense to this prima facie case under § 703(h).

Having determined that respondents' claim comes within the terms of Title VII, we must address the suggestion of petitioners and some *amici curiae* that we recognize an exception, either in the nature of an additional burden on plaintiffs seeking to establish a prima facie case or in the nature of an affirmative defense, for cases in which an employer has compensated for a discriminatory pass-fail barrier by hiring or promoting a sufficient number of black employees to reach a nondiscriminatory "bottom line." We reject this suggestion, which is in essence nothing more than a request that we redefine the protections guaranteed by Title VII.

■ NOTES AND QUESTIONS

1. The bottom-line defense demonstrates two different ways of looking at disparate impact law—whether the law should address discrimination against individuals specifically or protected groups as a whole. Which approach does the Court take here?

2. Is it fair to hold the employer liable where it has undertaken efforts to make certain that it has a proportionate workforce? Should the employer be entitled to an affirmative defense in such situations?

3. Is part of the problem here that the employer—in adopting a bottom-line defense—is advocating for a type of quota system usually disfavored by the legislature and courts?

4. An extensive dissent is omitted from the case above. The dissent takes more of a group-look at disparate impact law, and would not hold an employer liable where the "bottom-line" result of the employer's practices is a proportionate workforce.

⮌ *Interactive Problem*

Looking back at the interactive problem, would the employer have a valid defense to a disparate impact claim if it hired a disproportionately high number of women that satisfied the height and weight requirement to balance out its workforce? At a minimum, could such a strategy constitute an affirmative defense by the employer that it was trying to comply with the law?

2. Validation Studies as a Safe Harbor to Disparate Impact Claims

Validation studies have long been seen as an important way for employers to justify a test given to their employees. The authors below suggest that employers who carefully use these studies to "validate" their tests can insulate themselves from disparate impact liability:

> One [way for an employer to attain an affirmative defense to a disparate impact claim] would be a formal validation study. As we explain [], under the affirmative defense as we have described it, an employer that relied on a properly conducted formal validation study would probably not be liable for disparate impact. Although employers might sometimes be able to satisfy the affirmative defense even without formal validation studies, those studies might offer employers a safe harbor from disparate-impact liability. But this safe harbor would apply only when the employer did not also have independent evidence calling the test's validity into question. Once the employer had reason to doubt the test's validity—for example, because a plaintiff in a suit proffered evidence that the test was in fact invalid—the employer could not continue to rely on a validation study to avoid disparate-impact liability. For this reason, we refer to validation studies as a limited safe harbor.

Joseph A. Seiner & Benjamin N. Gutman, *Does* Ricci *Herald a New Disparate Impact?*, 90 B.U. L. Rev. 2181, 2209 (2010). A validation study is simply a way for employers to verify that the test that they are implementing actually accomplishes what it is intended to do. Thus, for example, an employer might commission a validation study on a promotion test for civil servants to see if the test actually measures factors that lead to successful performance in the new position. There are extensive guidelines and common practices on the best way to conduct these validation studies. Indeed, § 703(h) of Title VII provides specific criteria for this type of validation defense.

From a best practices standpoint, however, the bigger consideration is that employers should always contemplate having a validation study done any time that they are considering adopting a standardized test in the workplace. This type of study—if properly done—will help insulate employers from liability. Similarly, plaintiffs should attempt to identify whether an employer has conducted such a study, and if not, inquire as to why the employer has failed to do so. The level of "safe harbor" provided by such studies is still very much an issue to be decided by the courts. Nonetheless, these studies can be very valuable for employers when defending against disparate impact litigation. *See generally* Dennis Doverspike et al., *The Feasibility of Traditional Validation Procedures for Demonstrating Job-Relatedness*, 9 LAW & PSYCHOL. REV. 35 (1985).

E. Chapter-in-Review

At this point in the text, it is worth briefly reviewing the two primary ways in which discrimination claims can proceed. First, a claim can be brought as a disparate treatment—or intentional discrimination—claim. A disparate treatment claim is often considered through circumstantial evidence of discrimination and the factors outlined in the *McDonnell Douglas* test. If a plaintiff has direct evidence of discrimination, however, there is no need to proceed under this test. Supreme Court case law has called into question this strict divide between circumstantial and direct evidence, but the lower courts largely continue to apply this distinction. A number of specific types of disparate treatment cases require separate analysis, specifically: mixed-motives cases, after-acquired evidence cases, affirmative action policies, and class-action claims. This analysis was addressed extensively in Chapter 3.

Second, claims can proceed under a disparate impact analysis. For a disparate impact claim, a plaintiff must show that there is a policy or practice that has an adverse effect on a protected group. The employer then has the burden of persuasion of demonstrating that the policy is job related and consistent with business necessity. The plaintiff must then show that alternative policies or practices exist that have less discriminatory impact on the employer but still serve the employer's business goals. The bottom-line defense to disparate impact claims was soundly rejected by the Supreme Court. Employers utilizing testing procedures in the workplace can help defend against disparate impact claims by engaging in a carefully conducted validation study.

It is also important to note that disparate treatment and disparate impact are not mutually exclusive. Both claims can be—and often are—alleged in a particular case. A summary of the analytical framework for addressing employment discrimination claims is set forth below in graph form.

This analytical framework forms the basis of employment discrimination law. All claims of discrimination—including those based on race, color, sex, national origin, religion, age, and disability—proceed under this model. It is important to have a thorough understanding of how disparate treatment and disparate impact cases proceed before moving on to the specific categories of discrimination. Each category is nuanced, and there are slight variations to the framework discussed above for claims brought by each protected group. Those nuances will be addressed in the following chapters.

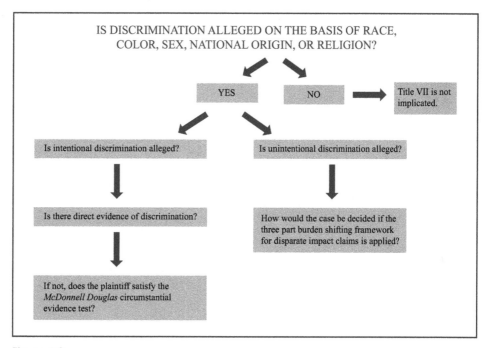

Figure 4.2

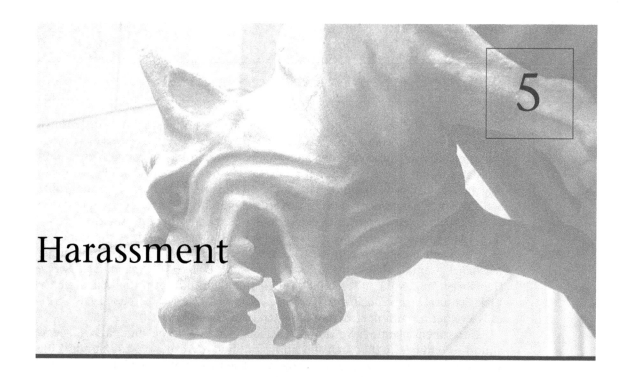

Harassment

 Interactive Problem

Sarah Server, a twenty-year old white female, worked as a waitress at "Gozangas Bar and Grill" for two years where her job was to serve food and drink to local patrons. Gozangas advertises itself as a "family restaurant," but its marketing campaigns tend to target adult males by highlighting their scantily clad female servers. The restaurant's entirely female waitstaff dresses in tight shirts and shorts, and is encouraged to "flirt" with the male customers. As one of the most attractive waitresses at the restaurant, Sarah is subjected to a number of comments about her breast size by managers and co-workers. The kitchen staff would also whistle at her when she picked up an order, and one member of the staff would touch her arm and back whenever she walked by. Sarah complained about all of this conduct, but the comments and touching persisted. In addition, Sarah would change into her work "uniform" from her street clothes in the restaurant changing room. As she removed her clothes one day, she could hear male laughter and noticed a "peep hole" in one of the walls. Sarah complained about the hole, which was subsequently covered up, but other holes continued to appear. Sarah eventually started changing in the restroom, where there was more privacy. All of this conduct really bothered Sarah, but she decided to "put up" with this "childish" behavior because the pay at Gozangas was substantial and she really needed the job.

Would Sarah have a cause of action under Title VII? What would her argument(s) be? How could Gozangas defend against a Title VII claim? *See generally* Ciesielski v. Hooters of Am., Inc., 94 Fair Empl. Prac. Cas. (BNA) 471 (2004).

A. Introduction

Harassment is a unique area of the law for a number of different reasons. Perhaps most importantly, harassment often takes place by employees without the knowledge of the company. Thus, harassers often harass co-workers or subordinates for their own "personal gain." Many harassers are completely aware that their behavior is inappropriate, and will thus try to conceal their improper actions. Since harassment is often driven underground at a company, it may be very difficult for an employer to detect, as compared to other forms of discrimination. Harassment is many times less about sex and more about power, as harassers often seek out and victimize those who they know (or hope) will not complain. *See generally* L. Camille Hebert, *Why Don't "Reasonable Women" Complain About Sexual Harassment?*, 82 IND. L.J. 711 (2007) (discussing definition of sexual harassment); Vicki Schultz, *Reconceptualizing Sexual Harassment*, 107 YALE L.J. 1683 (1998) (critically evaluating current structure of sexual harassment law).

Harassment claims have now been recognized for some time, and it seems almost second nature that such allegations can lead to a cause of action under Title VII. Such was not always the case, however. The theory of sexual harassment was identified in 1979 by Catharine A. MacKinnon in her well-known work, *The Sexual Harassment of Working Women*. In 1980, the EEOC developed guidelines clarifying protection against sexual harassment in the workplace under Title VII. As discussed later in this chapter, the hostile working environment theory was ultimately adopted by the Supreme Court in 1986 in *Meritor Savings Bank, FSB v. Vinson*, 477 U.S. 57. Early on, the courts divided sexual harassment claims into two broad categories. First, quid pro quo claims could be brought where a supervisor would use "sex" as a tool for either reward or punishment. Quid pro quo roughly translates to "something for something," mean-

ing that if you engaged in some type of sexual activity with your employer, you would receive some type of benefit (or suffer an adverse consequence if you failed to do so). As the terms, conditions, and privileges of employment are clearly implicated with quid pro quo claims, there has been little controversy as to whether these cases would fall within the ambit of Title VII.

More controversially, however, are the second type of harassment claims — hostile work environment cases. In a hostile work environment case, a plaintiff alleges that she has suffered a hostile atmosphere in the workplace, though not necessarily one that has had a direct economic impact. In such cases, there is no tangible employment action that has taken place. Rather, the plaintiff is

Anti-Sexual Harassment Poster

impacted in other ways — often psychologically — by the severity or pervasiveness of the inappropriate conduct taking place around her. The EEOC believed that such cases should be covered by Title VII. Others were more conflicted, however, and there were divergent opinions on this issue until it was ultimately resolved by the Supreme Court in *Meritor*. The major question in such cases is whether the plaintiff has suffered an adverse action even where no economic harm has occurred.

The scope of harassment claims has been one of several controversial topics in this area. A second issue that often arises is when (and how) employers can be held liable for such claims. This can be particularly problematic because many companies may have strict rules against engaging in harassing behavior, and may even be completely unaware that such conduct is occurring at its place of business. When is it fair to hold an employer liable for the conduct of its supervisors or other employees? Again, the courts were split on how such liability should be assessed, and the issue would have to be resolved by the Supreme Court. *See generally* STEPHEN MOREWITZ, SEXUAL HARASSMENT AND SOCIAL CHANGE IN AMERICAN SOCIETY (1996); CELIA MORRIS, BEARING WITNESS: SEXUAL HARASSMENT AND BEYOND (1994); ROSEMARIE SKAINE, POWER AND GENDER: ISSUES IN SEXUAL DOMINANCE AND HARASSMENT (1996).

B. The #MeToo Movement

The Me Too movement was established well before social media hashtags led to its national recognition. The movement began in 2006 through grassroots work and was created by Tarana Burke to "help survivors of sexual violence, particularly young women of color from low wealth communities, find pathways to healing." me too, https://metoomvmt.org/ (last visited June 27, 2018). Since Ms. Burke founded the movement, it has developed to help not only young women of color, but also adults of both genders who have experienced the trauma of sexual violence. The purpose of the movement is to de-stigmatize the survivors of sexual assault by bringing issues of sexual violence to the mainstream as well as building avenues for sexual assault survivors to find restorative justice. *See* Sandra E. Garcia, *The Woman Who Created #MeToo Long Before Hashtags*, N.Y. TIMES, Oct. 20, 2017.

The Me Too movement went viral with the hashtag #MeToo after Hollywood producer Harvey Weinstein was accused of sexual harassment by numerous actresses and workers. Prior to these accusations, Harvey Weinstein was regarded as one of the most influential film producers in Hollywood. Due, in part, to his immense power within the industry, he was able to coerce women into unwillingly performing sexual favors for him in order to boost their careers. *See Harvey Weinstein Timeline: How the Scandal Unfolded*, BBC NEWS (May 25, 2018), https://www.bbc.com/news/entertainment-arts-41594672.

The New York Times first broke the story involving Weinstein on October 5, 2017. The allegations stretched back decades and were made by actresses as well as former employees of the Weinstein Company and Miramax, businesses founded by Weinstein and his brother. Mr. Weinstein was fired from the Weinstein Company, resigned from the Weinstein Company's board, and has been ousted from the Academy of Motion Picture Arts and Sciences that awarded him five

Oscars for his films. *See* Daniel Victor, *How the Harvey Weinstein Story Has Unfolded*, N.Y. Times, Oct. 18, 2017, https://www.nytimes.com/2017/10/18/business/harvey-weinstein.html?action=click&contentCollection=U.S.&module=RelatedCoverage&region=EndOfArticle&pgtype=article.

This Weinstein scandal started a national discussion on harassment and sexual violence and allowed many others to add their voice and experience to the discussion. Many high-profile figures have now been accused of inappropriate sexual conduct. Among the most notable accused in the movement are politician Roy Moore, news anchor Tom Brokaw, comedian Louis C.K., Politician Al Franken, music producer Russell Simmons, chef Mario Batali, director Woody Allen, former USA gymnastics doctor Larry Nassar, singer R. Kelly, and a series of actors including Bill Cosby, Kevin Spacey, James Franco, Jeremy Piven, Morgan Freeman, and former "Today Show" anchor Matt Lauer. Following the myriad revelations of sexual harassment and sexual assault, *Time Magazine* named "Silence Breakers" its 2017 Person of the Year, citing a number of women who have spoken up about harassment and abuse as forces behind the movement.

In the midst of the Me Too movement, several high-profile companies have updated their sexual harassment policies. One company that made headlines for its new policy was Netflix. With the new policy, employees are banned from staring at a co-worker for more than five seconds or asking a co-worker for their phone number. Suzanne Lucas, *Netflix Has a New Sexual Harassment Policy. It's Like 7th Grade on Steroids*, Inc. (June 14, 2018), https://www.inc.com/suzanne-lucas/netflix-has-a-new-sexual-harassment-policy-its-like-7th-grade-on-steroids.html. However, one study shows that office sexual harassment policies may be lagging behind the #MeToo movement. The study found that while 90% of companies have a sexual harassment policy, more than 20% of those do not offer any sexual harassment training to prevent such incidents form occurring. The report also found that less than one-fifth of companies plan to offer bystander training to teach employees how to respond if they suspect a co-worker is being harassed at work. In addition, nearly 40% of companies polled think confidentiality or nondisclosure agreements, which have been in the news as part of the #MeToo movement, should be a part of sexual harassment settlements. Annie Nova, *Office Sexual Harassment Policies Lag Behind the #MeToo Movement*, CNBC (Apr. 19, 2018, 10:55 A.M.), https://www.cnbc.com/2018/04/19/office-sexual-harassment-policies-lag-behind-the-metoo-movement.html.

Larry Nassar's conviction for sexual assault proved to be the first "win" for the Me Too movement when he was sentenced to 175 years for molesting 168 young female gymnasts. Although a very extreme case, his conviction revealed that some justice can be served for those who have made sexual assault allegations, especially when victims report their assault to authorities. Matilda Dixon-Smith, Opinion, *Larry Nassar's 175-Year Sentence Feels Like a Victory for Me Too*, ABC News (Jan. 25, 2018), http://www.abc.net.au/news/2018-01-25/larry-nassars-huge-sentence-feels-like-a-victory-for-me-too/9360926. Another "win" for the Me Too movement occurred when Bill Cosby was convicted of sexual assault charges on April 26, 2018. Cosby, a household name and iconic actor, was accused of drugging and sexually assaulting a Temple University women's basketball director in 2004. Cosby has been accused of sexual assault by over sixty women since the first allegations were made against him. Manuel Roig-Franzia, *Bill Cosby Convicted on Three Counts of Sexual Assault*, Wash. Post, Apr. 26, 2018, https://www.washingtonpost.com/lifestyle/style/bill-cosby-convicted-on-three-counts-of-sexual-assault/2018/04/26/d740ef22-4885-11e8-827e-190efaf1f1ee_story.html?utm_term=.3115a83f9462.

The Me Too movement received further national attention when Alyssa Milano, a famous actress, promoted the hashtag #MeToo in order to give a voice to sexual abuse victims through a social media platform. Soon after, the hashtag was tweeted more than a million times within 48 hours. Anrea Park, *#MeToo Reaches 85 Countries with 1.7M Tweets*, CBS News (Oct. 24, 2017, 12:43 P.M.), https://www.cbsnews.com/news/metoo-reaches-85-countries-with-1-7-million-tweets/. On Facebook, there were more than 12 million posts relating to the Me Too movement. Associated Press, *More than 12M "Me Too" Facebook Posts, Comments, Reactions in 24 Hours*, CBS News (Oct. 17, 2017, 6:26 P.M.), https://www.cbsnews.com/news/metoo-more-than-12-million-facebook-posts-comments-reactions-24-hours/. Over 67,000 people have responded to Milano's tweet with their stories and words of support and encouragement for survivors. The response on Twitter include several posts from high-profile women including Gwyneth Paltrow, Jennifer Lawrence, and Uma Thurman.

The majority of responses to the Me Too movement demonstrate a shift from a narrative of sexual harassment claims that often included victim-shaming and blaming. After the Weinstein scandal and Cosby conviction, legal experts hope that more victims will speak up about assault and law enforcement agents will take sexual assault claims more seriously. The Bill Cosby case also evidenced a shift in the legal landscape, with states increasing the statute of limitations for both sexual assault and sexual harassment. Meredith Mandell, *Bill Cosby's Conviction Was Hailed as a #MeToo Victory. But Advocates Say More Needs to be Done*, NBC News (May 3, 2018, 12:36 P.M.), https://www.nbcnews.com/storyline/bill-cosby-scandal/bill-cosby-s-conviction-was-hailed-metoo-victory-advocates-say-n870796.

There is still much uncertainty as to how far-reaching the consequences of the Me Too movement will be in the workplace. Rebecca Shabad & Stephanie Perry, *Poll: Majority Says #MeToo Movement Has Helped Address Gender Inequality*, NBC News (Mar. 9, 2018, 4:33 A.M.), https://www.nbcnews.com/politics/politics-news/poll-majority-says-metoo-movement-has-helped-address-gender-inequality-n854576. More public awareness and discourse — both inside and out of the employment context — will continue to be critical to this debate. Employers must be vigilant in protecting against assault and harassment, and proactive in developing policies that will encourage victims and witnesses to speak up quickly.

C. Protected Categories of Harassment

Harassment is often thought of in the same context as "sexual harassment." Indeed, we often see sexual harassment claims dominate the news and the court system. Similarly, race harassment claims are also relatively common, and it has long been recognized that a cause of action can be brought on this basis as well.

The prohibited classes extend beyond race and sex, however, and companies must make certain not to discriminate against any group. Indeed, harassment causes of action have been recognized under every statute, and can occur on the basis of race, color, sex, national origin, religion, age, and disability. For example, claims of national origin harassment dramatically increased in the days and years following September 11, 2001. The case below examines whether disability can form the basis for a harassment claim.

Shaver v. Independent Stave Co.
350 F.3d 716 (8th Cir. 2003)

ARNOLD, Circuit Judge.

This is a harassment and retaliation case brought under the Americans with Disabilities Act (ADA), that comes to us on appeal from an order dismissing the plaintiff's claims on summary judgment.

We have suggested in dicta that it might be possible to bring a claim for a hostile work environment under the ADA, but we have never ruled directly on the matter. Today, for the reasons that follow, we join the other circuits that have decided the issue by holding that such claims are in fact actionable.

Even broad, remedial statutes such as the ADA do not give federal courts a license to create causes of action after the manner of the common law. Rather, our rulings must be disciplined by the text of the statute itself. The ADA states that "[n]o covered entity shall discriminate against a qualified individual with a disability because of the disability of such individual in regard to . . . terms, conditions, and privileges of employment." 42 U.S.C. § 12112(a). While the statute does not specifically mention hostile work environment, in construing a statute we must look at how its text was understood at the time that it was passed.

The drafters of the ADA borrowed the phrase "terms, conditions, and privileges of employment" directly from Title VII of the Civil Rights Act of 1964. As early as 1971, courts had construed the phrase in Title VII to create an action based on a hostile work environment, and by the time that the ADA was passed in 1991, this interpretation was clearly established as the controlling federal law on the subject. Thus, when Congress included the phrase "terms, conditions, and privileges of employment" in the ADA, it was using a legal term of art that prohibited a broad range of employment practices, including workplace harassment.

In determining whether a hostile work environment claim has been made out under the ADA, we think it proper to turn to standards developed elsewhere in our anti-discrimination law, adapting them to the unique requirements of the ADA. To be entitled to relief, it seems to us that [the plaintiff] must show that he is a member of the class of people protected by the statute, that he was subject to unwelcome harassment, that the harassment resulted from his membership in the protected class, and that the harassment was severe enough to affect the terms, conditions, or privileges of his employment.

■ NOTES AND QUESTIONS

1. In *Shaver*, the Eighth Circuit Court of Appeals acknowledged that individuals can avail themselves of disability harassment claims.

2. Generally speaking, the courts agree that harassment claims can be brought on the basis of race, color, sex, national origin, religion, age, and disability.

3. Would it be more difficult for a plaintiff to prevail on a disability harassment claim or a sexual harassment claim? Why? Would the courts view the claims differently?

4. In Chapter 10, we will explore more deeply whether the plaintiff in this case was "disabled" under the terms of the ADA. We will further consider whether the specific facts of this case were sufficient to create a cause of action for harassment under the statute.

5. **Harassment charge filing.** Men file significantly fewer sexual harassment claims than women. However, the percentage of charges filed by males with the EEOC has increased over the years. For example, the number of sexual harassment charges filed by males in the year 2000 was 13.6 percent. In 2017, that percentage had risen to 16.5 percent. *See* EEOC, Charges Alleging Sex-Based Harassment: FY 2010–FY 2017, http://www.eeoc.gov/eeoc/statistics/enforcement/sexual_harassment_new.cfm; EEOC, Sexual Harassment Charges EEOC & FEPAs Combined: FY 1997–FY 2011, http://www.eeoc.gov/eeoc/statistics/enforcement/sexual_harassment.cfm.

D. The Harassment Cause of Action

The elements of a harassment cause of action vary depending upon whether a tangible employment action or hostile work environment claim has been alleged. All claims of harassment have a single common thread, however — the action taken must be "because of" the protected characteristic. This "because of" determination was further defined by the Supreme Court in a case involving same-sex sexual harassment.

1. Because of Sex

Oncale v. Sundowner Offshore Services, Inc.
523 U.S. 75 (1998)

Justice Scalia delivered the opinion of the Court.

This case presents the question whether workplace harassment can violate Title VII's prohibition against "discriminat[ion] . . . because of . . . sex," 42 U.S.C. § 2000e–2(a)(1), when the harasser and the harassed employee are of the same sex.

The District Court having granted summary judgment for respondents, we must assume the facts to be as alleged by petitioner Joseph Oncale. The precise details are irrelevant to the legal point we must decide, and in the interest of both brevity and dignity we shall describe them only generally. In late October 1991, Oncale was working for respondent Sundowner Offshore Services, Inc., on a Chevron U.S.A., Inc., oil platform in the Gulf of Mexico. He was employed as a roustabout on an eight-man crew which included respondents John Lyons, Danny Pippen, and Brandon Johnson. Lyons, the crane operator, and Pippen, the driller, had supervisory authority. On several occasions, Oncale was forcibly subjected to sex-related, humiliating actions against him by Lyons, Pippen, and Johnson in the presence of the rest of the crew. Pippen and Lyons also physically assaulted Oncale in a sexual manner, and Lyons threatened him with rape.

Oncale's complaints to supervisory personnel produced no remedial action; in fact, the company's Safety Compliance Clerk, Valent Hohen, told Oncale that Lyons and Pippen "picked [on] him all the time too," and called him a name suggesting homosexuality. Oncale eventually quit — asking that his pink slip reflect that he "voluntarily left due to sexual harassment and verbal abuse." When asked at his deposition why he left Sundowner, Oncale stated: "I felt that if I didn't leave my job, that I would be raped or forced to have sex."

Oncale filed a complaint against Sundowner in the United States District Court for the Eastern District of Louisiana, alleging that he was discriminated against in his employment because of his sex. Relying on the Fifth Circuit's decision in *Garcia v. Elf Atochem North America*, 28 F.3d 446 (1994), the District Court held that "Mr. Oncale, a male, has no cause of action under Title VII for harassment by male co-workers." On appeal, a panel of the Fifth Circuit concluded that *Garcia* was binding Circuit precedent, and affirmed.

Oil Rig in Port Arthur, Texas

Title VII's prohibition of discrimination "because of . . . sex" protects men as well as women, and in the related context of racial discrimination in the workplace we have rejected any conclusive presumption that an employer will not discriminate against members of his own race. "Because of the many facets of human motivation, it would be unwise to presume as a matter of law that human beings of one definable group will not discriminate against other members of their group." *Castaneda v. Partida*, 430 U.S. 482, 499 (1977). In *Johnson v. Transportation Agency, Santa Clara Cty.*, 480 U.S. 616 (1987), a male employee claimed that his employer discriminated against him because of his sex when it preferred a female employee for promotion. Although we ultimately rejected the claim on other grounds, we did not consider it significant that the supervisor who made that decision was also a man. If our precedents leave any doubt on the question, we hold today that nothing in Title VII necessarily bars a claim of discrimination "because of . . . sex" merely because the plaintiff and the defendant (or the person charged with acting on behalf of the defendant) are of the same sex.

Courts have had little trouble with that principle in cases like *Johnson*, where an employee claims to have been passed over for a job or promotion. But when the issue arises in the context of a "hostile environment" sexual harassment claim, the state and federal courts have taken a bewildering variety of stances. Some, like the Fifth Circuit in this case, have held that same-sex sexual harassment claims are never cognizable under Title VII. Other decisions say that such claims are actionable only if the plaintiff can prove that the harasser is homosexual (and thus presumably motivated by sexual desire). Still others suggest that workplace harassment that is sexual in content is always actionable, regardless of the harasser's sex, sexual orientation, or motivations.

We see no justification in the statutory language or our precedents for a categorical rule excluding same-sex harassment claims from the coverage of Title VII. As some courts have observed, male-on-male sexual harassment in the workplace was assuredly not the principal evil Congress was concerned with when it enacted Title VII. But statutory prohibitions often go beyond the principal evil to cover reasonably comparable evils, and it is ultimately the provisions of our laws rather than the principal concerns of our legislators by which we are governed. Title VII prohibits "discriminat[ion] . . . because of . . . sex" in the "terms" or "conditions" of employment. Our holding that this includes sexual harassment must extend to sexual harassment of any kind that meets the statutory requirements.

Respondents and their *amici* contend that recognizing liability for same-sex harassment will transform Title VII into a general civility code for the American workplace. But that risk is no greater for same-sex than for opposite-sex harassment, and is adequately met by careful attention to the requirements of the statute.

> The courts often express reluctance with treating Title VII as a "civility code" for the workplace.

Title VII does not prohibit all verbal or physical harassment in the workplace; it is directed only at "*discriminat[ion]* . . . because of . . . sex." We have never held that workplace harassment, even harassment between men and women, is automatically discrimination because of sex merely because the words used have sexual content or connotations. "The critical issue, Title VII's text indicates, is whether members of one sex are exposed to disadvantageous terms or conditions of employment to which members of the other sex are not exposed." *Harris v. Forklift Systems, Inc.*, 510 U.S. 17, 25 (1993) (Ginsburg, J., concurring).

Courts and juries have found the inference of discrimination easy to draw in most male-female sexual harassment situations, because the challenged conduct typically involves explicit or implicit proposals of sexual activity; it is reasonable to assume those proposals would not have been made to someone of the same sex. The same chain of inference would be available to a plaintiff alleging same-sex harassment, if there were credible evidence that the harasser was homosexual. But harassing conduct need not be motivated by sexual desire to support an inference of discrimination on the basis of sex. A trier of fact might reasonably find such discrimination, for example, if a female victim is harassed in such sex-specific and derogatory terms by another woman as to make it clear that the harasser is motivated by general hostility to the presence of women in the workplace. A same-sex harassment plaintiff may also, of course, offer direct comparative evidence about how the alleged harasser treated members of both sexes in a mixed-sex workplace. Whatever evidentiary route the plaintiff chooses to follow, he or she must always prove that the conduct at issue was not merely tinged with offensive sexual connotations, but actually constituted "*discrimina[tion]* . . . because of . . . sex."

And there is another requirement that prevents Title VII from expanding into a general civility code: As we emphasized in *Meritor* and *Harris*, the statute does not reach genuine but innocuous differences in the ways men and women routinely interact with members of the same sex and of the opposite sex. The prohibition of harassment on the basis of sex requires neither asexuality nor androgyny in the workplace; it forbids only behavior so objectively offensive as to alter the "conditions" of the victim's employment. "Conduct that is not severe or pervasive enough to create an objectively hostile or abusive work environment — an environment that a reasonable person would find hostile or abusive — is beyond Title VII's purview." *Harris*, 510 U.S. at 21, citing *Meritor*, 477 U.S. at 67. We have always regarded that requirement as crucial, and as sufficient to ensure that courts and juries do not mistake ordinary socializing in the workplace — such as male-on-male horseplay or intersexual flirtation — for discriminatory "conditions of employment."

We have emphasized, moreover, that the objective severity of harassment should be judged from the perspective of a reasonable person in the plaintiff's position, considering "all the circumstances." *Harris*, *supra*, at 23. In same-sex (as in all) harassment cases, that inquiry requires careful consideration of the social context in which particular behavior occurs and is experienced by its target. A professional football player's working environment is not severely or pervasively abusive, for example, if the coach smacks him on the buttocks as he heads onto the field — even if the same behavior would reasonably be experienced as abusive by the coach's secretary (male or female) back at the office. The real social impact of workplace behavior often depends on a constellation of surrounding circumstances, expectations, and relationships which are not fully captured by a simple recitation of the words used or the physical acts performed. Common sense, and an appropriate sensitivity to social context, will enable courts and juries to distinguish between simple teasing or roughhousing among members of the same sex, and conduct which a reasonable person in the plaintiff's position would find severely hostile or abusive.

> The Court holds that "same-sex sexual harassment is actionable under Title VII" and enumerates several ways that such a claim could be established.

Because we conclude that sex discrimination consisting of same-sex sexual harassment is actionable under Title VII, the judgment of the Court of Appeals for the Fifth Circuit is reversed, and the case is remanded for further proceedings consistent with this opinion.

It is so ordered.

Justice THOMAS, concurring.

I concur because the Court stresses that in every sexual harassment case, the plaintiff must plead and ultimately prove Title VII's statutory requirement that there be discrimination "because of . . . sex."

■ NOTES AND QUESTIONS

1. The Supreme Court here holds, contrary to the finding of the lower court, that same-sex harassment claims are viable under Title VII. The defendants had argued that such a conclusion would turn Title VII into a civility code. Do you agree? The defendants further argue that the plaintiffs are bootstrapping sexual orientation claims beyond the text of the statute. Does this argument have merit?

2. In helping to define what "because of sex" means, the Supreme Court noted that there are three different circumstances in which this term can be established: (1) by showing that the harassment was sexual in nature; (2) by establishing that the company treated one sex with hostility; or (3) through comparative evidence showing that one sex was treated better than another. As the Court notes, this list is not exhaustive. What other ways might a plaintiff establish that an action was taken "because of sex" other than those specifically articulated by the Court? In Chapter 7, we will look at how advocates are using the Supreme Court's decision in *Price Waterhouse v. Hopkins* to potentially expand the meaning of "because of sex."

3. *Oncale* was brought as a sexual harassment claim. How could you show that harassment was "because of race," "disability," or some other protected characteristic?

4. As the Court notes, the case was remanded for further proceedings. If you were the judge on remand, would you conclude that there was sufficient evidence of harassment to allow the case to proceed? Is this harassment of the type prohibited by Title VII?

5. Claims that are sexual in nature seem to squarely fall within the harassment realm. But what type of evidence would a plaintiff need to establish that one sex is being treated with hostility?

6. Claims that involve allegations that are sexual in nature tend to lead to larger judgments than those that involve general hostility. Why would this be the case? *See* Eric Schnapper, *Some of Them Still Don't Get It: Hostile Work Environment Litigation in the Lower Courts*, 1999 U. Chi. Legal F. 277, 344 ("The appropriate response of the legal system to less severe forms of harassment should be the same as its response to less severe physical assaults — lower damages."); Caroline Vaile Wright & Louise F. Fitzgerald, *Correlates of Joining a Sexual Harassment Class Action*, 33 Law & Hum. Behavior 265, 268 (2009).

7. Justice Thomas's short concurrence emphasizes that for any harassment cause of action, the first question that must be asked is, "was the action taken because of a protected characteristic?" If the answer to this question is "no," the case will ultimately fail.

8. A 2011 poll produced for ABC News and the Washington Post by Langer Research Associates indicated that one in four women had experienced workplace sexual harassment. Additionally, one in ten men said they had experienced it, and a quarter of men said they fear being falsely accused of this type of workplace claim. *See One in Four U.S. Women Reports Workplace Harassment*, Langer Research (Nov. 16, 2011), http://www.langerresearch.com/uploads/1130a2Workplace Harassment.pdf.

Interactive Problem

Looking back at the facts of the interactive problem at the beginning of the chapter, assume that Sarah's direct supervisor is replaced by a female employee, Linda Loveless. Linda is jealous of how much male attention Sarah has been receiving at the workplace, and decides to take these jealousies out on her. Specifically, Linda cuts Sarah's hours by a third and refuses to allow her to work any weekend shifts, the most profitable days at the restaurant. Would Sarah have a cause of action under Title VII based on Linda's conduct?

The appellate courts also have struggled with how to determine when a decision is taken on the basis of sex. The Fourth Circuit Court of Appeals visited the question of what "because of sex" means in the controversial decision below, which contains disturbing allegations of harassment. This case illustrates how the courts grapple with harassment with respect to the question of whether certain conduct occurred "because of sex."

Ocheltree v. Scollon Productions Inc.

335 F.3d 325 (4th Cir. 2003) (en banc)

MICHAEL, Circuit Judge:

Scollon Productions makes costumes, including ones depicting university mascots and cartoon characters. The company has about fifty employees and is located in White Rock, South Carolina. The only persons with formal management authority at the company are Bill Scollon, the president, and Ellery Locklear, the senior vice president. The company's production facilities include a sewing room and what is called the production shop. The production shop itself is fairly small, with enough work tables to accommodate about a dozen employees, including the shop supervisor. Bill Scollon and Locklear have their offices near the production facilities.

Ocheltree was employed at Scollon Productions for eighteen months, from February 1994 until August 1995. She worked in the production shop making shoes. Ocheltree was the only female employee in the shop, working alongside ten or eleven men. In the early stages of her employment, the atmosphere in the shop was "fun" and "friendly," but this changed. During her first year there, coarse sexual talk and sexual antics by several of the men began to occur with increasing frequency. This misconduct worsened as time went on, especially after Ocheltree complained to the men and the shop supervisor, Harold Hirsch. The details of the sexual talk and conduct that Ocheltree heard and saw during her tenure in the production shop are as follows.

Scollon Productions has mannequins that are used in the production of its costumes. Some of the men in the production shop often used a female-form mannequin as a prop to engage in sexual antics in front of Ocheltree. Many times when Ocheltree was in sight of the mannequin, the men would fondle it or use it to demonstrate sexual techniques, including oral sex. One shop employee, Brian Hodge, noticed that "anytime [Ocheltree] was walking by just about they would

do something sexual to the mannequin in front of her." On one occasion, for example, two male shop
employees were positioned at the
mannequin when Ocheltree arrived
at work. One was pinching the mannequin's nipples, and the other was
on his knees simulating oral sex on
the mannequin. Ocheltree said to
the men, "You guys are disgusting,
this needs to stop." The incident
prompted Ocheltree to leave the
room. As she walked out, she heard laughter in the background.

On another occasion a male coworker came up to Ocheltree in the production
shop and sang the following song to her "like he was in the opera": "Come to me,
oh, baby come to me, your breath smells like c[o]m[e] to me." Ocheltree immediately told the man that he was disgusting. Nevertheless, the other men in the
production shop, including supervisor Hirsch, expressed their enjoyment of the
incident with much laughter. On still another occasion when Ocheltree was seated
at her work station, some of her male coworkers were looking at a book that
contained pictures of men with pierced genitalia. One coworker took the book,
approached Ocheltree, and opened it to the centerfold photograph showing a
man's crotch area. The scrotum was pierced with hoops, and there were chains
running up to the top of the penis. The coworker, with his male colleagues looking
on, said, "Lisa, what do you think about this?" Again, this generated laughter from
the men in the shop.

As time went on, Ocheltree's male coworkers subjected her to a daily stream
of discussion and conduct that was sex based or sexist. First, the men in the production shop used explicit sexual insults to needle each other in front of Ocheltree.
For example, "[g]uys would make hand gestures down at their private parts and
tell other guys to suck it." Some of the men at times suggested that two of their
number were involved in a homosexual relationship. The men engaging in this
sort of talk "pick[ed] on" their subjects by discussing the details of anal sex, saying
specifically that they "wonder[ed] who was on top and who took it up the ass."
There were also comments that one employee was having sex with a dog. Second,
Ocheltree's male coworkers constantly discussed their sexual exploits with their
wives and girlfriends in extremely graphic terms. The men talked every day about
their sexual experiences of the night before, making comments about their female
partners such as "she swallowed, she gave good head, [or] I fucked her all night
long." One employee announced that his girlfriend "gave good head[,] that she
likes to swallow, that she liked it from behind, [and] that she would do it anywhere
with him." He added that she "could suck a golf [ball] through a garden hose."
Another employee in the shop often "would speak of [his wife] sucking his dick
and swallowing and letting it run down the side of her face and stuff." Finally, on
one occasion, shop supervisor Hirsch said that he was interested in having sex
with young boys and that he "enjoyed . . . licking young boys['] dicks." Ocheltree
was convinced that Hirsch and other men in the shop engaged in sexual talk and

antics "in front of [her] because they enjoyed looking at [her] and seeing [her] reaction." Indeed, Hirsch frequently joined in the shoproom laughter that erupted at Ocheltree's expense. There were times when the sexual talk in the production shop got so far out of hand that Ocheltree would "turn red [and] would have to get up and leave [her] work area . . . just to get away from the atmosphere."

According to Bill Scollon, his company has a sexual harassment policy that is covered by the section entitled "Talking" in the employee handbook. Sexual harassment is not mentioned in the section. It only states that "[l]oud talking, yelling, uncontrolled laughter, swearing, and verbal abuse of co-workers, and supervisors is not acceptable. Verbal abuse, swearing, etc. are grounds for termination." The handbook's "Open Door Policy" directs that "[a]nyone having a complaint or problem should first try to resolve it with their immediate supervisor." The policy goes on to say that "Ellery [Locklear] or Bill [Scollon] are usually available throughout the day to help resolve complaints or problems not resolved by supervisors."

> Is the company's "sexual harassment policy" sufficient? In what ways could this policy be improved?

Ocheltree believed that she was being subjected to sexual harassment in her workplace, and she made attempts to register complaints as the employee handbook prescribed. She complained repeatedly to Hirsch, the shop supervisor, who ignored the problem. Ocheltree then attempted to register her concerns with Scollon and Locklear, but in Ocheltree's words, "[t]hey wouldn't give [her] the time of day." She went to Scollon's office several times and asked if he had a minute to talk with her. In each instance Scollon told her that he did not have time and that she should "go see Mr. Locklear" or "go back to work." Scollon acknowledges that on one occasion when Ocheltree attempted to speak with him, he told her it was not an appropriate time. He admits that he turned her away because he believed that whatever she wanted to talk about was not important. Locklear was likewise never available to hear Ocheltree's complaints. Once when Ocheltree went to Locklear's office, he was on the telephone; she put a note on his desk, saying: "Ellery, Need to talk to you, very important, Lisa." She underlined "very important." Locklear indicated that he saw the note, but he never talked with her. When Ocheltree left her work station because the sexual and sexist talk was getting out of hand, Hirsch would follow her to prevent her from speaking to Scollon or Locklear. For example, if she took refuge in the bathroom at these times, Hirsch would often be waiting when she emerged, telling her to go back to work. Ocheltree lost track of the number of times she tried to talk with Locklear, only to have Hirsch order her back to work. Ocheltree summed it up this way: "[Hirsch] knew [that] I was going to go and tell [Locklear or Scollon about the men's behavior] because he would not go forward with it. He would tell me to get back to work, that if I had something . . . to say to Bill or Ellery they would come to me and talk to me [and] that he would relay the message."

After Ocheltree had no success in voicing her complaints through regular channels, she decided to speak up at a safety meeting for the production shop. She knew that a supervisor would be taking minutes, and she believed the minutes would be passed along to Scollon and Locklear. Ocheltree "addressed everyone," saying that "the sexual conduct, pictures, the gestures, the imitating of sex to mannequins and all that" should stop. The offensive conduct ceased for two or three hours, but then resumed with the same intensity.

Her treatment at Scollon Productions left Ocheltree "embarrassed, humiliated, angered," and "totally down all the time." She found it hard to be around groups of people and, as a result, stopped attending functions and activities that her two children were involved in. She has been on and off antidepressants.

In April 1996 Ocheltree filed a complaint against Scollon Productions in the United States District Court for the District of South Carolina, asserting sex discrimination and retaliation claims under Title VII of the Civil Rights Act of 1964 and South Carolina state law. The district court granted summary judgment to Scollon Productions, and Ocheltree appealed. We vacated the judgment on the hostile work environment claim, concluding that there were genuine issues of material fact as to the imputation of liability element of that claim. Ocheltree's case went to trial after remand, and the jury returned a verdict in her favor, finding (in special interrogatories) that she had been subjected to a hostile work environment because of her sex. The jury awarded her $7280 in compensatory damages and $400,000 in punitive damages. The district court denied Scollon Productions' Rule 50 motion for judgment as a matter of law, but reduced the punitive damages to $42,720, bringing the total judgment in line with the $50,000 cap. Scollon Productions appealed, and a divided panel of this court held that the company was entitled to judgment as a matter of law because the offensive behavior directed at Ocheltree was neither because of her sex nor sufficiently severe or pervasive to constitute a hostile work environment. We vacated the panel decision and reheard the case en banc.

To establish a Title VII claim for sexual harassment in the workplace, a female plaintiff must prove that the offending conduct (1) was unwelcome, (2) was based on her sex, (3) was sufficiently severe or pervasive to alter the conditions of her employment and create an abusive work environment, and (4) was imputable to her employer.

The second element of the test requires proof that the offending conduct was based on the plaintiff's sex. This element comes straight from Title VII's "discriminat[ion] . . . because of . . . sex" requirement. 42 U.S.C. § 2000e–2(a)(1). "'The critical issue [in the "because of sex" inquiry] is whether members of one sex are exposed to disadvantageous terms or conditions of employment to which members of the other sex are not exposed.'" *Oncale,* 523 U.S. at 80 (quoting *Harris,* 510 U.S. at 25 (GINSBURG, J., concurring)). A woman may prove sex-based discrimination in the workplace even though she is not subjected to sexual advances or propositions. A trier of fact may reasonably find discrimination, for example, when a woman is the individual target of open hostility because of her sex, or when "a female victim is harassed in such sex-specific and derogatory terms . . . as to make it clear that the harasser is motivated by general hostility to the presence of women in the workplace," *Oncale,* 523 U.S. at 80.

The jury found specifically that Ocheltree's male coworkers engaged in the harassing conduct "because of [her] sex." Scollon Productions argues that the evidence does not support this finding because the conduct was not directed at Ocheltree (or at women in general) because of sex. The conduct was not directed at Ocheltree or women, the company says, because "it could have been heard [or seen] by anyone present in the shop" and "was equally offensive to some of the men." We conclude that the jury's "because of sex" finding is easily sustained. A reasonable jury could find that much of the sex-laden and sexist talk and conduct in the production shop was aimed at Ocheltree because of her sex — specifically, that the men behaved as they did to make her uncomfortable and self-conscious as the only woman in the workplace. Much of the conduct, a jury could find, was particularly offensive to women and was intended to provoke Ocheltree's reaction as a woman.

The disrespectful and degrading song that a coworker sang to Ocheltree in front of the men in the shop — "Come to me, oh, baby come to me, your breath smells like c[o]m[e] to me" — was by its words aimed at a woman. On the occasion when some of Ocheltree's male coworkers were looking at the book with pictures of men with pierced genitalia, one of the coworkers decided to take advantage of Ocheltree's presence. With his male colleagues watching, the man took the book over to Ocheltree's work station, held up the centerfold photograph (showing a hoop-pierced scrotum and a chained penis) for her to see, and said, "Lisa, what do you think about this?" No man in the shop was subjected to this same embarrassment, and no man there was called upon to offer a reaction to the photograph while the entire shop looked on. The sexual activity with the mannequin (from simulated oral sex to fondling) occurred repeatedly. Ocheltree's male coworkers did something sexual to the mannequin almost every time she was nearby. All of this conduct provoked much laughter from the men in the shop-laughter at Ocheltree's expense. Indeed, a jury could reasonably find that the men engaged in this conduct largely because they enjoyed watching and laughing at the reactions of the only woman in the shop.

The production shop talk that portrayed women as sexually subordinate to men was also calculated to disturb Ocheltree, a jury could reasonably find. We refer here to the almost daily accounts from some of the men who described their exploits with their wives and girlfriends in demeaning terms such as "she gave good head," "she likes to swallow," she "let[ ] [the semen] run down the side of her face," and "she like[s] it from behind." This kind of talk, as well as the sexual antics, got out of hand after Ocheltree's arrival in the production shop; it even escalated after she complained about it. It is true, as Scollon Productions points out, that at least a couple of the men were offended by the sexual talk and antics. There is no evidence, however, that this outrageous conduct was aimed at getting an embarrassed reaction from these men or that it was calculated to generate laughter at the expense of any man. No man was driven from the room because of the conduct, as was Ocheltree on occasion.

To sum up on this point, we conclude that a reasonable jury could find that Ocheltree was the individual target of harassment because of her sex. Moreover, a jury could find that the men in the production shop "harassed [Ocheltree] in such sex-specific and derogatory

> The court here concludes not only that there is evidence of a hostile environment, but that this hostility was specifically targeted at Ocheltree.

terms . . . as to make it clear that [they were] motivated by general hostility to the presence of [a] wom[a]n in the[ir] workplace." *Oncale*, 523 U.S. at 80. In all events, a reasonable jury could find, as did the jury in this case, that Ocheltree was harassed in her workplace because of her sex.

[The portion of the court's opinion discussing severity or pervasiveness of the conduct and whether the conduct can be imputed to the employer is omitted.]

Because there is a legally sufficient evidentiary basis for a reasonable jury to find that Ocheltree was the victim of sex-based employment discrimination, we conclude that the district court correctly denied Scollon Productions' motion for judgment as a matter of law on her basic Title VII claim. The evidence, however, was not legally sufficient for a jury to find that Scollon Productions had the knowledge required to be liable for punitive damages. Accordingly, we affirm the judgment for the amount awarded in compensatory damages, and we reverse the judgment for the amount awarded in punitive damages.

■ NOTES AND QUESTIONS

1. This decision looks specifically at the question of the meaning of "because of sex." The Fourth Circuit Court of Appeals had originally held that the facts presented here did not rise to the level of showing that the conduct was "because of sex," but the en banc panel reversed.

2. What if the sexual bantering that was taking place at this largely male-dominated workplace occurred before Ocheltree even arrived? If this bantering simply continued after she began work, could the conduct still be said to be because of sex?

3. How much of the inappropriate conduct here was actually directed at Ocheltree? Is this question at all relevant to the outcome of the case? Should it be?

4. Applying the Supreme Court's analysis in *Oncale*, was the conduct in this case sexual in nature? Was there hostility toward women generally? Would the employer have a defense that this was all simply "horseplay"?

5. The court's discussion of severity/pervasiveness was omitted from the facts above. Does the conduct outlined in the case appear egregious enough to warrant liability under Title VII?

6. Should the conduct in this case be imputed to the employer? Should the company be responsible for the conduct perpetrated by its employees?

7. What could the employer have done here to help prevent this type of situation from arising? What policies or procedures could it have put in place to prevent sexual harassment?

8. The en banc court here also concludes that there is insufficient knowledge on the part of the employer to warrant punitive damages. Is this a fair assessment? We will look at the standard for punitive damages in Chapter 12.

9. **The equal opportunity harasser.** If an employer harasses both men and women equally, can it evade liability under Title VII? While such harassment is possible in theory, in practice an employer is still likely to harass or treat one sex differently from another. *See* John D. Bible, *The "Equal Opportunity Harasser": The*

Slow Demise of a Strange Concept?, 61 LAB. L.J. (2010) (noting the absurdity of a rule that allows someone to harass more employees without being held liable for that conduct and noting that there has been a trend on the part of courts in recent years to find actionable harassment in cases in which both sexes were harassed); Steven Locke, *The Equal Opportunity Harasser as a Paradigm for Recognizing Sexual Harassment of Homosexuals Under Title VII*, 27 RUTGERS L.J. 383 (1996) (addressing the conundrum of the bisexual/equal opportunity harasser and proposing a modified test to be applied in sexual harassment cases that would resolve current inconsistencies); Ronald Turner, *Title VII and the Inequality-Enhancing Effects of the Bisexual and Equal Opportunity Harasser Defenses*, 7 U. PA. J. LAB. & EMP. L. 341 (2005) (examining the differing views and dissimilar results reached by courts in cases involving bisexual harassers and equal opportunity harassers).

Class Exercise: Defining "Because of Sex"

A female employee — Wanda Worker — works on a printing press for a nationally published newspaper. Her supervisor, a male, constantly makes sexually harassing remarks and comments to her over the course of the day. He even brushes up against her "inappropriately" when checking to make sure that she is stacking the papers correctly. The supervisor also makes sexually harassing remarks to just about all of his subordinates — men and women included. And, he has been seen "brushing" up against these workers as well. Breaking up into small groups, discuss whether Wanda would have a cause of action against the company. What other facts would you need to know to decide this question?

---

2. Unwelcome, and Severe or Pervasive

Establishing that the defendant's behavior was based on a protected characteristic is only the first element of any harassment case. For hostile work environment claims, the conduct must also be shown to be unwelcome, and severe or pervasive. These standards were developed by the Supreme Court in *Meritor Savings Bank, FSB v. Vinson*, which addressed — for the first time — whether hostile work environment claims are cognizable under Title VII.

Meritor Savings Bank, FSB v. Vinson
477 U.S. 57 (1986)

Justice REHNQUIST delivered the opinion of the Court.

This case presents important questions concerning claims of workplace "sexual harassment" brought under Title VII of the Civil Rights Act of 1964.

In 1974, respondent Mechelle Vinson met Sidney Taylor, a vice president of what is now petitioner Meritor Savings Bank (bank) and manager of one of its branch offices. When respondent asked whether she might obtain employment at the bank, Taylor gave her an application, which she completed and returned the next day; later that same day Taylor called her to say that she had been hired. With Taylor as her supervisor, respondent started as a teller-

trainee, and thereafter was promoted to teller, head teller, and assistant branch manager. She worked at the same branch for four years, and it is undisputed that her advancement there was based on merit alone. In September 1978, respondent notified Taylor that she was taking sick leave for an indefinite period. On November 1, 1978, the bank discharged her for excessive use of that leave.

Respondent brought this action against Taylor and the bank, claiming that during her four years at the bank she had "constantly been subjected to sexual harassment" by Taylor in violation of Title VII. She sought injunctive relief, compensatory and punitive damages against Taylor and the bank, and attorney's fees.

At the 11-day bench trial, the parties presented conflicting testimony about Taylor's behavior during respondent's employment. Respondent testified that during her probationary period as a teller-trainee, Taylor treated her in a fatherly way and made no sexual advances. Shortly thereafter, however, he invited her out to dinner and, during the course of the meal, suggested that they go to a motel to have sexual relations. At first she refused, but out of what she described as fear of losing her job she eventually agreed. According to respondent, Taylor thereafter made repeated demands upon her for sexual favors, usually at the branch, both during and after business hours; she estimated that over the next several years she had intercourse with him some 40 or 50 times. In addition, respondent testified that Taylor fondled her in front of other employees, followed her into the women's restroom when she went there alone, exposed himself to her, and even forcibly raped her on several occasions. These activities ceased after 1977, respondent stated, when she started going with a steady boyfriend.

Respondent also testified that Taylor touched and fondled other women employees of the bank, and she attempted to call witnesses to support this charge. But while some supporting testimony apparently was admitted without objection, the District Court did not allow her "to present wholesale evidence of a pattern and practice relating to sexual advances to other female employees in her case in chief, but advised her that she might well be able to present such evidence in rebuttal to the defendants' cases." Respondent did not offer such evidence in rebuttal. Finally, respondent testified that because she was afraid of Taylor she never reported his harassment to any of his supervisors and never attempted to use the bank's complaint procedure.

Taylor denied respondent's allegations of sexual activity, testifying that he never fondled her, never made suggestive remarks to her, never engaged in sexual intercourse with her, and never asked her to do so. He contended instead that respondent made her accusations in response to a business-related dispute. The bank also denied respondent's allegations and asserted that any sexual harassment by Taylor was unknown to the bank and engaged in without its consent or approval. The [district] court ultimately found that respondent "was not the victim of sexual harassment and was not the victim of sexual discrimination" while employed at the bank. The Court of Appeals for the District of Columbia Circuit reversed. [T]he court stated that a violation of Title VII may be predicated on either of two types of sexual harassment: harassment that involves the conditioning of concrete employment benefits on sexual favors, and harassment that, while not affecting economic benefits, creates a hostile or offensive working environment. The court drew additional support for this position from the Equal Employment Opportunity Commission's Guidelines on Discrimination Because of Sex, 29 C.F.R. § 1604.11(a) (1985), which set out these two types of sexual harassment claims.

Respondent argues, and the Court of Appeals held, that unwelcome sexual advances that create an offensive or hostile working environment violate Title VII. Without question, when a supervisor sexually harasses a subordinate because of the subordinate's sex, that supervisor "discriminate[s]" on the basis of sex. Petitioner apparently does not challenge this proposition. It contends instead that in prohibiting discrimination with respect to "compensation, terms, conditions, or privileges" of employment, Congress was concerned with what petitioner describes as "tangible loss" of "an economic character," not "purely psychological aspects of the workplace environment." In support of this claim petitioner observes that in both the legislative history of Title VII and this Court's Title VII decisions, the focus has been on tangible, economic barriers erected by discrimination.

> The fact that an adverse action need not have an economic component to be actionable was a major holding of the Court.

We reject petitioner's view. First, the language of Title VII is not limited to "economic" or "tangible" discrimination. The phrase "terms, conditions, or privileges of employment" evinces a congressional intent "'to strike at the entire spectrum of disparate treatment of men and women'" in employment. *Los Angeles Dept. of Water and Power v. Manhart*, 435 U.S. 702 (1978), quoting *Sprogis v. United Air Lines, Inc.*, 444 F.2d 1194 (CA 7 1971). Petitioner has pointed to nothing in the Act to suggest that Congress contemplated the limitation urged here.

Second, in 1980 the EEOC issued Guidelines specifying that "sexual harassment," as there defined, is a form of sex discrimination prohibited by Title VII. The EEOC Guidelines fully support the view that harassment leading to noneconomic injury can violate Title VII. In concluding that so-called "hostile environment" (i.e., non quid pro quo) harassment violates Title VII, the EEOC drew upon a substantial body of judicial decisions and EEOC precedent holding that Title VII affords employees the right to work in an environment free from discriminatory intimidation, ridicule, and insult. Since the Guidelines were issued, courts have uniformly held, and we agree, that a plaintiff may establish a violation of Title VII by proving that discrimination based on sex has created a hostile or abusive work environment.

Of course, not all workplace conduct that may be described as "harassment" affects a "term, condition, or privilege" of employment within the meaning of Title VII. For sexual harassment to be actionable, it must be sufficiently severe or pervasive "to alter the conditions of [the victim's] employment and create an abusive working environment." [*Henson v. Dundee*, 682 F.2d 897, 902 (1982).] Respondent's allegations in this case — which include not only pervasive harassment but also criminal conduct of the most serious nature — are plainly sufficient to state a claim for "hostile environment" sexual harassment.

> The Court is clear that to be actionable, the harassment must also be "severe or pervasive."

The question remains, however, whether the District Court's ultimate finding that respondent "was not the victim of sexual harassment," effectively disposed of respondent's claim. The Court of Appeals recognized, we think correctly, that this ultimate finding was likely based on one or both of two erroneous views of the law. First, the District Court apparently believed that a claim for sexual harassment will not lie absent an economic effect on the complainant's employment. Since it appears that the District Court made its findings without ever considering the "hostile environment" theory of sexual harassment, the Court of Appeals' decision to remand was correct.

Second, the District Court's conclusion that no actionable harassment occurred might have rested on its earlier "finding" that "[i]f [respondent] and Taylor did engage in an intimate or sexual relationship . . . , that relationship was a voluntary one." But the fact that sex-related conduct was "voluntary," in the sense that the complainant was not forced to participate against her will, is not a defense to a sexual harassment suit brought under Title VII. The gravamen of any sexual harassment claim is that the alleged sexual advances were "unwelcome." While the question whether particular conduct was indeed unwelcome presents difficult problems of proof and turns largely on credibility determinations committed to the trier of fact, the District Court in this case erroneously focused on the "voluntariness" of respondent's participation in the claimed sexual episodes. The correct inquiry is whether respondent by her conduct indicated that the alleged sexual advances were unwelcome, not whether her actual participation in sexual intercourse was voluntary.

Petitioner contends that even if this case must be remanded to the District Court, the Court of Appeals erred in one of the terms of its remand. Specifically, the Court of Appeals stated that testimony about respondent's "dress and personal fantasies," which the District Court apparently admitted into evidence, "had no place in this litigation." The apparent ground for this conclusion was that respondent's voluntariness *vel non* in submitting to Taylor's advances was immaterial to her sexual harassment claim. While "voluntariness" in the sense of consent is not a defense to such a claim, it does not follow that a complainant's sexually provocative speech or dress is irrelevant as a matter of law in determining whether he or she found particular sexual advances unwelcome. To the contrary, such evidence is obviously relevant.

Although the District Court concluded that respondent had not proved a violation of Title VII, it nevertheless went on to consider the question of the bank's liability. Finding that "the bank was without notice" of Taylor's alleged conduct, and that notice to Taylor was not the equivalent of notice to the bank, the court concluded that the bank therefore could not be held liable for Taylor's alleged actions. The Court of Appeals took the opposite view, holding that an employer is strictly liable for a hostile environment created by a supervisor's sexual advances, even though the employer neither knew nor reasonably could have known of the alleged misconduct. The court held that a supervisor, whether or not he possesses the authority to hire, fire, or promote, is necessarily an "agent" of his employer for all Title VII purposes, since "even the appearance" of such authority may enable him to impose himself on his subordinates.

In sum, we hold that a claim of "hostile environment" sex discrimination is actionable under Title VII, that the District Court's findings were insufficient to dispose of respondent's hostile environment claim, and that the District Court did not err in admitting testimony about respondent's sexually provocative speech and dress. As to employer liability, we conclude that the Court of Appeals was wrong to entirely disregard agency principles and impose absolute liability on employers for the acts of their supervisors, regardless of the circumstances of a particular case.

■ NOTES AND QUESTIONS

1. Perhaps the most important take away from *Meritor* is that the Supreme Court left little doubt that, in addition to so-called quid pro quo claims, plaintiffs could also allege an improper hostile work environment.

2. *Meritor* is also important in that it articulates some clear guidance on how to proceed when analyzing hostile work environment claims. Most notably, when a plaintiff alleges a hostile work environment claim, she must show that the behavior was (1) unwelcome and (2) severe or pervasive.

3. The Court is clear that unwelcome behavior does not equate with voluntary behavior. Thus, even though a plaintiff may go along with an employer's conduct, she may not welcome the activity. Can you articulate examples of conduct that is unwelcome even if the plaintiff submits to it voluntarily? How should a court go about determining whether conduct is welcome? The EEOC guidance on this question provides in part:

   When confronted with conflicting evidence as to welcomeness, the Commission looks "at the record as a whole and at the totality of circumstances . . . ." 29 C.F.R. § 1604.11(b), evaluating each situation on a case-by-case basis. When there is some indication of welcomeness or when the credibility of the parties is at issue, the charging party's claim will be considerably strengthened if she made a contemporaneous complaint or protest. Particularly when the alleged harasser may have some reason (*e.g.*, prior consensual relationship) to believe that the advances will be welcomed, it is important for the victim to communicate that the conduct is unwelcome. Generally, victims are well-advised to assert their right to a workplace free from sexual harassment. This may stop the harassment before it becomes more serious. A contemporaneous complaint or protest may also provide persuasive evidence that the sexual harassment in fact occurred as alleged. . . . Thus, in investigating sexual harassment charges, it is important to develop detailed evidence of the circumstances and nature of any such complaints or protests, whether to the alleged harasser, higher management, co-workers or others. While a complaint or protest is helpful to charging party's case, it is not a necessary element of the claim. Indeed, the Commission recognizes that victims may fear repercussions from complaining about the harassment and that such fear may explain a delay in opposing the conduct.

EEOC Enforcement Guidance: Policy Guidance on Current Issues of Sexual Harassment, EEOC Compl. Man. (CCH) Guidance § A (Mar. 19, 1990).

4. The Court notes that only conduct that is severe or pervasive can rise to the level of an actionable hostile work environment. The conduct need only be "severe OR pervasive," rather than "severe AND pervasive." The EEOC and the courts have suggested that in making this inquiry, there is a sliding scale for determining whether the test has been satisfied. Thus, the more severe the conduct is, the less pervasive it needs to be. And, the more pervasive it is, the less severe it must be. *See* EEOC v. Bimbo Bakeries USA, Inc., No. 1:09–CV–1872, 2010 WL 598641, at *5 n.5 (M.D. Pa. Feb. 17, 2010) ("[S]ome conduct, although isolated and sporadic, may be severe enough to contaminate the workplace; whereas, other, less objectionable, conduct must be pervasive in order to contaminate the workplace such that it meets the threshold under the second prong of a hostile work environment claim."); Allan H. Weitzman, *Employer Defenses to Sexual Harassment Claims*, 6 Duke J. Gender L. & Pol'y 27, 48 (1999) ("Although distinct elements, severity and pervasiveness must be considered in tandem; the more severe the incidents become, the less pervasive they need to be create [sic] a hostile environment.").

5. While sexual jokes and bantering can in and of themselves lead to a severe or pervasive environment, the courts have been particularly troubled by sexual conduct that involves physical contact and other such egregious activity. *See generally* Sara L. Johnson, Annotation, *When Is Work Environment Intimidating, Hostile, or Offensive, so as to Constitute Sexual Harassment in Violation of Title VII of Civil Rights Act of 1964, as amended (42 U.S.C.A. §§ 2000e et seq.)*, 78 A.L.R. 252 (1986); Eugene Volokh, *What Speech Does "Hostile Work Environment" Harassment Law Restrict?*, 85 Geo. L.J. 627 (1997). As we saw in the *Ocheltree* decision, the courts are particularly concerned with this type of egregious behavior.

6. The severity or pervasiveness question is often decisive in a hostile work environment case. The law of individual jurisdictions can vary greatly on what suffices as severe or pervasive. Not only is the law of each jurisdiction important on this question, the facts of the particular case will be critical in deciding whether this standard has been satisfied. *See, e.g.*, Heather L. Kleinschmidt, Note, *Reconsidering Severe or Pervasive: Aligning the Standard in Sexual Harassment and Racial Harassment Causes of Action*, 80 Ind. L.J. 1119, 1130 (2005).

7. Omitted from the opinion above is the Court's discussion of imputing liability to the employer. The Court stated that it would "decline the parties' invitation to issue a definitive rule on employer liability, but we do agree with the EEOC that Congress wanted courts to look to agency principles for guidance in this area." *Meritor*, 477 U.S. at 72. What agency principles would be helpful in deciding whether a company should be held liable for harassment? Are those principles satisfied in this case? As we will see in the subsequent Supreme Court case, the Court ultimately helped to define the important agency principles in the area.

8. The Court relied on the EEOC's guidelines on harassment, and noted that "the Guidelines provide that such sexual misconduct constitutes prohibited 'sexual harassment,' whether or not it is directly linked to the grant or denial of an economic quid pro quo, where 'such conduct has the purpose or effect of unreasonably interfering with an individual's work performance or creating an intimidating, hostile, or offensive working environment.'" *Meritor*, 477 U.S. at 65 (citing 29 C.F.R. § 1604.11(a)(3)). The guidelines are useful in helping employers (and individuals) determine whether conduct in the workplace is actionable.

9. The Court further weighed in on the extent to which a complaint policy can help insulate an employer from liability, stating that "we reject petitioner's view that the mere existence of a grievance procedure and a policy against discrimination, coupled with respondent's failure to invoke that procedure, must insulate petitioner from liability." If an employer implements an antiharassment policy in the workplace, should it still be held liable if harassment nonetheless takes place?

10. The Court does not restrict the introduction of an employee's speech or dress as evidence in the case. Can such evidence be relevant to a claim? Is it possible that an employee can "ask" to be harassed, simply by the way she dresses or talks? *See* Henry L. Chambers, Jr., *(Un)Welcome Conduct and the Sexually Hostile Environment*, 53 ALA. L. REV. 733 (2002); Grace S. Ho, *Not Quite Rights: How the Unwelcomeness Element in Sexual Harassment Law Undermines Title VII's Transformative Potential*, 20 YALE J.L. & FEMINISM 131 (2008); Lisa Dowlen Linton, *Past Sexual Conduct in Sexual Harassment Cases*, 75 CHI.-KENT L. REV. 179 (1999).

11. It is worth briefly summarizing the Supreme Court decisions thus far. After reviewing *Meritor* and *Oncale*, it is clear that quid pro quo sexual harassment will be actionable. At the same time, hostile work environment claims will be actionable where (1) the conduct is based on sex; (2) the conduct is unwelcome; (3) the conduct is severe or pervasive; and (4) the conduct can be imputed to the employer based on agency principles. The fourth element of this test will be discussed further below.

12. The severity or pervasiveness element of the hostile environment test is an important one, and has been developed in the lower courts. It is worth noting that there is both an objective and subjective component to this inquiry. Thus, the plaintiff must actually perceive that the behavior is severe or pervasive, and a reasonable person looking at the facts must also conclude that the standard has been met. As the EEOC has stated, "the objective standard should not be applied in a vacuum. . . . Consideration should be given to the context in which the alleged harassment took place." *EEOC Enforcement*

Guidance: Policy Guidance on Current Issues of Sexual Harassment, EEOC Compl. Man. (CCH) Guidance § A (Mar. 19, 1990).

13. *Meritor* provides a historical look at the type of harassment that took place years ago. It is interesting to see how harassment has evolved with changing technologies. Computers, cell phones, and other electronic devices have changed the way in which the facts of harassment cases now play out.

14. **Gaming and sexual harassment.** The prevalence of sexual harassment in the gaming community has risen dramatically in the past several years, possibly due to an increase in the female gaming population. Though this type of harassment arises outside of the employment context, it demonstrates how modern technologies have impacted women. Female video gamers find themselves subject to constant derogatory remarks made by male gamers regarding their sexuality and bodies. Some female gamers have even been victims of rape threats and death threats, against not only themselves, but their loved ones, as well. In one extreme situation, a female game developer was alleged to have used sex as a bargaining tool to achieve higher game ratings, leading to an influx of rape and death threats. Another female video game blogger left her home after receiving similar threats. While teasing and "trash talking" are typical in the gaming atmosphere, the sexual harassment against female gamers has far exceeded the limits of acceptability. *See* Brianna Wu, *Rape and Death Threats Are Terrorizing Female Gamers. Why Haven't Men in Tech Spoken Out?,* Wash. Post, Oct. 20, 2014; *Online Harassment Gets Real for Female Gamers,* NPR News (Aug. 8, 2012), http://www.npr.org/2012/08/08/158433079/virtual-harassment-gets-real-for-female-gamers; Corrine Segal, *Why Video Gamers Are Speaking Out Against Sexual Harassment,* PBS Newshour (Sept. 17, 2014, 10:54 a.m.), http://www.pbs.org/newshour/updates/gamers-speaking-sexual-harassment/.

Justice Clarence Thomas

15. **Historical note.** Before his confirmation to the U.S. Supreme Court by President George H. W. Bush, Justice Clarence Thomas served as Chair of the EEOC from 1982–1990, once earning praise for his role in the United States's *amicus* brief in *Meritor*, in which the Solicitor General argued that sexual harassment constituted discrimination under the Civil Rights Act. In October 1991, however, Thomas found himself the subject of sexual harassment allegations levied by Anita Hill, a female aide who worked with Thomas at the Department of Education and the EEOC before taking a position as assistant professor of law at Oral Roberts University. Hill alleged that Thomas had made unwelcome advances, stared at her, described in detail pornographic videos and his own sexual capability, and asked whether she had put a pubic hair on his can of soda.

These allegations were brought to national media attention, and after some national outrage at the absence of any investigation, the Senate Judiciary Commission held a special hearing televised nationally. Hill, Thomas, and several others testified. Some witnesses' testimony was for the apparent purpose of questioning Hill's credibility. Justice Thomas flatly refused to answer any questions on his personal life, and characterized the hearings as "a high-tech lynching for uppity blacks." *Hearing of the Senate Judiciary Committee on the Nomination of Clarence Thomas to the Supreme Court,* http://etext.lib.virginia.edu/etcbin/toccer-new-yitna?id=UsaThom&images=images/modeng&data=/lv6/workspace/yitna&tag=public&part=24. Politically, many Republicans, including those on the Senate Judiciary Committee, accused Hill of being a liar propped up by liberal special interests. The Senate would, of course, go on to confirm Thomas in a fifty-two to forty-eight vote. This vote would also highlight, in a public way, the under-representation of women in our national legislature. At the time, there were only two female U.S. senators (Nancy Kassebaum and Barbara Mikulski), one of whom voted for Thomas. Neither of these female senators were members of the Judiciary Committee. For an excellent and detailed look at this history, see JANE MAYER & JILL ANDERSON, STRANGE JUSTICE: THE SELLING OF CLARENCE THOMAS (1994).

Three years later, President Bill Clinton faced sexual harassment allegations from Paula Jones, who claimed that Clinton had touched her inappropriately, exposed himself, and propositioned her while serving as governor of Arkansas. This time, however, many supporters of the Democratic President claimed that Jones was a conservative ploy meant to discredit Clinton. Both episodes played out on the national stage, and each heightened public consciousness of sexual harassment. *See* STEPHEN MOREWITZ, SEXUAL HARASSMENT AND SOCIAL CHANGE IN AMERICAN SOCIETY (1996); ROSEMARIE SKAINE, POWER AND GENDER: ISSUES IN SEXUAL DOMINANCE AND HARASSMENT (1996).

President Bill Clinton

More recently, allegations of sexual abuse made headlines during the confirmation process of U.S. Supreme Court Justice Brett Kavanaugh. These allegations demonstrate the high-profile nature of the Me Too movement at all corporate and governmental levels.

Interactive Problem

Looking back at the facts of the interactive problem at the beginning of the chapter, assume that Sarah frequently makes sexual jokes and gestures over the course of her employment. She even shares these jokes with her supervisor and other restaurant management. And, one customer complains that Sarah made an inappropriate sexual joke while taking his order. Would these additional facts change the outcome of the problem?

The *Meritor* decision recognized that hostile environment actions can be pursued even where there is no economic component to the claim. In the case below, the Court considers whether evidence of psychological harm is necessary in a sexual harassment case, helping to further define the parameters of a hostile working environment.

Harris v. Forklift Systems, Inc.
510 U.S. 17 (1993)

Justice O'CONNOR delivered the opinion of the Court.

Teresa Harris worked as a manager at Forklift Systems, Inc., an equipment rental company, from April 1985 until October 1987. Charles Hardy was Forklift's president. The Magistrate found that, throughout Harris' time at Forklift, Hardy often insulted her because of her gender and often made her the target of unwanted sexual innuendos. Hardy told Harris on several occasions, in the presence of other employees, "You're a woman, what do you know" and "We need a man as the rental manager"; at least once, he told her she was "a dumb ass woman." Again in front of others, he suggested that the two of them "go to the Holiday Inn to negotiate [Harris'] raise." Hardy occasionally asked Harris and other female employees to get coins from his front pants pocket. He threw objects on the ground in front of Harris and other women, and asked them to pick the objects up. He made sexual innuendos about Harris' and other women's clothing.

In mid-August 1987, Harris complained to Hardy about his conduct. Hardy said he was surprised that Harris was offended, claimed he was only joking, and apologized. He also promised he would stop, and based on this assurance Harris stayed on the job. But in early September, Hardy began anew: While Harris was arranging a deal with one of Forklift's customers, he asked her, again in front of other employees, "What did you do, promise the guy . . . some [sex] Saturday night?" On October 1, Harris collected her paycheck and quit. Harris then sued Forklift, claiming that Hardy's conduct had created an abusive work environment for her because of her gender. The United States District Court for the Middle District of Tennessee, adopting the report and recommendation of the Magistrate, found this to be "a close case," but held that Hardy's conduct did not create an abusive environment. The court found that some of Hardy's comments "offended [Harris], and would offend the reasonable woman," but that they were not

> "so severe as to be expected to seriously affect [Harris's] psychological well-being. A reasonable woman manager under like circumstances would have been offended by Hardy, but his conduct would not have risen to the level of interfering with that person's work performance. . . .
>
> "Neither do I believe that [Harris] was subjectively so offended that she suffered injury. . . . Although Hardy may at times have genuinely offended [Harris], I do not believe that he created a working environment so poisoned as to be intimidating or abusive to [Harris]."

In focusing on the employee's psychological well-being, the District Court was following Circuit precedent. We granted certiorari, to resolve a conflict among the Circuits on whether conduct, to be actionable as "abusive work environment" harassment (no quid pro quo harassment issue is present here), must "seriously affect [an employee's] psychological well-being" or lead the plaintiff to "suffe[r] injury."

Title VII of the Civil Rights Act of 1964 makes it "an unlawful employment practice for an employer . . . to discriminate against any individual with respect to his compensation, terms, conditions, or privileges of employment, because of such individual's race, color, religion, sex, or national origin." As we made clear in *Meritor Savings Bank, FSB v. Vinson*, 477 U.S. 57 (1986), this language "is not limited to 'economic' or 'tangible' discrimination. The phrase 'terms, conditions, or privileges of employment' evinces a congressional intent 'to strike at the entire spectrum of disparate treatment of men and women' in employment," which includes requiring people to work in a discriminatorily

> The Court here emphasizes that a victim of harassment need *not* experience an emotional breakdown to establish a cause of action.

hostile or abusive environment. When the workplace is permeated with "discriminatory intimidation, ridicule, and insult," *Meritor*, 477 U.S. at 65, that is "sufficiently severe or pervasive to alter the conditions of the victim's employment and create an abusive working environment," *id.* at 67, Title VII is violated.

This standard, which we reaffirm today, takes a middle path between making actionable any conduct that is merely offensive and requiring the conduct to cause a tangible psychological injury. As we pointed out in *Meritor*, "mere utterance of an . . . epithet which engenders offensive feelings in a[n] employee," *ibid.* (internal quotation marks omitted) does not sufficiently affect the conditions of employment to implicate Title VII. Conduct that is not severe or pervasive enough to create an objectively hostile or abusive work environment — an environment that a reasonable person would find hostile or abusive — is beyond Title VII's purview. Likewise, if the victim does not subjectively perceive the environment to be abusive, the conduct has not actually altered the conditions of the victim's employment, and there is no Title VII violation.

But Title VII comes into play before the harassing conduct leads to a nervous breakdown. A discriminatorily abusive work environment, even one that does not seriously affect employees' psychological well-being, can and often will detract from employees' job performance, discourage employees from remaining on the job, or keep them from advancing in their careers. Moreover, even without regard to these tangible effects, the very fact that the discriminatory conduct was so severe or pervasive that it created a work environment abusive to employees because of their race, gender, religion, or national origin offends Title VII's broad rule of workplace equality. We therefore believe the District Court erred in relying on whether the conduct "seriously affect[ed] plaintiff's psychological well-being" or led her to "suffe[r] injury." Such an inquiry may needlessly focus the factfinder's attention on concrete psychological harm, an element Title VII does not require. Certainly Title VII bars conduct that would seriously affect a reasonable person's psychological well-being, but the statute is not limited to such conduct. So long as the environment would reasonably be perceived, and is perceived, as hostile or abusive, there is no need for it also to be psychologically injurious.

This is not, and by its nature cannot be, a mathematically precise test. But we can say that whether an environment is "hostile" or "abusive" can be determined only by looking at all the circumstances. These may include the frequency of the discriminatory conduct; its severity; whether it is physically threatening or humiliating, or a mere offensive utterance; and whether it unreasonably interferes with an employee's work performance. The effect on the employee's psychological well-being is, of course, relevant to determining whether the plaintiff actually found the environment abusive. But while psychological harm, like any other relevant factor, may be taken into account, no single factor is required.

Forklift, while conceding that a requirement that the conduct seriously affect psychological well-being is unfounded, argues that the District Court nonetheless correctly applied the *Meritor* standard. We disagree. Though the District Court did conclude that the work environment was not "intimidating or abusive to [Harris]," it did so only after finding that the conduct was not "so severe as to be expected to seriously affect plaintiff's psychological well-being," and that Harris was not "subjectively so offended that she suffered injury." The District Court's application of these incorrect standards may well have influenced its ultimate conclusion, especially given that the court found this to be a "close case." We therefore reverse the judgment of the Court of Appeals, and remand the case for further proceedings consistent with this opinion.

So ordered.

■ NOTES AND QUESTIONS

1. Was the conduct here sufficient to create a hostile work environment? Was it severe or pervasive? Why or why not?

2. The Court here emphasizes that a plaintiff need not demonstrate emotional harm to proceed on a cause of action for a hostile working environment.

3. While evidence of emotional harm is not necessary for a hostile work environment claim, it can help a plaintiff to enhance her damages. While not necessary to the claim, emotional damages are often present in sexual harassment cases.

4. In addition to the holding in *Harris* on psychological harm, the Court also stated, "When the workplace is permeated with 'discriminatory intimidation, ridicule, and insult,' that is 'sufficiently severe or pervasive to alter the conditions of the victim's employment and create an abusive working environment,' Title VII is violated." The lower courts frequently look to this guidance when applying the statute to harassment claims.

E. Imputing Liability

As the notes above reflect, the Supreme Court passed on the opportunity to decide the standard for employer liability in harassment cases in *Meritor*. The Court instead stated that it would "decline the parties' invitation to issue a definitive rule on employer liability, but we do agree with the EEOC that Congress wanted courts to look to agency principles for guidance in this area." *Meritor*, 477 U.S. at 72. The question of which agency principles should be looked to when resolving this question became a contentious question in the lower courts. *See* Maria M. Carrillo, *Hostile Environment Sexual Harassment by a Supervisor Under Title VII: Reassessment of Employer Liability in Light of the Civil Rights Act of 1991*, 24 COLUM. HUM. RTS. L. REV. 41 (1993); Ronald Turner, *Employer Liability Under Title VII for Hostile Environment Sexual Harassment by Supervisory Personnel: The Impact and Aftermath of* Meritor Savings Bank, 33 How. L.J. 1 (1990).

After *Meritor*, the lower courts struggled with how and when to hold an employer liable for harassment. The Supreme Court ultimately revisited that issue in a pair of companion cases issued on the same day.

Burlington Industries, Inc. v. Ellerth

524 U.S. 742 (1998)

Justice KENNEDY delivered the opinion of the Court.

We decide whether, under Title VII of the Civil Rights Act of 1964 an employee who refuses the unwelcome and threatening sexual advances of a supervisor, yet suffers no adverse, tangible job consequences, can recover against the employer without showing the employer is negligent or otherwise at fault for the supervisor's actions. Summary judgment was granted for the employer, so we must take the facts alleged by the employee to be true. The employer is Burlington Industries, the petitioner. The employee is Kimberly Ellerth, the respondent. From March 1993 until May 1994, Ellerth worked as a salesperson in one of Burlington's divisions in Chicago, Illinois. During her employment, she alleges, she was subjected to constant sexual harassment by her supervisor, one Ted Slowik.

In the hierarchy of Burlington's management structure, Slowik was a midlevel manager. Burlington has eight divisions, employing more than 22,000 people in some 50 plants around the United States. Slowik was a vice president in one of five business units within one of the divisions. He had authority to make hiring and promotion decisions subject to the approval of his supervisor, who signed the paperwork. According to Slowik's supervisor, his position was "not considered an upper-level management position," and he was "not amongst the decision-making or policy-making hierarchy." Slowik was not Ellerth's immediate supervisor. Ellerth worked in a two-person office in Chicago, and she answered to her office colleague, who in turn answered to Slowik in New York.

Against a background of repeated boorish and offensive remarks and gestures which Slowik allegedly made, Ellerth places particular emphasis on three alleged incidents where Slowik's comments could be construed as threats to deny her tangible job benefits. In the summer of 1993, while on a business trip, Slowik invited Ellerth to the hotel lounge, an invitation Ellerth felt compelled to accept because Slowik was her boss. When Ellerth gave no encouragement to remarks Slowik made about her breasts, he told her to "loosen up" and warned, "you know, Kim, I could make your life very hard or very easy at Burlington."

In March 1994, when Ellerth was being considered for a promotion, Slowik expressed reservations during the promotion interview because she was not "loose enough." The comment was followed by his reaching over and rubbing her knee. Ellerth did receive the promotion; but when Slowik called to announce it, he told Ellerth, "you're gonna be out there with men who work in factories, and they certainly like women with pretty butts/legs."

In May 1994, Ellerth called Slowik, asking permission to insert a customer's logo into a fabric sample. Slowik responded, "I don't have time for you right now, Kim . . . — unless you want to tell me what you're wearing." Ellerth told Slowik she had to go and ended the call. A day or two later, Ellerth called Slowik to ask permission again. This time he denied her request, but added something along the lines of, "are you wearing shorter skirts yet, Kim, because it would make your job a whole heck of a lot easier." A short time later, Ellerth's immediate supervisor cautioned her about returning telephone calls to customers in a prompt fashion. In response, Ellerth quit. She faxed a letter giving reasons unrelated to the alleged sexual harassment we have described. About three weeks later, however, she sent a letter explaining she quit because of Slowik's behavior.

During her tenure at Burlington, Ellerth did not inform anyone in authority about Slowik's conduct, despite knowing Burlington had a policy against sexual harassment. In fact, she chose not to inform her immediate supervisor (not Slowik) because "'it would be his duty as my supervisor to report any incidents of sexual harassment.'" On one occasion, she told Slowik a comment he made was inappropriate.

In October 1994, after receiving a right-to-sue letter from the EEOC, Ellerth filed suit in the United States District Court for the Northern District of Illinois, alleging Burlington engaged in sexual harassment and forced her constructive discharge, in violation of Title VII. The District Court granted summary judgment to Burlington. The court found Slowik's behavior, as described by Ellerth, severe and pervasive enough to create a hostile work environment, but found Burlington neither knew nor should have known about the conduct. There was no triable issue of fact on the latter point, and the court noted Ellerth had not used Burlington's internal complaint procedures. Although Ellerth's claim was framed as a hostile work environment complaint, the District Court observed there was a quid pro quo "component" to the hostile environment. Proceeding from the premise that an employer faces vicarious liability for quid pro quo harassment, the District Court thought it necessary to apply a negligence standard because the quid pro quo merely contributed to the hostile work environment. The Court of Appeals en banc reversed in a decision which produced eight separate opinions and no consensus for a controlling rationale. We granted certiorari.

At the outset, we assume an important proposition yet to be established before a trier of fact. It is a premise assumed as well, in explicit or implicit terms, in the various opinions by the judges of the Court of Appeals. The premise is: A trier of fact could find in Slowik's remarks numerous threats to retaliate against Ellerth if she denied some sexual liberties. The threats, however, were not carried out or fulfilled. Cases based on threats which are carried out are referred to often as quid pro quo cases, as distinct from bothersome attentions or sexual remarks that are sufficiently severe or pervasive to create a hostile work environment. The terms quid pro quo and hostile work environment are helpful, perhaps, in making a rough demarcation between cases in which threats are carried out and those where they are not or are absent altogether, but beyond this are of limited utility.

We do not suggest the terms quid pro quo and hostile work environment are irrelevant to Title VII litigation. To the extent they illustrate the distinction between cases involving a threat which is carried out and offensive conduct in general, the terms are relevant when there is a threshold question whether a plaintiff can prove discrimination in violation of Title VII. When a plaintiff proves that a tangible employment action resulted from a refusal to submit to a supervisor's sexual demands, he or she establishes that the employment decision itself constitutes a change in the terms and conditions of employment that is actionable under Title VII. For any sexual harassment preceding the employment decision to be actionable, however, the conduct must be severe or pervasive. Because Ellerth's claim involves only unfulfilled threats, it should be categorized as a hostile work environment claim which requires a showing of severe or pervasive conduct. See *Oncale v. Sundowner Offshore Services, Inc.*, 523 U.S. 75 (1998); *Harris v. Forklift Systems, Inc.*, 510 U.S. 17, 21 (1993). For purposes of this case, we accept the District Court's finding that the alleged conduct was severe or pervasive. The case before us involves numerous alleged threats, and we express no opinion as to whether a single unfulfilled threat is sufficient to constitute discrimination in the terms or conditions of employment.

When we assume discrimination can be proved, however, the factors we discuss below, and not the categories quid pro quo and hostile work environment, will be controlling on the issue of vicarious liability. That is the question we must resolve.

We must decide, then, whether an employer has vicarious liability when a supervisor creates a hostile work environment by making explicit threats to alter a subordinate's terms or conditions of employment, based on sex, but does not fulfill the threat. We turn to principles of agency law, for the term "employer" is defined

> **The Court looks to the principles of agency law to determine liability for sexual harassment.**

under Title VII to include "agents." 42 U.S.C. § 2000e(b). Section 219(1) of the Restatement sets out a central principle of agency law:

> "A master is subject to liability for the torts of his servants committed while acting in the scope of their employment."

An employer may be liable for both negligent and intentional torts committed by an employee within the scope of his or her employment. Sexual harassment under Title VII presupposes intentional conduct. While early decisions absolved employers of liability for the intentional torts of their employees, the law now imposes liability where the employee's "purpose, however misguided, is wholly or in part to further the master's business." W. Keeton, D. Dobbs, R. Keeton, & D. Owen, Prosser and Keeton on Law of Torts § 70, p. 505 (5th ed. 1984). In applying scope of employment principles to intentional torts, however, it is accepted that "it is less likely that a willful tort will properly be held to be in the course of employment and that the liability of the master for such torts will naturally be more limited." F. Mechem, Outlines of the Law of Agency § 394, p. 266 (P. Mechem 4th ed. 1952). The Restatement defines conduct, including an intentional tort, to be within the scope of employment when "actuated, at least in part, by a purpose to serve the [employer]," even if it is forbidden by the employer. Restatement §§ 228(1)(c), 230. For example, when a salesperson lies to a customer to make a sale, the tortious conduct is within the scope of employment because it benefits the employer by increasing sales, even though it may violate the employer's policies.

The concept of scope of employment has not always been construed to require a motive to serve the employer. Federal courts have nonetheless found similar limitations on employer liability when applying the agency laws of the States under the Federal Tort Claims Act, which makes the Federal Government liable for torts committed by employees within the scope of employment. The general rule is that sexual harassment by a supervisor is not conduct within the scope of employment.

Scope of employment does not define the only basis for employer liability under agency principles. In limited circumstances, agency principles impose liability on employers even where employees commit torts outside the scope of employment. Thus, although a supervisor's sexual harassment is outside the scope of employment because the conduct was for personal motives, an employer can be liable, nonetheless, where its own negligence is a cause of the harassment. An employer is negligent with respect to sexual harassment if it knew or should have known about the conduct and failed to stop it. Negligence sets a minimum standard for employer liability under Title VII; but Ellerth seeks to invoke the more stringent standard of vicarious liability.

> As acknowledged by the Court, employers can be liable, in certain situations, "even where employees commit torts outside the scope of employment."

Section 219(2)(d) concerns vicarious liability for intentional torts committed by an employee when the employee uses apparent authority (the apparent authority standard), or when the employee "was aided in accomplishing the tort by the existence of the agency relation" (the aided in the agency relation standard). As other federal decisions have done in discussing vicarious liability for supervisor harassment, we begin with § 291(2)(d).

As a general rule, apparent authority is relevant where the agent purports to exercise a power which he or she does not have. In the usual case, a supervisor's harassment involves misuse of actual power, not the false impression of its existence. Apparent authority analysis therefore is inappropriate in this context. If, in the unusual case, it is alleged there is a false impression that the actor was a supervisor, when he in fact was not, the victim's mistaken conclusion must be a reasonable one. When a party seeks to impose vicarious liability based on an agent's misuse of delegated authority, the Restatement's aided in the agency relation rule, rather than the apparent authority rule, appears to be the appropriate form of analysis.

We turn to the aided in the agency relation standard. In a sense, most workplace tortfeasors are aided in accomplishing their tortious objective by the existence of the agency relation: Proximity and regular contact may afford a captive pool of potential victims. Were this to satisfy the aided in the agency relation standard, an employer would be subject to vicarious liability not only for all supervisor harassment, but also for all co-worker harassment, a result enforced by neither the EEOC nor any court of appeals to have considered the issue. The aided in the agency relation standard, therefore, requires the existence of something more than the employment relation itself.

At the outset, we can identify a class of cases where, beyond question, more than the mere existence of the employment relation aids in commission of the harassment: when a supervisor takes a tangible employment action against the subordinate. Every Federal Court of Appeals to have considered the question has found vicarious liability when a discriminatory act results in a tangible employment action. Although few courts have elaborated how agency principles support this rule, we think it reflects a correct application of the aided in the agency relation standard.

In the context of this case, a tangible employment action would have taken the form of a denial of a raise or a promotion. The concept of a tangible employment action appears in numerous cases in the Courts of Appeals discussing claims involving race, age, and national origin discrimination, as well as sex discrimination. Without endorsing the specific results of those decisions, we think it prudent to import the concept of a tangible employment action for resolution of the vicarious liability issue we consider here. A tangible employment action constitutes a significant change in employment status, such as hiring, firing, failing to promote, reassignment with significantly different responsibilities, or a decision causing a significant change in benefits.

> As recognized by the Court, tangible employment actions include — but are not limited to —"hiring, firing, failing to promote, [and] reassignment with significantly different responsibilities."

When a supervisor makes a tangible employment decision, there is assurance the injury could not have been inflicted absent the agency relation. A tangible employment action in most cases inflicts direct economic harm. As a general proposition, only a supervisor, or other person acting with the authority of the company, can cause this sort of injury. A co-worker can break a co-worker's arm as easily as a supervisor, and anyone who has regular contact with an employee can inflict psychological injuries by his or her offensive conduct. But one co-worker (absent some elaborate scheme) cannot dock another's pay, nor can one co-worker demote another. Tangible employment actions fall within the special province of the supervisor. The supervisor has been empowered by the company as a distinct class of agent to make economic decisions affecting other employees under his or her control.

Whatever the exact contours of the aided in the agency relation standard, its requirements will always be met when a supervisor takes a tangible employment action against a subordinate. In that instance, it would be implausible to interpret agency principles to allow an employer to escape liability, as *Meritor* itself appeared to acknowledge.

Whether the agency relation aids in commission of supervisor harassment which does not culminate in a tangible employment action is less obvious. Application of the standard is made difficult by its malleable terminology, which can be read to either expand or limit liability in the context of supervisor harassment. On the one hand, a supervisor's power and authority invests his or her harassing conduct with a particular threatening character, and in this sense, a supervisor always is aided by the agency relation. On the other hand, there are acts of harassment a supervisor might commit which might be the same acts a coemployee would commit, and there may be some circumstances where the supervisor's status makes little difference.

It is this tension which, we think, has caused so much confusion among the Courts of Appeals which have sought to apply the aided in the agency relation standard to Title VII cases. The aided in the agency relation standard, however, is a developing feature of agency law, and we hesitate to render a definitive explanation of our understanding of the standard in an area where other important considerations must affect our judgment. In particular, we are bound by our holding in *Meritor* that agency principles constrain the imposition of vicarious liability in cases of supervisory harassment. Congress has not altered *Meritor*'s rule even though it has made significant amendments to Title VII in the interim.

In order to accommodate the agency principles of vicarious liability for harm caused by misuse of supervisory authority, as well as Title VII's equally basic policies of encouraging forethought by employers and saving action by objecting employees, we adopt the following holding in this case and in *Faragher v. Boca Raton*, 524 U.S. 775 (1998), also decided today. An employer is subject to vicarious liability to a victimized employee for an actionable hostile environment created by a supervisor with immediate (or successively higher) authority over the employee. When no tangible employment action is taken, a defending employer may raise an affirmative defense to liability or damages, subject to proof by a preponderance of the evidence, see Fed. Rule Civ. Proc. 8(c). The defense comprises two necessary elements: (a) that the employer exercised reasonable care to prevent and correct promptly any sexually harassing behavior, and (b) that the plaintiff employee unreasonably failed to take advantage of any preventive or corrective opportunities provided by the employer or to avoid harm otherwise. While proof that an employer had promulgated an antiharassment policy with complaint procedure is not necessary in every instance as a matter of law, the need for a stated policy suitable to the employment circumstances may appropriately be addressed in any case when litigating the first element of the defense. And while proof that an

> The Court creates an affirmative defense for employers to sexual harassment claims where no tangible employment action is taken.

employee failed to fulfill the corresponding obligation of reasonable care to avoid harm is not limited to showing any unreasonable failure to use any complaint procedure provided by the employer, a demonstration of such failure will normally suffice to satisfy the employer's burden under the second element of the defense. No affirmative defense is available, however, when the supervisor's harassment culminates in a tangible employment action, such as discharge, demotion, or undesirable reassignment.

Relying on existing case law which held out the promise of vicarious liability for all quid pro quo claims, Ellerth focused all her attention in the Court of Appeals on proving her claim fit within that category. Given our explanation that the labels quid pro quo and hostile work environment are not controlling for purposes of establishing employer liability, Ellerth should have an adequate opportunity to prove she has a claim for which Burlington is liable.

Although Ellerth has not alleged she suffered a tangible employment action at the hands of Slowik, which would deprive Burlington of the availability of the affirmative defense, this is not dispositive. In light of our decision, Burlington is still subject to vicarious liability for Slowik's activity, but Burlington should have an opportunity to assert and prove the affirmative defense to liability.

■ NOTES AND QUESTIONS

1. The *Ellerth* decision provides substantial guidance on how liability for harassment can be imputed to an employer. The Court relies heavily on agency principles to make this determination.

2. *Ellerth* makes clear that the legal landscape should put little emphasis on the "quid pro quo" determination. As the Court notes, "[t]he terms quid pro quo and hostile work environment are helpful, perhaps, in making a rough demarcation between cases in which threats are carried out and those where they are not or are absent altogether, but beyond this are of limited utility." *Ellerth*, 524 U.S. at 751.

3. Perhaps a more important distinction is whether there is a tangible employment action in the case, or a hostile work environment is involved.

4. What types of things constitute a tangible employment action? What does the Court suggest would rise to the level of a tangible employment action? Is this list exhaustive? According to the EEOC, "examples of tangible employment actions include: hiring and firing; promotion and failure to promote; demotion; undesirable reassignment; a decision causing a significant change in benefits; compensation decisions; and work assignment." *EEOC Enforcement Guidance: Vicarious Employer Liab. for Unlawful Harassment by Supervisors*, EEOC Compl. Man. (CCH) ¶ 3116, § IV(B) (June 18, 1999). Should anything else be added to this list?

5. The Court makes clear that where there is a tangible employment action, vicarious liability attaches. The Court states, "Every Federal Court of Appeals to have considered the question has found vicarious liability when a

discriminatory act results in a tangible employment action. Although few courts have elaborated how agency principles support this rule, we think it reflects a correct application of the aided in the agency relation standard." *Ellerth*, 524 U.S. at 760–761. Can a co-worker effectuate a tangible employment action? Does the Court weigh in on this issue?

6. Where no tangible employment action is involved in a case, and a supervisor has perpetrated the harassment, the employer can avail itself of a two-part affirmative defense by showing "(a) that the employer exercised reasonable care to prevent and correct promptly any sexually harassing behavior, and (b) that the plaintiff employee unreasonably failed to take advantage of any preventive or corrective opportunities provided by the employer or to avoid harm otherwise." *Ellerth*, 524 U.S. at 745.

7. The affirmative defense only applies where a supervisor is involved in the conduct. How would you define who is or is not a supervisor? Does the Court answer this question?

8. The affirmative defense requires that the employer show that it "exercised reasonable care" to stop the harassment. What does it mean to exercise reasonable care? For example, if an employer saw a supervisor inappropriately touching a subordinate and told him to "knock it off," would that be exercising reasonable care? Why or why not?

9. The Court notes that an anti-harassment policy can be useful in determining whether reasonable care was exercised, but that it is not "necessary in every instance." Given this language, how would you advise a client on whether it should adopt an anti-harassment policy? What would it include? How would it define harassment? Would it apply only to categories protected under federal law (sex, race, age, etc.) or would it go further? How should rank-and-file employees be trained? Should supervisors receive different training? Managers? Employees in the company's human resources department? Does it make any difference whether the employer is large or small?

10. Since *Ellerth*, the courts have been clear that simply having an anti-harassment policy is not enough. It must be an effective policy that is well maintained by the employer. What would this mean in practice?

11. The second part of the affirmative defense requires the employer to show that the plaintiff "unreasonably failed to take advantage of any preventive . . . opportunities." What does this mean in the context of a sexual harassment suit? If a complaint procedure is in place and it is not used by the plaintiff, does that end the case?

12. It is worth noting that the affirmative defense is a complete defense; if the employer is able to establish both elements, it will prevail in the case. Should the employer be permitted to avoid *all* liability by establishing these elements?

13. The affirmative defense also requires that the plaintiff "avoid harm otherwise." When would this language be applicable to a claim? What does this language mean?

14. Keep in mind that it is the employer that has the burden of proof to establish *both* elements of the two-part defense. Thus, even if the employer establishes that it had an effective policy, it can be subjected to liability if it does not properly respond to a worker's complaint under that policy.

15. **Historical note.** Mitsubishi Motors currently operates under a zero tolerance sexual harassment policy. This aggressive stance may be the result of its prior history of sexual harassment allegations. In 1998, the company paid $34 million to hundreds of female workers at its Normal, Illinois, plant after it was determined that the plant permitted widespread sexual harassment and a hostile work environment for women over the course of a decade. It is not unusual for sexual harassment claims to affect multiple workers and to result in high amounts of damages. Where an employer allows this type of environment to exist — or fails to properly detect it — it can negatively impact workers across the entire company. Stephen Braun, *Mitsubishi to Pay $34 Million in Sex Harassment Case*, L.A. Times, June 12, 1998, http://articles. latimes.com/ 1998/jun/12/news/mn-59249.

Practice and Procedural Tip

15: The Anti-Harassment Policy

Given the state of the law, all employers should have an anti-harassment policy in place. Indeed, most employers should have a broader antidiscrimination policy that prohibits its workers from discriminating and offers employees a mechanism to file complaints. But what would a good anti-harassment policy look like?

The key to any good policy is that it must be crafted to fit the specific organization. No two entities are exactly alike, and the policy should reflect the specific structure of the organization. The policy should include a discussion of what type of activities are prohibited — namely, discrimination on the basis of race, color, sex, national origin, and religion. Other considerations would include discrimination on the basis of sexual orientation, marital status, political affiliation, or appearance. A good policy will also discuss where an individual can go to complain if she feels that she has been discriminated against. The policy should offer a number of different avenues of complaint, in the event that the individual feels uncomfortable going to a particular person or part of the company. Thus, a policy might include an individual's supervisor, someone in the HR department, someone in corporate headquarters, and an anonymous 1-800 line as different places to file a complaint. Those who are named in the policy must be aware that they are contact persons, and should be well trained on how to address a complaint that is received.

The policy must be routinely updated. Employees frequently change within an organization, and the policy must thus reflect only those employees who are currently authorized to receive complaints. The policy must also be distributed to all employees. This can often be done as part of a new employee's orientation. Or, if a policy is adopted subsequent to this date, it can be given as part of a training session. It is important to maintain some type of documentation that the employees received the policy and had an adequate opportunity to review it. This can be a simple signature line that is maintained by the company.

Routine training can also be an important way of establishing that a company has exercised reasonable care. Either internal human resource managers or outside consultants can help train employees on how to recognize and prevent discrimination. Supervisors should receive special training in this regard, as should those who are authorized to receive complaints of discrimination. Again, documentation is key, and the company should maintain a sign-in list that reflects who attended antidiscrimination training.

In the end, there is no "magic" formula for how to adopt an anti-harassment policy. However, best practices usually require that a company maintain a number of avenues of complaint, and that there is some level of training on general antidiscrimination in the workplace. The benefits of adopting an antidiscrimination policy are numerous. In addition to the possible *Ellerth* defense discussed above, the company can also use a policy to argue that it should be exempt from punitive damages. And, employees will feel better about their working environment if they know that their employer is actively seeking to prevent discrimination. Simply having a policy is not enough — the policy must be effectively implemented and maintained. *See* Shirley Feldman-Summers, *Analyzing Anti-Harassment Policies and Complaint Procedures: Do They Encourage Victims to Come Forward?*, 16 Lab. Law. 307 (2000); Allan G. King, *Resist and Report: A Policy to Deter Quid Pro Quo Sexual Harassment*, 50 Baylor L. Rev. 333 (1998); Anna-Maria Marshall, *Idle Rights: Employees' Rights Consciousness and the Construction of Sexual Harassment Policies*, 39 Law & Soc'y Rev. 83 (2005); Tom R. Tyler, *Promoting Employee Policy Adherence and Rule Following in Work Settings: The Value of Self-Regulatory Approaches*, 70 Brook. L. Rev. 1287 (2005).

In a case decided the same day as *Ellerth*, the Supreme Court further defined the rules for imputing liability to an employer in harassment cases. The *Faragher* and *Ellerth* decisions go a long way toward defining the rules of agency for discrimination claims.

Faragher v. City of Boca Raton
524 U.S. 775 (1998)

Justice Souter delivered the opinion of the Court.

This case calls for identification of the circumstances under which an employer may be held liable under Title VII for the acts of a supervisory employee whose sexual harassment of subordinates has created a hostile work environment amounting to employment discrimination. We hold that an employer is vicariously liable for actionable discrimination caused by a supervisor, but subject to an affirmative defense looking to the reasonableness of the employer's conduct as well as that of a plaintiff victim.

Between 1985 and 1990, while attending college, petitioner Beth Ann Faragher worked part time and during the summers as an ocean lifeguard for the Marine Safety Section of the Parks and Recreation Department of respondent, the City of Boca Raton, Florida (City). During this period, Faragher's immediate supervisors were Bill Terry, David Silverman, and Robert Gordon. In June 1990, Faragher resigned.

In 1992, Faragher brought an action against Terry, Silverman, and the City, asserting claims under Title VII, 42 U.S.C. § 1983, and Florida law. So far as it concerns the Title VII claim, the complaint alleged that Terry and Silverman created a "sexually hostile atmosphere" at the beach by repeatedly subjecting Faragher and other female lifeguards to "uninvited and offensive touching," by making lewd remarks, and by speaking of women

in offensive terms. The complaint contained specific allegations that Terry once said that he would never promote a woman to the rank of lieutenant, and that Silverman had said to Faragher, "Date me or clean the toilets for a year." Asserting that Terry and Silverman were agents of the City, and that their conduct amounted to discrimination in the "terms, conditions, and privileges" of her employment, 42 U.S.C. § 2000e–2(a)(1), Faragher sought a judgment against the City for nominal damages, costs, and attorney's fees.

Following a bench trial, the United States District Court for the Southern District of Florida found that throughout Faragher's employment with the City, Terry served as Chief of the Marine Safety Division, with authority to hire new lifeguards (subject to the approval of higher management), to supervise all aspects of the lifeguards' work assignments, to engage in counseling, to deliver oral reprimands, and to make a record of any such discipline. Silverman was a Marine Safety lieutenant from 1985 until June 1989, when he became a captain. Gordon began the employment period as a lieutenant and at some point was promoted to the position of training captain. In these positions, Silverman and Gordon were responsible for making the lifeguards' daily assignments, and for supervising their work and fitness training.

The lifeguards and supervisors were stationed at the city beach and worked out of the Marine Safety Headquarters, a small one-story building containing an office, a meeting room, and a single, unisex locker room with a shower. Their work routine was structured in a "paramilitary configuration," with a clear chain of command. Lifeguards reported to lieutenants and captains, who reported to Terry. He was supervised by the Recreation Superintendent, who in turn reported to a Director of Parks and Recreation, answerable to the City Manager. The lifeguards had no significant contact with higher city officials like the Recreation Superintendent.

In February 1986, the City adopted a sexual harassment policy, which it stated in a memorandum from the City Manager addressed to all employees. In May 1990, the City revised the policy and reissued a statement of it. Although the City may actually have circulated the memos and statements to some employees, it completely failed to disseminate its policy

> As noted by the Court, the defendant in this case failed to properly distribute the sexual harassment policy to all of its workers.

among employees of the Marine Safety Section, with the result that Terry, Silverman, Gordon, and many lifeguards were unaware of it.

From time to time over the course of Faragher's tenure at the Marine Safety Section, between 4 and 6 of the 40 to 50 lifeguards were women. During that 5-year period, Terry repeatedly touched the bodies of female employees without invitation, would put his arm around Faragher, with his hand on her buttocks, and once made contact with another female lifeguard in a motion of sexual simulation. He made crudely demeaning references to women generally, and once commented disparagingly on Faragher's shape. During a job interview with a woman he hired as a lifeguard, Terry said that the female lifeguards had sex with their male counterparts and asked whether she would do the same.

Silverman behaved in similar ways. He once tackled Faragher and remarked that, but for a physical characteristic he found unattractive, he would readily have had sexual relations with her. Another time, he pantomimed an act of oral sex. Within earshot of the female lifeguards, Silverman made frequent, vulgar references to women and sexual matters, commented on the bodies of female lifeguards and beachgoers, and at least twice told female lifeguards that he would like to engage in sex with them.

Faragher did not complain to higher management about Terry or Silverman. Although she spoke of their behavior to Gordon, she did not regard these discussions as formal complaints to a supervisor but as conversations with a person she held in high esteem. Other female lifeguards had similarly informal talks with Gordon, but because Gordon did not feel that it was his place to do so, he did not report these complaints to Terry, his own supervisor, or to any other city official. Gordon responded to the complaints of one lifeguard by saying that "the City just [doesn't] care."

In April 1990, however, two months before Faragher's resignation, Nancy Ewanchew, a former lifeguard, wrote to Richard Bender, the City's Personnel Director, complaining that Terry and Silverman had harassed her and other female lifeguards. Following investigation of this complaint, the City found that Terry and Silverman had behaved improperly, reprimanded them, and required them to choose between a suspension without pay or the forfeiture of annual leave. On the basis of these findings, the District Court concluded that the conduct of Terry and Silverman was discriminatory harassment sufficiently serious to alter the conditions of Faragher's employment and constitute an abusive working environment. The District Court then ruled the City [was] liable for the harassment of its supervisory employees.

A panel of the Court of Appeals for the Eleventh Circuit reversed the judgment against the City. Although the panel had "no trouble concluding that Terry's and Silverman's conduct . . . was severe and pervasive enough to create an objectively abusive work environment." It overturned the District Court's conclusion that the City was liable. The panel ruled that Terry and Silverman were not acting within the scope of their employment when they engaged in the harassment, that they were not aided in their actions by the agency relationship, and that the City had no constructive knowledge of the harassment by virtue of its pervasiveness or Gordon's actual knowledge. In a 7-to-5 decision, the full Court of Appeals, sitting en banc, adopted the panel's conclusion. [T]he court rejected Faragher's Title VII claim against the City. We granted certiorari to address the divergence.

A "master is subject to liability for the torts of his servants committed while acting in the scope of their employment." Restatement § 219(1). This doctrine has traditionally defined the "scope of employment" as including conduct "of the kind [a servant] is employed to perform," occurring "substantially within the authorized time and space limits," and "actuated, at least in part, by a purpose to serve the master," but as excluding an intentional use of force "unexpectable by the master." *Id.* § 228(1).

The proper analysis here . . . calls not for a mechanical application of indefinite and malleable factors set forth in the Restatement, *see, e.g.*, §§ 219, 228, 229, but rather an inquiry into the reasons that would support a conclusion that harassing behavior ought to be held within the scope of a supervisor's employment, and the reasons for the opposite view. The Restatement itself points to such an approach, as in the commentary that the "ultimate question" in determining the scope of employment is "whether or not it is just that the loss resulting from the servant's acts should be considered as one of the normal risks to be borne by the business in which the servant is employed." *Id.* § 229, Comment a.

The agency relationship affords contact with an employee subjected to a supervisor's sexual harassment, and the victim may well be reluctant to accept the risks of blowing the whistle on a superior. When a person with supervisory authority discriminates in the terms and conditions of subordinates' employment, his actions necessarily draw upon his superior position over the people who report to him, or those under them, whereas an employee generally cannot check a supervisor's abusive conduct the same way that she might deal with abuse from a co-worker. When a fellow employee harasses, the victim can walk away or tell the offender where to go, but it may be difficult to offer such responses to a supervisor, whose "power to supervise — [which may be] to hire and fire, and to set work schedules and pay rates — does not disappear . . . when he chooses to harass through insults and offensive gestures rather than directly with threats of firing or promises of promotion."

> The Court here focuses on the distinction between supervisory harassment and co-worker harassment. Where a co-worker is involved, "the victim can walk away or tell the offender where to go."

Estrich, *Sex at Work*, 43 Stan. L. Rev. 813, 854 (1991). Recognition of employer liability when discriminatory misuse of supervisory authority alters the terms and conditions of a victim's employment is underscored by the fact that the employer has a greater opportunity to guard against misconduct by supervisors than by common workers; employers have greater opportunity and incentive to screen them, train them, and monitor their performance.

In sum, there are good reasons for vicarious liability for misuse of supervisory authority. That rationale must, however, satisfy one more condition. We are not entitled to recognize this theory under Title VII unless we can square it with *Meritor*'s holding that an employer is not "automatically" liable for harassment by a supervisor who creates the requisite degree of discrimination, and there is obviously some tension between that holding and the position that a supervisor's misconduct aided by supervisory authority subjects the employer to liability vicariously; if the "aid" may be the unspoken suggestion of retaliation by misuse of supervisory authority, the risk of automatic liability is high. To counter it, we think there are two basic alternatives, one being to require proof of some affirmative invocation of that authority by the harassing supervisor, the other to recognize an affirmative defense to liability in some circumstances, even when a supervisor has created the actionable environment. We think plaintiffs and defendants alike would be poorly served by an active-use rule.

The other basic alternative to automatic liability would allow an employer to show as an affirmative defense to liability that the employer had exercised reasonable care to avoid harassment and to eliminate it when it might occur, and that the complaining employee had failed to act with like reasonable care to take advantage of the employer's safeguards and otherwise to prevent harm that could have been avoided. This composite defense would, we think, implement the statute sensibly, for reasons that are not hard to fathom.

The requirement to show that the employee has failed in a coordinate duty to avoid or mitigate harm reflects an equally obvious policy imported from the general theory of damages, that a victim has a duty "to use such means as are reasonable under the circumstances to avoid or minimize the damages" that result from violations of the statute. Ford Motor Co. v. EEOC, 458 U.S. 219, 231, n. 15 (1982). An employer may, for example, have provided a proven, effective mechanism for reporting and resolving complaints of sexual harassment, available to the employee without undue risk or expense. If the plaintiff unreasonably failed to avail herself of the employer's preventive or remedial apparatus, she should not recover damages that could have been avoided if she had done so. If the victim could have avoided harm, no liability should be found against the employer who had taken reasonable care, and if damages could reasonably have been mitigated no award against a liable employer should reward a plaintiff for what her own efforts could have avoided.

In order to accommodate the principle of vicarious liability for harm caused by misuse of supervisory authority, as well as Title VII's equally basic policies of encouraging forethought by employers and saving action by objecting employees, we adopt the following holding in this case and in *Burlington Industries, Inc. v. Ellerth*, 524 U.S. 742 (1998), also decided today. An employer is subject to vicarious liability to a victimized employee for an actionable hostile environment created by a supervisor with immediate (or successively higher) authority over the employee. When no tangible employment action is taken, a defending employer may raise an affirmative defense to liability or damages, subject to proof by a preponderance of the evidence, see Fed. Rule Civ. Proc. 8(c). The defense comprises two necessary elements: (a) that the employer exercised reasonable care to prevent and correct promptly any sexually harassing behavior, and (b) that the plaintiff employee unreasonably failed to take advantage of any preventive or corrective opportunities provided by the employer or to avoid harm otherwise. While proof that an employer had promulgated an antiharassment policy with complaint procedure is not necessary in every instance as a matter of law, the need for a stated policy suitable to the employment circumstances may appropriately be addressed in any case when

> As emphasized again by the Court, no defense is available to the employer where a tangible employment action is taken because of sex.

litigating the first element of the defense. And while proof that an employee failed to fulfill the corresponding obligation of reasonable care to avoid harm is not limited to showing an unreasonable failure to use any complaint procedure provided by the employer, a demonstration of such failure will normally suffice to satisfy the employer's burden under the second element of the defense. No affirmative defense is available, however, when the supervisor's harassment culminates in a tangible employment action, such as discharge, demotion, or undesirable reassignment.

Applying these rules here, we believe that the judgment of the Court of Appeals must be reversed. The District Court found that the degree of hostility in the work environment rose to the actionable level and was attributable to Silverman and Terry. It is undisputed that these supervisors "were granted virtually unchecked authority" over their subordinates, "directly controll[ing] and supervis[ing] all aspects of [Faragher's] day-to-day activities." 111 F.3d at 1544 (BARKETT, J., dissenting in part and concurring in part). It is also clear that Faragher and her colleagues were "completely isolated from the City's higher management." *Id.* The City did not seek review of these findings.

While the City would have an opportunity to raise an affirmative defense if there were any serious prospect of its presenting one, it appears from the record that any such avenue is closed. The District Court found that the City had entirely failed to disseminate its policy against sexual harassment among the beach employees and that its officials made no attempt to keep track of the conduct of supervisors like Terry and Silverman. The record also makes clear that the City's policy did not include any assurance that the harassing supervisors could be bypassed in registering complaints. Under such circumstances, we hold as a matter of law that the City could not be found to have exercised reasonable care to prevent the supervisors' harassing conduct. Unlike the employer of a small work force, who might expect that sufficient care to prevent tortious behavior could be exercised informally, those responsible for city operations could not reasonably have thought that precautions against hostile environments in any one of many departments in far-flung locations could be effective without communicating some formal policy against harassment, with a sensible complaint procedure.

The City points to nothing that might justify a conclusion by the District Court on remand that the City had exercised reasonable care. Nor is there any reason to remand for consideration of Faragher's efforts to mitigate her own damages, since the award to her was solely nominal.

The Court of Appeals also rejected the possibility that it could hold the City liable for the reason that it knew of the harassment vicariously through the knowledge of its supervisors. We have no occasion to consider whether this was error, however. We are satisfied that liability on the ground of vicarious knowledge could not be determined without further factfinding on remand, whereas the reversal necessary on the theory of supervisory harassment renders any remand for consideration of imputed knowledge entirely unjustifiable (as would be any consideration of negligence as an alternative to a theory of vicarious liability here).

■ NOTES AND QUESTIONS

1. The *Faragher* decision talks extensively about the distinction between a supervisor and a co-worker. Why is this distinction important? Is it any more troubling to be harassed by a supervisor than by a co-worker? Why or why not?

2. In a portion of the decision that has been omitted above, the Court raises the possibility of so-called proxy liability. Such liability would apply where the discrimination occurs by someone so high up at the company (e.g., the CEO) that it is as if the company itself is acting. Assuming the validity of this theory, what types of officers could subject the company to proxy liability?

3. Looking back at the agency principles articulated in *Faragher* and *Ellerth*, do you agree with how the Court has applied this theory to harassment claims?

4. The Court here again references the affirmative defense that it announced in *Faragher*. Where in the statute or regulations can that defense be found? Was the Court wise to create the defense? Does the defense proactively prevent discrimination?

5. The plaintiff here ultimately prevails because while the company had a policy against harassment, it was poorly executed and distributed. What factors does the Court rely on to reject the defendant's policy? What steps would you advise an employer to take to ensure adequate execution and distribution?

6. Why is it important that a policy include multiple avenues of complaint? Who could have been included in the defendant's policy? How could the policy have been worded more effectively?

7. The EEOC has articulated a number of factors that should be present in an effective harassment policy. The agency states:

   An anti-harassment policy and complaint procedure should contain, at a minimum, the following elements:

   ■ A clear explanation of prohibited conduct;

   ■ Assurance that employees who make complaints of harassment or provide information related to such complaints will be protected against retaliation;

- A clearly described complaint process that provides accessible avenues of complaint;
- Assurance that the employer will protect the confidentiality of harassment complaints to the extent possible;
- A complaint process that provides a prompt, thorough, and impartial investigation; and
- Assurance that the employer will take immediate and appropriate corrective action when it determines that harassment has occurred.

EEOC Enforcement Guidance: Vicarious Employer Liab. for Unlawful Harassment by Supervisors, EEOC Compl. Man. (CCH) ¶ 3116, § II(C)(1) (June 18, 1999).

 Interactive Problem

Looking back at the facts of the interactive problem at the beginning of the chapter, assume that Sarah's claim against Gozangas is successful and she prevails before a jury that awards her a total of $300,000 in damages. Concerned about the possibility of other employee complaints, the company acts quickly to adopt an anti-harassment policy, which it has been meaning to put in place for years. How would such a policy look? What elements would you include?

1. Supervisor Harassment

There has often been substantial confusion on the question of who is or is not a supervisor under the terms of Title VII. As seen above, this question is critically important in cases of harassment, and directly impacts the way in which a case is analyzed. The Supreme Court addressed the supervisor standard in the case below. As the Court ultimately holds, the ability to effectuate a tangible employment action is critical to this inquiry.

Vance v. Ball State University
570 U.S. 421 (2013)

Justice ALITO delivered the opinion of the Court.

We hold that an employee is a "supervisor" for purposes of vicarious liability under Title VII if he or she is empowered by the employer to take tangible employment actions against the victim, and we therefore affirm the judgment of the Seventh Circuit. Maetta Vance, an African-American woman, began working for Ball State University (BSU) in 1989 as a substitute server in the University Banquet and Catering division of Dining Services. In 1991, BSU promoted Vance to a part-time catering assistant position, and in 2007 she applied and was selected for a position as a full-time catering assistant.

Over the course of her employment with BSU, Vance lodged numerous complaints of racial discrimination and retaliation, but most of those incidents are not at issue here. For present purposes, the only relevant incidents concern Vance's interactions with a fellow BSU employee, Saundra Davis. During the time in question, Davis, a white woman, was employed as a catering specialist in the Banquet and Catering division. The parties vigorously dispute the

Ball State University

precise nature and scope of Davis' duties, but they agree that Davis did not have the power to hire, fire, demote, promote, transfer, or discipline Vance.

In late 2005 and early 2006, Vance filed internal complaints with BSU and charges with the Equal Employment Opportunity Commission (EEOC), alleging racial harassment and discrimination, and many of these complaints and charges pertained to Davis. Vance complained that Davis "gave her a hard time at work by glaring at her, slamming pots and pans around her, and intimidating her." She alleged that she was "left alone in the kitchen with Davis, who smiled at her"; that Davis "blocked" her on an elevator and "stood there with her cart smiling"; and that Davis often gave her "weird" looks.

Vance's workplace strife persisted despite BSU's attempts to address the problem. As a result, Vance filed this lawsuit in 2006 in the United States District Court for the Southern District of Indiana, claiming, among other things, that she had been subjected to a racially hostile work environment in violation of Title VII. In her complaint, she alleged that Davis was her supervisor and that BSU was liable for Davis' creation of a racially hostile work environment.

Both parties moved for summary judgment, and the District Court entered summary judgment in favor of BSU. The court further held that BSU could not be liable in negligence because it responded reasonably to the incidents of which it was aware. The Seventh Circuit affirmed. It explained that, under its settled precedent, supervisor status requires " 'the power to hire, fire, demote, promote, transfer, or discipline an employee.' " The court concluded that Davis was not Vance's supervisor and thus that Vance could not recover from BSU unless she could prove negligence. Finding that BSU was not negligent with respect to Davis' conduct, the court affirmed.

We hold that an employer may be vicariously liable for an employee's unlawful harassment only when the employer has empowered that employee to take tangible employment actions against the victim, *i.e.*, to effect a "significant change in employment status, such as hiring, firing, failing to promote, reassignment with significantly different responsibilities, or a decision causing a significant change in benefits." *Burlington Indus., Inc. v. Ellerth*, 524 U.S. 742, 761 (1998). We reject the nebulous definition of a "supervisor" advocated in the EEOC Guidance and substantially adopted by several courts of appeals. Petitioner's reliance on colloquial uses of the term "supervisor" is misplaced, and her contention that our cases require the EEOC's abstract definition is simply wrong.

The *Ellerth/Faragher* framework represents what the Court saw as a workable compromise between the aided-in-the-accomplishment theory of vicarious liability and the legitimate interests of employers. The Seventh Circuit's understanding of the concept of a "supervisor," with which we agree, is easily workable; it can be applied without undue difficulty at both the summary judgment stage and at trial. The alternative, in many cases, would frustrate judges and confound jurors. Petitioner contends that her expansive understanding of the concept of a "supervisor" is supported by the meaning of the word in general usage and in other legal contexts, but this argument is both incorrect on its own terms and, in any event, misguided.

In general usage, the term "supervisor" lacks a sufficiently specific meaning to be helpful for present purposes. Petitioner is certainly right that the term is often used to refer to a person who has the authority to direct another's work. *See, e.g.,* 17 Oxford English Dictionary 245 (2d ed. 1989) (defining the term as applying to "one who inspects and directs the work of others"). But the term is also often closely tied to the authority to take what *Ellerth* and *Faragher* referred to as a "tangible employment action." *See, e.g.,* Webster's Third New International Dictionary 2296, def. 1(a) (1976) ("a person having authority delegated by an employer to hire, transfer, suspend, recall, promote, assign, or discharge another employee or to recommend such action").

If we look beyond general usage to the meaning of the term in other legal contexts, we find much the same situation. Sometimes the term is reserved for those in the upper echelons of the management hierarchy. But sometimes the term is used to refer to lower ranking individuals.

Although the meaning of the concept of a supervisor varies from one legal context to another, the law often contemplates that the ability to supervise includes the ability to take tangible employment actions. The interpretation of the concept of a supervisor that we adopt today is one that can be readily applied. In a great many cases, it will be known even before litigation is commenced whether an alleged harasser was a supervisor, and in others, the alleged harasser's status will become clear to both sides after discovery. And once this is known, the parties will be in a position to assess the strength of a case and to explore the possibility of resolving the dispute. Where this does not occur, supervisor status will generally be capable of resolution at summary judgment. By contrast, under the approach advocated by petitioner and the EEOC, supervisor status would very often be murky — as this case well illustrates.

Under the definition of "supervisor" that we adopt today, the question of supervisor status, when contested, can very often be resolved as a matter of law before trial. The elimination of this issue from the trial will focus the efforts of the parties, who will be able to present their cases in a way that conforms to the framework that the jury will apply. The plaintiff will know whether he or she must prove that the employer was negligent or whether the employer will have the burden of proving the elements of the *Ellerth/Faragher* affirmative defense. Perhaps even more important, the work of the jury, which is inevitably complicated in employment discrimination cases, will be simplified. The jurors can be given preliminary instructions that allow them to understand, as the evidence comes in, how each item of proof fits into the framework that they will ultimately be required to apply. And even where the issue of supervisor status cannot be eliminated from the trial (because there are genuine factual disputes about an alleged harasser's authority to take tangible employment actions), this preliminary question is relatively straightforward.

> The Court's decision makes the question of who is a supervisor one that is more for the judge than the jury.

The alternative approach advocated by petitioner and the United States would make matters far more complicated and difficult. The complexity of the standard they favor would impede the resolution of the issue before trial. With the issue still open when trial commences, the parties would be compelled to present evidence and argument on supervisor status, the affirmative defense, and the question of negligence, and the jury would have to grapple with all those issues as well. In addition, it would often be necessary for the jury to be instructed about two very different paths of analysis, *i.e.*, what to do if the alleged harasser was found to be a supervisor and what to do if the alleged harasser was found to be merely a co-worker.

Courts and commentators alike have opined on the need for reasonably clear jury instructions in employment discrimination cases. And the danger of juror confusion is particularly high where the jury is faced with instructions on alternative theories of liability under which different parties bear the burden of proof. By simplifying the process of determining who is a supervisor (and by extension, which liability rules apply to a given set of facts), the approach that we take will help to ensure that juries return verdicts that reflect the application of the correct legal rules to the facts.

Contrary to the dissent's suggestions, this approach will not leave employees unprotected against harassment by co-workers who possess the authority to inflict psychological injury by assigning unpleasant tasks or by altering the work environment in objectionable ways. In such cases, the victims will be able to prevail simply by showing that the employer was negligent in permitting this harassment to occur, and the jury should be instructed that the nature and degree of authority wielded by the harasser is an important factor to be considered in determining whether the employer was negligent. The nature and degree of authority possessed by harassing employees varies greatly, and as we explained above, the test proposed by petitioner and the United States is ill equipped to deal with the variety of situations that will inevitably arise. This variety presents no problem for the negligence standard, which is thought to provide adequate protection for tort plaintiffs in many other situations. There is no reason why this standard, if accompanied by proper instructions, cannot provide the same service in the context at issue here.

The dissent argues that the definition of a supervisor that we now adopt is out of touch with the realities of the workplace, where individuals with the power to assign daily tasks are often regarded by other employees as supervisors. But in reality it is the alternative that is out of touch. Particularly in modern organizations that have abandoned a highly hierarchical management structure, it is common for employees to have overlapping authority with respect to the assignment of work tasks. Members of a team may each have the responsibility for taking the lead with respect to a particular aspect of the work and thus may have the responsibility to direct each other in that area of responsibility.

Finally, petitioner argues that tying supervisor status to the authority to take tangible employment actions will encourage employers to attempt to insulate themselves from liability for workplace harassment by empowering only a handful of individuals to take tangible employment actions. But a broad definition of "supervisor" is not necessary to guard against this concern.

> The primary element the Court requires for supervisory status is "the ability to take tangible employment actions."

As an initial matter, an employer will always be liable when its negligence leads to the creation or continuation of a hostile work environment. And even if an employer concentrates all decisionmaking authority in a few individuals, it likely will not isolate itself from heightened liability under *Faragher* and *Ellerth*. If an employer does attempt to confine decisionmaking power to a small number of individuals, those individuals will have a limited ability to exercise independent discretion when making decisions and will likely rely on other workers who actually interact with the affected employee. Under those circumstances, the employer may be held to have effectively delegated the power to take tangible employment actions to the employees on whose recommendations it relies.

Importuning Congress, the dissent suggests that the standard we adopt today would cause the plaintiffs to lose in a handful of cases involving shocking allegations of harassment. However, the dissent does not mention *why* the plaintiffs would lose in those cases. It is not clear in any of those examples that the legal outcome hinges on the definition of "supervisor."

In any event, the dissent is wrong in claiming that our holding would preclude employer liability in other cases with facts similar to these. Assuming that a harasser is not a supervisor, a plaintiff could still prevail by showing that his or her employer was negligent in failing to prevent harassment from taking place. Evidence that an employer did not monitor the workplace, failed to respond to complaints, failed to provide a system for registering complaints, or effectively discouraged complaints from being filed would be relevant. Thus, it is not true, as the dissent asserts, that our holding "relieves scores of employers of responsibility" for the behavior of workers they employ.

Despite its rhetoric, the dissent acknowledges that Davis, the alleged harasser in this case, would probably not qualify as a supervisor even under the dissent's preferred approach. On that point, we agree. Petitioner did refer to Davis as a "supervisor" in some of the complaints that she filed, and Davis' job description does state that she supervises Kitchen Assistants and Substitutes and "[l]ead[s] and direct[s]" certain other employees. But under the dissent's preferred approach, supervisor status hinges not on formal job titles or "paper descriptions" but on "specific facts about the working relationship." *Post* (internal quotation marks omitted).

Turning to the "specific facts" of petitioner's and Davis' working relationship, there is simply no evidence that Davis directed petitioner's day-to-day activities. The record indicates that Bill Kimes (the general manager of the Catering Division) and the chef assigned petitioner's daily tasks, which were given to her on "prep lists." The fact that Davis sometimes may have handed prep lists to petitioner, is insufficient to confer supervisor status. And Kimes — *not* Davis — set petitioner's work schedule.

Because the dissent concedes that our approach in this case deprives petitioner of none of the protections that Title VII offers, the dissent's critique is based on nothing more than a hypothesis as to how our approach might affect the outcomes of *other* cases — cases where an employee who cannot take tangible employment actions, but who does direct the victim's daily work activities in a meaningful way, creates an unlawful hostile environment, and yet does not wield authority of such a degree and nature that the employer can be deemed negligent with respect to the harassment. We are skeptical that there are a great number of such cases. However, we are confident that, in every case, the approach we take today will be more easily administrable than the approach advocated by the dissent.

We hold that an employee is a "supervisor" for purposes of vicarious liability under Title VII if he or she is empowered by the employer to take tangible employment actions against the victim. Because there is no evidence that BSU empowered Davis to take any tangible employment actions against Vance, the judgment of the Seventh Circuit is affirmed.

Justice Ginsburg, with whom Justice Breyer, Justice Sotomayor, and Justice Kagan join, dissenting.

The Court today strikes from the supervisory category employees who control the day-to-day schedules and assignments of others, confining the category to those formally empowered to take tangible employment actions. The limitation the Court decrees diminishes the force of *Faragher* and *Ellerth*, ignores the conditions under which members of the work force labor, and disserves the objective of Title VII to prevent discrimination from infecting the Nation's workplaces. I would follow the EEOC's Guidance and hold that the authority to direct an employee's daily activities establishes supervisory status under Title VII.

The distinction *Faragher* and *Ellerth* drew between supervisors and co-workers corresponds to the realities of the workplace. Exposed to a fellow employee's harassment, one can walk away or tell the offender to "buzz off." A supervisor's slings and arrows, however, are not so easily avoided. An employee who confronts her harassing supervisor risks, for example, receiving an undesirable or unsafe work assignment or an unwanted transfer. She may be saddled with an excessive workload or with placement on a shift spanning hours disruptive of her family life. And she may be demoted or fired. Facing such dangers, she may be reluctant to blow the whistle on her superior, whose "power and authority invests

> The dissent appears primarily concerned that the majority's definition of supervisor does not include those "who control the day-to-day schedules and assignments of others."

his or her harassing conduct with a particular threatening character." *Ellerth*, 524 U.S. at 763.

While *Faragher* and *Ellerth* differentiated harassment by supervisors from harassment by co-workers, neither decision gave a definitive answer to the question: Who qualifies as a supervisor? Two views have emerged. One view, in line with the EEOC's Guidance, counts as a supervisor anyone with authority to take tangible employment actions or to direct an employee's daily work activities. The other view ranks as supervisors only those authorized to take tangible employment actions.

The . . . view taken by the Court today is out of accord with the agency principles that, *Faragher* and *Ellerth* affirmed, govern Title VII. It is blind to the realities of the workplace, and it discounts the guidance of the EEOC, the agency Congress established to interpret, and superintend the enforcement of, Title VII. Under that guidance, the appropriate question is: Has the employer given the alleged harasser authority to take tangible employment actions *or* to control the conditions under which subordinates do their daily work? If the answer to either inquiry is yes, vicarious liability is in order, for the superior-subordinate working arrangement facilitating the harassment is of the employer's making. Within a year after the Court's decisions in *Faragher* and *Ellerth*, the EEOC defined "supervisor" to include any employee with "authority to undertake or recommend tangible employment decisions," *or* with "authority to direct [another] employee's daily work activities." EEOC Guidance 405:7654. That definition should garner "respect proportional to its 'power to persuade.'" *United States v. Mead Corp.*, 533 U.S. 218, 235 (2001) (quoting *Skidmore v. Swift & Co.*, 323 U.S. 134, 140 (1944)). Furthermore, as the EEOC perceived, in assessing an employee's qualification as a supervisor, context is often key. I would accord the agency's judgment due respect.

Exhibiting remarkable resistance to the thrust of our prior decisions, workplace realities, and the EEOC's Guidance, the Court embraces a position that relieves scores of employers of responsibility for the behavior of the supervisors they employ. Trumpeting the virtues of simplicity and administrability, the Court restricts supervisor status to those with power to take tangible employment actions. In so restricting the definition of supervisor, the Court once again shuts from sight the "robust protection against workplace discrimination Congress intended Title VII to secure." *Ledbetter v. Goodyear Tire & Rubber Co.*, 550 U.S. 618, 660 (2007) (Ginsburg, J., dissenting).

Regrettably, the Court has seized upon Vance's thin case to narrow the definition of supervisor, and thereby manifestly limit Title VII's protections against workplace harassment. Not even Ball State, the defendant-employer in this case, has advanced the restrictive definition the Court adopts. Yet the Court, insistent on constructing artificial categories where context should be key, proceeds on an immoderate and unrestrained course to corral Title VII.

Congress has, in the recent past, intervened to correct this Court's wayward interpretations of Title VII. *See* Lilly Ledbetter Fair Pay Act of 2009, 123 Stat. 5, superseding *Ledbetter v. Goodyear Tire & Rubber Co.*, 550 U.S. 618 (2007). *See also* Civil Rights Act of 1991, 105 Stat. 1071, superseding in part, *Lorance v. AT & T Technologies, Inc.*, 490 U.S. 900 (1989); *Martin v. Wilks*, 490 U.S. 755 (1989); *Wards Cove Packing Co. v. Atonio*, 490 U.S. 642 (1989); and *Price Waterhouse v. Hopkins*,

490 U.S. 228 (1989). The ball is once again in Congress' court to correct the error into which this Court has fallen, and to restore the robust protections against workplace harassment the Court weakens today. For the reasons stated, I would reverse the judgment of the Seventh Circuit and remand the case for application of the proper standard for determining who qualifies as a supervisor.

■ NOTES AND QUESTIONS

1. *Vance* resolves an ambiguity left after *Faragher/Ellerth*: what it takes to qualify as a supervisor. The Court concludes that an "employer may be vicariously liable for an employee's unlawful harassment only when the employer has empowered that employee to take tangible employment actions against the victim, i.e., to effect a 'significant change in employment status, such as hiring, firing, failing to promote, reassignment with significantly different responsibilities, or a decision causing a significant change in benefits.'" *Vance*, 570 U.S. at 430–431. Do you agree with this definition?

2. The Court further holds that "[t]he ability to direct another employee's tasks is simply not sufficient [to be a supervisor under the law]. Employees with such powers are certainly capable of creating intolerable work environments." *Vance*, 570 U.S. at 439–440. This conclusion is the principle issue in the case with which the dissent disagrees. Which view more accurately reflects the realities of the workplace?

3. The majority notes that "[t]he dissent argues that the definition of a supervisor that we now adopt is out of touch with the realities of the workplace, where individuals with the power to assign daily tasks are often regarded by other employees as supervisors." *Vance*, 570 U.S. at 446–447. Do you agree? If an employee can assign another worker to perform onerous/undesired duties, and can further schedule the days and times that these duties are performed, is that employee a supervisor? Is the ability to take disciplinary action the Court's touchstone here? Does the ability to assign tasks give an individual supervisory authority?

4. The dissent notes that a major implication of the supervisor/co-worker distinction is that for co-worker harassment, "one can walk away or tell the offender to 'buzz off.'" *Vance*, 570 U.S. at 453–454. Would an employee feel comfortable telling someone responsible for assigning them daily tasks to buzz off? What about a co-worker at the same hierarchical level, but who is much more senior? Or a co-worker who is close friends or even sleeping with a direct supervisor?

5. The Court emphasizes that its definition of supervisor is straightforward and would help streamline the legal analysis. The dissent criticizes this argument, stating that it is simply "[t]rumpeting the virtues of simplicity and administrability," while restricting "supervisor status to those with power to take tangible employment actions." *Vance*, 570 U.S. at 463–464. How important is clarity and simplicity in the law? Is it more important to have a precise definition of who is a supervisor in every instance, or would it be more valuable to have the courts engage in a fact-specific inquiry?

6. The dissent accuses the majority of being "blind to the realities of the workplace." *Vance*, 570 U.S. at 454–455. Is this a fair charge? Why or why not?

7. Justice Ginsburg baits Congress to intervene and overturn the *Vance* decision. She states, "The ball is once again in Congress' court to correct the error into which this Court has fallen, and to restore the robust protections against workplace harassment the Court weakens today." *Vance*, 570 U.S. at 470–471. Is this the type of issue with which Congress should become involved? *See* Case Comment, *Title VII — Employer Liability for Supervisor Harassment —* Vance v. Ball State University, 127 Harv. L. Rev. 398 (2013).

 Interactive Problem

Looking back at the facts of the interactive problem at the beginning of the chapter, assume that the only two individuals who harassed Sarah were a cook and her shift manager. What additional facts would you need to know to determine whether these employees were supervisors as defined by the Court in *Vance*?

2. Co-Worker Harassment

Co-worker harassment occurs where a fellow employee is perpetrating the adverse conduct. As Justice Ginsburg notes in her dissent in *Vance*, it is often easier to tell such an employee "to buzz off." Different rules of agency apply where the individual is not cloaked with supervisory authority. The Court in *Ellerth* noted:

> Scope of employment does not define the only basis for employer liability under agency principles. In limited circumstances, agency principles impose liability on employers even where employees commit torts outside the scope of employment. . . . Thus, although a supervisor's sexual harassment is outside the scope of employment because the conduct was for personal motives, an employer can be liable, nonetheless, where its own negligence is a cause of the harassment. An employer is negligent with respect to sexual harassment if it knew or should have known about the conduct and failed to stop it. Negligence sets a minimum standard for employer liability under Title VII; but *Ellerth* seeks to invoke the more stringent standard of vicarious liability.

Ellerth, 524 U.S. at 758, 759 (some text omitted).

Similarly, in her dissent in *Vance*, Justice Ginsburg notes that "if the harassing employee is a co-worker, a negligence standard applies. To satisfy that standard, the complainant must show that the employer knew or should have known of the offensive conduct but failed to take appropriate corrective action." *Vance*, 570 U.S. at 453–454 (Ginsburg, J., dissenting).

After these decisions, it is clear that where a supervisor is not involved in the harassing conduct, the co-worker standard will apply. This co-worker standard follows a negligence test. The employer will be liable where it knew or should have known of the conduct, but failed to take appropriate remedial measures. As the *Ellerth* decision points out, this negligence test is the lowest level of liability that can be imposed on employers, and plaintiffs are better off pursuing a supervisory harassment claim if the facts permit it.

It is in many ways almost counterintuitive that the law would permit a negligence type claim in an employment discrimination case. These cases are almost always intentional in nature, and in many ways it seems unfair to put an employer on the hook where it did not cloak the harasser with any type of supervisory authority. Nonetheless, as we saw with disparate impact claims, this is one area where the courts have concluded that liability should exist. It can even be analogized to holding a landowner responsible for the actions of his or her invitees.

It can also be confusing to understand how the standard for co-worker and supervisory harassment differ. Most notably, why would the employer be able to avail itself of an affirmative defense in supervisory harassment claims, but not be entitled to the same defense in co-worker cases where a lower standard is being applied? The answer lies in the burden of proof. In many ways, the two-part test announced by the Court for the affirmative defense also applies to negligence cases, but it is the plaintiff that has the burden of proof. Thus, to show that an employer knew or should have known of the harassment, the plaintiff will often be required to establish that she complained pursuant to an employer-based anti-harassment policy. And, to argue that the employer did not take an appropriate remedial action, the plaintiff will further be required to establish that it did not act in accordance with its own policies. *See* Mark McLaughlin Hager, *Harassment as a Tort: Why Title VII Hostile Environment Liability Should Be Curtailed*, 30 CONN. L. REV. 375 (1998); Paul T. Sorensen, *A Fresh Look at Employer Liability for Sexual Harassment*, 27 T.M. COOLEY L. REV. 509 (2010); Kerri Lynn Stone, *License to Harass: Holding Defendants Accountable for Retaining Recidivist Harassers*, 41 AKRON L. REV. 1059 (2008).

There are myriad ways to establish co-worker harassment. And, constructive knowledge can certainly be inferred. Thus, an employer cannot simply "stick its head in the sand" in an attempt to avoid dealing with harassment. If harassment is rampant in the workplace, an employer must do something to correct the situation, even in the absence of a complaint. *See generally* Bailey Kuklin, *"You Should Have Known Better,"* 48 KAN. L. REV. 545 (2000).

Important distinctions exist between the supervisor and co-worker harassment tests. A supervisor is an individual who has the authority to effectuate a tangible employment action. Where supervisory harassment is present, the employer will be able to avoid liability if it can carry its burden of proof of establishing the two components of the affirmative defense. Where co-worker harassment is implicated, a negligence standard applies, and the plaintiff carries the burden of persuasion of showing that the employer knew or should have known of the conduct but failed to act.

Class Exercise: Customer Harassment

Wanda, a twenty-two-year old female, works as a pizza delivery person for a major fast-food chain. Every Friday night on her shift, she receives an order from a particular house where the owner treats her inappropriately. Specifically, when she delivers the pizza, the customer answers the door in nothing but his boxers, and, leering at Wanda, asks her if she remembered to bring "dessert." Wanda is disgusted by this behavior and complains to her managers about it. They laugh it off, and refuse to do anything about it. "The customer is always right," they say, so she will be fired if she refuses to deliver to this house.

Breaking up into small groups, discuss whether Wanda would have a cause of action against her company. What standard would apply? *See* Lockard v. Pizza Hut, Inc., 162 F.3d 1062 (10th Cir. 1998); Lori A. Tetreault, Annotation, *Liability of Employer, Under Title VII of Civil Rights Act of 1964 (42 U.S.C.A. §§ 2000e et seq.) for Sexual Harassment of Employee by Customer, Client, or Patron*, 163 A.L.R. Fed. 445 (2000).

---

3. Constructive Discharge

As discussed, the Supreme Court distinguishes between tangible employment actions and hostile work environments. Where a tangible employment action has been taken because of sex, vicarious liability attaches. Where a hostile work environment has been perpetrated by a supervisor, the defendant can still avoid liability by establishing the affirmative defense. Thus, whether or not a particular adverse act is considered to be a tangible employment action is a critical inquiry in the case.

The Supreme Court has listed several acts as constituting a tangible employment action: hiring, firing, failing to promote, reassignment with significantly different responsibilities, and a substantial change in benefits. One issue that often arises is whether a constructive discharge constitutes a tangible action. In a constructive discharge case, the plaintiff voluntarily quits her job under circumstances where a reasonable person would also have left the position. The courts have taken various approaches as to what constitutes a constructive discharge. For example, the Seventh Circuit Court of Appeals has said that the environment must be "hellish" to satisfy this standard. *See* Baskerville v. Culligan Int'l Co., 50 F.3d 428, 430 (7th Cir. 1995).

Though not weighing in on what actually constitutes a constructive discharge, the Supreme Court did decide — subsequent to *Faragher* and *Ellerth* — whether this type of adverse act is a tangible employment action.

Pennsylvania State Police v. Suders
542 U.S. 129 (2004)

Justice GINSBURG delivered the opinion of the Court.

Plaintiff-respondent Nancy Drew Suders alleged sexually harassing conduct by her supervisors, officers of the Pennsylvania State Police (PSP), of such severity she was forced to resign. The question presented concerns the proof burdens parties bear when a sexual harassment/constructive discharge claim of that character is asserted under Title VII of the Civil Rights Act of 1964. In March 1998, the PSP hired Suders as a police communications operator for the McConnellsburg barracks. Suders' supervisors were Sergeant Eric D. Easton, Station Commander at the McConnellsburg barracks, Patrol Corporal William D. Baker, and Corporal Eric B. Prendergast. Those three supervisors subjected Suders to a continuous barrage of sexual harassment that ceased only when she resigned from the force.

Easton "would bring up [the subject of] people having sex with animals" each time Suders entered his office. He told Prendergast, in front of Suders, that young girls should be given instruction in how to gratify men with oral sex. Easton also would sit down near Suders, wearing spandex shorts, and spread his legs apart. Apparently imitating a move popularized by television wrestling, Baker repeatedly made an obscene gesture in Suders' presence by grabbing his genitals and shouting out a vulgar comment inviting oral sex. Baker made this gesture as many as five-to-ten times per night throughout Suders' employment at the barracks. Suders once told Baker she "'d[id]n't think [he] should be doing this'"; Baker responded by jumping on a chair and again performing the gesture, with the accompanying vulgarity. Further, Baker would "rub his rear end in front of her and remark 'I have a nice ass, don't I?'" Prendergast told Suders "'the village idiot could do her job'"; wearing black gloves, he would pound on furniture to intimidate her.

In June 1998, Prendergast accused Suders of taking a missing accident file home with her. After that incident, Suders approached the PSP's Equal Employment Opportunity Officer, Virginia Smith-Elliott, and told her she "might need some help." Smith-Elliott gave Suders her telephone number, but neither woman followed up on the conversation. On August 18, 1998, Suders contacted Smith-Elliott again, this time stating that she was being harassed and was afraid. Smith-Elliott told Suders to file a complaint, but did not tell her how to obtain the necessary form. Smith-Elliott's response and the manner in which it was conveyed appeared to Suders insensitive and unhelpful.

Two days later, Suders' supervisors arrested her for theft, and Suders resigned from the force. The theft arrest occurred in the following circumstances. Suders had several times taken a computer-skills exam to satisfy a PSP job requirement. Each time, Suders' supervisors told her that she had failed. Suders one day came upon her exams in a set of drawers in the women's locker room. She concluded that her supervisors had never forwarded the tests for grading and that their reports of her failures were false. Regarding the tests as her property, Suders removed them from the locker room. Upon finding that the exams had been removed, Suders' supervisors devised a plan to arrest her for theft. The officers dusted the drawer in which the exams had been stored with a theft-detection powder that turns hands blue when touched. As anticipated by Easton, Baker, and Prendergast, Suders attempted to return the tests to the drawer, whereupon her hands turned telltale blue. The supervisors then apprehended and handcuffed her, photographed her blue hands, and commenced to question her. Suders had previously prepared a written resignation, which she tendered soon after the supervisors detained her. Nevertheless, the supervisors initially refused to release her. Instead, they brought her to an interrogation room, gave her warnings under Miranda v. Arizona, 384 U.S. 436 (1966), and continued to question her. Suders reiterated that she wanted to resign, and Easton then let her leave. The PSP never brought theft charges against her.

In September 2000, Suders sued the PSP in Federal District Court, alleging, *inter alia*, that she had been subjected to sexual harassment and constructively discharged, in violation of Title VII.

The Court of Appeals for the Third Circuit reversed and remanded the case for disposition on the merits. The Third Circuit agreed with the District Court that Suders had presented evidence sufficient for a trier of fact to conclude that the supervisors had engaged in a "pattern of sexual harassment that was pervasive and regular." But the appeals court disagreed with the District Court in two fundamental respects. First, the Court of Appeals held that, even assuming the PSP could assert the affirmative defense described in *Ellerth* and *Faragher*, genuine issues of material fact existed concerning the effectiveness of the PSP's "program . . . to address sexual harassment claims." Second, the appeals court held that the District Court erred in failing to recognize that Suders had stated a claim of constructive discharge due to the hostile work environment.

A plaintiff alleging constructive discharge in violation of Title VII, the Court of Appeals stated, must establish:

"(1) he or she suffered harassment or discrimination so intolerable that a reasonable person in the same position would have felt compelled to resign . . . ; and (2) the employee's reaction to the workplace situation — that is, his or her decision to resign — was reasonable given the totality of circumstances. . . ." Viewing the complaint in that context, the court determined that Suders had raised genuine issues of material fact relating to her claim of constructive discharge.

The Court of Appeals then made the ruling challenged here: It held that "a constructive discharge, when proved, constitutes a tangible employment action." Under *Ellerth* and *Faragher*, the court observed, such an action renders an employer strictly liable and precludes employer recourse to the affirmative defense announced in those decisions. The Third Circuit recognized that the Courts of Appeals for the Second and Sixth Circuits had ruled otherwise. This Court granted certiorari, to resolve the disagreement among the Circuits on the question whether a constructive discharge brought about by supervisor harassment ranks as a tangible employment action and therefore precludes assertion of the affirmative defense articulated in *Ellerth* and *Faragher*.

> Prior to this decision, there was a conflict in the courts as to whether a constructive discharge constitutes a tangible employment action.

Under the constructive discharge doctrine, an employee's reasonable decision to resign because of unendurable working conditions is assimilated to a formal discharge for remedial purposes. The inquiry is objective: Did working conditions become so intolerable that a reasonable person in the employee's position would have felt compelled to resign?

This case concerns an employer's liability for one subset of Title VII constructive discharge claims: constructive discharge resulting from sexual harassment, or "hostile work environment," attributable to a supervisor. The constructive discharge here at issue stems from, and can be regarded as an aggravated case of, sexual harassment or hostile work environment. For an atmosphere of sexual harassment or hostility to be actionable, we reiterate, the offending behavior "must be sufficiently severe or pervasive to alter the conditions of the victim's employment and create an abusive working environment." *Meritor*, 477 U.S. at 67 (internal quotation marks and brackets omitted). A hostile- environment constructive discharge claim entails something more: A plaintiff who advances such a compound claim must show working conditions so intolerable that a reasonable person would have felt compelled to resign.

Suders' claim is of the same genre as the hostile work environment claims the Court analyzed in *Ellerth* and *Faragher*. Essentially, Suders presents a "worse case" harassment scenario, harassment ratcheted up to the breaking point. Like the harassment considered in our pathmarking decisions, harassment so intolerable as to cause a resignation may be effected through co-worker conduct, unofficial supervisory conduct, or official company acts. Unlike an actual termination, which is *always* effected through an official act of the company, a constructive discharge need not be. A constructive discharge involves both an employee's decision to leave and precipitating conduct: The former involves no official action; the latter, like a harassment claim without any constructive discharge assertion, may or may not involve official action.

To be sure, a constructive discharge is functionally the same as an actual termination in damages-enhancing respects. As the Third Circuit observed, both "en[d] the employer-employee relationship," and both "inflic[t] . . . direct economic harm." 325 F.3d at 460 (internal quotation marks omitted). But when an official act does not underlie the constructive discharge, the *Ellerth* and *Faragher* analysis, we here hold, calls for extension of the affirmative defense

> The Court's decision here opens the door for employers to offer an affirmative defense in constructive discharge cases.

to the employer. As those leading decisions indicate, official directions and declarations are the acts most likely to be brought home to the employer, the measures over which the employer can exercise greatest control. Absent "an official act of the enterprise," as the last straw, the employer ordinarily would have no particular reason to suspect that a resignation is not the typical kind daily occurring in the work force. And as *Ellerth* and *Faragher* further point out, an official act reflected in company records — a demotion or a reduction in compensation, for example — shows "beyond question" that the supervisor has used his managerial or controlling position to the employee's disadvantage. Absent such an official act, the extent to which the supervisor's misconduct has been aided by the agency relation, as we earlier recounted, is less certain. That uncertainty, our precedent establishes, justifies affording the employer the chance to establish, through the *Ellerth/Faragher* affirmative defense, that it should not be held vicariously liable.

■ NOTES AND QUESTIONS

1. The Court here holds that where "an official act does not underlie the constructive discharge, the *Ellerth* and *Faragher* analysis . . . calls for extension of the affirmative defense to the employer." *Suders*, 542 U.S. at 148. The Court's holding means that in many (if not most) hostile work environment cases, a constructive discharge will not rise to the level of being a tangible employment action. The employer will have the opportunity in these cases to avoid liability through the use of the affirmative defense. Is this a fair assessment of the law, given that the employee is essentially being forced out of her job?

2. What type of factors could the defendant establish to show that it should not be held liable under the affirmative defense in a constructive discharge case?

3. Given the egregious facts that were present in this case, as a matter of policy, should the employer have the opportunity to avoid liability?

4. Assume that you are a human resources manager. An employee comes to you and says she wants to report sexual harassment, but will only do so if you promise confidentiality. What are the risks to the company if you agree to this request?

 Interactive Problem

Looking back at the facts of the interactive problem at the beginning of the chapter, assume that after Sarah complained of sexual harassment, she received an anonymous message on her cell phone stating that "she was no longer welcome at work, and if she returns, no one could guarantee her safety." If Sarah quit after receiving this message, could she claim constructive discharge?

Practice and Procedural Tip ▶ ## 16: Investigating Harassment Claims

One issue that frequently arises in harassment cases is how to investigate a harassment claim. There is no perfect model for conducting an investigation into harassment allegations. However, there are a number of considerations that should be kept in mind.

First, and foremost, it is critical that the person performing the investigation is a neutral party that has no bias in the matter. The allegations can often consist of he-said-she-said accusations, and any bias can stain the entire investigation. Thus, it is not unusual to have the investigation performed by someone from a completely separate part of the company — such as a human resources professional. Additionally, and particularly in smaller companies, it is not uncommon to have the investigation undertaken by someone from completely outside the organization, including a law firm or consulting group that is not a repeat player with the employer. By having a *truly* neutral third party conduct the investigation, there can be no argument in subsequent litigation that the investigation was conducted in an unfair or biased manner.

Second, it is important for the company not to have a "knee jerk" reaction against the alleged harasser. While quickly taking an adverse action against the alleged harasser may seem logical, it is not always the best course of action. Harassers who are punished without a fair investigation may themselves have claims that they can assert against the company, usually arising in the common law context. Such claims would include defamation and negligent (or intentional) infliction of emotional distress. Thus, any sanction against a party involved in the investigation should only come after careful consideration, and it should be proportional to the conduct involved.

Third, documentation is key at every step of the investigation. Thus, documenting conversations with relevant witnesses is critical, as is gathering any evidence that might be present. Email communications should be sought, and anyone with relevant information in the case should be interviewed.

Fourth, confidentiality cannot be guaranteed to witnesses in these matters. When questioning a party or witness, it is common for these individuals to ask, "Will you keep everything that I say confidential?" The investigator's response to this question simply *cannot* be "yes." Should the matter find its way into litigation, there is a strong likelihood that the interview will have to be revealed. And, the information may also have to be shared with corporate leaders so that an educated decision can be made on how to proceed. It is reasonable to assure the witness, however, that the material will be kept confidential to the extent possible. No absolute guarantees should ever be made in this regard.

Finally, if an outside third party investigates the harassment claim, the investigation may be considered a "credit report" under the Fair Credit Reporting Act. This would mean that the alleged harasser may be able to gain access to the investigator's report under federal law. Again, keep in mind that the investigation and report will not be confidential, and may have to be shared with others as the process unfolds.

The EEOC has provided some general guidance on the types of questions to ask the complainant, the alleged harasser, and witnesses when investigating harassment claims. This guidance should be considered:

Questions to Ask the Complainant

- Who, what, when, where, and how: Who committed the alleged harassment? What exactly occurred or was said? When did it occur and is it still ongoing? Where did it occur? How often did it occur? How did it affect you?
- How did you react? What response did you make when the incident(s) occurred or afterwards?
- How did the harassment affect you? Has your job been affected in any way?
- Are there any persons who have relevant information? Was anyone present when the alleged harassment occurred? Did you tell anyone about it? Did anyone see you immediately after episodes of alleged harassment?
- Did the person who harassed you harass anyone else? Do you know whether anyone complained about harassment by that person?
- Are there any notes, physical evidence, or other documentation regarding the incident(s)?

- How would you like to see the situation resolved?
- Do you know of any other relevant information?

Questions to Ask the Alleged Harasser

- What is your response to the allegations?
- If the harasser claims that the allegations are false, ask why the complainant might lie.
- Are there any persons who have relevant information?
- Are there any notes, physical evidence, or other documentation regarding the incident(s)?
- Do you know of any other relevant information?

Questions to Ask Third Parties

- What did you see or hear? When did this occur? Describe the alleged harasser's behavior toward the complainant and toward others in the workplace.
- What did the complainant tell you? When did he or she tell you this?
- Do you know of any other relevant information?
- Are there other persons who have relevant information?

EEOC Enforcement Guidance: Vicarious Employer Liab. for Unlawful Harassment by Supervisors, EEOC Compl. Man. (CCH) ¶ 3116 § V(C)(1)(e)(i) (June 18, 1999).

F. First Amendment Defense

As seen in this chapter, one common theme in the harassment context is that many claims that arise will be verbal in nature. It is not uncommon for employees to make racial or sexual jokes or comments in the workplace. Thus, many — but not all — cases turn primarily on words that are communicated in the workplace.

Where the alleged harassment is entirely verbal in nature, a natural question that arises is whether the employer can use a First Amendment defense to avoid liability under Title VII. In other words, does the employer have "freedom of speech" to make demeaning comments about a person's race, color, sex, national origin, or religion?

Lyle v. Warner Bros. Television Productions
38 Cal. 4th 264 (2006)

BAXTER, J.

Plaintiff was a comedy writers' assistant who worked on the production of a popular television show called *Friends.* The show revolved around a group of young, sexually active adults, featured adult-oriented sexual humor, and typically relied on sexual and anatomical language, innuendo, wordplay, and physical gestures to convey its humor. Before plaintiff was hired, she had been forewarned that the show dealt with sexual matters and that, as an assistant to the comedy writers, she would be listening to their sexual jokes and discussions about sex and transcribing the jokes and dialogue most likely to be used for scripts. After four months of employment, plaintiff was fired because of problems with her typing and transcription. She then filed this action against three of the male comedy writers and others, asserting among other things that the writers' use of sexually coarse and vulgar language and conduct, including the recounting of their own sexual experiences, constituted harassment based on sex within the meaning of the Fair Employment and Housing Act (the FEHA).

The Court of Appeal reversed the trial court's order granting summary judgment on plaintiff's sexual harassment action. We granted review to address whether the use of sexually coarse and vulgar language in the workplace can constitute harassment based on sex within the meaning of the FEHA, and if so, whether the imposition of liability under the FEHA for such speech would infringe on defendants' federal and state constitutional rights of free speech.

Here, the record discloses that most of the sexually coarse and vulgar language at issue did not involve and was not aimed at plaintiff or other women in the workplace. Based on the totality of the undisputed circumstances, particularly the fact the *Friends* production was a creative workplace focused on generating scripts for an adult-oriented comedy show featuring sexual themes, we find no reasonable trier of fact could conclude such language constituted harassment directed at plaintiff because of her sex within the meaning of the FEHA. Furthermore, to the extent triable issues of fact exist as to whether certain offensive comments were made about women other than plaintiff because of their sex, we find no reasonable trier of fact could conclude these particular comments were severe enough or sufficiently pervasive to create a work environment that was hostile or abusive to plaintiff in violation of the FEHA. Accordingly, we remand the matter with directions to affirm the summary judgment order insofar as it pertains to plaintiff's sexual harassment action, without addressing the potential of infringement on defendants' constitutional rights of free speech.

[The majority's analysis and discussion of the facts is omitted.]

Concurring Opinion by CHIN, J.

I agree that the trial court properly granted summary judgment in favor of defendants under the relevant statutes. I write separately to explain that any other result would violate free speech rights under the First Amendment of the United States Constitution and its California counterpart, article I, section 2 of the California Constitution (hereafter collectively the First Amendment).

This case has very little to do with sexual harassment and very much to do with core First Amendment free speech rights. The writers of the television show, *Friends*, were engaged in a *creative process* — writing adult comedy — when the alleged harassing conduct occurred. The First Amendment protects creativity. *Friends* was entertainment, but entertainment is fully entitled to First Amendment

> **Unlike the majority opinion, the concurrence addresses the First Amendment question head-on in this case.**

protection. Scripts of the *Friends* show "'are no less protected because they provide humorous rather than serious commentary.'" (*Comedy III Productions, Inc. v. Gary Saderup, Inc.* (2001) 25 Cal. 4th 387, 406.)

We have found that the First Amendment protects even threatening speech that does not rise to a criminal threat. (*In re George T.* (2004) 33 Cal. 4th 620 [dark poetry in school].) Similarly, we should protect the creative speech here. I do not suggest that the First Amendment protects all sexually harassing speech. Just as the First Amendment does not protect criminal threats, so too may the state proscribe sexual harassment. But the proscription must be carefully tailored to avoid infringing on First Amendment free speech rights in the creative process.

Balancing the compelling need to protect employees from sexual harassment with free speech rights can, in some contexts, present very difficult questions. For example, a potential, and sometimes real, tension between free speech and antiharassment laws exists even in the ordinary workplace. Debating these issues has kept academia occupied. Lawsuits like this one, directed at restricting the creative process in a workplace *whose very business is speech related*, present a clear and present danger to fundamental free speech rights. Even academics who generally defend antiharassment law against First Amendment attack recognize the importance of defending the First Amendment in a context like this.

The writers here did at times go to extremes in the creative process. They pushed the limits — hard. Some of what they did might be incomprehensible to people unfamiliar with the creative process. But that is what creative people sometimes have to do. As explained in an amicus curiae brief representing the Writers Guild of America, West, Inc.; the Directors Guild of America; the Screen Actors Guild; and 131 named individuals representing a "who's who" of television and motion picture writers and directors (hereafter the Writers Guild brief), "the process creators go through to capture the necessary magic is inexact, counterintuitive, nonlinear, often painful — and above all, delicate. And the problem is even more complicated for group writing." "Group writing," the brief explains, "requires an atmosphere of complete trust. Writers must feel not only that it's all right to fail, but also that they can share their most private and darkest thoughts without concern for ridicule or embarrassment or legal accountability." The brief quotes Steven Bochco, cocreator of *Hill Street Blues*, *L.A. Law*, and *NYPD Blue*, and one of the individuals the brief represents, as explaining that a "certain level of intimacy is required to do the work at its best, and so there is an implicit contract among the writers: what is said in the room, stays in the room." The brief further explains that "with adult audiences in particular, the characters, dialogue, and stories must ring true. That means on shows like *Law and Order*, *ER*, or *The Sopranos*, writers must tap into places in their experience or psyches that most of us are far too polite or self-conscious to bring up."

The creative process must be unfettered, especially because it can often take strange turns, as many bizarre and potentially offensive ideas are suggested, tried, and, in the end, either discarded or used. As the Writers Guild brief notes, "*All in the Family* pushed the limits in its day, but with race rather than sex." The brief quotes Norman Lear, *All in the Family*'s creator, and another of the individuals on whose behalf the brief was filed, as saying, "We were dealing with racism and constantly on dangerous ground. . . . We cleaned up a lot of what was said in the room, and some people *still* found it offensive." It is hard to imagine *All in the Family* having been successfully written if the writers and others involved in the creative process had to fear lawsuits by employees who claimed to be offended by the process of discovering what worked and did not work, what was funny and what was not funny, that led to the racial and ethnic humor actually used in the show.

"[S]peech may not be prohibited because it concerns subjects offending our sensibilities." (*Ashcroft v. Free Speech Coalition* (2002) 535 U.S. 234, 245.) We must not permit juries to dissect the creative process in order to determine what was *necessary* to achieve the final product and what was not, and to impose liability for sexual harassment for that portion deemed unnecessary. Creativity is, by its nature, creative. It is unpredictable. Much that is not obvious can be necessary to the creative process. Accordingly, courts may not constitutionally ask whether challenged speech was necessary for its intended purpose.

For this reason, it is meaningless to argue, as plaintiff does, that much of what occurred in this process did not make its way into the actual shows. The First Amendment also protects attempts at creativity that end in failure. That which ends up on the cutting room floor is also part of the creative process. An amicus curiae brief representing, among others, the American Booksellers Foundation for Free Expression explains: "To require the participants to justify after the fact the 'necessity' of minor segments of the creative process represents a misunderstanding of the creative process. That process usually includes many dead ends that are not reflected in the final work. But the dead ends are part of creating the final work; the fact that one approach or suggestion is not productive is part of the process of creatively reaching end result. In that sense the dead ends, as well as everything else in the creative process, are necessary."

The Writers Guild brief explains it similarly. "[T]he creative person tr[ies] one notion after another before coming up with the final product. Writers are like scavengers and get their ideas wherever they can: 'Ninety percent of everything doesn't work,' says Lear, 'That's why it's so hard, that's why you spend so much time there.' . . . Lear puts it this way: 'There were things we said we would never print. That's true of racism or any touchy subject. That's what it takes to make a great show: smart people sitting in a room, going wherever they want." As that brief notes, "It is impossible to imagine how writers, directors, and actors could work together if they had to worry about doing only what was 'creatively necessary' in order not to offend a worker on the set."

Does this mean that anything that occurs while writing a television show is permissible? Do employees involved in that process receive no protection? Of course not. Just as criminal threats are not protected, just as no one has the right to falsely shout "fire" in a crowded theater, limits exist as to what may occur in the writers' room. I agree with Professor Volokh that, even in this context, speech that is *directed*, or "aimed at a particular employee because of her race, sex, religion, or national origin," is not protected. (Eugene Volokh, *Freedom of Speech and Workplace Harassment*, 39 U.C.L.A. L. Rᴇᴠ. 1791, 1846 (1992)). "The state interest in assuring equality in the workplace would justify restricting directed speech. . . ." (*Ibid.*) Speech directed towards plaintiff *because* of her sex could not further the creative process.

Accordingly, I agree with the general test proposed in the amicus curiae brief of the California Newspaper Publishers Association et al.: "Where, as here, an employer's product is protected by the First Amendment — whether it be a television program, a newspaper, a book, or any other similar work — the challenged speech should not be actionable if the court finds that the speech arose in the context of the creative and/or editorial process, and it was not directed at or about the plaintiff." This test presents the proper balance. Often, free speech cases involve the very difficult balancing of important competing interests. But here, in the creative context, free speech is critical while the competing interest — protecting employees involved in the creative process against offensive language and conduct *not directed at them* — is, in comparison, minimal. Neither plaintiff nor anyone else is required to become part of a creative team. But those who choose to join a creative team should not be allowed to complain that some of the creativity was offensive or that behavior not directed at them was unnecessary to the creative process.

Cases like this, arising in a creative context, often can and should be decided on demurrer. Because even the taking of depositions could significantly chill the creative process, by destroying the mutual trust and confidentiality necessary to writing television shows like *Friends*, courts should independently review the allegations to ensure that First Amendment rights are not being violated. If the complaint does not allege that the offending conduct was pervasive and *directed at the plaintiff*, and include specific supporting facts that, if true, would establish those allegations, the court should grant a demurrer. The threat of litigation must not be permitted to stifle creativity.

We must "[a]lways remember[ ] that the widest scope of freedom is to be given to the adventurous and imaginative exercise of the human spirit. . . ." (*Kingsley Pictures Corp. v. Regents* (1959) 360 U.S. 684 (conc. opn. of FRANKFURTER, J.)) We must not tolerate laws that "lead to timidity and inertia and thereby discourage the boldness of expression indispensable for a progressive society." (*Ibid.*) The allegedly offending conduct in this case arose out of the protected creative process and was not directed at plaintiff. Accordingly, the trial court properly granted summary judgment in defendants' favor. The First Amendment demands no less.

■ NOTES AND QUESTIONS

1. The majority opinion — largely omitted above — does not resolve the case on First Amendment grounds. Why would the majority avoid this issue?

2. Should we examine the content of particular speech to determine whether it is potentially protected by the First Amendment? Here, the speech took place in a creative environment — should that grant additional protections to the defendant?

3. Is it important that the plaintiff was warned before starting the job that she would encounter vulgar speech as part of her position?

4. First Amendment defenses to harassment claims are interesting to debate. As the concurring opinion above demonstrates, law professors have written much on this topic. Nonetheless, the defense is not widely used in practice. Why?

5. The First Amendment defense — where it has been raised — typically fails. The courts have offered varying rationales for rejecting the defense, which include that the speech includes fighting words, that Title VII is narrowly tailored, and that the prohibition of harassing speech is limited in scope and time.

6. The concurrence suggests adopting a rule that "the challenged speech should not be actionable if the court finds that the speech arose in the context of the creative and/or editorial process, and it was not directed at or about the plaintiff." Would such a rule make sense in the workplace?

7. Employees generally may not waive their Title VII rights, or otherwise acquiesce to discriminatory conduct.

8. Should there be any differences in how the law treats working in a creative environment like the one here versus in a steel mill where male employees have historically used sexually explicit language and posted pornography on the walls?

 ## Interactive Problem

Looking back at the facts of the interactive problem at the beginning of the chapter, assume that Sarah decides that she is going to run for local office so that she can seek to enact more aggressive harassment laws. When her shift manager finds out about her plans to run for office, he states, "No one is going to vote for you. You are just a stupid woman." Could the employer successfully argue that this comment would be protected by the First Amendment and thus not be actionable under Title VII?

 # G. Chapter-in-Review

The law on harassment can be extraordinarily confusing. Even the federal courts and academics struggle with how to apply the various terms in this area of the law. The diagram below provides a useful resource when analyzing any claim of harassment. Though unique circumstances (such as proxy liability) can arise outside of the flowchart offered below, this diagram nonetheless provides a generalized summary of the analysis that should be undertaken for any harassment claim.

When analyzing harassment, the first critical question is whether the harassment was based on a protected characteristic. If it was not, the case should be dismissed. The next question that should be addressed is whether a tangible employment action is involved in the case. If a tangible employment action has occurred (and it was based on a protected characteristic), judgment should be entered in favor of the plaintiff. No affirmative defense is available.

Where no tangible employment action is present, there is still the potential for a hostile work environment claim. Initially, it should be considered whether the conduct at issue was welcomed by the plaintiff. As we know from *Meritor*, voluntariness does not equate with being welcome.

Next, it should be determined whether the facts present sufficient evidence of severity or pervasiveness. Typically, the most important inquiry for hostile work environment claims is whether or not the conduct at issue is severe or pervasive. A close analysis of jurisdictional law is important in making this determination. The courts vary widely when defining what is or is not severe or pervasive conduct, and this is often the decisive question in a hostile work environment case. As noted earlier, severity or pervasiveness is typically analyzed on a sliding scale. The more severe the conduct is, the less pervasive it must be to satisfy the legal standard.

If a hostile work environment is indeed present, the next critical question is whether or not a supervisor is involved in the harassment. As we learned in the *Vance* decision, a supervisor is one who has the authority to take a tangible employment action. Where a supervisor is implicated, the defendant will still have an affirmative defense available. Usually, this defense focuses on whether the employer has created and properly maintained an effective anti-harassment policy. Also, the defense examines whether the plaintiff properly availed herself of that policy.

Where a co-worker (rather than a supervisor) is involved, the lowest level of liability is in question — employer negligence. If the employer knew or should have known that the harassment was occurring, but failed to take appropriate remedial action, liability may attach. Typically, customer harassment claims are also considered under this negligence standard.

Finally, it is important to note that while sex harassment and race harassment claims are the most common, hostile work environments can arise under any protected category. Thus, an individual can bring a harassment claim based on age, disability, national origin, or religion in addition to the more common sex and race claims.

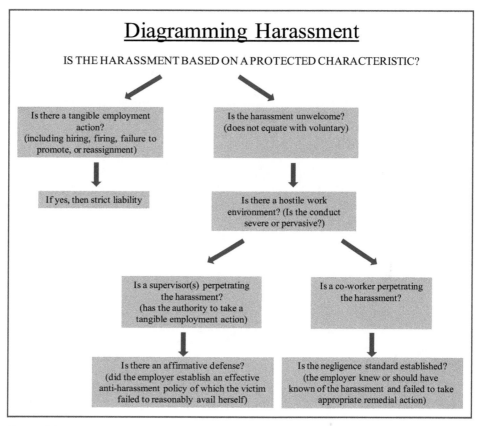

Figure 5.1

PART THREE

Enforcement by Protected Class

IT SEEMED LIKE REACHING FOR THE MOON.
BARBARA JOHNS

6

Race and Color Discrimination

 ## Interactive Problem

Alan Actor, an African-American male, pursued an acting career in Los Angeles for years with little success. While talking with his agent, he learned that Big Studios, Inc. was putting together a large-budget movie production on the life and times of George Washington. As a huge history buff, Alan believed that he would be great for this role, and he applied for the part. Based on his résumé, he was given an audition to read for the role. But when Alan showed up to audition for the part, the film's director appeared displeased with Alan's appearance. Before even allowing him to read a single line, the director exclaimed, "George Washington was white. You are black. How can you possibly ever expect to play this role? I can't believe you wasted everyone's time here today. Please don't ever try to audition for me again for any role — you won't get it." Saddened and disheartened by the director's reaction, Alan quickly became depressed and anxious that he would never work in Hollywood again. He decided to return to his hometown of Lincoln, Nebraska. On his way out of the city, however, he stopped by the local EEOC office. Will the EEOC tell Alan that he has a strong case against Big Studios, Inc.? Why or why not? What would be Alan's best arguments in the case? What would be the best arguments of Big Studios, Inc.?

A. Introduction

Race and color discrimination have been among the most pervasive forms of discrimination in the United States for years. Constant, egregious, and open race discrimination in the early 1960s was one of the motivating factors behind the passage of Title VII.

President Kennedy was sympathetic to the civil rights movement, but at the beginning of his presidency he was reticent to push for strong legislation. In April 1963, Martin Luther King, Jr., and other civil rights leaders led a series of peaceful demonstrations to protest deep-seated segregation. In May 1963, demonstrators marched into downtown Birmingham, where the local police, led by T. Eugene ("Bull") Connor, used such brutal tactics as dogs, fire hoses, and cattle prods to drive back or arrest protesters. The protests lasted several days, but despite mass public outcry, President Kennedy insisted the federal government could take no action in Birmingham because no federal law had been broken. On May 12, 1963, bombings at the home of A.D. King and the integration movement's headquarters caused full-scale violent riots.

The visceral images on television and in newsprint brought the harsh reality of segregation to a national audience, and public support moved steadily in favor of civil rights legislation thereafter. On May 31, 1963, President Kennedy announced in a televised address: "I shall ask the Congress of the United States to act, to make a commitment it has not fully made in this century to the proposition that race has no place in American life or law." Later, in a meeting of key civil rights leaders at the White House, when Bull Connor was mentioned derisively, the President retorted, "'Bull Connor' has done more for civil rights than

Civil Rights Leaders After a Meeting with President John F. Kennedy's Cabinet and Staff

anyone in this room." Robert D. Loevy, To End All Segregation: The Politics of the Passage of the Civil Rights Act of 1964 16, 17 (1990); Joseph L. Rauh, Jr., *The Role of the Leadership Conference on Civil Rights in the Civil Rights Struggle of 1963–1964*, in The Civil Rights Act of 1964: The Passage of the Law That Ended Racial Segregation 53 (Robert D. Loevy ed., 1997).

Given this history, the foundations of Title VII were largely targeted at preventing racial discrimination. Indeed, some of the exclusions found in employment discrimination law (such as the bona fide occupational qualification) do not apply to claims brought on the basis of race or color. Congress was clear that there is never an excuse or reason to discriminate on this basis. Nonetheless, race discrimination remains widespread, and typically comprises more than a third of all charges filed with the EEOC. The basis for federal protection against race and color discrimination arises in Title VII, § 2000e–2(a)(1), which provides:

> It shall be an unlawful employment practice for an employer . . . to fail or refuse to hire or to discharge any individual, or otherwise to discriminate against any individual with respect to his compensation, terms, conditions, or privileges of employment, because of such individual's race [or] color.

B. EEOC Guidance

The EEOC has long understood the problem of race and color discrimination in our society, and has provided substantial guidance on this issue. The EEOC defines race discrimination as including:

Ancestry: Employment discrimination because of racial or ethnic ancestry. Discrimination against a person because of his or her ancestry can violate Title VII's prohibition against race discrimination. Note that there can be considerable overlap between "race" and "national origin," but they are not identical. For example, discrimination against a Chinese American might be targeted at her Asian ancestry and not her Chinese national origin. In that case, she would have a claim of discrimination based on race, not national origin.

Physical Characteristics: Employment discrimination based on a person's physical characteristics associated with race, such as a person's color, hair, facial features, height and weight.

Race-linked Illness: Discrimination based on race-linked illnesses. For example, sickle cell anemia is a genetically-transmitted disease that affects primarily persons of African descent. Other diseases, while not linked directly to race or ethnicity, may nevertheless have a disproportionate impact. For example, Native Hawaiians have a disproportionately high incidence of diabetes. If the employer applies facially neutral standards to exclude treatment for conditions or risks that disproportionately affect employees on the basis of race or ethnicity, the employer must show that the standards are based on generally accepted medical criteria.

Culture: Employment discrimination because of cultural characteristics related to race or ethnicity. Title VII prohibits employment discrimination against a person because of cultural characteristics often linked to race or ethnicity, such as a person's name, cultural dress and grooming practices, or accent or manner of speech. For example, an employment decision based on a person having a so-called "Black accent," or "sounding White," violates Title VII if the accent or manner of speech does not materially interfere with the ability to perform job duties.

Perception: Employment discrimination against an individual based on a belief that the individual is a member of a particular racial group, regardless of how the individual identifies himself. Discrimination against an individual based on a perception of his or her race violates Title VII even if that perception is wrong.

Association: Employment discrimination against an individual because of his/her association with someone of a particular race. For example, it is unlawful to discriminate against a White person because he or she is married to an African American or has a multiracial child, or because he or she maintains friendships or otherwise associates with persons of a certain race.

Subgroup or "Race Plus": Title VII prohibits discrimination against a subgroup of persons in a racial group because they have certain attributes in addition to their race. Thus, for example, it would violate Title VII for an employer to reject Black women with preschool age children, while not rejecting other women with preschool age children.

EEOC Compl. Man. (CCH) ¶ 8710, § 15-II (2006).

While the courts take varying approaches as to whether such characteristics as culture, perception, and association can constitute race discrimination, from a more practical standpoint it is best for an employer to avoid relying on any of these factors when making an employment decision. An employer using these criteria to make a decision risks embroiling itself in time-consuming and expensive litigation.

Color discrimination is closely related to race discrimination, but focuses more on employment actions based on one's skin pigmentation. It is important to note that race and color are separated out in the statute, as discrimination on the basis of one does not necessarily imply discrimination on the basis of the other. Indeed, some color discrimination cases arise where there is discrimination by or in favor of someone in the same racial group. For example, a black person of darker complexion might discriminate against a black person of lighter complexion when making an employment decision. The EEOC has also addressed this type of discrimination, and defines color discrimination as that based on

pigmentation, complexion, or skin shade or tone. Thus, color discrimination occurs when a person is discriminated against based on the lightness, darkness, or other color characteristic of the person. Even though race and color clearly overlap, they are not synonymous. Thus, color discrimination can occur between persons of different races or ethnicities, or between persons of the same race or ethnicity.

EEOC Compl. Man. (CCH) ¶ 8720, § 15-III (2006).

It may not always be clear whether a particular act falls within the ambit of race or color discrimination, as there is certainly some ambiguity in this area. Nonetheless, in the vast majority of racial discrimination cases, it is fairly clear that the allegations would fall squarely under this category. For example, when a worker claims that she has been fired because she is black, there is no doubt that these allegations fall under a racial discrimination analysis.

As race discrimination claims comprised a large portion of the early Title VII cases, the law largely developed under these types of claims. For example, both the *McDonnell Douglas* and *Griggs* decisions were based on cases that involved allegations of race discrimination. The tests were founded on this protected characteristic. For that reason, the *McDonnell Douglas* test and disparate impact analysis clearly apply to race and color claims.

C. Discrimination — An Ongoing Problem

It is tempting to believe that race discrimination has largely been eradicated in American society. While there can be little doubt that the working environment has improved since the passage of Title VII, race discrimination is still present in our culture. Indeed, in fiscal year 2017, race discrimination claims accounted for a third of all charges filed with the EEOC, comprising more than 28,000 private sector workplace claims. *See* EEOC, Charge Statistics, FY 1997–FY 2017, http://eeoc.gov/eeoc/statistics/enforcement/charges.cfm.

It may be that much of this discrimination has been driven underground or is now largely subconscious. Nonetheless, cases are routinely filed, showing that race discrimination is still a persistent problem in our society. *See* Linda Hamilton Krieger & Susan T. Fiske, *Behavioral Realism in Employment Discrimination Law: Implicit Bias and Disparate Treatment*, 94 Calif. L. Rev. 997, 1033–1034 (2006); Charles R. Lawrence III, *The Id, the Ego, and Equal Protection: Reckoning with Unconscious Racism*, 39 Stan. L. Rev. 317 (1987); Kenneth B. Nunn, *Diversity as a Dead-End*, 35 Pepp. L. Rev. 705, 729 (2008); Terry Smith, *Speaking Against Norms: Public Discourse and the Economy of Racialization in the Workplace*, 57 Am. U. L. Rev. 523, 530 n.27 (2008); Amy L. Wax, *Discrimination as Accident*, 74 Ind. L.J. 1129 (1999).

For example, in the summer of 2013, three Hispanic former employees of a Target warehouse in California sued the retail giant for racial discrimination and harassment. The employees alleged that they were regularly harassed and discriminated against by their basically all-white management team, claiming that supervisors referred to the workers as "wetbacks" and made comments such as "you got to be a Mexican to work like this." The allegations also included a physical copy of a document printed on company letterhead and titled "Organization Effectiveness, Employee and Labor Relations Multi-Cultural Tips." The document included a demeaning list about Hispanic employees and stereotypes, including statements such as "Food: not everyone eats tacos and burritos" and "Music: not everyone dances to salsa." The document also stated that family is the highest priority for Hispanics and suggested that managers should try to take advantage of these strong familial tendencies to motivate the Hispanic workers. Target responded by arguing that this memorandum was used only during conversations at one distribution center and was not intended to be part of a formal, company-wide training procedure. While Target appeared apologetic and insisted that the memorandum was not reflective of what the company is, this document seems to be the type of "smoking gun" that generally helps win discrimination lawsuits. *See* Kim Bhasin, *Target Admits Reminding Managers That Not All Hispanics "Wear Sombreros,"* Huffington Post (July 10, 2013, 12:53 a.m.), http://www.huffingtonpost.com/2013/07/10/target-discrimination_n_3570717.html.

This example clearly shows that racial discrimination persists in American society. Similarly, the following case demonstrates that race discrimination is far from simply a vestige of the past.

EEOC v. Pipefitters Ass'n Local Union 597

334 F.3d 656 (7th Cir. 2003)

POSNER, J.

The EEOC brought suit against Foster Wheeler Constructors, the prime contractor on a project to construct a recycling plant in Robbins, Illinois, and a local of the pipefitters union that supplied workers to Foster Wheeler. The suit, based on Title VII and also on 42 U.S.C. § 1981 — but the standards are the same under the two statutes, at least so far as bears on this case — sought to affix liability to the defendants for the harassment of black pipefitters by their white coworkers. One of the eight pipefitters on whose behalf the EEOC had sued, James Ferguson, intervened in the suit as a plaintiff, as he was entitled to do, 42 U.S.C. § 2000e-5(f)(1), seeking higher damages than those sought on his behalf by the Commission. Foster Wheeler settled, but the case against the union proceeded to a bench trial, which the plaintiffs won. The judge awarded compensatory damages to the EEOC on behalf of the eight black workers totaling $105,000, punitive damages of $50,000, and an injunction against the union's "permitting a hostile work environment based on race to exist for its members at any job site." The union appeals.

The harassment consisted primarily of graffiti scrawled on the interior walls of portable toilets at the construction site — slogans such as "death to all niggers," "your grandmother is such a slut she even fucks niggers," "Fergie [plaintiff James Ferguson], if you don't want to be treated like a nigger, don't act like one," "The shines are ruining this country," and "Fuck Niggers." Additional acts of harassment included the placing of a swastika in a black pipefitter's toolbox, the hanging of a Ku Klux Klan poster in a trailer used by black pipefitters during breaks, and the display of a hangman's noose. That the effect of the graffiti and the other acts, considered together, was to create a hostile working environment for the black pipefitters is not in doubt. The only question is the union's legal responsibility.

> This case demonstrates some of the egregious racial comments and acts that allegedly still pervade the workplace.

Dennis Hahney, the union steward for the Robbins project and also Foster Wheeler's superintendent of pipefitting, and in the latter capacity essentially the superintendent of the pipefitters assigned to the project, was aware of the graffiti, but he did nothing about them until Ferguson complained about the ones that mentioned him. Hahney responded by ordering a foreman to paint over the graffiti; and this was done. Hahney testified that if he were aware of a safety problem he would take action, and indeed that if he had thought the portable toilets needed cleaning he would have seen to it that they were cleaned. But he didn't try to rid the toilets of graffiti. Another union official, Steven Toth, who also knew about the racially offensive graffiti, made no effort to eliminate them either, even though he had on his own initiative ordered the painting over of a drawing in one of the toilets of a penis and a vagina because he thought the drawing might be considered "a little offensive." None of the black pipefitters complained to the union about the racially hostile environment created by their white coworkers except Ferguson, and his complaint was narrowly focused on the graffiti that referred to him rather than on the ones that referred to blacks in general.

An employer who is aware of racial or sexual harassment that is making the workplace intolerable for the targets of the harassment, and does nothing to correct the situation, is guilty of violating Title VII. The EEOC argues that when the harassers and the targets are represented by a union, the union has exactly the same legal responsibility as the employer. Objections come quickly to mind. The employer is in a better position than the union to prevent or eliminate harassment because it can discipline its employees; the union cannot. If a worker complains to the union that he is being harassed, all the union can do is file a grievance on his behalf against the employer; the union cannot eliminate the harassment itself — that is the company's responsibility. Since the employer is both fully liable for failing to take effective measures against coworker harassment and far better positioned to apply such measures, what is to be gained, except litigation clutter, by imposing the same liability on the union? Foster Wheeler Constructors is a substantial firm and there is no suggestion that the EEOC could not obtain, on behalf of the eight black workers who were harassed, full relief against Foster Wheeler, which it also sued and which settled.

A further consideration is that members of different unions, or union and nonunion workers, often find themselves working at the same site. Although the portable toilets in which racial graffiti were found were intended for the use primarily of pipefitters, other workers had access to and sometimes used them and may have been responsible for some of the graffiti.

> The question in this case is not whether racial harassment occurred, but whether the union should be liable.

The pipefitters union had no control over workers belonging to other unions, or for that matter over the portable toilets.

Unimpressed by practical considerations — determined, it seems, to show itself as being as formalistic as any court — the EEOC points to section 703(c) of Title VII, which forbids a union "to exclude or to expel from its membership, *or otherwise to discriminate against*, any individual because of his race, color," etc. (emphasis added). It points out that the italicized words are similar to those in section 703(a), which forbids an employer "to fail or refuse to hire or to discharge any individual, or otherwise to discriminate against any individual with respect to his compensation, terms, conditions, or privileges of employment, because of such individual's race, color," etc. Therefore, the EEOC reasons, since an employer is guilty of discriminating if it unreasonably fails to correct a problem of coworker harassment, so must the union be. In other words, since the company is legally responsible for harassment by its employees, the union must be legally responsible for harassment by its members (more precisely, by members of the bargaining unit, since the union cannot insist that they become union members), even though they are the same people.

The asserted symmetry between employer and union is spurious. The duties of nondiscrimination imposed by sections 703(a) and (c) have reference to the respective roles of company and union in the workplace. The company, not the union, controls the workplace, including the portable toilets erected at the site for use by the workers. The union is not the company, but the workers' agent in dealing with the company. If it discriminates in the performance of its agency function, it violates Title VII, but not otherwise. Thus a union that refuses to accept blacks as members, or refuses to press their grievances, is guilty of discrimination. But if it merely fails to effectuate changes in the workplace — if for example it urges the company to take steps to prevent harassment and the company fails to do so — the union is not guilty of discrimination, though the company is. Notice that if the EEOC were right, the company would be liable for the union's discriminating against black employees in the grievance process.

The separate spheres, and correspondingly different responsibilities with regard to discrimination, of labor and management are blurred in the present case by the curious dual role of Hahney as union steward and supervising pipefitter. It seems doubtful, though the point is not pressed by any of the parties, that he was even legally eligible to be a union steward. In implementation of the National Labor Relations Act's prohibition against company unions, the Labor Board has ruled that a supervisory employee of the company cannot hold a union post that would create divided loyalty and thus undermine the union. Hahney's dual role as company supervisor and union steward may have run afoul of this rule, but the only point important to this case is that his dual role makes it unclear whether Ferguson was complaining to him in his capacity as a union steward or in his capacity as a company supervisor. But it is probably the latter. Remember that Hahney ordered a foreman to paint out the graffiti that Ferguson had complained about. When Hahney did this he was acting for the company, because a union official has no authority to order workers to do anything. A union official qua union official cannot order a company foreman to see to it that a portable toilet is repainted any more than he can order the foreman to build a portable toilet.

Ignoring Hahney's anomalous status for the moment, we think the EEOC would if pressed concede that a union is not guilty of discrimination for trying but failing to rectify workplace harassment, and would argue instead that the union must do what it can even if success cannot be guaranteed because the union does not operate the company. But inaction, unless invidious, is not discrimination in any accepted sense of the term. Most people don't take active measures to combat discrimination; their inaction does not condemn them as discriminators. Suppose that a union is lackluster, and while it will file a grievance if pressed to do so by a member of the collective bargaining unit, it will do nothing on its own initiative. We do not understand how such passivity, though it means the union will not take measures to prevent racial harassment on its own initiative, could be thought a form of racial discrimination; yet that is the EEOC's position. Unsurprisingly it has only limited judicial support. (The surprise is that it has any.) *Woods v. Graphic Communications*, 925 F.2d 1195, 1201 (9th Cir. 1991), says that an affirmative duty to prevent racial discrimination "may exist," but only *Howard v. International Molders & Allied Workers Union*, 779 F.2d 1546, 1553 (11th Cir. 1986), actually imposes such a duty. *Thorn v. Amalgamated Transit Union*, 305 F.3d 826, 832–33 (8th Cir. 2002), emphatically denies that there is such a duty; see also *Goodman v. Lukens Steel Co.*, 482 U.S. 656 (1987) (separate opinion). *York v. American Tel. & Tel. Co.*, 95 F.3d 948, 956–57 (10th Cir. 1996), while holding that a union may not "acquiesce" in the employer's unlawful discrimination, states that "mere inaction does not constitute acquiescence," though it is unclear what the court means by "mere inaction."

The dissent, omitted here, discusses how union liability in this context could create an additional watchful eye in the workplace. Does the majority disregard this policy consideration?

An affirmative duty of the union to investigate and rectify discrimination by the employer derives no support from the statutory language, as we have seen, and fills no gap in the remedial scheme that the statute creates. Imposing such a duty would make for factually messy cases because the union's power is so much more limited than the employer's when it comes to making changes in personnel or work rules. (More precisely, because, so far as the evidence suggests, this union's power over personnel and work rules is so much more limited than the employer's; other unions, operating under other collective bargaining agreements, might be delegated additional powers that would alter the analysis in this opinion.) Suppose only one worker is harassing blacks. The union is not his employer and cannot fire him, so the question would be whether it had done all it could to get the company to fire him, and that will often be an impossible question to answer by the methods of litigation. There is also the awkwardness of asking the union to take sides in a dispute between two employees both of whom it has a statutory duty to represent fairly in any disciplinary proceeding by the employer.

For all these reasons, we reject the EEOC's contention that unions have an affirmative duty to prevent racial harassment or other forms of unlawful discrimination in the workplace.

■ NOTES AND QUESTIONS

1. This case demonstrates that racial discrimination continues to be a problem in the workplace. The alleged events that occurred here were largely uncontested on appeal — the dispute was over the legal liability of what occurred.

2. As discussed in Chapter 5, two of the most common forms of harassment are those based on sex and race. This case directly implicates racial harassment.

3. Is it important that the plaintiff was unable to identify exactly who was behind the racially charged acts here?

4. The employer in this matter settled the case with the EEOC. Was this a wise decision? Would the plaintiff have been able to prevail against the employer at trial? On appeal?

5. Can an employer be liable for racial harassment that takes place in the workplace even where the plaintiff is unable to specifically identify who the harasser is? Isn't it possible that someone from the outside (a non-employee and non-union member) was doing the harassing?

6. Once the EEOC had reached a settlement with the employer, should it also be allowed to pursue a claim against the union? Wouldn't this present a double recovery?

7. What policy reasons might lead a court to hold the union liable in this case? Why does Judge Posner believe that policy suggests otherwise?

8. **Racial breakdown in the United States.** The United States has long been known as a melting pot, and one of our country's greatest strengths is its racial diversity. The chart below reflects the percentage of different races in this country as of 2016.

Race	Percent of Population
White alone	76.9
Black or African American alone	13.3
Asian alone	5.7
American Indian or Alaska Native alone	1.3
Native Hawaiian and Other Pacific Islander alone	0.2
Two or More Races	2.6
Hispanic or Latino*	17.8

*Hispanics may be of any race, so percentages are also included in applicable race-specific categories.
Source: U.S. Census Bureau (2016), https://www.census.gov/quickfacts/fact/table/US/PST045216.

Figure 6.1

9. **Historical note.** Martin Luther King, Jr., (1929–1968) played a key role in the American civil rights movement from the mid-1950s until his assassination in 1968. King sought to end racial discrimination, and to raise public consciousness of race-related issues. While his primary goal was racial equality, King plotted out a series of smaller goals that involved grassroots campaigns for equal rights for African Americans. In 1955, King became involved in his first major civil rights campaign in Montgomery, Alabama, where buses were racially segregated. When Rosa Parks, an African-American woman, refused to vacate her bus seat and was subsequently arrested for her civil disobedience, King mobilized Montgomery's African-American community to boycott the city's public transportation, and he successfully demanded equal rights for all citizens on public transportation there.

Martin Luther King, Jr., speaking at an anti-war demonstration in New York City

Subsequently, King gained substantial support for his movement. In 1963, President Kennedy proposed his civil rights bill, and in an effort to persuade Congress to support this bill, King, with other civil rights leaders, organized the legendary march on Washington, which attracted about a quarter million people. Following the march, where King made his famous "I Have a Dream" speech, Congress accepted Kennedy's civil rights bill, which became the 1964 Civil Rights Act. King then moved on to support a bill that would guarantee voting rights for African Americans, known as the 1965 Voting Rights Act. *See About Dr. King*, THE KING CENTER (2014), http://www.thekingcenter. org/about-dr-king.

 ## *Interactive Problem*

Looking back at the interactive problem, assume that Alan was a member of the Screen Actors Guild of America, and he notified the Guild of the comments made to him at his audition. Would the Guild have an obligation to pursue a claim on Alan's behalf under Title VII?

Class Exercise: Implicit Bias

Discrimination on the basis of race has evolved over the years. As we saw in *Griggs v. Duke Power*, it was not uncommon at one time for black workers to be openly discriminated against on the basis of their race. While such overt discrimination still occurs, many of our biases may now be more subconscious in nature. Do you believe that you have any biases against protected groups? One study attempts to measure just that. Working individually, go to the following website to take the race-based Implicit Association Test: https://implicit.harvard.edu/implicit/takeatest.html.

Allegations of blatant racial discrimination continue to pervade the courts. As seen below, these claims continue to be egregious in nature.

Henderson v. Irving Materials, Inc.

329 F. Supp. 2d 1002 (S.D. Ind. 2004)

HAMILTON, District Judge.

This Title VII case alleging a racially hostile environment is before the court on defendants' motion for summary judgment. Plaintiff Nathaniel Henderson, an African American, began working for SouthSide on April 9, 2001 as a concrete truck driver. Henderson was assigned to work at the Harding Street Plant in Indianapolis, Indiana. He was the first and only black person hired by SouthSide. Henderson's immediate supervisor was Willie Taylor, the plant manager for the Harding Street Plant.

Defendant Mitchell Santerre began working for SouthSide in 1987. Defendant Reed Moistner began working for SouthSide on April 27, 2001. Both defendants are white males and both worked with Henderson at the Harding Street Plant during the time in question. Plant manager Taylor's office was right next to the employee break room. The two rooms were separated by a wall with a window opening. Taylor would fraternize with employees in the break room. From his office, Taylor would also speak to employees and distribute work papers to them through the open window. Beginning in April 2001, Henderson heard Moistner telling racist jokes to co-workers, including Santerre. These episodes occurred in

the employee break room on a regular basis, as much as nine times per month. In these jokes, Moistner would use the terms "black," "nigger," "coon," and "spook." Henderson protested several times and told Moistner directly that he "didn't care to hear that mess." To no avail. The jokes continued until November when Moistner was transferred to a different facility. Plant manager Taylor was present when Moistner told racially disparaging jokes and when Henderson protested, and Taylor even laughed at the jokes himself.

As a truck driver for SouthSide, Henderson wore a uniform with his name on it. He kept some of his uniforms at work. In September or October 2001, someone cut the buttons off of several of his uniform work shirts. In September or October 2001, Santerre approached Henderson in the employee break room. He told Henderson that no one wanted Henderson working there and that Henderson should get another job. Moistner was present, as was plant manager Taylor.

Toward the beginning of October 2001 on a Saturday morning, Henderson found that his work truck had been vandalized. He was the only person at the plant assigned to drive that particular truck. Someone had put grease on the handle he used to get into the truck, on the inside knobs, on the water hose, on the back and bottom of his seat, and on several other places he routinely used to operate the truck. Henderson reported this incident to plant manager Taylor the following Monday.

Starting in October and continuing into November, Moistner began to insinuate to Henderson that Moistner belonged to the Ku Klux Klan. In November 2001, while Henderson was in the employee break room, Moistner stated that he was going to renew his membership in the KKK and that he knew the grand dragon of the KKK. Moistner said this in a conversation with Santerre and another person. Plant manager Taylor heard the comment. When Henderson asked Moistner whether he had actually been in the KKK, plant manager Taylor corrected Henderson's use of the past tense, saying that Moistner was still a member of the KKK.

In October 2001, Moistner, Santerre and another person were in the employee break room having a conversation in which Santerre or the other person mentioned Henderson's name. Moistner responded: "I'd like to drag him . . . down the street on the back of my pick-up truck." Moistner then spoke to Henderson directly and told Henderson to come out to the field in the back of the plant for a fight. Henderson told Moistner that he did not have time for Moistner's "mess." Plant manager Taylor heard the exchange. Although Moistner did not refer to Henderson by name initially, he made the explosive "dragging" statement in Henderson's presence and so that he could hear. A jury could easily infer that Henderson was the intended target of Moistner's threat.

In November 2001, Henderson's truck was parked in the parking lot at the plant and Henderson was climbing down the ladder on the side of the truck. Santerre drove through the parking lot at a high rate of speed and attempted to hit Henderson. Henderson reported the incident to plant manager Taylor, who said he would have a talk with Santerre. Santerre did this once more while Henderson was working at the Harding Street Plant.

Also in November 2001, Henderson began to notice an odor as he was driving his truck that he thought was coming from somewhere inside the truck. The smell persisted for a week. As Henderson was driving his truck on November 15th, a dead mouse fell into his lap. Upon further inspection, Henderson found three more dead mice wrapped in napkins that had been planted in his truck. Henderson reported the incident to plant manager Taylor, who removed one other dead mouse from Henderson's truck. Henderson's co-workers laughed at him when they realized he had discovered that the dead mice were the source of the odor. Shortly before this incident, Henderson had recorded Santerre on audio tape in the employee break room picking up a dead mouse from a mouse trap in the room and saying to the mouse "Don't you worry about a thing, I've got a home for you." Santerre then walked out of the break room carrying the mouse. Santerre had done the same thing with a dead mouse on the previous day as well.

According to Henderson, this was the last that he could take. He immediately complained to plant manager Taylor about the dead mice. In response, the company posted a sign at the plant to remind the drivers to keep their trucks clean to keep mice away. The sign also stated "Do not expose any other employee to rodents." On November 21, 2001, Henderson sent a letter of complaint to Goins, the general manager for SouthSide. In his complaint, Henderson listed incidents that he thought contributed to the hostile working environment, including the dead mice, Santerre's comment that no one wanted to work with him, the buttons cut from his work shirt, grease put on the inside of his truck, Moistner's comments about the KKK, and Moistner's expressed wish to drag Henderson from the back of his pick-up truck.

On November 26th, Henderson met with general manager Goins. At that meeting, Henderson complained of numerous other incidents, including Moistner's racially inappropriate jokes and comments and Santerre's picking up dead mice in the employee break room. On November 27, 2001, Goins issued a written warning to Moistner and to Santerre. Each warning restated Henderson's allegations with respect to each of the two individually and stated: "I am perplexed that such activity has gone on since June of 2001, without my knowledge. I am appalled by such destructive and violent behavior."

Just two days later, on November 29, 2001, Goins wrote letters to Moistner and to Santerre rescinding his reprimands and apologizing to both for overreacting. Goins stated in his letter, two days after his initial reprimands for months' worth of alleged harassment, that he was unable to substantiate Henderson's complaints against them both. In December 2001, Moistner and Santerre filed claims against Henderson in a small claims court stemming from Henderson's accusations against them. At some point after the claims were filed, Henderson and Moistner were at the small claims court when Moistner called Henderson a "f***ing nigger." Moistner later told Henderson that Moistner himself had reported the incident to Goins, who told Moistner to apologize to Henderson. Moistner did apologize to Henderson for the incident.

In March 2002, SouthSide, against Henderson's wishes, transferred Henderson to its Pittsboro Plant in Noblesville, Indiana. Henderson's job duties and benefits package remained the same. His pay increased.

[A]ll of the alleged incidents must be considered as a whole when analyzing Henderson's hostile work environment claim. Considering the totality of the circumstances, and giving Henderson the benefit of all reasonable inferences from the evidence, the incidents alleged are sufficient to allow a reasonable jury to find that plaintiff Henderson's work environment was severe, pervasive, and abusive, and was therefore actionable under Title VII. Once a Title VII plaintiff establishes that his work environment was both subjectively and objectively hostile, he must also establish a basis for employer liability. To establish employer liability where the harasser is a co-worker, plaintiff must show that the employer was negligent in either discovering or remedying the harassment

> The court here reviews the basic standards for a hostile work environment and concludes that the plaintiff has established sufficient evidence to proceed to trial on this question.

Defendants argue that plaintiff did not report to management several incidents, including Moistner's comment that he intended to renew his membership in the KKK, Moistner's racial jokes, and Moistner calling Henderson a "nigger" at the small claims court. However, plaintiff's evidence could convince a reasonable jury that Henderson's supervisor, plant manager Willie Taylor, was present and witnessed many of Moistner's racist jokes and comments, as well as his KKK membership renewal comment. There is no evidence that there was any company policy directing employees to report complaints to anyone other than Taylor, a supervisor with an actual presence at the plant. A jury could easily find on this record that plant manager Taylor was fully aware of the racist campaign against Henderson. The evidence is enough to support a finding that SouthSide management had actual notice of the incidents of which Henderson now complains, and that they did nothing about it for months.

Alternatively, defendants argue that the company took adequate corrective action. When Henderson reported to plant manager Taylor that Santerre had tried to hit him with his truck, Taylor spoke with Santerre, who denied the incident. That was the extent of the company's involvement with that incident. A reasonable jury could find that the company's response was insufficient. A reasonable jury could find, for instance, that more intervention and ultimately more supervision were necessary to control such physically dangerous conduct.

After Henderson found the dead mice, the company posted a statement that cautioned drivers to keep their trucks clean to keep mice away. A reasonable jury could find that the company's indirect poster about *hygiene* was insufficient to address the *deliberate* harassing behavior or to remedy the wrongs that Henderson suffered. The poster, moreover, addressed only one problem (and did so as if it had been the result of an oversight by Henderson rather than a deliberate act of others). It failed to address the dead mice as part of a larger campaign of harassment, except to suggest that employees not expose others to rodents. There is no evidence that the company had done anything prior to posting its statement to remedy the other problems alleged by plaintiff.

Also, Henderson reported the dead mice incident to SouthSide's general manager Goins at the same time that he reported so many of the other alleged harassing incidents that he had endured. The company's response was to reprimand the offenders — only to rescind the reprimands two days later. At the summary judgment stage, the court must assume that Henderson's account of the harassment directed against him is true. Based on that evidence, a reasonable jury could conclude that two days was not adequate time to launch and complete a reasonable investigation into the complaints by plaintiff.

On the issue of remedy, moreover, plaintiff's evidence would as noted above allow a reasonable jury to find that plant manager Willie Taylor was fully aware of the campaign of racial harassment against Henderson, and that he failed — for months — to take any meaningful steps to remedy the harassment. Taylor was the plant manager. He was the senior manager on site at the Harding Street facility. His failure to try to remedy the problems can be attributed to SouthSide, quite apart from the arguably feeble efforts made in response to Henderson's complaint to Goins. There is sufficient evidence to convince a reasonable jury that the defendant company was negligent in remedying the harassment.

■ NOTES AND QUESTIONS

1. Is it surprising that the conduct described in this case still takes place in our society? In light of the facts alleged in this case, how important is the enforcement of Title VII today?

2. As discussed in Chapter 5, harassment claims can be alleged on the basis of any protected characteristic, including race. Employers can be liable for harassment based on a negligence standard — if the employer was aware or should have been aware of harassing conduct and failed to take appropriate remedial action, liability can be imputed.

3. The court here believed that the company's response was insufficient given the complaints of the plaintiff. What should the company's response have been in the face of these allegations?

4. This case arose on a motion for summary judgment. The court held that the case should be permitted to proceed to trial. What evidence will the plaintiff put on to support its claim before the jury? How should the company attempt to defend its case?

5. Given the procedural posture of this case — immediately before trial — should an attempt be made to settle the case? What type of settlement would be appropriate? Who has more motivation to settle the claims involved, the defendant or the plaintiff?

6. If you were sitting on a jury and heard the facts as alleged here, what would your finding be? If you found for the plaintiff, what award would you believe appropriate?

7. What incident of racial harassment is the most disturbing in this case? How should the employer have responded to this particular incident?

An interesting question, which is revisited throughout this text, is whether discrimination based on one's appearance, or on a grooming or dress code, can violate federal laws. The case below examines this question in the context of race.

EEOC v. Catastrophe Management Solutions
852 F.3d 1018 (11th Cir. 2016)

Mr. JORDAN, Circuit Judge:

CMS, a claims processing company located in Mobile, Alabama, provides customer service support to insurance companies. In 2010, CMS announced that it was seeking candidates with basic computer knowledge and professional phone skills to work as customer service representatives. CMS' customer representatives do not have contact with the public, as they handle telephone calls in a large call room.

Ms. Jones, who is black, completed an online employment application for the customer service position in May of 2010, and was selected for an in-person interview. She arrived at CMS for her interview several days later dressed in a blue business suit and wearing her hair in short dreadlocks. After waiting with a number of other applicants, Ms. Jones interviewed with a company representative to discuss the requirements of the position. A short time later, Ms. Jones and other selected applicants were brought into a room as a group.

CMS' human resources manager, Jeannie Wilson—who is white—informed the applicants in the room, including Ms. Jones, that they had been hired. Ms. Wilson also told the successful applicants that they would have to complete scheduled lab tests and other paperwork before beginning their employment, and she offered to meet privately with anyone who had a conflict with CMS' schedule. As of this time no one had commented on Ms. Jones' hair. Following the meeting, Ms. Jones met with Ms. Wilson privately to discuss a scheduling conflict she had and to request to change her lab test date. Ms. Wilson told Ms. Jones that she could return at a different time for the lab test.

Before Ms. Jones got up to leave, Ms. Wilson asked her whether she had her hair in dreadlocks. Ms. Jones said yes, and Ms. Wilson replied that CMS could not hire her "with the dreadlocks." When Ms. Jones asked what the problem was, Ms. Wilson said "they tend to get messy, although I'm not saying yours are, but you know what I'm talking about." Ms. Wilson told Ms. Jones about a male applicant who was asked to cut off his dreadlocks in order to obtain a job with CMS. When Ms. Jones said that she would not cut her hair, Ms. Wilson told her that CMS could not hire her, and asked her to return the paperwork she had been given. Ms. Jones did as requested and left.

At the time, CMS had a race-neutral grooming policy which read as follows: "All personnel are expected to be dressed and groomed in a manner that projects a professional and businesslike image while adhering to company and industry standards and/or guidelines. . . . [H]airstyle should reflect a business/professional image. No excessive hairstyles or unusual colors are acceptable[.]"

Dreadlocks, according to the proposed amended complaint, are "a manner of wearing hair that is common for black people and suitable for black hair texture. Dreadlocks are formed in a black person's hair naturally, without any manipulation, or by manual manipulation of hair into larger coils." The EEOC alleged that the term dreadlock originated during the slave trade in the early history of the United States. "During the forced transportation of Africans across the ocean, their hair became matted with blood, feces, urine, sweat, tears, and dirt. Upon observing them, some slave traders referred to the slaves' hair as 'dreadful,'" and dreadlock became a "commonly used word to refer to the locks that had formed during the slaves' long trips across the ocean."

The proposed amended complaint also contained some legal conclusions about the concept of race. First, the EEOC stated that race "is a social construct and has no biological definition." Second, the EEOC asserted that "the concept of race is not limited to or defined by immutable physical characteristics." Third, according to the EEOC Compliance Manual, the "concept of race encompasses cultural characteristics related to race or ethnicity," including "grooming practices." Fourth, although some non-black persons "have a hair texture that would allow the hair to lock, dreadlocks are nonetheless a racial characteristic, just as skin color is a racial characteristic."

Playing off these legal conclusions, the proposed amended complaint set out allegations about black persons and their hair. The hair of black persons grows "in very tight coarse coils," which is different than the hair of white persons. "Historically, the texture of hair has been used as a substantial determiner of race," and "dreadlocks are a method of hair styling suitable for the texture of black hair and [are] culturally associated" with black persons. When black persons "choose to wear and display their hair in its natural texture in the workplace, rather than straightening it or hiding it, they are often stereotyped as not being 'teamplayers,' 'radicals,' 'troublemakers,' or not sufficiently assimilated into the corporate and professional world of employment." Significantly, the proposed amended complaint did not allege that dreadlocks are an immutable characteristic of black persons.

The EEOC claimed in its proposed amended complaint that a "prohibition of dreadlocks in the workplace constitutes race discrimination because dreadlocks are a manner of wearing the hair that is physiologically and culturally associated with people of African descent." So, according to the EEOC, the decision of CMS to "interpret its race-neutral written grooming policy to ban the wearing of dreadlocks constitutes an employment practice that discriminates on the basis of race."

The district court dismissed the initial complaint, and concluded that the proposed amended complaint was futile, because "Title VII prohibits discrimination on the basis of immutable characteristics, such as race, color, or natural origin," and "[a] hairstyle, even one more closely associated with a particular ethnic group, is a mutable characteristic." The district court was not swayed by the EEOC's contention that the allegations were sufficient because "hairstyle can be a determinant of racial identity," explaining that other courts had rejected that argument. The district court also declined the EEOC's invitation to discard the immutable/mutable distinction for Title VII race discrimination claims.

The EEOC advances a number of arguments on appeal in support of its position that denying a black person employment on the basis of her dreadlocks through the application of a race-neutral grooming policy constitutes intentional discrimination on the basis of race in violation of Title VII. The arguments, which build on each other, are that dreadlocks are a natural outgrowth of the immutable trait of black hair texture; that the dreadlocks hairstyle is directly associated with the immutable trait of race; that dreadlocks can be a symbolic expression of racial pride; and that targeting dreadlocks as a basis for employment can be a form of racial stereotyping. Before we address these arguments, we discuss an overarching problem concerning the EEOC's liability theory. Despite some loose language in its proposed amended complaint, the EEOC confirmed at oral argument that it is proceeding only on a disparate treatment theory [].

Despite its decision to assert only a disparate treatment claim, the EEOC at times conflates the two liability theories, making disparate impact arguments in support of its disparate treatment claim. The EEOC, for example, faults the district court for not allowing expert testimony on the "racial *impact* of a dreadlock ban" and for failing to acknowledge "the critical *disadvantage* at which the dreadlock ban places Black applicants." It also asserts that "the people most adversely and significantly *affected* by a dreadlocks ban, such as CMS', are African–Americans." (emphasis added). And it argues that "a policy which critically *disadvantages or affects* members of one group over another" can support an intentional discrimination claim. (emphasis added). Because this is a disparate treatment case, and only a disparate treatment case, we do not address further the EEOC's arguments that CMS' race-neutral grooming policy had (or potentially had) a disproportionate effect on other black job applicants.

Title VII does not define the term "race." And, in the more than 50 years since Title VII was enacted, the EEOC has not seen fit to issue a regulation defining the term. In the 1960s, as today, "race" was a complex concept that defied a single definition. Take, for example, the following discussion in a leading 1961 dictionary: "In technical discriminations, all more or less controversial and often lending themselves to great popular misunderstanding or misuse, RACE is anthropological and ethnological in force, usu[ally] implying a physical type with certain underlying characteristics, as a particular color of skin or shape of skull . . . although sometimes, and most controversially, other presumed factors are chosen, such as place of origin . . . or common root language." WEBSTER'S THIRD NEW INTERNATIONAL DICTIONARY OF THE ENGLISH LANGUAGE 1870 (unabridged 1961).

Nevertheless, most dictionaries at that time tied "race" to common physical characteristics or traits existing through ancestry, descent, or heredity. *See id.* (defining "race" as "the descendants of a common ancestor: a family, tribe, people, or nation belonging to the same stock" or "a class or kind of individuals with common characteristics, interests, appearance, or habits as if derived from a common ancestor," or "a division of mankind possessing traits that are transmissible by descent and sufficient to characterize it as a distinct human type (Caucasian ~) (Mongoloid ~)"); A DICTIONARY OF THE SOCIAL SCIENCES 569 (Julius Gould & William Kolb eds. 1964) ("A *race* is a subdivision of a species, individual members of which display with some frequency a number of hereditary attributes that have become associated with one another in some measure through considerable degree of in-breeding among the ancestors of the group during a substantial part of their recent evolution."); A DICTIONARY OF SOCIOLOGY 142 (G. Duncan Mitchell ed. 1968) ("Biologically speaking the concept of *race* refers to a population sharing a gene-pool giving rise to a characteristic distribution of physical characteristics determined by heredity. There are no clear cut boundaries between racial groups thus defined and considerable variations may be exhibited within races."). One specialty dictionary, while defining "race" as an "anthropological term denoting a large group of persons distinguished by significant hereditary physical traits," cautioned that "[a] common misconception is that cultural traits sufficiently differentiate races." DICTIONARY OF POLITICAL SCIENCE 440 (Joseph Dunne ed. 1964).

From the sources we have been able to review, it appears more likely than not that "race," as a matter of language and usage, referred to common physical characteristics shared by a group of people and transmitted by their ancestors over time. Although the period dictionaries did not use the word "immutable" to describe such common characteristics, it is not much of a linguistic stretch to think that such characteristics are a matter of birth, and not culture. There is little support for the position of the EEOC that the 1964 Congress meant for Title VII to protect "individual expression . . . tied to a protected race." Indeed, from a legal standpoint, it appears that "race" was then mostly understood in terms of inherited physical characteristics.

It may be that today "race" is recognized as a "social construct," rather than an absolute biological truth. But our possible current reality does not tell us what the country's collective zeitgeist was when Congress enacted Title VII half a century ago. If we assume, however, that the quest for the ordinary understanding of "race" in the 1960s does not have a clear winner, then we must look for answers elsewhere. Some cases from the former Fifth Circuit provide us with binding guidance, giving some credence to Felix Frankfurter's adage that "[n]o judge writes on a wholly clean slate." Walter Hamilton, *Preview of a Justice*, 48 YALE L.J. 819, 821 (1939) (quoting FELIX FRANKFURTER, THE COMMERCE CLAUSE UNDER MARSHALL, TANEY, AND WAITE 12 (1937)). As we explain below, those cases teach that Title VII protects against discrimination based on immutable characteristics.

In *Willingham v. Macon Tel. Publ'g Co.*, 507 F.2d 1084 (5th Cir. 1975) (en banc), we addressed a Title VII sex discrimination claim by a male job applicant who was denied a position because his hair was too long. Although the employer interpreted its neutral dress/grooming policy to prohibit the wearing of long hair only by men, and although the plaintiff argued that he was the victim of sexual stereotyping (i.e., the view that only women should have long hair), we affirmed the grant of summary judgment in favor of the employer.

We held in *Willingham* that "[e]qual employment opportunity," which was the purpose of Title VII, "may be secured only when employers are barred from discriminating against employees on the basis of immutable characteristics, such as race and national origin. Similarly, an employer cannot have one hiring policy for men and another for women *if* the distinction is based on some fundamental right. But a hiring policy that distinguishes on some other ground, such as grooming or length of hair, is related more closely to the employer's choice of how to run his business than equality of employment opportunity." We "adopt[ed] the view . . . that distinctions in employment practices between men and women on the basis of something other than immutable or protected characteristics do not inhibit employment *opportunity* in violation of [Title VII]." And we approved the district court's alternative ground for affirming the grant of summary judgment in favor of the employer—that because grooming and hair standards were also imposed on female employees, men and women were treated equally. In closing, we reiterated that "[p]rivate employers are prohibited from using different hiring policies for men and women only when the distinctions used relate to immutable characteristics or legally protected rights."

Willingham involved hair length in the context of a sex discrimination claim, but in *Garcia v. Gloor*, 618 F.2d 264 (5th Cir. 1980), we applied the immutable characteristic limitation to national origin, another of Title VII's protected categories. In *Garcia* a bilingual Mexican-American employee who worked as a salesperson was fired for speaking Spanish to a co-worker on the job in violation of his employer's English-only policy, and he alleged that his termination was based on his national origin in violation of Title VII (which we referred to as the "EEO Act"). We affirmed the district court's judgment in favor of the employer following a bench trial. We noted that an expert witness called by the employee had "testified that the Spanish language is the most important aspect of ethnic identification for Mexican–Americans, and it is to them what skin color is to others," and that testimony formed part of the basis for the claim that the employer's policy was unlawful. Although the district court had found that there were other reasons for the employee's dismissal, we assumed that the use of Spanish was a significant factor in the employer's decision.

We explained that neither Title VII nor common understanding "equates national origin with the language that one chooses to speak," and noted that the English-only rule was not applied to the employee as a "covert basis for national origin discrimination." Though the employee argued that he was discriminated against on the basis of national origin "because national origin influences or determines his language preference," we were unpersuaded because the employee was bilingual and was allowed to speak Spanish during breaks. And even if the employer had no genuine business need for the English-only policy, we said that "[n]ational origin must not be confused with ethnic or sociocultural traits or an unrelated status, such as citizenship or alienage." Citing *Willingham*, we emphasized that Title VII "focuses its laser of prohibition" on discriminatory acts based on matters "that are either beyond the victim's power to alter, or that impose a burden on an employee on one of the prohibited bases."

The employee in *Garcia* also argued that the employer's English-only policy was "discriminatory in impact, even if that result was not intentional, because it was likely to be violated only by Hispanic-Americans and that, therefore, they ha[d] a higher risk of incurring penalties." We rejected this argument as well because "there is no disparate impact if the rule is one that the affected employee can readily observe and nonobservance is a matter of individual preference," and Title VII "does not support an interpretation that equates the language an employee prefers to use with his national origin." *Id.*

What we take away from *Willingham* and *Garcia* is that, as a general matter, Title VII protects persons in covered categories with respect to their immutable characteristics, but not their cultural practices. We recognize that the distinction between immutable and mutable characteristics of race can sometimes be a fine (and difficult) one, but it is a line that courts have drawn. So, for example, discrimination on the basis of black hair texture (an immutable characteristic) is prohibited by Title VII, while adverse action on the basis of black hairstyle (a mutable choice) is not.

Critically, the EEOC's proposed amended complaint did not allege that dreadlocks themselves are an immutable characteristic of black persons, and in fact stated that black persons choose to wear dreadlocks because that hairstyle is historically, physiologically, and culturally associated with their race. That dreadlocks are a "natural outgrowth" of the texture of black hair does not make them an immutable characteristic of race. Under *Willingham* and *Garcia*, the EEOC failed to state a plausible claim that CMS intentionally discriminated against Ms. Jones on the basis of her race by asking her to cut her dreadlocks pursuant to its race-neutral grooming policy. The EEOC's allegations—individually or collectively—do not suggest that CMS used that policy as proxy for intentional racial discrimination.

Ms. Jones told CMS that she would not cut her dreadlocks in order to secure a job, and we respect that intensely personal decision and all it entails. But, for the reasons we have set out, the EEOC's original and proposed amended complaint did not state a plausible claim that CMS intentionally discriminated against Ms. Jones because of her race. The district court therefore did not err in dismissing the original complaint and in concluding that the proposed amended complaint was futile.

■ NOTES AND QUESTIONS

1. How is the term "race" properly defined? Do you agree with the court's approach to this question? *See* D. Wendy Greene, *Title VII: What's Hair (and Other Race-Based Characteristics) Got to Do With It?*, 79 U. Colo. L. Rev. 1355, 1385 (2008) ("Race includes physical appearances and behaviors that society, historically and presently, commonly associates with a particular racial group, even when the physical appearances and behavior are not 'uniquely' or 'exclusively' 'performed' by, or attributed to a particular racial group.") (as cited by the court in this case).

2. The court here rejects the EEOC's view that "denying a black person employment on the basis of her dreadlocks through the application of a race-neutral grooming policy constitutes intentional discrimination." Do you agree with the court's analysis?

3. Which analysis is more appropriate for this case—disparate treatment or disparate impact? How did the EEOC litigate the case? Was the EEOC's approach correct here?

4. A more thorough discussion of appearance discrimination/grooming standards is addressed in the chapter addressing sex discrimination. The issue can arise under any of the characteristics protected by Title VII.

> **Practice and Procedural Tip**

17: Discrimination in Hiring

Hiring discrimination can be particularly difficult for a plaintiff to establish. This is because a prospective employee will often have little information about the institution to which she is applying or the reason why the application was rejected. An applicant may not even know officially whether or not she is still being considered for a particular job. Thus, representing someone who believes that she has not been hired because of discriminatory reasons can be extremely difficult.

It is worth noting, however, that racial discrimination in hiring is extremely prevalent. While it can be difficult to establish these claims, studies have repeatedly shown that employers often discriminate on this basis. One well-known study performed by Harvard University and the University of Chicago sent out two identical résumés to employers — one with a "white" sounding name, and another with a "black" sounding name. The results were alarming.

> The percentages, which rose to the level of statistical significance, revealed that African-American applicants needed to send about *five additional* resumes to receive a callback than applicants with white-sounding names. A white-sounding name is a valuable credential, as it "yields as many more callbacks as an additional eight years of experience on a resume." And the study found that white applicants are better rewarded for having a higher-quality resume. Even the address on the resumes had an impact, as living in a wealthier (or more educated or Whiter) neighborhood increases callback rates. The study thus leaves little doubt as to the persistence of racial discrimination in our society, at least in the hiring context.

Joseph A. Seiner, *After* Iqbal, 45 Wake Forest L. Rev. 179, 201 (2010) (internal quotations and citations omitted) (citing Marianne Bertrand & Sendhil Mullainathan, *Are Emily and Greg More Employable than Lakisha and Jamal? A Field Experiment on Labor Market Discrimination*, 94 Am. Econ. Rev. 991, 992 (2004)).

Thus, prospective plaintiffs attorneys should be aware of the tendency of employers to discriminate — perhaps even unconsciously — on the basis of race when reviewing résumés and performing hiring duties. Similarly, when counseling clients on discrimination, employers should be made aware of the potential pitfalls of using race as a criteria in the hiring process.

D. Reverse Discrimination Claims

Another common form of discrimination that can arise is so-called reverse discrimination claims. The term "reverse discrimination" is largely a misnomer, as the statute clearly protects *all* classes (including the majority class) from discrimination in the workplace. Reverse discrimination claims occur when a white individual alleges that he has been discriminated against because of his race. The Supreme Court decided early on whether such claims should be protected under Title VII.

McDonald v. Santa Fe Trail Transportation Co.
427 U.S. 273 (1976)

Mr. Justice MARSHALL delivered the opinion of the Court.

Petitioners, L. N. McDonald and Raymond L. Laird, brought this action in the United States District Court for the Southern District of Texas seeking relief against Santa Fe Trail Transportation Co. (Santa Fe) and International Brotherhood of Teamsters Local 988 (Local 988), which represented Santa Fe's Houston employees, for alleged violations of the Civil Rights Act of 1866, 42 U.S.C. § 1981, and of Title VII of the Civil Rights Act of 1964, 42 U.S.C. § 2000e et seq., in connection with their discharge from Santa Fe's employment. The District Court dismissed the complaint on the pleadings. The Court of Appeals for the Fifth Circuit affirmed. In determining whether the decisions of these courts were correct, we must decide, first, whether a complaint alleging that white employees charged with misappropriating property from their employer were dismissed from employment, while a black employee similarly charged was not dismissed, states a claim under Title VII. Second, we must decide whether § 1981, which provides that "(a)ll persons . . . shall have the same right . . . to make and enforce contracts . . . as is enjoyed by white citizens . . ." affords protection from racial discrimination in private employment to white persons as well as nonwhites.

Because the District Court dismissed this case on the pleadings, we take as true the material facts alleged in petitioners' complaint. On September 26, 1970, petitioners, both white, and Charles Jackson, a Negro employee of Santa Fe, were jointly and severally charged with misappropriating 60 one-gallon cans of antifreeze which was part of a shipment Santa Fe was carrying for one of its customers. Six days later, petitioners were fired by Santa Fe, while Jackson was retained. A grievance was promptly filed with Local 988, pursuant to the collective-bargaining agreement between the two respondents, but grievance proceedings secured no relief. The following April, complaints were filed with the Equal Employment Opportunity Commission (EEOC) charging that Santa Fe had discriminated against both petitioners on the basis of their race in firing them, and that Local 988 had discriminated against McDonald on the basis of his race in failing properly to represent his interests in the grievance proceedings, all in violation of Title VII of the Civil Rights Act of 1964. Agency process proved equally unavailing for petitioners, however, and the EEOC notified them in July 1971 of their right under the Act to initiate a civil action in district court within 30 days. This suit followed, petitioners joining their § 1981 claim to their Title VII allegations.

Respondents moved to dismiss the complaint, and in June 1974 the District Court issued a final modified opinion and order dismissing petitioners' claims under both Title VII and § 1981. Turning first to the § 1981 claim, the District Court determined that § 1981 is wholly inapplicable to racial discrimination against white persons, and dismissed the claim for want of jurisdiction. Turning then to petitioners' claims under Title VII, the District Court concluded it had no jurisdiction over Laird's Title VII claim against Local 988, because Laird had not filed any charge against Local 988 with the EEOC. Respondent Santa Fe additionally contended that petitioners' EEOC charges against it, filed more than 90 days after their discharge, were untimely. Apparently relying upon Fifth Circuit authority for the proposition that the 90-day period for filing with the EEOC was tolled during the pendency of grievance proceedings, however, the District Court concluded that the question of timely filing with the EEOC could not be determined without a hearing on petitioners' allegations that they had not been notified until April 3, 1971, of the termination of the grievance proceedings. But the District Court found it unnecessary to hold such a hearing, since it concluded, quite apart from any timeliness problem, that "the dismissal of white employees charged with misappropriating company property while not dismissing a similarly charged Negro employee does not raise a claim upon which Title VII relief may be granted."

The Court of Appeals affirmed the dismissal. We granted certiorari [and] reverse.

Title VII prohibits the discharge of "any individual" because of "such individual's race." Its terms are not limited to discrimination against members of any particular race. Thus although we were not there confronted with racial discrimination against whites, we described the Act in *Griggs v. Duke Power Co.*, 401 U.S. 424 (1971), as prohibiting "(d)iscriminatory preference for *any* (racial) group, *minority or majority*" (emphasis added). Similarly the EEOC, whose interpretations are entitled to great deference, *id.* at 433–434, has consistently interpreted Title VII to proscribe racial discrimination in private employment against whites on the same terms as racial discrimination against nonwhites.

> Since the statute was first debated, there has been substantial controversy over the extent to which Title VII should protect white males.

This conclusion is in accord with uncontradicted legislative history to the effect that Title VII was intended to "cover white men and white women and all Americans," 110 Cong. Rec. 2578 (1964) (remarks of Rep. Celler), and create an "obligation not to discriminate against whites," *id.* at 7218 (memorandum of Sen. Clark). See also *id.* at 7213 (memorandum of Sens. Clark and Case); *id.* at 8912 (remarks of Sen. Williams). We therefore hold today that Title VII prohibits racial discrimination against the white petitioners in this case upon the same standards as would be applicable were they Negroes and Jackson white.

Respondents contend that, even though generally applicable to white persons, Title VII affords petitioners no protection in this case, because their dismissal was based upon their commission of a serious criminal offense against their employer. We think this argument is foreclosed by our decision in *McDonnell Douglas Corp. v. Green*, 411 U.S. 792 (1973).

We find this case indistinguishable from *McDonnell Douglas*. Fairly read, the complaint asserted that petitioners were discharged for their alleged participation in a misappropriation of cargo entrusted to Santa Fe, but that a fellow employee, likewise implicated, was not so disciplined, and that the reason for the discrepancy in discipline was that the favored employee is Negro while petitioners are white. See *Conley v. Gibson*, 355 U.S. 41, 45–46 (1957). While Santa Fe may decide that participation in a theft of cargo may render an employee unqualified for employment, this criterion must be "applied, alike to members of all races," and Title VII is violated if, as petitioners alleged, it was not.

We cannot accept respondents' argument that the principles of *McDonnell Douglas* are inapplicable where the discharge was based, as petitioners' complaint admitted, on participation in serious misconduct or crime directed against the employer. The Act prohibits *all* racial discrimination in employment, without exception for any group of particular employees, and while crime or other misconduct may be a legitimate basis for discharge, it is hardly one for racial discrimination. Indeed, the Title VII plaintiff in *McDonnell Douglas* had been convicted for a nontrivial offense against his former employer. It may be that theft of property entrusted to an employer for carriage is a more compelling basis for discharge than obstruction of an employer's traffic arteries, but this does not diminish the illogic in retaining guilty employees of one color while discharging those of another color.

At this stage of the litigation the claim against Local 988 must go with the claim against Santa Fe, for in substance the complaint alleges that the union shirked its duty properly to represent McDonald, and instead "acquiesced and/or joined in" Santa Fe's alleged racial discrimination against him. Local 988 argues that as a matter of law it should not be subject to liability under Title VII in a situation, such as this, where some but not all culpable employees are ultimately discharged on account of joint misconduct, because in representing all the affected employees in their relations with the employer, the union may necessarily have to compromise by securing retention of only some. We reject the argument. The same reasons which prohibit an employer from discriminating on the basis of race among the culpable employees apply equally to the union; and whatever factors the mechanisms of compromise may legitimately take into account in mitigating discipline of some employees, under Title VII race may not be among them.

Thus, we conclude that the District Court erred in dismissing both petitioners' Title VII claims against Santa Fe, and petitioner McDonald's Title VII claim against Local 988.

■ NOTES AND QUESTIONS

1. Title VII prohibits taking an adverse action against an employee because of that worker's race. This statutory language does not protect certain races. Rather, it protects *all* races. For this reason, even discrimination against the majority class is prohibited.

2. Race cases, like other claims, often turn on whether the plaintiff is able to show that a similarly situated employee of a different race was treated differently. Was that evidence present in this case?

3. Should the majority class receive protection against discrimination on the basis of race? Is discrimination against Caucasian workers really a pervasive problem that needs to be addressed? Was that the purpose behind the passage of Title VII?

4. What types of cases might involve discrimination against majority group members? For example, could males applying to be preschool teachers experience discrimination? What about a white athletic coach applying for a coaching position at a historically black inner-city school?

5. In 2013, the brokerage firm Merrill Lynch agreed to settle a class-action suit filed by an African-American employee for $160 million, making it one of the largest such employment discrimination settlements ever. The lead plaintiff alleged that the company's practices resulted in a workforce segregated on the basis of race, that the firm routinely assigned African Americans less favorable partners and accounts, and that the company pushed them into lower positions and subsequently reassigned their accounts. *See* Amanda Becker, *BofA's Merrill to Settle Racial Bias Suit for $160 Million*, Chi. Trib., Aug. 28, 2013, http://articles.chicagotribune.com/2013-08-28/business/sns-rt-us-merrillynch-20130827_1_black-brokers-bill-halldin-betty-dukes.

 Interactive Problem

Looking back at the interactive problem, assume all of the same facts except that Alan was a white actor who applied for a role as Martin Luther King. Would Alan's rejection on the basis of race be a stronger (or weaker) claim than the facts set forth in the original hypothetical?

Practice and Procedural Tip

18: "Reverse Discrimination" Claims — Discrimination Against the Majority Group

As we saw in the previous case, the statute protects all individuals from discrimination, regardless of race. As already noted, there really is no such thing as "reverse discrimination," because all discrimination is unlawful. Nonetheless, the courts have taken varying approaches to these so-called reverse discrimination claims.

Some courts have not altered the standard at all for these cases. These jurisdictions apply the same test found in *McDonnell Douglas* to claims brought by whites or male workers. Thus, the same analysis found in that test would apply to all races or sexes bringing a particular claim in these jurisdictions. *See, e.g.,* Charles A. Sullivan, *Circling Back to the Obvious: The Convergence of Traditional and Reverse Discrimination in Title VII Proof,* 46 Wm. & Mary L. Rev. 1031 (2004); *see also* Iadimarco v. Runyon, 190 F.3d 151, 160 (3d Cir. 1999); Young v. City of Houston, Tex., 906 F.2d 177 (5th Cir. 1990); E. Christi Cunningham, *The Rise of Identity Politics I: The Myth of the Protected Class in Title VII Disparate Treatment Cases,* 30 Conn. L. Rev. 441 (1998).

Other courts take a different view, however. These jurisdictions apply a more rigorous test to white workers who bring a race discrimination claim or to men who bring a sex discrimination claim. Often, these courts require that the plaintiff — in the first stage of the prima facie case — present "background circumstances" explaining why the employer would discriminate against the majority class. Thus, these courts make it more difficult to establish the prima facie case in these instances. This approach had been criticized as merging the final prong of the *McDonnell Douglas* analysis (the pretext prong) with the plaintiff's prima facie case. Nonetheless, the courts following this approach feel that such a requirement is justified as it would be unusual for these majority groups to face discrimination. *See, e.g.,* Angela Onwuachi-Willig, *When Different Means the Same: Applying a Different Standard of Proof to White Plaintiffs Under the* McDonnell Douglas *Prima Facie Case Test,* 50 Case W. Res. L. Rev. 53 (1999); *see also* Richard A. Primus, *Equal Protection and Disparate Impact: Round Three,* 117 Harv. L. Rev. 493 (2003); Parker v. Baltimore & Ohio R.R. Co., 652 F.2d 1012 (D.C. Cir. 1981); Murray v. Thistledown Racing Club, Inc., 770 F.2d 63 (6th Cir. 1985); Mills v. Health Care Serv. Corp., 171 F.3d 450, 456–457 (7th Cir. 1999).

From a procedural standpoint, the lesson here is simple: Know your case and know your jurisdiction. If you are representing a plaintiff who is in a jurisdiction that requires these "background circumstances," these facts should likely be pled as part of the initial case. Certainly, a plaintiff should strongly reconsider filing a claim at all if he is unable to establish these types of facts. All cases brought by a white or male worker on the basis of race or sex will ultimately turn in part on the ability to explain why that employee would be discriminated against despite being in the majority group. There is disagreement in the courts as to when in the litigation this explanation must take place, but ultimately, a plaintiff will not be able to prevail in the case without this explanation. Plaintiffs should be cautious of this potential procedural trap, and defendants should similarly look for opportunities to push the alleged victim to justify the case.

This is not to say that individuals from the majority class cannot prevail in a "reverse discrimination" claim. They can and do prevail in all jurisdictions. Some courts just look much more closely at these claims from the onset. It is important to understand how to litigate such cases in these particular courts.

E. Affirmative Action Plans

One specific race-related issue that often arises is the use of affirmative action plans. In many ways, an affirmative action plan is really direct evidence of discrimination, though the cases are not typically analyzed this way. With an affirmative action plan, an employer is acknowledging that it is using race as a factor in its hiring process. For this reason, these plans have been highly controversial. The legality of using such plans has frequently been litigated in the courts, with varying results.

In *United Steelworkers v. Weber*, 443 U.S. 193 (1979), the Supreme Court approved an affirmative action plan that was targeted at correcting the historical disadvantages of black workers at a company. The Court concluded that in certain instances, these types of plans were still consistent with the terms of Title VII. In the case set forth below, the Court further expanded on the criteria necessary to establish a valid affirmative action plan. Though the case arose in the context of a gender claim, the framework discussed applies to race claims as well.

Johnson v. Transportation Agency, Santa Clara County
480 U.S. 616 (1987)

Justice BRENNAN delivered the opinion of the Court.

Respondent, Transportation Agency of Santa Clara County, California, unilaterally promulgated an Affirmative Action Plan applicable, inter alia, to promotions of employees. In selecting applicants for the promotional position of road dispatcher, the Agency, pursuant to the Plan, passed over petitioner Paul Johnson, a male employee, and promoted a female employee applicant, Diane Joyce. The question for decision is whether in making the promotion the Agency impermissibly took into account the sex of the applicants in violation of Title VII. The District Court for the Northern District of California, in an action filed by petitioner following receipt of a right-to-sue letter from the [EEOC], held that respondent had violated Title VII. The Court of Appeals for the Ninth Circuit reversed. We granted certiorari [and] affirm.

In reviewing the composition of its work force, the Agency noted in its Plan that women were represented in numbers far less than their proportion of the County labor force in both the Agency as a whole and in five of seven job categories. Specifically, while women constituted 36.4% of the area labor market, they composed only 22.4% of Agency employees. Furthermore, women working at the Agency were concentrated largely in EEOC job categories traditionally held by women: women made up 76% of Office and Clerical Workers, but only 7.1% of Agency Officials and Administrators, 8.6% of Professionals, 9.7% of Technicians, and 22% of Service and Maintenance Workers. As for the job classification relevant to this case, none of the 238 Skilled Craft Worker positions was held by a woman. The Plan noted that this underrepresentation of women in part reflected the fact that women had not traditionally been employed in these positions, and that they had not been strongly motivated to seek training or employment in them "because of the limited opportunities that have existed in the past for them to work in such classifications." The Plan also observed that, while the proportion of ethnic minorities in the Agency as a whole exceeded the proportion of such minorities in the County work force, a smaller percentage of minority employees held management, professional, and technical positions.

The Agency stated that its Plan was intended to achieve "a statistically measurable yearly improvement in hiring, training and promotion of minorities and women throughout the Agency in all major job classifications where they are underrepresented." As a benchmark by which to evaluate progress, the Agency stated that its long-term goal was to attain a work force whose composition reflected the proportion of minorities and women in the area labor force. Thus, for the Skilled Craft category in which the road dispatcher position at issue here was classified, the Agency's aspiration was that eventually about 36% of the jobs would be occupied by women.

The Plan acknowledged that a number of factors might make it unrealistic to rely on the Agency's long-term goals in evaluating the Agency's progress in expanding job opportunities for minorities and women. Among the factors identified were low turnover rates in some classifications, the fact that some jobs involved heavy labor, the small number of positions within some job categories, the limited number of entry positions leading to the Technical and Skilled Craft classifications, and the limited number of minorities and women qualified for positions requiring specialized training and experience. As a result, the Plan counseled that short-range goals be established and annually adjusted to serve as the most realistic guide for actual employment decisions. Among the tasks identified as important in establishing such short-term goals was the acquisition of data "reflecting the ratio of minorities, women and handicapped persons who are working in the local area in major job classifications relating to those utilized by the County Administration," so as to determine the availability of members of such groups who "possess the desired qualifications or potential for placement." These data on qualified group members, along with predictions of position vacancies, were to serve as the basis for "realistic yearly employment goals for women, minorities and handicapped persons in each EEOC job category and major job classification."

The Agency's Plan thus set aside no specific number of positions for minorities or women, but authorized the consideration of ethnicity or sex as a factor when evaluating qualified candidates for jobs in which members of such groups were poorly represented. One such job was the road dispatcher position that is the subject of the dispute in this case.

On December 12, 1979, the Agency announced a vacancy for the promotional position of road dispatcher in the Agency's Roads Division. Dispatchers assign road crews, equipment, and materials, and maintain records pertaining to road maintenance jobs. The position requires at minimum four years of dispatch or road maintenance work experience for Santa Clara County. The EEOC job classification scheme designates a road dispatcher as a Skilled Craft Worker.

Twelve County employees applied for the promotion, including Joyce and Johnson. Joyce had worked for the County since 1970, serving as an account clerk until 1975. She had applied for a road dispatcher position in 1974, but was deemed ineligible because she had not served as a road maintenance worker. In 1975, Joyce transferred from a senior account clerk position to a road maintenance worker position, becoming the first woman to fill such a job. During her four years in that position, she occasionally worked out of class as a road dispatcher.

Petitioner Johnson began with the County in 1967 as a road yard clerk, after private employment that included working as a supervisor and dispatcher. He had also unsuccessfully applied for the road dispatcher opening in 1974. In 1977, his clerical position was downgraded, and he sought and received a transfer to the position of road maintenance worker. He also occasionally worked out of class as a dispatcher while performing that job.

Nine of the applicants, including Joyce and Johnson, were deemed qualified for the job, and were interviewed by a two-person board. Seven of the applicants scored above 70 on this interview, which meant that they were certified as eligible for selection by the appointing authority. The scores awarded ranged from 70 to 80. Johnson was tied for second with a score of 75, while Joyce ranked next with a score of 73. A second interview was conducted by three Agency supervisors, who ultimately recommended that Johnson be promoted. Prior to the second interview, Joyce had contacted the County's Affirmative Action Office because she feared that her application might not receive disinterested review. The Office in turn contacted the Agency's Affirmative Action Coordinator, whom the Agency's Plan makes responsible for, inter alia, keeping the Director informed of opportunities for the Agency to accomplish its objectives under the Plan. At the time, the Agency employed no women in any Skilled Craft position, and had never employed a woman as a road dispatcher. The Coordinator recommended to the Director of the Agency, James Graebner, that Joyce be promoted.

Graebner, authorized to choose any of the seven persons deemed eligible, thus had the benefit of suggestions by the second interview panel and by the Agency Coordinator in arriving at his decision. After deliberation, Graebner concluded that the promotion should be given to Joyce. As he testified: "I tried to look at the whole picture, the combination of her qualifications and Mr. Johnson's qualifications, their test scores, their expertise, their background, affirmative action matters, things like that. . . . I believe it was a combination of all those."

The certification form naming Joyce as the person promoted to the dispatcher position stated that both she and Johnson were rated as well qualified for the job. The evaluation of Joyce read: "Well qualified by virtue of 18 years of past clerical experience including 3 1/2 years at West Yard plus almost 5 years as a [road maintenance worker]." The evaluation of Johnson was as follows: "Well qualified applicant; two years of [road maintenance worker] experience plus 11 years of Road Yard Clerk. Has had previous outside Dispatch experience but was 13 years ago." Graebner testified that he did not regard as significant the fact that Johnson scored 75 and Joyce 73 when interviewed by the two-person board.

Petitioner Johnson filed a complaint with the EEOC alleging that he had been denied promotion on the basis of sex in violation of Title VII. He received a right-to-sue letter from the EEOC on March 10, 1981, and on March 20, 1981, filed suit in the United States District Court for the Northern District of California. The District Court found that Johnson was more qualified for the dispatcher position than Joyce, and that the sex of Joyce was the "determining factor in her selection." The court acknowledged that, since the Agency justified its decision on the basis of its Affirmative Action Plan, the criteria announced in *Steelworkers v. Weber*, 443 U.S. 193 (1979), should be applied in evaluating the validity of the Plan. It then found the Agency's Plan invalid on the ground that the evidence did not satisfy

Weber's criterion that the Plan be temporary. The Court of Appeals for the Ninth Circuit reversed, holding that the absence of an express termination date in the Plan was not dispositive, since the Plan repeatedly expressed its objective as the attainment, rather than the maintenance, of a work force mirroring the labor force in the County. The Court of Appeals added that the fact that the Plan established no fixed percentage of positions for minorities or women made it less essential that the Plan contain a relatively explicit deadline. The Court held further that the Agency's consideration of Joyce's sex in filling the road dispatcher position was lawful. The Agency Plan had been adopted, the court said, to address a conspicuous imbalance in the Agency's work force, and neither unnecessarily trammeled the rights of other employees, nor created an absolute bar to their advancement.

As a preliminary matter, we note that petitioner bears the burden of establishing the invalidity of the Agency's Plan. Only last Term, in *Wygant v. Jackson Board of Education*, 476 U.S. 267 (1986), we held that "[t]he ultimate burden remains with the employees to demonstrate the unconstitutionality of an affirmative-action program," and we see no basis for a different rule regarding a plan's alleged violation of Title VII. This case also fits readily within the analytical framework set forth in *McDonnell Douglas Corp. v. Green*, 411 U.S. 792 (1973). Once a plaintiff establishes a prima facie case that race or sex has been taken into account in an employer's employment decision, the burden shifts to the employer to articulate a nondiscriminatory rationale for its decision. The existence of an affirmative action plan provides such a rationale. If such a plan is articulated as the basis for the employer's decision, the burden shifts to the plaintiff to prove that the employer's justification is pretextual and the plan is invalid. As a practical matter, of course, an employer will generally seek to avoid a charge of pretext by presenting evidence in support of its plan. That does not mean, however, as petitioner suggests, that reliance on an affirmative action plan is to be treated as an affirmative defense requiring the employer to carry the burden of proving the validity of the plan. The burden of proving its invalidity remains on the plaintiff.

> The Court is clear that the burden of proof is with the employee to show that the affirmative action plan is invalid.

The assessment of the legality of the Agency Plan must be guided by our decision in *Weber, supra.* In that case, the Court addressed the question whether the employer violated Title VII by adopting a voluntary affirmative action plan designed to "eliminate manifest racial imbalances in traditionally segregated job categories." The respondent employee in that case challenged the employer's denial of his application for a position in a newly established craft training program, contending that the employer's selection process impermissibly took into account the race of the applicants. The selection process was guided by an affirmative action plan, which provided that 50% of the new trainees were to be black until the percentage of black skilled craftworkers in the employer's plant approximated the percentage of blacks in the local labor force. Adoption of the plan had been prompted by the fact that only 5 of 273, or 1.83%, of skilled craftworkers at the plant were black, even though the work force in the area was approximately 39% black. Because of the historical exclusion of blacks from craft positions, the employer regarded its former policy of hiring trained outsiders as inadequate to redress the imbalance in its work force.

We upheld the employer's decision to select less senior black applicants over the white respondent, for we found that taking race into account was consistent with Title VII's objective of "break[ing] down old patterns of racial segregation and hierarchy."

> The Court here sets forth its three-part test for assessing affirmative action plans in the private employer context.

We noted that the plan did not "unnecessarily trammel the interests of the white employees," since it did not require "the discharge of white workers and their replacement with new black hirees." Nor did the plan create "an absolute bar to the advancement of white employees," since half of those trained in the new program were to be white. Finally, we observed that the plan was a temporary measure, not designed to maintain racial balance, but to "eliminate a manifest racial imbalance." As Justice BLACKMUN's concurrence made clear, *Weber* held that an employer seeking to justify the adoption of a plan need not point to its own prior discriminatory practices, nor even to evidence of an "arguable violation" on its part. Rather, it need point only to a "conspicuous . . . imbalance in traditionally segregated job categories." Our decision was grounded in the recognition that voluntary employer action can play a crucial role in furthering Title VII's purpose of eliminating the effects of discrimination in the workplace, and that Title VII should not be read to thwart such efforts.

In reviewing the employment decision at issue in this case, we must first examine whether that decision was made pursuant to a plan prompted by concerns similar to those of the employer in *Weber*. Next, we must determine whether the effect of the Plan on males and nonminorities is comparable to the effect of the Plan in that case.

The first issue is therefore whether consideration of the sex of applicants for Skilled Craft jobs was justified by the existence of a "manifest imbalance" that reflected underrepresentation of women in "traditionally segregated job categories." [I]n determining whether an imbalance exists that would justify taking sex or race into account, a comparison of the percentage of minorities or women in the employer's work force with the percentage in the area labor market or general population is appropriate in analyzing jobs that require no special expertise, *see Teamsters v. United States*, 431 U.S. 324 (1977) (comparison between percentage of blacks in employer's work force and in general population proper in determining extent of imbalance in truck driving positions), or training programs designed to provide expertise, *see Steelworkers v. Weber*, 443 U.S. 193 (1979) (comparison between proportion of blacks working at plant and proportion of blacks in area labor force appropriate in calculating imbalance for purpose of establishing preferential admission to craft training program). Where a job requires special training, however, the comparison should be with those in the labor force who possess the relevant qualifications. *See Hazelwood School District v. United States*, 433 U.S. 299 (1977) (must compare percentage of blacks in employer's work ranks with percentage of qualified black teachers in area labor force in determining underrepresentation in teaching positions). The requirement that the "manifest imbalance" relate to a "traditionally segregated job category" provides assurance both that sex or race will be taken into account in a manner consistent with Title VII's purpose of eliminating the effects of employment discrimination, and that the interests of those employees not benefiting from the plan will not be unduly infringed.

A manifest imbalance need not be such that it would support a prima facie case against the employer, as suggested in Justice O'CONNOR's concurrence, since we do not regard as identical the constraints of Title VII and the Federal Constitution on voluntarily adopted affirmative action plans. Application of the "prima facie" standard in Title VII cases would be inconsistent with *Weber's* focus on statistical imbalance, and could inappropriately create a significant disincentive for employers to adopt an affirmative action plan. A corporation concerned with maximizing return on investment, for instance, is hardly likely to adopt a plan if in order to do so it must compile evidence that could be used to subject it to a colorable Title VII suit.

It is clear that the decision to hire Joyce was made pursuant to an Agency plan that directed that sex or race be taken into account for the purpose of remedying underrepresentation. The Agency Plan acknowledged the "limited opportunities that have existed in the past," for women to find employment in certain job classifications "where women have not been traditionally employed in significant numbers." As a result, observed the Plan, women were concentrated in traditionally female jobs in the Agency, and represented a lower percentage in other job classifications than would be expected if such traditional segregation had not occurred. Specifically, 9 of the 10 Para-Professionals and 110 of the 145 Office and Clerical Workers were women. By contrast, women were only 2 of the 28 Officials and Administrators, 5 of the 58 Professionals, 12 of the 124 Technicians, none of the Skilled Craft Workers, and 1 — who was Joyce — of the 110 Road Maintenance Workers. The Plan sought to remedy these imbalances through "hiring, training and promotion of . . . women throughout the Agency in all major job classifications where they are underrepresented."

As an initial matter, the Agency adopted as a benchmark for measuring progress in eliminating underrepresentation the long-term goal of a work force that mirrored in its major job classifications the percentage of women in the area labor market. Even as it did so, however, the Agency acknowledged that such a figure could not by itself necessarily justify taking into account the sex of applicants for positions in all job categories. For positions requiring specialized training and experience, the Plan observed that the number of minorities and women "who possess the qualifications required for entry into such job classifications is limited." The Plan therefore directed that annual short-term goals be formulated that would provide a more realistic indication of the degree to which sex should be taken into account in filling particular positions. The Plan stressed that such goals "should not be construed as 'quotas' that must be met," but as reasonable aspirations in correcting the imbalance in the Agency's work force. These goals were to take into account factors such as "turnover, layoffs, lateral transfers, new job openings, retirements and availability of minorities, women and handicapped persons in the area work force who possess the desired qualifications or potential for placement." The Plan specifically directed that, in establishing such goals, the Agency

> Why is it important — according to the Court — that the affirmative action plan not create a quota-like system?

work with the County Planning Department and other sources in attempting to compile data on the percentage of minorities and women in the local labor force that were actually working in the job classifications constituting the Agency work force. From the outset, therefore, the Plan sought annually to develop even more refined measures of the underrepresentation in each job category that required attention.

As the Agency Plan recognized, women were most egregiously underrepresented in the Skilled Craft job category, since none of the 238 positions was occupied by a woman. In mid-1980, when Joyce was selected for the road dispatcher position, the Agency was still in the process of refining its short-term goals for Skilled Craft Workers in accordance with the directive of the Plan. This process did not reach fruition until 1982, when the Agency established a short-term goal for that year of 3 women for the 55 expected openings in that job category — a modest goal of about 6% for that category.

We reject petitioner's argument that, since only the long-term goal was in place for Skilled Craft positions at the time of Joyce's promotion, it was inappropriate for the Director to take into account affirmative action considerations in filling the road dispatcher position. The Agency's Plan emphasized that the long-term goals were not to be taken as guides for actual hiring decisions, but that supervisors were to consider a host of practical factors in seeking to meet affirmative action objectives, including the fact that in some job categories women were not qualified in numbers comparable to their representation in the labor force.

By contrast, had the Plan simply calculated imbalances in all categories according to the proportion of women in the area labor pool, and then directed that hiring be governed solely by those figures, its validity fairly could be called into question. This is because analysis of a more specialized labor pool normally is necessary in determining underrepresentation in some positions. If a plan failed to take distinctions in qualifications into account in providing guidance for actual employment decisions, it would dictate mere blind hiring by the numbers, for it would hold supervisors to "achievement of a particular percentage of minority employment or membership . . . regardless of circumstances such as economic conditions or the number of available qualified minority applicants. . . ."

The Agency's Plan emphatically did not authorize such blind hiring. It expressly directed that numerous factors be taken into account in making hiring decisions, including specifically the qualifications of female applicants for particular jobs. Thus, despite the fact that no precise short-term goal was yet in place for the Skilled Craft category in mid-1980, the Agency's management nevertheless had been clearly instructed that they were not to hire solely by reference to statistics. The fact that only the long-term goal had been established for this category posed no danger that personnel decisions would be made by reflexive adherence to a numerical standard.

Furthermore, in considering the candidates for the road dispatcher position in 1980, the Agency hardly needed to rely on a refined short-term goal to realize that it had a significant problem of underrepresentation that required attention. Given the obvious imbalance in the Skilled Craft category, and given the Agency's commitment to eliminating such imbalances, it was plainly not unreasonable for the Agency to determine that it was appropriate to consider as one factor the sex of Ms. Joyce in making its decision. The promotion of Joyce thus satisfies the first requirement enunciated in *Weber*, since it was undertaken to further an affirmative action plan designed to eliminate Agency work force imbalances in traditionally segregated job categories.

We next consider whether the Agency Plan unnecessarily trammeled the rights of male employees or created an absolute bar to their advancement. In contrast to the plan in *Weber*, which provided that 50% of the positions in the craft training program were exclusively for blacks, and to the consent decree upheld last Term in *Firefighters v. Cleveland*, 478 U.S. 501 (1986), which required the promotion of specific numbers of minorities, the Plan sets aside no positions for women. The Plan expressly states that "[t]he 'goals' established for each Division should not be construed as 'quotas' that must be met." Rather, the Plan merely authorizes that consideration be given to affirmative action concerns when evaluating qualified applicants. As the Agency Director testified, the sex of Joyce was but one of numerous factors he took into account in arriving at his decision. The Plan thus resembles the "Harvard Plan" approvingly noted by Justice Powell in *Regents of University of California v. Bakke*, 438 U.S. 265 (1978), which considers race along with other criteria in determining admission to the college. As Justice POWELL observed: "In such an admissions program, race or ethnic background may be deemed a 'plus' in a particular applicant's file, yet it does not insulate the individual from comparison with all other candidates for the available seats." Similarly, the Agency Plan requires women to compete with all other qualified applicants. No persons are automatically excluded from consideration; all are able to have their qualifications weighed against those of other applicants.

In addition, petitioner had no absolute entitlement to the road dispatcher position. Seven of the applicants were classified as qualified and eligible, and the Agency Director was authorized to promote any of the seven. Thus, denial of the promotion unsettled no legitimate, firmly rooted expectation on the part of petitioner. Furthermore, while petitioner in this case was denied a promotion, he retained his employment with the Agency, at the same salary and with the same seniority, and remained eligible for other promotions.

Finally, the Agency's Plan was intended to attain a balanced work force, not to maintain one. The Plan contains 10 references to the Agency's desire to "attain" such a balance, but no reference whatsoever to a goal of maintaining it. The Director testified that, while the "broader goal" of affirmative action, defined as "the desire to hire, to promote, to give opportunity and training on an equitable, non-discriminatory basis," is something that is "a permanent part" of "the Agency's operating philosophy," that broader goal "is divorced, if you will, from specific numbers or percentages."

> The Court emphasizes that the affirmative action plan must seek to attain — rather than maintain — a balanced workforce.

The Agency acknowledged the difficulties that it would confront in remedying the imbalance in its work force, and it anticipated only gradual increases in the representation of minorities and women. It is thus unsurprising that the Plan contains no explicit end date, for the Agency's flexible, case-by-case approach was not expected to yield success in a brief period of time. Express assurance that a program is only temporary may be necessary if the program actually sets aside positions according to specific numbers. This is necessary both to minimize the effect of the program on other employees, and to ensure that the plan's goals "[are] not being used simply to achieve and maintain . . . balance, but rather as a benchmark against which" the employer may measure its progress in eliminating the underrepresentation of minorities and women. In this case, however, substantial evidence shows that the Agency has sought to take a moderate, gradual approach to eliminating the imbalance in its work force, one which establishes realistic guidance for employment decisions, and which visits minimal intrusion on the legitimate expectations of other employees. Given this fact, as well as the Agency's express commitment to "attain" a balanced work force, there is ample assurance that the Agency does not seek to use its Plan to maintain a permanent racial and sexual balance.

In evaluating the compliance of an affirmative action plan with Title VII's prohibition on discrimination, we must be mindful of "this Court's and Congress' consistent emphasis on 'the value of voluntary efforts to further the objectives of the law.'" *Wygant*, 476 U.S. at 290, (O'CONNOR, J., concurring in part and concurring in judgment) (quoting *Bakke, supra*, 438 U.S. at 364). The Agency in the case before us has undertaken such a voluntary effort, and has done so in full recognition of both the difficulties and the potential for intrusion on males and nonminorities. The Agency has identified a conspicuous imbalance in job categories traditionally segregated by race and sex. It has made clear from the outset, however, that employment decisions may not be justified solely by reference to this imbalance, but must rest on a multitude of practical, realistic factors. It has therefore committed itself to annual adjustment of goals so as to provide a reasonable guide for actual hiring and promotion decisions. The Agency earmarks no positions for anyone; sex is but one of several factors that may be taken into account in evaluating qualified applicants for a position. As both the Plan's language and its manner of operation attest, the Agency has no intention of establishing a work force whose permanent composition is dictated by rigid numerical standards.

We therefore hold that the Agency appropriately took into account as one factor the sex of Diane Joyce in determining that she should be promoted to the road dispatcher position. The decision to do so was made pursuant to an affirmative action plan that represents a moderate, flexible, case-by-case approach to effecting a gradual improvement in the representation of minorities and women in the Agency's work force. Such a plan is fully consistent with Title VII, for it embodies the contribution that voluntary employer action can make in eliminating the vestiges of discrimination in the workplace. Accordingly, the judgment of the Court of Appeals is Affirmed.

■ NOTES AND QUESTIONS

1. The *Johnson* decision does an excellent job of summarizing the legality of affirmative action plans in employment. As the decision reflects, such plans are considered under the traditional *McDonnell Douglas* analysis, and not as direct evidence of discrimination. Does this approach make sense?

2. The *Johnson* Court also emphasizes that it is the plaintiff that has the burden of establishing the invalidity of a particular affirmative action plan in the private employment context. Though the defendant here (the county) is a public entity, the constitutional claims were not considered on appeal. Courts analyzing affirmative action plans instituted by governmental entities will typically use a different standard from that set forth here.

3. Under *McDonnell Douglas*, the existence of an affirmative action plan will often satisfy the prima facie case of discrimination. The employer will then offer the plan as the legitimate nondiscriminatory rationale. The plaintiff would maintain the burden of showing that the plan was not valid. *See* Chris Engels, *Voluntary Affirmative Action in Employment for Women and Minorities Under Title VII of the Civil Rights Act: Extending Possibilities for Employers to Engage in Preferential Treatment to Achieve Equal Employment Opportunity*, 24 J. Marshall L. Rev. 731 (1991); Charles A. Sullivan, *Circling Back to the Obvious: The Convergence of Traditional and Reverse Discrimination in Title VII Proof*, 46 Wm. & Mary L. Rev. 1031 (2004).

4. Under the Court's analysis here, affirmative action plans implemented as part of the employment process typically must satisfy three different factors:

   a. The plan must be designed to break down old patterns of discrimination;

   b. The plan must not "unnecessarily trammel[ ] the rights of other employees, nor create[ ] an absolute bar to their advancement;" and

   c. The plan must be "a temporary measure, not designed to maintain racial balance, but to eliminate a manifest racial imbalance."

5. The factors articulated by the Court for determining whether an affirmative action plan is valid are somewhat ambiguous. How would you establish that a plan does not trammel the rights of other employees?

6. Given the factors outlined by the Court, should employers be hesitant to establish affirmative action plans? Why or why not? *See* Richard N. Appel, Alison L. Gray & Nilufer Loy, *Affirmative Action in the Workplace: Forty Years Later*, 22 Hofstra Lab. & Emp. L.J. 549 (2005).

Class Exercise: Developing an Affirmative Action Plan

Assume that you are hired as a new attorney at a major law firm in a nearby city. A client of your firm — a Fortune 500 company that produces computer software — recently received some bad publicity about the racial composition of its workforce. It decides to head off the controversy by implementing a company-wide affirmative action plan for the hiring of all of its new employees. The partner that works for the client has asked you to draft the policy.

What would the policy look like? How would you address the factors outlined in the Court's *Johnson* decision?

F. Chapter-in-Review

As this chapter demonstrates, racial discrimination in employment can be a substantial problem. The typical frameworks developed in *Griggs* and *McDonnell Douglas* were created with racial discrimination in mind, and squarely address these types of cases. Congress was clear that there is no reason to discriminate on the basis of race or color.

So-called reverse discrimination claims can provide a unique inquiry in race cases. When looking at race claims brought by white workers, some courts apply the traditional *McDonnell Douglas* test. Other courts, however, use a more rigid analysis at the first stage of the inquiry.

Affirmative action plans also frequently arise in the race context. Most private employers avoid the use of these plans. However, when utilized, employers must make sure that their plan complies with the framework set forth in the Supreme Court's *Johnson* decision.

Because a large percentage of charges of discrimination received by the EEOC involve race, employers must be particularly cognizant of this basis of discrimination. Clients should be counseled on preventing this type of discrimination before it ever occurs, and should understand how to address these issues when they present themselves.

The EEOC has done an excellent job of providing guidance on preventive issues when handling racial discrimination. The Commission has set forth its "best practices" for addressing the issue. These suggestions provide a nice summary of this chapter and further provide a valuable approach to addressing racial discrimination in the workplace:

- Develop a strong EEO policy that is embraced by the CEO and top executives, train managers and employees on its contents, enforce it, and hold company managers accountable.
- Make sure decisions are transparent (to the extent feasible) and documented. The reasons for employment decisions should be well explained to affected persons. Make sure managers maintain records for at least the statutorily required periods.
- Recruit, hire, and promote with EEO in mind, by implementing practices designed to widen and diversify the pool of candidates considered for employment openings, including openings in upper-level management.
- Monitor for EEO by conducting self-analyses to determine whether current employment practices disadvantage people of color, treat them differently, or leave uncorrected the effects of historical discrimination in the company.
- Analyze the duties, functions, and competencies relevant to jobs. Then create objective, job-related qualification standards related to those duties, functions, and competencies. Make sure they are consistently applied when choosing among candidates.
- Develop the potential of employees, supervisors, and executives with EEO in mind, by providing training and mentoring to give workers of all backgrounds the opportunity, skill, experience, and information

necessary to perform well, and to ascend to upper-level jobs. Make sure promotion criteria are made known, and that job openings are communicated to all eligible employees.

■ Monitor compensation practices and performance appraisal systems for patterns of potential discrimination. Make sure performance appraisals are based on employees' actual job performance.

■ Develop the potential of employees, supervisors, and executives with EEO in mind, by providing training and mentoring that provides workers of all backgrounds the opportunity, skill, experience, and information necessary to perform well, and to ascend to upper-level jobs.

■ Promote an inclusive culture in the workplace by inculcating an environment of professionalism and respect for personal differences. In addition, employees of all backgrounds should have equal access to workplace networks.

■ Foster open communication and early dispute resolution. This will minimize the chance of misunderstandings escalating into legally actionable EEO problems. In addition, an alternative dispute resolution (ADR) program can resolve EEO problems without the acrimony associated with an adversarial process.

■ Protect against retaliation. Provide clear and credible assurances that if employees make complaints or provide information related to complaints the employer will protect employees from retaliation, and consistently follow through on this guarantee.

EEOC Compl. Man. (CCH) ¶ 8780, § 15-IX (2006) (some text omitted).

The EEOC's recommendations are simply helpful guidelines, and not legal requirements. Each workplace environment should be individually tailored to help prevent discrimination. It can be useful to review the suggestions of the EEOC to better facilitate a discrimination-free workplace, and to make sure that everything is being done to prevent unfair treatment. Aggressive preventive measures — though expensive and time consuming — can be critical to avoiding even more expensive litigation.

Sex Discrimination

 Interactive Problem

Nancy Numbers has worked for several years as a certified public accountant at Bean Counters, Inc., the largest accounting firm in the country. Nancy was always very well regarded at the firm, and she often received praise from clients with whom she worked. Nancy also received excellent performance reviews every year that she worked at the firm. After ten years of employment at Bean Counters, Nancy submitted her name for partnership with the firm. The managing partner, and Nancy's mentor, Peter Partner, called her into his office to discuss her partnership application. Peter asked Nancy a number of questions that he deemed important regarding whether the firm should consider her for partnership. Initially, he asked Nancy whether she was currently "pregnant," because this was "relevant information" about how much time she would be able to spend at the firm. He also asked whether Nancy was married, and if not, what her future plans held in this regard. He noted that single women were far more productive than women that were "weighed down" with family responsibilities. Finally, he asked whether she would be comfortable heading up only accounts where the client was a female. Peter noted that "women are far more comfortable dealing with other women," and stated that her sex could be a significant advantage in this regard.

Were Peter's questions lawful? Could they lead to potential litigation under Title VII?

A. Introduction

The word "sex" was added to the Civil Rights Act of 1964 at the last minute by Representative Howard W. Smith. Critics believed that Smith, a Southern conservative who had previously gone on record as opposing any federal civil rights legislation, did so in an attempt to kill the entire Bill. Smith, however, claimed that he had amended the Bill in keeping with his support of Alice Paul (a well-known women's rights activist) and the National Women's Party with whom he had been working. Representative Martha W. Griffiths led the effort to keep the word "sex" in the Bill. Regardless of whether the word was added in good faith or whether Smith added it so that the Bill would have less chance of success, the law ultimately passed as amended and thus ensured that women have a remedy to fight employment discrimination. *See* Linda Napikoski, *How Women Became Part of the Civil Rights Act*, ABOUT.COM, http://womenshistory.about.com/od/laws/a/sex_and_civil_ rights_act.htm; *Teaching with Documents: The Civil Rights Act of 1964 and the Equal Employment Opportunity Commission*, NATIONAL ARCHIVES.GOV, http://www.archives. gov/ education/lessons/civil-rights-act/. For another interesting look at the historical roots of sex discrimination, see Cary Franklin, *Inventing the "Traditional Concept" of Sex Discrimination*, 125 HARV. L. REV. 1307 (2012).

Early Women's Employment Poster

Discrimination on the basis of sex is thus expressly prohibited under Title VII. The statute states that it is unlawful for an employer

> to fail or refuse to hire or to discharge any individual, or otherwise to discriminate against any individual with respect to his compensation, terms, conditions, or privileges of employment, because of such individual's . . . sex.

42 U.S.C. § 2000e–2(a)(1).

Sex discrimination is unique in a number of important ways that will be discussed in this chapter. One overriding theme of this chapter will be an examination of how "sex" is defined in the statute. Though it seems relatively straightforward, the meaning of the term has given rise to significant litigation. Sexual harassment is a separate topic that was covered earlier in this book. The Supreme Court helped provide guidance as to what constitutes sex discrimination in the same-sex sexual harassment context. In *Oncale v. Sundowner Offshore Services, Inc.*, 523 U.S. 75, 80–81 (1998), the Court stated that there are three different circumstances in which the statutory standard "because of sex" can be satisfied: (1) by showing that the employer's conduct was sexual in nature; (2) by establishing that the company treated one sex with hostility; or (3) through comparative evidence showing that one sex was treated better than the other. As the Court noted, this list is not exhaustive, and there are additional ways of establishing "sex" under the statute.

The Me Too Movement brought worldwide attention to the prevalence of sex discrimination, assault and sexual harassment that occurs in and outside the workplace. The movement gained momentum when people took to social media in 2017 to share personal experiences of sexual harassment and assault after numerous women accused Hollywood producer Harvey Weinstein of inappropriate sexual misconduct. The hashtag #MeToo was used over a million times on Facebook over a forty-eight-hour period alone.

With the increased use of technology, sexual harassment and assault in the workplace now extends well beyond the physical office space and traditional working hours. Texting, social media, and flexible work environments present numerous challenges for employers attempting to navigate workplace liability issues. As a result, employers are increasingly beginning to evaluate whether corporate policies and procedures for handling reports of sexual misconduct (such as zero-tolerance harassment policies and internal reporting mechanisms) are effective in addressing the widespread need for change.

A more thorough discussion of this movement, and its possible impact on employers and workers, is set forth in Chapter 5: Harassment.

Specific areas where "sex" is implicated in the employment discrimination context include discriminating on the basis of an employee's pregnancy, discriminating on the basis of an employee's sexual orientation, or failing to provide sufficient leave to allow the employee to care for him or herself or a family member. Sex discrimination also implicates specific issues related to pay, and includes specific exceptions under the statute.

B. Pregnancy as a Form of Sex Discrimination

When the statute was passed, it was unclear whether "pregnancy" was included as part of sex discrimination. On its face, it would appear that discrimination on the basis of pregnancy is indeed sex discrimination. Nonetheless, it can also be argued that discriminating on the basis of pregnancy is separate and apart from discriminating on the basis of sex. After all, not all women will become pregnant, or some female employees may have passed child-bearing age.

After Title VII was passed, the courts took varying approaches to when and whether pregnancy discrimination was a form of sex discrimination. The Pregnancy Discrimination Act (PDA) was passed in 1978 in response to two Supreme Court cases: *Geduldig v. Aiello* (1974) and *General Electric Co. v. Gilbert* (1976). Both decisions permitted employers to treat pregnant employees differently than non-pregnant disabled employees, particularly with respect to employment benefits.

Women's organizations and civil rights activists formed the Campaign to End Discrimination Against Pregnant Workers, seeking legislative reform from *Geduldig* and *Gilbert*. The PDA therefore overturned those Supreme Court decisions by mandating that pregnant women, or women affected by pregnancy-related conditions, be treated the same as other nonpregnant employees who were similarly unable to work. *See* Lorraine Hafer O'Hara, *An Overview of Federal and State Protections for Pregnant Workers*, 56 U. Cin. L. Rev. 757, 766 (1987); *PDA-Historical Perspective*, USLegal.com, http://pregnancydiscrim-inationact.uslegal.com/pda-historical-perspective/.

The PDA is not a separate statute, but instead amends Title VII and clarifies that the statute prohibits discrimination on the basis of pregnancy. The PDA — at section 701(k) of the statute — provides that:

> The terms "because of sex" or "on the basis of sex" include, but are not limited to, because of or on the basis of pregnancy, childbirth, or related medical conditions; and women affected by pregnancy, childbirth, or related medical conditions shall be treated the same for all employment-related purposes, including receipt of benefits under fringe benefit programs, as other persons not so affected but similar in their ability or inability to work. . . .

Thus, after the PDA was enacted, it was clear that discrimination on the basis of pregnancy was indeed sex discrimination under Title VII. Beyond pregnancy itself, the PDA also clearly includes childbirth and related medical conditions in its terms. Therefore, where an employer discriminates on the basis of the birth itself, or on the basis of related health issues, it will also be considered sex discrimination under Title VII. It is important to remember that Title VII only requires that employees not be treated differently on a protected basis. Thus, an employer cannot treat employees *worse* than other employees on the basis of sex or pregnancy. However, employers are also not required to treat pregnant workers *better* than other employees. Thus, under Title VII, employers can hold pregnant workers to the same standard as other employees.

A number of issues recently have arisen in this area, some of which focus on breast-feeding and lactation, and the extent to which employer discrimination on this basis runs afoul of Title VII. *See* Sarah Andrews, *Lactation Breaks in the Workplace: What Employers Need to Know About the Nursing Mothers Amendment to the FLSA*, 30 Hofstra Lab. & Emp. L.J. 121 (2012) (explaining the main requirements of the Nursing Mothers Amendment to the Fair Labor Standards Act (FLSA): that employees who are nursing are provided with reasonable break time to express breast milk; that the break, which can be unpaid, must be provided each time an employee has a need to express breast milk the first year following the birth of a child; and that the employer provide a workplace location for the purpose of expressing breast milk that is not a bathroom, is shielded from view, and is free from intrusion by co-workers and the public). This can be a surprisingly complex area that is still being navigated by the courts, governmental agencies, and legislatures.

Ames v. Nationwide Mutual Insurance Co.

747 F.3d 509 (8th Cir. 2014)

WOLLMAN, Circuit Judge.

[Angela] Ames was hired as a loss-mitigation specialist at Nationwide Mutual Insurance in October 2008. Timely completion of work is central to this position and "a high priority" for the loss-mitigation department as a whole. Brian Brinks was Ames's immediate supervisor, and Neel was the head of her department, as well as an associate vice president. Ames gave birth to her first child on May 2, 2009, and took eight weeks of maternity leave following his birth. In October 2009, Ames discovered that she was pregnant with her second child. Ames suffered pregnancy complications, and her doctor ordered her on bed rest in April 2010.

When Ames discussed her bed rest with [Karla] Neel, Neel rolled her eyes and said that she never had to go on bed rest when she was pregnant and that she never had complications with her pregnancies. Neel had previously expressed to Ames her belief that a woman should not have a baby shower while she is pregnant because the baby could die in utero. According to Ames, Brinks remarked to others in the office about Ames's maternity leave, stating, "Oh, yeah, I'm teasing her about only taking a week's worth of maternity leave. We're too busy for her to take off that much work." Nationwide trained Angie Ebensberger, who was a temporary employee at Nationwide Mutual Insurance, to fill Ames's position during her maternity leave.

Ames gave birth to her second child prematurely on May 18, 2010. Nationwide thereafter informed Ames that her Family Medical Leave Act (FMLA) maternity leave would expire on August 2, 2010. On June 16, 2010, Neel called Ames to inform her that there had been a mistake in calculating her FMLA maternity leave and that her maternity leave would expire on July 12, 2010. Neel also told Ames that she could take additional unpaid leave until August 2010, but that doing so would "cause[ ] red flags," that she "[didn't] want there to be any problems like that," and that she "[didn't] want there to be any issues down the road." Neel told Ames that she wanted to find a mutually agreeable date of return and offered to extend Ames's maternity leave an additional week.

Prior to returning to work, Ames asked a Nationwide disability case manager where she could express milk when she returned to work and was told that she could use a lactation room. Ames returned to work on July 19, 2010, when her son was two months old and breastfeeding every three hours. By the time Ames had arrived at work that morning, more than three hours had passed since her son had last nursed. Ames asked Neel about using a lactation room. Neel replied that it was not her responsibility to provide Ames with a lactation room. Ames then went to the security desk to inquire about the lactation rooms and was directed to see Sara Hallberg, the company nurse.

Hallberg informed Ames of Nationwide's lactation policy, which allowed employees to gain badge access to the company's lactation rooms after completing certain paperwork that required three days to be processed. The lactation policy was available to Nationwide's employees on the company's intranet, and Nationwide provided information regarding the policy at its quarterly maternity meetings. Ames's conversation with Hallberg was the first time that Ames had heard of the policy. Hallberg sent a copy of the lactation policy to Ames via email. Hallberg also requested that security "grant Angela Ames access to the lactation rooms as soon as possible." When Ames told Hallberg that she needed to express milk immediately, Hallberg suggested that Ames use a wellness room. Because the wellness room was occupied,

Would you be more careful if it was you that got pregnant?

Hallberg told Ames to return in fifteen or twenty minutes. Hallberg warned Ames that lactating in a wellness room might expose her breast milk to germs.

While waiting for the wellness room, Ames met with Brinks to discuss the status of her work. Brinks told Ames that none of her work had been completed while she was on maternity leave, that she had two weeks to complete that work, that she would have to work overtime to accomplish this, and that if she failed to catch up, she would be disciplined. After the meeting with Brinks, Ames returned to Neel's office to see if Neel could help her find a place to lactate. Neel again told Ames that she was unable to help. Neel testified that Ames was visibly upset and in tears. Neel then handed Ames a piece of paper and a pen and told Ames, "You know, I think it's best that you go home to be with your babies." Neel dictated to Ames what to write on the piece of paper to effectuate her resignation.

Ames sued Nationwide, alleging sex and pregnancy discrimination. Her complaint asserted that the unavailability of a lactation room, "her urgent need to express milk," and Nationwide's "unrealistic and unreasonable expectations about her work production" forced her to resign from her position. Nationwide moved for summary judgment, arguing that there was no genuine dispute of material fact that Nationwide discriminated against Ames. Specifically, Nationwide argued that Ames had not shown constructive discharge. Ames countered that she had set forth direct and indirect evidence of discrimination and that she had shown constructive discharge. Ames did not argue that Nationwide had actually discharged her. The district court granted Nationwide's motion, and this appeal followed.

> Does the comment "I think it's best that you go home to be with your babies" represent direct evidence of discrimination?

Title VII prohibits employment discrimination on the basis of sex. 42 U.S.C. § 2000e–2(a)(1). As amended by the Pregnancy Discrimination Act of 1978, sex-based discrimination under Title VII includes discrimination based on "pregnancy, childbirth, or related medical conditions." *Id.* § 2000e(k). Ames contends that she has presented sufficient evidence to demonstrate that Nationwide constructively discharged her.

"To prove a constructive discharge, an employee must show that the employer deliberately created intolerable working conditions with the intention of forcing her to quit." *Alvarez v. Des Moines Bolt Supply, Inc.*, 626 F.3d 410 (8th Cir. 2010). Ames argues that Nationwide treated her in a manner that would have caused any reasonable person to resign. Rather than presenting one event as the defining moment, Ames points to a number of incidents and circumstances that she claims collectively constitute constructive discharge. First, Neel and Brinks made negative statements regarding Ames's pregnancies. Second, Nationwide miscalculated the length of Ames's maternity leave, and Neel insisted that she return to work early or risk raising red flags. Third, Nationwide trained Angie Ebensberger to fill Ames's position during Ames's maternity leave. Fourth, Ames was not given immediate access to a lactation room and was told that she had to wait three days for badge access. Fifth, Brinks told Ames that none of her work had been completed while she was on maternity leave, that she had to work overtime to get caught up, and that if she did not catch up, she would be disciplined. Sixth, Neel did nothing to assist Ames in finding a place to lactate and instead told Ames, "I think it's best that you go home to be with your babies." And seventh, at the time Ames resigned, it had been more than five hours since she had last expressed milk and she was in considerable physical pain.

Nationwide's several attempts to accommodate Ames show its intent to maintain an employment relationship with Ames, not force her to quit. Although Nationwide incorrectly calculated Ames's FMLA leave, it made efforts to ameliorate the impact of its mistake. Neel did not discourage Ames from taking the FMLA leave to which Ames was entitled. Furthermore, even though Neel discouraged Ames from taking unpaid leave up to August, Neel gave Ames an extra week of maternity leave, which gave Ames more than thirty days to prepare for her return to work. Rather than intentionally rendering Ames's work conditions intolerable, the record shows that Nationwide sought to accommodate Ames's needs.

Moreover, Ames was denied immediate access to a lactation room only because she had not completed the paperwork to gain badge access. Every nursing mother was required to complete the same paperwork and was subjected to the same three-day waiting period. Further, Hallberg tried to accommodate Ames by allowing her to use a wellness room as soon as it was available and by requesting that Ames receive expedited access to the lactation rooms. During Ames's meeting with Brinks, Brinks relayed his expectations of her in the upcoming weeks and the consequences of failing to meet those expectations. Brinks's expectations of Ames were not unreasonable, for he expected all of his employees to keep their work current, given the high priority that timely work-completion is accorded within the loss-mitigation department. That Nationwide's policies treated all nursing mothers and loss-mitigation specialists alike demonstrates that Nationwide did not intend to force Ames to resign when it sought to enforce its policies.

While we are doubtful whether Neel's comment that it was best that Ames go home with her babies might support a finding of intent to force Ames to resign, assuming that it would, Ames's constructive discharge claim still fails because she did not give Nationwide a reasonable opportunity to address and ameliorate the conditions that she claims constituted a constructive discharge. The only way in which Ames attempted to alert Nationwide to the problem was by asking Neel twice about obtaining a lactation room and by approaching Hallberg about the same problem, all on the morning that Ames resigned. Moreover, when Ames approached Hallberg about the problem, Hallberg suggested to Ames a temporary solution. Although this solution may not have been immediately available or ideal, Ames had an obligation not to jump to the conclusion that the attempt would not work and that her only reasonable option was to resign. Ames also failed to avail herself of the channels of communication provided by Nationwide to deal with her problem. Nationwide's Compliance Statement, of which Ames was aware, provides: "If you have reason to believe that Nationwide is not in compliance with the law, contact your local HR professional, the Office of Ethics, or the Office of Associate Relations to report the circumstances immediately." By not attempting to return to Hallberg's office to determine the availability of a wellness room or to contact human resources, Ames acted unreasonably and failed to provide Nationwide with the necessary opportunity to remedy the problem she was experiencing. We thus conclude that Ames has not met her burden of demonstrating constructive discharge.

■ NOTES AND QUESTIONS

1. Do you agree with the court's analysis that there is no constructive discharge here? Would a reasonable person have left employment under these circumstances?

2. Irrespective of the outcome of this case, did the company properly handle this employee's pregnancy and subsequent childbirth? What would you have recommended that the company have done differently here?

3. How strong is the evidence that the plaintiff was told, "You know, I think it's best that you go home to be with your babies"? Did the court give enough weight to this comment?

4. Would a better claim have been that the plaintiff was actually discharged in this case, rather than constructively discharged?

5. Could the plaintiff have successfully argued for harassment based on her sex under the circumstances of this case?

6. The court does not ultimately address this issue, but was the employee's lactation a "related medical condition" to pregnancy? Was the PDA intended to extend this far? In *EEOC v. Houston Funding II, Ltd.*, which is excerpted in Chapter 2, the Fifth Circuit held, "Given our precedent, we hold the EEOC's

argument that [the defendant] discharged [the worker] because she was lactating or expressing milk states a cognizable Title VII sex discrimination claim." 717 F.3d 425, 428 (5th Cir. 2013).

7. Could the employee have been entitled to intermittent leave under the Family and Medical Leave Act to express milk? Consider this question as you read the following section.

8. The Patient Protection and Affordable Care Act amended § 7 of the FLSA to require employers to provide reasonable break time for an employee to express breast milk for one year after the nursing child's birth. The break time requirement became effective when the Affordable Care Act was signed into law on March 23, 2010. FLSA § 7(r) (as amended by the Affordable Care Act, Pub. L. No. 111–148); U.S. Dep't of Labor, Wage & Hour Division, Fact Sheet #73: Break Time for Nursing Mothers (Aug. 2013), http://www.dol.gov/whd/nursingmothers/.

 Interactive Problem

Looking back at the facts of the interactive problem, assume that shortly before seeking partnership at Bean Counters, Inc., Nancy Numbers revealed to her employers that she was pregnant. As a result of experiencing terrible morning sickness related to the pregnancy, Nancy missed several days of work. In fact, her absenteeism exceeded the amount allowed by company policy. If Peter Partner terminated Nancy as a result of this policy, would he run afoul of Title VII or the PDA?

Another issue that frequently arises in sex discrimination cases is what it means to treat pregnant women "similarly" to other employees. In *California Federal Savings & Loan Ass'n v. Guerra*, 479 U.S. 272 (1987), the Supreme Court emphasized the importance of this similar treatment. Despite this clear guidance, employers often face difficult questions when trying to determine how to treat pregnant workers. For example, where an employer gives light duty work to an individual with a temporary disability such as a broken leg, should that employer similarly provide light duty work to a pregnant worker when requested? The appellate courts have taken varying approaches to this issue, which was addressed by the Supreme Court in *Young v. United Parcel Service, Inc.*

Young v. United Parcel Service, Inc.

135 S. Ct. 1338 (2015)

Justice Breyer delivered the opinion of the Court.

The petitioner, Peggy Young, worked as a part-time driver for the respondent, United Parcel Service (UPS). Her responsibilities included pickup and delivery of packages that had arrived by air carrier the previous night. In 2006, after suffering several miscarriages, she became pregnant. Her doctor told her that she should not lift more than 20 pounds during the first 20 weeks of her pregnancy or more than 10 pounds thereafter. UPS required drivers like Young to be able to lift parcels weighing up to 70 pounds (and up to 150 pounds with assistance). UPS told Young she could not work while under a lifting restriction. Young consequently stayed home without pay during most of the time she was pregnant and eventually lost her employee medical coverage.

Young subsequently brought this federal lawsuit. We focus here on her claim that UPS acted unlawfully in refusing to accommodate her pregnancy-related lifting restriction. Young said that her co-workers were willing to help her with heavy packages. She also said that UPS accommodated other drivers who were "similar in their . . . inability to work." She accordingly concluded that UPS must accommodate her as well.

In 1978, Congress enacted the Pregnancy Discrimination Act, which added new language to Title VII. The first clause of the 1978 Act specifies that [the] "ter[m] 'because of sex' . . . include[s] . . . because of or on the basis of pregnancy, childbirth, or related medical conditions." § 2000e(k). The second clause says that

> women affected by pregnancy, childbirth, or related medical conditions shall be treated the same for all employment-related purposes . . . as other persons not so affected but similar in their ability or inability to work. . . .

This case requires us to consider the application of the second clause to a "disparate-treatment" claim — a claim that an employer intentionally treated a complainant less favorably than employees with the "complainant's qualifications" but outside the complainant's protected class. *McDonnell Douglas Corp. v. Green*, 411 U.S. 792, 802 (1973). We have said that "[l]iability in a disparate-treatment case depends on whether the protected trait actually motivated the employer's decision." *Raytheon Co. v. Hernandez*, 540 U.S. 44, 52 (2003) (ellipsis and internal quotation marks omitted). We have also made clear that a plaintiff can prove disparate treatment either (1) by direct evidence that a workplace policy, practice, or decision relies expressly on a protected characteristic, or (2) by using the burden-shifting framework set forth in *McDonnell Douglas. See Trans World Airlines, Inc. v. Thurston*, 469 U.S. 111, 121 (1985).

In *McDonnell Douglas*, we considered a claim of discriminatory hiring. We said that, to prove disparate treatment, an individual plaintiff must "carry the initial burden" of "establishing a prima facie case" of discrimination by showing

> (i) that he belongs to a . . . minority; (ii) that he applied and was qualified for a job for which the employer was seeking applicants; (iii) that, despite his qualifications, he was rejected; and (iv) that, after his rejection, the position remained open and the employer continued to seek applicants from persons of complainant's qualifications.

If a plaintiff makes this showing, then the employer must have an opportunity "to articulate some legitimate, nondiscriminatory reason for" treating employees outside the protected class better than employees within the protected class. If the employer articulates such a reason, the plaintiff then has "an opportunity to prove by a preponderance of the evidence that the legitimate reasons offered by the defendant [*i.e.,* the employer] were not its true reasons, but were a pretext for discrimination." *Texas Dept. of Community Affairs v. Burdine*, 450 U.S. 248, 253 (1981).

We note that employment discrimination law also creates what is called a "disparate-impact" claim. In evaluating a disparate-impact claim, courts focus on the *effects* of an employment practice, determining whether they are unlawful irrespective of motivation or intent. *See Raytheon, supra*, at 52–53; *see also Ricci v. DeStefano*, 557 U.S. 557, 578 (2009). But Young has not alleged a disparate impact claim. Nor has she asserted what we have called a "pattern-or-practice" claim. *See Teamsters v. United States*, 431 U.S. 324, 359 (1977).

In July 2007, Young filed a pregnancy discrimination charge with the Equal Employment Opportunity Commission (EEOC). In September 2008, the EEOC provided her with a right-to-sue letter. Young then filed this complaint in Federal District Court. She argued, among other things, that she could show by direct evidence that UPS had intended to discriminate against her because of her pregnancy and that, in any event, she could establish a prima facie case of disparate treatment under the *McDonnell Douglas* framework.

After discovery, UPS filed a motion for summary judgment. In reply, Young pointed to favorable facts that she believed were either undisputed or that, while disputed, she could prove. They include the following:

1. Young worked as a UPS driver, picking up and delivering packages carried by air.
2. Young was pregnant in the fall of 2006.
3. Young's doctor recommended that she "not be required to lift greater than 20 pounds for the first 20 weeks of pregnancy and no greater than 10 pounds thereafter."
4. UPS required drivers such as Young to be able to "[l]ift, lower, push, pull, leverage and manipulate . . . packages weighing up to 70 pounds" and to "[a]ssist in moving packages weighing up to 150 pounds."
5. UPS' occupational health manager, the official "responsible for most issues relating to employee health and ability to work" at Young's UPS facility, told Young that she could not return to work during her pregnancy because she could not satisfy UPS' lifting requirements.

6. The manager also determined that Young did not qualify for a temporary alternative work assignment.
7. UPS, in a collective-bargaining agreement, had promised to provide temporary alternative work assignments to employees "unable to perform their normal work assignments due to an *on-the-job injury.*"
8. The collective-bargaining agreement also provided that UPS would "make a good faith effort to comply . . . with requests for a reasonable accommodation because of a permanent disability" under the ADA.
9. The agreement further stated that UPS would give "inside" jobs to drivers who had lost their DOT certifications because of a failed medical exam, a lost driver's license, or involvement in a motor vehicle accident.
10. When Young later asked UPS' Capital Division Manager to accommodate her disability, he replied that, while she was pregnant, she was "too much of a liability" and could "not come back" until she " 'was no longer pregnant.' "
11. Young remained on a leave of absence (without pay) for much of her pregnancy.
12. Young returned to work as a driver in June 2007, about two months after her baby was born.

As direct evidence of intentional discrimination, Young relied, in significant part, on the statement of the Capital Division Manager (10 above). As evidence that she had made out a prima facie case under *McDonnell Douglas*, Young relied, in significant part, on evidence showing that UPS would accommodate workers injured on the job (7), those suffering from ADA disabilities (8), and those who had lost their DOT certifications (9). That evidence, she said, showed that UPS had a light-duty-for-injury policy with respect to numerous "other persons," but not with respect to pregnant workers. *See* Memorandum 29.

Young introduced further evidence indicating that UPS had accommodated several individuals when they suffered disabilities that created work restrictions similar to hers. UPS contests the correctness of some of these facts and the relevance of others. But because we are at the summary judgment stage, and because there is a genuine dispute as to these facts, we view this evidence in the light most favorable to Young, the nonmoving party:

13. Several employees received accommodations while suffering various similar or more serious disabilities incurred on the job.
14. Several employees received accommodations following injury, where the record is unclear as to whether the injury was incurred on or off the job.
15. Several employees received "inside" jobs after losing their DOT certifications.
16. Some employees were accommodated despite the fact that their disabilities had been incurred off the job.
17. According to a deposition of a UPS shop steward who had worked for UPS for roughly a decade, "the only light duty requested [due to physical] restrictions that became an issue" at UPS "were with women who were pregnant."

The District Court granted UPS' motion for summary judgment. On appeal, the Fourth Circuit affirmed. In light of lower-court uncertainty about the interpretation of the Act, we granted the petition [for certiorari]. The parties disagree about the interpretation of the Pregnancy Discrimination Act's second clause. As we have said, the Act's first clause specifies that discrimination " 'because of sex' " includes discrimination "because of . . . pregnancy." But the meaning of the second clause is less clear; it adds: "[W]omen affected by pregnancy, childbirth, or related medical conditions shall be treated the same for all employment-related purposes . . . as *other persons* not so affected but *similar in their ability or inability to work*." 42 U.S.C. § 2000e(k) (emphasis added). Does this clause mean that courts must compare workers *only* in respect to the work limitations that they suffer? Does it mean that courts must ignore all other similarities or differences between pregnant and nonpregnant workers? Or does it mean that courts, when deciding who the relevant "other persons" are, may consider other similarities and differences as well? If so, which ones?

The parties propose very different answers to this question. Young and the United States believe that the second clause of the Pregnancy Discrimination Act "requires an employer to provide the same accommodations to workplace disabilities caused by pregnancy that it provides to workplace disabilities that have other causes but have a similar effect on the ability to work." In other words, Young contends that the second clause means that whenever "an employer accommodates only a subset of workers with disabling conditions," a court should find a Title VII violation if "pregnant workers who are similar in the ability to work" do not "receive the same [accommodation] even if still other non-pregnant workers do not receive accommodations."

UPS takes an almost polar opposite view. It contends that the second clause does no more than define sex discrimination to include pregnancy discrimination. Under this view, courts would compare the accommodations an employer provides to pregnant women with the accommodations it provides to others *within* a facially neutral category (such as those with off-the-job injuries) to determine whether the employer has violated Title VII. The statute lends itself to an interpretation other than those that the parties advocate and that the dissent sets forth.

In our view, an individual pregnant worker who seeks to show disparate treatment through indirect evidence may do so through application of the *McDonnell Douglas* framework. That framework requires a plaintiff to make out a prima facie case of discrimination. But it is "not intended to be an inflexible rule." *Furnco Constr. Corp. v. Waters*, 438 U.S. 567, 575 (1978). Rather, an individual plaintiff may establish a prima facie case by "showing actions taken by the employer from which one can infer, if such actions remain unexplained, that it is more likely than not that such actions were based on a discriminatory criterion illegal under" Title VII. The burden of making this showing is "not onerous." In particular, making this showing is not as burdensome as succeeding on "an ultimate finding of fact as to" a discriminatory employment action. Neither does it require the plaintiff to show that those whom the employer favored and those whom the employer disfavored were similar in all but the protected ways.

Thus, a plaintiff alleging that the denial of an accommodation constituted disparate treatment under the Pregnancy Discrimination Act's second clause may make out a prima facie case by showing, as in *McDonnell Douglas*, that she belongs to the protected class, that she sought accommodation, that the employer did not accommodate her, and that the employer did accommodate others "similar in their ability or inability to work."

The employer may then seek to justify its refusal to accommodate the plaintiff by relying on "legitimate, nondiscriminatory" reasons for denying her accommodation. But, consistent with the Act's basic objective, that reason normally cannot consist simply of a claim that it is more expensive or less convenient to add pregnant women to the category of those ("similar in their ability or inability to work") whom the employer accommodates. After all, the employer in *Gilbert* could in all likelihood have made just such a claim. If the employer offers an apparently "legitimate, nondiscriminatory" reason for its actions, the plaintiff may in turn show that the employer's proffered reasons are in fact pretextual. We believe that the plaintiff may reach a jury on this issue by providing sufficient evidence that the employer's policies impose a significant burden on pregnant workers, and that the employer's "legitimate, nondiscriminatory" reasons are not sufficiently strong to justify the burden, but rather — when considered along with the burden imposed — give rise to an inference of intentional discrimination.

> Does the Court's requirement that the plaintiff provide "sufficient evidence" of a "significant burden" on the worker comport with its analyses in prior employment discrimination cases?

The plaintiff can create a genuine issue of material fact as to whether a significant burden exists by providing evidence that the employer accommodates a large percentage of nonpregnant workers while failing to accommodate a large percentage of pregnant workers. Here, for example, if the facts are as Young says they are, she can show that UPS accommodates most nonpregnant employees with lifting limitations while categorically failing to accommodate pregnant employees with lifting limitations. Young might also add that the fact that UPS has multiple policies that accommodate nonpregnant employees with lifting restrictions suggests that its reasons for failing to accommodate pregnant employees with lifting restrictions are not sufficiently strong — to the point that a jury could find that its reasons for failing to accommodate pregnant employees give rise to an inference of intentional discrimination.

This approach, though limited to the Pregnancy Discrimination Act context, is consistent with our longstanding rule that a plaintiff can use circumstantial proof to rebut an employer's apparently legitimate, nondiscriminatory reasons for treating individuals within a protected class differently than those outside the protected class. In particular, it is hardly anomalous (as the dissent makes it out to be) how a policy operates in practice. In *McDonnell Douglas* itself, we noted that an employer's "general policy and practice with respect to minority employment" — including "statistics as to" that policy and practice — could be evidence of pretext. Moreover, the continued focus on whether the plaintiff has introduced sufficient evidence to give rise to an inference of *intentional* discrimination avoids confusing the disparate-treatment and disparate impact doctrines.

Our interpretation of the Act is also, unlike the dissent's, consistent with Congress' intent to overrule *Gilbert*'s reasoning and result. The dissent says that "[i]f a pregnant woman is denied an accommodation under a policy that does not discriminate against pregnancy, she *has* been 'treated the same' as everyone else." This logic would have found no problem with the employer plan in *Gilbert*, which "denied an accommodation" to pregnant women on the same basis as it denied accommodations to other employees — *i.e.*, it accommodated only sicknesses and accidents, and pregnancy was neither of those. In arguing to the contrary, the dissent's discussion of *Gilbert* relies exclusively on the opinions of the dissenting Justices in that case. But Congress' intent in passing the Act was to overrule the *Gilbert majority* opinion, which viewed the employer's disability plan as denying coverage to pregnant employees on a neutral basis.

Under this interpretation of the Act, the judgment of the Fourth Circuit must be vacated. A party is entitled to summary judgment if there is "no genuine dispute as to any material fact and the movant is entitled to judgment as a matter of law." Fed. Rule Civ. Proc. 56(a). We have already outlined the evidence Young introduced. Viewing the record in the light most favorable to Young, there is a genuine dispute as to whether UPS provided more favorable treatment to at least some employees whose situation cannot reasonably be distinguished from Young's. In other words, Young created a genuine dispute of material fact as to the fourth prong of the *McDonnell Douglas* analysis.

Young also introduced evidence that UPS had three separate accommodation policies (on-the-job, ADA, DOT). Taken together, Young argued, these policies significantly burdened pregnant women. The Fourth Circuit did not consider the combined effects of these policies, nor did it consider the strength of UPS' justifications for each when combined. That is, why, when the employer accommodated so many, could it not accommodate pregnant women as well?

We do not determine whether Young created a genuine issue of material fact as to whether UPS' reasons for having treated Young less favorably than it treated these other nonpregnant employees were pretextual. We leave a final determination of that question for the Fourth Circuit to make on remand, in light of the interpretation of the Pregnancy Discrimination Act that we have set out above.

Justice SCALIA, with whom Justice KENNEDY and Justice THOMAS join, dissenting.

Faced with two conceivable readings of the Pregnancy Discrimination Act, the Court chooses neither. It crafts instead a new law that is splendidly unconnected with the text and even the legislative history of the Act. To "treat" pregnant workers "the same . . . as other persons," we are told, means refraining from adopting policies that impose "significant burden[s]" upon pregnant women without "sufficiently strong" justifications. Where do the "significant burden" and "sufficiently strong justification" requirements come from? Inventiveness posing as scholarship — which gives us an interpretation that is as dubious in principle as it is senseless in practice.

Dissatisfied with the only two readings that the words of the same-treatment clause could possibly bear, the Court decides that the clause means something in-between. It takes only a couple of waves of the Supreme Wand to produce the desired result. Poof!: The same-treatment clause means that a neutral reason for refusing to accommodate a pregnant woman is pretextual if "the employer's policies impose a significant burden on pregnant workers." Poof!: This is so only when the employer's reasons "are not sufficiently strong to justify the burden."

How we got here from the same-treatment clause is anyone's guess. There is no way to read "shall be treated the same" — or indeed anything else in the clause — to mean that courts must balance the significance of the burden on pregnant workers against the strength of the employer's justifications for the policy. That is presumably why the Court does not even *try* to connect the interpretation it adopts with the text it purports to interpret. The Court has forgotten that statutory purpose and the presumption against superfluity are tools for choosing among competing reasonable readings of a law, not authorizations for making up new readings that the law cannot reasonably bear.

The fun does not stop there. Having ignored the terms of the same-treatment clause, the Court proceeds to bungle the dichotomy between claims of disparate treatment and claims of disparate impact. Normally, liability for disparate treatment arises when an employment policy has a "discriminatory motive," while liability for disparate impact arises when the effects of an employment policy "fall more harshly on one group than another and cannot be justified by business necessity." *Teamsters*, 431 U.S., at 336, n. 15. In the topsy-turvy world created by today's decision, however, a pregnant woman can establish disparate *treatment* by showing that the *effects* of her employer's policy fall more harshly on pregnant women than on others (the policies "impose a significant burden on pregnant workers") and are inadequately justified (the "reasons are not sufficiently strong to justify the burden"). The change in labels may be small, but the change in results assuredly is not. Disparate treatment and disparate-impact claims come with different standards of liability, different defenses, and different remedies. For example, plaintiffs in disparate-treatment cases can get compensatory and punitive damages as well as equitable relief, but plaintiffs in disparate impact cases can get equitable relief only. A sound reading of the same-treatment clause would preserve the distinctions so carefully made elsewhere in the Act; the Court's reading makes a muddle of them.

But (believe it or not) it gets worse. In order to make sense of its conflation of disparate impact with disparate treatment, the Court claims that its new test is somehow "limited to the Pregnancy Discrimination Act context," yet at the same time "consistent with" the traditional use of circumstantial evidence to show intent to discriminate in Title VII cases. A court in a Title VII case, true enough, may consider a policy's effects and even its justifications — along with "'all of the [other] surrounding facts and circumstances'" — when trying to ferret out a policy's motive. *Hazelwood School Dist. v. United States*, 433 U.S. 299 (1977). The Court cannot possibly think, however, that its newfangled balancing test reflects this conventional inquiry. It has, after all, just marched up and down the hill telling us that the same-treatment clause is not (no-no!) "'superfluous, void, or insignificant.'" If the clause merely instructed courts to consider a policy's effects and justifications the way it considers other circumstantial evidence of motive, it *would* be superfluous. So the Court's balancing test must mean something else. Even if the effects and justifications of policies are not enough to show intent to discriminate under ordinary Title VII principles, they could (Poof!) still show intent to discriminate for purposes of the pregnancy same-treatment clause. Deliciously incoherent.

And all of this to what end? The difference between a routine circumstantial-evidence inquiry into motive and today's grotesque effects-and-justifications inquiry into motive, it would seem, is that today's approach requires judges to concentrate on effects and justifications to the exclusion of other considerations. But Title VII *already* has a framework that allows judges to home in on a policy's effects and justifications — disparate impact. Under that framework, it is *already* unlawful for an employer to use a practice that has a disparate impact on the basis of a protected trait, unless (among other things) the employer can show that the practice "is job related . . . and consistent with business necessity." § 2000e– 2(k)(1)(A)(i). The Court does not explain why we need (never mind how the Act could possibly be read to contain) today's ersatz disparate-impact test, under which the disparate-impact element gives way to the significant-burden criterion and the business-necessity defense gives way to the sufficiently strong-justification standard. Today's decision can thus serve only one purpose: allowing claims that belong under Title VII's disparate-impact provisions to be brought under its disparate-treatment provisions instead.

■ NOTES AND QUESTIONS

1. Is a pregnant employee similar to other workers who suffer short-term disabilities on the job? If such workers receive light duty work assignments from their employer, should pregnant workers receive light duty work assignments as well?

2. The PDA amended Title VII to provide that "women affected by pregnancy, childbirth, or related medical conditions shall be treated the same for all employment-related purposes . . . as other persons not so affected but similar in their ability or inability to work." *Young*, 135 S. Ct. at 1345. Does an employer that fails to provide light duty work run afoul of these statutory terms?

3. The Court here rejects the approaches offered by each of the parties and follows a separate analysis. Is the Court's reasoning grounded in the statute? Why or why not?

4. In Justice Scalia's animated dissent, he accuses the majority of conflating disparate impact and disparate treatment under the PDA. Has the Court merged the two frameworks in this case?

5. In reaching its decision, the majority states that "[t]he plaintiff may reach a jury on this issue by providing sufficient evidence that the employer's policies impose a significant burden on pregnant workers, and that the employer's 'legitimate, nondiscriminatory' reasons are not sufficiently strong to justify the burden, but rather — when considered along with the burden imposed — give rise to an inference of intentional discrimination." *Young*, 135 S. Ct. at 1343. How should a court or jury decide whether the plaintiff has established "sufficient evidence" in the case? Similarly, how should a court or jury determine whether the employer has provided a "sufficiently strong" reason for its action?

6. The Court here expressly limits the reasoning of its decision to the PDA. Can litigants still use the analysis of the Court's decision in areas of employment discrimination law other than pregnancy?

7. After this decision, how would you advise a client who asks whether it must provide a pregnant employee with light duty work? What other information would you want to know?

8. In a portion of the opinion omitted here, the Court discusses the possible implications of amendments to the ADA in this case:

> We note that statutory changes made after the time of Young's pregnancy may limit the future significance of our interpretation of the Act. In 2008, Congress expanded the definition of "disability" under the ADA to make clear that "physical or mental impairment[s] that substantially limi[t]" an individual's ability to lift, stand, or bend are ADA-covered disabilities. ADA Amendments Act of 2008. As interpreted by the EEOC, the new statutory definition requires employers to accommodate employees whose temporary lifting restrictions originate off the job. We express no view on these statutory and regulatory changes.

> *Young*, 135 S. Ct. at 1348.

We will address those amendments more fully in Chapter 10, on disability discrimination.

 ## *Interactive Problem*

Looking back at the facts of the interactive problem at the beginning of this chapter, assume that while being considered for partnership, Nancy becomes pregnant with twins. As a result of conditions related to her pregnancy, Nancy has difficulty traveling, and asks whether her work can be limited to the office. Her duties as an accountant typically involve frequent travel to existing and prospective clients. The firm has granted such requests to workers with temporary disabilities — such as broken arms, legs, or similar conditions — but has never exempted pregnant workers from travel. Should the firm grant Nancy's request? Why or why not?

 # C. The Family and Medical Leave Act

Closely related to pregnancy discrimination is the issue of employee leave. The PDA does not expressly permit leave, though its terms certainly contemplate that some leave should be given for childbirth or related conditions in certain situations. The Family and Medical Leave Act is much clearer on the issue of leave. A discussion of the FMLA could appear in numerous places within this text. It appears here, however, because leave time frequently arises with respect to pregnancy and the subsequent childbirth. The FMLA and Title VII are thus closely intertwined on this particular issue. It is important to note, however, that the FMLA applies much more broadly and is in no way limited to these specific areas.

Under the FMLA, covered and eligible employees are entitled to take twelve weeks of leave during a twelve-month period to care for a newborn child, to address a serious health condition, or to care for a close family member with a serious health condition. Family members included in the statute are one's spouse, child, or parent. The time off taken under the FMLA need not necessarily be sequential, and the regulations contemplate the use of intermittent leave taken over the course of the year in certain situations. It is important to note that the leave permitted under the FMLA is unpaid. Thus, while an employer is required to give an employee twelve weeks of leave to address serious health issues, it is not required to compensate an employee for that time off. In certain circumstances, however, an employer may require that the employee use vacation or sick leave as part of the worker's FMLA request, which will often result in some of the time off being paid.

To be covered by the statute, a private sector employer must employ fifty or more workers for twenty or more weeks of the current or prior calendar year. Public agencies are covered by the statute irrespective of the number of workers employed, as well as public and private elementary and secondary schools. The key coverage component of the statute is the fifty-worker threshold for private companies. This is a relatively substantial requirement, and far exceeds the coverage requirements of Title VII (fifteen workers), the ADA (fifteen workers), or the ADEA (twenty workers). The idea behind the larger threshold is that bigger employers will be better able to handle situations where employees are absent for extended periods of time. Smaller employers would have much more difficulty with these types of absences. *See* Engelhardt v. S.P. Richards Co., 472 F.3d 1, 5 (1st Cir. 2006) ("[W]e view the 50-employee exception as a threshold protecting smaller businesses from the onerous requirement of keeping an unproductive employee on the payroll in the form of redundant or absent employees, going without an employee for up to twelve weeks, or both.").

Because of the fifty-employee requirement, a large percentage of workers are not protected by the requirements of the FMLA. In some instances, state or local law will also step in to provide coverage where the FMLA fails to do so, or to provide additional protections or benefits for workers.

Not all employees working for a covered entity are protected by the statute. To be eligible for coverage, an employee must have been employed at a company for a minimum of twelve months before the protections of the FMLA will begin. Additionally, the employee must have worked for a minimum of 1,250 hours during the prior twelve-month period. And, the worker must be employed at a site where the company maintains fifty or more employees within a seventy-five-mile radius. Thus, not all individuals will be covered by the FMLA, and it is critical to make sure that an employer is large enough to be covered by the statute prior to seeking leave. Similarly, it is important to verify that an employee has been employed long enough by the company and worked a sufficient number of hours to be eligible for the benefits of the FMLA. In some narrow circumstances, certain employees can be considered central to the employer's operations and their presence too important to qualify for FMLA leave. The "key" employee exception under the FMLA permits employers to restrict certain critical workers from taking leave under the statute, though these employees must be highly paid and notified of their status by the employer.

Employees must also make certain to give employers sufficient notice of their intent to take FMLA-authorized leave. Generally speaking, workers must inform employers at least thirty days in advance of the anticipated leave. This type of advance notice will not always be possible, particularly in emergency-type situations or where the need for leave is not foreseeable. Where an employee is unable to provide thirty days' notice for a legitimate reason, she must give "notice as soon as possible and practicable under the circumstances." *See* U.S. Dep't of Labor, Wage and Hour Division, Fact Sheet #28: The Family and Medical Leave Act (2012), http://www.dol.gov/ whd/regs/compliance/whdfs28.htm.

The FMLA also includes an anti-retaliation provision under its terms. Thus, where an employee attempts to avail herself of her right to take leave under the statute, she cannot be retaliated against under the FMLA. If an employer does retaliate, the worker will have a separate cause of action under the statute.

Though the FMLA has provided substantial leave to thousands of workers, it has been criticized as being insufficient given the realities of the workplace. *See* Julie C. Suk, *Are Gender Stereotypes Bad for Women? Rethinking Antidiscrimination Law and Work-Family Conflict*, 110 Colum. L. Rev. 1, 7–8 (2010) ("Legal scholars have criticized the FMLA for being too limited to resolve most American workers' conflicts between work and family. First, the statute defines 'eligible employee' in a way that excludes many American employees from coverage . . . . Second, the FMLA is underutilized by covered employees because the leave guaranteed by the statute is unpaid.").

Many other countries have far surpassed the United States in this regard, and provide substantially more leave than is authorized in this country. *See* Robert B. Moberly, *Labor-Management Relations During the Clinton Administration*, 24 Hofstra Lab. & Emp. L.J. 31, 36 (2006) ("No matter how one looks at it, the United States legislation pales in comparison to most other industrialized countries. . . .") (quoting Marion G. Crain et al., Worklaw: Cases and Materials 670, 671 (2005) (citation omitted)). And, in many circumstances, the leave provided by other countries is paid. For example, the United Kingdom provides 280 days of paid maternity and paternity leave (90 percent pay for six weeks, flat rate after). Italy provides 140 days of paid maternity leave (80 percent pay), and France provides 112 days of paid maternity and paternity leave (100 percent pay). *See Paid Parental Leave: U.S. vs. The World*, Huffington Post (Feb. 21, 2013, 3:40 p.m.), http://www.huffingtonpost.com/2013/02/04/maternity-leave-paid-parental-leave-_n_2617284.html.

Makowski v. SmithAmundsen LLC

662 F.3d 818 (7th Cir. 2011)

Young, District Judge.

[Laura] Makowski was employed as Marketing Director for SmithAmundsen, a law firm, from January 17, 2005, through February 4, 2008. She reported to Glen Amundsen, Chair of the Executive Committee and Marketing Partner, and Michael

DeLargy, Chief Operating Officer. During each year of Makowski's employment with SmithAmundsen, she received an annual salary increase, as well as quarterly discretionary merit bonuses "based on individual performance and how the employee's contributions helped Defendant SmithAmundsen meet its objectives" for each quarter of Plaintiff's employment prior to beginning her leave under the FMLA.

In the summer of 2007, Makowski notified SmithAmundsen's management that she was pregnant and due in December. SmithAmundsen granted Makowski leave under the FMLA due to the pregnancy and birth. On November 5, 2007, Makowski's obstetrician placed her on bed rest for the remainder of her pregnancy as a result of a significant increase in her blood pressure. With SmithAmundsen's permission, Makowski worked from home until November 26, 2007, at which point she began FMLA leave. On December 2, 2007, Makowski gave birth.

In January 2008, the Executive Committee, comprised of Amundsen and four other men, conducted its yearly retreat to assess the overall structure of the firm and determine whether staffing changes were necessary. At this time, the Marketing Department consisted of Makowski, Marketing Director; Sarah Goddard, Marketing Project Manager; Lauren Siegel, Marketing Coordinator; and Kristi Fitzgerald, part-time Marketing Assistant. During a conversation before the retreat regarding restructuring of the Marketing Department, Amundsen told DeLargy that "[p]eople enjoyed working with [Goddard] more" and that Goddard would be a stronger lead person in the department than Makowski, which "was really what [SmithAmundsen] needed to focus a lot on." At the retreat, the Executive Committee ratified Amundsen's recommendation to eliminate Makowski's position and continue with Goddard as the leader of the Marketing Department. The Executive Committee charged DeLargy with the task of conferring with outside labor and employment counsel regarding Makowski's firing.

In an email sent at the conclusion of the retreat from DeLargy to Molly O'Gara, Director of Human Resources, DeLargy said that Makowski "doesn't fit into our culture." As the Director of Human Resources, O'Gara by her own admission was responsible for implementing and monitoring SmithAmundsen's compliance with human resources policies, as well as monitoring the firm's compliance with anti-discrimination laws. She is consulted regularly regarding decisions to eliminate positions and terminate employees, and considers herself "the boss" with respect to human resources policies and compliance. Fittingly, DeLargy delegated to O'Gara the task of consulting with outside counsel to discuss Makowski's firing, which she did prior to Makowski's termination.

On February 4, 2008, while Makowski was on maternity leave, Amundsen and DeLargy terminated her over the telephone, explaining that her position was being eliminated as part of an organizational restructuring. That same day, O'Gara fired the IT Director, Tuan Hoang. Additionally, Amundsen sent an email to all equity and non-equity members of SmithAmundsen informing them of the Executive Committee's decision to eliminate the IT Director and Director of Marketing positions and Hoang's and Makowski's terminations.

Later that day, Makowski came to the office to retrieve her belongings. As she was leaving, O'Gara met her in the elevator lobby. O'Gara told her that she (Makowski) "was let go because of the fact that [Makowski] was pregnant and . . .

took medical leave." Furthermore, O'Gara "believed that there were [sic] a group of people that were discriminated against because they were pregnant or because they took medical leave" and specifically mentioned Carrie Von Hoff, a former associate at the firm, as one of the victims of discrimination. O'Gara also advised Makowski that "it might be a good idea to speak with a lawyer [as there] might be a possibility of a class action." Regarding Hoang,

> A critical question in this case is whether the human resources director's comments are admissible and whether they constitute direct evidence of discrimination.

O'Gara said that "they were working to let Tuan [Hoang] go for performance-based reasons," but because Makowski was pregnant and on FMLA leave, outside counsel suggested labeling both Makowski's and Hoang's terminations as part of a reduction in force.

The day after Makowski's termination, Goddard resigned and accepted a position at another firm. Two days later, the Firm advertised for a position as Business Development and Marketing Manager, a role the Firm envisioned would have been filled by Goddard. In May 2008, the Firm rehired Goddard for the position.

Makowski filed this lawsuit on December 2, 2008, alleging violations under Title VII, as amended by the PDA, and the FMLA. Makowski first contends that the district court erred in excluding O'Gara's statements to Makowski concerning her termination and in failing to consider other evidence provided by Makowski. Second, Makowski argues that this evidence creates a genuine issue of material fact as to whether Makowski was terminated due to her pregnancy and her taking medical leave.

As we noted above, Makowski alleges that O'Gara told her that Makowski was terminated because she was pregnant and took medical leave, and informed her of the Firm's discriminatory treatment toward other pregnant employees. The district court ruled that O'Gara's statements were not admissions and excluded them as inadmissible hearsay. Makowski contends on appeal that O'Gara's statements were admissions and therefore should be admitted as evidence of discrimination.

O'Gara's statements fit squarely within the scope of her employment . . . and thus are admissible as nonhearsay under Rule 801(d)(2)(D). [These] statements . . . provide direct evidence that pregnancy was a motivating factor in Makowski's discharge. Although O'Gara denies having made the alleged statements, whether or not she made such admissions is a question for the jury.

Furthermore, Makowski presented additional circumstantial evidence that the district court inexplicably failed to address, such as suspicious timing, behavior toward other employees in the protected group, ambiguous oral and written statements, better treatment of similarly situated employees outside the protected class, and evidence that Makowski was qualified for her job but failed to receive the desired treatment. However, even with the exclusion of the circumstantial evidence, O'Gara's statements alone are direct evidence of a discriminatory intent. Accordingly, the district court's grant of summary judgment in favor of the defendants on Makowski's pregnancy discrimination claim is reversed.

Under the FMLA, it is "unlawful for any employer to discharge or in any other manner discriminate against any individual for opposing any practice made unlawful" by the FMLA. 29 U.S.C. § 2615(a)(2). Similar to a pregnancy discrimination claim, "[i]n asserting a charge of retaliation under the FMLA, a plaintiff may proceed under the direct or indirect methods of proof." Makowski has sufficiently asserted a charge of retaliation under the FMLA; therefore, summary judgment for the defendants on Makowski's FMLA retaliation claim is reversed.

■ NOTES AND QUESTIONS

1. Were the comments made by the human resources director direct evidence of discrimination? Why or why not?

2. The evidence in this case was sufficient to go to a jury on the questions of pregnancy discrimination and FMLA discrimination. What type of defense could the employer put on at trial in response to these claims?

3. As seen by this case, the FMLA's prohibition against retaliation is a critical component of the statute. It permits individuals to take medical leave without fear of reprisal.

4. Assuming that the human resources director's comments had never been made, would there be sufficient evidence to go to a jury? How often do you believe pregnancy or leave discrimination occurs that an employee is unable — or unwilling — to prove?

 Interactive Problem

Looking back at the facts of the interactive problem, assume that Nancy reveals to her employer that she is pregnant, and asks for twelve weeks of FMLA leave in advance of the partnership vote. In response to this request, Peter tells her, "Why don't you take the rest of your life off, as there is no longer any place for you here at this firm." What potential claims would Nancy have based on this evidence?

Practice and Procedural Tip   **19: Applying the FMLA**

There can be a tendency for many employers to want to adopt firm policies that can be applied to the entire workforce on many issues. The FMLA can be one such area where this occurs. Depending upon the size of the company, employers can receive hundreds or thousands of requests each year for family-related leave. For purposes of simplicity, employers often develop rigid guidelines and protocols to follow when administering leave requests. While developing these types of systems can be beneficial to the overall operation of the business, employers must make sure not to be too restrictive when considering FMLA requests.

To begin with, the FMLA itself is a relatively complex and cumbersome statute. It can thus be difficult to interpret and apply to a given factual situation. Because of the complexity of the statute, and because of the almost limitless factual situations that could arise, employers should approach leave questions with some degree of flexibility. When considering leave questions, a number of best practices points should be considered.

First, it is important to consider the federal regulations that were issued under the FMLA. These regulations are very "user friendly," and contemplate many different situations that can arise under the statute. Second, employers should further avail themselves of the Department of Labor website when addressing these issues (www.dol.gov). This website provides useful guidance on leave issues and is updated to contain the most current information. Third, employers should strongly consider having a single individual or office address leave requests. Consistency in the process is critical, and it is important to handle all leave issues in a similar manner. It is also important to have one corporate office responsible for maintaining all of the relevant information in this regard. Record keeping can be complex and cumbersome, and the rules are often changing. Finally, where the employer is unsure of what to do, it should seek advice from either the Department of Labor or legal counsel (or both). Seeking this advice may have some short-term costs associated with it, but it can save the employer enormous potential litigation fees over time.

FMLA issues can be problematic for employers, but if they proceed in a cautious manner they should be able to avoid costly litigation on the issue. A wealth of information exists on how to apply the statutory terms, and it is important for employers to access this information where necessary to address particular issues. Where employers are still unsure whether to grant a leave request, they should seek legal advice on how to handle the issue.

D. Sexual Orientation — A Protected Category?

Sexual orientation is not an *expressly* protected category under federal law for private workers. As will be seen in this section, however, the issue of whether Title VII covers sexual orientation discrimination is an area that remains in flux in the federal appellate courts.

Additionally, numerous states and local jurisdictions have passed provisions that protect gay and lesbian employees. For example, California state law protects employees in the private sector from discrimination on the basis of sexual orientation, gender identity, and/or gender expression. It also expressly protects employees of state and local governments from discrimination on the basis of sexual orientation, gender identity, and/or

Gay Pride Parade, San Francisco, CA

gender expression. *See* CAL. GOV'T CODE §§ 12920, 12940, 12926 & 12949. Indeed, several states — including Colorado, Connecticut, Delaware, Hawaii, Iowa, Maine, Massachusetts, Minnesota, Nevada, New Jersey, New Mexico, Oregon, Rhode Island, Vermont, Washington, and the District of Columbia have laws that prohibit sexual orientation discrimination in both the public and private employment sectors. *See In Your State,* LAMBDA LEGAL, http://www.lambdalegal.org/states-regions. Similarly, employees working in the federal sector have certain protections on the basis of sexual orientation.

Employers should thus verify how the courts in their particular jurisdiction have defined "sex" with regard to transgender employees or sexual orientation. Some courts have taken an expansive view which suggests further caution to employers attempting to discriminate against certain workers. *See* Neil Dishman, *The Expanding Rights of Transsexuals in the Workplace,* 21 LAB. LAW. 121, 124–125 (2005) (discussing five states — California, Maine, Minnesota, New Mexico, and Rhode Island — that include "transsexualism as a protected class under their civil-rights statutes"; noting that under "California's employment laws, 'sex' is defined to include 'a person's gender,' which is in turn defined to include 'a person's gender identity and gender related appearance and behavior . . .' ").

Additionally, employees have tried — with varying degrees of success — to gain protection for sexual orientation under the sexual stereotyping wing of the *Price Waterhouse v. Hopkins* decision. 490 U.S. 228 (1989). *See, e.g.,* Smith v. City of Salem, Ohio, 378 F.3d 566 (6th Cir. 2004). In *Price Waterhouse,* the plaintiff alleged sex discrimination against her employer who, *inter alia,* told her that to improve her chances for partnership, she should "walk more femininely, talk more femininely, dress more femininely, wear make-up, have her hair styled, and wear jewelry." 490 U.S. 228, 235 (1989). The Supreme Court held that the evidence was sufficient to establish that "sex stereotyping 'was permitted to play a part' in the evaluation of Hopkins as a candidate for the partnership." *Id.* at 255. There is a line of cases and scholarship that suggests that a plaintiff can use this type of gender stereotyping analysis to bring sexual orientation discrimination claims.

In other words, a homosexual plaintiff can bring a sexual orientation discrimination claim based on the fact that his employer made an adverse employment decision because the employee was acting "too gay," or "not enough like a man," similar to how in *Price Waterhouse* the employer told the plaintiff she was not acting enough like a woman. For instance, in 2012 a federal judge ruled that, even though Title VII does not explicitly protect against sexual orientation discrimination, a plaintiff can bring a claim under Title VII's ban on sex discrimination because an employer views the employee's sexual orientation as "not consistent with . . . perception of acceptable gender roles." Terveer v. Billington, No. CV 12-1290 (CKK), 2014 WL 1280301, at *9 (D.D.C. Mar. 31, 2014). In short, sexual orientation claims can now potentially be pursued under the gender stereotyping theory discussed in *Price Waterhouse.*

The exact scope of Title VII and its potential coverage with respect to sexual orientation remains unclear. The issue is ultimately one that will need to be resolved by the Supreme Court. The federal appellate courts are expressly conflicted on this question.

Evans v. Georgia Regional Hospital
850 F.3d 1248 (11th Cir. 2017)

MARTINEZ, District Judge:

Jameka Evans appeals the *sua sponte* dismissal of her employment discrimination complaint, filed pursuant to 42 U.S.C. § 2000e *et seq.*, in which she alleged that she was discriminated against because of her sexual orientation and gender non-conformity, and retaliated against after she lodged a complaint with her employer's human resources department. We have carefully reviewed the Appellant's and amicus curiae's initial and supplemental briefs, and have had the benefit of oral argument. For the reasons set forth below, we affirm the district court's dismissal order in part, and vacate and remand in part.

Evans filed a *pro se* complaint against Georgia Regional Hospital ("Hospital"), Chief Charles Moss, Lisa Clark, and Senior Human Resources Manager Jamekia Powers, alleging employment discrimination under Title VII in her job as a security officer at the Hospital. In her complaint, Evans alleged the following facts, which this Court accepts as true. Evans worked at the Hospital as a security officer from August 1, 2012, to October 11, 2013, when she left voluntarily. During her time at the Hospital, she was denied equal pay or work, harassed, and physically assaulted or battered. She was discriminated against on the basis of her sex and targeted for termination for failing to carry herself in a "traditional woman[ly] manner." Although she is a gay woman, she did not broadcast her sexuality. However, it was "evident" that she identified with the male gender, because of how she presented herself—"(male uniform, low male haircut, shoes, etc.")."

Evans had not met Powers before the harassment began and had never discussed her sexual preference with her. Yet, Evans was punished because her status as a gay female did not comport with Moss's gender stereotypes and this caused her to experience a hostile work environment. For example, a less qualified individual was appointed to be her direct supervisor. Moreover, internal e-mails provided evidence that Moss was trying to terminate Evans by making her employment unbearable, because she had too much information about his wrongdoing in the security department.

Evans also explained that her employers had violated some regulations or policies and that she had initiated an investigation. After Evans lodged her complaints about these violations, Powers asked Evans about her sexuality, causing Evans and "others" to infer that her sexuality was the basis of her harassment and that upper management had discussed it during the investigation. Finally, Evans provided that she was harassed and retaliated against because she spoke to human resources about Moss's discriminatory behavior. Evans also reserved the right to amend her complaint should new information arise.

Evans attached to her complaint a "Record of Incidents." This report stated that Moss had repeatedly closed a door on Evans in a rude manner, that she experienced scheduling issues and a shift change, and that a less qualified individual was promoted as her supervisor. She detailed the problems she had with her new supervisor, Corporal Shanika Johnson, and asserted that Johnson scrutinized and harassed her. Evans also asserted that someone had tampered with her equipment, including her radio, clip, and shoulder microphone.

Evans also included an e-mail from Harvey Sanchez Pegues, which stated that Moss had harassed Pegues on a daily basis, had a habit of favoritism, changed Pegues's schedule frequently, had created a tense and unpleasant work environment, and had a habit of targeting people for termination. Evans also attached a letter from Jalisia Bedgard, which stated that Johnson and Moss had expected Evans to quit because of Johnson's promotion and, if not, because of a bad shift change that would cause Evans scheduling conflicts. Another attached letter from Cheryl Sanders, Employee Relations Coordinator in the human resources department at the Hospital, indicated that the Hospital had investigated Evans's complaints of favoritism, inconsistent and unfair practices, and inappropriate conduct, and had found no evidence that she had been singled out and targeted for termination. Finally, Evans attached e-mail correspondence between Pegues and Evans, which indicated that: (1) Pegues believed that Moss was trying to target Evans for termination because she had substantial evidence of wrongdoing against him, and (2) Moss had changed the qualifications of a job to prevent other candidates from qualifying.

With regard to Evans's claim of discrimination based on gender nonconformity, the magistrate judge concluded that it was "just another way to claim discrimination based on sexual orientation," no matter how it was otherwise characterized. Additionally, [a] magistrate judge recommended dismissal of the retaliation claim on the basis that Evans failed to allege that she opposed an unlawful employment practice, given that sexual orientation was not protected under Title VII. Additionally, the R&R noted that Moss, Clark, and Powers were coworkers or supervisors sued in their individual capacities and, therefore, were not actionable defendants under Title VII.

The district court conducted a *de novo* review of the entire record and adopted—without further comment—the [Magistrate Court], dismissed the case with prejudice, and appointed counsel from Lambda Legal [Defense and Education Fund, Inc.] to represent Evans on appeal. On appeal, Evans, with the support of the EEOC as amicus curiae, argues that the district court erred in dismissing her claim that she was discriminated against for failing to conform to gender stereotypes, because an LGBT person may properly bring a separate discrimination claim for gender non-conformity in this Circuit. Evans also argues that, contrary to the district court's assertion, sexual orientation discrimination is, in fact, sex discrimination under Title VII.

Evans [] argues that she has stated a claim under Title VII by alleging that she endured workplace discrimination because of her sexual orientation. She has not. Our binding precedent forecloses such an action. *Blum v. Gulf Oil Corp.*, 597 F.2d 936, 938 (5th Cir. 1979) ("Discharge for homosexuality is not prohibited by Title VII . . . ."). "Under our prior precedent rule, we are bound to follow a binding precedent in this Circuit unless and until it is overruled by this court en banc or by the Supreme Court." *Offshore of the Palm Beaches, Inc. v. Lynch*, 741 F.3d 1251 (11th Cir. 2014) (internal quotations omitted).

The EEOC argues that the statement in *Blum* regarding discharge for homosexuality is dicta and not binding precedent. We disagree. Evans and the EEOC also argue that the Supreme Court decisions in *Price Waterhouse v. Hopkins*, 490

U.S. 228 (1989), and *Oncale v. Sundowner Offshore Servs., Inc.*, 523 U.S. 75 (1998), support a cause of action for sexual orientation discrimination under Title VII. Again, we disagree. The fact that claims for gender non-conformity and same-sex discrimination can be brought pursuant to Title VII does not permit us to depart from *Blum*. *Price Waterhouse* and *Oncale* are neither clearly on point nor contrary to *Blum*. These Supreme Court decisions do not squarely address whether sexual orientation discrimination is prohibited by Title VII.

Finally, even though they disagree with the decisions, Evans and the EEOC acknowledge that other circuits have held that sexual orientation discrimination is not actionable under Title VII. Evans and the EEOC question these decisions, in part, because of *Price Waterhouse* and *Oncale*. Whether those Supreme Court cases impact other circuit's decisions, many of which were decided after *Price Waterhouse* and *Oncale*, does not change our analysis that *Blum* is binding precedent that has not been overruled by a clearly contrary opinion of the Supreme Court or of this Court sitting en banc. Accordingly, we affirm the portion of the district court's order dismissing Evan's sexual orientation claim.

Pryor, Circuit Judge, concurring:
   I concur in the majority opinion, but I write separately to explain the error of the argument of the Equal Employment Opportunity Commission and the dissent that a person who experiences discrimination because of sexual orientation necessarily experiences discrimination for deviating from gender stereotypes. Although a person who experiences the former will sometimes also experience the latter, the two concepts are legally distinct. And the insistence otherwise by the Commission and the dissent relies on false stereotypes of gay individuals. I also write separately to explain that the dissent would create a new form of relief based on status that runs counter to binding precedent and would undermine the relationship between the doctrine of gender nonconformity and the enumerated classes protected by Title VII.

Rosenbaum, Circuit Judge, concurring in part and dissenting in part:
   A woman should be a "woman." She should wear dresses, be subservient to men, and be sexually attracted to only men. If she doesn't conform to this view of what a woman should be, an employer has every right to fire her.

   That was the law in 1963—before Congress enacted Title VII of the Civil Rights Act of 1964. But that is not the law now. And the rule that Title VII precludes discrimination on the basis of every stereotype of what a woman supposedly should be—including each of those stated above—has existed since the Supreme Court issued *Price Waterhouse v. Hopkins*, 490 U.S. 228 (1989), 28 years ago.

   Yet even today the panel ignores this clear mandate. To justify its position, the panel invokes 38-year-old precedent—issued ten years before *Price Waterhouse* necessarily abrogated it—and calls it binding precedent that ties our hands. I respectfully disagree.

   Plain and simple, when a woman alleges, as Evans has, that she has been discriminated against because she is a lesbian, she necessarily alleges that she has been discriminated against because she failed to conform to the employer's image of what women should be—specifically, that women should be sexually attracted to men only. And it is utter fiction to suggest that she was not discriminated against for failing to comport with her employer's stereotyped view of women. That is discrimination "because of . . . sex," 42 U.S.C. § 2000e-2(a)(1), and it clearly violates Title VII under *Price Waterhouse*.

So I dissent from [this part] of the panel's opinion. On remand, Evans should be allowed to amend her complaint to state such a claim.

■ NOTES AND QUESTIONS

1. Does the Supreme Court's decision in *Price Waterhouse* provide any insight on the scope of Title VII?

2. Does the *Oncale* decision suggest that sexual orientation should be covered by Title VII?

3. Is the court here bound by its prior precedent? How much reliance does it put on the view of other appellate courts?

4. Did Congress *intend* to include sexual orientation discrimination as part of Title VII when the statute was passed?

5. It is worth noting that there have been several attempts for workers to gain sexual orientation protection under federal law. While these attempts have been unsuccessful, there may at some future date be federal protection for gay and lesbian workers. The most high profile proposed legislation in this area is the Employment Non-Discrimination Act (ENDA), which would prohibit employers from discriminating on the basis of gender identity or sexual orientation. However, the proposed statute has not become law. *See* Emma Margolin, *"Let the Bells of Freedom Ring" — Senate Passes ENDA*, MSNBC (Nov. 8, 2013, 3:14 P.M.), http://www.msnbc.com/news-nation/let-the-bells-freedom-ring (noting that the Senate passed the ENDA in a 64 to 32 vote in November 2013 but discussing how there was little chance that the ENDA would go before the GOP-controlled House for further implementation).

6. **Historical Note.** There have been several past attempts to pass versions of the ENDA. Initially, efforts to end sexual orientation discrimination were a result of increasing activism by the Lesbian, Gay, Bisexual, and Transgender (LGBT) communities, following several protests throughout the country — including the well-known Stonewall riots — against police harassment and brutality directed at the LGBT population. Shortly after these protests, the Equality Act of 1974, which would ban discrimination against gay and lesbian (but not transgender) individuals in employment, was introduced into legislation. It was the first national piece of proposed legislation to end discrimination based on sexual orientation in the United States. However, despite the increasing media coverage of gay rights issues and the passage of the Civil Rights Act of 1964, the Equality Act of 1974 never earned enough support to become law. Similar bills and efforts failed in the late 1970s, and several political and social influences in the 1980s and early 1990s prevented equality measures from

gaining support nationally during these times. Lawmakers first introduced the ENDA in 1994; that version would have made it illegal to discriminate on the basis of a person's actual or perceived sexual orientation. Both the House and Senate versions of the ENDA died in committee in 1994. In 2007, lawmakers introduced the first version of the ENDA that included both sexual orientation and gender identity, but this inclusive version also failed to pass. A second attempt was made to move this version of the Bill forward, this time without the provisions that protected transgender workers, and the Bill was passed by the House in a vote of 235-184. However, the Senate did not vote on passage. Another version that included both gender identity and sexual orientation was introduced in 2009, but similarly failed to pass. While different versions of the Bill continue to be debated, such protections have yet to become federal law.

Other appellate courts have taken issue with the *Evans* decision and its holding with respect to the coverage of Title VII. These courts have taken a different approach from *Evans* with respect to the issue of sexual orientation discrimination.

Zarda v. Altitude Express, Inc.

883 F.3d 100 (2d Cir. 2018) (en banc)

Mr. KATZMANN, Chief Judge:

Donald Zarda, a skydiving instructor, brought a sex discrimination claim under Title VII of the Civil Rights Act of 1964 ("Title VII") alleging that he was fired from his job at Altitude Express, Inc., because he failed to conform to male sex stereotypes by referring to his sexual orientation. Although it is well-settled that gender stereotyping violates Title VII's prohibition on discrimination "because of . . . sex," we have previously held that sexual orientation discrimination claims, including claims that being gay or lesbian constitutes nonconformity with a gender stereotype, are not cognizable under Title VII. *See Simonton v. Runyon*, 232 F.3d 33 (2d Cir. 2000); *see also Dawson v. Bumble & Bumble*, 398 F.3d 211 (2d Cir. 2005).

At the time *Simonton* and *Dawson* were decided, and for many years since, this view was consistent with the consensus among our sister circuits and the position of the Equal Employment Opportunity Commission ("EEOC" or "Commission"). But legal doctrine evolves and in 2015 the EEOC held, for the first time, that "sexual orientation is inherently a 'sex-based consideration;' accordingly an allegation of discrimination based on sexual orientation is necessarily an allegation of sex discrimination under Title VII." *Baldwin v. Foxx*, EEOC Decision No. 0120133080, 2015 WL 4397641 (July 15, 2015) (quoting *Price Waterhouse v. Hopkins*, 490 U.S. 228 (1989) (plurality opinion)).

Since then, two circuits have revisited the question of whether claims of sexual orientation discrimination are viable under Title VII. In March 2017, a divided panel of the Eleventh Circuit declined to recognize such a claim, concluding that it was bound by *Blum*, 597 F.2d at 938, which "ha[s] not been overruled by a clearly contrary opinion of the Supreme Court or of [the Eleventh Circuit] sitting *en banc." Evans v. Ga. Reg'l Hosp.*, 850 F.3d 1248, 1257 (11th Cir.), *cert. denied,* _____ U.S. _____, 138 S. Ct. 557, 199 L. Ed. 2d 446 (2017). One month later, the Seventh Circuit, sitting en banc, took "a fresh look at [its] position in light of developments at the Supreme Court extending over two decades" and held that "discrimination on the basis of sexual orientation is a form of sex discrimination." *Hively*, 853 F.3d at 340–41.

Taking note of the potential persuasive force of these new decisions, we convened en banc to reevaluate *Simonton* and *Dawson* in light of arguments not previously considered by this Court. Having done so, we now hold that Title VII prohibits discrimination on the basis of sexual orientation as discrimination "because of . . . sex." To the extent that our prior precedents held otherwise, they are overruled.

In the summer of 2010, Donald Zarda, a gay man, worked as a sky-diving instructor at Altitude Express. As part of his job, he regularly participated in tandem skydives, strapped hip-to-hip and shoulder-to-shoulder with clients. In an environment where close physical proximity was common, Zarda's co-workers routinely referenced sexual orientation or made sexual jokes around clients, and Zarda sometimes told female clients about his sexual orientation to assuage any concern they might have about being strapped to a man for a tandem skydive. That June, Zarda told a female client with whom he was preparing for a tandem skydive that he was gay "and ha[d] an ex-husband to prove it." Although he later said this disclosure was intended simply to preempt any discomfort the client may have felt in being strapped to the body of an unfamiliar man, the client alleged that Zarda inappropriately touched her and disclosed his sexual orientation to excuse his behavior. After the jump was successfully completed, the client told her boyfriend about Zarda's alleged behavior and reference to his sexual orientation; the boyfriend in turn told Zarda's boss, who fired shortly Zarda thereafter. Zarda denied inappropriately touching the client and insisted he was fired solely because of his reference to his sexual orientation. One month later, Zarda filed a discrimination charge with the EEOC concerning his termination. Zarda claimed that "in addition to being discriminated against because of [his] sexual orientation, [he] was also discriminated against because of [his] gender." In particular, he claimed that "[a]ll of the men at [his workplace] made light of the intimate nature of being strapped to a member of the opposite sex," but that he was fired because he "honestly referred to [his] sexual orientation and did not conform to the straight male macho stereotype."

In September 2010, Zarda brought a lawsuit in federal court alleging, *inter alia*, sex stereotyping in violation of Title VII and sexual orientation discrimination in violation of New York law. Defendants moved for summary judgment arguing that Zarda's Title VII claim should be dismissed because, although "Plaintiff testifie[d] repeatedly that he believe[d] the reason he was terminated [was] because of his sexual orientation . . . [,] under Title VII, a gender stereotype cannot be predicated on sexual orientation." Dist. Ct. (citing *Simonton*, 232 F.3d at 35). In March 2014, the district court granted summary judgment to the defendants on the Title VII claim. As relevant here, the district court concluded that, although there was sufficient evidence to permit plaintiff to proceed with his claim for sexual orientation discrimination under New York law, plaintiff had failed to establish a prima facie case of gender stereotyping discrimination under Title VII.

While Zarda's remaining claims were still pending, the EEOC decided *Baldwin*, holding that "allegations of discrimination on the basis of sexual orientation necessarily state a claim of discrimination on the basis of sex." The Commission identified three ways to illustrate what it described as the "inescapable link between allegations of sexual orientation discrimination and sex discrimination." First, sexual orientation discrimination, such as suspending a lesbian employee for displaying a photo of her female spouse on her desk while not suspending a man for displaying a photo of his female spouse, "is sex discrimination because it necessarily entails treating an employee less favorably because of the employee's sex." Second, it is "associational discrimination" because "an employee alleging discrimination on the basis of sexual orientation is alleging that his or her employer took his or her sex into account by treating him or her differently for associating with a person of the same sex." Lastly, sexual orientation discrimination "necessarily involves discrimination based on gender stereotypes," most commonly "heterosexually defined gender norms." (internal quotation marks omitted). Shortly thereafter, Zarda moved to have his Title VII claim reinstated based on *Baldwin*. But, the district court denied the motion, concluding that *Simonton* remained binding precedent.

Zarda's surviving claims, which included his claim for sexual orientation discrimination under New York law, went to trial, where defendants prevailed. After judgment was entered for the defendants, Zarda appealed. As relevant here, Zarda argued that *Simonton* should be overturned because the EEOC's reasoning in *Baldwin* demonstrated that *Simonton* was incorrectly decided. By contrast, defendants argued that the court did not need to reach that issue because the jury found that they had not discriminated based on sexual orientation.

The panel held that "Zarda's [federal] sex-discrimination claim [was] properly before [it] because [his state law claim was tried under] a higher standard of causation than required by Title VII." However, the panel "decline[d] Zarda's invitation to revisit our precedent," which "can only be overturned by the entire Court sitting in banc." The Court subsequently ordered this rehearing en banc to revisit *Simonton* and *Dawson*'s holdings that claims of sexual orientation discrimination are not cognizable under Title VII.

We now conclude that sexual orientation discrimination is motivated, at least in part, by sex and is thus a subset of sex discrimination. Looking first to the text of Title VII, the most natural reading of the statute's prohibition on discrimination "because of . . . sex" is that it extends to sexual orientation discrimination because sex is necessarily a factor in sexual orientation. This statutory reading is reinforced by considering the question from the perspective of sex stereotyping because sexual orientation discrimination is predicated on assumptions about how persons of a certain sex can or should be, which is an impermissible basis for adverse employment actions. In addition, looking at the question from the perspective of associational discrimination, sexual orientation discrimination—which is motivated by an employer's opposition to romantic association between particular sexes—is discrimination based on the employee's own sex.

We begin by considering the nature of sexual orientation discrimination. The term "sexual orientation" refers to "[a] person's predisposition or inclination toward sexual activity or behavior with other males or females" and is commonly categorized as "heterosexuality, homosexuality, or bisexuality." *See Sexual Orientation, Black's Law Dictionary* (10th ed. 2014). To take one example, "homosexuality" is "characterized by sexual desire for a person of the same sex." *Homosexual, id.; see also Heterosexual, id.* ("Of, relating to, or characterized by sexual desire for a person of the opposite sex."); *Bisexual, id.* ("Of, relating to, or characterized by sexual desire for both males and females."). To operationalize this definition and identify the sexual orientation of a particular person, we need to know the sex of the person and that of the people to whom he or she is attracted. *Hively,* 853 F.3d at 358 (Flaum, J., concurring) ("One cannot consider a person's homosexuality without also accounting for their sex: doing so would render 'same' [sex] . . . meaningless."). Because one cannot fully define a person's sexual orientation without identifying his or her sex, sexual orientation is a function of sex. Indeed sexual orientation is doubly delineated by sex because it is a function of both a person's sex and the sex of those to whom he or she is attracted. Logically, because sexual orientation is a function of sex and sex is a protected characteristic under Title VII, it follows that sexual orientation is also protected. *See id.* ("[D]iscriminating against [an] employee because they are homosexual constitutes discriminating against an employee because of (A) the employee's sex, *and* (B) their sexual attraction to individuals of the *same sex.*").

The Supreme Court gave voice to this principle of construction when it held that Title VII barred male-on-male sexual harassment, which "was assuredly not the principal evil Congress was concerned with when it enacted Title VII," *Oncale v. Sundowner Offshore Servs., Inc.,* 523 U.S. 75, 79–80 (1998), and which few people in 1964 would likely have understood to be covered by the statutory text. But the Court was untroubled by these facts. "[S]tatutory prohibitions," it explained, "often go beyond the principal evil to cover reasonably comparable evils, and it is ultimately the provisions of our laws rather than the principal concerns of our legislators by which we are governed." *Id.* Applying this reasoning to the question at hand, the fact that Congress might not have contemplated that discrimination "because of . . . sex" would encompass sexual orientation discrimination does not limit the reach of the statute.

The dissent disagrees with this conclusion. It does not dispute our definition of the word "sex," nor does it argue that this word had a different meaning in 1964. Instead, it charges us with "misconceiv[ing] the fundamental public meaning of the language of" Title VII. (emphasis omitted). According to the dissent, the drafters included "sex" in Title VII to "secure the rights of women to equal protection in employment," and had no intention of prohibiting sexual orientation discrimination. We take no position on the substance of the dissent's discussion of the legislative history or the zeitgeist of the 1960s, but we respectfully disagree with its approach to interpreting Title VII as well as its conclusion that sexual orientation discrimination is not a "reasonably comparable evil," *Oncale,* 523 U.S. at 79, to sexual harassment and male-on-male harassment. Although legislative history most certainly has its uses, in ascertaining statutory meaning in a Title VII case, *Oncale* specifically rejects reliance on "the principal concerns of our legislators," *id.* at 79–80, 118 S. Ct. 998—the centerpiece of the dissent's statutory analysis.

Rather, *Oncale* instructs that the text is the lodestar of statutory interpretation, emphasizing that we are governed "by the provisions of our laws." *Id.* The text before us uses broad language, prohibiting discrimination "because of . . . sex," which Congress defined as making sex "a motivating factor." We give these words their full scope and conclude that, because sexual orientation discrimination is a function of sex, and is comparable to sexual harassment, gender stereotyping, and other evils long recognized as violating Title VII, the statute must prohibit it.

Our conclusion is reinforced by the Supreme Court's test for determining whether an employment practice constitutes sex discrimination. This approach, which we call the "comparative test," determines whether the trait that is the basis for discrimination is a function of sex by asking whether an employee's treatment would have been different "but for that person's sex." *City of Los Angeles, Dep't of Water & Power v. Manhart*, 435 U.S. 702, 711 (1978) (internal quotation marks omitted). To illustrate its application to sexual orientation, consider the facts of the recent Seventh Circuit case addressing a Title VII claim brought by Kimberly Hively, a lesbian professor who alleged that she was denied a promotion because of her sexual orientation. *Hively*, 853 F.3d at 341 (majority). Accepting that allegation as true at the motion-to-dismiss stage, the Seventh Circuit compared Hively, a female professor attracted to women (who was denied a promotion), with a hypothetical scenario in which Hively was a male who was attracted to women (and received a promotion). Under this scenario, the Seventh Circuit concluded that, as alleged, Hively would not have been denied a promotion but for her sex, and therefore sexual orientation is a function of sex. From this conclusion, it follows that sexual orientation discrimination is a subset of sex discrimination.

Having addressed the proper application of the comparative test, we conclude that the law is clear: To determine whether a trait operates as a proxy for sex, we ask whether the employee would have been treated differently "but for" his or her sex. In the context of sexual orientation, a woman who is subject to an adverse employment action because she is attracted to women would have been treated differently if she had been a man who was attracted to women. We can therefore conclude that sexual orientation is a function of sex and, by extension, sexual orientation discrimination is a subset of sex discrimination. Viewing the relationship between sexual orientation and sex through the lens of gender stereotyping provides yet another basis for concluding that sexual orientation discrimination is a subset of sex discrimination. Specifically, this framework demonstrates that sexual orientation discrimination is almost invariably rooted in stereotypes about men and women.

Since 1978, the Supreme Court has recognized that "employment decisions cannot be predicated on mere 'stereotyped' impressions about the characteristics of males or females," because Title VII "strike[s] at the entire spectrum of disparate treatment of men and women resulting from sex stereotypes." *Manhart*, 435 U.S. at 707 & n.13. This is true of stereotypes about both how the sexes are and how they should be. *Price Waterhouse*, 490 U.S. at 250, 109 S. Ct. 1775 ("[A]n employer who acts on the basis of a belief that a woman cannot . . . or must not [possess certain traits] has acted on the basis of gender.").

In *Price Waterhouse*, the Supreme Court concluded that adverse employment actions taken based on the belief that a female accountant should walk, talk, and dress femininely constituted impermissible sex discrimination. *See* 490 U.S. at 250–52 (plurality); *see also id.* at 259 (White, J., concurring in the judgment); *id.* at 272–73, 109 S. Ct. 1775 (O'Connor, J., concurring in the judgment). Similarly, *Manhart* stands for the proposition that "employment decisions cannot be predicated on mere 'stereotyped' impressions about the characteristics of males or females," and held that female employees could not, by virtue of their status as women, be discriminated against based on the gender stereotype that women generally outlive men. Under these principles, employees who experience adverse employment actions as a result of their employer's generalizations about members of their sex, *id.* at 708, or "as a result of their employer's animus toward their exhibition of behavior considered to be stereotypically inappropriate for their gender may have a claim under Title VII," *Dawson*, 398 F.3d at 218.

Applying *Price Waterhouse*'s reasoning to sexual orientation, we conclude that when, for example, "an employer . . . acts on the basis of a belief that [men] cannot be [attracted to men], or that [they] must not be," but takes no such action against women who are attracted to men, the employer "has acted on the basis of gender." *Cf.* 490 U.S. at 250. This conclusion is consistent with *Hively*'s holding that same-sex orientation "represents the ultimate case of failure to conform" to gender stereotypes, 853 F.3d at 346 (majority), and aligns with numerous district courts' observation that "stereotypes about homosexuality are directly related to our stereotypes about the proper roles of men and women. . . . The gender stereotype at work here is that 'real' men should date women, and not other men," *Centola v. Potter*, 183 F. Supp. 2d 403, 410 (D. Mass. 2002).

The conclusion that sexual orientation discrimination is a subset of sex discrimination is further reinforced by viewing this issue through the lens of associational discrimination. Consistent with the nature of sexual orientation, in most contexts where an employer discriminates based on sexual orientation, the employer's decision is predicated on opposition to romantic association between particular sexes. For example, when an employer fires a gay man based on the belief that men should not be attracted to other men, the employer discriminates based on the employee's own sex.

This Court recognized associational discrimination as a violation of Title VII in *Holcomb v. Iona College*, 521 F.3d 130, 139 (2d Cir. 2008), a case involving allegations of racial discrimination. Holcomb, a white man, alleged that he was fired from his job as the assistant coach of a college basketball team because his employer disapproved of his marriage to a black woman. This Court concluded that Holcomb had stated a viable claim, holding that "an employer may violate Title VII if it takes action against an employee because of the employee's association with a person of another race." *Id.* at 138. Although the Court considered the argument that the alleged discrimination was based on the race of Holcomb's wife rather than his own, it ultimately concluded that "where an employee is subjected to adverse action because an employer disapproves of interracial association, the employee suffers discrimination because of the employee's *own* race."

[W]e see no principled basis for recognizing a violation of Title VII for associational discrimination based on race but not on sex. Accordingly, we hold that sexual orientation discrimination, which is based on an employer's opposition to association between particular sexes and thereby discriminates against an employee based on their own sex, constitutes discrimination "because of . . . sex." Therefore, it is no less repugnant to Title VII than anti-miscegenation policies.

Since 1964, the legal framework for evaluating Title VII claims has evolved substantially. Under *Manhart*, traits that operate as a proxy for sex are an impermissible basis for disparate treatment of men and women. Under *Price Waterhouse*, discrimination on the basis of sex stereotypes is prohibited. Under *Holcomb*, building on *Loving v. Virginia*, 388 U.S. 1 (1967), it is unlawful to discriminate on the basis of an employee's association with persons of another race. Applying these precedents to sexual orientation discrimination, it is clear that there is "no justification in the statutory language . . . for a categorical rule excluding" such claims from the reach of Title VII. *Oncale*, 523 U.S. at 80.

Title VII's prohibition on sex discrimination applies to any practice in which sex is a motivating factor. As explained above, sexual orientation discrimination is a subset of sex discrimination because sexual orientation is *defined* by one's sex in relation to the sex of those to whom one is attracted, making it impossible for an employer to discriminate on the basis of sexual orientation without taking sex into account. Sexual orientation discrimination is also based on assumptions or stereotypes about how members of a particular gender should be, including to whom they should be attracted. Finally, sexual orientation discrimination is associational discrimination because an adverse employment action that is motivated by the employer's opposition to association between members of particular sexes discriminates against an employee on the basis of sex. Each of these three perspectives is sufficient to support this Court's conclusion and together they amply demonstrate that sexual orientation discrimination is a form of sex discrimination.

Although sexual orientation discrimination is "assuredly not the principal evil that Congress was concerned with when it enacted Title VII," "statutory prohibitions often go beyond the principal evil to cover reasonably comparable evils." *Oncale*, 523 U.S. at 80. In the context of Title VII, the statutory prohibition extends to all discrimination "because of . . . sex" and sexual orientation discrimination is an actionable subset of sex discrimination. We overturn our prior precedents to the contrary to the extent they conflict with this ruling.

Zarda has alleged that, by "honestly referr[ing] to his sexual orientation," he failed to "conform to the straight male macho stereotype." For this reason, he has alleged a claim of discrimination of the kind we now hold cognizable under Title VII. The district court held that there was sufficient evidence of sexual orientation discrimination to survive summary judgment on Zarda's state law claims. Even though Zarda lost his state sexual orientation discrimination claim at trial, that result does not preclude him from prevailing on his federal claim because his state law claim was tried under "a higher standard of causation than required by Title VII." *Zarda v. Altitude Express*, 855 F.3d 76, 81 (2d Cir. 2017). Thus, we hold that Zarda is entitled to bring a Title VII claim for discrimination based on sexual orientation.

[Concurring and dissenting opinions omitted.]

■ NOTES AND QUESTIONS

1. Which analysis do you find most persuasive, that of *Evans* or *Zarda*?

2. Do you agree with this court that "sexual orientation discrimination is motivated, at least in part, by sex and is thus a subset of sex discrimination"? Does *Price Waterhouse* support this conclusion?

3. Do you find the court's analysis of associational discrimination persuasive?

4. Given the conflicting views in this area, how would you respond to an employer that might ask whether the company can be sued for sexual orientation discrimination?

5. Should the Supreme Court weigh in on this area?

Class Exercise: Sexual Orientation and Local Law

As noted above many local jurisdictions have passed protections for workers on the basis of sexual orientation. Breaking up into small groups, draft a law that would protect a local city's workers from sexual orientation discrimination. How is your law worded? Who does it protect? Are *all* employers potentially liable for violations of your proposed statute?

E. The Bona Fide Occupational Qualification Exception

This text has already briefly addressed the importance of the bona fide occupational qualification (BFOQ) exception. In certain narrow circumstances, the BFOQ permits employers to discriminate on the basis of sex, national origin, or religion where such discrimination is a bona fide occupational qualification. Section 703e(1) of Title VII provides that

> [n]otwithstanding any other provision of this [title] . . . it shall not be an unlawful employment practice for an employer to hire and employ employees . . . on the basis of his religion, sex, or national origin in those certain instances where religion, sex, or national origin is a bona fide occupational qualification reasonably necessary to the normal operation of that particular business or enterprise. . . .

The statute has several important qualifiers in this language: It limits the categories that may be used as the basis of discrimination to religion, sex, and national origin. The statute also provides that the qualification is limited to those "certain instances" where the BFOQ is "reasonably necessary" to the operation of the business. Given these various qualifiers, it is clear that Congress intended only a narrow use of this exception. Over the years, the courts have interpreted the BFOQ by giving the exception very limited breadth.

It is also important to understand that the statute does not allow a BFOQ on the basis of race or color. Thus, under the clear terms of the statute, there is never a situation where an employer is allowed to discriminate on this basis, irrespective of the essence or central mission of the company at issue. *But see* Charles A. Shanor et al., *The Effect of the University of Michigan Cases on Affirmative Action in Employment: Proceedings of the 2004 Annual Meeting, Association of American Law Schools, Sections on Employment Discrimination Law, Labor Relations and Employment Law, and Minority Groups*, 8 Emp. Rts. & Emp. Pol'y J. 127, 144 (2004) (mentioning that there are some cases that allow a racial BFOQ, such as *Miller v. Texas State Board of Barber Examiners*, 615 F.2d 650 (5th Cir. 1980), and suggesting situations in which race may come into play, such as when a police department wants to investigate the Ku Klux Klan and is not going to send an African American police officer to do so). The legislative history behind Title VII reveals why race and color were omitted from the BFOQ exception. Indeed, the omission was intentional and not simply an oversight. Representative John Williams (D-MS) had proposed an amendment that would have included race and color in the BFOQ exception. Williams argued that including race and color would further client preferences; for instance, a traditionally African-American business would not have to be forced to hire white employees if that would destroy the business's identity as an African-American enterprise. Other representatives agreed with Williams, but the amendment ultimately failed. Many representatives opposed the amendment because it went against the purpose of the Civil Rights Act; namely, to prohibit black businesses from only hiring black employees and white businesses from only hiring white employees. This type of segregation, the representatives argued, was precisely the type of discrimination that Congress intended to eliminate with the Civil Rights Act. Representative Emanuel Celler (D-NY) stated, "We did not include the word 'race' because we felt that race would not be a bona fide qualification." Celler further noted that "the basic purpose of [T]itle VII is to prohibit discrimination in employment on the basis of race or color. Now the substitute amendment . . . would destroy this principle. It would permit discrimination on the basis of race and color. It would establish a loophole, that could well gut this [T]itle." *See* Clare Tower Putnam, Comment, *When Can a Law Firm Discriminate Among Its Own Employees to Meet a Client's Request? Reflections on the ACC's Call to Action*, 9 U. Pa. J. Lab. & Emp. L. 657, 663–664 (2007).

In the *Dothard* decision below, the Supreme Court addressed the applicability of the BFOQ to a case of sex discrimination. The facts of the case are more fully set forth in Chapter 4. In the case, a twenty-two-year old female was denied a position as a correctional counselor in the Alabama prison system because she failed to meet the state statutory requirements of weighing 120 pounds and measuring at least 5 feet 2 inches tall. The plaintiff in the case alleged both disparate impact and intentional sex discrimination.

Dothard v. Rawlinson
433 U.S. 321 (1977)

Mr. Justice STEWART delivered the opinion of the Court.

At the time [Diane Rawlinson] applied for a position as correctional counselor trainee, Rawlinson was a 22-year-old college graduate whose major course
of study had been correctional psychology. She was refused employment because
she failed to meet the minimum 120-pound weight requirement established by an
Alabama statute. The statute also establishes a height minimum of 5 feet 2 inches.

[The facts of the case are addressed in detail in Chapter 4.]

Unlike the statutory height and weight requirements, Regulation 204 explicitly discriminates against women on the basis of their sex. In defense of this overt
discrimination, the appellants rely on § 703(e) of Title VII, 42 U.S.C. § 2000e–2(e),
which permits sex-based discrimination "in those certain instances where . . . sex . . .
is a bona fide occupational qualifica-
tion reasonably necessary to the normal operation of that particular business or enterprise."

The District Court rejected the
bona-fide   occupational-qualification
(bfoq) defense, relying on the virtually uniform view of the federal courts
that § 703(e) provides only the narrowest of exceptions to the general
rule requiring equality of employment
opportunities. This view has been var-
iously formulated. [T]he federal courts
have agreed that it is impermissible under Title VII to refuse to hire an individual
woman or man on the basis of stereotyped characterizations of the sexes, and the
District Court in the present case held in effect that Regulation 204 is based on just
such stereotypical assumptions.

We are persuaded by the restrictive language of § 703(e), the relevant legislative
history, and the consistent interpretation of the Equal Employment Opportunity
Commission that the bfoq exception was in fact meant to be an extremely narrow exception to the general prohibition of discrimination on the basis of sex. In
the particular factual circumstances of this case, however, we conclude that the
District Court erred in rejecting the State's contention that Regulation 204 falls
within the narrow ambit of the bfoq exception.

The environment in Alabama's penitentiaries is a peculiarly inhospitable one for human
beings of whatever sex. Indeed, a Federal
District Court has held that the conditions of
confinement in the prisons of the State, characterized by "rampant violence" and a "jungle
atmosphere," are constitutionally intolerable.

> The rampant violence and
> jungle-like atmosphere
> at this prison distinguish
> it from most other
> correctional facilities.

Pugh v. Locke, 406 F. Supp. 318, 325 (MD Ala.). The record in the present case shows that because of inadequate staff and facilities, no attempt is made in the four maximum-security male penitentiaries to classify or segregate inmates according to their offense or level of dangerousness — a procedure that, according to expert testimony, is essential to effective penological administration. Consequently, the estimated 20% of the male prisoners who are sex offenders are scattered throughout the penitentiaries' dormitory facilities.

In this environment of violence and disorganization, it would be an oversimplification to characterize Regulation 204 as an exercise in "romantic paternalism." In the usual case, the argument that a particular job is too dangerous for women may appropriately be met by the rejoinder that it is the purpose of Title VII to allow the individual woman to make that choice for herself. More is at stake in this case, however, than an individual woman's decision to weigh and accept the risks of employment in a "contact" position in a maximum-security male prison.

The essence of a correctional counselor's job is to maintain prison security. A woman's relative ability to maintain order in a male, maximum-security, unclassified penitentiary of the type Alabama now runs could be directly reduced by her womanhood. There is a basis in fact for expecting that sex offenders who have criminally assaulted women in the past would be moved to do so again if access to women were established within the prison. There would also be a real risk that other inmates, deprived of a normal heterosexual environment, would assault women guards because they were women. In a prison system where violence is the order of the day, where inmate access to guards is facilitated by dormitory living arrangements, where every institution is understaffed, and where a substantial portion of the inmate population is composed of sex offenders mixed at random with other prisoners, there are few visible deterrents to inmate assaults on women custodians.

Appellee Rawlinson's own expert testified that dormitory housing for aggressive inmates poses a greater security problem than single-cell lockups, and further testified that it would be unwise to use women as guards in a prison where even 10% of the inmates had been convicted of sex crimes and were not segregated from the other prisoners. The likelihood that inmates would assault a woman because she was a woman would pose a real threat not only to the victim of the assault but also to the basic control of the penitentiary and protection of its inmates and the other security personnel. The employee's very womanhood would thus directly undermine her capacity to provide the security that is the essence of a correctional counselor's responsibility.

There was substantial testimony from experts on both sides of this litigation that the use of women as guards in "contact" positions under the existing conditions in Alabama maximum-security male penitentiaries would pose a substantial security problem, directly linked to the sex of the prison guard. On the basis of that evidence, we conclude that the

District Court was in error in ruling that being male is not a bona fide occupational qualification for the job of correctional counselor in a "contact" position in an Alabama male maximum-security penitentiary.

The judgment is accordingly affirmed in part and reversed in part, and the case is remanded to the District Court for further proceedings consistent with this opinion.

It is so ordered.

Mr. Justice MARSHALL, with whom Mr. Justice BRENNAN joins, concurring in part and dissenting in part.

I must . . . respectfully disagree with the Court's application of the bfoq exception in this case. The Court properly rejects two proffered justifications for denying women jobs as prison guards. It is simply irrelevant here that a guard's occupation is dangerous and that some women might be unable to protect themselves adequately. Those themes permeate the testimony of the state officials below, but as the Court holds, "the argument that a particular job is too dangerous for women" is refuted by the "purpose of Title VII to allow the individual woman to make that choice for herself." Some women, like some men, undoubtedly are not qualified and do not wish to serve as prison guards, but that does not justify the exclusion of all women from this employment opportunity. Thus, "(i)n the usual case," the Court's interpretation of the bfoq exception would mandate hiring qualified women for guard jobs in maximum-security institutions. The highly successful experiences of other States allowing such job opportunities, see briefs for the States of California and Washington, as amici curiae, confirm that absolute disqualification of women is not, in the words of Title VII, "reasonably necessary to the normal operation" of a maximum security prison.

What would otherwise be considered unlawful discrimination against women is justified by the Court, however, on the basis of the "barbaric and inhumane" conditions in Alabama prisons, conditions so bad that state officials have conceded that they violate the Constitution. To me, this analysis sounds distressingly like saying two wrongs make a right. It is refuted by the plain words of § 703(e). The statute requires that a bfoq be "reasonably necessary to the normal operation of that particular business or enterprise." But no governmental "business" may operate "normally" in violation of the Constitution. Every action of government is constrained by constitutional limitations. While those limits may be violated more frequently than we would wish, no one disputes that the "normal operation" of all government functions takes place within them. A prison system operating in blatant violation of the Eighth Amendment is an exception that should be remedied with all possible speed. In the meantime, the existence of such violations should not be legitimatized by calling them "normal." Nor should the Court accept them as justifying conduct that would otherwise violate a statute intended to remedy age-old discrimination.

The Court's error in statutory construction is less objectionable, however, than the attitude it displays toward women. Though the Court recognizes that possible harm to women guards is an unacceptable reason for disqualifying women, it relies instead on an equally speculative threat to prison discipline supposedly generated by the sexuality of female guards. There is simply no evidence in the record to show that women guards would create any danger to security in Alabama prisons significantly greater than that which already exists. All of the dangers with one exception discussed below are inherent in a prison setting, whatever the gender of the guards.

The Court first sees women guards as a threat to security because "there are few visible deterrents to inmate assaults on women custodians." In fact, any prison guard is constantly subject to the threat of attack by inmates, and "invisible" deterrents are the guard's only real protection. No prison guard relies primarily on his or her ability to ward off an inmate attack to maintain order. Guards are typically unarmed and sheer numbers of inmates could overcome the normal complement. Rather, like all other law enforcement officers, prison guards must rely primarily on the moral authority of their office and the threat of future punishment for miscreants. As one expert testified below, common sense, fairness, and mental and emotional stability are the qualities a guard needs to cope with the dangers of the job. Well qualified and properly trained women, no less than men, have these psychological weapons at their disposal.

The particular severity of discipline problems in the Alabama maximum-security prisons is also no justification for the discrimination sanctioned by the Court. If male guards face an impossible situation, it is difficult to see how women could make the problem worse, unless one relies on precisely the type of generalized bias against women that the Court agrees Title VII was intended to outlaw. For example, much of the testimony of appellants' witnesses ignores individual differences among members of each sex and reads like "ancient canards about the proper role of women." *Phillips v. Martin Marietta Corp.*, 400 U.S. at 545 at 498. The witnesses claimed that women guards are not strict disciplinarians; that they are physically less capable of protecting themselves and subduing unruly inmates; that inmates take advantage of them as they did their mothers, while male guards are strong father figures who easily maintain discipline, and so on. Yet the record shows that the presence of women guards has not led to a single incident amounting to a serious breach of security in any Alabama institution. And, in any event, "(g)uards rarely enter the cell blocks and dormitories," where the danger of inmate attacks is the greatest.

It appears that the real disqualifying factor in the Court's view is "(t)he employee's very womanhood." The Court refers to the large number of sex offenders in Alabama prisons, and to "(t)he likelihood that inmates would assault a woman because she was a woman." In short, the fundamental justification for the decision is that women as guards will generate sexual assaults. With all respect, this rationale regrettably perpetuates one of the most insidious of the old myths about women — that women, wittingly or not, are seductive sexual objects. The effect of the decision, made I am sure with the best of intentions, is to punish women because their very presence might provoke sexual assaults. It is women who are made to pay the price in lost job opportunities for the threat of depraved conduct by prison inmates. Once again, "(t)he pedestal upon which women have been placed has . . . , upon closer inspection, been revealed as a cage." Sail'er Inn, Inc.

> Is the majority opinion—as the dissent maintains— treating women as "seductive sexual objects"?

v. Kirby, 5 Cal. 3d 1, 20 (1971). It is particularly ironic that the cage is erected here in response to feared misbehavior by imprisoned criminals.

The Court points to no evidence in the record to support the asserted "likelihood that inmates would assault a woman because she was a woman." Perhaps the Court relies upon common sense, or "innate recognition." But the danger in this emotionally laden context is that common sense will be used to mask the "romantic paternalism" and persisting discriminatory attitudes that the Court properly eschews. To me, the only matter of innate recognition is that the incidence of sexually motivated attacks on guards will be minute compared to the "likelihood that inmates will assault" a guard because he or she is a guard.

The proper response to inevitable attacks on both female and male guards is not to limit the employment opportunities of law[]abiding women who wish to contribute to their community, but to take swift and sure punitive action against the inmate offenders. Presumably, one of the goals of the Alabama prison system is the eradication of inmates' antisocial behavior patterns so that prisoners will be able to live one day in free society. Sex offenders can begin this process by learning to relate to women guards in a socially acceptable manner. To deprive women of job opportunities because of the threatened behavior of convicted criminals is to turn our social priorities upside down.

Although I do not countenance the sex discrimination condoned by the majority, it is fortunate that the Court's decision is carefully limited to the facts before it. I trust the lower courts will recognize that the decision was impelled by the shockingly inhuman conditions in Alabama prisons, and thus that the "extremely narrow (bfoq) exception" recognized here, will not be allowed "to swallow the rule" against sex discrimination. Expansion of today's decision beyond its narrow factual basis would erect a serious roadblock to economic equality for women.

■ NOTES AND QUESTIONS

1. Is the Court's application of the BFOQ here paternalistic? Shouldn't women be permitted to decide for themselves whether to take on the risk associated with the prison job?

2. The Court concludes that "[i]n this environment of violence and disorganization, it would be an oversimplification to characterize [the Regulation] as an exercise in 'romantic paternalism.'" Should an employer be allowed to evade the requirements of Title VII by permitting this type of environment to exist?

3. The Court notes that "the conditions of confinement in the prisons of the State" were "characterized by 'rampant violence' and a 'jungle atmosphere.'" Should these facts have any significant bearing on the application of the BFOQ?

It is worth noting that while the Court applied the BFOQ to prison guards in this case, other courts have tended to distinguish the *Dothard* decision in the prison setting, noting that the decision was heavily based on a "jungle atmosphere" not present in most prisons. *See* Gunter v. Iowa State Men's Reformatory, 612 F.2d 1079, 1085–1086 (8th Cir.), *cert. denied*, 446 U.S. 966 (1980) (holding that the BFOQ could not be applied to exclude females from prison guard positions where the conditions were not like those in Alabama's institutions). Given the passage of time and tendency for the lower courts to distinguish the case, fair concern exists as to whether *Dothard* is even "good law."

4. The dissent notes, "I trust the lower courts will recognize that the decision was impelled by the shockingly inhuman conditions in Alabama prisons, and thus that the 'extremely narrow [BFOQ] exception' recognized here . . . will not be allowed 'to swallow the rule' against sex discrimination."

5. Though the Court applies the BFOQ to the facts of this case, it does recognize that "the [BFOQ] exception was in fact meant to be an extremely narrow exception to the general prohibition of discrimination on the basis of sex."

6. Can any general principles be drawn from this case on when the BFOQ would be applicable to a particular factual setting? Does the Court articulate any general standards for applying the BFOQ?

7. Irrespective of your view on the scope of Title VII, it is undeniable that this case squarely addresses a question of health and safety. When these types of safety concerns are implicated, should an employer be given some leeway in making employment decisions that it believes best protects the lives of its workers?

8. The dissent states that "[t]he Court points to no evidence in the record to support the asserted 'likelihood that inmates would assault a woman because she was a woman.' . . . Perhaps the Court relies upon common sense, or 'innate recognition.'" Is it common sense to believe that women would be singled out for aggressive behavior?

9. The dissent further maintains that "[t]he proper response to inevitable attacks on both female and male guards is not to limit the employment opportunities of law-abiding women who wish to contribute to their community, but to take swift and sure punitive action against the inmate offenders." Wouldn't such a response come after an attack? Wouldn't the damage already be done at this point?

10. Does the dissent's argument that "[t]o deprive women of job opportunities because of the threatened behavior of convicted criminals is to turn our social priorities upside down" carry any weight here? Should safety concerns outweigh societal priorities in this case?

11. Is the BFOQ as applied in this case too sweeping in its scope? Would a prisoner be more likely to attack all women? What if the hiring choice were between a short woman that was highly trained in the martial arts or an overweight former male security guard that just satisfied the height standard?

12. The federal regulations specifically permit sex to be used for purposes of authenticity.

> Where it is necessary for the purpose of authenticity or genuineness, the Commission will consider sex to be a bona fide occupational qualification, e.g., an actor or actress.

29 C.F.R. § 1604.2(a)(2).

The legislative history of the BFOQ further notes that it would be permissible for the owner of an Italian restaurant to advertise for and hire an Italian cook, because "he would hardly be doing his business justice by advertising for a Turk to cook spaghetti." 110 Cong. Rec. 2549 (1964) (remarks of Representative Dent).

13. The *Dothard* case was also addressed in our discussion of disparate impact in Chapter 4. Is this case more appropriately considered as an intentional or unintentional case of discrimination? Why?

 Interactive Problem

Looking back at the facts of the interactive problem, assume that Nancy decides to change careers and uses her accounting background to attain her high school teaching certificate in mathematics. When she applies for a job at the most prestigious private school in the state, Bloomington Preparatory School for Boys, she is told that she will not be considered for the job. The recruiting coordinator at Bloomington Prep explains to Nancy that the school provides an all-male environment, and that employing any females at the school is strictly prohibited. If Nancy decided to sue the school under Title VII, could the school defend itself on the basis of the BFOQ?

The contours of the BFOQ have led to substantial confusion in the courts. Over the years, the courts have disagreed on the scope and breadth of this exception. In the decision below, the Supreme Court provides some much-needed guidance on how to apply this standard.

International Union, United Automobile Workers v. Johnson Controls, Inc.

499 U.S. 187 (1991)

Justice Blackmun delivered the opinion of the Court.

In this case we are concerned with an employer's gender-based fetal-protection policy. May an employer exclude a fertile female employee from certain jobs because of its concern for the health of the fetus the woman might conceive? Respondent Johnson Controls, Inc., manufactures batteries. In the manufacturing process, the element lead is a primary ingredient. Occupational exposure to lead entails health risks, including the risk of harm to any fetus carried by a female employee.

Before the Civil Rights Act of 1964 became law, Johnson Controls did not employ any woman in a battery-manufacturing job. In June 1977, however, it announced its first official policy concerning its employment of women in lead-exposure work:

> "[P]rotection of the health of the unborn child is the immediate and direct responsibility of the prospective parents. While the medical profession and the company can support them in the exercise of this responsibility, it cannot assume it for them without simultaneously infringing their rights as persons.
>
> ". . . . Since not all women who can become mothers wish to become mothers (or will become mothers), it would appear to be illegal discrimination to treat all who are capable of pregnancy as though they will become pregnant."

Consistent with that view, Johnson Controls "stopped short of excluding women capable of bearing children from lead exposure," but emphasized that a woman who expected to have a child should not choose a job in which she would have such exposure. The company also required a woman who wished to be considered for employment to sign a statement that she had been advised of the risk of having a child while she was exposed to lead. The statement informed the woman that although there was evidence "that women exposed to lead have a higher rate of abortion," this evidence was "not as clear . . . as the relationship between cigarette smoking and cancer," but that it was, "medically speaking, just good sense not to run that risk if you want children and do not want to expose the unborn child to risk, however small. . . ."

Five years later, in 1982, Johnson Controls shifted from a policy of warning to a policy of exclusion. Between 1979 and 1983, eight employees became pregnant while maintaining blood lead levels in excess of 30 micrograms per deciliter. This appeared to be the critical level noted by the Occupational Safety and Health Administration (OSHA) for a worker who was planning to have a family. *See* 29 CFR § 1910.1025 (1990). The company responded by announcing a broad exclusion of women from jobs that exposed them to lead:

> ". . . [I]t is [Johnson Controls'] policy that women who are pregnant or who are capable of bearing children will not be placed into jobs involving lead exposure or which could expose them to lead through the exercise of job bidding, bumping, transfer or promotion rights."

The policy defined "women . . . capable of bearing children" as "[a]ll women except those whose inability to bear children is medically documented." It further stated that an unacceptable work station was one where, "over the past year," an employee had recorded a blood lead level of more than 30 micrograms per deciliter or the work site had yielded an air sample containing a lead level in excess of 30 micrograms per cubic meter.

In April 1984, petitioners filed in the United States District Court for the Eastern District of Wisconsin a class action challenging Johnson Controls' fetal-protection policy as sex discrimination that violated Title VII of the Civil Rights Act of 1964. The District Court granted summary judgment for defendant-respondent Johnson Controls. The Court of Appeals for the Seventh Circuit, sitting en banc, affirmed the summary judgment by a 7-to-4 vote. The majority held that the proper standard for evaluating the fetal-protection policy was the defense of business necessity;

that Johnson Controls was entitled to summary judgment under that defense; and that even if the proper standard was a BFOQ, Johnson Controls still was entitled to summary judgment.

The bias in Johnson Controls' policy is obvious. Fertile men, but not fertile women, are given a choice as to whether they wish to risk their reproductive health for a particular job. Section 703(a) of the Civil Rights Act of 1964 prohibits sex-based classifications in terms and conditions of employment, in hiring and discharging decisions, and in other employment decisions that adversely affect an employee's status. Respondent's fetal-protection policy explicitly discriminates against women on the basis of their sex. The policy excludes women with child-bearing capacity from lead-exposed jobs and so creates a facial classification based on gender. Respondent assumes as much in its brief before this Court.

Nevertheless, the Court of Appeals assumed, as did the two appellate courts that already had confronted the issue, that sex-specific fetal-protection policies do not involve facial discrimination. These courts analyzed the policies as though they were facially neutral, and had only a discriminatory effect upon the employment opportunities of women. Consequently, the courts looked to see if each employer in question had established that its policy was justified as a business necessity. The business necessity standard is more lenient for the employer than the statutory BFOQ defense. The Court of Appeals here went one step further and invoked the burden-shifting framework set forth in *Wards Cove Packing Co. v. Atonio*, 490 U.S. 642 (1989), thus requiring petitioners to bear the burden of persuasion on all questions. The court assumed that because the asserted reason for the sex-based exclusion (protecting women's unconceived offspring) was ostensibly benign, the policy was not sex-based discrimination. That assumption, however, was incorrect.

Johnson Controls' policy classifies on the basis of gender and childbearing capacity, rather than fertility alone. Respondent does not seek to protect the unconceived children of all its employees. Despite evidence in the record about the debilitating effect of lead exposure on the male reproductive system, Johnson Controls is concerned only with the harms that may befall the unborn offspring of its female employees. Johnson Controls' policy is facially discriminatory because it requires only a female employee to produce proof that she is not capable of reproducing.

We concluded above that Johnson Controls' policy is not neutral because it does not apply to the reproductive capacity of the company's male employees in the same way as it applies to that of the females. Moreover, the absence of a malevolent motive does not convert a facially discriminatory policy into a neutral policy with a discriminatory effect. Whether an employment practice involves disparate treatment through explicit facial discrimination does not depend on why the employer discriminates but rather on the explicit terms of the discrimination. The beneficence of an employer's purpose does not undermine the conclusion that an explicit gender-based policy is sex discrimination under § 703(a) and thus may be defended only as a BFOQ.

Under § 703(e)(1) of Title VII, an employer may discriminate on the basis of "religion, sex, or national origin in those certain instances where religion, sex, or national origin is a bona fide occupational qualification reasonably necessary to the normal operation of that particular business or enterprise." 42 U.S.C. § 2000e–2(e)(1).

We therefore turn to the question whether Johnson Controls' fetal-protection policy is one of those "certain instances" that come within the BFOQ exception.

The BFOQ defense is written narrowly, and this Court has read it narrowly. The wording of the BFOQ defense contains several terms of restriction that indicate that the exception reaches only special situations. The statute thus limits the situations in which discrimination is permissible to "certain instances" where sex discrimination is "reasonably necessary" to the "normal operation" of the "particular" busi-

> The Court here emphasizes the "narrow" terms set forth in the statutory language that gives rise to the BFOQ.

ness. Each one of these terms — certain, normal, particular — prevents the use of general subjective standards and favors an objective, verifiable requirement. But the most telling term is "occupational"; this indicates that these objective, verifiable requirements must concern job-related skills and aptitudes. By modifying "qualification" with "occupational," Congress narrowed the term to qualifications that affect an employee's ability to do the job.

Johnson Controls argues that its fetal-protection policy falls within the so-called safety exception to the BFOQ. Our cases have stressed that discrimination on the basis of sex because of safety concerns is allowed only in narrow circumstances. In *Dothard v. Rawlinson*, this Court indicated that danger to a woman herself does not justify discrimination. We there allowed the employer to hire only male guards in contact areas of maximum-security male penitentiaries only because more was at stake than the "individual woman's decision to weigh and accept the risks of employment." We found sex to be a BFOQ inasmuch as the employment of a female guard would create real risks of safety to others if violence broke out because the guard was a woman. Sex discrimination was tolerated because sex was related to the guard's ability to do the job-maintaining prison security. We also required in *Dothard* a high correlation between sex and ability to perform job functions and refused to allow employers to use sex as a proxy for strength although it might be a fairly accurate one.

We considered safety to third parties in *Western Airlines, Inc. v. Criswell*, 472 U.S. 400 (1985), in the context of the ADEA. We focused upon "the nature of the flight engineer's tasks," and the "actual capabilities of persons over age 60" in relation to those tasks. 472 U.S. at 406. Our safety concerns were not independent of the individual's ability to perform the assigned tasks, but rather involved the possibility that, because of age-connected debility, a flight engineer might not properly assist the pilot, and might thereby cause a safety emergency. Furthermore, although we considered the safety of third parties in *Dothard* and *Criswell*, those third parties were indispensable to the particular business at issue. In *Dothard*, the third parties were the inmates; in *Criswell*, the third parties were the passengers on the plane. We stressed that in order to qualify as a BFOQ, a job qualification must relate to the " 'essence,' " *Dothard*, 433 U.S. at 333 (emphasis deleted), or to the "central mission of the employer's business," *Criswell*, 472 U.S. at 413.

Justice White ignores the "essence of the business" test and so concludes that "protecting fetal safety while carrying out the duties of battery manufacturing is as much a legitimate concern as is safety to third parties in guarding prisons (*Dothard*) or flying airplanes (*Criswell*)." By limiting his discussion to cost and safety concerns and rejecting the "essence of the business" test that our case law has established, he seeks to expand what is now the narrow BFOQ defense. Third-party safety considerations properly entered into the BFOQ analysis in *Dothard* and *Criswell* because they went to the core of the employee's job

> To fall within the contours of the BFOQ, the qualification standard must be job related and go to the essence or central mission of the employer's business.

performance. Moreover, that performance involved the central purpose of the enterprise. *Dothard*, 433 U.S. at 335 ("The essence of a correctional counselor's job is to maintain prison security"); *Criswell*, 472 U.S. at 413 (the central mission of the airline's business was the safe transportation of its passengers). Justice White attempts to transform this case into one of customer safety. The unconceived fetuses of Johnson Controls' female employees, however, are neither customers nor third parties whose safety is essential to the business of battery manufacturing. No one can disregard the possibility of injury to future children; the BFOQ, however, is not so broad that it transforms this deep social concern into an essential aspect of battery making.

Our case law, therefore, makes clear that the safety exception is limited to instances in which sex or pregnancy actually interferes with the employee's ability to perform the job. This approach is consistent with the language of the BFOQ provision itself, for it suggests that permissible distinctions based on sex must relate to ability to perform the duties of the job. Johnson Controls suggests, however, that we expand the exception to allow fetal-protection policies that mandate particular standards for pregnant or fertile women. We decline to do so. Such an expansion contradicts not only the language of the BFOQ and the narrowness of its exception, but also the plain language and history of the PDA.

We conclude that the language of both the BFOQ provision and the PDA which amended it, as well as the legislative history and the case law, prohibit an employer from discriminating against a woman because of her capacity to become pregnant unless her reproductive potential prevents her from performing the duties of her job. We reiterate our holdings in *Criswell* and *Dothard* that an employer must direct its concerns about a woman's ability to perform her job safely and efficiently to those aspects of the woman's job-related activities that fall within the "essence" of the particular business.

We have no difficulty concluding that Johnson Controls cannot establish a BFOQ. Fertile women, as far as appears in the record, participate in the manufacture of batteries as efficiently as anyone else. Johnson Controls' professed moral and ethical concerns about the welfare of the next generation do not suffice to establish a BFOQ of female sterility. Decisions about the welfare of future children must be left to the parents who conceive, bear, support, and raise them rather than to the employers who hire those parents. Congress has mandated this choice through Title VII, as amended by the PDA. Johnson Controls has attempted to exclude women because of their reproductive capacity. Title VII and the PDA simply do not allow a woman's dismissal because of her failure to submit to sterilization.

Nor can concerns about the welfare of the next generation be considered a part of the "essence" of Johnson Controls' business.

A word about tort liability and the increased cost of fertile women in the workplace is perhaps necessary. One of the dissenting judges in this case expressed concern about an employer's tort liability and concluded that liability for a potential injury to a fetus is a social cost that Title VII does not require a company to ignore. It is correct to say that Title VII does not prevent the employer from having a conscience. The statute, however, does prevent sex-specific fetal-protection policies. These two aspects of Title VII do not conflict.

More than 40 States currently recognize a right to recover for a prenatal injury based either on negligence or on wrongful death. According to Johnson Controls, however, the company complies with the lead standard developed by OSHA and warns its female employees about the damaging effects of lead. It is worth noting that OSHA gave the problem of lead lengthy consideration and concluded that "there is no basis whatsoever for the claim that women of childbearing age should be excluded from the workplace in order to protect the fetus or the course of pregnancy." 43 Fed. Reg. 52952, 52966 (1978). Although the issue is not before us, Justice White observes that "it is far from clear that compliance with Title VII will pre-empt state tort liability." The cases relied upon by him to support his prediction, however, are inapposite.

> What role, if any, does state tort law play in Title VII?

If state tort law furthers discrimination in the workplace and prevents employers from hiring women who are capable of manufacturing the product as efficiently as men, then it will impede the accomplishment of Congress' goals in enacting Title VII. Because Johnson Controls has not argued that it faces any costs from tort liability, not to mention crippling ones, the pre-emption question is not before us. We therefore say no more than that the concurrence's speculation appears unfounded as well as premature.

The tort-liability argument reduces to two equally unpersuasive propositions. First, Johnson Controls attempts to solve the problem of reproductive health hazards by resorting to an exclusionary policy. Title VII plainly forbids illegal sex discrimination as a method of diverting attention from an employer's obligation to police the workplace. Second, the specter of an award of damages reflects a fear that hiring fertile women will cost more. The extra cost of employing members of one sex, however, does not provide an affirmative Title VII defense for a discriminatory refusal to hire members of that gender. We, of course, are not presented with, nor do we decide, a case in which costs would be so prohibitive as to threaten the survival of the employer's business. We merely reiterate our prior holdings that the incremental cost of hiring women cannot justify discriminating against them.

Our holding today that Title VII, as so amended, forbids sex-specific fetal-protection policies is neither remarkable nor unprecedented. Concern for a woman's existing or potential offspring historically has been the excuse for denying women equal employment opportunities. Congress in the PDA prohibited discrimination on the basis of a woman's ability to become pregnant. We do no more than hold that the PDA means what it says.

Justice WHITE, with whom THE CHIEF Justice and Justice KENNEDY join, concurring in part and concurring in the judgment.

The Court properly holds that Johnson Controls' fetal-protection policy overtly discriminates against women, and thus is prohibited by Title VII of the Civil Rights Act of 1964 unless it falls within the BFOQ exception.

[A] fetal-protection policy would be justified under the terms of the statute if, for example, an employer could show that exclusion of women from certain jobs was reasonably necessary to avoid substantial tort liability. Common sense tells us that it is part of the normal operation of business concerns to avoid causing injury to third parties, as well as to employees, if for no other reason than to avoid tort liability and its substantial costs. This possibility of tort liability is not hypothetical; every State currently allows children born alive to recover in tort for prenatal injuries caused by third parties, *see* W. Keeton, D. Dobbs, R. Keeton, & D. Owen, Prosser and Keeton on Law of Torts § 55, p. 368 (5th ed. 1984), and an increasing number of courts have recognized a right to recover even for prenatal injuries caused by torts committed prior to conception.

The Court dismisses the possibility of tort liability by no more than speculating that if "Title VII bans sex-specific fetal-protection policies, the employer fully informs the woman of the risk, and the employer has not acted negligently, the basis for holding an employer liable seems remote at best." Such speculation will be small comfort to employers. First, it is far from clear that compliance with Title VII will pre-empt state tort liability, and the Court offers no support for that proposition. Second, although warnings may preclude claims by injured *employees*, they will not preclude claims by injured children because the general rule is that parents cannot waive causes of action on behalf of their children, and the parents' negligence will not be imputed to the children. Finally, although state tort liability for prenatal injuries generally requires negligence, it will be difficult for employers to determine in advance what will constitute negligence. Compliance with OSHA standards, for example, has been held not to be a defense to state tort or criminal liability.

[T]he Court contends that tort liability cannot justify a fetal-protection policy because the extra costs of hiring women is not a defense under Title VII. Prior decisions construing the BFOQ defense confirm that the defense is broad enough to include considerations of cost and safety of the sort that could form the basis for an employer's adoption of a fetal-protection policy.

Dothard and *Criswell* make clear that avoidance of substantial safety risks to third parties is *inherently* part of both an employee's ability to perform a job and an employer's "normal operation" of its business. *Dothard* and *Criswell* also confirm that costs are relevant in determining whether a discriminatory policy is reasonably necessary for the normal operation of a business.

In enacting the BFOQ standard, "Congress did not ignore the public interest in safety." *Criswell*, 472 U.S. at 419. The Court's narrow interpretation of the BFOQ defense in this case, however, means that an employer cannot exclude even *pregnant* women from an environment highly toxic to their fetuses. It is foolish to think that Congress intended such a result, and neither the language of the BFOQ exception nor our cases require it.

■ NOTES AND QUESTIONS

1. The Court in this decision emphasizes that the BFOQ was intended to be a narrow defense. By and large, the lower courts have narrowly applied the defense as well, rarely permitting the employer to invoke this exception. *See, e.g.,* White v. Dep't of Corr. Servs., 814 F. Supp. 2d 374 (S.D.N.Y. 2011) (applying the BFOQ narrowly to deny the defendant's motion for summary judgment dismissing the plaintiff's Title VII claim).

2. The two opinions in this case conflict on whether *Dothard* is distinguishable from the facts of this case. Does *Dothard* present a distinguishable factual scenario? If so, how?

3. The majority opinion essentially adopts a two-part test for evaluating whether the BFOQ applies: First, the discrimination must be job related. Second, the necessary discrimination must go to the essence or central mission of what the employer does. Do you agree that the discrimination in *Dothard* was job related while the discrimination in *Johnson Controls* was not?

4. Is the Court disregarding the concerns over safety in this case? Shouldn't an employer be permitted to have the safety of its workers at heart? The majority concludes that "[t]he beneficence of an employer's purpose does not undermine the conclusion that an explicit gender-based policy is sex discrimination under § 703(a) and thus may be defended only as a BFOQ." Shouldn't the "beneficence of an employer's purpose" be an important inquiry under the statute?

5. The Court notes that "the safety exception is limited to instances in which sex or pregnancy actually interferes with the employee's ability to perform the job." If women are actually injured by performing the job, wouldn't this constitute such an interference?

6. Is the bigger consideration here that the company gave men a choice as to whether to continue employment in these jobs, but did not offer women the same choice?

7. The two opinions also seem to conflict on the question of potential tort liability. Is that an important consideration here? Why or why not? Could the employer simply have its employees sign a waiver in this regard?

8. Privacy BFOQ. Justice White notes that "[t]he lower federal courts . . . have consistently recognized that privacy interests may justify sex-based requirements for certain jobs." While there is a substantial amount of debate on this issue, a number of lower courts have indeed recognized the so-called privacy-based BFOQ. This BFOQ applies to certain sensitive areas of employment that interact with an individual's right to privacy. Thus, for example, in the home health care industry many individuals may feel uncomfortable being bathed or dressed by an individual of the opposite sex. In these very limited circumstances, some courts have applied the privacy BFOQ. *See* Emily Gold Waldman, *The Case of the Male OB-GYN: A Proposal for Expansion of the Privacy BFOQ in the Healthcare Context*, 6 U. Pa. J. Lab. & Emp. L. 357 (2004) (explaining the privacy BFOQ exception in depth).

9. **Customer preference BFOQ.** At the same time, in a broader sense, the courts have made clear that there is no customer preference BFOQ. Thus, for example, an employer cannot employ more women simply because its clients are more comfortable with female workers. *See* Diaz v. Pan Am. World Airways, Inc., 442 F.2d 385 (5th Cir. 1971) (holding that Pan Am's practice of hiring only female flight attendants was unlawful discrimination against males, despite the fact that Pan Am's customers preferred women attendants); EEOC v. HI 40 Corp., 953 F. Supp. 301, 305 (W.D. Mo. 1996) ("[P]references by customers have little, if any, legitimate role in making determinations of the legitimacy of discrimination under Title VII."); *see generally* Michael L. Sirota, *Sex Discrimination: Title VII and the Bona Fide Occupational Qualification*, 55 Tex. L. Rev. 1025, 1055–1056 (1977).

10. At the end of the day, it is important to understand the lesson from *Johnson Controls* that the BFOQ is an extremely narrow exception. It is narrowly applied by the courts and is not intended to provide an end-run around Title VII for employers.

Class Exercise: Customer Preference

Assume that a restaurant chain operates on the basis of providing its largely male clientele with attractive female waitresses that wear very tight-fitting shirts and extremely short skirts. If a male that applied for a waitress position were rejected for "not fitting this mold," could the company defend a lawsuit on the basis of the BFOQ? Breaking up into small groups, how would you argue in favor of the BFOQ if you were an attorney representing the restaurant? How would you argue against it?

Note: In the late 1990s, Hooters — a restaurant chain known for scantily clad female bartenders and waitresses — agreed to pay $3.75 million to settle a lawsuit filed by men who were denied employment because of their gender. The settlement still allows Hooters to continue with a majority female staff, but the restaurant agreed to create a few additional support jobs, such as bartenders and hosts, that must be filled without consideration of sex. *See Hooters Settles Suit by Men Denied Jobs*, N.Y. Times, Oct. 1, 1997, http://www.nytimes.com/1997/10/01/us/hooters-settles-suit-by-men-denied-jobs.html.

F. Grooming and Appearance Standards

The courts have also faced numerous questions regarding whether employers can apply different grooming and appearance standards to their male and female employees. After all, men and women traditionally wear different business attire and take varying amounts of time to groom themselves each day. Is it discrimination to have different standards for men and women in this regard? Can men be required to wear a shirt and tie while women must wear a skirt? Can men be required to have short hair while longer hair is permitted for females?

The short answer is that the courts have generally allowed different grooming standards for male and female employees, where the differing standards comply with general social norms. While there is no express basis for this distinction in the statute, the courts largely see these different standards as de minimis and not worthy of Title VII concerns. Similarly, the EEOC has looked at the issue from the perspective of possible racial discrimination, and has advised that "[a]ppearance standards generally must be neutral, adopted for nondiscriminatory reasons, consistently applied to persons of all racial and ethnic groups, and, if the standard has a disparate impact, it must be job-related and consistent with business necessity." EEOC Compl. Man. (CCH) § 15-VII(B.5) (2006). With limited exceptions, then, dress and grooming standards do not typically present a problem for employers, particularly in the sex discrimination context. If the employer complies with societal norms, it will usually be deemed in compliance with the statute. *See* Pecenka v. Fareway Stores, Inc., 672 N.W.2d 800, 804 (Iowa 2003) ("[T]itle VII . . . [was] not meant to prohibit employers from instituting personal grooming codes which have a de minimis [e]ffect on employment."); *see also* Harper v. Blockbuster Entm't Corp., 139 F.3d 1385, 1388 (11th Cir. 1998) (finding that a personal grooming code that prohibited men but not women from wearing long hair was nondiscriminatory under Title VII); Kleinsorge v. Eyeland Corp., 81 Fair Empl. Prac. Cas. (BNA) 1601 (E.D. Pa. 2000) (holding that a personal grooming code that allowed females to wear earrings but not men did not constitute a violation of Title VII); *but see* D. Wendy Greene, *Black Women Can't Have Blonde Hair . . . in the Workplace*, 14 J. Gender Race & Just. 405 (2011) (examining several "hair stories" involving black employees and arguing that hair proscriptions, which are largely viewed by courts as irrelevant to equal employment opportunity, are in fact critical to black women's ability to acquire and maintain employment).

Another issue that often arises is where employers prefer attractive workers over unattractive workers. *See* Ann C. McGinley, *Trouble in Sin City: Protecting Sexy Workers' Civil Rights*, 23 Stan. L. & Pol'y Rev. 253 (2012) (examining the legal issues surrounding the hyper-sexualization of women workers in casinos, pool clubs, and nightclubs, specifically with regards to women workers' legal rights to be free of sex discrimination and sexual harassment while at work). This issue is a bit more difficult. On its face, choosing attractive workers over unattractive ones does not run afoul of Title VII. Nothing in the statute focuses on appearance generally. Nonetheless, there are a couple of areas where employers can get themselves into trouble on this issue. First, some employers might correlate younger workers with being more attractive — doing so might implicate potential issues of age discrimination and the provisions of the ADEA. Second, if employers do use attractiveness as a basis to hire, they must make sure that they apply this standard equally to both males and females. Failure to do so would constitute sex discrimination under Title VII. Finally, employers must make certain that state or local laws do not prohibit this type of practice. Though federal law does not expressly prohibit appearance discrimination, a number of jurisdictions do have local laws that outlaw these considerations. For example, Washington, D.C.'s employment discrimination statute, § 2-1402.11, makes it illegal to discriminate based on personal appearance.

In the decision below, a federal appellate court looked at whether a casino's appearance policies violated sex discrimination law. The case provides an excellent example of how Title VII can be implicated when an employer adopts a standard for a worker's appearance.

Jespersen v. Harrah's Operating Co.
392 F.3d 1076 (9th Cir. 2004)

TASHIMA, Circuit Judge:

Darlene Jespersen was a bartender at the sports bar in Harrah's Casino in Reno, Nevada, for nearly 20 years. She was an outstanding employee. Over the years, Jespersen's supervisors commented that she was "highly effective," that her attitude was "very positive," and that she made a "positive impression" on Harrah's guests. Harrah's customers repeatedly praised Jespersen on employee feedback forms, writing that Jespersen's excellent service and good attitude enhanced their experience at the sports bar and encouraged them to come back.

Throughout the 1980s and '90s Harrah's encouraged its female beverage servers to wear makeup, but wearing makeup was not a formal requirement. Although Jespersen never cared for makeup, she tried wearing it for a short period of time in the 1980s. But she found that wearing makeup made her feel sick, degraded, exposed, and violated. Jespersen felt that wearing makeup "forced her to be feminine" and to become "dolled up" like a sexual object, and that wearing makeup actually interfered with her ability to be an effective bartender (which sometimes required her to deal with unruly, intoxicated guests) because it "took away [her] credibility as an individual and as a person." After a few weeks, Jespersen stopped wearing makeup because it was so harmful to her dignity and her effectiveness behind the bar that she could no longer do her job. Harrah's did not object to Jespersen's choice not to wear makeup and Jespersen continued to work at the sports bar and receive positive performance reviews for over a decade.

Harrah's Hotel and Casino

In February 2000, Harrah's implemented its "Beverage Department Image Transformation" program at 20 Harrah's locations, including its casino in Reno. The goal of the program was to create a "brand standard of excellence" throughout Harrah's operations, with an emphasis on guest service positions. The program imposed specific "appearance standards" on each of its employees in guest services, including heightened requirements for beverage servers. All beverage servers were required to be "well groomed, appealing to the eye, be firm and body toned, and be comfortable with maintaining this look while wearing the specified uniform." In addition to these general appearance standards applicable to both sexes, there were gender-specific standards for male and female beverage servers. Female beverage servers were required to wear stockings and colored nail polish, and they were required to wear their hair "teased, curled, or styled." Male beverage servers were prohibited from wearing makeup or colored nail polish, and they were required to maintain short haircuts and neatly trimmed fingernails.

The text of the appearance standards provides, in relevant part, as follows:

> All Beverage Service Personnel, in addition to being friendly, polite, courteous and responsive to our customer's needs, must possess the ability to physically perform the essential factors of the job as set forth in the standard job descriptions. They must be well groomed, appealing to the eye, be firm and body toned, and be comfortable with maintaining this look while wearing the specified uniform. Additional factors to be considered include, but are not limited to, hair styles, overall body contour, and degree of comfort the employee projects while wearing the uniform.

Beverage Bartenders and Barbacks will adhere to these additional guidelines:

Overall Guidelines (applied equally to male/female):

- Appearance: Must maintain Personal Best Image portrayed at time
- Jewelry, if issued, must be worn. Otherwise, tasteful and simple jewelry is permitted; no large chokers, chains or bracelets.
- No faddish hairstyles or unnatural colors are permitted.

Males:

- Hair must not extend below top of shirt collar. Ponytails are prohibited.
- Hands and fingernails must be clean and nails neatly trimmed at all times. No colored polish is permitted.
- Eye and facial makeup is not permitted.
- Shoes will be solid black leather or leather type with rubber (non skid) soles.

Females:

- Hair must be teased, curled, or styled every day you work. Hair must be worn down at all times, no exceptions.
- Stockings are to be of nude or natural color consistent with employee's skin tone. No runs.
- Nail polish can be clear, white, pink or red color only. No exotic nail art or length.
- Shoes will be solid black leather or leather type with rubber (non skid) soles.

Harrah's called its new appearance standards the "Personal Best" program. In order to enforce the "Personal Best" standards, Harrah's required each beverage service employee to attend "Personal Best Image Training" prior to his or her final uniform fitting. At the training, "Personal Best Image Facilitators" instructed Harrah's employees on how to adhere to the standards of the program and tested their proficiency. At the conclusion of the training, two photographs (one portrait and one full body) were taken of the employee looking his or her "Personal Best." Each employee's "Personal Best" photographs were placed in his or her file and distributed to his or her supervisor. The supervisors used the "Personal Best" photographs as an "appearance measurement" tool, holding each employee accountable to look his or her "Personal Best" on a daily basis. Jespersen acknowledged receipt of the policy and committed to adhere to the appearance standards for her position as a beverage bartender in March 2000.

Shortly thereafter, however, the "Personal Best" standards were amended such that in addition to the existing appearance standards, all female beverage servers (including beverage bartenders) were required to wear makeup. As before, male beverage servers were prohibited from wearing makeup. Because of her objection to wearing makeup, Jespersen refused to comply with the new policy. In July 2000, Harrah's told Jespersen that the makeup requirement was mandatory for female beverage service employees and gave

> Does the casino's rigid appearance standard violate Title VII by treating men and women differently?

her 30 days to apply for a position that did not require makeup to be worn. At the expiration of the 30-day period, Jespersen had not applied for another job, and she was terminated.

After exhausting her administrative remedies with the Equal Employment Opportunity Commission, Jespersen brought this action alleging that Harrah's makeup requirement for female beverage servers constituted disparate treatment sex discrimination. The district court granted Harrah's motion for summary judgment.

In order to prevail on a Title VII disparate treatment sex discrimination claim, an employee need only establish that, but for his or her sex, he or she would have been treated differently. Although the employee must prove that the employer acted intentionally, the intent need not have been malevolent.

Pursuant to the "Personal Best" program, women are required to wear makeup, while men are prohibited from doing so. Women are required to wear their hair "teased, curled, or styled" each day, whereas men are only required to maintain short haircuts. We must decide whether these standards are discriminatory; whether they are "based on a policy which on its face applies less favorably to one gender. . . ." If so, then Harrah's would have discriminated against Jespersen "because of . . . sex." 42 U.S.C. § 2000e–2(a)(1).

We have previously held that grooming and appearance standards that apply differently to women and men do not constitute discrimination on the basis of sex. We concluded that grooming and dress standards were entirely outside the purview of Title VII because Congress intended that Title VII only prohibit discrimination based on "immutable characteristics" associated with a worker's sex. Because grooming and dress standards regulated "mutable" characteristics such as hair length, we reasoned, employers that made compliance with such standards a condition of employment discriminated on the basis of their employees' appearance, not their sex.

Our later cases recognized, however, that an employer's imposition of more stringent appearance standards on one sex than the other constitutes sex discrimination even where the appearance standards regulate only "mutable" characteristics such as weight. Although employers are free to adopt *different* appearance standards for each sex, they may not adopt standards that impose a greater burden on one sex than the other.

In order to evaluate the relative burdens the "Personal Best" policy imposes, we must assess the actual impact that it has on both male and female employees. In doing so we must weigh the cost and time necessary for employees of each sex to comply with the policy. Harrah's contends that the burden of the makeup requirement must be evaluated with reference to all of the requirements of the policy, including those that burden men only, such as the requirement that men maintain short haircuts and neatly trimmed nails. Jespersen contends that the only meaningful appearance standard against which the makeup requirement can be measured is the corresponding "no makeup" requirement for men. We agree with Harrah's approach. Because employers are permitted to apply different appearance standards to each sex so long as those standards are equal, our task in applying the "unequal burdens" test to grooming and dress requirements must some-

times involve weighing the relative burdens that particular requirements impose on workers of one sex against the distinct requirements imposed on workers of the other sex.

Jespersen contends that the makeup requirement imposes "innumerable" tangible burdens on women that men do not share because cosmetics can cost hundreds of dollars per year and putting on makeup requires a significant investment in time. There is, however, no evidence in the record in support of this contention. Jespersen cites to academic literature discussing the cost and time burdens of cosmetics generally, but she presents no evidence as to the cost or time burdens that must be borne by female bartenders in

order to comply with the makeup requirement. Even if we were to take judicial notice of the fact that the application of makeup requires *some* expenditure of time and money, Jespersen would still have the burden of producing some evidence that the burdens associated with the makeup requirement are greater than the burdens the "Personal Best" policy imposes on male bartenders, and exceed whatever "burden" is associated with ordinary good-grooming standards. Because there is no evidence in the record from which we can assess the burdens that the "Personal Best" policy imposes on male bartenders either, Jespersen's claim fails for that reason alone.

Although [the Supreme Court's decision in] *Price Waterhouse v. Hopkins*, 490 U.S. 228 (1989), held that Title VII bans discrimination against an employee on the basis of that employee's failure to dress and behave according to the stereotype corresponding with her gender, it did not address the specific question of whether an employer can impose sex-differentiated appearance and grooming standards on its male and female employees. Nor have our subsequent cases invalidated the "unequal burdens" test as a means of assessing whether sex-differentiated appearance standards discriminate on the basis of sex. In short, although we have applied the reasoning of *Price Waterhouse* to sexual harassment cases, we have not done so in the context of appearance and grooming standards cases, and we decline to do so here.

We hold that under the "unequal burdens" test, which is this Circuit's test for evaluating whether an employer's sex-differentiated appearance standards constitute sex discrimination in violation of Title VII, Jespersen failed to introduce evidence raising a triable issue of fact as to whether Harrah's "Personal Best" policy imposes unequal burdens on male and female employees.

THOMAS, Circuit Judge, dissenting.

I respectfully dissent.

Harrah's required Darlene Jespersen to wear makeup to work. She refused because the cost — measured in time, money, and personal dignity — was too high. Harrah's fired her. The majority holds that Jespersen failed to raise a triable issue of fact as to whether Harrah's policy imposes unequal burdens on men and women. In fact, Jespersen easily satisfied her burden. A reasonable factfinder could determine that Harrah's acted because of Jespersen's sex under not just one theory, but two. First, Harrah's fired Jespersen because of her failure to conform to sex stereotypes, which is discrimination based on sex and is therefore impermissible under Title VII. Second, Jespersen created a triable issue of fact as to whether the policy imposed unequal burdens on men and women, because the policy imposes a requirement on women that is not only time-consuming and expensive, but burdensome for its requirement that women conform to outdated and impermissible sex stereotypes.

A reasonable factfinder could conclude that the Harrah's makeup requirement imposes an unequal burden on women, that Jespersen was fired for failure to conform to a sex stereotype, or both. Darlene Jespersen should be allowed to present her case to a jury.

■ NOTES AND QUESTIONS

1. Does the "Personal Best" program put a more onerous burden on women than men? Does it constitute sex discrimination in violation of Title VII?

2. Do you agree with the "unequal burdens" test established by the court? Is there an unequal burden placed on female employees?

3. Is the company engaging in sex stereotyping with its requirements? Do the requirements set forth in the program pigeonhole individuals on the basis of sex?

4. Does wearing makeup constitute an essential function of the job? Why would the employer impose this requirement on workers?

5. As a general matter, does our society require more in terms of grooming standards for women than men? Does appearing in a professional manner cost women more money (and take additional time) compared to their male counterparts?

6. Should this case have gone to a jury on the question of whether the company created an unequal burden on women? Why is the court permitted to resolve this apparent factual issue?

7. Do you agree with the dissent's characterization that the company is requiring females to "conform to outdated and impermissible sex stereotypes"? *See generally* Zachary A. Kramer, *The New Sex Discrimination*, 63 Duke L.J. 891, 893–896 (2014) (discussing *Jespersen* and arguing that sex discrimination law has not kept pace with the lived experience of sex discrimination, which is highly individualized).

8. A related "casino" appearance case involves the Borgata Hotel Casino & Spa located in Atlantic City, New Jersey. The women who work as cocktail waitresses in this casino are known as "Borgata Babes." The "Borgata Babes" position is described as "part fashion model, part beverage server, part charming host and hostess. All impossibly lovely." The contract that the female employees sign at the beginning of their employment includes a weight policy, which requires periodic weigh-ins and limits the employee's weight gain to 7 percent of her body weight upon hire. If an employee gains too much weight while being employed at the resort, she is suspended from the job. Twenty-two of these former "Borgata Babes" filed a lawsuit alleging sex discrimination. The complainants argued that they were treated like sex objects under the resort's weight and appearance policy. However, because the employees had read and signed their contracts, the court concluded that the women agreed to the weight policy and, basically, assumed the risk of the position. *See* Kate Rogers, N.J. *Judge Rules Employer Can Limit Weight Gain*, Fox Business (July 30, 2013), http://www.foxbusiness.com/personal-finance/2013/07/30/nj-judge-rules-employer-can-limit-weight-gain/ (last visited July 1, 2018); Josh Sanburn, *Too Big to Cocktail? Judge Upholds Weight Discrimination in the Workplace*, Time (July 26, 2013), http://nation.time.com/2013/07/26/too-big-to-cocktail-judge-upholds-weight-discrimination-in-the-workplace/.

 *Interactive Problem*

Looking back at the facts of the interactive problem, assume that Peter calls Nancy into his office and tells her, "If you want to be a partner here, I'm going to need you to be more lady-like. You should wear more makeup, dress and walk more femininely, and buy more jewelry." Would such comments run afoul of Title VII? Why or why not?

G. The Equal Pay Act and the Lilly Ledbetter Fair Pay Act

The Equal Pay Act (EPA) is a separate statute that requires that men and women be paid the same for performing equal work. The EPA is separate and apart from Title VII, though claims can be brought under both statutes. The EPA is much narrower than Title VII, as it addresses only (1) pay discrimination specifically in the context of (2) gender discrimination. Title VII can also include wage discrimination against any protected class, including females. The EPA states:

> No employer . . . shall discriminate . . . between employees on the basis of sex by paying wages to employees in such establishment at a rate less than the rate at which he pays wages to employees of the opposite sex in such establishment for equal work on jobs the performance of which requires equal skill, effort, and responsibility, and which are performed under similar working conditions. . . .

29 U.S.C. § 206(d)(1).

There are a number of important distinctions between Title VII and the EPA. Perhaps most importantly, claims brought under the EPA do *not* require a showing of intent. Most claims brought under Title VII, by contrast, do mandate that the plaintiff establish that the discrimination was intentional. This lack of intent can be an important distinction between the two causes of action. If a worker can establish that the employer paid male and female employees differently for performing the same work, the employer can be held liable under the EPA irrespective of its motivations. Though the articulation of the prima facie case for an EPA claim varies from court to court, a typical showing requires that the plaintiff establish the following three factors:

> (1) the plaintiff was performing work which was substantially equal to that of employees of the opposite sex, taking into consideration the skills, duties, supervision, effort and responsibilities of the jobs; (2) the conditions where the work was performed were basically the same; (3) employees of the opposite sex were paid more under such circumstances.

Mickelson v. New York Life Ins. Co., 460 F.3d 1305, 1311 (10th Cir. 2006) (citing Miller v. Automobile Club of N.M., Inc., 420 F.3d 1098, 1119 (2005)).

Once the plaintiff establishes this prima facie case, the burden of persuasion shifts to the employer to establish one of the statutory exceptions. These four exceptions include that the wage differential was made on the basis of "(i) a seniority system; (ii) a merit system; (iii) a system which measures earnings by quantity or quality of production; or (iv) a differential based on any other factor other than sex. . . ." 29 U.S.C. § 206(d). It is worth noting that these exceptions also now apply to Title VII wage discrimination claims.

The typical EPA prima facie case thus proceeds in two parts. First, the plaintiff must establish that she is being paid less for performing substantially similar work to a comparable male employee. In making this determination, the courts will examine whether the two positions were indeed equivalent. This inquiry looks at the skills, duties, and responsibilities of the job, as well as the conditions under which the job was performed. If the plaintiff satisfies this showing, the defendant must establish that it was operating pursuant to a valid statutory exception — essentially showing that the pay differential was "based on any other factor other than sex." The critical distinction between the EPA and Title VII, then, is that the EPA does not require a showing of intent. In Title VII cases, a plaintiff need not establish that the working conditions were similar, but instead must show that a woman is being paid less because she is a woman.

Another important distinction between Title VII and EPA claims is the charge filing process. Under Title VII, a private plaintiff must file a charge with the EEOC within 180/300 days of the discriminatory wage payment. By contrast, no charge must be filed under the EPA and plaintiffs have two years to file a claim (or three years if the violation was willful). Though not necessary under the EPA, a plaintiff may elect to file a charge if she is also pursuing a Title VII cause of action. Thus, no administrative process is required for EPA claims.

The damages are also different under the EPA and Title VII. Damages are carefully proscribed by the statutes. However, generally speaking, a plaintiff will be entitled to a salary increase and backpay, as well as liquidated damages (absent a showing of good faith on the part of the employer) under the EPA. No compensatory or punitive damages are available under the EPA. Under Title VII, however, plaintiffs can receive compensatory and punitive damages up to the statutory cap.

 ## Interactive Problem

Looking back at the facts of the interactive problem, assume that Nancy Numbers learns that she receives less pay than any male accountant at the firm. Indeed, Nancy learns that her pay is $500 less per month than the lowest-paid accountant — despite the fact that her work record compares favorably with the best employees at the firm. What causes of action would Nancy be able to pursue? What proof would she have to show? What damages would she be entitled to?

Pay discrimination claims can arise under both Title VII and the EPA. In the controversial decision below, the Supreme Court examines when the statutory clock for pay discrimination begins to run. This decision attempted to resolve a circuit split that existed on the issue.

Ledbetter v. Goodyear Tire & Rubber Co.
550 U.S. 618 (2007)

Justice Aʟɪᴛᴏ delivered the opinion of the Court.

Petitioner Lilly Ledbetter (Ledbetter) worked for respondent Goodyear Tire & Rubber Company (Goodyear) at its Gadsden, Alabama, plant from 1979 until 1998. During much of this time, salaried employees at the plant were given or denied raises based on their supervisors' evaluation of their performance. In March 1998, Ledbetter submitted a questionnaire to the EEOC alleging certain acts of sex discrimination, and in July of that year she filed a formal EEOC charge. After taking early retirement in November 1998, Ledbetter commenced this action, in which she asserted, among other claims, a Title VII pay discrimination claim and a claim under the Equal Pay Act of 1963 (EPA).

The District Court granted summary judgment in favor of Goodyear on several of Ledbetter's claims, including her EPA claim, but allowed others, including her Title VII pay discrimination claim, to proceed to trial. In support of this latter claim, Ledbetter introduced evidence that during the course of her employment several supervisors had given her poor evaluations because of her sex, that as a result of these evaluations her pay was not increased as much as it would have been if she had been evaluated fairly, and that these past pay decisions continued to affect the amount of her pay throughout her employment. Toward the end of her time with Goodyear, she was being paid significantly less than any of her male colleagues. Goodyear maintained that the evaluations had been non-discriminatory, but the jury found for Ledbetter and awarded her backpay and damages.

> Alabama had no state or local equivalent EEO agency at the time of this case, and thus the statute of limitations was 180 as opposed to 300 days.

On appeal, Goodyear contended that Ledbetter's pay discrimination claim was time barred with respect to all pay decisions made prior to September 26, 1997 — that is, 180 days before the filing of her EEOC questionnaire. And Goodyear argued that no discriminatory act relating to Ledbetter's pay occurred after that date.

The Court of Appeals for the Eleventh Circuit reversed, holding that a Title VII pay discrimination claim cannot be based on any pay decision that occurred prior to the last pay decision that affected the employee's pay during the EEOC charging period. The Court of Appeals then concluded that there was insufficient evidence to prove that Goodyear had acted with discriminatory intent in making the only two pay decisions that occurred within that time span, namely, a decision made in 1997 to deny Ledbetter a raise and a similar decision made in 1998.

An individual wishing to challenge an employment practice under [Title VII] must first file a charge with the EEOC. § 2000e–5(e)(1). Such a charge must be filed within a specified period (either 180 or 300 days, depending on the State) "after the alleged unlawful employment practice occurred," *ibid.,* and if the employee does not submit a timely EEOC charge, the employee may not challenge that practice in court, § 2000e–5(f)(1).

In addressing the issue whether an EEOC charge was filed on time, we have stressed the need to identify with care the specific employment practice that is at issue. *National Railroad Passenger Corporation v. Morgan*, 536 U.S. 101 (2002). Ledbetter points to two different employment practices as possible candidates. Primarily, she urges us to focus on the paychecks that were issued to her during the EEOC charging period (the 180-day period preceding the filing of her EEOC questionnaire), each of which, she contends, was a separate act of discrimination. Alternatively, Ledbetter directs us to the 1998 decision denying her a raise, and she argues that this decision was "unlawful because it carried forward intentionally discriminatory disparities from prior years." Reply Brief for Petitioner 20. Both of these arguments fail because they would require us in effect to jettison the defining element of the legal claim on which her Title VII recovery was based.

Ledbetter asserted disparate treatment, the central element of which is discriminatory intent. However, Ledbetter does not assert that the relevant Goodyear decisionmakers acted with actual discriminatory intent either when they issued her checks during the EEOC charging period or when they denied her a raise in 1998. Rather, she argues that the paychecks were unlawful because they would have been larger if she had been evaluated in a nondiscriminatory manner prior to the EEOC charging period. Similarly, she maintains that the 1998 decision was unlawful because it "carried forward" the effects of prior, uncharged discrimination decisions. In essence, she suggests that it is sufficient that discriminatory acts that occurred prior to the charging period had continuing effects during that period. This argument is squarely foreclosed by our precedents.

In *United Air Lines, Inc. v. Evans*, 431 U.S. 553 (1977), we rejected an argument that is basically the same as Ledbetter's. Evans was forced to resign because the airline refused to employ married flight attendants, but she did not file an EEOC charge regarding her termination. Some years later, the airline rehired her but treated her as a new employee for seniority purposes. Evans then sued, arguing that, while any suit based on the original discrimination was time barred, the airline's refusal to give her credit for her prior service gave "present effect to [its] past illegal act and therefore perpetuate[d] the consequences of forbidden discrimination." We agreed with Evans that the airline's "seniority system [did] indeed have a continuing impact on her pay and fringe benefits," but we noted that "the critical question [was] whether any present *violation* exist[ed]," (emphasis in original). We concluded that the continuing effects of the precharging period discrimination did not make out a present violation.

Equally instructive is *Delaware State College v. Ricks*, 449 U.S. 250 (1980), which concerned a college professor, Ricks, who alleged that he had been discharged because of national origin. In March 1974, Ricks was denied tenure, but he was given a final, nonrenewable 1-year contract that expired on June 30, 1975. Ricks delayed filing a charge with the EEOC until April 1975, but he argued that the EEOC charging period ran from the date of his actual termination rather than from the date when tenure was denied. In rejecting this argument, we recognized that "one of the *effects* of the denial of tenure," namely, his ultimate termination, "did not occur until later." (emphasis in original). But because Ricks failed to identify any specific discriminatory act "that continued until, or occurred at the time of, the actual termination of his employment," we held that the EEOC charging period ran from "the time the tenure decision was made and communicated to Ricks."

In *Morgan*, we explained that the statutory term "employment practice" generally refers to "a discrete act or single 'occurrence'" that takes place at a particular point in time. 536 U.S. at 110–111. We pointed to "termination, failure to promote, denial of transfer, [and] refusal to hire" as examples of such "discrete" acts, and we held that a Title VII plaintiff "can only file a charge to cover discrete acts that 'occurred' within the appropriate time period."

The instruction provided by [these cases] is clear. The EEOC charging period is triggered when a discrete unlawful practice takes place. A new violation does not occur, and a new charging period does not commence, upon the occurrence of subsequent nondiscriminatory acts that entail adverse effects resulting from the past discrimination. But of course, if an employer engages in a series of acts each of which is intentionally discriminatory, then a fresh violation takes place when each act is committed.

Ledbetter's arguments here — that the paychecks that she received during the charging period and the 1998 raise denial each violated Title VII and triggered a new EEOC charging period — cannot be reconciled with [these cases]. Ledbetter, as noted, makes

Circa 1920. Cartoon Depicting Women's Progress

no claim that intentionally discriminatory conduct occurred during the charging period or that discriminatory decisions that occurred prior to that period were not communicated to her. Instead, she argues simply that Goodyear's conduct during the charging period gave present effect to discriminatory conduct outside of that period. But current effects alone cannot breathe life into prior, uncharged discrimination; as we held in *Evans*, such effects in themselves have "no present legal consequences." 431 U.S. at 558. Ledbetter should have filed an EEOC charge within 180 days after each allegedly discriminatory pay decision was made and communicated to her. She did not do so, and the paychecks that were issued to her during the 180 days prior to the filing of her EEOC charge do not provide a basis for overcoming that prior failure.

Ledbetter's attempt to take the intent associated with the prior pay decisions and shift it to the 1998 pay decision is unsound. It would shift intent from one act (the act that consummates the discriminatory employment practice) to a later act that was not performed with bias or discriminatory motive. The effect of this shift would be to impose liability in the absence of the requisite intent.

Statutes of limitations serve a policy of repose. Certainly, the 180-day EEOC charging deadline, 42 U.S.C. § 2000e–5(e)(1), is short by any measure, but "[b]y choosing what are obviously quite short deadlines, Congress clearly intended to encourage the prompt processing of all charges of employment discrimination." This short deadline reflects Congress' strong preference for the prompt resolution of employment discrimination allegations through voluntary conciliation and cooperation.

In advancing her two theories Ledbetter does not seriously contest the logic of [our prior cases] as set out above, but rather argues that our decision in *Bazemore v. Friday*, 478 U.S. 385 (1986) [is controlling].

Ledbetter focuses specifically on our statement that "[e]ach week's paycheck that delivers less to a black than to a similarly situated white is a wrong actionable under Title VII." She argues that in *Bazemore* we adopted a "paycheck accrual rule" under which each paycheck, even if not accompanied by discriminatory intent, triggers a new EEOC charging period during which the complainant may properly challenge

> Do you find the Court's distinction of the *Bazemore* decision convincing? The applicability of that decision is central to this case.

any prior discriminatory conduct that impacted the amount of that paycheck, no matter how long ago the discrimination occurred.

Bazemore concerned a disparate-treatment pay claim brought against the North Carolina Agricultural Extension Service (Service). Service employees were originally segregated into "a white branch" and "a 'Negro branch,'" with the latter receiving less pay, but in 1965 the two branches were merged. After Title VII was extended to public employees in 1972, black employees brought suit claiming that pay disparities attributable to the old dual pay scale persisted.

Far from adopting the approach that Ledbetter advances here, [*Bazemore*] made a point that was "too obvious to warrant extended discussion," namely, that when an employer adopts a facially discriminatory pay structure that puts some employees on a lower scale because of race, the employer engages in intentional discrimination whenever it issues a check to one of these disfavored employees. An employer that adopts and intentionally retains such a pay structure can surely be regarded as intending to discriminate on the basis of race as long as the structure is used.

Bazemore thus is entirely consistent with our prior precedents, as Justice Brennan's opinion took care to point out. *Bazemore* stands for the proposition that an employer violates Title VII and triggers a new EEOC charging period whenever the employer issues paychecks using a discriminatory pay structure. But a new Title VII violation does not occur and a new charging period is not triggered when an employer issues paychecks pursuant to a system that is "facially nondiscriminatory and neutrally applied." The fact that precharging period discrimination adversely affects the calculation of a neutral factor (like seniority) that is used in determining future pay does not mean that each new paycheck constitutes a new violation and restarts the EEOC charging period.

The dissent also argues that pay claims are different. Its principal argument is that a pay discrimination claim is like a hostile work environment claim because both types of claims are "'based on the cumulative effect of individual acts,'" but this analogy overlooks the critical conceptual distinction between these two types of claims. And although the dissent relies heavily on *Morgan*, the dissent's argument is fundamentally inconsistent with *Morgan*'s reasoning.

Contrary to the dissent's assertion, what Ledbetter alleged was not a single wrong consisting of a succession of acts. Instead, she alleged a series of discrete discriminatory acts (arguing that payment of each paycheck constituted a separate violation of Title VII), each of which was independently identifiable and actionable, and *Morgan* is perfectly clear that when an employee alleges "serial violations," *i.e.,* a series of actionable wrongs, a timely EEOC charge must be filed with respect to each discrete alleged violation.

> The Court declines to address Ledbetter's policy arguments in the case. Why?

Ledbetter places significant weight on the EPA, which was enacted contemporaneously with Title VII and prohibits paying unequal wages for equal work because of sex. 29 U.S.C. § 206(d). Stating that "the lower courts routinely hear [EPA] claims challenging pay disparities that first arose outside the limitations period," Ledbetter suggests that we should hold that Title VII is violated each time an employee receives a paycheck that reflects past discrimination. The simple answer to this argument is that the EPA and Title VII are not the same. In particular, the EPA does not require the filing of a charge with the EEOC or proof of intentional discrimination. Ledbetter originally asserted an EPA claim, but that claim was dismissed by the District Court and is not before us. If Ledbetter had pursued her EPA claim, she would not face the Title VII obstacles that she now confronts.

Ledbetter, finally, makes a variety of policy arguments in favor of giving the alleged victims of pay discrimination more time before they are required to file a charge with the EEOC. Among other things, she claims that pay discrimination is harder to detect than other forms of employment discrimination. We are not in a position to evaluate Ledbetter's policy arguments, and it is not our prerogative to change the way in which Title VII balances the interests of aggrieved employees against the interest in encouraging the "prompt processing of all charges of employment discrimination," and the interest in repose. For these reasons, the judgment of the Court of Appeals for the Eleventh Circuit is affirmed.

Justice GINSBURG, with whom Justice STEVENS, Justice SOUTER, and Justice BREYER join, dissenting.

Lilly Ledbetter was a supervisor at Goodyear Tire & Rubber's plant in Gadsden, Alabama, from 1979 until her retirement in 1998. For most of those years, she worked as an area manager, a position largely occupied by men. Initially, Ledbetter's salary was in line with the salaries of men performing substantially similar work. Over time, however, her pay slipped in comparison to the pay of male area managers with equal or less seniority. By the end of 1997, Ledbetter was the only woman working as an area manager and the pay discrepancy between Ledbetter and her 15

> In what way is the dissent's factual articulation of the case different from the majority's?

male counterparts was stark: Ledbetter was paid $3,727 per month; the lowest paid male area manager received $4,286 per month, the highest paid, $5,236.

Ledbetter launched charges of discrimination before the Equal Employment Opportunity Commission (EEOC) in March 1998. Her formal administrative complaint specified that, in violation of Title VII, Goodyear paid her a discriminatorily low salary because of her sex. That charge was eventually tried to a jury, which found it "more likely than not that [Goodyear] paid [Ledbetter] a[n] unequal salary because of her sex." In accord with the jury's liability determination, the District Court entered judgment for Ledbetter for backpay and damages, plus counsel fees and costs.

The Court of Appeals for the Eleventh Circuit reversed [and the Supreme Court affirms that decision today]. The Court's insistence on immediate contest overlooks common characteristics of pay discrimination. Pay disparities often occur, as they did in Ledbetter's case, in small increments; cause to suspect that discrimination is at work develops only over time. Comparative pay information, moreover, is often hidden from the employee's view. Employers may keep under wraps the pay differentials maintained among supervisors, no less the reasons for those differentials. Small initial discrepancies may not be seen as meet for a federal case, particularly when the employee, trying to succeed in a nontraditional environment, is averse to making waves.

Pay disparities are thus significantly different from adverse actions "such as termination, failure to promote, . . . or refusal to hire," all involving fully communicated discrete acts, "easy to identify" as discriminatory. It is only when the disparity becomes apparent and sizable, *e.g.*, through future raises calculated as a percentage of current salaries, that an employee in Ledbetter's situation is likely to comprehend her plight and, therefore, to complain. Her initial readiness to give her employer the benefit of the doubt should not preclude her from later challenging the then current and continuing payment of a wage depressed on account of her sex.

In *Bazemore*, we unanimously held that an employer, the North Carolina Agricultural Extension Service, committed an unlawful employment practice each time it paid black employees less than similarly situated white employees. 478 U.S. at 395 (opinion of Brennan, J.). Paychecks perpetuating past discrimination, we thus recognized, are actionable not simply because they are "related" to a decision made outside the charge-filing period, but because they discriminate anew each time they issue.

Subsequently, in *Morgan*, we set apart, for purposes of Title VII's timely filing requirement, unlawful employment actions of two kinds: "discrete acts" that are "easy to identify" as discriminatory, and acts that recur and are cumulative in impact. "[D]ifferent in kind from discrete acts," we made clear, are "claims . . . based on the cumulative effect of individual acts." The *Morgan* decision placed hostile work environment claims in that category.

Pay disparities, of the kind Ledbetter experienced, have a closer kinship to hostile work environment claims than to charges of a single episode of discrimination. Ledbetter's claim, resembling Morgan's, rested not on one particular paycheck, but on "the cumulative effect of individual acts." She charged insidious discrimination building up slowly but steadily. Initially in line with the salaries of men performing substantially the same work, Ledbetter's salary fell 15 to 40 percent behind her male counterparts only after successive evaluations and percentage-based pay adjustments. Over time, she alleged and proved, the repetition of pay decisions undervaluing her work gave rise to the current discrimination of which she complained. Though component acts fell outside the charge-filing period, with each new paycheck, Goodyear contributed incrementally to the accumulating harm.

The realities of the workplace reveal why the discrimination with respect to compensation that Ledbetter suffered does not fit within the category of singular discrete acts "easy to identify." A worker

> The dissent relies heavily on various policy rationales in the case.

knows immediately if she is denied a promotion or transfer, if she is fired or refused employment. And promotions, transfers, hirings, and firings are generally public events, known to co-workers. When an employer makes a decision of such open and definitive character, an employee can immediately seek out an explanation and evaluate it for pretext. Compensation disparities, in contrast, are often hidden from sight. It is not unusual, decisions in point illustrate, for management to decline to publish employee pay levels, or for employees to keep private their own salaries.

The problem of concealed pay discrimination is particularly acute where the disparity arises not because the female employee is flatly denied a raise but because male counterparts are given larger raises. Having received a pay increase, the female employee is unlikely to discern at once that she has experienced an adverse employment decision. She may have little reason even to suspect discrimination until a pattern develops incrementally and she ultimately becomes aware of the disparity. Even if an employee suspects that the reason for a comparatively low raise is not performance but sex (or another protected ground), the amount involved may seem too small, or the employer's intent too ambiguous, to make the issue immediately actionable — or winnable.

Further separating pay claims from the discrete employment actions identified in *Morgan*, an employer gains from sex-based pay disparities in a way it does not from a discriminatory denial of promotion, hiring, or transfer. When a male employee is selected over a female for a higher level position, someone still gets the promotion and is paid a higher salary; the employer is not enriched. But when a woman is paid less than a similarly situated man, the employer reduces its costs each time the pay differential is implemented. Furthermore, decisions on promotions, like decisions installing seniority systems, often implicate the interests of third-party employees in a way that pay differentials do not. Disparate pay, by contrast, can be remedied at any time solely at the expense of the employer who acts in a discriminatory fashion.

In light of the significant differences between pay disparities and discrete employment decisions of the type identified in *Morgan*, the cases on which the Court relies hold no sway. *Evans* and *Ricks* both involved a single, immediately identifiable act of discrimination: in *Evans*, a constructive discharge, 431 U.S. at 554; in *Ricks*, a denial of tenure, 449 U.S. at 252. No repetitive, cumulative discriminatory employment practice was at issue in either case. Similarly in line with the real-world characteristics of pay discrimination, the EEOC — the federal agency responsible for enforcing Title VII, *see, e.g.,* 42 U.S.C. §§ 2000e–5(f), 2000e–12(a) — has interpreted the Act to permit employees to challenge disparate pay each time it is received.

The Court asserts that treating pay discrimination as a discrete act, limited to each particular pay-setting decision, is necessary to "protec[t] employers from the burden of defending claims arising from employment decisions that are long past." But the discrimination of which Ledbetter complained is not long past. As she alleged, and as the jury found, Goodyear continued to treat Ledbetter differently because of sex each pay period, with mounting harm. Allowing employees to challenge discrimination "that extend[s] over long periods of time," into the charge-filing period, we have previously explained, "does not leave employers defenseless" against unreasonable or prejudicial delay. *Morgan*, 536 U.S. at 121. Employers disadvantaged by such delay may raise various defenses. Doctrines such as "waiver, estoppel, and equitable tolling" "allow us to honor Title VII's remedial purpose without negating the particular purpose of the filing requirement, to give prompt notice to the employer." *Id.* at 121 [quotation omitted].

Ledbetter, the Court observes, dropped an alternative remedy she could have pursued: Had she persisted in pressing her claim under the Equal Pay Act of 1963 (EPA), she would not have encountered a time bar. Notably, the EPA provides no relief when the pay discrimination charged is based on race, religion, national origin, age, or disability. Thus, in truncating the Title VII rule this Court announced in *Bazemore*, the Court does not disarm female workers from achieving redress for unequal pay, but it does impede racial and other minorities from gaining similar relief.

This is not the first time the Court has ordered a cramped interpretation of Title VII, incompatible with the statute's broad remedial purpose. *See also Wards Cove Packing Co. v. Atonio*, 490 U.S. 642 (1989) (superseded in part by the Civil Rights Act of 1991); *Price Waterhouse v. Hopkins*, 490 U.S. 228 (1989) (plurality opinion) (same); 1 B. Lindemann & P. Grossman, Employment Discrimination Law 2 (3d ed. 1996) ("A spate of Court decisions in the late 1980s drew congressional fire and resulted in demands for legislative change[,]" culminating in the 1991 Civil Rights Act (footnote omitted)). Once again, the ball is in Congress' court. As in 1991, the Legislature may act to correct this Court's parsimonious reading of Title VII.

■ NOTES AND QUESTIONS

1. The majority and dissent disagree strongly on the meaning of *Ricks* and *Evans*. Do you agree with the majority that those two decisions would apply to the facts of this case?

2. Is pay discrimination a discrete act — as the majority suggests — or more akin to a hostile work environment as argued by the dissent? Recall that in the *Morgan* decision, the Supreme Court distinguished between discrete acts and continuing violations. For hostile work environment claims, which involve continuing violations, a claim is timely if it is filed with the EEOC within 180/300 days of the last event comprising the hostile environment.

3. What are the policy concerns over maintaining a short statute of limitations as invoked by the majority? What policy concerns does the dissent raise? *See generally* Michelle A. Travis, *Disabling the Gender Pay Gap: Lessons from the Social Model of Disability*, 91 Denv. U. L. Rev. 893 (2014) (discussing the potential benefits of borrowing the social model approach from the disability rights movement to reframe the discussion about women's pay).

4. The following passage from *Bazemore* is at the heart of the disagreement between the majority and the dissent: "Each week's paycheck that delivers less to a black than to a similarly situated white is a wrong actionable under Title VII, regardless of the fact that this pattern was begun prior to the effective date of Title VII." Should this passage be the beginning and end of the case?

5. Should the majority have given more weight to the view of the EEOC in this case? Why or why not?

6. Justice Ginsburg read this dissent from the bench (an unusual practice), possibly because the case negatively impacted women's rights. The Justice clearly took strong issue with the Court's decision. *See* Robert Barnes, *Over Ginsburg's Dissent, Court Limits Bias Suits*, WASH. POST, May 30, 2007, http://www.washingtonpost.com/wp-dyn/content/article/2007/05/29/AR2007052900740.html.

7. Do you agree with the dissent that pay discrimination is easier to conceal and more difficult to identify than other forms of discrimination?

8. Why did Ledbetter choose not to pursue her Equal Pay Act claim after it was dismissed by the district court on summary judgement? Had she appealed that dismissal, would she have avoided "the Title VII obstacles that she now confronts"?

9. Does the EPA avoid the problems created by this case, which revolve around the issue of discriminatory intent? What limitations does the EPA have that would restrict the scope of recovery?

10. **The Lilly Ledbetter Fair Pay Act.** At the conclusion of her dissent, Justice Ginsburg attempted to get the attention of Congress. She noted that "the ball is in Congress' court. As in 1991, the Legislature may act to correct this Court's parsimonious reading of Title VII." Congress quickly took the bait and stepped in to largely overturn the Court's decision. The Lilly Ledbetter Fair Pay Act of 2009 was the first Bill signed by President Barack Obama. The Act, which amends Title VII, provides that

    > an unlawful employment practice occurs, with respect to discrimination in compensation in violation of this title, when a discriminatory compensation decision or other practice is adopted, when an individual becomes subject to a discriminatory compensation decision or other practice, or when an individual is affected by application of a discriminatory compensation decision or other practice, including each time wages, benefits, or other compensation is paid. . . .

    Pub. L. No. 111–2 (Jan. 29, 2009) (amending Title VII at 42 U.S.C. § 2000e–5).
    The statute thus makes clear that each time a discriminatory paycheck is issued, a separate violation of Title VII has occurred. And, this language applies not only to paychecks related to sex discrimination, but also to paychecks affected by race, color, national origin, or religious discrimination. The Lilly Ledbetter Fair Pay Act goes beyond Title VII, however. The Act amends the ADA and the ADEA in similar ways. *See* Pub. L. No. 111–2 (Jan. 29, 2009).

11. **Historical note.** Even after the Lilly Ledbetter Fair Pay Act was signed into law in 2009, Ledbetter's fight for pay equality has remained in the spotlight. Ledbetter spoke at the Democratic National Convention in both 2008 and 2012, focusing on her fight for equal pay for women. Likewise, Ledbetter gives similar speeches throughout the country. Additionally, Ledbetter published a co-written memoir, *Grace and Grit*, in the spring of 2012, and in the

spring of 2013, Ledbetter's attorney announced that Ledbetter had signed with a Hollywood filmmaker and agreed to make a movie about her story. *See* Bob Carlton, *Lilly Ledbetter, the Alabama Woman Who Fought for Equal Pay, Will Be the Subject of Hollywood Movie*, Alabama Media Group (Feb. 11, 2013, 3:00 p.m.), www.al.com/entertainment/index.ssf/2013/02/lilly_ledbetter_the_gadsden_wo.html; Stephanie Francis Ward, *Lilly Ledbetter's Story to Be Made into a Movie*, Aba J. (Feb. 11, 2013, 5:00 p.m.), www .abajournal.com/news/article/lilly_ledbetters_story_to_be_made_into_a_movie/.

12. **The glass ceiling.** Over the years, there has been substantial debate about the so-called glass ceiling for women. The concern has been that it is far more difficult for women to advance within a corporation than it is to be hired initially. *See generally* Deborah Thompson Eisenberg, *Shattering the Equal Pay Act's Glass Ceiling*, 63 SMU L. Rev. 17 (2010) (arguing that as women climb the occupational ladder, the way in which many federal courts interpret the EPA imposes a wage glass ceiling, shutting out women in non-standardized jobs from its protection). This can lead to a growing pay disparity over time, as the chart below reflects:

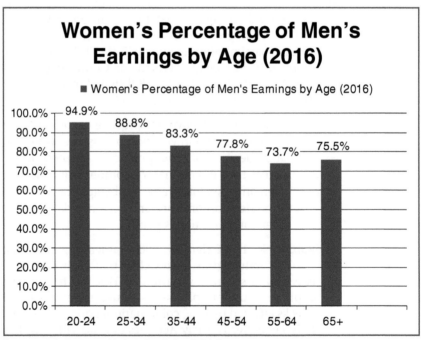

Source: U.S. Bureau of Labor Statistics (2016).
Figure 7.1

Pay discrimination claims are difficult to prove, as evidence showing pay disparities can be hard to uncover. In the case below, the Seventh Circuit Court of Appeals discusses some data reflecting the pay differences of a company's employees. Accessing this type of pay information can be instrumental in helping to establish a Title VII violation.

King v. Acosta Sales & Marketing, Inc.

678 F.3d 470 (7th Cir. 2012)

EASTERBROOK, Chief Judge.

Acosta Sales and Marketing is a food broker, which represents producers that seek to sell to supermarkets and other bulk purchasers. In 2001 Acosta's midwest operation hired Susan King as one of its business managers — a term that Acosta uses for people who represent a group of producers. (McCormick & Co., which sells spices and spiced foods, was one of King's major clients.) After quitting in 2007, King charged Acosta with two kinds of sex discrimination: that Acosta maintained a hostile work environment in which conditions for women were inferior to those for men, and that Acosta paid women less than men for the same work. Both kinds of discrimination violate Title VII of the Civil Rights Act of 1964, and discrimination in pay also violates the Equal Pay Act, 29 U.S.C. § 206(d).

The district court granted summary judgment to Acosta on King's claims under federal law. King contends that the work environment at Acosta was hostile to her throughout her employment. The district judge broke that contention into two, asking first whether working conditions were actionable during the 300 days before King filed her charge with the EEOC (the judge gave a negative answer) and then whether acts that preceded the 300-day window could be attributed to the employer. That approach misapplied *National Railroad Passenger Corp. v. Morgan*, 536 U.S. 101 (2002), which holds that an employee may rest a hostile-working-environment claim on acts any time during her employment. *Morgan* concludes that, when an assertedly unlawful employment practice occurs as a pattern over time rather than in one discrete act, it does not matter when the individual deeds contributing to the pattern occurred, if the pattern continued into the 300 days before the charge's filing.

The district court's error does not require a remand, however, because King's evidence does not establish a pattern of hostility that continued into the 300 days before her charge. Most of the obnoxious acts were committed by Thomas Connelly, another of Acosta's business managers, between 2001 and 2004. Connelly distributed pornographic materials at work and in February 2002 showed King a picture of himself wearing only a trench coat, tight swimming trunks, and a dildo. Three months later Connelly gave King a pornographic video tape and a nine-inch dildo. In September 2004 he called her a "cunt" during a business meeting. King promptly complained to her supervisor. Connelly was disciplined and instructed to clean up his act; he did not harass King again before quitting in 2005, approximately two years before King filed her charge with the EEOC.

King's working environment was markedly better after September 2004. There were still events that King found unwelcome. One supervisor made a pass at her; another called her "Suzie Big Hair" and referred to one of King's co-workers as a "tramp" and another as "Pass-Around Patti." When a representative of one of Acosta's clients made a crude

> Do you agree with the court that the events detailed here are not "severe"?

sexual remark, King's supervisor let the incident pass. All of this may have been unpleasant, but none of it was severe, and a few incidents at the rate of one every four to six months (which is what King's evidence shows) cannot be called pervasive. Once Connelly desisted, King's working environment was not marked by severe or pervasive hostility toward women. (We need not decide whether Connelly's behavior, which long predated the period of limitations, would satisfy the Supreme Court's hostile-working-conditions doctrine.)

Pay is a different matter. Even a dollar's difference based on sex violates both Title VII and the Equal Pay Act — and King established much larger differences. Some men in the same job classification, doing the same work under the same conditions, received more than twice her pay. Here's a table, with women's names in italics:

Business Manager	Starting Year	Starting Salary	2007 or Final Salary
Thomas Connelly	1998	$91,000.08	$122,004.00
Thomas Robaczewski	2000	$95,000.00	$101,921.00
Tim Wilson	2004	$85,000.01	$99,500.11
Helmut Fritz	2001	$94,999.99	$97,635.55
Edgar Perez	2006	$93,000.00	$93,000.00
Mario Saracco	1998	$69,448.56	$81,502.73
Steven Blanchard	2002	$77,182.51	$79,881.10
Dennis Muhr	1998	$72,799.92	$79,598.69
Matthew Marron	1998	$63,000.00	$72,375.05
Rosanne Maschek	2001	$38,666.64	$60,399.62
Brett Lanford	2007	$60,000.00	$60,000.00
Christopher Pfister	2005	$40,000.01	$60,000.00
John Czarnik	2007	$55,000.00	$55,000.00
Pearl Martinez	2005	$40,000.01	$52,299.77
Susan King	2001	$40,000.01	$46,850.23
Elizabeth Wood	2005	$45,000.00	$46,350.00
Michelle Carroll	2007	$42,500.64	$42,500.64
Carrie Mengel	2007	$40,000.42	$40,000.42
Mary Anne Sapp	2001	$64,000.01	$37,752.00
Nancy Rogers	2001	$38,092.01	$26,624.00

The difference between men and women is striking. All of the men were paid more than all but one of the women — and that one woman achieved her $60,000 salary only after six years on the job, while men exceeded the $60,000 line faster. "Business manager" was a sales job, and the pay of many salespersons is strongly influenced by customers' purchases. But Acosta does not contend that the difference in business managers' pay can be accounted for by the volume of sales; indeed, it concedes that King was one of its most successful sales executives, on a par with Connelly, who was paid almost three times as much. But if sales don't explain the disparity revealed by the table, what does? Acosta contends that education and experience account for the men's salaries. All have college degrees; King does not. (The record does not show whether other women do.) Education and experience often increase the pay that employers offer, and Acosta had to match or exceed what other firms would pay in order to hire a capable staff. Neither Title VII nor the Equal Pay Act requires employers to ignore the compensation that workers could receive in other jobs, which in the language of the Equal Pay Act is a "factor other than sex" (29 U.S.C. § 206(d)(1)).

The district court made a legal error at this step of the analysis. The court thought it enough for Acosta to articulate education and experience as potentially explanatory variables, without proving that they *actually* account for the difference; the court wrote that King must show that Acosta's explanation is a pretext for discrimination. That's part of the burden-shifting approach under Title VII, but is not the way the Equal Pay Act is written. An employee's only burden under the Equal Pay Act is to show a difference in pay for "equal work on jobs the performance of which requires equal skill, effort, and responsibility, and which are performed under similar working conditions" (§ 206(d)(1)). An employer asserting that the difference is the result of a "factor other than sex" must present this contention as an affirmative defense — and the proponent of an affirmative defense has the burdens of both production and persuasion.

King's claim under the Equal Pay Act must be returned to the district court for a trial at which Acosta will need to prove, and not just assert, that education and experience account for these differences. The Title VII claim also must be tried, because King has marshalled evidence that would permit a trier of fact to conclude that Acosta's explanations are smokescreens.

Let us suppose that education and experience (which imply greater pay at other firms, with which Acosta is competing for talent) explain some or even all of the difference in the *starting* salaries reflected in the table. There is no reason why they should explain increases in pay while a person is employed by Acosta. Changes in salary at most firms depend on how well a person performs at work. Education and experience may predict on-the-job performance, but the prediction affects the starting wage, just as scores on the LSAT predict grades in law school and thus affect the probability of admission. Once a person has been admitted to a given law school, however, it is performance on exams, or in writing papers, not the LSAT, that determines grades; and grades plus extracurricular activities, not the LSAT score, affect who is hired by which law firms; after that, performance on the job, not the LSAT or grades in law school, determines who makes partner and how much each lawyer is paid. Similarly, if men arrive at Acosta with higher salaries because of education, but men and women are equally good on the job, women should get more rapid raises after employment and the salaries should tend to converge. Law firms may pay extra to people with better credentials, which they can tout to clients, and perhaps Acosta also did this, but this is compatible with salary convergence during employment.

Look at the difference between the starting salary column in the table and the 2007 or final salary column. Men receive substantially greater increases in pay. Salaries did not converge after business managers began work; they diverged. King worked at Acosta for six years, and her salary rose by less than $7,000; Tim Wilson's salary, by contrast, rose more than $14,000 in three years. Christopher Pfister was hired at $40,000, the same as King's starting wage; but within two years Pfister was at $60,000, while in six years King never topped $50,000. These numbers can't be explained by education and experience at the time of hire, which should matter less as years pass on the job. Differences in the rate of change might be explained by different on-the-job performance, but as we've already mentioned King was one of Acosta's top producers yet was not rewarded accordingly.

> The court places heavy emphasis on the salary data articulated by the plaintiffs. Do you find it convincing?

Gary Moe, Acosta's general manager for the midwest region, set the business managers' salaries. He testified by deposition that King's sales were "comparable" to that of men who were paid twice as much. When asked how he set salaries, Moe testified that the process was "subjective"; he could not, or would not, elaborate on the reasons why he set any particular business manager's salary where he did. Acosta's national management set pay scales that were supposed to constrain the discretion of the regional general managers. In 2007 the pay scale for business managers ran from $51,600 to $88,400 a year, with a target median of $73,700. King and all but one of the other women were paid less than the low end of the scale, and all were paid less than the target median. Five men were paid more than the top end of the scale, and seven received more than the target median. Moe had no explanation for how men's salaries had become so far out of line, or why women were not paid even the minimum. King has an explanation — sex discrimination — and a reasonable juror could conclude that King is right.

At oral argument, Acosta's lawyer suggested that Moe may have set salaries haphazardly or irrationally. Random decision is a factor other than sex. If Moe had acted randomly, however, then the entries for men and women in the table should be jumbled together. The actual distribution is not random. It is difficult to see how every man could be paid more than all but one woman, and why men received greater raises, if Moe were pulling numbers out of a jar.

The judgment is affirmed with respect to working conditions and reversed with respect to salaries, and the case is remanded for trial.

■ NOTES AND QUESTIONS

1. The court notes that "[e]ven a dollar's difference based on sex violates both Title VII and the Equal Pay Act." Would a dollar pay differential truly be sufficient to rise to the level of an adverse action under these statutes?

2. This case demonstrates the importance of the intent requirement of Title VII. As the court properly notes, there is no such requirement in the EPA. Where intent is difficult to establish, the EPA can be an attractive claim to raise. The pay discrimination claim was permitted to proceed under both statutes here. Do you agree?

3. The court relies heavily on the pay table set forth in the case, noting that "[t]he difference between men and women is striking." How convincing is this evidence in the case?

4. The court disregards the defendant's argument that the company "may have set salaries haphazardly or irrationally." Should this argument have been given greater weight?

5. How convincing is the defendant's argument that "education and experience" explained the differential in pay? What type of evidence would the defendant need to introduce to establish this defense in the district court?

6. Do you agree with the court's dismissal of the hostile work environment claim? Was the claim beyond the statute of limitations?

7. Even though the court dismissed the hostile work environment claim, some of the facts that gave rise to this claim may still be able to come into evidence as "background circumstances." How would introduction of such evidence potentially impact the case?

Class Exercise: Preventing Salary Discrimination

Assume that you are the chief financial officer for a Fortune 500 company. You have just read Judge Easterbrook's decision in the prior case, and are concerned that your company could similarly be liable for pay discrimination. What steps could you take to evaluate whether such discrimination is taking place at your business? What policies could you implement going forward that would help prevent this type of discrimination?

Practice and Procedural Tip

20: Pay Discrimination

As discussed in this chapter, discrimination on the basis of pay can give rise to claims under both Title VII and the Equal Pay Act. Similarly, paying workers incorrect amounts of base or overtime pay can give employees a cause of action under the Fair Labor Standards Act. When it comes to pay issues, then, employers must be very cautious.

Employers should be advised to carefully monitor and periodically check their pay practices for compliance with the law. If any questions arise, companies should verify their pay practices with legal counsel before proceeding further. While this is true with any legal question, it is particularly important in the pay context. As noted, pay disparity claims can give workers multiple sources of litigation under numerous statutes. Perhaps most importantly, however, decisions made on the basis of pay often affect more than a single worker. Thus, an employer's pay structure can, and often does, affect hundreds or thousands of employees across its workforce. If an employer makes an error or discriminates in some way, it can result in expensive class-action litigation. Even small errors, when multiplied by hundreds of employees (and combined with liquidated damages and attorneys' fees) can create an overwhelming burden for employers.

The *Wal-Mart* litigation, Wal-Mart Stores, Inc. v. Dukes, 564 U.S. 338 (2011), discussed earlier in this text, provides an excellent example of this compound effect. Though Wal-Mart was ultimately successful in preventing a class of over a million women from being certified, this litigation was unquestionably an expensive endeavor. And many of the alleged victims in that case were still free to pursue individual litigation against the company. At the end of the day, the lesson here is simple. It is always important to use caution when dealing with employment issues. This is especially true when pay is involved in the equation.

H. Chapter-in-Review

Sex discrimination is an important and constantly evolving area of the law. The typical *McDonnell Douglas* and disparate impact models discussed earlier will apply to these claims. Pregnancy claims require a unique analysis and determination of whether an adverse act was taken because of pregnancy, childbirth, or related medical conditions. When considering pregnancy or other leave issues, the FMLA must also be considered for larger employers that must provide twelve weeks of unpaid leave to employees to care for a newborn child, or to address their own serious health condition or that of a close family member. Sexual orientation discrimination is an evolving area of Title VII law, and there are conflicting federal appellate court decisions on the question of the scope of the statute's coverage in this area.

The BFOQ frequently arises in sex discrimination cases and applies where the employer can show that the applicant's sex is job related and goes to the essence or central mission of the company. The BFOQ is an affirmative defense for employers, and the exception is not widely used.

Grooming and appearance standards also provide a unique inquiry in sex discrimination cases. The critical question in these cases is whether men and women are being treated in a different way that is more than simply de minimis or a reflection of the cultural norms.

Finally, the EPA is a statute separate and apart from Title VII that addresses pay disparities between men and women when performing equal work under similar conditions. The statute has different procedural requirements and a different relief structure, and it does not require a showing of discriminatory intent.

National Origin Discrimination

 Interactive Problem

Osama Hussein was born in India and lived for many years in Fiji where he was brought up as a Muslim. Hussein came to the United States in 1999 and was hired as a pilot for Big Plane Airlines in Detroit. On September 15, 2001, an executive at Big Plane received an anonymous call stating that the caller had seen a pilot in a Big Plane Airlines uniform at a bar on September 11, 2001, wearing an identification tag with the name "Hussein." The caller indicated that "Hussein was acting in an unusual manner and was expressing his support for the terrorist attacks that occurred that day." The anonymous report also prompted an FBI investigation into the matter. Hussein flatly denied making any remarks or gestures that could have been construed as endorsing the terrorist acts, and stated that he found the attacks "contemptible and horrific." He also stated that he may have been smiling when he was at the bar because he found out only hours before that his wife was pregnant. When the Big Plane executive later learned of the FBI investigation, he terminated Hussein, even though he had never actually met him or personally interviewed him about the incident. Hussein brought a claim of national origin discrimination, as well as race and religion discrimination, under Title VII. *See* EEOC v. Trans States Airlines, Inc., 462 F.3d 987 (8th Cir. 2006).

Would Hussein have a strong claim for national origin discrimination? How would you litigate such a claim if you represented Hussein? How would you defend it if you represented the Airlines?

A. Introduction

Discrimination on the basis of national origin is expressly prohibited by Title VII. The statute provides that

> [i]t shall be an unlawful employment practice for an employer . . . to fail or refuse to hire or to discharge any individual, or otherwise to discriminate against any individual with respect to his compensation, terms, conditions, or privileges of employment, because of such individual's . . . national origin.

42 U.S.C. § 2000e–(2)(a).

As the EEOC provides, "[g]enerally, national origin discrimination means treating someone less favorably because that individual (or his or her ancestors) is from a certain place or belongs to a particular national origin group." EEOC Compl. Man. (CCH) § 13-II (2002). National origin discrimination has a long and storied history. Many nations have not experienced the same degree of national origin discrimination that individuals have faced in the United States. This is because of the substantial diversity that exists in our nation. Though the obvious benefits of such diversity are great, it also comes with it the inherent problem of discrimination. *See* Mark L. Adams, *Fear of Foreigners: Nativism and Workplace Language Restrictions*, 74 Or. L. Rev. 849 (1995); Kenneth L. Karst, *Paths to Belonging: The Constitution and Cultural Identity*, 64 N.C. L. Rev. 303, 305 (1986).

National origin discrimination also has experienced both peaks and valleys over time. Irish immigrants at the turn of the twentieth century often encountered "Irish Need Not Apply" signs. *See* Sylvia R. Lazos Vargas, *Deconstructing Homo[genous] Americanus: The White Ethnic Immigrant Narrative and Its Exclusionary Effect*, 72 Tul. L. Rev. 1493,

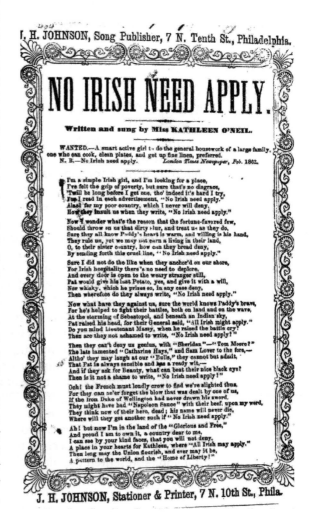

1524, 1540 (1998) (discussing the use of "No Irish Need Apply" signs as a means of excluding Irish immigrants from employment opportunities); Antonin Scalia, *The Disease as Cure: "In Order to Get Beyond Racism, We Must First Take Account of Race,"* 1979 WASH. U. L.Q. 147 ("If I can recall in my lifetime the obnoxious 'White Trade Only' signs in shops in Washington, D.C., others can recall 'Irish Need Not Apply' signs in Boston, three or four decades earlier."). During World War II, Japanese Americans often had difficulty finding employment as a result of national origin stereotypes. And after 9/11, Americans of Middle Eastern descent have experienced widespread discrimination. *See* Steven Greenhouse, *Muslims Report Rising Discrimination at Work*, N.Y. TIMES, Sept. 23, 2010, at B1; Carol Morello, *Muslim Americans Say Life Is More Difficult Since 9/11*, WASH. POST, Aug. 30, 2011. This discrimination has been created by animus arising on the basis of a combination of religion and national origin.

National origin discrimination thus takes many forms, and it is important to be able to identify and analyze this type of bias. The same disparate impact and disparate treatment frameworks that were discussed in Chapters 3 and 4 apply to national origin claims. There are some unique considerations that arise in these cases, however, that will be addressed here.

B. The Meaning of National Origin

National origin discrimination claims can be substantially different from other forms of employment litigation. One aspect that can arise is the meaning of national origin. This is typically not a problem in many other protected categories, but there can be obvious ambiguities as to what constitutes a particular national origin: How do we define our national origin?

Not surprisingly, the courts have taken varying approaches to this particular issue. Some jurisdictions take a narrow approach to what constitutes national origin. Others are much more expansive. *See* Juan F. Perea, *Ethnicity and Prejudice: Reevaluating "National Origin" Discrimination Under Title VII*, 35 WM. & MARY L. REV. 805, 822–830 (1994) (summarizing court interpretations of the meaning of "national origin"). The EEOC takes a broad approach to defining national origin discrimination:

> **Ethnicity:** Employment discrimination against members of an ethnic group, for example, discrimination against someone because he is Arab. National origin discrimination also includes discrimination against anyone who does not belong to a particular ethnic group, for example, less favorable treatment of anyone who is not Hispanic.

> **Physical, linguistic, or cultural traits:** Employment discrimination against an individual because she has physical, linguistic, and/or cultural characteristics closely associated with a national origin group, for example, discrimination against someone based on her traditional African style of dress.

> **Perception:** Employment discrimination against an individual based on the employer's belief that he is a member of a particular national origin group,

for example, discrimination against someone perceived as being Arab based on his speech, mannerisms, and appearance, regardless of how he identifies himself or whether he is, in fact, of Arab ethnicity.

EEOC Compl. Man. (CCH) ¶ 8504, § 13-II(B) (2002).

The EEOC further notes that "[a] 'national origin group,' often referred to as an 'ethnic group,' is a group of people sharing a common language, culture, ancestry, and/or other similar social characteristics. Title VII prohibits employment discrimination against any national origin group, including larger ethnic groups, such as Hispanics and Arabs, and smaller ethnic groups, such as Kurds or Roma (Gypsies). National origin discrimination includes discrimination against American Indians or members of a particular tribe." *Id.*

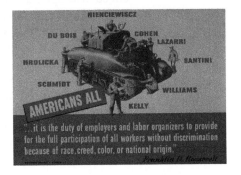

The EEOC's definition is quite expansive, as it includes things such as perception and association with a national origin group. Not all courts would agree that such traits fall within the confines of national origin discrimination. Nonetheless, as a best practices consideration, employers should be cautioned against discriminating on a basis that can be construed as national origin discrimination by the EEOC. And, if litigation results from alleged discrimination, an understanding of the jurisdiction's definition of national origin may be critical to the case.

The Supreme Court has not provided any substantial guidance on this issue. However, the Court has provided some basic guidelines on what does constitute a national origin.

Espinoza v. Farah Manufacturing Co.

414 U.S. 86 (1973)

Mr. Justice MARSHALL delivered the opinion of the Court.

This case involves interpretation of the phrase "national origin" in Tit. VII of the Civil Rights Act of 1964. Petitioner Cecilia Espinoza is a lawfully admitted resident alien who was born in and remains a citizen of Mexico. She resides in San Antonio, Texas, with her husband, Rudolfo Espinoza, a United States citizen. In July 1969, Mrs. Espinoza sought employment as a seamstress at the San Antonio division of respondent Farah Manufacturing Co. Her employment application was rejected on the basis of a longstanding company policy against the employment of aliens. After exhausting their administrative remedies with the Equal Employment Opportunity Commission petitioners commenced this suit in the District Court alleging that respondent had discriminated against Mrs. Espinoza because of her "national origin" in violation of [Title VII]. The District Court granted petitioners' motion for summary judgment, holding that a refusal to hire because of lack of citizenship constitutes discrimination on the basis of "national origin." 343 F. Supp. 1205. The

Court of Appeals reversed, concluding that the statutory phrase "national origin" did not embrace citizenship. 462 F.2d 1331. We granted the writ to resolve this question of statutory construction, 411 U.S. 946, and now affirm.

Section 703 makes it "an unlawful employment practice for an employer . . . to fail or refuse to hire . . . any individual . . . because of such individual's race, color, religion, sex, or national origin." Certainly the plain language of the statute supports the result reached by the Court of Appeals. The term "national origin" on its face refers to the country where a person was born, or, more broadly, the country from which his or her ancestors came.

> As the Court notes, national origin includes "where a person was born, or, more broadly, the country from which his or her ancestors came."

The statute's legislative history, though quite meager in this respect, fully supports this construction. The only direct definition given the phrase "national origin" is the following remark made on the floor of the House of Representatives by Congressman Roosevelt, Chairman of the House Subcommittee which reported the bill: "It means the country from which you or your forebears came. . . . You may come from Poland, Czechoslovakia, England, France, or any other country." 110 Cong. Rec. 2549 (1964). We also note that an earlier version of § 703 had referred to discrimination because of "race, color, religion, national origin, or *ancestry*." H.R. 7152, 88th Cong., 1st Sess., § 804, Oct. 2, 1963 (Comm. print) (emphasis added). The deletion of the word "ancestry" from the final version was not intended as a material change, suggesting that the terms "national origin" and "ancestry" were considered synonymous.

There are other compelling reasons to believe that Congress did not intend the term "national origin" to embrace citizenship requirements. Since 1914, the Federal Government itself, through Civil Service Commission regulations, has engaged in what amounts to discrimination against aliens by denying them the right to enter competitive examination for federal employment. But it has never been suggested that the citizenship requirement for federal employment constitutes discrimination because of national origin, even though since 1943, various Executive Orders have expressly prohibited discrimination on the basis of national origin in Federal Government employment.

To interpret the term "national origin" to embrace citizenship requirements would require us to conclude that Congress itself has repeatedly flouted its own declaration of policy. This Court cannot lightly find such a breach of faith. So far as federal employment is concerned, we think it plain that Congress has assumed that the ban on national-origin discrimination [] did not affect the historical practice of requiring citizenship as a condition of employment. And there is no reason to believe Congress intended the term "national origin" in [Title VII] to have any broader scope.

Petitioners have suggested that the statutes and regulations discriminating against noncitizens in federal employment are unconstitutional under the Due Process Clause of the Fifth Amendment. We need not address that question here, for the issue presented in this case is not whether Congress has the power to discriminate against aliens in federal employment, but rather, whether Congress intended to prohibit such discrimination in private employment. Suffice it to say that we cannot conclude Congress would at once continue the practice of requiring citizenship as a condition of federal employment and, at the same time, prevent private employers from doing likewise. Interpreting § 703 as petitioners suggest would achieve the rather bizarre result of preventing Farah from insisting on United States citizenship as a condition of employment while the very agency charged with enforcement of Tit. VII would itself be required by Congress to place such a condition on its own personnel.

The District Court drew primary support for its holding from an interpretative guideline issued by the Equal Employment Opportunity Commission which provides:

> Because discrimination on the basis of citizenship has the effect of discriminating on the basis of national origin, a lawfully immigrated alien who is domiciled or residing in this country may not be discriminated against on the basis of his citizenship. . . .

29 CFR § 1606.1(d) (1972).

Like the Court of Appeals, we have no occasion here to question the general validity of this guideline insofar as it can be read as an expression of the Commission's belief that there may be many situations where discrimination on the basis of citizenship would have the effect of discriminating on the basis of national origin. In some instances, for example, a citizenship requirement might be but one part of a wider scheme of unlawful national-origin discrimination. In other cases, an employer might use a citizenship test as a pretext to disguise what is in fact national-origin discrimination. Certainly Tit. VII prohibits discrimination on the basis of citizenship whenever it has the purpose or effect of discriminating on the basis of national origin.

> The level of deference given to the EEOC in interpreting Title VII and other antidiscrimination statutes has always been an issue of debate in the Supreme Court.

It is equally clear, however, that these principles lend no support to petitioners in this case. There is no indication in the record that Farah's policy against employment of aliens had the purpose or effect of discriminating against persons of Mexican national origin. It is conceded that Farah accepts employees of Mexican origin, provided the individual concerned has become an American citizen. Indeed, the District Court found that persons of Mexican ancestry make up more than 96% of the employees at the company's San Antonio division, and 97% of those doing the work for which Mrs. Espinoza applied. While statistics such as these do not automatically shield an employer from a charge of unlawful discrimination, the plain fact of the matter is that Farah does not discriminate against persons of Mexican national origin with respect to employment in the job Mrs. Espinoza sought. She was denied employment, not because of the country of her origin, but because she had not yet achieved United States citizenship. In fact, the record shows that the worker hired in place of Mrs. Espinoza was a citizen with a Spanish surname.

The Commission's guideline may have significance for a wide range of situations, but not for a case such as this where its very premise — that discrimination on the basis of citizenship has the effect of discrimination on the basis of national origin — is not borne out. It is also significant to note that the Commission itself once held a different view as to the meaning of the phrase "national origin." When first confronted with the question, the Commission, through its General Counsel, said: "'National origin' refers to the country from which the individual or his forebears came . . . , not to whether or not he is a United States citizen. . . ." The Commission's more recent interpretation of the statute in the guideline relied on by the District Court is no doubt entitled to great deference, but that deference must have limits where, as here, application of the guideline would be inconsistent with an obvious congressional intent not to reach the employment practice in question. Courts need not defer to an administrative construction of a statute where there are "compelling indications that it is wrong." Red Lion Broadcasting Co. v. FCC, 395 U.S. 367 (1969).

We agree with the Court of Appeals that neither the language of the Act, nor its history, nor the specific facts of this case indicate that respondent has engaged in unlawful discrimination because of national origin.

Affirmed.

Mr. Justice Douglas, dissenting.

It is odd that the Court which holds that a State may not bar an alien from the practice of law or deny employment to aliens can read a federal statute that prohibits discrimination in employment on account of "national origin" so as to permit discrimination against aliens. Alienage results from one condition only: being born outside the United States. Those born within the country are citizens from birth. It could not be more clear that Farah's policy of excluding aliens is

> The dissent raises a novel concern over the definition of "alienage."

de facto a policy of preferring those who were born in this country. Therefore the construction placed upon the "national origin" provision is inconsistent with the construction this Court has placed upon the same Act's protections for persons denied employment on account of race or sex.

In connection with racial discrimination we have said that the Act prohibits "practices, procedures, or tests neutral on their face, and even neutral in terms of intent," if they create "artificial, arbitrary, and unnecessary barriers to employment when the barriers operate invidiously to discriminate on the basis of racial *or other impermissible classification*." Griggs v. Duke Power Co., 401 U.S. 424 (1971) (emphasis added). There we found that the employer could not use test or diploma requirements which on their face were racially neutral, when in fact those requirements had a de facto discriminatory result and the employer was unable to justify them as related to job performance. The tests involved in *Griggs* did not eliminate all blacks seeking employment, just as the citizenship requirement here does not eliminate all applicants of foreign origin. Respondent here explicitly conceded that the citizenship requirement is imposed without regard to the alien's qualifications for the job.

These petitioners against whom discrimination is charged are Chicanos. But whether brown, yellow, black, or white, the thrust of the Act is clear: alienage is no barrier to employment here. *Griggs*, as I understood it until today, extends its protective principles to all, not to blacks alone. Our cases on sex discrimination under the Act yield the same result as *Griggs*.

The construction placed upon the statute in the majority opinion is an extraordinary departure from prior cases, and it is opposed by the Equal Employment Opportunity Commission, the agency provided by law with the responsibility of enforcing the Act's protections. The Commission takes the only permissible position: that discrimination on the basis of alienage always has the effect of discrimination on the basis of national origin. Refusing to hire an individual because he is an alien "is discrimination based on birth outside the United States and is thus discrimination based on national origin in violation of Title VII." Brief for Commission as Amicus Curiae. The Commission's interpretation of the statute is entitled to great weight. There is no legislative history to cast doubt on this construction.

Mrs. Espinoza is a permanent resident alien, married to an American citizen, and her children will be native-born American citizens. But that first generation has the greatest adjustments to make to their new country. Their unfamiliarity with America makes them the most vulnerable to exploitation and discriminatory treatment. They, of course, have the same obligation as American citizens to pay taxes, and they are subject to the draft on the same basis. But they have never received equal treatment in the job market. The majority decides today that in passing sweeping legislation guaranteeing equal job opportunities, the Congress intended to help only the immigrant's children, excluding those "for whom there (is) no place at all." I cannot impute that niggardly an intent to Congress.

■ NOTES AND QUESTIONS

1. The Court notes that the term "ancestry" was originally in a draft of the statute, but was later removed. Why would Congress have eliminated this provision?

2. In a footnote omitted from the text above, the Court notes "a general understanding that the term 'national origin' does not embrace a requirement of United States citizenship." Is this a fair statement of our understanding of national origin?

3. The Court here makes a clear distinction between discrimination on the basis of citizenship and discrimination on the basis of national origin. The former is permitted while the latter is forbidden under Title VII. Does this result make sense? Are national origin and citizenship often closely linked?

4. Could an employer that discriminates on the basis of citizenship open itself up to a potential disparate impact claim?

5. Could an employer use citizenship as an excuse to discriminate on the basis of national origin?

6. In describing what national origin means, the Supreme Court gives us some guidance on its definition, stating that "[t]he term 'national origin' on its face refers to the country where a person was born, or, more broadly, the country from which his or her ancestors came." *Espinoza*, 414 U.S. at 88. This is important language from the Court's decision. After *Espinoza*, it is clear, at a minimum,

that one's national origin is made up of at least (1) where that individual was born; and (2) where that individual's parents were born. Many courts (and certainly the EEOC) have defined national origin much more expansively than this. Nonetheless, this language creates a "floor" for national origin claims, and provides some clarity to the definition.

7. **The Immigration Reform and Control Act of 1986.** This statutory provision, which is separate and distinct from Title VII, provides for certain discrimination claims on the basis of national origin and citizenship.

8. **Historical note.** In the nineteenth century, thousands of Chinese workers were imported into California to work for capitalists who were in search of cheap labor, mainly on the transcontinental railroad and gold mining projects. From the moment they arrived — in ships as dirty and packed as full "as those used in the African slave trade" — the Chinese workers were treated brutally,

PACIFIC CHIVALRY.
Encouragement to Chinese Immigration.

reinforcing the idea that the Chinese immigrants were a subservient people to the dominant white employers. *See* Kathy Knechtges, *Forgotten Victims — American Workers Immiserated by Chinese Immigration in Nineteenth Century California*, VDARE.COM (Sept. 22, 2013, 7:05 A.M.), http://www.vdare.com/articles/forgotten-victims-american-workers-immiserated-by-chinese-immigration- in-nineteenth-century; *The Anti-Chinese Movement and Chinese Exclusion*, THE BANCROFT LIBRARY, http://bancroft.berkeley.edu/collections/chineseinca/antichinese.html.

 Interactive Problem

Looking back at the interactive problem, recall that the plaintiff was born in India and raised in Fiji. Also assume that the plaintiff's parents were born in Iraq and China. Under the Supreme Court's ruling in *Espinoza*, what are the plaintiff's national origin(s)?

C. English-Only Rules

While English was once the predominant language spoken in the home in the United States, recent surveys have revealed that millions of Americans now converse in a different language. Though these trends are difficult to quantify, research reveals the following breakdown of the number of homes that speak a language other than English:

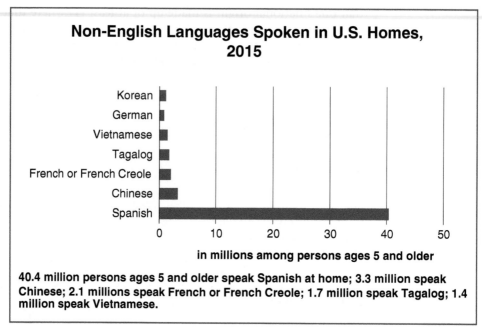

Non-English Languages Spoken in U.S. Homes, 2015

in millions among persons ages 5 and older

40.4 million persons ages 5 and older speak Spanish at home; 3.3 million speak Chinese; 2.1 millions speak French or French Creole; 1.7 million speak Tagalog; 1.4 million speak Vietnamese.

Figure 8.1

Given the widespread use of languages other than English in this country, it is not surprising that language is a source of substantial litigation in the employment context. Indeed, it is difficult to separate language from national origin, and it is common for individuals to associate their language with their ancestry.

Perhaps one of the most controversial areas in all of employment discrimination law is an employer's implementation of English-only rules. These employer policies take many different forms, but all place some restrictions on the ability of employees to speak anything other than English in the workplace. English-only policies can vary from rules that require workers to speak English during certain working hours of the day, to rules that completely prohibit workers from speaking anything other than English at the workplace at any time.

The EEOC has expressed concern over such policies, and has issued clear regulations on the use of these rules. The regulations vary depending upon whether the employer's policy is applied to some working time, or if it applies at all times. These provisions are set forth below:

(a) When applied at all times. A rule requiring employees to speak only English at all times in the workplace is a burdensome term and condition of employment. The primary language of an individual is often an essential national origin characteristic. Prohibiting employees at all times, in the workplace, from speaking their primary language or the language they speak most comfortably, disadvantages an individual's employment opportunities on the basis of national origin. It may also create an atmosphere of inferiority, isolation and intimidation based on national origin which could result in a discriminatory working environment. Therefore, the Commission will presume that such a rule violates [T]itle VII and will closely scrutinize it.

(b) When applied only at certain times. An employer may have a rule requiring that employees speak only in English at certain times where the employer can show that the rule is justified by business necessity.

29 C.F.R. § 1606.7.

Under subsection (a), this rule presumes that Title VII has been violated where an English-only rule applies at all times. Under subsection (b), a more limited rule that applies at more specific times will be seen as having a disparate impact against workers, but can be rebutted by business necessity. The Commission also set forth the importance of providing sufficient notice of the rule to a company's employees:

(c) Notice of the rule. It is common for individuals whose primary language is not English to inadvertently change from speaking English to speaking their primary language. Therefore, if an employer believes it has a business necessity for a speak-English-only rule at certain times, the employer should inform its employees of the general circumstances when speaking only in English is required and of the consequences of violating the rule. If an employer fails to effectively notify its employees of the rule and makes an adverse employment decision against an individual based on a violation of the rule, the Commission will consider the employer's application of the rule as evidence of discrimination on the basis of national origin.

Id.

Thus, where an employer does implement such a policy, it must make certain to provide notice to its workers that the policy is in accordance with the EEOC guidelines. The EEOC rules are fairly clear in English-only cases. However, these regulations have met with differing opinions in the federal courts.

Garcia v. Spun Steak Co.
998 F.2d 1480 (9th Cir. 1993)

O'SCANNLAIN, Circuit Judge:

We are called upon to decide whether an employer violates Title VII of the Civil Rights Act of 1964 in requiring its bilingual workers to speak only English while working on the job.

Spun Steak Company ("Spun Steak") is a California corporation that produces poultry and meat products in South San Francisco for wholesale distribution. Spun Steak employs thirty-three workers, twenty-four of whom are Spanish-speaking. Virtually all of the Spanish-speaking employees are Hispanic. While two employees speak no English, the others have varying degrees of proficiency in English. Spun Steak has never required job applicants to speak or to understand English as a condition of employment.

Approximately two-thirds of Spun Steak's employees are production line workers or otherwise involved in the production process. Appellees Garcia and Buitrago are production line workers; they stand before a conveyor belt, remove poultry or other meat products from the belt and place the product into cases or trays for resale. Their work is done individually. Both Garcia and Buitrago are fully bilingual, speaking both English and Spanish.

> Note the mundane nature of the plaintiff's work in this case.

Appellee Local 115, United Food and Commercial Workers International Union, AFL-CIO ("Local 115"), is the collective bargaining agent representing the employees at Spun Steak.

Prior to September 1990, these Spun Steak employees spoke Spanish freely to their co-workers during work hours. After receiving complaints that some workers were using their bilingual capabilities to harass and to insult other workers in a language they could not understand, Spun Steak began to investigate the possibility of requiring its employees to speak only English in the workplace. Specifically, Spun Steak received complaints that Garcia and Buitrago made derogatory, racist comments in Spanish about two co-workers, one of whom is African-American and the other Chinese-American.

The company's president, Kenneth Bertelson, concluded that an English-only rule would promote racial harmony in the workplace. In addition, he concluded that the English-only rule would enhance worker safety because some employees who did not understand Spanish claimed that the use of Spanish distracted them while they were operating machinery, and would enhance product quality because the U.S.D.A. inspector in the plant spoke only English and thus could not understand if a product-related concern was raised in Spanish. Accordingly, the following rule was adopted:

> The English-only policy adopted by the company here does not apply at all hours of the workday — there are certain exceptions.

> [I]t is hereafter the policy of this Company that only English will be spoken in connection with work. During lunch, breaks, and employees' own time, they are obviously free to speak Spanish if they wish. However, we urge all of you not to use your fluency in Spanish in a fashion which may lead other employees to suffer humiliation.

In addition to the English-only policy, Spun Steak adopted a rule forbidding offensive racial, sexual, or personal remarks of any kind.

It is unclear from the record whether Spun Steak strictly enforced the English-only rule. According to the plaintiffs-appellees, some workers continued to speak Spanish without incident. Spun Steak issued written exceptions to the policy allowing its clean-up crew to speak Spanish, allowing its foreman to speak Spanish, and authorizing certain workers to speak Spanish to the foreman at the foreman's discretion. One of the two employees who speak only Spanish is a member of the clean-up crew and thus is unaffected by the policy.

In November 1990, Garcia and Buitrago received warning letters for speaking Spanish during working hours. For approximately two months thereafter, they were not permitted to work next to each other. Local 115 protested the English-only policy and requested that it be rescinded but to no avail.

On May 6, 1991, Garcia, Buitrago, and Local 115 filed charges of discrimination against Spun Steak with the U.S. Equal Employment Opportunity Commission

("EEOC"). The EEOC conducted an investigation and determined that "there is reasonable cause to believe [Spun Steak] violated Title VII of the Civil Rights Act of 1964, as amended, with respect to its adoption of an English-only rule and with respect to retaliation when [Garcia, Buitrago, and Local 115] complained."

Garcia, Buitrago, and Local 115, on behalf of all Spanish-speaking employees of Spun Steak (collectively, "the Spanish-speaking employees"), filed suit, alleging that the English-only policy violated Title VII. On September 6, 1991, the parties filed cross-motions for summary judgment. The district court denied Spun Steak's motion and granted the Spanish-speaking employees' motion for summary judgment, concluding that the English-only policy disparately impacted Hispanic workers without sufficient business justification, and thus violated Title VII. Spun Steak filed this timely appeal and the EEOC filed a brief amicus curiae and participated in oral argument.

It is well-settled that Title VII is concerned not only with intentional discrimination, but also with employment practices and policies that lead to disparities in the treatment of classes of workers. Thus, a plaintiff alleging discrimination under Title VII may proceed under two theories of liability: disparate treatment or disparate impact. While the disparate treatment theory requires proof of discriminatory intent, intent is irrelevant to a disparate impact theory.

The Spanish-speaking employees do not contend that Spun Steak intentionally discriminated against them in enacting the English-only policy. Rather, they contend that the policy had a discriminatory impact on them because it imposes a burdensome term or condition of employment exclusively upon Hispanic workers and denies them a privilege of employment that non-Spanish-speaking workers enjoy. Because their claim focuses on disparities in the terms, conditions, and privileges of employment, and not on barriers to hiring or promotion, it is outside the mainstream of disparate impact cases decided thus far. As a threshold matter, therefore, we must determine whether the disparate impact theory can be made applicable at all.

The disparate impact cause of action developed out of the language in section 703(a)(2) prohibiting discrimination based on deprivation of employment opportunities, such as the opportunity to be hired or promoted. Our court's disparate impact cases fall squarely within the language of section 703(a)(2). The cases in which we have concluded that the plaintiff has proved discrimination based on a disparate impact theory have all involved plaintiffs who claimed that they were denied employment opportunities as the result of artificial, arbitrary, and unnecessary barriers that excluded members of a protected group from being hired or promoted, not plaintiffs contending that they were subjected to harsher working conditions than the general employee population.

This case, by contrast, does not fall within the language of section 703(a)(2). While policies that serve as barriers to hiring or promotion clearly deprive applicants of employment opportunities, we cannot conclude that a burdensome term or condition of employment or the denial of a privilege would "limit, segregate, or classify" employees in a way that would "deprive any individual of employment opportunities" or "otherwise adversely affect his status as an employee" in violation of section 703(a)(2). Such claims, therefore, must be brought directly under section 703(a)(1). We have never expressly considered, however, whether disparate impact theory applies to claims under section 703(a)(1), and the Supreme Court has explicitly reserved the issue.

Nevertheless, we are called upon to decide the issue in this case notwithstanding the parties' failure to brief it. Our decision is simple: we see no reason to restrict the application of the disparate impact theory to the denial of employment opportunities under section 703(a)(2). Regardless whether a company's decisions about whom to hire or to promote are infected with discrimination, policies or practices that impose significantly harsher burdens on a protected group than on the employee population in general may operate as barriers to equality in the workplace and, if unsupported by a business justification, may be considered "discriminatory." We are satisfied that a disparate impact claim may be based upon a challenge to a practice or policy that has a significant adverse impact on the "terms, conditions, or privileges" of the employment of a protected group under section 703(a)(1).

To make out a prima facie case of discriminatory impact, a plaintiff must identify a specific, seemingly neutral practice or policy that has a significantly adverse impact on persons of a protected class.

We first consider whether the Spanish-speaking employees have made out the prima facie case. "[T]he requirements of a prima facie disparate impact case . . . are in some respects more exacting than those of a disparate treatment case." In the disparate treatment context, a plaintiff can make out a prima facie case merely by presenting evidence sufficient to give rise to an inference of discrimination. In a disparate impact case, by contrast, plaintiffs must do more than merely raise an inference of discrimination before the burden shifts; they "must actually prove the discriminatory impact at issue." In the typical disparate impact case, in which the plaintiff argues that a selection criterion excludes protected applicants from jobs or promotions, the plaintiff proves discriminatory impact by showing statistical disparities between the number of protected class members in the qualified applicant group and those in the relevant segment of the workforce. While such statistics are often difficult to compile, whether the protected group has been disadvantaged turns on quantifiable data. When the alleged disparate impact is on the conditions, terms, or privileges of employment, however, determining whether the protected group has been adversely affected may depend on subjective factors not easily quantified. The fact that the alleged effects are subjective, however, does not relieve the plaintiff of the burden of proving disparate impact. The plaintiff may not merely assert that the policy has harmed members of the group to which he or she belongs. Instead, the plaintiff must prove the existence of adverse effects of the policy, must prove that

> The majority outlines the prima facie case for disparate impact in this case, and concludes that the plaintiff has failed to make this showing.

the impact of the policy is on terms, conditions, or privileges of employment of the protected class, must prove that the adverse effects are significant, and must prove that the employee population in general is not affected by the policy to the same degree.

It is beyond dispute that, in this case, if the English-only policy causes any adverse effects, those effects will be suffered disproportionately by those of Hispanic origin. The vast majority of those workers at Spun Steak who speak a language other than English — and virtually all those employees for whom English is not a first language — are Hispanic. It is of no consequence that not all Hispanic employees of Spun Steak speak Spanish; nor is it relevant that some non-Hispanic workers may speak Spanish. If the adverse effects are proved, it is enough under Title VII that Hispanics are disproportionately impacted.

> The plaintiffs argue that the employer's policy had an adverse effect upon them for the three different reasons outlined by the court.

The crux of the dispute between Spun Steak and the Spanish-speaking employees, however, is not over whether Hispanic workers will disproportionately bear any adverse effects of the policy; rather, the dispute centers on whether the policy causes any adverse effects at all, and if it does, whether the effects are significant. The Spanish-speaking employees argue that the policy adversely affects them in the following ways: (1) it denies them the ability to express their cultural heritage on the job; (2) it denies them a privilege of employment that is enjoyed by monolingual speakers of English; and (3) it creates an atmosphere of inferiority, isolation, and intimidation. We discuss each of these contentions in turn.

The employees argue that denying them the ability to speak Spanish on the job denies them the right to cultural expression. It cannot be gainsaid that an individual's primary language can be an important link to his ethnic culture and identity. Title VII, however, does not protect the ability of workers to express their cultural heritage at the workplace. Title VII is concerned only with disparities in the treatment of workers; it does not confer substantive privileges. It is axiomatic that an employee must often sacrifice individual self-expression during working hours. Just as a private employer is not required to allow other types of self-expression, there is nothing in Title VII which requires an employer to allow employees to express their cultural identity.

Next, the Spanish-speaking employees argue that the English-only policy has a disparate impact on them because it deprives them of a privilege given by the employer to native-English speakers: the ability to converse on the job in the language with which they feel most comfortable. It is undisputed that Spun Steak allows its employees to converse on the job. The ability to converse — especially to make small talk — is a privilege of employment, and may in fact be a significant privilege of employment in an assembly-line job. It is inaccurate, however, to describe the privilege as broadly as the Spanish-speaking employees urge us to do.

The employees have attempted to define the privilege as the ability to speak in the language of their choice. A privilege, however, is by definition given at the employer's discretion; an employer has the right to define its contours. Thus, an employer may allow employees to converse on the job, but only during certain times of the day or during the performance of certain tasks. The employer may proscribe certain topics as inappropriate during working hours or may even forbid the use of certain words, such as profanity.

Here, as is its prerogative, the employer has defined the privilege narrowly. When the privilege is defined at its narrowest (as merely the ability to speak on the job), we cannot conclude that those employees fluent in both English and Spanish are adversely impacted by the policy. Because they are able to speak English, bilingual employees can engage in conversation on the job. It is axiomatic that "the language a person who is multi-lingual elects to speak at a particular time is . . . a matter of choice." *Garcia*, 618 F.2d at 270. The bilingual employee can readily comply with the English-only rule and still enjoy the privilege of speaking on the job. "There is no disparate impact" with respect to a privilege of employment "if the rule is one that the affected employee can readily observe and nonobservance is a matter of individual preference." *Id.*

> The court notes that, in certain instances, bilingual employees may not consciously be aware that they are switching languages.

The Spanish-speaking employees argue that fully bilingual employees are hampered in the enjoyment of the privilege because for them, switching from one language to another is not fully volitional. Whether a bilingual speaker can control which language is used in a given circumstance is a factual issue that cannot be resolved at the summary judgment stage. However, we fail to see the relevance of the assertion, even assuming that it can be proved. Title VII is not meant to protect against rules that merely inconvenience some employees, even if the inconvenience falls regularly on a protected class. Rather, Title VII protects against only those policies that have a significant impact. The fact that an employee may have to catch himself or herself from occasionally slipping into Spanish does not impose a burden significant enough to amount to the denial of equal opportunity. This is not a case in which the employees have alleged that the company is enforcing the policy in such a way as to impose penalties for minor slips of the tongue. The fact that a bilingual employee may, on occasion, unconsciously substitute a Spanish word in the place of an English one does not override our conclusion that the bilingual employee can easily comply with the rule. In short, we conclude that a bilingual employee is not denied a privilege of employment by the English-only policy.

By contrast, non-English speakers cannot enjoy the privilege of conversing on the job if conversation is limited to a language they cannot speak. As applied "[t]o a person who speaks only one tongue or to a person who has difficulty using another language than the one spoken in his home," an English-only rule might well have an adverse impact. *Garcia*, 618 F.2d at 270. Indeed, counsel for Spun Steak conceded at oral argument that the policy would have an adverse impact on an employee unable to speak English. There is only one employee at Spun Steak affected by the policy who is unable to speak any English. Even with regard to her, however, summary judgment was improper because a genuine issue of material fact exists as to whether she has been adversely affected by the policy. She stated in her deposition that she was not bothered by the rule because she preferred not to make small talk on the job, but rather preferred to work in peace. Furthermore, there is some evidence suggesting that she is not required to comply with the policy when she chooses to speak. For example, she is allowed to speak Spanish to her supervisor. Remand is necessary to determine whether she has suffered adverse effects from the policy. It is unclear from the record whether there are any other employees who have such limited proficiency in English that they are effectively denied the privilege of speaking on the job. Whether an employee speaks such little English as to be effectively denied the privilege is a question of fact for which summary judgment is improper.

Finally, the Spanish-speaking employees argue that the policy creates an atmosphere of inferiority, isolation, and intimidation. Under this theory, the employees do not assert that the policy directly affects a term, condition, or privilege of employment. Instead, the argument must be that the policy causes the work environment to become infused with ethnic tensions. The tense environment, the argument goes, itself amounts to a condition of employment.

The Supreme Court in *Meritor Savings Bank v. Vinson*, 477 U.S. 57, 66 (1985) held that an abusive work environment may, in some circumstances, amount to a condition of employment giving rise to a violation of Title VII. Although *Vinson* is a sexual harassment case in which the individual incidents involved behavior that was arguably intentionally discriminatory, its rationale applies equally to cases in which seemingly neutral policies of a company infuse the atmosphere of the workplace with discrimination. The *Vinson* Court emphasized, however, that discriminatory practices must be pervasive before an employee has a Title VII claim under a hostile environment theory.

Here, the employees urge us to adopt a per se rule that English-only policies always infect the working environment to such a degree as to amount to a hostile or abusive work environment. This we cannot do. Whether a working environment is infused with discrimination is a factual question, one for which a per se rule is particularly inappropriate. The dynamics of an individual workplace are enormously complex; we cannot conclude, as a matter of law, that the introduction of an English-only policy, in every workplace, will always have the same effect.

The Spanish-speaking employees in this case have presented no evidence other than conclusory statements that the policy has contributed to an atmosphere of "isolation, inferiority or intimidation." The bilingual employees are able to comply with the rule, and there is no evidence to show that the atmosphere at Spun Steak in general is infused with hostility toward Hispanic workers.

> What type of evidence could establish that an English-only policy created "isolation, inferiority or intimidation"? Was that evidence present here?

Indeed, there is substantial evidence in the record demonstrating that the policy was enacted to prevent the employees from intentionally using their fluency in Spanish to isolate and to intimidate members of other ethnic groups. In light of the specific factual context of this case, we conclude that the bilingual employees have not raised a genuine issue of material fact that the effect is so pronounced as to amount to a hostile environment.

We do not foreclose the prospect that in some circumstances English-only rules can exacerbate existing tensions, or, when combined with other discriminatory behavior, contribute to an overall environment of discrimination. Likewise, we can envision a case in which such rules are enforced in such a draconian manner that the enforcement itself amounts to harassment. In evaluating such a claim, however, a court must look to the totality of the circumstances in the particular factual context in which the claim arises.

In holding that the enactment of an English-only while working policy does not inexorably lead to an abusive environment for those whose primary language is not English, we reach a conclusion opposite to the EEOC's long standing position. The EEOC Guidelines provide that an employee meets the prima facie case in a disparate impact cause of action merely by proving the existence of the English-only policy. *See* 29 C.F.R. § 1606.7(a) & (b) (1991). Under the EEOC's scheme, an employer must always provide a business justification for such a rule. The EEOC enacted this scheme in part because of its conclusion that English-only rules may "create an atmosphere of inferiority, isolation and intimidation based on national origin which could result in a discriminatory working environment." 29 C.F.R. § 1606.7(a). We do not reject the English-only rule Guideline lightly. We will not defer to an administrative construction of a statute where there are compelling indications that it is wrong. [quotations and citations omitted].

> The court here rejects the EEOC's English-only regulation. Why does it not afford greater deference to the agency?

We have been impressed by Judge Rubin's pre-Guidelines analysis for the Fifth Circuit in *Garcia*, which we follow today. *Garcia*, 618 F.2d 264. Nothing in the plain language of section 703(a)(1) supports EEOC's English-only rule Guideline. "Title VII could not have been enacted into law without substantial support from legislators in both Houses who traditionally resisted federal regulation of private business." *United Steelworkers of America, AFL-CIO v. Weber*, 443 U.S. 193 (1979). "Those legislators demanded as a price for their support that." *Id.*

It is clear that Congress intended a balance to be struck in preventing discrimination and preserving the independence of the employer. In striking that balance, the Supreme Court has held that a plaintiff in a disparate impact case must prove the alleged discriminatory effect before the burden shifts to the employer. The EEOC Guideline at issue here contravenes that policy by presuming that an English-only policy has a disparate impact in the absence of proof. We are not aware of, nor has counsel shown us, anything in the legislative history to Title VII that indicates that English-only policies are to be presumed discriminatory. Indeed, nowhere in the legislative history is there a discussion of English-only policies at all.

Because the bilingual employees have failed to make out a prima facie case, we need not consider the business justifications offered for the policy as applied to them. On remand, if Local 115 is able to make out a prima facie case with regard to employees with limited proficiency in English, the district court could then consider any business justification offered by Spun Steak.

In sum, we conclude that the bilingual employees have not made out a prima facie case and that Spun Steak has not violated Title VII in adopting an English-only rule as to them. Thus, we reverse the grant of summary judgment in favor of Garcia, Buitrago, and Local 115 to the extent it represents the bilingual employees, and remand with instructions to grant summary judgment in favor of Spun Steak on their claims. A genuine issue of material fact exists as to whether there are one or more employees represented by Local 115 with limited proficiency in English who were adversely impacted by the policy. As to such employee or employees, we reverse the grant of summary judgment in favor of Local 115, and remand for further proceedings.

Reversed and Remanded.

BOOCHEVER, Circuit Judge, dissenting in part:

I agree with most of the majority's carefully crafted opinion. I dissent, however, from the majority's rejection of the EEOC guidelines. The guidelines provide that an employee establishes a prima facie case in a disparate impact claim by proving the existence of an English-

> The dissent argues for greater deference to the EEOC's regulations.

only policy, thereby shifting the burden to the employer to show a business necessity for the rule. I would defer to the Commission's expertise in construing the Act, by virtue of which it concluded that English-only rules may "create an atmosphere of inferiority, isolation and intimidation based on national origin which could result in a discriminatory working environment."

As the majority indicates, proof of such an effect of English-only rules requires analysis of subjective factors. It is hard to envision how the burden of proving such an effect would be met other than by conclusory self-serving statements of the Spanish-speaking employees or possibly by expert testimony of psychologists. The difficulty of meeting such a burden may well have been one of the reasons for the promulgation of the guideline. On the other hand, it should not be difficult for an employer to give specific reasons for the policy, such as the safety reasons advanced in this case.

It is true that EEOC regulations are entitled to somewhat less weight than those promulgated by an agency with Congressionally delegated rulemaking authority. Nevertheless, the EEOC guideline is entitled to "great deference" in the absence of "compelling indications that it is wrong." *Espinoza v. Farah Mfg. Co.*, 414 U.S. 86 (1973). While one may reasonably differ with the EEOC's position as a matter of policy, I can find no such "compelling indications" in this case. The lack of directly supporting language in § 703(a)(1) or the legislative history of Title VII, relied on by the majority, does not in my opinion make the guideline "inconsistent with an obvious congressional intent not to reach the employment practice in question."

I conclude that if appropriate deference is given to the administrative interpretation of the Act, we should follow the guideline and uphold the district court's decision that a prima facie case was established. I believe, however, that triable issues were presented whether Spun Steak established a business justification for the rule, and I would remand for trial of that issue.

◼ NOTES AND QUESTIONS

1. *Spun Steak* is one of the leading cases considering the validity of the EEOC's guidelines on English-only rules. The decision represents only one opinion, however, and others have reached differing conclusions. *See* Kania v. Archdiocese of Phila., 14 F. Supp. 2d 730 (E.D. Pa. 1998) (discussing the disagreement among courts).

2. The court notes that, as part of their job, workers "stand before a conveyor belt, remove poultry or other meat products from the belt and place the product into cases or trays for resale." Is it really critical to speak only English in such a position?

3. Plaintiffs argue that there are three reasons why they have suffered an adverse action in this case: "(1) it denies them the ability to express their cultural heritage on the job; (2) it denies them a privilege of employment that is enjoyed by monolingual speakers of English; and (3) it creates an atmosphere of inferiority, isolation, and intimidation." The court systematically rejects each rationale. Do you agree?

4. Where a job is extremely mundane, such as the one in this case, is the ability of an employee to speak his native language a privilege of employment? Does it make a difference here that the workers were permitted to speak any language during their break time?

5. Is the ability to express your cultural heritage on the job protected by federal law? Why or why not? In a dissent from a petition for rehearing en banc in this case, Judge Reinhardt states:

   > Language is intimately tied to national origin and cultural identity: its discriminatory suppression cannot be dismissed as an "inconvenience" to the affected employees, as Spun Steak asserts. Even when an individual learns English and becomes assimilated into American society, his native language remains an important manifestation of his ethnic identity and a means of affirming links to his original culture. English-only rules not only symbolize a rejection of the excluded language and the culture it embodies, but also a denial of that side of an individual's personality.

   13 F.3d 296, 298 (9th Cir. 1993). Do you agree?

6. Is it intimidating for workers to be told that they cannot speak a language with which they are most comfortable?

7. The plaintiffs in this case argued that even though a person is bilingual, changing between languages "is not fully volitional." Is this true? Studies have found "code switching" to be a reality; often bilingual workers may not know that they have changed languages while speaking. *See* EEOC v. Premier Operator Servs., Inc., 113 F. Supp. 2d 1066, 1070 (N.D. Tex. 2000) ("Credible and persuasive evidence was presented . . . regarding research of psycho linguists in the late 1990's, which concludes that code switching cannot typically be 'turned

off'; and that a person cannot be forced to refrain from uttering a word of the primary language simply upon direction or request, because this switching is, or can be an unconscious act."). Would it be fair to discipline a worker for failing to speak English when that worker was unintentionally speaking another language?

8. Is this case properly analyzed as a disparate impact case, rather than as a disparate treatment case? As Judge Reinhold observed in his dissent from rehearing en banc, "it should be noted that the imposition of an English-only rule may mask intentional discrimination on the basis of national origin . . . [a]s . . . the urge to repress another's language is rarely, if ever, driven by benevolent impulses." 13 F.3d at 298. Was intentional discrimination present here?

9. The court here rejects the EEOC's regulation on English-only rules. Has the court given the federal agency sufficient deference?

10. The court here rejected the prima facie case of the plaintiffs, meaning that the employer was not required to show that the policy was job related and consistent with business necessity. Would the court have found that the employer had satisfied its burden if it had reached this question? Was the policy job related and consistent with business necessity?

11. What are some of the common business justifications for adopting English-only rules? *See* James Leonard, *Title VII and the Protection of Minority Languages in the American Workplace: The Search for a Justification*, 72 Mo. L. Rev. 745, 792 (2007) (arguing that the EEOC guidelines against "English Only" rules interfere with valid business objectives).

12. Certain jobs tend to lend themselves more toward using a common language than others. It may be easier to justify an English-only rule, for example, where the employment involves emergency issues or public safety. Regardless, the specific factual setting and necessity of the rule must be fully considered.

13. English proficiency. It is also worth noting that where employers apply an English proficiency test requiring a certain level of language skills of its employees, workers often challenge such exams on a disparate impact theory. *See* Trivedi v. N.Y.S. Unified Court Sys. Office of Court Admin., 818 F. Supp. 2d 712 (S.D.N.Y. 2011) (finding that the court interpreters who were terminated after they failed required English proficiency exams established a prima facie case of discrimination under Title VII). *But see* Kim v. Commandant, Def. Language Inst., Foreign Language Ctr., 772 F.2d 521 (9th Cir. 1985) (holding that the candidate failed to demonstrate that English language oral proficiency test had a disparate impact upon nonnative English speakers). If workers are able to satisfy the prima facie case, the defendant would have the burden in such cases to establish that the policy is job related and consistent with business necessity.

14. One interesting example of an English-only rule in practice involved Whole Foods. The company was threatened with a national boycott — one online petition gathered more than 15,000 signatures — after two Spanish-speaking workers claimed that they were suspended for complaining about the English-only language policy for employees. Whole Foods officials claimed

that the employees were suspended based on their behavior alone — that they were rude and disrespectful on the job — and not because they spoke Spanish to each other. A Whole Foods executive marketing coordinator explained that the policy provided that all English-speaking workers must speak English to customers and other employees while on the clock, unless the customer speaks another language; that the employees are free to speak any language they choose during their breaks; and that the policy does not prevent employees from speaking Spanish if all parties present agree that a different language is preferred. Nonetheless, Whole Foods officials delivered a timely apology for the unclear language of the English-only policy and changed the wording of the section accordingly. *See* Bruce Horovitz, *Whole Foods Revises Wording of English-Only Policy*, Usa Today (June 16, 2013, 2:34 A.M.), http://usat.ly/11PjfOD; Martha White, *Whole Foods Changes English-Only Store Policy*, NBC News (June 17, 2013, 5:03 P.M.), http://www.cnbc.com/id/100822119#.

 ## Interactive Problem

Looking back at the interactive problem, assume that Big Plane Airlines has been experiencing trouble with its pilots speaking a language other than English when they communicate with the tower and other ground communication centers. If the Airlines adopted an "English-only rule" that applied from the time pilots stepped onto a plane until the time they stepped off, could such a rule be enforced? How would it be analyzed?

The *Garcia* case was highly controversial, particularly in its interpretation of the EEOC's English-only guidelines. As seen in the case below, not all courts have followed the approach adopted by *Garcia*. Indeed, the appellate courts have taken varying approaches on the issue of English-only rules.

Maldonado v. City of Altus
433 F.3d 1294 (10th Cir. 2006)

Hartz, Circuit Judge.

Plaintiffs are employees of the City of Altus, Oklahoma (City). They appeal the district court's grant of summary judgment dismissing all their claims against the City, the City Administrator, and the Street Commissioner (collectively referred to as Defendants). All claims arise out of the City's English-only policy for its employees. Asserting claims of both disparate-impact and disparate-treatment, Plaintiffs contend that the English-only policy discriminates against them on the basis of race and national origin in violation of Titles VI and VII of the Civil Rights Act of 1964. We reverse and remand with respect to Plaintiffs' claims against the City alleging disparate impact and disparate treatment under Title VII; intentional discrimination under § 1981; and violation of equal protection under 42 U.S.C. § 1983. We affirm summary judgment for Defendants on all other claims.

Plaintiffs' claims stem from the City's promulgation of an English-only policy. Approximately 29 City employees are Hispanic, the only significant national-origin minority group affected by the policy. All Plaintiffs are Hispanic and bilingual, each speaking fluent English and Spanish.

In the spring of 2002 the City's Street Commissioner, Defendant Holmes Willis, received a complaint that because Street Department employees were speaking Spanish, other employees could not understand what was being said on the City radio. Willis informed the City's Human Resources Director, Candy Richardson, of the complaint, and she advised Willis that he could direct his employees to speak only English when using the radio for City business.

> The origin of a policy is always a critical question: Here, employee complaints led to the adoption of the English-only rule.

Plaintiffs claim that Willis instead told the Street Department employees that they could not speak Spanish at work at all and informed them that the City would soon implement an official English-only policy. On June 18, 2002, Plaintiff Tommy Sanchez wrote a letter to Ms. Richardson and the City Administrator, Defendant Michael Nettles, expressing concerns about the new Street Department English-only policy and the proposed citywide policy. Sanchez was particularly concerned that his subordinates, Plaintiffs Ruben Rios and Lloyd Lopez, had been told of a policy that he knew nothing about. Citing the City's Personnel Policies and Procedures Manual, the letter informed Nettles that employees had not been given proper notice if this was a new administrative policy and questioned whether Willis and the City had followed proper procedures in implementing the new policy. Sanchez reported that Willis had told him that the reason Hispanics speak Spanish "is because [of] . . . insecurities," and that Willis had suggested that he (Sanchez) "would feel uncomfortable if another race would speak their native language in front of [him]." The letter requested that "the City of Altus understand that we Hispanics are proud of our heritage and do not feel that our ability to communicate in a bilingual manner is a hindrance or an embarrassment. There has never been a time that because I spoke Spanish to another Spanish speaking individual, I was unable to perform our job duties and requirements." At the end of the letter Rios and Lopez signed a paragraph stating that "[t]he purpose of this correspondence is to serve as a discrimination complaint in accordance with the City of Altus Personnel Policies and Procedures Manual Section 102, in which we are requesting that an investigation be conducted into these charges and that a report be issue[d] within two weeks." *Id.* Another employee (Leticia Sanchez) also complained orally to Richardson about Willis's instructing employees not to speak Spanish in any circumstances during work hours.

In July 2002 the City promulgated the following official policy signed by Nettles:

> To insure effective communications among and between employees and various departments of the City, to prevent misunderstandings and to promote

and enhance safe work practices, all work related and business communications during the work day shall be conducted in the English language with the exception of those circumstances where it is necessary or prudent to communicate with a citizen, business owner, organization or criminal suspect in his or her native language due to the person or entity's limited English language skills. The use of the English language during work hours and while engaged in City business includes face to face communication of work orders and directions as well as communications utilizing telephones, mobile telephones, cellular telephones, radios, computer or e-mail transmissions and all written forms of communications. If an employee or applicant for employment believes that he or she cannot understand communications due to limited English language skills, the employee is to discuss the situation with the department head and the Human Resources Director to determine what accommodation is required and feasible. This policy does not apply to strictly private communications between co-workers while they are on approved lunch hours or breaks or before or after work hours while the employees are still on City property if City property is not being used for the communication. Further, this policy does not apply to strictly private communication between an employee and a family member so long as the communications are limited in time and are not disruptive to the work environment. Employees are encouraged to be sensitive to the feelings of their fellow employees, including a possible feeling of exclusion if a co-worker cannot understand what is being said in his or her presence when a language other than English is being utilized.

Defendants state three primary reasons for adopting the policy:

1) workers and supervisors could not understand what was being said over the City's radios . . . ; 2) non-Spanish speaking employees, both before and after the adoption of the Policy, informed management that they felt uncomfortable when their co-workers were speaking in front of them in a language they could not understand because they did not know if their co-workers were speaking about them; and 3) there were safety concerns with a non-common language being used around heavy equipment.

Although the district court observed "that there was no written record of any communication problems, morale problems or safety problems resulting from the use of languages other than English prior to implementation of the policy," it noted that Willis had testified that at least one employee complained about the use of Spanish by his co-workers before implementation of the policy and other non-Spanish speaking employees subsequently made similar complaints. Those city officials who were deposed could recount no incidents of safety problems caused by the use of a language other than English, but the district court found that some Plaintiffs were aware "that employee safety was one reason for the adoption of the policy." The court also stated that "it does not seem necessary that the City await an accident before acting."

> In what way does safety play a role in the use of languages other than English in this case?

Defendants offered evidence that the restrictions in the written policy were actually relaxed to allow workers to speak Spanish during work hours and on City property if everyone present understood Spanish. But Plaintiffs offered evidence that employees were told that the restrictions went beyond the written policy and prohibited all use of Spanish if a non-Spanish speaker was present, even during breaks, lunch hours, and private telephone conversations. Plaintiff Lloyd Lopez stated in his deposition that "we were told that the only time we could speak Spanish is when two of us are in a break room by ourselves, and if anybody other than Hispanic comes in, we are to change our language." In addition he said, "We no longer can speak about anything in general in Spanish around anybody. Even if we were on the phone talking to our wives and we were having a private conversation with them and somebody happened to walk by, we were to change our language because it would offend whoever was walking by." Lopez understood, however, that the policy permitted him to speak Spanish if he was alone in a truck with another Spanish-speaking co-worker. Plaintiff Ruben Rios testified in his deposition that he similarly understood the policy to exclude the use of Spanish during breaks and the lunch hour if non-Hispanic co-workers were present. When asked specifically whether he understood that the policy allowed Spanish to be spoken between co-workers during lunch or other breaks, he stated that "[a]s long as there was another Hispanic person, we could speak in Spanish but away from other individuals, non-Hispanic people." And Plaintiff Tommy Sanchez testified that he was told that he could not speak Spanish at all, but added that Richardson explained to him that "[t]hat's not the way [the City] meant it." The City has not disciplined anyone for violating the English-only policy.

Plaintiffs allege that the policy created a hostile environment for Hispanic employees, causing them "fear and uncertainty in their employment," and subjecting them to racial and ethnic taunting. They contend "that the English-only rule created a hostile environment because it pervasively — every hour of every work day — burdened, threatened and demeaned the [Plaintiffs] because of their Hispanic origin.

Evidence of ethnic taunting included Plaintiffs' affidavits stating that they had "personally been teased and made the subject of jokes directly because of the English-only policy[,]" and that they were "aware of other Hispanic co-workers being teased and made the subject of jokes because of the English-only policy." Plaintiff Tommy Sanchez testified in his deposition that each time he went to the City of Altus he was reminded of the restrictions on his speech by non-Hispanic employees. He stated that these other employees of the City of Altus "would pull up and laugh, start saying stuff in Spanish to us and said, 'They didn't tell us we couldn't stop. They just told you.'" Sanchez also testified that an Altus police officer taunted him about not being allowed to speak Spanish by saying, "'Don't let me hear you talk Spanish.'" He further testified that "some of the guys from the street department would . . . poke fun out of it [the policy]" and that when he went to other departments "they would bring it up constantly." As evidence that such taunting was not unexpected by management, Lloyd Lopez recounted in his deposition that Street Commissioner Willis told Ruben Rios and him that he was informing them of the English-only policy in private because Willis had concerns about "the other guys making fun of [them]." Plaintiffs also provided evidence that

Mayor Gramling was "quoted in a newspaper article as referring to the Spanish language as 'garbage,'" although the Mayor claims that he used the word garble and was misquoted.

> To what extent — if any — did the "garbage" comment by the Mayor drive the result of the case?

Each Plaintiff filed a discrimination charge with the EEOC, complaining that the English-only policy constituted national-origin discrimination. Plaintiffs Danny Maldonado and Tommy Sanchez also alleged retaliation in their charges, and Danny Maldonado and Freddie Perez claimed that they had been subjected to "harassment and intimidation resulting in a hostile work environment."

After an investigation the EEOC determined that the City "ha[d] committed a per se violation of [Title VII] with respect to the establishment of its overly broad and discriminatory English-only policy." The EEOC attempted to resolve the dispute informally, but these efforts were unsuccessful. Each Plaintiff received a right-to-sue letter and this litigation commenced. Defendants do not claim that Plaintiffs failed to exhaust administrative remedies.

In district court Plaintiffs brought disparate-treatment, disparate-impact, and retaliation claims under Title VII, raising a hostile-work-environment theory as part of their disparate-treatment and disparate-impact claims; the district court granted summary judgment in favor of Defendants on all claims.

One might say that Plaintiffs have not been subjected to an unlawful employment practice because they are treated identically to non-Hispanics. They claim no discrimination with respect to their pay or benefits, their hours of work, or their job duties. And every employee, not just Hispanics, must abide by the English-only policy. But the Supreme Court has "repeatedly made clear that although Title VII mentions specific employment decisions with immediate consequences, the scope of the prohibition is not limited to economic or tangible discrimination, and that it covers more than terms and conditions in the narrow contractual sense." *Nat'l R.R. Passenger Corp. v. Morgan*, 536 U.S. 101, 115–16 (2002) (internal brackets, quotation marks, and citation omitted). The conditions of work encompass the workplace atmosphere as well as the more tangible elements of the job. Title VII does not tolerate, for example, a racist or sexist work environment "that is sufficiently severe or pervasive to alter the conditions of the victim's employment and create an abusive working environment[.]" *Harris v. Forklift Sys., Inc.*, 510 U.S. 17, 21, (1993) (internal quotation marks omitted). In their disparate-impact claim Plaintiffs allege that the City's English-only policy has created such an environment for Hispanic workers. Discrimination against Hispanics can be characterized as being based on either race or national origin.

To prevail on these claims, Plaintiffs need not show that the policy was created with discriminatory intent. In the leading case on the subject, *Griggs v. Duke Power Co.*, 401 U.S. 424, 431 (1971), the Supreme Court held that Title VII "proscribes not only overt discrimination but also practices that are fair in form, but discriminatory in operation." These kinds of claims, known as disparate-impact claims, "involve employment practices that are facially neutral in their treatment of different groups but that in fact fall more harshly on one group than another and cannot be justified by business necessity." *Int'l Bhd. of Teamsters v. United States*,

431 U.S. 324, 335–36 n. 15 (1977). To be sure, claims based on a hostile work environment commonly are disparate-treatment claims, which do require proof of discriminatory intent. Indeed, Plaintiffs here bring such a disparate-treatment claim as well as this discriminatory-impact claim. But there is no reason to prohibit discriminatory-impact claims predicated on a hostile work environment.

The allocation of the burdens of proof in disparate-impact cases is set forth in 42 U.S.C. § 2000e–2(k), enacted in 1991 after the Supreme Court's opinion in *Wards Cove Packing Co. v. Atonio*, 490 U.S. 642 (1989), imposed a heavier burden on plaintiffs. Under the statute a plaintiff first must "demonstrate[ ] that a respondent uses a particular employment practice that causes a disparate impact on the basis of race, color, religion, sex, or national origin." 42 U.S.C. § 2000e–2(k)(1)(A)(i). "This prima facie case, in many respects, is more rigorous than in a disparate treatment case because a plaintiff must not merely show circumstances raising an inference of discriminatory impact but must demonstrate the discriminatory impact at issue." *Bullington*, 186 F.3d at 1312. If the plaintiff establishes a prima facie case, the burden then shifts to the defendant to "demonstrate that the challenged practice is job related for the position in question and consistent with business necessity." 42 U.S.C. § 2000e–2(k)(1)(A)(I).

The district court, relying principally on *Garcia v. Spun Steak Co.*, 998 F.2d 1480 (9th Cir. 1993), concluded that Plaintiffs had "not shown that requiring them to use the English language in the workplace imposed significant, adverse effects on the terms, conditions or privileges of their employment, so as to create a prima facie case of disparate impact discrimination under Title VII." Even under *Spun Steak*, however, English-only policies are not always permissible; each case turns on its facts. Here, Plaintiffs have produced evidence that the English-only policy created a hostile atmosphere for Hispanics in their workplace. As previously set forth, all the Plaintiffs stated that they had experienced ethnic taunting as a result of the policy and that the policy made them feel like second-class citizens. Tommy Sanchez testified to instances of taunting by an Altus Police officer, Street Department employees, and other non-Hispanic employees of the City. As evidence that such harassment would be an expected consequence of the policy, Lloyd Lopez testified that Street Commissioner Willis told him that he was notifying him of the policy in private because of concern that other employees would tease Hispanic employees about the policy if they learned of it.

Some of this evidence, as the district court pointed out, has diluted persuasive power because of the absence of specifics — who made what comment when and where. In a typical hostile-work-environment case, we might conclude that the evidence of co-worker taunting did not reach the threshold necessary for a Title VII claim.

There are, however, other considerations with respect to a *policy* that allegedly creates a hostile work environment. The policy itself, and not just the effect of the policy in evoking hostility by co-workers, may create or contribute to the hostility of the work environment. A policy requiring each employee to wear a badge noting his or her religion, for example, might well engender extreme discomfort in a reasonable employee who belongs to a minority religion, even if no co-worker utters a word on the matter. Here, the very fact that the City would forbid Hispanics from using their preferred language could reasonably be construed as an expression of hostility to Hispanics. At least that could be a reasonable inference if there was no apparent legitimate purpose for the restrictions. It would be unreasonable to take offense at a requirement that all pilots flying into an airport speak English in communications with the tower or between planes; but hostility would be a reasonable inference to draw from a requirement that an employee calling home during a work break speak only in English. The less the apparent justification for mandating English, the more reasonable it is to infer hostility toward employees whose ethnic group or nationality favors another language. For example, Plaintiffs presented evidence that the English-only policy extended beyond its written terms to include lunch hours, breaks, and even private telephone conversations, if non-Spanish-speaking co-workers were nearby. Absent a legitimate reason for such a restriction, the inference of hostility may be reasonable.

Our task in this appeal is not to determine whether Plaintiffs have established that they were subjected to a hostile work environment. Rather, in reviewing the grant of summary judgment to Defendants, we are to decide only whether a rational juror could find on this record that the impact of the English-only policy on Hispanic workers was "sufficiently severe or persuasive to alter the conditions of [their] employment and create an abusive working environment." *Harris*, 510 U.S. at 21.

It is in this context that we consider the EEOC guideline on English-only workplace rules, 29 C.F.R. § 1606.7. Under the relevant provisions of the guideline: (1) an English-only rule that applies at all times is considered "a burdensome term and condition of employment," § 1606.7(a), presumptively constituting a Title VII violation; and (2) an English-only rule that applies only at certain times does not violate Title VII if the employer can justify the rule by showing business necessity, § 1606.7(b). The EEOC rationales for the guideline are: (1) English-only policies "may 'create an atmosphere of inferiority, isolation, and intimidation' that could make a 'discriminatory working environment,'" EEOC Br. at 13 (quoting § 1606.7(a)); (2) "English-only rules adversely impact employees with limited or no English skills . . . by denying them a privilege enjoyed by native English speakers: the opportunity to speak at work," *id.* at 14; (3) "English-only rules create barriers to employment for employees with limited or no English skills," *id.*; (4) "English-only rules prevent bilingual employees whose first language is not English from speaking in their most effective language," *id.* at 15; and (5) "the risk of discipline and termination for violating English-only rules falls disproportionately on bilingual employees as well as persons with limited English skills," *id.* at 16.

> The Court here gives far more deference to the EEOC's regulation than the prior court did in *Spun Steak*. Why is this the case?

EEOC guidelines, "while not controlling upon the courts by reason of their authority, do constitute a body of experience and informed judgment to which courts and litigants may properly resort for guidance." *Meritor Sav. Bank, F.S.B. v. Vinson*, 477 U.S. 57, 65 (1986) (internal quotation marks omitted). In *Spun Steak* the Ninth Circuit rejected the English-only guideline outright because, in its view, nothing in the plain text or the legislative history of Title VII supported the guideline's presumption of a disparate impact. *See* 998 F.2d at 1489–90. But we need not resolve the validity of that presumption. For our purposes, it is enough that the EEOC, based on its expertise and experience, has consistently concluded that an English-only policy, at least when no business need for the policy is shown, is likely in itself to "create an atmosphere of inferiority, isolation, and intimidation" that constitutes a "discriminatory working environment." § 1606.7(a). (We recognize that several of the EEOC's other grounds for its guidelines do not apply here. For example, there is no evidence that the policy prevented any of the Plaintiffs from speaking at work, because all are bilingual.) We believe that these conclusions are entitled to respect, not as interpretations of the governing law, but as an indication of what a reasonable, informed person may think about the impact of an English-only work rule on minority employees, even if we might not draw the same inference. Assuming the reasonableness of the EEOC on the matter, we cannot say that on the record before us it would be unreasonable for a juror to agree that the City's English-only policy created a hostile work environment for its Hispanic employees. We are not suggesting that the guideline is evidence admissible at trial or should be incorporated in a jury instruction. What we are saying is only that a juror presented with the evidence presently on the record in this case would not be unreasonable in finding that a hostile work environment existed.

As an alternative ground for granting summary judgment on the disparate-impact claim, the district court held that Defendants "offered sufficient proof of business justification." It found "that city officials had received complaints that some employees could not understand what was being said on the City's radio frequency because other employees were speaking Spanish . . . [and] that city officials received complaints from non-Spanish speaking employees who felt uncomfortable when their co-workers spoke Spanish in front of them." Based on these justifications, it concluded that "Defendants have met any burden they may have to demonstrate that the City's English-only policy was supported by an adequate business justification."

We disagree. One of Congress's stated purposes in passing the 1991 amendments to the Civil Rights Act was "to codify the concepts of 'business necessity' and 'job related' enunciated by the Supreme Court in *Griggs v. Duke Power Co.*, 401 U.S. 424 (1971), and in the other Supreme Court decisions prior to *Wards Cove Packing Co. v. Atonio*, 490 U.S. 642 (1989)." Civil Rights Act of 1991, Pub. L. No. 102–166, Sec. 3, 105 Stat. 1071 (1991). In *Griggs* the Supreme Court held that "Congress has placed on the employer the burden of showing that any given requirement must have a manifest relationship to the employment in question." 401 U.S. at 432. The Court stressed that "[t]he touchstone is business necessity. If an employment practice which operates to [discriminate against a protected minority] cannot be shown to be related to job performance, the practice is prohibited." *Id.* at 431.

Defendants' evidence of business necessity in this case is scant. As observed by the district court, "[T]here was no written record of any communication problems, morale problems or safety problems resulting from the use of languages other than English prior to implementation of the policy." And there was little undocumented evidence. Defendants cited only one example of an employee's complaining about the use of Spanish prior to implementation of the policy. Mr. Willis admitted that he had no knowledge of City business being disrupted or delayed because Spanish was used on the radio. In addition, "city officials who were deposed could give no specific examples of safety problems resulting from the use of languages other than English. . . ." Moreover, Plaintiffs produced evidence that the policy encompassed lunch hours, breaks, and private phone conversations; and Defendants conceded that there would be no business reason for such a restriction.

On this record we are not able to affirm summary judgment based on a business necessity for the English-only policy. A reasonable person could find from this evidence that Defendants had failed to establish a business necessity for the English-only rule.

Plaintiffs [further] allege that the City engaged in intentional discrimination. As previously noted, Title VII bars discrimination in employment on the basis of race or national origin. The same analytical framework is applicable to all Plaintiffs' theories of intentional discrimination. "[I]n [disparate-treatment] discrimination suits, the elements of a plaintiff's case are the same . . . whether that case is brought under §§ 1981 or 1983 or Title VII." To prevail under a disparate-treatment theory, "a plaintiff must show, through either direct or indirect evidence, that the discrimination complained of was intentional."

Plaintiffs contend that they were intentionally discriminated against by the creation of a hostile work environment. We have already held that there is sufficient evidence to support a finding of a hostile work environment. The issue remaining, therefore, is whether those who established the English-only policy did so with the intent to create a hostile work environment.

To begin with, the disparate impact of the English-only rule (creation of a hostile work environment) is in itself evidence of intent. As the Supreme Court stated in *International Brotherhood of Teamsters*, 431 U.S. at 335, in a disparate-treatment case, "Proof of discriminatory motive . . . can in some situations be inferred from the mere fact of differences in treatment."

Here, Plaintiffs can rely on more than just that inference. First, there is evidence that management realized that the English-only policy would likely lead to taunting of Hispanic employees: Street Commissioner Willis allegedly told two Hispanic employees about the policy in private because of concern that non-Hispanic employees would tease them if they learned of it. Also, a jury could find that there were no substantial work-related reasons for the policy (particularly if it believed Plaintiffs' evidence that the policy extended to nonwork periods), suggesting that the true reason was illegitimate. Further, the policy was adopted without prior consultation with Hispanic employees, or even prior disclosure to a consultant to the City who was conducting an investigation of alleged anti-Hispanic discrimination during the period when the English-only policy was under consideration. Finally, there is evidence that during a news interview the Mayor referred to the Spanish language as "garbage."

In our view, the record contains sufficient evidence of intent to create a hostile environment that the summary judgment on those claims must be set aside.

■ NOTES AND QUESTIONS

1. How would you evaluate the appropriateness of the English-only policy as implemented by the City? The policy states that it "does not apply to strictly private communications between co-workers while they are on approved lunch hours or breaks or before or after work hours while the employees are still on City property." Would this limitation on the policy make it more likely that § 1606.7(a) or (b) would apply to this case? Why?

2. Isn't it a fair concern for a city to want to maintain a uniform language of communication over the airwaves? How is such a policy discriminatory? Is safety a legitimate rationale for the policy here?

3. Was the policy being used by employees as a way to intimidate and/or humiliate other workers?

4. Does this case seem more like a disparate impact or disparate treatment case, or is it both? Was the policy implemented neutral? How powerful is the evidence that the Mayor called the Spanish language "garbage"?

5. The Tenth Circuit gives the EEOC's English-only regulation far more deference than the Fifth Circuit. Which court's analysis is correct? Is the regulation properly viewed as "an indication of what a reasonable, informed person may think about the impact of an English-only work rule on minority employees"? *City of Altus*, 433 F.3d at 1306.

6. The policy in *City of Altus* appears much more thorough and thought-out than the policy at issue in *Spun Steak*. Additionally, the *Altus* policy seems to be better justified — the importance of having a uniform language spoken over public airwaves seems greater than the need for line workers to refrain from speaking Spanish. Despite these facts, the Court in *Altus* questioned the policy while the court in *Spun Steak* upheld the policy. What accounts for the difference in the decisions of these courts?

7. How did the Tenth Circuit in this case distinguish *Spun Steak*, if at all?

Class Exercise: English-Only Policies

Breaking up into small groups, assume that you represent an employer in southern Texas that operates one of the nation's largest construction companies. Because of the nature of the work, this employer would like to adopt an English-only rule to be used where construction is taking place. The employer is concerned that in the event of an emergency — or when important instructions are given — the use of any foreign language would enhance the potential for danger. What advice would you give this employer? How would you draft such a policy? What other information would you need to gather?

21: Implementing English-Only Rules in the Workplace

As *City of Altus* and *Spun Steak* clearly demonstrate, the use of English-only policies in the workplace is highly controversial. Employers should thus proceed with extreme caution when attempting to implement such a policy. A few practical considerations should be highlighted with respect to these policies.

First, employers should ask whether the policy is absolutely necessary. An English-only policy has the potential to result in expensive and time-consuming litigation for employers. Does the benefit of adopting the policy outweigh the risk of a lawsuit?

Second, where an employer decides to proceed with an English-only policy, has it clearly documented its rationale for doing so? As we saw in *City of Altus*, a case can turn on the defendant's articulation of business necessity for the policy. What is the relevant business issue for the employer? Workplace safety? Increased harmony among workers?

Third, employers should ask whether the policy as implemented and enforced is the least restrictive possible. It should be no more burdensome to workers than necessary. Thus, if there are certain times, days, or locations where the policy can be lifted, employers should make every effort to do so. A more narrow, targeted policy is much more likely to be upheld by the courts (and not challenged in the first instance by employees or the government).

Fourth, as demonstrated by 29 C.F.R. § 1606.7(c), employers must make certain to notify all workers of the policy. Employers should document when notification occurs, and if possible, retain some form of written acknowledgment from employees. As a matter of best practices, employers should also clearly inform workers of the exact parameters of the policy, and articulate why the policy is being adopted by the company.

Finally, as we saw in both *Spun Steak* and *City of Altus*, workers can use the policies as a basis to harass or make fun of employees whose primary language is something other than English. Employers should make certain that no management employees are taking part in this type of activity, and also discipline other workers that use the policy as a basis to harass certain individuals. As will be discussed later in this text, even if management does not specifically endorse this type of harassing conduct, the company can still be held liable where it knows (or should have known) about it and fails to act.

The bottom-line take away from these cases is that the courts have taken differing views on the validity of English-only rules. This type of uncertainty can create difficulties for employers trying to adopt an English-only policy. Employers should ensure that a policy is necessary for their workplace before proceeding. And where a company does adopt such a policy, it should carefully craft the policy to make sure that it complies with the law of the jurisdiction.

D. Accent Discrimination

Accent is closely tied to national origin, and discrimination against someone based on his accent can thus constitute national origin discrimination. Employers should thus be cautious when taking an adverse action against a worker (or prospective worker) on this basis. The EEOC has provided guidance on the issue of accent discrimination, noting that

> [b]ecause linguistic characteristics are a component of national origin, employers should carefully scrutinize employment decisions that are based on accent to ensure that they do not violate Title VII.
>
> An employment decision based on foreign accent does not violate Title VII if an individual's accent materially interferes with the ability to perform job duties. This assessment depends upon the specific duties of the position in question and the extent to which the individual's accent affects his or her ability to perform job duties. Employers should distinguish between a merely discernible foreign accent and one that interferes with communication skills necessary to perform job duties. Generally, an employer may only base an employment decision on accent if effective oral communication in English is required to perform job duties and the individual's foreign accent materially interferes with his or her ability to communicate orally in English. Positions for which effective oral communication in English may be required include teaching, customer service, and telemarketing. Even for these positions, an employer must still determine whether the particular individual's accent interferes with the ability to perform job duties.

EEOC Compl. Man. (CCH) ¶ 8530 § 13-V(A) (Dec. 2, 2002).

The federal regulations are equally clear that discrimination on the basis of accent may also be national origin discrimination. As 29 C.F.R. § 1606.1 provides, "national origin discrimination includ[es], but [is] not limited to, the denial of equal employment opportunity . . . because an individual has the . . . linguistic characteristics of a national origin group." Not all accent discrimination runs afoul of Title VII, however, and as the EEOC's guidance above notes, it is acceptable for an employer to use accent as a basis to deny employment in certain jobs that require "effective oral communication in English." The courts have unquestionably taken different positions on when it may be appropriate to deny an individual employment on the basis of accent.

Fragante v. City & County of Honolulu

888 F.2d 591 (9th Cir. 1989)

TROTT, Circuit Judge:

In April 1981, at the age of sixty, [Manuel] Fragante emigrated from the Philippines to Hawaii. In response to a newspaper ad, he applied in November of 1981 for the job at issue in this appeal — an entry level Civil Service Clerk SR-8 job for the City of Honolulu's Division of Motor Vehicles and Licensing. The SR-8 clerk position involved such tasks as filing, processing mail, cashiering, orally providing routine information to the "sometimes contentious" public over the telephone and at an information counter, and obtaining supplies. Fragante scored the highest of 721 test takers on the written SR-8 Civil Service Examination which tested, among other things, word usage, grammar and spelling. Accordingly, he was ranked first on a certified list of eligibles for two SR-8 clerk positions, an achievement of which he is understandably quite proud.

Fragante then was interviewed in the normal course of the selection process — as were other applicants — by George Kuwahara, the assistant licensing administrator, and Kalani McCandless, the division secretary. Both Kuwahara and McCandless were personally familiar with the demands of the position at issue, and both had extensive experience interviewing applicants to the division. During the interview, Kuwahara stressed that the position involved constant public contact and that the ability to speak clearly was one of the most important skills required for the position.

Both Kuwahara and McCandless had difficulty understanding Fragante due to his pronounced Filipino accent, and they determined on the basis of the oral interview that he would be difficult to understand both at the information counter and over the telephone. Accordingly, both interviewers gave Fragante a negative recommendation. They noted he had a very pronounced accent and was difficult to understand. It was their judgment that this would interfere with his performance of certain aspects of the job. As a consequence, Mr. Fragante dropped from number one to number three on the list of eligibles for the position.

> The plaintiff's heavy accent substantially hurt his chances of receiving the position, despite his exceptional performance on the written examination.

Under the city's civil service rules, the Department of Motor Vehicles and Licensing, as the appointing authority, is allowed discretion in selecting applicants for the clerk vacancies. City Civil Service Rule 4.2(d) allows the defendants to select any of the top five eligibles without regard to their rank order. The essence of this rule was clearly stated in the employment announcement posted for the SR-8 position:

> The names of the "top five" qualified applicants with the highest examination grades will be referred to the employing agency in the order of their examination grade and availability for employment according to Civil Service Rules. The employing agency may select any one of the eligibles referred. Those not selected will remain on the list for at least one year for future referrals.

In accord with this process, the two other applicants who were judged more qualified than Fragante and who therefore placed higher than he on the final list got the two available jobs, and he was so notified by mail. After exhausting administrative remedies, Fragante filed a claim under Title VII of the Civil Rights Act against the City and County of Honolulu, alleging he was discriminated against because of his accent. The district court relied on the results of the oral interview and found that Fragante's oral skills were "hampered by his accent or manner of speaking." The court found no evidence of unlawful discrimination in violation of Title VII, concluding that Fragante lacked the "bona fide occupational requirement" of being able to communicate effectively with the public, and dismissed his claim.

Defendants first argue Fragante failed to meet his burden of proving a prima facie case [of intentional discrimination] because he failed to show he was actually qualified for the SR-8 clerk position, a position which requires the applicant to be able to communicate clearly and effectively. Fragante, on the other hand, contends he was qualified for the position. As proof he points to his exceptional score on the objective written examination, and he argues that his speech, though heavily accented, was deemed comprehensible by two expert witnesses at trial. Fragante's position is supported by the approach taken by the Equal Employment Opportunity Commission which submits that a plaintiff who proves he has been discriminated against solely because of his accent does establish a prima facie case of national origin discrimination. This contention is further supported by EEOC guidelines which define discrimination to include "the denial of equal employment opportunity . . . because an individual has the . . . linguistic characteristics of a national origin group." 29 C.F.R. § 1606.1 (1988). Furthermore, Fragante was never advised that he was not qualified for the job: he was only told that he was less-qualified than his competition.

Because we find that Fragante did not carry the ultimate burden of proving national origin discrimination, however, the issue of whether Fragante established a prima facie case of discrimination is not significant, and we assume without deciding that he did.

Preliminarily, we do well to remember that this country was founded and has been built in large measure by people from other lands, many of whom came here — especially after our early beginnings — with a limited knowledge of English. This flow of immigrants has continued and has been encouraged over the years. From its inception, the United States of America has been a dream to many around the world. We hold out promises of freedom, equality, and economic opportunity to many who only know these words as concepts. It would be more than ironic if we followed up our invitation to people such as Manuel Fragante with a closed economic door based on national origin discrimination. It is no surprise that Title VII speaks to this issue and clearly articulates the policy of our nation: unlawful discrimination based on national origin shall not be permitted to exist in the workplace. But, it is also true that there is another important aspect of Title VII: the "preservation of an employer's remaining freedom of choice." *Price Waterhouse v. Ann B. Hopkins*, 490 U.S. 228 (1989).

We turn our discussion to whether defendants articulated a legitimate, nondiscriminatory reason for Fragante's nonselection. We find that they did, but to this finding we add a note of caution to the trial courts. Accent and national origin are obviously inextricably intertwined in many cases. It would therefore be an easy refuge in this context for an employer unlawfully discriminating against someone based on national origin to state falsely that it was not the person's national origin that caused the employment or promotion problem, but the candidate's inability to measure up to the communications skills demanded by the job. We encourage a very searching look by the district courts at such a claim.

An adverse employment decision may be predicated upon an individual's accent when — but only when — it interferes materially with job performance. There is nothing improper about an employer making an honest assessment of the oral communications skills of a candidate for a job when such skills are reasonably related to job performance.

The defendants advertised for applicants to fill SR-8 vacancies. The initial job announcement listed the ability to "deal tactfully and effectively with the public" as one of the areas to be tested. There is no doubt from the record that the oral ability to communicate effectively in English is reasonably related to the normal operation of the clerk's office. A clerk must be able to respond to the public's questions in a manner which the public can understand. In this regard, the district court in its Findings of Fact and Conclusions of Law and Order made the following significant observations:

> The job is a difficult one because it involves dealing with a great number of disgruntled members of the public. The clerk must deal with 200-300 people a day, many of whom are angry or complaining and who do not want to hear what the clerk may have to explain concerning their applications or an answer to their questions. It is a high turnover position where people leave quickly because of the high stress involving daily contact with contentious people.

What must next be determined is whether defendants established a factual basis for believing that Fragante would be hampered in performing this requirement. Defendants submit that because his accent made Fragante difficult to understand as determined by the interview, he would be less able to perform the job than other applicants. Fragante, on the other hand, contends he is able to communicate effectively in English as established by two expert witnesses at trial and by his responses in open court. In essence, he argues his non-selection was effectively based upon national origin discrimination.

After the interview, Kuwahara and McCandless scored Fragante on a rating sheet that was used for all applicants. Applicants were scored in the categories of appearance, speech, self-confidence, emotional control, alertness, initiative, personality, attitude, work experience, and overall fitness for the job. A scale of 1-10 was used. Kuwahara gave Fragante a score of 3 for speech, and noted: "very pronounced accent, difficult to understand." Although McCandless did not enter a score in the speech category, she noted: "Heavy Filipino accent. Would be difficult to understand over the telephone."

> In evaluating the plaintiff, the employer openly acknowledged that it believed his heavy accent would be problematic for the position.

After the interviews were scored, Kuwahara and McCandless reviewed the scores, discussed the applicants, and decided on their hiring recommendation to finance director Peter Leong. In making the recommendation, written examination scores were given no consideration. Kuwahara prepared the written recommendation to Leong, dated April 13, 1982, recommending two others for selection. Fragante in his position as Number 3 on the final list was described as follows:

> 3. Manuel Fragante — Retired Phillippine (sic) army officer. Speaks with very pronounced accent which is difficult to understand. He has 37 years of experience in management administration and appears more qualified for professional rather than clerical work. However, because of his accent, I would not recommend him for this position.

McCandless then notified Fragante that he was not selected for either of the clerk position vacancies. Pursuant to a request from Fragante, Kuwahara then reduced the matter to writing. In a letter, dated June 28, 1982, the reasons why he was not selected were articulated as follows:

> As to the reason for your non-selection, we felt the two selected applicants were both superior in their verbal communication ability. As we indicated in your interview, our clerks are constantly dealing with the public and the ability to speak clearly is one of the most important skills required for the position. Therefore, while we were impressed with your educational and employment history, we felt the applicants selected would be better able to work in our office because of their communication skills.

Thus, the interviewers' record discloses Fragante's third place ranking was based on his "pronounced accent which is difficult to understand." Indeed, Fragante can point to no facts which indicate that his ranking was based on factors other than his inability to communicate effectively with the public. This view was shared by the district court.

Although the district court determined that the interview lacked some formality as to standards, instructions, guidelines, or criteria for its conduct and that the rating sheet was inadequate, the court also found that these "insufficiencies" were irrelevant with respect to plaintiff's complaint of unlawful discrimination. A review of the record reveals nothing that would impeach this assessment. Kuwahara and McCandless recorded their evaluation of Fragante's problem in separate written remarks on their rating sheets. As such, a legitimate factual basis for this conclusion that Fragante would be less able than his competition to perform the required duties was established.

Fragante argues the district court erred in considering "listener prejudice" as a legitimate, nondiscriminatory reason for failure to hire. We find, however, that the district court did not determine defendants refused to hire Fragante on the basis that some listeners would "turn off" a Filipino accent. The district court after trial noted that: "Fragante, in fact, has a difficult manner of pronunciation and the Court further finds as a fact from his general testimony that he would often not respond directly to the questions as propounded. He maintains much of his military bearing." We regard the last sentence of the court's comment to be little more than a stray remark of no moment.

We do not find the court's conclusion clearly erroneous. We find support for our view in *Fernandez v. Wynn Oil*, 653 F.2d 1273, 1275 (9th Cir. 1981), where this court held inability to communicate effectively to be one valid ground for finding a job applicant not qualified.

Having established that defendants articulated a legitimate reason for Fragante's non-selection, our next inquiry is whether the reason was a mere pretext for discrimination. Fragante essentially argues that defendant's selection and evaluation procedures were so deficient as to render the proffered reason for non-selection nothing more than a pretext for national origin discrimination. The problem with this argument, however, is that on examination it is only a charge without substance. The process may not have been perfect, but it reveals no discriminatory motive or intent. Search as we have, we have not been able to find even a hint of a mixed motive such as existed in *Price Waterhouse*. Instead, it appears that defendants were motivated exclusively by reasonable business necessity.

Fragante's counsel attempts to cast this case as one in which his client was denied a job simply because he had a difficult accent. This materially alters what actually happened. Fragante failed to get the job because two competitors had superior qualifications with respect to a relevant task performed by a government clerk. Insofar as this implicates "the interest of the State, as an employer, in promoting the efficiency of the public services it performs through its employees . . . ," *Pickering v. Board of Education*, 391 U.S. 563 (1968), it is not something we are permitted to ignore. Title VII does not stand for the proposition that a person in a protected class — or a person with a foreign accent — shall enjoy a position of advantage thereby when competing for a job against others not similarly protected. And, the record does not show that the jobs went to persons less qualified than Fragante: to the contrary.

In sum, the record conclusively shows that Fragante was passed over because of the deleterious *effect* of his Filipino accent on his ability to communicate orally, not merely because he had such an accent.

■ NOTES AND QUESTIONS

1. On the written examination for the position, Fragante scored the highest out of over 700 total applicants. Given how qualified he was for the job, is it fair to deny Fragante the position because he has a heavy accent?

2. Given this particular job as a clerk, would Fragante's heavy accent truly impair his performance? Would there be a way to modify the job duties so that accent was no longer a problem?

3. It is important to note that whether a foreign accent materially interferes with an individual's ability to perform a job is often a heavily subjective inquiry. It is thus not surprising that the courts have reached different opinions on the question of when accent may be used to deny employment. *See, e.g.*, Hasham v. Cal. State Bd. of Equalization, 200 F.3d 1035 (7th Cir. 2000); *In re* Rodriguez v. FedEx Freight E., Inc., 487 F.3d 1001 (6th Cir. 2007).

4. The court in *Fragante* went out of its way to note that "this country was founded and has been built in large measure by people from other lands, many of whom came here — especially after our early beginnings — with a limited knowledge of English." Is the court largely disregarding this important fact? *See* Mari J. Matsuda, *Voices of America: Accent, Antidiscrimination Law, and a Jurisprudence for the Last Reconstruction*, 100 YALE L.J. 1329 (1991).

5. If someone were denied a job because of a heavy New York accent or a heavy Southern accent, could that individual allege discrimination under Title VII? *See* Curtsinger v. Gober, No. APL 01A05360, 2001 WL 45655, at *2 (EEOC Jan. 12, 2001) (finding that a claim of national origin discrimination cannot be based on the fact that the complainant comes from a certain region of the United States, such as the South, and thus has a Southern accent).

6. One interesting example of this area of the law in practice involves the education system. An Arizona elementary school teacher filed a complaint with the EEOC after being informed that she would not be allowed to teach students who were learning English because of her accent. The teacher, who was an immigrant from northern Mexico, argued that she had the same credentials as all the other teachers and that it was unfair that she was being singled out solely because of her accent. The State Department of Education countered her argument by claiming that teaching with accents leads to a pattern of misuses of the language or mispronunciation of the language that was being taught. The federal investigation into possible civil rights violations prompted Arizona to alter its policy regarding teachers with accents. *See* Marc Lacey, *In Arizona, Complaints That an Accent Can Hinder a Teacher's Career*, N.Y. TIMES, Sept. 25, 2011, at A18.

 Interactive Problem

Looking back at the interactive problem, assume that, after being terminated, Osama Hussein applied for a job as a "global airline pilot" at another air carrier. In considering his application, the prospective airline ultimately rejected it as Hussein had a heavy foreign accent that might interfere with in-flight communications when dealing with ground crew in other countries. Could this rejection constitute national origin discrimination?

Class Exercise: Telemarketer Discrimination

Breaking up into small groups, consider the following factual scenario: An employer is seeking to hire several telemarketers to sell computer supplies to the general public. Because communication is critical to this job, the employer does not want to hire anyone with a heavy foreign accent.

With your classmates, try to develop the various factors the employer might use to screen applicants. Are these factors lawful? What factors might the employer consider that would help assure that its selection complies with Title VII?

E. Undocumented Worker Status

One factor that is often tied to the question of national origin discrimination is the issue of undocumented worker status. If an employee from another country is working in the United States illegally, can that worker still avail herself of the civil rights laws? Are employers bound by the same standards as they would be with legally employed workers?

The Supreme Court has never addressed this question under Title VII. As discussed earlier in this text, the Immigration Reform and Control Act (IRCA) addresses some of the same issues of national origin and citizenship discrimination. The Supreme Court has provided some guidance under IRCA and the National Labor Relations Act on the question of the applicability of these laws to those workers in the country illegally.

Hoffman Plastic Compounds, Inc. v. NLRB
535 U.S. 137 (2002)

Chief Justice REHNQUIST delivered the opinion of the Court.

The National Labor Relations Board (Board) awarded backpay to an undocumented alien who has never been legally authorized to work in the United States. We hold that such relief is foreclosed by federal immigration policy, as expressed by Congress in the Immigration Reform and Control Act of 1986 (IRCA).

Petitioner Hoffman Plastic Compounds, Inc. (petitioner or Hoffman), custom-formulates chemical compounds for businesses that manufacture pharmaceutical, construction, and household products. In May 1988, petitioner hired Jose Castro to operate various blending machines that "mix and cook" the particular formulas per customer order. Before being hired for this position, Castro presented documents that appeared to verify his authorization to work in the United States. In December 1988, the United Rubber, Cork, Linoleum, and Plastic Workers of America, AFL-CIO, began a union-organizing campaign at petitioner's production plant. Castro and several other employees supported the organizing campaign and distributed authorization cards to co-workers. In January 1989, Hoffman laid off Castro and other employees engaged in these organizing activities.

Three years later, in January 1992, respondent Board found that Hoffman unlawfully selected four employees, including Castro, for layoff "in order to rid itself of known union supporters" in violation of § 8(a)(3) of the National Labor Relations Act (NLRA). To remedy this violation, the Board ordered that Hoffman (1) cease and desist from further violations of the NLRA, (2) post a detailed notice to its employees regarding the remedial order, and (3) offer reinstatement and backpay to the four affected employees. Hoffman entered into a stipulation with the Board's General Counsel and agreed to abide by the Board's order.

In June 1993, the parties proceeded to a compliance hearing before an Administrative Law Judge (ALJ) to determine the amount of backpay owed to each discriminatee. On the final day of the hearing, Castro testified that he was born in Mexico and that he had never been legally admitted to, or authorized to work in, the United States. He admitted gaining employment with Hoffman only after tendering a birth certificate belonging to a friend who was born in Texas. He also admitted that he used this birth certificate to fraudulently obtain a California driver's license and a Social Security card, and to fraudulently obtain employment following his layoff by Hoffman. Neither Castro nor the Board's General Counsel offered any evidence that Castro had applied or intended to apply for legal authorization to work in the United States. Based on this testimony, the ALJ found the Board precluded from awarding Castro backpay or reinstatement as such relief would be contrary to *Sure-Tan, Inc. v. NLRB,* 467 U.S. 883 (1984), and in conflict with IRCA, which makes it unlawful for employers knowingly to hire undocumented workers or for employees to use fraudulent documents to establish employment eligibility.

In September 1998, four years after the ALJ's decision, and nine years after Castro was fired, the Board reversed with respect to backpay. Citing its earlier decision in *A.P.R.A. Fuel Oil Buyers Group, Inc.,* 320 N.L.R.B. 408 (1995), the Board determined that "the most effective way to accommodate and further the immigration policies embodied in [IRCA] is to provide the protections and remedies of the [NLRA] to undocumented workers in the same manner as to other employees." The Board thus found that Castro was entitled to $66,951 of backpay, plus interest. It calculated this backpay award from the date of Castro's termination to the date Hoffman first learned of Castro's undocumented status, a period of 4 1/2 years. A dissenting Board member would have affirmed the ALJ and denied Castro all backpay.

Hoffman filed a petition for review of the Board's order in the Court of Appeals. A panel of the Court of Appeals denied the petition for review. After rehearing the case en banc, the court again denied the petition for review and enforced the Board's order. We granted certiorari, and now reverse.

This case exemplifies the principle that the Board's discretion to select and fashion remedies for violations of the NLRA, though generally broad, is not unlimited. Since the Board's inception, we have consistently set aside awards of reinstatement or backpay to employees found guilty of serious illegal conduct in connection with their employment.

The parties and the lower courts focus much of their attention on *Sure-Tan,* particularly its express limitation of backpay to aliens "lawfully entitled to be present and employed in the United States." 467 U.S. at 903. All agree that as a matter of plain language, this limitation forecloses the award of backpay to Castro. Castro was never lawfully entitled to be present or employed in the United States, and thus, under the plain language of *Sure-Tan,* he has no right to claim backpay. The Board takes the view, however, that read in context, this limitation applies only to aliens who left the United States and thus cannot claim backpay without lawful reentry. The Court of Appeals agreed with this view. Another Court of Appeals, however, agrees with Hoffman, and concludes that *Sure-Tan* simply meant what it said, i.e., that any alien who is "not lawfully entitled to be present and employed in the United States" cannot claim backpay. We need not resolve this controversy. For whether isolated sentences from *Sure-Tan* definitively control, or count merely as persuasive dicta in support of petitioner, we think the question presented here better analyzed through a wider lens, focused as it must be on a legal landscape now significantly changed.

[Our] line of cases [has] established that where the Board's chosen remedy trenches upon a federal statute or policy outside the Board's competence to administer, the Board's remedy may be required to yield. Whether or not this was the situation at the time of

> The ultimate question that the Court addresses here is the extent to which an individual not legally present in this country can still avail himself of federal law.

Sure-Tan, it is precisely the situation today. In 1986, two years after *Sure-Tan*, Congress enacted IRCA, a comprehensive scheme prohibiting the employment of illegal aliens in the United States. § 101(a)(1), 100 Stat. 3360, 8 U.S.C. § 1324a. As we have previously noted, IRCA "forcefully" made combating the employment of illegal aliens central to "[t]he policy of immigration law." *INS v. National Center for Immigrants' Rights, Inc.*, 502 U.S. 183, 194, and n. 8 (1991). It did so by establishing an extensive "employment verification system," § 1324a(a)(1), designed to deny employment to aliens who (a) are not lawfully present in the United States, or (b) are not lawfully authorized to work in the United States, § 1324a(h)(3). This verification system is critical to the IRCA regime. To enforce it, IRCA mandates that employers verify the identity and eligibility of all new hires by examining specified documents before they begin work. § 1324a(b). If an alien applicant is unable to present the required documentation, the unauthorized alien cannot be hired.

Similarly, if an employer unknowingly hires an unauthorized alien, or if the alien becomes unauthorized while employed, the employer is compelled to discharge the worker upon discovery of the worker's undocumented status. § 1324a(a)(2). Employers who violate IRCA are punished by civil fines, § 1324a(e)(4)(A), and may be subject to criminal prosecution, § 1324a(f)(1). IRCA also makes it a crime for an unauthorized alien to subvert the employer verification system by tendering fraudulent documents. § 1324c(a). It thus prohibits aliens from using or attempting to use "any forged, counterfeit, altered, or falsely made document" or "any document lawfully issued to or with respect to a person other than the possessor" for purposes of obtaining employment in the United States. §§ 1324c(a)(1)–(3). Aliens who use or attempt to use such documents are subject to fines and criminal prosecution. 18 U.S.C. § 1546(b). There is no dispute that Castro's use of false documents to obtain employment with Hoffman violated these provisions.

Under the IRCA regime, it is impossible for an undocumented alien to obtain employment in the United States without some party directly contravening explicit congressional policies. Either the undocumented alien tenders fraudulent identification, which subverts the cornerstone of IRCA's enforcement mechanism, or the employer knowingly hires the undocumented alien in direct contradiction of its IRCA obligations. The Board asks that we overlook this fact and allow it to award backpay to an illegal alien for years of work not performed, for wages that could not lawfully have been earned, and for a job obtained in the first instance by a criminal fraud. We find, however, that awarding backpay to illegal aliens runs counter to policies underlying IRCA, policies the Board has no authority to enforce or administer. Therefore, as we have consistently held in like circumstances, the award lies beyond the bounds of the Board's remedial discretion.

The Board contends that awarding limited backpay to Castro "reasonably accommodates" IRCA, because, in the Board's view, such an award is not "inconsistent" with IRCA. The Board argues that because the backpay period was closed as of the date Hoffman learned of Castro's illegal status, Hoffman could have employed Castro during the backpay period without violating IRCA. The Board further argues that while IRCA criminalized the misuse of documents, "it did not make violators ineligible for back pay awards or other compensation flowing from employment secured by the misuse of such documents." This latter statement, of course, proves little[.] What matters here, and what sinks both of the Board's claims, is that Congress has expressly made it criminally punishable for an alien to obtain employment with false documents. There is no reason to think that Congress nonetheless intended to permit backpay where but for an employer's unfair labor practices, an alien-employee would have remained in the United States illegally, and continued to work illegally, all the while successfully evading apprehension by immigration authorities. Far from "accommodating" IRCA, the Board's position, recognizing employer misconduct but discounting the misconduct of illegal alien employees, subverts it.

Indeed, awarding backpay in a case like this not only trivializes the immigration laws, it also condones and encourages future violations. The Board admits that had the INS detained Castro, or had Castro obeyed the law and departed to Mexico, Castro would have lost his right to backpay. Castro thus qualifies for the Board's award only by remaining inside the United States illegally. Similarly, Castro cannot mitigate damages, a duty our cases require without triggering new IRCA violations, either by tendering false documents to employers or by finding employers willing to ignore IRCA and hire illegal workers. The Board here has failed to even consider this tension.

We therefore conclude that allowing the Board to award backpay to illegal aliens would unduly trench upon explicit statutory prohibitions critical to federal immigration policy, as expressed in IRCA. It would encourage the successful evasion of apprehension by immigration authorities, condone prior violations of the immigration laws, and encourage future violations. However broad the Board's discretion to fashion remedies when dealing only with the NLRA, it is not so unbounded as to authorize this sort of an award.

Lack of authority to award backpay does not mean that the employer gets off scot-free. The Board here has already imposed other significant sanctions against Hoffman — sanctions Hoffman does not challenge. These include orders that Hoffman cease and desist its violations of the NLRA, and that it conspicuously post a notice to employees setting forth their rights under the NLRA and detailing its prior unfair practices. Hoffman will be subject to contempt proceedings should it fail to comply with these orders. We have deemed such "traditional remedies" sufficient to effectuate national labor policy regardless of whether the "spur and catalyst" of backpay accompanies them.

■ NOTES AND QUESTIONS

1. The Court holds that "allowing the Board to award backpay to illegal aliens would unduly trench upon explicit statutory prohibitions critical to federal immigration policy." *Hoffman Plastic*, 535 U.S. at 151. Do you agree with this conclusion?

2. Does *Hoffman Plastic* make it easier for employers to discriminate against workers? Does it encourage them to employ illegal aliens?

3. *Hoffman Plastic* arises in the context of the NLRA. Would it apply to Title VII and other employment discrimination statutes? There are several different views as to whether *Hoffman Plastic* applies in these other contexts, and the issue has yet to be resolved. Ultimately, the Supreme Court may have to revisit the question in the Title VII context. *See* Christopher Ho & Jennifer C. Chang, *Drawing the Line After* Hoffman Plastic Compounds, Inc. v. NLRB: *Strategies for Protecting Undocumented Workers in the Title VII Context and Beyond*, 22 Hofstra Lab. & Emp. L.J. 473, 476 (2005) (arguing that the *Hoffman* analysis cannot "be generically extended to other statutes," including Title VII); Crespo v. Evergo Corp., 841 A.2d 471, 475 (N.J. App. Div. 2004) (discussing how *Hoffman* "has not been expanded beyond its specific focus").

4. *Hoffman Plastic* holds that the NLRB cannot award backpay to illegal workers under the NLRA. As already noted, the issue of whether *Hoffman Plastic* applies to Title VII is still unresolved. Following this decision, the EEOC issued the following statement:

> In light of the Supreme Court's decision in Hoffman Plastic Compounds, Inc. v. National Labor Relations Board, [535 U.S. 137] (2002), the Commission is reexamining its position on remedies for undocumented workers . . . .
>
> The Court's holding [in *Hoffman Plastic*] bars an award of backpay under the NLRA to an undocumented worker for any period following the termination of his or her employment. Because the Commission's [previous] Guidance relied on NLRA cases to conclude that undocumented workers are entitled to all forms of monetary relief — including post-discharge backpay — under the federal employment discrimination statutes, the Commission has decided to rescind that Guidance. The Commission will evaluate the effect *Hoffman* may have on the availability of monetary remedies to undocumented workers under the federal employment discrimination statutes.
>
> The Supreme Court's decision in *Hoffman* in no way calls into question the settled principle that undocumented workers are covered by the federal employment discrimination statutes and that it is as illegal for employers to discriminate against them as it is to discriminate against individuals authorized to work. When enforcing these laws, EEOC will not, on its own initiative, inquire into a worker's immigration status. Nor will EEOC consider an individual's immigration status when examining the underlying merits of a charge. The Commission will continue vigorously to pursue charges filed by any worker covered by the federal employment discrimination laws, including charges brought by undocumented workers, and will seek appropriate relief consistent with the Supreme Court's ruling in *Hoffman*. Enforcing the law to protect vulnerable workers, particularly low income and immigrant workers, remains a priority for EEOC.

Rescission of Enforcement Guidance on Remedies Available to Undocumented Workers Under Federal Employment Discrimination Laws, EEOC Compl. Man. (CCH) ¶ 3811 app. 622-B (June 27, 2002).

The EEOC thus maintains that "undocumented workers are covered by the federal employment statutes" even after *Hoffman Plastic*. Is that a fair assessment of the current state of the law?

5. As discussed by the Supreme Court, and as noted earlier in this text, the Immigration Reform and Control Act (IRCA) provides for certain discrimination claims on the basis of national origin. This statute is separate and apart from any prohibitions in Title VII. While citizenship status discrimination is not specifically protected under Title VII, the administrative procedures under IRCA do prohibit discrimination against a person with legal status but no citizenship.

 ## *Interactive Problem*

Look back at the facts of the interactive problem. Assume that after Hussein filed a case of national origin discrimination, it was revealed in discovery that he was an illegal undocumented worker. Would the company be liable under Title VII, or would the case be dismissed?

F. Chapter-in-Review

The typical *McDonnell Douglas* test and disparate impact analyses apply to national origin discrimination claims. This area is unique, however, as defining what someone's national origin is will not always be a straightforward inquiry. While the courts have applied varying tests, it is clear, at a minimum, that one's national origin includes where that individual was born and where her parents were born.

English-only rules are another area that requires specific attention. The EEOC guidelines on these rules can provide substantial assistance to employers, but they are not followed in every jurisdiction. When adopting these rules, employers should be advised to limit the scope of the rule as much as practicable and to make sure to have a job-related reason for the policy that is consistent with business necessity.

Accent discrimination should also be closely examined. Employers should not consider an individual's accent when making an employment decision, unless the employer can show that the worker's speech directly impairs the ability to perform the job. Courts have developed different inquiries for analyzing this question.

Finally, the question of the applicability of Title VII to undocumented workers is still evolving. *Hoffman Plastic* provides some guidance on the issue, but the case arises outside of the Title VII context. Subsequent decisions and regulations will help formulate the law in this area.

9

Religious Discrimination

 ## *Interactive Problem*

Krista Christian was hired to work on the assembly line of Big Cars, Inc., in Detroit, Michigan, where she helped to assemble the new Condor 5000 automobile. Krista was initially hired to work the shift beginning at 7 A.M. and ending at 3 P.M., Monday through Friday. Sales of the Condor 5000 were much better than expected, and the company began having difficulty keeping up with demand. Big Cars, Inc., thus decided to add weekend shifts, and required that all employees work at least one weekend a month as part of their new job assignments. Like all other employees, Krista was notified that she would be required to work on a Saturday at least once a month. As a devout Seventh-Day Adventist, Krista believed that working on Saturday would interfere with her religious beliefs. She thus asked her manager whether it would be possible for her to receive an exemption from the Saturday requirement so that she would not face this religious conflict. In response, her boss simply gave her a disgusted look and said, "Absolutely not." Krista further inquired as to whether it would be possible to see if any other employees might want to work some extra hours by taking on her additional Saturday shift, to which her boss stated only, "You have two options — work the weekend shift, or go stand in the unemployment line. We are not making any special exceptions for you or anyone else, and we are not going to waste anyone's time with this type of request."

Would Krista have a cause of action for religious discrimination? Would the company have a defense against a religious discrimination claim?

A. Introduction

Religious discrimination is perhaps the most unique area of employment discrimination law. The law in this area is often unsettled, and specific questions that arise must closely be examined under the rulings of a particular jurisdiction. On its face, the prohibition against religious discrimination is like that of any other protected basis. The statute, Title VII, § 2000e–2(a)(1), provides that

> [i]t shall be an unlawful employment practice for an employer . . . to fail or refuse to hire or to discharge any individual, or otherwise to discriminate against any individual with respect to his compensation, terms, conditions, or privileges of employment, because of such individual's . . . religion.

Just like the other protected categories, then, religious discrimination cases can proceed under a disparate treatment or disparate impact analysis. For reasons that will be discussed later in this chapter, however, disparate treatment claims are far more prevalent than disparate impact claims.

Though there are many similarities between religious discrimination claims and other areas of employment discrimination law, there are also many differences. Perhaps the most obvious reason for this difference is the constitutional implications of religious discrimination. The First Amendment to the U.S. Constitution states that "Congress shall make no law respecting an establishment of religion, or prohibiting the free exercise thereof; or abridging the freedom of speech, or of the press; or the right of the people peaceably to assemble, and to petition the Government for a redress of grievances." Because religion is so directly tied to constitutional rights, this overlay makes religious discrimination claims particularly difficult to analyze. While Title VII certainly prohibits discrimination on the basis of religion, the Constitution also prohibits the government from entangling itself in religion.

Prayer at Meeting of House of Representatives

Many companies closely integrate religion into the business itself. For instance, several big-name companies have identified themselves with Christianity. The founder of the fast-food chain Chick-fil-A made religion part of the corporation's identity. At Chick-fil-A's corporate headquarters in Atlanta, company meetings often include prayer, and all Chick-fil-A stores are required to close on Sundays. Similarly, Hobby Lobby, a litigant in a major Supreme Court decision on religion and the Affordable Care Act (*Burwell v. Hobby Lobby Stores, Inc.*, 134 S. Ct. 2751 (2014)), is a crafts and home decorations store that manages its business according to the Bible and is also closed every Sunday.

B. What Is Religion?

One area where religion is unique from other areas of discrimination law is that religion itself is not always easy to categorize. What makes something a religion? Title VII defines the term as encompassing "all aspects of religious observance and practice, as well as belief, unless an employer demonstrates that he is unable to reasonably accommodate an employee's or prospective employee's religious observance or practice without undue hardship on the conduct of the employer's business." 42 U.S.C. § 2000e(j). As will be discussed in greater detail below, this definition specifically requires that employers accommodate a particular employee's religious beliefs, up to the threshold of undue hardship.

Not every case raises the issue of whether a practice or belief is religious in nature. Beliefs or practices centered around more traditional religions are infrequently challenged on this basis. However, where a particular belief is more novel in nature, the question of whether religion is even implicated in the case can arise. The EEOC has provided an excellent summary of how inclusive Title VII should be in the religious context:

> Religion includes not only traditional, organized religions such as Christianity, Judaism, Islam, Hinduism, and Buddhism, but also religious beliefs that are new, uncommon, not part of a formal church or sect, only subscribed to by a small number of people, or that seem illogical or unreasonable to others. Further, a person's religious beliefs "need not be confined in either source or content to traditional or parochial concepts of religion." A belief is "religious" for Title VII purposes if it is "'religious' in the person's own scheme of things," *i.e.*, it is "a sincere and meaningful belief that occupies in the life of its possessor a place parallel to that filled by . . . God." An employee's belief or practice can be "religious" under Title VII even if the employee is affiliated with a religious group that does not espouse or recognize that individual's belief or practice, or if few — or no — other people adhere to it.
>
> Religious beliefs include theistic beliefs as well as non-theistic "moral or ethical beliefs as to what is right and wrong which are sincerely held with the strength of traditional religious views." Although courts generally resolve doubts about particular beliefs in favor of finding that they are religious, beliefs are not protected merely because they are strongly held. Rather, religion typically concerns "ultimate ideas" about "life, purpose, and death." Social, political, or economic philosophies, as well as mere personal preferences, are not "religious" beliefs protected by Title VII.

Religious observances or practices include, for example, attending worship services, praying, wearing religious garb or symbols, displaying religious objects, adhering to certain dietary rules, proselytizing or other forms of religious expression, or refraining from certain activities. Determining whether a practice is religious turns not on the nature of the activity, but on the employee's motivation. The same practice might be engaged in by one person for religious reasons and by another person for purely secular reasons. Whether or not the practice is "religious" is therefore a situational, case-by-case inquiry.

EEOC Compl. Man. ¶ 8310, § 12-I(A)(1) (July 22, 2008).

The EEOC's definition of religion is likely broader than that adopted by many courts. Nonetheless, this articulation of the standard is helpful initially to evaluate whether a particular belief, practice, or observance falls within Title VII's strictures. The question of what is or is not a religion can vary among the jurisdictions, and even among the district courts.

EEOC v. Red Robin Gourmet Burgers, Inc.

No. C04-1291JLR, 2005 WL 2090677 (W.D. Wash. Aug. 29, 2005)

ROBART, J.

Plaintiffs Equal Employment Opportunity Commission and Edward Rangel (collectively "Plaintiffs") filed suit against Rangel's former employer, Defendant Red Robin Gourmet Burgers, Inc. ("Red Robin"), alleging religious discrimination in violation of Title VII. Red Robin terminated Rangel when he refused to cover his tattoos, allegedly obtained for religious reasons, in violation of Red Robin's dress code policy. Defendant now moves for summary judgment on Rangel's claims.

Rangel practices Kemetecism, a religion with roots in ancient Egypt, or "Kemet." With an interest in joining the priesthood, Rangel obtained two tattoos, encircling his wrists, which are less than a quarter-inch wide. Written in Coptic, the tattoos translated in English state, "My Father Ra is Lord. I am the son who exists of his Father; I am the Father who exists of his son." Rangel received the tattoos during a religious ceremony after undergoing a rite of passage involving communal prayer, meditation, and ritual. The tattoos allegedly represent his servitude to Ra, the Egyptian god of the sun, and his commitment to his faith. Rangel believes that intentionally covering them is a sin, while incidentally covering them, such as when wearing a long-sleeve shirt or gloves, is not a sin. For Rangel, the key difference is whether he intends to cover them, which only happened during the month of Mesura, when Rangel believes Ra died and was reborn. According to Rangel, binding his wrists (and thereby covering his tattoos) represents his grief and servitude to Ra.

Rangel began working in December 2001 for Red Robin's Bellevue, Washington location as a server. Upon being hired, Rangel signed Red Robin's "Uniform/Appearance" policy which provides in part, "[b]ody piercings and tattoos must not be visible." Rangel, as well as other servers, worked at the Bellevue location with their tattoos uncovered until May 2002 when the assistant manager, Brad Holmes, told him to cover his tattoos. Rangel alleges that he explained the religious significance of his tattoos to Holmes who "basically said, 'Okay, cool,'" and allowed him to continue working with the tattoos uncovered.

In June 2002, Rangel attended an orientation for Red Robin's new restaurant location in Bellevue. During the orientation, Red Robin's general manager and senior regional operations director approached Rangel about his tattoos, telling him to cover them. According to Holly Hogan, one of the managers, Rangel gave a "lengthy explanation" about his faith, his reasons for having the tattoos, and his belief against covering them. Although Hogan and the other manager, Stephanie DeFrancisco, suggested Rangel could cover the tattoos with wrist bands or bracelets (contrary to Red Robin policy which limits jewelry to two rings and earrings), Rangel refused and was escorted out. When Rangel returned for his second scheduled shift at the new location, Hogan and DeFrancisco asked him again to cover his tattoos and he refused. After Hogan and DeFrancisco presented him with the option of covering his tattoos and working, or leaving them uncovered and going home, Rangel maintained his refusal to cover them and DeFrancisco escorted him out. Rangel immediately called DeFrancisco's supervisor, Ernie Sapiro, who looked into the matter and upheld the managers' decision. Red Robin officially terminated Rangel on June 17, 2002.

Title VII prohibits employers from discharging an employee based on the individual's "religion." Broadly defined, "religion" includes "all aspects of religious observances and practice, as well as belief" unless the employer demonstrates it is unable to reasonably accommodate an employee's religious observance or practice without "undue hardship on the conduct of the employer's business." 42 U.S.C. § 2000e(j).

It is undisputed that Rangel notified Red Robin of the conflict between his religious belief and its dress code policy, and that Red Robin discharged him based on his violation of the policy, thereby establishing the second and third elements of a prima facie case. The parties strongly dispute, however, whether Rangel possesses a bona fide religious belief against intentionally covering the tattooed name of Ra (his Creator) on his wrists. Red Robin argues that Rangel's tattoos lack historical and textual support, and that Rangel's belief is both "inconsistent and arbitrary" in application, focusing on Rangel's practice of covering his tattoos during Mesura (when Ra allegedly died and was reborn), when he is cold, and while wearing long-sleeve clothing and costumes. In response, Plaintiffs distinguish Rangel's belief against intentionally covering his tattoos, which they call "sacrilegious concealment," from "incidental covering" that occurs while wearing a long-sleeve shirt or gloves. Further, Plaintiffs explain that Rangel covers his tattoos during Mesura as a sign of his grief and servitude to Ra. Viewing the evidence in the light most favorable to Plaintiffs as the court must on summary judgment, the court finds that Rangel has brought forth sufficient evidence to demonstrate that he possessed a bona fide religious belief, and thereby established a prima facie case of religious discrimination for failure to accommodate.

Red Robin's first argument, that "sincerity is a threshold issue that must be resolved in every religious discrimination case," relying on *United States v. Seeger*, 380 U.S. 163 (1965), misstates the law. In *Seeger*, the Supreme Court considered the claims of conscientious objectors seeking to avoid military service. Although the Court held that "the threshold question of sincerity . . . must be resolved in every case," it specifically limited this holding in the next sentence (which Red Robin omits) to "every claim for exemption as a conscientious objector." Contrary to Red Robin's suggestion, the Court did not indicate that sincerity is a threshold issue arising in every religious discrimination case, nor did it mention Title VII which Congress had enacted only one year prior.

While Red Robin characterizes Rangel's religious belief as an unprotected "personal preference," similar to that expressed by the plaintiff in *Tiano v. Dillard Dep't Stores, Inc.*, 139 F.3d 679 (9th Cir. 1998), the court finds this comparison unavailing. In *Tiano*, the Ninth Circuit held that an employee's alleged religious belief that she attend a specific pilgrimage during a certain time frame, was a "personal preference" because she offered one "lone unilateral statement" in support of her belief, without any further corroborating testimony of her own, and despite a record "replete" with contradictory evidence. This evidence included Tiano's failure to complain about the alleged discrimination until after she learned that her plane ticket was non-refundable and her friend's testimony that they both decided to go on the pilgrimage after they "talked about it" and "thought it would be interesting to go on." In light of this evidence, the Ninth Circuit held that Tiano's professed belief was "hardly a religious calling" and dismissed her case for failure to establish the first element of a prima facie case.

Turning to the facts of this case, the court finds that Rangel, unlike Tiano, offered multiple statements in his deposition about his faith, how he received his tattoos, and his belief that intentionally covering his tattoos amounts to sacrilege. Rangel explained that he based his belief on both scripture and Egyptian history. Further, he answered repeated questions about his reasons for covering his tattoos during Mesura and the distinction that exists for him between incidentally and intentionally covering his tattoos. The contradictory evidence before the court in *Tiano*, suggesting a financial motive and failing to corroborate plaintiff's belief, is absent here. Rangel's deposition testimony, along with his decision to sacrifice his job rather than cover his tattoos, is sufficient to demonstrate a bona fide religious belief.

■ NOTES AND QUESTIONS

1. The Supreme Court has not provided much guidance on what constitutes a religion. However, the Court has stated that it "is not merely a matter of personal preference, but one of deep religious conviction, shared by an organized group, and intimately related to daily living." Wisconsin v. Yoder, 406 U.S. 205 (1972). Is this definition helpful? Can you improve on it?

2. Does the plaintiff's religion fit the definition in *Wisconsin v. Yoder*? Is a religion involved here or are the tattoos merely a matter of personal preference?

3. Would someone who actively practices witchcraft be able to claim protection under Title VII's religious tenets? *See generally* Dettmer v. Landon, 799 F.2d 929 (1986) (holding "that religion based on witchcraft was a 'religion' for free exercise clause purposes but . . . contraband materials were properly denied to inmates as reasonably threatening to prison security").

4. The portion of the case excerpted above only addresses whether the plaintiff had an actual religious belief, which is only the first stage of the prima facie case. Thus, the plaintiff must still establish that she was discriminated against (or not reasonably accommodated by her employer up to the point of undue hardship). Would the plaintiff ultimately prevail in this case? The court denied the defendant's motion for summary judgment in the case, and allowed the matter to proceed on the accommodation issue.

5. As the EEOC indicated in a press release, the *Red Robin* case was subsequently settled, and the defendants agreed to "pay $150,000 and make substantial policy and procedural changes." Press Release, EEOC, Burger Chain to Pay $150,000 to Resolve EEOC Religious Discrimination Suit (Sept. 16, 2005), http://www.eeoc.gov/eeoc/newsroom/release/9-16-05.cfm. If you represented the defendant in this case, would you have settled the matter or taken it to trial?

6. For other examples of whether certain conduct is religious in nature, compare McGlothin v. Jackson Mun. Separate Sch. Dist., 829 F. Supp. 853 (S.D. Miss. 1992) (holding that the discharged employee failed to establish that she wore African-style head wraps based on her religious beliefs and therefore failed to prove a violation of Title VII), with EEOC v. Starlight, LLC, No. CV-06-3075-EFS, 2008 WL 3095254 (E.D. Wash. Aug. 4, 2008) (holding that it was discriminatory to refuse to promote a server to a more desirable shift because she wore a Muslim headdress).

7. Over the years, employees have tried to argue for the existence of rather unusual religious beliefs, usually with little success in the courts. *See, e.g.*, Brown v. Pena, 441 F. Supp. 1382 (S.D. Fla. 1977) (employee alleging a "personal religious creed" that Kozy Kitten Cat Food contributed significantly to his state of well-being and his overall work performance by increasing his energy); Bellamy v. Mason's Stores, Inc., 508 F.2d 504 (4th Cir. 1974) (employee alleging that membership in Ku Klux Klan constitutes a religion); Storey v. Burns Int'l Security Servs., 390 F.3d 760 (3d Cir. 2004) (employee alleging that his display of the Confederate flag in the workplace was because of his self-proclaimed religious identity as

a "Confederate Southern-American"); Friedman v. S. Cal. Permanente Med. Grp., 102 Cal. App. 4th 39 (2002) (employee alleging that veganism is a religious creed that prohibited him from being immunized against mumps, the vaccine for which is grown in chicken embryos); Brown v. Dade Christian Sch., Inc., 556 F.2d 310 (5th Cir. 1977) (school alleging that its racial separation was adopted in the exercise of religion).

8. **Historical note.** Prior to the enactment of Title VII, which explicitly included protections from religious discrimination in the workplace, a safeguard for employees from religious discrimination did not fully exist. The First Amendment of the Constitution obviously provides some safeguards to religious discrimination. However, the First Amendment generally "restricts [only] those acting on behalf of the government" and the Amendment "is relevant [mostly] to a discussion of religious protections in the public sector." Thus, the protections provided by the First Amendment do not fully apply to private employers. Title VII, therefore, greatly expanded the scope of protection that was previously afforded under the Constitution. *See* Robert J. Friedman, *Religious Discrimination in the Workplace: The Persistent Polarized Struggle*, 11 TENN. J. BUS. L. 143, 146 n.14 (2010).

9. *Hobby Lobby.* On June 30, 2014, the Supreme Court ruled that "family-owned corporations do not have to pay for insurance coverage for contraception under the ACA." The landmark decision, *Burwell v. Hobby Lobby Stores, Inc.*, 134 S. Ct. 2751 (2014), "concerned the arts-and-crafts chain Hobby Lobby, which is owned and operated by an evangelical Christian family." The company claimed that because its religious beliefs are "morally  opposed to these birth control methods and therefore they should not be forced to help provide" this type of coverage. The Supreme Court agreed. The ruling, however, is limited in several respects: (1) it does not apply to other insurance mandates for vital healthcare services (e.g., insurance for blood transfusions or vaccinations); (2) it only applies to "closely held" corporations — i.e., "five or fewer people own more than half" of the company — and companies with owners who "have clearly established" and sincere religious beliefs; and (3) the ruling does not mean that "[c]ompanies cannot deny coverage [for certain birth control] simply because they do not want to pay for it; they must have a legitimate religious objection." Even with these limitations, the decision clearly impacts the health of the women who are employed by these companies, and the ability of such female employees to access certain contraceptives. *See* Sarah Tardo et al., *Point/Counterpoint: Two Perspectives on the Hobby Lobby Ruling*, HEADCOUNT BLOG (July 1, 2014), http://www.headcount.org/ pointcounterpoint-two-perspectives-on-the-hobby-lobby-ruling/; Burwell v. Hobby Lobby Stores, Inc., 134 S. Ct. 2751 (2014).

Interactive Problem

Looking back at the facts of the interactive problem at the beginning of the chapter, assume that rather than being a member of the Seventh-Day Adventist Church, Krista belongs to the "Church of Sundays off," of which she is currently the only member. This religion, as Krista describes, holds as its primary religious tenet that no one should work on Sunday, and should instead devote the entire day to watching television and eating greasy foods. Would Krista have a claim against her employer if it refused to give her Sunday off to observe her religion? Why or why not? Would you need additional information to answer this question?

 ## C. Disparate Treatment Cases

The typical *McDonnell Douglas* model applies to religious discrimination cases, though fewer cases are brought in this context. To make a showing of intentional discrimination under this model, the plaintiff must establish that she was treated differently by the employer because of her religion. Thus, just like any other protected category, employers cannot use religion as a basis for which to take an adverse action.

EEOC v. Preferred Management Corp.
216 F. Supp. 2d 763 (S.D. Ind. 2002)

BARKER, District Judge.

This is an employment discrimination case involving alleged religious harassment and disparate treatment in violation of Title VII. The case is before us on defendant's motion for summary judgment as to all claims. The Preferred companies consist of four operating companies, a real estate company, and a management company. Michael Pyatt was employed by PMC [Preferred Management Company] as Director of Human Resources from October 1994 through 1998. He was a member of the executive management team.

Preferred's guiding hand is Jackie Steuerwald, the company's co-owner and chief executive officer. Ms. Steuerwald identifies herself as a practicing Christian who adheres to a literal interpretation of the Bible, which she reads daily. She professes a concept of salvation by the grace of God and that she is "born again." Ms. Steuerwald believes that God directed her to establish [part of the company] in Vincennes and that Preferred is God's home health care agency. She openly shares these beliefs with her employees. Ms. Steuerwald has prepared a narrative entitled "The Transfiguration of Preferred," a brief history of the company's formation, which discusses her belief that God was involved in Preferred's establishment and is involved in Preferred's direction.

Ms. Steuerwald believes in "The Great Commission," a religious directive to go into the world to share her faith. "The world" includes the work place. Asked whether she believes that religion is appropriate in the workplace, Ms. Steuerwald responded: "I don't believe it can be . . . If you're a person of faith, it can't be separated." She added by way of explanation: "Well, in Him I live and breathe and have my being, and I don't leave my faith at the door when I go to work. It's who I am. It permeates my thinking, my decisions."

Agricultural Workers Union Opens with a Prayer, 1940

Ms. Steuerwald anoints new branch offices with olive oil and asks God's blessing on each new office. When a new office is anointed, the ceremony is conducted during working hours. Ms. Steuerwald also has anointed two existing facilities, in Terre Haute and Evansville, because of strife and discord in those offices. Ms. Steuerwald testified that she discerned demons in those offices and that by anointing them she believed she was able to rid the offices of the demons. Ms. Steuerwald also has anointed individual employees of Preferred for healing purposes. She believes that anointing has healing power.

Ms. Steuerwald defines Preferred's mission as presenting God and his Son, Jesus Christ, to all of Preferred's employees. Preferred's mission statement includes that its primary mission is "to be a Christian dedicated provider of quality health care." Preferred employs an "evangelism and discipleship" subcommittee, whose members have prayed for the salvation of employees.

Beginning in June 1995, Preferred has required its employees, as a condition of employment, to sign a statement that includes the words: "I have examined myself and I agree that I have respected and actively supported Preferred's Mission and Values during this past year of employment and I agree to respect and actively support Preferred's Mission and Values for the coming year." Preferred's managers and supervisors are instructed to use the company's values in disciplining employees because values are considered a standard of performance. Preferred employees are evaluated according to the Mission and Values Statement. They are also disciplined on the basis of the Mission and Values Statement. Religious references are made on employee evaluations. Employees were terminated for violating the values in the Mission and Values Statement.

Preferred's corporate organizational chart is known as "the wheel." At its center is the name "Jesus," who represents the rock upon which Preferred professes to be built. From this center, all of Preferred's departments radiate as spokes. During comprehensive orientation or a management meeting, Ms. Steuerwald had a wheel on the board with Jesus in the middle and employees' names on the spokes. She told those in attendance that, with Jesus as the foundation of Preferred and the employees there providing the care, Preferred would grow and benefit. During the comprehensive orientation that [an employee] attended, Ms. Steuerwald said that it was a vision of hers that the conference room at Preferred would some day be a church and that people could come there and pray.

Preferred gives copies of the company's mission statement, statement of values, definitions, "the wheel," and the "Transfiguration" to all applicants as they apply for employment. Applicants are informed that Preferred is a Christian organization and that prayers are recited at the company; they are asked how they feel about working for a Christian organization. Former branch manager Sondra Sievers testified that Ms. Steuerwald told her and others that a candidate for employment who said that there was no room in the work place for religion did not belong at Preferred. A Mormon who also was a candidate for employment, was not hired. The chaplain who interviewed the candidate told others who had been present at the interview that Mormonism is a "cult."

> Though the facts of all employment cases are critical, the background of the case is particularly important in religious discrimination cases given the statutory and constitutional considerations that are often involved.

Preferred offers religious gatherings, which it refers to as "devotions," to its employees on a weekly basis. The devotions are facilitated by two staff chaplains. Preferred states that there was no corporate-wide policy of mandatory attendance at devotions. By contrast, Ann Parker testified that, as a manager she was required to be a "role model," which meant, among other things, that she was "expected" to attend and was required to embody and exemplify corporate policy. Ms. Parker also testified that she discussed the manager's responsibilities with Sherry Stute when Preferred was going to open an Evansville facility and one responsibility was to attend devotions. Accordingly, she perceived devotions to be mandatory.

Human Resources Director Michael Pyatt professes to be a follower of Jesus Christ. Mr. Pyatt testified that he is saved or born again and that all of the churches he has attended are fundamentalist. On two occasions, Mr. Pyatt conducted devotions at a branch office. Prayer and "script devotion" on various themes are conducted at the weekly devotions. Ms. Steuerwald sometimes commented about employees' attendance at devotions. Employees are not told that they may leave meetings before prayer is conducted. The handwritten document, "Expectations of Branch Manager," included the following items: (1) actively demonstrate company values, behavior standards of branch manager (attached) and (2) devotions are held weekly at a scheduled time.

The EEOC alleges that Sondra Sievers was the victim of religious discrimination in that she was demoted from her position as branch manager at Vincennes and subsequently discharged because she failed to subscribe to Jackie Steuerwald's religious preferences or that she was discharged

School Day Opens with Prayer at Private School, 1940

in retaliation for having complained about religious discrimination. Preferred argues that the demotion and discharge were justified by Ms. Sievers' inadequate work performance.

Ms. Steuerwald says that she demoted Ms. Sievers because of the results of the employee survey — "Your Opinion Counts" — conducted by Mike Pyatt in October 1995. The details of the survey are recounted in our statement of facts. Suffice to say here that the survey included the question: "Are the Company's Values actively promoted and modeled by supervisors and managers?" And the request: "Please make any other comments or suggestions that you believe would help Preferred be more effective and be a better place to work and serve the Lord and our customers," providing space for comments.

As Mr. Pyatt distributed the survey to the Vincennes employees, he said in response to an employee's question that management was looking at all the managers and "if they weren't where they thought they should be, there would be changes made."

Mr. Pyatt distributed fifty-nine surveys; thirty-four employees responded. Three of the employee responses included the following negative comments about Ms. Sievers: (1) "We have lost a lot of very good, kind, caring office and field staff because of the branch manager and it sure is a shame;" (2) "Sondra does not respect our opinion. If we voice our opinion she will usually disagree and then she will be angry"; (3) "Sondra has us all very unhappy with her lack of responsibility, caring or understanding"; (4) "Sondra does not like others, is either [sic] revengeful with field staff, clients and families"; and (5) "If a person isn't liked or if a person does a job well, branch manager will do anything to create problems for the person."

After receiving the results of the survey, on November 14, 1995, Ms. Steuerwald and Mr. Pyatt went to Vincennes to inform Ms. Sievers of her demotion. Ms. Sievers met with Mr. Pyatt who addressed the survey results and told Ms. Sievers that she would be removed from her position, placed in the Leader in the Making program with Nellie Foster, and re-evaluated by December 31, 1995. He also gave Ms. Sievers three documents. The first outlined the "qualifications" of a Leader in the Making as (1) having a teachable spirit[;] (2) having love for one another[;] (3) honoring others above self; (4) being approachable; (5) willing to ask others other for help and advice; and (6) willing to invest in others. The second, entitled "Confess-Repent-Turn," outlined what Ms. Sievers needed to accomplish by December 31, including (1) restoring broken relationships with Cherie Deem, referral sources, patients and staff; (2) submitting to authority; (3) regaining trust and respect of the staff and community; and (4) consistently walking in a blameless way to be above reproach. The third document was called "Characteristics of Broken People Prepared for Revival." After the meeting, Mr. Pyatt told Ms. Sievers to take three days off and pray and think about things.

Preferred argues that Ms. Steuerwald based her decision to demote Ms. Sievers on the results of the survey. It argues that Ms. Steuerwald "honestly believed" that, based on the survey, Ms. Sievers' work performance was deficient and that we have no authority to second-guess honestly held business decisions. But we do second-guess employment decisions in virtually every employment discrimination case. We test employers' decisions to determine whether they are, indeed, "honestly held" or whether a jury might determine that they are pretextual. Preferred's argument may well be true and we would expect Preferred to present it to the jury. But a jury would not be compelled to believe it. Accordingly, we cannot conclusively determine its truth and grant summary judgment on Ms. Sievers' demotion claim.

In addition to the reasons we outlined earlier explaining why Preferred's employment practices and Ms. Steuerwald's comments raise genuine issues of material fact with respect to her motivation in making employment decisions, we also note the following. First, assuming that Ms. Steuerwald based her decision on the results of the survey — or, more precisely, on the negative comments of three employees about Ms. Sievers — the decision was "performance related" only in the sense that religious beliefs and practices are part and parcel of Preferred's understanding of "performance." In other words, Preferred used an unlawful determinant of "performance."

Second, Ann Parker, Ms. Sievers' supervisor at the time, testified that she thought the survey had been designed to obtained negative results about Ms. Sievers. This is strong testimony from a management employee, especially one who was in favor with upper management for a considerable period. Third, Ms. Steuerwald replaced Ms. Sievers with Sue Klein. Where Ms. Sievers had several years of managerial experience with satisfactory (and more than satisfactory) performance evaluations, Ms. Klein had no management experience whatever. Third, as we described in considerable detail earlier, Ms. Klein's religious views and practices were demonstrably consistent with Ms. Steuerwald's.

In view of these facts, as well as those recited earlier, there is a genuine issue of material fact as to whether Ms. Steuerwald demoted Ms. Sievers on the basis of religion. Accordingly, we cannot say as a matter of law that Preferred's demotion of Ms. Sievers was not motivated by religion.

After Ms. Sievers' demotion, she was assigned to Nellie Foster's Leader in the Making program for training to remedy her alleged performance deficiencies. Ms. Foster was going to customize a training program for Ms. Sievers' circumstances. The customized training involved meetings between Ms. Sievers and Ms. Foster on December 5 and 6, 1995. Both were religiously-oriented. At the December 6 meeting, Ms. Foster presented the "Lordship Ladder" to Ms. Sievers and asked such questions as: "What was the last sin you committed?" and "What was the last thing you asked God forgiveness for?" Ms. Sievers responded, "I am a Catholic, and I discuss my sins with my priest," and began crying.

Ms. Foster concluded from these meetings that Ms. Sievers was not a candidate for leadership training and that she should not be returned to her branch manager position. She conveyed these conclusions to Ms. Steuerwald, who decided to offer Ms. Sievers a position in quality assurance instead. On March 8, 1996, three months later, Ms. Steuerwald fired her.

Preferred argues that the decision to terminate Ms. Sievers was, like the decision to demote her, based on Ms. Sievers' performance. It argues that, during Ms. Steuerwald's investigation of [another employee's] role in [alleged patient misconduct], she learned that [the other employee] had discharged a patient under questionable circumstances and that Ms. Sievers did not intervene to correct the matter. Indeed, according to Ms. Steuerwald's "sources," Ms. Sievers "actually hung-up on the client when the client called." According to Preferred, Ms. Steuerwald also believed that Ms. Sievers was directly responsible for the loss of business as a result of separate incidents involving two clients and a referral source. In addition, Darlene Wright told Ms. Steuerwald that Ms. Sievers had approved the hiring of [another employee] even though [that employee] did not meet the company's minimum experience requirements for a field nurse. Finally, "Ms. Steuerwald believed that Ms. Sievers' conduct while she was the branch manager was inimical to PHHC's values of treating people with respect and dignity and honoring others."

> Like any other case analyzed under *McDonnell Douglas,* the defendant must articulate a legitimate nondiscriminatory reason after the prima facie case is established.

While these explanations of an employment decision might ordinarily carry considerable weight on summary judgment, here they are counterbalanced by all of the evidence that supports the EEOC's argument that Ms. Steuerwald had a powerful propensity to make employment decisions on the basis of religion.

We note in addition that Darlene Wright [personnel director for the southern district of Preferred], who apparently criticized Ms. Sievers for hiring [another employee] even though [that employee] did not have the proper qualifications, was the same Ms. Wright who recommended [the same employee] for the job for which she was hired. Besides, by the time Ms. Steuerwald fired Ms. Sievers, [the other employee] had been employed for two years. She had received favorable employment evaluations. The decision to terminate Ms. Sievers because of a decision she participated in two years earlier raises an eyebrow as to suspicious timing.

We also note that Ms. Sievers' alleged loss of a referral source is questionable. At first Ms. Steuerwald could not identify which referral source Ms. Sievers allegedly lost. Then, she identified the referral source as the Vincennes Housing Authority. It turned out, however, that the Vincennes Housing Authority was not a source of referrals.

Additionally, one of Ms. Steuerwald's express reasons for discharging Ms. Sievers was that Ms. Sievers' performance as branch manager was "inimical" to Preferred's values. Coupled with Ms. Steuerwald's earlier findings that Ms. Sievers was irredeemable as a leader and that Ms. Sievers did not exemplify such characteristics as "a teachable spirit," we cannot separate religious reasons from the secular reasons, or subjective reasons from objective reasons in a sufficiently conclusive manner so as to grant summary judgment.

Both the decision to demote Ms. Sievers and the decision to discharge Ms. Sievers were made, at least in part, on the basis of subjective factors: "attitude," "caring," "management style," and the like. Federal courts, including the Seventh Circuit, have routinely held that an employer may base adverse employment actions on subjective factors. They have also held, however, that subjective explanations are more susceptible of abuse and may mask discrimination more effectively than objective, testable explanations.

The EEOC's evidence is sufficient to raise a reasonable inference that Ms. Sievers' demotion and termination were based on religion and that they were, therefore, in violation of Title VII.

■ NOTES AND QUESTIONS

1. The facts of the court decision above have been heavily edited, and the case involved several other alleged victims and specific claims, including religious harassment. Would the facts as presented here create an environment of religious harassment?

2. If the company is privately owned, as the company is here, wouldn't it have an absolute constitutional right to include religion as part of its operational mission?

3. Does the First Amendment prohibit the government from intervening in the employer's actions?

4. Do you agree with the court's conclusion that Sievers was demoted and discharged because of her religion? Does the court give enough deference to the defendant's poor performance rationales?

5. Would the traditional *McDonnell Douglas* model work in analyzing this particular case?

 Interactive Problem

Looking back at the facts of the interactive problem at the beginning of the chapter, assume that Krista's direct manager was of the Muslim faith, and that he had been heard stating to another supervisor that "he never really felt comfortable working with Christians." Would this evidence strengthen Krista's case against the company? Would it constitute direct evidence of discrimination?

Class Exercise: The Religious Employer

It is common for a private employer to have very strongly held religious convictions, and many well-known companies openly advocate their religious views. Assume that you represent just such a client, who operates a large chain of movie theaters. The client would like some advice on what types of activities it can and cannot participate in when advocating its evangelical religious beliefs. In particular, the company would like to make the following changes to its business structure: (1) shutting its theaters down on Sundays so that its employees do not have to work on the Sabbath; (2) only showing family-oriented movies with an overall rating of PG-13 or lower; (3) not hiring anyone to work in its various facilities that does not share in its religious beliefs; and (4) for those non-religious workers currently employed by the company, enacting a "reform period" by which the workers can convert to the employer's religious faith within ninety days to save their jobs. The employer believes that this would be a wonderful business decision for two reasons. First, it would align perfectly with the religious views of the company. Second, the policies would be highly controversial and bring a lot of attention (and possibly business) to the employer. How would you advise the client on the legality of its proposed actions?

As already noted, the statutory text of Title VII applies directly to religion. The statute expressly makes it unlawful for an employer to take an adverse action "because of such individual's . . . religion." Though this language is fairly straightforward, the exact meaning of these words has been challenged. An interesting and important decision of the U.S. Court of Appeals for the Seventh Circuit closely examined this statutory text.

Moranski v. General Motors Corp.

433 F.3d 537 (7th Cir. 2005)

WILLIAMS, Circuit Judge.

Several years ago, General Motors developed what is now known as its Affinity Group program. The program, which makes company resources available to recognized groups, began as an outgrowth of the company's efforts to support employees from diverse backgrounds and improve company performance. General Motors's Affinity Group Guidelines prohibit the conferral of Affinity Group status on any group promoting or advocating a religious position. Citing these Guidelines, General Motors declined to grant Affinity Group status to employee John Moranski's proposed Christian Employee Network. We agree with the district court that General Motors's

General Motors, Detroit, Michigan

denial of Affinity Group status to Moranski's proposed group did not discriminate against him on the basis of his religion, as the program treats equally all groups with religious positions. Therefore, we affirm the district court's decision to dismiss Moranski's complaint for failure to state a claim upon which relief could be granted.

The allegations that follow are set forth in the complaint and in the General Motors Affinity Group Guidelines attached as an exhibit to the complaint. General Motors ("GM") instituted its Affinity Group program in 1999. The program resulted from efforts to make diverse constituencies feel more welcomed and valued at GM, remove barriers to productivity for all employees, and increase market share and customer enthusiasm in diverse market segments. According to the Guidelines, Affinity Groups "are typically created around an aspect of common social identity that influences how others see them at GM." Affinity Groups are eligible to receive resources including the use of company facilities and equipment for group activities and funds to support the group's mission.

In order to receive Affinity Group status, General Motors must approve the proposed group's request for registration. The Guidelines provide that the company will not recognize as Affinity Groups entities organized only as the result of a common interest or activity, such as golf or theater. The Guidelines also explicitly list other groups that GM will not approve for Affinity Group status, including, as relevant here, groups that "promote or advocate particular religious or political positions." General Motors currently recognizes nine Affinity Groups: People with Disabilities, the General Motors African Ancestry Network, GM Plus (for gay and lesbian persons), the North American Women's Advisory Council, the GM Hispanic Initiative Team, the GM Asian Indian Affinity Group, the GM Chinese Affinity Group, the GM Mid-East/South-East Asian Affinity Group, and the Veterans Affinity Group. Membership is voluntary and must be open to all current, salaried, full-time employees who share a group's goals.

John Moranski works as a desktop computing architect at GM's Allison Transmission unit in Indianapolis, Indiana. He is a born-again Christian. In December 2002, Moranski submitted an application for recognition of the "GM Christian Employee Network" as an Affinity Group. The application stated that the Christian Employee Network would be an interdenominational group and would not promote a particular church or religious denomination in the work-place. General Motors denied Moranski's application, stating the company's Affinity Group Guidelines preclude groups that promote or advocate religious positions from receiving Affinity Group status.

Moranski filed a complaint with the Equal Employment Opportunity Commission and received a Notification of Right to Sue letter. He then filed suit in federal court, alleging that General Motors discriminated against him on the basis of his religion when it denied his request for Affinity Group recognition. The district court granted General Motors's motion to dismiss for failure to state a claim upon which relief could be granted, and Moranski appeals.

Employer-sponsored diversity initiatives have become increasingly popular. "[M]ajor American businesses have made clear that the skills needed in today's increasingly global marketplace can only be developed through exposure to widely diverse people, cultures, ideas, and viewpoints." *Grutter v. Bollinger,* 539 U.S. 306, 330 (2003) (citing amici briefs submitted by leading American corporations). In an effort to, among other things, support employees of diverse backgrounds, some employers officially recognize employee groups organized on the basis of aspects of social identity. Some of these companies, including Intel (which recognizes groups including the Intel Baha'i Group, Intel Bible-Based Christian Network, Intel Jewish Community, and Intel Muslim Employee Group) and Texas Instruments (the company supports diversity initiatives including the Christian Values Initiative and Muslim Initiative) recognize groups that, although open to both members and nonmembers of the religion, are organized on the basis of a religious affinity.

General Motors, although it has an Affinity Group program to support employee-organized groups organized around aspects of social identity, declines to sanction any group that promotes a religious position. As a result, when Moranski sought Affinity Group status for the "GM Christian Employee Network," General Motors denied his request. Moranski contends that this denial constituted unlawful discrimination against him on the basis of his Christian religion, in violation of Title VII.

> **The key dispute in this case is whether GM's decision to "decline[] to sanction any group that promotes a religious position" runs afoul of Title VII's religious protections.**

Title VII defines "religion" to include "all aspects of religious observance and practice, as well as belief." 42 U.S.C. § 2000e(j). The statute makes it unlawful for an employer "to discriminate against any individual with respect to his compensation, terms, conditions, or privileges of employment, because of such individual's race, color, religion, sex, or national origin." 42 U.S.C. § 2000e-2(a)(1). It is well-established that "[t]he central question in any employment-discrimination case is whether the employer would have taken the same action had the employee been of a different race (age, sex, religion, national origin, etc.) and everything else had remained the same." *Carson v. Bethlehem Steel Corp.*, 82 F.3d 157, 158 (7th Cir. 1996). Here, the allegations in Moranski's complaint make clear that General Motors would have taken the same action had he possessed a different religious position.

Although General Motors currently recognizes nine Affinity Groups, Moranski acknowledges that the company has never approved an Affinity Group based on any other religion, nor would the Guidelines allow it to do so. Instead, Moranski argues that General Motors's refusal to grant Affinity Group status to any group that promotes or advocates a religious position means that it treats "nonreligious" employees more favorably than religious employees. General Motors, however, has never recognized an Affinity Group that promotes or advocates any religious position, even one of religious indifference or opposition to religion. Nor, as Moranski acknowledges, would the Guidelines allow it to do so. The Guidelines preclude recognition of Affinity Groups based on any religious "position," including agnosticism, atheism, and secular humanism. The Guidelines also prohibit General Motors from recognizing, in Moranski's terms, a group organized on the basis of "nonreligion." Simply stated, General Motors's Affinity Group policy treats all religious positions alike — it excludes them all from serving as the basis of a company-recognized Affinity Group. The company's decision to treat all religious positions alike in its Affinity Group program does not constitute impermissible "discrimination" under Title VII.

It is true, as Moranski points out, that General Motors does recognize Affinity Groups based on race, color, sex, and national origin, the other categories protected by Title VII. It does not follow, however, that the company's decision to exclude all groups formed on the basis of religious positions violates Title VII. Unsurprisingly, Moranski does not point us to any authority for his proposition that a court should use cross-categorical comparisons when evaluating Title VII claims. His logic would mean that a company would violate Title VII if it recognized an Affinity Group on the basis of religion but not sex, or granted status to a group on the basis of sex but not to one based on ethnicity. Yet even Moranski concedes Title VII law does not stretch this far, replying instead that a company must allow recognition of a group organized on the basis of whatever an employee deems his or her "main identifying characteristic." This argument does not help Moranski. It has no basis in Title VII law, nor do the Affinity Group Guidelines make any reference to an employee's "main identifying characteristic."

Rather than looking to what an employee might deem his or her "main identifying characteristic," we return again to the language of Title VII, which makes it unlawful for an employer to *"discriminate . . . because of* such individual's race, color, religion, sex, or national origin." 42 U.S.C. § 2000e–2(a)(1) (emphasis added). As we have said before, this statutory text means that the "touchstone of Title VII is, of course, discrimination or disparate treatment." *Holman v. Indiana*, 211 F.3d 399 (7th Cir. 2000). In *Holman*, we held a Title VII claim failed where the employer treated men and women equally[.]

Similarly here, Moranski's complaint contains allegations making clear that General Motors refuses to grant Affinity Group status to any group on the basis of any position with respect to religion. It makes no difference that, as Moranski stressed, all employees have a race or gender, but not all might identify with a religion. The Affinity Group Guidelines treat employees with all religious positions identically: any employee with any religious position may join any of the recognized Affinity Groups, but the company will not recognize as an Affinity Group a group organized on the basis of a religious position. This is not discrimination "because of" religion, and the district court properly granted General Motors's motion to dismiss for failure to state a claim upon which relief could be granted. Our conclusion on this point makes it unnecessary for us to consider the other arguments General Motors raised in support of the district court's decision.

For the foregoing reasons, the district court's grant of General Motors's motion to dismiss for failure to state a claim upon which relief could be granted is Affirmed.

■ NOTES AND QUESTIONS

1. The court notes that "Moranski's complaint contains allegations making clear that General Motors refuses to grant Affinity Group status to any group on the basis of any position with respect to religion." How decisive is this fact in the case?

2. Is the court's basic conclusion here that as long as everyone is discriminated against on the basis of religion, no one is being discriminated against? Does this conclusion fall within the spirit of Title VII?

3. The court also raises the question of the so-called equal opportunity harasser, whereby there is no claim of discrimination if both sexes are treated poorly and in an equal manner. Does this comparison apply to the religion context?

4. If it could be established that General Motors had a particular distrust of Muslim employees, and, on that basis, decided to prohibit all Affinity Groups formed on the basis of religion, would the company run afoul of Title VII?

5. The statute makes it unlawful "to discriminate against any individual with respect to his . . . religion." How important is the word "individual" to the outcome of this case?

6. It is clear that the court here believes that there was no intentional discrimination in the case. Could it be argued that there was a failure to accommodate religion on the part of General Motors? A discussion of failure to accommodate claims is set forth below.

7. The United States has a rich history of religious tolerance and diversity. The chart below reflects the different religions of individuals in this country:

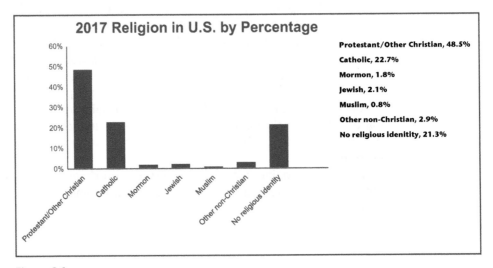

Figure 9.1
Source: Gallup (2017).

 *Interactive Problem*

Looking back at the interactive problem at the beginning of the chapter, assume that Big Cars, Inc., can establish that it has never made any changes to an employee's work schedule on the basis of religion. Thus, the company is able to establish that it has treated all religions the same — poorly — by not working with religious employees to accommodate their schedules. Would this fact affect the outcome of the case?

 # D. Failure to Accommodate Cases

While many religious discrimination cases are brought as intentional disparate treatment claims, many other cases are pursued under the failure to accommodate theory. *But see* Roberto L. Corrada, *Toward an Integrated Disparate Treatment and Accommodation Framework for Title VII Religion Cases*, 77 U. CIN. L. REV. 1411 (2009) (exploring the interrelationship between accommodation and discrimination in religion cases and arguing that the two should not always be considered distinct). The statute provides that an employer must "reasonably accommodate an employee's or prospective employee's religious observance or practice without undue hardship on the conduct of the employer's business." 42 U.S.C. § 2000e(j). For the first time in this text, then, we see the statute treating individuals *differently*. While Title VII was passed to equalize the playing field among workers, in this specific context, the law asks that certain differences are acknowledged as well.

As the statute provides, there are two critical components to any reasonable accommodation claim. First, the accommodation itself must be reasonable. Second, the accommodation must not rise to the level of undue hardship for the employer. It is important to keep in mind, as we review the cases below, that these requirements and terms have been interpreted uniquely in the religious discrimination context. Thus, the terms "reasonable" and "undue hardship" will have different meanings when we visit the accommodation topic again later in this text in our discussion of disability discrimination.

The majority of religious employment discrimination cases do not arise as pure *McDonnell Douglas* disparate treatment claims. Rather, most cases arise where there is some type of conflict between an individual's religion and that employee's job responsibilities. Though the courts vary on how to analyze these types of claims, a typical formulation is as follows:

(1) she had a bona fide religious belief, the practice of which conflicted with an employment duty; (2) she informed her employer of the belief and conflict; and (3) the employer threatened her or subjected her to discriminatory treatment, including discharge, because of her inability to fulfill the job

requirements. If the employee proves a prima facie case of discrimination, the burden shifts to the employer to show either that it initiated good faith efforts to accommodate reasonably the employee's religious practices or that it could not reasonably accommodate the employee without undue hardship.

Tiano v. Dillard Dep't Stores, Inc., 139 F.3d 679, 681 (9th Cir. 1998).

Thus, the courts initially look to whether there was a valid religious belief that conflicted with an employment duty; whether the conflict was communicated to the employer; and whether there was the threat of (or actual) adverse treatment of the worker. If these elements are satisfied, the employer must then show that the accommodation created an undue hardship.

The terms "reasonable" and "undue hardship" are thus critical to analyzing a failure to accommodate claim. The courts have had varying interpretations of these terms, though the Supreme Court has provided some clarity on these issues.

Trans World Airlines, Inc. v. Hardison
432 U.S. 63 (1986)

Mr. Justice WHITE delivered the opinion of the Court.

Petitioner Trans World Airlines (TWA) operates a large maintenance and overhaul base in Kansas City, Mo. On June 5, 1967, respondent Larry G. Hardison was hired by TWA to work as a clerk in the Stores Department at its Kansas City base. Because of its essential role in the Kansas City operation, the Stores Department must operate 24 hours per day, 365 days per year, and whenever an employee's job in that department is not filled, an employee must be shifted from another department, or a supervisor must cover the job, even if the work in other areas may suffer.

Hardison, like other employees at the Kansas City base, was subject to a seniority system contained in a collective-bargaining agreement that TWA maintains with petitioner International Association of Machinists and Aerospace Workers (IAM).

The seniority system is implemented by the union steward through a system of bidding by employees for particular shift assignments as they become available. The most senior employees have first choice for job and shift assignments, and the most junior employees are required to work when the union steward is unable to find enough people willing to work at a particular time or in a particular job to fill TWA's needs.

In the spring of 1968 Hardison began to study the religion known as the Worldwide Church of God. One of the tenets of that religion is that one must observe the Sabbath by refraining from performing any work from sunset

on Friday until sunset on Saturday. The religion also proscribes work on certain specified religious holidays.

When Hardison informed Everett Kussman, the manager of the Stores Department, of his religious conviction regarding observance of the Sabbath, Kussman agreed that the union steward should seek a job swap for Hardison or a change of days off; that Hardison would have his religious holidays off whenever possible if Hardison agreed to work the traditional holidays when asked; and that Kussman would try to find Hardison another job that would be more compatible with his religious beliefs. The problem was temporarily solved when Hardison transferred to the 11 P.M.-7 A.M. shift. Working this shift permitted Hardison to observe his Sabbath.

The problem soon reappeared when Hardison bid for and received a transfer from Building 1, where he had been employed, to Building 2, where he would work the day shift. The two buildings had entirely separate seniority lists; and while in Building 1 Hardison had sufficient seniority to observe the Sabbath regularly, he was second from the bottom on the Building 2 seniority list.

In Building 2 Hardison was asked to work Saturdays when a fellow employee went on vacation. TWA agreed to permit the union to seek a change of work assignments for Hardison, but the union was not willing to violate the seniority provisions set out in the collective-bargaining contract, and Hardison had insufficient seniority to bid for a shift having Saturdays off.

A proposal that Hardison work only four days a week was rejected by the company. Hardison's job was essential and on weekends he was the only available person on his shift to perform it. To leave the position empty would have impaired supply shop functions, which were critical to airline operations; to fill Hardison's position with a supervisor or an employee from another area would simply have undermanned another operation; and to employ someone not regularly assigned to work Saturdays would have required TWA to pay premium wages.

When an accommodation was not reached, Hardison refused to report for work on Saturdays. A transfer to the twilight shift proved unavailing since that scheduled still required Hardison to work past sundown on Fridays. After a hearing, Hardison was discharged on grounds of insubordination for refusing to work during his designated shift.

Hardison, having first invoked the administrative remedy provided by Title VII, brought this action for injunctive relief in the United States District Court against TWA and IAM, claiming that his discharge by TWA constituted religious discrimination in violation of Title VII. He also charged that the union had discriminated against him by failing to represent him adequately in his dispute with TWA and by depriving him of his right to exercise his religious beliefs. Hardison's claim of religious discrimination rested on 1967 EEOC guidelines requiring employers "to make reasonable accommodations to the religious needs of employees" whenever such accommodation would not work an "undue hardship," 29 CFR § 1605.1 (1968), and on similar language adopted by Congress in the 1972 amendments to Title VII.

After a bench trial, the District Court ruled in favor of the defendants. Turning first to the claim against the union, the District Court ruled that although the 1967 EEOC guidelines were applicable to unions, the union's duty to accommodate Hardison's belief did not require it to ignore its seniority system as Hardison appeared to claim. As for Hardison's claim against TWA, the District Court rejected at the outset TWA's contention that requiring it in any way to accommodate the religious needs of its employees would constitute an unconstitutional establishment of religion. As the District Court construed the Act, however, TWA had satisfied its "reasonable accommodations" obligation, and any further accommodation would have worked an undue hardship on the company.

The Court of Appeals for the Eighth Circuit reversed the judgment for TWA. It agreed with the District Court's constitutional ruling, but held that TWA had not satisfied its duty to accommodate. Because it did not appear that Hardison had attacked directly the judgment in favor of the union, the Court of Appeals affirmed that judgment without ruling on its substantive merits.

We disagree with the Court of Appeals in all relevant respects. It is our view that TWA made reasonable efforts to accommodate and that each of the Court of Appeals' suggested alternatives would have been an undue hardship within the meaning of the statute as construed by the EEOC guidelines.

> The Court analyzes all of the suggested accommodations and finds each one to be an undue hardship.

It might be inferred from the Court of Appeals' opinion and from the brief of the EEOC in this Court that TWA's efforts to accommodate were no more than negligible. The findings of the District Court, supported by the record, are to the contrary. In summarizing its more detailed findings, the District Court observed:

> TWA established as a matter of fact that it did take appropriate action to accommodate as required by Title VII. It held several meetings with plaintiff at which it attempted to find a solution to plaintiff's problems. It did accommodate plaintiff's observance of his special religious holidays. It authorized the union steward to search for someone who would swap shifts, which apparently was normal procedure.

It is also true that TWA itself attempted without success to find Hardison another job. The District Court's view was that TWA had done all that could reasonably be expected within the bounds of the seniority system.

The Court of Appeals observed, however, that the possibility of a variance from the seniority system was never really posed to the union. This is contrary to the District Court's findings and to the record. The District Court found that when TWA first learned of Hardison's religious observances in April 1968, it agreed to permit the union's steward to seek a swap of shifts or days off but that "the steward reported that he was unable to work out scheduling changes and that he understood that no one was willing to swap days with plaintiff." Later, in March 1969, at a meeting held just two days before Hardison first failed to report for his Saturday shift, TWA again "offered to accommodate plaintiff's religious observance by agreeing to any trade of shifts or change of shifts that plaintiff and the union could work out. . . . Any shift or change was impossible within the seniority framework and the union was not willing to violate the seniority provisions set out in the contract to make a shift or change." As the record shows, Hardison himself testified that Kussman was willing, but the union was not, to work out a shift or job trade with another employee.

We shall say more about the seniority system, but at this juncture it appears to us that the system itself represented a significant accommodation to the needs, both religious and secular, of all of TWA's employees. As will become apparent, the seniority system represents a neutral way of minimizing the number of occasions when an employee must work on a day that he would prefer to have off. Additionally, recognizing that weekend work schedules are the least popular, the company made further accommodation by reducing its work force to a bare minimum on those days.

We are also convinced, contrary to the Court of Appeals, that TWA itself cannot be faulted for having failed to work out a shift or job swap for Hardison. Both the union and TWA had agreed to the seniority system; the union was unwilling to entertain a variance over the objections of men senior to Hardison; and for TWA to have arranged unilaterally for a swap would have amounted to a breach of the collective-bargaining agreement.

Hardison and the EEOC insist that the statutory obligation to accommodate religious needs takes precedence over both the collective-bargaining contract and the seniority rights of TWA's other employees. We agree that neither a collective-bargaining contract nor a seniority system may be employed to violate the statute, but we do not believe that the duty to accommodate requires TWA to take steps inconsistent with the otherwise valid agreement. Collective bargaining, aimed at effecting workable and enforceable agreements between management and labor, lies at the core of our national labor policy, and seniority provisions are universally included in these contracts. Without a clear and express indication from Congress, we cannot agree with Hardison and the EEOC that an agreed-upon seniority system must give way when necessary to accommodate religious observances. The issue is important and warrants some discussion.

Any employer who, like TWA, conducts an around-the-clock operation is presented with the choice of allocating work schedules either in accordance with the preferences of its employees or by involuntary assignment. Insofar as the varying shift preferences of its employees complement each other, TWA could meet its manpower needs through voluntary work scheduling. In the present case, for example, Hardison's supervisor foresaw little difficulty in giving Hardison his religious holidays off since they fell on days that most other employees preferred to work, while Hardison was willing to work on the traditional holidays that most other employees preferred to have off.

Whenever there are not enough employees who choose to work a particular shift, however, some employees must be assigned to that shift even though it is not their first choice. Such was evidently the case with regard to Saturday work;

even though TWA cut back its weekend work force to a skeleton crew, not enough employees chose those days off to staff the Stores Department through voluntary scheduling. In these circumstances, TWA and IAM agreed to give first preference to employees who had worked in a particular department the longest.

Had TWA nevertheless circumvented the seniority system by relieving Hardison of Saturday work and ordering a senior employee to replace him, it would have denied the latter his shift preference so that Hardison could be given his. The senior employee would also have been deprived of his contractual rights under the collective-bargaining agreement.

It was essential to TWA's business to require Saturday and Sunday work from at least a few employees even though most employees preferred those days off. Allocating the burdens of weekend work was a matter for collective bargaining. In considering criteria to govern this allocation, TWA and the union had two alternatives: adopt a neutral system, such as seniority, a lottery, or rotating shifts; or allocate days off in accordance with the religious needs of its employees. TWA would have had to adopt the latter in order to assure Hardison and others like him of getting the days off necessary for strict observance of their religion, but it could have done so only at the expense of others who had strong, but perhaps nonreligious, reasons for not working on weekends. There were no volunteers to relieve Hardison on Saturdays, and to give Hardison Saturdays off, TWA would have had to deprive another employee of his shift preference at least in part because he did not adhere to a religion that observed the Saturday Sabbath.

Title VII does not contemplate such unequal treatment. The repeated, unequivocal emphasis of both the language and the legislative history of Title VII is on eliminating discrimination in employment, and such discrimination is proscribed when it is directed against majorities as well as minorities. Indeed, the foundation of Hardison's claim is that TWA and IAM engaged in religious discrimination in violation of § 703(a)(1) when they failed to arrange for him to have Saturdays off. It would be anomalous to conclude that by "reasonable accommodation" Congress meant that an employer must deny the shift and job preference of some employees, as well as deprive them of their contractual rights, in order to accommodate or prefer the religious needs of others, and we conclude that Title VII does not require an employer to go that far. Our conclusion is supported by the fact that seniority systems are afforded special treatment under Title VII itself [under § 703(h)].

There has been no suggestion of discriminatory intent in this case. "The seniority system was not designed with the intention to discriminate against religion nor did it act to lock members of any religion into a pattern wherein their freedom to exercise their religion was limited. It was coincidental that in plaintiff's case the seniority system acted to compound his problems in exercising his religion." The Court of Appeals' conclusion that TWA was not limited by the terms of its seniority system was in substance nothing more than a ruling that operation of the seniority system was itself an unlawful employment practice even though no discriminatory purpose had been shown. That ruling is plainly inconsistent with the dictates of § 703(h), both on its face and as interpreted in the recent decisions of this Court.

As we have said, TWA was not required by Title VII to carve out a special exception to its seniority system in order to help Hardison to meet his religious obligations.

The Court of Appeals also suggested that TWA could have permitted Hardison to work a four-day week if necessary in order to avoid working on his Sabbath. Recognizing that this might have left TWA short-handed on the one shift each week that Hardison did not work, the court still concluded that TWA would suffer no undue hardship if it were required to replace Hardison either with supervisory personnel or with qualified personnel from other departments. Alternatively, the Court of Appeals suggested that TWA could have replaced Hardison on his Saturday shift with other available employees through the payment of premium wages. Both of these alternatives would involve costs to TWA, either in the form of lost efficiency in other jobs or higher wages.

To require TWA to bear more than a de minimis cost in order to give Hardison Saturdays off is an undue hardship. Like abandonment of the seniority system, to require TWA to bear additional costs when no such costs are incurred to give other employees the days off that they want would involve unequal treatment of employees on the basis of their religion. By suggesting that TWA should incur certain costs in order to give Hardison Saturdays off the Court of Appeals would in effect require TWA to finance an additional Saturday off and then to choose the employee

> **The de minimis cost standard is now widely applied in all Title VII religious accommodation cases.**

who will enjoy it on the basis of his religious beliefs. While incurring extra costs to secure a replacement for Hardison might remove the necessity of compelling another employee to work involuntarily[] in Hardison's place, it would not change the fact that the privilege of having Saturdays off would be allocated according to religious beliefs.

As we have seen, the paramount concern of Congress in enacting Title VII was the elimination of discrimination in employment. In the absence of clear statutory language or legislative history to the contrary, we will not readily construe the statute to require an employer to discriminate against some employees in order to enable others to observe their Sabbath.

Reversed.

Mr. Justice MARSHALL, with whom Mr. Justice BRENNAN joins, dissenting.

One of the most intractable problems arising under Title VII has been whether an employer is guilty of religious discrimination when he discharges an employee (or refuses to hire a job applicant) because of the employee's religious practices. Particularly troublesome has been the plight of adherents to minority faiths who do not observe the holy days on which most businesses are closed[—]Sundays, Christmas, and Easter[—]but who need time off for their own days of religious observance. The Equal Employment Opportunity Commission has grappled with this problem in two sets of regulations, and in a long line of decisions. Initially the Commission concluded that an employer was "free under Title VII to establish a normal workweek . . . generally applicable to all employees," and that an employee could not "demand any alteration in (his work schedule) to accommodate his religious needs." Eventually, however, the Commission changed its view and decided that employers must reasonably accommodate such requested schedule changes except where "undue hardship" would result[—]for example, "where the employee's needed work cannot be performed by another employee of substantially similar qualifications during the period of absence."

In amending Title VII in 1972 Congress confronted the same problem and adopted the second position of the EEOC. Both before and after the 1972 amendment the lower courts have considered at length the circumstances in which employers must accommodate the religious practices of employees, reaching what the Court correctly describes as conflicting results. And on two occasions this Court has attempted to provide guidance to the lower courts, only to find ourselves evenly divided.

Today's decision deals a fatal blow to all efforts under Title VII to accommodate work requirements to religious practices. The Court holds, in essence, that although the EEOC regulations and the Act state that an employer must make reasonable adjustments in his work demands to take account of religious observances, the regulation and Act do not really mean what they say. An employer, the Court concludes, need not grant even the most minor special privilege to religious observers to enable them to follow their faith. As a question of social policy, this result is deeply troubling, for a society that truly values religious pluralism cannot compel adherents of minority religions to make the cruel choice of surrendering their religion or their job. And as a matter of law today's result is intolerable, for the Court adopts the very position that Congress expressly rejected in 1972, as if we were free to disregard congressional choices that a majority of this Court thinks unwise. I therefore dissent.

What makes today's decision most tragic, however, is not that respondent Hardison has been needlessly deprived of his livelihood simply because he chose to follow the dictates of his conscience. Nor is the tragedy exhausted by the impact it will have on thousands of Americans like Hardison who could be forced to live on welfare as the price they must pay for worshiping their God. The ultimate tragedy is that despite Congress' best efforts, one of this Nation's pillars of strength[—] our hospitality to religious diversity has been seriously eroded. All Americans will be a little poorer until today's decision is erased.

I respectfully dissent.

■ NOTES AND QUESTIONS

1. Perhaps the most important aspect of *Hardison* is the Court's observance that "[t]o require TWA to bear more than a de minimis cost in order to give Hardison Saturdays off is an undue hardship." In light of the Court's analysis in this case, it is now widely considered the standard in religious accommodation cases that anything more than a "de minimis cost" would create an undue hardship for the employer.

2. What does it mean to have a "de minimis cost"? Is *any* substantive financial burden on the employer necessarily an undue hardship? What would it have cost TWA to have accommodated Hardison?

3. The test for undue hardship is different in religious and disability discrimination cases. It is often considered to be far easier to satisfy the religious accommodation requirements than the disability accommodation test. Why would this difference exist? Why do courts interpret identical language differently? The Establishment Clause of the First Amendment makes religious accommodation claims far more complex than disability accommodation claims. This distinction will be discussed in greater detail in Chapter 10, Disability Discrimination.

4. The Court specifically rejected the three accommodations offered by Hardison: the four-day week, premium overtime pay to other substitute workers, and an employee shift swap. Do you agree that each of these three accommodations was unworkable?

5. How important is the collective bargaining agreement to the outcome of the case? If there were no such agreement in place, would it have been easier for the plaintiff to argue that the proposed accommodations did not create an undue hardship? What if the employer had a practice of following seniority, but the employees were not organized and there was no collective bargaining agreement compelling the employer to do so?

6. The Court relies heavily on the fact that TWA "agreed to permit the union's steward to seek a swap of shifts or days off." Is allowing the union steward to seek (but not require) a shift swap really much of an accommodation?

7. The dissent argues that the "decision deals a fatal blow to all efforts under Title VII to accommodate work requirements to religious practices." Is this a fair assessment of the case? Have religious accommodation rights gone extinct after *Hardison*?

8. In his dissent, Justice Marshall further observes that "[t]he ultimate tragedy is that despite Congress' best efforts, one of this Nation's pillars of strength[—] our   hospitality to religious diversity[—]has been seriously eroded. All Americans will be a little poorer until today's decision is erased." To what extent — if any — do you believe that the majority's opinion "seriously erodes" religious discrimination protections? Would a contrary result erode the rights of employers to effectively manage the workplace?

9. The EEOC provides some guidance on when an accommodation poses an undue hardship, stating that factors relevant to undue hardship

> may include the type of workplace, the nature of the employee's duties, the identifiable cost of the accommodation in relation to the size and operating costs of the employer, and the number of employees who will in fact need a particular accommodation. . . . Costs to consider include not only direct monetary costs but also the burden on the conduct of the employer's business. For example, courts have found undue hardship where the accommodation diminishes efficiency in other jobs, infringes on other employees' job rights or benefits, impairs workplace safety, or causes co-workers to carry the accommodated employee's share of potentially hazardous or burdensome work.

EEOC Compl. Man. (CCH) ¶ 8340, § 12-IV(B)(1) & (B)(2) (July 22, 2008).

10. When attempting to determine whether a particular accommodation is appropriate, it is important to look closely at the decisions of the Supreme Court and the local jurisdiction. The federal appellate courts have issued countless decisions on this question arising in a variety of factual scenarios. *See, e.g.,* Peterson v. Hewlett-Packard Co., 358 F.3d 599 (9th Cir. 2004) (holding that employer was not required to accommodate a devout Christian employee by allowing him to post messages intended to demean and harass homosexual co-workers; additionally, employer was not required to accommodate employee by excluding sexual orientation from its workplace diversity programs); Cloutier v. Costco Wholesale Corp., 390 F.3d 126 (1st Cir. 2004) (holding that employer did not have to accommodate an employee who claimed that her religion, the Church of Body Modification, required her to wear multiple facial piercings in violation of the employer's no facial jewelry policy); Bahtia v. Chevron U.S.A., Inc., 734 F.2d 1382 (9th Cir. 1984) (holding that employer did not have to accommodate a Sikh employee by allowing him to wear a beard when the appearance policy was based solely on safety reasons, particularly, the necessity of wearing a respirator with a gas-tight face seal).

 Interactive Problem

Looking back to the interactive problem at the beginning of the chapter, assume that Krista decides that it would not create a religious conflict for her to work on Saturday as long as she is able to go to church in the morning. Her local church has services from 11 A.M. to noon. If she attended this service, she could combine it with her lunch break and only miss about a half hour of work that day. If she were to offer this as an accommodation to her employer, would Big Cars, Inc. be required to accept it?

Practice and Procedural Tip   **22: Reasonable Accommodations and Undue Hardship**

It is not uncommon for employers to seek the advice of legal counsel on whether they should accommodate a particular employee's request for a religious accommodation. When it comes to these types of requests, one important key is to make sure to research: (1) the type of accommodation being requested; (2) the jurisdiction where the request is being sought; and (3) whether the accomodation requested is religious in nature. This may not always be possible; accommodations are very fact specific and it may be that you simply have to offer an employer the best advice possible with possible caveats as to the existing uncertainty in the law.

One important thing to consider, however, is that there are often two separate inquiries when it comes to making reasonable accommodations. First, does the employer have a legal obligation to agree to the employee's request? Second, and perhaps more important, even if there is no legal obligation, should the employer nonetheless attempt to accommodate the employee? Certainly, where a legal obligation is present, there is no question that the accommodation should be made. However, even absent such a requirement, there may be several reasons why an employer may still want to accommodate. First, by accommodating a worker's religious beliefs, it will make that employee more loyal to the company that is trying to work with the employee's request. Our religious beliefs are often very important in our daily lives, and an employer that is sympathetic to this will develop substantial goodwill with its workforce. Second, accommodations are typically inexpensive. Many requests will simply involve slight adjustments to an employee's work schedules for a short period of time. If this is the case, there may be very few negative consequences to making the concession. Finally, even if there is no legal obligation to accommodate, denying a request can often invite litigation. Even where such litigation is unsuccessful, it can still be expensive. Thus, in considering the advice to give an employer with respect to religious accommodations, it is important to use your best legal judgment. Beyond this, however, there is a certain amount of practicality that goes into the decision, and these considerations should also be discussed with the employer.

From the other side of the equation, if an employee seeks your advice on whether an employer has violated her rights by refusing to provide a religious accommodation, it is equally important to research the law in your jurisdiction. The courts vary tremendously regarding the types of accommodations that must be provided. Before jumping to litigation, it may be possible to simply send a letter or email to the employer letting the company know that the worker has sought counsel and that you would hope to work out some type of accommodation. This approach will often be successful. It is important to keep in mind that it will not be difficult for an employer to satisfy the de minimis standard articulated by the Court in *Hardison*. Thus, where an employer is not willing to make an accommodation, litigating a religious accommodation case can be an uphill battle for employees. Nonetheless, where an employer is disregarding an employee's statutory rights, and is nonresponsive to follow-up from opposing counsel, litigation may be necessary and can be successful.

In the *Hardison* case, the Court evaluated the potential viability of several religious accommodation requests proposed by the worker. In the decision below, the Court revisited this approach and decided whether each accommodation request must be evaluated by the employer. This case provides employers with additional important guidance on accommodation requests brought in the religious context.

Ansonia Board of Education v. Philbrook
479 U.S. 60 (1986)

Chief Justice REHNQUIST delivered the opinion of the Court.

Petitioner Ansonia Board of Education has employed respondent Ronald Philbrook since 1962 to teach high school business and typing classes in Ansonia, Connecticut. In 1968, Philbrook was baptized into the Worldwide Church of God. The tenets of the church require members to refrain from secular employment during designated holy days, a practice that has caused respondent to miss approximately six

> As in *Hardison*, the facts here include a collective bargaining agreement that impacts the ability of the employer to accommodate the worker.

schooldays each year. We are asked to determine whether the employer's efforts to adjust respondent's work schedule in light of his beliefs fulfill its obligation under § 701(j) of the Civil Rights Act of 1964, to "reasonably accommodate to an employee's . . . religious observance or practice without undue hardship on the conduct of the employer's business."

Since the 1967–1968 school year, the school board's collective-bargaining agreements with the Ansonia Federation of Teachers have granted to each teacher 18 days of leave per year for illness, cumulative to 150 and later to 180 days. Accumulated leave may be used for purposes other than illness as specified in the agreement. A teacher may accordingly use five days' leave for a death in the immediate family, one day for attendance at a wedding, three days per year for attendance as an official delegate to a national veterans organization, and the like. With the exception of the agreement covering the 1967–1968 school year, each contract has specifically provided three days' annual leave for observance of mandatory religious holidays, as defined in the contract. Unlike other categories for which leave is permitted, absences for religious holidays are not charged against the teacher's annual or accumulated leave.

The school board has also agreed that teachers may use up to three days of accumulated leave each school year for "necessary personal business." Recent contracts limited permissible personal leave to those uses not otherwise specified in the contract. This limitation dictated, for example, that an employee who wanted more than three leave days to attend the convention of a national veterans organization could not use personal leave to gain extra days for that purpose. Likewise, an employee already absent three days for mandatory religious observances could not later use personal leave for "[a]ny religious activity," or "[a]ny religious observance." Since the 1978–1979 school year, teachers have been allowed to take one of the three personal days without prior approval; use of the remaining two days requires advance approval by the school principal.

The limitations on the use of personal business leave spawned this litigation. Until the 1976–1977 year, Philbrook observed mandatory holy days by using the three days granted in the contract and then taking unauthorized leave. His pay was reduced accordingly. In 1976, however, respondent stopped taking unauthorized leave for religious reasons, and began scheduling required hospital visits on church holy days. He also worked on several holy days. Dissatisfied with this arrangement, Philbrook repeatedly asked the school board to adopt one of two alternatives. His preferred alternative would allow use of personal business leave for religious observance, effectively giving him three additional days of paid leave for that purpose. Short of this arrangement, respondent suggested that he pay the cost of a substitute and receive full pay for additional days off for religious observances. Petitioner has consistently rejected both proposals.

After a 2-day trial, the District Court concluded that Philbrook had failed to prove a case of religious discrimination because he had not been placed by the school board in a position of violating his religion or losing his job. The Court of Appeals for the Second Circuit reversed and remanded for further proceedings.

[W]e are asked to address whether the Court of Appeals erred in finding that Philbrook established a prima facie case of religious discrimination and in opining that an employer must accept the employee's preferred accommodation absent proof of undue hardship. We find little support in the statute for the approach adopted by the Court of Appeals, but we agree that the ultimate issue of reasonable accommodation cannot be resolved without further factual inquiry. We accordingly affirm the judgment of the Court of Appeals remanding the case to the District Court for additional findings.

As we noted in our only previous consideration of § 701(j), its language was added to the 1972 amendments on the floor of the Senate with little discussion. *Trans World Airlines, Inc. v. Hardison*, 432 U.S. 63 (1977). In *Hardison*, we determined that an accommodation causes "undue hardship" whenever that accommodation results in "more than a de minimis cost" to the employer. Hardison had been discharged because his religious beliefs would not allow him to work on Saturdays and claimed that this action violated the employer's duty to effect a reasonable accommodation of his beliefs. Because we concluded that each of the suggested accommodations would impose on the employer an undue hardship, we had no occasion to consider the bounds of a prima facie case in the religious accommodation context or whether an employer is required to choose from available accommodations the alternative preferred by the employee. The employer in *Hardison* simply argued that all conceivable accommodations would result in undue hardship, and we agreed.

Petitioner asks us to establish for religious accommodation claims a proof scheme analogous to that developed in other Title VII contexts, delineating the plaintiff's prima facie case and shifting production burdens. But the present case raises no such issue. As in *United States Postal Service Board of Governors v. Aikens*, 460 U.S. 711 (1983), the defendant here failed to persuade the District Court to dismiss the action for want of a prima facie case, and the case was fully tried on the merits. We held in *Aikens* that these circumstances place the ultimate Title VII question of discrimination vel non directly before the court. "Where the defendant has done everything that would be required of him if the plaintiff had properly made out a prima facie case, whether the plaintiff really did so is no longer relevant." We may therefore proceed to the question whether the employer's proposed accommodation of respondent's religious practices comports with the statutory mandate of § 701(j).

In addressing this question, the Court of Appeals assumed that the employer had offered a reasonable accommodation of Philbrook's religious beliefs. This alone, however, was insufficient in that court's view to allow resolution of the dispute. The court observed that the duty to accommodate "cannot be defined without reference to undue hardship." *Philbrook v. Ansonia Bd. of Educ.*, 757 F.2d 476 (1985). It accordingly determined that the accommodation obligation includes a duty to accept "the proposal the employee prefers unless that accommodation causes undue hardship on the employer's conduct of his business." Because the District Court had not considered whether Philbrook's proposals would impose undue hardship, the Court of Appeals remanded for further consideration of those proposals.

We find no basis in either the statute or its legislative history for requiring an employer to choose any particular reasonable accommodation. By its very terms the statute directs that any reasonable accommodation by the employer is sufficient to meet its accommodation obligation. The employer violates the statute unless it "demonstrates that [it] is unable to reasonably accommodate . . . an employee's . . . religious observance or practice without undue hardship on the conduct of the employer's business." 42 U.S.C. § 2000e(j). Thus, where the employer has already reasonably accommodated the employee's religious needs, the statutory inquiry is at an end. The employer need not further show that each of the employee's alternative accommodations would result in undue hardship. As *Hardison* illustrates, the extent of undue hardship on the employer's business is at issue only where the employer claims that it is unable to offer any reasonable accommodation without such hardship. Once the Court of Appeals assumed that the school board had offered to Philbrook a reasonable alternative, it erred by requiring the Board to nonetheless demonstrate the hardship of Philbrook's alternatives.

The legislative history of § 701(j), as we noted in *Hardison*, is of little help in defining the employer's accommodation obligation. To the extent it provides any indication of congressional intent, however, we think that the history supports our conclusion. Senator Randolph, the sponsor of the amendment that became § 701(j), expressed his hope that accommodation would be made with "flexibility" and "a desire to achieve an adjustment." 118 Cong. Rec. 706 (1972). Consistent with these goals, courts have noted that "bilateral cooperation is appropriate in the search for an acceptable reconciliation of the needs of the employee's religion and the exigencies of the employer's business." *Brener v. Diagnostic Center Hospital*, 671 F.2d 141, 145–146 (CA5 1982). Under the approach articulated by the Court of Appeals, however, the employee is given every incentive to hold out for the most beneficial accommodation, despite the fact that an employer offers a reasonable resolution of the conflict. This approach, we think, conflicts with both the language of the statute and the views that led to its enactment. We accordingly hold that an employer has met its obligation under § 701(j) when it demonstrates that it has offered a reasonable accommodation to the employee.

The remaining issue in the case is whether the school board's leave policy constitutes a reasonable accommodation of Philbrook's religious beliefs. Because both the District Court and the Court of Appeals applied what we hold to be an erroneous view of the law, neither explicitly considered this question. We think that there are insufficient factual findings as to the manner in which the collective-bargaining agreements have been interpreted in order for us to make that judgment initially. We think that the school board policy in this case, requiring respondent

> The Court here leaves open the possibility that religion is being treated differently by the employer for purposes of granting leave.

to take unpaid leave for holy day observance that exceeded the amount allowed by the collective-bargaining agreement, would generally be a reasonable one. In enacting § 701(j), Congress was understandably motivated by a desire to assure the individual additional opportunity to observe religious practices, but it did not impose a duty on the employer to accommodate at all costs. *Trans World Airlines, Inc. v. Hardison*, 432 U.S. 63 (1977). The provision of unpaid leave eliminates the conflict between employment requirements and religious practices by allowing the individual to observe fully religious holy days and requires him only to give up compensation for a day that he did not in fact work.

But unpaid leave is not a reasonable accommodation when paid leave is provided for all purposes except religious ones. A provision for paid leave "that is part and parcel of the employment relationship may not be doled out in a discriminatory fashion, even if the employer would be free . . . not to provide the benefit at all." *Hishon v. King & Spalding*, 467 U.S. 69 (1984). Such an arrangement would display a discrimination against religious practices that is the antithesis of reasonableness. Whether the policy here violates this teaching turns on factual inquiry into past and present administration of the personal business leave provisions of the collective-bargaining agreement. The school board contends that the necessary personal business category in the agreement, like other leave provisions, defines a limited purpose leave. Philbrook, on the other hand, asserts that the necessary personal leave category is not so limited, operating as an open-ended leave provision that may be used for a wide range of secular purposes in addition to those specifically provided for in the contract, but not for similar religious purposes. We do not think that the record is sufficiently clear on this point for us to make the necessary factual findings, and we therefore affirm the judgment of the Court of Appeals remanding the case to the District Court.

It is so ordered.

Justice Marshall, concurring in part and dissenting in part.

I agree with the Court's conclusion that, if the school board provides paid leave "for all purposes except religious ones," its accommodation of Philbrook's religious needs would be unreasonable and thus violate Title VII. But I do not find the specificity of the personal business leave, or the possibility that it may be used for activities similar to the religious activities Philbrook seeks leave to pursue, necessarily dispositive of whether the Board has satisfied its affirmative duty under § 701(j), 42 U.S.C. § 2000e(j), to reasonably accommodate Philbrook's religious needs. Even if the District Court should find that the personal leave is restricted to specific secular uses having no similarity with Philbrook's religious activities, Philbrook would still encounter a conflict between his religious needs and work requirements. In my view, the question would remain whether, without imposing an undue hardship on the conduct of its educational program, the school board could further reasonably accommodate Philbrook's need for additional religious leave.

The Court suggests that requiring an employer to consider an employee's proposals would enable the employee to hold his employer hostage in exchange for a particular accommodation. If the employer has offered a reasonable accommodation that fully resolves the conflict between the employee's work and religious requirements, I agree that no further consideration of the employee's proposals would normally be warranted. But if the accommodation offered by the employer does not completely resolve the employee's conflict, I would hold that the employer remains under an obligation to consider whatever reasonable proposals the employee may submit.

The Court's analysis in *Trans World Airlines, Inc. v. Hardison*, 432 U.S. 63 (1977), is difficult to reconcile with its holding today. In *Hardison*, the Court held that the employer's chosen work schedule was a reasonable accommodation but nonetheless went on to consider and reject each of the alternative suggested accommodations. The course followed in *Hardison* should have been adopted here as well. "Once it is determined that the duty to accommodate sometimes requires that an employee be exempted from an otherwise valid work requirement, the only remaining question is. . . . Did [the employer] prove that *it exhausted all reasonable accommodations*, and that the *only remaining alternatives would have caused undue hardship* on [the employer's] business?" *Id.* at 91 (Marshall, J., dissenting) (emphasis added).

Accordingly, I would remand this case for factual findings on both the intended scope of the school board's leave provision and the reasonableness and expected hardship of Philbrook's proposals.

■ NOTES AND QUESTIONS

1. The basic holding of this case is that an employer need not agree to the particular accommodation that is offered by the employee; as long as a reasonable accommodation is offered by the employer, that is sufficient to satisfy the statute. Should this be the standard? Would it be a better standard for the employee and employer to collaborate on finding the best accommodation available?

2. Philbrook offered two possible accommodations here — allowing the use of personal days for religious observance or allowing him to pay for a substitute to cover his classes. Don't both of these alternatives seem very reasonable? Why doesn't the Court assess the validity of these suggestions? Is the accommodation offered by the employer a better accommodation?

3. In his dissent, Justice Marshall notes that "[t]he Court's analysis in *Trans World Airlines, Inc. v. Hardison* . . . is difficult to reconcile with its holding today."

In *Hardison*, the Court closely examined each of the alternatives offered by the plaintiff, rejecting each along the way. In this case, however, the Court did not assess the validity of the plaintiff's offered accommodations, and concluded that the defendant had satisfied its statutory obligation once it had offered a reasonable accommodation. Is Justice Marshall correct that the Court's approach in *Hardison* is inconsistent with its decision in *Ansonia*?

4. While the Court rejected the plaintiff's accommodation claim, the Court did hold that "unpaid leave is not a reasonable accommodation when paid leave is provided for all purposes except religious ones." The Court thus remanded the case to more fully develop the record on this point. Was the employer discriminating on the basis of religion in how it allowed the paid leave to be used? If it discriminated against all religious activities in this regard, would it still run afoul of the statute? Can you reconcile the *Moranski* decision discussed earlier — where the Seventh Circuit found that it was not discrimination to prohibit all religious affinity groups — with the Court's statements in this case?

5. In general, "an employer does not have to accommodate an employee's religious beliefs or practices if doing so would cause undue hardship to the employer," such as if the accommodation is "costly, compromises workplace safety, decreases workplace efficiency, infringes on the rights of other employees, or requires other employees to do more than their share of potentially hazardous or burdensome work." EEOC, *Religious Discrimination*, http://www.eeoc.gov/laws/types/religion.cfm. *See* Yeager v. FirstEnergy Generation Corp., No. 5:14-CV-567, 2014 WL 2919288, at *1 (N.D. Ohio June 27, 2014) (holding that employer did not have to accommodate employee who refused to provide a social security number when filling out his new-employee paperwork because it would have caused him to have the "mark of the beast"). *See also* Baltgalvis v. Newport News Shipbuilding Inc., 132 F. Supp. 2d 414 (E.D. Va. 2000) (holding that an employer may terminate or refuse to hire an employee who refuses to provide a social security number as required by federal law).

Religious accommodation claims can be unique from other areas of the law because an employee may not necessarily inform the employer of the need for the accommodation. In the interesting case below, the Supreme Court addressed the question of whether an employer must accommodate a religious belief or practice even where the applicant (or employee) has not specifically informed the company of the needed accommodation. The Court's decision helps provide some much needed guidance to this important area of the law.

EEOC v. Abercrombie & Fitch Stores, Inc.
135 S. Ct. 2028 (2015)

JUSTICE SCALIA delivered the opinion of the Court.

Title VII of the Civil Rights Act of 1964 prohibits a prospective employer from refusing to hire an applicant in order to avoid accommodating a religious practice that it could accommodate without undue hardship. The question presented is whether this prohibition applies only where an applicant has informed the employer of his need for an accommodation.

We summarize the facts in the light most favorable to the Equal Employment Opportunity Commission (EEOC), against whom the Tenth Circuit granted summary judgment. Respondent Abercrombie & Fitch Stores, Inc., operates several lines of clothing stores, each with its own "style." Consistent with the image Abercrombie seeks to project for each store, the company imposes a Look Policy that governs its employees' dress. The Look Policy prohibits "caps" — a term the Policy does not define — as too informal for Abercrombie's desired image.

Samantha Elauf is a practicing Muslim who, consistent with her understanding of her religion's requirements, wears a headscarf. She applied for a position in an Abercrombie store, and was interviewed by Heather Cooke, the store's assistant manager. Using Abercrombie's ordinary system for evaluating applicants, Cooke gave Elauf a rating that qualified her to be hired; Cooke was concerned, however, that Elauf's headscarf would conflict with the store's Look Policy.

> How does the company define its Look Policy here? Shouldn't the company be able to adopt such a policy under its normal business practices?

Cooke sought the store manager's guidance to clarify whether the headscarf was a forbidden "cap." When this yielded no answer, Cooke turned to Randall Johnson, the district manager. Cooke informed Johnson that she believed Elauf wore her headscarf because of her faith. Johnson told Cooke that Elauf's headscarf would violate the Look Policy, as would all other headwear, religious or otherwise, and directed Cooke not to hire Elauf.

The EEOC sued Abercrombie on Elauf's behalf, claiming that its refusal to hire Elauf violated Title VII. The District Court granted the EEOC summary judgment on the issue of liability, held a trial on damages, and awarded $20,000. The Tenth Circuit reversed and awarded Abercrombie summary judgment. It concluded that ordinarily an employer cannot be liable under Title VII for failing to accommodate a religious practice until the applicant (or employee) provides the employer with actual knowledge of his need for an accommodation. We granted certiorari.

Abercrombie's primary argument is that an applicant cannot show disparate treatment without first showing that an employer has "actual knowledge" of the applicant's need for an accommodation. We disagree. Instead, an applicant need only show that his need for an accommodation was a motivating factor in the employer's decision.

The disparate-treatment provision forbids employers to: (1) "fail . . . to hire" an applicant (2) "because of" (3) "such individual's . . . religion" (which includes his religious practice). Here, of course, Abercrombie (1) failed to hire Elauf. The parties concede that (if Elauf sincerely believes that her religion so requires) Elauf's wearing of a head-scarf is (3) a "religious practice." All that remains is whether she was not hired (2) "because of" her religious practice.

The term "because of" appears frequently in antidiscrimination laws. It typically imports, at a minimum, the traditional standard of but-for causation. *University of Tex. Southwestern Medical Center* v. *Nassar*, 133 S. Ct. 2517 (2013). Title VII relaxes this standard, however, to prohibit even making a protected characteristic a "motivating factor" in an employment decision.

It is significant that [the statute] does not impose a knowledge requirement. [T]he intentional discrimination provision prohibits certain *motives*, regardless of the state of the actor's knowledge. Motive and knowledge are separate concepts. An employer who has actual knowledge of the need for an accommodation does not violate Title VII by refusing to hire an applicant if avoiding that accommodation is not his *motive*. Conversely, an employer who acts with the motive of avoiding accommodation may violate Title VII even if he has no more than an unsubstantiated suspicion that accommodation would be needed.

Thus, the rule for disparate-treatment claims based on a failure to accommodate a religious practice is straightforward: An employer may not make an applicant's religious practice, confirmed or otherwise, a factor in employment decisions. For example, suppose that an employer thinks (though he does not know for certain) that a job applicant may be an orthodox Jew who will observe the Sabbath, and thus be unable to work on Saturdays. If the applicant actually requires an accommodation of that religious practice, and the employer's desire to avoid the prospective accommodation is a motivating factor in his decision, the employer violates Title VII.

Abercrombie urges this Court to adopt the Tenth Circuit's rule "allocat[ing] the burden of raising a religious conflict." This would require the employer to have actual knowledge of a conflict between an applicant's religious practice and a work rule. The problem with this approach is the one that inheres in most incorrect interpretations of statutes: It asks us to add words to the law to produce what is thought to be a desirable result. That is Congress's province. We construe Title VII's silence as exactly that: silence. Its disparate-treatment provision prohibits actions taken with the *motive* of avoiding the need for accommodating a religious practice. A request for accommodation, or the employer's certainty that the practice exists, may make it easier to infer motive, but is not a necessary condition of liability.

> **The Court rejects the argument that the Look Policy should be analyzed under disparate impact theory. Why?**

Abercrombie argues in the alternative that a claim based on a failure to accommodate an applicant's religious practice must be raised as a disparate-impact claim, not a disparate-treatment claim. We think not. That might have been true if Congress had limited the meaning of "religion" in Title VII to religious *belief* — so that discriminating against a particular religious *practice* would not be disparate treatment though it might have disparate impact. In fact, however, Congress defined "religion," for Title VII's purposes, as "includ[ing] all aspects of religious observance and practice, as well as belief." 42 U.S.C. § 2000e(j). Thus, religious practice is one of the protected characteristics that cannot be accorded disparate treatment and must be accommodated.

Nor does the statute limit disparate-treatment claims to only those employer policies that treat religious practices less favorably than similar secular practices. Abercrombie's argument that a neutral policy cannot constitute "intentional discrimination" may make sense in other contexts. But Title VII does not demand mere neutrality with regard to religious practices — that they be treated no worse than other practices. Rather, it gives them favored treatment, affirmatively obligating employers not "to fail or refuse to hire or discharge any individual . . . because of such individual's" "religious observance and practice." An employer is surely entitled to have, for example, a no-headwear policy as an ordinary matter. But when an applicant requires an accommodation as an "aspec[t] of religious . . . practice," it is no response that the subsequent "fail[ure] . . . to hire" was due to an otherwise-neutral policy. Title VII requires otherwise-neutral policies to give way to the need for an accommodation. We reverse [the appellate court's] judgment and remand the case for further consideration consistent with this opinion.

It is so ordered.

[Concurrence of Justice Alito, and Concurrence and Dissent of Justice Thomas omitted.]

■ NOTES AND QUESTIONS

1. The Supreme Court decides here that "[m]otive and knowledge are separate concepts. An employer who has actual knowledge of the need for an accommodation does not violate Title VII by refusing to hire an applicant if avoiding that accommodation is not his *motive*. Conversely, an employer who acts with the motive of avoiding accommodation may violate Title VII even if he has no more than an unsubstantiated suspicion that accommodation would be needed." Do you find this distinction between motive and knowledge persuasive?

2. The Supreme Court articulates what it believes to be a "straightforward" rule for disparate treatment claims that are connected to a failure to accommodate in the religious context: "An employer may not make an applicant's religious practice, confirmed or otherwise, a factor in employment decisions. For example, suppose that an employer thinks (though he does not know for certain) that a job applicant may be an orthodox Jew who will observe the Sabbath, and thus be unable to work on Saturdays. If the applicant actually requires an accommodation of that religious practice, and the employer's desire to avoid the prospective accommodation is a motivating factor in his decision, the employer violates Title VII." Should it be enough that there is a motivating factor in these cases, or should but-for causation be required?

3. The company asked that the Court adopt the appellate court's view that the employer must "have actual knowledge of a conflict between an applicant's religious practice and a work rule." The Court rejected this approach as inconsistent with the wording of the statute. Do you agree?

4. The Court rejects the defendant's argument that the claim here should have been raised as one of disparate impact as it involves a discriminatory practice. How should a court decide whether such a claim invokes intentional or unintentional discrimination?

5. The company here has presumptively generated a lot of money through its Look Policy, which in turn has led to increased profits and enhanced employment opportunities for workers. Should federal law—and the Supreme Court—be interfering with practices that may ultimately be good for the economy as a whole? Should the courts be acting as super-personnel departments that are second-guessing the decisions of employers?

6. Though this argument was not made in the case, could the Look Policy be seen as a BFOQ in the religious context? Is having a certain attractive look job related? Does it go to the essence or central mission of the company?

7. Does the Court treat the claim here as a failure-to-accommodate cause of action or as a disparate treatment claim? Does it make a difference? Why?

8. The company here is not the first to adopt such a policy on appearance. As we saw in earlier chapters, companies routinely attempt to apply such requirements that may impact individuals on the basis of sex, race, national origin, or age. Employers should proceed with extreme caution before implementing such a policy. As we see here, the Supreme Court has serious concerns about the way Abercrombie implemented the policy in question.

One issue that often arises in religious accommodation cases is whether the religious beliefs of the employee are "sincere." Under Title VII, employers are required to accommodate only those beliefs that are "sincerely held" by the employees. Though sincerity of belief is not often a question in a particular matter, it can present difficulties in certain cases. The courts vary tremendously regarding the extent to which they evaluate the sincerity question.

EEOC v. Unión Independiente de la Autoridad de Acueductos y Alcantarillados de Puerto Rico

279 F.3d 49 (1st Cir. 2002)

TORRUELLA, Circuit Judge.

David Cruz-Carrillo ("Cruz") is a member of the Seventh-Day Adventist Church who claims that the tenets of his religion prohibit him from joining a labor organization. Cruz was hired by the Autoridad de Acueductos y Alcantarillados of the Commonwealth of Puerto Rico ("AAA") as a temporary employee in 1986. When he applied for employment with AAA, he never disclosed that his religious beliefs forbid him from becoming a member of a labor organization. However, his application for employment at AAA reveals that Cruz attended Seventh-Day Adventist schools and graduated from a Seventh-Day Adventist college.

Defendant Unión Independiente de la Autoridad de Acueductos y Alcantarillados ("UIA" or "Union") is a labor organization created in accordance with the Puerto Rico Labor Relations Act. UIA represents several categories of employees, including operations and maintenance workers of AAA. UIA maintained a Collective Bargaining Agreement (CBA) with AAA that contains a union security clause, pursuant to which all permanent employees of the appropriate bargaining unit must belong to the Union.

On December 5, 1988, Cruz became a permanent employee of AAA. He was given written notification of the conditions under which he would be employed, including his obligation to join UIA and pay union dues. According to UIA, Cruz did not state his objection to union membership outright at that time. Instead, he objected only to specific union practices, each of which UIA contends it was willing to accommodate. For example, Cruz objected at various points to attending Saturday union meetings, joining union demonstrations or strikes, taking the Union's loyalty oath, and paying union dues. Through a series of correspondence, meetings, and administrative procedures, UIA expressed its willingness to exempt Cruz from Saturday meetings and public strikes or picketing, to paraphrase its loyalty oath to an affirmation, and to transfer his dues to a nonprofit organization (but retain the share used to pay his fringe benefits). Only after Cruz rejected these proposals, contends UIA, did he assert his objection to union membership in any form. Cruz disputes this version of events and maintains that his opposition to union membership was steadfast and unqualified.

On March 27, 1991, the Board of Directors of UIA initiated disciplinary proceedings against Cruz for his refusal to become a UIA member. At the end of these proceedings, UIA requested that AAA suspend Cruz from employment in accordance with the union security clause. Cruz appealed the resolution to the Executive Central Committee of UIA, which affirmed the proposed disciplinary measures. Cruz avers that throughout the course of these proceedings he was declared "persona non grata" by the UIA.

The requirement that the employee have a "bona fide religious belief" is an essential element of a religious accommodation claim. In order to satisfy this element, the plaintiff must demonstrate both that the belief or practice is religious and that it is sincerely held.

As noted above, Title VII's capacious definition of "religion" includes "all aspects of religious observance and practice, as well as belief. . . ." 42 U.S.C. § 2000e(j). The statute thus leaves little room for a party to challenge the religious nature of an employee's professed beliefs. Plus, in this case, the religious foundation of the Seventh-Day Adventist faith's opposition to union membership has long been recognized in the opinions of this court and those of our sister circuits. The religious nature of Cruz's professed belief therefore cannot seriously be disputed, nor has UIA mounted such a challenge.

Yet, "[w]hile the 'truth' of a belief is not open to question, there remains the significant question of whether it is 'truly held.'" *United States v. Seeger*, 380 U.S. 163 (1965). The element of sincerity is fundamental, since "if the religious beliefs that apparently prompted a request are not sincerely held, there has been no showing of a religious observance or practice that conflicts with an employment requirement." *EEOC v. Ilona of Hungary, Inc.*, 108 F.3d 1569 (7th Cir. 1997). The finding on this issue generally will depend on the factfinder's assessment of the employee's credibility. In this case, UIA has by no means conceded that Cruz's opposition to union membership was the product of a sincerely held belief. Instead, it has adduced specific undisputed evidence of conduct on Cruz's

> The Court here acknowledges that measuring an individual's religious sincerity is "a delicate business."

part that is contrary to the tenets of his professed religious belief. For example, there is record evidence that Cruz lied on an employment application; that he is divorced; that he took an oath before a notary upon becoming a public employee; and that he works five days a week (instead of the six days required by his faith). Evidence tending to show that an employee acted in a manner inconsistent with his professed religious belief is, of course, relevant to the factfinder's evaluation of sincerity. UIA also points to disputed evidence that, when viewed in the light most favorable to UIA, shows that the alleged conflict between Cruz's beliefs and union membership was a moving target: at first, Cruz objected only to certain membership requirements, and he only voiced his opposition to any form of union membership after UIA agreed to accommodate him with respect to each practice he had identified earlier. Such evidence, if credited by the factfinder, could also bear on the sincerity of Cruz's beliefs. We therefore conclude that UIA raised a triable issue of fact, making summary judgment inappropriate.

To be sure, assessing the bona fides of an employee's religious belief is a delicate business. On the one hand, the defendant is entitled to hold the plaintiff to his burden, making it "entirely appropriate, indeed necessary, for a court to engage in analysis of the sincerity of someone's religious beliefs. . . ." *Protos v. Volkswagen of Am., Inc.*, 797 F.2d 129, 137 (3d Cir. 1986) [quotation omitted]. On the other hand, "[s]incerity analysis is exceedingly amorphous, requiring the factfinder to delve into the [employee's] most veiled motivations and vigilantly separate the issue of sincerity from the factfinder's perception of the religious nature of the [employee's] beliefs." *Patrick v. LeFevre*, 745 F.2d 153 (2d Cir. 1984).

We believe that a jury, acting under proper instructions from the trial judge, is fully capable of evaluating the parties' evidence and making the appropriate factual determination.

■ NOTES AND QUESTIONS

1. Why is it important to have a "sincerity" requirement for accommodation claims?

2. As the court notes, "assessing the bona fides of an employee's religious belief is a delicate business." How does a court go about assessing the sincerity of an individual's beliefs? Is this a role for the jury?

3. The court noted several inconsistencies between the plaintiff's religion and his conduct, notably that he "lied on an employment application; that he is divorced; that he took an oath before a notary upon becoming a public employee; and that he works five days a week (instead of the six days required by his faith)." Do these inconsistencies necessarily mean that the plaintiff is not sincere about his religious beliefs? Don't many individuals struggle to maintain the teachings of their particular religions? If so, does this make their beliefs any less sincere? How should courts treat recent converts who likely have a history inconsistent with their new beliefs?

4. The sincerity of an individual's religious beliefs has given rise to several interesting decisions of the lower courts. *See, e.g.,* EEOC v. Chemsico, Inc., 216 F. Supp. 2d 940, 950 (E.D. Miss. 2002) (finding that an employee who failed to observe many of the tenets of her religion — by failing to attend regular church services, making an inaccurate statement that the Sabbath begins at sunup Saturday rather than at sundown Friday, failing to observe prohibition on work during other holy days, and having a child out of wedlock — could still hold a sincere religious belief preventing her from working on Saturdays); Franks v. Nat'l Lime & Stone Co., 740 N.E.2d 694, 698 (Ohio Ct. App. 2000) (finding that the employee's failure to fully and honestly disclose a religious conflict in an initial interview calls into question the extent to which the religious belief was sincerely held by the employee); McCrory v. Rapides Reg'l Med. Ctr., 635 F. Supp. 975, 979 (W.D. La. 1986) (finding that employees who were discharged because of the disruption caused by their extramarital affairs could not claim a sincere religious belief in a right to commit adultery when their Baptist faith specifically forbade such behavior).

 Interactive Problem

Looking back at the interactive problem at the beginning of the chapter, assume that Krista's employer hired a private investigator to follow her, and it was revealed that Krista had secured a second job working on Sundays as part of a cleaning team that worked in local businesses. Would this additional fact alter the analysis of Krista's accommodation request?

The EEOC has also offered substantial guidance as to the "best practices" for both employees and employers for handling religious accommodation requests. That guidance is set forth below. Though such guidance does not have the force of law, courts often look to it when reviewing discrimination claims, and it should provide a valuable starting point for employers when contemplating how to approach a particular request:

Employer Best Practices

Reasonable Accommodation — Generally

Employers should inform employees that they will make reasonable efforts to accommodate the employees' religious practices. . . .
 Employers should individually assess each request and avoid assumptions or stereotypes about what constitutes a religious belief or practice or what type of accommodation is appropriate. . . .

Undue Hardship — Generally

The de minimis undue hardship standard refers to the legal requirement. As with all aspects of employee relations, employers can go beyond the requirements of the law and should be flexible in evaluating whether or not an accommodation is feasible.

An employer should not assume that an accommodation will conflict with the terms of a seniority system or CBA without first checking if there are any exceptions for religious accommodation. . . .

Schedule Changes

Employers should work with employees who need an adjustment to their work schedule to accommodate their religious practices. . . .

Employers should consider adopting flexible leave and scheduling policies and procedures that will often allow employees to meet their religious and other personal needs. . . .

Modifying Workplace Practices, Policies, and Procedures

Employers should make efforts to accommodate an employee's desire to wear a yarmulke, hijab, or other religious garb. If the employer is concerned about uniform appearance in a position which involves interaction with the public, it may be appropriate to consider whether the employee's religious views would permit him to resolve the religious conflict by, for example, wearing the item of religious garb in the company uniform color(s). . . .

Permitting Prayer, Proselytizing, and Other Forms of Religious Expression

Employers should train managers to gauge the actual disruption posed by religious expression in the workplace, rather than merely speculating that disruption may result. Employers should also train managers to identify alternative accommodations that might be offered to avoid actual disruption. . . .

Employers should incorporate a discussion of religious expression, and the need for all employees to be sensitive to the beliefs or non-beliefs of others, into any anti-harassment training provided to managers and employees.

EEOC Compl. Man. (CCH) ¶ 8340, § 12-IV(C)(7) (July 22, 2008).

E. Exceptions to Religious Discrimination Claims

Unlike the other areas of employment discrimination, religious claims are particularly unique in that there are a number of exceptions that can apply. Though the exceptions are varied, there are four primary exceptions that will be highlighted in the text below: (1) the educational exception; (2) the religious employer exception found in § 702(a); (3) the bona fide occupational qualification; and (4) the ministerial exception. If one of these exceptions applies to a particular situation, the employer may discriminate on the basis of religion without violating Title VII. In particular, the exceptions do provide complete immunity in specific situations, but do so only with respect to activities that are religious in nature.

1. The Educational Exception

The educational exception for employment discrimination claims states that

> it shall not be an unlawful employment practice for a school, college, university, or other educational institution or institution of learning to hire and employ employees of a particular religion if such school, college, university, or other educational institution or institution of learning is, in whole or in substantial part, owned, supported, controlled, or managed by a particular religion or by a particular religious corporation, association, or society, or if the curriculum of such school, college, university, or other educational institution or institution of learning is directed toward the propagation of a particular religion.

University of Notre Dame

42 U.S.C. § 2000e–2(e).

Thus, where a school is religious in nature and satisfies the terms of the statute, that institution can choose to hire individuals who share a common faith without running afoul of the statute. Note the primary limitation of the statute, however — the exception applies only to educational institutions. Thus, to fit within the contours of this exception, an entity must have education as one of its primary missions.

2. The Religious Employer Exception

The religious employer exception to religious discrimination (commonly known as the 702(a) exception) can be found at 42 U.S.C. § 2000e–1(a) and provides:

> This subchapter shall not apply to an employer with respect to the employment of aliens outside any State, or to a religious corporation, association, educational institution, or society with respect to the employment of individuals of a particular religion to perform work connected with the carrying on by such corporation, association, educational institution, or society of its activities.

This exemption overlaps with the educational exception discussed above. Both exceptions would apply to situations where a religious educational institution is involved in the inquiry.

To be covered by the religious employer exception, the employer must satisfy the terms of the statute outlined above. Generally speaking, this means that the employer must satisfy the following two tests: (1) the employer itself must be religious, and (2) the discrimination that is being exercised must be religious in nature. Thus, only where the organization itself is religious, and where the employer attempts to discriminate on the basis of religion, will an exception be found. A religious employer that discriminates on the basis of race, color, sex, or national origin will not be protected by this provision. Similarly, an organization that does not have a religious mission — but nonetheless attempts to discriminate on the basis of religion — will not be protected.

The EEOC has issued guidance on the scope of this exception, which is outlined below:

> Under Title VII, religious organizations are permitted to give employment preference to members of their own religion. The exception applies only to those institutions whose "purpose and character are primarily religious." That determination is to be based on "[a]ll significant religious and secular characteristics." Although no one factor is dispositive, significant factors to consider that would indicate whether an entity is religious include:
>
> ■ Do its articles of incorporation state a religious purpose?
> ■ Are its day-to-day operations religious (e.g., are the services the entity performs, the product it produces, or the educational curriculum it provides directed toward propagation of the religion)?
> ■ Is it not-for-profit?
> ■ Is it affiliated with or supported by a church or other religious organization?
>
> This exception is not limited to religious activities of the organization. However, it only allows religious organizations to prefer to employ individuals who share their religion. The exception does not allow religious organizations otherwise to discriminate in employment on protected bases other than religion, such as race, color, national origin, sex, age, or disability.

EEOC Compl. Man. (CCH) ¶ 8310, § 12-I(C)(1) (July 22, 2008).

The religious employer exception has been interesting in application. In 2006, for example, the EEOC determined that a private Catholic school engaged in unlawful pregnancy discrimination by firing a teacher after she informed the school that she was pregnant and unmarried. The school argued that the teacher was terminated because she violated the school's religious principles by becoming pregnant while unmarried. The New York Civil Liberties Union filed a complaint with the EEOC, arguing that the school had engaged in sex discrimination and pregnancy discrimination by firing the teacher because she had engaged in nonmarital sex, even though the school did not have a similar policy concerning male employees. The EEOC agreed, maintaining that while there is a religious employer exception, the scope of this exception does not allow termination based on sex or pregnancy discrimination. *See Catholic School Cannot Discriminate Against Unwed Pregnant Teacher, EEOC Rules*, NYCLU.com (Oct. 11, 2006), http://www .nyclu.org/ news/catholic-school-cannot-discriminate-against-unwed-pregnant-teacher-eeoc-rules.

3. The BFOQ

Perhaps the narrowest statutory exception for religious discrimination claims comes in the form of the bona fide occupation qualification. The BFOQ provides:

> Notwithstanding any other provision of this subchapter . . . it shall not be an unlawful employment practice for an employer to hire and employ employees . . . on the basis of his religion . . . where religion . . . is a bona fide occupational qualification reasonably necessary to the normal operation of that particular business or enterprise.

42 U.S.C. § 2000e–2(e)(1).

As discussed throughout this text, the BFOQ has been narrowly applied and is narrowly interpreted by the courts. The BFOQ has tended to apply primarily to claims brought in the sex or national origin context, and it is rarely used in the religious discrimination setting. This may be because the other exceptions discussed here tend to be broader and are more likely to apply. As the EEOC provides:

> Religious organizations do not typically need to rely on this BFOQ defense . . . because the "religious organization" exception in Title VII permits them to prefer their co-religionists. It is well settled that for employers that are not religious organizations and therefore seek to rely on the BFOQ defense to justify a religious preference, the defense is a narrow one and can rarely be successfully invoked.

EEOC Compl. Man. (CCH) ¶ 8320, § 2-II(D) (July 22, 2008).

Nonetheless, the statute clearly anticipates that situations will arise where religion may be job related and go to the essence or central mission of the entity. *See* Andrew H. Friedman, Litigating Employment Discrimination Cases § 2-142, 2-223 (2005) (noting "there have been relatively few cases to address the BFOQ defense in the context of religious discrimination claims").

4. The Ministerial Exception

As already discussed, several statutory exceptions apply to claims of religious discrimination. These exceptions are in many ways both broad and narrow. The courts have expanded upon the scope of the religious exceptions and have created an additional exemption for leaders within a religious organization. This so-called ministerial exception thus applies where a minister within an organization alleges discrimination. The basic idea behind the ministerial exception is that the government should not be interfering too closely in the affairs of religious organizations and their ministerial employees. To do so could run afoul of the excessive entanglement provisions of the First Amendment, which separates the activities of church and state. Thus, the courts have generally held that where a religious employer takes an adverse action against a ministerial employee, that employee will not have a cause of action under Title VII.

The ministerial exception is in many ways much broader than the other exceptions discussed above. This is because the ministerial exception applies to other categories of discrimination, including race, color, sex, and national origin. If a religious organization refuses to hire female ministers, for example, a female applicant would not have a cause of action if the ministerial exception could be applied.

The ministerial exception is entirely judicially created, and cannot be found in the statute itself. Because it has no statutory underpinning, the exception has been applied in varying ways across the different jurisdictions. Thus, for example, some courts have taken a more restrictive view on whether this exception could apply to claims of sexual harassment, which can certainly be controversial in the religious employer setting. *See, e.g.,* Bollard v. Cal. Province of Soc'y of Jesus, 196 F.3d 940 (9th Cir. 1999) (holding that the ministerial exception does not apply to a sexual harassment cause of action); Prince of Peace Lutheran Church v. Linklater, 28 A.3d 1171 (Md. 2011) (holding that the ministerial exception did not apply to claims of sexual harassment and hostile work environment).

More importantly, how the term "minister" is defined can vary dramatically as well. The Fourth Circuit has stated that a ministerial exception can be found where "the employee's primary duties consist of teaching, spreading the faith, church governance, supervision of a religious order, or supervision or participation in religious ritual and worship." *See* Rayburn v. Gen. Conference of Seventh-Day Adventists, 772 F.2d 1164, 1169 (4th Cir. 1985). While this definition generally encompasses the views of the lower courts, the specific contours of the exception differ substantially. *See* Jamie Darin Prenkert, *Liberty, Diversity, Academic Freedom, and Survival: Preferential Hiring Among Religiously-Affiliated Institutions of Higher Education,* 22 Hofstra Lab. & Emp. L.J. 1, 38 (2004) (noting that defining what qualifies an employee as a minister is not always logically apparent; discussing how "ordination is neither necessary nor, by itself, sufficient to qualify an employee as a minister" and how the definition of a minister instead "focuses largely on the functioning role of the employee within the organization"). For the first time, the Supreme Court visited the question of the scope of the ministerial exception, and provided some guidance on the issue in the case below.

Hosanna-Tabor Evangelical Lutheran Church v. EEOC

565 U.S. 171 (2012)

Chief Justice Roberts delivered the opinion of the Court.

Certain employment discrimination laws authorize employees who have been wrongfully terminated to sue their employers for reinstatement and damages. The question presented is whether the Establishment and Free Exercise Clauses of the First Amendment bar such an action when the employer is a religious group and the employee is one of the group's ministers.

Petitioner Hosanna-Tabor Evangelical Lutheran Church and School is a member congregation of the Lutheran Church–Missouri Synod, the second largest Lutheran denomination in America. Hosanna-Tabor operated a small school in Redford, Michigan, offering a "Christ-centered education" to students in kindergarten through eighth grade. The Synod classifies teachers into two categories: "called" and "lay." "Called" teachers are regarded as having been called to their vocation by God through a congregation. To be eligible to receive a call from a congregation, a teacher must satisfy certain academic requirements. One way of doing so is by completing a "colloquy" program at a Lutheran college or university. The program requires candidates to take eight courses of theological study, obtain the endorsement of their local Synod district, and pass an oral examination by a faculty committee. A teacher who meets these requirements may be called by a congregation. Once called, a teacher receives the formal title "Minister of Religion, Commissioned." A commissioned minister serves for an open-ended term; at Hosanna-Tabor, a call could be rescinded only for cause and by a super-majority vote of the congregation.

"Lay" or "contract" teachers, by contrast, are not required to be trained by the Synod or even to be Lutheran. At Hosanna-Tabor, they were appointed by the school board, without a vote of the congregation, to one-year renewable terms. Although teachers at the school generally performed the same duties regardless of whether they were lay or called, lay teachers were hired only when called teachers were unavailable.

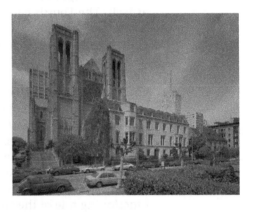

Respondent Cheryl Perich was first employed by Hosanna-Tabor as a lay teacher in 1999. After Perich completed her colloquy later that school year, Hosanna-Tabor asked her to become a called teacher. Perich accepted the call and received a "diploma of vocation" designating her a commissioned minister.

Perich taught kindergarten during her first four years at Hosanna-Tabor and fourth grade during the 2003–2004 school year. She taught math, language arts, social studies, science, gym, art, and music. She also taught a religion class four days a week, led the students in prayer and devotional exercises each day, and attended a weekly school-wide chapel service. Perich led the chapel service herself about twice a year.

Perich became ill in June 2004 with what was eventually diagnosed as narcolepsy. Symptoms included sudden and deep sleeps from which she could not be roused. Because of her illness, Perich began the 2004–2005 school year on disability leave. On January 27, 2005, however, Perich notified the school principal, Stacey Hoeft, that she would be able to report to work the following month. Hoeft responded that the school had already contracted with a lay teacher to fill Perich's position for the remainder of the school year. Hoeft also expressed concern that Perich was not yet ready to return to the classroom.

On January 30, Hosanna-Tabor held a meeting of its congregation at which school administrators stated that Perich was unlikely to be physically capable of returning to work that school year or the next. The congregation voted to offer Perich a "peaceful release" from her call, whereby the congregation would pay a portion of her health insurance premiums in exchange for her resignation as a called teacher. Perich refused to resign and produced a note from her doctor stating that she would be able to return to work on February 22. The school board urged Perich to reconsider, informing her that the school no longer had a position for her, but Perich stood by her decision not to resign.

On the morning of February 22 — the first day she was medically cleared to return to work — Perich presented herself at the school. Hoeft asked her to leave but she would not do so until she obtained written documentation that she had reported to work. Later that afternoon, Hoeft called Perich at home and told her that she would likely be fired. Perich responded that she had spoken with an attorney and intended to assert her legal rights.

Following a school board meeting that evening, board chairman Scott Salo sent Perich a letter stating that Hosanna-Tabor was reviewing the process for rescinding her call in light of her "regrettable" actions. Salo subsequently followed up with a letter advising Perich that the congregation would consider whether to rescind her call at its next meeting. As grounds for termination, the letter cited Perich's "insubordination and disruptive behavior" on February 22, as well as the damage she had done to her "working relationship" with the school by "threatening to take legal action." The congregation voted to rescind Perich's call on April 10, and Hosanna-Tabor sent her a letter of termination the next day.

The EEOC brought suit against Hosanna-Tabor, alleging that Perich had been fired in retaliation for threatening to file an [Americans with Disabilities Act] lawsuit. Perich intervened in the litigation, claiming unlawful retaliation under both the ADA and the Michigan Persons with Disabilities Civil Rights Act, Mich. Comp. Laws § 37.1602(a) (1979). The EEOC and Perich sought Perich's reinstatement to her former position (or frontpay in lieu thereof), along with backpay, compensatory and punitive damages, attorney's fees, and other injunctive relief.

Hosanna-Tabor moved for summary judgment. Invoking what is known as the "ministerial exception," the Church argued that the suit was barred by the First Amendment because the claims at issue concerned the employment relationship between a religious institution and one of its ministers. According to the Church, Perich was a minister, and she had been fired for a religious reason — namely, that her threat to sue the Church violated the Synod's belief that Christians should resolve their disputes internally.

The District Court agreed that the suit was barred by the ministerial exception and granted summary judgment in Hosanna-Tabor's favor.

> As the Court recognizes here, the ministerial exception is grounded in the First Amendment rather than any federal or state statute.

The court explained that "Hosanna-Tabor treated Perich like a minister and held her out to the world as such long before this litigation began," and that the "facts surrounding Perich's employment in a religious school with a sectarian mission" supported the Church's characterization. EEOC v. Hosanna-Tabor Evangelical Lutheran, 582 F. Supp. 2d 881, 891–92 (E.D. Mich. 2008). In light of that determination, the court concluded that it could "inquire no further into her claims of retaliation."

The Court of Appeals for the Sixth Circuit vacated and remanded, directing the District Court to proceed to the merits of Perich's retaliation claims. The Court of Appeals recognized the existence of a ministerial exception barring certain employment discrimination claims against religious institutions — an exception "rooted in the First Amendment's guarantees of religious freedom." EEOC v. Hosanna-Tabor Evangelical Lutheran, 597 F.3d 769 (6th Cir. 2010). The court concluded, however, that Perich did not qualify as a "minister" under the exception, noting in particular that her duties as a called teacher were identical to her duties as a lay teacher. Judge White concurred. She viewed the question whether Perich qualified as a minister to be closer than did the majority, but agreed that the "fact that the duties of the contract teachers are the same as the duties of the called teachers is telling."

The First Amendment provides, in part, that "Congress shall make no law respecting an establishment of religion, or prohibiting the free exercise thereof." We have said that these two Clauses "often exert conflicting pressures," Cutter v. Wilkinson, 544 U.S. 709, 719 (2005), and that there can be "internal tension . . . between the Establishment Clause and the Free Exercise Clause," Tilton v. Richardson, 403 U.S. 672 (1971) (plurality opinion). Not so here. Both Religion Clauses bar the government from interfering with the decision of a religious group to fire one of its ministers.

Until today, we have not had occasion to consider whether this freedom of a religious organization to select its ministers is implicated by a suit alleging discrimination in employment. The Courts of Appeals, in contrast, have had extensive experience with this issue. Since the passage of Title VII of the Civil Rights Act of 1964, 42 U.S.C. § 2000e et seq., and other employment discrimination laws, the Courts of Appeals have uniformly recognized the existence of a "ministerial exception," grounded in the First Amendment, that precludes application of such legislation to claims concerning the employment relationship between a religious institution and its ministers.

We agree that there is such a ministerial exception. The members of a religious group put their faith in the hands of their ministers. Requiring a church to accept or retain an unwanted minister, or punishing a church for failing to do so, intrudes upon more than a mere employment decision. Such action interferes with the internal governance of the church, depriving the church of control over the selection of those who will personify its beliefs. By imposing an unwanted minister, the state infringes the Free Exercise Clause, which protects a religious group's right to shape its own faith and mission through its appointments. According the state the power to determine which individuals will

> For the first time, the Supreme Court here recognizes the existence of the "ministerial exception" for Title VII cases.

minister to the faithful also violates the Establishment Clause, which prohibits government involvement in such ecclesiastical decisions.

The EEOC and Perich acknowledge that employment discrimination laws would be unconstitutional as applied to religious groups in certain circumstances. They grant, for example, that it would violate the First Amendment for courts to apply such laws to compel the ordination of women by the Catholic Church or by an Orthodox Jewish seminary. According to the EEOC and Perich, religious organizations could successfully defend against employment discrimination claims in those circumstances by invoking the constitutional right to freedom of association — a right "implicit" in the First Amendment. The EEOC and Perich thus see no need — and no basis — for a special rule for ministers grounded in the Religion Clauses themselves.

We find this position untenable. The right to freedom of association is a right enjoyed by religious and secular groups alike. It follows under the EEOC's and Perich's view that the First Amendment analysis should be the same, whether the association in question is the Lutheran Church, a labor union, or a social club. That result is hard to square with the text of the First Amendment itself, which gives special solicitude to the rights of religious organizations. We cannot accept the remarkable view that the Religion Clauses have nothing to say about a religious organization's freedom to select its own ministers.

The EEOC and Perich also contend that our decision in Employment Div., Dept. of Human Resources of Ore. v. Smith, 494 U.S. 872 (1990), precludes recognition of a ministerial exception. In *Smith*, two members of the Native American Church were denied state unemployment benefits after it was determined that they had been fired from their jobs for ingesting peyote, a crime under Oregon law. We held that this did not violate the Free Exercise Clause, even though the peyote had been ingested for sacramental purposes, because the "right of free exercise does not relieve an individual of the obligation to comply with a valid and neutral law of general applicability on the ground that the law proscribes (or prescribes) conduct that his religion prescribes (or proscribes)." *Id.* at 879 (internal quotation marks omitted).

It is true that the ADA's prohibition on retaliation, like Oregon's prohibition on peyote use, is a valid and neutral law of general applicability. But a church's selection of its ministers is unlike an individual's ingestion of peyote. *Smith* involved government regulation of only outward physical acts. The present case, in contrast, concerns government interference with an internal church decision that affects the faith and mission of the church itself. See *id.* at 877, 110 S. Ct. 1595 (distinguishing the government's regulation of "physical acts" from its "lend[ing] its power to one or the other side in controversies over religious authority or dogma"). The contention that *Smith* forecloses recognition of a ministerial exception rooted in the Religion Clauses has no merit.

Having concluded that there is a ministerial exception grounded in the Religion Clauses of the First Amendment, we consider whether the exception applies in this case. We hold that it does.

Every Court of Appeals to have considered the question has concluded that the ministerial exception is not limited to the head of a religious congregation, and we agree. We are reluctant, however, to adopt a rigid formula for

> The Court here declined to adopt a "rigid formula" for defining ministerial employees.

deciding when an employee qualifies as a minister. It is enough for us to conclude, in this our first case involving the ministerial exception, that the exception covers Perich, given all the circumstances of her employment.

To begin with, Hosanna-Tabor held Perich out as a minister, with a role distinct from that of most of its members. When Hosanna-Tabor extended her a call, it issued her a "diploma of vocation" according her the title "Minister of Religion, Commissioned." She was tasked with performing that office "according to the Word of God and the confessional standards of the Evangelical Lutheran Church as drawn from the Sacred Scriptures." The congregation prayed that God "bless [her] ministrations to the glory of His holy name, [and] the building of His church." In a supplement to the diploma, the congregation undertook to periodically review Perich's "skills of ministry" and "ministerial responsibilities," and to provide for her "continuing education as a professional person in the ministry of the Gospel."

Perich's title as a minister reflected a significant degree of religious training followed by a formal process of commissioning. To be eligible to become a commissioned minister, Perich had to complete eight college-level courses in subjects including biblical interpretation, church doctrine, and the ministry of the Lutheran teacher. She also had to obtain the endorsement of her local Synod district by submitting a petition that contained her academic transcripts, letters of recommendation, personal statement, and written answers to various ministry-related questions. Finally, she had to pass an oral examination by a faculty committee at a Lutheran college. It took Perich six years to fulfill these requirements. And when she eventually did, she was commissioned as a minister only upon election by the congregation, which recognized God's call to her to teach. At that point, her call could be rescinded only upon a supermajority vote of the congregation — a protection designed to allow her to "preach the Word of God boldly."

Perich held herself out as a minister of the Church by accepting the formal call to religious service, according to its terms. She did so in other ways as well. For example, she claimed a special housing allowance on her taxes that was available only to employees earning their compensation "'in the exercise of the ministry.'" ("If you are not conducting activities 'in the exercise of the ministry,' you cannot take advantage of the parsonage or housing allowance exclusion" (quoting Lutheran Church–Missouri Synod Brochure on Whether the IRS Considers Employees as a Minister (2007)).) In a form she submitted to the Synod following her termination, Perich again indicated that she regarded herself as a minister at Hosanna-Tabor, stating: "I feel that God is leading me to serve in the teaching ministry. . . . I am anxious to be in the teaching ministry again soon."

Perich's job duties reflected a role in conveying the Church's message and carrying out its mission. Hosanna-Tabor expressly charged her with "lead[ing] others toward Christian maturity" and "teach[ing] faithfully the Word of God, the Sacred Scriptures, in its truth and purity and as set forth in all the symbolical books of the Evangelical Lutheran Church." In fulfilling these responsibilities, Perich taught her students religion four days a week, and led them in prayer three times a day. Once a week, she took her students to a school-wide chapel service, and — about twice a year — she took her turn leading it, choosing the liturgy, selecting the hymns, and delivering a short message based on verses from the Bible. During her last year of teaching, Perich also led her fourth graders in a brief devotional exercise each morning. As a source of religious instruction, Perich performed an important role in transmitting the Lutheran faith to the next generation.

In light of these considerations — the formal title given Perich by the Church, the substance reflected in that title, her own use of that title, and the important religious functions she performed for the Church — we conclude that Perich was a minister covered by the ministerial exception.

> The Court considered many factors in determining whether Perich was a ministerial employee— including her title, the use of the title, the substance of her job, and the religious functions that she actually performed.

In reaching a contrary conclusion, the Court of Appeals committed three errors. First, the Sixth Circuit failed to see any relevance in the fact that Perich was a commissioned minister. Although such a title, by itself, does not automatically ensure coverage, the fact that an employee has been ordained or commissioned as a minister is surely relevant, as is the fact that significant religious training and a recognized religious mission underlie the description of the employee's position. It was wrong for the Court of Appeals — and Perich, who has adopted the court's view — to say that an employee's title does not matter.

Second, the Sixth Circuit gave too much weight to the fact that lay teachers at the school performed the same religious duties as Perich. We express no view on whether someone with Perich's duties would be covered by the ministerial exception in the absence of the other considerations we have discussed. But though relevant, it cannot be dispositive that others not formally recognized as ministers by the church perform the same functions — particularly when, as here, they did so only because commissioned ministers were unavailable.

Third, the Sixth Circuit placed too much emphasis on Perich's performance of secular duties. It is true that her religious duties consumed only 45 minutes of each workday, and that the rest of her day was devoted to teaching secular subjects. The EEOC regards that as conclusive, contending that any ministerial exception "should be limited to those employees who perform exclusively religious functions." We cannot accept that view. Indeed, we are unsure whether any such employees exist. The heads of congregations themselves often have a mix of duties, including secular ones such as helping to manage the congregation's finances, supervising purely secular personnel, and overseeing the upkeep of facilities.

Although the Sixth Circuit did not adopt the extreme position pressed here by the EEOC, it did regard the relative amount of time Perich spent performing religious functions as largely determinative. The issue before us, however, is not one that can be resolved by a stopwatch. The amount of time an employee spends on particular activities is relevant in assessing that employee's status, but that factor cannot be considered in isolation, without regard to the nature of the religious functions performed and the other considerations discussed above. Because Perich was a minister within the meaning of the exception, the First Amendment requires dismissal of this employment discrimination suit against her religious employer. The EEOC and Perich originally sought an order reinstating Perich to her former position as a called teacher. By requiring the Church to accept a minister it did not want, such an order would have plainly violated the Church's freedom under the Religion Clauses to select its own ministers.

Perich no longer seeks reinstatement, having abandoned that relief before this Court. But that is immaterial. Perich continues to seek frontpay in lieu of reinstatement, backpay, compensatory and punitive damages, and attorney's fees. An award of such relief would operate as a penalty on the Church for terminating an unwanted minister, and would be no less prohibited by the First Amendment than an order overturning the termination. Such relief would depend on a determination that Hosanna-Tabor was wrong to have relieved Perich of her position, and it is precisely such a ruling that is barred by the ministerial exception.

The EEOC and Perich suggest that Hosanna-Tabor's asserted religious reason for firing Perich — that she violated the Synod's commitment to internal dispute resolution — was pretextual. That suggestion misses the point of the ministerial exception. The purpose of the exception is not to safeguard a church's decision to fire a minister only when it is made for a religious reason. The exception instead ensures that the authority to select and control who will minister to the faithful — a matter "strictly ecclesiastical" — is the church's alone [citation omitted].

The EEOC and Perich foresee a parade of horribles that will follow our recognition of a ministerial exception to employment discrimination suits. According to the EEOC and Perich, such an exception could protect religious organizations from liability for retaliating against employees for reporting criminal misconduct or for testifying before a grand jury or in a criminal trial. What is more, the EEOC contends, the logic of the exception would confer on religious employers "unfettered discretion" to violate employment laws by, for example, hiring children or aliens not authorized to work in the United States.

Hosanna-Tabor responds that the ministerial exception would not in any way bar criminal prosecutions for interfering with law enforcement investigations or other proceedings. Nor, according to the Church, would the exception bar government enforcement of general laws restricting eligibility for employment, because the exception applies only to suits by or on behalf of ministers themselves. Hosanna-Tabor also notes that the ministerial exception has been around in the lower courts for 40 years, and has not given rise to the dire consequences predicted by the EEOC and Perich.

The case before us is an employment discrimination suit brought on behalf of a minister, challenging her church's decision to fire her. Today we hold only that the ministerial exception bars such a suit. We express no view on whether the exception bars other types of suits, including actions by employees alleging breach of contract or tortious conduct by their religious employers. There will be time enough to address the applicability of the exception to other circumstances if and when they arise.

The interest of society in the enforcement of employment discrimination statutes is undoubtedly important. But so too is the interest of religious groups in choosing who will preach their beliefs, teach their faith, and carry out their mission. When a minister who has been fired sues her church alleging that her termination was discriminatory, the First Amendment has struck the balance for us. The church must be free to choose those who will guide it on its way.

■ NOTES AND QUESTIONS

1. Prior to *Hosanna-Tabor*, it was unclear whether the ministerial exception properly existed. The Supreme Court resolved that issue, finding that the exception is an important exclusion for religious discrimination claims and helps balance the discrimination statutes with the First Amendment.

2. Though *Hosanna-Tabor* arose in the context of a disability case, it would likely apply to Title VII claims as well.

3. Beyond recognizing this religious exception, the Court goes even further and helps define the contours of the exception. In doing so, however, we are not given a bright-line test. The Court specifically notes that it is "reluctant . . . to adopt a rigid formula for deciding when an employee qualifies as a minister. It is enough for us to conclude, in this our first case involving the ministerial exception, that the exception covers [the employee], given all the circumstances of her employment." *Hosanna-Tabor*, 565 U.S. at 190-191.

4. Though the Court declines to adopt a bright-line test for ministerial employees, the specific facts of the case can be insightful as to when the exception will apply in future cases. The Court holds that in considering "the formal title given [the employee] by the Church, the substance reflected in that title, her own use of that title, and the important religious functions she performed for the Church — we conclude that [the employee] was a minister covered by the ministerial exception." Thus, important factors to consider when addressing the exception include: (1) the title of the employee, (2) whether/how the employee uses that title, and (3) the religious functions performed by the employee.

5. In addition to the factors discussed by the Court, what other factors might be considered when determining whether a worker is a ministerial employee under the statute?

6. **Historical note.** Prior to *Hosanna-Tabor*, several lower courts had used the "ministerial exception" to exempt religious employers from both antidiscrimination laws and other statutes regulating how employers manage their workers. In fact, the lower courts had recognized the "ministerial exception" for approximately forty years. However, the Supreme Court had never recognized the doctrine or ruled on its constitutionality. Thus, *Hosanna-Tabor* was extremely significant in creating primary, mandatory authority and guidance for lower courts to finally be able to explicitly follow. Ira C. Lupu et al., *In Brief:* Hosanna-Tabor v. EEOC: *The Court's Unanimous Decision*, Pew Research Center (Jan. 11, 2012), http://www.pewforum.org/2012/01/11/the-supreme-court-takes-up-church-employment-disputes-and-the-ministerial-exception/.

 Interactive Problem

Looking back at the facts of the interactive problem at the beginning of the chapter, assume that the company president of Big Cars, Inc., becomes aware of Krista's request for a religious accommodation based on her beliefs. The president, a very active Catholic, states, "Not only will we not grant her request, she must be fired immediately. I never knew that she was a Seventh-Day Adventist, and I only like members of my own faith working here." Would the president's decision to fire Krista be protected under any of the exceptions discussed in this chapter?

Class Exercise: Ministerial Employees

Janie Kowlinski works as a cafeteria worker at a Protestant elementary school. Janie's primary duties include preparing and distributing the afternoon lunch to the students. When the principal of the school learns that Janie is pregnant out of wedlock, he decides to terminate her, as this type of pregnancy is inconsistent with the religious tenets of the school. Breaking up into small groups, discuss whether Janie would have a cause of action against the school. Would the case for the school be stronger if Janie were a teacher at the school? A school administrator? What if, every day, she led students in a pre-meal prayer?

Practice and Procedural Tip

23: The Proselytizing Problem

One particular issue that can often arise in religious discrimination cases is an employee who believes that it is her religious obligation to convert other workers to a particular religion or religious point of view. It is not uncommon for a religion to include proselytizing as one of its basic tenets. And it is also not uncommon for workers to share their religious views with others in the workplace.

The proselytizing employee can present a serious problem for the employer, however. Most notably, as already discussed, the statute requires that the employer accommodate an employee's religious beliefs and practices. This would mean that in certain circumstances, an employer may have to permit an employee to share her religious views and beliefs with others. On the other side of the coin, however, employers also have a duty to prevent a hostile work environment on the basis of religion. A non-religious employee, or an employee of another faith, might feel that she is being subjected to a hostile work environment where she is frequently subjected to attempts from co-workers or supervisors to convert her to a particular religion.

This tension — the obligation to accommodate an employee's religious beliefs, and the obligation to prevent a hostile work environment — can put the employer in a Catch-22 situation. If the employer prohibits the proselytizing, it could find itself subjected to a failure to accommodate claim under Title VII. If the employer instead chooses to ignore the issue, it could find itself subjected to a hostile work environment claim under the same statute.

So how is an employer to proceed in these situations? Two words capture the appropriate way to proceed — delicately and carefully. As discussed above, the obligation to accommodate an employee is only a de minimis burden, so where an employee is creating a hostile work environment, there is certainly no need to accommodate the worker. Still, the cost of even defending this type of claim can be substantial. Employers should thoroughly investigate these situations and address them with the employees involved. Is there a way that the proselytizing can be done after hours where other employees can leave if they feel uncomfortable? And, where an employee has made clear that such attempts at religious conversion make him feel uncomfortable, the proselytizing worker should be told not to persist in these efforts.

In the end, this issue can create a difficult situation for employers. The bottom-line best practices advice is for employers to be cognizant of the potential litigation that can arise from the issue. And, employers must be aware of the environment, and address specific issues where they arise. When receiving specific complaints, or where it is clear that such activity is present, employers should investigate the matter and handle it in an appropriate and sensitive manner. If any discipline is enacted, it should be well documented and clearly articulated to the employees involved. Employers should thus proceed with caution in this area, as the case law is replete with expensive and time-consuming litigation on this very question. *See* Knight v. Conn. Dep't of Pub. Health, 275 F.3d 156 (2d Cir. 2001) (holding that accommodating two employees' requests to proselytize to clients was an undue burden on the employer that would disrupt the agencies' efficient provision of services); Chalmers v. Tulon Co. of Richmond, 101 F.3d 1012, 1021 (4th Cir. 1996) (noting that "where an employee contends that she has a religious need to impose personally and directly on fellow employees . . . the employer is placed between a rock and a hard place" but holding that the employee's conduct — accusing co-workers of immoral conduct — was not the sort of conduct that employers could accommodate without unduly burdening other employees); Wilson v. U.S. West Commc'ns, 58 F.3d 1337, 1342 (8th Cir. 1995) ("Title VII does not require an employer to allow an employee to impose his religious views on others.").

F. Chapter-in-Review

The analysis of religious discrimination cases frequently involves knowing more about the exceptions involved than the actual rule. These exceptions are interpreted in varying ways across jurisdictions, and are both statutory and constitutional. Before advising a client on a question of religious discrimination, careful attention must be paid to the law of the particular court. Very few issues are straightforward in the religious discrimination context, and the specific facts of each case and the nature of the institution involved are critical questions that must be addressed. The chart below summarizes some of the more important exceptions in this area:

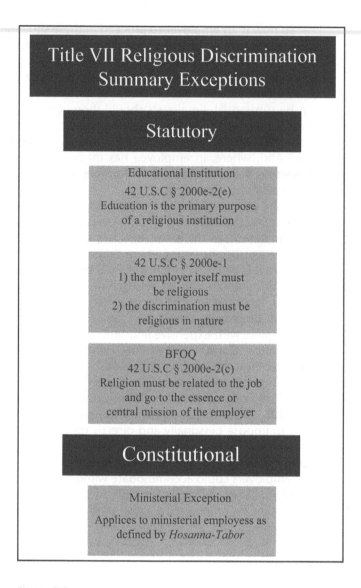

Figure 9.2

The same disparate treatment model found in *McDonnell Douglas* can be applied to religious discrimination cases where individuals are being treated differently on the basis of their faith. Where a religious conflict exists, however, a modified prima facie test is used, which looks at whether the worker (a) had a belief that conflicted with a workplace duty; (b) the worker made the company aware of the belief and conflict; and (c) there was an adverse action (or threat of an adverse action) because of the conflict.

Religion is unique as a Title VII protected category in that there is a statutory duty to accommodate the religious beliefs of employees up to the point of undue hardship. This obligation does not create more than a de minimis burden on employees.

Finally, employers must proceed cautiously when addressing the issue of proselytizing in the workplace. Employers must balance the First Amendment rights of workers with the protection other employees have against harassment. Religious discrimination is unique in that it is often difficult to determine exactly what a "religion" is. This question is often jurisdiction specific, and the Supreme Court has been clear that religious beliefs involve more than simply a matter of personal preference.

Disability Discrimination

 Interactive Problem

Tina Teacher worked as an elementary school teacher for a private school. Over the course of her employment, she began to gain significant weight, because, as she tells her friends, she "just really likes food," but she could "lose the weight if she wanted to." By the time Tina had worked at the school for ten years, she weighed 350 pounds despite being only five foot three inches tall. Tina began to notice that she was having some problems entering into the restroom because the doorway was too narrow. She asked the school principal whether he would consider widening the bathroom entry so that she could have better access. In discussing this possibility, Tina also mentioned that she was having difficulty walking more than a few steps without stopping for rest. After considering the situation, the principal denied the request to widen the bathroom doorway and further terminated Tina because she would be unable to assist students in evacuating the building in the event of a fire. In letting Tina go, the principal stated, "You're just too large to be able to walk fast enough in case of a fire, and that is a major liability risk for us. We have to put the children first in this situation."

Would Tina have a cause of action under the Americans with Disabilities Act? Is she disabled? Can she perform the essential functions of her job? What other information would be helpful to have in deciding this case?

A. Introduction

The Americans with Disabilities Act (ADA) was passed much later than those federal statutes addressing race, color, sex, national origin, religion, or age. Unlike many other civil rights statutes, the ADA had widespread support from business groups, employee advocates, and political powers. Indeed, the ADA was passed with overwhelming support in the U.S. House of Representatives and the U.S. Senate, and was signed into law by George H.W. Bush on July 26, 1990. *See* Stephen F. Befort & Holly Lindquist Thomas, *The ADA in Turmoil: Judicial Dissonance, the Supreme Court's Response, and the Future of Disability Discrimination Law*, 78 OR. L. REV. 27, 27 (1999) ("The [ADA] was enacted in 1990 with considerable fanfare and support.") (citations omitted).

The ADA was the result of extensive participation of disability organizations, bipartisan members of the House and Senate, the Leadership Conference on Civil Rights, and the business community. The ADA also received remarkable support from American society as a whole. Parents of disabled children, community members who simply wanted to eliminate the societal barriers and prejudices that excluded people with disabilities from the community and workplace, and many others all worked together to lead a movement in this area. Local advocate groups arranged sit-ins in federal buildings (especially Department of Health, Education, and Welfare buildings), obstructed the movement of inaccessible buses, and participated in marches to protest disability discrimination. Judith Heumann, *Celebrating the Americans with Disabilities Act (ADA) at Home and Abroad*, DISABILITY BLOG (July 25, 2011), http://www.tilrc.org/assests/news/0711news/0711rights25.html; Arlene Mayerson, *The History of the Americans with Disabilities Act: A Movement Perspective*, DISABILITY RIGHTS EDUCATION & DEFENSE FUND (1992), http://dredf.org/news/publications/the-history-of-the-ada/.

The operative language of the ADA makes it unlawful for an employer to "discriminate against a qualified individual on the basis of disability in regard to job application procedures, the hiring, advancement, or discharge of employees, employee compensation, job training, and other terms, conditions, and privileges of employment." 42 U.S.C. § 12112(a). Similarly, it is unlawful under the ADA for an employer to fail to provide "reasonable accommodations to the known physical or mental limitations of an otherwise qualified individual with a disability who is an applicant or employee, unless such covered entity can demonstrate that the accommodation would impose an undue hardship on the operation of the business of such covered entity." 42 U.S.C. § 12112(b)(5)(A). Much of the terminology of the ADA comes directly from the Rehabilitation Act of 1973.

Section 504 of the Rehabilitation Act of 1973 (Rehab Act) influenced the creation of the ADA in several ways. First, Congress believed that the Rehab Act, on its own, was not preventing discrimination against all individuals with disabilities in the United States. Second, Congress clarified in the ADA that it intended to legislate broader protection than courts may have previously provided when interpreting § 504 narrowly. Finally, the ADA was based in large part on § 504 and its regulations. Likewise, the ADA influenced the Rehab Act when it was amended in 1992. The Rehab Act was amended primarily to include similar language, goals, and objectives as provided in the ADA. The two Acts share a critical belief — that individuals with disabilities, even severe disabilities, can work — and both Acts require employers to accommodate an individual's disability up to the point of undue hardship. The two Acts also share many similar terms, including the definition of "disability." While the Rehab Act applies to the federal workforce, the ADA provides coverage for private workers. *See* DEBORAH LEUCHOVIUS, PACER CENTER, ACTION SHEET: PHP-C51F, ADA Q&A . . . THE REHABILITATION ACT AND THE ADA CONNECTION (2003).

Helen Keller, Holding the Hand of Her Teacher, Anne Mansfield Sullivan

The language of the ADA contains a number of phrases that have become "terms of art" defined by the federal regulations and case law. In particular, the terms "qualified," "disabled," "reasonable," and "undue hardship" have been well litigated in the courts. The ADA is different from other areas of employment discrimination law in that it focuses heavily on definitional terms. Whether an employee falls within the protected class is a critical inquiry in these cases.

1. Elements of the Cause of Action

Unlike any other area of employment discrimination law, a plaintiff may pursue four different causes of action under the ADA: (1) disparate treatment discrimination; (2) failure to make reasonable accommodations; (3) unlawful medical inquiries; and (4) unlawful disparate impact discrimination. This section will focus on one of the most widely pursued claims under the ADA, disparate treatment discrimination. Like other areas of discrimination law, it is unlawful to treat someone with a disability different from other workers. While failure to accommodate claims are perhaps the most commonly raised issue under the ADA, disparate treatment claims are equally problematic for employers and can lead to substantial damages.

Cases brought under the ADA are analyzed under the typical *McDonnell Douglas* approach used for Title VII cases, though the precise analysis used varies from these more traditional claims. While the individual courts and jurisdictions vary as to the exact formulation of the prima facie case, there is widespread agreement over some of the more common elements. Thus, under the ADA, plaintiffs must establish that they: (1) are disabled, (2) are qualified to perform the essential functions of the job with or without a reasonable accommodation, and (3) have suffered an adverse action. Once the plaintiff has established this prima facie case, the employer carries the burden of production of articulating a legitimate nondiscriminatory reason for the adverse action in question. After the employer meets this standard, the plaintiff — who carries the burden of persuasion throughout the case — must establish that the legitimate nondiscriminatory reason is pretextual. The courts have applied varying tests for satisfying these burdens in disparate treatment cases, and have articulated the prima facie case in different ways. Nonetheless, all courts follow this same basic framework for analyzing ADA cases.

2. Disability and Qualified Defined

Perhaps the most substantive difference between the ADA and other areas of discrimination law is the different threshold terminology for pursuing a claim. Most notably, a plaintiff cannot proceed in an ADA action unless she is "a qualified individual with a disability." There are different statutory standards that have been formulated to determine whether a plaintiff is disabled and whether she is qualified. Both of these standards must be met before a plaintiff can proceed in the case.

For a plaintiff to establish that she is a "qualified individual," she must show first that she "can perform the essential functions of the employment position that" the plaintiff "holds or desires." 42 U.S.C. § 12111(8). In addition to demonstrating that she is qualified for a position, the plaintiff must also establish that she is disabled under the terms of the statute. There are three different ways to show disability. The plaintiff can establish that she has

(A) a physical or mental impairment that substantially limits one or more major life activities of such individual;
(B) a record of such an impairment; or
(C) [is] regarded as having such an impairment

42 U.S.C. § 12102(1).

If a plaintiff is able to establish any of these three prongs of the disability definition, she will be considered disabled for purposes of the statute. Thus, if she can show an actual disability, a history of a disability, or a perceived disability, she will be permitted to proceed in the case. Whether someone is disabled is a critical inquiry in many ADA cases, and the courts have taken varying approaches to how the statutory terms are interpreted. In the *Sutton* case below, the Supreme Court defines some of this terminology.

B. Actual, Perceived, and Record of a Disability

Sutton v. United Air Lines, Inc.
527 U.S. 471 (1999)

Justice O'CONNOR delivered the opinion of the Court.

Petitioners are twin sisters, both of whom have severe myopia. Each petitioner's uncorrected visual acuity is 20/200 or worse in her right eye and 20/400 or worse in her left eye, but "[w]ith the use of corrective lenses, each . . . has vision that is 20/20 or better." Consequently, without corrective lenses, each "effectively cannot see to conduct numerous activities such as driving a vehicle, watching television or shopping in public stores," but with corrective measures, such as glasses or contact lenses, both "function identically to individuals without a similar impairment."

In 1992, petitioners applied to respondent for employment as commercial airline pilots. They met respondent's basic age, education, experience, and Federal Aviation Administration certification qualifications. After submitting their applications for employment, both petitioners were invited by respondent to an interview and to flight simulator tests. Both were told during their interviews, however, that a mistake had been made in inviting them to interview because petitioners did not meet respondent's minimum vision requirement, which was uncorrected visual acuity of 20/100 or better. Due to their failure to meet this requirement, petitioners' interviews were terminated, and neither was offered a pilot position.

In light of respondent's proffered reason for rejecting them, petitioners filed a charge of disability discrimination under the ADA with the Equal Employment Opportunity Commission (EEOC). After receiving a right to sue letter, petitioners filed suit in the United States District Court for the District of Colorado, alleging that respondent had discriminated against them "on the basis of their disability, or because [respondent] regarded [petitioners] as having a disability" in violation of the ADA. Specifically, petitioners alleged that due to their severe myopia they actually have a substantially limiting impairment or are regarded as having such an impairment, and are thus disabled under the Act.

The District Court dismissed petitioners' complaint for failure to state a claim upon which relief could be granted. Because petitioners could fully correct their visual impairments, the court held that they were not actually substantially limited in any major life activity and thus had not stated a claim that they were disabled within the meaning of the ADA. The court also determined that petitioners had not made allegations sufficient to support their claim that they were "regarded" by respondent as having an impairment that substantially limits a major life activity. The court observed that "[t]he statutory reference to a substantial limitation indicates . . . that an employer regards an employee as handicapped in his or her ability to work by finding the employee's impairment to foreclose generally the type of employment involved." But petitioners had alleged only that respondent regarded them as unable to satisfy the requirements of a particular job, global airline pilot. Consequently, the court held that petitioners had not stated a claim that they were regarded as substantially limited in the major life activity of working. Employing similar logic, the Court of Appeals for the Tenth Circuit affirmed the District Court's judgment. We granted certiorari.

The ADA prohibits discrimination by covered entities, including private employers, against qualified individuals with a disability. Specifically, it provides that no covered employer "shall discriminate against a qualified individual with a disability because of the disability of such individual in regard to job application procedures, the hiring, advancement, or discharge of employees, employee compensation, job training, and other terms, conditions, and privileges of employment." 42 U.S.C. § 12112(a); *see also* § 12111(2) ("The term 'covered entity' means an employer, employment agency, labor organization, or joint labor-management committee"). A "qualified individual with a disability" is identified as "an individual with a disability who, with or without reasonable accommodation, can perform the essential functions of the employment position that such individual holds or desires." § 12111(8). In turn, a "disability" is defined as:

"(A) a physical or mental impairment that substantially limits one or more of the major life activities of such individual;
"(B) a record of such an impairment; or
"(C) being regarded as having such an impairment." § 12102(2).

Accordingly, to fall within this definition one must have an actual disability (subsection (A)), have a record of a disability (subsection (B)), or be regarded as having one (subsection (C)).

Under the regulations, a "physical impairment" includes "[a]ny physiological disorder, or condition, cosmetic disfigurement, or anatomical loss affecting one or more of the following body systems: neurological, musculoskeletal, special sense organs, respiratory (including speech organs), cardiovascular, reproductive, digestive, genitourinary, hemic and lymphatic, skin, and endocrine." § 1630.2(h)(1). The term "substantially limits" means, among other things, "[u]nable to perform a major life activity that the average person in the general population can perform";

> The Supreme Court sets forth here the three-part test that forms the statutory basis for the definition of disability under the ADA.

or "[s]ignificantly restricted as to the condition, manner or duration under which an individual can perform a particular major life activity as compared to the condition, manner, or duration under which the average person in the general population can perform that same major life activity." § 1630.2(j). Finally, "[m]ajor [l]ife [a]ctivities means functions such as caring for oneself, performing manual tasks, walking, seeing, hearing, speaking, breathing, learning, and working." § 1630.2(i). Because both parties accept these regulations as valid, and determining their validity is not necessary to decide this case, we have no occasion to consider what deference they are due, if any.

With this statutory and regulatory framework in mind, we turn first to the question whether petitioners have stated a claim under subsection (A) of the disability definition, that is, whether they have alleged that they possess a physical impairment that substantially limits them in one or more major life activities. *See* 42 U.S.C. § 12102(2)(A). Because petitioners allege that with corrective measures their vision "is 20/20 or better," they are not actually disabled within the meaning of the Act if the "disability" determination is made with reference to these measures. Consequently, with respect to subsection (A) of the disability definition, our decision turns on whether disability is to be determined with or without reference to corrective measures.

We conclude that respondent is correct that the approach adopted by the agency guidelines — that persons are to be evaluated in their hypothetical uncorrected state — is an impermissible interpretation of the ADA. Looking at the Act as a whole, it is apparent that if a person is taking measures to correct for, or mitigate, a physical or mental impairment, the effects of those measures — both positive and negative — must be taken into account when judging whether that person is "substantially limited" in a major life activity and thus "disabled" under the Act. Justice Stevens relies on the legislative history of the ADA for the contrary proposition that individuals should be examined in their uncorrected state. Because we decide that, by its terms, the ADA cannot be read in this manner, we have no reason to consider the ADA's legislative history.

Three separate provisions of the ADA, read in concert, lead us to this conclusion. The Act defines a "disability" as "a physical or mental impairment that *substantially limits* one or more of the major life activities" of an individual. § 12102(2)(A) (emphasis added). Because the phrase "substantially limits" appears in the Act in the present indicative verb form, we think the language is properly read as requiring that a person be presently — not potentially or hypothetically — substantially limited in order to demonstrate a disability. A "disability" exists only where an impairment "substantially limits" a major life activity, not where it "might," "could," or "would" be substantially limiting if mitigating measures were not taken. A person whose physical or mental impairment is corrected by medication or other measures does not have an impairment that presently "substantially limits" a major life activity. To be sure, a person whose physical or mental impairment is corrected by mitigating measures still has an impairment, but if the impairment is corrected it does not "substantially limi[t]" a major life activity.

> Congress and the courts have repeatedly made clear that disability claims should be considered with respect to the specific individual involved—generalizations should not be made across groups.

The definition of disability also requires that disabilities be evaluated "with respect to an individual" and be determined based on whether an impairment substantially limits the "major life activities of such individual." § 12102(2). Thus, whether a person has a disability under the ADA is an individualized inquiry. The agency guidelines' directive that persons be judged in their uncorrected or unmitigated state runs directly counter to the individualized inquiry mandated by the ADA. The agency approach would often require courts and employers to speculate about a person's condition and would, in many cases, force them to make a disability determination based on general information about how an uncorrected impairment usually affects individuals, rather than on the individual's actual condition. For instance, under this view, courts would almost certainly find all diabetics to be disabled, because if they failed to monitor their blood sugar levels and administer insulin, they would almost certainly be substantially limited in one or more major life activities. A diabetic whose illness does not impair his or her daily activities would therefore be considered disabled simply because he or she has diabetes. Thus, the guidelines approach would create a system in which persons often must be treated as members of a group of people with similar impairments, rather than as individuals. This is contrary to both the letter and the spirit of the ADA.

The guidelines approach could also lead to the anomalous result that in determining whether an individual is disabled, courts and employers could not consider any negative side effects suffered by an individual resulting from the use of mitigating measures, even when those side effects are very severe. Finally, and critically, findings enacted as part of the ADA require the conclusion that Congress did not intend to bring under the statute's protection all those whose uncorrected conditions amount to disabilities. Congress found that "some 43,000,000 Americans have one or more physical or mental disabilities,

> At the time the ADA was passed, Congress was clear that "43,000,000 Americans have one or more physical or mental disabilities."

and this number is increasing as the population as a whole is growing older." § 12101(a)(1). This figure is inconsistent with the definition of disability pressed by petitioners.

[T]he exact source of the 43 million figure is not clear. Regardless of its exact source, however, the 43 million figure reflects an understanding that those whose impairments are largely corrected by medication or other devices are not "disabled" within the meaning of the ADA. The estimate is consistent with the numbers produced by studies performed during this same time period that took a similar functional approach to determining disability. Because it is included in the ADA's text, the finding that 43 million individuals are disabled gives content to the ADA's terms, specifically the term "disability." Had Congress intended to include all persons with corrected physical limitations among those covered by the Act, it undoubtedly would have cited a much higher number of disabled persons in the findings. That it did not is evidence that the ADA's coverage is restricted to only those whose impairments are not mitigated by corrective measures.

The use of a corrective device does not, by itself, relieve one's disability. Rather, one has a disability under subsection (A) if, notwithstanding the use of a corrective device, that individual is substantially limited in a major life activity. For example, individuals who use prosthetic limbs or wheelchairs may be mobile and capable of functioning in society but still be disabled because of a substantial limitation on their ability to walk or run. The same may be true of individuals who take medicine to lessen the symptoms of an impairment so that they can function but nevertheless remain substantially limited. Alternatively, one whose high blood pressure is "cured" by medication may be regarded as disabled by a covered entity, and thus disabled under subsection (C) of the definition. The use or nonuse of a corrective device does not determine whether an individual is disabled; that determination depends on whether the limitations an individual with an impairment actually faces are in fact substantially limiting.

Applying this reading of the Act to the case at hand, we conclude that the Court of Appeals correctly resolved the issue of disability in respondent's favor. As noted above, petitioners allege that with corrective measures, their visual acuity is 20/20, and that they "function identically to individuals without a similar impairment." In addition, petitioners concede that they "do not argue that the use of corrective lenses in itself demonstrates a substantially limiting impairment." Accordingly, because we decide that disability under the Act is to be determined with reference to corrective measures, we agree with the courts below that petitioners have not stated a claim that they are substantially limited in any major life activity.

Our conclusion that petitioners have failed to state a claim that they are actually disabled under subsection (A) of the disability definition does not end our inquiry. Under subsection (C), individuals who are "regarded as" having a disability are disabled within the meaning of the ADA. *See* § 12102(2)(C). Subsection (C) provides that having a disability includes "being regarded as having," § 12102(2)(C), "a physical or mental impairment that substantially limits one or more of the major life activities of such individual," § 12102(2)(A). There are two apparent ways in which individuals may fall within this statutory definition: (1) a covered entity mistakenly believes that a person has a physical impairment that substantially limits one or more major life activities, or (2) a covered entity mistakenly believes that an actual, nonlimiting impairment substantially limits one or more major life activities. In both cases, it is necessary that a covered entity entertain misperceptions about the individual — it must believe either that one has a substantially limiting impairment that one does not have or that one has a substantially limiting impairment when, in fact, the impairment is not so limiting.

> In the more recent amendments to the ADA, Congress rejected the EEOC's prior definition of "substantially limits."

There is no dispute that petitioners are physically impaired. Petitioners do not make the obvious argument that they are regarded due to their impairments as substantially limited in the major life activity of seeing. They contend only that respondent mistakenly believes their physical impairments substantially limit them in the major life activity of working. To support this claim, petitioners allege that respondent has a vision requirement that is allegedly based on myth and stereotype. Further, this requirement substantially limits their ability to engage in the major life activity of working by precluding them from obtaining the job of global airline pilot, which they argue is a "class of employment." In reply, respondent argues that the position of global airline pilot is not a class of jobs and therefore petitioners have not stated a claim that they are regarded as substantially limited in the major life activity of working.

Considering the allegations of the amended complaint in tandem, petitioners have not stated a claim that respondent regards their impairment as substantially limiting their ability to work. The ADA does not define "substantially limits," but "substantially" suggests "considerable" or "specified to a large degree." The EEOC has codified regulations interpreting the term "substantially limits" in this manner, defining the term to mean "[u]nable to perform" or "[s]ignificantly restricted." *See* 29 CFR §§ 1630.2(j)(1)(i), (ii) (1998).

When the major life activity under consideration is that of working, the statutory phrase "substantially limits" requires, at a minimum, that plaintiffs allege they are unable to work in a broad class of jobs. Reflecting this requirement, the EEOC uses a specialized definition of the term "substantially limits" when referring to the major life activity of working:

> significantly restricted in the ability to perform either a class of jobs or a broad range of jobs in various classes as compared to the average person having comparable training, skills and abilities. The inability to perform a single, particular job does not constitute a substantial limitation in the major life activity of working. § 1630.2(j)(3)(i).

The EEOC further identifies several factors that courts should consider when determining whether an individual is substantially limited in the major life activity of working, including the geographical area to which the individual has reasonable access, and "the number and types of jobs utilizing similar training, knowledge, skills or abilities, within the geographical area, from which the individual is also disqualified." §§ 1630.2(j)(3)(ii)(A), (B). To be substantially limited in the major life activity of working, then, one must be precluded from more than one type of job, a specialized job, or a particular job of choice. If jobs utilizing an individual's skills (but perhaps not his or her unique talents) are available, one is not precluded from a substantial class of jobs. Similarly, if a host of different types of jobs are available, one is not precluded from a broad range of jobs. Because the parties accept that the term "major life activities" includes working, we do not determine the validity of the cited regulations. We note, however, that there may be some conceptual difficulty in defining "major life activities" to include work. Assuming without deciding that working is a major life activity and that the EEOC regulations interpreting the term "substantially limits" are reasonable, petitioners have failed to allege adequately that their poor eyesight is regarded as an impairment that substantially limits them in the major life activity of working. They allege only that respondent regards their poor vision as precluding them from holding positions as a "global airline pilot." Because the position of global airline pilot is a single job, this allegation does not support the claim that respondent regards petitioners as having a substantially limiting impairment. *See* 29 CFR § 1630.2(j)(3)(i) (1998) ("The inability to perform a single, particular job does not constitute a substantial limitation in the major life activity of working"). Indeed, there are a number of other positions utilizing petitioners' skills, such as regional pilot and pilot instructor to name a few, that are available to them.

Petitioners also argue that if one were to assume that a substantial number of airline carriers have similar vision requirements, they would be substantially limited in the major life activity of working. Even assuming for the sake of argument that the adoption of similar vision requirements by other carriers would represent a substantial limitation on the major life activity of working, the argument is nevertheless flawed. It is not enough to say that if the physical criteria of a single employer were imputed to all similar employers one would be regarded as substantially limited in the major life activity of working only as a result of this imputation. An otherwise valid job requirement, such as a height requirement, does not become invalid simply because it would limit a person's employment opportunities in a substantial way if it were adopted by a substantial number of employers. Because petitioners have not alleged, and cannot demonstrate, that respondent's vision requirement reflects a belief that petitioners' vision substantially limits them, we agree with the decision of the Court of Appeals affirming the dismissal of petitioners' claim that they are regarded as disabled.

For these reasons, the judgment of the Court of Appeals for the Tenth Circuit is affirmed.

It is so ordered.

Justice STEVENS, with whom Justice BREYER joins, dissenting.

When it enacted the ADA, Congress certainly did not intend to require United Air Lines to hire unsafe or unqualified pilots. Nor, in all likelihood, did it view every person who wears glasses as a member of a "discrete and insular minority." Indeed, by reason of legislative myopia it may not have foreseen that its definition of "disability" might theoretically encompass, not just "some 43,000,000 Americans," 42 U.S.C. § 12101(a)(1), but perhaps two or three times that number. Nevertheless, if we apply customary tools of statutory construction, it is quite clear that the threshold question whether an individual is "disabled" within the meaning of the Act — and, therefore, is entitled to the basic assurances that the Act affords — focuses on her past or present physical condition without regard to mitigation that has resulted from rehabilitation, self-improvement, prosthetic devices, or medication. One might reasonably argue that the general rule should not apply to an impairment that merely requires a nearsighted person to wear glasses. But I believe that, in order to be faithful to the remedial purpose of the Act, we should give it a generous, rather than a miserly, construction.

> Justice Stevens's accusations of the majority's "miserly [] construction" of the ADA took hold with Congress, which subsequently amended the statute.

There are many individuals who have lost one or more limbs in industrial accidents, or perhaps in the service of their country in places like Iwo Jima. With the aid of prostheses, coupled with courageous determination and physical therapy, many of these hardy individuals can perform all of their major life activities just as efficiently as an average couch potato. If the Act were just concerned with their present ability to participate in society, many of these individuals' physical impairments would not be viewed as disabilities. Similarly, if the statute were solely concerned with whether these individuals viewed themselves as disabled — or with whether a majority of employers regarded them as unable to perform most jobs — many of these individuals would lack statutory protection from discrimination based on their prostheses.

The sweep of the statute's three-pronged definition, however, makes it pellucidly clear that Congress intended the Act to cover such persons. The fact that a prosthetic device, such as an artificial leg, has restored one's ability to perform major life activities surely cannot mean that subsection (A) of the definition is inapplicable. Nor should the fact that the individual considers himself (or actually is) "cured," or that a prospective employer considers him generally employable, mean that subsections (B) or (C) are inapplicable. [I]f I correctly understand the Court's opinion, it holds that one who continues to wear a hearing aid that she has worn all her life might not be covered — fully cured impairments are covered, but merely treatable ones are not. The text of the Act surely does not require such a bizarre result.

■ NOTES AND QUESTIONS

1. *Sutton* does a nice job of explaining the statutory terms for pursuing a disability claim. It also clearly demonstrates the difference between an actual and a perceived disability.

2. The major holding in the case is that mitigating measures should not be taken into account when deciding whether an individual is actually disabled. Do you agree? How persuasive is the dissent's position that veterans with prosthetics may not be covered by the statute?

3. In 2008, Congress amended the statute with the ADA Amendments Act (ADAAA). The ADAAA was passed, in part, to respond to the overly rigid interpretation of "disability" the Supreme Court had applied to the statute. Congress specifically stated in its findings that "the holdings of the Supreme Court in *Sutton* . . . and its companion cases have narrowed the broad scope of protection intended to be afforded by the ADA, thus eliminating protection for many individuals whom Congress intended to protect." ADA Amendments Act of 2008, Pub. L. No. 110-325, § 2(a)(4), 122 Stat. 3553, 3553 (2008).

4. As part of the ADAAA, the statute now provides that mitigating measures may not be taken into account when determining whether an individual is disabled. The statute provides for two exceptions to this general rule, however: ordinary eyeglasses and contact lenses. 42 U.S.C. § 12102. Under the revised statute, then, the outcome of the *Sutton* case would have been the same, though the broader holding was rejected by Congress.

5. Why did the plaintiffs not argue that they were perceived as disabled in the major life activity of seeing? Would this have been a better argument?

6. *Sutton* is also instructive in that it focuses on the regulatory terms of the statute. As defined by the EEOC, an impairment includes "[a]ny physiological disorder or condition, cosmetic disfigurement, or anatomical loss affecting one or more body systems, such as neurological, musculoskeletal, special sense organs, respiratory (including speech organs), cardiovascular, reproductive, digestive, genitourinary, immune, circulatory, hemic, lymphatic, skin, and endocrine" or "any mental or psychological disorder." 29 C.F.R. § 1630.2(h)(1), (2).

7. The "major life activities" under the statute have been revised pursuant to the ADAAA, and now specifically include "working." The statute provides that these activities "include, but are not limited to" "[c]aring for oneself, performing manual tasks, seeing, hearing, eating, sleeping, walking, standing, sitting, reaching, lifting, bending, speaking, breathing, learning, reading, concentrating, thinking, communicating, interacting with others, and working." 29 C.F.R. § 1630.2(i)(1)(i).

8. Congress specifically rejected the EEOC's interpretation of the term "substantially limits." The agency subsequently revised its regulations, which now provide in part that "[t]he term 'substantially limits' shall be construed broadly in favor of expansive coverage, to the maximum extent permitted by the terms of the ADA. 'Substantially limits' is not meant to be a demanding standard." 29 C.F.R. § 1630.2(j)(1)(i). The agency also notes that "[a]n impairment is a disability within the meaning of this section if it substantially limits the ability of an individual to perform a major life activity as compared to most people in the general population." *Id.* at (ii).

9. The ADAAA also included several additional important changes to the statute. Notably, the revised statute:

   ■ clarifies that an impairment that is episodic or in remission is a disability if it would substantially limit a major life activity when active;
   ■ changes the definition of "regarded as" so that it no longer requires a showing that the employer perceived the individual to be substantially limited in a major life activity, and instead says that an applicant or employee is "regarded as" disabled if he or she is subject to an action prohibited by the ADA (e.g., failure to hire or termination) based on an impairment that is not transitory and minor;
   ■ provides that individuals covered only under the "regarded as" prong are not entitled to reasonable accommodation.

   EEOC, *Notice Concerning the Americans with Disabilities Act (ADA) Amendments Act of 2008*, http://www.eeoc.gov/laws/statutes/adaaa_notice.cfm. For a discussion on the major changes to the ADA by the ADAAA, see Joseph A. Seiner, *Pleading Disability*, 51 B.C. L. Rev. 95 (2010).

10. **Obesity.** In June 2013, the American Medical Association (AMA) voted to classify obesity as a disease. Commentators and lawyers noted that this will have legal consequences, potentially "expand[ing] the reach of the ADA further." While the general understanding has been that common obesity, if not linked to an underlying medical condition, is not a disability protected under the ADA, the decision by the AMA will likely open the door for protection of not just severe obesity connected to an "underlying medical condition such as diabetes," which has already been found to be protected under the ADA, but also for protection of common, ordinary obesity. Michele Bowman, *Obesity Likely to Become "Disability" Under ADA*, Lawyers. com Blog (July 10, 2013), http://blogs.lawyers.com/2013/07/obesity-to-become-disability/.

The way obesity is viewed also varies in different countries around the world. For example, the European Court of Justice ruled that severely overweight workers "could be called disabled if their condition prevents a 'full and effective participation in professional life.'" *See* Susan Milligan, *Calling in Overweight to Work?*, U.S. NEWS & WORLD REPORT (Dec. 18, 2014, 1:00 P.M.), http://www.usnews.com/opinion/blogs/susan-milligan/2014/12/18/european-court-rules-obesity-could-be-a-disability.

 ## Interactive Problem

Looking back at the facts of the interactive problem at the beginning of the chapter, assume that Tina also informed her employer that she also was suffering from diabetes, though this condition was under complete control through the use of insulin. Would this condition satisfy the definition of being an actual disability under the reasoning of *Sutton*? Under the ADAAA?

As already noted, the ADAAA specifically includes "working" as a major life activity. In the following case, the Tenth Circuit Court of Appeals considered the situation where a worker alleged that the employer *perceived* that she was substantially limited in the major life activity of working.

EEOC v. Heartway Corp.
466 F.3d 1156 (10th Cir. 2006)

EBEL, Circuit Judge.

Janet Edwards has been diagnosed with hepatitis C, a viral disease that is transmitted by blood-to-blood contact. Edwards began regular medical treatment in 2000 and by January 2001 there was no detectable amount of the hepatitis C virus in her blood, although according to her physician she will always have chronic hepatitis. Edwards continued to be treated and monitored for hepatitis through at least July 2003.

On August 13, 2001, Edwards applied for a job at York Manor Nursing Center, a nursing home in Muskogee, Oklahoma. The application process included completing a "Physical Requirements Questionnaire" that included the following item: "In order that we may protect our residents from disease, please indicate if you are under a doctor's care or taking medications now." Despite the ongoing monitoring of her hepatitis, Edwards checked the "no" box. She was subsequently hired as a "dietary aide" and eventually became a cook for the York Manor residents and employees.

York Manor first learned that Edwards had hepatitis on April 1, 2002. That day, Edwards accidentally cut her hand at work. Edwards's sister — who also worked at York Manor — sought out Theresa Raines, York Manor's director of nursing, and told her both that Edwards had cut herself and that Edwards had hepatitis. After work, Edwards herself asked to talk to Raines, "off the record," and told Raines about her hepatitis. Two days later, Raines called Edwards and informed her that she would not be allowed to return to work without a doctor's permission. Edwards promptly asked her doctor for a letter clearing her to return to work; he mailed her such a letter, which arrived at her house on April 5. However, that evening, before Edwards had a chance to bring the letter to York Manor, Edwards's kitchen supervisor called to tell her that she was fired.

The next week, Edwards took her doctor's note to Mitchell Townsend, York Manor's facility administrator, and asked to be reinstated as a cook. According to Edwards, Townsend refused, saying: "Well, Janet, you having Hepatitis C, you will not work in our kitchen." When Edwards asked him if she was being terminated because of her hepatitis, according to Edwards he replied, "No, I'm firing you because you falsified information on your [job] application." Townsend then ended the conversation. In June 2002, Edwards filed a discrimination charge with the EEOC. An EEOC investigator recorded that when he called Townsend to discuss Edwards's complaint, Townsend responded by asking: "How would you like to eat food containing her blood, if she ever cut her finger?" The investigator also reported that Townsend "stated that if this got out to their clients they[] would have a mass exodus from their nursing home."

In September 2003, the EEOC filed a complaint on Edwards's behalf against Heartway Corporation. The complaint alleged that Heartway violated Title I of the ADA by firing Edwards "because it regarded her as disabled." The case was eventually tried to a jury. At the close of the EEOC's case in chief, Heartway moved for judgment as a matter of law. Part of Heartway's motion was a challenge to the sufficiency of the evidence showing that Heartway discriminated against Edwards. The district court denied this part of the motion. Heartway's motion also sought judgment as a matter of law on the issue of punitive damages, claiming that there was no evidence that Heartway exhibited malice or reckless indifference. Over the EEOC's objection, the court granted this portion of Heartway's motion, saying that it saw "no basis under [Supreme Court precedent] or under the ADA or under the evidence to send the issue of punitive damages to the jury."

The case was then submitted to the jury, which found "by a preponderance of the evidence that Heartway discriminated against Janet Edwards due to perceived disability." The jury awarded Edwards $20,000 in compensatory damages and recommended an award of back pay, which the district court awarded in the amount of $1,240. Following the jury verdict, Heartway renewed its motion for judgment as a matter of law, again contending that the evidence was insufficient to prove the EEOC's prima facie case. The district court denied Heartway's renewed motion.

The EEOC timely filed a notice of appeal and now argues that the district court erred in withholding the issue of punitive damages from the jury. Heartway timely cross-appealed the district court's denial of its motion for judgment as a matter of law as to the claim of discrimination.

To prove that Heartway violated the ADA by firing Edwards, the EEOC was required to prove, inter alia, that Edwards had a disability. In claiming that Edwards had a disability, the EEOC has never asserted that either of the first two parts of the above definition apply (*i.e.*, that Edwards *actually* had a qualifying impairment or record of impairment); rather, it has consistently argued only that Heartway *regarded* Edwards as having a substantially limiting impairment. The applicable EEOC regulations specify that the "regarded as" standard may be met when a person "[h]as a physical or mental impairment that does not substantially limit major life activities but is treated by a covered entity as constituting such limitation." 29 C.F.R. § 1630.2(l). Heartway apparently does not dispute that Edwards's hepatitis is a "physical . . . impairment that does not substantially limit [her] major life activities." Thus, the question is whether Heartway nonetheless treated Edwards's hepatitis as "substantially limiting" one or more of her "major life activities."

The only major life activity at issue in this case is the activity of working. The EEOC regulations state that "[w]ith respect to the major life activity of working," [t]he term "substantially limit[ed]" means significantly restricted in the ability to perform either a class of jobs or a broad range of jobs in various classes as compared to the average person having comparable training, skills and abilities. The inability to perform a single, particular job does not constitute a substantial limitation in the major life activity of working.

> "Working" has always been a controversial major life activity, but it was given a statutory basis in the 2009 amendments to the ADA.

[F]or an employee to prevail on a "regarded as" claim with respect to the major life activity of working, there must be sufficient evidence that the employer *subjectively* believed the employee to be significantly restricted as to a class of jobs or broad range of jobs in various classes. There will often not be evidence on this point, but it is not an insurmountable showing.

Furthermore, although the above inquiry is strongly subjective, the question of *what constitutes* a "class of jobs" or "broad range of jobs in various classes" is an objective question. That is, there need not be evidence that the employer knew or believed that the group of jobs from which the employer viewed the employee as restricted constituted (or included) a "class of jobs" or a "broad range of jobs in various classes." However, that the inquiry is an objective one does not mean that there are bright-line standards as to what a "class of jobs" is.

Looking to . . . broad language from the EEOC regulations, we have noted that [a] "class of jobs" is defined as "[t]he job from which the individual has been disqualified because of an impairment, and the number and types of jobs utilizing similar training, knowledge, skills or abilities, within that geographical area, from which the individual is also disqualified because of the impairment." 29 C.F.R. § 1630.2(j)(3)(ii)(B). A "broad range of jobs in various classes" is defined as "[t]he job from which the individual has been disqualified because of an impairment, and the number and types of other jobs not utilizing similar training, knowledge, skills or abilities, within that geographical area, from which the individual is also disqualified because of the impairment." 29 C.F.R. § 1630.2(j)[(3)](ii)(C).

The question we face . . . is whether or not there was a "legally sufficient evidentiary basis" for a reasonable jury to conclude that Heartway treated Edwards's hepatitis as significantly restricting her ability to perform either a class of jobs or a broad range of jobs in various classes. [citation omitted] We conclude that there was.

Because Townsend was the one who made the decision to fire Edwards, his beliefs regarding Edwards's hepatitis is the relevant inquiry.

As to the first part of our inquiry, there was sufficient evidence to show that Townsend viewed Edwards as substantially limited in her ability to perform her job at York Manor. His comments to Edwards ("you having Hepat[i]tis C, you will not work in our kitchen") and the EEOC investigator ("How would you like to eat food containing her blood . . . ?") could be taken by a reasonable jury to indicate that Townsend thought it would be unsafe or unsanitary for Edwards to continue cooking food for the nursing home residents and staff. This is evidence that Townsend treated Edwards as limited in her "ability to perform" the job of nursing home cook. Similarly, Townsend's expression of concern about a "mass exodus" is evidence that he thought that Edwards could not properly perform her job because of how others might react to her perceived disability. Therefore, there was sufficient evidence for a reasonable jury to conclude that Townsend viewed Edwards as significantly restricted in her ability to perform her job at York Manor.

This evidence was also sufficient for a jury to conclude that Townsend treated Edwards as significantly restricted in her ability to perform other jobs, in addition to the job she held at York Manor. Specifically, a jury could reasonably view the testimony as showing that Townsend believed Edwards was restricted in her ability to do any kitchen job ("you have Hepatitis C, you will not work in our kitchen") and any other job where there is a chance of bleeding and thereby transmitting hepatitis ("How would you like to eat food containing her blood, if she ever cut her finger?").

Finally, we conclude that the jobs from which Edwards was regarded as restricted constituted a "class of jobs." As noted earlier, the EEOC regulations define a "class of jobs" as the job from which one is disqualified and "jobs utilizing similar training, knowledge, skills or abilities, within that geographical area." 29 C.F.R. § 1630.2(j)(3)(ii)(B).

The EEOC's expert witness, Elvira Sisolak, testified that jobs in the "health care support" and "food preparation and food serving" census job groups — in the geographical area — required training, knowledge, and skills similar to those utilized in Edwards's job at York Manor. Many — if not most — of these jobs (*e.g.*, operating room assistant, first aid nurse, cook, waitress) would require kitchen work and/or present the risk of cuts and contamination. It is reasonable to conclude, based on this expert evidence and the reasonable inferences to be drawn from Townsend's comments, that Townsend viewed Edwards as significantly restricted in her ability to perform a class of such jobs. Therefore, we hold that there was a "legally sufficient evidentiary basis" for a jury to conclude that Edwards had a disability as defined by the ADA.

To prove that Heartway violated the ADA, the EEOC was also required to prove that

> **Beyond showing coverage under the statute, a plaintiff must further demonstrate that the adverse action was taken because of a disability.**

Edwards was terminated *because of* her disability. We conclude that there was sufficient evidence to support the jury's conclusion that Heartway did indeed terminate Edwards because of her disability.

Edwards testified that Townsend told her "you having Hepatitis C, you will not work in our kitchen." Although this is arguably an ambiguous statement, a jury could reasonably take it to mean that Edwards was being fired *because* she had hepatitis and was therefore (in Townsend's mind) unable to perform her job or other jobs in the same class. Similarly, Townsend's expression of concern to the EEOC investigator that there would be "mass exodus" if the clients found out that the cook had hepatitis supports a finding that Edwards was therefore fired because she had that disease and was thus restricted in her ability to perform her job and other jobs in the same class.

Heartway spends several pages of its brief trying to show that Edwards actually did lie on her job application and that this provided a sufficient non-discriminatory justification for terminating her. However, even assuming that Edwards did indeed lie, and even assuming that this would have provided a valid reason for terminating her under the applicable law, a reasonable jury could have nonetheless concluded that she was *actually* fired because of her disability.

Heartway points to the allegedly "uncontroverted" testimony that Townsend fired Edwards for dishonesty, not for having a disability. At trial, Townsend stated: "I fired her for being untruthful on her application for employment." When asked "Did you fire Miss Edwards because you thought she was disabled?" he responded "No." His testimony also included this exchange:

Q. Is untruthfulness a basis for termination at Heartway?
A. Yes.
Q. And if you discover any untruthfulness, your common practice is to terminate that employee?
A. Yes.

Similarly, Edwards testified that when she asked Townsend if she was being fired for having hepatitis, Townsend replied "No, I'm firing you because you falsified information on your application." Although this testimony certainly could lead a jury to agree with Heartway's version of the facts, the jury was also entitled to conclude that Townsend was not entirely truthful at trial and that he misled Edwards when he told her that she was being fired for lying on her application. Heartway is not entitled to judgment as a matter of law just because there was evidence that, if believed, would have weighed heavily in favor of Heartway. Based on Townsend's statements to Edwards and to the EEOC investigator, and despite the contrary testimony at trial, a reasonable jury could conclude that Edwards was fired for having a disability, rather than for Heartway's proffered reason.

Therefore, because there was a "legally sufficient evidentiary basis" for concluding that Edwards had a disability (defined as "regarded as having an impairment") and that she was fired because of her disability, the district court did not err in denying Heartway's motion for judgment as a matter of law. We therefore affirm that denial.

■ NOTES AND QUESTIONS

1. *Heartway* provides an excellent example of a situation where an employer may have "regarded" an employee as disabled. Did Heartway *regard* Edwards as unable to perform a class or broad range of jobs, or did it simply believe that she was unable to work at this one particular facility?

2. The ADAAA incorporated working as a major life activity. The EEOC also made regulatory revisions as to what constitutes substantially limited in "working" under the statute. Why was Edwards able to show that she was unable to perform a class or broad range of jobs, while the plaintiffs in *Sutton* fell short on this task? What distinguishes the two cases?

3. The federal regulations were revised after the ADAAA. The new regulations do not include the "class" or "broad range of jobs" language. The appendix to the regulations make clear that where used, these terms should not be as rigorously interpreted as they have been in the past. *See* 29 C.F.R. § 1630 app. ("as used in this section the terms 'class of jobs' and 'broad range of jobs in various classes' will be applied in a more straightforward and simple manner than they were applied by the courts prior to the Amendments Act").

4. Why did the EEOC allege that the employer perceived Edwards as unable to work? Why didn't the Commission choose a different major life activity?

5. *Heartway* also underscores the point that a plaintiff must show more than that she is disabled. She must further demonstrate that an adverse action was taken because of her disability or that the employer failed to provide a reasonable accommodation. Here, the court explores the sufficiency of the evidence that shows that Heartway acted *because of* Edwards' disability.

Class Exercise: Working as a Major Life Activity

Breaking up into small groups, develop a set of facts that would establish that an employer at a Fortune 500 company perceived that an employee (a secretary) was substantially limited in the major life activity of working. Was it difficult to develop such facts? Why or why not? As a general matter, is it hard to show that someone is perceived as disabled under the major life activity of working?

As discussed, the ADAAA was intended to broaden the scope of coverage of the statute, and to expand the meaning of the term "disability." In the following case, a federal district court applies this new standard to a matter involving an individual with head injuries. This case helps provide some guidance on the revisions to the ADA.

Graham v. St. John's United Methodist Church
913 F. Supp. 2d 650 (S.D. Ill. 2012)

Memorandum and Order

REAGAN, District Judge.

The complaint alleges the following facts. In 1996, Graham was the victim of a serious beating in which he suffered multiple concussions, multiple fractures including parts of his face, and severe contusions over a substantial portion of his body. Graham's head injuries resulted in a permanent disability of his cognitive processes leaving him with difficulty articulating his thoughts and comprehending, especially in stressful situations. In August 2008, Graham was hired as a part-time custodian at St. John's [United Methodist Church] and was told that he would work 25 hours a week. A short time after Graham began his employment, the other part-time custodian left, and Graham assumed all custodial duties at the church. He performed his duties in a satisfactory manner. Palmer told Graham that regardless of the extra work load and the number of hours worked, he would only be paid for 25 hours a week.

Methodist Church in Illinois

As a result of his head injuries, Graham is a very acquiescent individual, especially with authority figures like Palmer. Palmer took advantage of Graham's disability and required him to work seven days a week, averaging 35 to 40 hours, while only allowing him to put approximately 25 hours on his timesheet. [Reverend Sheryl] Palmer called Graham "stupid" and "retard" and allowed other members to call him these names as well. She yelled at Graham in front of others in order to embarrass him.

About June 6, 2011, Julia and Darol Holsman, who were members of St. John's and advocates for Graham's employment, asked [for an investigation of] Palmer's mistreatment of Graham. The Holsmans also assisted Graham in filing a complaint with the Illinois Department of Labor ("IDOL").

Graham repeatedly asked Palmer and St. John's for accommodation for his mental challenges, but they refused to accommodate him. In July 2011, the Holsmans told Palmer and St. John's that Graham was ill and scheduled for surgery. On August 15, 2011, Palmer unilaterally scheduled Graham to return to work. In a letter dated August 17, 2011, Palmer told Graham that if he did not notify St. John's of his health status by August 23, 2011, St. John's would "assume [he] resigned his position." On August 23, 2011, Graham was discharged.

St. John's contends that Graham has not sufficiently pleaded that he has a disability that substantially limits one or more major life activities, as is required to state a claim under the ADA. Specifically, St. John's maintains that Graham fails to allege a mental impairment that substantially limits a major life activity, a record of such an impairment or that he was regarded as having such an impairment.

Graham was hired as a custodian for St. John's in August 2008 and was discharged in August 2011. Consequently, he began his employment prior to the effective date of the ADA Amendments Act of 2008 ("ADAAA"), January 1, 2009, but continued in his employment after the Act became effective.

In order to allege disability discrimination, Graham must claim that (1) he is disabled within the meaning of the ADA; (2) he is qualified to perform the essential functions of the job, either with or without a reasonable accommodation; and (3) he suffered from an adverse employment action because of his disability. St. John's asserts that Graham's claims fail at the first prong of the test — that he is not an individual with a disability within the meaning of the ADA.

The ADAAA provides more generous coverage than the ADA by providing that the definition of disability "shall be construed in favor of broad coverage of individuals . . . to the maximum extent permitted by the terms of [the Act.]" 42 U.S.C. § 12102(4)(A). The associated regulations instruct courts to be liberal in determining whether a plaintiff is substantially limited: "[t]he term 'substantially limits' shall be construed broadly in favor of expansive coverage, to the maximum extent permitted by the terms of the ADA. 'Substantially limits' is not meant to be a demanding standard." 29 C.F.R. § 1630.2(j)(1)(i).

> The amendments to the ADA were intended to expand its coverage. The statute now provides that it should "be construed in favor of broad coverage of individuals . . . to the maximum extent permitted."

Graham alleges that he has permanent brain damage which causes him difficulty articulating his thoughts, slowness to comprehend and difficulty challenging anyone he views as a figure of authority. As such, he has alleged sufficient facts to meet the definition of an individual with a disability. His claims are detailed enough to meet the requirements of *Twombly* and, consequently, sufficient to survive St. John's motion to dismiss.

Furthermore, accepting as true all well-pleaded factual allegations and drawing all reasonable inferences in Graham's favor, he has sufficiently pleaded that he was regarded as an individual with a disability. Being "regarded as" having a disability "means that the individual has been subjected to an action prohibited by the ADA as amended because of an actual or perceived impairment. . . ." 29 CFR § 1630.2(g)(ii).

Graham claims that Palmer called him a "retard" on multiple occasions as well as allowing other staff members to call him by that epithet. Graham also claims that Palmer took advantage of his mental impairment by requiring him to work seven days a week and to do both custodial work and personal chores for her. Moreover, Graham claims that Palmer asked the Holsmans to act as advocates for him with respect to his employment at St. John's after she learned of his impairment. These allegations are sufficient to survive St. John's motion to dismiss on the issue of whether Palmer regarded Graham as an individual with a disability.

■ NOTES AND QUESTIONS

1. Were Palmer's comments to Graham sufficient to demonstrate that the employer perceived him as disabled? Was there any evidence beyond these comments that helped support this conclusion?

2. The court here concludes that Graham is regarded as disabled. Is there enough evidence in the case to determine whether the plaintiff was actually disabled?

3. To demonstrate a perceived disability, the plaintiff must show that he is regarded as substantially limited in a major life activity by the employer.

4. Coverage under the actual, perceived, or "record of" prongs of the statute is sufficient to satisfy the first element of the prima facie case in a disparate treatment disability claim.

5. The court here concludes that the plaintiff has satisfied coverage under the statute. Will the plaintiff further be able to show that he was discriminated against because of his disability?

6. Based on the facts as presented here, what would be the plaintiff's best cause of action? Failure to accommodate? Discriminatory discharge? Unlawful harassment? What additional facts might you need to establish these potential claims?

7. The Fair Labor Standards Act (FLSA) is beyond the scope of this text. It is worth noting, however, that the facts as presented here could give rise to a claim under the FLSA, which gives workers guarantees on several different aspects of wages.

8. **Disability claims over the past decade.** Like many areas of the law, disability claims have ebbed and flowed over the years. The chart below reflects the peaks and valleys of charges of disability discrimination with the EEOC over more than a decade, as reflected on the EEOC's website.

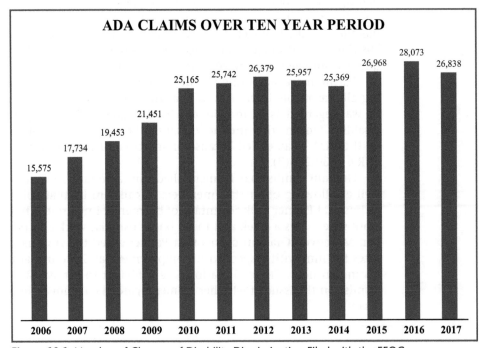

Figure 10.1: Number of Charges of Disability Discrimination Filed with the EEOC

9. One interesting example of this area of the law in practice occurred in in Ohio, where a high school languages teacher maintained that she was discriminated against on the basis of her disability. The teacher, who had worked successfully for decades in the school district, was reassigned to a junior high school classroom. Because she suffered from pedophobia — a fear of young children — the teacher had made a previous agreement with the district not to have to teach these younger students. The disorder is a recognized condition in the medical literature, and being in the presence of young students results in stress and anxiety for the educator. Would this teacher have a viable claim under the ADA? Is her condition a disability under the statute? *See* Denise Smith Amos, *Ohio Teacher Claims Discrimination over Fear of Kids*, USA Today (Jan. 15, 2013, 7:35 A.M.), http://www.usatoday.com/story/news/nation/2013/01/15/teacher-sues-discrimination-fear-kids/1835363/.

C. History of a Disability

In addition to an actual or perceived disability, an individual can gain coverage under the statute by establishing a history of a disability. This "record of" prong of the statute allows employees to show that at one time they had a physical or mental impairment that substantially limited a major life activity. The following case explores the meaning of this prong of the definition.

Shaver v. Independent Stave Co.
350 F.3d 716 (8th Cir. 2003)

Morris Sheppard Arnold, Circuit Judge.

Christopher Shaver has suffered from nocturnal epilepsy since he was a teenager. After an operation in which part of his brain was removed and replaced by a metal plate, he was able to get a job working at the timber mill of Salem Wood Products Company. After being fired, allegedly for insubordination, Mr. Shaver sued Salem under various theories.

In determining whether a hostile work environment claim has been made out under the ADA, we think it proper to turn to standards developed elsewhere in our anti-discrimination law, adapting them to the unique requirements of the ADA. To be entitled to relief, it seems to us that Mr. Shaver must show that he is a member of the class of people protected by the statute, that he was subject to unwelcome harassment, that the harassment resulted from his membership in the protected class, and that the harassment was severe enough to affect the terms, conditions, or privileges of his employment. *Cf. Reedy v. Quebecor Printing Eagle, Inc.*, 333 F.3d 906, 907–08 (8th Cir. 2003).

The ADA's employment provisions protect people who are "qualified individual[s] with a disability." 42 U.S.C. §§ 12111(8), 12112(a). In this case, neither party disputes that Mr. Shaver was qualified for his job at Salem's lumber mill. Salem does argue, however, that Mr. Shaver is not "disabled" within the meaning of the statute. A disability is an "impairment that substantially limits one or more . . . major life activities." *See* 42 U.S.C. § 12102(2)(A). Furthermore, one can be within the statute if one is regarded (accurately or inaccurately) as having such an impairment or if one has a record of such an impairment in the past. *See* 42 U.S.C. § 12102(2)(B)–(C).

Lumberyard

Before his operation, it is undisputed that Mr. Shaver's epilepsy caused severe seizures of the kind and frequency that this court has held impair "major life activities" such as speaking, walking, or seeing. He thus has a record of impairment. Our review of the record also persuades us that at least some of his co-workers regarded Mr. Shaver as "stupid" and "not playing with a full deck" because of his epilepsy and resulting operation. And, since thinking is a major life activity, we conclude as well that a jury could find that Mr. Shaver qualifies as disabled because he was regarded as disabled.

Our review of the record indicates that there is no real factual dispute about whether Mr. Shaver was harassed. (The severity and legal consequence of that harassment are separate questions that we deal with below.) There is ample evidence, for instance, that he was routinely referred to as "platehead." Salem argues that the harassment was not the result of

Moving Logs at a Lumberyard

his disability, claiming that the name "platehead" was linked to the physical fact that Mr. Shaver has a plate in his skull, rather than with any impairment as such. We think that this distinction may be too fine for us, but in any case the meaning of the statements (that is, what inference to draw from the words used) is properly a matter for the jury. There is certainly nothing in the record to suggest that those who called Mr. Shaver "platehead" made the distinction suggested by Salem. The distinction itself, moreover, may well be meaningless: Even if one calls a person "pegleg" because he has a peg leg rather than because he has trouble walking, it is nevertheless the case that the nickname was chosen because the person was disabled.

With the question of the effect of the harassment on the "terms, conditions, and privileges" of Mr. Shaver's employment we come to the heart of this case. In order to be actionable, harassment must be both subjectively hostile or abusive to the victim and "severe and pervasive enough to create an objectively hostile or abusive work environment — an environment that a reasonable person would find hostile or abusive." *Harris v. Forklift Sys., Inc.,* 510 U.S. 17 (1993). On the other hand, we have repeatedly emphasized that anti-discrimination laws do not create a general civility code. Conduct that is merely rude, abrasive, unkind, or insensitive does not come within the scope of the law.

Taking the evidence in the light most favorable to Mr. Shaver, we have little difficulty concluding that a jury could find that he found the harassment by his co-workers hostile or abusive. The more difficult question is whether the behavior fell within the elusive category of "objectively . . . offensive," *see Faragher v. City of Boca Raton*, 524 U.S. 775 (1998). Mr. Shaver's co-workers referred to him as "platehead" over a period of about two years. Some of the co-workers were supervisors, and some were not. Some of the co-workers stopped using the name when Mr. Shaver asked them to, and others did not. Use of nicknames is widespread at the mill, and while this fact does not render the name applied to Mr. Shaver inoffensive, it might reduce its offensiveness. Several co-workers suggested that Mr. Shaver was stupid. On one occasion, a co-worker said that Mr. Shaver "pissed in his pants when the microwave was on," but this uglier statement seems to have occurred outside of Mr. Shaver's presence, a fact that lessens but does not undo its offensiveness.

Taken as a whole, we conclude that the verbal harassment here does not rise to the same level as that in cases where we have granted relief. While Mr. Shaver was upset about the harassment at work, it was not so severe as to result in any psychological treatment. In *Reedy*, 333 F.3d at 909–10, we upheld a hostile work environment claim based on harassing words, but the words at issue were death threats directed specifically at the plaintiff over a sustained period of time. In contrast, there is no allegation or evidence in this case to suggest that any of the harassment of Mr. Shaver was explicitly or implicitly threatening. Nor does this case involve harassing conduct of a physical nature as was found actionable in many of the cases that Mr. Shaver cites.

> How would the claim of disability harassment here fit within the harassment framework discussed in Chapter 5?

■ NOTES AND QUESTIONS

1. The *Shaver* case presents an interesting example of where a plaintiff may not be actually disabled, but is regarded as disabled and has a history of a disability. There can be little question in this case that Shaver was disabled at one time, given the severity of his epilepsy.

2. The *Shaver* decision was issued prior to the ADAAA. Would the amendments to the ADA have impacted the question of whether Shaver was actually disabled?

3. This decision highlights the importance of not only showing that the plaintiff is disabled, but of proving that the plaintiff was discriminated against *because of* his disability.

4. As discussed in Chapter 5, harassment can be on the basis of any protected characteristic. In Chapter 5, this text looked at the *Shaver* decision and whether the federal courts have accepted disability harassment claims. While this court acknowledged that such a claim could exist, it found that the facts were not severe or pervasive enough to create a claim. What type of facts would be necessary for the court here to conclude that the plaintiff established a disability harassment cause of action?

5. Do you agree with the court that the evidence was insufficient for Shaver to show that he was harassed on the basis of his disability? Is the pervasive nature of the comments enough to establish a hostile work environment? Does the court too quickly disregard the Supreme Court holding in *Harris*, discussed in Chapter 5, that psychological trauma need not be established in a hostile work environment case?

6. Though the court does not address this issue, is it important that the harassment was primarily based on the plate in Mr. Shaver's head? Thus, can an ADA harassment claim be based on conduct that targets the corrective measure, rather than the disability?

7. In a portion of the decision omitted above, the court went on to rule in favor of Mr. Shaver on a claim of retaliation for conduct that took place after the plaintiff was no longer employed by the company. From the court:

> When contacted by Mr. Shaver's acquaintances, [his former supervisor] told them that he could not recommend Mr. Shaver because he had "a get rich quick scheme involving suing companies." . . . Contrary to [the employer's] arguments, negative job references can constitute adverse, retaliatory action as a matter of law. . . . [I]t is for a jury to decide whether [the supervisor] is to be believed, whether his interpretation of events is consistent with the rest of the evidence, and whether his recommendations caused prospective employers to reject Mr. Shaver's applications.

Shaver, 350 F.3d at 723, 725.

These allegations demonstrate the importance of preventing retaliation in the workplace, and of counseling employers against such retaliation. Even though the employer won the underlying claim, it was still vulnerable on the retaliation cause of action.

 Interactive Problem

Looking back at the facts of the interactive problem at the beginning of the chapter, assume that Tina Teacher had severe high blood pressure for several years when she began teaching, and that this condition persisted for over a decade. The employer was never aware of this condition. Would Tina be able to establish that she has a history of a disability? If so, would it impact the outcome of the case?

D. Accommodation Requirement and the Interactive Process

As already discussed, there are multiple claims a plaintiff can raise under the ADA. Thus far, this text has addressed a disparate treatment claim under the statute. One other area that can be pursued, however, is a failure to accommodate cause of action. Alleging that the employer failed to accommodate the plaintiff is a separate cause of action under the statute. The ADA requires that an employer make "reasonable accommodations to the known physical or mental limitations of an otherwise qualified individual with a disability who is an applicant or employee, unless [the employer can show that the] accommodation would impose an undue hardship." 42 U.S.C. § 12112(b)(5)(A).

Based on the statutory text, there is a basic two-part test for failure to accommodate claims: (1) the employee must establish that she suggested an accommodation that was reasonable; and (2) if a reasonable accommodation exists, the employer must establish that it results in an undue hardship on the business. Though different jurisdictions have applied different tests and burdens to the accommodation inquiry, most courts have followed this basic two-part test.

The only other area of employment discrimination law to require reasonable accommodations is in the religious discrimination context. However, the disability accommodation requirement has far more bite than the religious accommodation requirement. This is likely because there are no First Amendment concerns in the disability context. In the religion context, the courts are reluctant to require too much of an employer, which could run afoul of excessive government entanglement. *See* S. Elizabeth Wilbourn Malloy, *Something Borrowed, Something Blue: Why Disability Law Claims Are Different*, 33 Conn. L. Rev. 603, 627–628 (2001) (discussing how the Supreme Court interpreted Title VII's religious accommodation requirement narrowly but how disability accommodations are broader, because there is no First Amendment issue involved). Moreover, aware of the requirements in the religious accommodation context, some legislators debating the ADA attempted to make clear the more rigorous burdens inherent in the disability accommodation. H.R. Rep. No. 101–485, pt. 2, at 68 (1990) (providing that "[t]he Committee wishes to make it clear that the principles enunciated by the Supreme Court in TWA v. Hardison, [432] U.S. 63 (1977), are not applicable to this legislation").

Because First Amendment concerns are not present in the disability context, the courts tend to be more demanding of the employer when accommodating employees in the workplace. Indeed, the de minimis standard that applies to religious accommodation claims has not been adopted in the ADA context. Instead, the courts have applied a more stringent meaning to the undue hardship analysis. In the case below, the Supreme Court provides some guidance on how the accommodation requirement is defined under the ADA.

U.S. Airways, Inc. v. Barnett
535 U.S. 391 (2002)

Justice Breyer delivered the opinion of the Court.

In 1990, Robert Barnett, the plaintiff and respondent here, injured his back while working in a cargo-handling position at petitioner U.S. Airways, Inc. He invoked seniority rights and transferred to a less physically demanding mailroom position. Under U.S. Airways' seniority system, that position, like others, periodically became open to seniority-based employee bidding. In 1992, Barnett learned that at least two employees senior to him intended to bid for the mailroom job. He asked U.S. Airways to accommodate his disability-imposed limitations by making an exception that would allow him to remain in the mailroom. After permitting Barnett to continue his mailroom work for five months while it considered the matter, U.S. Airways eventually decided not to make an exception. And Barnett lost his job.

U.S. Airways, Tempe, AZ

Barnett then brought this ADA suit claiming, among other things, that he was an "individual with a disability" capable of performing the essential functions of the mailroom job, that the mailroom job amounted to a "reasonable accommodation" of his disability, and that U.S. Airways, in refusing to assign him the job, unlawfully discriminated against him. U.S. Airways moved for summary judgment. It supported its motion with appropriate affidavits, Fed. Rule Civ. Proc. 56, contending that its "well-established" seniority system granted other employees the right to obtain the mailroom position.

The District Court found that the undisputed facts about seniority warranted summary judgment in U.S. Airways' favor. The Act says that an employer who fails to make "reasonable accommodations to the known physical or mental limitations of an [employee] with a disability" discriminates *"unless"* the employer "can demonstrate that the accommodation would impose an *undue hardship* on the operation of [its] business." 42 U.S.C. § 12112(b)(5)(A) (emphasis added). The court said:

> "[T]he uncontroverted evidence shows that the U.S. Air seniority system has been in place for 'decades' and governs over 14,000 U.S. Air Agents. Moreover, seniority policies such as the one at issue in this case are common to the airline industry. Given this context, it seems clear that the U.S. Air employees were justified in relying upon the policy. As such, any significant alteration of that policy would result in undue hardship to both the company and its non-disabled employees."

An en banc panel of the United States Court of Appeals for the Ninth Circuit reversed. It said that the presence of a seniority system is merely "a factor in the undue hardship analysis." *Barnett v. U.S. Air, Inc.*, 228 F.3d 1105 (9th Cir. 2000). And it held that "[a] case-by-case fact intensive analysis is required to determine whether any particular reassignment would constitute an undue hardship to the employer." *Ibid.* U.S. Airways petitioned for certiorari, asking us to decide whether "the [ADA] requires an employer to reassign a disabled employee to a position as a 'reasonable accommodation' even though another employee is entitled to hold the position under the employer's bona fide and established seniority system." We agreed to answer U.S. Airways' question.

In answering the question presented, we must consider the following statutory provisions. First, the ADA says that an employer may not "discriminate against a qualified individual with a disability." 42 U.S.C. § 12112(a). Second, the ADA says that a "qualified" individual includes "an individual with a disability who, *with* or without *reasonable accommodation*, can perform the essential functions of" the relevant "employment position." § 12111(8) (emphasis added). Third, the ADA says that "discrimination" includes an employer's "*not making reasonable accommodations* to the known physical or mental limitations of an otherwise qualified . . . employee, *unless* [the employer] can demonstrate that the accommodation would impose an *undue hardship* on the operation of [its] business." § 12112(b)(5)(A) (emphasis added). Fourth, the ADA says that the term " 'reasonable accommodation' may include . . . reassignment to a vacant position." § 12111(9)(B).

U.S. Airways' claim that a seniority system virtually always trumps a conflicting accommodation demand rests primarily upon its view of how the Act treats workplace "preferences." Insofar as a requested accommodation violates a disability-neutral workplace rule, such as a seniority rule, it grants the employee with a disability treatment that other workers could not receive. Yet the Act, U.S. Airways says, seeks only "equal" treatment for those with disabilities. Hence it does not require the employer to grant a request that, in violating a disability-neutral rule, would provide a preference.

> The presence of a seniority system in this case is a substantial factor underlying the Court's decision.

While linguistically logical, this argument fails to recognize what the Act specifies, namely, that preferences will sometimes prove necessary to achieve the Act's basic equal opportunity goal. The Act requires preferences in the form of "reasonable accommodations" that are needed for those with disabilities to obtain the same workplace opportunities that those without disabilities automatically enjoy. By definition any special "accommodation" requires the employer to treat an employee with a disability differently, i.e., preferentially. And the fact that the difference in treatment violates an employer's disability-neutral rule cannot by itself place the accommodation beyond the Act's potential reach.

Were that not so, the "reasonable accommodation" provision could not accomplish its intended objective. Neutral office assignment rules would automatically prevent the accommodation of an employee whose disability-imposed limitations require him to work on the ground floor. Neutral "break-from-work" rules would automatically prevent the accommodation of an individual who needs additional breaks from work, perhaps to permit medical visits. Neutral furniture budget rules would automatically prevent the accommodation of an individual who needs a different kind of chair or desk. Many employers will have neutral rules governing the kinds of actions most needed to reasonably accommodate a worker with a disability. Yet Congress [] said nothing suggesting that the presence of such neutral rules would create an automatic exemption. Nor have the lower courts made any such suggestion.

In sum, the nature of the "reasonable accommodation" requirement, the statutory examples, and the Act's silence about the exempting effect of neutral rules together convince us that the Act does not create any such automatic exemption. The simple fact that an accommodation would provide a "preference" — in the sense that it would permit the worker with a disability to violate a rule that others must obey — cannot, *in and of itself*, automatically show that the accommodation is not "reasonable." As a result, we reject the position taken by U.S. Airways and Justice Scalia to the contrary.

U.S. Airways also points to the ADA provisions stating that a "'reasonable accommodation' may include . . . reassignment to a *vacant* position." § 12111(9)(B) (emphasis added). And it claims that the fact that an established seniority system would assign that position to another worker automatically and always means that the position is not a "vacant" one. Nothing in the Act, however, suggests that Congress intended the word "vacant" to have a specialized meaning. And in ordinary English, a seniority system can give employees seniority rights allowing them to bid for a "vacant" position. The position in this case was held, at the time of suit, by Barnett, not by some other worker; and that position, under the U.S. Airways seniority system, became an "open" one. Moreover, U.S. Airways has said that it "reserves the right to change any and all" portions of the seniority system at will. Consequently, we cannot agree with U.S. Airways about the position's vacancy; nor do we agree that the Act would automatically deny Barnett's accommodation request for that reason.

Barnett argues that the statutory words "reasonable accommodation" mean only "effective accommodation," authorizing a court to consider the requested accommodation's ability to meet an individual's disability-related needs, and nothing more. On this view, a seniority rule violation, having nothing to do with the accommodation's effectiveness, has nothing to do with its "reasonableness." It might, at most, help to prove an "undue hardship on the operation of the business." But, he adds, that is a matter that the statute requires the employer to demonstrate, case by case.

[We are not] persuade[d] that Barnett's legal interpretation of "reasonable" is correct. For one thing, in ordinary English the word "reasonable" does not mean "effective." It is the word "accommodation," not the word "reasonable," that conveys the need for effectiveness. An ineffective "modification" or "adjustment" will not accommodate a disabled individual's limitations. Nor does an ordinary English meaning of the term "reasonable accommodation" make of it a simple, redundant mirror image of the term "undue hardship." The statute refers to an "undue hardship on the operation of the business." 42 U.S.C. § 12112(b)(5)(A). Yet a demand for an effective accommodation could prove unreasonable because of its impact, not on business operations, but on fellow employees — say, because it will lead to dismissals, relocations, or modification of employee benefits to which an employer, looking at the matter from the perspective of the business itself, may be relatively indifferent.

Neither does the statute's primary purpose require Barnett's special reading. The statute seeks to diminish or to eliminate the stereotypical thought processes, the thoughtless actions, and the hostile reactions that far too often bar those with disabilities from participating fully in the Nation's life, including the workplace. *See generally* §§ 12101(a) and (b). These objectives demand unprejudiced thought and reasonable responsive reaction on the part of employers and fellow workers alike. They will sometimes require affirmative conduct to promote entry of disabled people into the work force. They do not, however, demand action beyond the realm of the reasonable.

Neither has Congress indicated in the statute, or elsewhere, that the word "reasonable" means no more than "effective." The EEOC regulations do say that reasonable accommodations "enable" a person with a disability to perform the essential functions of a task. But that phrasing simply emphasizes the statutory provision's basic objective. The regulations do not say that "enable" and "reasonable" mean the same thing. And as discussed below, no court of appeals has so read them.

Finally, an ordinary language interpretation of the word "reasonable" does not create the "burden of proof" dilemma to which Barnett points. Many of the lower courts, while rejecting both U.S. Airways' and Barnett's more absolute views, have reconciled the phrases "reasonable accommodation" and "undue hardship" in a practical way.

They have held that a plaintiff/employee (to defeat a defendant/employer's motion for summary judgment) need only show that an "accommodation" seems reasonable on its face, *i.e.*, ordinarily or in the run of cases. Once the plaintiff has made this showing, the defendant/employer then must show special (typically case-specific) circumstances that demonstrate undue hardship in the particular circumstances. Not every court has used the same language, but their results are functionally similar. In our opinion, that practical view of the statute, applied consistently with ordinary summary judgment principles, *see* Fed. Rule Civ. Proc. 56, avoids Barnett's burden of proof dilemma, while reconciling the two statutory phrases ("reasonable accommodation" and "undue hardship").

> The "reasonable on its face" or "in the run of cases" language articulated in this case has been widely used in the lower courts.

The question in the present case focuses on the relationship between seniority systems and the plaintiff's need to show that an "accommodation" seems reasonable on its face, i.e., ordinarily or in the run of cases. We must assume that the plaintiff, an employee, is an "individual with a disability." He has requested assignment to a mailroom position as a "reasonable accommodation." We also assume that normally such a request would be reasonable within the meaning of the statute, were it not for one circumstance, namely, that the assignment would violate the rules of a seniority system. *See* § 12111(9) ("reasonable accommodation" may include "reassignment to a vacant position"). Does that circumstance mean that the proposed accommodation is not a "reasonable" one?

In our view, the answer to this question ordinarily is "yes." The statute does not require proof on a case-by-case basis that a seniority system should prevail. That is because it would not be reasonable in the run of cases that the assignment in question trump the rules of a seniority system. To the contrary, it will ordinarily be unreasonable for the assignment to prevail.

Several factors support our conclusion that a proposed accommodation will not be reasonable in the run of cases. Analogous case law supports this conclusion, for it has recognized the importance of seniority to employee-management relations. This Court has held that, in the context of a Title VII religious discrimination case, an employer need not adapt to an employee's special worship schedule as a "reasonable accommodation" where doing so would conflict with the seniority rights of other employees.

Most important for present purposes, to require the typical employer to show more than the existence of a seniority system might well undermine the employees' expectations of consistent, uniform treatment — expectations upon which the seniority system's benefits depend. That is because such a rule would substitute a complex case-specific "accommodation" decision made by management for the more uniform, impersonal operation of seniority rules. Such management decisionmaking, with its inevitable discretionary elements, would involve a matter of the greatest importance to employees, namely, layoffs; it would take place outside, as well as inside, the confines of a court case; and it might well take place fairly often. Cf. ADA, 42 U.S.C. § 12101(a)(1) (estimating that some 43 million Americans suffer from physical or mental disabilities). We can find nothing in the statute that suggests Congress intended to undermine seniority systems in this way. And we consequently conclude that the employer's showing of violation of the rules of a seniority system is by itself ordinarily sufficient.

The plaintiff (here the employee) nonetheless remains free to show that special circumstances warrant a finding that, despite the presence of a seniority system (which the ADA may not trump in the run of cases), the requested "accommodation" is "reasonable" on the particular facts. That is because special circumstances might alter the important expectations described above.

Justice O'CONNOR, concurring.

I agree with portions of the opinion of the Court, but I find problematic the Court's test for determining whether the fact that a job reassignment violates a seniority system makes the reassignment an unreasonable accommodation under the Americans with Disabilities Act of 1990 (ADA or Act), 42 U.S.C. § 12101 et seq. (1994 ed. and Supp. V). Although a seniority system plays an important role in the workplace . . . I would prefer to say that the effect of a seniority system on the reasonableness of a reassignment as an accommodation for purposes of the ADA depends on whether the seniority system is legally enforceable. "Were it possible for me to adhere to [this belief] in my vote, and for the Court at the same time to [adopt a majority rule]," I would do so. *Screws v. United States*, 325 U.S. 91, 134, (1945) (Rutledge, J., concurring in result). "The Court, however, is divided in opinion," *ibid.*, and if each Member voted consistently with his or her beliefs, we would not agree on a resolution of the question presented in this case. Yet "[s]talemate should not prevail," *ibid.*, particularly in a case in which we are merely interpreting a statute. Accordingly, in order that the Court may adopt a rule, and because I believe the Court's rule will often lead to the same outcome as the one I would have adopted, I join the Court's opinion despite my concerns.

Justice SCALIA, with whom Justice THOMAS joins, dissenting.

The question presented asks whether the "reasonable accommodation" mandate of the Americans with Disabilities Act of 1990 (ADA or Act) requires reassignment of a disabled employee to a position that "another employee is entitled to hold . . . under the employer's bona fide and established seniority system." Indulging its penchant for eschewing clear rules that might avoid litigation the Court answers "maybe." It creates a presumption that an exception to a seniority rule is an "unreasonable" accommodation, but allows that presumption to be rebutted by showing that the exception "will not likely make a difference."

The principal defect of today's opinion, however, goes well beyond the uncertainty it produces regarding the relationship between the ADA and the infinite variety of seniority systems. The conclusion that any seniority system can ever be overridden is merely one consequence of a mistaken interpretation of the ADA that makes all employment rules and practices — even those which (like a seniority system) pose no distinctive obstacle to the disabled — subject to suspension when that is (in

a court's view) a "reasonable" means of enabling a disabled employee to keep his job. That is a far cry from what I believe the accommodation provision of the ADA requires: the suspension (within reason) of those employment rules and practices that the employee's disability prevents him from observing.

In particular cases, seniority rules may have a harsher effect upon the disabled employee than upon his co-workers. If the disabled employee is physically capable of performing only one task in the workplace, seniority rules may be, for him, the difference between employment and unemployment. But that does not make the seniority system a disability-related obstacle, any more than harsher impact upon the more needy disabled employee renders the salary system a disability-related obstacle. When one departs from this understanding, the ADA's accommodation provision becomes a standardless grab bag — leaving it to the courts to decide which workplace preferences (higher salary, longer vacations, reassignment to positions to which others are entitled) can be deemed "reasonable" to "make up for" the particular employee's disability.

Because the Court's opinion leaves the question whether a seniority system must be disregarded in order to accommodate a disabled employee in a state of uncertainty that can be resolved only by constant litigation; and because it adopts an interpretation of the ADA that incorrectly subjects all employer rules and practices to the requirement of reasonable accommodation; I respectfully dissent.

Justice SOUTER, with whom Justice GINSBURG joins, dissenting.

"[R]eassignment to a vacant position," 42 U.S.C. § 12111(9) (1994 ed.), is one way an employer may "reasonabl[y] accommodat[e]" disabled employees under the [ADA]. The Court today holds that a request for reassignment will nonetheless most likely be unreasonable when it would violate the terms of a seniority system imposed by an employer. Although I concur in the Court's appreciation of the value and importance of seniority systems, I do not believe my hand is free to accept the majority's result and therefore respectfully dissent.

Nothing in the ADA insulates seniority rules from the "reasonable accommodation" requirement, in marked contrast to Title VII and the [ADEA], each of which has an explicit protection for seniority. Because Congress modeled several of the ADA's provisions on Title VII, its failure to replicate Title VII's exemption for seniority systems leaves the statute ambiguous, albeit with more than a hint that seniority rules do not inevitably carry the day.

In any event, the statute's legislative history resolves the ambiguity. The Committee Reports from both the House of Representatives and the Senate explain that seniority protections contained in a collective-bargaining agreement should not amount to more than "a factor" when it comes to deciding whether some accommodation at odds with the seniority rules is "reasonable" nevertheless. Because a unilaterally imposed seniority system enjoys no special protection under the ADA, a consideration of facts peculiar to this very case is needed to gauge whether Barnett has carried the burden of showing his proposed accommodation to be a "reasonable" one despite the policy in force at U.S. Airways. The majority describes this as a burden to show the accommodation is "plausible" or "feasible," and I believe Barnett has met it.

With U.S. Airways itself insisting that its seniority system was noncontractual and modifiable at will, there is no reason to think that Barnett's accommodation would have resulted in anything more than minimal disruption to U.S. Airways's operations, if that. Barnett has shown his requested accommodation to be "reasonable," and the burden ought to shift to U.S. Airways if it wishes to claim that, in spite of surface appearances, violation of the seniority scheme would have worked an undue hardship. I would therefore affirm the Ninth Circuit.

■ NOTES AND QUESTIONS

1. What does it mean for an accommodation to be reasonable? How would you define what is or is not a reasonable accommodation? Does the Court define the term in this case? *See* Nicole Buonocore Porter, *Martinizing Title I of the Americans with Disabilities Act,* 47 Ga. L. Rev. 527 (2013) (discussing the scope of an employer's obligation to provide a reasonable accommodation to an individual with a disability).

2. The Supreme Court stated that a reasonable accommodation is one that "seems reasonable on its face, i.e., ordinarily or in the run of cases." U.S. Airways, Inc. v. Barnett, 535 U.S. 391, 402 (2002). Does that comport with your definition? Is this definition circular?

3. The EEOC has said that a reasonable accommodation is one that is "feasible" or "plausible." "An accommodation also must be effective in meeting the needs of the individual. In the context of job performance, this means that a reasonable accommodation enables the individual to perform the essential functions of the position." EEOC Enforcement Guidance: Reasonable Accommodation and Undue Hardship Under the Americans with Disabilities Act, EEOC Notice No. 915.002 (Oct. 17, 2002). Do these statements provide more guidance than the Supreme Court does?

4. The Justices offer varying interpretations of what a reasonable accommodation means in the context of a seniority agreement. Which opinion do you find most persuasive?

5. The seniority provision here was not in a collective bargaining agreement (which would have been protected under the NLRA), but rather was part of a system unilaterally implemented by the employer. Why should that system be given the same weight as a collective bargaining agreement negotiated pursuant to a federal statute? *See generally* Michael Ashley Stein, Anita Silvers, Bradley A. Areheart, & Leslie Pickering Francis, *Accommodating Every Body,* 81 U. Chi. L. Rev. 689 (2014) (arguing that "workplace accommodations should be predicated on need or effectiveness instead of group-identity status").

6. Barnett's co-workers knew he would lose his job if they applied for transfer to the vacant position, but they applied anyway. What does this say about the harmony of the workforce? Could providing a worker with an accommodation disrupt the harmony of the workplace as a general matter? Will some workers be angry or jealous when they learn of the accommodation? Nicole Buonocore Porter, *Mutual Marginalization: Individuals with Disabilities and Workers with Caregiving Responsibilities,* 66 Fla. L. Rev. 1099 (2014) (discussing the "special treatment stigma" that results from resentment by co-workers because of the special benefits workers with disabilities and caregiving responsibilities get from accommodations).

7. Does the holding of the case leave the ADA a "standardless grab bag," as the dissent maintains?

8. Is Barnett "disabled" in this case? Would you need any additional facts to answer this question, or is all of the relevant information provided in the decision?

9. **Regarded as disabled.** A plaintiff must be considered "disabled" under the statutory definition before she is entitled to an accommodation. At one time, there was a substantial debate as to whether an employer must accommodate a plaintiff with a perceived — rather than an actual — disability. The ADAAA resolved that debate, and it is now clear that an employer need not accommodate an employee that only satisfies the "perceived" prong of the disability definition.

10. For an in-depth discussion of *Barnett*, including an analysis of the answers provided by the Court in *Barnett* as well as many of the questions that remained unanswered after the decision, see Stephen F. Befort, *Reasonable Accommodation and Reassignment Under the Americans with Disabilities Act: Answers, Questions and Suggested Solutions After* U.S. Airways, Inc. v. Barnett, 45 ARIZ. L. REV. 931 (2003).

 ## Interactive Problem

Looking back at the facts of the interactive problem at the beginning of the chapter, assume that Tina asked that the employer provide her a Segway electric scooter that she could use to help students evacuate the building in the event of an emergency. Would such a request be reasonable? Would it create an undue hardship on the employer?

Working at home has always been a controversial accommodation request for those with disabilities. The decision below examines this particular request for a disabled worker. When reading this case, keep in mind that over a decade has passed since the decision, and work-at-home technologies have continued to evolve dramatically in that time.

Rauen v. U.S. Tobacco Manufacturing Ltd. Partnership
319 F.3d 891 (7th Cir. 2003)

KANNE, Circuit Judge.

[Beverly] Rauen began working as a secretary for UST, a smokeless tobacco manufacturer, immediately after graduating high school in 1968. While working for UST, she was able to obtain a college degree in 1977 through UST's tuition reimbursement program. She received various promotions, including one in 1987 when UST made her a software engineer in its Nashville, Tennessee facility. After four years of work in Nashville, Rauen moved to the company's plant in Franklin Park, Illinois. She remained in Franklin Park as a software engineer from approximately 1991 until the present litigation.

According to UST's Software Engineer Position Profile, Rauen is expected to spend 60% of her time managing capital projects at the Franklin Park facility; 20% of her time serving as a liaison between UST's Nashville and Franklin Park facilities; and the remaining 20% ensuring that various systems and programs are performing as designed. Both parties agree that Rauen's primary duties involve monitoring contractors' work at the Franklin Park facility, answering contractors' questions as they arise, and ensuring that the contractors' work does not interfere with the manufacturing process.

In April 1996, Rauen was diagnosed with rectal cancer. She had to have several surgeries and undergo radiation and chemotherapy treatments. Unable to work as a result of these treatments, Rauen went on short-term disability leave from April to October 1996, and then on long-term leave from October to December 1996. UST held her job open during this leave. Rauen returned to work in January 1997 and was able to work without further leaves of absence or accommodations throughout that year. Unfortunately, in January 1998, Rauen was diagnosed with breast cancer and had to undergo various treatments that again left her unable to work. UST again accommodated Rauen's condition by granting her short-term disability leave from January to July 1998 and long-term disability leave from August 1998 to January 1999. She returned to work on January 13, 1999, and was able to work full time, without further leave, from January 1999 through October 2001.

According to Rauen, her sickness and treatments have taken their toll, making it more difficult for her to perform various daily activities. For instance, because she is without a portion of her small intestine and must take in two liters of IV fluids daily, she has to use the bathroom up to fourteen times a day. The fluid intake and rapid flow through her system requires her to wear an ostomy appliance that must be emptied frequently. Because of her small size, the appliance does not fit her properly and often leaks, causing skin rashes. Her condition also produces overwhelming fatigue, forcing her to lie down and rest often. Getting to work can be difficult because she sometimes must stop and use the restroom on the way, and the fatigue she experiences increases her chances of falling asleep behind the wheel.

Because of these complications, upon returning to work in January 1999, Rauen presented UST with a letter from her doctor stating that it would be beneficial for her to work from a home office. In response to this letter, UST requested that Rauen sign a release form permitting its independent contractor health and disability consultant, Dr. Cassidy, to obtain Rauen's medical information in order to review her accommodation request. Rauen, however, refused to sign the release. Her refusal, she informs us, stemmed from concern over the fact that Dr. Cassidy, in addition to being a medical doctor, also held a law degree, and she did not feel comfortable giving her medical records to a lawyer who worked for UST. Thus, no further action was taken by either party pursuant to this initial accommodation request, and Rauen continued to work full time at the office. In May 1999, she presented UST with another letter, renewing her request to work at home. Although she had still not signed the medical release, UST agreed to meet with her on May

6, 1999, to discuss possible accommodations. Rauen made detailed notes of this meeting. Both parties agree that her notes accurately reflect the events that transpired. The relevant portions of those notes are reproduced below:

> They asked how this home office would work. How many days would I be at home. I said I would be at the plant as needed — that my job was not routine, it was project oriented, so that, as projects required it, I would be here 7 days a week, that, in the past, I have worked 20-hour days. . . . But if there were no reason to be here, then I would be home. They said they felt that some structure was needed, maybe coming to work 1 day each week. I said I could see no reason to do that for the sake of doing that. They said they felt that things going on in the Plant would affect my projects and that I needed to be here to know what's going on. I said I could do that by phone and, when I felt it was necessary, I would go to the Plant. So they said you want a home office in its entirety, that a partial home office was not acceptable. I said yes. . . .
>
> They asked who would determine when I came to work. I said if John wanted me for a meeting or other reason, I would be here. If I had meetings I would be here. John said, "but you would determine when you would be here, right. Right now, I don't know what time you get to work or what time you leave work, do I?" I said no, that's right; for the most part, I would determine when I would be here.
>
> They asked me if there was any accommodation they could make at work for me. I said No. They said we could provide you with private facilities. I said that would not help. They said we could give you a place to rest during the day. I said if I want to rest I can lay down on the floor in my office. They asked what it was that made it difficult for me to come to work everyday. I said that if I could stay home, there are things that I would not have to do everyday that I have to do now, that I get very tired, and that I have Leukopenia.

It is apparent from these notes that the accommodation Rauen sought was a home office "in its entirety." According to her, she would accept nothing less than being allowed to work from home when she thought she was not needed at the office.

After the meeting, no further discussions about her accommodation request took place for over a year. UST did not inquire further about Rauen's ability to do the essential functions of her job at home, and it did not formally refuse her request to do so. Rauen did not seek further discussions, nor did she sign the medical release form that would have allowed UST's health and disability consultant to review her request.

In August 1999, four months after the meeting, Rauen filed a charge of disability discrimination with the EEOC. She did not inform UST that she was filing the charge, nor did she modify her initial request for a home office. Rather, she immediately sought a right-to-sue letter, and, on October 25, 1999, she filed this action alleging, among other things, that UST violated the ADA by not granting her a home office accommodation.

The next communication between Rauen and UST about an accommodation occurred in September 2000, when she sent UST another letter from her doctor asserting that it would benefit her to work at home. The parties never met concerning this request, each blaming the other for the failure to get together.

The district court granted UST's motion for summary judgment on the ADA claim in October 2001, basing its decision on the fact that Rauen could and did perform all essential aspects of her job without accommodation. Rauen worked full-time at the office throughout the entire period from January 1999, when she returned to work following her second leave of absence, to October 2001, when the district court ruled against her. In fact, Rauen maintains, and UST agrees, that despite not receiving the requested home office accommodation, she continued to perform the essential functions of her job as a Software Engineer exceedingly well. Moreover, both parties agree that she was actually performing duties "above and beyond that of a software engineer," in that she was also doing many duties of a project engineer.

The district court held that since Rauen could perform the essential aspects of her job without accommodation that she was not entitled to any accommodation. Rauen now appeals that decision. We affirm the district court's decision, but we reach our conclusion through different analysis.

Rauen requested a home office as an accommodation for her disability. Specifically, she asked that she be allowed to work at home when she was not needed at the office, and that generally, she would determine when it was necessary for her to come to work. Indeed, she plainly rejected all other possible accommodations suggested by UST, including their suggestion that she come to the office only once a week. She made clear that any sort of "partial home office" was out of the question, and that the only acceptable option to her was "a home office in its entirety." Rauen points to nowhere in the record where she backed away from this position or ever requested anything other than a home office on her terms. Thus, we must decide whether this sort of home office would have been a reasonable accommodation for Rauen.

> Is working at home as a reasonable accommodation a fact-specific issue? If so, what facts would help or hurt Rauen in this case?

We have stated that the issue of "[w]hether a requested accommodation is reasonable or not is a highly fact-specific inquiry and requires balancing the needs of the parties." In conducting this balance, we first note, as we held in *Vande Zande v. Wis. Dep't of Admin.*, that a home office is rarely a reasonable accommodation. 44 F.3d 538 (7th Cir. 1995).

The reason working at home is rarely a reasonable accommodation is because most jobs require the kind of teamwork, personal interaction, and supervision that simply cannot be had in a home office situation. Rauen's situation does not present the type of "very extraordinary case" where a home office would be reasonable. The central components of Rauen's job require her to be at the office. Even she admits that her primary job responsibilities involve monitoring contractors' work, answering contractors' questions as they arise, and ensuring that the contractors' work does not interfere with the manufacturing process. It is difficult to understand how these sorts of tasks could be performed from home. Rauen asserts that she would be at work when it was necessary, but she also made clear that she would determine when it was necessary for her to be there. Further, in the type of project and production work that Rauen's job involves, problems requiring immediate resolution would undoubtedly arise on the spur of the moment. Every description of Rauen's duties that either party has presented in the record shows that hers is the kind of job that requires teamwork, interaction, and coordination of the type that requires being in the work place. Thus, her situation does not present the exceptional case where a work-at-home accommodation would be reasonable.

Tipping the scales even further against the reasonableness of Rauen's home office accommodation request is the fact that Rauen can perform all essential elements of her job without any accommodation. [W]e do not answer the question today of whether any accommodation could ever be reasonable for an employee who can perform all essential job functions without accommodation. But Rauen's ability to perform the essential functions of the job without accommodation surely weighs against the reasonableness of an accommodation. In other words, while it might not be impossible for a person that can perform all essential functions to show that an accommodation is reasonable, it is surely more difficult. Therefore, given that Rauen can perform the essential functions of her job without accommodation and given that she seeks a home office, which we have held is almost never reasonable, we find that the scales of the reasonable accommodation balance weigh against Rauen.

■ NOTES AND QUESTIONS

1. The court here states that the accommodation requested by Rauen was not reasonable. Do you agree? Is the question that the accommodation was not reasonable, or that it caused an undue hardship?

2. Based on the facts of the case, is Rauen disabled? Does she have an actual disability, a perceived disability, or a history of a disability?

3. The court notes that "working at home is rarely a reasonable accommodation." This decision, however, was issued in 2003. Has technology — and workplace practice — changed substantially in intervening years to call this statement into question? In what way?

4. If Rauen would have established that her request were reasonable, what type of evidence could the employer have introduced to show that the accommodation would have resulted in an undue hardship? The statute provides a number of factors that should be considered, which are set forth below. How would they be applied in this case?

In determining whether an accommodation would impose an undue hardship on a covered entity, factors to be considered include —

(i) the nature and cost of the accommodation needed under this chapter;

(ii) the overall financial resources of the facility or facilities involved in the provision of the reasonable accommodation; the number of persons employed at such facility; the effect on expenses and resources, or the impact otherwise of such accommodation upon the operation of the facility;

(iii) the overall financial resources of the covered entity; the overall size of the business of a covered entity with respect to the number of its employees; the number, type, and location of its facilities; and

(iv) the type of operation or operations of the covered entity, including the composition, structure, and functions of the workforce of such entity; the geographic separateness, administrative, or fiscal relationship of the facility or facilities in question to the covered entity.

42 U.S.C. § 12111(10)(B).

5. From the facts of the case, it is clear that Rauen and her employer discussed the parameters of a possible accommodation for her disability. Should such a discussion be required by law?

6. This area of the law is constantly changing, and the courts seem to be increasingly receptive to the idea of individuals working at home in certain circumstances. *See, e.g.,* EEOC v. Ford Motor Co., 752 F.3d 634, 641 (6th Cir. 2014) ("as technology has advanced in the intervening decades, and an ever-greater number of employers and employees utilize remote work arrangements, attendance at the workplace can no longer be assumed to mean attendance at the employer's physical location").

Practice and Procedural Tip **24: The Interactive Process**

The federal regulations anticipate that when an accommodation is requested, there will be an "interactive process" between the employer and employee to determine the most appropriate measures to implement. The regulations provide:

Once an individual with a disability has requested . . . a reasonable accommodation, the employer must make a reasonable effort to determine the appropriate accommodation. The appropriate reasonable accommodation is best determined through a flexible, interactive process that involves both the employer and the individual with a disability. Although this process is described below in terms of accommodations that enable the individual with a disability to perform the essential functions of the position held or desired, it is equally applicable to accommodations involving the job application process, and to accommodations that enable the individual with a disability to enjoy equal benefits and privileges of employment.

29 C.F.R. §§ 1630 app., 1630.9.

From a procedural/best practices standpoint, it is thus best for the employer to sit down and engage the employee in a discussion of what accommodation would best work for both the employer and the employee. Many organizations have established a particular person or office to handle and address such requests. Even if an employer is inclined to reject an accommodation, that employer should first discuss the request with the employee, and attempt to find a possible resolution to any barriers that might exist.

The employer is not required to accept the accommodation offered by the employee, and may instead offer another reasonable accommodation in its place. Similarly, an employer will typically be permitted to choose between many reasonable accommodations. *See id.* ("employer providing the accommodation has the ultimate discretion to choose between effective accommodations"). Nonetheless, from a best practices standpoint, an employer should communicate with an employee over the best accommodation available, and give preference to the wishes of the individual worker where possible.

Additionally, employers should resist the temptation to reject an accommodation request out of hand. Many accommodation requests are quite inexpensive, and the organization will often bear little to no extra costs to implement such requests. *See* Helen A. Schartz et al., *Workplace Accommodations: Evidence-Based Outcomes*, 27 WORK 345 (2006) ("The average cost of an accommodation decreased after implementation of the ADA. From 1978 to 1992, the average direct cost of an accommodation was $121. From 1993 to 1997, the average direct cost of an accommodation was $45."); *see also* EEOC's Regulations to Implement the Equal Employment Provisions of the Americans with Disabilities Act, as Amended, Emp. Guide (BNA) ¶ 5329 (Mar. 24, 2011) (discussing how Professor Peter Blanck, a co-author of the above study, filed public comments clarifying the study's data and arguing that the Commission overstated the cost of accommodations because the preliminary analysis used a "mean" rather than a "median"; according to Blanck, the median is a better measure of the cost of accommodations because so many accommodations have no cost; based on Blanck's research, 49.4 percent of accommodations had zero direct costs, such that for all accommodations, the median cost is only $25). Thus, at a minimum, employers should make certain to engage in the interactive process with workers who request a particular accommodation. And, where inexpensive, employers should strongly consider agreeing to the requested accommodation. The cost of the request will almost always be more affordable than the cost of imminent federal litigation on the issue.

Class Exercise: The Interactive Process

Break up into small groups with those around you, with some students representing an employee and others the employer. Assume that the employee — who suffers from diabetes — needs ten minutes off twice a day to take an insulin shot. The employer, who operates an automotive assembly line business, is reluctant to accede to this request because it would disrupt operations. Engaging in the interactive process, how could you reach an amicable result?

E. Direct Threat Defense and Qualification Standards

The ADA provides that an employer cannot discriminate against a "qualified individual" with a disability. A qualified individual is one "who, with or without reasonable accommodation, can perform the essential functions of the employment position that such individual holds or desires." 42 U.S.C. § 12111.

The statute further states that an individual may not be qualified if she presents a direct threat in the workplace. 42 U.S.C. § 12113(b). The ADA defines direct threat to mean "a significant risk to the health or safety of others that cannot be eliminated by reasonable accommodation." 42 U.S.C. § 12111(3). Thus, an employee may not be qualified for the job if she presents a direct threat to her place of employment.

The federal regulations have more fully defined who constitutes a "direct threat." These guidelines provide that when assessing an individual's qualifications, the evaluation should be performed "on a reasonable medical judgment" that considers "the most current medical knowledge and/or on the best available objective evidence." 29 C.F.R. § 1630.2(r). The regulations further provide that four factors should be weighed when deciding whether an employee poses a direct threat to the workplace. These factors include (1) the duration of the risk; (2) the nature and severity of the potential harm; (3) the likelihood that the potential harm will occur; and (4) the imminence of the potential harm. 29 C.F.R. § 1630.2(r).

There is some question as to where the burden of proof lies on the direct threat issue. On the one hand, plaintiffs typically have the burden of establishing that they are qualified for a job. On the other hand, the direct threat inquiry appears under the defenses section of the statute, and is in many ways akin to an affirmative defense. The Supreme Court has never addressed this question, and it may be that the answer to which party carries the burden of proof will vary depending upon the jurisdiction or the facts of the case.

Another issue that arose in the years following passage of the ADA was the question of whether an employee who presents a potential risk to himself — but not to other employees — qualifies as a direct threat. The Supreme Court ultimately resolved this issue in the case below.

Chevron U.S.A., Inc. v. Echazabal
536 U.S. 73 (2002)

Justice SOUTER delivered the opinion of the Court.

Beginning in 1972, respondent Mario Echazabal worked for independent contractors at an oil refinery owned by petitioner Chevron U.S.A. Inc. Twice he applied for a job directly with Chevron, which offered to hire him if he could pass the company's physical examination. Each time, the exam showed liver abnormality or damage, the cause eventually being identified as Hepatitis C, which Chevron's doctors said would be aggravated by continued exposure to toxins at Chevron's refinery. In each instance, the company withdrew the offer, and the second time it asked the contractor employing Echazabal either to reassign him to a job without exposure to harmful chemicals or to remove him from the refinery altogether. The contractor laid him off in early 1996.

Echazabal filed suit, ultimately removed to federal court, claiming, among other things, that Chevron violated the ADA in refusing to hire him, or even to let him continue working in the plant, because of a disability, his liver condition. Chevron defended under a regulation of the EEOC permitting the defense that a worker's disability on the job would pose a "direct threat" to his health. Although two medical witnesses disputed Chevron's judgment that Echazabal's liver function was impaired and subject to further damage under the job conditions in the refinery, the District Court granted summary judgment for Chevron. It held that Echazabal raised no genuine issue of material fact as to whether the company acted reasonably in relying on its own doctors' medical advice, regardless of its accuracy.

On appeal, the Ninth Circuit asked for briefs on a threshold question not raised before, whether the EEOC's regulation recognizing a threat-to-self defense, exceeded the scope of permissible rulemaking under the ADA. 226 F.3d 1063 (9th Cir. 2000). The Circuit held that it did and reversed the summary judgment. We granted certiorari and now reverse.

Section 102 of the ADA prohibits "discriminat[ion] against a qualified individual with a disability because of the disability . . . in regard to" a number of actions by an employer, including "hiring." 42 U.S.C. § 12112(a). The statutory definition of "discriminat[ion]" covers a number of things an employer might do to block a disabled person from advancing in the workplace, such as "using qualification standards . . . that screen out or tend to screen out an individual with a disability." § 12112(b)(6). By that same definition, *ibid.*, as well as by separate provision, § 12113(a), the Act creates an affirmative defense for action under a qualification standard "shown to be job-related for the position in question and . . . consistent with business necessity." Such a standard may include "a requirement that an individual shall not pose a direct threat to the health or safety of other individuals in the workplace," § 12113(b), if the individual cannot perform the job safely with reasonable accommodation, § 12113(a). By regulation, the EEOC carries the defense one step further, in allowing an employer to screen out a potential worker with a disability not only for risks that he would pose to others in the workplace but for risks on the job to his own health or safety as well: "The term 'qualification standard' may include a requirement that an individual shall not pose a direct threat to the health or safety of the individual or others in the workplace." 29 CFR § 1630.15(b)(2) (2001). Chevron relies on the regulation here, since it says a job in the refinery would pose a "direct threat" to Echazabal's health.

Since Congress has not spoken exhaustively on threats to a worker's own health, the agency regulation can claim adherence under the rule in *Chevron U.S.A. Inc. v. Natural Resources Defense Council, Inc.*, 467 U.S. 837, 843 (1984), so long as it makes sense of the statutory defense for qualification standards that are "job-related and consistent with business necessity." 42 U.S.C. § 12113(a). Chevron's reasons for calling the regulation reasonable are unsurprising: moral concerns aside, it wishes to avoid time lost to sickness, excessive turnover from medical retirement or death, litigation under state tort law, and the risk of violating the national Occupational Safety and Health Act of 1970. Although Echazabal claims that none of these reasons is legitimate, focusing on the concern with OSHA will be enough to show that the regulation is entitled to survive.

Echazabal points out that there is no known instance of OSHA enforcement, or even threatened enforcement, against an employer who relied on the ADA to hire a worker willing to accept a risk to himself from his disability on the job. In Echazabal's mind, this shows that invoking OSHA policy and possible OSHA liability is just a red herring to excuse covert discrimination. But there is another side to this. The text of OSHA itself says its point is "to assure so far as possible every working man and woman in the Nation safe and healthful working conditions," § 651(b), and Congress specifically obligated an employer to "furnish to each of his employees employment and a place of employment which are free from recognized hazards that are causing or are likely to cause death or serious physical harm to his employees," § 654(a)(1). Although there may be an open question whether an employer would actually be liable under OSHA for hiring an individual who knowingly consented to the particular dangers the job would pose to him, there is no denying that the employer would be asking for trouble: his decision to hire would put Congress's policy in the ADA, a disabled individual's right to operate on equal terms within the workplace, at loggerheads with the competing policy of OSHA, to ensure the safety of "each" and "every" worker. Courts would, of course, resolve the tension if there were no agency action, but the EEOC's resolution exemplifies the substantive choices that agencies are expected to make when Congress leaves the intersection of competing objectives both imprecisely marked but subject to the administrative leeway found in 42 U.S.C. § 12113(a).

Nor can the EEOC's resolution be fairly called unreasonable as allowing the kind of workplace paternalism the ADA was meant to outlaw. It is true that Congress had paternalism in its sights when it passed the ADA, *see* § 12101(a)(5) (recognizing "overprotective rules and policies" as a form of discrimination). But the EEOC has taken this to mean that Congress was not aiming at an employer's refusal to place disabled workers at a specifically demonstrated risk, but was trying to get at refusals to give an even break to classes of disabled people, while claiming to act for their own good in reliance on untested and pretextual stereotypes. Its regulation disallows just this sort of sham protection, through demands for a particularized enquiry into the harms the employee would probably face. The direct threat defense must be "based on a reasonable medical judgment that relies on the most current medical knowledge and/ or the best available objective evidence," and upon an expressly "individualized assessment

> The Court gives substantial weight to the EEOC's interpretation of the statute.

of the individual's present ability to safely perform the essential functions of the job," reached after considering, among other things, the imminence of the risk and the severity of the harm portended. 29 CFR § 1630.2(r) (2001). The EEOC was certainly acting within the reasonable zone when it saw a difference between rejecting workplace paternalism and ignoring specific and documented risks to the employee himself, even if the employee would take his chances for the sake of getting a job.

Finally, our conclusions that some regulation is permissible and this one is reasonable are not open to Echazabal's objection that they reduce the direct threat provision to "surplusage[.]" The mere fact that a threat-to-self defense reasonably falls within the general "job related" and "business necessity" standard does not mean that Congress accomplished nothing with its explicit provision for a defense based on threats to others. The provision made a conclusion clear that might otherwise have been fought over in litigation or administrative rulemaking. It did not lack a job to do merely because the EEOC might have adopted the same rule later in applying the general defense provisions, nor was its job any less responsible simply because the agency was left with the option to go a step further. A provision can be useful even without congressional attention being indispensable.

Accordingly, we reverse the judgment of the Court of Appeals and remand the case for proceedings consistent with this opinion.

■ NOTES AND QUESTIONS

1. The Court here adopts the approach of the EEOC and extends the definition of the direct threat to include a threat to oneself. Is this approach too paternalistic? Shouldn't individuals be permitted to decide for themselves whether employment is worth the risk? Is it consistent with § 12113(b)? Is it relevant that prior to passage of the ADA, the identical issue had arisen in the context of the Rehabilitation Act, and yet Congress chose *not* to include the "oneself" language in the ADA?

2. How do you reconcile this case with the Supreme Court's decision in *Johnson Controls* discussed in Chapter 7, on sex discrimination? In that case, the Court concluded that it was too paternalistic to allow employers to prevent women from participating in employment that might present a risk to their fetus. The Court concluded that this decision should be left to the women themselves. How is this case different? Is the distinction that there is no direct threat defense written into Title VII?

3. Could the employer simply require employees wanting to engage in the particular hazardous employment to sign a waiver before beginning work? Would such a waiver insulate the employer from liability?

4. Applying the four factors set forth in the regulations and addressed above, was Echazabal a direct threat to himself? How would these factors be applied?

 Interactive Problem

Looking back to the facts of the interactive problem at the beginning of the chapter, assume that there is no reasonable accommodation available that would help Tina perform the essential functions of her job. Is Tina a direct threat to herself or others? How would a court weigh the four factors set forth in the federal regulations?

Practice and Procedural Tip   **25: The Direct Threat Defense**

While the direct threat defense is a very real statutory tool, for employers, it should only be used with extreme caution. Employers must be advised that they cannot use the direct threat simply as an excuse to discriminate against employees that they would prefer not to have in the workplace. Instead, employers must proceed with a cautious, well-considered plan before prohibiting workers from employment on this basis.

Employers cannot act under the guise of the direct threat defense to make a decision based on myths, fears, or stereotypes. An employer's baseless fears or unfounded concerns will not be enough to establish this defense in court. Before making a decision pursuant to this defense, the employer should apply the four factors set forth in the regulations to the situation at issue. What is the duration of the risk? How likely is the harm to occur? What is the nature and severity of the harm? What is the imminence of this threat? Employers may want to act quickly based on a desire to "protect the workplace," but these concerns must be carefully considered and evaluated in the context of the regulations and case law.

Similarly, before acting pursuant to direct threat concerns, the employer will likely want to seek expert medical advice on the issue. What does a reasoned medical opinion on the issue suggest is the potential risk at hand? How certain is the expert on the opinion being offered, and will other experts likely disagree with the opinion? As the Supreme Court in *Echazabal* emphasized, the federal regulations contemplate that any decision must be "based on a reasonable medical judgment that relies on the most current medical knowledge and/or the best available objective evidence." Only after seeking this kind of expert opinion, and carefully considering the possible ramifications of the defense, should an employer prohibit a worker from employment on this basis. Even then, there is a substantial risk of litigation, and the employer must be proactive in attempting to insulate itself from liability on this issue.

F. Disparate Impact Claims

Just like any other area of employment discrimination law, individuals can bring disparate impact claims under the ADA. As with Title VII, plaintiffs must establish that a facially neutral policy or practice discriminates against individuals with disabilities. The key distinction with these cases is that unintentional acts can be called into question and no intentional discrimination need be established.

This chapter will thus not explore an analysis of how to proceed with disparate impact claims — a subject that was thoroughly discussed in Chapter 4 on unintentional discrimination. However, it is worth highlighting one specific area that is unique to disparate impact claims brought in the disability context. Specifically, under the ADA, individuals need not show that the questioned policy or practice discriminates against the *entire protected group*. *See* 42 U.S.C. § 12112(b)(6) (making it unlawful to use "qualification standards, employment tests or other selection criteria that screen out or tend to screen out an individual with a disability or a class of individuals with disabilities unless the standard, test or other selection criteria . . . is shown to be job-related for the position in question and is consistent with business necessity").

Rather, it is sufficient to establish that a particular policy or practice has an adverse effect on a specific disability. This requirement is consistent with Congress's focus on the individualized nature of the disability inquiry as part of the ADA. *See generally* Michael Ashley Stein & Michael E. Waterstone, *Disability, Disparate Impact, and Class Actions*, 56 Duke L.J. 861, 887–894 (2006); Mary Crossley, *Reasonable Accommodation as Part and Parcel of the Antidiscrimination Project*, 35 Rutgers L.J. 861, 898–919 (2004). For example, in *Gonzales v. City of New Braunfels, Texas*, the Fifth Circuit recognized that to win an ADA disparate impact claim, the plaintiff must satisfy the same elements required to prevail on a Title VII disparate impact claim. 176 F.3d 834, 839 n.26 (5th Cir. 1999). However, the court concluded that in an ADA case, the employee can satisfy the disparate impact requirements by simply demonstrating an adverse impact on the plaintiff alone, rather than on an entire group, as required by Title VII. *Id.*

G. Unlawful Medical Inquiries and Examinations

In all areas of employment law, it is not advisable to ask questions during the hiring process as to whether someone is in a particular protected class. For example, asking someone's age or whether they are pregnant during an interview could lead to subsequent litigation. These questions are evidence of a discriminatory motive. However, the questions in and of themselves are not unlawful. Under the ADA, however, the statute gives individuals a separate cause of action to pursue employers who have asked an improper medical question or have performed an unlawful medical examination. 42 U.S.C. § 12112(d) provides that the definition of discrimination includes unlawful "medical examinations and inquiries." Thus, unlike the other employment discrimination statutes, simply asking the wrong question can create a cause of action in and of itself under the ADA.

The best way to proceed when interviewing applicants for a job is to completely avoid asking medical-related questions if possible. However, there may be certain situations where an employer has a particular need to know this information, or where the applicant displays an obvious disability that will likely impede her ability to perform the job. Employers should proceed carefully in these situations, closely reviewing the statute, regulations, and case law to make sure that their questions and/or examinations are in compliance.

As a general rule, there are three different stages of the hiring process with which employers may be concerned. At each stage, different rules apply as to the ability to ask medical questions or require medical examinations. Initially, employers will be concerned with what questions they may ask applicants before extending them an offer of employment. During this pre-employment stage of the process, employers must avoid asking about any disabilities or requiring individuals to undergo a medical examination. There are some exceptions to this general rule under the ADA, however. First, an employer can ask whether an applicant has the ability to perform all of the functions of the job, provided that the employer asks this same question of all applicants for the job. Second, the employer can ask that prospective employees demonstrate how they would carry out the essential duties of the position, as long as this inquiry is made of all applicants. Third, if the applicant has a disability that is obvious (or known by the employer), the employer may inquire as to what type of accommodation the applicant may need to perform the essential job functions. Finally, employers can inquire about the prospective worker's education, prior employment, and licenses or other non-medical qualifications for the particular job. Thus, while disability-related inquiries are not permitted at this stage of the process, there are still numerous questions employers can ask to determine whether a prospective employee is qualified for the position. *See* EEOC Enforcement Guidance: Preemployment Disability-Related Questions and Medical Examinations, EEOC Notice No. 915.002 (Oct. 10, 1995); EEOC Enforcement Guidance, Disability-Related Inquiries and Medical Examinations of Employees Under the Americans with Disabilities Act, EEOC Notice No. 915.002 (July 27, 2000).

After an applicant has received an offer of employment, employers may have additional questions that they would like to ask the worker. At this post-offer stage of the process, but before the individual begins work at the company, the statute permits the employer to inquire about a worker's disabilities and to require that the worker submit to a medical examination. Any medical-related questions or examinations must be required of all workers, however, and certain individuals cannot be singled out for this requirement. If an employer determines that an individual cannot commence work at the company because of the results of an examination or because of the answer to a disability-related question, the employer will be required to show that the worker's dismissal was "job-related and consistent with business necessity." And, if the employer believes that the worker poses safety concerns, the company will be required to establish the direct threat defense already discussed in this chapter. Though there are very limited exceptions, all medical information collected from workers must be kept strictly confidential.

Once an employee begins work, there are other limitations. For current employees, the statute provides that employers "shall not require a medical examination and shall not make inquiries of an employee as to whether such employee is an individual with a disability or as to the nature or severity of the disability, unless such examination or inquiry is shown to be job-related and consistent with business necessity." 42 U.S.C. § 12112(d)(4). Thus, post-employment, employers may not ask medical questions or require medical exams unless doing so is job related and consistent with business necessity. According to the EEOC, these medical inquiries can be "job-related and consistent with business necessity" when the company "has a reasonable belief, based on objective evidence, that: (1) an employee's ability to perform essential job functions will be impaired by a medical condition; or (2) an employee will pose a direct threat due to a medical condition." EEOC Enforcement Guidance, Disability-Related Inquiries and Medical Examinations of Employees Under the Americans with Disabilities Act, EEOC Notice No. 915.002 (July 27, 2000). Additionally, where an employee requests a reasonable accommodation, it may be lawful for the employer to ask certain follow-up medical questions.

Thus, the statute begins from the standpoint that medical questions or medical examinations are unlawful. It permits these exams or requirements in certain instances, however. What is permitted varies depending upon the particular stage of the individual's employment.

There are some basic questions that an employer may ask of an employee at any stage of the employment process. General questions about how the employee is doing will not run afoul of the statute. Inquiries about non-disability-related conditions (such as a broken arm) are also permitted. Employers may ask about whether an applicant is currently using illegal drugs. An employer may also solicit contact information from the applicant for use in a medical emergency.

 ## Interactive Problem

Looking back at the facts of the interactive problem at the beginning of the chapter, assume that Tina becomes frustrated with her current employer and applies for a position with a private school. During her interview, the employer says, "We notice that you are a bit overweight — has this resulted in any medical problems for you?" Would such a question be lawful under the ADA?

Class Exercise: Interviews and the ADA

Assume that Big Construction, Inc., is a major home builder in the Southeast. An area supervisor of the company is hiring several construction workers who will need to be able to: (1) lift heavy objects; (2) work with industrial machinery; (3) move quickly around a construction site; and (4) read and quickly understand plan documents and instructions. Breaking up into small groups, decide what questions you would like to ask prospective employees that might potentially be disability related. Is there a way to ask these questions that would comply with the statute? How would you, as a prospective worker, answer the questions if you wanted to avoid revealing an existing disability?

 ## H. The Genetic Information Nondiscrimination Act

On November 21, 2009, the Genetic Information Nondiscrimination Act (GINA) went into effect, prohibiting the unlawful use of genetic information. Title II of the statute specifically restricts the use of genetic information in the workplace. The statute provides that it is unlawful for an employer to take an adverse action against an individual "because of genetic information with respect to the employee." Genetic Information Nondiscrimination Act of 2008, 42 U.S.C. § 2000ff–1(a) (2008). Genetic information is broadly defined under the statute, and includes any "information about an individual's genetic tests and the genetic tests of an individual's family members, as well as information about the manifestation of a disease or disorder in an individual's family members (i.e., family medical history)." EEOC, *Genetic Information Discrimination*, http://www.eeoc.gov/laws/types/genetic.cfm. Thus, the statute extends genetic information beyond an individual's own personal information and includes one's family history in this regard.

Beyond the basic prohibitions against making employment decisions on the basis of genetic information, GINA also includes additional restrictions against the use of genetic information in the workplace. Thus, it is also unlawful for an employer to harass an employee on the basis of any genetic information. And, an employer may also not retaliate against a worker who has alleged discrimination on the basis of genetic information. Except in very limited circumstances, the employer is further prohibited from gathering any genetic information on an employee. And, even where the employer is permitted to maintain genetic information (for example, where an employee has requested FMLA leave to assist a sick family member), the statute provides strict rules on keeping such information confidential.

In addition to the prohibitions in this federal law, numerous other issues arise as to an employer's use of genetic information. Invasion of privacy concerns, as well as state, local, and common laws can be implicated where an employer attempts to use this information. Additionally, other federal statutes, such as the Health Insurance Portability and Accountability Act, can be implicated where an employer gathers genetic information. Similarly, as the use of genetic information can have a disparate impact on certain minority groups, an employer that attempts to use this data can also run afoul of Title VII. It is clearly unlawful for an employer to use genetic information in the employment setting, and an employer should be strongly advised to steer clear of these unlawful employment practices.

I. Chapter-in-Review

As seen throughout this chapter, disability is a unique form of employment discrimination that implicates several different issues. The chart below illustrates the three major causes of action that can arise from intentional disability claims. As noted above, there are also disparate impact type cases that can be brought where a facially neutral policy or practice discriminates against individuals with a disability. The potential *intentional* discrimination claims are summarized in Figure 10.2 below.

When considering these claims, defining the term "disability" is a critical first step. The statute is clear that this can be shown through an actual, perceived, or historical disability. The ADAAA was specifically enacted to help broaden this definition, and to expand coverage of the statute.

The accommodation requirement of the ADA has much more teeth than the same requirement in the religious context. Employers must make reasonable accommodations up to the point of undue hardship. This requires more than simply a de minimis burden.

Employers can refuse to employ individuals who pose a direct threat to themselves or others in the workplace. Before availing themselves of this defense, however, employers must make certain they have complied with the statutory and regulatory requirements of the defense. This typically involves seeking the best available objective medical advice on the question.

Following the enactment of GINA, employers must be cautious about ever using genetic information in the workplace. This practice is now specifically prohibited by federal law.

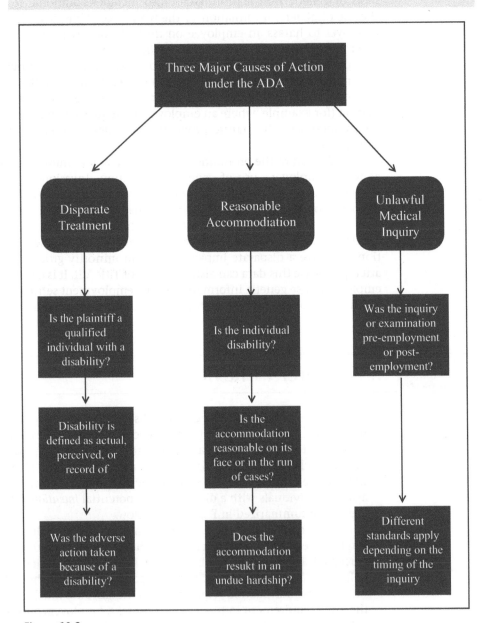

Figure 10.2

11

Age Discrimination

Interactive Problem

Peter Programmer, a forty-eight-year-old computer programmer, has worked for over a decade at "Computers-R-Us," the biggest software company in the nation. Peter has always received excellent employee evaluations and has steadily received pay increases throughout his career. When Peter's supervisor announced his retirement, Peter applied for the vacant position. Instead of receiving the promotion, however, Yanni Younguy, a twenty-nine-year-old recent graduate of an Ivy League school, was hired to fill the position. On his first day of work, Yanni announced that he planned "to clean house" at Computers-R-Us by getting rid of some of the "dead wood" that currently existed there. Yanni also scheduled a discussion with each of his new employees and expressed some concerns to Peter about his background. In particular, Yanni asked Peter whether he thought he had been working at the company "too long to come up with any new ideas," and asked him whether he considered himself to be a "computer dinosaur" in light of all of the recent changes in technology that had occurred over the last few years. When Peter explained to Yanni that he had actively kept up with the modern technology, Yanni simply laughed and said, "I really love old people, they are so funny." Over the coming months, Peter began to notice that he was receiving fewer and fewer assignments. When six months had passed, Peter received a visit from a human resources manager who told him that the company was downsizing and that he would be terminated in two weeks. Peter received a three-month severance package as part of his dismissal.

Will Peter have a cause of action against the company for age discrimination? Will the company be able to defend against the claim? What other evidence would be useful to know in evaluating this potential case?

What other employees were fired? Ages?

A. Introduction

In addition to Title VII's protections for workers on the basis of race, color, sex, national origin, and religion, Congress debated legislation at the time that would outlaw age-based discrimination as well. Early attempts to include age discrimination as part of Title VII were unsuccessful. As discussed below, instead of including age as part of this earlier statute, the Secretary of Labor was charged with conducting a study on the issue to determine the extent of the problem.

Age discrimination has long been a recognized problem in the workplace. Older workers typically have more difficulty securing employment and may be perceived by their employers as being less productive than their younger counterparts. Charges under the Age Discrimination in Employment Act (ADEA) filed with the EEOC have varied over time:

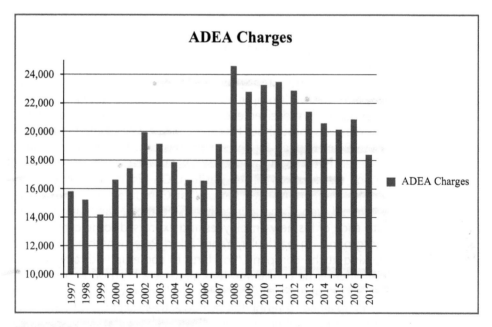

Figure 11.1
Source: EEOC, AGE DISCRIMINATION IN EMPLOYMENT ACT FY 1997–FY 2017, http://www.eeoc.gov/eeoc/statistics/enforcement/adea.cfm

Several states had passed some sort of age discrimination laws long before federal legislation was put in place on this issue. The state of Colorado, which passed legislation as early as 1903, was the first of about twenty states to implement age discrimination laws by 1965. The first attempt to eliminate age discrimination on a federal level came in 1962, with the proposed Equal Employment Opportunity Act. This "act would have prohibited employment discrimination on the basis of age, race, color, national origin, or ancestry." The Act, however, did not pass. In 1964, debate emerged as to whether age should be added to the list of prohibited bases for discrimination as part of the Civil Rights Act. While this addition was never made, the "Civil Rights Act of 1964 did . . . require the Secretary of Labor to study the problem of age discrimination in the workplace" and issue a corresponding report to Congress. The Secretary's report revealed widespread discrimination on the basis of age that was mainly due to stereotypes and not actual worker performance. This well-known report, *The Older American Worker: Age Discrimination in Employment*, was presented to Congress in 1965 and fueled passage of the Age Discrimination in Employment Act of 1967. Unlike the contentious passage of Title VII, there was virtually no opposition to the bill establishing the ADEA that was introduced in 1967. *See* Kelli A. Webb, Note, *Learning How to Stand on Its Own: Will the Supreme Court's Attempt to Distinguish the ADEA from Title VII Save Employers from Increased Litigation?*, 66 Ohio St. L.J. 1375, 1379–1382 (2005).

As discussed throughout this text, Title VII of the Civil Rights Act of 1964 prohibits discrimination on the basis of race, color, sex, national origin, and religion. The ADEA is a completely separate statute, and prohibits discrimination on the basis of age. As a separate law, the ADEA has unique statutory terms, and it has been interpreted differently from Title VII by the courts in several respects. The operative language of the ADEA is very similar to Title VII, and provides:

> It shall be unlawful for an employer . . . to fail or refuse to hire or to discharge any individual or otherwise discriminate against any individual with respect to his compensation, terms, conditions, or privileges of employment, *because of such individual's age.*

29 U.S.C. § 623(a)(1) (emphasis added).

The statute further establishes the threshold for the age of those that can bring a claim under the ADEA. The statute provides that "[t]he prohibitions in this chapter shall be limited to individuals who are at least forty years of age." 29 U.S.C. § 631(a). Thus, under federal law, discrimination claims can be brought only by those who are forty or older. Those under this age will have no cause of action pursuant to the ADEA. To have an actionable claim under the ADEA, an employer must also have twenty or more employees to satisfy the statutory threshold. By comparison, Title VII and the ADA require only fifteen employees for coverage. There are also several states that have *no* minimum age requirement for discrimination claims, thus departing substantially from federal law; for example, Florida, Maine, Maryland, and New Hampshire. Some other states protect workers eighteen years of age or older; for example, Iowa, Minnesota, New Jersey, Oregon, and Vermont.

B. Disparate Treatment Claims

As set forth above, the prohibitive language of the ADEA closely mirrors Title VII. The prima facie case for age discrimination claims is articulated somewhat differently by each court. However, a traditional analysis of an ADEA claim would require the employee to establish that

> (1) he is over 40 years old, (2) he met the applicable job qualifications, (3) he suffered an adverse employment action, and (4) there is some additional evidence that age was a factor in the employer's termination decision.

Rahlf v. Mo-Tech Corp., 642 F.3d 633, 637 (8th Cir. 2011).

Just as in Title VII cases, "[o]nce the plaintiff establishes a prima facie case, the burden of production shifts to the employer to articulate a legitimate, nondiscriminatory reason for its adverse employment action." *Id.* And if the defendant makes this articulation, "the plaintiff must show that the employer's proffered reason was pretext for discrimination." *Id.*

Despite the similarities to Title VII, the courts have treated age claims somewhat differently. In *Hazen Paper*, the Supreme Court provided substantial guidance on how to analyze these claims.

[handwritten left margin: Burden of Proof]

Hazen Paper Co. v. Biggins

507 U.S. 604 (1993)

[handwritten annotations: Years of service pertaining to retirement benefits ≠ Age (must be older than 40)] [handwritten right: "Analytically distinct"]

Justice O'CONNOR delivered the opinion of the Court.

Petitioner Hazen Paper Company manufactures coated, laminated, and printed paper and paperboard. The company is owned and operated by two cousins, petitioners Robert Hazen and Thomas N. Hazen. The Hazens hired respondent Walter F. Biggins as their technical director in 1977. They fired him in 1986, when he was 62 years old.

Respondent brought suit against petitioners in the United States District Court for the District of Massachusetts, alleging a violation of the ADEA. He claimed that age had been a determinative factor in petitioners' decision to fire him. Petitioners contested this claim, asserting instead that respondent had been fired for doing business with competitors of Hazen Paper. The case was tried before a jury, which rendered a verdict for respondent on his ADEA claim and also found violations of the Employee Retirement Income Security Act of 1974 (ERISA) and state law. On the ADEA count, the jury specifically found that petitioners "willfully" violated the statute. Under § 7(b) of the ADEA, 29 U.S.C. § 626(b), a "willful" violation gives rise to liquidated damages.

Petitioners moved for judgment notwithstanding the verdict. The District Court granted the motion with respect to a state-law claim and the finding of "willfulness" but otherwise denied it. An appeal ensued. The United States Court of Appeals for the First Circuit affirmed judgment for respondent on both the

ADEA and ERISA counts, and reversed judgment notwithstanding the verdict for petitioners as to "willfulness."

In affirming the judgments of liability, the Court of Appeals relied heavily on the evidence that petitioners had fired respondent in order to prevent his pension benefits from vesting. That evidence, as construed most favorably to respondent by the court, showed that the Hazen Paper pension plan had a 10-year vesting period and that respondent would have reached the 10-year mark had he worked "a few more weeks" after being fired. There was also testimony that petitioners had offered to retain respondent as a consultant to Hazen Paper, in which capacity he would not have been entitled to receive pension benefits. The Court of Appeals found this evidence of pension interference to be sufficient for ERISA liability, and also gave it considerable emphasis in upholding ADEA liability. We granted certiorari.

The Courts of Appeals repeatedly have faced the question whether an employer violates the ADEA by acting on the basis of a factor, such as an employee's pension status or seniority, that is empirically correlated with age. We now clarify that there is no disparate treatment under the ADEA when the factor motivating the employer is some feature other than the employee's age.

Whatever the employer's decisionmaking process, a disparate treatment claim cannot succeed unless the employee's protected trait actually played a role in that process and had a determinative influence on the outcome. Disparate treatment, thus defined, captures the essence of what Congress sought to prohibit in the ADEA. It is the very essence of age discrimination for an older employee to be fired because the employer believes that productivity and competence decline with old age. Congress' promulgation of the ADEA was prompted by its concern that older workers were being deprived of employment on the basis of inaccurate and stigmatizing stereotypes.

Thus the ADEA commands that "employers are to evaluate [older] employees . . . on their merits and not their age." *Western Air Lines, Inc. v. Criswell,* 472 U.S. 400 (1985). The employer cannot rely on age as a proxy for an employee's remaining characteristics, such as productivity, but must instead focus on those factors directly.

When the employer's decision is wholly motivated by factors other than age, the problem of inaccurate and stigmatizing stereotypes disappears. This is true even if the motivating factor is correlated with age, as pension status typically is. Pension plans typically provide that an employee's accrued benefits will become nonforfeitable, or "vested," once the employee completes a certain number of years of service with the employer. On average, an older employee has had more years in the work force than a younger employee, and thus may well have accumulated more years of service with a particular employer. Yet an employee's age is analytically distinct from his years of service.

An employee who is younger than 40, and therefore outside the class of older workers as defined by the ADEA, see 29 U.S.C. § 631(a), may have worked for a particular employer his entire career, while an older worker may have been newly hired. Because age and years of

> The Court here establishes the well-known "analytically distinct" standard for age claims.

service are analytically distinct, an employer can take account of one while ignoring the other, and thus it is incorrect to say that a decision based on years of service is necessarily "age based."

The instant case is illustrative. Under the Hazen Paper pension plan, as construed by the Court of Appeals, an employee's pension benefits vest after the employee completes 10 years of service with the company. Perhaps it is true that older employees of Hazen Paper are more likely to be "close to vesting" than younger employees. Yet a decision by the company to fire an older employee solely because he has nine-plus years of service and therefore is "close to vesting" would not constitute discriminatory treatment on the basis of age. The prohibited stereotype ("Older employees are likely to be _____") would not have figured in this decision, and the attendant stigma would not ensue. The decision would not be the result of an inaccurate and denigrating generalization about age, but would rather represent an accurate judgment about the employee — that he indeed is "close to vesting."

We do not mean to suggest that an employer lawfully could fire an employee in order to prevent his pension benefits from vesting. Such conduct is actionable under § 510 of ERISA, as the Court of Appeals rightly found in affirming judgment for respondent under that statute. But it would not, without more, violate the ADEA. That law requires the employer to ignore an employee's age (absent a statutory exemption or defense); it does not specify further characteristics that an employer must also ignore. Although some language in our prior decisions might be read to mean that an employer violates the ADEA whenever its reason for firing an employee is improper in any respect, this reading is obviously incorrect. For example, it cannot be true that an employer who fires an older black worker because the worker is black thereby violates the ADEA. The employee's race is an improper reason, but it is improper under Title VII, not the ADEA.

We do not preclude the possibility that an employer who targets employees with a particular pension status on the assumption that these employees are likely to be older thereby engages in age discrimination. Pension status may be a proxy for age, not in the sense that the ADEA makes the two factors equivalent, but in the sense that the employer may suppose a correlation between the two factors and act accordingly. Nor do we rule out the possibility of dual liability under ERISA and the ADEA where the decision to fire the employee was motivated both by the employee's age and by his pension status. Finally, we do not consider the special case where an employee is about to vest in pension benefits as a result of his age, rather than years of service, and the employer fires the employee in order to prevent vesting. That case is not presented here. Our holding is simply that an employer does not violate the ADEA just by interfering with an older employee's pension benefits that would have vested by virtue of the employee's years of service.

Besides the evidence of pension interference, the Court of Appeals cited some additional evidentiary support for ADEA liability. Although there was no direct evidence of

> The Supreme Court remands this case and instructs the lower court to reconsider other discriminatory evidence.

[Handwritten margin notes: "close to vesting benefits alone isn't enough to implicate ADEA"; "ADEA doesn't consider race"; "Rule"]

petitioners' motivation, except for two isolated comments by the Hazens, the Court of Appeals did note the following indirect evidence: Respondent was asked to sign a confidentiality agreement, even though no other employee had been required to do so, and his replacement was a younger man who was given a less onerous agreement. In the ordinary ADEA case, indirect evidence of this kind may well suffice to support liability if the plaintiff also shows that the employer's explanation for its decision . . . is "'unworthy of credence.'" But inferring age-motivation from the implausibility of the employer's explanation may be problematic in cases where other unsavory motives, such as pension interference, were present. This issue is now before us in the Title VII context, see *Hicks v. St. Mary's Honor Center*, 970 F.2d 487 (8th Cir. 1992), *cert. granted*, 506 U.S. 1042 (1993), and we will not address it prematurely. We therefore remand the case for the Court of Appeals to reconsider whether the jury had sufficient evidence to find an ADEA violation.

[handwritten margin notes: "Indirect evidence is sufficient +"; "Dispositive /"; "(whether the confidentiality agreement is sufficient evidence)"]

■ NOTES AND QUESTIONS

1. The Court notes that a worker's age and years of service are "analytically distinct," and thus discrimination on the basis of years of service is not necessarily the same as discrimination on the basis of age. Would age and years of service still be "analytically distinct" if a worker did not vest in her pension until twenty-five years of service?

2. How should a court determine whether a particular factor is analytically distinct from age? Would gray hair be analytically distinct? What about being "overqualified" for a position? What if an employee were fired for being overpaid? *See* Mary Ellen Maatman, *Choosing Words and Creating Worlds: The Supreme Court's Rhetoric and Its Constitutive Effects on Employment Discrimination Law*, 60 U. Pitt. L. Rev. 1, 31 (1998) (referring to the phrasing of "analytically distinct" as "syllogistic rhetoric and highly abstract").

3. As already discussed, the ADEA is a separate and distinct statute from Title VII. For this reason, we see the "analytically distinct" language applied to the ADEA. Could the "analytically distinct" analysis ever apply to Title VII? Why or why not?

4. The Court remands the matter to more fully consider the record on the intentional discrimination claim. The Court asked the lower court to revisit the fact that the plaintiff "was asked to sign a confidentiality agreement" when "no other employee had been required to do so," and the fact that the plaintiff's "replacement was a younger man who was given a less onerous agreement." *Hazen*, 507 U.S. at 613. Would these facts support a finding of age discrimination?

5. This case also implicated ERISA, which is a statute that addresses certain benefit protections of employees. ERISA protects employees from, among other things,

[handwritten margin note: "Erisa protections"]

being fired by an employer with the intent of avoiding pension obligations. Even where certain conduct may not run afoul of Title VII, other federal statutes may still come into play.

6. **Historical note.** Congress specifically did not include age as a protected category in Title VII because it recognized that discrimination based on age is different from discrimination based on race or sex, in that there are sometimes both legitimate and non-legitimate reasons for making employment decisions based on age. Instead of including age as a protected class, therefore, Congress directed the Secretary of Labor to conduct a study on the issue and thereafter recommend remedial legislation to Congress (as noted earlier in this chapter). The Secretary of Labor found that age discrimination was widespread in employment, but that it was different from discrimination based on race. The report noted that discrimination based on race exists because of prejudices against individuals that are wholly unrelated to their ability to perform their job, whereas discrimination based on age exists because of unfounded assumptions that elderly workers are unable to perform their job as well as younger workers. Thus, age was treated differently from the protected classes in Title VII because Congress wanted to take a closer look at age discrimination in employment. More pragmatically, there were concerns at the time from some that adding age as a protected category to Title VII would have enhanced opposition to the legislation. *See* General Dynamics Land Sys., Inc. v. Cline, 540 U.S. 581, 587 n.2 (2004); REPORT OF THE SECRETARY OF LABOR, THE OLDER AMERICAN WORKER: AGE DISCRIMINATION IN EMPLOYMENT 2 (1965); Jennifer L. Thompson, Comment, *Civil Rights — Employment Discrimination: The Standard of Review in State-Based Employment Discrimination Claims: The North Dakota Supreme Court Redefines the Standard of Review in Employment Discrimination Claims,* 72 N.D. L. REV. 411, 413 n.24 (1996) (citing EEOC v. Wyoming, 460 U.S. 226 (1983)).

 Interactive Problem

Looking back at the facts of the interactive problem at the beginning of the chapter, assume that Computers-R-Us could establish that it had fired Peter because the computer classes he took in college were "outdated" and that the company was looking to employ only those workers "with the most modern training at well-respected institutes of higher learning." Would this basis for terminating Peter be analytically distinct from age?

Age discrimination claims are often established through offensive comments or other evidence of discrimination. In the case below, the U.S. Court of Appeals for the Fifth Circuit concluded that an internal company memorandum constituted *direct* evidence of discrimination.

Palasota v. Haggar Clothing Co.

342 F.3d 569 (5th Cir. 2003)

Before DAVIS, SMITH and DUHÉ, Circuit Judges.

Per Curiam:

The sole issue before us in this age discrimination in employment case is whether the district court erred in granting Judgment as a Matter of Law to Defendant, Haggar Clothing Co. ("Haggar") after the jury returned a verdict in favor of Plaintiff Jimmy Palasota ("Palasota"). Our review of the record convinces us that the district court did err. Accordingly, we reverse the judgment of the district court, reinstate the jury verdict in favor of Palasota and remand for further proceedings.

Palasota was employed as a Sales Associate by Haggar for twenty-eight years. When terminated on May 10, 1996, he was fifty-one years old. For most of his career, Palasota oversaw one of Haggar's key accounts, Dillard's Department Stores. Palasota also serviced eight J.C. Penney's key accounts and various trade accounts. He was considered an "outstanding" employee who "had great relationships with customers" and "was second to none in his sales professionalism."

In the 1990s, Haggar's management sought to portray a younger image for the company. Haggar created the Retail Marketing Associate ("RMA") program, and transferred many of the sales functions previously performed by Sales Associates to the RMA employees. Indeed, ninety-five percent of the RMAs were females in their late twenties and early thirties, whereas ninety-five percent of the Sales Associates were males between forty-five and fifty-five years of age. From 1993 to 1996, Haggar hired between 32 and 51 sales people, all of them RMAs and all, but four, of whom were under forty years of age. During this same period, Haggar terminated 17 Sales Associates, all of whom were males over forty years of age. Between December 1, 1996, and March 31, 1998, Haggar terminated 12 Sales Associates forty years of age or older, including Palasota, while hiring 13 new RMAs, only one of whom was over forty years of age. Haggar's chief financial officer testified that the increase in the number of RMAs and the decrease in the number of Sales Associates were related and offset each other in the company's sales budget.

In late 1995, Haggar lost its account with Dillard's which comprised approximately 85% of Palasota's commissions. National Sales Manager James Thompson created a new territory consisting of J.C. Penney stores in Houston, San Antonio, and Austin, that would have generated 85% to 90% of Palasota's 1995 commission amount. However, Thompson left Haggar in December of 1995. Palasota contends that Thompson's replacement, Alan Burks, and Vice President of Sales/ Casual Tim Lyons, refused to grant him the territory proposed by Thompson, relegating him to less lucrative trade accounts in East Texas and Louisiana.

On February 23, 1996, Lyons told Palasota that he could accept the trade account territory or a severance package. Palasota declined the severance offer and refused to resign. On February 23, 1996, after the meeting, Lyons sent a memo to four other members of Haggar's management. After noting Palasota's 28 years of service and his refusal to accept the severance package, Lyons wrote that "we have approximately 14 associates with this same amount of tenure who are in their early fifties or older. I strongly recommend that Human Resources look at developing a severance package for these individuals. . . . This could provide us the ability to thin the ranks in a fashion that will create good will and ease the anxiety of this transition period . . . ." The memo concluded that "[t]he end result will be a sales organization that has its best people in a healthy account environment. . . ." Of the 14 associates listed in the memo, all but two subsequently ended their employment with Haggar.

In March of 1996, without denying that the additional J.C. Penney stores were available, Lyons informed Palasota that he would be terminated. On April 29, 1996, Palasota was notified in writing that his position was being "eliminated" due to a "reconfiguration of the sales force." Following Palasota's termination, other Sales Associates were given the J.C. Penney account that Thompson had slated for Palasota, and in 1997, these Sales Associates were terminated and replaced by younger RMAs.

Haggar portrays Palasota's termination as an effective resignation, resulting from his dissatisfaction with the low commission yield of his new territory and the severance package offer. Haggar notes that Palasota never told management that he believed the company was treating him unfairly or that RMAs were taking over his position. Palasota's only complaint was that he wanted 28 months' severance, rather than the standard 12 months'. Haggar disputes Palasota's testimony that Thompson and other members of management promised Palasota additional J.C. Penney stores in San Antonio, Austin, or Houston. Haggar contends that Vice President of Retail Merchandising Ray Pierce, with whom Palasota never spoke about the subject, retained sole authority to open J.C. Penney stores to Haggar's Sales Associates.

Palasota produced further evidence that Haggar's management was concerned with the appearance of its aging sales force. In late 1995, Haggar's President, Frank Bracken, stated that he wanted "race horses" and not "plow horses," while telling Palasota that he was out of the "old school" of selling. Bracken announced at a sales meeting that there was a significant "graying of the sales force." Alan Burks, a member of management, stated at a sales executive meeting: "Hey, fellows, let's face it, we've got an ageing, graying sales force out there. Sales are bad, and we've got to figure out a way to get through it." After his termination, Palasota filed a charge of age and sex discrimination with the EEOC, which issued a determination finding cause on the age claim. At trial, a jury found Haggar liable under the Age Discrimination in Employment Act (ADEA), 29 U.S.C. § 621 *et seq.*, awarding Palasota $842,218.96 in backpay; the jury found no liability as to Palasota's Title VII claim.

Some months after the verdict, the district court granted Haggar's Motion for Judgment as a Matter of Law. The district court found that Palasota failed to demonstrate that Haggar had given preferential treatment to a younger employee and that evidence of treatment of other Sales Associates after Palasota left Haggar was not probative of whether age was a determinative factor in Palasota's discharge. Relying on a case predating *Reeves v. Sanderson Plumbing Prods., Inc.,*

530 U.S. 133 (2000), the court ruled that a reasonable jury could not conclude "without any inferences or presumptions" that age was a determinative factor in the company's termination decision. Further, the court found that all of the age-related comments made by Haggar's management were "stray remarks" and therefore not probative of discriminatory intent.

Our reading of the record and the district court's opinions convinces us that it erred by: (1) holding that Palasota was required to show that a younger employee was given preferential treatment; (2) ignoring much evidence which supports the jury's verdict, including the February 23, 1996 memo; and (3) discounting the probative value of management's remarks, despite Palasota's establishment of a prima facie case. Under *Reeves*, Palasota's establishment of a prima facie case combined with doubt cast on Haggar's proffered supposed non-discriminatory explanation for termination — that Palasota voluntarily resigned — are sufficient to support liability.

In earlier denying Haggar's Motion for Summary Judgment, the district court correctly found that Palasota established a prima facie case: (1) he was discharged; (2) he qualified for the position; (3) he was a member of a protected class; and (4) there was a material issue of fact as to whether he was discharged because of his age. On appeal, Haggar does not argue that Palasota failed to establish a prima facie case, nor, as discussed below, does it defend the district court's mistaken observation that Palasota was required to demonstrate preferential treatment of a younger employee. Instead, Haggar argues that Palasota's stated dissatisfaction with the loss of his Dillard's account and request for severance prove that he voluntarily resigned. Yet, the April 26, 1996, termination letter states that Palasota's "position has been eliminated" as a means of "re-configuring the sales staff." Haggar explains this inconsistency by contending that termination language was necessary for Palasota to receive extended medical benefits and severance pay. However, given the plain language of the termination letter, Palasota's previous rejection of Haggar's severance offer, and Haggar's refusal to link the loss of the Dillard's account to an overall down-sizing in its sales staff (the only other plausible non-discriminatory explanation for Palasota's termination), a reasonable jury could have "infer[red] from the falsity of the explanation that the employer is dissembling to cover up a discriminatory purpose."

The court also erred by holding that Palasota had to show that Haggar had given preferential treatment to a younger employee under "nearly identical" circumstances. Without discussing evidence favorable to Palasota, the court summarily concluded that his theory of the case — that Haggar sought to replace its largely older, male sales force with a younger female sales force — was insufficient to prove disparate treatment. The court stated that Palasota's "attempted comparison with the RMAs, general and conclusory as it was, does not" show preferential treatment under "nearly identical circumstances."

Treating younger workers more favorably is not the only way to prove age discrimination. A plaintiff must show that "(1) he was discharged; (2) he was qualified for the position; (3) he was within the protected class at the time of discharge; and (4) he was either i) replaced by someone outside the protected class, ii) replaced by someone younger, or iii) otherwise discharged because of his age." *Bodenheimer v. PPG Indus., Inc.*, 5 F.3d 955 (5th Cir. 1993). Accepting Haggar's characterization of this dispute as a reduction-in-force case, the plaintiff need only show "evidence, circumstantial or direct, from which a factfinder might reasonably conclude that the employer intended to discriminate in reaching the decision at issue." *Nichols v. Loral Vought Sys. Corp.*, 81 F.3d 38 (5th Cir. 1996) (citation omitted)). Therefore, Palasota was not required to demonstrate that the Sales Associates and RMAs were given preferential treatment or that he was immediately replaced by an RMA.

The district court observed that, though replacement by a younger worker was not a necessary component of Palasota's prima facie case, Palasota still "[a]t the end of the day . . . has to compare himself to a younger worker under 'nearly identical' circumstances to show that he was treated 'disparately' because of his age." This runs counter to *Reeves*, 530 U.S. at 147, which holds that the establishment of a prima facie case and evidence casting doubt on the veracity of the employer's explanation is sufficient to find liability.

Palasota produced evidence which the district court did not address from which a reasonable juror could conclude that he was terminated as part of Haggar's plan to turn Sales Associate duties over to younger RMAs. For example, it did not address the February 23, 1996, memorandum from Tim Lyons to Haggar executives Frank Bracken, Joe Haggar, III, and Alan Burks. In that memo, Lyons discusses Palasota's displeasure with the company's offer of a standard severance package. Lyons then shifts focus, recommending severance packages for fourteen named Sales Associates, all of whom are specifically identified as over fifty years of age, in order to "thin the ranks" as part of a transition period. The memo states that, by eliminating employees over fifty years of age, "we will have the flexibility to bring on some new players that can help us achieve our growth plans."

To qualify as direct evidence, a document must be (1) age related, (2) proximate in time to the termination, (3) made by an individual with authority over the termination, and (4) related to the employment decision. *Brown v. CSC Logic, Inc.*, 82 F.3d 651 (5th Cir. 1996). The memo, which is undeniably age-related, was composed approximately two months before Palasota's termination. Lyons, Vice President of Sales/Casual, was empowered to terminate Palasota, as well as offer severance packages to other employees. In no uncertain terms, the memo discusses a broad plan to "thin the ranks" of older Sales Associates in order to "ease the anxiety of this transition period."

> The court sets forth here the generally accepted four-part test to determine whether certain evidence constitutes "direct evidence" of discrimination.

Haggar contends the memo merely discusses the possibility of providing severance packages to three employees requesting them, including Palasota. This ignores the fact that 14 employees over fifty years of age, at least 11 of whom did not request severance packages, were targeted for offers. Haggar does not explain why, as part of its plan to "reconfigure" its sales staff, only older associates were selected, nor why RMAs were simultaneously hired to perform sales duties.

Though the offer of a severance package is not, by itself, evidence of age discrimination, such offers assume that employees "may decline the [early retirement] offer and keep working under lawful conditions." Within two months after Palasota refused to accept the severance package, he was "eliminated"; the stated reason for termination was a "reconfiguration of the sales force." Between December 1, 1996, and March 31, 1998, Haggar terminated twelve Sales Associates, including Palasota. Within one year after Palasota's termination, the Sales Associates assigned to the J.C. Penney's account were terminated and replaced by RMAs. Ninety-five percent of the Sales Associates were males over the age forty, while ninety-five percent of the RMAs were females under forty. Haggar's chief financial officer testified that increases in the number of RMAs and declines in Sales Associates were designed to offset one another. The former head of Haggar's J.C. Penney account testified that "there was no difference" between the RMAs and Sales Associates, and that the transition was part of a plan to shift sales responsibilities to the younger, predominantly female, RMAs. Coupled with Haggar's mid-1990s campaign to present a more youthful image, a reasonable juror could conclude that Palasota was terminated because of his age. The district court also erred by discounting age-related remarks attributed to National Sales Manager Alan Burks and President Frank Bracken as "stray remarks." After *Reeves* . . . so long as remarks are not the only evidence of pretext, they are probative of discriminatory intent.

Haggar argues that Bracken's comment that Haggar needs race horses, not plow horses, is not probative because "[r]acehorses and plowhorses can be young or old." Similarly, the company argues that Bracken's comment that Palasota's sales techniques were out of the "old school" of selling relates to traditional practices, not age. As to Bracken's sales meeting comment that there was a "graying of the sales force" and Burks's statement that "we've got to find a way to get through it," Haggar contends these are objective observations, ambiguous, and insufficient to infer discrimination; the statements were also unconnected in time to Palasota's termination.

Post-*Reeves*, this court has taken a more "cautious" view of the stray remark doctrine. Age-related remarks "are appropriately taken into account when analyzing the evidence supporting the jury's verdict," even where the comment is not in the direct context of the termination and even if uttered by one other than the formal decision maker, provided that the individual is in a position to influence the decision. Bracken and Burks, both members of upper management, were in such a position. The jury was entitled to believe Palasota's theory that older Sales Associates were pushed out in favor of younger RMAs as part of a plan to bring a more youthful appearance to Haggar. Alongside Palasota's establishment of a prima facie case and a fact issue as to the veracity of Haggar's stated grounds for termination, Bracken's and Burks's remarks were probative of discriminatory intent.

The district court erred in granting Judgment as a Matter of Law. The judgment of the district court is reversed, the verdict of the jury is reinstated, and the case is remanded to the district court.

■ NOTES AND QUESTIONS

1. The *Palasota* decision presents an excellent example of how to analyze a disparate treatment age discrimination case. This court discusses the multi-factor analysis that is typically used.

2. The appellate court reversed the district court's ruling, and concluded that there was sufficient evidence to support the jury's verdict of age discrimination. Do you agree?

3. Is the company president's comment that he wanted more "race horses" and fewer "plow horses" discriminatory? In what way? Is it an age-related comment?

4. Was the employer's memorandum stating that it wanted to "thin the ranks" and "bring on some new players" direct evidence of discrimination? Does it leave room for inference or doubt as to whether age discrimination occurred in this instance?

Class Exercise: The Prima Facie Case

The court's articulation of the prima facie case in *Palasota* is slightly different than that articulated earlier in this chapter. It is important to note that each jurisdiction maintains its own method of formulating the prima facie case of discrimination. Breaking up into small groups, discuss how you would articulate the prima facie case for age discrimination. Does it matter whether the case involves a reduction in force?

Though some might argue that age discrimination is largely a thing of the past, such claims are routinely brought in this country. As the case below demonstrates, some claims still present alarming allegations of age discrimination.

Dediol v. Best Chevrolet, Inc.
655 F.3d 435 (5th Cir. 2011)

Carl E. Stewart, Circuit Judge:

[Milan] Dediol was employed at Best Chevrolet from June 1, 2007, until August 30, 2007. During his tenure, he worked directly under Donald Clay ("Clay"), Best Chevrolet's Used Car Sales Manager. Dediol was 65 years old during his employment with Best Chevrolet, and he was also a practicing born-again Christian. Dediol alleges that, on July 3, 2007, friction surfaced between him and Clay when he requested permission to take off from work for the next morning — July 4, 2007 — to volunteer at a church event. Dediol received permission from Clay's assistant manager, Tommy Melady ("Melady"), but Clay overruled Melady in derogatory terms. Dediol alleges that Clay told him, "You old mother******, you are not going over there tomorrow" and "if you go over there, [I'll] fire your f*****g ass."

Dediol claims that after his request to take off from work for the morning of July 4th, Clay never again referred to him by his given name, instead calling him names like "old mother******," "old man," and "pops." Clay would employ these terms for Dediol up to a half-dozen times a day from on or around July 3, 2007, until the end of his employment. Dediol also claims that "[Clay] stole a couple of deals from me[,]" and directed them towards younger salespersons.

According to Dediol, Clay also began to make comments related to Dediol's religion. Examples of these comments include "go to your God and [God] would save your job;" "God would not put food on your plate"; and "[G]o to your f****ng God and see if he can save your job." Clay disparaged Dediol's religion approximately twelve times over the two months leading up to Clay's departure from Best Chevrolet. At one point, Clay instructed Dediol to go out to the lot to make sales by saying, "Get your ass out on the floor." Dediol responded to this instruction by stating he was busy reading the Bible. To this, Clay responded "Get outside and catch a customer. I don't have anybody in the lot. Go get outside." Clay also allegedly provoked fights with Dediol. On many occasions, there were incidents of physical intimidation and/or violence between Clay and Dediol. According to Dediol, Clay would threaten him in a variety of ways, including threats that Clay was going to "kick [Dediol's] ass." On one occasion, Clay took off his shirt, and stated to Dediol, "You don't know who you are talking to. See these scars. I was shot and was in jail."

Much of the complained-of conduct occurred in front of Melady. According to Dediol, by the end of July 2007, he requested permission from the acting General Manager (and New Car Manager), John Oliver ("Oliver"), to move to the New Car Department. To wit, Dediol also repeated the offending language in

> If true, is any of the conduct alleged in this case *criminal* in nature?

front of Oliver in the days leading up to, and when he made his request to change departments. Dediol avers that his request was precipitated by Clay's conduct. This request was preliminarily approved by Melady. Yet, when Clay learned of Dediol's request, Clay denied Dediol's transfer and stated, "Get your old f*****g ass over here. You are not going to work with new cars."

Tensions escalated and reached a climax at an office meeting on August 29, 2007. During an increasingly volatile exchange, Clay proclaimed, "I am going to beat the 'F' out of you," and "charged" toward Dediol in the presence of nine to ten employees. Dediol continued working the balance of that day and the next. Allegedly, the next day, Dediol grew tired of his employment at Best Chevrolet and working under Clay. In a subsequent meeting with managers, Dediol stated, "I cannot work under these conditions — you are good people, but I cannot work under these conditions. It's getting too much for me." Dediol stopped coming to work after August 30, 2007, after which he was terminated for abandoning his job. Dediol filed a complaint with the Equal Employment Opportunity Commission ("EEOC") and he received his Right-To-Sue letter from the EEOC on July 8, 2008.

On August 22, 2008, Dediol filed suit in the Eastern District of Louisiana alleging the following claims: hostile work environment based on age, religion harassment and constructive discharge, and state law claims of assault, stemming from the

August 29, 2007 incident. Best Chevrolet and Clay filed a motion for summary judg-ment, which the district court granted on July 20, 2010. Dediol timely appealed.

We now hold that a plaintiff's hostile work environment claim based on age discrimination under the ADEA may be advanced in this court. A plaintiff advances such a claim by establishing that (1) he was over the age of 40; (2) the employee was subjected to harassment, either through words or actions, based on age; (3) the nature of the harassment was such that it created an objectively intimi-dating, hostile, or offensive work environment; and (4) there exists some basis for liability on the part of the employer.

In order to satisfy the third element of a prima facie case of hostile work environment, a plaintiff must demonstrate that the harassment was objectively unreasonable. *Id.* A workplace environment is hostile when it is "permeated with discriminatory intimidation, ridicule, and insult, that is sufficiently pervasive to alter the conditions of the victim's employment." *Alaniz v. Zamora-Quezada*, 591 F.3d 761 (5th Cir. 2009). Moreover, the complained-of conduct must be both objectively and subjectively offensive. *EEOC v. WC&M Enters.*, 496 F.3d 393 (5th Cir. 2007). This means that not only must a plaintiff perceive the environment to be hostile, but it must appear hostile or abusive to a reasonable person. *Id.* To determine whether conduct is objectively offensive, the totality of the circum-stances is considered, including: "(1) the frequency of the discriminatory conduct; (2) its severity; (3) whether it is physically threatening or humiliating, or merely an offensive utterance; and (4) whether it interferes with an employee's work perfor-mance." *Id.*

Having established that a discrimination claim for hostile work environment based on the ADEA may be pursued in this circuit, we next consider, based on the record below, whether the district court's grant of summary judgment in favor of Best Chevrolet was in error. We conclude that it was.

Here, Dediol's age satisfies the first prong of the ADEA/hostile work envi-ronment framework. Similarly, Dediol satisfies the second prong of the analysis. Dediol asserts various incidents, many of which were witnessed by Melady, which he claims were harassment. He was called names like "old mother******," "old man," and "pops." He also claims that after his request for time off on July 4, Clay never used Dediol's given name to refer to him but instead only called him by these insults. These allegations satisfy the second element. Moreover, as stated above, the record indicates that Dediol was called these names a half-dozen times daily from early July until the conclusion of his tenure at Best Chevrolet.

Here, the third factor is critical. In order to successfully challenge the district court's summary judgment against him, Dediol must establish a genuine issue of material fact that the conduct was both objectively and subjectively offensive. Here, the comments were subjectively offensive, as evidenced by Dediol's reaction in the workplace and ultimately by his leaving the car dealership.

Our discussion of objective offensiveness concerns a consideration of the total-ity of the circumstances. Here, the comments were frequent, when compared to the complained of conduct in *WC&M*. In that case, this court reversed the district court's grant of summary judgment for a defendant-employer. A panel of this court held that a plaintiff-employee of Indian descent, who worked as a car sales-man for defendant, had been subject to national origin discrimination based on comments made "multiple times a day." *Id.* at 396. The plaintiff in *WC&M* was called names like "Taliban" on the day of and those immediately following the

September 11, 2001, terrorist attacks on New York and Washington, D.C. He also tolerated implications that he was involved in the attacks. *Id.* at 396–97.

Furthermore, when considered against *Farpella-Crosby v. Horizon Health Care*, 97 F.3d 803, 806–08 (5th Cir. 1996), Dediol's complaint of frequently harassing comments satisfies the first prong of the *WC&M* framework to determine whether a work environment was objectively offensive. In *Farpella-Crosby*, this court found frequency based on sexually harassing comments two to three times a week for six months. 97 F.3d at 806–08. Yet, the question for the court at this phase of the proceedings is whether the relationship between the frequency of the comments and their severity created a genuine issue of material fact precluding summary judgment. We conclude that it did.

This court in *WC&M* held that a "continuous pattern of much less severe incidents can create an actionable claim." *WC&M*, 496 F.3d at 400. Put differently, the required level of severity or seriousness varies inversely with the pervasiveness or frequency of the conduct. *Id.* Here, the half-dozen daily times of remarks here support an actionable claim for age harassment. Yet, for Dediol to continue, he must establish that the comments were in and of themselves severe or pervasive.

Here, Clay's repeated profane references to Dediol, and the strident age-related comments about Dediol used by Clay on almost a daily basis within the work setting, are sufficient to create a genuine issue of material fact concerning Dediol's ADEA-based claim for hostile work environment discrimination.

Dediol also presented evidence indicating that workplace conduct was physically threatening or humiliating. Here, the record is replete with incidents of physically threatening behavior by Clay towards Dediol. First, Clay "charged" at Dediol at a staff meeting on August 29, 2007. Second, Clay would often threaten to "kick [Dediol's] ass." Next, Clay allegedly removed his shirt, and stated to Dediol, "You don't know who you are talking to. See these scars. I was shot and was in jail." The tenor of these comments and physical actions support the inference that the conduct was physically threatening.

The last prong of the *WC&M* objectively offensive analysis requires the court to consider whether the harassment interfered with Dediol's work performance. Dediol claims that because of his age, Clay steered certain deals away from him and towards younger salespersons. On this issue, the facts are conflicting, and better suited for resolution by a trier of fact. While hostile work environment jurisprudence is not designed to "prohibit all verbal or physical harassment in the workplace," *Oncale v. Sundowner Offshore Servs., Inc.*, 523 U.S. 75 (1998), the record supports Dediol's assertion that he endured a pattern of name-calling of a half-dozen times daily and that it may have interfered with his pecuniary interests. Moreover, Clay's behavior in threatening to beat up Dediol, "charging" at Dediol on August 29, removing his shirt, and stating to Dediol "You don't know who you are talking to. See these scars. I was shot and was in jail," underscore our conclusion that at the very least, there is a genuine issue of material fact on this claim. These allegations are for the trier of fact to resolve and summary judgment was granted in error on Dediol's claim of hostile work environment based on age.

Dediol's third and last basis for appeal is the district court's grant of summary judgment for Best Chevrolet on his claim of constructive discharge. To prove constructive discharge, a party must show that "a reasonable party in his shoes would have felt compelled to resign." *Benningfield v. City of Houston*, 157 F.3d 369 (5th Cir. 1998). The claim requires a "greater severity of pervasiveness or harassment than the minimum required to prove a hostile work environment." *Id.* To determine if a reasonable employee would feel compelled to resign, courts consider the relevancy of the following events: (1) demotion; (2) reduction in salary; (3) reduction in job responsibility; (4) reassignment to menial or degrading work; (5) reassignment to work under a younger supervisor; (6) badgering harassment, or humiliation by the employer calculated to encourage the employee's resignation; or (7) offers of early retirement or continued employment on terms less favorable than the employee's former status.

Our review of the record yields a genuine issue of material fact on this issue, too. For example, in the eight-week span between the July 3rd incident and his resignation from Best Chevrolet, tensions escalated into a physical altercation in front of others, which precipitated Dediol's departure from Best Chevrolet. The record illustrates a difficult — and at times volatile — relationship Dediol shared with Clay. Unhappy in the Used Cars department, Dediol sought to maintain his employment with Best Chevrolet, but in a different department. When this request was rejected, the situation erupted, eventually compelling Dediol to resign. We conclude that in this case, these allegations survive summary judgment.

■ NOTES AND QUESTIONS

1. This case involves some pretty harsh language. The court, for example, notes that the plaintiff was called "old mother ******," "old man," and "pops." How prevalent do you believe this type of language is in the workplace today?

2. Everyone gets older, and most individuals will find themselves protected by the ADEA at some point in their working lives. Because we are all subject to the hands of time, does that make age discrimination seem somewhat more permissible on a societal level? Is it less morally blameworthy in some way? Does it seem at least statistically fair that the discrimination will be evenly distributed over time if everyone (or most working people) will be subjected to age discrimination at some point in their careers?

3. Is the alleged conduct of the supervisor here actually discriminatory, or is it more in line with workplace bullying and an abusive attitude? Does such a distinction make a difference?

4. The plaintiff here stated that "I cannot work under these conditions — you are good people, but I cannot work under these conditions. It's getting too much for me." Should the voluntary relinquishing of one's job preclude a discrimination claim? Why or why not?

5. The court here does not completely resolve the issue, but rather reverses the grant of summary judgment. What standard should be applied in considering whether summary judgment is appropriate? When the case proceeds to trial, what evidence will each side present to support their case?

6. For constructive discharge claims, most courts apply an objective reasonableness test — would a reasonable person have left under similar circumstances? Does the plaintiff satisfy the standard for constructive discharge in this case? Would a reasonable person have left the job under the facts of this case?

7. Given our previous review of harassment claims in this text, do you agree that there was enough evidence here to permit an ADEA harassment claim to go to trial?

8. This case again emphasizes the important point that harassment claims are broader than simply race or sex. Harassment claims have been permitted to proceed under the ADEA and the ADA, as well as all protected categories of Title VII.

9. As technology and social media advance, the potential for age discrimination increases exponentially, especially in start-up companies whose management often consists of young professionals. For instance, in 2014, a former Twitter employee sued the social media company for age discrimination. The employee, who was fifty-seven at the time he was fired, alleged that he was terminated from his managerial position with no warning and only a month after he had undergone kidney stone surgery. The employee argued that he had satisfied the company's standards and that his work was instrumental in saving millions of dollars for the company during a period of expansion. The employee further claimed that he was terminated and replaced by far younger individuals. As evidence of discrimination, he alleged that his supervisor made at least one critical comment regarding his age during his termination. *See* Riley Snyder, *Former Twitter Employee Alleges Age Discrimination in Lawsuit*, L.A. TIMES (July 15, 2014, 3:11 P.M.), http://www.latimes.com/business/technology/la-fi-tn-twitter-lawsuit-20140715-story.html.

 Interactive Problem

Looking back at the facts of the interactive problem at the beginning of the chapter, which plaintiff has a better cause of action under the ADEA — Peter Programmer or the plaintiff in the *Dediol* case just discussed? Would Programmer have an ADEA harassment claim similar to Dediol's? Why or why not?

C. The Meaning of "Age"

Age can have many different meanings when used in different contexts. One common question that has often arisen is whether an employer can discriminate against a younger employee in favor of an older employee. If the younger employee is under forty, the answer is unquestionably "yes." If the employee is over forty, the question becomes more difficult. As we learned earlier in the text, these so-called reverse discrimination claims are viable in the context of race or sex. Age discrimination arises in a separate statute, however, and this question deserves a special inquiry.

General Dynamics Land Systems, Inc. v. Cline
540 U.S. 581 (2004)

Justice Souter delivered the opinion of the Court.

The ADEA forbids discriminatory preference for the young over the old. The question in this case is whether it also prohibits favoring the old over the young. We hold it does not.

In 1997, a collective-bargaining agreement between petitioner General Dynamics and the United Auto Workers eliminated the company's obligation to provide health benefits to subsequently retired employees, except as to then-current workers at least 50 years old. Respondents (collectively, Cline) were then at least 40 and thus protected by the Act, *see* 29 U.S.C. § 631(a), but under 50 and so without promise of the benefits. All of them objected to the new terms, although some had retired before the change in order to get the prior advantage, some retired afterwards with no benefit, and some worked on, knowing the new contract would give them no health coverage when they were through.

General Dynamics Shipyard, Quincy, Mass.

Before the Equal Employment Opportunity Commission (EEOC or Commission) they claimed that the agreement violated the ADEA, because it "discriminate[d against them] . . . with respect to . . . compensation, terms, conditions, or privileges of employment, because of [their] age," § 623(a)(1). The EEOC agreed, and invited General Dynamics and the union to settle informally with Cline.

When they failed, Cline brought this action against General Dynamics, combining claims under the ADEA and state law. The District Court called the federal claim one of "reverse age discrimination," upon which, it observed, no court had ever granted relief under the ADEA. It dismissed in reliance on the Seventh Circuit's opinion in *Hamilton v. Caterpillar Inc.*, 966 F.2d 1226 (1992), that "the ADEA 'does not protect . . . the younger against the older.'" *Id.* at 1227 (citation omitted).

A divided panel of the Sixth Circuit reversed, 296 F.3d 466 (2002), with the majority reasoning that the prohibition of § 623(a)(1), covering discrimination against "any individual . . . because of such individual's age," is so clear on its face that if Congress had meant to limit its coverage to protect only the older worker against the younger, it would have said so. The court acknowledged the conflict of its ruling with earlier cases, but it criticized the cases going the other way for paying too much attention to the "hortatory, generalized language" of the congressional findings incorporated in the ADEA. The Sixth Circuit drew support for its view from the position taken by the EEOC in an interpretive regulation. We granted certiorari.

The common ground in this case is the generalization that the ADEA's prohibition covers "discriminat[ion] . . . because of [an] individual's age," 29 U.S.C. § 623(a)(1), that helps the younger by hurting the older. In the abstract, the phrase is open to an argument for a broader construction, since reference to "age" carries no express modifier and the word could be read to look two ways. This more expansive possible understanding does not, however, square with the natural reading of the whole provision prohibiting discrimination, and in fact Congress's interpretive clues speak almost unanimously to an understanding of discrimination as directed against workers who are older than the ones getting treated better.

The testimony at both hearings [of Congress] dwelled on unjustified assumptions about the effect of age on ability to work. . . . The [Congressional] Record thus reflects the common facts that an individual's chances to find and keep a job get worse over time; as between any two people, the younger is in the stronger position, the older more apt to be tagged with demeaning stereotype. Not surprisingly, from the voluminous records of the hearings, we have found (and Cline has cited) nothing suggesting that any workers were registering complaints about discrimination in favor of their seniors.

The prefatory provisions and their legislative history make a case that we think is beyond reasonable doubt, that the ADEA was concerned to protect a relatively old worker from discrimination that works to the advantage of the relatively young.

Nor is it remarkable that the record is devoid of any evidence that younger workers were suffering at the expense of their elders, let alone that a social problem required a federal statute to place a younger worker in parity with an older one. Common experience is to the contrary, and the testimony, reports, and congressional findings simply confirm that Congress used the phrase "discriminat[ion] . . . because of [an] individual's age" the same way that ordinary people in common usage might speak of age discrimination any day of the week. One commonplace conception of American society in recent decades is its character as a "youth culture," and in a world where younger is better, talk about discrimination because of age is naturally understood to refer to discrimination against the older.

> Do you agree with the Court's view that our society promotes a "youth culture"?

This same, idiomatic sense of the statutory phrase is confirmed by the statute's restriction of the protected class to those 40 and above. If Congress had been worrying about protecting the younger against the older, it would not likely have ignored everyone under 40. The youthful deficiencies of inexperience and unsteadiness invite stereotypical and discriminatory thinking about those a lot younger than 40, and prejudice suffered by a 40-year-old is not typically owing to youth, as 40-year-olds sadly tend to find out. The enemy of 40 is 30, not 50. Thus, the 40-year threshold makes sense as identifying a class requiring protection against preference for their juniors, not as defining a class that might be threatened by favoritism toward seniors.

[One criticism of] our reading is the dictionary argument that "age" means the length of a person's life, with the phrase "because of such individual's age" stating a simple test of causation: "discriminat[ion] . . . because of [an] individual's age" is treatment that would not have occurred if the individual's span of years had been longer or shorter. The case for this reading calls attention to the other instances of "age" in the ADEA that are not limited to old age, such as 29 U.S.C. § 623(f), which gives an employer a defense to charges of age discrimination when "age is a bona fide occupational qualification." Cline and the EEOC argue that if "age" meant old age, § 623(f) would then provide a defense (old age is a bona fide qualification) only for an employer's action that on our reading would never clash with the statute (because preferring the older is not forbidden).

The argument rests on two mistakes. First, it assumes that the word "age" has the same meaning wherever the ADEA uses it. But this is not so, and Cline simply misemploys the "presumption that identical words used in different parts of the same act are intended to have the same meaning." *Atlantic Cleaners & Dyers, Inc. v. United States*, 286 U.S. 427 (1932). Cline forgets that "the presumption is not rigid and readily yields whenever there is such variation in the connection in which the words are used as reasonably to warrant the conclusion that they were employed in different parts of the act with different intent." *Ibid.* The presumption of uniform usage thus relents when a word used has several commonly understood meanings among which a speaker can alternate in the course of an ordinary conversation, without being confused or getting confusing.

"Age" is that kind of word. As Justice Thomas agrees, the word "age" standing alone can be readily understood either as pointing to any number of years lived, or as common shorthand for the longer span and concurrent aches that make youth look good. Which alternative was probably intended is a matter of context; we understand the different choices of meaning that lie behind a sentence like "Age can be shown by a driver's license," and the statement, "Age has left him a shut-in." So it is easy to understand that Congress chose different meanings at different places in the ADEA, as the different settings readily show. Hence the second flaw in Cline's argument for uniform usage: it ignores the cardinal rule that "[s]tatutory language must be read in context [since] a phrase 'gathers meaning from the words around it.'" *Jones v. United States*, 527 U.S. 373, 389 (1999) (citation omitted). The point here is that we are not asking an abstract question about the meaning of "age"; we are seeking the meaning of the whole phrase "discriminate . . . because of such individual's age," where it occurs in the ADEA, 29 U.S.C. § 623(a)(1). As we have said, social history emphatically reveals an understanding of age discrimination as aimed against the old, and the statutory reference to age discrimination in this idiomatic sense is confirmed by legislative history. For the very reason that reference to context shows that "age" means "old age" when teamed with "discrimination," the provision of an affirmative defense when age is a bona fide occupational qualification readily shows that "age" as a qualification means comparative youth. As context tells us that "age" means one thing in § 623(a)(1) and another in § 623(f), so it also tells us that the presumption of uniformity cannot sensibly operate here.

We see the text, structure, purpose, and history of the ADEA, along with its relationship to other federal statutes, as showing that the statute does not mean

> The Court discusses the meaning of "age" at great length. How would you define age? What does age mean to the average person?

to stop an employer from favoring an older employee over a younger one. The judgment of the Court of Appeals is Reversed.

Justice SCALIA, dissenting.

The ADEA makes it unlawful for an employer to "discriminate against any individual with respect to his compensation, terms, conditions, or privileges of employment, because of such individual's age." § 623(a)(1). The question in this case is whether, in the absence of an affirmative defense, the ADEA prohibits an employer from favoring older over younger workers when both are protected by the Act, i.e., are 40 years of age or older.

The EEOC has answered this question in the affirmative. In 1981, the agency adopted a regulation which states, in pertinent part:

> "It is unlawful in situations where this Act applies, for an employer to discriminate in hiring or in any other way by giving preference because of age between individuals 40 and over. Thus, if two people apply for the same position, and one is 42 and the other 52, the employer may not lawfully turn down either one on the basis of age, but must make such decision on the basis of some other factor." 29 C.F.R. § 1625.2(a) (2003).

This regulation represents the interpretation of the agency tasked by Congress with enforcing the ADEA. *See* 29 U.S.C. § 628.

Because § 623(a) "does not unambiguously require a different interpretation, and . . . the [EEOC's] regulation is an entirely reasonable interpretation of the text," *Barnhart v. Thomas*, 540 U.S. 20, 29–30 (2003), I would defer to the agency's authoritative conclusion. I respectfully dissent.

Justice THOMAS, with whom Justice KENNEDY joins, dissenting.

This should have been an easy case. The plain language of 29 U.S.C. § 623(a)(1) mandates a particular outcome: that the respondents are able to sue for discrimination against them in favor of older workers. The agency charged with enforcing the statute has adopted a regulation and issued an opinion as an adjudicator, both of which adopt this natural interpretation of the provision. And the only portion of legislative history relevant to the question before us is consistent with this outcome. Despite the fact that these traditional tools of statutory interpretation lead inexorably to the conclusion that respondents can state a claim for discrimination against the relatively young, the Court, apparently disappointed by this result, today adopts a different interpretation. In doing so, the Court, of necessity, creates a new tool of statutory interpretation, and then proceeds to give this newly created "social history" analysis dispositive weight. Because I cannot agree with the Court's new approach to interpreting antidiscrimination statutes, I respectfully dissent.

"The starting point for [the] interpretation of a statute is always its language," *Community for Creative Non-Violence v. Reid*, 490 U.S. 730, 739 (1989), and "courts must presume that a legislature says in a statute what it means and means in a statute what it says there," *Connecticut Nat. Bank v. Germain*, 503 U.S. 249, 253–254 (1992). Thus, rather than looking through the historical background of the ADEA,

I would instead start with the text of § 623(a)(1) itself, and if "the words of [the] statute are unambiguous," my "judicial inquiry [would be] complete." *Id.* at 254 (internal quotation marks omitted).

The plain language of the ADEA clearly allows for suits brought by the relatively young when discriminated against in favor of the relatively old. The phrase "discriminate . . . because of such individual's age," 29 U.S.C. § 623(a)(1), is not restricted to discrimination because of relatively older age. If an employer fired a worker for the sole reason that the worker was under 45, it would be entirely natural to say that the worker had been discriminated against because of his age. I struggle to think of what other phrase I would use to describe such behavior. I wonder how the Court would describe such incidents, because the Court apparently considers such usage to be unusual, atypical, or aberrant.

The parties do identify a possible ambiguity, centering on the multiple meanings of the word "age." As the parties note, "age" does have an alternative meaning, namely, "[t]he state of being old; old age." American Heritage Dictionary 33 (3d ed. 1992); *see also* Oxford American Dictionary 18 (1999); Webster's Third New International Dictionary 40 (1993). First, this secondary meaning is, of course, less commonly used than the primary meaning, and appears restricted to those few instances where it is clear in the immediate context of the phrase that it could have no other meaning. The phrases "hair white with age," American Heritage Dictionary, *supra*, at 33, or "eyes . . . dim with age," Random House Dictionary of the English Language 37 (2d ed. 1987), cannot possibly be using "age" to include "young age," unlike a phrase such as "he fired her because of her age." Second, the use of the word "age" in other portions of the statute effectively destroys any doubt. The ADEA's advertising prohibition, 29 U.S.C. § 623(e), and the bona fide occupational qualification defense, § 623(f)(1), would both be rendered incoherent if the term "age" in those provisions were read to mean only "older age." Although it is true that the "'presumption that identical words used in different parts of the same act are intended to have the same meaning'" is not "rigid" and can be overcome when the context is clear, the presumption is not rebutted here. As noted, the plain and common reading of the phrase "such individual's age" refers to the individual's chronological age. At the very least, it is manifestly unclear that it bars only discrimination against the relatively older. Only by incorrectly concluding that § 623(a)(1) clearly and unequivocally bars only discrimination as "against the older," can the Court then conclude that the "context" of §§ 623(f)(1) and 623(e) allows for an alternative meaning of the term "age."

This plain reading of the ADEA is bolstered by the interpretation of the agency charged with administering the statute. A regulation issued by the Equal Employment Opportunity Commission (EEOC) adopts the view contrary to the Court's, 29 CFR § 1625.2(a) (2003), and the only binding EEOC decision that addresses the question before us also adopted the view contrary to the Court's, see *Garrett v. Runyon*, Appeal No. 01960422, 1997 WL 574739, *1 (EEOC, Sept. 5, 1997).

As the ADEA clearly prohibits discrimination because of an individual's age, whether the individual is too old or too young, I would affirm the Court of Appeals. Because the Court resorts to interpretive sleight of hand to avoid addressing the plain language of the ADEA, I respectfully dissent.

■ NOTES AND QUESTIONS

1. In contrast to Title VII, the Court here found that there are no reverse age discrimination claims under the ADEA. Why would the ADEA be interpreted differently from Title VII in this regard?

2. The Court believes that in a "world where younger is better, talk about discrimination because of age is naturally understood to refer to discrimination against the older." *General Dynamics*, 540 U.S. at 591. Is this a fair understanding of age discrimination?

3. The Court further concludes that the "reference to context shows that 'age' means 'old age'" in the statute, *General Dynamics*, 540 U.S. at 596. Is it clear that the statute uses age in this way? The Court further maintains that "[t]he enemy of 40 is 30, not 50." 540 U.S. at 591. Is that what the drafters of the statute had in mind when they used the term "age"?

4. The dissent believes that the majority disregards the plain meaning of the ADEA, which states that it is unlawful to take an adverse action against an employee "because of such individual's age." The dissent argues that this phrase "clearly allows for suits brought by the relatively young when discriminated against in favor of the relatively old . . . [and it] is not restricted to discrimination because of relatively *older* age." *General Dynamics*, 540 U.S. at 604. Is the statute unambiguous on its face? Should the EEOC's interpretation of the statute be given deference?

5. Does the majority believe that the statute is ambiguous? If not, why does the Court resort to looking at the Congressional Record and social history to help interpret the ADEA? *See* Ramona L. Paetzold, *Supreme Court's 2003–04 Term Employment Law Cases: Clarifying Aspects of Anti-Discrimination Law and ERISA*, 8 Emp. Rts. & Emp. Pol'y J. 195, 202–208, 229–234 (2004) (providing in-depth discussion of *General Dynamics* decision); *see generally* D. Aaron Lacy, *You Are Not Quite as Old as You Think: Making the Case for Reverse Age Discrimination Under the ADEA*, 26 Berkeley J. Emp. & Lab. L. 363 (2005) (arguing that the Supreme Court's decision regarding reverse age discrimination in *General Dynamics* is incorrect and inconsistent with the plain meaning of the ADEA and the Court's interpretation of other antidiscrimination jurisprudence).

6. As discussed in *General Dynamics*, "reverse" age discrimination is not unlawful under the ADEA. In more pragmatic terms, employers can give significant benefits to a group of "older" old workers. The Court notes that there was little concern in the statute about protecting younger workers. Although some countries do provide protections for younger workers, such federal legislation has never been seriously considered in this country. Indeed, there was very little — if any — debate about prohibiting all age discrimination in the ADEA. One notable exception involved a group of airline stewardesses, who believed that the forty-year age requirement was too high. Why are younger workers not as active in demanding protections from discrimination as their counterparts in other countries? *See generally* Joseph A. Seiner, *Understanding the Unrest of France's Younger Workers: The Price of American Ambivalence*, 38 Ariz. St. L.J. 1053, 1100–1101 (2006).

Interactive Problem

Looking back at the facts of the interactive problem at the beginning of the chapter, assume that the company CEO decides to replace Peter with a fifty-five-year old employee who recently received an advanced degree in computer studies from a respected college. In making the new hire, the CEO states, "It is part of our mission here at Computers-R-Us to help older workers. Sometimes this comes at the cost of younger employees, but ultimately they will have other options available to them in the workplace." Would the CEO's statement give rise to a possible cause of action? *No! It's not unlawful to engage in reverse age discrim.*

Practice and Procedural Tip

26: *Consolidated Coin* and "Substantially Younger"

One issue that frequently arises in determining the meaning of "age discrimination" is the age differential necessary between employees to give rise to a cause of action. Thus, when one employee is terminated and replaced by another employee, courts often look to whether the new worker is "substantially younger" than the outgoing employee as a consideration regarding whether the fourth element of the prima facie case has been satisfied. While hiring a substantially younger employee may not necessarily be a requirement in an age discrimination case, it can be an important consideration. After all, why would an employer discriminate against an employee on the basis of age only to hire an even older worker or a worker of similar age?

The practical question often arises, then, as to what it means to be "substantially younger." The Supreme Court has not provided any clear guidance on this question. In *Consolidated Coin*, the Court considered whether a fifty-six-year-old employee could bring a claim where he was replaced by a forty-year-old worker. As both employees were protected by age under the ADEA, the question became whether the plaintiff could bring a cause of action under the statute. The Court held:

> Perhaps some courts have been induced to adopt the principle urged by respondent in order to avoid creating a prima facie case on the basis of very thin evidence — for example, the replacement of a 68-year-old by a 65-year-old. While the respondent's principle theoretically permits such thin evidence (consider the example above of a 40-year-old replaced by a 39-year-old), as a practical matter it will rarely do so, since the vast majority of age-discrimination claims come from older employees. . . . Because the ADEA prohibits discrimination on the basis of age and not class membership, the fact that a replacement is substantially younger than the plaintiff is a far more reliable indicator of age discrimination than is the fact that the plaintiff was replaced by someone outside the protected class.

O'Connor v. Consolidated Coin Caterers Corp., 517 U.S. 308, 312–313 (1996). Thus, from this case, we know that having a replacement that is substantially younger than the plaintiff will suffice to satisfy the prima facie case. And we know that a sixteen-year age differential is enough to satisfy this standard. Beyond this, however, there has not been unanimity in the lower courts as to what it means to be "substantially younger." Indeed, "[s]ome courts have held that the 'magic number' is ten years, [and] others have said that five is not enough. To this point, there has been no resolution as to what age difference 'substantially younger' requires." Amanda Zaremba, Comment and Casenote, *The ADEA and Reverse Age Discrimination: The Realities and Implications of* Cline v. General Dynamics Land Systems, Inc., 72 U. CIN. L. REV. 389, 396 (2003). *See* Barber v. CSX Distribution Servs., 68 F.3d 694, 699 (3d Cir. 1995) ("There is no magical formula to measure a particular age gap and determine if it is sufficiently wide to give rise to an inference of discrimination[;] however, case law assists our inquiry.").

The primary practice point from this discussion is to understand the importance of the jurisdiction-specific nature of this inquiry. What "substantially younger" actually means will be determined by where the plaintiff resides. Research on this question is critical to properly handling the case. And, from a procedural perspective, a case should not be filed at all where the age differential between the plaintiff and her replacement does not satisfy the jurisdiction's standard, unless there is some additional evidence of discrimination present.

Satisfying the substantially younger requirement is thus sufficient to meet the prima facie case. And, each jurisdiction will have its own definition as to how this requirement is met. Nonetheless, the substantially younger requirement is only one way of meeting the prima facie case. Even where there is not a substantial age differential between the plaintiff and the replacement, there still may be sufficient "other evidence" of discrimination (such as discriminatory comments) to proceed with the case.

Class Exercise: Applying *Consolidated Coin*

As the Supreme Court made clear in *Consolidated Coin*, there can be evidence of discrimination where the plaintiff is replaced by someone that is substantially younger. And, as noted, this determination is jurisdiction specific. If you were developing the rules for your jurisdiction, what age differential would you require? Would a forty-nine-year-old plaintiff who is replaced with a forty-year-old worker be able to satisfy the test in your jurisdiction?

Remember that age discrimination cases arise under a completely different statute from Title VII. For this reason, there can be differences in how age claims are analyzed from other employment cases. In the case below, the Supreme Court considers whether the "mixed-motives" language from Title VII should apply to ADEA claims.

Gross v. FBL Financial Services, Inc.

557 U.S. 167 (2009)

Justice THOMAS delivered the opinion of the Court.

The question presented by the petitioner in this case is whether a plaintiff must present direct evidence of age discrimination in order to obtain a mixed-motives jury instruction in a suit brought under the ADEA. Because we hold that such a jury instruction is never proper in an ADEA case, we vacate the decision below.

Petitioner Jack Gross began working for respondent FBL Financial Group, Inc. (FBL), in 1971. As of 2001, Gross held the position of claims administration director. But in 2003, when he was 54 years old, Gross was reassigned to the position of claims project coordinator. At that same time, FBL transferred many of Gross' job responsibilities to a newly created position — claims administration manager. That position was given to Lisa Kneeskern, who had previously been supervised by Gross and who was then in her early forties. Although Gross (in his new position) and Kneeskern received the same compensation, Gross considered the reassignment a demotion because of FBL's reallocation of his former job responsibilities to Kneeskern.

In April 2004, Gross filed suit in District Court, alleging that his reassignment to the position of claims project coordinator violated the ADEA, which makes it unlawful for an employer to take adverse action against an employee "because of such individual's age." 29 U.S.C. § 623(a). The case proceeded to trial, where Gross introduced evidence suggesting that his reassignment was based at least in part on his age. FBL defended its decision on the grounds that Gross' reassignment was part of a corporate restructuring and that Gross' new position was better suited to his skills.

At the close of trial, and over FBL's objections, the District Court instructed the jury that it must return a verdict for Gross if he proved, by a preponderance of the evidence, that FBL "demoted [him] to claims projec[t] coordinator" and that his "age was a motivating factor" in FBL's decision to demote him. The jury was further instructed that Gross' age would qualify as a "'motivating factor,' if [it] played a part or a role in [FBL]'s decision to demote [him]." The jury was also instructed regarding FBL's burden of proof. According to the District Court, the "verdict must be for [FBL] . . . if it has been proved by the preponderance of the evidence that [FBL] would have demoted [Gross] regardless of his age." The jury returned a verdict for Gross, awarding him $46,945 in lost compensation.

FBL challenged the jury instructions on appeal. The United States Court of Appeals for the Eighth Circuit reversed and remanded for a new trial. We granted certiorari, 555 U.S. 1066 (2008), and now vacate the decision of the Court of Appeals. The parties have asked us to decide whether a plaintiff must "present direct evidence of discrimination in order to obtain a mixed-motive instruction in a non-Title VII discrimination case." Before reaching this question, however, we must first determine whether the burden of persuasion ever shifts to the party defending an alleged mixed-motives discrimination claim brought under the ADEA. We hold

[handwritten margin notes: "Jury instructions"; "only burden of production, not persuasion"]

that it does not. Petitioner relies on this Court's decisions construing Title VII for his interpretation of the ADEA. Because Title VII is materially different with respect to the relevant burden of persuasion, however, these decisions do not control our construction of the ADEA.

In *Price Waterhouse*, a plurality of the Court and two Justices concurring in the judgment determined that once a "plaintiff in a Title VII case proves that [the plaintiff's membership in a protected class] played a motivating part in an employment decision, the defendant may avoid a finding of liability only by proving by a preponderance of the evidence that it would have made the same decision even if it had not taken [that factor] into account." 490 U.S., at 258; *see also id.* at 259–260 (opinion of WHITE, J.); *id.* at 276 (opinion of O'CONNOR, J.). But as we explained in *Desert Palace, Inc. v. Costa*, 539 U.S. 90, 94–95 (2003), Congress has since amended Title VII by explicitly authorizing discrimination claims in which an improper consideration was "a motivating factor" for an adverse employment decision. *See* 42 U.S.C. § 2000e–2(m) (providing that "an unlawful employment practice is established when the complaining party demonstrates that race, color, religion, sex, or national origin was *a motivating factor* for any employment practice, even though other factors also motivated the practice" (emphasis added)); § 2000e–5(g)(2)(B) (restricting the remedies available to plaintiffs proving violations of § 2000e–2(m)).

This Court has never held that this burden-shifting framework applies to ADEA claims. And, we decline to do so now. When conducting statutory interpretation, we "must be careful not to apply rules applicable under one statute to a different statute without careful and critical examination." *Federal Express Corp. v. Holowecki*, 552 U.S. 389, 393 (2008). Unlike Title VII, the ADEA's text does not provide that a plaintiff may establish discrimination by showing that age was simply a motivating factor. Moreover, Congress neglected to add such a provision to the ADEA when it amended Title VII to add §§ 2000e–2(m) and 2000e–5(g)(2)(B), even though it contemporaneously amended the ADEA in several ways, Civil Rights Act of 1991, § 115, 105 Stat. 1079; *id.*, § 302 at 1088.

Our inquiry therefore must focus on the text of the ADEA to decide whether it authorizes a mixed-motives age discrimination claim. It does not. The ADEA provides, in relevant part, that "[i]t shall be unlawful for an employer . . . to fail or refuse to hire or to discharge any individual or otherwise discriminate against any individual with respect to his compensation, terms, conditions, or privileges of employment, *because of* such individual's age." 29 U.S.C. § 623(a)(1) (emphasis added).

The words "because of" mean "by reason of: on account of." 1 Webster's Third New International Dictionary 194 (1966); see also 1 Oxford English Dictionary 746 (1933) (defining "because of" to mean "By reason *of*, on account *of*" (italics in original)); The Random House Dictionary of the English Language 132 (1966) (defining "because" to mean "by reason; on account"). Thus, the ordinary meaning of the ADEA's requirement that an employer took adverse action "because of" age is that age was the "reason" that the employer decided to act. See *Hazen Paper Co. v. Biggins*, 507 U.S. 604, 610 (1993) (explaining that the claim "cannot succeed unless the employee's protected trait actually played a role in [the employer's decision-making] process *and had a determinative influence on the outcome*" (emphasis added)). To establish a disparate-treatment claim under the plain language of the ADEA, therefore, a plaintiff must prove that age was the "but-for" cause of the employer's adverse decision.

It follows, then, that under § 623(a)(1), the plaintiff retains the burden of persuasion to establish that age was the "but-for" cause of the employer's adverse action. Indeed, we have previously held that the burden is allocated in this manner in ADEA cases. And nothing in the statute's text indicates that Congress has carved out an exception to that rule for a subset of ADEA cases. Hence, the burden of persuasion necessary to establish employer liability is the same in alleged mixed-motives cases as in any other ADEA disparate-treatment action. A plaintiff must prove by a preponderance of the evidence (which may be direct or circumstantial), that age was the "but-for" cause of the challenged employer decision.

> Do you agree with the Court's reading of the ADEA to conclude that the statute does not permit mixed-motives claims?

Finally, we reject petitioner's contention that our interpretation of the ADEA is controlled by *Price Waterhouse*, which initially established that the burden of persuasion shifted in alleged mixed-motives Title VII claims. In any event, it is far from clear that the Court would have the same approach were it to consider the question today in the first instance. Whatever the deficiencies of *Price Waterhouse* in retrospect, it has become evident in the years since that case was decided that its burden-shifting framework is difficult to apply.

We hold that a plaintiff bringing a disparate-treatment claim pursuant to the ADEA must prove, by a preponderance of the evidence, that age was the "but-for" cause of the challenged adverse employment action. The burden of persuasion does not shift to the employer to show that it would have taken the action regardless of age, even when a plaintiff has produced some evidence that age was one motivating factor in that decision. Accordingly, we vacate the judgment of the Court of Appeals and remand the case for further proceedings consistent with this opinion.

It is so ordered.

■ NOTES AND QUESTIONS

1. The Supreme Court's decision in *Gross* makes clear that there are no "mixed motives" decisions in the age context. Thus, "but-for" causation must always be established by plaintiffs in age cases. How harmful is it to plaintiffs not to have the option to pursue mixed-motives claims under the ADEA?

2. Does the lack of a mixed-motives jury instruction make it easier for companies to defend these cases?

3. Why didn't Congress put "motivating factor" language in the ADEA as part of the Civil Rights Act of 1991? Why would the legislative body have only amended Title VII in this regard? *See* William R. Corbett, *Babbling About Employment Discrimination Law: Does the Master Builder Understand the Blueprint for the Great Tower?*, 12 U. Pa. J. Bus. L. 683 (2010); Michael C. Harper, *ADEA Doctrinal Impediments to the Fulfillment of the Wirtz Report Agenda*, 31 U. Rich. L. Rev. 757, 772 n.61 (1997); Howard Eglit, *The Age Discrimination in Employment Act, Title VII, and the Civil Rights Act of 1991: Three Acts and a Dog That Didn't Bark*, 39 Wayne L. Rev. 1093 (1993).

 Interactive Problem

Looking back at the facts of the interactive problem at the beginning of the chapter, assume that two weeks prior to his dismissal, Peter had made a major error on a software project that cost the company several thousand dollars. Would Peter be able to establish "but-for" causation for his dismissal under these facts? *No — no longer the only reason for the adverse employment decision*

D. RFOA Defense and a Note About the BFOQ

The ADEA is unique in many respects that have already been discussed in this chapter. The age act also contains a defense that does not appear in Title VII. Specifically, the statute provides that it is acceptable to make an employment decision where that decision is based on a reasonable factor other than age — or what is commonly known as the RFOA defense. The statute specifically states:

> It shall not be unlawful for an employer, employment agency, or labor organization to take any action otherwise prohibited under [this statute] where age is . . . reasonably necessary to the normal operation of the particular business, or where the differentiation is based on reasonable factors other than age.

29 U.S.C. § 623(f)(1).

The RFOA defense is an affirmative defense through which the employer bears the burden of proof. It is often not a popular defense for employers to pursue, given that they must carry this burden. Under the more traditional *McDonnell Douglas* analysis, it is the plaintiff that carries the burden of proof throughout the case. Nonetheless, it is an important defense that can impact a particular case. *See* Arthur Gutnam et al., EEO Law and Personnel Practices 279 (3d ed. 2010) ("In general, the . . . RFOA defense[] [is] rare in ADEA disparate treatment cases because [it has] an affirmative burden of *persuasion (proof)*, whereas the *McDonnell-Burdine* scenario requires the lesser burden of *production (explanation)*.").

The RFOA defense may have led to the Supreme Court's "analytically distinct" language in *Hazen Paper*. As the RFOA defense allows employers to make decisions that are separate and apart from age, the "analytically distinct" analysis also permits employers to make employment decisions that are based on factors other than age. *See* Judith Johnson, *Semantic Cover for Age Discrimination: Twilight of the ADEA*, 42 Wayne L. Rev. 1, 6 (1995) ("Although the Supreme Court did not explicitly mention the defense of RFOA in *Hazen Paper*, the decision leaves little room to interpret the RFOA defense as meaning anything except '*any* factor other than age.'").

Finally, in *Meacham v. Knolls Atomic Power Laboratory*, 554 U.S. 84 (2008), the Supreme Court clarified that RFOA, like the BFOQ, is an affirmative defense. The Court stated that "we find it impossible to look at the text and structure of the ADEA and imagine that the RFOA clause works differently from the BFOQ clause next to it. Both exempt otherwise illegal conduct by reference to a further item of proof, thereby creating a defense for which the burden of persuasion falls on . . . the employer." *Id.* at 93. Thus, the RFOA defense is an affirmative defense, and employers bear the burden of proof of establishing its provisions.

The same statutory provision addressing RFOA also permits employers to discriminate "where age is a bona fide occupational qualification reasonably necessary to the normal operation of the particular business." 29 U.S.C. § 623(f)(1). Thus, in addition to the RFOA defense, an employer does have the opportunity to show that age is a BFOQ. If the employer can show that age is job related and that it goes to the essence or central mission of the employer's business, the company can discriminate on this basis. Like RFOA, the BFOQ is an affirmative defense, and it must be established by the employer in order for the company to prevail. Like its interpretation in other contexts, the BFOQ defense is narrowly applied — and rarely used — in age cases. Nonetheless, it is a viable defense that should be considered by employers in the appropriate case.

Handwritten margin note: RFOA operates the same as BFOQ

E. Disparate Impact Claims

Since *Griggs*, it has been clear that disparate impact claims are a viable and important way of proving Title VII claims where a facially neutral policy or practice is involved in the case. Though the courts chipped away at many of the protections offered by *Griggs* in subsequent years, Congress restored these protections as part of the Civil Rights Act of 1991.

The viability of disparate impact claims in the ADEA was not as clear, however. *Griggs* was a case brought specifically under Title VII, and Congress did not include a specific disparate impact provision in the ADEA as part of the Civil Rights Act of 1991. Ultimately, the Supreme Court resolved the issue.

In *Smith v. City of Jackson*, 544 U.S. 228 (2006), the Supreme Court addressed a city's pay plan that allegedly had a disparate impact on older workers. The plan gave pay increases to all workers, but "[t]hose who had less than five years of tenure received proportionately greater raises when compared to their former pay than those with more seniority. Although some officers over the age of 40 had less than five years of service, most of the older officers had more." *Smith*, 544 U.S. at

231. In determining whether disparate impact claims are even viable under the ADEA, the Supreme Court reasoned that

> for over two decades after our decision in *Griggs*, the Courts of Appeals uniformly interpreted the ADEA as authorizing recovery on a "disparate-impact" theory in appropriate cases. It was only after our decision in *Hazen Paper Co. v. Biggins*, 507 U.S. 604 (1993), that some of those courts concluded that the ADEA did not authorize a disparate-impact theory of liability. Our opinion in *Hazen Paper*, however, did not address or comment on the issue we decide today. While we noted that disparate treatment "captures the essence of what Congress sought to prohibit in the ADEA," *id.* at 610, we were careful to explain that we were not deciding "whether a disparate impact theory of liability is available under the ADEA . . . ," *ibid.* In sum, there is nothing in our opinion in *Hazen Paper* that precludes an interpretation of the ADEA that parallels our holding in *Griggs*.
>
> The text of the statute, as interpreted in *Griggs*, the RFOA provision, and the EEOC regulations all support petitioners' view. We therefore conclude that it was error for the Court of Appeals to hold that the disparate-impact theory of liability is categorically unavailable under the ADEA.
>
> Two textual differences between the ADEA and Title VII make it clear that even though both statutes authorize recovery on a disparate-impact theory, the scope of disparate-impact liability under ADEA is narrower than under Title VII. The first is the RFOA provision, which we have already identified. The second is the amendment to Title VII contained in the Civil Rights Act of 1991, 105 Stat. 1071. One of the purposes of that amendment was to modify the Court's holding in *Wards Cove Packing Co. v. Atonio*, 490 U.S. 642 (1989), a case in which we narrowly construed the employer's exposure to liability on a disparate-impact theory. *See* Civil Rights Act of 1991, § 2, 105 Stat. 1071. While the relevant 1991 amendments expanded the coverage of Title VII, they did not amend the ADEA or speak to the subject of age discrimination. Hence, *Wards Cove's* pre-1991 interpretation of Title VII's identical language remains applicable to the ADEA.
>
> Congress' decision to limit the coverage of the ADEA by including the RFOA provision is consistent with the fact that age, unlike race or other classifications protected by Title VII, not uncommonly has relevance to an individual's capacity to engage in certain types of employment. To be sure, Congress recognized that this is not always the case, and that society may perceive those differences to be larger or more consequential than they are in fact. However, as Secretary Wirtz noted in his report, "certain circumstances . . . unquestionably affect older workers more strongly, as a group, than they do younger workers."

Smith, 544 U.S. at 236–241.

As *Smith* makes clear, then, disparate impact claims are viable in the age discrimination context. The decision thus recognized this theory and resolved a circuit split on the issue. Nonetheless, *Smith* also raised some questions on the strength of disparate impact age claims. The decision highlights that the Civil Rights Act of 1991 failed to "overturn" the *Wards Cove* decision as to the ADEA. Thus, the *Wards Cove* analysis, which makes it more difficult for plaintiffs to prevail in disparate impact claims, would still likely apply to age cases. Similarly, the Court notes that the availability of the RFOA language also provides a defense for employers that is not available under Title VII. Thus, while disparate impact claims are definitively available to plaintiffs in age cases, *Smith* makes clear that it may be more difficult for plaintiffs to prevail in these cases. *See* Joanna Grossman, *The Supreme Court's New Age Discrimination Ruling: Good News and Bad News for Both Employers and Older Workers*, FINDLAW (Apr. 19, 2005), http://writ.news.find-law.com/grossman/20050419.html (discussing why ADEA claims will be harder to win after *Smith*).

F. Exceptions for Police and Firefighters

The ADEA also recognizes certain exceptions for individuals who work in positions involving public safety. In this regard, the statute provides:

(j) Employment as firefighter or law enforcement officer

It shall not be unlawful for an employer which is a State, a political sub-division of a State, an agency or instru-mentality of a State or a political subdi-vision of a State, or an interstate agency to fail or refuse to hire or to discharge any individual because of such individual's age if such action is taken —

(1) with respect to the employment of an individual as a firefighter or as a law enforcement officer, the employer has complied with section 3(d)(2) of the Age Discrimination in Employment Amendments of 1996 if the individual was discharged after the date described in such section, and the individual has attained —

(A) the age of hiring or retirement, respectively, in effect under applica-ble State or local law on March 3, 1983; or

(B)(i) if the individual was not hired, the age of hiring in effect on the date of such failure or refusal to hire under applicable State or local law enacted after September 30, 1996; or

(ii) if applicable State or local law was enacted after September 30, 1996, and the individual was discharged, the higher of —

(I) the age of retirement in effect on the date of such discharge under such law; and

(II) age 55; and

(2) pursuant to a bona fide hiring or retirement plan that is not a subter-fuge to evade the purposes of this chapter.

29 U.S.C. § 623(j).

Thus, the statute states that local jurisdictions can set mandatory retirement ages for police and firefighters, as long as: (1) the minimum retirement age is at least fifty-five years of age; and (2) the retirement age is part of a valid retirement plan.

There can certainly be debate as to whether there should be such age exceptions for public safety officers. However, Congress intervened in this debate to resolve the issue and permit discrimination in these circumstances, provided that the other requirements of the statute are met. The Congressional Record sheds light on Congress's intent with these provisions: particularly, that the public safety exception to the mandatory retirement rule is warranted because police and firefighter jobs involve a sufficiently high degree of public danger. *See, e.g.,* 141 CONG. REC. H3822, H3823 (statement of Rep. Hoyer) ("Ultimately, this bill seeks to clear up the confusion which has come about due to differing court decisions throughout the country on this issue. . . . All of us know how physically demanding firefighting is. We also recognize the importance of protecting our communities. Mr. Speaker, the ability for firefighters and law enforcement officials to perform their duties at peak level is literally a matter of life and death for each and every American.").

It is important to note the limitations of the mandatory retirement provisions, and that they *only apply* in a public safety context. In an interesting case brought by the EEOC against a major Chicago law firm, Sidley Austin LLP, the government challenged the mandatory retirement age for partners at the firm. The firm settled the case with the government, and agreed to compensate thirty-two former partners a total of $27.5 million dollars. *See* Press Release, EEOC, $27.5 Million Consent Decree Resolves EEOC Age Bias Suit Against Sidley Austin (Oct. 5, 2007). Thus, the context of a mandatory retirement policy will directly impact whether that policy is valid or actionable. Those policies arising outside of the public safety context will likely be subject to attack by both the government and private individuals.

G. Damages

As will be discussed in Chapter 12 on relief, the ADEA maintains a system of damages much different from Title VII. It is worth briefly highlighting those differences in this chapter.

Most notably, the ADEA does not contain any provision for compensatory or punitive damages. Instead, the age act allows for liquidated damages. Liquidated damages provide a "doubling" of the backpay due to the employee. These damages are only available in cases where there has been a "willful" violation.

Like Title VII claims, the ADEA also allows for awards of backpay, front pay (or reinstatement), and attorneys' fees. Thus, the key distinction between the two statutes is the availability of liquidated damages, as opposed to compensatory or punitive relief. *See generally* 29 U.S.C. § 626(b) (2012) (ADEA damages provision). The chart below summarizes the damages available in age cases, and distinguishes these damages from Title VII claims (differences in red):

Title VII Damages	ADEA Damages

Back Pay
• Wages and Salary
  o Includes overtime, shift differentials, commissions, tips, cost-of-living increases, merit increases, and raises due to promotion
• Fringe Benefits
  o Includes vacation pay, pension and retirement benefits, stock options and bonus plans, savings plan contributions, cafeteria plan benefits, profit-sharing benefits, and medical and life insurance benefits
• Pre-judgment Interest
	Back Pay
	• Wages and Salary
	  o Includes overtime, shift differentials, commissions, tips, cost-of-living increases, merit increases, and raises due to promotion
	• Fringe Benefits
	  o Includes vacation pay, pension and retirement benefits, stock options and bonus plans, savings plan contributions, cafeteria plan benefits, profit-sharing benefits, and medical and life insurance benefits
	• Pre-judgment Interest

Front Pay (or Reinstatement) • Front pay compensates for the future effects of discrimination when reinstatement would be an appropriate, but not feasible, remedy or for the estimated length period before the plaintiff could return to her former position	Front Pay (or Reinstatement) • Front pay compensates for the future effects of discrimination when reinstatement would be an appropriate, but not feasible, remedy or for the estimated length period before the plaintiff could return to her former position
Compensatory & Punitive Damages • Compensatory damages: Awarded for future pecuniary losses, emotional pain, suffering, inconvenience, mental anguish, loss of enjoyment of life, and other nonpecuniary losses • Punitive damages: Awarded when defendant acts with malice or reckless disregard	Liquidated Damages • Available up to the amount of back pay for willful violations of the ADEA • The ADEA allows damages only for pecuniary benefits connected to the job, but not compensatory damages for mental anguish, pain, suffering, humiliation, and loss of employment
Attorneys' Fees • Reasonable attorneys' fees are available to the prevailing pa rty	Attorneys' Fees • Reasonable attorneys' fees are available to the prevailing party

Figure 11.2

Source: Barbara L. Johnson, *Types of Damages Available in Employment Cases,* http ://www.americanbar.org/content/dam/aba/administrative/labor_law/meetings/2011/annual meeting/004.authcheckdam.pdf.

Interactive Problem

Looking back at the facts of the interactive problem at the beginning of the chapter, assume that after a bench trial, the trial judge concluded that the company had violated the ADEA. The judge believes that Peter should receive $10,000 in backpay, reasonable attorneys' fees, and reinstatement with the employer. Would Peter be entitled to any additional relief in the case? If so, how much? What additional information (if any) would we need to know?

liquidation damages, if it's a "willful violation"

 ## H. Chapter-in-Review

> The ADEA is a separate and distinct statute from Title VII. It prohibits discrimination in employment against those forty years of age or older. The traditional *McDonnell Douglas* disparate treatment analysis applies to age discrimination claims. The Supreme Court has acknowledged that there are also disparate impact claims under the ADEA, though the more watered-down *Wards Cove* analysis likely applies to these cases.
>
> One unique aspect of ADEA claims is that employers can avoid liability by establishing that an adverse action was taken on the basis of a factor that is "analytically distinct" from age. This analytically distinct language is exclusive to ADEA claims, and cannot be used in the Title VII context. It likely arises from the RFOA statutory language found in the ADEA.
>
> The ADEA does include a special exception for public safety officials. In this regard, local governments can enact mandatory retirement ages for police or firefighters where doing so complies with all other aspects of the statute.
>
> The ADEA also has a different damages scheme from Title VII. Most notably, the age act allows for liquidated damages, rather than compensatory or punitive relief.

PART FOUR

Remedies

Relief in Discrimination Cases

 ## Interactive Problem

Wendy Worker, an employee at Big Company U.S.A., believes that she is being discriminated against on the basis of her gender, and files a charge of discrimination with the EEOC. Within days of learning of this charge, the employer fires Wendy for "poor performance." As her supervisor, Barry Boss, tells her, "your work was never up to par at this company." During its investigation of the charge, the EEOC asks Barry Boss whether Wendy was fired for filing a charge of discrimination. Barry Boss responded that "he would never do that because it would be a violation of Title VII to act in that manner." Barry Boss further indicated that he had received extensive training on antidiscrimination law, and was careful to treat all workers in an even-handed manner. Wendy has had substantial difficulty finding another equivalent job, given that she was making a substantial salary — $80,000 a year — as a customer service manager at Big Company. Though Barry Boss "feels bad" about Wendy's difficulties in securing other employment, he believes firmly that the company could not continue to employ someone "with such questionable performance issues."

Assume that Wendy files a Title VII action in federal court alleging sex discrimination and retaliation against Big Company. Wendy loses the sex discrimination claim, but prevails on her allegations of retaliation. What damages would she be entitled to?

A. Introduction

In the study of employment discrimination law, remedies are often given far too little attention. While a critical part of any case is certainly whether an employer can be held liable for its conduct, damages can be equally as important. From a practical standpoint, the remedies available can be even more important. Damages often drive the litigation. If the potential relief available to a  plaintiff is very small, an employer may be far less likely to settle a case with a worker. Where the potential damages are great, however, employers may take a claim much more seriously and take proactive steps to make sure that the unlawful conduct is not repeated at the company. Where the potential damages are small, employee-claimants are unlikely to be able to find a lawyer to take their claim on a contingency basis. Additionally, few workers who have recently suffered a major adverse employment action can afford to pay a lawyer's hourly rate out of pocket. Unfortunately, as damages in employment cases usually are a function of wages, this often means that low-income employees are the least able to pursue their employment discrimination claims.

Assessing damages in a case is much more of an art than a science. It can be extremely difficult to ascertain the potential dollar value of a particular claim, and even more difficult to guess what a judge or jury will do with a particular case. Nonetheless, the ability to realistically assess potential damages is a critical skill for both plaintiff and defense attorneys. Knowing what a claim is worth will be a crucial inquiry for determining whether to take on a case. And advising a client on his potential liability for a given claim is equally important in determining whether to settle the case or to defend against the litigation.

In sum, then, all employment attorneys should have a working knowledge and thorough understanding of the various ways that damages are assessed in discrimination cases. These damages will vary depending upon the statute in question, the facts of the case, and the jurisdiction where the claim has been filed. The critical components to consider when addressing discrimination damages are: (1) whether reinstatement is available; (2) whether front pay should be awarded in lieu of reinstatement; (3) whether backpay is appropriate; (4) whether compensatory and/or punitive damages should be awarded; and (5) whether attorneys' fees should be granted. We will assess each consideration in turn.

B. Reinstatement

Termination is one of the more common adverse actions in employment discrimination cases. When an employee loses her job through unlawful discrimination, that worker will often desire to be reinstated to her former position. Reinstatement is thus one of the most frequently sought remedies in employment discrimination cases. This form of equitable relief is specifically authorized under Title VII:

> If the court finds . . . an unlawful employment practice . . . the court may . . . order such affirmative action as may be appropriate, which may include, but is not limited to, reinstatement or hiring of employees. . . .

42 U.S.C. § 2000(e)(5)(g)(1).

Reinstatement is considered the "preferred" remedy for an unlawful termination, and courts seek to put workers back in the position that they were in prior to the discrimination that was suffered. Courts have deemed reinstatement to be appropriate in many cases because it sufficiently makes the plaintiff whole again (i.e., restores the employee to the position he would have held but for the unlawful employment discrimination). In this sense, courts view reinstatement as the best avenue to satisfy the policy objectives of the statutes. *See* Peter Janovsky, Note, *Front Pay: A Necessary Alternative to Reinstatement Under the Age Discrimination in Employment Act*, 53 FORDHAM L. REV. 579, 598 (1984); Elizabeth Papacek, *Sexual Harassment and the Struggle for Equal Treatment Under Title VII: Front Pay as an Appropriate Remedy*, 24 WM. MITCHELL L. REV. 743, 773–775 (1998). As one court has observed:

> This rule of presumptive reinstatement is justified by reason as well as precedent. When a person loses his job, it is at best disingenuous to say that money damages can suffice to make that person whole. The psychological benefits of work are intangible, yet they are real and cannot be ignored. Yet at the same time, there is a high probability that reinstatement will engender personal friction of one sort or another in almost every case in which a public employee is discharged for a constitutionally infirm reason. Unless we are willing to withhold full relief from all or most successful plaintiffs in discharge cases, and we are not, we cannot allow actual or expected ill-feeling alone to justify nonreinstatement. We also note that reinstatement is an effective deterrent in preventing employer retaliation against employees who exercise their constitutional rights. If an employer's best efforts to remove an employee for unconstitutional reasons are presumptively unlikely to succeed, there is, of course, less incentive to use employment decisions to chill the exercise of constitutional rights.

Allen v. Autauga Cnty. Bd. of Educ., 685 F.2d 1302, 1306 (11th Cir. 1982).

Though reinstatement is preferred, in practice, it is not frequently used by the federal courts (though labor arbitrators often apply this remedy). The courts have recognized numerous circumstances where reinstatement is not possible. There are typically three situations where the courts will consider that reinstatement is not "feasible" under the facts.

First, if there is too much hostility or animosity between the parties, the courts will consider it inappropriate to reinstate the worker. As is frequently the case with litigants, hostility grows over the course of the proceedings, and it may simply be an unworkable solution to put an employee back into her former position. *See*

Benjamin W. Wolkinson & Victor W. Nichol, *The Illusion of Make-Whole Relief: The Exclusion of the Reinstatement Remedy in Hostility-Based Discrimination Cases*, 8 Lab. Law. 157 (1992). Second, the position previously held by the worker may no longer exist at the company. Circumstances change over time, as do the structure of corporations. It is not uncommon for litigation to go on for years, and at the end of this time, the individual's position may no longer exist. Third, while the case has proceeded, the employer may have hired another worker to fill the prior worker's position at the company. If this is the case, many courts will not require that the new, "innocent" employee be "bumped" out of the position. *See* Larry M. Parsons, Note, *Title VII Remedies: Reinstatement and the Innocent Incumbent Employee*, 42 Vand. L. Rev. 1441 (1989). Many courts take this position, even where discrimination has been found.

In the landmark Supreme Court decision in *Price Waterhouse v. Hopkins*, 490 U.S. 228 (1989), excerpted in Chapter 3, the Court awarded the plaintiff, Ann Hopkins, the promotion that she alleged she was denied because of her sex. Hopkins was nominated for partnership for the accounting firm and, out of all the nominees, she had generated the most new business and secured the most multimillion-dollar contracts for the company. Yet, her promotion was denied. Evidence was produced at trial that several male partners referred to Hopkins as overly aggressive and "macho," and that the men suggested Hopkins behave more femininely if she wanted to increase her chances of being promoted. The case ultimately found its way to the Supreme Court. Throughout the process, Hopkins's attorney cautioned her several times that if she insisted on reinstatement, her case would be harder to win. Hopkins remained firm, however, that her primary goal was to be reinstated, not to receive front pay or other remedies. Her insistence paid off, as the Court ultimately awarded Hopkins reinstatement as a partner. *See* Ann Branigar Hopkins, So Ordered: Making Partner the Hard Way (1996).

Where reinstatement is not a feasible remedy, the courts will typically award front pay in its place.

C. Front Pay

Where reinstatement is not feasible in a case of unlawful termination, the courts will frequently award money damages in its place. These damages are known as "front pay," and are considered another form of equitable relief. Front pay is usually measured from the date of the unlawful judgment to some unspecified date in the future. Front pay may be awarded in addition to compensatory damages, as discussed later in this chapter. As the Supreme Court has summarized, "[a]lthough courts have defined 'front pay' in numerous ways, front pay is simply money awarded for lost compensation during the period between judgment and reinstatement or in lieu of reinstatement." Pollard v. E.I. du Pont de Nemours & Co., 532 U.S. 843, 846 (2001). Front pay can also be awarded in cases involving a wrongful failure to promote an employee. There is some dispute in the courts as to whether front pay is an award determined by the court or whether a jury should make this determination.

Awarding front pay is much more of an art than a science, and often involves a substantial amount of speculation. Essentially, courts are being asked to calculate damages based on future events, which is a task that will inherently be inexact at best. Courts vary on how far after judgment they are willing to award damages, and this is often a highly fact-intensive inquiry. Indeed, the "cases reveal that front pay awards range from a few months to over a decade [and] the dollar amounts of front pay awards range widely" as well. Susan K. Grebeldinger, *The Role of Workplace Hostility in Determining Prospective Remedies for Employment Discrimination: A Call for Greater Judicial Discretion in Awarding Front Pay*, 1996 U. ILL. L. REV. 319, 348–349. With wide differences in how great of an award to expect, and how far into the future front pay will be awarded, this form of relief is often a guessing game for the parties.

Nonetheless, courts do their best to be as precise as possible. The plaintiff's salary in a particular case will be perhaps the most important factor in weighing the amount of front pay that is awarded. How long a period that the court will allow front pay will vary with the circumstances of the case and will depend on numerous factors such as the proximity of the plaintiff to retirement and on the availability and likelihood of securing other employment. In this regard, a plaintiff is expected to "mitigate" her damages, and must attempt to find other comparable employment to replace her former job. A plaintiff is not required to accept any position available, but should seek a job that is equivalent to her former job.

Another factor that can be considered in front pay cases is the ability of the employee to perform the job. If, through the passage of time, the plaintiff is no longer able or qualified to adequately perform her prior position, this may also impact the amount of front pay damages available. In cases brought under the ADA, for example, a plaintiff's worsening condition may make it unlikely that she could return to her former position. Similarly, an individual's license status or other important qualifications may change over time and make reemployment unlikely, thus also affecting a front pay award.

 ## Interactive Problem

Looking back at the facts of the interactive problem at the beginning of the chapter, assume that during the litigation of the case, Wendy developed a serious medical condition that makes it impossible for her to leave her home. How will this condition affect her entitlement to reinstatement or front pay, if at all?

Class Exercise: Appropriate Relief

Breaking up into small groups, discuss what type of relief would be appropriate in a case where a worker is discharged from her job as a secretary at a Fortune 500 company because of her race. Should front pay be awarded? If so, for how long? What about reinstatement?

D. Backpay

Closely related to the concept of front pay is the award of backpay, which is also authorized under Title VII. Where discrimination is found, backpay is typically awarded from the date the discrimination occurred to the date of judgment in the case, though courts vary as to the exact definition of the concept. The statute also prohibits an award of backpay that is "more than two years prior to the filing of a charge with the Commission." 42 U.S.C. § 2000e–5(g)(1). Thus, there is a statutory limitation to the time period for which backpay may be awarded.

Generally speaking, then, backpay damages award a plaintiff for the loss of income she suffered as a result of the discrimination. This calculation looks specifically at the period immediately following the discrimination until the time of judgment. Like front pay, the calculation of backpay damages is not always precise. This determination involves more than looking simply at lost wages in a particular case. Courts also examine things such as lost benefits, commissions, and other sources of income that a plaintiff may have been forced to forgo as a result of the discrimination.

Like front pay, when calculating backpay, mitigation is considered. Again, a plaintiff need not accept any available employment opportunity. A plaintiff should, however, attempt to find equivalent employment and should accept such employment when it is available.

EEOC v. E.I. DuPont de Nemours & Co.

406 F. Supp. 2d 645 (E.D. La. 2005)

Vance, District Judge.

Laura Barrios is a 56 year-old woman with severe scoliosis of the lumbar spine, lumbar disc disease with sciatica, lumbar spinal stenosis with compression neuropathy, neurogenic bladder, cervical spondylosis, and previous cervical disc disease with surgical fusions. Barrios has considerable difficulty walking. Barrios began to work for E.I. DuPont de Nemours in its LaPlace chemical plant as a lab operator in 1981. In 1986, Barrios became a lab trainer/operator. In March of 1997, DuPont transferred Barrios to the sedentary position of lab clerk under a number of medical restrictions, such as no standing for more than ten minutes at a time and no walking more than 100 feet without rest.

In May of 1999, the DuPont plant physician ordered Barrios to undergo [a] functional capacity evaluation (FCE). On July 6, 1999, DuPont received the results of the FCE. On July 7, 1999, DuPont restricted Barrios from walking anywhere on the plant site. At that time, DuPont placed Barrios on short-term disability leave and ultimately discharged her on Total and Permanent disability.

> The jury's million-dollar award was reduced to comply with the statutory caps discussed later in this chapter.

On June 5, 2003, the Equal Employment Opportunity Commission sued DuPont on Barrios's behalf. In October of 2004, the Court held a three-day jury trial in the matter. DuPont moved the Court for judgment as a matter of law at the close of the EEOC's evidence and at the close of all of the evidence. The Court denied both motions, and the case went to the jury. The jury found that DuPont discharged Barrios in violation of the ADA. As a result, the jury awarded Barrios $91,000.00 in back pay, $200,000.00 in front pay, and $1,000,000.00 in punitive damages. The Court later reduced the punitive damages award to the $300,000.00 statutory cap. The jury did not find that DuPont required Barrios to undergo an FCE in violation of the ADA.

DuPont moves the Court for post-trial relief on several grounds.

(1) BACK PAY

Back pay is an equitable remedy available to claimants under the ADA. The Court typically decides the availability of equitable relief, such as back pay. Under Federal Rule of Civil Procedure 39(c), however, the parties may consent to a trial by jury on the issue of back pay even though the ADA does not expressly authorize one. Here, the parties requested a trial by jury on all issues, with the exception of front pay. The jury awarded Barrios $91,000.00 in back pay. At the time of her discharge, Barrios earned $48,000.00 per year. In the five years since her termination, Barrios earned approximately $28,000.00 per year in benefits. This means that the jury awarded Barrios approximately $20,000.00 per year in back pay.

DuPont Power Plant Facility

DuPont contends that the award of back pay is either incorrect or excessive because [a doctor] testified that Barrios would have been unable to work beginning in June of 2001. But [this doctor] later testified that Barrios's back is stable, and her real limitation comes from the pain associated with her impairment. Moreover, Barrios testified that if she could have worked during that time without losing her benefits, she would have. Although there is a conflict in the evidence as to whether Barrios could have worked beyond June of 2001, the jury could have reasonably concluded that she could have. Furthermore, the amount of back pay that the jury awarded has a sufficient basis in the evidence. Accordingly, DuPont's objection to the award of back pay is without merit.

(2) REINSTATEMENT AND FRONT PAY

DuPont argues that an award of front pay is inappropriate because, according to DuPont, the EEOC presented no evidence as to whether reinstatement was appropriate. The Court decides the availability of equitable relief such as reinstatement and front pay. When there is discord or hostility between the parties, however, reinstatement may not be feasible. The Court finds that reinstatement is not a feasible remedy in this case because the relationship between the parties is hostile. For example, Barrios testified that [] the person who made the ultimate decision to discharge her, stated that he did not want to see her "crippled, crooked self going down the hall, hugging the walls anymore." According to both Barrios and her husband, DuPont tried repeatedly to force Barrios out on Total and Permanent disability. DuPont first suggested it in 1986, and continued to "harass" Barrios about retiring on disability for the rest of her tenure at DuPont. When she married Raymond Barrios, DuPont increased the pressure on her to retire on Total and Permanent disability, asserting that she would be entitled to her husband's health benefits.

Moreover, the evidence shows that Barrios suffered an emotional toll as a result of DuPont's discrimination against her. The emotional baggage that Barrios carries as a result of DuPont's discrimination would likely affect her work performance to such an extent that reinstatement is not an adequate remedy. For example, Barrios testified that she has had nightmares about getting fired ever since she left the plant in 1999. Before she returned to DuPont for the EEOC site review in 2003, Barrios experienced stress for several weeks, and she had difficulty sleeping for several nights leading up to it. Furthermore, the evidence that DuPont recklessly disregarded Barrios's rights under the ADA, discussed in depth below in connection with the punitive damages award, only confirms that reinstatement is not a feasible option. Finally, DuPont maintained throughout the course of the litigation that Barrios is not qualified to work at DuPont. Even though the jury found that Barrios is, in fact, qualified to work at DuPont, DuPont's hostile position, along with all of the other evidence of the relationship between Barrios and DuPont, precludes the Court from imposing a remedy of reinstatement.

Because reinstatement is not feasible, the Court must determine whether Barrios is entitled to front pay. As noted *supra*, the Court decides the issue of the availability and the amount of front pay damages. The Fifth Circuit has held, however, that a district court may determine the availability and amount of front pay with the assistance of an advisory jury. Given the speculative nature of front pay damages and that "[t]he courts must employ intelligent guesswork to arrive at the best answer," [citation omitted] the Court submitted the issue of front pay to the jury on an

> The court awarded front pay rather than reinstatement, which it did not find feasible in this case.

advisory basis. Here, the jury recommended a front pay award of $200,000.00. The Court finds that the jury's award was reasonable, and the Court adopts it.

Front pay "compensates the plaintiff for lost income from the date of judgment to the date the plaintiff obtains the position she would have occupied but for the discrimination." *Floca v. Homcare Health Svs., Inc.*, 845 F.2d 108, 112 (5th Cir. 1988). As the Court instructed the jury, in determining an award of front pay, relevant factors include how long Barrios worked at DuPont, the permanency of her position, the nature of her work, her age, her physical condition, possible consolidation of jobs, and any other factor that may have impacted her employment relationship with DuPont.

The first issue that the Court must determine with regard to front pay is the length of time for which Barrios is entitled to compensation. The Court finds that an award of front pay until Barrios reaches age 65 is reasonable, and the Court notes that the jury's award reflects such a determination. This is because Barrios would have remained at DuPont for the rest of her working life. Barrios worked at DuPont for 18 years before DuPont illegally discharged her. Additionally, the work history of other DuPont employees who testified at trial indicates that it is not uncommon for DuPont employees to be career employees. Barrios's age combined with her tenure at DuPont and the evidence that shows that career employees are not unusual at DuPont indicates that Barrios would have likely remained at DuPont until she reached retirement age.

Additionally, the Court finds that Barrios would not have been subject to termination for poor work performance. This is because Barrios successfully performed her job duties as a lab clerk. Moreover, Barrios likely would have continued to work despite her physical impairment. Significantly, Barrios's trial testimony revealed her to be both committed and hard-working. Additionally, although [a doctor] questioned whether Barrios would have been able to continue working because of her severe pain, he testified that her back condition is stable. Furthermore, the evidence showed that Barrios has a high tolerance for pain.

Not only does the Court find it unlikely that Barrios would have stopped working for DuPont due to her impairment, but also the Court finds it unlikely that Barrios would have left DuPont to pursue other opportunities. Barrios testified that there is no other business within her local area where she could work for pay comparable to what she received at DuPont, and DuPont offered nothing to refute Barrios's testimony. Significantly, DuPont treats lab clerks, who essentially function as secretaries, the same in terms of pay and seniority as lab operators, who are skilled technical industrial operators and whose jobs are significantly more physically demanding. Therefore, it is unlikely that Barrios would have left DuPont in pursuit of other opportunities. Accordingly, the Court finds that an award of front pay until Barrios reaches age 65, i.e., an award covering nine years, is reasonable in this case.

Barrios made $48,000.00 per year when DuPont discharged her. There was evidence that Barrios received regular pay increases during her tenure at DuPont. For example, Barrios started at DuPont in 1981 making $8.89 per hour. Within her first five years, Barrios received six step progressions and ultimately made $14.66 per hour in 1985. At 40 hours per week, this comes out to approximately $30,492.00 per year. From 1985 to 1999, when her salary was $48,000.00 per year, Barrios's pay increased by an average of approximately $1,250 per year. On the basis of this evidence, it was reasonable for the jury to adjust Barrios's front pay award to reflect modest pay increases.

Additionally, as the Court instructed the jury, future income, such as Barrios's annual disability benefits, must be subtracted from the front pay award. Furthermore, the Court instructed the jury to discount Barrios's front pay award to present value by considering the interest that Barrios could earn on the award if she made a relatively risk-free investment. Ultimately, the jury arrived at an award of $200,000.00. Taking all relevant factors into account, including reduction to present value at a rate of approximately two percent, the jury's figure is reasonable. Accordingly, the Court adopts it.

DuPont argues that the jury's award is excessive because, according to DuPont, the jury awarded Barrios ten years of front pay at $20,000.00 per year, without reducing to present value. DuPont's characterization of the front pay award is incorrect, as the jury's award reflects consideration of the proper factors. Therefore, the Court rejects DuPont's objection to the front pay award.

(3) MITIGATION

DuPont contends that any award for wage loss is incorrect because, according to DuPont, Barrios failed to mitigate her damages. This is because Barrios did not get another job after DuPont discharged her on Total and Permanent disability. Plaintiffs have a responsibility to exercise reasonable diligence under the circumstances to minimize their damages. Therefore, plaintiffs have the duty to accept alternative employment that is substantially equivalent to their former job in terms of opportunities, compensation, working conditions, and status. DuPont bore the burden to prove that Barrios failed to mitigate her damages. To meet its burden, DuPont must have shown that substantially equivalent work was available to Barrios and that Barrios did not exercise reasonable efforts to obtain it. If, however, DuPont proved that Barrios did not use reasonable efforts to mitigate her damages, DuPont does not have to show that there was substantially equivalent work available to Barrios.

There is sufficient evidence to show that Barrios mitigated her damages. First, Barrios tried repeatedly to get her job at DuPont back after DuPont illegally discharged her. For example, Barrios offered to buy her own wheelchair or golf cart, or even ride a bicycle at work. DuPont refused her requests. Barrios also asked to demonstrate to DuPont that she could, in fact, walk the evacuation route, but DuPont refused her request. Barrios's attempts to get her job back are a form of mitigation.

In addition to trying to get her job back, Barrios mitigated her damages by accepting disability benefits. Significantly, Barrios testified that there were no opportunities in the LaPlace, Louisiana area in which she could make an amount of money comparable to the amount she was making at DuPont. As noted *supra*, lab clerks are equivalent in the DuPont hierarchy in terms of pay and seniority to skilled technical industrial operators whose jobs are more physically demanding. Barrios's testimony that, as a person in her 50's, she could not have started afresh in a secretarial position with a new employer in the same area of Louisiana area making close to $50,000.00 per year is not unreasonable. Indeed, the Court notes that before she started at DuPont, Barrios made only $21,000.00 per year. Barrios further explained that if she had taken another job with a lesser salary, she would have been at risk of losing her disability benefits. The outcome of such a situation is that Barrios would have made less money if she sought alternative employment than she would have received on disability benefits. Accordingly, DuPont's argument that Barrios failed to mitigate her damages is not supported by the record. Furthermore, DuPont offered nothing to controvert Barrios's testimony, and James Gregg, a DuPont personnel relations consultant, admitted that Barrios could have lost some of her disability benefits had she sought alternative employment. The

Court finds that accepting disability benefits was a reasonable alternative to seeking a position with another employer in light of Barrios's particular circumstances. Accordingly, the Court finds that DuPont did not carry its burden on mitigation.

■ NOTES AND QUESTIONS

1. Is the jury's award of backpay in this case proper? Is five years of backpay an excessive award? Should the court have given more consideration to the argument that Ms. Barrios may not have been able to perform her job? Do you agree with the way that the court calculated front pay?

2. Do you agree with the court's assessment that reinstatement was not feasible in this case? Was the evidence of hostility between the parties convincing?

3. The court here concluded that an "award of front pay until Barrios reaches age 65 is reasonable." Is that a fair conclusion in this case? How long a period of front pay did the court ultimately award here? Do you agree with the way the court calculated the damages?

4. Did Barrios sufficiently mitigate her damages? Is her willingness to accept disability benefits a form of mitigation? Should the disability benefits she received be used to offset her damages?

5. Shouldn't the court have required that Barrios attempt to find employment elsewhere? Would it have been difficult for her to find a similar position?

6. The jury here also awarded a substantial amount of punitive damages. Are punitive damages appropriate in this case?

7. Does the decision maker's comment in this case that he did not want to see Barrios's "crippled, crooked self going down the hall, hugging the walls anymore" support the award of punitive damages?

8. The EEOC has been very successful in obtaining monetary relief for victims of employment discrimination. Figure 12.1 looks at the EEOC's recovery data over several years.

Year	Monetary Benefit (in millions)
1997	$114.7
1998	$95.6
1999	$98.7
2000	$52.2
2001	$49.8
2002	$56.2
2003	$146.6
2004	$168.6
2005	$104.8
2006	$44.3
2007	$54.8
2008	$102.2
2009	$82.1
2010	$85.1
2011	$91.0
2012	$44.2
2013	$38.6
2014	$22.5
2015	$65.3
2016	$52.2
2017	$42.4

Figure 12.1 EEOC Recovery Data, FY 1997–FY 2017
Source: EEOC Litigation Statistics, HTTPS://WWW.EEOC.GOV/EEOC/STATISTICS/ENFORCEMENT/LITIGATION.CFM (LAST VISITED JUNE 28, 2018)

E. Compensatory Damages

Compensatory damages have a unique meaning under Title VII. In the classic torts context, compensatory damages are meant to measure actual harm that a plaintiff suffers. This is not the case under Title VII, however, as backpay and front pay usually provide this type of relief. Instead, under Title VII, compensatory damages provide plaintiffs with damages for emotional pain and suffering. The statute provides that compensatory damages include "future pecuniary losses, emotional pain, suffering, inconvenience, mental anguish, loss of enjoyment of life, and other nonpecuniary losses." 42 U.S.C. § 1981a(b)(3). Backpay is specifically excluded from the statutory definition of compensatory damages, as this type of relief is provided elsewhere in the statute. *Id.* at (b)(2).

Thus, under Title VII, compensatory damages do not measure actual harm that the plaintiff suffers. Instead, this form of relief focuses more on the pain and suffering endured by the victim of discrimination. And, as noted in greater detail below, compensatory damages are capped in Title VII cases, with the total amount allowed varying by the size of the employer.

 Interactive Problem

Looking back at the facts of the interactive problem at the beginning of the chapter, what type of evidence would you seek to establish that Wendy was entitled to compensatory damages under the statute?

The district court must always carefully analyze the evidence to determine what — if any — relief should be awarded in a particular case. As you review the court's decision in the following case, consider whether you agree with the remedies awarded by the court.

Whitten v. Cross Garage Corp.
2003 WL 21744088, No. 00 Civ. 5333 JSM FM (S.D.N.Y. July 9, 2003)

MAAS, Magistrate J.

In this action, plaintiff Julius Whitten ("Whitten") alleges that defendants Cross Garage Corporation ("Cross Garage") and Joseph Vassallo ("Vassallo") (together, the "defendants"), unlawfully terminated his employment in violation of Title VII and the Age Discrimination in Employment Act. [A default judgment was entered against the defendant in this case.]

On January 17, 2003, I held an inquest hearing to determine the amount of compensatory and punitive damages, if any, that Whitten should be awarded. Two witnesses testified at that hearing: Whitten and his wife, Flora Whitten. For the reasons set forth below, I recommend that unless the default judgment is vacated, Whitten be awarded judgment in the amount of $148,466.48, consisting of backpay and prejudgment interest in the amount of $57,702.67, front pay in the

> Why are the facts here being determined by a magistrate judge rather than a jury?

amount of $12,490.40, compensatory and punitive damages in the amount of $60,000, attorney's fees in the amount of $17,949.50, and costs in the amount of $323.91.

In light of the defendants' default, Whitten's well-pleaded allegations concerning issues other than damages must be accepted as true. On the basis of the complaint, the inquest papers, and the testimony given by Whitten and his wife at the inquest hearing, I find that the facts are as follows:

Whitten is a resident of the Bronx who was employed in Manhattan at all relevant times. He is an African-American male, born on May 17, 1949. Defendant Cross Garage is a corporation organized and existing under the laws of the State of New York, with its principal office located in Manhattan. Defendant Vassallo is the principal owner of Cross Garage. Whitten was employed as a parking attendant at a garage located on 445 East 80th Street, New York, New York ("Garage"), for a period of approximately 28 years, commencing in 1971. From 1971 until June 1995, the Garage was managed by Claremont South Garage Co. In or around June 1995, management of the Garage was taken over by Cross Garage, which was owned or controlled by Vassallo, who owns or controls a number of other parking garages.

When Cross Garage became the manager, Whitten was one of three Garage employees, all of whom were African-American, over fifty years of age, and members of Local 272 of the Garage Employees Union. In or around July 1995, Vassallo stated that he was going to terminate, force the retirement of, or transfer these employees, including [Whitten], to another location, and . . . that if they did not like it, they could quit. Whitten contacted his union regarding Vassallo's statements, and shortly thereafter, Vassallo confronted Whitten in the Garage. He told Whitten that he did not want union workers and referred to Whitten under his breath as a "nigger." As a result of Vassallo's statements and threats, the other two employees decide to retire, and Vassallo hired younger inexperienced employees. Subsequently, Whitten became the target of daily verbal abuse, which included derogatory racial remarks, made in front of customers and employees. Vassallo also refused to pay Whitten the salary increase to which he was entitled.

In 1997, Vassallo converted the employees' locker room and adjacent toilet at the Garage into his private office. Because the Garage employees had no available toilet facilities, they began using the Garage drains as urinals and putting human feces wrapped in newspaper in the garbage cans. When Whitten complained to Vassallo about the conditions, Vassallo told him, "[H]ey, . . . you nigger bastard, if you don't like it, . . . you can just find yourself another job."

In February 1999, Whitten called the Department of Health and reported the unsanitary conditions and lack of toilet facilities. As a result of this complaint, inspectors from the Department of Health came to the garage, inspected the premises, and issued a Notice of Violation to Cross Garage and Vassallo.

Whitten took a vacation from June 26 to July 18, 1999. Upon his return to work on July 19, 1999, Vassallo told him, "You are terminated." When asked the reason, Vassallo replied, "You nigger bastard, I know it was you who called the Department of Health, but I have you in black and white pissing on the floor." Whitten was replaced by someone younger. On March 21, 2000, Whitten filed a timely Charge of Discrimination with the United States Equal Employment Opportunities Commission ("EEOC"). On May 31, 2000, the EEOC issued a written determination concluding that there was "reasonable cause to believe" that Whitten's allegations of race and age discrimination were true. On June 9, 2000, the EEOC issued Whitten a "right to sue" letter. This suit was timely filed on July 18, 2000.

A plaintiff successful in a Title VII suit is entitled to an award of back pay. See 42 U.S.C. § 2000e–5(g)(1). "An award of backpay is the rule, not the exception." *Carrero v. New York City Housing Authority*, 890 F.2d 569, 580 (2d Cir. 1989). Title VII plaintiffs are entitled to back pay from the date of termination until the date of judgment, as well as prejudgment interest on the back pay award. When Whitten was terminated, he was working approximately 40 hours per week, at an hourly rate of $12.01 per hour, for a weekly gross wage of $480.40. The default judgment was entered on July 31, 2001. Thus, from the date of discharge to the date of judgment, 106 weeks and one day elapsed. Accordingly, Whitten should be awarded $51,018.48 in backpay ($480.40/week × 106 weeks + $12.01/hour × 8 hours).

At the time of his termination, the defendants also owed Whitten one week's pay of $480.40 for the last week in June and six days of vacation totaling $576.48 ($12.01/hour × 8 hours × 6 days). In addition, had he not been improperly terminated, Whitten would have earned a $300 bonus for 1999. He therefore is entitled to an additional $1,356.88 through the date of judgment.

The rate at which prejudgment interest is to be calculated is within the Court's discretion. In this case, Whitten has requested interest at the statutory rate of nine percent per year set forth in Section 5004 of the New York Civil Practice and Rules. This, however, is more than double the prevailing interest rates on conservative financial investments during the same period. Accordingly, I find that a five percent interest rate is more in accordance with reality. The per diem interest rate is therefore $7.17 ($52,375.36 × 0.05 ÷ 365), and Whitten is entitled to prejudgment interest for a period of 743 days, for a total of $5,327.31.

Front pay is an equitable remedy available to prevailing Title VII plaintiffs, and is generally understood to be an award for lost compensation for the period between judgment and reinstatement. Thus, front pay helps make a discharged employee whole. However, such compensation is not mandatory, and it is within the court's discretion to "award front pay, reinstate the plaintiff's employment, or do nothing at all with regard to future employment." *Vernon v. Port Authority of N.Y. and N.J.*, 220 F. Supp. 2d 223, 236 (S.D.N.Y. 2002). Further, an award of front pay should be discounted to its present value.

In 1998, prior to his termination, Whitten began working part-time at another garage managed by Rudin Management ("Rudin"). In or around April 1999, Whitten began working full-time for Rudin in addition to his full-time position at Cross Garage. At the inquest hearing, Whitten testified that the reason he began working two full-time jobs was that he knew "it wouldn't be long before Joseph [Vassallo], you know, let me go, so I just went on and prepared myself."

There is no need to consider reinstatement as a remedy in this case because Whitten's employment at Rudin actually pays him a higher wage. Moreover, that employment is full-time. Had he not been summarily terminated on July 19, 1999, Whitten could theoretically have continued working two full-time jobs. It is more likely, however, that Whitten would have voluntarily left his job at Cross Garage before too long since he had a higher paying job at Rudin. In these circumstances, I find that six months of front pay, amounting to $12,490.40 ($480.40/week × 26 weeks), is reasonably sufficient to make Whitten whole. Although usually such an award should be discounted to present value, it is unnecessary to do so here because six months from the date of judgment has long since passed.

Under Title VII, a court may also award a sum of money as compensation for "emotional pain, suffering, inconvenience, mental anguish, loss of enjoyment of life, and other nonpecuniary losses." 42 U.S.C. § 1981a(b)(3). A prevailing Title VII plaintiff may also recover punitive damages if he "demonstrates that the [defendant] engaged in a discriminatory practice or discriminatory practices with malice or with reckless indifference." *Id.* § 1981a(b)(1). However, Title VII imposes a cap on the maximum compensatory and punitive damage award that a plaintiff can recover which is based on the size of the employer's staff. Assuming that Cross Garage had more than 14, but fewer than 101 employees, as appears likely, Title VII places a cap of $50,000 on Whitten's compensatory and punitive damages. *See id.* § 1981a(b)(3)(A). Under the New York Human Rights Law, however, an award of compensatory damages is not subject to any limitation. Similarly, there is no statutory limitation on the maximum amount of punitive damages awardable under the New York City Human Rights Law.

In cases involving "typical" emotional distress, some courts have remitted jury awards for emotional distress to between $5,000 and $30,000. *Kuper v. Empire Blue Cross & Blue Shield*, 2003 WL 359462, at *12 (S.D.N.Y. Feb. 18, 2003) (collecting cases). In other similar cases, courts have remitted such awards to between $30,000 and $75,000, even though "the only evidence of emotional distress has been the plaintiff's testimony, [and] the plaintiff claims no physical manifestations." *Id.* at *13 (collecting cases).

> Note the distinction here between the statutory caps for state and federal law.

Here, Whitten testified that due to Vassallo's constant racial epithets, he felt "belittled" and "angry." Whitten's wife also testified that the racial slurs made her husband "feel much less than human." She stated that Vassallo's constant derogatory remarks made Whitten feel "mad" and "angry," and that this affected his ability to have a relationship with the children. *Id.* In light of this testimony, I find that an award of $40,000 in compensatory damages is appropriate.

Although there is no limit on an award of punitive damages under the New York City Human Rights Law, the $50,000 cap for compensatory and punitive damages under 42 U.S.C. § 1981a(b)(3) serves as a useful guidepost. Thus, if Section 1981a(b)(3) were controlling, Whitten would be entitled to a maximum of $10,000 in punitive damages ($50,000 − $40,000). Under that statute, a plaintiff need not show that the defendants' conduct was "extraordinarily egregious" in order to recover punitive damages. *Luciano v. Olsten Corp.*, 110 F.3d 210, 220 (2d Cir. 1997). Here, even if one were to find that Vassallo's racial epithets were garden variety (which I do not), the deprivation of toilet facilities to which he was subjected would not be tolerated in a jail, and is nothing short of shocking. For that reason, I find that he should be awarded an additional $20,000 in punitive damages.

A plaintiff prevailing in a Title VII suit is entitled to recover his attorney's reasonable fees and costs. 42 U.S.C. § 2000e–5(k). Attorney's fees are determined using the lodestar method, which entails multiplying the number of hours reasonably spent by a reasonable hourly rate. In the Second Circuit, a party seeking an award of attorney's fees must support that request with contemporaneous time records that show, "for each attorney, the date, the hours expended, and the nature of the work done." *New York State Ass'n for Retarded Children, Inc. v. Carey*, 711 F.2d 1136, 1154 (2d Cir. 1983). Fee applications that do not contain such supporting data "should normally be disallowed." *Id.* at 1154. Furthermore, the Court has a great deal of discretion in awarding attorney's fees and can deduct hours from the lodestar calculation if it finds that the hours charged are superfluous or unreasonable.

In prosecuting this action, Whitten engaged the services of Daniel, Siegel & Bimbler LLP, which merged with the law firm of Cowan, DeBaets, Abrahams & Sheppard LLP in November 2002. At both firms, the attorney handling this matter was Al J. Daniel, Jr., who has submitted an affidavit and a supplemental declaration setting forth: (a) his professional experience; (b) the number of hours he devoted to this action and the nature of the work performed; and (c) the billing rate at which he seeks to be compensated. Based upon my review, both the number of hours expended and the hourly rates for these legal services generally seem reasonable. Mr. Daniel, however, also billed at his customary hourly rate for services more appropriately handled by a paralegal. I have therefore reduced his hourly rate to $75 for the approximately five hours that he spent performing such routine tasks as traveling to court to file papers, ensuring that service was effected, and forwarding copies of documents. Following that minimal adjustment, I recommend that Whitten be awarded attorney's fees in the amount of $16,392 for services rendered prior to the inquest hearing ($285/hour × 56.2 hours + $75/hour × 5 hours), plus an additional $1,557.50 for services rendered in connection with the hearing ($350/hour × 4.45 hours), for a total of $17,949.50.

For the reasons set forth above, I recommend that Whitten be awarded damages, including attorney's fees and costs, totaling $148,466.48.

■ NOTES AND QUESTIONS

1. The facts of this case are being driven by the defendant's failure to respond. If the garage were able to put on an adequate defense, how would the damages potentially be affected?

2. Do you agree with the magistrate judge's calculation of backpay in this case? Why or why not?

3. Do you agree with the magistrate judge's calculation of front pay in this case? If the plaintiff had another full-time job, why is any front pay appropriate at all here?

4. Do the facts of this case support a finding for $40,000 in compensatory damages? What type of evidence of emotional pain and suffering support this conclusion?

5. The facts here seem particularly egregious. The plaintiff was subjected to unsanitary health conditions and extremely offensive racial language. Given these facts, would a greater award than $20,000 in punitive damages be appropriate? Why does Title VII limit the amount of damages available to plaintiffs? Should the court use these limits as a guideline for state law decisions?

6. The court also awarded attorneys' fees in this case. Are attorneys' fees typical in a Title VII action? Do the attorneys' fees seem reasonable here?

 Interactive Problem

Looking back at the facts of the interactive problem at the beginning of the chapter, assume that Wendy received a judgment in her favor exactly two years after she was unlawfully terminated under Title VII. How much backpay would Wendy be entitled to?

 F. Punitive Damages

In addition to compensatory damages, the Civil Rights Act of 1991 also amended Title VII to provide for punitive damages. Punitive damages are available where the plaintiff successfully shows that the employer

> engaged in a discriminatory practice or discriminatory practices with malice or with reckless indifference to the federally protected rights of an aggrieved individual.

42 U.S.C. § 1981a(b)(1).

The award of punitive damages thus focuses on whether the defendant acted with malice or reckless disregard to the plaintiff's rights under Title VII. As addressed by the Supreme Court in the *Kolstad* case below, this determination is not made on the basis of egregiousness. Rather, the question is whether the defendant was aware of the plaintiff's rights under the statute and chose to discriminate in the face of this knowledge. A careful assessment of the case law in this area reveals that there are three elements that must be considered when determining whether a plaintiff is entitled to punitive relief:

1. whether the employer had knowledge of its obligations under Title VII;
2. whether the unlawful conduct can be imputed to the employer; and
3. whether the employer can establish that it was acting in good faith under the statute (the affirmative defense).

Knowledge of Title VII is a key element in any punitive damages award. It establishes that the employer was aware of its obligations pursuant to the statute. Similarly, this knowledge, and the unlawful conduct, must be imputed to the employer. This typically means that the unlawful conduct must have been perpetrated by a manager or supervisor at the company who was acting within the scope of her employment. And, this manager must have been aware of the prohibitions under Title VII. Finally, even where a plaintiff is able to establish these elements, the defendant still has an affirmative defense. If the employer can establish that it was acting in good faith under the statute, it can avoid liability for punitive damages. This defense only extends to punitive damages, however, and does not allow the employer to avoid liability under the statute.

One other consideration when calculating compensatory and punitive damages are the statutory caps. There is no cap on the amount of backpay or front pay that a plaintiff may receive. Title VII does limit the combined amount of punitive and compensatory relief, however. Pursuant to the statute, there is a sliding scale based on the size of the employer for these damages. The statute provides that

> [P]unitive damages awarded under this section, shall not exceed, for each complaining party —
>> **(A)** in the case of a respondent who has more than 14 and fewer than 101 employees . . . $50,000;
>> **(B)** in the case of a respondent who has more than 100 and fewer than 201 employees . . . $100,000; and
>> **(C)** in the case of a respondent who has more than 200 and fewer than 501 employees . . . $200,000; and
>> **(D)** in the case of a respondent who has more than 500 employees . . . $300,000.

42 U.S.C. § 1981a(b)(3).

Based on this sliding scale, then, for the largest employers, plaintiffs may receive up to $300,000 in punitive and compensatory damages combined. These caps have remained in place since the Civil Rights Act amended Title VII in 1991. The impact of these damages has waned over time as the effect of inflation has substantially reduced the financial effects of this form of relief.

Attempts to raise and/or eliminate these caps have been made in Congress, but these attempts have failed. The compromise of statutory caps allowed Congress to recognize that punitive damages should be recoverable in employment discrimination cases, but that such relief should not be unlimited. When the Civil Rights Act was passed, many senators were opposed to the statutory caps. Both major political parties explained that they accepted the Act with the caps in place because of the overriding importance of protecting employees from employment discrimination. Only a week after President Bush signed the 1991 Act into law, however, senators from both the Democratic and Republican parties proposed bills to lift the caps on punitive and compensatory damages. Republican Senator Orrin Hatch proposed the Employee Equality and Job Preservation Act of 1991, which would have lifted all caps on compensatory and punitive damages, unless the employer involved had less than 100 employees. On the same day, Democratic Senator Ted Kennedy proposed the Equal Remedies Act of 1991, which would have lifted all caps regardless of the employer's size. Despite these efforts, the caps have remained unchanged in amount since the statute was passed over two decades ago. *See* Michael W. Roskiewicz, *Title VII Remedies: Lifting the Statutory Caps from the Civil Rights Act of 1991 to Achieve Equal Remedies for Employment Discrimination*, 43 Wash. U. J. Urb. & Contemp. L. 391, 407–409 (1993).

Kolstad v. American Dental Ass'n

527 U.S. 526 (1999)

Justice O'Connor delivered the opinion of the Court.

In September 1992, Jack O'Donnell announced that he would be retiring as the Director of Legislation and Legislative Policy and Director of the Council on Government Affairs and Federal Dental Services for respondent, American Dental Association (respondent or Association). Petitioner, Carole Kolstad, was employed with O'Donnell in respondent's Washington, D.C., office, where she was serving as respondent's Director of Federal Agency Relations. When she learned of O'Donnell's retirement, she expressed an interest in filling his position. Also interested in replacing O'Donnell was Tom Spangler, another employee in respondent's Washington office. At this time, Spangler was serving as the Association's Legislative Counsel, a position that involved him in respondent's legislative lobbying 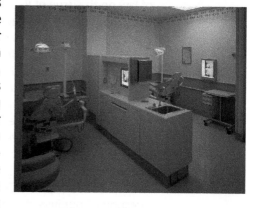 efforts. Both petitioner and Spangler had worked directly with O'Donnell, and both had received "distinguished" performance ratings by the acting head of the Washington office, Leonard Wheat.

Both petitioner and Spangler formally applied for O'Donnell's position, and Wheat requested that Dr. William Allen, then serving as respondent's Executive Director in the Association's Chicago office, make the ultimate promotion decision. After interviewing both petitioner and Spangler, Wheat recommended that

Allen select Spangler for O'Donnell's post. Allen notified petitioner in December 1992 that he had, in fact, selected Spangler to serve as O'Donnell's replacement. Petitioner's challenge to this employment decision forms the basis of the instant action.

After first exhausting her avenues for relief before the Equal Employment Opportunity Commission, petitioner filed suit against the Association in Federal District Court, alleging that respondent's decision to promote Spangler was an act of employment discrimination proscribed under Title VII. In petitioner's view, the entire selection process was a sham. Counsel for petitioner urged the jury to conclude that Allen's stated reasons for selecting Spangler were pretext for gender discrimination, and that Spangler had been chosen for the position before the formal selection process began. Among the evidence offered in support of this view, there was testimony to the effect that Allen modified the description of O'Donnell's post to track aspects of the job description used to hire Spangler. In petitioner's view, this "preselection" procedure suggested an intent by the Association to discriminate on the basis of sex. Petitioner also introduced testimony at trial that Wheat told sexually offensive jokes and that he had referred to certain prominent professional women in derogatory terms. Moreover, Wheat allegedly refused to meet with petitioner for several weeks regarding her interest in O'Donnell's position. Petitioner testified, in fact, that she had historically experienced difficulty gaining access to meet with Wheat. Allen, for his part, testified that he conducted informal meetings regarding O'Donnell's position with both petitioner and Spangler, although petitioner stated that Allen did not discuss the position with her.

The District Court denied petitioner's request for a jury instruction on punitive damages. The jury concluded that respondent had discriminated against petitioner on the basis of sex and awarded her back pay totaling $52,718. Although the District Court subsequently denied respondent's motion for judgment as a matter of law on the issue of liability, the court made clear that it had not been persuaded that respondent had selected Spangler over petitioner on the basis of sex, and the court denied petitioner's requests for reinstatement and for attorney's fees.

Petitioner appealed from the District Court's decisions denying her requested jury instruction on punitive damages and her request for reinstatement and attorney's fees. Respondent cross-appealed from the denial of its motion for judgment as a matter of law. In a split decision, a panel of the Court of Appeals for the District of Columbia reversed the District Court's decision denying petitioner's request for an instruction on punitive damages.

The Court of Appeals subsequently agreed to rehear the case en banc, limited to the punitive damages question. In a divided opinion, the court affirmed the decision of the District Court. The en banc majority concluded that, "before the question of punitive damages can go to the jury, the evidence of the defendant's culpability must exceed what is needed to show intentional discrimination." Based on the 1991 Act's structure and legislative history, the court determined, specifically, that a defendant must be shown to have engaged in some "egregious" misconduct before the jury is permitted to consider a request for punitive damages. Although the court declined to set out the "egregiousness" requirement in any detail, it concluded that petitioner failed to make the requisite showing in the instant case. Judge Randolph concurred, relying chiefly on § 1981a's structure as evidence of a congressional intent to "limi[t] punitive damages to exceptional cases." Judge Tatel wrote in dissent for five judges, who agreed generally with the panel majority. We granted certiorari.

The [Civil Rights Act of 1991] limits compensatory and punitive damages awards [] to cases of "intentional discrimination" — that is, cases that do not rely on the "disparate impact" theory of discrimination. 42 U.S.C. § 1981a(a)(1). Section 1981a(b)(1) further qualifies the availability of punitive awards:

> "A complaining party may recover punitive damages under this section against a respondent (other than a government, government agency or political subdivision) if the complaining party demonstrates that the respondent engaged in a discriminatory practice or discriminatory practices with malice or with reckless indifference to the federally protected rights of an aggrieved individual." (Emphasis added).

The very structure of § 1981a suggests a congressional intent to authorize punitive awards in only a subset of cases involving intentional discrimination. Section 1981a(a)(1) limits compensatory and punitive awards to instances of intentional discrimination, while § 1981a(b)(1) requires plaintiffs to make an additional "demonstrat[ion]" of their eligibility for punitive damages. Congress plainly sought to impose two standards of liability — one for establishing a right to compensatory damages and another, higher standard that a plaintiff must satisfy to qualify for a punitive award.

The Court of Appeals sought to give life to this two-tiered structure by limiting punitive awards to cases involving intentional discrimination of an "egregious" nature. We credit the en banc majority's effort to effectuate congressional intent, but, in the end, we reject its conclusion that eligibility for punitive damages can only be described in terms of an employer's "egregious" misconduct. The terms "malice" and "reckless" ultimately focus on the actor's state of mind. While egregious misconduct is evidence of the requisite mental state, § 1981a does not limit plaintiffs to this form of evidence, and the section does not require a showing of egregious or outrageous discrimination independent of the employer's state of mind. Nor does the statute's structure imply an independent role for "egregiousness" in the face of congressional silence. On the contrary, the view that § 1981a provides for punitive awards based solely on an employer's state of mind is consistent with the 1991 Act's distinction between equitable and compensatory relief. Intent determines which remedies are open to a plaintiff here as well; compensatory awards are available only where the employer has engaged in "*intentional* discrimination." § 1981a(a)(1) (emphasis added).

> After this decision, it is clear that egregiousness is no longer a necessary element for punitive damages under Title VII or the ADA.

Moreover, § 1981a's focus on the employer's state of mind gives some effect to Congress' apparent intent to narrow the class of cases for which punitive awards are available to a subset of those involving intentional discrimination. The employer must act with "malice or with reckless indifference *to the [plaintiff's] federally protected rights."* § 1981a(b)(1) (emphasis added). The terms "malice" or "reckless indifference" pertain to the employer's knowledge that it may be acting in violation of federal law, not its awareness that it is engaging in discrimination. [I]n the context of § 1981a, an employer must at least discriminate in the face of a perceived risk that its actions will violate federal law to be liable in punitive damages.

There will be circumstances where intentional discrimination does not give rise to punitive damages liability under this standard. In some instances, the employer may simply be unaware of the relevant federal prohibition. There will be cases, moreover, in which the employer discriminates with the distinct belief that its discrimination is lawful. The underlying theory of discrimination may be novel or otherwise poorly recognized, or an employer may reasonably believe that its discrimination satisfies a bona fide occupational qualification defense or other statutory exception to liability.

Egregious misconduct is often associated with the award of punitive damages, but the reprehensible character of the conduct is not generally considered apart from the requisite state of mind. Conduct warranting punitive awards has been characterized as "egregious," for example, because of the defendant's mental state. That conduct committed with the specified mental state may be characterized as egregious, however, is not to say that employers must engage in conduct with some independent, "egregious" quality before being subject to a punitive award.

The inquiry does not end with a showing of the requisite "malice or . . . reckless indifference" on the part of certain individuals, however. 42 U.S.C. § 1981a(b)(1). The plaintiff must impute liability for punitive damages to respondent. The Restatement provides that the principal may be liable for punitive damages if it authorizes or ratifies the agent's tortious act, or if it acts recklessly in employing the malfeasing agent. The Restatement also contemplates liability for punitive awards where an employee serving in a "managerial capacity" committed the wrong while "acting in the scope of employment." Restatement (Second) of Agency [§ 217 C].

Holding employers liable for punitive damages when they engage in good faith efforts to comply with Title VII, however, is in some tension with the very principles underlying common law limitations on vicarious liability for punitive damages. . . . Applying the Restatement of Agency's "scope of employment" rule in the Title VII punitive damages context, moreover, would reduce the incentive for employers to implement antidiscrimination programs. In fact, such a rule would likely exacerbate concerns among employers that § 1981a's "malice" and "reckless indifference" standard penalizes those employers who educate themselves and their employees on Title VII's prohibitions. Dissuading employers from implementing programs or policies to prevent discrimination in the workplace is directly contrary to the purposes underlying Title VII. The purposes underlying Title VII are . . . advanced where employers are encouraged to adopt antidiscrimination policies and to educate their personnel on Title VII's prohibitions.

In light of the perverse incentives that the Restatement's "scope of employment" rules create, we are compelled to modify these principles to avoid undermining the objectives underlying Title VII. Recognizing Title VII as an effort to promote prevention as well as remediation, and observing the very principles underlying the Restatements' strict limits on vicarious liability for punitive damages, we agree that, in the punitive damages context, an employer may not be vicariously liable for the discriminatory employment decisions of managerial

> **The Court here establishes an affirmative good faith defense for employers to avoid a punitive damages award.**

agents where these decisions are contrary to the employer's "good-faith efforts to comply with Title VII." Kolstad v. Am. Dental Ass'n, 139 F.3d 958, 974 (D.C. Cir. 1998) (TATEL, J., dissenting). As the dissent recognized, "[g]iving punitive damages protection to employers who make good-faith efforts to prevent discrimination in the workplace accomplishes" Title VII's objective of "motivat[ing] employers to detect and deter Title VII violations." *Ibid.*

We have concluded that an employer's conduct need not be independently "egregious" to satisfy § 1981a's requirements for a punitive damages award, although evidence of egregious misconduct may be used to meet the plaintiff's burden of proof. We leave for remand the question whether petitioner can identify facts sufficient to support an inference that the requisite mental state can be imputed to respondent. The parties have not yet had an opportunity to marshal the record evidence in support of their views on the application of agency principles in the instant case, and the en banc majority had no reason to resolve the issue because it concluded that petitioner had failed to demonstrate the requisite "egregious" misconduct. Although trial testimony established that Allen made the ultimate decision to promote Spangler while serving as petitioner's interim executive director, respondent's highest position, it remains to be seen whether petitioner can make a sufficient showing that Allen acted with malice or reckless indifference to petitioner's Title VII rights. Even if it could be established that Wheat effectively selected O'Donnell's replacement, moreover, several questions would remain, *e.g.*, whether Wheat was serving in a "managerial capacity" and whether he behaved with malice or reckless indifference to petitioner's rights. It may also be necessary to determine whether the Association had been making good faith efforts to enforce an antidiscrimination policy. We leave these issues for resolution on remand.

■ NOTES AND QUESTIONS

1. The Court in *Kolstad* made clear that there is no "egregiousness" requirement for punitive damages under Title VII. What role, if any, does egregiousness still play in a Title VII case?

2. The Court notes that to warrant punitive damages, the conduct must be imputed to the employer through traditional agency principles. How is this accomplished in a traditional Title VII case? Are the same agency principles used for imputing liability in sexual harassment cases (Chapter 5) applicable here?

3. The Court establishes a "good faith" exception where an employer can prevent the imposition of punitive damages. How would an employer demonstrate good faith?

4. The good faith defense is an affirmative defense. It relieves the employer only of punitive damages; the employer is still responsible for other damages in the case, as well as potential attorneys' fees. Interestingly, the good faith defense was not briefed or argued before the Court. *See* Erwin Chemerinsky, *The Supremes: The New Judicial Activism*, CAL. LAW., Feb. 2000.

5. In portions of the decision omitted here, the Court analogizes the good faith defense to the *Faragher/Ellerth* defense for sexual harassment. How is the defense similar? How is it different?

6. The Court notes that not all intentional discrimination warrants punitive damages. As examples of this, it suggests that where the employer is unaware of the statute or where the particular form of discrimination is "novel or otherwise poorly recognized," *Kolstad*, 527 U.S. at 537, punitive relief may not be appropriate. Can you suggest any other types of intentional discrimination that do not warrant punitive damages?

7. Generally speaking, after *Kolstad*, courts apply the three-part test for punitive damages discussed above. A plaintiff must first establish that the employer was aware of Title VII's prohibitions, and the unlawful conduct must be imputed to the employer. Finally, the employer will still have the opportunity to establish a good faith defense.

8. The statutory caps have been very controversial in Title VII cases. It is interesting to note that, given inflation, it would take $552,452.45 in the year 2018 to have the same monetary impact on an employer as $300,000 did in 1991. *See* U.S. DEP'T OF LABOR, BUREAU OF LABOR STATISTICS, INFLATION CALCULATOR, http://data.bls.gov/cgi-bin/cpicalc.pl.

9. Do you agree that statutory caps are necessary as part of Title VII litigation? Should they be raised? Should they be eliminated altogether?

10. In some instances, plaintiffs' attorneys may choose to litigate in state court rather than federal court to avoid these statutory caps. For example, New Jersey's Punitive Damages Act, N.J. STAT. ANN. §§ 2A:15–5.9 *et seq.* (2013), provides for a punitive damages cap of $35,000; however, the state's Law Against Discrimination, N.J. STAT. ANN. §§ 10:5–1 *et seq.* (West 2002), is explicitly excepted from that cap. Similarly, Ohio's Anti-Discrimination Law, OHIO REV. CODE ANN. § 4112.00 (2001), allows for punitive damages, and does not provide a cap for such relief. *See* Rice v. CertainTeed Corp., 704 N.E.2d 1217, 1219 n.1 (Ohio 1999). And, Missouri's Human Rights Act includes no limit on punitive damages. *See* MO. REV. STAT. § 213.111(2) (2014); Brady v. Curators of Univ. of Mo., 213 S.W.3d 101, 111 (Mo. Ct. App. 2006) ("Under the MHRA, punitive damages may be assessed against a defendant with no stated limit.").

11. Having an effective antidiscrimination policy in place can help relieve an employer of liability for harassment under Title VII. It can also help demonstrate good faith for purposes of avoiding punitive damages. There are thus

numerous reasons why employers should make certain to be proactive in preventing discrimination. And, defense counsel should strongly recommend that an employer effectively implement and maintain an antidiscrimination policy in the workplace.

12. **Historical note.** The plaintiff's attorney in *Kolstad*, Joseph Albert "Chip" Yablonski, Jr., is a prominent Washington, D.C. lawyer. He attended law school at the University of Pittsburgh School of Law, clerked for Chief Judge Austin Staley on the U.S. Court of Appeals for the Third Circuit, and later worked as an attorney for the National Labor Relations Board. Chip's father, Jock Yablonski, was a well-known union activist and labor leader who repeatedly tried to reform the United Mine Workers of America (UMWA) in the 1960s. In a major political crime on New Year's Eve of 1969, Jock, his wife, and their daughter were murdered by three assassins hired by the UMWA. The assassination was ordered by the UMWA president at the time, after Jock had run against him and lost in a fraudulent election. The murders led to the election being overturned, and the new president appointed Chip as general counsel for the UMWA. After Chip resigned from the UMWA a few years later, he formed a private practice focusing on labor law and union advocacy. He has also earned success as a civil trial lawyer, and his performance in *Kolstad* is one of his most well-known accomplishments. *See* Richard Robbins, *1969 Yablonski Murders Spurred Union Reforms*, TribLive (Dec. 27, 2009), http://triblive.com/x/pittsburghtrib/news/regional/s_659597.html#axzz3HxlNsZ1P; Joseph Yablonski's Attorney Profile, Law Offices of Joseph A. Yablonski, P.L.L.C., http://www.yablonskilaw.com/profile/.

 Interactive Problem

Looking back at the facts of the interactive problem at the beginning of the chapter, would Wendy be entitled to punitive damages under Title VII based on Barry Boss's conduct? Is there any other information we would need to know to make this determination?

Practice and Procedural Tip
27: Litigating Punitive Damages: Knowledge Requirement and Statutory Caps

Litigating punitive damages in the employment discrimination context can be a difficult task. From a practical standpoint, most juries will be swayed by the egregious nature of an employer's conduct. From a legal standpoint, such conduct is not overly relevant to the issue of the employer's liability for such damages. When litigating a case involving punitive damages, it is important to be cognizant of the three-part test typically applied by the circuits: knowledge of the statute, conduct imputable to the employer, and the good faith defense.

Of these elements, the knowledge requirement can be the most tricky to apply. How can a plaintiff demonstrate that the employer had knowledge that its conduct was unlawful? Though this may sound like a difficult inquiry on its face, getting this type of evidence can be relatively straightforward in deposition testimony or at trial. Generally speaking, employers are more than willing to acknowledge that they are aware of Title VII and its obligations. In fact, most employers will indicate that they are aware of the prohibitions against employment discrimination, and that they have not violated these prohibitions in any way.

The key takeaway from this issue, then, is that plaintiffs must be certain to properly develop the record and ask the correct questions if they are seeking to pursue punitive relief. For example, a plaintiff's counsel might ask: "Manager Smith, were you aware at the time of Ms. Jones's employment that sexual harassment was unlawful?" Or, "Ms. Thompson, have you ever had any training — in this job or in previous employment — on the topic of race discrimination?" Such questions help demonstrate the knowledge requirement and go to the issue of whether the employer's conduct was not only intentional, but in willful disregard of the plaintiff's federally protected rights.

From a procedural standpoint, juries are not typically instructed on the statutory caps in employment discrimination cases. Rather, juries are free to award plaintiffs any amount that they deem appropriate. Assuming that the jury's verdict is in excess of the statutory caps, the court will typically reduce the award to comply with these caps before the judgment is issued.

The Supreme Court's punitive damages jurisprudence extends well beyond employment discrimination case law. In the decision below, the Court looks at whether harm caused to third parties by a company can be used by a plaintiff to bolster a punitive damages claim. As discussed below, this issue has important implications for employment discrimination cases.

Philip Morris USA v. Williams

549 U.S. 346 (2007)

Justice BREYER delivered the opinion of the Court.

This lawsuit arises out of the death of Jesse Williams, a heavy cigarette smoker. Respondent, Williams' widow, represents his estate in this state lawsuit for negligence and deceit against Philip Morris, the manufacturer of Marlboro, the brand that Williams favored. A jury found that Williams' death was caused by smoking; that Williams smoked in significant part because he thought it was safe to do so; and that Philip Morris knowingly and falsely led him to believe that this was so. The jury ultimately found that Philip Morris was negligent (as was Williams) and that Philip Morris had engaged in deceit. In respect to deceit, the claim at issue here, it awarded compensatory damages of about $821,000 (about $21,000 economic and $800,000 noneconomic) along with $79.5 million in punitive damages.

The trial judge subsequently found the $79.5 million punitive damages award "excessive," *see, e.g., BMW of North America, Inc. v. Gore*, 517 U.S. 559 (1996), and reduced it to $32 million. Both sides appealed. The Oregon Court of

Appeals rejected Philip Morris' arguments and restored the $79.5 million jury award. Subsequently, Philip Morris sought review in the Oregon Supreme Court (which denied review) and then here. We remanded the case in light of *State Farm Mut. Automobile Ins. Co. v. Campbell*, 538 U.S. 408 (2003). The Oregon Court of Appeals adhered to its original views. And Philip Morris sought, and this time obtained, review in the Oregon Supreme Court.

Philip Morris [argued that] the trial court should have accepted, but did not accept, a proposed "punitive damages" instruction that specified the jury could not seek to punish Philip Morris for injury to other persons not before the court. In particular, Philip Morris pointed out that the plaintiff's attorney had told the jury to "think about how many other Jesse Williams in the last 40 years in the State of Oregon there have been. . . . In Oregon, how many people do we see outside, driving home . . . smoking cigarettes? . . . [C]igarettes . . . are going to kill ten [of every hundred]. [And] the market share of Marlboros [*i.e.*, Philip Morris] is one-third [*i.e.*, one of every three killed]." In light of this argument, Philip Morris asked the trial court to tell the jury that "you may consider the extent of harm suffered by others in determining what [the] reasonable relationship is" between any punitive award and "the harm caused to Jesse Williams" by Philip Morris' misconduct, "[but] you are not to punish the defendant for the impact of its alleged misconduct on other persons, who may bring lawsuits of their own in which other juries can resolve their claims . . . . " The judge rejected this proposal and instead told the jury that "[p]unitive damages are awarded against a defendant to punish misconduct and to deter misconduct," and "are not intended to compensate the plaintiff or anyone else for damages caused by the defendant's conduct." In Philip Morris' view, the result was a significant likelihood that a portion of the $79.5 million award represented punishment for its having harmed others, a punishment that the Due Process Clause would here forbid.

The Oregon Supreme Court rejected [this argument]. We granted certiorari. For reasons we shall set forth, we consider only the first of these questions. We vacate the Oregon Supreme Court's judgment, and we remand the case for further proceedings.

In our view, the Constitution's Due Process Clause forbids a State to use a punitive damages award to punish a defendant for injury that it inflicts upon nonparties or those whom they directly represent, *i.e.*, injury that it inflicts upon those who are, essentially, strangers to the litigation. For one thing, the Due Process Clause prohibits a State from punishing an individual without first providing that individual with "an opportunity to present every available defense." *Lindsey v. Normet*, 405 U.S. 56 (1972) (internal quotation marks omitted). Yet a defendant threatened with punishment for injuring a nonparty victim has no opportunity

> The Court holds here that third-party harm is an inappropriate consideration for punitive damages.

to defend against the charge, by showing, for example in a case such as this, that the other victim was not entitled to damages because he or she knew that smoking was dangerous or did not rely upon the defendant's statements to the contrary.

For another, to permit punishment for injuring a nonparty victim would add a near standardless dimension to the punitive damages equation. How many such victims are there? How seriously were they injured? Under what circumstances did injury occur? The trial will not likely answer such questions as to nonparty victims. The jury will be left to speculate. And the fundamental due process concerns to which our punitive damages cases refer — risks of arbitrariness, uncertainty, and lack of notice — will be magnified.

Finally, we can find no authority supporting the use of punitive damages awards for the purpose of punishing a defendant for harming others. We have said that it may be appropriate to consider the reasonableness of a punitive damages award in light of the *potential* harm the defendant's conduct could have caused. But we have made clear that the potential harm at issue was harm potentially caused *the plaintiff*.

Respondent argues that she is free to show harm to other victims because it is relevant to a different part of the punitive damages constitutional equation, namely, reprehensibility. That is to say, harm to others shows more reprehensible conduct. Philip Morris, in turn, does not deny that a plaintiff may show harm to others in order to demonstrate reprehensibility. Nor do we. Evidence of actual harm to nonparties can help to show that the conduct that harmed the plaintiff also posed a substantial risk of harm to the general public, and so was particularly reprehensible — although counsel may argue in a particular case that conduct resulting in no harm to others nonetheless posed a grave risk to the public, or the converse. Yet for the reasons given above, a jury may not go further than this and use a punitive damages verdict to punish a defendant directly on account of harms it is alleged to have visited on nonparties.

Given the risks of unfairness that we have mentioned, it is constitutionally important for a court to provide assurance that the jury will ask the right question, not the wrong one. And given the risks of arbitrariness, the concern for adequate notice, and the risk that punitive damages awards can, in practice, impose one State's (or one jury's) policies (*e.g.*, banning cigarettes) upon other States — all of which accompany awards that, today, may be many times the size of such awards in the 18th and 19th centuries — it is particularly important that States avoid procedure that unnecessarily deprives juries of proper legal guidance. We therefore conclude that the Due Process Clause requires States to provide assurance that juries are not asking the wrong question, *i.e.*, seeking, not simply to determine reprehensibility, but also to punish for harm caused strangers.

■ NOTES AND QUESTIONS

1. This case arose outside of the employment discrimination context. Would it have any possible impact on employment discrimination claims?

2. The plaintiff here was not allowed to argue for an enhanced punitive damages award based on harm caused to third parties. If an employer discriminated against many individuals in the workplace, but only one brought suit, would that individual be prohibited from arguing that the employer's overall conduct warranted a greater punitive damages award?

3. The Court here maintains that allowing punishment for harm to third parties "would add a near standardless dimension to the punitive damages equation." Do you agree?

4. The Court allows the use of third-party harm to show "reprehensibility." How could a worker show that an employer's conduct toward third parties was reprehensible?

5. In one sexual harassment and retaliation case, a federal jury returned a verdict for over $20 million to eight former employees of a Florida vacation agency, an award that was later reduced to comply with the statutory caps. The female employees were exposed to egregious sexual harassment daily, including unwelcome advances, touching, constant propositions for sex, and power imbalances between the female and male employees. The EEOC attorney who litigated the case noted that the punitive damages award was justified because the women were exposed to unimaginably adverse conditions that greatly affected both their work and personal lives. *See* Press Release, EEOC, EEOC Wins Jury Verdict of More Than $20 Million for Sexual Harassment and Retaliation (May 1, 2013), http://www.eeoc.gov/eeoc/newsroom/release/5-1-13a.cfm.

 Interactive Problem

Looking back at the facts of the interactive problem at the beginning of the chapter, assume that there is evidence that many of Wendy's co-workers were discriminated against on the basis of their sex, but none brought suit. Could Wendy use this evidence to argue for a larger punitive damages award against the company?

Practice and Procedural Tip   **28: Ratios and Punitive Damages**

In *State Farm Mutual Automobile Insurance Co. v. Campbell*, the Supreme Court considered the issue of the ratio of punitive damages to actual harm. The Court concluded that "[s]ingle-digit multipliers are more likely to comport with due process, while still achieving the State's goals of deterrence and retribution, than awards with [much higher] ratios." 538 U.S. 408, 425 (2003). Like *Philip Morris*, the *State Farm* decision arose outside of the employment discrimination context, and there is thus a substantial question as to the extent to which this case applies to Title VII. The federal courts have yet to issue any unified guidance of the issue. For example, the Second Circuit has held that "[a]n award of actual or nominal damages is not a prerequisite for an award of punitive damages in Title VII cases." Cush-Crawford v. Adchem Corp., 271 F.3d 352, 357 (2d Cir. 2001). By contrast, the First Circuit has concluded that a "punitive damages award must be vacated absent either a compensatory damages award, or a timely request for nominal damages, on the federal claims." Kerr-Selgas v. Am. Airlines, Inc., 69 F.3d 1205 (1995).

Whether a "single-digit" ratio should apply to cases brought under Title VII will dramatically impact the amount of damages to which a plaintiff may be entitled. Typically speaking, if a court is willing to consider the "ratio" argument, that court will compare the amount of punitive damages awarded in a case to the amount of actual damages awarded. These "actual" damages will include not only compensatory damages, but other damages such as backpay. An argument can be made, however, that (consistent with the Second Circuit's decision above) such ratios are inapplicable to Title VII cases. Most notably, the Supreme Court case law in this regard examines whether excessive ratios run afoul of the due process component of the Constitution. In Title VII claims, however, employers have received sufficient notice that if they discriminate, they can be subjected to compensatory and punitive damages of $300,000.

Punitive damages awards can raise interesting practical and procedural issues in Title VII cases. The outcome of these questions depends largely on the jurisdiction where the suit is brought, and many of these issues are still evolving in the federal courts. *See generally* Joseph A. Seiner, *Punitive Damages, Due Process, and Employment Discrimination*, 97 Iowa L. Rev. 473 (2012).

G. Other Damages

Title VII provides for various damages other than those discussed in this chapter. These other forms of relief tend to be equitable. Courts routinely impose numerous sanctions on employers, including requiring them to "provide anti-discrimination training, prohibiting the continuation of certain discriminatory practices, requiring new hiring practices to remedy past discrimination, and removing damaging information from an employee's file." Sandra Sperino, *The New Calculus of Punitive Damages for Employment Discrimination Cases*, 62 Okla. L. Rev. 701, 707 (2010). Thus, Title VII authorizes far more than simply monetary relief, and it is not uncommon for the courts to impose training requirements, hiring requirements, or other forward-looking relief in a particular case.

For example, in a case brought under the ADA (which mirrors the damages provisions of Title VII), the EEOC obtained widespread injunctive relief against American Tool & Mold, LLC (ATM). The federal district court judge in the case required the company "to conduct a functional job analysis and create written job descriptions for each position subject to a post-offer medical examination. ATM must also ensure that any third-party medical contractors it uses for post-offer medical examinations conducts them in a manner consistent with the ADA. Finally, ATM must report to the EEOC twice a year concerning individuals not hired or terminated as a result of employment medical screenings and people who make complaints of disability discrimination." *See* Press Release, EEOC, Court

Enters Permanent Injunction Against American Tool & Mold in EEOC Disability Case (May 20, 2014), http://www.eeoc.gov/eeoc/newsroom/release/5-20-14.cfm. This type of injunctive relief is fairly common in a case where the plaintiff prevails in a claim brought under one of the employment discrimination statutes.

 Interactive Problem

Looking back at the facts of the interactive problem at the beginning of the chapter, what types of non-monetary, equitable relief would be appropriate in this particular case? What types of injunctive relief would Wendy want to seek in her particular case?

 # H. Liquidated Damages and the ADEA

This chapter has focused almost exclusively on the damages authorized under Title VII. The ADA largely adopts the damages requirement of this statute as well. *See* EEOC v. Waffle House, Inc., 534 U.S. 279, 285 (2002) ("Congress has directed the EEOC to exercise the same enforcement powers, remedies, and procedures that are set forth in Title VII of the Civil Rights Act of 1964 when it is enforcing the ADA's prohibitions against employment discrimination on the basis of disability."). The ADEA, however, provides for a different form of relief. Most notably, the ADEA does not contain any provision for compensatory or punitive damages. Instead, the age act allows for liquidated damages. Liquidated damages provide a "doubling" of the backpay due to the employee. Front pay is not included in the "doubling" of the award. These liquidated damages are only available in cases where there has been a "willful" violation. "[L]iquidated damages are defined by the statute as a sum equal to the amount owing, which includes unpaid wages or unpaid overtime compensation. In effect, therefore, liquidated damages double the back-pay award." Justin A. Walters, Note, *Drawing a Line: The Need to Rethink Remedies Under the Age Discrimination in Employment Act*, 2012 U. ILL. L. REV. 255, 261.

Like Title VII claims, the ADEA also allows awards of backpay, front pay (or reinstatement), as well as attorneys' fees. 29 U.S.C. § 626(b) (ADEA remedies provision). Thus, the key distinction between the two statutes is the availability of liquidated damages, as opposed to compensatory or punitive relief. As noted, this liquidated relief doubles the amount of the backpay award where the employer's violation is willful.

Though it may seem as though Title VII is far more generous than the ADEA when it comes to the question of damages, this is not actually the case. It is true that Title VII permits compensatory and punitive damages, where the ADEA does not. However, empirically speaking, ADEA cases often yield larger financial rewards. This is likely because older workers at the end of their career are often making more than younger workers, making these cases a higher dollar proposition. A doubling of backpay in these instances — with no statutory cap — can make age discrimination cases very profitable for successful plaintiff attorneys. *See generally* Joseph A. Seiner, *The Failure of Punitive Damages in Employment Discrimination Cases: A Call for Change*, 50 WM. & MARY L. REV. 735 (2008).

I. Attorneys' Fees

In addition to reinstatement, front pay, backpay, compensatory damages, and punitive damages, an important remedy under Title VII is the ability to recover reasonable attorneys' fees. Because prevailing plaintiffs are awarded attorneys' fees, employers who lose a discrimination lawsuit may be responsible not only for monetary damages, but for a sizable amount of legal fees as well. This remedy subjects the losing party to the costs of the reasonable legal services rendered by the opposing side. One court has even suggested that employers may be responsible for paying a plaintiff's attorneys' fees when the case has not proceeded to trial. *See* Smith v. Thomas, 725 F.2d 354 (5th Cir. 1984) (holding that plaintiff is considered a prevailing party entitled to attorneys' fees where defendant abandoned its efforts to terminate the plaintiff and did not oppose a temporary restraining order under which plaintiff returned to work). While prevailing plaintiffs are entitled to attorneys' fees, prevailing defendants can be entitled to attorneys' fees as well. However, "an employer must not only be the prevailing party, but must show that the . . . employee's claim was frivolous" in order to be entitled to fee recovery. *See* Corporate Counsel's Guide to Legal Aspects of Employee Handbooks and Policies § 22:6 (Thomson Reuters ed., 2014).

A prevailing party in a Title VII action is therefore authorized under the statute to seek attorneys' fees. The statute provides that under Title VII,

> the court, in its discretion, may allow the prevailing party, other than the Commission or the United States, a reasonable attorney's fee (including expert fees) as part of the costs, and the Commission and the United States shall be liable for costs the same as a private person.

42 U.S.C. § 2000e-5(k).

Thus, reasonable attorneys' fees are available to both employers and employees in a given case, depending upon which side is the "prevailing party." This determination is not always clear cut, and the question of whether a particular party "prevails" can also be a question for the courts. *See, e.g.,* Spencer v. Wal-Mart Stores, Inc., 469 F.3d 311, 318 (3d Cir. 2006) ("In an employment discrimination case . . . [t]he prevailing party can be either the plaintiff or the defendant. The former must "'succeed on any significant issue in litigation which achieves some of the benefit . . . sought in bringing suit.'"") (quotation and internal citations omitted). As a general rule, "a plaintiff must substantially prevail on a 'significant claim' pertaining to the lawsuit; otherwise the court will limit the award commensurate with the plaintiff's success on the claim." *Sexual Discrimination Claims Under Title VII of the Civil Rights Act of 1964*, 12 Geo. J. Gender & L. 577, 603 (Frances Cheever & Jina Moon eds., 2011).

Similarly, which fees are "reasonable" can also be the subject of debate. Generally speaking, the district court will be in the best position to assess the reasonableness of a given fee request, as it has overseen the course of the parties' litigation in the matter.

The attorneys' fee provision has often been criticized as insufficient in its ability to allow access to justice to low-income workers. Attorneys' fees are not always awarded in employment discrimination cases, and the provision is not adjusted to reflect the risk of loss. Only the prevailing party is entitled to this form of relief.

For these reasons, and others, low-income workers may have difficulty securing adequate representation in employment discrimination cases.

Class Exercise: Litigation to "Make a Point"

Assume that you represent the plaintiff in a race discrimination suit brought under Title VII against a major employer. Though the plaintiff in the case was terminated, she quickly secured other employment for much higher pay. The defendant in the case has offered $50,000 to make it "go away." The plaintiff is offended, however, and wants to see the case through trial to "make a point" that discrimination should never be tolerated. How would you advise this client? How would your understanding of the damages available in a Title VII case potentially affect your advice?

J. Chapter-in-Review

The relief available in the various employment discrimination statutes can be confusing. The litigants and courts often struggle with how and when to apply these damages. The chart below highlights and summarizes the remedies available under the various federal employment discrimination laws, emphasizing the differences in Title VII, ADA, and ADEA cases.

DAMAGES

Title VII/ADA	**ADEA**

• Backpay
  – from date unlawful conduct occurs to date of judgment
	• Backpay
	  – from date unlawful conduct occurs to date of judgment

• Reinstatement (preferred remedy)	• Reinstatement (preferred remedy)

• Front Pay
  – only available where reinstatement is unavailable
  – from date of judgment to unspecified date in future
	• Front Pay
	  – only available where reinstatement is unavailable
	  – from date of judgment to unspecified date in future

• Compensatory Damages
  – subject to caps, not to exceed $300,000 with punitives
	• Liquidated Damages
	  – double backpay for willful violations

• Punitive Damages
  – subject to caps, not to exceed $300,000 with compensatory damages
  – subject to good faith defense of employer
	• Attorney's Fees and Costs

• Attorney's Fees & Costs	

RED TEXT DENOTES DIFFERENCES BETWEEN STATUTES

Figure 12.2

PART FIVE

Best Practices

Handling Employment Discrimination Claims: Best Practices

13

 ## Interactive Problem

Sarah Secretary works as an administrative assistant for a large software manufacturer — Computers-R-Us. After several years of successful employment at the company, she begins dating her co-worker, Peter Programmer. The couple decides to keep their relationship quiet, because they are aware of the company's "no-dating policy," which prohibits employees from entering into a romantic relationship with other workers.

Ned Nosey, Sarah's direct supervisor, routinely listens in on Sarah's phone conversations and monitors her computer communications. Opening up a file on her computer marked "Personal Information," Ned discovers that Sarah has been dating Peter for several months. He immediately calls Sarah into his office, and notifies her that she will be suspended for a week without pay for violating the company's no fraternization policy. Sarah pleads with Ned to go easy on Peter, to which Ned responds, "That's no problem at all — we are mainly concerned with women engaging in this type of unethical behavior. You can't really blame Peter — he's just being a typical guy."

Does the company's no-dating policy violate federal law? If so, how should Sarah go about complaining?

A. Introduction

This book has thus far provided a comprehensive review of the laws that comprise federal employment discrimination. As we have seen, these laws are complex and span several statutes, each with its own nuances. The law also varies by jurisdiction, as the courts differ on how they choose to apply the various statutory and regulatory provisions. There can be no doubt, then, that these laws are complex both in theory and in application.

There is more to the practice of labor and employment than the law, however. While the law certainly provides guidelines to attorneys and the parties, it also has its limitations. Indeed, most corporate clients will expect not only to prevail in a lawsuit under the applicable laws, but also to avoid litigation altogether. This is not to say that it is possible to avoid run-ins with the law completely. Nonetheless, careful attention to detail can maximize a party's likelihood of success should litigation occur.

In this regard, this section looks beyond the applicable law and examines the "best practices" that currently exist in the employment discrimination area. These practices include the generally accepted policies and procedures for addressing a discrimination claim. Indeed, best practices often become implicated in a given situation long before litigation is ever contemplated. Dealing with employees in an equitable and well-considered manner is the key to avoiding a lawsuit. Following the best practices in this area will help a company to prevail even where litigation does occur.

This chapter explores several critical areas where employers and employees can follow a best practices approach to optimize their positions. The best practices identified cover a range of different areas, both pre- and post-litigation. It is important to note, however, that this list is not (nor is it intended to be) exhaustive in nature. Rather, this chapter identifies a few critical concepts to consider, in hopes of spurring further discussion of different topics and issues. The instructor — and students — will likely be able to identify numerous other areas where standard procedures can be adopted to better achieve the result an employee or employer desires. To the extent these additional areas are identified, you should feel comfortable raising and discussing other approaches that employers and employees can use to establish a more positive working environment.

This chapter breaks the discussion down into two primary areas. First, it explores various "best practices" that employees should follow in the discrimination field. Next, this chapter examines the policies and procedures that employers should follow in this area. Finally, it should be noted that the best practices suggested here are merely guidelines. Through knowledge and experience, some attorneys might disagree with the basic methodologies offered. What is important, however, is that employers and employees begin to consider the optimal approach to the employment relationship *before* litigation enters into the equation.

B. The Employee

A variety of workplace issues can arise that the employee — and her attorneys — should be prepared to handle. These issues vary in time and scope, and can arise in many different factual scenarios. Workplace questions can be presented before the employment relationship ever begins, and can also occur throughout one's employment. Even after an individual separates from her position, numerous other issues can come into play. This section of the text looks at a few of the common questions that employees face, and explores the best way for workers to address these situations.

1. When to Complain of Discrimination

It can be quite perplexing for a worker to determine when — and if — she should complain of discrimination. The timelines discussed in this book provide some of the more definite guidelines:

- As a general matter, workers have 180 calendar days to file a discrimination charge with the EEOC. This timeline is extended to 300 days if a state or local agency is also present in the jurisdiction where the discrimination occurs. The vast majority of states have some type of local agency in place.
- It is important to note that these deadlines apply primarily to private sector workers. Different rules thus apply to government workers. For example, federal employees have only 45 days to contact an EEOC counselor at the agency.
- Irrespective of these deadlines, from a best practices standpoint, workers should file a discrimination charge as soon as they determine that this is the best course of action to pursue. Waiting to file is generally not beneficial.
- It is also important for workers to recognize that if they are attempting to resolve the allegations more informally (through mediation, arbitration, or a grievance procedure), the time limits will not be tolled or extended. Workers should thus make sure that they are not lulled into a sense of complacency, inadvertently missing the charge filing deadline.
- With the exception of continuing violations (such as harassment), the 180/300-day deadline applies to each independent discrete act of discrimination. Thus, where multiple discriminatory events have taken place, the employee must file a charge for each separate event.
- From a best practices standpoint, it is best to make certain that the charge is actually received by the agency within the 180/300-day window, usually by physical receipt or some other tracking mechanism. It is best not to rely on the "mailbox rule" if possible.

These general guidelines can be very useful when employees are attempting to navigate the charge filing process. Nonetheless, there can be times where ambiguity is still present. It is not always obvious when an actual discriminatory event has occurred. The courts have also added to this confusion. *See* EEOC, Time Limits for Filing a Charge, http://www.eeoc.gov/employees/timeliness.cfm. The case below looks at the question of when an employee should complain of perceived harassment.

Jordan v. Alternative Resources Corp.
458 F.3d 332 (4th Cir. 2006)

Niemeyer, Circuit Judge.

In his complaint, Jordan alleges that in October 2002, he was employed jointly by ARC and IBM in Montgomery County, Maryland, because of the business relationship between the companies. He had entered into an at-will employment relationship with ARC in December 1998 as a network technician and, before October 2002, had been assigned to work at the IBM office in Gaithersburg, Montgomery County, Maryland. Jordan alleges that, while in the network room at IBM's office on October 23, 2002, he heard his co-worker, Jay Farjah, who was watching television, exclaim — not directly to Jordan but in his presence — "They should put those two black monkeys in a cage with a bunch of black apes and let the apes f-k them." Farjah was speaking to the television in response to a report that John Allen Muhammad and Lee Boyd Malvo had been captured.

Snipers Fashioned a Firing Port in Their Vehicle's Trunk. Courtesy FBI

Over a period of three weeks, Muhammad and Malvo shot 13 people in public places in the greater Washington, D.C. metropolitan area from hidden positions. They killed 10 people and seriously wounded 3. Soon after the snipers' names and a description of their car were released by Montgomery County police late on October 23, Malvo and Muhammad were arrested. Jordan and Farjah were watching this breaking news report on a television at the IBM facility.

In his complaint, Jordan states that he was offended by Farjah's statement and reported it to two IBM supervisors, Mary Ellen Gillard and C.J. Huang, explaining that he believed that Farjah should not utter racist comments in the office. After Gillard spoke with Farjah, who claimed that he only said, "They should put those two monkeys in a cage," Jordan told Gillard he was going to raise his complaint with Ron Thompson, IBM's site manager. Jordan also complained to ARC manager Sheri Mathers.

Jordan alleges that during the month following his complaints about Farjah's inappropriate statement, Gillard delayed Jordan's work shift by two-and-a-half hours and gave him additional work assignments. Jordan also alleges that Huang made a derogatory remark and gestured toward Jordan at an office Thanksgiving party. On November 21, 2002, ARC manager Mathers telephoned Jordan and fired him because, as Jordan alleges, he was "disruptive," his position "had come to an end," and IBM employees and officials "don't like you and you don't like them."

Alleging retaliatory discharge in violation of 42 U.S.C. § 2000e–3(a), 42 U.S.C. § 1981, and related state laws, Jordan sued IBM and ARC based on his claim that they fired him for complaining about Farjah's statement. IBM and ARC filed a motion under Federal Rule of Civil Procedure 12(b)(6), alleging that the complaint failed to state a claim upon which relief can be granted. While the defendants' motion to dismiss was pending, Jordan filed a motion for leave to file an amended complaint to add an allegation that after hearing Farjah's remark, he discussed it with several co-workers, and "[a]t least two of the co-workers told Jordan that they had heard Farjah make similar offensive comments many times before." The district court granted the defendants' motion to dismiss.

At the heart of Jordan's complaint is the allegation that IBM and ARC retaliated against him because he complained about Farjah's racist exclamation, made in response to a television report that the two snipers had been captured. Farjah's comment, directed at the news report, was the only time that Jordan had ever heard a racist comment from Farjah. Moreover, Jordan does not complain of any other similar statements made to him by others or heard by him in the workplace.

IBM and ARC contend that Title VII protects an employee against retaliation for opposing workplace conduct only if the employee had both a subjective belief and an objectively reasonable belief that the employer had engaged in activity that violated the discrimination statutes. The defendants argue that on the facts alleged in this complaint, Jordan's belief could not have been objectively reasonable because "a plethora of authority holds squarely to the contrary . . . [that] a single verbal incident in the workplace, no matter how racially charged, is [in]sufficient to create a racially hostile work environment." They assert that "because the law on this point is so clear, Jordan [could not] have held an objectively reasonable belief to the contrary."

Unlike other, more direct and discrete unlawful employment practices, hostile work environments generally result only after an accumulation of discrete instances of harassment. In this case, both Jordan and the defendants agree that Jordan's complaint to IBM and ARC's managers was opposition activity and that the only conceivable unlawful employment practice that Jordan could have been opposing was a hostile work environment. Thus, the question reduces to whether Jordan complained about an actual hostile work environment or, if there was not one, whether Jordan could reasonably have believed there was one.

On the question of whether Jordan was complaining of an actual hostile work environment made unlawful by Title VII, we conclude that he was not. While Farjah's comment on October 23, 2002 (or October 24) was unacceptably crude and racist, it was an isolated response directed at the snipers through the television set when Farjah heard the report that they had been arrested. Because the remark was rhetorical insofar as its object was beyond the workplace, it was not directed at any fellow employee. Moreover, it was a singular and isolated exclamation, having not been repeated to Jordan or in his presence before or after October 23, 2002. Jordan does not and cannot allege in his complaint that Farjah's comment altered the terms and conditions of his employment. Based on all that Jordan knew, Jordan concluded that the remark reflected unacceptable racism and should not have been made. And while we agree with Jordan's sentiment, we conclude that such an allegation is a far cry from alleging an environment of crude and racist conditions so severe or pervasive that they altered the conditions of Jordan's employment with IBM or ARC. The complaint does not describe a workplace permeated by racism, by threats of violence, by improper interference with work, or by conduct resulting in psychological harm.

The question of whether Jordan could *reasonably have believed* that he was complaining of a hostile work environment made unlawful by Title VII requires more discussion and must be determined through an objective-reasonableness inquiry. In this case, Jordan argues that he had an objectively reasonable belief that Title VII was about to be violated because "had [Farjah] continued, unabated, his conduct would at some point have ripened into [a] racially hostile work environment." While in the abstract, continued repetition of racial comments of the kind Farjah made might have led to a hostile work environment, no allegation in the complaint suggests that a plan was in motion to create such an environment, let alone that such an environment was even likely to occur.

When considering the facts alleged by Jordan in his complaint, no objectively reasonable person could have believed that IBM's Montgomery County office was in the grips of a hostile work environment or that one was taking shape. That is, no objectively reasonable person could have believed that the IBM office was, or was soon going to be, infected by severe or pervasive racist, threatening, or humiliating harassment. Jordan had been employed at the location for four years and had not complained of any racist or abusive incidents. On the day in question, Jordan overheard Farjah speak a single abhorrent slur prompted by — though not excused by — a breaking news report. As Jordan acknowledges in his complaint, Farjah was in Jordan's presence at the time, but he was not talking directly to Jordan or to any employee. Although Jordan could reasonably have concluded that only a racist would resort to such crudity even in times when emotions run high, the mere fact that one's *coworker* has revealed himself to be racist is not enough to support an objectively reasonable conclusion that the *workplace* has likewise become racist.

> The court seems to emphasize the "isolated" nature of the comment at issue here. Could any *single* remark ever be enough to create a hostile work environment?

Jordan's proposed amended complaint added allegations that, after hearing Farjah's comment, Jordan spoke to several coworkers and two of them referred to some similar statements made by Farjah in the past. But Jordan never experienced them, nor did he witness a workplace affected by them. From his coworkers' vague references, Jordan did not know about where or when such statements were made, or what Farjah said except that the statements were similar. There is, moreover, no allegation that any of those earlier statements interfered with Jordan's or any other employee's work performance, were complained about, or gave rise to a hostile environment at Jordan's workplace. Although these observations tended to confirm that Farjah makes racist comments, no allegation reasonably supports the inference that they were likely to recur at a level sufficient to create a hostile work environment. Jordan rests his case on the assumption that Farjah would repeat the remarks that he made on October 23 more frequently than his past history indicates; Jordan makes no allegations justifying this assumption.

Arguing for a rule that would protect virtually any complaint about a racist remark, Jordan maintains that, as a policy matter, "it is imperative that employees report harassment early" and that, in this case, he "was acting to prevent a hostile environment from arising." Employees, Jordan argues, are left in "a double bind — risking firing by reporting harassing conduct early, or waiting to report upon pain of having an otherwise valid claim dismissed."

Jordan's dilemma, that the law is inconsistent by both encouraging and discouraging "early" reporting, is presented too abstractly. Jordan overlooks the fact, which is fundamental to Title VII jurisprudence, that there is a difference between an isolated racial slur, which is always and everywhere inappropriate, and the sort of severe or pervasive conduct that creates a hostile work environment. "Title VII does not prohibit all verbal or physical harassment in the workplace." *Oncale v. Sundowner Offshore Servs., Inc.,* 523 U.S. 75, 80 (1998). Although the distinction between a racial slur and a hostile workplace may at a highly abstract level seem a difficult one for employees to manage, the distinction should not be conceived of in the abstract but rather in light of the *EEOC v. Navy Federal Credit Union,* 424 F.3d 397 (4th Cir. 2005), objective reasonableness standard, which serves to protect an employee's judgment in a close case. Objectively reasonable employees can and do recognize that not every offensive comment will by itself transform a workplace into an abusive one. Therefore it sometimes will not be reasonable for an employee to believe that the isolated harassing event he has witnessed is a component of a hostile workplace that is permeated with discriminatory intimidation, ridicule, and insult.

As the law stands, employees are not subject to conflicting incentives. Complaining employees are protected by Title VII once they have an objectively reasonable belief that a Title VII violation has occurred, and they have a reasonable amount of time in which to bring their concern to their employers' attention if they want to protect their right to sue their employers. Only at an impermissibly high level of generality, where meaningful distinctions can no longer be observed, can it be argued that the law inconsistently encourages employees to report and at the same time not to report violations, and Jordan's argument, if accepted, would lead to the adoption of a new rule that protects employees who have no reasonable belief that a Title VII violation has occurred, contrary to the statutory limits of the law. When considered in actual application, the objective reasonableness standard *protects* the reporting employee.

KING, Circuit Judge, dissenting:

My colleagues of the panel majority have today concluded that, as a matter of law, it was not reasonable for an African-American employee to think that the on-the-job remark made by his IBM co-worker — "[t]hey should put those two black monkeys in a cage with a bunch of black apes and let the apes fuck them" — warranted being reported to his employers as a potential Title VII violation. And, in the majority's view, Plaintiff Robert Jordan has not sufficiently alleged that IBM's decision to fire him for making that report was racially motivated. I disagree and write separately to elaborate on my position.

To begin with, the severity of Farjah's racially hostile "black monkeys" comment merits our consideration. It is plain that a reference to our African-American fellow citizens as "monkeys" reflects the speaker's deep hostility towards them — on the sole basis of their color. And it is equally clear that such comments constitute profound insults to our friends in the African-American community. By referring to African-Americans as "monkeys," the speaker plays on historic, bigoted stereotypes that have characterized them as uncivilized, non-human creatures who are intellectually and culturally inferior to whites. Indeed, our Court probably understated the impact of such racially charged references in recently observing that " '[t]o suggest that a human being's physical appearance is essentially a caricature of a jungle beast goes far beyond the merely unflattering; it is degrading and humiliating in the extreme.' " *White v. BFI Waste Servs., LLC,* 375 F.3d 288, 298 (4th Cir. 2004) (quoting *Spriggs v. Diamond Auto Glass,* 242 F.3d 179, 185 (4th Cir. 2001)).

> The dissent focuses more on the severity of the comment at issue. Is the statement here so offensive as to inherently create a cause of action?

In his "black monkeys" comment, Farjah openly opined that the "black monkeys" should be put in a "cage with a bunch of black apes" so that the "apes" could "fuck them." While we must endeavor to do so, our panel is scarcely qualified to comprehend the impact such a remark would have on the reasonable African-American listener. Suffice it to say that, in a single breath, Farjah equated African-Americans with "black monkeys" and "black apes," and implied a savage, bestial sexual predilection acutely insulting to members of the African-American community.

In this case, Jordan contends, *inter alia*, that IBM and ARC fired him for reporting Farjah's "black monkeys" comment to IBM's managers, and that his firing contravened Title VII. The district court ruled that his Complaint and Amended Complaint each failed to state a claim of Title VII retaliation. On appeal, the primary issue we face is whether Jordan has alleged facts sufficient to show that, in reporting the "black monkeys" comment to IBM management, he was engaged in a Title VII protected activity.

Jordan maintains that, in reporting the "black monkeys" comment to IBM and ARC, he was reasonably opposing a potential racially hostile work environment. Title VII has been consistently interpreted as prohibiting conduct that is "so severe or pervasive as to alter the conditions of the victim's employment and create an abusive working environment." *Faragher v. City of Boca Raton,* 524 U.S. 775 (1998) (internal quotation marks and alteration omitted). An employee who opposes a hostile work environment is engaged in a "protected activity" and cannot be retaliated against. [W]e have recognized that a plaintiff pursuing a Title VII retaliation claim need not show that the activity he opposed has, in fact, contravened some aspect of Title VII. Rather, he must simply have a reasonable belief that Title VII has been — or is in the process of being — violated by the activity being opposed. Accordingly, we are obliged to vacate the district court's ruling if Jordan was engaged in a protected activity when he complained to IBM, i.e., if he reasonably believed that Title VII was being contravened when Farjah made his "black monkeys" comment.

In the majority's view, Jordan is not protected by Title VII, and IBM and ARC were thus free to fire him for reporting Farjah's "black monkeys" comment. The majority's conclusion on this point, however, relies on its misapprehension of Jordan's allegations and its misapplication of the controlling legal principles. As a result, its decision has placed employees like Jordan in an untenable position, requiring them to report racially hostile conduct, but leaving them entirely at the employer's mercy when they do so.

Our inquiry must focus on Jordan, and whether it was reasonable for him to believe that Title VII was in the process of being violated when Farjah's "black monkeys" comment was made. Even if the "black monkeys" comment was prompted by a news report and not specifically aimed at Jordan or anyone else in the room, a reasonable person could readily conclude that, if not confronted, Farjah's conduct would continue unabated, altering the working conditions of IBM's African-American employees. Indeed, Farjah apparently offered no apology or explanation (such as that supplied today by the majority) to manifest any remorse or regret for having made his "black monkeys" comment. Responding to such blatant and unabashed racism in his workplace, Jordan "immediately reported [Farjah's] remark to several co-workers," and at least two of them advised Jordan "that they had heard Farjah make *similar offensive comments many times before.*" That information confirmed Jordan's initial concerns, thereby providing substantial (and ample) support for his reasonable conclusion that African-American workers at IBM's facility were regularly exposed to conduct akin to the "black monkeys" comment, and that such conduct would continue unless Farjah was confronted.

In the majority's view, the information provided by Jordan's co-workers, coupled with the "black monkeys" comment, did not allow Jordan to reasonably believe that Farjah's conduct would be repeated. As the majority sees it, a reasonable person could not make heads or tails out of what his co-workers meant because (1) Jordan had not experienced the other comments personally, and (2) he "did not know about where or when such statements were made, or what Farjah said except that the statements were similar." Taking the co-workers' reports at face value, however, nothing was vague — Farjah had openly referred to African-Americans as "black monkeys," and he had made "similar offensive comments many times before." That the specific content, dates, and conditions of Farjah's earlier offensive remarks may not have been communicated to Jordan is beside the point. The reasonable employee — like Jordan, an

African-American — would have no need to question his co-workers to determine that Farjah had previously voiced racially hostile comments, and that he was likely to continue doing so. Accepting Jordan's allegations as true, he possessed an objectively valid basis for believing that Farjah had made comments of "similar offens[e]" to his "black monkeys" comment "many times before." Jordan was thus entitled to conclude that what he had witnessed and heard in the television room was simply "par for the course."

Next, as a matter of law, I do not subscribe to the majority's view that an employee lacks Title VII protection for reporting racially charged conduct, unless he has "an objectively reasonable belief that a violation is actually occurring." On this point, the majority implies that the employee cannot meet that burden without allegations that "a plan was in motion to create [a hostile work] environment." This position is simply incorrect, for at least two reasons. First, requiring an employee to show that a hostile work environment was being planned imagines a fanciful world where bigots announce their intentions to repeatedly belittle racial minorities at the outset, and it ignores the possibility that a hostile work environment could evolve without some specific intention to alter the working conditions of African-Americans through racial harassment. Second, and relatedly, it fails to take into account the cumulative nature of a hostile work environment, and is thus at odds with the broad application of Title VII's anti-retaliation provision prescribed by the Supreme Court.

By opposing racially charged conduct that he reasonably believes could be part and parcel of a hostile work environment, a reporting employee has opposed the impermissible whole, even absent an independent basis for believing the conduct might be repeated. Only a tortured reading of Title VII can validate the proposition that an employee who has taken a step necessary to avoid complicity in a Title VII violation has not "opposed any practice made an unlawful employment practice." § 2000e–3(a).

Without question, Farjah's "black monkeys" comment is the stuff of which a racially hostile work environment is made. *See White v. BFI Waste Servs., LLC,* 375 F.3d 288 (4th Cir. 2004) (recognizing pervasive use of terms including "boy," "jigaboo," "nigger," "porch monkey," "Mighty Joe Young," and "Zulu warrior" created triable issue of fact on hostile work environment claim); *Spriggs v. Diamond Auto Glass,* 242 F.3d 179 (4th Cir. 2001) (same for repeated use of racial slurs, including "niggers," "monkeys," and "black bitch"). On the allegations here, it was entirely reasonable for Jordan to believe that, in reporting the racially charged "black monkeys" comment to his employers, he was opposing a racially hostile work environment. IBM and ARC nonetheless fired him — for simply reporting this outrageous comment to them — and they thereby contravened his Title VII rights.

As a result of today's decision, employees in this Circuit who experience racially harassing conduct are faced with a "Catch-22." They may report such conduct to their employer at their peril (as Jordan did), or they may remain quiet and work in a racially hostile and degrading work environment, with no legal recourse beyond resignation.

■ NOTES AND QUESTIONS

1. The majority concludes that no reasonable person could have believed that Jordan was subjected to a hostile work environment. Is this an accurate assessment of the situation? Does it place too high a burden on the average person's understanding of the law?

2. Would the average person believe that the "black monkeys" comment was bad enough to warrant a complaint to human resources or management?

3. The majority found it important that the racist remark here was "not directed" at the employee. Is this an important fact in the case?

4. From a policy standpoint, does this decision discourage "early" reporting? Shouldn't employers be encouraged to uncover and correct this type of offensive behavior before it becomes more problematic?

5. The dissent maintains that this decision "place[s] employees who experience racially discriminatory conduct in a classic 'Catch-22' situation." *Jordan*, 485 F.3d at 349. In what way has a Catch-22 situation been created?

6. In an eloquent part of the dissent omitted above, Judge King states that "Farjah's 'black monkeys' comment opened a window into his soul, revealing to Jordan a racial animus as ignorant as it was virulent. It is, in my view, entirely reasonable to believe that a person who — even in a moment of extreme frustration — equates African-Americans with 'black monkeys' and 'black apes,' and implies that they have a bestial sexual appetite, possesses a deep disdain for the entire black community and would likely repeat his offending conduct." *Jordan*, 485 F.3d at 349. Is this view putting too much weight on an isolated comment or is such a remark truly a window to someone's soul?

7. The dissent further maintains that the decision discourages employee complaints, thus foreclosing the "room for the employee cooperation the Supreme Court has just explained as being critical to Title VII's effectiveness." *Jordan*, 485 F.3d at 356. Does this decision discourage employee cooperation in preventing discrimination?

8. The case here was decided on a motion to dismiss. Should the case have at least been allowed to proceed to discovery? Why or why not?

9. In retrospect, what should the plaintiff in this case have done after hearing the racist remark? Should he have waited to complain until there were further discriminatory comments or actions? At what point would this conduct become a Title VII violation? Should a typical employee be expected to know when there is enough discriminatory conduct present to warrant a complaint?

10. Are certain words or phrases — in and of themselves — so offensive as to violate Title VII? *See* Leora F. Eisenstadt, *The N-Word at Work: Contextualizing Language in the Workplace*, 33 Berkeley J. Emp. & Lab. L. 299 (2012) (arguing that in deciding if and how to punish employees for their words, employers should consider the context in which the word was used, including the identity of

the speaker); Julie A. Seaman, *Form and (Dys)function in Sexual Harassment Law: Biology, Culture, and the Spandrels of Title VII*, 37 Ariz. St. L.J. 321, 419 (2005) (noting that the harassment must be "severe or pervasive" to violate Title VII, such that a few instances of racial slurs being uttered or mere insults alone are not violations); Eugene Volokh, *Freedom of Speech and Appellate Review in Workplace Harassment Cases*, 90 Nw. U. L. Rev. 1009 (1996) (noting that offensive words that in and of themselves do not constitute a violation of Title VII can, when considered in combination with other isolated offenses, become actionable).

11. If the individual in this case had gone to the EEOC to complain rather than complaining internally, would he have been protected under the statute?

 ## Interactive Problem

Looking back at the facts of the interactive problem at the beginning of the chapter, assume that rather than suspending Sarah for her infraction, Ned terminates her. During the meeting where Ned informs Sarah of her termination, he tells her that Peter had insisted that "making love to her was like making love to the Grand Canyon." If Sarah complained about such a comment to the human resources department, would she be protected from retaliation by Title VII? Why or why not?

Practice and Procedural Tip   29: When to Complain of Discrimination

Understanding when to complain of discrimination can be a difficult endeavor for both attorneys and workers. As the *Jordan* case demonstrates, if an employee complains too soon about a hostile work environment, she risks forgoing Title VII's protections against retaliation. Waiting to complain, however, also has risks. It may suggest, for example, that the individual does not actually object to the conduct in question.

It is important to remember that the *Jordan* case primarily addressed the issue of a hostile work environment, which is a continuing violation. In the vast majority of workplace discrimination cases, however, discrete acts are involved. There will often be less scrutiny over whether such discrete acts rise to the level of a Title VII violation. Indeed, complaints regarding demotions, transfers, or pay disparities will likely fall squarely within the ambit of the statute.

At the end of the day, plaintiffs should proceed with caution when deciding whether to file a claim of discrimination with their employer. Workers should be cognizant of the fact that if they complain too early, they may not be protected from an adverse action by their employer. In certain narrow situations, employees may want to wait until the conduct involved clearly runs afoul of Title VII before deciding to complain. In this regard, plaintiffs will want to make sure that they retain protection from retaliation.

Additionally, it is not entirely clear that all jurisdictions would reach the same conclusion as the Fourth Circuit did in this case. *See generally* Gwendolyn

Leachman, Jordan v. Alternative Res. Corp.*: The Fourth Circuit Limits Protection from Retaliation for Employees Reporting a Hostile Work Environment,* 28 Berkeley J. Emp. & Lab. L. 599 (2007); Lynn Ridgeway Zehrt, *Retaliation's Changing Landscape,* 20 Geo. Mason U. Civ. Rts. L.J. 143 (2010). Indeed, as the vigorous dissent makes clear in this case, there is certainly room for disagreement among reasonable minds. Thus, individuals should verify the law of their particular jurisdiction if there is a question as to the timing of the complaint. It also makes sense to err on the side of waiting to complain if there is any ambiguity in a particular situation. Though this may not be the best approach from a policy standpoint, it maximizes the protections available to the individual employee.

From a more practical perspective, it is also worth noting that employers should be cautious about relying too much on the *Jordan* decision. While the employer may not have been liable in this particular case, the environment created by these remarks was unfortunate. Employers that permit these types of hostile environments to persist — even where they are not actionable under the law — risk upsetting their workforce. Additionally, employers should be proactive about ferreting out discrimination and identifying hostile work environments early in the process. By being proactive in this regard, employers can help insulate themselves from liability further down the road. Monitoring the workforce and maintaining strong antidiscrimination policies can help employers to identify discrimination before it becomes actionable.

Thus, while *Jordan* does give some flexibility to employers in addressing discrimination claims, companies should be cautious and alert to discrimination or hostile work environments present in the workforce.

2. How and Where to Complain of Discrimination

It can be overwhelming for an individual to attempt to determine how to actually pursue a complaint of discrimination. The law in this area varies by jurisdiction, but there are a few fundamental principles to consider:

- It is likely best to start with the company's antidiscrimination policies. Is there a way to handle the issue informally, without bringing a state or federal entity into the picture? Employers are often unaware of the conduct in question, and an informal internal complaint can often quickly and effectively remedy the situation.
- Internal complaints at a company are often received by the human resources department, or by an individual's supervisor. Look to the employee handbook or manual to determine the preferred method of complaint.

Sometimes, complaining internally does not effectively remedy the discrimination. In some instances, it can even make it worse. Under these circumstances, a worker may want to go to his local state or federal agency to complain. When doing so, there are a few considerations to keep in mind:

- It is almost always better to file as early as possible.
- The EEOC requires that the charge be filed in person or by letter; state agencies may permit electronic filing or filing over the phone.

- Make sure to document any relevant information, and to keep any documents, emails, etc. that may be helpful to an investigator.
- It will also be helpful to the investigator if you can identify the names of relevant witnesses in the case, and the identities of any individuals involved in the discrimination. It is also important to keep close track of any dates or times of important events.
- Individuals should also keep any relevant workplace policies, employee handbooks, or other employer regulations. It can also be helpful to maintain pay records and performance evaluations.
- You should provide the EEOC with the relevant information in the case. It should be clear and concise, thus allowing the agency to determine the validity of the allegations. Basic guidelines suggest that you should provide the agency with the who, what, when, where, and why of your cause of action.
- It can also be helpful to explain to the EEOC why you believe you were discriminated against. Additionally, it can be useful to identify similarly situated individuals at the company who have been treated differently.
- It is also important to stay in contact with the EEOC, and to follow up with the agency to check on the status of your case. Also, you may still pursue internal resolution of the matter while your charge is pending.
- It may be helpful for you or your attorney to remind your employer of the prohibitions against retaliation for filing a charge with the EEOC.

Generally speaking, individuals may choose whether to file a charge of discrimination with their local state agency or with the nearest office of the EEOC. This may simply be a matter of preference to the individual, or to any attorneys who might be involved. Quick research on the internet can reveal the location of these offices. The EEOC field map can be found at http://www.eeoc.gov/field/index.cfm. The EEOC currently maintains fifty-three different field offices. It is generally best to file your claim with the EEOC office that is closest to your place of work, though you may file with any branch of the EEOC. Most likely, the charge will be investigated by the nearest office of the agency.

A sample charge of discrimination is set forth in Chapter 2, Figure 2.1 and is a simple one-page summary of the events that occurred.

Class Exercise: The Charge of Discrimination

Breaking up into small groups, prepare a charge of discrimination in a case where a female executive alleges pay discrimination. This employee maintains that the other male executives are all paid more, and that the previous two workers to hold her current job (both males) also received higher pay. What information would you include in your charge? What other information would you try to uncover?

3. Drafting the Complaint

Until recently, brevity was a valued component of filing a case of discrimination. There was little need to go into great detail about the allegations. Instead, a basic description of the claim was usually enough to survive dismissal. As Judge Easterbrook eloquently stated, "[b]ecause racial discrimination in employment is 'a claim upon which relief can be granted'. . . . 'I was turned down for a job because of my race' is all a complaint has to say." Bennett v. Schmidt, 153 F.3d 516, 518 (7th Cir. 1998).

In recent years, however, the standard for complaints seems to have become much more rigorous. As discussed earlier in this text, the Supreme Court's decisions in *Twombly* and *Iqbal* have muddied the waters for pleading employment discrimination claims. At a minimum, there is much more uncertainty on the issue of what must be included in a Title VII complaint. The empirical research in this area is mixed, and it is unclear to what extent these decisions have changed the playing field. Given this uncertainty, practical considerations may suggest that plaintiffs over-plead their case in an abundance of caution. Many individual cases interpreting the plausibility standard support this approach, as many judges have been very demanding of plaintiffs following the Supreme Court's decisions.

Mangum v. Town of Holly Springs
551 F. Supp. 2d 439 (E.D.N.C. 2008)

W. Earl Britt, Senior District Judge.

This matter is before the court on defendant's motion to dismiss plaintiff's claims pursuant to Federal Rules of Civil Procedure 12(b)(1) and 12(b)(6). Plaintiff has filed a response and defendant has replied. Accordingly, this matter is ripe for disposition. In this action, plaintiff alleges gender discrimination in the form of hostile work environment, disparate treatment, and retaliation in violation of Title VII. Plaintiff was employed by defendant from 1995 until 16 July 2006 as an administrative assistant and then as an emergency medical technician. From 16 July 2006 until 10 March 2007, plaintiff was employed by defendant as a firefighter.

After applying for a position as a firefighter with defendant's fire department, plaintiff was offered the job on 12 July 2006. Prior to accepting the position, plaintiff was told by several employees that she needed "to make sure" she knew what she was "getting into" before accepting the job as a firefighter. Plaintiff was also told that defendant's engineer for the Fire Department, Eric Wood, had said that

"he was not comfortable with Plaintiff as a female firefighter and that he would refuse to engage in a fire suppression service call with Plaintiff on his team." At the time plaintiff was offered the position as a firefighter, defendant employed 30 other firefighters, all of whom were men. Before she accepted the position, plaintiff wrote a letter to Chief Cecil Parker to complain about Wood's comments and apparent gender discrimination. Parker told plaintiff that if Wood wanted to keep his job, then he would have to fight fire with plaintiff. Parker also told plaintiff that instead of filing a discrimination complaint, she should meet with Wood "one-on-one" and say, "Hey mother f-ker . . . what problem do you have with me." Plaintiff then told Parker that if she accepted the job, she did not want to work on the "A shift" with Wood.

The following day plaintiff again talked to Parker and told him that she would be fearful for her life if she was on the same shift as Wood and was called to a fire. Plaintiff also told Parker that she heard that the other male firefighters did not want to work with her because she was female. Parker responded that plaintiff would be required to work with Wood. As a result, plaintiff informed Parker that she would not accept the job.

While typing her rejection letter, plaintiff received a telephone call from defendant's human resources director, who arranged for plaintiff to meet with both the director and Parker to discuss the firefighter position. At the meeting, plaintiff accepted the job on the condition that she be placed on the "C shift," to avoid working with Wood. Following the meeting, Parker asked plaintiff if anything was bothering her, to which plaintiff responded that she was bothered at the prospect of working in a place where "filthy and vile" words that she finds offensive are often used. During the previous 18-month period, plaintiff had already complained about the use of vulgar language by firefighters, including the words, "mother f-ker, f-ker, c-ksucker, son-of-b-ch, p-ssy, and G-damn."

Following the meeting with Parker and the human resources director, plaintiff met with the assistant town manager, Chuck Simmons, to discuss her concerns about use of foul language in the workplace. Simmons agreed that the language violated the town policy, but stated that "it ain't against the rules to be a jerk — only to use sexually charged language."

On 16 July 2006, plaintiff reported to Fire Station 1 for her first day of work as a firefighter, and was informed by Captain Jamie Holland that she would be moving to Station 2. Although most of the firefighters were assigned to Station 1, only one firefighter and one engineer were assigned to Station 2. Plaintiff alleges that other probationary firefighters were assigned to Station 1; therefore, she missed out on training opportunities, fellowship with colleagues, and advancement opportunities by being assigned to Station 2. Plaintiff also contends that defendant delayed in issuing her a gas mask and fire coat for responding to emergency calls. Wood was not disciplined for his alleged discriminatory comments about working with plaintiff, but was instead promoted to Station Supervisor.

On 27 July 2006, plaintiff again complained to Parker and the Town Manager about the habitual use of profanity by some of the other firefighters in plaintiff's presence as well as being told that she needed to "watch her back" because she had complained. Plaintiff made other complaints regarding the offensive language to Parker, the human resources director, and the Town Manager between 16 July 2006 and 15 November 2006. After complaining, plaintiff noticed that more male firefighters began using profanity in her presence. On 30 October 2006 plaintiff again complained to Parker about profanity being used while she was teaching a training class, specifically, when several firefighters fell asleep during the class, Captain Chuck Horton yelled, "wake the f-ck up" to those firefighters. Additionally, she told Parker that while teaching a different class, Assistant Chief John Jones stated out loud during a quiz, "G-damn, how do I know where this stuff is?"

On approximately 15 November 2006 plaintiff left work pursuant to the Family Medical Leave Act ("FMLA") to relieve her mental anguish over her work environment and to care for her ailing parents. Upon the expiration of her FMLA leave, on or about 1 March 2007, plaintiff resigned from her employment with defendant. On 31 July 2006 plaintiff filed a charge of discrimination with the EEOC concerning the alleged gender discrimination.

The court may dismiss any claim brought under Title VII when a plaintiff has failed to exhaust his or her administrative remedies. Prior to filing a Title VII lawsuit, a plaintiff must file a charge with the EEOC. The court may then entertain "claims stated in the initial charge, those reasonably related to the original complaint, and those developed by reasonable investigation of the original complaint." *Evans v. Technologies Applications & Serv. Co.*, 80 F.3d 954 (4th Cir. 1996). Claims that exceed the scope of this standard are procedurally barred.

When evaluating a motion to dismiss under Federal Rule of Civil Procedure 12(b)(6), the court must construe the facts in the complaint and draw all reasonable inferences in the light most favorable to the plaintiff. Federal Rule of Civil Procedure 8 requires that the complaint contain only a "short and plain statement of the claim showing that the pleader is entitled to relief." Fed. R. Civ. P. 8(a). If a claim has been adequately stated in the complaint, "it may be supported by showing any set of facts consistent with the allegations in the complaint." *Bell Atlantic Corp. v. Twombly*, 550 U.S. 544 (2007). However, the factual allegations in plaintiff's complaint "must

> As noted by the district court here, the Supreme Court's *Twombly* decision requires that the facts in a complaint rise to the level of "plausibility" to survive dismissal.

be enough to raise a right to relief above the speculative level." The claims alleged must not be merely conceivable, but must be plausible.

Plaintiff alleges that defendant violated Title VII by subjecting her to a hostile work environment. Specifically, plaintiff claims that she worked in an environment where the male firefighters used vulgar and profane words and expressed open concerns about working with plaintiff because of her gender. Additionally, plaintiff contends that defendant's failure to investigate her complaints, discipline the male firefighters, provide training programs on Title VII, and provide her with proper equipment to perform her duties as a firefighter created a hostile working environment based on her gender.

Defendant contends that plaintiff is unable to show, under any plausible reading of the facts, that the conduct complained of was sufficiently severe or pervasive to create a hostile or abusive work environment. The court agrees. To establish this element, the offending conduct must be both *objectively and subjectively* severe and pervasive to create an abusive and hostile working environment — an environment that altered the terms and conditions of plaintiff's employment. While plaintiff may subjectively believe that the offending conduct created a hostile work environment, "[c]onduct that is not severe or pervasive enough to create an *objectively* hostile or abusive work environment — an environment that a reasonable person would find hostile or abusive — is beyond Title VII's purview." *Harris v. Forklift Systems, Inc.*, 510 U.S. 17, 21 (1993) (emphasis added). The court looks to the totality of the circumstances in making this determination, including the frequency and severity of the offending conduct, whether plaintiff was physically threatened or humiliated or merely subjected to an offensive utterance, and whether the conduct unreasonably interferes with plaintiff's work performance. The purpose of this standard is to "filter out complaints attacking the ordinary tribulations of the workplace, such as the sporadic use of abusive language, gender-related jokes, and occasional teasing." *Faragher v. City of Boca Raton*, 524 U.S. 775, 788 (1998) (citations omitted). Further, "the conduct must be extreme to amount to a change in the terms and conditions of employment." *Id.*

Here, plaintiff's complaint regarding the male firefighters not wanting to work with her is based on hearsay comments of other individuals and not actual comments by the male firefighters directed to her. Additionally, the vulgar and profane language that plaintiff complains of may have been uncivilized and unprofessional, but it does not create an objectively hostile work environment under Title VII. The language was not gender specific nor was it even spoken to plaintiff. This court does not have a duty to regulate civility in the workplace. *Oncale v. Sundowner Offshore Servs. Inc.*, 523 U.S. 75, 81 (1998). Further, although plaintiff contends that the vulgar language was sexually charged, "workplace harassment" between men and women is not automatically considered gender discrimination "merely because the words used have sexual content or connotations." Although plaintiff subjectively feared that her life would be in danger if she were to respond to a fire emergency with her male counterparts, there is no concrete evidence to support that contention, only hearsay. Plaintiff was not physically threatened and there is no indication that plaintiff's work performance suffered. Finally, plaintiff's complaints about defendant's failure to investigate her complaints, discipline male firefighters, provide training, and provide plaintiff will proper equipment do not rise to the level of an objectively hostile work environment. Plaintiff's work environment, while perhaps unpleasant, is simply not a situation that an objectively reasonable person would find hostile or abusive such that it altered the terms of plaintiff's employment.

Because plaintiff has not alleged facts that, if true, would establish the third element of her claim under any plausible reading of her complaint, the court need not address the other elements. The facts plaintiff has alleged simply do not rise to the level of unlawful gender discrimination based on hostile work environment in violation of Title VII, and defendant's motion to dismiss with respect to this claim will be granted.

■ NOTES AND QUESTIONS

1. Does the court here apply too rigid a plausibility standard to the case?

2. Does the court make too many assumptions here of the evidence? Should the case at least be allowed to proceed to discovery?

3. What information could the plaintiff have alleged that would have allowed her to prevail on this motion?

4. In this case, the plaintiff alleges that she was told that other firefighters did not want to work with her because of her sex. There was also a specific threat to her safety and an articulated reluctance to help her in an emergency situation. Finally, the workplace was permeated with sexually derogatory comments, including use of the terms "mother f-ker, f-ker, c-ksucker, son-of-b-ch, p-ssy, and G-damn." Looking back at the sexual harassment standards set forth in previous chapters, is this evidence sufficient to survive a motion to dismiss? Is there a plausible argument that a hostile work environment exists under these facts?

5. The court dismissed the complaint here because the conduct was not directed at the plaintiff. Is this true? Is this asking too much of the plaintiff prior to any discovery in the case? Is the specific threat enough to overcome this hurdle?

6. Even assuming this case was properly dismissed, how should the fire department treat the situation? Even though it prevailed on this claim, would it want to take any steps to alter the workplace environment?

7. Does the test articulated by the court here for surviving dismissal demand more than the test set forth by Judge Easterbrook earlier in this chapter? How much more is being demanded here than simply stating, "I was turned down for a job because of my race"?

8. A related issue that arises when drafting a complaint is what other claims, in addition to employment discrimination, the plaintiff wants to plead. *See* Timothy P. Glynn, *The Limited Viability of Negligent Supervision, Retention, Hiring, and Infliction of Emotional Distress Claims in Employment Discrimination Cases in Minnesota*, 24 WM. MITCHELL L. REV. 581, 632–633 (1998) (concluding that supplemental claims like "[n]egligent supervision, negligent retention, negligent hiring, and negligent infliction of emotional distress" . . . "are only viable in discrimination cases involving severe forms of harassment — namely, acts rising to the level of an assault, battery, or other physically threatening conduct").

9. **Historical note.** Following the *Twombly* and *Iqbal* decisions both houses of Congress introduced measures aimed at reducing the potentially negative consequences of the new standard. Specifically, in 2009, Former Senator Arlen Specter, D-PA, introduced the Notice Pleading Restoration Act of 2009 (S. 1504, 111th Cong. (2009)), which would essentially codify the *Conley* standard — a more simplified notice pleading standard — and require that

> [f]ederal courts shall not dismiss complaints under rule 12(b)(6) or (e) of the Federal Rules of Civil Procedure, except under the standards set forth by the Supreme Court of the United States in Conley v. Gibson, 355 U.S. 41 (1957).

The House of Representatives introduced the same measure, known as the Open Access to the Courts Act of 2009 (H.R. 4115, 111th Cong. (2009)). However, neither proposal ever made it out of committee. *See* Angela K. Herring, Note, *Untangling the* Twombly-McDonnell *Knot: The Substantive Impact of Procedural Rules in Title VII Cases,* 86 N.Y.U. L. Rev. 1083 (2011).

 ## Interactive Problem

Looking back at the facts of the interactive problem at the beginning of the chapter, how could Sarah Secretary draft a complaint alleging Title VII disparate treatment? How would you argue that such a complaint survives the plausibility test? How would you argue that it does not?

The federal courts have struggled with how to apply the Supreme Court's plausibility standard. In the decision below, the Seventh Circuit Court of Appeals addresses this issue in an employment discrimination case considered shortly after the *Twombly* decision.

EEOC v. Concentra Health Services, Inc.
496 F.3d 773 (7th Cir. 2007)

Cudahy, Circuit Judge.

In 2003, Charles Horn filed a charge of discrimination with the Equal Employment Opportunity Commission (EEOC). In it he alleged that, while working as an Assistant Center Administrator for Concentra Health Services, Inc. (Concentra) in August 2001, he discovered that his supervisor and another employee were having a sexual affair. In April 2002 Horn further learned that the supervisor was giving the employee preferential treatment because of this relationship. The charge stated that on April 25, 2002, Horn reported the situation to Concentra's brass. Concentra allegedly responded by, among other things, firing Horn on a pretext.

The EEOC investigated Horn's charge and sued Concentra under Title VII of the Civil Rights Act of 1964. Its terse complaint alleged that Concentra had retaliated against Horn because he "opposed [a] practice made an unlawful employment practice" by Title VII, in violation of 42 U.S.C. § 2000e–3(a). The complaint also laid out the broad details alleged in Horn's charge: Horn reported to Concentra's Director of Human Resources that "his female supervisor gave a male subordinate, with whom she was having an inappropriate sexual relationship, preferential treatment over similarly situated employees with respect to his employment," and Concentra responded by firing Horn.

The district court granted Concentra's motion to dismiss the complaint for failure to state a claim upon which relief can be granted. It reasoned that employees are protected against retaliation only when they reasonably believe that the activities they oppose violate Title VII, and that it was clear at the time Horn reported the affair that favoring a subordinate because of a sexual relationship did not, without more, violate Title VII. The court concluded that, assuming Horn had believed that the affair violated Title VII, his belief was not reasonable, and that the EEOC's complaint therefore did not state a claim of illegal retaliation.

The dismissal was without prejudice and rather than stand on its complaint and challenge the district court's interpretation of Title VII, the EEOC chose to file an amended complaint that is the subject of this appeal. It differs from the original in only one respect: the seventh paragraph, which sets forth the EEOC's claim, is conspicuously less detailed and specific[:]

> Since at least 2001, Defendant has engaged in unlawful employment practices at its Elk Grove location, in violation of Section 704(a) of Title VII, 42 U.S.C. § 2000e–3(a). Such unlawful employment practices include, but are not limited to, retaliating against Horn after he opposed conduct in the workplace that he objectively and reasonably believed in good faith violated Title VII by reporting the conduct to Concentra's Director of Human Resources. Concentra's retaliation includes, but is not limited to, issuing Horn unwarranted negative evaluations and terminating him.

(Am. Compl. ¶ 7.) Thus, the amended complaint does not specify the nature of the conduct Horn reported to the Human Resources Director other than to indicate that Horn reasonably believed that it violated Title VII.

Concentra again moved to dismiss. The district court, noting that the "amended complaint is even more vague than the original," granted the motion with prejudice, offering two alternative and radically different (indeed logically inconsistent) bases for its decision. First, it concluded that the complaint did not provide sufficient notice of the nature of the EEOC's claim "because it offers only a conclusory allegation rather than offering any facts to support the claim," and more specifically because it does not "specify what conduct Horn believed to violate Title VII." Second, it concluded that Horn's EEOC charge is "central to [the EEOC's] claim" (in that a charge is a statutory prerequisite to the EEOC's suit) and consequently should be considered part of the complaint, even though it was not physically attached to the complaint. The court reasoned that because the amended complaint refers to the charge, the EEOC must adopt all of the charge's allegations and plead itself out of court again. The EEOC now appeals.

Rule 12(b)(6) permits a motion to dismiss a complaint for failure to state a claim upon which relief can be granted. To state such a claim, the complaint need only contain a "short and plain statement of the claim showing that the pleader is entitled to relief." Fed. R. Civ. P. 8(a)(2). The Supreme Court has interpreted that language to impose two easy-to-clear hurdles. First, the complaint must describe the claim in sufficient detail to give the defendant "fair notice of what the . . . claim is and the grounds upon which it rests." *Bell Atlantic Corp. v. Twombly*, 550 U.S. 544 (2007) (*quoting Conley v. Gibson*, 355 U.S. 41, 47 (1957)) (alteration in *Bell Atlantic*). Second, its allegations must plausibly suggest that the plaintiff has a right to relief, raising that possibility above a "speculative level"; if they do not, the plaintiff pleads itself out of court. *Bell Atlantic*, 127 S. Ct. at 1965, 1973 n. 14. Concentra argues in the alternative that the EEOC's complaint has failed to meet either of these requirements; we discuss the latter first.

One reason Concentra offers for affirming the dismissal of the EEOC's amended complaint is that the EEOC has pleaded itself out of court by alleging that Horn reported his supervisor's favoritism to a lover. This argument reflects a fond nostalgia for the EEOC's original complaint, which alleged those facts and was dismissed because the allegations neither constituted a violation of Title VII nor "suggest[ed]" such a violation. That original dismissal was probably correct. True, while the original complaint stressed the rejected "favoring a paramour" theory, it did not logically foreclose the possibility that some other aspect of Horn's report might have furnished a ground for relief. Perhaps, as Concentra now suggests, the reported affair was not consensual but rather the result of quid-pro-quo sexual harassment. Some of our cases suggest that such a possibility is enough to avoid dismissal.

Those cases, however, are no longer valid in light of the Supreme Court's recent rejection of the famous remark in *Conley v. Gibson* from which they derive, that "a complaint should not be dismissed for failure to state a claim unless it appears beyond doubt that the plaintiff can prove no set of facts in support of his claim which would entitle him to relief." *Bell Atlantic*, 127 S. Ct. at 1968 (*quoting Conley*, 355 U.S. at 45–46, 78 S. Ct. 99). As the *Bell Atlantic* Court explained, it is not enough for a complaint to *avoid foreclosing* possible bases for relief; it must actually *suggest* that the plaintiff has a right to relief, *id.* at 1968–69, by providing allegations that

> As noted by the court, one major result of the *Twombly* decision was the abrogation of the " no set of facts" language from *Conley*.

"raise a right to relief above the speculative level," *id.* at 1965. Horn's report of a sexual affair is logically consistent with the possibility that the affair was caused by quid-pro-quo sexual harassment, but it does not *suggest* that possibility any more than money changing hands suggests robbery. Dismissal was probably correct.

But enough of this trip down memory lane; why are allegations contained in the original complaint relevant to this appeal? The original complaint was dismissed and the EEOC does not seek to resurrect it. The amended complaint does not contain the specifics of Horn's report, which the EEOC undoubtedly excluded precisely to avoid pleading itself out of court. Concentra does not contend that the bare allegations of the amended complaint's seventh paragraph fail to plausibly suggest a right to relief. Neither does it argue that the EEOC is still bound by the allegations of its original complaint, which it is not.

Concentra does argue that the EEOC is bound by Horn's EEOC charge. Concentra's argument does not work because while the defendant the EEOC sues must be named as a respondent in a charge, the facts it seeks to prove need not be listed there. The charge triggers the investigation, but "if the investigation turns up additional violations, the [EEOC] can add them to its suit"; there is no need for the EEOC's complaint to be "closely related to the charge." *EEOC v. Caterpillar, Inc.*, 409 F.3d 831, 833 (7th Cir. 2005). Given that flexibility, the charge need not be "central" to the complaint, and consequently need not be considered part of it.

In the present case, the EEOC referred to Horn's charge not to catalogue the facts it hoped to prove at trial, but only to show that "[a]ll conditions precedent to the institution of this lawsuit have been fulfilled," in other words, that a charge naming Concentra as respondent had been filed. The EEOC's considerate decision to include this fact in its complaint did not compel it to adopt the charge's statements as its own and thereby plead itself out of court.

This leaves the second ground on which Concentra urges us to affirm the dismissal of the complaint: that it fails to specify the conduct that Horn reported to the Director of Human Resources (except, of course, to say that Horn reasonably believed it violated Title VII). Rule 8(a)(2)'s "short and plain statement of the claim" must contain a minimal level of factual detail, although that level is indeed very minimal. *See Bell Atlantic*, 127 S. Ct. at 1964–65 & n. 3 (2007). The classic verbal formula is that a complaint need only be sufficiently detailed to "give the defendant fair notice of what the . . . claim is and the grounds upon which it rests." *Id.* at 1964 (*quoting Conley v. Gibson*, 355 U.S. 41, 47 (1957)) (alteration in *Bell Atlantic*). This formula captures a mood of liberal pleading that is enough to settle the sufficiency of most federal complaints, but "it isn't anything that we can use with any precision." Charles E. Clark, *Pleading Under the Federal Rules*, 12 Wʏᴏ. L.J. 177, 181 (1957–1958). "[T]o determine exactly what is 'enough'" in a rare close case, a court must attend closely to the purpose of the federal pleading rules and the guidance offered by prior decisions. *McCormick v. City of Chicago*, 230 F.3d 319, 323–26 (7th Cir. 2000).

As the EEOC asserts, "[t]he intent of the liberal notice pleading system is to ensure that claims are determined on their merits rather than through missteps in pleading." Requiring a plaintiff to plead detailed facts interferes with that goal in multiple ways. First, and most importantly, the number of factual details potentially relevant to any case is astronomical, and requiring a plaintiff to plead facts that are not obviously important and easy to catalogue would result in "needless controversies" about what is required that could serve only to delay or prevent trial. Most details are more efficiently learned through the flexible discovery process. Second, a plaintiff might sometimes have a right to relief without knowing every factual detail supporting its right; requiring the plaintiff to plead those unknown details before discovery would improperly deny the plaintiff the opportunity to prove its claim.

But a pleading standard designed to protect litigants and their lawyers from needless, counterproductive technicality is less convincingly invoked by a government agency seeking to simply step around a more informative complaint that has been dismissed for failure to state a claim. The rules do not require unnecessary detail, but neither do they promote vagueness or reward deliberate obfuscation.

In the present case the EEOC's lawyers failed to persuade the district court that the facts it originally pleaded stated a claim, so it deleted enough information to disguise the nature of its claim before the court. This gambit is not necessarily fatal to a claimant, but such obfuscation certainly does not intuitively

> The court here accuses the EEOC of engaging in "obfuscation" with its amended complaint. Do you agree?

comport with the purposes of notice pleading. A complaint should contain information that one *can* provide and that is clearly important; the EEOC has removed information that it *did* provide and that showed that its prior allegations did not state a claim. The one redeeming possibility is that the original complaint contained detail that was not easily provided or obviously helpful. In general that is not an unlikely possibility; federal complaints are more often than not prolix far beyond anything Rule 8 requires. But in the present case the EEOC's original complaint was a model of economy. The claim itself was set forth in less than a page and the critical details were contained in a single eight-line paragraph, the very paragraph targeted for excision in the amended complaint. There was no fat to trim. The EEOC should have been seriously concerned that its amended complaint sliced away the very meat of its claim.

Precedent confirms that a plaintiff like the EEOC alleging illegal retaliation on account of protected conduct must provide some specific description of that conduct beyond the mere fact that it is protected. [T]he EEOC's amended complaint fails to provide the notice required by Rule 8(a)(2); it must further specify the "conduct in the workplace" that Horn reported. [S]urely Horn must remember in some detail what he said to the Human Resources Director and must have relayed that information to the EEOC during its investigation. (Of course, as the EEOC cagily observed at oral argument, there is nothing in the complaint itself to indicate the full extent of what Horn told it, but the EEOC cannot avoid a requirement to provide limited detail simply by failing to provide it and suggesting — not even asserting! — that it cannot do so.)

[W]e are unaware of any court that has approved a retaliation complaint as stripped-down as the EEOC's; one court has merely suggested, in dicta, that it might. *See Rochon v. Gonzales*, 438 F.3d 1211, 1220 (D.C. Cir. 2006) (suggesting that a Title VII retaliation plaintiff need only allege that the defendant "retaliated against me because I engaged in protected activity"). It is rarely proper to draw analogies between complaints alleging different sorts of claims; the type of facts that must be alleged depend upon the legal contours of the claim. [T]o require a more detailed complaint in the present case is neither to adopt fact pleading nor to impose the heightened pleading required in some instances by Rule 9(b); it is only to insist upon easily provided, clearly important facts. The proper analogue for the present complaint is not a complaint alleging racial discrimination in hiring; it is a complaint in which the plaintiff withholds the basis upon which she suspects her employer acted: "I was turned down for a job for a reason forbidden by Title VII." To permit the EEOC's complaint would reward obfuscation, a perverse result.

Failure to provide fair notice should not normally warrant a dismissal *with prejudice*. Rule 8(a)(2) does not seek detail that a plaintiff cannot provide, so a plaintiff should be able to re-plead successfully. But the EEOC has not argued that the district court should have permitted a second amended complaint, so we need not address that issue. We need only affirm.

For the foregoing reasons, we affirm the judgment of the district court.

FLAUM, Circuit Judge, concurring.

I join the majority's final conclusions that the EEOC's complaint does not meet the notice pleading standards of Rule 8(a) of the Federal Rules of Civil Procedure and that the EEOC did not plead itself out of court by referring to the charge in its complaint. I respectfully disagree, however, that the complaint was insufficient under our pre-*Bell Atlantic* case law.

In my judgment, the EEOC's complaint — which alleged that Concentra retaliated against Horn because he reported a colorable Title VII violation — was sufficient before *Bell Atlantic*, as I find it difficult to distinguish from other equally sparse pleadings that this Court previously approved. Although I conclude that the EEOC's complaint would have been sufficient under this and other circuits' pre-*Bell Atlantic* case law, I am unable to share the majority's view that *Bell Atlantic* left our notice pleading jurisprudence intact. Indeed, as I read *Bell Atlantic*, the Supreme Court in interpreting Rule 8(a) required that a plaintiff plead enough facts to demonstrate a plausible claim. *Bell Atlantic*, 127 S. Ct. at 1959 ("Factual allegations must be enough to raise a right to relief above the speculative level."). Because in my view the EEOC's complaint did not meet that threshold, I concur in the majority's decision to affirm the district court's dismissal.

■ NOTES AND QUESTIONS

1. Was the EEOC's complaint specific enough to survive dismissal? What types of facts should the agency have included in its allegations to state a plausible claim?

2. Why would the government have made its complaint less specific after the first dismissal? Was it attempting to hide the ball in the case? If the Commission believed that a more detailed complaint would be stricken, why would it believe that it would eventually be able to uncover enough facts to go to trial?

3. Should the case have been permitted to proceed to discovery? What facts might discovery have revealed that would have given the EEOC a viable claim?

4. As Judge Flaum's concurrence makes clear, the court is struggling to interpret the *Twombly* decision. The Supreme Court's decision in that case came down shortly before oral argument in this matter, and this case is one of the first rulings to apply the plausibility standard to a Title VII case. Did the court properly apply that standard?

5. Do you agree with the concurrence, which indicates that the EEOC's complaint would have survived before the *Twombly* decision? If so, was it fair for the court to have dismissed the case with prejudice? Should the Commission have been given an opportunity to re-plead in light of the new case law?

30: Filing a Complaint

Filing a complaint has historically not been a challenging process for employment discrimination plaintiffs. The standard for surviving dismissal has been relatively low and plaintiffs have been permitted to proceed where "any set of facts" might reasonably support their claims. The *Twombly* and *Iqbal* decisions have changed all of this, however, and plaintiffs must now establish that there is a plausible basis to bring their claims.

What this means in practice for employment discrimination plaintiffs is a bit more complex. What plausible means to one court may not be the same as what it means to another. Thus, there is substantial ambiguity over the definition of plausibility in the civil rights context. It will likely take a number of years for district court and appellate decisions to help clarify this area of the law. In the meantime, plaintiffs should be particularly cautious when considering the information that they put into a complaint. It is currently the better approach to err on the side of inclusiveness at this stage of the proceedings. There is always the danger of "pleading one's self out of court" by alleging too much in the complaint. Nonetheless, given the uncertainty of the plausibility standard, it is probably a better practice for plaintiffs to include all relevant facts in the allegations that will help support the cause of action.

At a minimum, plaintiffs should strongly consider alleging a *McDonnell Douglas* prima facie case of discrimination. Consider the following approach:

> The proposed new pleading model for Title VII discrimination claims set forth above has five components. To be sure that the plaintiff has stated a plausible claim in light of *Twombly*, a Title VII litigant should make certain that the allegations clearly provide the following facts:
>
> 1. The victim or victims of the alleged discrimination;
> 2. The protected characteristic or characteristics of the plaintiff;
> 3. The nature of the discrimination suffered;
> 4. The approximate time that the discrimination occurred; and
> 5. That the discrimination by the employer was because of the plaintiff's protected characteristic.
>
> If a plaintiff has properly alleged these five facts, there can be little doubt that the plaintiff has stated a claim of discrimination under Title VII. Similarly, there can be no doubt that a defendant who is provided with this information will have notice of the claim and will be able to properly respond to or move to dismiss the complaint.

Joseph A. Seiner, *The Trouble with* Twombly: *A Proposed Pleading Standard for Employment Discrimination Cases*, 2009 U. Ill. L. Rev. 1011, 1047–1048. *See also* Charles A. Sullivan, *Plausibility Pleading Employment Discrimination*, 52 Wm. & Mary L. Rev. 1613, 1650–1677 (2011) (discussing plaintiffs' pleading requirements following Supreme Court plausibility decisions).

As the quoted article points out, the test and standard for proceeding with an employment discrimination case need not be onerous. The bigger challenge is making sure that all of the key elements of the claim are well supported with factual allegations. These allegations must still be taken in the light most favorable to the plaintiff and considered as true for purposes of the pleadings. The *McDonnell Douglas* factors provide an excellent framework for assuring that all of the elements of the claim are supported by the pleadings.

There will certainly be some instances where it is difficult or impossible for plaintiffs to allege all of the *McDonnell Douglas* factors. Indeed, in many cases discovery may be necessary to uncover some of this information. If this is the case, plaintiffs have little choice but to simply allege all of the information available to them and to argue that a plausible claim has been set forth in the pleadings. One developing question in this area is whether the Supreme Court's decision in *Swierkiewicz* remains good law. That decision holds that a Title VII plaintiff need not plead a prima facie case to survive a dismissal motion. The validity of that decision is still being debated in the appellate courts and the academic scholarship. *Compare* Fowler v. UPMC Shadyside, 578 F.3d 203, 211 (3d Cir. 2009) (affirming the dismissal of a complaint and holding that, to the extent that *Swierkiewicz* relies on the Supreme Court's decision in *Conley v. Gibson*, it is overruled), *with* Swanson v. Citibank, 614 F.3d 400, 404 (7th Cir. 2010) (overturning the dismissal of a complaint and noting the continued "validity of *Swierkiewicz*, which was cited with approval in *Twombly*").

Similarly, defendants should be aggressive during this period of uncertainty in seeking motions to dismiss. As the plausibility standard is still developing, there is an opportunity for defendants to have Title VII claims dismissed at an earlier stage of the proceedings. Defendants should carefully review a plaintiff's complaint and move for dismissal if one of the *McDonnell Douglas* factors is not properly alleged. The Supreme Court's recent decisions on the plausibility standard have provided defendants with an additional opportunity to prevail in workplace claims. From a best practices standpoint, then, defendants should routinely *consider* seeking dismissal based on the pleadings in the case.

4. Protecting Against Retaliation

One common concern employees often have when bringing a complaint of discrimination is fear of retaliation. For this reason, Congress gave employment discrimination plaintiffs greater protections from retaliation than it did from the underlying discrimination itself. The concern was that if plaintiffs were too afraid to bring a claim, their rights would be chilled and the statute would become largely ineffective.

From a best practices standpoint, plaintiffs must be well aware of the protections that they have against retaliation. They should further be cognizant of an employer's conduct once a discrimination charge has been filed. If an individual is represented by counsel, it may even be advisable for that attorney to remind the employer — in writing — of the prohibitions against retaliation.

The standard for retaliation is set forth in Chapter 3. Not all negative conduct will rise to the level of retaliation. Where an employer's conduct would reasonably dissuade an individual from filing a Title VII claim, that conduct will be actionable. The Supreme Court made clear that not all negative employer actions will satisfy this standard. Petty slights and other low-level conduct likely will not create such a claim.

If an individual believes that she has been retaliated against, the best course of action is often to bring the conduct to the attention of the employer. The company may have a completely innocent and viable explanation for its actions. Or, the company may simply be acting unconsciously in its treatment of the worker. Either way, simply bringing the issue to the attention of the employer is often a quick and inexpensive way of resolving the dispute. Where the employer is unable to justify its actions or is unwilling to acknowledge its misconduct, the employee should consider contacting the EEOC. It is important to remember that retaliation is a separate and distinct discrimination claim. Thus, a separate charge filing time period is involved, and the clock begins to run once the retaliatory act has occurred. An employee must make certain to exhaust the administrative process not only as to the underlying claim, but as to the allegations of retaliation as well.

Similarly, employers should take precautions to make sure that they are in compliance with the statute once a discrimination complaint has been received. Confidentiality is key in this regard, and only those who need to know the allegations should be informed. Those that do learn of the complaint should be advised not to treat the employee involved any differently. It is very common for those who have been accused of discrimination to become upset over the allegations. This is particularly true where the allegations are untrue or unfounded. Employers should be aware that, in many ways, it is only human nature to retaliate against someone who has made these types of accusations, and they must, therefore, take proactive steps to make sure that this type of retaliation does not occur. The courts are replete with cases where the underlying charge of discrimination fails, but an allegation of retaliation is allowed to proceed. *See, e.g.*, Shaver v. Indep. Stave Co., 350 F.3d 716 (8th Cir. 2003) (rejecting ADA hostile work environment claim, but permitting retaliation cause of action); Westendorf v. West Coast Contractors of Nev., Inc., 712 F.3d 417 (9th Cir. 2013) (holding that a Title VII retaliation suit could proceed despite the failure of the underlying hostile work environment claim); Lipphardt v. Durango Steakhouse of Brandon, Inc., 267 F.3d 1183 (11th Cir. 2001) (dismissing the plaintiff's sexual harassment claims but returning a jury verdict in favor of the plaintiff's retaliation claim); Farias v. Instructional Sys., Inc., 259 F.3d 91 (2d Cir. 2001) (granting summary judgment on the plaintiff's race discrimination claims but upholding the jury's award of damages for the plaintiff's retaliation claim); Forman v. Small, 271 F.3d 285 (D.C. Cir. 2001) (granting summary judgment on the plaintiff's age discrimination claim, but allowing the retaliation claim to proceed to trial).

 Interactive Problem

Looking back at the facts of the interactive problem at the beginning of the chapter, assume that Sarah files a charge of discrimination with the EEOC alleging that the company's no-dating policy violates federal law. As the EEOC begins to investigate this matter, what should the company be doing in response? Should the employer act any differently toward Sarah in the workplace?

C. The Employer

As seen above, there are a number of different issues that employees should be concerned with when facing employment discrimination. Similarly, employers should be aware of a variety of different issues that may need to be addressed in the workplace. Making certain not to violate a worker's individual rights may be difficult for employers in some situations. Formulating policies or employment practices is often more of an art than a science, and can present a potential Title VII trap for some businesses.

There is frequently no clear-cut advice that will completely insulate an employer from Title VII liability. Rather, employers are often left with efforts to survey the legal landscape and to proceed as best they can. This section will attempt to raise some of the issues that an employer may face in the workplace. A best practices approach is offered, but there is often disagreement as how best to proceed on these more difficult issues. Again, space constraints limit an examination of all the issues an employer may face. Nonetheless, some of the more common difficulties are addressed below.

While there are various policies, programs, and practices that employers can adopt and implement to limit potential liability, there is one overriding maxim that should always be kept in mind: *Nosce te ipsum*, Latin for know thyself. Employers should always remember that no single policy or practice will work for every company or workplace. A practice must be individually tailored to the particular company involved. Each workplace will have its own nuances and particular issues of concern. Employers must not get too caught up in what policies or practices are being adopted in other workplace environments. Rather, there should be an emphasis on creating an optimal environment for the particular employer in question. Workplaces and industries will vary widely in numerous aspects. No single approach to discrimination claims can be carved out across these employers. Individualization is thus key in this area.

1. Effective Employer Policies

There are numerous practices and policies that employers can implement across the workforce. These policies vary depending upon the industry involved and the nature of the issue that needs to be addressed. Whenever an employer contemplates implementing a policy, it should strongly consider any potential legal implications that may be involved. There are numerous legal concerns that can arise from a workplace policy or practice, and many of these concerns originate from the employment statutes discussed in this book. For example, as set forth in detail in previous chapters, a workplace policy or practice can have an unlawful disparate impact in violation of Title VII if it discriminates on the basis of race, color, sex, national origin, or religion.

One employer policy that should be given special consideration is an employer practice regarding dating in the workplace.

a. Dating Policies

Dating policies must be carefully reviewed by employers because of the potential these policies have to run afoul of Title VII sex discrimination law. When implementing a dating policy, employers should exercise extreme caution. Indeed, employers may want to consider whether such a policy will be beneficial for the company. The primary benefit of implementing such a policy is the avoidance of interpersonal relationships in the workplace. Such relationships can distract from employee productivity, create issues of favoritism, and even lead to sexual harassment claims. Thus, it is reasonable for companies to want to prevent these relationships where possible and to create policies in the workplace that forbid employees from dating one another.

Despite these benefits, there are substantial risks involved with implementing such a policy. Most notably, employers may be subject to a sex discrimination claim if they apply the policy more harshly to one particular sex. Even if such disparate treatment is unintentional, it can result in a Title VII claim. In many ways, adopting a no-dating policy invites this type of litigation. It is very difficult to treat everyone equally even where an employer intends to do so. Thus, where an employer does adopt a dating policy in the workplace, it must make every effort to apply the policy consistently across its workforce. Failing to do so can subject the company to a Title VII disparate treatment or disparate impact claim.

Similarly, it is unrealistic to believe that workers will not date one another simply because of the creation of a no-dating policy. Employees are working longer hours than ever, and spending substantial time with their co-workers. It is only human nature for personal relationships to develop out of these working relationships. When this occurs, employees may try to conceal their relationship from the employer. By driving the relationship underground, the employer loses the ability to monitor any wrongdoing that may occur. Thus, a supervisor may be treating an employee better because of a personal relationship that exists, yet such preferential treatment may go undetected because there is no knowledge of the relationship itself. Were the relationship to be out in the open, an employer could make sure to separate those employees who are dating. Similarly, when a personal relationship deteriorates, the employer may be vulnerable to a subsequent sexual harassment claim if the "spurned" worker attempts to get back at his or her colleague. By encouraging workers to remain silent about their relationships, then, employers may lose the ability to address issues that arise from such behavior. Any employer that believes that a no-dating policy will actually result in no dating in the workplace is likely deluding itself.

One middle-of-the-road approach is to consider restricting dating only involving supervisors and subordinates. These types of relationships can be particularly problematic as they can lead to claims of favoritism. Similarly, if problems develop in the relationship, it can spill over into the working environment. By limiting the no-dating policy to direct reports, employees will not be as afraid to reveal the relationship to the employer. Where such a relationship does exist, individuals can be reassigned to a new supervisor rather than being terminated from the company. And, when individuals do reveal an ongoing relationship to their employer, the employer can also act proactively in monitoring the environment for potential harassment or favoritism claims. The employer can also remind those employees who are dating of their responsibilities and obligations under the law. This may even include written disclosures to employees who are engaged in a relationship with one another.

At the end of the day, there is no single best approach to handling workplace dating. Employers should be cognizant that such relationships can lead to claims of favoritism and sexual harassment. An employer should craft any policy to fit the particular workplace environment. Employers can consider completely restricting workplace dating, though, as noted, this type of policy comes with great risk. A less intrusive approach is to restrict dating within the chain of command. And, employers may also contemplate not adopting any policy, and simply monitoring the workplace for disparate treatment. Regardless of which approach is adopted, however, the employer must make every effort possible to make certain that the policy is equitably applied to all workers and sexes. Finally, employers should also consider that relationships can develop within an organization from a variety of different avenues. Thus, to the extent a policy is developed, the employer should consider applying it to outside vendors, independent contractors, and others with whom the employer might do business. *See* Mindy Chapman, *No-Dating Policies: How Far Should Yours Go?*, Bus. Mgmt., May 22, 2008, http://www.businessmanagementdaily.com/18598/no-dating-policies-how-far-should-yours-go#; Chas Rampenthal, *Is Workplace Dating Really Off Limits?*, Inc. (Sept. 18, 2012), http://www.inc.com/chas-rampenthal/dating-in-the-office-is-it-legal.html.

Sarsha v. Sears, Roebuck & Co.

3 F.3d 1035 (7th Cir. 1993)

Kanne, Circuit Judge.

In December 1987, Gary Taylor, manager of the Sears retail store in Springfield, Illinois, determined that Sarsha, the store's operating manager and second-in-command, was dating a subordinate by the name of Rebecca Schaertl. The next month, after consulting the company's regional office in St. Louis, Taylor fired Sarsha for alleged "willful misconduct," specifically, dating Schaertl after being warned by his supervisors not to date co-workers. Sarsha sued, charging age and gender discrimination. He claimed that Sears had no policy or long standing practice preventing managers from dating subordinates,

and protested that he was never warned, on threat of his job, to refrain from dating a co-worker. According to Sarsha, he was discharged because of his age (46) and because he was a male; Sears did not discharge his inamorata.

The district court found, and the parties agree, that Sarsha established a prima facie case of age discrimination. The question, therefore, is whether Sarsha has created a genuine issue concerning the sincerity of the proffered reasons for his discharge.

The following is supported by the record in this case. Taylor believed Sarsha's relationship with Schaertl compromised his effectiveness as a manager and exposed Sears to potential liability in the form of a sexual harassment suit. He claims he informed Sarsha that Sears's policy prohibits relationships between staff members and employees of the opposite sex, and instructed him to refrain from such relationships. Because Sarsha refused to comply, Taylor contacted Stephen Allen, the company's regional director in St. Louis.

After reviewing [the situation], Allen consulted with Taylor and David Rich, the current regional personnel manager. They concluded that Sarsha's relationship with Schaertl compromised his effectiveness as a manager and amounted to insubordination in light of Taylor's and Zimmerman's alleged previous warnings. Taylor subsequently fired Sarsha in accordance with instructions from Rich.

Sarsha, for his part, admits to the affair with Schaertl, but contends that the true reason for his termination lies elsewhere. In attacking Sears's reason for terminating him, Sarsha argues that the company had no policy prohibiting employees from dating. Indeed, the deposition testimony of Allen, Taylor, Zimmerman, and Gordon Fifer, the Springfield store's manager from 1977–87, demonstrates that Sears does not have any written policy. Sarsha also claims the company did not have an informal policy. Fifer testified during his deposition that, during the time he was the manager of the Springfield store, he never heard of a policy pertaining to dating. In an affidavit attached to his Memorandum in Opposition to Defendant's Motion for Summary Judgment, Sarsha claims he met his second wife while they were both employed at the Springfield store and dated her openly. Indeed, Sears threw a party for the couple prior to their marriage.

Based on the record, we believe that a material issue of fact exists as to whether or not Sears has a policy against employee dating. Allen, the company's regional director, testified in his deposition that Sears's policy would permit Sarsha to have a nonsexual social relationship with a co-worker depending on "the

> **Whether the no dating policy actually existed was a critical issue in this case.**

general perception of inappropriate activity or conduct in that particular case." Zimmerman's testimony suggests the policy would allow employees to become more involved (go out on dates and perhaps engage in sexual foreplay), up to the point they were informed it was creating a problem at work. We cannot say, based on the statements of Sears's local and regional management, that the company's decision to terminate Sarsha was rooted in a coherent formal or informal policy, or even a "long standing practice," of prohibiting dating between managers and subordinates. When the existence of a uniform policy or practice is in doubt, it cannot serve as a reason for discharging Sarsha.

This does not end the matter, however, for Sears may still discharge Sarsha if, as the district court found, the record shows that he "was repeatedly taken aside and warned of the disruptive aspects of his behavior." Sarsha admits that he openly dated a Sears security guard in 1986; his boss, Fifer, knew of the relationship but apparently did not object.

Stripped down, this is a case of one party's word against the other. It is clear that whether or not Sarsha disregarded instructions to break off his relationship with Schaertl or was "repeatedly taken aside and warned of the disruptive aspects of his behavior" depends, in turn, on whether or not the testimony of Taylor and Zimmerman should be credited over that of Sarsha. Taylor and Zimmerman insist Sarsha was warned to stop dating or be fired, and that he disobeyed; Sarsha responds that he received no such warning and thus did not disobey. We cannot resolve the conflict between these two positions without deciding which side to believe. On summary judgment, a court can neither make a credibility determination nor choose between competing inferences.

We think that Sarsha has satisfied his evidentiary task. His affidavit does not rehash the facts alleged in his complaint. Rather, it describes three conversations with two supervisors over a period of roughly a year and a half. Dating was discussed during these conversations, but Sarsha contends he was never told it was a prohibited activity or he could lose his job.

The material issue in dispute, of course, is whether Zimmerman and Taylor intended in their conversations with Sarsha to bring home the point that, after the security guard, further dating would result in dismissal. The cold record does not provide the answer either way, and any doubts we have must be resolved in Sarsha's favor. We are mindful that summary judgment is particularly inappropriate for settling issues of intent or motivation, especially where, as here, the claim is brought under a statute that allows for trial by jury.

> As with many employment discrimination cases, the facts in this case are in dispute and should be addressed by a jury rather than a judge to determine whose testimony is more credible.

Taking Sarsha's allegations as true, we conclude a material issue of fact exists concerning whether or not he was warned that dating in general, or his relationship with Schaertl in particular, would result in dismissal. The evidence presented by Sears in support of its motion for summary judgment conflicts with Sarsha's version of events, and the result is a genuine dispute in this case. Disposition of the ADEA claim by summary judgment was inappropriate.

Sarsha also contends that Sears discriminated against him on the basis of his sex. The crux of his complaint is that he, but not Schaertl, was fired. According to Sarsha, if Sears had a policy forbidding a supervisor from dating a subordinate, ipso facto the policy must also forbid a subordinate from dating a supervisor. Thus, the failure to discipline or discharge Schaertl is proof of unequal treatment based on sex.

We need not tarry over this claim. Sears is entitled to enforce a no dating policy (if one exists) against supervisors, who by virtue of their managerial positions are expected to know better, rather than subordinates. This court does not sit to review a company's business judgments; unless Sarsha's gender mattered to Sears — that is, unless, under the circumstances, he would have been kept on in a management position if he were a woman — he is not entitled to relief under Title VII.

Sarsha does not allege that he has been treated differently from a similarly situated female. Moreover, he was presented no direct evidence that gender was a motivating factor in Sears's decision to fire him. His claim of gender discrimination must therefore fail.

■ NOTES AND QUESTIONS

1. This case demonstrates the difficulty that employers can face when attempting to implement a no-dating policy. Whether a policy is beneficial to the company or not, it is critical to enforce such a policy equally across the workforce.

2. This case further makes clear that a company must treat workers equally on all bases when enforcing this type of policy. While a sex discrimination claim is probably the most common to arise from a no-dating policy, we can see an age claim brought here as well.

3. It appears in this case that the company did not have a written policy in place. Is it beneficial to put such a policy in writing, or is it better to make such policies more informal (and flexible) in nature?

4. As this case demonstrates, no-dating policies can be difficult to resolve on summary judgment, as they will inherently be fact intensive in nature.

 Interactive Problem

Looking back at the facts of the interactive problem at the beginning of the chapter, assume that the company decides to terminate both Sarah and Peter for violating the no fraternization policy. Would either Sarah or Peter have a potential cause of action against the company for their termination? Is there a better way for the company to handle dating in the workplace? Would you write its policy any differently?

b. Computer/Electronic Device Policies

The dawn of the computer age, email, mobile electronic devices, and other technological advances have created dramatic changes in the workplace. Employees are now no longer bound to their desks, and the ability to communicate while outside the office has grown exponentially. Title VII, the ADA, and the ADEA were developed at a time when electronic communication was in its infancy. Thus, many of the rules and regulations prohibiting employment discrimination were put in place without any contemplation of some of the technological advances that were to come. *See generally* Helen Norton, *Regulating Cyberharassment: Some Thoughts on Sexual Harassment 2.0*, 1 Denv. U. L. Rev. Online 11 (2010) (arguing that Title VII and other existing civil rights laws do not capture and address cyberharassment's harms and suggesting that a new civil rights law is required).

Employers should consider all of the various ways that electronic media can influence its workforce. There are a number of possible ways that computer usage can lead to an employment discrimination claim. Someone might, for example, post disparaging remarks on a Facebook page that could lead to legal problems for the company. When it comes to electronic media, there is no clear-cut approach to prevent all problems from developing. Again, employers must consider their own particular workforce when determining how to monitor employee devices.

Employers cannot simply turn a blind eye to this problem. Failing to monitor the workplace can lead to claims of negligence or sexual harassment if the employer should have known of unlawful conduct. From a best practices standpoint, then, a prudent employer should develop an electronic device policy in the workplace. The contours of that policy will depend heavily on the type of company at issue and the industry that is implicated. Legal counsel can be very helpful in preparing this type of document. The employer should consider a number of different factors when putting together such a policy. First, what conduct is the employer seeking to prohibit? Will all non-work computer usage be prohibited? Or will employees be permitted to use employer-provided electronic devices for personal reasons? Second, how will a policy be communicated to employees? Will there be a uniform way of informing workers about the policy? Third, how will the employer monitor compliance with the policy? Will there be technical support that monitors the usage of electronic devices? Or will monitoring be much less formal? Finally, what will the consequences be for employees who fail to comply with the company policy? How will the employer make sure to apply this policy consistently across the workforce?

When considering the monitoring of employee devices, whether an employee works for a public or private entity may involve different questions. This may be particularly true where employers are attempting to uncover personal email or cell phone texts in the workplace. As a general rule, it will be easier for employers to monitor the electronic communications of private employees rather than public employees, though this line now appears to be somewhat blurred. *See* City of Ontario v. Quon, 560 U.S. 746 (2010). Also, employers should be cognizant of other workplace laws that can restrict the monitoring of employee computer usage. For example, companies must make sure to comply with the Wiretap Act and Stored Communications Act, as well as other state and local laws.

There are numerous resources available that discuss the best practices available for developing policies related to electronic devices. One interesting approach recommends a consideration of the following ten practices to assure proper employee internet usage:

Top 10 Best Practices to Maximize Compliance and Minimize E-Mail and Web Risk:

1. Put Acceptable Usage Policies in Writing.
2. Educate Employees About Risks, Policies, and Compliance.
3. Establish E-Mail Business Record Retention Guidelines.
4. Set Rules for Personal Use.
5. Recap Harassment, Discrimination, Ethics, Confidentiality, Security, and Other Policies.
6. Stress Compliance with Sexual Harassment Policy.
7. Address Monitoring and Privacy.
8. Enforce Content Rules.
9. Support Acceptable Usage Policies with Technology.
10. Don't Allow Employees to Dismiss Policy as Unenforceable.

See Nancy Flynn, *ePolicy Best Practices: A Business Guide to Clean and Compliant, Safe and Secure E-mail and Web Usage Content*, MESSAGELABS, 2006, http ://www.epolicyin-stitute.com/docs/ePolicyInstitute~ML~EmailBestPractices.pdf.

The potential employment implications of employee computer usage is well beyond the scope of this book. Needless to say, electronic devices now touch upon almost every aspect of the employment relationship. Nonetheless, computers, cell phones, and other electronic devices are frequently used to discriminate or harass workers. As a best practices approach, then, employers should develop policies that encourage the monitoring of electronic communications. Such policies will inherently vary from employer to employer, but all companies should keep in mind the potential misuse that can result in discrimination or harassment claims. When developing these policies, employers should make certain to consult with their attorneys or seek outside legal advice.

Cargo v. Kansas City Southern Railway Co.

2012 WL 4596757 (W.D. La. Oct. 1, 2012)

HICKS, JR., District Judge.

Stanley, an African American male, began working for the defendant, KCS, on June 28, 1998. Stanley was initially hired as a customer service representative, where his duties required, among other things, that he work daily on a computer and be knowledgeable of the KCS computer systems. KCS had specific policies governing computer use as well as policies prohibiting harassment. In October 1998, Stanley was personally counseled by KCS after sending an email containing a sexually explicit joke that violated KCS's computer use policy. Nevertheless, in September of 2000, Stanley was promoted to Assistant Manager of the Customer Service Center; he was again promoted in August 2002 to the position of Manager of Production Control in the Customer Service Center ("CSC"). This position was created especially for him and resulted in approximately a 17.5% pay raise. There were no other employees at KCS who held an identical management position.

During his tenure from June 1998 through October 2002, Stanley received a total of 4 pay raises.

As a manager in the CSC, Stanley was again required to operate a workplace computer in accordance with KCS's policy governing computer use. Additionally, KCS had policies that prohibited harassment of any kind and mandated that all employees comply with all regulations and laws. Stanley admits to having signed a written authorization confirming receipt of said rules. Stanley's knowledge of KCS's computer policy is further demonstrated by the repeated warnings he gave to co-workers that they should not be transmitting personal messages via KCS computers. Stanley also received a written notice from manager Janice McNeal reminding him of the prohibition against inappropriate emails.

During a company-wide email audit, KCS discovered that Stanley sent more than 46 non-business, inappropriate emails, many of which were sexually explicit and/or specifically directed toward a specific subordinate female employee. Despite Stanley's knowledge that his conduct violated KCS's policy, Stanley repeatedly sent sexually explicit or harassing emails. Examples of the personal, inappropriate emails sent from Stanley's workplace computer include a barrage of sexual advances toward a subordinate female employee and an email containing moving animations of cartoon characters, such as Fred Flintstone, Homer Simpson, and the Simpson children engaging in sexual acts. In fact, Stanley has even admitted the emails were "inappropriate" and "lewd" and does not dispute that his 46 emails at issue were a violation of KCS's computer use and anti-harassment policies. The moving party, KCS, has clearly shown that there is no material issue of fact as to either the content of the 46 emails or whether Stanley violated KCS's computer use and harassment policies.

It is apparent from both the statement of material facts admitted by Stanley and the parties' briefs that this claim of discriminatory discharge rests on the fourth element of the *McDonnell* framework, as there is no dispute over elements one through three. Stanley must show that other KCS employees were similarly situated yet received more favorable treatment. Stanley has failed to satisfy this requirement, as he did not provide the Court with adequate evidence to show that there is a genuine question of fact regarding whether [any of the] individuals proffered as comparators are similarly situated.

> As with any policy implemented at a company, an employer must make sure that its rules are evenly applied across the workforce.

Even if Stanley were able to establish a *prima facie* case of discrimination, KCS has provided a legitimate and non-discriminatory reason for his discharge. KCS's claim that Stanley continued to send out sexually explicit emails despite being specifically warned not to do so, remains unchallenged. Additionally, Stanley sent sexually explicit personal emails to a subordinate employee in violation of KCS's anti-harassment policy potentially exposing KCS to liability. Rule violations are legitimate non-discriminatory reasons for discharging an employee. Stanley admitted responsibility for transmitting over 46 non-business, pornographic, harassing and inappropriate emails via the KCS email system. Transmitting the sexually explicit Flintstones/Simpson email, which included cartoon characters of children engaging in sexual activity was, in itself, a terminable offense. The overwhelming number of inappropriate and/or sexually explicit emails sent in direct violation of KCS's policies and federal law more than justify Stanley's dismissal. KCS asserts that as a result of Stanley's actions, he has violated its trust in his ability to manage subordinate employees. This is further substantiated by the SBA's review of the evidence and decision to uphold Stanley's removal. Stanley has presented no evidence that his termination was motivated by anything other than his repeated and serious violation of KCS policies.

■ NOTES AND QUESTIONS

1. The court here notes that the company "had specific policies governing computer use as well as policies prohibiting harassment." How important were those policies in upholding the discharge?

2. Even assuming that the company did not have a computer policy in place, could it still have terminated the plaintiff for his purported behavior?

3. Was the plaintiff's behavior sufficient to warrant his discharge? If you were outside counsel for the corporation reviewing the behavior, would you recommend termination?

4. What type of evidence would the plaintiff need to present to prevail on this claim? How would he show that he was disparately treated based on the policy? Is it important whether or not others at the company violated the policy as well but were treated differently?

5. It is also interesting to note that the technological sector of the economy has frequently been criticized for discriminating on the basis of age. Silicon Valley is well known for having a "youth" culture that it promotes to its workforce. Indeed, the EEOC has been critical of many tech companies that advertise for new or recent grads, which may be a proxy for age discrimination. *See* Verne Kopytoff, *Tech Industry Job Ads: Older Workers Need Not Apply*, Fortune (June 19, 2014), http://fortune.com/2014/06/19/tech-job-ads-discrimination/.

6. Social media sites — such as Facebook, personal blogs, Twitter, etc. — "have become popular forums for bullying and harassment." One of the many consequences of increased cyber-bullying is that employers may be held liable under Title VII for harassment claims that result from cyber-bullying among employees. Consider an example where a disabled employee found himself a victim of cyber-bullying on a personal blog created by another employee. The disabled employee had reported misconduct on the part of some of his co-workers, and as a result the co-workers created a blog referring to the disabled employee as a "rat." Additionally, the blog posts referred to the disabled employee's disfigured right hand as "the claw" and "one blogger promise[d] to pay $100 to anyone who captured a photograph of 'the claw.'" "The posts gr[e]w increasingly vulgar" over time and, inevitably, "the cyber-bullying and harassment spread from the blog to the workplace." The disabled employee informed his employer several

times but no action was ever taken. In the end, "the employer was found liable for having knowledge of the [cyber-bullying and] harassment but failing to take corrective action." *See* Lindsay Schenk, *Employers Beware: Cyber-Bullying Could Wreak Havoc in Your Workplace*, FROSTBROWNTODD (Oct. 5, 2012), http://www.frost-browntodd.com/resources-1520.html; *see also* Paul M. Secunda, *Blogging While (Publicly) Employed: Some First Amendment Implications*, 47 U. LOUISVILLE L. REV. 679 (2009) (discussing public-sector employee's First Amendment free speech protection for their blogging activities relating the workplace).

Class Exercise: Crafting a Computer Policy

Assume that you have been brought in as a newly hired associate at a law firm to help craft an electronic communications policy for a large automobile manufacturer. Breaking up into small groups, determine how you would craft such a policy. Consider who the policy would apply to, what devices would be implicated, and how you would go about monitoring the workplace.

---

c. Antidiscrimination Policies

Antidiscrimination policies are critical for any workplace environment. Best practices suggest that all employers — regardless of size — should adopt and effectively implement a nondiscriminatory employment policy. As discussed in this text, simply adopting an antidiscrimination policy is insufficient. Employers must actively maintain and enforce these policies.

Education is also critical to any good workplace policy. The entire workforce should be trained on the meaning of discrimination and harassment, and informed of how to identify and report discriminatory behavior. Managers and supervisors should be given special attention in this regard, and those who are named in the harassment policy should also receive training on how to receive complaints and address improper behavior. Discrimination policies should be reviewed frequently to make sure that they are current and up to date. The organizational structure of the workplace changes periodically, as do management level employees. A stale policy will be largely ineffective under the eyes of the law, and employers must take care to update these provisions.

Structuring a proper antidiscrimination policy is largely dependent on the particular company and industry involved. This text has already set forth some of the key considerations employers should focus on when adopting such a policy. At the end of the day, the major consideration should be whether the particular policy fits with the company in question. Beyond this, however, there are some major issues that should be addressed by most workplace antidiscrimination policies. An acceptable policy will typically include

- multiple channels of complaint available;
- an opportunity to complain to various individuals from different areas of the company, usually including a supervisor and the HR department;

- a definition of discrimination, harassment, and protected categories;
- assurances of protection from retaliation for complaining employees;
- special attention for disability issues, including requests for accommodation; and
- a basic discussion of training and enforcement of the policy itself.

Just like all policies that are adopted in the workplace, it is critical that an antidiscrimination policy be applied equally to all workers. Failure to consistently apply these policies can also result in claims of preferential treatment and Title VII discrimination. It is important to remember that these policies should apply to all of the terms and conditions of employment, and not just to hiring and firing decisions.

Beyond providing an opportunity to ferret out and prevent discrimination and harassment in the workplace, antidiscrimination policies have numerous legal benefits that are addressed in this text. As noted, these policies can help prevent a harassment claim from being imputed to the employer through agency principles. Additionally, a good antidiscrimination policy can help an employer to avoid punitive damages for a Title VII violation. One federal court decision, *Sackett v. ITC Deltacom, Inc.*, 374 F. Supp. 2d 602 (E.D. Tenn. 2005), provided a nice summary of the various approaches that the appellate courts have used in determining whether a company's policy was sufficient:

> Other than their disagreement on the characterization of the good faith efforts prong, the courts of appeal have approached this analysis in much the same way, focusing on the implementation, rather than the mere existence, of any antidiscrimination policy. However, the circuits are not in agreement in the breadth of their evaluation of the employer's antidiscrimination efforts. Some circuits concentrate only on the facts relevant to the plaintiff's case at hand. *See, e.g.*, Hertzberg v. SRAM Corp., 261 F.3d 651, 663–64 (7th Cir. 2001) (employer did not make good faith efforts to implement its sexual harassment policy where record contained evidence plaintiff complained about gender-based harassment to her immediate supervisor, who told her she was being "too emotional," and to the manager of the plant where she worked, who "seemed to shrug it off" and did not follow company policy of putting her complaints in writing); Ogden v. Wax Works, Inc., 214 F.3d 999, 1009 (8th Cir. 2000) (jury award of punitive damages upheld where employer submitted evidence of its written sexual harassment policy and policy of encouraging employees with grievances to contact the home office, but plaintiff showed the company minimized her complaints of sexual harassment, performed a cursory investigation that focused on her performance rather than the harasser's behavior, and forced her to resign rather than discipline the harasser); Cadena v. Pacesetter Corp., 224 F.3d 1203, 1210 (10th Cir. 2000) (employer's claims of strong antidiscrimination policy and monthly employee training on its policy and relevant statutes as good faith efforts to comply with Title VII contradicted by employee testimony including clearly incorrect ideas of what constitutes sexual harassment, testimony no such training actually took place, and evidence in the record showing employer knew plaintiff was being sexually harassed but failed to take any action to stop

it); Deffenbaugh-Williams v. Wal-Mart Stores, Inc., 188 F.3d 278, 286 (5th Cir. 1999) (employer's evidence of good faith efforts was insufficient to defeat punitive damages where employer merely represented it encouraged employees to contact higher management with grievances, but plaintiff presented substantial evidence employer failed to respond to her complaints about her manager's racial animus).

Other circuits assess the employer's practices as a whole, including any prevention of and response to, or lack thereof, other claims of discrimination not involving the plaintiff or the case at hand. *See, e.g.,* Madison v. IBP, Inc., 257 F.3d 780, 795–796 (8th Cir. 2001) (although employer had a corporate policy prohibiting racial and sexual discrimination and harassment and put on an annual two-hour training session for plant managers on the "Legal Aspects of Supervision," record contained evidence these policies were not carried out at the plant at issue, where management did not investigate or remedy a substantial number of complaints of civil rights violations, failed to record reprimands for harassing conduct in employees' personnel files, and maintained policies that punished harassment victims by telling an alleged harasser the identity of a complainant and putting "counseling for sexual harassment" notations in the personnel files of any complaining employee); Romano v. U-Haul Int'l, 233 F.3d 655, 670 (1st Cir. 2000) (jury's award of punitive damages upheld where employer, although it put forth evidence it distributed materials and instructed managers regarding nondiscriminatory hiring and termination policies did not show it had any active mechanism for renewing employees' awareness of these policies and did not present examples showing antidiscrimination policies actually were followed); Lowery v. Circuit City Stores, Inc., 206 F.3d 431, 445 (4th Cir. 2000) (jury award of punitive damages affirmed although employer had disseminated antidiscrimination policy through posters, its employee handbook, and some training and allegedly had three avenues available for employees to complain about discrimination, since plaintiff showed two top executives harbored racial animosity toward minorities, buried internal reports showing the employer had a negative attitude against minorities, and took no action to remedy these issues; employees feared retaliation if they used any of the three avenues to complain about discrimination; and the employer had a subjective, unstructured promotional system instituted by one of the executives who harbored racial animosity toward minorities).

Sackett, 374 F. Supp. 2d at 616–617.

 Interactive Problem

Looking back at the facts of the interactive problem at the beginning of the chapter, assume that Computers-R-Us does not currently have any policies or procedures that expressly prohibit discrimination or harassment in the workplace. Should the employer adopt these policies? What are some of the pros and cons of doing so? What workplace considerations should be examined prior to crafting such a policy or strategy?

d. Anti-Bullying Policies

There is a fine line between bullying and harassment. Harassment, if it is based on a category protected by federal statute, is unlawful. Bullying, however, is a much broader concept. Bullying is not necessarily linked to a protected category. Moreover, bullying by itself is not unlawful. There has been proposed legislation outlawing bullying in numerous states. As of yet, no state has adopted such legislation. There is also no federal legislation prohibiting this type of behavior. Anti-bullying legislation has been more popular abroad. Canada and France, for example, have outlawed bullying in certain instances. *See* Katherine Lippel, *The Law of Workplace Bullying: An International Overview*, 32 COMP. LAB. L. & POL'Y J. 1, 6 (2010) ("Specific legal prohibitions on workplace bullying exist in France, Belgium, Québec, South Australia, and Sweden. . . .").

Even though bullying is not necessarily unlawful, employers should be cognizant of this type of behavior and should strongly consider prohibiting it. Bullying has become the focus of substantial attention in the education context, and is also coming under fire by some employers. The same types of power imbalances that often lead to claims of harassment may also be involved when individuals bully specific workers. Where an individual is bullied by a member of a different protected class, the conduct involved can be used to help support a claim of harassment.

Therefore, employers should strongly consider adopting anti-bullying policies. Such policies may help prevent harassment claims and lead to a more harmonious working environment. The Workplace Bullying Institute defines bullying to include

> repeated, health-harming mistreatment of one or more persons (the targets) by one or more perpetrators. It is abusive conduct that is:
>
> - Threatening, humiliating, or intimidating, or
> - Work interference — sabotage — which prevents work from getting done, or
> - Verbal abuse

The WBI Definition of Workplace Bullying, WORKPLACE BULLYING INST., http://www.workplacebullying.org/individuals/problem/definition/.

When crafting anti-bullying policies, employers should consider many of the same elements included in an anti-harassment policy. Indeed, it may be appropriate to integrate the two policies together. Keeping the policy current, training and educating employees and supervisors, and monitoring the workplace is critical to effectively maintaining this type of policy. As bullying behavior is only recently coming under intense criticism, it is even more important to educate workers on the types of behavior that are prohibited. A good policy will include examples of inappropriate conduct. Insulting language, obscene gestures, and workplace sabotage are typical types of behavior seen in bullies. Special attention should also be given to identifying and reporting bullying. By its nature, bullies often target those individuals who are less likely to complain. An effective reporting mechanism and means of monitoring the workplace are particularly important for a proper policy.

Interactive Problem

Looking back at the facts of the interactive problem at the beginning of the chapter, assume that Ned Nosey changes his mind about whether Peter Programmer's behavior is inappropriate. Ned calls Peter into his office and screams at the top of his lungs, "How can you violate our no-dating policy? You are a silly, silly man and a fool for trying to hide your relationship." He repeatedly pounds his fist on the desk and demands that Peter stop dating Sarah. Ned also informs Peter that, as a punishment for his indiscretion, he will not be able to use his company computer for a month. Would this conduct violate a typical anti-bullying policy? Would it constitute harassment actionable under Title VII? Why or why not?

e. Responding to Reference Requests

Many employers have developed policies on responding to reference requests concerning their current or previous employees. This can be a very delicate issue for employers. Many companies want to give as good a reference as possible to allow their workers to obtain suitable employment elsewhere. At the same time, employers may be hesitant to provide negative references for employees even where an individual's work has not been satisfactory.

This text does not address some of the substantial issues and concerns that can arise when responding to reference requests. *See, e.g.*, Bradley Saxton, *Flaws in the Laws Governing Employment References: Problems of "Overdeterrence" and a Proposal for Reform*, 13 YALE L. & POL'Y REV. 45 (1995). Employers that give questionable references can be subject to claims of defamation under state law. Similarly, an employer that does not adequately check an employee's background can be subject to a claim of negligence. Other state law claims may be available to employees when their former employer gives a false or defamatory assessment of their prior work.

These types of claims fall more under the broad category of employment law than employment discrimination practice. Nonetheless, employers must be cognizant of the provisions of federal employment discrimination law when giving reference requests. In particular, if an employer gives a request that is related to a current employee's race, color, sex, national origin, religion, age, or disability, that employer may find itself subject to an employment discrimination claim. Perhaps more problematically, employers must be conscious of the type of reference that is given for workers who may already have filed a claim of discrimination against the company. If an employer gives a negative reference regarding a litigious worker, it may be subjected to a retaliation action under one of the federal antidiscrimination statutes. Where an employee or former employee has filed a charge of discrimination, then, employers must be particularly careful in making sure that the response to a reference request is accurate.

The National Association of College and University Attorneys recommend the following for employers responding to reference requests:

1. Understand your institution's policy on responding to such requests, and follow it.
2. If your institution does not require an authorization form, inquire whether the employer seeking a reference has required or sought an authorization for release of personnel information from the employee.

3. Give thoughtful responses rather than a hurried, incomplete or off-the-cuff response.
4. If you respond to a reference request orally rather than in writing, make a complete note for your files of the date and time of your conversation, who you spoke to, and what you said.
5. When responding to a reference request and not dealing with strictly factual information about an employee, be sure to characterize your statements as your opinion, and where possible support your opinion with specific examples and illustrations.
6. Try to limit references to information and factors related to job performance that can be measured and defended if later subjected to scrutiny.
7. Remember there really is no such thing as an "off-the-record" or "confidential" conversation with someone seeking an employee reference. Don't say anything in such conversations that you would not otherwise say were the conversation "on-the-record."
8. You do not have to respond to each question posed by a person seeking an employee reference. Don't speculate about matters when you don't know the answer, and don't answer questions you think are inappropriate. Be accurate and truthful in those statements you do choose to make, and don't mislead a potential employer by failing to tell them about serious misconduct by an employee.
9. Don't hesitate to contact your institution's Office of Human Resources or General Counsel office for guidance.

Nat'l Ass'n of Coll. & Univ. Attorneys, *Some Guidelines for Administrators and Faculty: Responding to Requests for Employment References* (some text omitted).

This is good general guidance for all employers. It is important to note, however, that there is no uniform approach that will completely insulate an employer from liability. Many employers now refuse to provide anything other than basic information about their employees to prospective employers for fear of litigation. From a best practices standpoint, employers should be aware that giving erroneous reference information can not only lead to state law claims, but potentially to claims of retaliation under federal discrimination laws as well.

Matthews v. Wisconsin Energy Corp.
534 F.3d 547 (7th Cir. 2008)

FLAUM, Circuit Judge.

Bernadine Matthews began working for Wisconsin Energy, then known as Wisconsin Gas Company in 1980. Matthews soon became a "commercial service representative," a customer-service position that required in-person dealings with Wisconsin Energy's customers. After an unfortunate workplace injury in 1996 — a disgruntled customer attacked her — Matthews took a leave of absence. A number of things then happened while Matthews was on leave that put her at odds with Wisconsin Energy. The first was that she was a member of a class action alleging that Wisconsin Energy had redlined the customers in the Wisconsin metro area, where she lived. Then she disputed a claimed shortage in her pension fund. And lastly, in 1998, Matthews filed a discrimination claim against Wisconsin Energy, a dispute the parties eventually settled. Matthews never ended up returning to Wisconsin Energy, and in April 1999, she and the company executed their first Separation Agreement. Matthews didn't immediately seek another job, instead earning a four-year degree from the University of Wisconsin–Milwaukee. Shortly before earning her degree in 2003, Matthews plotted her return to the market, applying to local companies that in turn sought employment references from Wisconsin Energy.

That's when the troubles, and this case, began. As part of the 1999 Separation Agreement, Wisconsin Energy agreed to provide employment references for Matthews as the need arose. Dissatisfied with the responses that Wisconsin Energy was providing — she says Wisconsin Energy denied she had ever worked there — Matthews filed suit in 2003. In her complaint, she alleged both violations of the 1999 separation agreement and intentional interference with prospective contractual relations. The parties soon settled the dispute, and a new settlement agreement was forthcoming in December 2003. The Agreement required Wisconsin Energy to provide an employment reference for Matthews and also contained an attorney-fees provision in the event of a future lawsuit.

Before the parties inked this agreement, Wisconsin Energy's in-house attorney, Lynne English, recited the terms into the record in open court. In so doing, she characterized the company's "policy" to be "what you call name, rank, and serial number." That is, the company would "confirm people worked there, the dates of employment, and their position or at least their last position." Here on appeal, the company describes a similar reference policy. The company only confirms dates of employment, final salary, and the last position that the employee held. Reliance on this objective data prevents the disclosure of "subjective information" regarding the former employee. Although the reference itself is fairly basic, getting to the relevant information may require an involved search. Former employees come in a number of categories, and Wisconsin Energy stores information for these kinds of former employee in a number of different databases. The information for those who, like Matthews, left before the 2000 merger of Wisconsin Energy and Wisconsin Gas has its own database. And searching this database comes last in the process for providing references.

> It is not uncommon for employers to agree to give their former workers neutral or positive employment references as part of a separation agreement.

Wisconsin Energy claims that this last fact caused some problems when companies came calling to get a reference for Matthews, several of which followed from late 2004 to the end of 2005. Financial Management Services conducted one such check in October 2004. This check initially resulted in Wisconsin Energy saying that Matthews had never worked there, although the company eventually confirmed she had. Wisconsin Energy blamed the initial error on the tortuous process of searching through several databases to confirm employment information. In addition, following the request, Wisconsin Energy said that Matthews had worked as a "credit specialist" and not as a "commercial service representative."

As part of a reorganization during Matthews's leave of absence, the company had, unbeknownst to her, changed her old position to this new name. So, when queried, the database provided this job title as the last position held. FMS then relayed this information to Matthews.

Also in May 2005, Matthews enrolled in a program through the Social Security Administration called the "Ticket to Work Program." This program allows those individuals receiving social-security benefits to work while continuing to receive their benefits. To find available jobs, Matthews hired Howard Schwartz, a consultant who specializes in helping disabled individuals seek employment through the program. After performing a review of his client's capabilities, he would then put them into contact with prospective employers. As part of his assessment, Schwartz mailed a letter to the Wisconsin Energy's Vice President of human resources on October 15, 2005. The letter explained Schwartz's role and the program and asked Wisconsin Energy to "confirm [Matthews's] work history . . . and provide comments regarding work performance." No response was forthcoming and a follow-up phone call to Wisconsin Energy's human-resources department went nowhere.

But Wisconsin Energy had received the letter. Given that the VP of human resources did not typically handle reference requests, Schwartz's letter eventually landed on the desk of Lynne English, the in-house attorney who had handled the 2003 settlement agreement with Matthews. On October 19, 2005, English called Schwartz on the phone to discuss the reference. English and Schwartz provided slightly conflicting versions of the phone call during their respective depositions. Schwartz described an "uncomfortable" phone call in which English asked, with an "obvious sense of distrust," why he had sent the letter to the VP of human resources. She then characterized his requested reference as a "sensitive issue to discuss," informing him that Matthews "had been involved in at least one, if not more legal actions against the company." English then asked questions regarding Matthews's social-security benefits, which Schwartz interpreted as being a question whether Matthews "was really entitled to them or [whether she was] cheating the system." English then told him that she would only provide a basic verification of employment, and she would only provide that if she had a written release from Matthews.

English's version differs somewhat. She agreed that she wanted to know why someone would send a reference request to the VP of human resources. And she also agreed that she asked about the social-security program Matthews had enrolled in, although she characterized her request as being motivated more by curiosity than suspicion. English told Schwartz that she was committed to Matthews getting a job after which, she says, Schwartz began pressing his request for a reference. When English said that she could not respond to the letter over the phone, Schwartz asked why — at which point [English] told him "we are in litigation with Ms. Matthews regarding how we respond to reference requests." English testified that it was "possible" that she said that Matthews had sued twice, but she said the exchange was more lighthearted. In the end, English told Schwartz that he would need to send in an authorization from Matthews for the reference, after which Wisconsin Energy would send the basic reference discussed above. Both sides agree that a few days later Schwartz received a confirmation that Matthews had worked at Wisconsin Energy and that she had worked as a "commercial service representative" before her reclassification as a "credit specialist."

Matthews claims that the poor treatment continued when Wisconsin Energy gave her a negative reference in October 2005. She had applied for a management position at Midwest Airlines. When she received the call telling her that she had not been selected, Matthews claims that one of the stated reasons was a poor reference from Wisconsin Energy. And she suspects that similar poor references scuttled several later applications for other jobs in the Washington D.C. area as well.

Title VII prohibits an employer from retaliating against its employees for "oppos[ing]" discrimination, 42 U.S.C. § 2000e-3(a), and this ban extends to acts of retaliation against former employees. An "adverse employment action" is an employment action that is likely to "dissuade a reasonable worker from making or supporting a charge of discrimination." *Burlington Northern*, 548 U.S. at 68. In the context of negative employment references, we have defined this to mean "the dissemination of false reference information that a prospective employer would view as material to its hiring decision."

> As set forth in our prior discussion of retaliation, the Supreme Court has defined an adverse action as any act that would dissuade a reasonable employee from complaining of discrimination.

Here, a number of Matthews's purported acts of retaliation fail because they were not "adverse." With respect to the statements made to FMS, Wisconsin Energy did not provide any false information. Her last position was a "credit specialist." And even if the company initially denied the fact of Matthews's employment, it corrected its mistake, meaning that FMS would not have left with any false impression regarding Matthews's previous employment. As for Midwest, for the reasons stated above, there is no admissible evidence that Midwest ever talked with Wisconsin Energy regarding Matthews's employment. So this theory falls short as well.

Matthews also fails to prove that the substance of English's conversation with Schwartz was retaliatory. In the first place, her prior litigation history was objectively true, so English's disclosure of this fact was not adverse. In addition, she has not shown that English's questions regarding her social-security benefits constituted a negative employment reference. Schwartz left the conversation with the impression that English thought Matthews was gaming the system. But English never explicitly made this claim. Her questions regarding social security arose based on Schwartz's job, which is to place workers receiving social security with employers. Nor did English ever link this "suspicion" — such as it was — to Matthews's previous performance at Wisconsin Energy or to other incidents of her employment. Notably, after the conversation between English and Schwartz, Wisconsin Energy sent along a reference that complied with its policies and that was objectively neutral.

Schwartz's impression after responding to English's questions about his relationship to Matthews is too undefined to have "dissuaded a reasonable worker from making or supporting a charge of discrimination." *Burlington Northern*, 548 U.S. at 68. And in context, English's questions followed naturally from the details surrounding Schwartz's request. If there was a basis for Schwartz's impression, Matthews's conveying such a suspicion may have been uncalled for. But such an interpersonal slight does not constitute an adverse employment action in the context of this conversation. Because showing an "adverse employment action" is a necessary condition under either the direct or indirect methods and Matthews has failed to show one, her claims here must fail.

■ NOTES AND QUESTIONS

1. The court here defines an adverse action to mean "the dissemination of false reference information that a prospective employer would view as material to its hiring decision." *Matthews*, 534 F.3d at 558. Do you agree with this definition?

2. The court further noted that a discussion of the plaintiff's "prior litigation history was objectively true," and her employer's "disclosure of this fact was not adverse." *Matthews*, 534 F.3d at 559. Would an individual's litigious nature hurt her future employment prospects? Should the disclosure of this fact constitute retaliation under Title VII?

3. The court here refers to an "interpersonal slight" that occurred in the discussion between English and Schwartz. *Matthews*, 534 F.3d at 559. To what is the court referring? Should this "slight" rise to the level of an adverse employment action?

4. How difficult is it for a plaintiff to gather evidence establishing that an employer provided a negative reference? How would the plaintiff go about establishing such a claim?

5. Can an individual "test" an employer's reference by having a friend contact the former employer under the guise of being a prospective employer? Would such evidence be admissible in a Title VII retaliation case? *See* Enforcement Guidance: Whether "Testers" Can File Charges and Litigate Claims of Employment Discrimination, EEOC Notice No. 915.002, 2 EEOC Compl. Man. (BNA) (May 22, 1996), http://www.eeoc.gov/policy/docs/testers.html.

6. The key take away from this case — and others like it — is that an employer must be particularly cautious when giving a reference for an employee who has filed a federal employment discrimination claim. If a negative reference is given because of the lawsuit, the individual may have a cause of action. Though the employer here ultimately won the case, defending against this type of litigation was both costly and time-consuming. From a best practices standpoint, employers will want to be cautious to try to avoid this type of situation.

Interactive Problem

Looking back at the facts of the interactive problem at the beginning of the chapter, assume that Sarah applies for a position at P.C. World, a major computer company. P.C. World contacts Computers-R-Us for a reference request about Sarah. Ned Nosey responds that Sarah is an "excellent" employee, but that he would not recommend hiring her. Ned further describes Sarah as a "gold digger" who filed a discrimination claim against the company for a silly dispute about dating in the workplace. Would Sarah have any claims against the company under Title VII?

f. Caregiving Responsibilities

The FMLA is not a primary focus of this book. Family leave tends to fall under the broader category of individual employment law rather than employment discrimination. Nonetheless, treating caregivers disparately can lead to claims of sex discrimination. Many workplace laws were created with an eye toward a traditional "male" sole income environment, and did not contemplate the dual-income family that is much more common today. Employers must make sure not to fall into the trap of coming down too harshly on those with caregiver responsibilities and thus treating individuals differently on the basis of their sex in violation of Title VII.

A full discussion of the contours of the FMLA is beyond the scope of this book. Generally speaking, it is enough to know here that for larger employers federal law requires providing employees twelve weeks of unpaid leave to care for themselves, a newborn, or a close family member with a serious medical condition. This leave can be taken on a consistent or intermittent basis. Though this book only touches on these family responsibilities, it is worth highlighting a few considerations when adopting a caregiving policy in the workplace. Again, such policies can help protect employers from claims of sex discrimination.

When adopting a family leave policy, the employer should become familiar with the FMLA provisions as well as its regulations. The employer should also research applicable state and local law, which frequently give additional protections and benefits to workers with medical issues. These protections can vary based on public or private sector employment. It is also important to have a company's policy reviewed by corporate counsel or independent attorneys. It may be worthwhile to specifically protect caregivers with a policy in the workplace. According to the EEOC, such a policy should:

- Define relevant terms ("caregiver," "caregiving responsibilities," "family")
- Describe common stereotypes or biases about caregivers that may result in unlawful conduct
- Provide examples of prohibited conduct related to workers' caregiving responsibilities
- Prohibit retaliation against individuals who report discrimination or harassment based on caregiving responsibilities or who provide information related to such complaints

- Identify an office or person that staff may contact if they have questions or need to file a complaint related to caregiver discrimination
- Ensure that managers at all levels are aware of, and comply with, the organization's work-life policies
- Respond to complaints of caregiver discrimination efficiently and effectively
- Protect against retaliation

EEOC, *Best Practices for Workers with Caregiving Responsibilities*, http://www.eeoc.gov/policy/docs/caregiver-best-practices.html (last modified Jan. 9, 2011) (some text omitted).

The EEOC also recommends that employers focus on worker qualifications rather than family status during a job interview. The agency advises not to "ask questions about the applicant's or employee's children, plans to start a family, pregnancy, or other caregiving-related issues during interviews or performance reviews." *Id.* Similarly, when job responsibilities are created, they should be related to the duties of the job and should avoid gender stereotyping. To the extent possible, employers should make their workplace friendly for those needing to take extended leaves of absence. Employers should further examine an individual's specific job duties to determine if flexible work arrangements can be created. Job sharing or part-time employment may make it easier for employees with caregiving responsibilities. It is further a best practices approach to provide adequate sick and vacation leave to employees to address caregiving and other responsibilities.

Finally, the employer should make certain that its leave policies comply with state and federal law. If covered, the employer must make certain to provide adequate leave under the FMLA. And the employer should also be familiar with the relevant regulations under the statute. The workplace is becoming much more family-friendly. Employers that remain too rigid on leave time for family issues will be left behind. And, in certain instances, these employers may also run afoul of the law.

Johnson v. University of Iowa

431 F.3d 325 (8th Cir. 2005)

MELLOY, Circuit Judge.

In 2002, [David] Johnson and his wife, Jennie Embree, were expecting a baby girl. At that time, Johnson worked full-time in the Office of the Registrar at the University, and Embree worked part-time in the University's College of Nursing. While attending a class that explained the details of the University's Parental Leave Policy, Johnson was told that he, unlike Embree, could not use accrued sick leave to be paid for absences after the birth of their daughter.

Johnson disagreed with the class instructor's interpretation of the policy, so he sought clarification from other representatives from the University's human resources department as well as the president of the University. After being consistently told that biological fathers were not allowed to use accrued paid sick leave for absences following the birth of a child, Johnson filed a complaint with the Iowa Civil Rights Commission and the Equal Employment Opportunity Commission. He obtained right-to-sue letters and initiated this case in the district court. He was subsequently certified to represent the class of similarly-situated biological fathers employed by the University.

Johnson argues that the University's Parental Leave Policy is discriminatory on its face because it allows biological mothers and adoptive parents to use accrued sick leave after the birth or arrival of a new child without extending a similar benefit to biological fathers. Johnson also contends that the policy is discriminatory as applied because the University denied his request to use accrued sick leave but granted Embree's request for what Johnson deems "caregiving" leave.

The University's Parental Leave Policy provides biological mothers and adoptive parents of both genders with the ability to use accrued paid sick leave for time away from work that is related to the addition of a child. Johnson argues that the policy is unlawful because the University does not extend this benefit to biological fathers. All of Johnson's claims of discrimination rely on this premise.

> It is not uncommon for universities to have progressive leave policies for both male and female employees.

As the district court correctly noted, to determine whether biological fathers are being unlawfully discriminated against, we must separately compare them to the two groups allowed to use accrued paid sick leave: 1) biological mothers and 2) adoptive parents of both genders. We decline to adopt Johnson's repeated characterization that the Parental Leave Policy contains a "biological father exclusion." Rather, the policy provides two different sets of benefits to two different groups. The University did not provide these benefits to Johnson because he is not a member of either group designated to receive benefits. It did not exclude him on the basis that he is a biological father.

The University provides biological mothers with the option of using up to six weeks of accrued paid sick leave after birth. Although only women are eligible to receive this benefit, the policy does not necessarily present "gender-plus" discrimination. If the leave given to biological mothers is granted due to the physical trauma they sustain giving birth, then it is conferred for a valid reason wholly separate from gender. If the leave is instead designed to provide time to care for, and bond with, a newborn, then there is no legitimate reason for biological fathers to be denied the same benefit. Thus, the primary question for us to consider is whether the leave given to biological mothers is in fact disability leave.

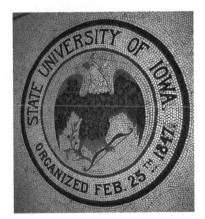

[The] policy language does not allow mothers to use accrued sick leave after their period of disability has ended. Thus, the period away from work constitutes disability leave, even though mothers are likely caring for their newborns during this period. Allowing biological mothers pregnancy-related disability leave on the same terms as employees with other disabilities is not only permissible, but is required by the Pregnancy Discrimination Act of 1978.

Johnson argues that the University's paid maternity leave cannot be interpreted as disability leave because the University does not require proof of a disability when the leave taken after giving birth is six weeks or less. We reject this argument because it is not unreasonable for the University to establish a period of presumptive disability so that it does not need to review medical records for each and every employee who gives birth. In support of its motion for summary judgment, the University provided testimony that a six-week period of disability after childbirth is supported by medical evidence. Although Johnson submitted Embree's affidavit claiming that she was fully recovered from childbirth after four weeks, he has offered no medical evidence indicating that the general period of recovery is less than six weeks. For all of these reasons, we find that the policy's provisions distinguishing between biological mothers and biological fathers are not facially invalid.

> This case again raises the issue of whether a neutral policy has been applied disparately to different groups of workers.

Johnson also contends that even if these provisions are facially valid, they are discriminatory as applied. He claims that Embree was given four weeks of medical leave and then two weeks of paid "parental leave," but that his request to take any paid leave was denied. Embree's affidavit asserts that she decided to take four weeks of medical leave and then an additional two weeks of partial leave "for the exclusive purpose of spending time with and caring for [her] newborn child." Embree's affidavit also contends that she made the reasons for her requested leave known to a supervisor.

We are only concerned with the University's motivation in granting the leave. The University required Embree to obtain a medical release before she voluntarily returned to work on a part-time basis four weeks after giving birth. Johnson contends that this release proves that the subsequent two weeks of part-time leave granted to Embree were for "caregiving" purposes and not disability leave. This argument fails to consider the possibility of partial disability leave. In the fifth and sixth weeks after giving birth, Embree worked only ten hours per week. Furthermore, she worked from home. Thus, it is not a reasonable inference to assume that Embree demonstrated that she was medically cleared to return to work full-time without any restrictions, but was then still allowed to continue to take paid leave.

Even if we assume that the University did allow Embree to use accrued sick leave solely for the purpose of caring for her newborn, Johnson cannot establish that the policy was improperly applied to him in a discriminatory fashion. To demonstrate that the University's stated reasons for treating Johnson and Embree differently are pretextual — and that Johnson's gender was the real reason he was discriminated against — Johnson would have to show that he was treated differently than a "similarly situated" female employee.

Johnson and Embree are not similarly situated. They had different job responsibilities, worked in different departments and reported to different supervisors. Most significantly, Johnson was a full-time employee and Embree was a part-time employee. Generally, part-time employees are not similarly situated to full-time employees. Furthermore, even if Embree and Johnson were similarly situated from an employment perspective, at the time Embree allegedly received parental leave for caregiving purposes, she was only a month removed from childbirth. Even if Embree was medically released to begin working from home on a part-time basis, the fact that she had recently gone through the physical trauma of labor is a distinguishing characteristic between her and Johnson. Accordingly, Johnson's "as applied" challenge to the biological mother classification fails.

The Parental Leave Policy's classification allowing adoptive parents to use accrued sick leave [also] does not discriminate on the basis of gender. It provides exactly the same benefits to adoptive fathers as to adoptive mothers.

■ NOTES AND QUESTIONS

1. Does the policy at issue here discriminate against male employees? Why are male workers not permitted to take parental leave while female workers are allowed this time off?

2. Does the court properly construe the leave permitted by the University as disability leave? Why is this determination important?

3. The court also finds that Johnson and Embree are not similarly situated. Do you agree? Why or why not?

4. Putting Title VII aside, from a best practices standpoint, should an employer provide parental leave to both male and female workers?

5. This case again demonstrates the importance of treating workers similarly and fairly. When employers begin to treat different classes of workers differently, they can be subject to litigation. Though this litigation may not necessarily be successful, it can be expensive and time-consuming.

6. Employers considering a parental leave policy should closely follow the FMLA and Title VII to assure that the proposed policy is compliant with these statutes and is fairly applied.

7. The FMLA is enforced by the Department of Labor while Title VII is enforced by the EEOC. Questions of parental leave can arise under both statutes.

Class Exercise: Providing Leave to Workers

As noted in this section, the FMLA requires that larger employers with fifty or more employees provide twelve weeks of unpaid leave to workers to care for themselves or close family members. Many states have altered these requirements, providing more generous leave provisions. Breaking up into small groups, discuss whether the state in which you reside should provide more than twelve weeks of leave. Should any/all of the leave be paid? Would you recommend a lower threshold for coverage? If your proposed leave would be more generous than the FMLA, how would you recommend paying for it?

2. Training Employees on Discrimination

From a best practices standpoint, effective training on antidiscrimination is critical in the workplace. Employers should conduct regular training of management and other personnel in these areas. While it is important to have substantive antidiscrimination policies in place, proper training can help bring these policies to life and give them new meaning. Training will help employees to understand the importance of these policies and to understand how to address problems that might arise in the workplace.

While training can be done by almost anyone with a thorough understanding of antidiscrimination law, employers should strongly consider having an experienced attorney conduct the sessions. Someone with a legal background in this particular area can help focus the training on important issues and address any particular concerns for the company in question. With this in mind, particular attention should be given to any recurring issues that an employer may be experiencing.

Training should also occur regularly at a company. It should not be a one-time event. Companies often hire new employees, and existing employees often change positions. It is important to make sure that all employees have received proper training on discrimination. Moreover, the dynamics and issues of a particular company change over time. It is important that the training remains up to date and occurs on a regular basis.

Training also demonstrates an employer's dedication to preventing discrimination. As noted throughout this text, this commitment can help limit an employer's liability for discrimination and help restrict the imposition of punitive damages. More fundamentally, employees who are aware of an employer's commitment to antidiscrimination will be less likely to engage in prohibited conduct. And, some workers may truly not even be aware that certain behavior is unlawful — education thus provides an important incentive to conduct training.

Like any other issue that can arise in the employment discrimination context, proper training must be crafted to the individual workplace. Employers vary dramatically from one another, and effective training will focus on these differences. There is no one-size-fits-all approach to these issues. Training gives an employer the opportunity to highlight the company's antidiscrimination policies. It also allows the employer to reinforce its dedication to equality in the workplace. And, it provides a mechanism for educating workers on civil rights. From a best practices standpoint, then, all workplaces should participate in this type of training. When in doubt, the training should be conducted by attorneys who are well experienced in the field.

 *Interactive Problem*

Looking back at the facts of the interactive problem at the beginning of the chapter, consider what type of training programs the employer might implement for its workforce. Are there any issues in the computer field that should be specifically addressed? Who at the company should conduct the training? What types of issues should the training include? Given the facts in the interactive problem, are there any specific topics that you would include in the training?

3. Documentation, Discipline, and Investigations

In addition to implementing proper policies and training in the workforce, employers should be well versed in how to handle issues when they do arise. This can be particularly challenging to employers who are facing an issue for the first time. It is often difficult to know where to start on these issues. Again, there is no single approach that will effectively address a case of discrimination in the workplace. Nonetheless, there are many general guidelines that should be followed when investigating a claim and disciplining an employee.

This text cannot address all of the potential issues that can arise when investigating a claim of discrimination. There are many excellent sources that provide an in-depth review of how to properly handle an investigation. *See, e.g.,* Deborah C. England, The Essential Guide to Handling Workplace Harassment and Discrimination (2d ed. 2012). There are also a number of issues that come readily to mind when addressing these questions.

First and foremost, employers often make the mistake of treating workplace discrimination too informally. One key to effective workplace management is to document any questionable conduct that may occur. There are numerous legal reasons for employers to make certain to document this type of behavior. Though an incident may seem small or trivial, over time, continued inappropriate behavior can be problematic. It may be necessary to have documentation to establish a pattern of improper behavior. Documentation also helps establish that an employer was cognizant of the issue when it arose, and took the proper steps to correct the behavior. Documentation can also be used to help support taking an adverse action against an employee.

Documentation need not always be extensive. It can often be as simple as typing out a short statement and placing it in a separate file. The documentation should include all of the relevant facts of the incident involved. It should specify all of the employees at issue. It should also include the relevant dates and times of all incidents that occurred. It should further be shared with anyone who would have a need to know the information, including the human resources department. It is important not only to document an incident, but to document immediately after the event occurred while the information is still fresh in the mind of the supervisor. When documenting behavior, supervisors should not be vague and generic, or too conclusory. Documentation should be as specific as possible and relate to specific facts. *See, e.g.*, Thadford Felton, *Best Practices in Documenting Employee Discipline*, Workforce, Jan. 15, 2009, http://www.workforce.com/articles/best-practices-in-documenting-employee-discipline.

Performing an investigation of a discrimination claim can also be another complex issue that many employers face. The nature of the investigation will largely depend on the severity of the behavior in question and the type of improper conduct alleged. When performing an investigation, the employer should follow a few basic rules. Ten basic guidelines should be considered when conducting any investigation.

First, the importance of selecting the investigator should not be overlooked. An investigator should be chosen who is completely impartial and in no way involved in the complaint itself. Investigators should also be adequately trained and have the qualifications necessary to conduct the review. It can often be best to choose an investigator from the human resources department or a completely separate part of the corporation. Indeed, having outside counsel or an independent agency perform the investigation can also have numerous benefits. And, in certain instances, it may be best to have more than one investigator.

Second, the investigation must be prompt. Delay can cause numerous problems. It suggests that the company is not taking the issue seriously. And, as time passes, it will become increasingly difficult to collect the necessary information surrounding the event.

Third, the complainant (as well as the target of the investigation, if any) should be kept apprised of the status of the review. This will allow the parties involved to be well informed of where the investigation stands.

Fourth, to the extent possible the investigation should remain confidential. Only those with a need to know should be informed of the investigation, and these individuals should be advised of the importance of keeping the information confidential. At the same time, it is important for investigators to understand that confidentiality can never be promised to the parties involved. Any information that is uncovered could subsequently be revealed in a lawsuit and disclosed in public records.

Fifth, the institution should make every effort to assure that retaliation does not occur against the claimant. As noted throughout this text, retaliation can be an enormous problem for those alleging claims of discrimination.

Sixth, the scope of the investigation should be thorough. All individuals with pertinent information should be interviewed. For a sexual harassment claim, then, the harasser, victim, and witnesses should all be interviewed.

Seventh, relevant documentation should be sought. Individuals who are interviewed should be asked whether they have any documents that might support or refute any claims that have been made. Email correspondence, voicemail messages, handwritten notes, or any other documentation should be collected and maintained.

Eighth, the investigator should accurately and contemporaneously document all relevant aspects of the investigation itself. This can be challenging, particularly when interviewing witnesses, but there are many techniques that can be used to make sure that the record is accurately reflected in the investigation notes.

Ninth, the institution and the investigator should fairly review the facts and weigh the credibility of the witnesses. A conclusion should not be drawn until all of the facts have been explored and all of the relevant witnesses have been interviewed. If there is concern about ongoing discrimination or harassment while the investigation proceeds, it is always possible to separate the individuals involved or to place employees on paid administrative leave. Finally, the complainant (and target of the investigation, if applicable) should be advised of the conclusions of the investigation. These results should typically be conveyed in writing after the review of corporate counsel.

Again, each investigation must be approached strategically and independently. Following these basic guidelines, however, will help ensure that the investigation is performed quickly and fairly. Harassment claims are frequently investigated by employers and these cases are notoriously complex. The same basic guidelines discussed above would apply to these claims. It is important to note, however, that these allegations should be handled particularly delicately. One excellent summary of harassment investigations advises that an investigator should:

- Avoid excessive delay in beginning the investigation.
- Choose qualified and trained investigators.
- Never "guarantee" confidentiality.
- Assure the complainant and witnesses that the institution takes its anti-retaliation policy seriously.
- Assure the complainant and witnesses that confidentiality will be preserved to the extent permitted and required by law.
- [N]ot give out information regarding the investigation to anyone who does not have an absolute need to know, except as required by law or protected by attorney/client privilege. . . .
- Provide appropriate feedback to the complainant, the respondent, and the respondent's supervisor throughout the process.
- Effect fairness to the respondent and, at the very least, provide any due process required by law or institutional policy.
- Document as appropriate, and conduct a prompt, thorough, and complete investigation.

Elsa Kircher Cole et al., *How to Conduct a Sexual Harassment Investigation*, NACUA (2006).

Once the investigation is complete, a determination should be made as to whether any disciplinary or other action needs to be taken. Disciplining a worker can be difficult for employers, particularly where there has been a good working relationship with the employee. When determining whether to discipline a worker, the results of the investigation should be fairly weighed. The human resources department, and even legal counsel, should be consulted in the decision. The employer should not make a rash judgment, and any serious discipline should be well thought out before being implemented.

It is also important that the discipline is proportionate to the inappropriate conduct. The employer should not be afraid to respond with harsh discipline for severe conduct, but should impose lighter sanctions for more borderline behavior. For example, an oral reprimand might be appropriate for a simple inappropriate joke that is overheard by the supervisor. Discharge, however, could certainly be recommended for something more severe like a sexual assault. The discipline should also be consistent with similar infractions involving other individuals at the company in the past. If the employer treats employees differently based on the same conduct, it risks a potential discrimination claim.

Individuals should be advised of the discipline in writing. This written explanation should thoroughly document the reasons for the adverse action, and clearly explain what the resulting sanctions will be. Where the discipline is severe or results in discharge, the employer should make certain to have multiple individuals present when conducting the discipline. It is important to have more than one witness present in the event that there is a dispute over what transpired. It may also be appropriate for at least one company representative to take contemporaneous notes during this meeting. The employer should also consider whether a collective bargaining agreement or progressive disciplinary policy is in place. If so, the employer must make certain that it has complied with these agreements. In the union setting, it is also common for workers to have a union representative present when receiving a disciplinary sanction.

Prior to implementing discipline, employers should also contemplate any potential legal action that may result. For example, where an individual is discharged for sexual harassment, that individual may bring a defamation claim or a cause of action for negligent infliction of emotional distress. The employer should make sure that it has assessed this risk and is prepared to respond to these types of claims. The employer should also consider how to actually effectuate the discharge. Important questions that should be considered are whether to allow the employee to work for any additional amount of time, whether security should be present for the incident, and how to make sure that company files, documents, or electronic information are not sabotaged.

An excellent summary of issues to weigh when disciplining a worker suggests that the company should do the following:

- Evaluate the mitigating and aggravating factors
  - Mitigating factors include long service with the company, history of satisfactory appraisals, prior commendations or awards, etc.
  - Aggravating factors include short length of service, history of unsatisfactory performance, prior instances of performance/conduct/attendance problems, etc.
- Consider the risk associated with retaining the employee
  - That the employee will engage in future misconduct resulting in employer liability
  - That the employee's attitude will deteriorate because he thinks he has "gotten away with something"
  - That the morale of other employees will be harmed
  - The risk of "setting a precedent" that other employees will expect you to follow in the future
- Consider the harm associated with discharging or severely disciplining the employee
  - Evaluate the risk that the employee will claim discrimination on the basis of membership in a protected group

ANNE H. WILLIAMS, HOW TO DISCIPLINE AND DOCUMENT EMPLOYEE BEHAVIOR 11–12 (2002) (some text omitted).

The following case looks at how one investigation of discrimination was performed. Though the case arises outside of the employment context, it addresses the importance of performing a fair and equitable investigation.

Toliver v. Alaska State Commission for Human Rights

279 P.3d 619 (Alaska 2012)

MATTHEWS, Senior Justice.

William M. Toliver II is an African-American man in his sixties; he has litigated pro se throughout these proceedings. During 2007 and 2008, Toliver shopped at two Brown Jug liquor stores — Store 32 and Store 55 — located in the Mountain View neighborhood of Anchorage.

On August 21, 2007, Toliver entered Store 32 and was approached by the assistant manager, Crystal Dockter. After a

heated verbal exchange of some sort, Dockter "86ed" — banned — Toliver from Store 32. In the store's incident log for that evening, Dockter wrote that she had banned Toliver "for causing problems and for cursing me out." Toliver later disputed this version of events. He continued to shop at Store 55, where he was not banned.

In late June 2008 Toliver called O. C. Madden III, Brown Jug's vice-president for human resources, and complained that Brown Jug was discriminating against him and other members of racial minority groups in Mountain View. Madden and Ed O'Neill — Brown Jug's co-owner — invited Toliver to meet with them in person at their offices. During the meeting Toliver expressed frustration over Dockter's behavior and stated that members of the Mountain View community considered Store 32 to be a "[w]hites only" store.

Madden and O'Neill spoke with their staff in response to Toliver's allegations. They eventually told Toliver that he would be allowed to continue shopping at Store 55 but would be banned from Store 32. Madden and O'Neill also organized a public meeting at a community center to address Toliver's claim that members of the Mountain View community believed Brown Jug employees had racially discriminated against them.

On August 29, 2008, Toliver filed a complaint with the Commission. He alleged that Brown Jug had denied him "rights and privileges as a customer" on the basis of race.

On December 5, 2008, Brown Jug filed a letter with the Commission responding to Toliver's complaint. Brown Jug contended that Toliver's allegations were "meritless" and "unsupported" and that the facts showed "Brown Jug refused service to Toliver at one of its stores after Toliver verbally abused and physically threatened the store's assistant manager." Brown Jug also pointed out that after meeting with Toliver and listening to his concerns, Brown Jug allowed him to make purchases at a different store in the same area.

After receiving Brown Jug's statement of position the investigator assigned by the Commission to the case called Toliver to review Brown Jug's position statement with him. Toliver denied threatening or cursing at Dockter. Toliver mentioned the manager at Brown Jug Store 55, Richard Senior, as a potential witness, alleging that Senior had told Toliver that he thought what was occurring was wrong. Toliver also stated that the manager at Store 32 "shook his head and said what the heck is going on here." Toliver further stated that the people who had signed the petition were also witnesses.

On December 10, 2008, the investigator wrote to Brown Jug's attorney requesting copies of incident logs and information about, among other things, Brown Jug's policy for denying customer service. She also requested interviews with Dockter, Madden, O'Neill, and the managers of Stores 32 and 55. The investigator did interview Dockter and Madden, but did not interview Senior (the manager of Store 55), nor the manager of Store 32, nor any of the individuals who signed Toliver's petition.

On April 21, 2009, the investigator issued a written determination based on her investigation. She concluded that Toliver was denied the right to shop at Brown Jug Store 32 "because he verbally abused and threatened employees." She observed that customers of other races had been denied service for similar reasons and that the evidence did not show that Toliver was denied service because of his race. The investigator reviewed the determination with Toliver, who vigorously disputed the version of events advanced by Brown Jug and again alleged that Senior had agreed banning Toliver from Store 32 was wrong.

Ultimately, the investigator concluded that Toliver's allegations were "not supported by substantial evidence." On the same day that this report was issued, the executive director of the Commission issued an order closing the case because the "[i]nvestigation did not find substantial evidence to support allegations in the complaint."

Toliver appealed the closing order to the superior court, arguing in part that the investigation was incomplete because the investigator did not interview any of the individuals who signed Toliver's petition. The superior court affirmed the order in a seven-page written decision. The court concluded that it was not necessary for the investigator to interview the petitioners because "the record does not demonstrate that any of the petitioners on the list were present when Toliver's incidents occurred."

The investigatory duties of the Commission [require]: "The executive director or a member of the commission's staff designated by the executive director shall informally investigate the matters set out in a filed complaint, promptly and impartially." This language explicitly requires that the Commission conduct an impartial investigation of each complaint.

Here, the Commission's investigation consisted of an intake interview with Toliver, interviews with Dockter and Madden, and a few telephone conversations with Toliver that he initiated. Significantly, the investigator did not interview any of the individuals who, according to Toliver, would corroborate his claim of discrimination.

The investigator did ask Toliver to provide the names of specific individuals who had witnessed the alleged discrimination taking place. Toliver claimed at oral argument before

> As this case demonstrates, simply performing an investigation is not enough. Investigations must be thorough, unbiased, and equitable.

the superior court that he provided the investigator with the names of three individuals, but the agency record does not corroborate this claim. Even without these specific names, however, it would have taken little effort for the investigator to contact at least a few of the 24 individuals who signed the petition and provided telephone numbers.

Further, it is unclear why the investigator retreated from her stated intention to interview the managers of Stores 55 and 32. Her failure to interview Senior — the manager of Store 55 — is particularly troubling. Toliver alleged that Senior had agreed that Brown Jug's actions were racially motivated. If verified, Senior's agreement would mark him as a witness who has potentially relevant information. We conclude, therefore, that as a result of its failure to make an effort to interview at least some of the witnesses identified by Toliver, the Commission breached its duty to conduct an impartial investigation.

The Commission's regulations authorize it to "determine the nature and scope" of each investigation. We agree that this authority is properly committed to agency discretion subject only to review for abuse of discretion. We do not require by this decision that the Commission interview all alleged witnesses to discrimination, nor do we substantially restrict the Commission's ability to guide its own investigations. We merely hold that the Commission abuses its discretion when it interviews witnesses who can be expected to be favorable to the respondent but makes no effort to interview any witnesses listed by the complainant. In such a case the Commission may not dismiss a complaint for lack of substantial evidence because an investigation which is "abbreviated and one-sided" does not supply a reasonable basis for making such a determination.

■ NOTES AND QUESTIONS

1. This case arose outside of the employment context, but it demonstrates the importance of fairly addressing a claim of discrimination.

2. The court here finds the failure to interview witnesses to be a basis for an improper investigation. What witnesses should be questioned in a typical discrimination claim?

3. Aside from interviewing the relevant witnesses, what conduct would constitute a fair and equitable discrimination investigation? What documents should be examined? Should any computer usage be reviewed? What are the hallmarks of a fair and unbiased investigation?

4. Who should conduct an unbiased discrimination investigation? Should an investigation be performed by an outside party? Should it be conducted by an internal investigator? What are the advantages and disadvantages of each?

5. One important take away from this case is that simply performing an investigation may not be enough. The investigation should be thorough and it should be fair. Failure to conduct an unbiased investigation can lead to difficulties under the federal discrimination statutes.

 ## *Interactive Problem*

Looking back at the facts of the interactive problem at the beginning of the chapter, assume that Sarah files a claim of discrimination against the company. How would the employer go about investigating this type of claim? Who should be interviewed, and what questions should be asked? If the company decides that Ned has acted inappropriately, should he be disciplined? What sanction would be appropriate under the circumstances?

Class Exercise: Sexual Harassment Investigations

Breaking up into small groups, discuss what elements should determine whether an employer has performed an effective sexual harassment investigation. What should an employer do to assure a full and fair investigation into the situation? What mistakes could employers make in their investigation? How would you help avoid these mistakes?

---

4. Insulation from Liability

One issue that has recently been considered by the courts is the extent to which employers may attempt to insulate themselves from liability by involving multiple individuals in a decision to discipline a worker. Where employers involve decision makers from outside the ordinary chain of command, those employers can claim that the decision was made by neutral parties that would have no incentive to discriminate against the worker. This so-called "cat's paw" theory was recently considered by the Supreme Court in the context of a military leave law.

Staub v. Proctor Hospital
562 U.S. 411 (2011)

Justice SCALIA delivered the opinion of the Court.

We consider the circumstances under which an employer may be held liable for employment discrimination based on the discriminatory animus of an employee who influenced, but did not make, the ultimate employment decision.

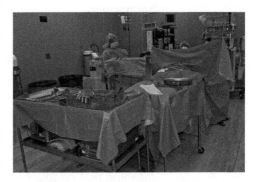

Petitioner Vincent Staub worked as an angiography technician for respondent Proctor Hospital until 2004, when he was fired. Staub and Proctor hotly dispute the facts surrounding the firing, but because a jury found for Staub in his claim of employment discrimination against Proctor, we describe the facts viewed in the light most favorable to him.

While employed by Proctor, Staub was a member of the United States Army Reserve, which required him to attend drill one weekend per month and to train full time for two to three weeks a year. Both Janice Mulally, Staub's immediate supervisor, and Michael Korenchuk, Mulally's supervisor, were hostile to Staub's military obligations. Mulally scheduled Staub for additional shifts without notice so that he would "'pa[y] back the department for everyone else having to bend over backwards to cover [his] schedule for the Reserves.'" 560 F.3d 647, 652 (C.A.7 2009). She also informed Staub's co-worker, Leslie Sweborg, that Staub's "'military duty had been a strain on th[e] department,'" and asked Sweborg to help her "'get rid of him'" *Ibid.* Korenchuk referred to Staub's military obligations as "'a b[u]nch of smoking and joking and [a] waste of taxpayers['] money.'" *Ibid.* He was also aware that Mulally was "'out to get'" Staub. *Ibid.*

In January 2004, Mulally issued Staub a "Corrective Action" disciplinary warning for purportedly violating a company rule requiring him to stay in his work area whenever he was not working with a patient. The Corrective Action included a directive requiring Staub to report to Mulally or Korenchuk "'when [he] ha[d] no patients and [the angio] cases [we]re complete[d].'" *Id.* at 653. According to Staub, Mulally's justification for the Corrective Action was false for two reasons: First, the company rule invoked by Mulally did not exist; and second, even if it did, Staub did not violate it.

On April 2, 2004, Angie Day, Staub's co-worker, complained to Linda Buck, Proctor's vice president of human resources, and Garrett McGowan, Proctor's chief operating officer, about Staub's frequent unavailability and abruptness. McGowan directed Korenchuk and Buck to create a plan that would solve Staub's "'availability' problems." *Id.* at 654. But three weeks later, before they had time to do so, Korenchuk informed Buck that Staub had left his desk without informing a supervisor, in violation of the January Corrective Action. Staub now contends this accusation was false: he had left Korenchuk a voice-mail notification that he was leaving his desk. Buck relied on Korenchuk's accusation, however, and after reviewing Staub's personnel file, she decided to fire him. The termination notice stated that Staub had ignored the directive issued in the January 2004 Corrective Action.

Staub challenged his firing through Proctor's grievance process, claiming that Mulally had fabricated the allegation underlying the Corrective Action out of hostility toward his military obligations. Buck did not follow up with Mulally about this claim. After discussing the matter with another personnel officer, Buck adhered to her decision.

Staub sued Proctor under the Uniformed Services Employment and Reemployment Rights Act of 1994 [USERRA] claiming that his discharge was motivated by hostility to his obligations as a military reservist. His contention was not that Buck had any such hostility but that Mulally and Korenchuk did, and that their actions influenced Buck's ultimate employment decision. A jury found that Staub's "military status was a motivating factor in [Proctor's] decision to discharge him," and awarded $57,640 in damages.

The Seventh Circuit reversed, holding that Proctor was entitled to judgment as a matter of law. The court observed that Staub had brought a "'cat's paw' case," meaning that he sought to hold his employer liable for the animus of a supervisor who was not charged with making the ultimate employment decision. It explained that under Seventh Circuit precedent, a "cat's paw" case could not succeed unless the nondecisionmaker exercised such "'singular influence'" over the decisionmaker that the decision to terminate was the product of "blind reliance." It then noted that "Buck looked beyond what Mulally and Korenchuk said," relying in part on her conversation with Day and her review of Staub's personnel file. The court "admit[ted] that Buck's investigation could have been more robust," since it "failed to pursue Staub's theory that Mulally fabricated the write-up." But the court said that the "'singular influence'" rule "does not require the decisionmaker to be a paragon of independence": "It is enough that the decisionmaker is not wholly dependent on a single source of information and conducts her own investigation into the facts relevant to the decision." Because the undisputed evidence established that Buck was not wholly dependent on the advice of Korenchuk and Mulally, the court held that Proctor was entitled to judgment.

When a decision to fire is made with no unlawful animus on the part of the firing agent, but partly on the basis of a report prompted (unbeknownst to that agent) by discrimination, discrimination might perhaps be called a "factor" or a "causal factor" in the decision; but it seems to us a considerable stretch to call it "a motivating factor." Proctor, on the other hand, contends that the employer is not liable unless the *de facto* decisionmaker (the technical decisionmaker or the agent for whom he is the "cat's paw") is motivated by discriminatory animus. This avoids the aggregation of animus and adverse action, but it seems to us not the only application of general tort law that can do so. Animus and responsibility for the adverse action can both be attributed to the earlier agent (here, Staub's supervisors) if the adverse action is the intended consequence of that agent's discriminatory conduct. So long as the agent intends, for discriminatory reasons, that the adverse action occur, he has the scienter required to be liable under USERRA. And it is axiomatic under tort law that the exercise of judgment by the decisionmaker does not prevent the earlier agent's action (and hence the earlier agent's discriminatory animus) from being the proximate cause of the harm. Proximate cause requires only "some direct relation between the injury asserted and the injurious conduct alleged," and excludes only those "link[s] that are too remote, purely contingent, or indirect." *Hemi Group, LLC v. City of New York*, 130 S. Ct. 983 (2010) (internal quotation marks omitted). We do not think that the ultimate decisionmaker's exercise of judgment automatically renders the link to the supervisor's bias "remote" or "purely contingent." The decisionmaker's exercise of judgment is *also* a proximate cause of the employment decision, but it is common for injuries to have multiple proximate causes. Nor can the ultimate decisionmaker's judgment be deemed a superseding cause of the harm. A cause can be thought "superseding" only if it is a "cause of independent origin that was not foreseeable." *Exxon Co., U.S.A. v. Sofec, Inc.*, 517 U.S. 830, 837 (1996) (internal quotation marks omitted).

Moreover, the approach urged upon us by Proctor gives an unlikely meaning to a provision designed to prevent employer discrimination. An employer's authority to reward, punish, or dismiss is often allocated among multiple agents. The one who makes the ultimate decision does so on the basis of performance assessments by other supervisors. Proctor's view would have the improbable consequence that if an employer isolates a personnel official from an employee's supervisors, vests the decision to take adverse employment actions in that official, and asks that official to review the employee's personnel file before taking the adverse action, then the employer will be effectively shielded from discriminatory acts and recommendations of supervisors that were *designed and intended* to produce the adverse action. That seems to us an implausible meaning of the text, and one that is not compelled by its words.

Proctor suggests that even if the decisionmaker's mere exercise of independent judgment does not suffice to negate the effect of the prior discrimination, at least the decisionmaker's independent investigation (and rejection) of the employee's allegations of discriminatory animus ought to do so. We decline to adopt such a hard-and-fast rule. As we have already acknowledged, the requirement that the biased supervisor's action be a causal factor of the ultimate employment action incorporates the traditional tort-law concept of proximate cause. Thus, if the employer's investigation results in an adverse action for reasons unrelated to the supervisor's original biased action (by the terms of USERRA it is the employer's burden to establish that), then the employer will not be liable. But the supervisor's biased report may remain a causal factor if the independent investigation takes it into account without determining that the adverse action was, apart from the supervisor's recommendation, entirely justified. We are aware of no principle in tort or agency law under which an employer's mere conduct of an independent investigation has a claim-preclusive effect. Nor do we think the independent investigation somehow relieves the employer of "fault." The employer is at fault because one of its agents committed an action based on discriminatory animus that was intended to cause, and did in fact cause, an adverse employment decision.

We therefore hold that if a supervisor performs an act motivated by antimilitary animus that is *intended* by the supervisor to cause an adverse employment action, and if that act is a proximate cause of the ultimate employment action, then the employer is liable under USERRA.

Applying our analysis to the facts of this case, it is clear that the Seventh Circuit's judgment must be reversed. Both Mulally and Korenchuk were acting within the scope of their employment when they took the actions that allegedly caused Buck to fire Staub. A "reprimand . . . for workplace failings" constitutes conduct within the scope of an agent's employment. *Faragher v. Boca Raton*, 524 U.S. 775, 798–799 (1998). As the Seventh Circuit recognized, there was evidence that Mulally's and Korenchuk's actions

> The Court here holds that "if a supervisor performs an act intended by the supervisor to cause an adverse employment action, and if that act is a proximate cause of the . . . action, then the employer is liable."

were motivated by hostility toward Staub's military obligations. There was also evidence that Mulally's and Korenchuk's actions were causal factors underlying Buck's decision to fire Staub. Buck's termination notice expressly stated that Staub was terminated because he had "ignored" the directive in the Corrective Action. Finally, there was evidence that both Mulally and Korenchuk had the specific intent to cause Staub to be terminated. Mulally stated she was trying to "'get rid of'" Staub, and Korenchuk was aware that Mulally was "'out to get'" Staub. Moreover, Korenchuk informed Buck, Proctor's personnel officer responsible for terminating employees, of Staub's alleged noncompliance with Mulally's Corrective Action, and Buck fired Staub immediately thereafter; a reasonable jury could infer that Korenchuk intended that Staub be fired. The Seventh Circuit therefore erred in holding that Proctor was entitled to judgment as a matter of law.

■ NOTES AND QUESTIONS

1. This case arose in the context of military leave law. Will the same principles discussed here apply to a case brought under Title VII? *See generally* Stephen F. Befort & Alison L. Olig, *Within the Grasp of the Cat's Paw: Delineating the Scope of Subordinate Bias Liability Under Federal Antidiscrimination Statutes*, 60 S.C. L. Rev. 383 (2008) (discussing imputed liability and the "cat's paw" theory).

2. The Court held that an "employer is at fault because one of its agents committed an action based on discriminatory animus that was intended to cause, and did in fact cause, an adverse employment decision." *Staub*, 562 U.S. 421. If a supervisor recommends a subordinate's termination based on racial animus, will the company be liable under Title VII if it adopts the supervisor's recommendation?

3. It is clear from this opinion that an employer can be liable where its decision is somehow tinged by discriminatory animus. Nonetheless, is it still more difficult to ultimately prove discrimination where the decision maker is removed from the day-to-day activities of the employee?

4. After this decision, how would you recommend an employer proceed if it wants to terminate an employee? Who should ultimately be responsible for the discharge decision? How can the employer help break the causal link of discrimination?

Practice and Procedural Tip

31: The Discharge Decision

The *Staub* case highlights the importance of making a nondiscriminatory decision when discharging an employee. Because employers may be acting with unconscious discriminatory motivations, or may be accepting recommendations from employees who are acting with discriminatory animus, a company may subject itself to litigation even where it tries to avoid improper conduct. There are many ways that an employer can attempt to protect itself from Title VII litigation. The Supreme Court's decision in *Staub* raises one potential avenue that employers can use to avoid these types of claims.

More specifically, when an employer is making a discharge decision, it should carefully review its motivations. Involving multiple company officials — including human resources personnel — can help assure that the decision is based on performance rather than the employee's protected characteristic. And, where an employee challenges her discharge, it will be much more difficult to establish discrimination if there are multiple decision makers in the process. This is not to say that it will be impossible for a plaintiff to establish discrimination under the circumstances. Indeed, *Staub* provides an excellent example of how a company can still be held liable for improper conduct where many people are involved in the termination. However, it can be more challenging for a plaintiff to establish a causal link where several individuals are involved in the discharge.

From a best practices standpoint, then, employers should strongly consider involving multiple individuals in any employment decision that will result in termination. From a practical perspective, this type of system will provide a checks-and-balances approach that can help avoid a decision based on discrimination. And, from a legal perspective, it will be more difficult for plaintiffs to challenge actions taken by multiple decision makers.

As others have noted, "[a]lthough an employer's impartial internal review of important personnel decisions, such as discharges, will not always provide an iron-clad defense to liability as might have been the case in some circuits prior to *Staub*, it is still good practice. Independent review may disclose irregularities in process or inadequate consideration of the substance of such important decisions. Moreover, independent review may yet provide a potent defense in some cases, depending on the facts." Neal Mollen & Mitchell Mosvick, *An Employment Decision Can Be Discriminatory Even If the Decision-Maker Has No Discriminatory Intent, Supreme Court Rules*, PAUL HASTINGS: STAY CURRENT (Mar. 2011), https://www.paulhastings.com/docs/default-source/PDFs/1849.pdf.

 Interactive Problem

Looking back at the facts of the interactive problem at the beginning of the chapter, assume that the company decides to terminate Sarah and Peter for violating the no-dating policy. Given the Supreme Court's decision in *Staub*, how could the company involve multiple decision makers in the process to help avoid any potential liability?

D. Chapter-in-Review

Unlike many other fields, employment discrimination law often requires handling certain issues with a great deal of sensitivity. While legal considerations frequently come into play here, practical concerns are often just as important. Employers can be "in the right," but still end up with a costly legal defense if they do not handle a matter carefully.

This chapter addresses some of the best practices for handling common issues that arise in the workplace setting. For employees, this includes when, where, and how to complain of discrimination, as well as how to draft a complaint and avoid retaliation.

For employers, common concerns often involve how to adopt workplace policies to maximize employee productivity and enhance worker harmony. Such policies include dating in the workplace, computer and electronic device usage, anti-bullying policies, and guidelines on responding to reference requests. Employers often face issues when training employees on how to address discrimination, as well as on how to investigate complaints and discipline wrong-doers.

All of these issues must be handled delicately and with an eye toward maintaining a harmonious working environment. This chapter touches on some of the more practical ways to handle these types of issues that may arise. There are obviously no cookie-cutter approaches to tackling these difficult considerations, and this chapter simply offers some practical advice on how to best approach these sensitive topics. In addition to the areas addressed here, many other common issues can and do arise. The key to addressing any workplace topic is to approach the issue with a complete understanding of the law. Beyond the law, however, employers must also use a common-sense approach that integrates the best practices of the industry involved.